The PRAIRIE WEST

Paul Chase

The PRAIRIE WEST
Historical Readings

Second Edition,
Revised and Expanded

EDITED BY

R. Douglas Francis

Howard Palmer

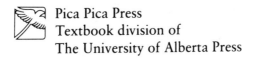

Pica Pica Press
Textbook division of
The University of Alberta Press

First published by
Pica Pica Press
Textbook division of
The University of Alberta Press
Athabasca Hall
Edmonton, Alberta
Canada T6G 2E8

Copyright © Pica Pica Press 1992
Second printing 1995
ISBN 0-88864-227-X

Canadian Cataloguing in Publication Data

Main entry under title:
The Prairie West

Includes bibliographical references.
ISBN 0-88864-227-X

1. Prairie Provinces—History.   I. Francis, R. D.
(R. Douglas), 1944-   II. Palmer, Howard, 1946-1991.
FC3237.P73 1992   971.2   C92-091246-X
F1060.P73 1992

Typesetting by Pièce de Résistance Ltée., Edmonton, Alberta, Canada
Printed on acid-free paper.
Printed by Transcontinental Printing

Permissions

"Historical Writing on the Prairie West" by Gerald Friesen is copyright 1992 by the author and printed with his permission.

"A Century of Plain and Parkland" by W.L. Morton is from *Alberta Historical Review* 17 (Spring 1969): 1-10 and is reprinted by permission of Mrs. W.L. Morton.

"A Historical Reconstruction for the Northwestern Plains" by Olive Patricia Dickason is from *Prairie Forum* 5 (Spring 1980): 19-37 and is reprinted by permission of the author and the Canadian Plains Research Centre, University of Regina.

"Traders and Indians" by Daniel Francis is Chapter 3 from his *Battle for the West: Fur Traders and the Birth of Western Canada* (Edmonton: Hurtig, 1982) and is reprinted by permission of the author.

"The Indian and the Fur Trade: A Review of Literature" by Jacqueline Peterson with John Anfinson is from *Manitoba History* 10 (Autumn 1985): 10-18 and is reprinted by permission of the authors and Manitoba History.

"The Metis: Genesis and Rebirth" by Jennifer S.H. Brown is from *Native People, Native Lands*, edited by Bruce Cox (Ottawa: Carleton University Press, 1988), pp. 136-47 and is reprinted by permission of Carleton University Press and the author. This paper is based on an article in *The Canadian Encyclopedia*, Hurtig Publishers, a McClelland and Stewart Company.

"The Manitoba Land Question, 1870-1882" by D.N. Sprague is from the *Journal of Canadian Studies/Revue d'étude canadiennes* 15, no. 3 (Fall 1980): 74-84 and is reprinted by permission of the Journal of Canadian Studies/Revue d'étude canadiennes.

"Dispossession or Adaptation? Migration and Persistence of the Red River Metis, 1835-1890" by Gerhard Ens is from *CHA Historical Papers 1988 Communications Historiques* (Ottawa: Canadian Historical Association/Le Société Historique de Canada, 1988), pp. 120-44 and is reprinted by permission of the Canadian Historical Association/Le Société Historique de Canada and the author.

" 'Conspiracy and Treason' ": The Red River Resistance From an Expansionist Perspective" by Doug Owram is from *Prairie Forum* 3, no. 2 (1978): 157-74 and is reprinted by permission of the Canadian Plains Research Centre, University of Regina.

"From Riel to the Metis" by J.R. Miller is from *Canadian Historical Review* 69, no. 1 (March 1988): 1-20 and is reprinted by permission of the University of Toronto Press.

"Protection,Civilization, Assimilation: An Outline History of Canada's Indian Policy" by John L. Tobias is from *Western Canadian Journal of Anthropology* 6, no. 2 (1976): 13-30 and is reprinted by permission of the Western Canadian Journal of Anthropology, Department of Anthropology, University of Alberta.

"Canadianizing the West: The North-West Mounted Police as Agents of the National Policy, 1873-1905" by R.C. Macleod is from *Essays on Western History*, edited by Lewis H. Thomas (Edmonton: University of Alberta Press, 1876), pp. 101-10 and is reprinted with permission of the University of Alberta Press.

"The National Policy and the Rate of Prairie Settlement: A Review" by Kenneth H. Norrie is from the *Journal of Canadian Studies/Revue d'étude canadiennes* 14 (Fall 1979): 63-76 and is reprinted by permission of the Journal of Canadian Studies/Revue d'étude canadiennes.

"Western Canada and the Burden of National Transportation Policies" by T.D. Regehr is from *Canada and the Burden of Unity*, edited by D.J. Bercuson (Toronto: Gage, 1977), pp. 115-44 and is reprinted by permission of D.J. Bercuson and the author.

"The Schooling Experience of Ukrainians in Manitoba, 1896-1916" by Stella M. Hryniuk and Neil G. McDonald is from *Schools in the West: Essays in Canadian Educational History*, edited by Nancy Sheehan, Donald Wilson and David Jones (Calgary: Detselig Enterprises, 1986), pp. 155-73 and is reprinted by permission of Detselig Enterprises.

"Strangers and Stereotypes: The Rise of Nativism, 1880-1920" by Howard Palmer is from Howard Palmer's *Patterns of Prejudice: A History of Nativism in Alberta* (Toronto: McClelland and Stewart, 1982), pp. 17-60 is reprinted by permission of the Canadian Publishers, McClelland and Stewart and was abridged by the author for this edition.

"The Old Homestead: Romance and Reality" by Wilfrid Eggleston is from *The Settlement of the West*, edited by Howard Palmer (Calgary: Comprint, 1977), pp. 114-29 and is reprinted by permission of Mrs. Wilfrid Eggleston.

"Utopian Ideals and Community Settlements in Western Canada, 1880-1914" by A.W. Rasporich is from *The Settlement of the West*, edited by Howard Palmer (Calgary: Comprint, 1977), pp. 114-29 and is reprinted by permission of the author.

"The 'Autonomy Question' and the Creation of Alberta and Saskatchewan, 1905" by J. William Brennan is from *The New Provinces: Alberta and Saskatchewan*, edited by H. Palmer and D.B. Smith, B.C. Geographical Series (Vancouver: Tantalus Research Limited, 1980), pp. 43-63 and is reprinted by permission of the author and the B.C. Geographical Series, Geography Department, University of British Columbia.

"Pulling in Double Harness or Hauling a Double Load: Women, Work and Feminism on the Canadian Prairie" by Veronica Strong-Boag is from the *Journal of Canadian Studies/Revue d'étude canadiennes* 21, no. 3 (Fall 1986): 32-52 and is reprinted by permission of the Journal of Canadian Studies/Revue d'étude canadiennes.

"Amelia Turner and Calgary Labour Women, 1919-1935" by Patricia Roome is from *Beyond the Vote: Canadian Women and Politics*, edited by Linda Kealey and Joan Sangster (Toronto: University of Toronto Press, 1989), pp. 89-117 and is reprinted by permission of the University of Toronto Press.

"'There Is Some Power About the Land'—The Western Agrarian Press and Country Life Ideology" by David C. Jones is from the *Journal of Canadian Studies/Revue d'étude canadiennes* 17, no. 3 (Fall 1982): 96-109 and is reprinted by permission of the Journal of Canadian Studies/Revue d'étude canadiennes and the author.

"The Business of Agriculture: Prairie Farmers and the Adoption of 'Business Methods,' 1880-1950" by Ian MacPherson and John Herd Thompson is from *Canadian Papers in Business History*, Volume I, edited by Peter Baskerville (Victoria: Public History Group, University of Victoria, 1989), pp. 245-69 and is reprinted by permission of the Public History Group, University of Victoria.

"Rural Local History and the Prairie West" by Paul Voisey is from *Prairie Forum* 10, no. 2 (Autumn 1985): 327-38 and is reprinted by permission of the Canadian Plains Research Centre, University of Regina.

"Boosterism and the Development of Prairie Cities, 1871-1913" by Alan F.J. Artibise is from *Town and City: Aspects of Western Canadian Urban Development*, edited by Alan F.J. Artibise (Regina: Canadian Plains Research Centre, 1981), pp. 209-35 and is reprinted by permission of the Canadian Plains Research Centre, University of Regina.

Early Working-Class Life on the Prairies by Joe Cherwinski is from a series on Canada's Visual History, Vol. 69, and is reprinted by permission of the Canadian Museum of Civilization (formerly the National Museum of Man) and the National Film Board of Canada. The complete work includes 30 slides with commentaries.

"The Social Gospel as the Religion of the Agrarian Revolt" by Richard Allen is from *The West and the Nation: Essays in Honour of W.L. Morton*, edited by C. Berger and R. Cook (Toronto: McClelland and Stewart, 1976), pp. 174-86 is reprinted by permission of the editors and the author.

"Crypto-Liberalism" by David Laycock is Chapter 2 from *Populism and Democratic Thought in the Canadian Prairies, 1910 to 1945* (Toronto: University of Toronto Press, 1990): 23-68 and is reprinted with permission of the University of Toronto Press.

"Our World Stopped and We Got Off" by James Gray is Chapter 1 from James Gray's *The Winter Years* (Toronto: Macmillan, 1966): 8-18 and is reprinted by permission of Macmillan of Canada, a division of Canada Publishing Corporation.

"The Pattern of Prairie Politics" by Nelson Wiseman was originally from *Queen's Quarterly* 88, no. 2 (Summer 1981) and will appear in a future edition of *Party Politics in Canada*, edited by Hugh Thorburn. This revised version is printed with the permission of the author.

"Alberta Social Credit Reappraised: The Radical Character of the Early Social Credit Movement" by Alvin Finkel is from *Prairie Forum* 11, no. 1 (Spring 1986): 69-86 and is reprinted by permission of the Canadian Plains Research Centre, University of Regina.

"Political Discontent in the Prairie West: Patterns of Continuity and Change" by Roger Gibbins is from *Transactions of the Royal Society of Canada*, Series V, Vol. I (1986), pp. 19-30 and is reprinted by permission of the Royal Society of Canada.

"A Regional Economic Overview of the West Since 1945" by Kenneth H. Norrie pp. 63-78 is from *The Making of the Modern West: Western Canada Since 1945*, edited by A.W. Rasporich (Calgary: University of Calgary Press, 1984) and is reprinted by permission of the University of Calgary Press.

"Changing Images of the West" by R. Douglas Francis is from the *Journal of Canadian Studies/Revue d'étude canadiennes* 17, no. 3 (Fall 1982): 5-19 and is reprinted by permission of the Journal of Canadian Studies/Revue d'étude canadiennes.

"Fictions of the American and Canadian Wests" by Dick Harrison is from *Prairie Forum* 8, no. 1 (1983): 89-97 and is reprinted by permission of the Canadian Plains Research Centre, University of Regina and the author.

CONTENTS

PREFACE

In the second edition of *The Prairie West: Historical Readings*, as in the first edition, we provide students with a collection of articles on key topics in the history of prairie Canada. Some of the topics and many of the readings have changed in our effort to provide articles of current research and interest. As a result, we have had to eliminate, with regret, several worthwhile readings that appeared in the first edition. Still, we believe that this edition will continue to meet the needs of students in western Canadian history.

The fifteen topics are introduced by short essays, setting the topics within the context of western Canadian history and the individual articles within the framework of particular topics. A "Selected Bibliography" in each introductory essay lists other relevant books and articles on the topic. This new edition of *Prairie West* should continue to contribute to tutorial discussions and complement course lectures and, where applicable, textbooks.

We appreciate the help of several colleagues at our own and other universities in making the final selection, and acknowledge with thanks the willingness of those western Canadian historians who consented to let their writings be included in this book. A special thanks to our colleagues, Donald Smith and Gerald Friesen, for assisting with the introductions and "Selected Bibliography" sections. At the Press, Mary Mahoney-Robson has been a helpful and resourceful editor.

It is with a heavy heart that I recall the death of my co-editor, Howard Palmer, during the time of the revision of this edition. By his death, the history profession has lost a great scholar, western Canada has lost an insightful commentator and critic, the History Department at the University of Calgary has lost a willing and able colleague, and I have lost a dear friend. The dedication of this volume to him is a small token of appreciation for his great contribution to the study of Western Canadian History.

Royalties for this book are being contributed to the Howard Palmer Memorial Fund, which will provide scholarships for undergraduate students of Canadian history at the University of Calgary. Others wishing to contribute to this fund are encouraged to do so. Donations can be sent directly to the Department of History at the University of Calgary.

R. Douglas Francis
Department of History
University of Calgary

I

INTERPRETATIONS AND HISTORIOGRAPHY

Since the nineteenth century, western Canadian historians have chronicled and analyzed the patterns of life that emerged on the prairies. Early residents such as Donald Gunn, Alexander Begg, and George Bryce, recounted developments such as the fur trade, the growth of the Red River community, and the birth of Manitoba as a province. They saw western history as the struggle of human beings against nature, and as the story of the advancement of "civilization." These works were, in the words of historian Ted Regehr, "chronicles of heroic men subduing and civilizing the western wilderness." Western historical writing in the early part of the twentieth century focused on what was seen as the romantic period of western Canadian history—the opening of the west to settlement, with numerous histories of the Mounted Police, ranching, and the building of the Canadian Pacific Railway (CPR).

A more mature scholarship dates back to the interwar years, an era which saw the growth of farm protest movements. The emergence of several studies in the 1930s of the roots of farm protest and farm organizations marked the coming of age of western Canadian history. A series of cooperative studies by geographers, economists, historians, sociologists, and political scientists in the multi-volume *Canadian Frontiers of Settlement* dealt with the problems of pioneering on the prairies in a full, detailed manner. Twenty years later, in the 1950s, came the Social Credit in Alberta series—ten volumes on the immediate background and rise of Social Credit in early twentieth century western Canada.

Until the 1960s, the Red River Resistance of 1869/70, the North West Rebellion of 1885, the railways, the North-West Mounted Police, pioneering, the wheat economy and political protest constituted western Canadian historians' dominant concerns. The last twenty years have witnessed an expansion of research not only on these topics, but also on many long neglected aspects of western Canadian history. The earlier economic and institutional histories of the fur trade were given a new social dimension. Heightened interest in the history of agriculture, labour, immigration, women, native people, social reform, and the cities have resulted as well in new publications. Gerald Friesen presents an overview of this research in "Historical Writing on the Prairie West." This article presents a synthesis of many of the main interpretive ideas which provide the framework for his survey, *The Canadian Prairies: A History* (1984).

One of the most prolific and skilled interpreters of the prairie region, W.L. Morton, published his first major work on western history, *The Progressive Party in Canada* in 1950. He followed this with a series of articles and books which dealt with many different aspects of prairie history. In "A Century of Plain and Parkland," originally published in 1967, Morton surveyed the main themes and unique features in prairie history. Morton stressed the importance of a stable economy, the plural nature of western society, the adaptation of institutions and social aspirations to the limits of a new environment, and the distinctive character of prairie political life. Friesen and Morton both delineated the major time periods in the development of western history.

In his writing, Morton tried to balance two competing theories of western historical development—frontierism and metropolitanism. The frontier thesis stresses environmental and local (frontier) influences in the development of a new society, while metropolitanism stresses the impact of outside traditions and influences on that development. Morton attempted to synthesize some of the major characteristics of prairie society, but there are many other perspectives on what constitutes the distinctive characteristics of prairie society. There are also many different perspectives on whether frontier or metropolitan influences have been more important in shaping the nature of prairie society.

SELECTED BIBLIOGRAPHY

For an overview of historical writing on the fur trade era, see L.G. Thomas, "The Historiography of the Fur Trade Era," in Richard Allen, ed., *A Region of the Mind* (Regina, 1973), pp. 73-86; for an assessment of historical research on the period from 1870 to the early 1970s, see T.D. Regehr, "Historiography of the Canadian Plains after 1870," in R. Allen, ed., *A Region of the Mind,* pp. 87-101. L.G. Thomas has also written a thoughtful essay on "The Writing of History in Western Canada," in D.J. Bercuson and Philip Buckner, eds., *Eastern and Western Perspectives* (Toronto, 1981), pp. 69-84. W.L. Morton's major articles have been collected in A.B. McKillop, ed., *Contexts of Canada's Past: Selected Essays of W.L. Morton* (Toronto, 1980). For an analysis of Morton's writings, see the essay by Carl

Berger, "William Morton: The Delicate Balance of Region and Nation," in Carl Berger and Ramsay Cook, eds., *The West and the Nation* (Toronto, 1976), pp. 9-32.

Books and articles which deal with the frontier thesis and metropolitanism include: J.M.S. Careless, "Frontierism, Metropolitanism and Canadian History," *Canadian Historical Review* 35 (March, 1954): 1-21; S.D. Clark, *The Developing Canadian Community*, 2nd ed. (Toronto, 1968); R. Cook, *The Maple Leaf Forever* (Toronto, 1971); W.L. Morton, "The Bias of Prairie Politics," *Transactions,* Royal Society of Canada, Vol. 49, Ser. III, Sec. 2 (June, 1955): 57-66; also in Donald Swainson, *Historical Essays on the Prairie Provinces* (Toronto, 1970), pp. 289-300; and G.F.G. Stanley, "The Western Canadian Mystique," in David P. Gagan, ed., *Prairie Perspectives* (Toronto, 1970), pp. 6-29.

There are good provincial histories of the prairie provinces. On Manitoba, see W.L. Morton, *Manitoba: A History* (Toronto, 1957; 2nd ed., 1967); on Saskatchewan, see John Archer, *Saskatchewan: A History* (Saskatoon, 1980); on Alberta, see Howard and Tamara Palmer, *Alberta: A New History* (Edmonton, 1990), as well as James G. MacGregor, *A History of Alberta,* rev. ed. (Edmonton, 1981).

The following periodicals regularly contain articles dealing with the history of the prairie provinces:

Alberta: Studies in the Arts and Sciences, 1988-1992
Alberta Geographer, 1964-
Alberta Historical Review, 1953-1975 (Renamed *Alberta History* in 1975.)
The Beaver, 1920-
Canadian Ethnic Studies, 1968-
Canadian Historical Review, 1920-
Canadian Historical Association Report/Historical Papers, 1920-
Manitoba History, 1980-
Prairie Forum, 1976-
Saskatchewan History, 1948-
Transactions of the Historical and Scientific Society of Manitoba, Third Series, 1944-1979
Western Canadian Journal of Anthropology, 1969-

Several different bibliographies and bibliographical guides have been published which the student of western Canadian history will find indispensable. One pioneering attempt is the bibliography by Bruce Peel, *A Bibliography of the Prairie Provinces to 1953* (Toronto, 1956); *Supplement,* (Toronto, 1963). For a more up-to-date guide see Alan Artibise, *Western Canada Since 1970: A Select Bibliography* (Vancouver, 1978). For a guide to both research material and writing on Manitoba history see Gerald Friesen and Barry Potyondi, *A Guide to the Study of Manitoba Local History* (Winnipeg, 1981) and annual updates in *Manitoba History*. John Archer's overview history, *Saskatchewan, A History* (Saskatoon, 1980) contains an excellent bibliographic essay on Saskatchewan history. On Alberta history, see the bibliographies by Pat Roome and Leslie Robinson, "Alberta," *Communique* 4 (Autumn, 1980); and Gloria Strathern, *Alberta 1954–1979, A Provincial Bibliography* (Edmonton, 1982).

GERALD FRIESEN

1 Historical Writing on the Prairie West

The prairie west has long been a favourite subject of Canadian historians. Substantial volumes on the region's history appeared as early as the 1880s and 1890s and many more were added in the first half of this century. Despite the long list of historical works published before 1960, the flood of publications after that date is still remarkable. A recent western Canadian bibliography listed four thousand items, of which at least two-thirds bore imprints from the 1970s and the pace has quickened since its appearance. Community-sponsored local histories alone sustained a small industry in the 1970s. Government-funded research projects, such as those of Parks Canada and the provincial departments of culture, have added new sources of funding for prairie historical study. If historical writing is a measure of cultural maturity, the region has been blessed in the decades after 1960.

Early prairie scholars were especially interested in the fur trade. They favoured the French or the North-West Company or the Hudson's Bay Company, depending upon their predilections and their patron—for the HBC itself sponsored one publishing venture, the Hudson's Bay Record Society—and they viewed the West as a distinct theatre of British imperial history. The great achievement of this research was Arthur Silver Morton's *A History of the Canadian West to 1870-71*.[1] Next in importance as a field of study was the era of transition to Canadian rule, including the Mounted Police, the railway and the disturbances associated with Louis Riel. The era of agricultural settlement received special attention because of the Canadian Frontiers of Settlement series, a multi-volume project undertaken by the American Geographical Society and the Social Science Research Council in the 1930s. And the political behaviour of Albertans, in particular, became the object of a similarly ambitious research project in the 1940s, the Social Credit in Alberta series directed by S.D. Clark. The eight volumes of the Frontier group and the ten volumes related to Social Credit represented a very large proportion of prairie scholarship on twentieth-century topics. Thus, the selection of these subjects for special attention by funding agencies determined, to a large degree, the shape of pre-1960 prairie scholarship.[2]

The historical discipline changed considerably after 1960. New approaches, especially the widespread interest in social history as opposed to political and economic analysis, happened to become popular just as Canadian universities were growing rapidly and training increasing numbers of history specialists. And, after a generation when national topics were the chief concern of Canadian historians, regional, class and ethnic subjects were coming into vogue. The result was a dramatically-revised version of western Canadian history.

Native history or ethnohistory, ignored to a large degree by such scholars as A.S. Morton, achieved prominence in the 1970s. The landmark work on the western interior was A.J. Ray's *Indians in the Fur Trade*[3] but this one volume was complemented by Ray and Donald Freeman's *Give Us Good Measure*,[4] Abe Rotstein's dissertation on the relationship between native trade and diplomatic alliances,[5] Charles Bishop's study of the northern Ojibway,[6] the re-issue of David Mandelbaum's *Plains Cree*,[7] and John Milloy's *The Plains Cree: Trade, Diplomacy and War, 1790 to 1870*.[8] These authors had in common a determination to examine pre-treaty, pre-Reserve native history from the native perspective and thus to examine an entire and distinctive society. They demonstrated that there was considerable native cultural and economic autonomy in the first years of contact with whites. They showed, too, that the Indians of the western interior, unlike some of their eastern counterparts, were partners of the Europeans in the fur trade for several centuries. Indians adapted slowly to the introduction of European trade goods, in this view, and retained considerable independence for at least a century and a half after serious trading began in the 1680s. By examining native population movements before and after white contact, these recent historical works demonstrated how the European trade could be integrated into native culture without drastic dislocation and, indeed, that particular native alliances were able to control the direction and pace of the trade.[9]

Contemporaneous with their revisions of native history, scholars also established new approaches to fur trade company studies. Where A.S. Morton and E.E. Rich were concerned with company organization, market share, geographical determinants and the effect of reliance upon staple exploitation, recent works by Van Kirk, Brown, Foster and Payne concentrated upon the traders in the field.[10] A most important change in perspective resulted: the fur posts were no longer regarded merely as isolated extensions of Britain in Canada; rather, these scholars were suggesting that the native-white relationships constituted a distinctive society in the western interior—a "fur trade society"—which encompassed traders, laborers, hunters, women and children. This society had several variants—Hudson's Bay Company and North West Company and French models—with different patterns of upward mobility in the fur trade hierarchy, different relationships with aboriginal people, particularly with aboriginal women, and different family structures and child-raising customs. The history of this society acquired its own chronology, too, based upon the eras when native women were favoured as wives (before 1780), when metis women were preferred (1780-1830) and, finally, when a few influential white women were introduced (1820-1850). What was striking about this chronology or periodisation was that it parallelled changes in the position of natives and whites in the trade, where three eras also had been delineated: first, when Indian customs dominated trade practice (before 1770); second, when trade reflected a combination of European and native customs (1770-1820); and, third, when European direction became overwhelming (post 1821).

Little attention has been paid to the question of when this fur trade society gave way to the agricultural society that has dominated the southern prairies ever since. The delineation of a brief era of transition, seen most clearly in Professor W.L. Morton's work, suggested that the transition from old order to new occurred between 1857 and 1870.[11] Recent interpretations blurred this picture, it would seem, and yet promised a new and fascinating consensus. Sylvia Van Kirk, for example, suggested that the European wives who arrived in the western interior in the 1830s and 1840s had a significant impact upon fur trade society because they relegated native and metis women to a distinctly inferior position. Similarly, Frits Pannekoek emphasized the arrival in the same era of European clergy, Protestant and Catholic, but especially those from the Church Missionary Society, and argued that they created instability in Red River that could lead only to social disintegration.[12] Irene Spry and Carol Judd preferred to concentrate upon economic opportunity and upward mobility in their treatment of the events that brought about the transformation of prairie society.[13] Doug Owram discussed the conscious campaign of a handful of Ontario expansionists to change the image of the west from wilderness to promised land in the 1856-60 era.[14] These interpretations had in common an emphasis upon the changing cultural perspective of Europeans, Canadians, and those of mixed cultural origin. They implied that, among Europeans whose perspectives were shaped by nineteenth century industrial capitalism, coexistence with aboriginal society in an unchanging fur economy was no longer acceptable. Thus, like the studies of eastern Canadian workers, these historical works pre-figured a new consensus in Canadian history. Based upon developments in the social history of England and Europe, in which the Industrial Revolution assumed a centrality once reserved for the Renaissance and the rise of the nation state, this consensus divided the history of the nation, and of the western interior, at some point near the middle of the nineteenth century when the industrial capitalist way of life became the dominant social force in Canada.[15]

The transition which began in the decades around the middle of the nineteenth century proceeded with amazing rapidity. For Indians, the story included treaty-making,[16] economic crises, and official interventions by government and church and police to hasten their cultural adaptation.[17] The aboriginal response to these developments is only slowly emerging from the documentary record but it seems to have been remarkably patient, given the insensitive (though often well-intentioned) treatment that Indians received at the hands of European Canadians.[18] Recent analysis of Metis society has also resulted in important new interpretations. The conventional wisdom of past generations, created by Marcel Giraud and George Stanley, emphasized French-English differences in the mixed-blood population and argued that the French Metis, in particular, who were said to be closer to their native cultural roots, found it difficult to make the shift from fur trade to agriculture and experienced serious conflicts with the incoming civilization.[19] W.L. Morton emphasized the Canadian context of the Red River resistance of 1869, suggesting that the French Metis were merely resisting Ontario English-speaking newcomers; that is, though Morton rejected the thesis of a clash between frontier and civilization, he did not revise the broader picture of French-English differences among the Metis.[20]

Writing on the Metis has flourished in the past decade and historical debates have been intense. The key areas of debate have been the circumstances in Manitoba after 1870 and the origins of the Northwest uprising of 1885. It is clear that the old Red River settlement adjusted with difficulty to the new order, that violence was common, and that many people of mixed race migrated westward during the 1870s. Whether this was a result of economic opportunities on the western plains, of "government lawlessness," or of Ontarian bigotry has not been resolved.[21] One consequence was a period of instability in Manitoba which was reflected in local politics and society. However, the French and English-speaking Metis of Manitoba's "old order" made common cause in defence of their interests until the collapse of their political coalition in 1879.[22]

Debates about the 1885 uprising have been similarly fruitful. They have been enriched by a five-volume edition of Louis Riel's collected writings, a publishing and editing feat that alters our view of Riel's thought in the 1880s and raises new questions about his activity in the Northwest in 1884-85.[23] Where earlier discussions of the uprising juxtaposed Riel's alleged "madness" and Territorial political and economic grievances, Thomas Flanagan treated Riel as a prophet and the rebellion as a millenarian movement. This view does seem to be supported by the newly-published Riel writings. But as his research proceeded, Flanagan adopted a harsher judgment of Riel. He concluded that mental instability was no defence for the actions of Riel or his followers.[24] Moreover, he argued that the Canadian government was in the process of resolving the land disputes that lay behind unrest in the Northwest just when the rebellion broke out. This has provoked several critical responses.[25]

The imposition of a Canadian institutional and economic structure upon the western interior was controlled largely by the federal government and, as historians have recognized for many years, its central features were the treaties, the Mounted Police and the Pacific railway.[26] The customary interpretations of the National Policy described it as a positive element in western development.[27] The first challenge to this view was presented by V.C. Fowke, who characterized these policies and the protective tariff which accompanied them as an instrument created by eastern Canadian imperialists to exploit a western hinterland.[28] John Dales raised further discussion by suggesting that the three pillars of the National Policy, taken together, constituted neither an integrated nor a positive contribution to Canadian economic development.[29] But the vexing question as to why, with an institutional structure in place, the West failed to experience a sustained boom in the last quarter of the nineteenth century was not discussed except by reference to the international depression of 1873-96. Having discredited that concept of a monolithic depression, recent economic histories re-examined the timing and nature of western settlement, and after an interesting and fruitful dialogue, produced elements of a new consensus.[30] According to Kenneth Norrie, the National Policy did not significantly affect the rate and timing of western settlement; the crucial factors, instead, were the exhaustion of the preferable sub-humid lands in the United States, the development of dry farming techniques, the post-1896 rise in world wheat prices, and the movements of relative real wages in Canada, the United States and the United Kingdom.[31]

Norrie also raised the possibility that the National Policy, especially free land and railway land grants, actually induced settlement and rail construction before it was economically viable and thus resulted in the "misallocation of scarce resources" and a good deal of human misery.[32] These significant challenges to the conventional wisdom were reinforced by several empirical studies, two by Donald Loveridge on rural municipalities in Manitoba,[33] and another by Lyle Dick who studied the district near Abernethy, Assiniboia 1880-1900.[34] These works suggested there were no simple answers to the question of why individuals selected their particular plot of land, but they also argued that federal policies might well have resulted in the inefficient allocation of resources. In pursuing these questions, the authors also developed a new scholarly theme, the nature of rural society. Dick, in particular, emphasized the class basis of the new communities. He was challenged by Paul Voisey, whose study of a district in rural Alberta concentrated on the classlessness of a business-oriented frontier and the universality of a free enterprise philosophy.[35]

Debate over the rate and timing of western settlement was accompanied by an equally stimulating dispute in which economic historians questioned the regional consequences of the National Policy. The alleged "central Canadian imperialism" of Macdonald's policy was the focus of this debate. As in the discussions of the rate of settlement, the discussion began in the work of Creighton, Fowke and Dales. The traditional view of the matter, as presented in Creighton's works, was that the National Policy created the framework for an integrated, prosperous national economy. Fowke argued instead that the Ottawa government viewed the West as a resource hinterland subservient to the commercial and industrial interests of the East and, thus, that individual incomes on the prairies were lower than would have been possible under an alternative policy structure. Dales suggested simply that the National Policy was a "dismal failure" because it created an inefficient and inappropriately-sized Canadian economy. Until very recently it was customary, in prairie academic circles at least, to endorse a version of the Fowke interpretation.[36] But Kenneth Norrie challenged this convention in an important series of articles. He agreed that the issue of "regional impacts of national economic policies" was important and should be examined, but he concluded that individuals resident on the Prairies did not suffer unfair "economic and non-economic costs of adjustment solely because of their geographical location." Moreover, he argued that the absence of industrial development on the prairies, a crucial matter in today's debates about the future of Confederation, was not the result of Ottawa's tariff and rail freight rate policies. And, finally, he suggested that, though the tariff did redistribute income among regions (*to* manufacturing and *from* resource regions), it did not redistribute income among regions in an *unfair* fashion.[37] Norrie's argument rested on his definition of economic and political justice: he assumed that tariffs were in place before settlement began and thus were part of the economic calculation of the immigrant. He did not suggest that westerners were misguided in their attempts to change federal tariff policy or to alter freight rate structure. After all, prairie success in these protest campaigns would increase the relative income of prairie citizens. But, Norrie continued, these prairie people did not suffer, as was often alleged, "actual out-of-pocket transfers"; rather they failed to appropriate capital gains on a regional basis. Though he did not convince his colleagues on all points, Norrie established the terms for the debate on the National Policy. Local empirical studies may take over from macro-economic analysis in the discussion of the rate, timing and strategy of settlement, but new social science techniques such as econometric models and new approaches such as counterfactual propositions will now be the prevailing approaches to the debate over prairie economic structure. And Norrie's refreshing insistence upon the use of the concept of "comparative advantage" when dealing with the failure of the prairies to achieve significant industrial development will undoubtedly shape the thinking of his future critics.

The era of transition from a nonindustrial to an industrial capitalist society in western Canada extended from some point around the mid-nineteenth century to about the last decade of the century. By the 1890s, the native way of life had been altered irrevocably, the Metis had lost political power, and the economic structure and intellectual assumptions of a western European and, more precisely, a British-Ontario society had been set in place. The new West differed sufficiently from its parents to warrant description as a distinct region, but the elements it shared with its founding societies were profound. Of these, the most important was prairie acceptance of a local version of industrial society's class structure. Thus, Rod Macleod's study of the North West Mounted Police, Alan Artibise's work on Winnipeg and David Breen's work on ranchers,[38] to cite just three contributions to this theme, emphasized that prairie social leaders assumed they were part of the "better element" and that they must control the "lower elements" around them. From their selection of house type and creation of segregated residential districts to their foundation of historical societies, schools, private clubs, and other voluntary agencies of cultural improvement, the members of the respectable class set the proper tone for prairie life.[39] The danger they anticipated was not class war of the Marxian type but an Indian uprising or frontier violence or disrespectful—even downright disgusting—public behaviour. Thus, the recent literature demonstrated that class affiliation and class ideals were very much a part of prairie society and played an important role in the social history of the last two decades of the nineteenth century. Though the definition of these class assumptions was far from satisfactory, the presence of such class lines was no longer disputed.

The prairie world changed drastically around the turn of the twentieth century. Population numbers rose sharply, ethnic diversity became almost unmanageable—or so it seemed to many—and the conventions of the preceding generation, including worker-management relations, the place of the prairie farmer in the national economic and political order, the place of women in the home and in public life, and even the structure and role of the churches, were called into question. Recent scholarship reinforced the thesis of a sharp change in prairie society around 1900. Many of the recent studies began in the 1890s or in the first decade of the twentieth century and, by implication, suggested sharp differences between the western interior in, say, 1886, and that same territory in the decades after 1905. This was particularly true in Saskatchewan and Alberta, where the population influx simply inundated the small society of the pre-1900 era, but it was also applicable in Manitoba, where the impact of post-1898 immigrants upon Winnipeg and rural districts alike was quite extraordinary.

The important social changes were not simply the result of demographic factors. They were also evident in the rise of a myriad of social and economic reform movements which produced intense debate about the appropriate distribution of wealth and exercise of power in prairie and, indeed, Canadian society. City government reform, women's suffrage, direct legislation, prohibition, progressive education, cooperative elevators and similar issues were aspects of an attempt to make government more democratic, to make the distribution of wealth more equitable, and to ensure that the new Canada would be a more decent and humane society than other parts of the nation and the world. Recent historical writing focused upon these social and political tensions with results that were extremely interesting. They can best be discussed under five headings: first, where western political protest had once been described as agrarian, recent work emphasized the importance of the union, the construction camp and the company town; second, where prairie society had been seen as primarily agricultural, recent studies on urban centres demonstrated the importance of cities and towns in the social fabric; third, the study of rural ideas and farm protest—once included in institutional analysis of the Progressives and the cooperatives—itself moved to another level with the adoption of new political concepts to describe the tactics and goals of these organizations. Fourth, ethnic group history came of age and transformed our impressions of pioneer days. Finally, the realization that much of this story, typically written by males, created a picture of a male-oriented world, has encouraged a belated rethinking of the prairie past. The goal of this revisionism is to place women's history and men's history on the same plane.

The lives of working people and their children were distinguished by clear social divisions, by poverty and, often, by wretched working conditions. In the 1970s scholars debated the root cause of western labour radicalism, a phenomenon which they attributed to the national policy, to the stifled hopes of immigrants or to socialist agitation, but which came to be seen as a plea for western distinctiveness or western "exceptionalism." In the 1980s the writing focused rather on specific unions, communities and industries. The differences were small: the important lesson was that the experience of working men and women and of their families had become an important part of prairie history.[40] Bercuson had once argued that the western labour movement was betrayed by a handful of radicals in 1919.[41] This was not so clear after further scholarly work was completed. Avery and McCormack demonstrated the depth and extent of worker dissatisfaction; Bercuson chronicled the rise and collapse of the workers' "revolutionary" vehicle, the One Big Union.[42] Several authors suggested that the radical leadership was actually overtaken by the tide of worker unrest in 1919.[43] Rather than being able to direct the workers' energies toward an eventual revolution, these works argued, the leaders of the militants were forced to go along with the ill-prepared strikes which broke out after the declaration of the Winnipeg general strike. Left wing factionalism, arrests, government intervention, AFL re-organizing efforts, and business resistance did the rest.[44] The radical movement never came together again.

Recent work on the urban scene complemented this perspective. As Artibise demonstrated in the case of Winnipeg, businessmen dominated civic governments and determined the policies of the city councils.[45] This business influence accounted for the politicians' interest in immigration and cheap electricity and their failure to respond to the need of public housing, public health measures and social amenities for the urban labourer. And, as Bercuson suggested, the roots of the Winnipeg general strike lay not simply in the wartime and post-war situation, but in social conditions and labour-management relations that had been breeding class division for at least two decades.[46] Finally, J.E. Rea demonstrated conclusively that the Winnipeg strike simply hardened these class lines so that over the next 50 years—indeed to this day—Winnipeg political support was divided into two camps along class and neighbourhood lines.[47] Winnipeg is probably unique in the degree of political consciousness among its working class households but the story of class allegiances in other prairie cities has yet to be told.

Fewer historians have been interested in the "middle class," though several have written on middle class membership in social reform movements. Recent work on prairie cities has noted the role of the social gospel in protestant churches.[48] It also noted the emergence of a "culture of professionalism" in business and education and government.[49] Scholars contended that the religious revival and the human and social sciences produced an extraordinary range of important reform movements. Studies of lawyers and law also promised new insights. John Thompson singled out the prohibition and women's suffrage movements for special attention and, by so doing, demonstrated how important was urban British Canadian support for the achievement of their goals. Other historians discussed technical high schools and agricultural schools and the child welfare system but, in the process, made the same point that Thompson had emphasized: a city-based professional class had emerged in prairie society just as it had in the rest of North America.[50]

Studies of the professional class, political reform and radicalism may lead to a reconsideration of the Progressive revolt of 1919-25. The Progressive movement had once been seen as the culmination of grain growers' unrest in western Canada.[51] Thus, despite their obvious support in the Maritimes and Ontario and among urban reformers in the West, the Progressives were described as a regional and occupational protest movement. As a result of recent contributions, progressivism has been placed in a broader context. Forbes revised eastern Progressive history[52] and a number of scholars discovered that "populism," as defined by Lawrence Goodwyn in particular, provided an interesting context for political reform movements on the prairies.[53] Rather than confine their discussions to group government and cooperatives, these students apparently concluded that both farm and city reform movements were built upon a widespread dissent from industrial capitalism and that both groups, like the revolutionary labourers, wanted to build an alternate society. Thus, adopting Goodwyn's definition of the American Populist movements of the 1890s, Ian MacPherson suggested that the various types of Canadian progressive envisioned "a new society based on decentralized political and economic institutions, direct democracy and a cooperative ethos."[54] In his view, the cooperatives and the United Church and the Wheat Pool and the Prohibition movements shared a critique of contemporary North America and a vision of an ideal alternative.[55] Jeffery

Taylor was much less complimentary to the agrarian reformers, arguing that their analysis was shaped by the dominant liberal capitalist ideology.[56] And David Laycock distinguished four threads in prairie populist thought in his volume, *Populism and Democratic Thought in the Canadian Prairies, 1910 to 1945.*[57]

Revision of progressive historiography led in turn to reconsideration of Social Credit and the Cooperative Commonwealth Federation. The most important contribution to this discussion was John Richards and Larry Pratt's *Prairie Capitalism*, which took up the old chestnut of prairie studies, "why did Saskatchewan go socialist and Alberta Social Credit?" Their interesting solution was to suggest that Western Canada experienced two variants, a left-wing and a right-wing of the populist strategy: the left supported farm-labour alliances against capitalists; the right preferred a regional common front of all classes; the left attacked all sectors of corporate capitalism whereas the right concentrated its attention upon banks; the left relied heavily upon cooperatives as the basis for an alternate economic system and happily advocated government regulation or ownership; the right, on the other hand, had few links to the coop movement and preferred open competition except where banks were concerned. The authors did not claim that the prairie political movements were consistently "left" or "right" but they did suggest that, by the accidents of political history, new provincial governments came from the right in Alberta and from the left in Saskatchewan.[58] Their conclusions have not been sustained by two new studies of Alberta, one on Premier Aberhart and the other on the Social Credit government which he founded. They emphasize, instead, the reformism of the early Socred years and its later transformation into a conservative political force.[59] One might add, judging from John Kendle's study of Premier John Bracken, that the Manitoba "coalition" governments from 1922 to 1958 were more determined to avoid ideological discussions than were their counterparts in Alberta and Saskatchewan. Bracken established a pragmatic government with no ideological commitment beyond the maintenance of the status quo at minimal cost to the taxpayer.[60] These recent works suggested that a reexamination of prairie Progressivism was under way and that the study of reform politics in the 1920s and 1930s, particularly the striking differences in the three provincial political systems, would soon appear in a new light.[61]

An examination of trends in prairie historiography in the early twentieth century within the categories of labour, urban society and populism, neglects a fourth vital strand of historical writing, that dealing with ethnic groups. As in native history, so in ethnic history, scholars provided two different perspectives upon their subject: some were most concerned to address the evolution of the ethnic group itself;[62] others preferred to examine the reaction of Canadian society to the presence of these newcomers.[63] These works suggested a different rhythm and a different periodisation for every ethnic community and every wave of immigration. They suggested, too, that the transition from parent to prairie society must be the first theme in the story.[64] The second theme, undoubtedly, was the process of adaptation.[65]

The other perspective upon ethnic history, that from the host Canadian society, became clearer with every passing year. Not only did individual ethnic histories touch upon relations with the larger society, but a number of general works dealt precisely with attitudes to ethnic minorities. As the writings of J.S. Woodsworth revealed long ago, there was a continuum from the welcome extended to Scandinavians, at one extreme, to the hostility expressed towards Orientals, at the other.[66] The study was more descriptive of the host than of the newcomer, to be sure, but it did suggest the context within which the immigrant encountered Canadian society.

No such neat observations can be made about the history of women or of relations between the sexes in prairie society. These matters have been given very little attention by students of the region. Moreover, as the implications of male historians' cultural blindness are articulated, scholars increasingly recognize that a dramatic revision of our picture of the past must now be undertaken. One illustration must suffice. Historians have long believed that the women's rights campaign faltered and failed in the 1920s after it had secured women the right to vote. Their explanations were diverse: the movement's goals had been achieved; women did not value or deserve the franchise; middle class feminists betrayed their working-class colleagues; the more radical women moved into new areas of political action where class, not gender, was the issue. Each of these explanations smack of male political biases, according to Veronica Strong-Boag. She argues, instead, that women continued to seek reform but that their revitalized campaign was "the feminism of the workplace, of day-to-day life." Because they carried a double load, an inequitable load, "they could not enlarge their contribution to society." Nevertheless, their recognition of their oppression contributed to the survival of their feminism: "It continued, as always, to be far more than a debate about a share in public spoils; its arguments went to the heart of human relationships, in the home and the family."[67] The rewriting of prairie history to acknowledge the force of this perspective in every era and every culture will require the labour of a generation.[68]

Just as the nature of prairie society changed in the mid-nineteenth century and again at the end of the century, so it altered during the course of the twentieth century. In his discussion of recent events in the western interior, W.L. Morton distinguished the era after 1947 from the one before, thinking perhaps of the oil bonanza in Alberta;[69] John Thompson noted that, in 1941, for the first time, half of prairie farms had tractors;[70] J.H. Archer emphasized the fact that Saskatchewan elected a CCF government in 1944;[71] Morris Zaslow emphasized the impact of the Second World War;[72] others noted that rural-to-urban migration became a significant social phenomenon in the 1940s.[73] Each of these indices, in brief, suggested that the 1940s could be the point of demarcation between the third and fourth eras of prairie history.

Not surprisingly, the historiography of the modern era was sparse. Oil inspired a number of volumes but, aside from the very important Richards-Pratt study of Alberta and Saskatchewan resource politics, was not the subject of significant business histories. The modern grain trade was, remarkably, almost untouched by scholarship; students of these two topics turned to journalism to learn a little more about the operation of these important industries.[74] There were a few scholarly works on agriculture, petroleum and coops but, given the role of such institutions in the prairie west, this was a remarkably brief list.[75] Social studies were more numerous, especially those dealing with ethnic groups, but their conclusions did not readily fit into a synthesis upon ethnicity in the west.[76] Native issues were attracting much more attention and the number of useful volumes increased rapidly in the 1980s.[77] Literary criticism prospered but the relationship between literature and history was not clear-cut; indeed, some scholars contended that fiction created the environment and, thus, that historical events were of little importance in shaping prairie literature.[78] Cultural history, fuelled by the galleries as well as by the changing perspectives of international scholarship, made its appearance.[79] But the gaps in the scholarly literature, as is apparent, were considerable.

Western political behaviour and the issue of "western alienation" did receive a great deal of scholarly attention. One of the broadest of the recent political studies was Roger Gibbins's *Prairie Politics and Society: Regionalism in Decline*.[80] Gibbins contended that the prairies had ceased to be a political region and, instead, like central Canada, consisted of several provincial empires fighting for advantage in a federal state. His conclusion was useful because it impressed upon the reader that regions were not static places with fixed boundaries. Rather, they were communities which coalesced and disappeared with changes in the political, economic and intellectual environment.[81] And, as the writing of provincial histories suggested, provincial identities were replacing regional loyalties in the post-1940 prairie west.

Recent historical writing has produced significant new perspectives upon the prairie west. Not that it is "better" than the scholarship of the preceding generations, for it is not; contemporary historians will have difficulty matching the great accomplishments of A.S. Morton and V.C. Fowke, to cite just two of many examples. But every generation writes its own history and, in doing so, responds to the changing interests and values of its age.[82] In recent work, prairie scholars were more concerned than their predecessors with social and cultural themes. As a consequence, "ordinary people" and literary and artistic production appeared more often in their work. If the frontier myth of social equality was sometimes applied to the prairie west in earlier decades, the concepts of social hierarchy and social class were more influential in recent scholarship. Aboriginal subjects and concerns were, for the first time, receiving a great deal of attention. The integration of the history of women into the story of the prairies remained a significant challenge. The idea of a prairie region, once a static and environmentally-determined approach, was now a flexible descriptive device. Above all, the history of the prairie west was the subject of vigorous debate in these decades, as it had been for almost a century.

NOTES
1. Arthur Silver Morton, *A History of the Canadian West to 1870-71*, Lewis G. Thomas, ed., second edition (Toronto, 1973). First published 1939.
2. Surveys of this writing are L.G. Thomas, "Historiography of the Fur Trade Era," and T.D. Regehr, "Historiography of the Canadian Plains after 1870," in Richard Allen, ed., *A Region of the Mind* (Regina, 1973); essays by two important historians are collected in A.B. McKillop, ed., *Contexts of Canada's Past: Selected Essays of W.L. Morton* (Toronto, 1980) and Patrick A. Dunae, ed., *Ranchers' Legacy: Alberta Essays by Lewis G. Thomas* (Edmonton, 1986); interviews with Morton and Thomas appear in *Heritage of the Great Plains* 22, no. 4 (1989) and 23, no. 1 (1990), Emporia State University, Kansas.
3. Arthur J. Ray, *Indians in the Fur Trade: Their role as hunters, trappers and middlemen in the lands southwest of Hudson Bay* (Toronto, 1974).
4. Arthur J. Ray and Donald Freeman, *"Give Us Good Measure": An Economic analysis of relations between the Indians and the Hudson's Bay Company before 1763* (Toronto, 1978).
5. A. Rotstein, "Fur Trade and Empire: An Institutional Analysis," Ph.D. dissertation, University of Toronto, 1967.
6. Charles A. Bishop, *The Northern Ojibwa and the Fur Trade: An Historical and Ecological Study* (Toronto, 1974).
7. David G. Mandelbaum, *The Plains Cree: An Ethnographic, Historical Comparative Study* (Regina, 1979; first published in 1940).
8. John S. Milloy, *The Plains Cree: Trade, Diplomacy and War, 1790 to 1870* (Winnipeg, 1988).
9. A useful survey of this literature is Jacqueline Peterson and John Anfinson, "The Indian and the Fur Trade: A Review of Recent Literature" *Manitoba History* 10 (Autumn 1985): 10-18 (Chapter 5 in this volume). Other useful works include Daniel Francis and Toby Morantz, *Partners in Furs: A History of the Fur Trade in Eastern James Bay 1600 - 1870* (Kingston, 1983), Jennifer S.H. Brown and Robert Brightman, eds., *"The Orders of the Dreamed": George Nelson on Cree and Northern Ojibwa Religion and Myth, 1823* (Winnipeg 1988), and Paul C. Thistle, *Indian-European Trade Relations in the Lower Saskatchewan River Region to 1840* (Winnipeg, 1986). The most recent synthesis in this field is J.R. Miller, *Skyscrapers Hide the Heavens: A History of Indian-White Relations in Canada* (Toronto, 1989).
10. John Foster has written useful introductions to these themes in his essays for the slide sets in "Canada's Visual History / L'Histoire du Canada en Images." The main works include Sylvia Van Kirk, *"Many Tender Ties": Women in Fur-Trade Society in Western Canada, 1670-1870* (Winnipeg, 1980); Jennifer S.H. Brown, *Strangers in Blood: Fur Trade Families in Indian Country* (Vancouver, 1980); J.E. Foster, "The Origins of the Mixed Bloods in the Canadian West"

in L.H. Thomas, ed., *Essays on Western History* (Edmonton, 1976); Michael Payne, *The Most Respectable Place in the Territory: Everyday Life in Hudson's Bay Company Service, York Factory, 1788 to 1870* (Ottawa, 1989); James Parker, *Emporium of the North: Fort Chipewyan and the Fur Trade to 1835* (Regina, 1987); J.M. Bumsted, ed., *The Collected Writings of Lord Selkirk I, 1799-1809* and *II, 1810-1820* (Winnipeg, 1984 and 1987).

11. W.L. Morton, *Manitoba: A History* (Toronto, 1957).

12. Frits Pannekoek, "The Anglican Church and the Disintegration of Red River Society, 1818-1870" in Carl Berger and Ramsay Cook, eds., *The West and the Nation: Essays in Honour of W.L. Morton* (Toronto, 1976); also relevant is Barry Cooper, *Alexander Kennedy Isbister: A Respectable Critic of the Honourable Company* (Ottawa, 1988).

13. Carol Judd, "Native labour and social stratification in the Hudson's Bay Company's Northern Department, 1770-1870," *Canadian Review of Sociology and Anthropology* 17, no. 4 (1980): 305-14; and "'Mixt Bands of Many Nations': 1821-1870" in Carol M. Judd and Arthur J. Ray, eds., *Old Trails and New Directions: Papers of the Third North American Fur Trade Conference* (Toronto, 1980), 127-46; Irene M. Spry, "The 'Private Adventurers' of Rupert's Land" in John E. Foster, ed., *The Developing West: Essays on Canadian History in Honor of Lewis H. Thomas* (Edmonton, 1983): 49-70. One volume that offers a survey of much of this literature is Jacqueline Peterson and Jennifer S.H. Brown, eds., *The New Peoples: Being and Becoming Metis in North America* (Winnipeg, 1985).

14. Doug Owram, *Promise of Eden: The Canadian Expansionist Movement and the Idea of the West* (Toronto, 1980).

15. The best representative of this new perspective in social history is Gerhard J. Ens, "Kinship, Ethnicity, Class and the Red River Metis: The Parishes of St. Francois Xavier and St. Andrew's," Ph.D. dissertation, University of Alberta, 1989.

16. Jean Friesen, "Magnificent Gifts: The Treaties of Canada with the Indians of the Northwest, 1869-1876," *Transactions of the Royal Society of Canada*, series 5, volume 1 (1986): 41-51; Richard Price, ed., *The Spirit of the Alberta Indian Treaties* (Edmonton, 1979; 1987); John Leonard Taylor, "The Development of an Indian Policy for the Canadian North-West 1869-79," Ph.D. dissertation, Queen's University, 1975.

17. The most extensive analysis of the theme is Sarah Carter, *Lost Harvests: Prairie Indian Reserve Farmers and Government Policy* (Montreal, 1990). Also useful are A.J. Looy, "The Indian Agent and His Role in the Administration of the North-West Superintendency 1876-1893," Ph.D. dissertation, Queen's University, 1977; and Jacqueline Gresko [Kennedy], "Qu'Appelle Industrial School: White 'Rites' for the Indians of the Old North West," MA thesis, Carleton University, 1970. A more recent period is covered in E. Brian Titley, *A Narrow Vision: Duncan Campbell Scott and the Administration of Indian Affairs in Canada* (Vancouver, 1986). Another perspective is offered by H. Samek, *The Blackfoot Confederacy 1880-1920: A Comparative Study of Canadian and U.S. Indian Policy* (Albuquerque, 1987).

18. In addition to Carter and Titley, works include John Tobias, "Canada's Subjugation of the Plains Cree, 1879-1885," *Canadian Historical Review* 64, no.

4 (1983): 519-48; Peter Douglas Elias, *The Dakota of the Canadian Northwest: Lessons for Survival* (Winnipeg, 1988); Hugh Dempsey, *Big Bear: The End of Freedom* (Vancouver, 1984); Hugh Dempsey, *Crowfoot, Chief of the Blackfeet* (Norman, 1972). The modern fur trade is discussed in Arthur J. Ray, *The Canadian Fur Trade in the Industrial Age* (Toronto, 1990). Another very useful source is Frank Tough, "Native People and the Regional Economy of Northern Manitoba: 1870-1930s," Ph.D. dissertation, York University, 1987; in the modern era, see James B. Waldram, *As Long as the Rivers Run: Hydroelectric Development and Native Communities in Western Canada* (Winnipeg, 1988).

19. Marcel Giraud, *Le Métis Canadien: Son Role dans l'Histoire des Provinces de l'Ouest* (Paris, 1945), translated by George Woodcock under the title *The Métis in the Canadian West*, 2 volumes (Edmonton, 1986); George F.G. Stanley, *The Birth of Western Canada: A History of the Riel Rebellions* (Toronto 1936; 1960); the Metis view was recorded by A.-H de Tremaudan, *L'Histoire de la Nation Metisse dans L'Ouest Canadien* (1936, 1979), which appeared in English as Elizabeth Maguet, trans., *Hold High Your Heads: History of the Metis Nation in Western Canada* (Winnipeg,1982).

20. W.L. Morton, ed., *Alexander Begg's Red River Journal* (Toronto, 1956), and W.L. Morton, ed., *Manitoba: The Birth of a Province* (Altona, 1965).

21. Gerhard Ens, "Dispossession or Adaptation? Migration and Persistence of the Red River Metis, 1835-1890," *CHA Historical Papers* (1988) (Chapter 8 in this volume); D.N. Sprague, "The Manitoba Land Question, 1870-1882," *Journal of Canadian Studies* 15, no. 4 (Fall 1980): 74-84 (Chapter 7 in this volume); and D.N. Sprague, *Canada and the Metis, 1869-1885* (Waterloo, 1988); Allen Ronaghan, "The Confrontation at Riviere aux Ilets de Bois," *Prairie Forum* 14, no. 1 (1989): 1-9; Allen Ronaghan, "James Farquharson—Agent and Agitator," *Manitoba History* 17 (Spring 1989); and Allen Ronaghan, "The Archibald Administration in Manitoba 1870-72," Ph.D. dissertation, University of Manitoba, 1987; Thomas Flanagan's *Metis Lands in Manitoba* (Calgary, 1991) supplements this material.

22. Gerhard Ens, "Metis Lands in Manitoba," *Manitoba History* 5 (1983): 2-11; Gerald Friesen, "Homeland to Hinterland: Political Transition in Manitoba, 1870 to 1879," Canadian Historical Association, *Historical Papers* (1979): 33-47.

23. G.F.G. Stanley et. al., eds., *The Collected Writings of Louis Riel/Les ecrits complets de Louis Riel*, 5 volumes (Edmonton, 1986).

24. Lewis Herbert Thomas, *The Struggle for Responsible Government in the North-West Territories 1870-1897* (Toronto 1956, 1978); Stanley *Birth of Western Canada*; Thomas Flanagan, *Louis "David" Riel: Prophet of the New World* (Toronto, 1979); Flanagan's conclusion to this book, he tells us, is his "Louis Riel: Was He Really Crazy?" in F. Laurie Barron and James B. Waldram, eds., *1885 and After: Native Society in Transition* (Regina, 1986); the rest of his argument is in Flanagan, *Riel and the Rebellion: 1885 Reconsidered* (Saskatoon, 1983) and in "Metis Land Claims at St. Laurent: Old Arguments and New Evidence," *Prairie Forum* 12, no. 2 (1987): 245-56; another view is Gilles Martel, *Le Messianisme de Louis Riel* (Waterloo, 1984).

25. The literature is reviewed in J.R. Miller, "From Riel to the Metis," *Canadian Historical Review* 69, no. 1 (March 1988) (Chapter 10 in this volume) and in J.S.H. Brown, "People of Myth, People of History: A Look at Recent Writings on the Metis," *Acadiensis* 17 (Fall 1987). A sampling of recent perspectives appears in Barron and Waldram, eds., *1885 and After*. The most recent volume is Diane Paulette Payment, *"The Free People—Otipemisiwak": Batoche, Saskatchewan 1870-1930* (Ottawa, 1990).

A general account of the uprising is Bob Beal and Rod Macleod, *Prairie Fire: The 1885 North-West Rebellion* (Edmonton, 1984). A military history is Walter Hildebrandt, *The Battle of Batoche: British Small Warfare and the Entrenched Metis* (Ottawa, 1985).

26. Donald Creighton, *Dominion of the North* (Toronto, 1944). The most recent volume on the railways is John A. Eagle, *The Canadian Pacific Railway and the Development of Western Canada, 1896-1914* (Montreal, 1989).

27. Donald Creighton, *John A. Macdonald*, II *The Old Chieftain* (Toronto, 1955).

28. Vernon C. Fowke, *The National Policy and the Wheat Economy* (Toronto, 1957).

29. John H. Dales, "Some Historical and Theoretical Comments on Canada's National Policies," *Queen's Quarterly* 71, no. 3 (Autumn, 1964): 297-316.

30. Kenneth H. Norrie, "The National Policy and the Rate of Prairie Settlement: A Review," *Journal of Canadian Studies* 14, no. 3 (Fall 1979) 63-76.

31. Ibid.

32. Ibid.

33. Donald Merwin Loveridge, "The Settlement of the Rural Municipality of Sifton 1881-1920," MA thesis, University of Manitoba, 1977; Donald M. Loveridge, "The Garden of Manitoba: The Settlement and Agricultural Development of the Rock Lake District and the Municipality of Louise, 1878-1902," Ph.D. dissertation, University of Toronto, 1986.

34. Lyle Dick, *Farmers "Making Good": The Development of Abernethy District, Saskatchewan, 1880-1920* (Ottawa, 1989); a different perspective is in David C. Jones, *Empire of Dust: Settling and Abandoning the Prairie Dry Belt* (Edmonton, 1987).

35. Paul Voisey, *Vulcan: The Making of a Prairie Community* (Toronto, 1988). A related theme is addressed by J.H. Thompson and Ian MacPherson, "The Business of Agriculture: Prairie Farmers and the Adoption of 'Business Methods,' 1890-1950," *Canadian Papers in Business History*, 1 (Public History Group, University of Victoria, 1989) (Chapter 23 in this volume); a survey of recent approaches is David C. Jones and Ian MacPherson, eds., *Building Beyond the Homestead: Rural History on the Prairies* (Calgary, 1985); *Prairie Forum* 11, no. 2 (1986) which focuses on prairie agriculture; see also Ray D. Bollman and Philip Ehrensaft, "Changing Farm Size Distribution on the Prairies Over the Past One Hundred Years," *Prairie Forum* 13, no. 1 (1988): 43-66; useful comparative perspectives are Carl E. Solberg, *The Prairies and the Pampas: Agrarian Policy in Canada and Argentina, 1880-1930* (Stanford, 1987) and Jeremy Adelman, "Frontier Development: Land, Labour and Capital on the Wheatlands of Argentina and Canada, 1890-1914," D.Phil. dissertation, Oxford University, 1989; and Wendy Owen, ed., *The Wheat King: Selected Letters and Papers of A.J. Cotton 1888-1913* (Winnipeg, 1985).

36. See the Introduction to David Jay Bercuson, ed., *Canada and the Burden of Unity* (Toronto, 1977): 1-18.

37. Kenneth H. Norrie, "The National Policy and Prairie Economic Discrimination, 1870-1930" in Donald H. Akenson, ed., *Canadian Papers in Rural History* I (Gananoque, 1978).

38. R.C. Macleod, *The NWMP and Law Enforcement* (Toronto, 1976); Alan F.J. Artibise, *Winnipeg: A social history of urban growth, 1874-1914* (Montreal, 1975); David H. Breen, *The Canadian Prairie West and the Ranching Frontier 1874-1924* (Toronto, 1983); for discussion of changing prairie trade patterns, see Andy den Otter, "Transportation, Trade and Regional Identity in the Southwestern Prairies," *Prairie Forum* 15, no. 1 (1990): 1-24 and Gerald Friesen, "Imports and Exports in the Manitoba Economy 1870-1890," *Manitoba History* 16 (Autumn 1988): 31-41.

39. There are variety of ways to examine this theme. One is through David Hall, *Clifford Sifton*, I *The Young Napoleon 1861-1900* (Vancouver, 1981) and *Clifford Sifton*, II *A Lonely Eminence 1901-1929* (Vancouver, 1984); Louis Knafla, ed., *Law and Justice in a New Land: Essays in Western Canadian Legal History* (Toronto, 1986); D.R. Babcock, *Alexander Cameron Rutherford: A Gentleman of Strathcona* (Calgary, 1989); Gerald Friesen, "The Manitoba Historical Society: A Centennial History," *Manitoba History* 4 (1982): 2-9; A.A. den Otter, *Civilizing the West: The Galts and the Development of Western Canada* (Edmonton, 1982); Morris Mott and John Allardyce, *Curling Capital: Winnipeg and the Roarin' Game 1876 to 1988* (Winnipeg, 1989); Morris Mott, "Manly Sports and Manitobans: Settlement Days to World War One," Ph.D. dissertation, Queen's University, 1980; E.A. Corbet and A.W. Rasporich, eds., *Winter Sports in the West* (Calgary, 1990).

40. Examples include the special issues of *Labour/Le Travail* on the Winnipeg General Strike, volume 13 (1984) and on Labour in Alberta, volume 16 (1985). Other articles in *Labour/Le Travail* include Robert Robson, "Strike in the Single Enterprise Community: Flin Flon, Manitoba-1934" 12 (1983); J.H. Tuck, "The United Brotherhood of Railway Employees in Western Canada, 1898-1905," 11 (1983); W.M. Baker, "The Miners and the Mediator: The 1906 Lethbridge Strike and Mackenzie King," 11 (1983); G. Makahonuk, "Class Conflict in a Prairie City: The Saskatoon Working-Class Response to Prairie Capitalism, 1906-19," 19 (1987); S. Reilly, "Robert Kell and the Art of the Winnipeg General Strike" 20 (1988); D. Schulze, "The Industrial Workers of the World and the Unemployed in Edmonton and Calgary in the Depression of 1913-15," 25 (1989). Labour history also appears in the provincial historical journals. Two pictorial surveys are Doug Smith, *Let Us Rise! An Illustrated History of the Manitoba Labour Movement* (Vancouver, 1985) and Warren Caragata, *Alberta Labour: A Heritage Untold* (Toronto, 1979).

41. David J. Bercuson, "Western Labour Radicalism and the One Big Union: Myths and Realities" in S.M. Trofimenkoff, ed., *The Twenties in Western Canada* (Ottawa, 1972): 32-49.

42. David J. Bercuson, *Fools and Wise Men: The Rise and Fall of the One Big Union* (Toronto, 1978); A. Ross McCormack, *Reformers, Rebels and Revolutionaries: The Western Canadian Radical Movement 1899-1919* (Toronto, 1977);

Donald Avery, *"Dangerous Foreigners": European Immigrant Workers and Labour Radicalism in Canada 1896-1932* (Toronto,1979).

43. Gerald Friesen, "'Yours in Revolt': The Socialist Party of Canada and the Western Canadian Labour Movement," *Labour/Le Travailleur* I (1976): 139-57.

44. David Jay Bercuson, *Fools and Wise Men* (Toronto, 1978) and David Jay Bercuson, ed., *Alberta's Coal Industry 1919* (Calgary, 1978).

45. Alan F.J. Artibise, *Winnipeg: a social history of urban growth 1874-1914* (Montreal 1975); also Alan F.J. Artibise, ed., *Town and City: Aspects of Western Canadian Urban Development* (Regina, 1981); Robert Robson; "Wilderness Suburbs: Boom and Gloom on the Prairies, 1945-1986," *Prairie Forum* 13, no. 2 (1988); several volumes in the series of illustrated histories of Canadian cities deal with prairie centres, including Winnipeg (A. Artibise), Regina (W. Brennan) and Calgary (M. Foran); also Tom Mitchell "'A Square Deal for All and No Railroading': Labour and Politics in Brandon, 1900-1920," *Prairie Forum* 15, no. 1 (1990): 45-66; Carl Betke, "The Original City of Edmonton: A Derivative Prairie Urban Community" in Artibise, ed., *Town and City,* pp. 309-45; Don Kerr and Stan Hanson, *Saskatoon: The First Half-Century* (Edmonton, 1982).

46. David Jay Bercuson, *Confrontation at Winnipeg: Labour, Industrial Relations, and the General Strike* (Montreal, 1974).

47. J.E. Rea, "The Politics of Class: Winnipeg City Council, 1919-1945" in Carl Berger and Ramsay Cook, eds., *The West and the Nation: Essays in Honour of W.L. Morton* (Toronto, 1976): 232-49.

48. Richard Allen, *The Social Passion: Religion and Social Reform in Canada 1914-28* (Toronto, 1971) and Richard Allen, ed., *The Social Gospel in Canada* (Ottawa, 1972). A broader canvas is painted by Benjamin G. Smillie, ed., *Visions of the New Jerusalem: Religious settlement on the prairies* (Edmonton, 1983).

49. David C. Jones, Nancy M. Sheehan and Robert M. Stamp, eds., *Shaping the Schools of the Canadian West* (Calgary, 1979); for an American example, see Burton J. Bledstein, *The Culture of Professionalism: The middle class and the development of higher education in America* (New York, 1976). University histories have been written for Manitoba, Winnipeg, Regina, Saskatchewan and Alberta.

50. John Herd Thompson, *The Harvests of War: The Prairie West, 1914-1918* (Toronto, 1978). A different perspective is presented in Jeffery Taylor, "Professionalism, Intellectual Practice, and the Educational State Structure in Manitoba Agriculture, 1890-1925," *Manitoba History* 18 (1989): 36-45; the Canadian Legal History Project and the Legal Research Institute at the University of Manitoba and similar groups at the University of Regina, University of Alberta and University of Calgary promised to bring police, courts and crime into the study of prairie society.

51. W.L. Morton, *The Progressive Party in Canada* (Toronto, 1950).

52. Ernest R. Forbes, *The Maritime Rights Movement, 1919-1927: A Study in Canadian Regionalism* (Montreal, 1979).

53. Lawrence Goodwyn, *The Populist Moment: A Short History of the Agrarian Revolt in America* (Oxford, 1978).

54. Ian MacPherson, "Selected Borrowings: The American Impact upon the Prairie Co-operative Movement, 1920-1939," *Canadian Review of American Studies* 10, no. 2 (Fall 1979).

55. Ian MacPherson, *Each for All: A History of the Co-operative Movement in English Canada, 1900-1945* (Toronto, 1979).

56. Jeffery Taylor, "The Language of Agrarianism in Manitoba, 1890-1925," *Labour/Le Travail* 23 (1989): 91-118 and "Dominant and Popular Ideologies in the Making of Rural Manitobans, 1890-1925," Ph.D. dissertation, University of Manitoba, 1988.

57. David Laycock, *Populism and Democratic Thought in the Canadian Prairies, 1910 to 1945* (Toronto, 1990).

58. John Richards and Larry Pratt, *Prairie Capitalism: Power and Influence in the New West* (Toronto, 1979); J. William Brennan, *"Building the Commonwealth": Essays on the Democratic Socialist Tradition in Canada* (Regina, 1985).

59. Alvin Finkel, *The Social Credit Phenomenon in Alberta* (Toronto, 1989); David R. Elliott and Iris Miller, *Bible Bill: A Biography of William Aberhart* (Edmonton, 1987).

60. John Kendle, *John Bracken: A Political Biography* (Toronto, 1979); Christopher Dunn, "The Manitoba Cabinet in the Liberal-Progressive Era, 1922-1958," *Prairie Forum* 15, no. 1 (1990): 85-102.

61. Carlo Caldarola, ed., *Society and Politics in Alberta: Research Papers* (Toronto, 1979); Evelyn Eager, *Saskatchewan Government: Politics and Pragmatism* (Saskatoon, 1980); Lewis H. Thomas, "The CCF Victory in Saskatchewan, 1944," *Saskatchewan History* 34, no. 1 (Winter 1981): 1-16; David E. Smith, *Prairie Liberalism: The Liberal Party in Saskatchewan 1905-71* (Toronto, 1975); David E. Smith, *The Regional Decline of a National Party: Liberals on the Prairies* (Toronto, 1981); Thomas Peterson, "Manitoba: Ethnic and Class Politics," in Martin Robin, ed., *Canadian Provincial Politics; The Party Systems of the Ten Provinces*, second edition (Scarborough, 1978): 61-119; J.F. Conway, "The Prairie Populist Resistance to the National Policy: Some Reconsiderations," *Journal of Canadian Studies* 14, no. 3 (Fall 1979): 77-91; Anthony Mardiros, *William Irvine: The Life of a Prairie Radical* (Toronto, 1979); Norman Ward and David E. Smith, *James G. Gardiner* (Toronto, 1989); Douglas R. Owram, ed., *The Formation of Alberta: A Documentary History* (Calgary, 1979).

62. Alan B. Anderson, "Prairie Ethnic Studies and Research: Review and Assessment," *Prairie Forum* 7, no. 2 (Fall 1982): 155-70; Howard Palmer, "Canadian Immigration and Ethnic History in the 1970s and 1980s," *Journal of Canadian Studies* 17, no. 2 (Spring 1982): 35-50. The writing of ethnic group histories was stimulated by the Multiculturalism Directorate of the Department of the Secretary of State, Canada, through the "Generations" publishing project. Its capstone volume is Jean R. Burnet with Howard Palmer, *"Coming Canadians": An Introduction to a History of Canada's Peoples* (Ottawa, 1988). Among its twenty-odd volumes, one might note Manoly R. Lupul, ed., *A Heritage in Transition: Essays in the History of Ukrainians in Canada* (Ottawa, 1982). Another valuable project was sponsored by the Mennonite community; its first two volumes are Frank Epp, *Mennonites in Canada, I 1786-1920: The History of a Separate People* (Toronto, 1974) and *II 1920-1940: A People's Struggle for Survival* (Toronto, 1982). The broadest survey is Howard and Tamara Palmer, eds., *Peoples of Alberta: Portraits of Cultural Diversity* (Saskatoon, 1985).

63. Howard Palmer, *Patterns of Prejudice: A History of Nativism in Alberta* (Toronto, 1982).

64. The most complete analysis of this theme is Royden Loewen, "Family, Church and Market: A History of a Mennonite Community Transplanted from Russia to Canada and the United States, 1850-1930," Ph.D. dissertation, University of Manitoba, 1990; Orest T. Martynowych, "The Ukrainian Bloc Settlement in East Central Alberta, 1890-1930: A History," Alberta Culture, Historic Sites Service (Edmonton,1985); Frances Ann Swyripa, "From Princess Olha to Baba: Images, Roles and Myths in the History of Ukrainian Women in Canada," Ph.D. dissertation, University of Alberta, 1988.

65. Alan B. Anderson, "Linguistic Trends Among Saskatchewan's Ethnic Groups" in Martin L. Kovacs, ed., *Ethnic Canadians: Culture and Education* (Regina, 1978); Ross McCormack, "Cloth Caps and Jobs: The Ethnicity of English Immigrants in Canada, 1900-1914" in Jorgen Dahlie and Tissa Fernando, eds., *Ethnicity, Power and Politics in Canada* (Toronto, 1981); Nelson Wiseman, "The Politics of Manitoba's Ukrainians Between the Wars," *Prairie Forum* 12, no. 1 (1987): 95-122; Tamara Palmer, "Ethnic Response to the Canadian Prairies, 1900-1950: A Literary Perspective on Perceptions of the Physical and Social Environment," *Prairie Forum* 12, no. 1 (1987): 49-74.

66. James S. Woodsworth, *Strangers Within Our Gates: or Coming Canadians* (Toronto, 1909; 1972).

67. Veronica Strong-Boag, "Pulling in Double Harness or Hauling a Double Load: Women, Work and Feminism on the Canadian Prairie," *Journal of Canadian Studies* 21, no. 3 (1986): 32-52 (Chapter 20 in this volume).

68. Mary Kinnear and Vera Fast, *Planting the Garden: An Annotated Archival Bibliography of the History of Women in Manitoba* (Winnipeg, 1987); Allison Prentice et. al., *Canadian Women: A History* (Toronto, 1988); Carol Lee Bacchi, *Liberation Deferred? The Ideas of the English Canadian Suffragists, 1877-1918* (Toronto, 1983); Eliane Silverman, *The Last Best West: Women on the Alberta Frontier, 1880-1930* (Montreal, 1984); Meg Luxton, *More than a Labour of Love: Three Generations of Women's Work in the Home* (Toronto, 1980); Veronica Strong-Boag, *The New Day Recalled: Lives of Girls and Women in English Canada, 1919-1939* (Toronto, 1988); Susan Jackel, ed., *A Flannel Shirt and Liberty: British Emigrant Gentlewomen in the Canadian West, 1880-1914* (Vancouver, 1982); Mary Kinnear, ed., *First Days, Fighting Days: Women in Manitoba History* (Regina, 1987); Mary Kinnear, *Margaret McWilliams* (forthcoming).

69. W.L. Morton, "A Century of Plain and Parkland" in Richard Allen, ed., *A Region of the Mind* (Regina, 1973) (Chapter 2 in this volume).

70. Robert E. Ankli, H. Dan Helsberg and John Herd Thompson, "The Adoption of the Gasoline Tractor in Western Canada" in Donald H. Akenson, ed., *Canadian Papers in Rural History* III (Gananoque, 1980): 9-39.

71. John Archer, *Saskatchewan: A History* (Saskatoon, 1980).

72. Morris Zaslow, *The Northward Expansion of Canada 1914-1967* (Toronto, 1988); both this and his earlier Centenary series volume, *The Opening of the Canadian North 1870-1914* (Toronto, 1971) contain much of relevance to prairie historians.

73. Marc-Adelard Tremblay and Walton J. Anderson, eds., *Rural Canada in Transition* (Ottawa, 1966); Barry Wilson, *Beyond the Harvest: Canadian Grain at the Crossroads* (Saskatoon, 1981).

74. David Breen addresses this situation in *Alberta's Petroleum Industry and the Petroleum and Natural Gas Conservation Board* (Edmonton, forthcoming); see David Breen, ed., *William Stewart Herron: Father of the Petroleum Industry in Alberta* (Calgary, 1984); and David Breen, "Anglo-American Rivalry and the Evolution of Canadian Petroleum Policy to 1930," *Canadian Historical Review* 62, no. 3 (1981): 283-305; and the chapter in Michael Bliss, *Northern Enterprise: Five Centuries of Canadian Business* (Toronto, 1987); Barry K. Wilson, *Farming the System: How Politicians and Producers Shape Canadian Agricultural Policy* (Saskatoon, 1990); G.A. Basran and D.A. Hay, eds., *The Political Economy of Agriculture in Western Canada* (Toronto, 1988); Brett Fairbairn, *Building a Dream: The Co-operative Retailing System in Western Canada, 1928-1988* (Saskatoon, 1989); Brewster Kneen, *Trading Up: How Cargill, the World's Largest Grain Company, is Changing Canadian Agriculture* (Toronto, 1990); Peter Foster, *The Blue-Eyed Sheiks: The Canadian Oil Establishment* (Toronto, 1979); J.D. House, *The Last of the Free Enterprisers: The Oilmen of Calgary* (Toronto, 1980); Dan Morgan, *Merchants of Grain* (New York, 1979; 1980).

75. C.F. Wilson, *A Century of Canadian Grain: Government Policy to 1951* (Saskatoon, 1978); Barry Wilson, *Beyond the Harvest: Canadian Grain at the Crossroads* (Saskatoon, 1981); G.E. Britnell and V.C. Fowke, *Canadian Agriculture in War and Peace 1935-1950* (Stanford, 1962); Terry Veeman and Michele Veeman, *The Future of Grain: Canada's Prospects for Grains, Oilseeds and Related Industries* (Toronto, 1984); William E. Morriss, *Chosen Instrument: A History of the Canadian Wheat Board: The McIvor Years* (Edmonton, 1987); Barry Glen Ferguson, *Athabasca Oil Sands: Northern Resource Exploration 1875-1951* (Regina, 1985).

76. Reginald W. Bibby, *Mosaic Madness: The Poverty and Potential of Life in Canada* (Toronto, 1990); Leo Driedger, "Multicultural Regionalism: Toward Understanding the Canadian West," in A.W. Rasporich, ed., *The Making of the Modern West: Western Canada Since 1945* (Calgary, 1984); J.E. Rea, "The Roots of Prairie Society" in David P. Gagan, ed., *Prairie Perspectives* (Toronto, 1970): 46-57; Jim Silver and Jeremy Hull, eds., *The Political Economy of Manitoba* (Regina, 1990).

77. Joseph Dion, *My Tribe the Crees* (Calgary, 1979); Sally M. Weaver, *Making Canadian Indian Policy: The Hidden Agenda 1968-1970* (Toronto, 1981); Frank Cassidy and Robert L. Bish, *Indian Government: Its Meaning in Practice* (Halifax, 1989); Kent McNeil, *Common Law Aboriginal Title* (Oxford, 1989); Yngve George Lithman, *The Community Apart: A Case Study of a Canadian Indian Reserve Community* (Winnipeg, 1984); B.W. Morse, ed., *Aboriginal Peoples and the Law: Indian, Metis and Inuit Rights in Canada* (Ottawa, 1985); Menno Boldt and J. Anthony Long, eds., *The Quest for Justice: Aboriginal Peoples and Aboriginal Rights* (Toronto, 1985); J. Richard Ponting and Roger Gibbins, *Out of Irrelevance: A socio-political introduction to Indian Affairs in Canada* (Toronto, 1980); Ian A.L. Getty and Antoine S. Lussier, eds., *As Long As The Sun Shines and Water Flows: A Reader in Canadian Native Studies* (Vancouver, 1983).

78. Dick Harrison, *Unnamed Country: The Struggle for a Canadian Prairie Fiction* (Edmonton, 1977); Dick Harrison, ed., *Crossing Frontiers: Papers on the Literature of the American and Canadian Wests* (Edmonton, 1979); Laurence Ricou, *Vertical Man/Horizontal World: Man and Landscape in Canadian Prairie Fiction* (Vancouver, 1973); Eli Mandel, *Another Time* (Erin, Ontario, 1977); *Alberta: Studies in the Arts and Sciences*, edited by Dick Harrison and John Foster, devotes its 1990 issues (Volume 2, numbers 1 and 2) to Popular Culture in Alberta; Gerald Friesen, "Three generations of fiction: an introduction to prairie cultural history" in David Jay Bercuson and Phillip A. Buckner, eds., *Eastern and Western Perspectives* (Toronto, 1981).

79. The publications of the Glenbow Museum, Calgary, lead the list. One example is Patricia Ainslie, *Inglis Sheldon-Williams* (Calgary, 1981). Various presses have published volumes on individual artists, including W.J. Phillips, Ivan Eyre, C.W. Jeffreys, Illingworth Kerr and Ernest Lindner. Two surveys are Christopher Varley "Winnipeg West: The Postwar Development of Art in Western Canada" in A.W. Rasporich, ed., *The Making of the Modern West: Western Canada Since 1945* (Calgary, 1984) and Ronald Rees, *Land of Earth and Sky: Landscape Painting of Western Canada* (Saskatoon, 1984); a different approach is taken by Angela Davis in a series of articles in *Manitoba History* and in "Business, Art and Labour: Brigden's and the Growth of the Graphic Arts Industry 1870-1950," Ph.D. dissertation, University of Manitoba, 1986. Original material is collected and interpreted in R. Douglas Francis, *Images of the West: Changing Perceptions of the Prairies, 1690-1960* (Saskatoon, 1989).

80. Roger Gibbins, *Prairie Politics and Society: Regionalism in Decline* (Toronto, 1980); David E. Smith, *The Regional Decline of a National Party: Liberals on the Prairies* (Toronto, 1981); Patrick Kyba, *Alvin: A Biography of the Honourable Alvin Hamilton P.C.* (Regina, 1989); Don Braid and Sydney Sharpe, *Breakup: Why the West Feels Left Out of Canada* (Toronto, 1990); Larry Pratt and Garth Stevenson, eds., *Western Separatism: The Myths, Realities and Dangers* (Edmonton, 1981); Barry Wilson, *Politics of Defeat: The Decline of the Liberal Party in Saskatchewan* (Saskatoon, 1980); Dale Eisler, *Rumours of Glory: Saskatchewan and the Thatcher Years* (Edmonton, 1987); Roger Gibbins, ed., *Meech Lake and Canada: Perspectives from the West* (Edmonton, 1988); Larry Pratt, ed., *Democracy and Socialism in Alberta: Essays in Honour of Grant Notley* (Edmonton, 1986); Nelson Wiseman, *Social Democracy in Manitoba: A History of the CCF-NDP* (Winnipeg, 1986); James A. McAllister, *The Government of Edward Schreyer: Democratic Socialism in Manitoba* (Kingston, 1984).

81. Roger Gibbins, *Regionalism: Territorial Politics in Canada and the United States* (Toronto, 1982).

82. Three surveys are Gerald Friesen, *The Canadian Prairies: A History* (Toronto, 1984); J.F. Conway, *The West: The History of a Region in Confederation* (Toronto, 1983); J. Arthur Lower, *Western Canada: An Outline History* (Vancouver, 1983). The context of heritage interpretation and material culture is presented in Alan F.J. Artibise and Jean Friesen, eds., "Heritage Conservation," a special issue of *Prairie Forum* 15, no. 2 (1990).

W.L. MORTON

2 A Century of Plain and Parkland

I

One hundred years ago the prairies, the lands rolling upward from the Red River to the foothills of the Rockies, were primitive, with little trace of human habitation. No rut scored the sod, no furrow scarred the long roll of the prairie. The 'pitching' tracks of the Indians, the cart trails of the fur freighters were scarcely to be seen. The plains were as thousands of years of geological and climatic change had made them. Men had hardly touched them, for man himself was primitive, in that he had adapted himself to nature, and not nature to himself. The grasses flowed, the prairie fires ran in the wind; the buffalo grazed like cloud shadows in the plain; the buffalo hunt raised a flurry of dust in the diamond summer light; the rivers sought the distant sea unchecked; summer made green, autumn bronze, winter white, spring gray, the august monotony of the plains, *secula seculorum*. What had been wrought, green grass on dry grass, day on night turning, lay unchanged until it became the setting for the last frontier.

Primitive the plains were in 1867, to man at least, although the processed outcome of a majestic evolutionary logic. Yet man, the Indian, the fur trader, and the first farmers had already put the plain and parkland to their uses. But their uses were archaic, adapted to nature, and not imposed upon the orchestral rhythms of plains ecology. The plains tribes of the short grass buffalo plains had created a hunting economy and a civilization based upon the plains' chief product, the sea-like, inexhaustible, ever-renewable buffalo herds. This they had done by means of the pound and the horse, come since 1740 to the Canadian plains, and the buffalo skin teepee, the easy product of the herds. Few men have ever known an ampler adaptation to what nature had prepared; few men have known, in a life of endless challenge, a greater security, a more conscious independence.

Whom Catlin, Parkman, and Kane have drawn, let no man attempt to sketch. More apt to this theme is the neo-archaic uses to which the fur trader and the settler had put the plains by 1867. To the fur trade the plains were chiefly the source of provisions, the dried meat and pemmican that were the produce of the buffalo hunt. His provision posts—also fur trading posts, for there were few absolutes in practice—lined the fringe of prairie and forest from Fort Garry by the Qu'Appelle posts and Carlton to Edmonton. In them the spoils of the buffalo hunt by the semi-Indian *métis*, the dried meat and pemmican of the summer hunts, the fresh meat of the fall hunt, were stored in warehouses and frozen in ice-cellars. In the plains provisions were the margin of safety for the posts, the boat brigades of the forest rivers, the cart brigades of the prairie trails. The slow winter collection, the long summer freighting, of furs rested firmly on the provisions afforded by the plains. The fur trade, no less than the plains tribes, depended on the stomachs of the buffalo churning grass to flesh.

So also did the Woods tribes pressing on to the plains, much as the white poplar ran its sub-surface shoots beneath the sod, to rise in green-gold bluffs across the northern plains. The parkland was a zone of conflict, swaying to and fro with the wet and dry seasons, between the grasses and the poplars, the prairie fires and the sloughs, the Plains Indians and the Woods until in the neo-archaic age the gun from the East gave the Woods tribes an advantage that carried the Crees onto the Plains and the Assiniboines to the Rockies.

Even where agriculture appeared, in the river-lots of the Red and the Assiniboine, and in the gardens of the fur posts, it never escaped from the neo-archaic to the modern. Not only was agriculture introduced to the plains by fugitive peasants from the Scots Highlands and the "freemen" from the seigneuries of Quebec; it had to adapt its slovenly methods, its traditional practices, to the short summer, variable rainfall, and the neo-archaic economy of the plains. The farmer grew what he could; he might sell, for want of transport, only to the fur trade. Potatoes and vegetables served the local market, wheat flour and butter the fur posts, mandan corn and cattle his own table. For him, too, there was no escape from the still prevailing ecology of the plains. Even his wheat was but a superior prairie grass, thriving only as it could face the swift prairie summers, and use the long hours of a burning northern sun.

The prairies until 1867 therefore remained, at most neo-archaic. They remained, for modern civilization, a virgin *tabula rasa*, a blank sheet with no writing, an unmarked parchment, unscraped, unoiled, unprepared.

Only in the community of Red River did a transition from the neo-archaic to the modern occur. Fort Garry, grown into Winnipeg, is perhaps the only organic community in the West which has a continuous and unbroken growth from the old times before 1867 to the new. Edmonton might have been such a community, but is not, because its remoteness caused a break between its neo-archaic past and its modern being. It is, like all other prairie communities, one created *de novo* from the virgin prairie.

The plains remained archaic and neo-archaic until a century ago because they were even more isolated then than the Arctic North is today. They were to be reached only by the Hudson's Bay Company's annual ship to York Factory, or the occasional canoe coming in summer from Fort William, or by the cart brigades creaking their slow way from St. Paul in summer and autumn, when the prairie grass fed the ponies. That, and the odd courier or traveller marching by toboggan or cariole to St. Paul. From the Pacific across the mountains little came, for the Pacific before the Panama Canal was an outlet rather than an inlet to the West. The prairie region was, therefore, not integrated with the continent, but rather by sea with the British Isles—a reminder the prairies were, to a degree are still, a maritime rather than a continental hinterland.

The isolation, however, was ended by 1867. Not only had Lorin Blodget with his *Climatology of North America*, and Hind and Palliser by their expeditions, ended the myth of the sub-arctic character of prairie climate; the new route to St. Paul had since 1844 been drawing the West into the pattern of continental integration. Beyond St. Paul lay the network of rivers, canals, and railways that was making North America a trading unit. The volume of the St. Paul trade, after the admission of free trade in furs throughout the southeastern prairies by the outcome of the Sayer trial in 1849, drew the West towards the American Union and the modern period. Continental integration had begun; the isolation of the prairies was ending; the coming of modern civilization, the railway, the town, agriculture and industry, was inevitable. The already apparent dwindling of the buffalo herds was only an anticipation, historically apt, biologically sad, of what was inevitable.

Such matters were not, however, only economic and ecological; they were also political. The beginning of the integration of the prairies into the continental pattern was one of the principal causes of Confederation. The jarring Canadas and the about to be depressed Maritimes could face the future neither in their existing state, nor even in a united future, unless they had a hinterland for expansion. The lands to the north afforded none; the shorelines and fisheries of the Gulf of St. Lawrence little, only the prairies offered the expansion that was necessary to union. Confederation was, therefore, in part only, but also in essential fact, a prelude and preparation for the annexation of the prairies to the Canadian version of continental integration.

Nothing seemed more easy, once Confederation had been arranged. An eagerly acquiescent Britain was only too impatient to devolve upon the new Confederation its unwanted title to the northern half of the continent, including the fertile prairies. Canada, accustomed to dealing with Britain, but not with the West, calmly prepared the transfer in London, forgetting that it had also to be accomplished on the banks of the Red and the Saskatchewan. The result was the resistance by the *Métis*, and, indeed, to some degree, by all the native people of the West, to being transferred unconsulted. The resistance, however, was headed by the *Métis*, the people who were the most distinct and the most excitable of the neo-archaic Westerners. That their missionaries feared civilization for their flock, that their leader, Louis Riel, was of almost pure French blood and educated in Quebec, meant that Western resistance found an ally in French-Canadian ultramontane nationalism. The diplomatic situation, combined with the Canadian winter and the straitness of the Winnipeg gateway to the West, gave their resistance a weight neither their own numbers, nor the importance of their cause merited. The integration of the West with Confederation had nevertheless to be made on terms with its neo-archaic past. The result was the province of Manitoba, in its political form a Canadian province but in substance a neo-archaic and organic community—crudely put, a half breed reserve. Itself a gateway between East and West, it was also a gateway between the past and future, the archaic and the modern.

As a Canadian province, however, it had itself no justification; it was a concession to the past and to French missionary interests. It was not so much to set the patterns of integration into Confederation as to have itself to conform to that pattern as it emerged. The creation of Manitoba served its purposes; it opened the gateway to the West and preserved the West for "the purposes of the Dominion." The political preparations had been made for the replacement of the neo-archaic by the modern.

II

Modern civilization came to the plains and parkland in the 1870s, but in a specific form, that of Ontario settlement. The next generation was to be dominated by the introduction of the institutions and mores of Ontario into the prairies. A solid body of agricultural practice, a sharp commercial sense, a rigidly utilitarian approach to life, excessive caution, and a dour self-depreciation—these were new things on the prairies and they were to be the spirit in which the prairies were civilized.

It was true that Ontario was not to have it all its own way in the next decade, nor, indeed, did it desire to do so. There was still the ethnic duality of Manitoba until 1890, and something of the same was to survive in the Territories and the later provinces. The new settlers brought with them a core of idealism, based on their religious faiths and their agrarian experience, which looked to found a new and juster society for plain people. This idealism was the core of organizations such as the Farmers' Union, the Patrons of Industry, and of men like the Ontario-born E.A. Partridge and J.S. Woodsworth. They were not to find their reward in the immediate future, but were to mark the farther future when allies arrived. In the short run, as marked in the passage of the Manitoba School Act, the Ontario immigrants were to impose the harsher side of their character on the civilizing of the plains.

Their influences, democratic, rational, and utilitarian, were vastly rein-forced by the coming of the railway. Not only did the St. Paul and Manitoba end the long isolation of the West by the southern plains route in 1878, and the Canadian Pacific by the Lakes route in 1882; the railway, by crossing the plains from Winnipeg to the Rockies, both ended the neo-archaic cart and boat brigades by the northern route and also made the plains one as they had not been before.

The old union of provisions plains and fur forest continued, of course, but ceased to be the dominant pattern of the West. The West was both integrated into and subdued to the continental structure of the new Canada. Ontario had largely provided the drive and credit for the creation of Con-federation, even if the construction of the railway had fallen to Montrealers like Stephen and Smith; so now Ontario people themselves were settling the prairies and giving them Ontario institutions, making them the extension of Ontario just as the northern tier of states was an expansion of New England.

The process was, of course, a complex one. It was not a matter of rail-way construction and the spread of settlement. Just as in Manitoba the neo-archaic, allied with the political weight of Quebec, had left its traces in the Manitoba Act, so the advance across the prairies had to encounter and deal with the relics of the neo-archaic. With the Indians, the treaty regime won a success from the Lake of the Woods to the Rockies that was a tribute, scarcely to be adequately valued, to the diplomacy of the Canadian govern-ment, and to the influence of the Hudson's Bay Company, of the mission-aries and of the long traditions of Indian friendship with the Crown. But in those arch-representatives of the neo-archaic, the *Métis*, the policy of pacification and compensation met disaster. The compromise of the Manitoba Act, with the acceptance of French institutions and the French language, and the land grants to the *Métis*, had failed to settle those semi-nomadic people. Many had trekked to the Saskatchewan. In this respect, as in that of French institutions, the Manitoba Act had failed before 1890, so that it is little wonder that the Ontario settlers came to regard it as devoid of practical meaning.

That failure is, perhaps, the explanation, although not a justification, of the Saskatchewan Rebellion. The successful resistance of 1870, and its compromise of the fears of the old order and the needs of the new, had not stilled those fears. The coming of the railway and the failure of the buffalo herds, each a tremendous portent in the life of the plains, could only inflame the dark broodings of the hunter and the tripman whose traditional way of life was crumbling. Something of this kind explains the Rebellion, a purely neo-archaic rising, not at first united, as that of 1869 was, with French nationalism, but which was united with that ferment later only by the acci-dents of Quebec and Ontario politics.

Because the rising of the Saskatchewan *Métis* and the Plains Crees was incomplete, it was easily crushed. The hanging of Riel was a symbol only of the end of the neo-archaic on the prairies; the Rebellion at bottom had nothing to do, as the Red River resistance had, with the relations of the English and French in Canada, although it had much to do with the subsequent, and novel separation of the Indian and the *Métis* from the main stream of Canadian life.

The result of the Rebellion, then, was both the completion of the Canadian Pacific Railway, and the further political integration of the prairies into Confederation, with the grant of representation to the Territories in Parliament.

As in politics the prairies were also being integrated into Canadian agriculture, but by adaption rather than by extension of known practices. In Manitoba, the Ontario and the French farmers had brought modern methods for the day. Apart from difficulties in obtaining mould-boards that would scour in the prairie gumbo, in finding wood and fuel for fences, and in procuring water on the plains, there were few adaptations to be made. American prairie experience, in fact, furnished the remedies for most difficulties in the chilled steel mould-board, barbwire, and the windmill.

As the farmers moved westward with the railway to the second prairie steppe, however, the some time hazards of old Manitoba, frost and drought, became more marked. The farmers were forced to turn, particularly in the dry years of the middle eighties, to agricultural science and to novel adaptations. Dryland farming made its beginning with the use of summer fallow, the short season crop with the introduction of Red Fife. Agricultural science appeared in the West with the founding of the Brandon Experimental Station in 1886. The advance onto the plains, led by the spearhead of the Canadian Pacific Railway, had begun on the broad front of settlement, to Indian Head, to Regina, until the dusty core of Palliser's Triangle was reached, and the farming front advancing from the east was stopped by the ranching front advancing from the south. The farmer and the cowman were to be neighbours until the next generation.

The Ontario immigration, however, failed to fill the prairies at the pace the development of national policy required. Expansive as Ontario had been, great as was its head of popular steam, the opening of the West, the demands of new industries, and the drain of population to the United States, reduced the pressure and drew off its surplus farmers' sons. In addition the prolonged depression from 1882 to 1896 shrank the whole economy and froze people in their places, however unattractive. Security, however bleak, was preferred to adventure certain to be unrewarding. Ontario, even with the help of the Maritimes and Quebec, the Icelanders and the Mennonites, had failed to settle the prairies. From its beach-head in Manitoba, it had occupied, it had not peopled them.

It had, however, given them its institutions, after 1890 even in Manitoba, and decisively, despite the vestigial separate schools of the Territories. Yet even these institutions were to fail. The county vanished from Manitoba, disintegrating into the rural municipality. The towns mostly became tank towns; those that throve, market towns at best; local industries were few and struggling, most to perish. Only the local school district possessed the vitality of its Ontario model.

Moreover, the great assertion of Ontario democracy, the Manitoba School Act, disastrously affected the national institutions of Canada. Accidental as the duality of Manitoba was, it was not the less historically valid for being accidental—what, in history, is not to some degree? Even the accidents rested on historical elements too little studied by the more pontifical of Canadian historians. Further more, it offered an opportunity for French participation with English Canadians in settling the West. It was an opportunity that the French, despite the heroic efforts of Tache and his fellow bishops, failed to take, turning rather to the sterile wastes of the Gaspé and the Laurentides, or to the Ontario side of the Ottawa and the mills of Massachusetts. The maintenance by the Privy Council of the School Act completed the already far advanced destruction by judicial process of the national constitution of 1867. Thus the imposition of Ontario's character on Manitoba replaced the original constitution by the federal structure in which the provinces had risen to a provincial and popular sovereignty little imagined in 1867. This backlash from the prairies had now reduced the federal government of Canada to the paralysis of today.

III

The settlement of the West by the Ontario migration, then, had brought the institutions of civilization to the prairies, law, police, agriculture, commerce, education. It had incorporated the West into the political struc-ture of Canada. Yet it had failed either to people the plains or to create a civilization adapted to the character of the plains. Neither had it incor-porated the new society into the old in a way congenial to the character of the old.

The failure had always been described as an essentially superficial one, an economic failure caused by the great depression of the 1880s and 1890s. That, however, was only an aggravation of the deeper failure caused by the fact that the settlement of the prairies was attempted in the main by only one province, and in a provincial, not a federal, and in one sense not a national, way. Moreover, the failure was not only a failure to people, it was a failure to adapt. Only in its initial and incomplete settlement, and in its political institutions, was the West an off-shoot of Ontario. The final and fundamental task of creating a civilization suitable to the character of the plains and parklands had only been begun, and had largely still to be done.

It cannot be said, either, that it was to be done by the next immigration, the vast Amero-European influx of the next generation. Such an influx had always been sought, and with special urgency and direct apppeal since the early 1890s. Immigration from Europe and the United States, however, reached no significant volume until the end of that decade, when, by reason of the ending of the supply of free land in the United States, the Canadian West became a real alternative, the only successor of the American West. The new immigration when it began, however, neither carried on or amplified what the Ontario immigration had done. Neither did it as much, except to a degree through the American settler, carry significantly further the process of adaptation to Western conditions begun in the 1880s. What it did do, however, was first to introduce new social and popular assumptions into the process of settlement, and then encounter and contend with, in a far more creative struggle, the basic conditions of prairie settlement. By the end of the generation, in 1927, the prairie civilization in temper and institutions had been established, if not tested.

The characteristics of the new settlers who produced these changes are readily discernible. The Americans, although often returning Canadians or their sons, carried with them that curious American trait of readily accepting strange institutions and customs while remaining quietly and consciously American. They thus made excellent settlers, as everyone agreed; they did not challenge the Canadian institutions of the West, as many feared. They did, however, preserve, on the one hand, a latent republicanism with their family and business ties with the States, not a revolutionary republicanism but a republican simplicity, and, on the other, a deep doubt of the utility of politics and the state, except as an occasional convenience. This scepticism, when combined with their quiet refusal to accept the whole spirit of Canadian politics, including Canadian political parties, helped prepare the way for the later independence of national political parties, and the final apolitical outlook of many prairie people.

Equally, if not more important, was their contribution of a generation of agricultural experience of dryland farming on the plains, of third party movements and of agrarian politics. They were to reinforce heavily the agrarianism first experienced in the West by the Farmers' Union in the 1880s and the Patrons of Industry in the 1890s, the least noted and most important attempts of the Ontario migration to meet the needs of western settlement, although they, too, were failures.

The European immigrants were more various than the American, and some were less prepared for the conditions of prairie settlement. Some, of course, were not; the Ukrainians from the Carpathian foothills found a familiar habitat in the parklands; the Russians and Russo-Germans, one on the prairies. Despite their variety, they also possessed certain common traits.

One was their strong national—or group—persistence. For the Germans, this was an old characteristic. Ausland Deutsch in central and eastern Europe had always preserved their identity by group settlement, by following family rather than commercial, private rather than political, lives. The central Europeans, particularly the Austrian Ukrainians, were usually extraordinary examples of an unrealized, and therefore especially dear nationality. To that coherent bond was added the strangeness in Canadian experience of Slavonic speech, and the use of the vernacular by the churches of the Greek rite. They, too, by group settlement and preoccupation with farming persisted in their own ways, and either avoided political life, or joined it on their own terms to promote their interests as groups. They could better, therefore, fit into a new pattern of civilization to which they had made a contribution rather than be assimilated to an old and only partly established one.

One strange and very different strain some of them brought with them, that of Social Democratic ideas. While most were conservative and withdrawn from political life, a few were politically active and liberal, some part were active and convinced Social Democrats, holders of the only political conviction other than Populism that had been meaningful to the Central and Eastern European peasant and intellectual. Thus, they brought one additional factor to impede association with the political parties and acceptance of the Ontario ideal of the classless, middle class farming community served by professionals, business people, and workmen of essentially the same outlook. It was one more pebble, to add to the weight against accepting the established parties and the building of a conventional Canadian society on the prairies.

The third group, the British, though politically so germane to the older settlement of the prairies, was in fact, even more various and more difficult to define than the American and the European immigrants. English, Irish, Scots, and Welsh, they were not any more than the others to be brought under one sufficient definition. Two characteristics were, however, of importance in the context of the settlement of the prairies at the beginning of this century. One is, perhaps, best called chauvinism. They were the children, after all, of the hectic imperialism of late Victorian and Edwardian times. Being British, the last thing they expected was to assimilated in a British colony—a sad, if natural, misreading of the true nature of Canada. They, therefore, constituted another drag on assimilation to the Ontario establishment on the prairies, including in some cases the established political parties. The latter trait occurred because a good number of them were Labor people, and even Socialists, who found little welcome for their ideas in Canadian society or in Canadian politics. Not actually allies of the Social Democrats, they had the same effect of challenging the existing political conventions. Among them, were founders of the Labor Party and the Co-operative Commonwealth Federation.

Such were the three great strains of the new immigration that was to make the West for almost two generations, until the immigration after the last was significantly different in its population from the rest of Canada. Such were the characteristics of the people who, imposed on the Ontario settlement were to contribute to the formation of the character and spirit of western Canadian civilization. Had these three great strains anything in common other than land hunger and a desire for a new life?

It may be that they had. Two things at least were common to all. One was the desire to escape the closing of the frontier in the United States and the fragmentation of land holdings in Europe—the same thing—and the poverty and recurrent unemployment of the great industrial cities of an England that had passed its economic prime. The second was, perhaps, less widely common, certainly it is far more difficult to define, because it was a matter of the spirit. It was the hope that the West might be a practical, a really viable, utopia. Utopianism the first half of the nineteenth century had seen, and it was readily definable as the result of certain religious or socialist ideas. The sources of the utopianism in the West, at the beginning of this century, are less discernible. The Socialist dream was part of it; so was the semi-scientific literature of H.G. Wells and writers influenced by him. But something of it was native to Canadian democracy, the democratic dream that men might be free and independent, particularly, as transmitted by the young women who taught school in Ontario and the West. But whatever its origins, it was a fact, however curious, in a society commercial and utilitarian, and the most important fact in the creation of the civilization of the West. Without it, men would not have toiled and ventured as they did.

The West, however, was more than people. The people, old and new, used the land to produce what the land and climate were specially qualified to produce, hard spring wheat. The successor to prairie grass and the buffalo was wheat and beef, as the freight trains were successors to the cart brigades. The wheat economy replaced the buffalo economy; the plains fed, not the fur trade, but the industrial cities overseas. This vast, monolithic economy, however, although tied now to a trade in necessities rather than luxuries, to bread, not fur, was as vulnerable to hazards of climate and market as the old was to the vagaries of fashion and price, the equally to the costs of transport. The West, transformed, was still the West, distant and mono-economic. What buffers could be devised, what bulwarks built, against the crushing impact of drought, frost and depression.

Nor could such a see-saw economy, now up, now down, endure the tortures of depression as well as a more diversified society. Neither were its people disposed to do so. There was a strong disposition rather to try radical measures. Not only was there the American influence of the International Workers of the World, and the West's own reaction to it and to Canadian unionism in the One Big Union; there was, also, the growth of non-partisanship, or apoliticalism, fed by the agrarian strains from Ontario and the States, and by the political experience of the Territories. From the beginning of the century there was much social ferment, both in the great shipping centres, the cities, and in the rapidly filling stretches of the country.

From the ferment came the great agrarian organization of the Grain Growers, and after the shock of the First World War, the Farmers' Unions, the Progressive Party, and the Wheat Pools. Out of it came the Winnipeg General Strike, the West's one world-rippling event; and out of the strike the Labor Party and Labor members of Parliament, some Ontario-born, most of British birth.

In that tremendous generation, a generation of fierce action and hard decisions, the West with heavy strokes forged its own institutions, declared its own identity, and created its own sense of semi-political independence. It affirmed its own newly discovered and deeply felt sense of novelty. Its people had realized that the West was indeed a clean sheet on which a new story might be written. The West was no longer attempting to be Ontario on the prairies, it had declared its spiritual independence; it was persuaded of its own difference.

IV

The West then had formed and discovered itself by 1927, and half a century from Confederation. The open prairie, the bluff-strewn parkland, had been incised like a vast copper bowl into squares and triangles by railway and road allowances, embossed and punctuated by the red phalli of grain elevators and railway tanks. The stopping points had been determined and the roads opened for the crawling grain wagons and the brisk Tin Lizzies. The provincial legislatures were farmer-dominated, and "Wheat Pool" and "Saskatchewan Co-operative" matched the Winnipeg and Vancouver grain company names in the stiff parade of elevators by the long sidings. The farmer and labour revolt of the post-war years had fruited in the peculiarly Western institutions of the farmers' apolitical, non-partisan parties and the great producers' co-operatives.

On this enormous achievement of a decade, not yet settled into place, not yet hardened in use and routine, fell the tremendous blows of the great depression and drought of 1929 to 1939. The shattering disillusion of those events are forgotten except by the now aging survivors. In perspective, two things seem to emerge above all others. The first was that the depression and the drought completed the revolt of the West against the imported and the conventional. The old economic institutions and habits of thought were condemned and had to be discarded. The West, if it was to be, had to be what it was shaping itself to be; there was no going back on the revolutionary post-war decade. The second was that the West was nearly destroyed by the combination of drought and depression, and perhaps could not have survived by itself. It was saved, and it is a sobering thought for Westerners, by the federal government.

A third event, perhaps more important in the long run, but less evident and ambiguous, lay in the field of agricultural practice. The considerable beginnings of power farming and the mechanization of agriculture was delayed by the depression; capital was not available for the purchase of tractors and machinery. The drought forced an acceleration and increase of the adaptation of tillage practices to prairie conditions. Strip farming, the replacement of the plough by the disc, treeplanting, are only examples of the ecological revolution in prairie agriculture.

Closely related in governmental and economic practice was a fourth change, the use of government—federal, be it noted again—to provide the back-stop necessary if the farmers were to survive drought and crop failure until the rains came again. The Prairie Farm Rehabilitation Act and the Prairie Farm Assistance Act, with the restoration of the Wheat Board, placed the stability and skills of government behind the farmer gambling with the unpredictable chances of an area of marginal rainfall and of a world market. The last two measures were, of course, that blend of government stability and independent individual action and individual payment for service that the western farmer and his allies, the prairie townsmen, had desired. The legislation might be federal, the spirit and the concept were Western.

Definitely national, however, was the governmental action that set about the salvaging of the institutions and public finances of the West. The Bank of Canada's studies and the Royal Commission on Federal-Provincial Relations (Rowell-Sirois) were in large part a response to the practical dereliction of the West. Thus, the West, independent in spirit but of federal creation, largely set in train that revival of federal power, which the Second World War increased, and which led to the federal-provincial equalization payments of 1947. This was the long delayed national answer to the West's protest against the unequal incidence of the National Policy of east-west transportation and the protective tariff.

By such ambivalent logic did the West escape from the decade of drought and depression. It remained, however, restless and radical in its political attitudes; became, indeed, more independent than ever of conventional Canadian politics in Saskatchewan and Alberta. In Manitoba, the outcome of the farmers' revolt of 1920, the Bracken Government, remained in power. That it did so was an indication that even relatively conservative Manitoba had come to set reasonably good administration above the excitement, and possible abuses, of conventional parliamentary government by parties. The Bracken Government was not only without politics; it was even without ideas. It turned back the new political movements of the Co-operative Commonwealth Federation and Social Credit, but the strains it suffered in doing so forced it slowly towards that catch-all of Canadian politics, the Liberal party. With Bracken's departure to federal politics in 1942, it became, in effect, a Liberal party, in wartime coalition. Manitoba, as the gateway to the West, as it was still in spirit, could not too boldly adopt the new movements by which the West was to express itself.

That fell to the other provinces to do. In Saskatchewan, latent non-partisanship and overt economic distress finally drove the electorate to return the C.C.F. to power, although not until 1944. The C.C.F., organized in 1932, had sought national rather than provincial office. It had incorporated the persons, the ideas and the hopes of the agrarian and labor movements of the 1920s. These had shown themselves in all provinces, especially Ontario, but they had remained centered in the prairie West, where the basic radicalism and the hope of novelty gave the movement its origin and natural home. But the provincial victory in Saskatchewan was not so much a victory for a socialist or even a radical party as of prairie apoliticism, the determination to throw off conventional shackles and make government the direct administrative agent of the people. The school teacher leaders might experiment in socialism but their essential work was to use the provincial government positively to meet the expressed needs of the people. This was an old Canadian tradition, and especially, a western one.

Apparently much less in the Canadian tradition, but actually very much so, and even more expressive of the peculiar traditions of the West, was the Social Credit movement. The tidal spread of that doctrine over Alberta in the early 1930s was, of course, one more incoming of the perennial revolt of the debtor community against the creditor. That it should have come on the parkland frontier of the West and in the greatest depression and drought in North American history was not in the least surprising. That it should have allied itself readily with religious fundamentalism was not surprising either, for the debtor is more likely than the creditor to be a fundamentalist.

What is surprising is that the Social Credit doctrine should have jumped, like an erratic electrical charge, from its place of fermentation in England to Alberta. Social Credit was, as a study of its origin reveals, an attempt to deal with the problem of distribution in an industrial economy by means of changes in the concept and use of credit rather than by political revolution. From this came its appeal to many religious people, and still more to benevolent intellectuals, particularly those with no economic or political training. It was its essentially non-partisan, apolitical character that formed the links with Alberta quite as much as its appeal to a debtor community. Hence, C.B. Macpherson was only partly right—gave only the first stroke of the scalpel that was to open the way to truth—when he called it a "quasi-party." It was, in fact, not a political party at all; it was an apolitical—or anti-political—movement.

When Social Credit was returned to power in 1935, it demanded, at bottom, good administration by honest men who were by profession and practice *not* politicians. Social Credit could, therefore, give the community what use it required of the state while keeping state action limited. It thus combined social use of the state with free enterprise. The West, therefore, acquired in the administration of Alberta the reconciliation of state action with free enterprise—the individual firm and business concern working in

an institutional environment that the West had been seeking for a generation and which Alberta itself has now enjoyed for a generation. It is, at the
moment, impossible to see any end, except in gross incompetence, to an
administration which perfectly reflects an anti-political community. Social
Credit was the end of politics in Alberta; it was the beginning of popular
administration. The general will of Jean-Jacques Rousseau had been realized and implemented. May I be at the learned conference in the next world
where that vindicated philosopher and Mr. Manning meet!

Thus, despite the differences of the three provincial regimes, from 1935
to 1958 (when party government returned to Manitoba) the West was largely
an anti-political community. Something of the vast monotony of the grasslands prevailed in its public life.

That extraordinary harmony of public and private life was increased by
the balancing of the tariff by the equalization grants, by the wartime and
postwar prosperity. Prosperity made possible the delayed triumph of
machine-powered agriculture, a triumph redoubled by the use of artificial
fertilizers and a long succession of years of abundant or sufficient rain. In
this prosperity, the new ecology of agriculture and institutional life with the
basic conditions of the plains came to its full development. The process was
re-inforced by the state reshaped as the state assistant and ancillary to free
enterprise, a role which could be easily expanded in the less prosperous
provinces—in Saskatchewan by the C.C.F. government, and in Manitoba
even under a party government. The second decade of the period 1927 to
1947 saw the forming of institutions and the firming of conventions by which
the West had succeeded in expressing its own needs and aspirations.

V

The last twenty years of the past century, then, from 1948 to the present
were years of fulfilment in the civilization of the West. They saw the matur-
ing of the wheat economy, a maturity relieved of its earlier dependence on
the narrow and uncertain markets in the wheat-growing countries of Europe
by the beginning of large, long term sales to markets in Asia. The West, by
the fact, ceased to be an economic colony of Europe in political subordina-
tion to Eastern Canada. In the Saskatchewan Dam the scientific agricultural
economy of the prairies developed its working symbol, a symbol also of that
rural electrification which gave abundant power to rural and to urban
industry.

The years also—how neat it is that 1947 should also be the year of the
Leduc oil strike!—saw the enormous broadening of the primary economy
of the West, first by the oil and gas discoveries, and then by the beginning
of potash mining in Saskatchewan. To a basic food stuff, the West now added
basic sources of power and of food growing. The West, by these accessions

to its developed resources carried further its integration with the continental and the world economy.

The same process of broadening and deepening the foundations of the West's ecological economy and institutions went on in the service industries, trucking, marketing, manufacturing. The monolithic wheat economy was now buttressed by a wide perimeter of associated industries, recalling the subdued diversity of the majestic monotony of the plains.

From their fulfilment of a way of life, partly groped for, partly foreseen, came a revival of that sense of independence in association which had always marked the West in its Canadian role. Federally created, the West was self-defined. Always mindful of its creator and salvation, the West knew in its bones that it was an independent creature which had determined its own life within known and accepted limits. Even the return of party politics in federal Manitoba public life under Conservative leadership was only an assertion, necessitated in its expression by federal and provincial needs, of the West's essentially anti-political character—expressed as in Quebec by bloc voting—and of the assistant and developmental character of the Western provincial state, carried further by the party government of Duff Roblin than by any other western administration.

It is easy, therefore, to see in the West today the emergence of a distinctive civilization—a sub-civilization, to speak with some preciseness. What are the characteristics of that way of life?

The first is its obvious and deliberate ecological character. Agricultural technics and political administration have been purposefully reduced to complete co-operation by scientific research and instruction and by an usually wide and deep diffusion of political power in western society. Simple in both social and economic structure, the West is a striking example of the adaptation of ideas, institutions and social aspirations to the limits and potentialities of a distinctive environment.

The second is the apolitical, or even anti-political, character of its public life. This development began in the assertion of the sectional needs of the West; it found fullest expression in Alberta through Social Credit as a medium of expression of religious fundamentation, sectionalism, and the sense of novelty, of the possibility of new beginnings.

The third characteristic is the reduction of government to administration, and of the state to the role of assistant and ancillary to individual and community enterprise and development. As the settler had to come to terms with the plains, so the state had to come to terms with the voter. The dignity of government is much diminished, its utility greatly increased.

These three things, the ecological community, the anti-political society, the ancillary state, are the three chief features of the century long development of civilization in the West. These distinguish it; what gave it its special character in Canadian history at least, was the sense of novelty, the belief that the prairies were a *tabula rasa*. Does that sense remain? To attempt an answer would be to pass from the revelation of the past proper to the historian to the criticism of the present proper to the publicist. Perhaps one may, as a layman, remark that in a civilization as materialistic as that of the West, and as prone to smugness in success as any other community, there still remains place for a sense that new beginnings are possible also in the art and taste that are the bloom of civilization.

II

NATIVE PEOPLES AND
THE FUR TRADE

Amerindians had lived on the Canadian prairies for over 10,000 years by the time of European contact. Initially using only spears, sticks and bows and arrows and then, by the early eighteenth century, the horse for hunting the buffalo, the Plains Indians had developed an independent way of life at the time of European contact. The Plains Indians were, however, drawn into trade with the French, who were working out of their colony in New France, in the late seventeenth century and with the British, who had established posts along Hudson Bay. This trade had a great impact on the native people.

Much of our knowledge of native history before European contact and even at the time of contact comes from archaeological research, particularly the artifacts at buffalo jumps where the Indians herded buffalo over cliffs. At the base of the cliff, they set up camps where they butchered meat. Olive Dickason summarizes much of the recent archaeological research on the Plains Indians in "A Historical Reconstruction for the Northwest Plains."

The French and the British each established fur trading companies in the region which vied for the profits which could be made from selling furs. The Hudson's Bay Company (HBC) had begun its operations via Hudson Bay in 1670, having secured a monopoly from the English crown to conduct trade in Rupert's Land, the region roughly defined as territory whose rivers drained into Hudson Bay. The French rivalled the British through their St. Lawrence–Great Lakes–Saskatchewan River route. After the British Conquest of New France in 1760, a new Montreal-based trading system, initially known as the Pedlars and then a larger North West Company (NWC), emerged to rival the Hudson's Bay Company. This new North West Company was headed by British (predominantly Scottish) managers but utilized French-Canadian canoemen for transporting the furs.

These two rival fur trading companies, the Hudson's Bay Company and the North West Company, had different forms of organization, patterns of trade, personnel, social patterns and relations with the Indians. Daniel Francis contrasts the two companies in "Traders and Indians," excerpted from his *Battle for the West: Fur Traders and the Birth of Western Canada*.

Fur trade history has undergone a revolutionary change since 1960. Historians have moved away from the earlier focus on institutional developments and trading policies to study the social life of the people involved in the fur trade. How did the fur trade affect the native people's way of life? What was the role of women in the fur trade, and what was family life like for children of mixed marriages? Jacqueline Peterson and John Anfinson review works in the field of fur trade history in "The Indian and the Fur Trade: A Review of Literature."

SELECTED BIBLIOGRAPHY

Studies on the early archaeology of the prairies include H.M. Wormington and Richard Forbis, *An Introduction to the Archaeology of Alberta, Canada* (Denver, 1965); T.A. Moore, ed., *Alberta Archaeology: Prospect and Retrospect* (Lethbridge, 1981); and the popular synthesis: Liz Bryan, *The Buffalo People: Prehistoric Archeology on the Canadian Plains* (Edmonton, 1991). Henry T. Epp, *Long Ago Today: The Story of Saskatchewan's Earliest Peoples* (Saskatoon, 1991) summarizes archaeological research on Saskatchewan. Gerald Friesen's *The Canadian Prairies: A History* (Toronto, 1985), pp. 10-65, contains summaries on native peoples, and the impact of the fur trade on them.

Useful studies on the Cree Indians in the region include David C. Mandelbaum, *The Plains Cree: An Ethnographic, Historical Comparative Study* (1940) (Regina, 1979), and John Milloy, *The Plains Cree: Trade, Diplomacy and War, 1790 to 1870* (Winnipeg, 1988). Dale Russell provides a new look at tribal movements in *Eighteenth-Century Western Cree and Their Neighbours* (Hull, Quebec, 1991).

For the Blackfoot-speaking tribes, John C. Ewers's, *The Blackfeet* (Norman, 1958) is invaluable, as are the two biographies by Hugh Dempsey, *Crowfoot* (Edmonton, 1972) and *Red Crow: Warrior Chief* (Saskatoon, 1980). Peter Douglas Elias has completed a study of the Sioux or Dakota Indians in Canada, *The Dakota of the Canadian Northwest* (Winnipeg, 1988).

Hugh Dempsey's survey *Indian Tribes of Alberta*, 2nd ed. (Calgary, 1986) provides a good general overview. Donald Smith's chapter, "The Original Peoples of Alberta," in Howard and Tamara Palmer, eds., *Peoples of Alberta* (Saskatoon, 1985), pp. 50-82, 476-86, summarizes the existing research to the early 1980s, and includes an extensive bibliography.

For general accounts of the fur trade see Daniel Francis, *Battle for the*

West: Fur Traders and the Birth of Western Canada (Edmonton, 1982); A.S. Morton, *A History of the Canadian West to 1870–71* (1939), 2nd edition, edited by L.G. Thomas (Toronto, 1973); E.E. Rich, *The Fur Trade and the North West to 1857* (Toronto, 1967); and Frits Pannekoek, *The Fur Trade and Western Canadian Society, 1670–1870,* Canadian Historical Association Booklet No. 43 (Ottawa, 1987).

Important collections of papers on the fur trade have been published: see Malvina Bolus, ed., *People and Pelts: Selected Papers of the North American Fur Trade Conference* (Winnipeg, 1972); *Western Canadian Journal of Anthropology,* Special Issue: "The Fur Trade in Canada," III, 1 (1972); Carol Judd and Arthur J. Ray, eds., *Old Trails and New Directions: Papers of the Third North American Fur Trade Conference* (Toronto, 1980); and Bruce G. Trigger et al., *Le Castor Fait Tout: Selected Papers of the Fifth North American Fur Trade Conference, 1985* (1987).

Of particular importance on the subject of Indians and the fur trade are Arthur J. Ray, *Indians in the Fur Trade: Their Role as Trappers, Hunters and Middlemen in the Lands Southwest of Hudson Bay 1660-1870* (Toronto, 1974); Arthur Ray and Conrad Heidenrich, *The Early Fur Traders: A Study in Cultural Interaction* (Toronto, 1976); Arthur Ray and Donald B. Freeman, *"Give Us Good Measure": An Economic Analysis of Relations between the Indians and the Hudson's Bay Company before 1763* (Toronto, 1978). A study of a specific region is Paul C. Thistle's *Indian-European Trade Relations in the Lower Saskatchewan River Region to 1840* (Winnipeg, 1986).

Much of the new work on fur trade social history is discussed by Sylvia Van Kirk in "Fur Trade Social History: Some Recent Trends," in Carol Judd and Arthur Ray, eds., *Old Trails and New Directions* (Toronto, 1980), pp. 160-73. For further information and more recent publications in family and community in the fur trade see Sylvia Van Kirk's, *"Many Tender Ties": Women in Fur Trade Society in Western Canada* (Winnipeg, 1980); "Women and the Fur Trade," *The Beaver* (Winter, 1972): 4-21; "'The Custom of the Country': An Examination of Fur Trade Marriage Practices," in L.H. Thomas, ed., *Essays in Western History* (Edmonton, 1976), pp. 49-68; and Jennifer S.H. Brown, *Strangers in Blood: Fur Trade Company Families in Indian Country* (Vancouver, 1980); "A Colony of Very Useful Hands," *The Beaver* (Spring, 1977): 39-45; and "Ultimate Respectability: Fur Trade Children in the 'Civilized World'," Pts. I and II, *The Beaver* (Winter, 1977): 4-10, and (Spring, 1978): 48-55.

For a detailed account of Fort Chipewyan, an important fur trade post, see James Parker, *Emporium of the North: Fort Chipewyan and the Fur Trade to 1835* (Regina, 1987). See also two useful biographies: J.S. Galbraith, *The Little Emperor: Governor Simpson of the Hudson's Bay Company* (Toronto, 1976) and J.G. McGregor, *John Rowand: Czar of the Prairies* (Saskatoon, 1979).

For a more detailed annotated bibliography on the history of the fur trade see two lists of books and articles by Glyndwr Williams in *The Beaver* (Autumn, 1970): 60-63; and *The Beaver* (Autumn, 1983): 83-86. Original fur traders' journals and letters have been published by both the Hudson's Bay Record Society and the Champlain Society.

Important maps and historical commentary appear in the *Historical Atlas of Canada,* Vol. 1 (From the Beginning to 1800), edited by R. Cole Harris (Toronto, 1987). A second important book on the early cartography of the North West is Richard I. Ruggles, *A Country So Interesting: The Hudson's Bay Company and Two Centuries of Mapping, 1670–1870* (Montreal and Kingston, 1991).

OLIVE PATRICIA DICKASON

3 A Historical Reconstruction for the Northwestern Plains

ABSTRACT. There is now no doubt as to the considerable time span of human habitation on the northwestern plains of North America. Indeed, some of our most ancient archaeological records have been discovered here. However, archaeological evidence has not been found to support the hypothesis that early migrating Siberians found a corridor in the open lands east of the mountains; those historic plains tribes which did originate in the northwest—all Athapaskan-speakers—arrived comparatively recently. Ancient Amerindians of the plains appear to have had more connections, however remote, indirect and sporadic, with the eastern and northeastern woodlands, as well as with the civilizations of the Mississippi, the pueblos of the southwest, and even tenuously with Mexico. We would do well to re-evaluate our perception of Canada as a "new world" without traditions of civilization before the arrival of Europeans.[1]

Reconstructing the early history of the people of the northwestern plains of North America has been so difficult for the historian that the task is still far from completed. Because the written record began very recently, historians have had to place a heavy, and professionally uncharacteristic, reliance on unwritten resources. In effect, this has meant a dependence upon archaeology, which has been very useful up to a point. But the plains have not been kind to archaeologists either, especially in Alberta and southwestern Saskatchewan where the record has been particularly difficult to decipher.[2]

It is perhaps not surprising, under these circumstances, that it came to be believed that the plains had not been inhabited to any extent before the appearance of the European-introduced horse. Such an eminent authority as Clark Wissler wrote in 1907, "the peopling of the plains proper was a recent phenomenon due in part to the introduction of the horse and the displacement of tribes by white settlement."[3] Even as late as 1939, A.L. Kroeber concurred, adding that in his view, the plains had developed culturally "only since the taking over of the horse from Europeans."[4] These two authorities were writing principally of the plains south of the forty-ninth parallel. If their interpretation was correct for the south, so the reasoning went, how much truer must it have been for the north?

Today, we know that such views were heavily conditioned by the inability of most nineteenth-century scholars, as well as some in the twentieth century, to envision man as having been capable of wresting a living from the plains before the advent of the horse and gun.[5] Here archaeology has helped to set the record straight. It is on the plains, including those of the northwest, that some of our earliest evidence of human presence in North America has been found. The great advances in archaeology during recent years have dramatically lengthened our historical perspective of man in the Americas. The world that Europeans labelled "New" when they became aware of it in the fifteenth century has turned out to be anything but new; and the people who inhabited it, considered by Europeans to be such a young race as to be still in their cultural ABCs,[6] have a history that can claim the dignified label of "ancient."

It is also a complex history. The development of stone and bone tools represented one of man's great strides forward into technological sophistication; and while such a technology can in a way be regarded as "simple," it was viable only because of acute and careful observation of nature—still a basic requirement today. As a general rule, a "simple" technology is effective in proportion as it is based upon sharp and accurate observation on the one hand, and supported by a workable social organization on the other. In other words, the intelligent manipulation of nature backed by supportive social structures makes possible man's survival under extremely difficult conditions. The process is a dynamic one; although the rates of change can and do vary, at no time can a living culture be regarded as static. As far back as we have traced the presence of man in America, his story has been one of adaptation and alteration—so slow as to be all but imperceptible in the beginning, but ever so gradually gaining momentum. This process was not characterized by a consistent rate of change, but rather by spurts or leaps alternating with "idling" periods. In this context, the arrival of Europeans, horses and all, is to be viewed as part of an ongoing process; the intrusion may have accelerated or altered patterns of change, but it did not initiate change in itself.

The story of this change on the northwestern plains is the concern of this paper. Because the time span is so long, from early prehistoric to European-Amerindian contact, it will be possible to trace events only in their broad outlines, but with the hope that this will be sufficient to reveal something of underlying patterns. The term "northwestern plains" includes the southern halves of Alberta and Saskatchewan, the eastern two-thirds of

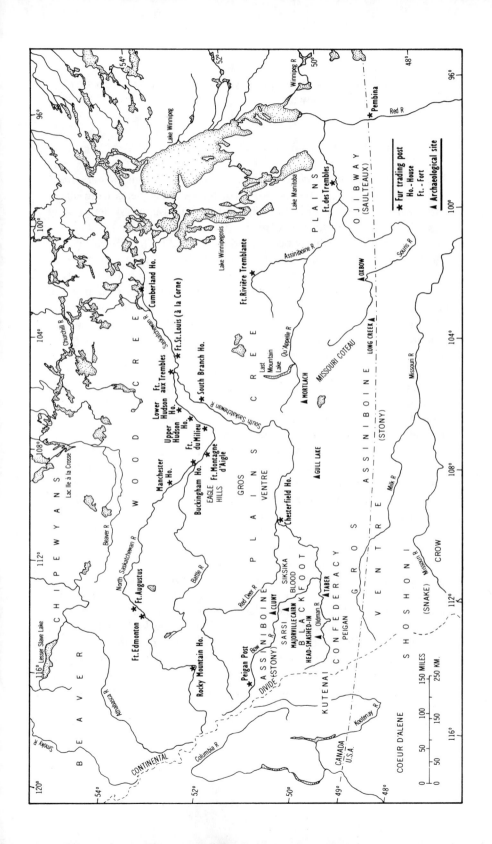

Montana and the northern third of Wyoming; however, the focus will be on Alberta and Saskatchewan.

EARLY BIG-GAME HUNTERS (17,000-5,000 B.C.)[7]

The earliest consistent evidence of man on the Great Plains clusters in the period of 17,000 to 7,000 years ago. We do have some evidence from earlier dates, perhaps even as far back as 30,000 B.C.,[8] although a skeleton of an infant found under glacial till in Taber, Alberta,[9] which had suggested considerable antiquity has now been dated to about 2,000 B.C. With the big-game hunters of 12,000 or so years ago we are on firm ground. Our knowledge of their activities is derived from sites associated with kills of mammoth, contemporaries of giant beaver and giant wolves, of camels and horses, species which disappeared during the late Pleistocene megafaunal extinctions of about 11,000 years ago. We know that long before the invention of the bow and arrow, paleo-Amerindians hunted with spears tipped with bone or with fluted stone points. Very early—at least by the time of the extinctions—the "atlatl," or thrower, appeared, enabling hunters to hurl their spears with great force.[10] Used in this manner, spears have been aptly described as "guided missiles"; their effectiveness has been dramatically illustrated by the discovery of points embedded in bone, such as the rib of a mastodon or the scapula of a giant bison.

Sites associated with bison hunting date from more than 10,000 years ago; the earliest buffalo drive of which we have a record was a jump at Bonfire Shelter in southwestern Texas from about that time.[11] The greatest number of jump sites have been found in the foothills of the Rocky Mountains, where they outnumber pounds. The latter were apparently more commonly used on the plains,[12] particularly in such areas as the Missouri Coteau. Drive sites are most frequent in Saskatchewan, Alberta, Montana and Wyoming. By whatever means the herds were harvested, the archaeological record indicates that buffalo hunting has provided the basis for life on the plains for at least as long as drives have been used. It also tells us that our previously held and much cherished picture of early hunters perpetually facing starvation does not equate with what we now know to have been the case. Although lean times certainly alternated with periods of plenty, such cycles were prepared for from a very early period by drying or otherwise preserving meat. Oddly enough, the dog does not seem to have accompanied man in the Americas during distant prehistoric days;[13] the earliest indications of its presence—and these are not undisputed—date from about 5,000 B.C.

PLAINS ARCHAIC (5,000 B.C. TO B.C./A.D.)

After 5,000 B.C., seasonal migration continued, largely based on bison as a food resource. However, there was a long period called the Altithermal (5,000-2,500 B.C.), in which bison appear to have been scarce or even absent, and during which human presence also seems to have been much reduced, particularly in short-grass areas.[14] The Altithermal is believed to have been marked by higher temperatures and increased aridity which decimated the herds of giant buffalo by cutting down on their food supply. Before the Altithermal, hunters pursued giant bison; afterward, the bison available was of the smaller variety with which we are familiar.[15]

The end of the Altithermal period saw the growing elaboration of the buffalo drive, such as the jump at Head-Smashed-In, Alberta, and as indicated by campsites at Oxbow and Long Creek in Saskatchewan. In fact, sites in general increased throughout the two provinces; about 12,000 have been recorded in Alberta alone, believed to be a small proportion of those that existed;[16] their numbers reflect substantial increases in population. From this period too we can date the appearance of elaborate surface assemblages which probably indicate eastern influence.[17] Some sites include several hundred tipi rings which extend for miles; it has been estimated that there are more than a million such rings scattered throughout Alberta.[18] They may be mute testimony to the annual cycle of buffalo hunters, who in historic times gathered seasonally in large camps, as these sites were usually excellent observation posts for watching the movement of game, a characteristic which they share with medicine wheels.[19] Wheels found on the Canadian plains, largely in Alberta, seldom exceed 30 feet in diameter; those dating from the proto-historic period characteristically have four spokes; earlier ones may have five or even more.[20] Those found south of the forty-ninth parallel are usually more complicated in form but are far fewer in number.

All these features were associated, particularly in the later phase, with the appearance of the small-point weapons system to which the bow and arrow belongs. This new weaponry may have been introduced by peoples filtering down from the north, such as the Athapaskans, who reached the southern limits of the plains sometime before the sixteenth century.[21] These were probably the people described by Spaniards during the first half of that century as "dog nomads," appearing at pueblos with as many as five hundred dogs loaded with the products of the buffalo hunt to trade for farm produce as well as for manufactured items.

PLAINS WOODLANDS (250 B.C.-950 A.D.)

This was the period when plains cultures, as we know them, began to develop patterns resembling their proto-historical forms. This seems to have resulted from an accelerated infusion of eastern influences.[22] The northern plains continued as the centre for bison hunting. Pottery was now seen for the first time; its evidence indicates that ancestral Kutenai occupied southern Alberta as long as 2,000 years ago, supporting oral traditions reported by David Thompson.[23]

It was also the period in which agricultural communities appeared in those areas of the plains where rainfall and the growing season allowed—factors which still have to be contended with. The Adena and the later Hopewell cultural complexes, each named from Ohio sites where their distinctive characteristics were first identified, spread in from the south. Hopewell extended further north than Adena: mounds and burials after the pattern of Hopewell have been found in Ontario, Manitoba and Saskatchewan. Such traces are also seen in ceramics, some of which have been found in southern Alberta. In the northwestern grasslands generally, hunting and gathering persisted in cultural manifestations such as the intrusive Besant and the indigenous Avonlea. At those sites especially, the developing complexities of ritualized, planned buffalo drives have been traced.[24]

PLAINS VILLAGE (900 A.D.-1750 A.D.)

These social units were characterized by multi-family lodges at fixed locations; permanent settlements fortified with dry moats and stockades; underground storage pits, pottery, and a wide range of artifacts in stone, bone, horn, shell and other materials. The Cluny Earth Lodge village at Blackfoot Crossing, about 70 miles east of Calgary, may have been the northernmost manifestation of this phase; according to Blackfoot legend, it was built by the Crow, in which case it would be proto-historic.[25] In any event, village life on the high plains was discouraged by recurrent droughts, to the point of disappearing entirely during the fifteenth century; surviving villages in peripheral areas, such as the aspen parklands, provide mute testimony to what once had been.[26] It is interesting that all historic farming peoples of the plains speak a Hokan-Siouan tongue; this language group may well be the oldest in North America.

Bison populations recovered more rapidly than human populations from these droughts. At about this time the herds reached the immense sizes reported by Francisco Vasquez Coronado in the south (1541), by Father Simon Le Moyne in the Great Lakes region (1654) and Henry Kelsey on the Saskatchewan (1690). Their spread east of the Mississippi appears to have been comparatively recent, if one is to judge from the tenuous evidence of Spanish accounts; and it was not until the late eighteenth century that they were seen on the Peace River west of Lesser Slave Lake.[27] These herds could well have prevented the return of village farmers to the high plains.[28] For instance, Hernando De Soto reported in 1541 that the Amerindians of Caluca in north-central Arkansas

. . . stated that thence toward the north, the country, being very cold, was very thinly populated; that cattle were in such plenty, no maize-field could be protected from them, and the inhabitants lived upon the meat.[29]

Colonists who tried to farm the plains before the extermination of the herds discovered to their sorrow that they were as vulnerable to depredations by bison as their Amerindian predecessors had been. Not only did the animals eat and trample crops, they were even reported to have demolished a settler's cabin in Pennsylvania about 1770.[30] The movements of such great herds rendered permanent settlements extremely precarious, both from the physical as well as the economic point of view, and they were also dangerous to hunters on foot. Canadian-born explorer Louis Jolliet, with Jesuit Jacques Marquette in 1673, reported bison as being "very fierce . . . not a year passes without their killing some savages." Amerindian appreciation of these dangers is graphically presented in a Caddo legend which tells how buffalo ceased to eat humans.[31]

PROTO-HISTORIC BISON HUNTERS

The bison-hunting way of life on the plains which today is considered "traditional" crystallized between 1600 and 1750, depending on locality; in southern Alberta and Saskatchewan, it seems to have appeared during the first half of the eighteenth century. It was, of course, based upon horses, which not only altered the hunt, transportation and warfare, but also, and perhaps most importantly of all, trade routes. Interestingly, horses did not generally become a source of subsistence in themselves, as they had in Asia.[32] However, to view the changes that did occur with the introduction of the horse as simply superficial, as some have done, is to misunderstand the process of cultural evolution. Technologies change faster than institutions, and institutions change faster than ideologies. In less than two centuries on the northwestern plains, the horse in conjunction with the fur trade had heavily altered the principal institutions of plains Amerindian society; given more time, more profound ideological modifications would probably have been effected as well.[33]

While there is no doubt that horses were first reintroduced into the Americas by the Spaniards, there is considerable question as to when Amerindians began to ride and own them. In 1541 Viceroy Antonio de Mendoza provided mounts for Mexican allies during a campaign in central Mexico; about 1567, the Amerindians of Sonora rode horses and used them for food.[34] Spanish stock-raising settlements in the southwest, particularly in the neighborhood of Santa Fe, were apparently points of diffusion;[35] as for the Atlantic seaboard, where horses had been present since early in the seventeenth century, they do not seem to have crossed the Alleghenies until later.

On the southern plains, Amerindians owned horses by 1630, and may well have had some as early as 1600. Athapaskan-speaking Apache were riding on horseback by mid-seventeenth century;[36] indeed, they evolved Amerindian techniques for mounted warfare, and also had become the prototype of the mounted bison hunter.

Although horses had such a radical effect on buffalo hunting, they were not universally suited to their new role. Some could not overcome their fear of buffalo and so could not be trained as hunters; among the Cree during the last days of bison hunting, only one tipi in ten had a good buffalo horse, although nearly all had riding and transport animals. While running buffalo became universally favoured as a hunting technique, horses were also used for surrounds, which became more efficient as a result.[37] Jumps began to fall into disuse between 1840 and 1850; the last known use was by the Blackfoot in 1873.[38] Pounds, on the other hand, continued to be used until the end of the herds. Another effect of the horse was to eliminate women from direct participation in bison drives, turning their attention exclusively to the preparation of meat and hides.

Apart from its usefulness for hunting and transport, the horse both extended and altered trade routes. As a consequence of all this, it became a symbol of wealth in its own right and, as usual with the growth of affluence, polarized economic status both between individuals as well as between tribes. For example, in 1833 a Peigan chief, Sackomaph, was reported to own between 4,000 and 5,000 horses, 150 of which were killed upon his death. Among tribes, the Assiniboine and Plains Cree had fewer horses than the Blackfoot. However, they were highly skilled as horse raiders; David Thompson described a spectacular raid in which a band of Assiniboines disguised as antelope made off with fifty horses from Rocky Mountain House.[39]

The Shoshoni (Snake, Gens du Serpent), seasonal residents of grasslands and plateau, are generally believed to have been the first to acquire horses on the northwestern plains.[40] Their sources were their relatives to the south, the Comanche, as well as neighbours, such as the Coeur d'Alene and Flathead from the western plateau and Columbia River, who were early large-scale herders.[41] The Shoshoni may have employed their horses at first principally for the hunt, presaging, as the Apache had done earlier, the emergence of the buffalo-based "horse cultures." By the 1730s the Shoshoni were using horses for raiding, and during the following decades they were feared mounted warriors of the plains.[42] Under the circumstances, word quickly spread of the strange animal, "swift as a deer." A Cree, Saukamapee, described to David Thompson his first encounter with the new arrival, which occurred while he and some fellow tribesmen were hunting in the territory of the Peigan, westernmost and most southerly of the four tribes of the Blackfoot Confederacy. Attacking a lone Shoshoni, the Cree succeeded in killing his mount, and crowded in wonder around the fallen animal which, like the dog, was a slave to man and carried his burdens. So they called it

"Misstutim," "big dog";[43] later, the Blackfoot were to name it "Ponokamita," "elk dog," in recognition of its size and usefulness.[44]

HISTORIC RESIDENTS

At this time, all of the year-round residents of the northwestern plains were Algonkian or Siouan speakers except the Sarsi, who spoke an Athapaskan language and who had broken away from the Beaver, apparently not long before the arrival of Europeans. Eventually, they became part of the Blackfoot Confederacy, along with the Siksika (Blackfoot proper), Blood and Peigan.[45] Linguistic evidence indicates a great time span of occupation for the Algonkian-speaking Blackfoot and Gros Ventre, much of it in isolation from their own language group. Speech similarities between the Blackfoot and the Kutenai may hark back to the time when the latter also lived in the area. In any event, the Blackfoot were probably the first to arrive of all the historic peoples still in the region; cultural indications are that they came from the eastern woodlands,[46] the source of much immigration to the northwestern plains. Directly to the east of the Confederacy were the allied Gros Ventre (Atsina, originally a division of the Arapaho) who may have been second to arrive in the region.[47] They share with the Blackfoot the probability of being the "Archithinue" or "Archithine" reported by Anthony Henday in 1754.[48] If we except the Plains Ojibway (Saulteaux, Bungi), who reached Saskatchewan by the late eighteenth century, but who did not establish a major presence on the high plains,[49] the newest arrivals on the northwestern plains are the Plains Cree. Their presence dates from some time during the seventeenth century; their arrival may have been in association with their close allies, the Siouan Assiniboine, who probably preceded them. To the south were the Siouan Crow, who were described in their territory of the middle Yellowstone by the Nor'Wester Francois Larocque in 1805. It has been estimated that at the beginning of the historic period the population of the northwestern plains averaged less than one person per 10 square miles.[50] However, there were considerable fluctuations. Tribes from surrounding areas made forays on to the plains for hunting and warfare, such forays increasing in frequency as the bison herds declined and then disappeared from their eastern ranges after 1850, until their final extermination in Alberta in the 1880s.[51] All of these peoples, with the exception of the Gros Ventre and Crow (Hidatsa),[52] had been hunters and gatherers from time immemorial, so that their shift to plains life was from one form of hunting to another.

The opening of the historic period saw the southwestern parts of the region being dominated by the raiding Shoshoni. They appear to have been an aggressive people even when they were on foot; horses enabled them to extend their field of operations. According to Saukamapee's description of some of their raids during the first half of the eighteenth century,[53] the Shoshoni wore six-ply quilted leather armour and carried shields, but did not at that time have firearms, as they had "no Traders among them."[54] What trading connections they had were with the south, and Spaniards were reluctant to include arms in such transactions. However, the Shoshoni sinew-backed bow was an efficient weapon, particularly when used with metal-tipped arrows, and was both more accurate and more reliable than guns until about the middle of the nineteenth century. With the principal exception of the Cree, but also of the Assiniboine and Saulteaux, it was usually preferred by Amerindians for buffalo hunting. In 1811, Alexander Henry the Younger reported that Peigans would trade a horse or a gun for such a bow.[55] The principal economic purpose of the Shoshoni raids seems to have been the acquisition of captives, who as slaves were useful to both Amerindians and Spaniards as well as to the French, and so had high trading value.

SHIFTING POWER BALANCES

The acquisition of the gun by the Comanche, from the French pushing west of the Mississippi early in the eighteenth century, inaugurated the final phase of shifting Amerindian power balances on the plains. The gun, for all its inadequacies at that time, had been quickly adopted for warfare for its psychological effect as well as for the damage it could do; for one thing, it rendered Amerindian armour ineffective. Within twenty years the Comanche had driven the still gunless Apache south of the River Platte.[56] In the north, the Shoshoni had no such luck; they first encountered guns in the hands of their enemy the Cree, about the same time as their southern kinsmen, the Comanche, were acquiring them in trade. The Cree were blessed with two sources of the new weaponry: the English, who by that time were established on Hudson Bay, and the French, whose St. Lawrence and Great Lakes network of posts had by 1753 reached into the northwest with the establishment of Fort St. Louis on the Saskatchewan River. The Shoshoni quickly discovered that this new weapon seriously diminished the advantage they had gained from the horse.[57] But before they could gain regular access to firearms, the French and Indian War had broken out, interrupting such trade in the West. By 1770, British traders were back on the Upper Mississippi and the Saskatchewan, and were beginning to penetrate into the far northwest; but France as a power had all but disappeared from North America, and her jurisdiction over Louisiana had been transferred to Spain. This dealt a severe blow to whatever hopes the Shoshoni might have had of obtaining enough guns to face their enemies. As the Blackfoot, now mounted, already had access to British firearms, the Shoshoni were pushed off the plains by the end of the eighteenth century.[58] In achieving this, the Blackfoot were powerfully aided by epidemics, especially that of 1781-1782, which took a particularly heavy toll of the Shoshoni.[59] By the turn of the century, the victorious Peigans, who had been the tribe of the Blackfoot confederates mainly involved in the struggle, were referring to the once-dreaded Shoshoni as miserable old women whom they could defeat with sticks and stones.[60] With the removal of the Shoshoni threat, the fragile alliance of the Confederacy with Assiniboine and Cree lost its principal motivation, and the two expanding power groups came into collision.

Before this happened, and while they were still allies, the Blackfoot had obtained their first trade items from the Assiniboine and Cree, rather than directly from Europeans. Linguistic evidence hints that the first white men they met were French, as they designated them as "Real (or Original) Old Man People;" their term for whites in general was "Napikawan," "Old Man Person."[61] While the furthest west of the French establishments, Fort St. Louis (later Fort à la Corne), was located east of the forks of the Saskatchewan and thus outside Blackfoot territory, it would have been easily accessible to them. However, the first recorded meeting is the well-known encounter with Anthony Henday in 1754-1755. It has been estimated that by that time the Blackfoot were all mounted; but Henday's report that they had horses was greeted with disbelief by the English on the Bay.[62] By then, the Blackfoot were well into their period of expansion; as the Peigan pushed the Shoshoni south and west, the Sarsi moved into the North Saskatchewan basin and the Gros Ventre occupied territories vacated by the Blackfoot around the Eagle Hills. By 1770, the territory along the eastern Rockies north of Yellowstone was controlled by the Blackfoot Confederacy and its allies. It was about this time that the Crow (Hidatsa) first appeared in the southern part of this region; they also took up the fight against the Shoshoni.[63]

The Blackfoot never took to trading with Europeans as had the Cree and the Assiniboine; neither Henday nor, later, Matthew Cocking had been able to persuade them, or the Gros Ventre, to make the arduous journey to the Bay. This resistance was due partly to the fact that they were already receiving trade goods through the Cree and the Assiniboine, and partly to a conflict of the demands of the fur trade with those of buffalo hunting, which provided so bountifully for them. Late fall and early winter was the best season for trapping, as pelts were then in their prime; it was also the best time for killing bison and preparing winter provisions. From the social aspect, trapping was a family affair, whereas buffalo hunting involved the whole community. Of the Blackfoot confederates, the Peigan had the most beaver in their territory, and consequently became the most active as trappers; the others, as well as their allies, were to become provisioners for the trade rather than trappers for furs. This independence of the Blackfoot and Gros Ventre helped convince the Hudson's Bay Company to build Cumberland House (near The Pas) in 1774 and Hudson House (west of Prince Albert) in 1779. These posts were, however, outside Blackfoot territory. By the time the Nor'Westers built

Fort Augustus on the North Saskatchewan in 1795, and the Hudson's Bay Company had countered with Fort Edmonton that same year, Blackfoot territory was ringed with trading posts.[64] It was not until 1799, when the Nor'Westers built the first Rocky Mountain House, that a post was established within the Blackfoot sphere of control.

TRADING SITUATION

The trading situation on the plains was complex, compounded by rivalries between tribes, between traders, between traders and Amerindians, as well as between Canada and the U.S.A. Despite their unwillingness to meet the fur trade on its own terms, the Blackfoot and Gros Ventre felt that they were not as well treated in trade as their enemies, the Cree, particularly in the case of firearms.[65] The traders, especially the independents, did not help when they treated Amerindians badly, as happened all too frequently. The resultant tensions sometimes led to trouble, as in 1781 when Amerindians burned the prairie around the posts, which the traders believed was done to scare game away.[66] When the Nor'Westers sought to cross the mountains and make contact with the Kutenai and other plateau peoples, the Blackfoot became seriously alarmed. David Thompson finally succeeded in building a post in Kutenai territory in 1807, which moved the Peigans, already disturbed by the killing of two of their tribesmen by members of the Lewis and Clark expedition shortly before, to raise a war party. Although Thompson was able to negotiate a peaceful settlement, the unfortunate result for him was that famous delay which cost the Nor'Westers the right to claim the mouth of the Columbia for Britain.[67] That same year (1807), a band of Bloods and Atsina pillaged the first Fort Augustus, and when the Hudson's Bay Company built Peigan Post (Old Bow Fort) in 1832 in territory controlled by the Bloods, the latter refused to allow their allies to trade there, forcing the closing of the post two years later.[68] Nor did it take long for the Blackfoot to take advantage of the new international boundary; they became adept at raiding posts built in that part of their territory claimed by the United States and then selling the proceeds to posts north of the border.[69] The situation was aggravated by the American custom of sending out white trappers instead of relying on Amerindian sources—an act which the Blackfoot considered trespassing.

It was a change in the character of the trade which brought about better relations between the Blackfoot and traders. In Canada, this developed because of the opening of the Athabaska region for furs, which resulted in a greatly increased demand for pemmican to provision lengthening supply lines. Pemmican, a highly concentrated food, was particularly suitable for the transportation facilities of the northern routes which depended upon the canoe. In the U.S., the growing importance of buffalo robes, encouraged by the development of transportation facilities, made it practicable to traffic in the bulky, heavy hides. In either case, increasing affluence was manifested in the size of tipis, which by the 1830s, could be large enough to accommodate as many as 100 persons.[70] The new commerce placed a premium upon the services of women, who prepared both pemmican and hides. This encouraged polygyny, as well as a younger age for brides. Where plains Amerindian women had usually married in their late teens, girls as young as twelve now did so. Rarely could a man afford to buy a wife before he was 35, however. As polygyny increased, a hierarchy developed among wives, with the senior wife usually directing the others.[71] Women taken in raids now tended to be retained by their captors rather than to be sold, a trend that became particularly evident after the first third of the nineteenth century.

Commercialism and its concomitant emphasis on wealth affected other social institutions as well. A great many societies appeared, the best known of which were connected with war and the maintenance of camp and hunt disciplines. War as a way of life was a comparatively late development; for the Blackfoot, it became a means of accumulating wealth, which in turn was a route to prestige. Still, something of the old ways persisted, for although the Blackfoot were a major military power on the northwestern plains for more than a century, it remained possible in their society to become a chief without going on the warpath.[72] Bravery and generosity were the requisites, as they were among the Plains Cree and others.

ALLIES AND ENEMIES

The Gros Ventre, who were established between the forks of the Saskatchewan River when Matthew Cocking visited them in 1772—he referred to them as one of the tribes of "equestrian natives"—were the easternmost of the Blackfoot allies. The expression "Gros Ventre" was first recorded by Edward Umfreville, who was in their territory from 1784 to 1788.[73] The Blackfoot term for these Algonkian-speaking agriculturalists-turned-hunters was "Atsina," "gut people"; they called themselves "Haaninin," "chalk-men" or "men of soft white stone." They impressed Cocking not only with their skill as buffalo hunters, but also in their customs and manners, which he found more like those of Europeans.[74] A later fur trader, however, described them as "lazy" and "treacherous," good only at stealing horses,[75] an opinion probably based on nothing more substantial than poor trading relations. Weakened by the ravages of the great epidemic of 1781-1782, the Gros Ventre began to be pushed south and east by the Assiniboine and Cree. In 1793, a key battle was fought near South Branch House, when Cree wiped out a Gros Ventre band which had numbered sixteen lodges. Apparently their alliance with the Blackfoot was not on a very secure basis,[76] as they received little, if any, help from them.

Such incidents greatly exacerbated the resentment shared by the Gros Ventre and the Blackfoot toward the trading success of the Cree and Assiniboine, which made possible the latter's superiority in firearms. In the eyes of the Gros Ventre, the traders were in effect allies of their enemies, so they responded to the Cree raid by attacking fur trade posts such as Manchester House (on Pine Island, North Saskatchewan River), which they looted in 1793, and in the destruction of the Hudson's Bay Company's South Branch House the following year. In both cases, nearby Nor'Wester forts had been able to defend themselves. Such raids, of course, only compounded the trading difficulties of the Gros Ventre, who apparently were responsible for pillaging Chesterfield House at the mouth of the Red Deer River in 1826; in any event, groups of them subsequently fled south to the headwaters of the Missouri, where they joined their Arapaho kinsmen.[77] The disappearance of the Gros Ventre from the Saskatchewan basin meant that there was no longer a buffer between Blackfoot and the Assiniboine-Cree, who were thus in direct conflict.

The first European mention of Cree and their allies, the Assiniboines (Stoneys), is in the Jesuit Relations for 1640, when the latter are referred to first as the "Assinipour" and later (1657) as "Assinipoualak," "Warriors of Rock." The Assiniboines came to the attention of the French because of their connection with the Ottawa River trading system.[78] A Siouan-speaking people, they apparently broke off from the Yanktonai Dakota sometime around 1600, moving north and west, establishing themselves on the Red and Assiniboine Rivers, and along the Saskatchewan River to the foothills;[79] others moved northeastward into the boreal forest. According to David Thompson, the rupture had not been peaceful. As the Assiniboines became more firmly associated with the fur trade, their alliance with the Cree and other Algonkian speakers strengthened, as did their hostility to their kinsmen, the Sioux.

The Cree, the most widespread of northern Amerindians, were first identified by the French as "Kristinaux" or "Killistinaux"; like the Assiniboine, they were connected with the Ottawa and Huron trading systems. Soon, however, they were in direct trading contact with the French in what is now northern Quebec, to the east of Hudson Bay, as well as north of Lake Superior. By 1684, the French had built a post on Lake Nipigon to trade with the Cree and their Assiniboine allies in the area;[80] by that time, other bands of Cree were actively trading with the English on the Bay.[81] Kelsey noted in 1690 that both Cree and Assiniboine were well armed, a situation which encouraged an already evident trend toward expansion. By 1730, Pierre Gaultier de Varennes et de La Vérendrye reported a detachment of Cree south of the Saskatchewan, which the stories of Saukamapee support.[82] The Cree probably entered the northwestern plains by two routes, the Saskatchewan to the north and the Assiniboine and its tributaries to the south. That they flourished in the plains environment despite the decimations of the smallpox epidemic of 1776-1777 and later is witnessed by the number of bands which developed between the Qu'Appelle Valley and Edmonton—eight, all told.[83] In the forests of the north, the Cree were finally stopped and pushed back by the Chipewyans, although bands raided as far as the Mackenzie basin in 1820, the farthest point of their expansion.[84] In the southwest, they were stopped by the Blackfoot, with whom they had once been in sporadic alliance when the Shoshoni were a common enemy. By the early nineteenth century, Cree and Blackfoot considered each other their worst foe.

Whether or not the Cree were introduced to plains life by the Assiniboine, as some have maintained, underlying similarities between customs of northeastern woodlands and northwestern plains meant that adaptation was not difficult. By 1772, Cree were impounding bison, but preferred the gun to the bow for the hunt, in contrast to peoples longer established on the grasslands. However, buffalo hunting lessened dependence upon the fur trade; bands of Cree acting as hunters for particular posts, known as the "home guard," were more a phenomenon of the northern forests,[85] although they were not unknown at the posts of the parklands or prairies, as for example at Fort Pembina.

Reduced dependence on the fur trade affected relationships with traders, and it was the Plains Cree who were involved in one of the most widely remembered confrontations. It occurred in 1779 in reaction to the callous behaviour of a group of independent traders at Fort Montagne d'Aigle (Eagle Hills Fort), on the Saskatchewan between Eagle Hill Creek and Battle River. Two traders were killed and the rest forced to flee; the post was abandoned, and was apparently never permanently reoccupied. The incident also caused the abandonment that same year of the Nor'Wester Fort du Milieu and Upper Hudson House of the Hudson's Bay Company. Nor was this an isolated occurrence. For just one more example, it was the Cree who were participants in a *mêlée* in 1781 at Fort des Trembles on the Assiniboine that resulted in the death of three traders and between 15 and 30 Amerindians. Only the outbreak of the 1781-1782 smallpox epidemic prevented large scale retaliations against the traders.[86] The much-vaunted peaceful cooperation considered to be characteristic of the fur trade in the northern forests was not so evident on the plains.

In spite of this, the converging influences of the horse and the fur trade fostered an efflorescence of plains cultures, whose golden years in the northwest are usually dated from 1750 to 1880. The horse facilitated the exploitation of the bison herds and the extension of overland routes; the fur trade made available a new range of goods, but even more importantly, provided new markets for products of the hunt. This meant that as long as the herds lasted, plains Amerindians were able to hold their own and indeed to reach new heights of cultural expression as their societies became increasingly complex. They were even able to overcome to a large extent the demographic disasters of introduced diseases. But they did not have time to make their own accommodations to the disappearance of the herds upon which all this was based; it was the dramatic suddenness of that event which catapulted matters beyond their control.

This flourishing of a culture soon to die was not unique to the plains. It had previously occurred in the eastern woodlands, for example, among the Ojibway, Woods Cree and Iroquois; and it occurred simultaneously and continued somewhat later on the west coast, where one of its more spectacular manifestations was the burgeoning of totem poles, not to mention the appearance of button blankets and argillite carving. But in sheer artistry of dress, the mounted plainsman achieved an elegance which has never been surpassed; as an expression of the migratory bison-hunting way of life, he was his own *pièce de résistance*.

SUMMARY

To conclude, there is now no doubt as to the considerable time span of human habitation on the northwestern plains. Indeed, some of our most ancient archaeological records have been discovered here. In Alberta, for instance, there is Head-Smashed-In Buffalo Jump and the Majorville Cairn and Medicine Wheel site, both of which have yielded evidence of continuous human use for 6,000 years or more. In Saskatchewan, Oxbow and Long Creek campsites show a similar length of habitation. However, archaeological evidence has not been found to support the hypothesis that early migrating Siberians found a corridor in the open lands east of the mountains;[87] those historic plains tribes which did originate in the northwest, all Athapaskan-speakers, arrived comparatively recently. Ancient Amerindians of the plains appear to have had more connections, however remote, indirect and sporadic, with the eastern and northeastern woodlands, as well as with the civilizations of the Mississippi, the pueblos of the southwest, and even tenuously with Mexico. Similarly, when the horse and European trade goods appeared on the northwestern plains, they filtered in from the south as well as from the east and northeast. When Europeans first began to colonize mainland America during the sixteenth century, they often compared Amerindians with what they imagined their own Stone Age ancestors to have been like, and even sometimes with the peoples of classical antiquity. In the hurly-burly of conquering the land, that more generous perspective was often overlooked. As archaeology reveals the richness and antiquity of our prehistoric heritage, and as its links with the historic present are slowly traced out, we would do well to re-evaluate our perception of Canada as a "new world" without traditions of civilization before the arrival of Europeans.

NOTES

1. This paper was presented in a slightly different form to the Edmonton Branch of the Alberta Historical Society, December 6, 1979. I would like to thank Dr. Paul F. Donahue, acting director of the Archaeological Survey, Historical Resources Division, Alberta Culture, for his generous assistance, as well as Dr. L.H. Thomas and Dr. John Honsaker, both of the University of Alberta, for their thoughtful and informed comments. The conception and line of thought is entirely my responsibility.

2. H.M. Wormington, and Richard G. Forbis, *An Introduction to the Archaeology of Alberta*, Denver, Proceedings of the Denver Museum of Natural History #11, 1965, 198-99.

3. Clark Wissler, "Diffusion of Culture in the Plains of North America," *International Congress of Americanists*, 15th session (Quebec, 1906), 39-52; also cited by William Mulloy, *A Preliminary Historical Outline for the Northwestern Plains,* Laramie, Wyoming, University of Wyoming Publications, XXII #1 (July, 1958), 6. However, Wissler later modified this view. See Edward Adamson Hoebel, *The Plains Indians: a critical bibliography,* Bloomington, Indiana University Press, 1977, 8-10.

4. A.L. Kroeber, *Cultural and Natural Areas of Native North America*, Berkeley, University of California, 1939, 76; also cited in Mulloy, *Preliminary Historical Outline*, 6.

5. Waldo R. Wedel, *Prehistoric Man on the Great Plains*, Norman, University of Oklahoma Press, 1961, 243-244, 256. Also, by the same author, "The High Plains and their Utilization by the Indian," *American Antiquity*, XXIX #1 (1963), 1-16.

6. Michel de Montaigne, *The Complete Works of Montaigne*, trans. by Donald M. Frame, Stanford, California, Stanford University Press, 1957, 693.

7. The classification I am using was suggested by that of Waldo R. Wedel in the "The Prehistoric Plains," *Ancient Native Americans*, ed., Jesse D. Jennings, San Francisco, W.H. Freeman, 1978, 183-219.

8. Hoebel, *Plains Indians*, 12; Zenon S. Pohorecky, "Archaeology and Prehistory: The Saskatchewan Case," in *Region of the Mind*, ed. Richard Allen, Regina, Canadian Plains Research Centre, 1973, 47-72. Such an early date has recently received indirect support from the discovery of a hunters' camp in Western Pennsylvania which has been dated to 19,000 B.C. (J.M. Adovasio and R.C. Carlisle, "An Indian Hunters' Camp for 20,000 Years," Scientific American (1984), 130-136).

9. "Scientists find skeleton bones," Edmonton Journal, 19 March 1982. For earlier speculations that it might be older, see "Infant Skeleton may hold elusive answer" (Edmonton Journal, 17 October 1981), and Brian O.K. Reeves, "The Southern Alberta Paleo-Cultural Paleo-Environmental Sequence," in *Post-Pleistocene Man and His Environment on the Northern Plains*, Calgary, University of Calgary Archaeological Association, 1969, 21.

10. H.M. Wormington, *Ancient Man in North America.* Denver, The Denver Museum of Natural History, 1964, 149. "Atlatl" is a Nahuatl word, as it was in Mexico that the instrument was first identified.

11. George W. Arthur, *An introduction to the ecology of early historic communal bison hunting among the Northern Plains Indians*, Ottawa, National Museums of Canada, 1975, 71.

12. *Ibid.*, 72; Reeves, *Post-Pleistocene*, 22; Thomas F. and Alice B. Kehoe, "Saskatchewan," in *The Northwestern Plains: A Symposium*, ed., Warren W. Caldwell, Billings, Montana, Centre for Indian Studies, Rocky Mountain College, 1968, 21. See also Thomas F. Kehoe, *The Gull Lake Site*, Milwaukee, Milwaukee Public Museum, 1973.

13. Wedel, *Prehistoric*, 249.

14. There is always the possibility—even probability—that this reduction is more apparent than real. As archaeological techniques develop, traces of man's presence become more evident. For other aspects of the problem, see Brian Reeves, "The Concept of an Altithermal Cultural Hiatus in Northern Plains Prehistory," *American Anthropologist* LXXV (1973), 1221-53; and W.R. Hurt, "The Altithermal and the Prehistory of the Northern Plains," *Quaternia* VIII (1966) 101-13.

15. Jennings, *Ancient Native*, 202.

16. So far the Archaeological Survey of Alberta has examined about 5 percent of the province's surface.

17. James M. Calder, *The Majorville Cairn and Medicine Wheel Site, Alberta*, Ottawa, National Museum of Man (Mercury Series #62), 1977, 202. See also two reports by Boyd Wettlaufer, *The Long Creek Site*, Regina, Saskatchewan Museum of Natural History, 1960, and *The Mortlach Site in The Besant Valley of Central Saskatchewan*, Regina, Department of Natural Resources, 1955; and one by Robert W. Nero and Bruce A. McCorquodale, "Report of and Excavation at the Oxbow Dam Site," *The Blue Jay*, XVI #2 (1958), 82-90.

18. Richard G. Forbis, *A Review of Alberta Archaeology to 1964*, Ottawa, National Museum of Canada, 1970, 27.

19. Arthur, *Introduction*, 110ff; Forbis, *Review*, 29. See also Thomas F. Kehoe, *Indian Boulder Effigies*, Regina, Saskatchewan Museum of Natural History, 1965.

20. Forbis, *Review*, 27. On the significance of the circle, Calder cited Hyemeyohsts Storm: "It is the mirror in which everything is reflected, it is the universe and the cycle of all things that exist," and added that it represented understanding, knowledge and perception. The four great powers of the circle found at the four cardinal points are wisdom, innocence, illumination and introspection (Calder, *Majorville Cairn*, 207).

21. Kehoe, "Saskatchewan," 30.

22. Jennings, *Ancient Native*, 203. Ceramic evidence also supports this hypothesis. See William J. Byrne, *The Archaeology and Prehistory of Southern Alberta as Reflected by Ceramics*, 3 vols., Ottawa, National Museum of Man (Mercury Series #14), 1973, II: 561.

23. *Ibid.*, II: 554; Richard Glover, ed., *David Thompson's Narrative*, Toronto, Champlain Society, 1962, 240.

24. Reeves, *Post-Pleistocene*, 34-36.

25. Richard G. Forbis, "Alberta," in *Northwest Plains Symposium*, 44. An earth village described by Peter Fidler, who was in Saskatchewan late in the 18th century, has not been located (Kehoe, "Saskatchewan," 32).

26. Population on the high plains during the post-glacial period has been estimated at 0.2 to 0.3 persons per square mile. (Reeves, *Post-Pleistocene*, 37).

27. Dolores A. Gunnerson, "Man and Bison on the Plains in the Protohistoric Period," *Plains Anthropologist* XVII #55 (1972), 3-4, 5-6. See also F.G. Roe, *The North American Buffalo*, Toronto, University of Toronto Press, 1972, 228-56 and 283-333.

28. *Ibid.*, 2. It has been estimated that the buffalo may have numbered as many as 60,000,000 at their peak (Arthur, *Introduction*, 11-12; F.G. Roe, *The North American Buffalo*, Toronto, University of Toronto Press, 1951, 518-19).

29. T.H. Lewis, ed., "The Narrative of the Expedition of Hernando de Soto by the Gentleman of Elvas," in *Spanish Exploreres in the Southern United States 1528-1543*, ed., Frederick W. Hodge, N.Y., Scribner's, 1907, 213.

30. Roe, *American Buffalo*, 235, 843-44; Gunnerson, "Man and Bison," 2. Buffalo also destroyed small trees and pushed over telephone poles. Arthur, *Introduction*, 15-16.

31. R.G. Thwaites, ed., *The Jesuit Relations and Allied Documents*, 73 vols., Cleveland, Burrows Bros., 1896-1901, LIX, 113; Gunnerson, "Man and Bison," 2-3, citing G.A. Dorsey, *Traditions of the Caddo*, Washington, Carnegie Institution of Washington, 1905, 50-55, 109-11.

32. Joseph Jablow, *The Cheyenne in Plains Indian Trade Relations 1795-1840*, Monograph of the American Ethnological Society, XIX, Seattle and London, University of Washington Press, 1950, 14; Robert H. Lowrie, *Indians of the Plains*, New York, American Museum of Natural History, 1963, 45.

33. William Duncan Strong, "The Plains Culture Area in the Light of Archaeology," *American Anthropologist* XXXV (1933), held that horse nomadism represented no more than a "thin and strikingly uniform veneer" on earlier cultural manifestations. For the lack of specific rites among the Plains Cree for the increase of horses even though they were the symbol of wealth, see David G. Mandelbaum, *The Plains Cree*, New York, American Museum of Natural History Anthropological Papers #37, Pt. 2, 1940, 195-96. Mandelbaum's work has recently been reprinted by the Canadian Plains Research Center, Regina.

34. F.G. Roe, *The Indian and the Horse*, Norman, University of Oklahoma Press, 1951, 54.

35. John C. Ewers, *The Horse in Blackfoot Indian Culture*, Washington, Smithsonian Institution Press, 1955, 2-3.

36. Roe, *Indian and Horse*, 74-75.

37. Arthur, *Introduction*, 66; Elliott Coues, ed., *History of the Expedition Under the Command of Lewis and Clark*, 4 vols., New York, Harper, 1893, III: 1148.

38. Arthur, *Introduction*, 72.

39. Oscar Lewis, *The Effects of White Contact Upon Blackfoot Culture With Special References to the Fur Trade*, Monographs of the American Ethnological Society #6, New York, Augustin, 1942, 39-40; Bernard Mishkin, *Rank and Warfare Among Plains Indians*, Monographs of the American Ethnological Society #3, Seattle and London, University of Washington Press, 1940, 10; Glover, *David Thompson*, 267-68. For other such raids, see A.S. Morton, ed., *The Journal of Duncan M'Gillivray of the Northwest Company at Fort George on the Saskatchewan, 1794-1795*, Toronto, MacMillan, 1979, 27.

40. Glover, *David Thompson*, 241-42; Frank Raymond Secoy, *Changing Military Patterns on the Great Plains*, Monographs of the American Ethnological Society XXI, Seattle and London, University of Washington Press, 1953, 33; Lewis,

White Contact, 11; George E. Hyde, *Indians of the High Plains*, Norman, University of Oklahoma Press, 1959, 121, 133-34.

41. James Teit, "The Salishan Tribes of the Western Plateaus," *45th Annual Report, U.S. Bureau of American Ethnology (1927-1928)*, Washington, 1930, 109-10; Mishkin, *Rank and Warfare*, 9.

42. Secoy, *Military Patterns*, 36-38.

43. Glover, *David Thompson*, 244.

44. John C. Ewers, *The Blackfeet*, Norman, University of Oklahoma Press, 1958, 22.

45. John C. Ewers, "Was There a Northwestern Plains Sub-Culture? An Ethnographic Appraisal," *Northwest Plains Symposium*, 71. See also Hugh A. Dempsey, *Indian Tribes of Alberta*, Calgary, Glenbow-Alberta Institute, 1978.

46. Ewers, *Blackfeet*, 6-7; Hoebel, *Plains Indians*, 37; Lewis, *White Contact*, 7-9.

47. Ewers, "Ethnographic Appraisal," 73.

48. Ewers, *Blackfeet*, 24-25.

49. Cf. James Henri Howard, *The Plains-Ojibwa or Bungi, Hunters and Warriors of the Northern Prairie*, Vermillion, S.D., South Dakota Museum, University of South Dakota, 1965. Also Edwin Thompson Denig, *Five Indian Tribes of the Upper Missouri*, ed., John C. Ewers, Norman, University of Oklahoma Press, 1961, 100. Denig says that the Ojibwa and Cree were so intermingled as to be difficult to consider separately.

50. Ewers, "Ethnographic Appraisal," 71.

51. *Ibid.*, 72.

52. Symmes C. Oliver, *Ecology and Cultural Continuity as Contributing Factors in the Social Organization of the Plains Indians*, Berkeley and Los Angeles, University of California Press, 1962, 46.

53. Glover, *David Thompson*, 241-42; Hyde, *High Plains*, 133-34; and Secoy, *Military Patterns*, 36-37.

54. Glover, *David Thompson*, 245.

55. Elliott Coues, ed., *New Light on the Early History of the Great Northwest, 1799-1814*, 3 vols., New York, Harper, 1897. II: 713-14. For a Spanish governor's ingenious argument in favor of providing guns to *indios barbaros* in order to make them less formidable, see Max L. Moorhead, *The Apache Frontier*, Norman, University of Oklahoma Press, 1968, 127-28.

56. Hyde, *High Plains*, 146.

57. Secoy, *Military Patterns*, 52.

58. Glover, *David Thompson*, 107, 240.

59. Hyde, *High Plains*, 164-65.

60. Coues, *New Light*, II: 726.

61. Ewers, *Blackfeet*, 19; 24.

62. Glyndwr Williams, "The Puzzle of Anthony Henday's Journal, 1754-55," *The Beaver*, Outfit 309:3 (Winter, 1978), 53.

63. Lewis, *White Contact*, 14.

64. *Ibid.*, 17-18.

65. Morton, *Duncan M'Gillivray*, 31.

66. E.E. Rich, *The Fur Trade in the Northwest to 1857*, Toronto, McClelland and Stewart, 1967, 158. For the Amerindian use of fire to control both plant and animal life, see Henry T. Lewis, *A Time for Burning*. (Edmonton, Boreal

Institute for Northern Studies, 1982); and Stephen J. Pyne, "Our Grandfather Fire: Fire and the American Indian," in *Fire in America* (Princeton, Princeton University Press, 1982), 71-83. Arthur discusses Amerindian uses of fire to hunt bison in *Introduction*, 10-30.

67. Lewis, *White Contact*, 23.
68. J.B. Tyrrell, ed., *David Thompson's Narrative of his Explorations in Western America*, Toronto, Champlain Society, 1916, xc; for a different version, see J.E.A. Macleod, "Peigan Post and the Blackfoot Trade," *Canadian Historical Review*, XXIV #3 (1943), 273-79.
69. Lewis, *White Contact*, 24.
70. *Ibid.*, 35-36.
71. Mandelbaum, *Plains Cree* (1940), 246; Lewis says that among the Blackfoot, the third or fourth wife had such an inferior status that she was referred to as a "slave" (*White Contact*, 39-40).
72. *Ibid.*, 57.
73. Regina Flannery, *The Gros Ventres of Montana, Part I: Social Life*, Anthropological Series #15, Washington, The Catholic University of America Press, 1953, 4-5.
74. *Ibid.*, 5; Alfred L. Kroeber, *Ethnology of the Gros Ventre*, New York, Anthropological Papers of the American Museum of Natural History, I, 1908, 145.
75. Morton, *Duncan M'Gillivray;* 26-27, 73-74.
76. *Ibid.*, 62-63; Arthur J. Ray, *Indians in the Fur Trade*, Toronto, University of Toronto Press, 1974, 98; Kroeber, *Ethnology*, 146.
77. Flannery, *Gros Ventres*, 9.
78. Thwaites, *Jesuit Relations* XVIII: 231; XLIV; 249; Ray, Fur Trade, 11.
79. Glover, *David Thompson*, 164.
80. Thwaites, *Jesuit Relations* XVIII: 229; Ray, *Fur Trade*, 11.
81. Apparently the English on the Bay, on the advice of Medard Chouart de Groseilliers and Pierre Radisson, had entered into ceremonial alliances with the local Cree, which were ritually renewed annually with feasting and gift exchanges. One observer saw this as paying "rent" (Denig, *Five Tribes*, 112).
82. Glover, *David Thompson*, 240ff; L.J. Burpee, ed., *Journals and Letters by Pierre Gaultier de Varennes de La Verendrye*, Toronto, Champlain Society, 1927, 25.
83. David G. Mandelbaum, *Anthropology and People: the World of the Plains Cree*, University Lectures #12, Saskatoon, University of Saskatchewan, 1967, 7.
84. Mandelbaum, *Plains Cree* (1940), 183.
85. Mandelbaum, *Anthropology*, 6.
86. Coues, *New Light*, I: 292-93; II: 498-99; Alexander Mackenzie, *Voyages from Montreal on the River St. Lawrence Through the Continent of America*, London, 1801, xiii-xiv.
87. Wormington and Forbis, *Introduction*, 183.

4 Traders and Indians

The rivalry between the North West Company and the Hudson's Bay Company for control of the western fur country was as old as La Verendrye and the French *coureurs*. Peter Pond, Samuel Hearne, and the others were following the tracks laid down by generations of traders before them. The problems they encountered were the same problems of distance and diplomacy encountered by Anthony Henday and Legardeur de Saint-Pierre. Their solutions were unique but they grew out of experience in the Indian trade and a growing knowledge of the contours of the western interior. Indeed, the rivalry was not really between two commercial enterprises at all; rather it was a rivalry between two great geographic possibilities. Would the resources of the western hinterland flow southeastward across the Great Lakes and down the Ottawa River to Canada? Or would they take the shorter route north and east through the stunted forest of the Shield to the swampy shores of Hudson Bay? For almost half a century the answer hung in the balance.

A glance at the map would suggest that the Hudson Bay route made the most sense. After all, the Bay was over two thousand kilometres closer to the best fur country and well connected by navigable waterways to the main arteries of the western trade. Yet the map is deceiving. It does not indicate the pride of a trading tradition, the ambitions of a rising commercial class, the enterprise of a group of traders linked by family ties and dreams of personal wealth. Nor does it show the more prosaic facts: the unequal distribution of the valuable birch tree or the maddening tendency of the British armed forces to conscript manpower which otherwise might have ended up in the employ of the Hudson's Bay Company. And so traders from Canada were able to corner an increasing share of the western furs despite the distances they had to travel. With the creation of the North West Company, the Canadian trading system reached its peak and the struggle for the fur empire was joined in earnest.

The Hudson's Bay Company and the North West Company both dealt in furs but they were as different as two trading companies possibly could be. They were organized differently; their employees were drawn from different places; they approached the native people differently; for the most part they even spoke different languages. The Hudson's Bay Company was in the traditional mould of the imperial trading company, chartered by the British monarch and given a monopoly to exploit the resources of its far-flung possessions. Headquartered in London, it was directed by men who had almost no first-hand knowledge of the fur trade. As a result they were cautious, even timid, and as the pressure of competition grew they were sometimes slow to grasp an opportunity or take a bold initiative. The Company drew its men at first from the English working class and increasingly from the Scottish islands. These men were called "servants" and the term suggests the deference employees were expected to show their "officers." Chances of promotion into the top ranks were slight, and there was little incentive for men to exert themselves unduly on the Company's behalf. But if the Hudson's Bay Company was at times sluggish, it was never inert. Rigor mortis was not setting in. When it embarked in new directions the Company moved forward relentlessly, and all its advantages of organization and experience made it a formidable competitor.

On the other hand the North West Company was a restive partnership of aggressive colonial merchants. Far from being cumbersome like its opponent, the Canadian concern was flexible and ever-changing as different partners joined and fell away. Most of its leading lights cut their teeth on the western trade and knew every aspect of the business. The upper ranks of the Company, the Nor'Westers proper, were recruited primarily in Scotland and England. After serving in the "Indian country" as clerks, they could graduate to a full partnership in the Company, sharing materially in its profits and psychologically in its triumphs over all competitors. So many of these men were related to each other that it seemed that the old "Marquis," Simon McTavish, who directed the company until his death in 1804, was presiding over a family affair. The McGillivray brothers, one of whom, William, succeeded McTavish as chief, were all his nephews. Alexander Mackenzie was a cousin to Roderic Mackenzie who was the brother-in-law of McTavish's wife. Angus Shaw, a prominent western trader for many years, was a nephew-in-law; Simon Fraser was a cousin; David Thompson was a brother-in-law to a nephew; and so it went. The result was a degree of enthusiasm and enterprise that, for a time, completely dominated the western fur trade.

The lower ranks of the North West Company were filled by the French-Canadian *voyageurs* who paddled the canoes, hauled supplies, built the posts, and generally did the scut work. With few exceptions, they never became partners in the Company, remaining instead an unruly mob of salaried employees. *Voyageurs* have become the romantic figures of the trade, so much more colorful than the dour Scots who worked for the

Hudson's Bay Company. We see them in our school books, dressed in their bright costumes and fearlessly shooting the foaming rapids with a song on their lips. (A collection of these songs, by the way, was once deemed unfit for publication because they were so obscene.) But the reverse side of their independence and pride was a tendency to resist the authority of their employer, and a North West Company post was often riven by squabbling between French *voyageurs* and English *bourgeois*. If a Hudson's Bay Company trading house resembled a military barracks, a Nor'Wester establishment had more in common with a rowdy tavern.

Unlike the monolithic Hudson's Bay Company, the North West Company had a kind of split personality. In Montreal the merchant partners looked after marketing the furs and importing the mountain of goods which fueled the trade. Each winter they supervised the packing of ironware, guns, kegs of powder and bags of lead shot, tobacco, woollens and linens, blankets, and liquor. As well they hired the guides, interpreters, clerks, and paddlers who went with the canoes to the interior. At the other end of the system, in the interior, "wintering" partners supervised trading in the various districts. The conduct of business was in their hands. They sought out distant Indian groups; they developed new transport routes; they even altered the prices being offered for furs. Competion made such flexibility necessary. When opponents were settled nearby, prices could be lowered and bribes of liquor and tobacco handed out freely; when the field was clear, partners could drive a harder bargain. The ability to react quickly to changes in the local situation was a big advantage for the North West Company.

Every summer the two ends of the North West Company's operations converged on the hinge of the Canadian trade, the depot at Grand Portage at the head of Lake Superior. (After 1801 the depot moved to Fort William, sixty kilometres to the north.) This fourteen-kilometre portage, separating the Pigeon River from Lake Superior, also separated the relatively unobstructed navigation of the Great Lakes from the swifter, shallower waterways of the interior. As well, the Grand Portage separated two ways of life; the itinerant, unsupervised, violent, elemental life of the Northwest and the more genteel society of the St. Lawrence settlements. The northmen best expressed this sense of crossing over into a different world. They were the *voyageurs* who manned the canoes from the interior, and for several years at a stretch they would not go east of the portage. A mystique, fed by their own boasting, grew up around the exploits of these inland travellers, and they loudly proclaimed their contempt for the soft life of their Montreal brothers. To keep the peace at Grand Portage, the two groups tented in separate camps divided by a small stream.

But business, not bragging, was the purpose of the annual rendezvous. Furs and supplies had to be carried across the portage and a partner up from Montreal brought news of the fur auctions, the activities of the competition and plans being made at headquarters. Alexander Mackenzie described how "the proprietors, clerks, guides and interpreters, mess together, to a number of sometimes an hundred, at several tables, in one large hall, the provision consisting of bread, salt pork, tea, spirits, wine, etc. and plenty of milk, for which purpose several milch cows are constantly kept." Canoemen, however, kept to their own tents and their usual diet of boiled corn and fat. Once the goods had been trans-shipped and business matters attended to, a banquet and dance was held in the main hall at the post, and then the canoes hurried off east and west to make their destinations before the ice began to form.

From Montreal the trip had been made in the giant *canots du maitres*, eleven metres long, propelled by eight to ten *voyageurs*, but at Grand Portage, travellers switched to the smaller North canoes, about seven metres in length and manned by a crew of four or five. The inland brigades made their arduous way through the country of the border lakes and down the Winnipeg River to the open waters of Lake Winnipeg. Along the way *voyageurs* fed on the familiar stew of boiled corn or wild rice flavoured with pork fat, but at Lake Winnipeg canoes were stocked with bags of pemmican, a mixture of powdered buffalo meat and fat which had become the staple item in a western traveller's diet. Pemmican was traded from the Plains Indians and stockpiled at key provisioning posts along the main transport routes. It provided a concentrated yet nutritious food supply which travelled well and did not spoil. Quite simply, the fur trade would have been impossible without it. As much as twenty thousand kilograms of pemmican were gathered along the Saskatchewan River alone each spring simply to feed the brigades moving up the river and north to Athabasca. During the winter buffalo meat continued to feed the people at the trading posts and a single post might consume a couple of hundred kilograms every day. As rival posts proliferated across the West, it is safe to assume that several million kilograms of pemmican were consumed in the fur country each year.

At Lake Winnipeg the brigades veered off toward their different destinations. Some canoes swung south into the Red River, continuing past the forty-ninth parallel or turning west up the Assiniboine to the posts which encroached in the southern plains. Others travelled up Lake Winnipeg, then hived off through a network of lakes and portages to the Swan River district. The Saskatchewan brigade continued northward to the top of Lake Winnipeg where it entered the mouth of the great river via the Grand Rapids and Cedar Lake. By now the Nor'Westers would have crossed paths with some Hudson's Bay Company canoes which came inland from York Fort up the Hayes and Nelson rivers. York Fort was to the Hudson's Bay Company trading system what Grand Portage was to the Nor'Westers. Like the mouth of a funnel, York sat at the outlet of a vast network of Indian canoe routes leading from the northern forest and the southern plains. Each summer, ships from Europe unloaded their supplies at this depot and collected the fur packs which had been brought from the interior. At times

York controlled the trade of a hinterland which encompassed most of what today are the three prairie provinces and a large part of the Northwest Territories. Yet despite the size of the empire at its back, York Fort was a wretched place. "Nine months of winter varied by three of rain and mosquitoes," grumbled one unhappy resident. The post was set back from the bank of the Hayes River about ten kilometres inland from the shores of Hudson Bay. It looked out across a dismal landscape of bog and stunted forest with trees so small a grown man could see over them. In the winter there was no escaping the cold; the snow drifted as high as the roof eaves, and ice actually formed on the inside walls of the log dwellings. In the summer came oppressive heat and voracious mosquitoes which filled the nose and screamed in the ear. In the fall cold fogs rolled in off the Bay, and in the spring the ground was such a quagmire of mud that buildings had to be perched on pilings and everyone went about on board sidewalks. York Fort? "The very name gives me Colick," wrote one trader, "and the worst news I could now receive would be that I was again to winter there."

As the inland brigades toiled westward up the Saskatchewan, the low, marshy shoreline gradually gave way to higher, wooded banks edged here and there by a beach of sand and rock. Not long after passing Cumberland House the brigades entered the "tracking ground" where the current picked up speed and the river was broken by a series of rapids. Amid much grumbling, *voyageurs* spilled onto the shore and for several days tracked their loaded canoes upriver by hauling on long ropes. The heat was stifling and the hunched, sweating bodies of the men were enveloped in clouds of mosquitoes. Stumbling on the slippery rocks, sinking thigh deep into the mud and sand, the *voyageurs* struggled against the brown current from sunup to sundown. "This part of the River is an object of terror to the whole band," allowed the inland trader Duncan McGillivray.

Near the present site of Prince Albert, Saskatchewan, the brigade reached level ground, the current slackened, and with relief the men re-embarked in their canoes. Now the open prairie was coming into view. "The face of the Country here assumes a different appearance," wrote McGillivray, "hitherto our way has been obstructed by thick woods, on each side of the River but now extensive plains interspersed with only a few tufts of wood, open themselves to view, and extend to the utmost extremity of your sight round the Horizon, which appears as plain as in the midst of the Ocean in a perfect calm." Mosquitoes became less troublesome, but were replaced by a fine sand which blew off the steep banks into the eyes of the paddlers. The river followed a confused path through a labyrinth of sandbanks and willow islands and only the most experienced guide could keep the brigade from wandering into false channels and dead ends. The high banks were scarred with paths worn smooth by the buffalo which migrated across the river in huge herds. Running headlong over the escarpment down into the water, the animals were mindless of human intruders, and *voyageurs* who could not fend them off with paddles were swamped. At a spot on the river called *La Montee*, later the site of Fort Carlton, a few members of the brigade exchanged their canoes for horses traded from the Indians. Ranging across the grasslands, these outriders brought in a daily ration of freshly butchered meat to feed the *voyageurs* on the last leg of their exhausting voyage.

The north branch of the Saskatchewan River marked the approximate boundary between wooded country to the north and grassland prairie to the south. Posts along its banks were strategically situated to gather furs from the Cree who inhabited the woods, while at the same time trading buffalo meat and horses from the Indians who inhabited the beaver-poor plains. Driven by a restless ambition, rival traders chased each other westward up the river, pausing every now and again to put up a draughty habitation before moving on, until the entire length of the waterway from Lake Winnipeg to the Rockies was dotted with posts like beads on a string. Similarly, major rivers like the Assiniboine, the Qu'Appelle, the Swan, and the Red were thickly inhabited by trading establishments. In fact, most rivers which provided a navigable canoe route and access to profitable hunting grounds were eventually settled by the ubiquitous traders, who, by the turn of the century, were drawing goods from every Indian group east of the mountains.

Trading posts were erected by the men themselves, so they had to be simply constructed and made of materials found on site. Buildings were set in a cleared quadrangle beside the river. In the middle stood the "main house," often a two-storey structure, made of logs plastered with mud and whitewashed. Inside, space was divided between a trading room and living quarters for the senior men. Floors were made of planks, and rooms were heated with stone fireplaces. Furniture was primitive. Other buildings were ranged along the sides of the quadrangle and contained the men's quarters, workshops, and storerooms. The entire establishment was enclosed by a stockade of pointed logs with bastions in opposite corners and gates open in two directions. Outside the stockade there was sometimes a vegetable garden, a corral for the livestock, and the "plantation" where the Indians pitched their tents when they arrived to trade.

The actual trade was surrounded by a formal ritual that varied little from post to post whether the traders were from Canada or Hudson Bay. Indians were not shoppers in the modern sense. They visited the posts not only to obtain goods but also to indulge their love of ceremony, to renew friendships, and to emphasize their position of equality with the white strangers. Duncan McGillivray described the trading procedure which evolved.

When a Band of Indians approach near the Fort it is customary for the Chiefs to send a few young men before them to announce their arrival, and to procure a few articles which they are accustomed to receive on these occasions—such as Powder, a Piece of Tobacco and a little paint to besmear their faces, an operation which they seldom fail to perform previous to their presenting themselves before the *White People*. At a few yards distance from the gate they salute us with several discharges of their guns, which is answered by hoisting a flag and firing a few guns. On entering the house they are disarmed, treated with a few drams and a bit of tobacco, and after the pipe has been plyed about for some time they relate the news with great deliberation and ceremony. . . . When their lodges are erected by the women they receive a present of Rum proportioned to the Nation and quality of their Chiefs and the whole Band drink during 24 hours and sometimes much longer for nothing. . . . When the drinking match has subsided they begin to trade.

Traders honoured leaders of the bands by dressing them in scarlet coats, trousers, laced hats with colored feathers, and linen shirts, and by giving them extra presents of tobacco and liquor. By giving a boost to a leader's authority, traders hoped to increase his prestige among his people which would in turn increase the amount of trade he brought to the post. Since rival companies indulged in gift-giving, it was not long before, in the words of one Nor'Wester, "every man who killed a few skins was considered a chief and treated accordingly; there was scarcely a common buck to be seen, all wore scarlet coats. . . ."

The fur trade had no use for money. It was a barter trade, goods exchanged for goods. Still, a recognized standard of value had to be set if any business was going to be done. Therefore the beaver pelt became the accepted unit of "currency." A single prime pelt was called a *Made Beaver*, and all other items were measured against it. For instance, a gun might be worth fourteen Made Beaver, a blanket seven Made Beaver, a hatchet one Made Beaver, and so on. Many other types of pelts were traded and they were given an equivalent value in beaver skins—a marten equalled half a beaver, an otter one beaver, a bear three beaver. The result was that the total value of an Indian's furs could be given a Made Beaver value and theoretically he could then get an equivalent value in trade goods. Yet it is misleading to know these prices because they were seldom adhered to. The trade was too competitive and changeable for a fixed price list. In practice the standard was a minimum, and each trader worked to increase his take by means both fair and larcenous. First of all, he could arbitrarily raise prices, a move that did not please the Indians, who usually knew the old price, and that therefore, wasn't very successful when competitors lived nearby. Secondly, he could haggle over the quality of the furs, claiming they were too worn, too small or too thin to bring full value. Thirdly, he could simply cheat the Indians by putting his thumb on the scale when weighing out shot, by using a short rule when measuring cloth, by diluting the brandy with water, and by substituting second-hand or second-rate goods for the top of the line. Cheating was so common that it was an accepted part of the trade. Profits made from it were entered on the account books and the Indians themselves knew how the traders operated. "You told me last year to bring many Indians to trade, which I promised to," announced one leader,

> you see I have not lied; here are a great many young men come with me; use them kindly, I say; let them trade good goods I say! We lived hard last winter and hungry, the powder being short measure and bad; being short measure and bad, I say! Tell your servants to fill the measure, and not to put their thumbs within the brim. . . . The guns are bad, let us trade light guns, small in the hand, and well shaped, with locks that will not freeze in the winter, and red gun cases. . . . Give us good measure of cloth; let us see the old measure; do you mind me?

"Give us good measure," the Indians said, asking for fair treatment. Yet the traders continued to charge what the market would bear. After all, they reasoned, the Indians were given no end of presents every time they visited the post, so why not balance the books with a little overcharging? Furthermore, since the Indians did not like to see prices changing every year, the value of their furs could not fluctuate with prices in the European market. Neither could the traders refuse to take furs in periods of glut. In other words, the conventional economics of supply and demand did not apply. As a result, traders used informal methods of compensating for a relatively inflexible price system.

The Indians were not defenceless when it came to trading. They were as expert at haggling as the white man, and they could simply refuse to trade their furs if they couldn't strike a deal. This threat was given special force when rival traders were in business nearby. Then the Indian with his furs had a choice and could play one against the other to get a better price for his goods. Neither were the Indians averse to practising some petty larceny of their own. Credit was an important part of the trading system and had been almost from the beginning. Indians were "trusted" with a quantity of goods in the fall on the understanding that they would repay their debt in the spring when they had trapped some furs. Yet the Indians sometimes refused to pay up, pleading poverty or sickness, and if a trader pressed the issue the debtor could simply decamp for another post where he might start with a clean slate. In theory credit seemed very much in the trader's interest. What better way of controlling Indian behaviour than by keeping him in debt to the Company? But in practice the Indians did not always recognize these economic obligations and refused to be kept under the trader's thumb.

What all of this makes clear is that the fur trade was a unique economic system. It was not a system invented by merchants in the Old World and imposed on the New. Instead it evolved out of conditions in the North West and the cultural needs of the people who lived there. A shopkeeper in Montreal or London would have been bewildered if he had been expected to treat his customers to a smoke and a drink, sit through a long speech in which he was alternately beseeched and berated, and then dress them in fine clothes so they would be sure to bring him their business next time. But gift-giving and oration were very much a part of Indian "commerce" and so they became part of the fur trade. The trade was carried on according to certain rules, which were systematically broken. At first glance the whole enterprise seems farcical. There was a price standard which was ignored, debts which were not repaid, and cheating which was openly declared. But each of these elements was part of the compromise between Indian and European trader which characterized the trade. Elements of farce are perhaps inevitable when economies and cultures as different as these meet and attempt to do business.

Although Canadians and Europeans came into the West to collect furs, the actual trading period only occupied a few days in the spring and fall. In summer, traders were on the move between their inland posts and the depots at Grand Portage and Hudson Bay. The rest of the time was marked by monotony rather than the high adventure we have come to associate with the fur trade. The men subsisted on fish and wild game, and most of their time was taken up with hunting and fishing. Still, a great deal of their food was bartered from the Indians; without this supply of buffalo and moose meat the newcomers would have starved. When they weren't out hunting, they were gathering wood to feed their insatiable fires or patching up the dilapidated houses. But through the dark, cold days of winter there was much free time for gambling, reading, writing letters, and brooding on distant places and half-forgotten friends. It was a time an active trader hated, a time of depression and lethargy, broken by nervous outbursts of violence and drunkenness.

Life at a Hudson's Bay Company post differed from life at a North West Company establishment. The English company expected its men to be obedient and sober. Early in its history the Company had recruited from among the laboring classes of the large British cities but these men were thought to be unsuitable because they were "acquainted with the ways and debaucheries of the town." Instead, an apprenticeship system was introduced. Young boys, sometimes only twelve years old, were taken from orphanages and charity schools and bound to the Company's service for up to seven years. They received a small salary and a chance to learn the skills of the trade, and when their term ran out many signed on as regular servants. The result was a pool of "Company men," experienced, disciplined, and obedient. Early in the eighteenth century the Company began to recruit its laborers from the Orkney Islands. These men, raised on the marginal farms and in the fishing villages of the rocky islands, were used to working hard for not much reward, and were able to endure much without complaint. Scots "are a hardy people both to endure hunger, and cold, and are subject to obedience," said an early Hudson's Bay Company governor. No wonder they appealed to a company looking for tractable employees. For their part, the Orkneymen were attracted to the fur trade by the chance to earn good wages and by a thirst for adventure. Orkneymen fulfilled the expectations held for them. Fathers brought in their sons and brother recruited brothers until by 1800 about three-quarters of the Hudson's Bay company men were from the Islands. Many of these men later settled in the West and formed an important Scottish element in the unique society taking shape there.

A North West Company post was a much less disciplined place. The wintering partners were never able to assert the same degree of authority over their French-Canadian *voyageurs*. This was much in keeping with the less structured, more democratic organization of the Canadian company in general. There seems to have been no love lost between the English-speaking partners and clerks and the French canoemen. The former may have respected the latters' abilities with the paddle but they had little patience for them as wintering companies. "With a slight education, if any, and no books, when in their wintering houses they passed their time in card playing, gambling and dancing," reported David Thompson, "which brought on disputes, quarrels and all respect was lost. Goods beyond the extent of their wages were taken by the men to pay their gambling debts, and every festival of the church of Rome was an excuse to get drunk. . . ." This behaviour has become part of the *voyageurs'* colorful legend today, but many of the Nor'Westers had only contempt for it. Daniel Harmon, with a party of *voyageurs*, came to the Swan River in 1800 to trade. He was the only Englishman in the group and there was not a soul at the post for him to talk to for weeks on end. He consoled himself with the thought that "what conversation would an illiterate ignorant Canadian be able to keep up. All of their chat is about Horses, Dogs, Canoes and Women, and strong Men who can fight a good battle." It was disingenuous of David Thompson to blame *voyageurs* for running up debts with the Company; the mark-up on goods from the Company stores was very high and it was well known that the *bourgeois* encouraged their men to go into debt as a way of keeping a hold over them. It is no wonder that the French were sometimes restless under the command of their highminded, often priggish employers. It has been tempting for romantically-inclined historians to present the fur trade as an example of French and English working together to develop the resources of the continent, but if the fur trade is an example of anything it is of the uneasy relations between the two groups which have so often plagued the country.

While traders were absorbed by their business concerns, the Indians of the West went about their own lives in many ways unaffected by the presence of so many newcomers to their lands. The two groups met briefly at the posts to exchange goods, each receiving from the other things it could not produce for itself. Then they parted, the Indians returning to a world the trader never entered or understood, a world with its own patterns of trade, its own religion and social relations, its own wars and alliances. Traders from Canada and

Europe obviously affected events in this world. They introduced new goods into it and disrupted its balance of power. But for the most part the traders were peripheral to the real concerns of the Indian people.

Until quite recently it was fashionable to emphasize the dependence of Indians on the traders. Native people quickly saw the superiority of European trade goods, such as ironware, cloth, and guns, abandoned their traditional ways of doing things, and fell headlong into an abject reliance on the trading post. At least that is how the argument goes, as if an entire civilization could be bought off with a kettle and a gun.

This interpretation is wrong for two reasons. First of all, it neglects to point out that traders were far more dependent on the Indians than vice versa. Aside from supplying furs, native people supplied most of the food without which the traders would have been forced to leave the country. As well, they helped transport goods, made snowshoes and canoes, and guided the newcomers through the bewildering maze of waterways to distant fur grounds. All of these chores were vital to the success of the fur trade. Nothing the traders offered in return, except perhaps guns, can be considered vital to the welfare of the Indians.

Secondly, to believe in the dependence of the Indians is to overlook the opinions of the traders themselves, who were always regretting their own lack of influence. Ever since Anthony Henday had visited the Blackfoot at mid-century, traders had complained that the western Indians would rather hunt buffalo, steal horses, and make war than produce furs for the white man. Duncan McGillivray summed up the situation from his post on the Saskatchewan. In his opinion, the Plains people lived "very happily independent of our assistance. They are surrounded with innumerable herds of various kinds of animals . . . and they have invented so many methods for the destruction of Animals, that they stand in no need of ammunition to provide a sufficiency for these purposes." McGillivray pointed out that the traders had only liquor, tobacco, and ammunition to attract the Indians. "The rest of our commodities are indeed useful to the Natives, when they can afford to purchase them, but if they had hitherto lived unacquainted with European productions it would not I believe diminish their felicity."

The impact of the trade was different for every Indian group. McGillivray was speaking about the Plains Indians who, because of their reliable food supply, could afford to be more independent of the traders than could their Woodland neighbours who specialized in hunting furs. Nonetheless, the fur trade did not destroy native culture. Indians were participants in the trade, not its victims. And they participated as independent people with a keen sense of their own needs, not as dupes who sold their birthright for a mess of beads and trinkets.

The traders from away did not bring any women with them into the West. The fur business was for men only. But this did not mean that they lived celibate lives. Indian women were numerous and it was a rare trader who did not have a "country wife" to share his lodgings. These relationships were far more than sexual affairs; they were as affectionate and durable as European-style marriages. Indeed, many liaisons led to marriage of a kind. According to the "custom of the country," borrowed from the native people, a trader took a wife by obtaining the permission of her parents and paying the "bride price" set by her relatives. These marriages *a la facon du pays* did not have the benefit of clergy but they were solemnized by Indian ritual and recognized as valid.

The Hudson's Bay Company feared these marriages and banned them, with little success. Its rival had a more pragmatic view. The Canadian partners knew from experience that, sex and romance aside, marriage was the best way to cement a trade alliance. If a trader wanted to be sure that an Indian leader brought his furs to the post each year, there was no better way than to marry his daughter. North West partners also were not above acting as pimps, stealing Indian women in payment for debts owed by fathers or husbands, "then selling them to their men [for] from five hundred to two thousand *livres* and if the Father or Husband or any of them resist the only satisfaction they get is a beating. . . ." However, force was not usually needed since the Indians saw the advantages of being linked by marriage to the strangers and frequently forced their women upon them.

Eventually the Hudson's Bay Company recognized the wisdom of country marriages and relaxed its restrictions, not only for reasons of trade but also because women were already proving valuable, if unofficial employees. "They clean and put into a state of preservation all Beaver and Otter skins brought by the Indians undried and in bad Condition," explained a letter from the Bay in 1802. "They prepare Line for Snow shoes and knit them also without which your Honors servants could not give efficient opposition to the Canadian traders they make Leather shoes for the men who are obliged to travel about in search of Indians and furs and are useful in a variety of other instances, in short they are Virtually your Honors Servants and as such we hope you will Consider them." The result was that western fur trade posts were filled with children and all the confusion of family life.

Yet for all that Indians and traders intermarried and intermingled, relations between them were strained, marked by suspicion, and punctuated by outbursts of violence and murder. As the brigades moved slowly up the Saskatchewan River each season, they were watched over by armed men on horseback who patrolled the high banks on the lookout for Indian ambush. At more than one post, people lived in terror of their lives. Sometimes the problem was local, caused by the stupidity or brutality of an individual trader. This was the case in 1780 on the Saskatchewan when one of the pedlars, renowned for his double-dealing, was murdered by Indians and the whole trading community retreated down the river in fear of an uprising that never came. More basic was the system of Indian alliances which the newcomers did not understand. The traders bartered guns to some Indian groups which then used the new weapons to make war on their neighbours. Naturally enough, traders were then seen as allies of their trading partners, and as such became the enemies of their enemies. On the plains, for example, the Gros Ventres came to hate the people who supplied their Cree enemies with guns, and in the Red River area the Sioux from the south terrorized the posts frequented by their enemies, the Ojibwa. There is evidence in the traders' journals that plans were brewing in 1780 to drive the newcomers from the Northwest. The Plains Indians were not as interested in trading as their Woodland neighbours, and, according to John Macdonell, a Nor'Wester in southern Manitoba, the Indians were developing plans "of cutting off all the white men in the interior country." It is possible that had the small pox not swept the plains at this point, with drastic results for the native people, the fur trade in the West might have been brought to a violent close.

In the next decade the Gros Ventres took the offensive. "They are an audacious, turbulent race," thought Alexander Henry the Younger, "and have repeatedly attempted to menace us." Their first move was to plunder a Hudson's Bay Company post on the North Saskatchewan. Then, in July 1794, the Gros Ventres attacked a North West Company post on the south branch of the river. The alarm was raised, however, and the post was securely locked. After exchanging gunfire for half an hour the warriors shifted their attention to a Hudson's Bay Company post not far away. They were able to take the small settlement totally by surprise, killing three men and five or six women and children before setting the buildings ablaze. One man managed to escape by hiding in a pile of rubbish, then scurrying under cover of smoke to a canoe and making his way downriver with news of the attack. However, this was the extent of the "uprising." The Gros Ventres withdrew, and though for several years rumours that they were coming again to attack the traders flew up and down the river, they eventually made their peace with the white men. The Indians were not united enough to drive the traders from the Northwest. And as time passed there appeared to be less and less reason to do so. Traders were too valuable to be evicted. The goods they imported were extremely useful to the Indians, both in peace and in war, and it would have been unlikely that the native people would destroy a trading system which served their interests.

As the century drew to a close the battle for the furs of the Northwest was going decidedly in the favour of the upstart company from Canada. In two decades the Nor'Westers had come to control over seventy-eight per cent of the trade, leaving a paltry amount for their older rival the Hudsons' Bay Company to share with the few independent traders still in the field. The British company was matching the Canadian post for post across the West, but there was no matching the ruthless energy of the Nor'Westers. Hudson's

Bay Company men carried on business on the Saskatchewan "as if it were drawn by a dead Horse," crowed their rivals. They were shorthanded, lacked drive, and feared the Indians. All of which led Duncan McGillivray to suggest that the venerable company should "adopt some terms of agreement" with the Nor'Westers' in other words, throw in the towel.

However, it was a little early for surrender. McGillivray was a few years ahead of his time; there would be no union yet. Even as the Nor'Westers seemed to be getting the best of the Bay Company, new competitors were getting ready in Montreal to join the struggle for the fur trade empire. These competitors were experienced, wealthy, and equal to the knock-about aggressiveness of the Nor'Westers. As the new century opened, the old rivalry was put aside for a while to meet this formidable challenge.

JACQUELINE PETERSON with

JOHN ANFINSON

5 The Indian and the Fur Trade
A Review of Literature

In the 1970s and 80s a multitude of books and articles on the fur trade in North America have appeared. Two important conclusions may be drawn from them. First, as Daniel Francis and Toby Morantz persuasively argue in *Partners in Fur*, the term itself is an oversimplification.[1] There were actually numerous fur trades, differing over time and across a vast cultural and ecological landscape. Secondly, the fur trade was far more than a first-stage colonial extractive industry forecasting the European settlement and national development of the United States and Canada, views which were propounded by Frederick Jackson Turner in 1891 and by Harold A. Innis in 1930, and which are still cherished by many historians of the West and North.[2] Rather, the fur trade, properly phrased, was an "Indian trade." It was a process of human interaction in which the economic exchange of raw commodities for manufactured goods figured as a vehicle and symbol for a much wider set of contacts between Indian and white. Although some fur trade history continues to be written otherwise, a binding characteristic of much of the literature published in the U.S. and Canada over the past fifteen years is the recognition of Indian centrality or, as Arthur J. Ray succinctly put it in 1978, of "Fur Trade History as an Aspect of Native History."[3]

Much of the impetus behind the recent work and its orientation derives from the maturation of a new subdiscipline, ethnohistory, which applies the perspectives of anthropology to the reconstruction of the history of non-western peoples. Until the 1960s, historians and anthropologists interested in the fur trade and its impact upon native people tracked separate courses, rarely intersecting to shape a debate. Since then, however, a number of trends have combined to make the fur trade a testing ground for a sophisticated analysis of Indian-white contact and particularly of Indian economic motivation and behavior in the trade. The appearance in 1974 of two major works, Charles A. Bishop's *The Northern Ojibway and the Fur Trade*, and Arthur J. Ray's *Indians in the Fur Trade*, signaled by their titles alone the emphasis now to be accorded to Indian peoples in a significant revision of fur trade history.[4]

It is noteworthy, perhaps, that in addition to historians and anthropologists, fur trade studies have recently engaged the attentions of economists, political scientists and, especially, geographers. Whatever the immediate concerns and foci of these diverse authors, all have attempted to answer several fundamental questions: Why, in what fashion, and to what degree did tribal peoples across northern North America engage in the fur trade? How was the trade shaped and what did it signify? How rapidly and in what ways did native involvement in the trade alter the patterns of precontact tribal societies? What were the results of such changes?

Not unexpectedly, the earliest and still most vital debate concerning Indian participation in the trade rose out of the older treatment of fur trade history as an aspect of business or economic history. Prior to the 1960s it had not occurred to scholars such as Harold A. Innis and George T. Hunt, writing from an unqualified neoclassical perspective, to ask "why" there was Indian involvement. The answer was self-evident. Indian hunters, like their white trader counterparts, were rational economic men driven by the profit motive and susceptible to the forces of the marketplace. While tacitly recognizing that most tribal economies were subsistence-oriented and that Indian tribes placed a peculiarly high value upon generosity and gift-giving, this view assumed that any original differences in tribal economic beliefs or practices were quickly subordinated by the desire for new sources of wealth and superior European commodities.[5]

Beginning in the 1960s, these assumptions increasingly came under fire as scholars took a closer look at the behavior of Indian hunters and traders. E. E. Rich, the first person to delve deeply into the riches of the Hudson's Bay Company archives, took a major step away from Innis and Hunt in a 1960 essay by acknowledging that Subarctic people did not maximize, accumulate, or take profit as classical theory predicted, but rather had "limited consumer demands." Rich noted, moreover, that Indian attitudes about reciprocity and gift-giving helped to shape and define the trade in ways which were formal and social rather than purely economic. While recognizing that Indians responded differently to exchange opportunities than Europeans, however, Rich was unable to explain why this was so, nor did he question the assumption that the irresistible superiority of European trade goods rendered Indians economically dependent.[6]

The suggestion that classical economic theory did not readily explain Indian trade behavior led Iroquoian scholars to reevaluate Hunt's thesis that competition over beaver resources underlay seventeenth century Huron-Iroquois warfare. In "The Iroquois and the Western Fur Trade: A Problem in Interpretation," Alan W. Trelease argued that social institutions such as the blood feud and the traditional pursuit of male prestige explained Iroquois activity in the fur trade wars as much if not more than economic opportunism.[7] Bruce G. Trigger, in his two-volume *The Children of Aataentsic*, similarly denied that Huron behavior was motivated exclusively by economic opportunities presented and controlled by white outsiders, or that by their participation the Huron were quickly rendered dependent and stripped of their aboriginal beliefs. Rather, in a model and painstaking portrait, Trigger recreated the intricate web of institutions, values and relationships which informed the actions of various groups and individuals within a native society whose attachment to trade long antedated the arrival of Europeans and European trade goods.[8]

Trelease and Trigger, while breaking with Hunt in an effort to emphasize the interplay and importance of social and cultural institutions, did not deny that economic motivations were present in tribal societies, however different these might appear from European economic motivations. Their work represents a transition from the blunt economic determinism of the 1930s to a period beginning in the early 1970s in which a number of scholars rejected outright the application of classical economic theory to American Indian societies' involvement in the trade. In opposition to neoclassicists or formalists, who themselves have tried to temper economic explanations with cultural ingredients, a new group, sometimes calling themselves substantivists, have argued that North American Indian peoples neither believed nor behaved as Europeans and that what appeared to be economically motivated activity may have had other causes and meanings. This position was first advanced in Abraham Rotstein's 1972 article, "Trade and Politics: An Institutional Approach," which maintained that from a tribal perspective the fur trade was subordinate to the politics of security, i.e., that economy was embedded in the institution of politics.[9] Bruce M. White subsequently attempted to enlarge this approach by linking trade to the institutions of gift-giving and kinship in" 'Give Us a Little Milk'."[10]

The most engaging substantivist approach has come from Calvin Martin. In *Keepers of the Game: Indian-Animal Relationships in the Fur Trade*, and in a supporting article, Martin suggests that rather than conceiving of animals as potential commodities, northern hunters regarded game animals as close spiritual relatives. Animals allowed themselves to be caught upon the condition that they be treated with reverence before, during, and after the kill. As long as Indians in northeastern North America held to these beliefs they could not have participated in a commercial enterprise predicated upon the slaughter of animals for personal gain. Because post-contact Indian hunters did just this, in Martin's view aboriginal Indian religion must have suffered a catastrophic blow.[11]

Virgin soil epidemics, racing far in advance of European traders, left Indian hunters questioning their belief systems. According to Martin, the most convincing explanation they found for the devastating diseases was that the animals had turned on their human relatives, launching a war of extermination, and that the humans, in self-defense, must eliminate the animals first. With their traditional world view thus thrown into disarray, Indian hunters were susceptible to the economic lures of the fur trade. Economic activity was by this process separated from religion and this resulted in a different kind of Indian, one who overkilled rather than conserved.

Unfortunately, empirical support for this intriguing and elegantly crafted thesis is thin. Moreover, while Martin deserves congratulations for drawing fur trade scholars' attention to the connection between native hunters' behavior and their religious beliefs, it is unfortunate that *Keepers of the Game* has overshadowed the more solidly grounded study by Adrian Tanner, *Bringing Home Animals*, from which, in its dissertation form, much of Martin's understanding of the spiritual relationship between animals and northern hunters was derived.[12] In fact Tanner's impressive work and that of Harvey Feit point to a conclusion contrary to the one reached by Martin. Feit and Tanner demonstrate the persistence and vitality of a world view Martin pronounced dead as well as the ability of the Cree to "manage" rather than wantonly slaughter their animal resources, even when they engaged in hunting for the commercial fur trade. Further proof of forest hunters' continued sensitivity to fluctuating animal populations is provided in Jeanne Kay's study of nineteenth century Menomini and Winnebago, which shows these Wisconsin Indians rotating their trade-related hunting activities in accordance with species availability.[13]

Not surprisingly Martin's *Keepers of the Game* provoked considerable discussion. *Indians, Animals, and the Fur Trade: A Critique of Keepers of the Game*, edited by Shepard Krech III, contains a series of articles which confront Martin's analysis in two respects. First, most of the authors, who happen to be anthropologists, question historian Martin's analysis of the meaning of the relationship between animals and Cree and Ojibway hunters and reject the idea that his thesis is likely to apply to other Indian groups. Secondly, they generally argue that Indian hunters made economic decisions based upon material rather than spiritualistic premises. Although both criticisms are well-aimed, Krech's slim volume provides little new information and does not challenge the theoretical potential of the substantivist position, as Martin's final comment suggests.[14]

Neoclassicists or formalists have provided stronger responses to the nonmaterialist interpretations of Rotstein and Martin. Since neoclassicists believe that the same economic rationality underlies all human actions, regardless of time or space, no catastrophic explanations such as epidemic disease or spiritual apostasy are necessary to account for readjustments in Indian decision-making as a result of participation in the fur trade. They would argue that if Indian economic behavior appears irrational or inefficient, scholars simply have not yet identified the correct neoclassical method of analysis, or they have been misled by the historical record.

John McManus's 1972 article, "An Economic Analysis of Indian Behavior in the North American Fur Trade," represented an unpersuasive attempt to explain the underlying rationale of the Montagnais-Naskapi economy.[15] Far more successful in using the formalist approach has been Canadian geographer Ray. In "Indians as Consumers in the Eighteenth Century," Ray depicts the Cree and Assiniboine as shrewd buyers, fully the equals of their European trading partners, who knew how to take advantage of Anglo-French competition in order to obtain the highest quality at the best price possible, and whose precise demands stimulated technological innovation among European manufacturers of Indian trade goods. In "Competition and Conservation in the Early Subarctic Fur Trade," as in *Indians in the Fur Trade*, Ray focuses on western Cree middlemen who manipulated the fur trade to meet their own needs and thereby frustrated both the English at the Bay and the interior tribes who were forced to accept used goods at high mark-ups.[16] This vigorous portrait of Subarctic middlemen traders keenly aware of profit has not gone unchallenged. Bruce Cox reassesses their behavior in his "Indian Middlemen and the Early Fur Trade: Reconsidering the Position of the Hudson's Bay Company's 'Trading Indians'."[17] On the other hand, clear evidence of entrepreneurial activity drawn from a later period and from a different culture area, the North West Coast, is presented in Robert L. Whitner's interesting "Makah Commercial Sealing, 1869-1897."[18]

Ray's most persuasive critique of the substantivist school and particularly of Rotstein's notion of politically motivated or "treaty" trade appears in *'Give Us Good Measure'*, coauthored with Donald B. Freeman. Subarctic Indians were not organized into sufficiently large or cohesive political units to carry on treaty trade, they insist, and a far more accurate rendering of Indian behavior in the fur trade results from applying marketplace theory. Ray and Freeman's assertions are based upon an inventive statistical analysis of Hudson's Bay Company post documents which they believe should lay to rest several persistent misconceptions about Indian attitudes toward price and profit. For example, scholars formerly believed that fixed prices obtained over long periods, from which they deduced that Indians were not profit-oriented. Ray and Freeman demonstrate, however, that earlier researchers were misled by the complex method developed by HBC post officials to exact a profit from the trade. Once the "overplus" system is understood, they argue, significant fluctuations in price over time are revealed, as are concerted native attempts to secure "full measure" for their furs.[19]

Until recently, most of the debate over Indian participation in the fur trade has centered on exchange behavior. While representatives of the neoclassical and the substantivist schools disagree over the influence of Indian culture and belief in the economic sphere, they agree that it is in the exchange process that Indian motivations and activities in the fur trade are best understood. Production aspects of the trade, as a result, have generally been slighted.

The importance of the production sphere has lately gained recognition, however, and in the 1980s neo-Marxist interpretations of the fur trade should prove a stimulating alternative to substantivism and neoclassicism. Representative of early forays in this direction is Harold Hickerson's "Fur Trade Colonialism and the North American Indian," which recasts the Indians into the role of a wilderness proletariat. Like colonized people elsewhere, Hickerson argues, Indians who linked their economies to the fur trade lost control of the means of production and, as a result, became dependent upon their colonizers.[20]

A transition from an aboriginal mode of production (in which natives controlled the means and produced food and domestic manufactures for their use-value only) to a "fur trade" or capitalist mode (in which Europeans controlled the means of production and Indians were forced to produce goods for their market value) is outlined in Patricia A. McCormack, "The Transformation to a Fur Trade Mode of Production at Fort Chipewyan."[21] Rapid alterations in the productive activities of Subarctic hunters brought on by changes in the forces of production—game depletions and other ecological crises, new technologies, and specialization—are also outlined by Charles A. Bishop, who argues that a dramatic change in mode of production could and did precede observable changes in social structure on ideology among the Western James Bay Cree.[22] Toby Morantz, however, concludes on the basis of archaeological evidence and an exhaustive compilation of hunter "profiles" over many decades that for the James Bay Cree Inlanders, at least, involvement in the fur trade did not produce structural realignments in their mode of production during the eighteenth century. They remained subsistence hunters.[23] The keen attention to ecological context and to the complex interplay between environmental factors and the productive and consumptive behavior of native hunters, evident in Bishop's and Morantz's work, also informs Robert Jarvanpa and Hetty Jo Brumbach's, "The Microeconomics of Southern Chipewyan Fur-Trade History," a welcome late nineteenth century case study.[24]

The impact of the shift to a market economy upon the status and productive roles of tribal women in particular has recently been explored by Eleanor Leacock, Patricia C. Albers and Alan Klein. Klein's article, although lean in documentation, makes a compelling case for the analysis of gender-specific and group-specific responses to the fur trade. On the Plains, he argues, men grew in wealth, status, warlike proclivities, and political dominance at the expense of their women once the horse and hide trades replaced domestic production for use as the primary subsistence strategies.[25]

Alternatively, Sylvia Van Kirk in *"Many Tender Ties"* argues that, at least for the first century of fur trade expansion in the Canadian Northwest, tribal women were essential economic producers depended on and valued for their skills as provisioners of small game, fish and cultigens, as makers of snowshoes and moccasins, as house-builders, transporters, guides, inter-preters and, occasionally, traders. Van Kirk pays insufficient attention to the varying tribal and cultural backgrounds of the native women she describes; however, *"Many Tender Ties"* broke new ground when published in 1980 and remains the most comprehensive treatment of Indian women's roles in the fur trade.[26]

With regard to northern hunters, the most sophisticated analysis to date of the influence of market economy upon mode of production is Adrian Tanner's *Bringing Home Animals*. Tanner combines religious ideology with material and ecological constraints to explain the nature and extent of Mistassini Cree involvement in the fur trade. Contrary to scholars still inclined to paint Indian involvement in absolute terms, Tanner is impressed, as is Toby Morantz in "The Fur Trade and the Cree of James Bay," by the degree of flexibility the Cree still exhibited in the 1970s in their pursuits. The Mistassini, Tanner observes, practiced two modes of production simultaneously, hunting for furs for the external world and hunting for subsistence to sustain the interior traditional world. Of the two modes, hunting for subsistence, with all of its spiritual prescriptions intact, was clearly dominant.[27]

Other researchers such as David V. Burley have also argued that the oppor-tunity to trade furs for manufactured goods and foodstuffs added to the store of available subsistence strategies, particularly among marginal northeastern horticulturists.[28] On the other hand D. W. Moodie has noted that the oppor-tunity to trade did not wean tribes like the Ottawa and Sauk from their corn fields, but rather caused them to place more emphasis on agriculture because fur trade expansion depended upon Indian provisions. Herman G. Sprenger has made a similar point in demonstrating that prior to 1870 the Metis rejected agriculture in favor of pemmican provisioning for sound economic and ecological reasons.[29] That provisioning could serve as an alternative tribal strategy is revealed in Lynn Ceci's interesting dissertation on Indians in colonial New York. Ceci contends that, when animal resources dwindled, semi-sedentary coastal tribes turned to sedentary agricultural production and wampum manufacture in an effort to reap the benefits of a triangular trade with Europeans and inland hunters, as well as to defend their remain-ing lands and autonomy from European encroachment.[30]

The idea that Indians may have over-hunted in a short-term fur and hide trade in an effort to forestall the outbreak of war with Europeans has been explored by both Richard C. Haan and Charles Hudson.[31] That such action often weakened the subsistence base of participating tribal societies did not necessarily indicate short-sightedness. As Peter A. Thomas has recently argued, Indians of the seventeenth and eighteenth centuries lacked the benefit of hindsight possessed by modern scholars and should not be criticized today for adopting what appeared to them at the time as sensible strategies of survival, accommodation, and even material enrichment.[32]

Since the early 1970s works focusing on the economic aspects of the fur trade have become increasingly detailed and complex; however, all point to the inescapable conclusion that there were many fur trades, both within the same tribal and linguistic group as Francis and Morantz show for the Cree, and within the same ecological zone as Ray reveals in *Indians in the Fur Trade.*[33] Unfortunately, despite the previously mentioned book-length works of Francis and Morantz, Tanner, and Bishop, and articles by Krech, and Jarvanpa and Brumbach, detailed treatments of the historic involvement of individual tribes in the fur trade are still lacking.[34]

Other publications which have approached the study of the fur trade from a regional, company, personnel group, or biographical perspective have taken as a whole, only inferentially cast light on the motivations and roles of tribal participants. They have, however, contributed to an understanding of the nature and chronology of change within the oldest and most durable industry involving the cooperation of Indian and white in North America. At least implicit in these studies and in most other recent writing on the fur trade has been the question: what were the effects of this partnership?

Few scholars would argue that tribal societies in the United States and Canada were not modified by their involvement in the trade, or that the trade itself did not spawn a new complex of behaviors and materials adopted on the part of both Indians and whites. Changes in material culture, for example, have been amply illustrated by a number of well-conceived and beautifully produced fur trade exhibit catalogs,[35] and especially by archaeological site reports of fur trade post excavations. In addition to Lyle M. Stone's comprehensive *Fort Michilimackinac, 1715-1781*, archaeological studies which shed light on the material aspects of fur trade culture in a variety of regional, temporal, and company contexts include *Voices from the Rapids* by Robert C. Wheeler and others, John A. Hussey's two volume *Fort Vancouver Historic Structure Report*, and C. S. "Paddy" Reid, ed., *Northern Ontario Fur Trade Archaeology: Recent Research*. Of additional interest is Alice B. Kehoe's brief "Ethnicity at a Pedlar's Post in Saskatchewan," which applies a gender analysis to the artifacts of fur trade post life, and the careful, detailed studies of culture change among the Huron by Trigger and among the Northern Ojibway by Bishop. George Irving Quimby's *Indian Culture and European Trade Goods* still commands attention, particularly for its insight into the development of a Pan-Indian fur trade culture in the Upper Great Lakes.[36]

By and large, historic archaeologists have offered few conclusions about the impact of European trade goods upon tribal societies; however, Trigger and Bishop have engaged directly the larger question of Indian dependency and loss of autonomy, which scholars such as E. E. Rich claimed were the immediate consequences of fur trade involvement. Bishop, in his 1974 study, while not denying that the Northern Ojibway were substantially changed

by participation in the trade, pushed the timetable forward, dating accelerating dependency and loss of autonomy from the 1821 merger of the two
major British companies. Viewed in this context, Donald F. Bibeau's claim
that Bishop is an advocate of the dependency school does not seem wholly
fair.[37] Actually, Bishop's most recent work on the Western James Bay Cree,
while positing early and abrupt alterations in the aboriginal mode of production as a result of fur trade participation, backs away, as does that of Morantz
and Krech, from a simplistic cultural-breakdown-versus-cultural persistence
model of history change. He argues instead that post-contact adaptations
are a synthesis of the old and new, a gradual shifting configuration in which
one can find both persistence and change.[38]

Ultimately, however, according to Bishop, cumulative change did result
in cultural discontinuity and dependency. Just when this dependency set in
and how it relates to the fur trade is the subject of considerable debate.
Perhaps in reaction to a vocal minority of western American historians who
would argue that the fur trade had a devastating and demoralizing impact
upon tribal societies of the Plains, Howard Lamar has noted that in contrast
to other frontiers, that of the fur trade was marked by peaceful communication, and that Plains tribes traded with whites for fully seven generations
without losing their cultural or tribal integrity. Similarly, James R. Gibson
has pointed out that in the far Northwest it was Russian traders who were
dependent, not their Aleut hunters.[39]

The dependence of white fur trade personnel upon native provisioners
was most keenly felt, of course, in the Subarctic and Arctic regions. The
problem of supply especially plagued the Russian fur trade and is the subject of an important book-length work by the geographer Gibson. In an
article published after his book, Gibson elaborates upon the significant
economic role played by native provisioners, as do Donald A. Harris and
George C. Ingram in a study on New Caledonia, Shepard Krech on the
Eastern Kutchin, and Carol Judd on the "Homeguard" Cree goose-hunters
of southern James Bay.[40]

The rapid decimation of the Aleut population under Russian rule would
seem to contradict Gibson's assertions of Russian-Aleut interdependence.
However, the persistence of autonomy and cultural integrity among the
neighboring Tlingit is demonstrated by Natalie B. Stoddard and enlarged
to encompass the native peoples of British Columbia in Robin Fisher's
Contact and Conflict.[41] Fisher's work, which traces the history of Indian-
white relations in British Columbia to 1890, concludes that white settlement
and missionary activity were far more injurious to tribal autonomy than the
fur trade and that dependency did not set in until after the trade's decline.
This conclusion has recently been extended to the Cree by Francis and
Morantz in *Partners in Furs*, and by Morantz in "The Fur Trade and the
Cree of James Bay."

Mutual dependency is the theme of Harris and Ingram's "New Caledonia and the Fur Trade." In the forbidding isolation of interior British Columbia—the "Siberia" of Canada—transportation and provisioning problems mitigated against full involvement in and dependency upon the trade by the Carrier Indians. Moreover, as Bishop's biography of a native trading captain demonstrates, the fur trade in New Caledonia posed opportunities for, rather than limitations upon, the expression of traditional Carrier values and leadership roles.[42]

Michael I. Asch, like Harris and Ingram, views technology, transport, and isolation as important variables in the timing and extent of Indian involvement in the trade. Asch maintains that the Slavey Indians remained virtually independent of the trade until 1870 when steam and rail transport, steel traps, higher prices for furs, and a better assortment of trade goods motivated them to work for HBC traders. Cultural transformation and dependency followed swiftly thereafter, however, Asch concludes. In contrast, James W. Van Stone has argued that the Yukon River Ingalik altered their traditional subsistence patterns in order to hunt fur bearers almost immediately after the introduction of trade goods.[43]

Among the Slaveys and Dogribs trading at Fort Simpson in the 1820s, fur trapping for commodities did not supplant trapping for subsistence nor did it result in immediate dependence upon European goods. Nonetheless, the trade did interfere with traditional subsistence activities by bringing disease, by spawning interethnic conflict and by breeding desire for manufactured goods which led to longer and, perhaps, inopportune visits to the post. It is within this broader historical context, Shepard Krech would argue, that the dependency question should be addressed.[44]

Ray's *Indians in the Fur Trade*, and Francis and Morantz's *Partners in Furs* have been particularly successful in depicting Native American peoples as active and intelligent decision-makers in matters affecting the rate and extent of change within their own cultures. Dependency, loss of autonomy, and even participation in the trade itself, were not foregone conclusions. On the Plains, the Assiniboine and numerous other tribes rejected the call of the fur trade in favor of an economy and material culture revolving around the bison hunt. Among the Cree of Eastern James Bay, Francis and Morantz point out, different groups—Coasters, mixed-bloods, and Inlanders—chose to participate in varying degrees and thus were affected differentially. Even the main producers among the Cree did not depend entirely upon their "earnings" from the trade and maintained a greater level of autonomy than historians usually notice.

In addition to the larger concern with dependency versus autonomy, scholars have begun to look at the impact of the fur trade upon the political organizations of tribes involved, as well as upon intertribal relations. Bishop, Ray, Judd, and Francis and Morantz have all noted the emergence of a new leadership role, the "trading captain," whose influence, while dependent upon traditional skills, also was derived from Euro-American support and acknowledgement. These authors have also described the evolution of a new band structure among the Cree, the "Homeguard," whose activities as provisioners and employees for the Hudson's Bay Company and intermarriages with Hudson's Bay Company personnel set them apart from their migratory hunter-cousins in the interior. Judd's dual biography, "Sakie, Esquanwenoe, and the foundation of a Dual-Native Tradition at Moose factory," provides an interesting study in contrasts between a Homeguard and an Upland Cree hunting captain. Such patterns, while perhaps unique to the Subarctic, deserve testing in other regions of fur trade activity.[45]

The close relationship between an expanding fur trade and intertribal warfare continues to be probed, particularly by Iroquian scholars such as Trigger. In an interesting reversal, however, James G. E. Smith has argued that the endemic warfare between autonomous and ethnocentric brands west of Hudson Bay diminished as the fur trade broke down barriers of isolation and mistrust, transforming bands into tribes.[46]

The most recent developments in fur trade studies fall under the rubric "fur trade social history." Whatever the fur trade may have meant, and whatever economic, political, and cultural changes were wrought within tribal societies as a result of their involvement, the trade was built upon and cemented by an enlarging web of social interactions and compacts between Indian and white men and, as is now recognized, between native women and white men. In the aggregate, and over time, such compacts were to generate what Sylvia Van Kirk first termed a "fur trade society."

The native demand for rituals of reciprocity such as gift-giving as a prelude to formal trade was noted by Rich in "Trade Habits and Economic Motivation Among the Indians of North America." Only recently, however, have scholars such as Bruce M. White in "'Give Us a Little Milk'" interpreted such rituals as a metaphor for the creation of fictive kinship ties between trader and Indian. The importance of the social sphere and especially kinship has lately been recognized by a number of scholars, including Ray.[47] However, other than Jennifer S.H. Brown's "'Man in His Natural State',," few publications have yet focused upon the mechanisms by which white traders were integrated into a tribal kinship system, or on the perceived or actual behaviors a kinship relationship between white and native males necessitated.[48]

Instead, most of the literature concerning social relations, which recently has been summarized by Van Kirk and critically evaluated by Ray, looks at marriages between native women and white men of the trade, at the roles and motivations of native "women in between," and at the families and communities which such unions produced.[49] In addition to the seminal book-length works of Brown and Van Kirk, intermarriage is the subject of other items by Harry H. Anderson, John Elgin Foster, Jacqueline Peterson, and William F. Swagerty.[50] These writers generally concur that white traders were motivated by the economic benefits to be gained from an alliance with a woman's male kin, as well as by the skills and companionship of a native woman herself. The motivations of Indian women are less clearly understood, particularly since, as Brown points out, native wives of white fur trade personnel exposed themselves to the rigors of more frequent childbirth and the risks of infectious European diseases.[51] Van Kirk emphasizes the attractions of heightened material comfort and role enlargement to tribal women throughout western Canada.[52] Jacqueline Peterson finds evidence of similar motivations in the Great Lakes region; however, she cautions against generalizing about native wives, suggesting that outmarriage must be viewed from within the individual tribal context. While women who married whites took on exceptional roles, it may be that their behavior was sanctioned by traditional means, such as dreams or visions.[53]

During the early years of fur trade expansion, marriages occurred primarily between white men and native women reared within a tribal setting. This was as true of the Great Lakes region and western Canada in the seventeenth and eighteenth centuries as it was in the American West and the Far North in the nineteenth century. Such marriages did not ordinarily occur in the presence of a priest or justice of the peace, and often they proved ephemeral. Increasingly, however, as fur trade personnel took their native wives to live in a trading post or fort and as stable family relationships developed, customary marriage or "marriage à la facon du pays" took on the force of law. This institution, as Van Kirk in *"Many Tender Ties"* perceptively argues, was the sign of an emergent fur trade society, composed of an interrelated network of fur trade families spread over a vast region, and by a set of norms and values unique to the fur trade country.

Van Kirk, Brown, Peterson, Swagerty, Judd, Anderson, and John Long have all detailed the rising numbers of children of mixed descent as a result of fur trade intermarriages.[54] As these studies of diverse regions and periods suggest, this phenomenon was by no means limited to the Canadian fur trade or to French-speaking personnel.

Van Kirk, Brown and Peterson have attempted to establish a chronology for the development of a fur trade society in the Canadian West and the American Great Lakes regions. Brown, in *Strangers in Blood*, points to two lines of development growing out of the separate traditions and behavioral patterns of Hudson's Bay Company and North West Company personnel. These authors agree that by 1800 daughters of mixed descent, the product of two cultures, had replaced native women as the preferred mates of fur trade personnel and that fur trade society was becoming increasingly endogamous.

The growth of multicultural residential communities inhabited by fur trade families paralleled the spread of a set of social norms and institutions in the fur trade country. A regional network of such towns has been described by Peterson for the Great Lakes region.[55] Elsewhere, on James Bay, on the Plains, in the Southwest, and in the Pacific Northwest, similar communities gathered themselves, even where the trade was of relatively short duration. Previously mentioned articles by Swagerty and Anderson are revealing in this regard. On the Southern Plains, traders out of St. Louis and Santa Fe-Taos formed marital alliances with native women from a wide range of tribal backgrounds as well as with Spanish-speaking New Mexican women. Some, like members of the Chouteau family described by Thorne, contributed to a sizeable mixed-blood constituency within a powerful tribe, while others, as detailed by Janet LeCompte in her award-winning *Pueblo, Hardscrabble, Greenhorn*, joined forces to found composite settlements within Indian country.[56]

The most important of the multicultural communities spawned by the fur trade was the Selkirk or Red River Colony near present-day Winnipeg, designed as a place of refuge for retired Hudson's Bay Company employees and their native families. A full-length study of this important community, from its inception in 1815 to its absorption in Canada by the Manitoba Act of 1870, is still wanting. However, both Van Kirk and Brown have illuminated the growing tensions within fur trade society following the introduction of white wives by Company officers and missionaries after 1820, and have at least outlined the causes for the collapse of the society itself.

The ultimate consequences of wide-spread intermarriage accompanying the fur trade are to be seen in the persistence and vitality of a native population and identity termed "Métis." Métis history has recently established itself as a separate field of study and is perforce beyond the scope of this essay. However, to the degree that the Métis are in a very real sense the human legacy of the fur trade, a short list of articles deserves mention. As a beginning John Elgin Foster's "The Métis: The People and the Term," provides a useful introduction to a group identity which was formerly reserved for those of mixed tribal and French descent and linked historically to the Red River Colony, but which is now extended to those of mixed ancestry generally.[57] A sampling of the most recent work on a wide variety of Métis communities in the U.S. and Canada is Peterson and Brown, eds., *The New People: Being Métis in North America*.

The roots of Metis identity and nationality are still poorly understood. Jennifer Brown has examined the impact of a racial classification system imposed by Hudson's Bay Company officials which cast children of mixed descent as a separate group within western Canadian fur trade society.[58] Olive P. Dickason, in a supporting article, has argued that despite significant French-native intermarriage in the Northeast during the French regime, Métis group consciousness did not coalesce until the British period and then on the western Canadian prairies.[59] Jacqueline Peterson has suggested, alternatively, that Métis identity was not only a reaction to Anglo-American pressures, but the culmination of nearly a century of community-building and cultural hybridization in the Great Lakes region.[60] However, even where substantial intermarriage occurred and residential communities were established, Métis identity did not necessarily follow. As Brown and Judd both have demonstrated, neither the "Homeguard" Cree nor the "country-born," both the result of English-native intermarriage, identified themselves as Métis, but rather as native, Half-Breed, or English-Canadian.[61] According to John Long, the Halfbreeds of James Bay have only recently begun to identify themselves with the term "Métis."[62] Within the continental United States after 1820, Métis identity was stifled by a governmental policy which categorized persons as white or native, leaving those of mixed descent with an awkward choice. Canada followed suit, but too late to snuff out a well-established way of life and group identity, which is now recognized under the Aboriginal Rights provision of the Constitution Act of 1982.

That there were children of many fur trades, following divergent paths and adopting different identities is amply illustrated in Jennifer Brown's "Children of the Early Fur Trades." Elsewhere, Brown suggests that those calling themselves Metis were drawn from children of French-speaking fathers who were oriented toward their native mothers' sphere, whereas children of British fathers were actively pushed toward integration within the larger Anglo community after 1820.[63] That these latter children were, in the racist climate of mid-nineteenth century Victorian North America, often caught between two worlds, unable either to view themselves as Métis and identify with Métis national aspirations or to gain full acceptance as whites, is the subject of Sylvia Van Kirk's poignant "'What if Mama is an Indian?'"[64]

Fur trade history as an aspect of native history continues to attract scholars from many disciplines and is perhaps unique among aspects of North American native history generally in that five international conferences have been devoted to the subject. Interested readers may turn to the published proceedings of three of these conferences, as well as to *Cultural Ecology: Readings on the Canadian Indians and Eskimos*, edited by Bruce Cox, for additional contributions.[65] In future, one hopes that the scholarly chorus will be joined by native voices. To date, only Donald F. Bibeau has offered an Indian perspective on a history still not owned by Indians themselves.[66]

NOTES

*   An earlier version of this essay, which gave greater attention to U.S. materials, was published in W.R. Swagerty, ed., *Scholars and the Indian Experience: Critical Reviews of Recent Writing in the Social Sciences* (Bloomington: Indiana University Press, 1984), pp. 223-257.

1. Daniel Francis and Toby Morantz, *Partners in Furs: A History of the Fur Trade in Eastern James Bay 1600-1870* (Kingston and Montreal: McGill-Queen's University Press, 1983).

2. Frederick Jackson Turner, *The Character and Influence of the Indian Trade in Wisconsin: A Study of the Trading Post as an Institution* (Baltimore: John Hopkins Press, 1891), reprinted David Harry Miller and William W. Savage,

Jr., eds. (Norman: University of Oklahoma Press, 1977); Harold A. Innis, *The Fur Trade in Canada: An Introduction to Canadian Economic History* (New Haven: Yale University Press, 1930), revised eds. (Toronto: University of Toronto Press, 1956, 1970).

3. Arthur J. Ray, "Fur Trade History as an Aspect of Native History," in Ian A.L. Getty and Donald B. Smith (eds.), *One Century Later: Western Canadian Reserve Indians Since Treaty 7* (Vancouver: University of British Columbia Press, 1978).

4. Charles A. Bishop, The Northern Ojibway and the Fur Trade: An Historical and Ecological Study (Toronto and Montreal: Holt, Rinehart and Winston of Canada, Ltd., 1974); Ray, *Indians in the Fur Trade: Their Role as Hunters, Trappers and Middlemen in the Lands Southwest of Hudson Bay, 1660-1870* (Toronto and Buffalo: University of Toronto Press, 1974).

5. Innis, *The Fur Trade in Canada;* George T. Hunt, *The Wars of the Iroquois, A Study in Intertribal Relations* (Madison: University of Wisconsin Press, 1940, new edition 1967).

6. E.E. Rich, "Trade Habits and Economic Motivation Among the Indians of North America," *Canadian Journal of Economics and Political Science,* 26 (1960), 35-53.

7. Alan W. Trelease, "The Iroquois and the Western Fur Trade: A Problem of Interpretation," *Mississippi Valley Historical Review* 49 (1962), 32-51.

8. Bruce G. Trigger, *The Children of Aataentsic,* 2 vols. (Montreal: McGill-Queen's University Press, 1976).

9. Abraham Rotstein, "Trade and Politics: An Institutional Approach," *Western Canadian Journal of Anthropology* 3, no. 1 (1972), 1-28.

10. Bruce M. White, "'Give Us a Little Milk': The Social and Cultural Significance of Gift Giving in the Lake Superior Fur Trade," in Thomas C. Buckley (ed.), *Rendezvous: Selected Papers of the Fourth North American Fur Trade Conference, 1981* (St. Paul: North American Fur Trade Conference, 1983), pp. 185-198.

11. Calvin Martin, *Keepers of the Game: Indian-Animal Relationships and the Fur Trade* (Berkeley, Los Angeles and London: University of California Press, 1978); Martin, "Subarctic Indians and Wildlife," in Carol M. Judd and Ray (eds.), *Old Trails and New Directions: Papers of the Third North American Fur Trade Conference* (Toronto, Buffalo and London: University of Toronto Press, 1980), pp. 73-81.

12. Adrian Tanner, *Bringing Home Animals: Religious Ideology and Mode of Production of the Mistassini Cree Hunters* (New York: St. Martin's Press, 1979).

13. *Ibid.;* Tanner, "The Significance of Hunting Territories Today," in Bruce Cox (ed.), *Cultural Ecology: Readings on the Canadian Indians and Eskimos* (Toronto: McClelland and Stewart Ltd., 1973), pp. 101-114; Harvey A. Feit, "The Ethno-Ecology of the Waswanipi Cree; or How Hunters Can Manage Their Resources," in *ibid.,* pp .115-128; Jeanne Kay, "Wisconsin Indian Hunting Patterns, 1634-1836," *Annals of the Association of American Geographers,* 69 (1979), 402-418.

14. Shepard Krech, III (ed.), *Indians, Animals, and the Fur Trade: A Critique of Keepers of the Game* (Athens, Ga.: University of Georgia Press, 1981).

15. John McManus, "An Economic Analysis of Indian Behavior in the North American Fur Trade," *Journal of Economic History*, 32 (1972), 36-53.

16. Ray, *Indians in the Fur Trade;* Ray, "Indians as Consumers in the Eighteenth Century," in Judd and Ray, *Old Trails and New Directions*, pp. 255-271; Ray, "Competition and Conservation in the Early Subarctic Fur Trade," *Ethnohistory*, 25 (1978), 347-357.

17. Bruce Cox, "Indian Middlemen and the Early Fur Trade: Reconsidering the Position of the Hudson's Bay Company's 'Trading Indians'," in Buckley, *Rendezvous*, pp. 93-100.

18. Robert L. Whitner, "Makah Commercial Sealing, 1869-1897," in *ibid.*, pp. 121-130.

19. Ray and Donald B. Freeman, *'Give Us Good Measure': An Economic Analysis of Relations Between the Indians and the Hudson's Bay Company Before 1763* (Toronto, Buffalo and London: University of Toronto Press, 1978).

20. Harold Hickerson, "Fur Trade Colonialism and the North American Indian," *Journal of Ethnic Studies*, 1, no. 2 (1973), 15-44.

21. Patricia A. McCormack, "The Transformation to a Fur Trade Mode of Production at Fort Chipewyan," in Buckley, *Rendezvous*, pp. 155-176.

22. Bishop, "The First Century: Adaptive Changes Among the Western James Bay Cree Between the Early Seventeenth and Early Eighteenth Centuries," in Krech (ed.); *The Subarctic Fur Trade: Native Social and Economic Adaptations* (Vancouver: University of British Columbia Press, 1984), pp. 21-54.

23. Morantz, "Economic and Social Accommodations of the James Bay Inlanders to the Fur Trade," in *ibid.*, pp. 55-80.

24. Robert Jarvanpa and Hetty Jo Brumbach, "The Micro-economics of Southern Chipewyan Fur-Trade History," in *ibid.*, pp. 147-183.

25. Eleanor Leacock, Introduction to Mona Etienne and Leacock (eds.), *Women and Colonization: Anthropological Perspectives* (New York: Praeger Publishers and J. F. Bergen Publishers, Inc., 1980); Leacock, "Women's Status in Egalitarian Society: Implications for Social Evolution," *Current Anthropology*, 19 (1978), 247-255; Patricia C. Albers, "Sioux Women in Transition: A Study of Their Changing Status in Domestic and Capitalist Sectors of Production," in Albers and Beatrice Medicine (eds.), *The Hidden Half: Studies of Plains Indian Women* (Washington, D.C.: University Press of America, Inc., 1983), pp. 175-223; Alan Klein, "The Political Economy of Gender: A 19th Century Plains Indian Case Study," in *ibid.*, pp. 143-173.

26. Sylvia Van Kirk, *"Many Tender Ties": Women in Fur-Trade Society in Western Canada, 1670-1870* (Winnipeg: Watson and Dwyer Ltd., 1980).

27. Tanner, *Bringing Home Animals*; Morantz, "The Fur Trade and the Cree of James Bay," in Judd and Ray, *Old Trails and New Directions*, pp. 39-58.

28. David V. Burley, "Proto-Historical Ecological Effects of the Fur Trade on Micmac Culture in Northeastern New Brunswick," *Ethnohistory*, 28 (1981), 203-216.

29. D.W. Moodie, "Agriculture and the Fur Trade," in Judd and Ray, *Old Trails and New Directions,* pp. 39-58; Herman G. Sprenger, "Metis Nation: Buffalo Hunting vs. Agriculture in the Red River Settlement (Circa, 1810-1870)," *Western Canadian Journal of Anthropology*, 3, no. 1 (1972), 158-178.

30. Lynn Ceci, "The Effect of European Contact and Trade on the Settlement Patterns of Indians in Colonial New York, 1524-1665: The Archaeological and Documentary Evidence" (Ph.D. dissertation, City University of New York, 1977).

31. Richard L. Haan "The 'Trade Do's Not Flourish as Formerly': The Ecological Origins of the Yamassee War of 1715," *Ethnohistory*, 28 (1981), 341-358; Hudson in Krech, *Indians, Animals and the Fur Trade*.

32. Peter A. Thomas, "The Fur Trade, Indian Land and the Need to Define Adequate Environmental Parameters," *Ethnohistory*, 28 (1981), 359-379.

33. Frances and Morantz, *Partners in Furs*; Morantz, "Economic and Social Accommodations of James Bay Inlanders"; Ray, *Indians in the Fur Trade*.

34. Shepard Krech, III, "The Eastern Kutchin and the Fur Trade, 1800-1860," *Ethnohistory*, 23 (1976), 213-235; Krech, "The Trade of the Slavey and Dogrib at Fort Simpson in the Early Nineteenth Century," in Krech, *The Subarctic Fur Trade*, pp. 99-146; James W. Van Stone, "The Yukon River Ingalik: Subsistence, the Fur Trade, and a Changing Resource Base," *Ethnohistory* 23 (1976), 199-212; Jarvanpa and Brumbach, "The Microeconomics of Southern Chipewyan Fur Trade History."

35. See for example Carolyn Gilman, *Where Two Worlds Meet: The Great Lakes Fur Trade* (St. Paul: Minnesota Historical Society, 1982), and Thomas Vaughn and Bill Holm, eds., *Soft Gold: The Fur Trade and Cultural Exchange on the Northwest Coast of America* (Salem, Oregon: Oregon Historical Society, 1982).

36. Lyle M. Stone, *Fort Michilimackinac, 1715-1781: An Archaeological Perspective on the Revolutionary Frontier* (East Lansing, Mich.: Michigan State University Anthropological Series, in cooperation with the Mackinac Island State Park Commission, 1974); Robert C. Wheeler, Walter A. Kenyon, Alan R. Woolworth and Douglas A. Birk, *Voices from the Rapids: An Underwater Search for Fur Trade Artifacts, 1960-73* (St. Paul: Minnesota Historical Society, 1975); John A. Hussey, *Fort Vancouver Historic Structure Report—Historical Data*, volumes I, II (Denver: National Park Service, 1972,1976): C.S. "Paddy" Reid, ed., *Northern Ontario Fur Trade Archaeology: Recent Research* (Toronto: Historical Planning and Research Branch, Ontario Ministry of Culture and Recreation, 1980); Alice B. Kehoe, "Ethnicity at a Pedlar's Post in Saskatchewan," *Western Canadian Journal of Anthropology*, 6 no. 1 (1976), 52-60; Trigger, *Children of Aataentsic;* Bishop, *The Northern Ojibway;* George Irving Quimby, *Indian Culture and European Trade Goods: The Archaeology of the Historic Period in the Western Great Lakes Region* (Madison: University of Wisconsin Press, 1966).

37. Donald F. Bibeau, "Fur Trade Literature from a Tribal Point of View: A Critique," in Buckley, *Rendezvous*, pp. 83-92.

38. Bishop, "The First Century"; Morantz, "Economic and Social Accommodations of the James Bay Inlanders"; Krech, "The Fur Trade of the Slavey and Dogrib."

39. Howard R. Lamar, *The Trader on the American Frontier: Myth's Victim* (College Station and London: Texas A & M University Press, 1977); James R. Gibson, "European Dependence Upon American Natives: The Case of Russian America," *Ethnohistory*, 25 (1978), 359-385.

40. Gibson, *Imperial Russia in Frontier America: The Changing Geography of Supply of Russian America, 1784-1867* (New York: Oxford University Press, 1976); Gibson, "The Russian Fur Trade," in Judd and Ray, *Old Trails and New Directions*, pp. 217-230; Donald A. Harris and George C. Ingram, "New Caledonia and the Fur Trade: A Status Report," *Western Canadian Journal of Anthropology*, 3, no. 1 (1972), 179-194; Krech, "The Eastern Kutchin and the Fur Trade"; Judd, 'Mixed Bloods of Moose Factory, 1730-1981: A Socio-Economic Study," *American Indian Culture and Research Journal*, 6, no. 2 (1982), 65-88.

41. Natalie B. Stoddard, "Some Ethnological Aspects of the Russian Fur Trade," in Malvina Bolus (ed.), *People and Pelts: Selected Papers of the Second North American Fur Trade Conference* (Winnipeg: Peguis Publishers, 1972), pp. 39-58; Robin Fisher, *Contact and Conflict: Indian-European Relations in British Columbia, 1774-1890* (Vancouver, University of British Columbia Press, 1977).

42. Harris and Ingram, "New Caledonia and the Fur Trade"; Bishop, "Kwah: A Carrier Chief," in Judd and Ray, *Old Trails and New Directions*, pp. 191-294.

43. Michael I. Asch, "Some Effects of the Late Nineteenth Century Modernization of the Fur Trade on the Economy of the Slavey Indians," *Western Canadian Journal of Anthropology*, 6, no. 4 (1976), 7-15; Van Stone, "The Yukon River Ingalik."

44. Krech, "The Trade of the Slavey and Dogrib."

45. Judd, "Sakie, Esquanwenoe, and the Foundation of a Dual-Native Tradition at Moose Factory" in Krech, *The Subarctic Fur Trade*, pp. 81-98.

46. James G.E. Smith, "Chipewyan, Cree and Inuit Relations West of Hudson Bay, 1714-1855," *Ethnohistory*, 28 (1981), 133-155.

47. Ray, "Reflections on Fur Trade Social History and Métis History in Canada," *American Indian Culture and Research Journal*, 6 no. 2 (1982), 91-107.

48. Jennifer S.H. Brown, "'Man in His Natural State': The Indian Worlds of George Nelson," in Buckley, *Rendezvous*, pp. 199-206.

49. Van Kirk, "Fur Trade Social History: Some Recent Trends," in Judd and Ray, *Old Trails and New Directions*, pp. 160-173; Ray, "Reflections on Fur Trade History and Métis History."

50. Brown, *Strangers in Blood: Fur Trade Company Families in Indian Country* (Vancouver and London: University of British Columbia Press, 1980); Van Kirk, *"Many Tender Ties"*; Harry N. Anderson, "Fur Traders as Fathers: The Origins of the Mixed-Blood Community Among the Rosebud Sioux," *South Dakota History*, 3 (1973), 233-270; John Elgin Foster, "Some Questions and Perspectives on the Problems of Métis Roots," in Jacqueline Peterson and Brown (eds.), *The New Peoples: Being and Becoming Métis in North America* (Winnipeg: University of Manitoba Press, 1985), pp. 73-92; Peterson "The People in Between: Indian-White Marriage and the Genesis of a Métis Society and Culture in the Great Lakes Region, 1680-1830" (Ph.D. dissertation, University of Illinois at Chicago, 1981); Peterson, "Ethnogenesis: The Settlement and Growth of a 'New People' in the Great Lakes Region, 1702-1815," *American Indian Culture and Research Journal* 6, no. 2 (1982), 23-64, revised and reprinted in Peterson and Brown, *The New Peoples;* Tanis Chapman Thorne, "The Chouteau Family and the Osage Trade: A Generational Study," in Buckley, *Rendezvous*, pp. 109-120; William R. Swagerty, "Marriage and Settlement Patterns of Rocky Mountain Trappers and Traders," *Western Historical Quarterly*, 11(1980), 159-180.

51. Brown, "A Demographic Transition in the Fur Trade Country: Family Sizes and Futility of Company Officers and Country Wives, ca. 1750-1800," *Western Canadian Journal of Anthropology*, 6, no. 1 (1976), 61-71.
52. Van Kirk, *"Many Tender Ties."*
53. Peterson, *"The People in Between."*
54. Van Kirk, *"Many Tender Ties"*: Brown, *Strangers in Blood;* Brown, "A Demographic Transition"; Peterson, "Prelude to Red River: A Social Portrait of the Great Lakes Métis," *Ethnohistory*, 25 (1978), 41-67; Peterson, "People in Between"; Peterson, "Ethnogenesis"; Swagerty, "Marriage and Settlement Patterns of Rocky Mountain Trappers and Traders"; Anderson, "Fur Traders as Fathers"; John S. Long, "Treaty No. 9 and Fur Trade Company Families: Northeastern Ontario's Halfbreeds, Indians, Petitioners and Métis," in Peterson and Brown, *The New Peoples*, pp. 137-162.
55. Peterson, "Prelude to Red River"; Peterson, "Ethnogenesis."
56. Thorne, "The Chouteau Family and the Osage Trade"; Janet LeCompte, *Pueblo, Hardscrabble, Greenhorn: The Upper Arkansas, 1832-1856* (Norman: University of Oklahoma Press, 1978).
57. John Elgin Foster, "The Métis: The People and the Term," *Prairie Forum*, 3 (1978), 79-90.
58. Brown, "Linguistic Solitudes and Changing Social Categories," in Judd and Ray, *Old Trails and New Directions*, pp. 147-159.
59. Olive Patricia Dickason, "From 'One Nation' in the Northeast to 'New Nation' in the Northwest: A Look at the Emergence of the Métis," in Peterson and Brown, *The New Peoples*.
60. Peterson, *"The People in Between"*; Peterson, *"Ethnogenesis."*
61. Brown, *Strangers in Blood;* Judd, "Mixed Bloods of Moose Factory."
62. Long, "Treaty No. 9 and Fur Trade Company Families."
63. Brown, "Children of the Early Fur Trades"; Brown, "Women as Centre and Symbol in the Emergence of Métis Communities," *Canadian Journal of Native Studies*, 3, no. 1 (1983), 39-46.
64. Van Kirk, "'What if Mama is an Indian?' The Cultural Ambivalence of the Alexander Ross Family, in Foster (ed.), *The Developing West: Essays on Canadian History in Honor of Lewis H. Thomas* (Edmonton: University of Alberta Press, 1983), pp. 123-136.
65. Bolus, *People and Pelts;* Judd and Ray, *Old Trails and New Directions;* Buckley, *Rendezvous;* Cox, *Cultural Ecology.*
66. Bibeau, "Fur Trade Literature from a Tribal Point of View."

III

THE MÉTIS, THE RED RIVER COLONY, AND CANADA

The Red River Colony, the first permanent European agricultural settlement in western Canada, formed the core around which the future province of Manitoba developed. The colony brought together several different groups—Scottish immigrants, fur traders, and the mixed-blood population. Two separate mixed-blood groups emerged. One was the offspring of marriages between French Canadians of the North West Company and Indian wives. This group, the Métis, formed the largest mixed-blood group on the plains. The other group is today also called Métis, but in references to the nineteenth century a number of historians have termed them the "Country-born." They were the descendents of intermarriages between Highland Scots, Orkney, and English traders, who worked for the Hudson's Bay Company, and Indian women. In "The Métis: Genesis and Rebirth," Jennifer Brown notes the origins of the Métis in the Great Lakes Region, and describes their development as a socio-political entity in Manitoba.

The French-speaking Métis strongly opposed the Selkirk settlers who came to the Red River Valley in 1812 under the auspices of the Hudson's Bay Company to establish an agricultural colony. This agricultural settlement threatened the Métis buffalo hunt, and challenged the North West Company for trade. The resulting conflict marked the final stage in a continuing trade war between the Hudson's Bay Company and the North West Company. In 1821, the rival companies merged. Thereafter the colony developed as the founder Lord Selkirk had envisioned: becoming an agricultural centre furnishing food supplies for the Hudson's Bay Company's fur trading posts and brigades, as a place of retirement for traders and their families, and as a home for employees or "servants" of the company.

Substantial economic and social changes occurred among the Métis and in the Red River settlement after the merger in 1821. The upheaval culminated in the seizure of Upper Fort Garry in 1869 by the Métis under the leadership of Louis Riel. Although Riel succeeded in obtaining provincial status for Manitoba within Canada, and acquiring land grants for the Métis, few Métis stayed in Manitoba. Instead they moved westward into present-day Saskatchewan and Alberta. Historians differ on the reasons for this westward movement. In "The Manitoba Land Question, 1870-1882," D.N. Sprague claims a "virtual conspiracy existed on the part of the federal government to fleece the land from the Métis," while at the same time new laws made it extremely difficult for them to fend off land speculators. Thus, the Métis were forced to leave Manitoba as a result of both the formal and informal actions of the federal government. In "Dispossession or Adaptation: Migration and Persistence of the Red River Métis, 1835-1890," Gerhard Ens argues to the contrary that changed economic conditions surrounding the buffalo fur trade had necessitated a westward movement of the Métis well before the resistance of 1869.

SELECTED BIBLIOGRAPHY

Jacqueline Peterson and Jennifer Brown, eds., *The New Peoples: Being and Becoming Métis in North America* (Winnipeg, 1985) presents recent interpretations on the origins and development of the Métis. For a review of the historiography of the Red River Colony, see Frits Pannekoek, "The Historiography of the Red River Settlement," *Prairie Forum* 6 (1981): 75-85; and the "Historiographical Introduction" to D.N. Sprague, *Canada and the Métis, 1869-1885* (Waterloo, 1988), pp. 1-17. General accounts include the relevant sections of W.L. Morton's *Manitoba: A History* (Toronto, 1957); E.E. Rich's *The Fur Trade and the Northwest to 1857* (Toronto, 1967); and Gerald Friesen's *The Canadian Prairies: A History* (Toronto, 1987). John Gray provides a useful biography of the founder of the Red River Colony in *Lord Selkirk of Red River* (Toronto, 1963). M. Giraud's *Le Métis Canadien: Son role dans l'histoire des provinces de l'Ouest* (1945) has been translated into English by George Woodcock as *The Métis in the Canadian West,* 2 vols. (Edmonton, 1986).

For a study of the origins of the Métis in the West, see J.E. Foster, "The Origins of the Mixed Bloods in the Canadian West," in L.H. Thomas, ed., *Essays in Western History* (Edmonton, 1976); his article, "The Plains Métis," in *Native Peoples, The Canadian Experience,* edited by R. Bruce Morrison and C. Roderick Wilson (Toronto, 1986), pp. 375-403; and his collection of documents in L.G. Thomas, ed., *The Prairie West to 1905* (Toronto, 1975): 19-72; as well as D.N. Sprague and R.P. Frye, compilers, *The Genealogy of the First Métis Nation: The Development and Dispersal of the Red River Settlement 1820-1900* (Winnipeg, 1983).

On life in the Red River Colony, see W.L. Morton and M. Macleod,

Cuthbert Grant of Grantown: Warden of the Plains of Red River (1963) (Toronto, 1974); Sylvia Van Kirk, "'What if Mama is an Indian?': The Cultural Ambivalence of the Alexander Ross Family," in John E. Foster, ed., *The Developing West: Essays in Canadian History in Honour of Lewis H. Thomas* (Edmonton, 1983), pp. 123-36; and the following articles by Frits Pannekoek: "The Anglican Church and the Disintegration of Red River Society, 1818-1870," in Carl Berger and Ramsay Cook, ed., *The West and the Nation: Essays in Honour of W.L. Morton* (Toronto, 1976), pp. 72-90; "Some Comments on the Social Origins of the Riel Protest of 1869," *Historical and Scientific Society of Manitoba,* Series III, 34 (1977-78): 39-48; and "The Reverend Griffiths Owen Corbett and the Red River Civil War of 1869-70," *Canadian Historical Review* 57 (June, 1976): 133-49. Pannekoek has recently summarized his research on the Red River in *A Snug Little Flock: The Social Origins of the Riel Resistance, 1869-70* (Winnipeg, 1991).

For a contemporary account of the Red River, see Alexander Ross, *The Red River Settlement: Its Rise, Progress and Present State* (1856; reprinted Edmonton, 1972).

JENNIFER S.H. BROWN

6 The Métis
Genesis and Rebirth

Métis, derived from an old French word meaning "mixed," is one of several terms (michif, *bois-brûlé*, *chicot*, half-breed, country-born, mixed-blood) that have been used to designate people of mixed Amerindian-European descent. Since the 1970s, the use of this French term, formerly used mainly for people of French-Indian background in Western Canada, has increased exponentially among anglophone writers.[2] However, since many such writers (along with politicians and others) either have not been explicit about, or have not achieved consensus on exactly which historical and present-day groups and categories of people of mixed ancestry may properly be defined as "Métis", it is necessary to explain how the term is used in this essay.

Written with a small "m" and italicized, *métis* is used here in the general French sense for all people of dual Amerindian-White ancestry. Capitalized, "Métis" is therefore not a generic term for all persons of biracial descent; it refers to those people who are agreed to possess a distinctive socio-cultural heritage and a sense of ethnic self-identification. Alternatively, the capitalized English form may signify a political and legal category, more or less narrowly defined, as in, for example, Alberta's Métis Betterment Act of 1938, or else left undefined, as in Canada's new Constitution Act, 1982 which recognized the Métis along with (status) Indians and Inuit as distinct native peoples.

Biologically speaking, racial mixing (French, *métissage*) has gone on since the earliest European-Indian contacts along the Atlantic coast. *Métissage* by itself, however, does not determine a person's social, ethnic, or political identity. Many North American whites have some Indian ancestry, and rates of European genetic admixture among status Indian groups in eastern and central Canada and New England range in some instances from 20 to over 40 percent.[3] Over time, and in different areas, people of mixed ancestry have grown up and lived out their lives in a vast variety of circumstances, leading them and their descendants to be categorized and to classify themselves by many different criteria.[4]

ACADIA AND NEW FRANCE

On Canada's Atlantic seaboard, *métis* families and communities were identifiable in the 1600s, although not classified according to race. Early and often casual unions between European fishermen and native women from Acadia to Labrador produced progeny who matured as Indians among their maternal relatives. Those among the Maliseet were sometimes described as "Malouidit" because so many of their fathers came from St. Malo on the Brittany coast of France. In Acadia, many French took Indian wives, and some communities became largely biracial. The *capitaines des sauvages*, who served the French governors as interpreters, intermediaries and distributors of annual presents to the Indians, were commonly of mixed parentage. A writer at Louisbourg in 1756 praised these *métis* as "generally hardy, inured to the fatigues of the chase and war, and . . . serviceable subjects in their way."[5]

Some biracial offspring were born of formal church marriages, as Acadian families such as the Denys and d'Entremonts forged both kinship and trading ties with the Micmac.[6] During the seventeenth century French officials supported such marriages in hopes of furthering their policy of frenchification, converting the Indians, and building up the population of New France. "Our young men will marry your daughters and we shall be one people," Samuel de Champlain reportedly told his Indian allies; and some subsequent administrators such as LaMothe Cadillac at Detroit in 1701 continued to encourage those mixed unions which were church-sanctified.[7]

Problems arose, however. Some officials such as Governor Vaudreuil had strong doubts about *métissage* as producing inferior offspring.[8] Further, there was concern that both the Indians and the French traders who sojourned among them had a distressing tolerance for unions unblessed by Christian rite, and that many Frenchmen took up savage ways themselves. As New France began its second century, crown policy shifted against intermarriage—reflecting, too, the increased availability of White wives within the colony, both *filles du roi* (French women deliberately imported to marry bachelor settlers) and native-born. The ideal of "one people" (French, incorporating Indian and *métis*) faded. Countless families, both French and Indian, had become genetically mixed, but Indian communities, as such, were not assimilated. Nor did biological *métissage* in New France yield a biracial population that persisted as socio-culturally or politically distinct. Indeed, despite their numbers, people of mixed descent are difficult to identify in early records of New France; they either remained among their mothers' kin as Indians, or were baptized with French names and in almost all instances went on record solely as French.[9]

MÉTIS COMMUNITIES IN THE GREAT LAKES REGION

The official discouraging of mixed unions in eighteenth century New France was probably one among many factors that fostered the growth of the first distinguishably *métis* communities around and beyond the Great Lakes. From the 1690s on, these settlements were increasingly remarked upon by clergymen, travelers, and others. Many men who evidently preferred the freedom and opportunities of life in the Indian country to the regulation of church and state in the home colony found livelihoods and new homes around the trading and military posts that were carrying French influence into the interior of the continent. Their native families, whom they might or might not legitimize in the missionaries' terms, had formed nuclei of settlement at several dozen localities by the time the British conquered Canada in 1763. Numerous American and Canadian towns and cities, for example Detroit and Michilimackinac in Michigan; Sault Ste. Marie at the juncture of Lakes Superior and Huron; Chicago and Peoria in Illinois; Milwaukee, Green Bay, and Prairie du Chien in Wisconsin, had their origins in these informal biracial communities. The sizes of these populations are sporadically reported, but some soon became substantial. As of 1700, the Jesuit missionary Étienne de Carheil was deploring the lewdness and apostasy of the hundred or more voyageurs and *coureurs de bois* residing with native women around Michilimackinac.[10]

Carheil and other outsider-critics to the contrary, these communities achieved a moral and social order of their own. French Catholicism remained a part of their heritage, even if attenuated by isolation. Indian constraints also set moral limits. Unions with Indian women involved commitments to and reciprocities with Indian kin and neighbours and earned their own descriptive term, marriage *à la façon du pays*, "according to the custom of the country." Fathers often lived out their lives with these families, whether formally employed at the forts, or subsisting as *gens libres*, freemen who provisioned the posts and served intermittently as guides, interpreters, or voyageurs. Game, fish, wild rice, and maple sugar furnished sustenance, supplemented by the small-scale slash-and-burn or "burnt-stump" agriculture that may have caused Great Lakes *métis* to be labelled *bois-brûlés* or *chicots*.[11]

"NATIVES OF HUDSON'S BAY"

While these communities were growing during the 1700s, a biracial population of a rather different character was becoming noticeable to the north of the Great Lakes watershed. In 1670, the enormous region draining into Hudson Bay was granted by Charles II of England to his cousin Prince Rupert and other speculators for the exclusive trade of the new Hudson's Bay Company (HBC). After the Treaty of Utrecht in 1713 granted Hudson Bay to the British, numerous HBC posts in Rupert's Land, as the area became known, grew into enclaves among the predominantly Cree Indians, who, as "Home Guard" traders and provisioners, were basic to the company's survival and success.[12] As around the Great Lakes, White women were absent; and Indians eager to consolidate trade and friendship offered wives to the Europeans in "the custom of the country." HBC employees, however, violated strict company rules if they accepted. The HBC directors in London, strongly aware of the costs and problems of maintaining posts so remote from their home base in so northern an environment, sought rigid controls on the numbers of post dependants. Needs to maintain security at the forts, and to minimize expenses and sources of friction with the Indians, reinforced company concerns to maintain servants' celibacy and chastity; and servants in turn attempted to keep their transgressions off the record. By the 1740s, however, when officer James Isham reported that traders' native offspring around the posts had become "pretty Numerious", the HBC London Committee had to acknowledge the limits of its control. By 1810, the Company had given some attention to both the responsibilities and the rewards of educating and training these progeny into "a colony of very useful hands."[13]

These early "natives of Hudson's Bay" did not become classed as a separate ethnic/racial entity in those years. Even if the company could not suppress its servants' marriages, it could and did suppress the growth of dependent post communities and free traders by removing from the Bay all British servants who retired or were dismissed, and by encouraging Indians to disperse to their hunting grounds each winter. A very few HBC officers' native sons gained permission to travel to Britain; but most offspring were assimilated among the Home Guard Cree, and a few became Company servants, by 1800, sometimes classed as "Natives of Hudson's Bay", or even as "English" as for example, was Charles, the half-Cree son of James Isham.

The HBC data from the period before 1810 show that biological mixing in itself was insufficient to occasion "ethnogenesis", as Jacqueline Peterson has termed the Great Lakes and Red River *métis'* rise to recognition and self-consciousness. The HBC offspring lacked the distinct community and economic base upon which to build a separate identity. Through much of the eighteenth century, Company rules gave their trader-fathers good reason to be circumspect about their existence, while at the same time, Cree maternal relatives seem to have readily incorporated the offspring among themselves. HBC word usage also muted their distinctiveness. It was in New France, and in British Canada after 1763, that *métis, bois-brûlé,* and later, "half-breed," came into use; HBC men lacked such terms until they picked them up from the Montreal-based traders in the early 1800s. If language is any guide to thought, perhaps HBC writers also lacked (although they later acquired) the increasingly judgemental racial consciousness evident among some of their fur trade counterparts (and among numerous European thinkers) during the early nineteenth century.[14]

Events of the late 1700s brought accelerating changes for both British and Montreal-based fur traders. Around the Great Lakes, the British conquest of New France in 1763 may have heightened a *métis* sense of separateness. As the North West Company gained strength in the 1780s, the British (mainly Highland Scots) took over the leadership of the Montreal fur trade. Most francophones, although their experience and skills continued to be fundamental to the fur trade, were relegated to lower ranks. In 1794, Jay's Treaty fixed the US-Canadian border around the Great Lakes. In the following decades, American settlers and governments displaced and disorganized numerous *métis* communities around the lower lakes, leading many to migrate northwest towards Minnesota and Manitoba.[15]

ETHNOGENESIS IN RED RIVER

It was in Manitoba that the Métis became conspicuous as a socio-political entity in Canadian history. By 1810 they had established roles as buffalo hunters and provisioners to the North West Company (NWC). As supply lines lengthened to Athabasca and beyond, the NWC fur traders became more and more dependent on the pemmican (processed buffalo meat and fat) supplied by the Red River heartland. When in 1811, Thomas Douglas, Fifth Earl of Selkirk, reached an agreement with the HBC to found the colony of Assiniboia with a band of Scottish settlers, the Nor'Westers and their native-born employees and associates saw it as a direct threat to their trade, livelihood and territorial interests.

Events of the next decade are well known: the Pemmican War (1814-15), the killing of Governor Robert Semple and several colonists at Seven Oaks in 1816, the often violent conflicts between the HBC and NWC, and the final merger of the two companies in 1821. Less recognized is the fact that each company's Red River Colony involvement was intensified by the existence of its own native-born constituency. The growing numbers of "Hudson's Bay natives" were a factor in the HBC decision to support the colony. Servants with native wives and families lobbied for the establishment of a community where they could retire and have lands, livelihoods, schools, churches, and other amenities. The HBC itself hoped to reduce costs by relocating dependent populations in a place where, under company governance, they could become self-supporting.

The Nor'Westers and their Métis associates had a more complex relationship. The NWC claimed less control over its Métis and freemen, many of whose biracial connections stretched to both the Great Lakes and the Prairies, and long predated its arrival in the northwest. In the conflict around Red River, this fact served the NWC well, for no matter what support it actually gave to Cuthbert Grant, Jr. (North West Company clerk, local leader, and native-born son of an old NWC partner) and his cohorts, it could and did argue that these men were defending an identity and interest of their own. Leading Nor'Wester William McGillivray admitted in a letter of March 14, 1818 that Grant and the others were linked to the NWC by occupation and kinship. "Yet," he emphasized, "they one and all look upon themselves as members of an independent tribe of natives, entitled to a property in the soil, to a flag of their own, and to protection from the British government." Further, it was well proved "that the half-breeds under the denomination of *bois brûlés* and *métifs* [alternative form of *métis*] have formed a separate and distinct tribe of Indians for a considerable time back."[16]

McGillivray's statement (although he was an interested party) helps to document the maturation of a network of communities amounting, probably, to several hundred people who resided in the Red River and Assiniboine River drainages, from the Pembina and Brandon areas to Lake Winnipeg. By 1818, when these communities were gaining attention from McGillivray and others as a distinct native people, the concept of a Métis Nation was already taking root.

RED RIVER TO THE 1870s

From 1821 (when the North West and Hudson's Bay companies merged) to 1870, Red River's overwhelmingly mixed-descent population continued to reflect its dual origins: Montreal, the Great Lakes and Prairies, and the NWC; and Great Britain, the Orkney Islands (a major HBC recruiting ground), and Rupert's Land. The extent to which these subgroups were allied is debated. Some argue for their solidarity on the basis of their numerous intermarriages, business ties, and shared involvements in the buffalo hunt, the HBC transport brigades, and Louis Riel's provisional government of 1869-70.[17] A contrary view emphasizes the split between the Roman Catholic francophones and the Protestant anglophone "country-born"[18] as they were sometimes known. The debate reflects in part the complexity of the evidence and in part the fact that many individuals, such as members of the Alexander Ross family, suffered personal ambivalence about their Indian heritage and about Métis political activism.[19]

Whatever their internal ties and tensions, the rapidly growing population of "half-breeds" in the northwest was, by the 1830s, increasingly seen as an aggregate, as racial interpretations of human behaviour gained ground in nineteenth century European thought and writing.[20] As such, they were often stereotyped and disparaged. For example, in his characterizations of the Company's "half-breed" clerks and postmasters, HBC Governor George Simpson, from the mid-1820s to 1832, showed biases that were common among other Europeans (clergy, colonists) arriving in the Red River region, and among numerous scientific and popular writers of the period. Attributes of race or "blood" were linked with cultural and behavioural traits to produce judgements that science later proved untenable. Such views, applied to biracial groups, covered a wide range; hybrids were everything from "faulty stock" or a "spurious breed"[21] to "the natural link between civilization and barbarism," as Alexis de Tocqueville put it in the 1830s.[22] Daniel Wilson, writing of the Red River half-breeds in 1876, offered a contrast to racial determinism, noting that racial traits did not set limits to adaptiveness or potential. Besides demonstrating "a remarkable aptitude for self-government" in their organization of the buffalo hunt, the Red River Métis showed "capacity for all the higher duties of a settled, industrious community."[23]

Events of the decade in which Wilson wrote offered few outlets for the qualities that he perceived. The 1840s had seen a rising entrepreneurial spirit in Red River.[24] New challenges to the HBC trade and administrative monopoly in Red River were expressed in the trial and freeing of trader Pierre-Guillaume Sayer in 1849, and, in the 1840s and 1850s the anti-HBC lobbying efforts in London by Alexander Kennedy Isbister, the part-Cree grandson of HBC Chief Factor Alexander Kennedy. Other events, however, soon overshadowed the free traders' gains and the issue of HBC power. Eastern Canadian interest in developing the West was heightened by Henry Y. Hind's glowing report of its agricultural potential. The subsequent planned transfer of Rupert's Land from the Hudson's Bay Company to the new Canadian government in 1869 led surveyors to begin to map Red River without regard for local residents' holdings. This touched off Louis Riel's establishment, in 1869-70, of a provisional government in Red River. The Canadian government's bargaining with Riel led in 1870 to the passage of the Manitoba Act, which secured the admittance of a small portion of Manitoba to Canada and provincial status and, most important for the Métis, stated that 1,400,000 acres of land would be allotted for their children.

This promised land was lost in the next decade, however. The settlers and troops who arrived in the new province from 1870 on were hostile to the prior inhabitants, many of whom were "beaten and outraged by a small but noisy section"[25] of the newcomers, according to a report by the new governor, Adams Archibald. Métis landholders were harassed, while new laws and amendments to the Manitoba Act undermined their power to fend off speculators and new settlers.[26] Of the approximately ten thousand people of mixed descent in Manitoba in 1870, two-thirds or more are estimated to have departed in the next several years. While some went north and some went south to the United States (where they already had ties through the Red River cart trade to St. Paul, Minnesota, and the buffalo hunts to Montana), most headed west to the Catholic mission settlements around Fort Edmonton (Lac Ste. Anne, St. Albert, Lac La Biche), and to the South Saskatchewan River where they founded or joined such settlements as St. Laurent (now St. Laurent-Grandin), Batoche, and Duck Lake.[27]

As they grew, the Saskatchewan River communities sought to secure clear titles to their river lots from the Canadian government, in the face of governmental efforts to survey the whole region into squared sections. Lieutenant Governor Alexander Morris thought in 1880 that the claimants' land case was clear: "They will, of course, be recognized as possessors of the soil and confirmed by the Government in their holdings." He urged that the Métis who still depended on the buffalo hunt have lands assigned to them since that resource had increasingly failed.[28] The government, however, ignored or responded very slowly to Métis concerns, while at the same time negotiating the major western Indian treaties and pre-empting land for the railways. The relative blame for subsequent events has been variously assigned by researchers to government incompetence or connivance, to agents fostering Canadian Pacific Railways, and other interests, and to poor guidance of the Métis' interests by their own priests and leaders.[29] Whatever the precise importance of these various factors, they probably all contributed toward building the crisis in which the Saskatchewan Métis, in deep frustration, took up arms under Louis Riel and Gabriel Dumont in the Northwest Rebellion of 1885.

AFTER 1885

The Métis defeat at Batoche, and the execution of Riel in the same year set off a second dispersal, particularly to Alberta, and a renewed weakening of Métis political influence and cohesiveness. Sir John A. Macdonald in 1885 viewed them as without distinct standing: "If they are Indians, they go with the tribe; if they are half-breeds they are Whites,"[30] in contrast to his 1870 acceptance of their distinctness.[31] Where Métis individuals did receive land allowances, or money equivalents, these were usually granted in scrip or transferable certificates which unscrupulous speculators often pressured them to sell cheaply on the spot. The "scrip hunters" who followed the Treaty 8 Half-Breed Commission as it made its awards to Métis in the Dene (Northern Athapascan) settlements, for example, bought up many $240 scrip certificates for cash amounts of $70 to $130.[32]

From 1885 into the mid-1900s, poverty, demoralization, and the opprobrium commonly attached to being "half-breed" led many people of Indian descent if they could, to deny or suppress that part of their heritage.[33] In 1896, Father Albert Lacombe, concerned for Métis interests, founded St. Paul des Métis, northeast of Edmonton, on land furnished by the government. For financial and other reasons, by 1908, the colony had failed as a formal entity, and settlers from Quebec began to dominate the area.[34] Here, as elsewhere, the Métis who remained found themselves on the lower socio-economic levels.

Some other developments after 1900, however, were more positive. In 1909, the Union Nationale St-Joseph de Manitoba, founded by former associates of Riel and others, began to retrieve from documents and memories their own history of the events of 1869-70 and 1885, resulting in A.-H. de Tremaudan's *History of the Métis Nation in Western Canada*.[35] The 1920s and 1930s saw the rise of new leaders—notably James Patrick (Jim) Brady and Malcolm Norris—who, as prairie socialist activists, built a new political and organizational base to defend their people's interests. Many Métis and ex-treaty Indians had been squatters on Crown lands in north-central Alberta. Threatened by a federal plan to place these lands under provincial jurisdiction, Joseph Dion and others organized petitions and delegations to the Alberta government to seek land title for the squatters. After Brady and Norris joined the movement in 1932, the first of several provincially based organizations was founded—the Métis Association of Alberta, open to all persons of Indian ancestry.[36] Its efforts led, in 1934-35, to the province's appointment of the Ewing Commission to "make enquiry into the condition of the Half-breed population of Alberta." Despite reverses, the association eventually secured land for Métis settlements and passage of the Métis Betterment Act in 1938. In the same year, the Saskatchewan Métis Society (later the Association of Métis and Non-Status Indians of Saskatchewan) was founded.

From the mid-1960s on, Métis political activity intensified with the founding of numerous other organizations such as the Manitoba Métis Federation, the Ontario Métis and Non-Status Indian Association, and the Louis Riel Métis Association of British Columbia. Confronting such issues as the federal government's White Paper of 1969 and the Constitution of 1982, Métis representatives repeatedly faced questions about whether to pursue their concerns jointly with status and/or non-status Indians, or on their own. From 1970 to 1983, the Native Council of Canada (NCC) alone represented Métis interests on the national level. For the 1983 First Ministers' Conference, however, the two NCC seats were both allocated to non-status Indian delegates; and the Métis National Council was formed to secure distinct Métis representation there and elsewhere.

Reflecting the historical diversity of their communities across Canada, people who identify themselves and are accepted as Métis (or in some localities, half-breeds) have not necessarily shared a consensus about what organization may best represent them in Ottawa. Western Métis who view themselves as "a distinct indigenous nation with a history, culture and and homeland in western Canada"[37] are generally affiliated with the Métis National Council. Those who define their claims as based more on aboriginal than national rights, and whose *métis* roots may reach to Quebec, Ontario, the Maritimes, or elsewhere, rather than to the prairie heartland of Louis Riel and Gabriel Dumont, appear more inclined to affiliate (as Métis or Non-Status Indians) with the Native Council of Canada.[38] The open-ended recognition, and non-definition, of Métis in the Constitution Act, 1982, present new issues, challenges, and opportunities which will be explored and tested for many years to come.[39]

MÉTIS RENAISSANCE: THE 1980s

Whatever courses the Métis may follow in their evolving political history, the late twentieth century has been a time for their revival and renewal in both Canada and the northern United States. In Canada's 1981 federal census, nearly 100,000 people identified themselves as Métis, and many thousands more may legitimately be able to rediscover past histories and affiliations, suppressed or forgotten, through which they may link themselves to Métis communities. In 1985, the Manitoba Métis Federation (which has claimed a population base of between 80,000 and 100,000 people in Manitoba alone) launched proceedings to pursue land claims dating from the Manitoba Act, 1870.

In the United States, where governments have given no recognition to ethnic categories between those of Indian and White, people of mixed descent have been obliged to establish either Indian or White identities.[40] Yet there, too, Métisism (to use a recently coined Alberta Métis term) has gained ground among the many thousands of people with Canadian Métis roots and connections who live in Michigan, Minnesota, North Dakota, Montana, and Washington,[41] generating a cultural resurgence with political overtones.

Expressions of Métisism range far beyond the political. In literature, both Métis and non-Métis authors have brought the past and present lives of Métis people to centre stage with varying success. Maria Campbell's *Halfbreed*[42] (1973) and Beatrice Culleton's novel, *In Search of April Raintree*[43] (1983) stand out.[44] Winnipeg is home to a publisher that is Métis in both focus and management—Pemmican Publications. Métis language and linguistics are growing fields of study.[45] Arts and artisanry that are now recognized to be distinctively Métis rather than tribal or simply "Indian" have received long-delayed recognition in Alberta's Glenbow Museum exhibition, "Métis," which toured Canada in 1985-86.[46] Film and television attention to Métis themes has increased; 1986-87 saw the launching of a new four-part National Film Board dramatic series, "Daughters of the Country," and media commemorations of the 1885 centenary were widespread. Métis historical sites have become foci of intensive research, restoration, and reconstruction.[47]

It seems fair to speak of a Métis renaissance giving new vitality to communities who have experienced long periods of relative invisibility, economic hardship, and prejudice. Social currents of the 1970s and 1980s have legitimized ethnicity and ethnic pride on a broad scale all across North America, and many Métis people, as the centenary of Batoche approached, were drawn to rediscover and reconstruct their past.

Shifting intellectual currents have also helped; new modes of social history and ethnohistorical analysis have placed ordinary people of all kinds in the mainstream of recent historical writing. As an example, the perspectives of women's history have reinforced the attention paid to Métis history and origins: as long as western Canadian history was European-oriented, patricentric, and patrilineally directed in the reconstruction of its genealogies, native origins and components of those families were readily screened out because the native women from whom they were derived were overlooked. Younger generations, however, are retracing these origins and connections with enthusiasm.

Probably these development have occurred partly because the Indians and "half-breeds" of a century ago have become safely exotic, and many of their descendants have been able to put aside the vulnerability and insecurity long associated with their plight. But there is more to it than this. In a very positive sense, a sea change may finally be occurring in Canadians' views of their nation's Indian past and native heritage. The Métis, along with Canada's other native peoples, are earning attention as integral parts of our past and present, rather than residing, as formerly, on the shadowy margins of colonial and frontier history. Neither scholars, nor the media, nor the Métis themselves, are likely to allow this trend to be reversed.

NOTES

1. This essay is a revised and expanded version of the article, "Métis," which appeared in *The Canadian Encyclopedia* (Edmonton: Hurtig, 1985): 1124-27, by permission.

2. Two recent guides to sources on Métis history are: John W. Friesen and Terry Lusty, *The Métis of Canada: An Annotated Bibliography* (Toronto: OISE Press, 1980) and D.F.K. Madill, *Selected Annotated Bibliography on Métis History and Claims* (Ottawa: Indian and Northern Affairs Canada, 1983). The *Canadian Journal of Native Studies*, vol. 3, no. 1 (1983), appeared as a special issue on the Métis since 1870, and contains useful articles on Métis history, claims, language, and other topics. Similarly, *Canadian Ethnic Studies*, vol. 17, no. 2 (1985) was a special issue, entitled "The Métis: Past and Present."

3. Emoke J.E. Szathmary and Franklin Auger, "Biological Distances and Genetic Relationships with Algonkians," in *Boreal Forest Adaptations: The Northern Algonkians*, edited by A. Theodore Steegmann Jr. (New York: Plenum Press, 1983), 298-99.

4. Jacqueline Peterson and Jennifer S.H. Brown, eds., *The New Peoples: Being and Becoming Métis in North America* (Winnipeg: University of Manitoba Press, 1985).

5. Cornelius Jaenen, *The French Relationship with the Native Peoples of New France and Acadia* (Ottawa: Indian and Northern Affairs, 1984), 72.

6. Olive Patricia Dickason, "From 'One Nation' in the Northeast to 'New Nation' in the Northwest: A Look at the Emergence of the Métis," in *New Peoples*, edited by Peterson and Brown, 26.

7. Jaenen, *French Relationship*, 74.

8. *Ibid.*, 74-75.

9. Dickason, "One Nation," 20-23.

10. Jacqueline Peterson, "Many Roads to Red River: Métis Genesis in the Great Lakes Region, 1680-1815," in *New Peoples*, edited by Peterson and Brown, 38-43.

11. Jacqueline Peterson, "Prelude to Red River: A Social Portrait of the Great Lakes Métis," *Ethnohistory*, vol. 25, no. 1 (1978).

12. Daniel Francis and Toby Morantz, *Partners in Furs: A History of the Fur Trade in Eastern James Bay 1600-1870* (Kingston and Montreal: McGill-Queen's University Press, 1983).

13. Jennifer S. H. Brown, *Strangers in Blood: Fur Trade Company Families in Indian Country* (Vancouver: University of British Columbia Press, 1980).

14. Jennifer S.H. Brown, "Linguistic Solitudes and Changing Social Categories," in *Old Trails and New Directions: Papers of the Third North American Fur Trade Conference*, edited by C.M. Judd and A.J. Ray (Toronto: University of Toronto Press, 1980).

15. Peterson, "Prelude to Red River."

16. Jennifer S.H. Brown, "Woman as Centre and Symbol in the Emergence of Métis Communities," *Canadian Journal of Native Studies*, vol. 3, no. 1 (1983):43-44.

17. Irene M. Spry, "The Métis and Mixed-bloods of Rupert's Land before 1870," in *New Peoples*, edited by Peterson and Brown.

18. Frits Pannekoek, "The Rev. Griffiths Owen Corbett and the Red River Civil War of 1869-70," *Canadian Historical Review*, vol. 57, no. 2 (1976): 133-49.

19. Sylvia Van Kirk, "'What if Mama is an Indian?': The Cultural Ambivalence of the Alexander Ross Family," in *New Peoples*, edited by Peterson and Brown.

20. Robert E. Bieder, "Scientific Attitudes toward Indian Mixed-bloods in Early Nineteenth Century America," *Journal of Ethnic Studies*, vol. 8, no. 7 (1980).

21. Lewis O. Saum, *The Fur Trader and the Indian* (Seattle: University of Washington Press, 1965), 206.

22. Bieder, *Scientific Attitudes*, 20.

23. Daniel Wilson, *Prehistoric Man: Researches into the Origin of Civilisation in the Old and the New World*, vol. 2 (London, 1876), 264, 265.

24. Irene M. Spry, "The 'Private Adventurers' of Rupert's Land," in *The Developing West*, edited by John E. Foster (Edmonton: University of Alberta Press, 1983).

25. Arthur S. Morton, *A History of the Canadian West to 1870-71*, 2nd ed. (Toronto: University of Toronto Press, 1973), 920.

26. Douglas N. Sprague, "Government Lawlessness in the Administration of Manitoba Land Claims 1870-1887," *Manitoba Law Journal* 10 (1980).

27. Murray Dobbin, *The One-and-a-half Men: The Story of Jim Brady and Malcolm Morris* (Vancouver: New Star Books, 1981), 23.

28. Alexander Morris, *The Treaties of Canada with the Indians* (Toronto, 1880), 294-95.

29. Compare, for example, Bob Beal and Rod MacLeod, *Prairie Fire: The 1885 NorthWest Rebellion* (Edmonton: Hurtig Press, 1984); Martin Shulman and Don McLean, "Lawrence Clarke: Architect of Revolt," *Canadian Journal of Native Studies*, vol. 3, no. 1 (1983); Thomas Flanagan, *Riel and the Rebellion: 1885 Reconsidered* (Saskatoon: Western Producer Prairie Books, 1983).

30. Quoted in Joe Sawchuk, *The Métis of Manitoba: Reformulation of an Ethnic Identity* (Toronto: Peter Martin Associates, 1978), 33.

31. Flanagan, *Riel and the Rebellion*, 62.

32. René Fumoleau, *As Long as this Land Shall Last: A History of Treaty 8 and Treaty 11, 1870-1939* (Toronto: McClelland and Stewart, 1974), 76.

33. Jean H. Lagassé, director, *The People of Indian Ancestry in Manitoba*, 3 vols. (Winnipeg: Department of Agriculture and Immigration, 1959).

34. James G. MacGregor, *Father Lacombe* (Edmonton: Hurtig, 1975), 306-308; Dobbin, *One-and-a-half Men*, 42-43.

35. A.-H. de Tremaudan, *Hold High Your Heads*, translated by Elizabeth Maguet (originally published as *History of the Métis Nation in Western Canada*, 1936; Winnipeg: Pemmican Publications, 1982).

36. Dobbin, *One-and-a-half Men*, 61.

37. Peterson and Brown, eds., *New Peoples*, 6.

38. *Ibid.*

39. For a good discussion of these issues and controversies, see Joe Sawchuk, "The Métis, Non-Status Indians and the New Aboriginality: Government Influence on Native Political Alliances and Identity," *Canadian Ethnic Studies*, vol. 17, no. 2 (1985).

40. Verne Dusenberry, "Waiting for a Day that Never Comes: The Dispossessed Métis of Montana," in *New Peoples*, edited by Peterson and Brown.

41. Peterson and Brown, eds., *New Peoples*, 7.

42. Maria Campbell, *Halfbreed* (Toronto: McClelland and Stewart, 1973).

43. Beatrice Culleton, *In Search of April Raintree* (Winnipeg: Pemmican Publications, 1983).

44. For a recent overview of such literature, see Emma LaRocque, "The Métis in English Literature," *Canadian Journal of Native Studies*, vol. 3, no. 1 (1983).

45. John C. Crawford, "What is Michif? Language in the Métis Tradition," in *New Peoples*, edited by Peterson and Brown; Patline Laverdure and Ida Rose Allard, *The Michif Dictionary: Turtle Mountain Chippewa Cree*, edited by John Crawford (Winnipeg: Pemmican Publications, 1983); Patrick C. Douaud, *Ethnolinguistic Profile of the Canadian Métis*, National Museum of Man, Mercury Series, Canadian Ethnology Service Paper, no. 99 (Ottawa, I 985).

46. Ted J. Brasser, "In Search of Métis Art," in *New Peoples*, edited by Peterson and Brown.

47. Two of the best known sites are the house of the Riel family in Winnipeg and Batoche in Saskatchewan, both under the care of the Canadian Parks Service. Diane Payment, who carried out major site research on Batoche, is the author of an important work on that community, *"The Free People—Otipemisiwak": Batoche, Saskatchewan 1870-1930* (Ottawa: Studies in Archaeology, Architecture and History, National Historic Parks and Sites, Parks Service, 1990). Numerous local and family histories with a Metis focus have appeared in the last decade for other communities across the prairie west.

7 The Manitoba Land Question, 1870-1882

One of the more interesting dynamics in Canadian history is the way strong provinces can fulfill their provincial interests by successful manipulation of national institutions. The earliest example is the case of Ontario and its interest in territorial expansion, an interest which was one of the primary reasons for Confederation in the first place. The story is well known. In the 1850s, 'Canadians' were frustrated in their attempts to acquire Rupert's Land from the Hudson's Bay Company; as a means to this (and other ends) they sought a union of all of British North America. Once they were successful in this step, Ontario became optimistic about expansion west, particularly in 1869 with the apparent completion of negotiations with the Hudson's Bay Company which secured Rupert's Land not to Ontario alone but at least to Canada. Then came the Riel disturbance.

All of Ontario had expected that the west would have to be colonized before any consideration of new provinces would come up. Furthermore, since Ontario was the province which was adjacent to the new land, it was expected that the new western provinces which would eventually emerge should resemble the one from which settlers were most likely to come. But the Riel disturbance in 1869-70 threatened to defeat Ontario's declared destiny. The predominantly Metis population south of Lake Winnipeg demanded recognition as a province with rights equal to the others. The government of John A. Macdonald and George Cartier felt obliged to listen to the demands of this largely Catholic and French-speaking nationality. To do otherwise would invite a bitter controversy between Protestants and Catholics, English and French in Canada at large over questions too fundamental for the frail federation to debate openly at this time.

Still, negotiations between Canada and a western delegation in the spring of 1870 were successful for both sides. The Canadians recognized the most essential of the westerners' rights; and they did so without sacrificing much territory. They drafted a statute "to establish and Provide for the government of Manitoba" which mentioned two official languages, denominational schools, and promised acreage to every man, woman and child in this part of Rupert's Land, a small 'postage stamp' of a province, no more than a few percentage points of the area of the west over all. Still, the debate on the Manitoba Act early in May of 1870 was ferocious. Ontario members of Parliament—especially those with Orange Lodge associations—complained that Canada had been humiliated.[1] National honour demanded punishment rather than favours for these western rebels. On the other side of the house, government spokesmen emphasized that the sacrifice of a few acres and some small points of principle to secure the vast domain remaining was a great deal cheaper than the alternative. It was said that they had two choices: "either they had to send an army to conquer these people and force them to submit, or to consider their claims as put forward by their delegates."[2] In view of the relatively trivial amount of land which was sacrificed, the latter course seemed wiser to Francis Hincks. Besides, Hincks went further and hinted that the Manitoba Act was really no more than a gesture: "those delegates should return with the impression that justice had been done."[3] They should have the impression that they were not about to lose their land. Meanwhile, behind the debate in the House of Commons, a leader more prominent than Hincks was hinting that the Manitoba Act would have little force. John A. Macdonald wrote that the Metis were "impulsive" and "spoilt," a people to be "kept down by a strong hand until they are swamped by the influx of settlers."[4]

Thus, the introduction of the Manitoba Act was duplicitous to say the least. With the notable exceptions of George Cartier and a few other French Canadian or Roman Catholic members of the government, there was no positive support for it in principle. More importantly, there was private repudiation of the interpretation of the act which the delegates from Manitoba were supposed to take back to their associates at home. The leading members of the government believed that Canada could—and should—change the face of the province they recognized in 1870, to recreate Manitoba in the image of Ontario. The dis-establishment of French as an official language and the removal of public support for denominational schools were parts of this process which have been described fully elsewhere. In what follows, the focus is upon an even more basic element in the transformation of Manitoba. Here, the focus is upon the dispossession and dispersal of the Metis population, despite promises of secure tenure of their land in Sections 31 and 32 of the Manitoba Act.

In the first year of the administration of the new province, several steps were taken to further the interests of Ontario and nullify the Manitoba Act. First, Canada sent a military force of about 1,200 troops (roughly equal to the adult Metis male population) to pacify a people who were now declared to be in a state of rebellion and each volunteer soldier from Canada was awarded a free grant of 160 acres of the province so occupied. Then, while enumerating Manitobans for census purposes in the autumn of 1870, the population was sorted into two groups, one the 'Insurgents' and the other, the 'Loyalists.' Loyalists received cash indemnities and political patronage.[5] There was nothing for the general Insurgent population. On the contrary, in March of 1871, an Order-in-Council encouraged prospective settlers from Canada to emigrate to Manitoba to take up land as squatters. They were told that a homestead law was forthcoming and in the meantime, in the event of trespass, interlopers were promised protection and the full support of the government.

Contrary to this strategy of flooding the province with a tide of new settlers, however, the first Lieutenant Governor of Manitoba, Adams G. Archibald, a Nova Scotian who seems to have interpreted the Manitoba Act along the lines of the Manitoba delegation, began to make plans for the implementation of the two sections of the law which made land promises to the original citizens of the province. Section 31 called for the distribution of "one million four hundred thousand acres . . . for the benefit of the families of half-breed residents." Since the census of 1870 indicated that the "Half-breed" population included about 10,000 people, just as the enumeration was being reported, Archibald proposed a method for granting each partly Indian person his allotment of 140 acres.[6] At the same time, Archibald talked to Archbishop Taché about the best location for these grants and the two men agreed that the allotments should come from the lands immediately behind the river lots.[7] In this way, families would not be dispersed all over the province but remain fairly well concentrated in the twenty-four parishes along the Red and Assiniboine rivers.

Archibald also proposed a scheme for administering Section 32, the part of the law which assured Manitobans that the land they already occupied would not be jeopardized by the transfer of the west to Canada. The preamble to the section stated that it was intended "for the quieting of titles, and assuring to the settlers in the Province the peaceable possession of the lands now held by them. To Archibald this meant that "the intention of the Act was to give assurance to all those who . . . held land . . . that their possession should be assured as proof of right."[8] To this end, he proposed that Manitoba be recognized as a province like the others with the same jurisdiction over property and civil rights to administer the distribution of assurances to river-lot occupants in the parishes. Early in 1871, Archibald wrote the Secretary of State suggesting "local legislation" could be drafted to implement Section 32 and thus avoid a thousand difficulties which might arise from administration in Ottawa. "It would be easy to frame a local statute," he said, "whereby a party applying to be enrolled and treated as owner of a defined lot should put up certain notices of his intended application. In case no opposition to his claim should be made within a prescribed time, he would be considered as entitled." This was certainly in accord with the useage of the country to date. So also was the remedy which Archibald proposed for settling conflicting claims locally: "one inquiry should be held; the facts reported, and the title declared according to the evidence."[9] In this way, the whole problem could be disposed of in a single year.

But Archibald's suggestion was flatly rejected. Section 30 of the Manitoba Act clearly placed "all ungranted or waste lands in the Province" under the jurisdiction of the Government of Canada "for the purposes of the Dominion." In Ontario, this meant all of Manitoba was 'Dominion Land.' No one in Ottawa was receptive to Archibald's distinction between parish land, which was already settled, and territory outside the settlement belt, which was the ungranted part. Archibald was dismissed, and two successive governments in Ottawa took ten years to administer that which Archibald wished to accomplish in a single season.[10] To date, most historians have suggested that these delays were inadvertent: the governments of John A. Macdonald and Alexander Mackenzie were simply too preoccupied with other matters. If they administered the Manitoba Act poorly, it was because of their preoccupation with these other important questions, for instance, railways. But officials in Ottawa, from the ministerial to clerical level, did keep constantly informed of the status of the Manitoba land question. In fact, a whole new branch of the government, the Department of the Interior, came into existence to look after Dominion Lands. Judging by its annual reports in the Sessional Papers between 1873 and 1880, the Manitoba land question was the dominant, in some years, indeed, almost the exclusive preoccupation of this department.

The first point, therefore, is that Manitoba was not neglected in the sense of being ignored. When the voluminous flow of communication on this issue is followed more thoroughly than through the Sessional Papers, however, a second point emerges. The first hint of this is discovering that the Department of Justice was extraordinarily preoccupied and active in the administration of the Manitoba Act, tied into a bureaucratic relationship which was neither well publicized nor equal. Justice was superior and supreme even though the Deputy Minister liked to give ordinary citizens the impression that other departments had all authority over the distribution of public lands.[11] Thousands of secret letters, memos, draft copies of Orders-in-Council and statutes show that the Department of Justice was clearly in charge.[12] In other words, the Department of the Interior was the bureaucracy to which the public was referred but all internal referrals stopped finally at the Minister of Justice because the rest of the government was denied the luxury of autonomous legal opinion. The Department of Justice was the department in charge of the other departments—and also some of the provinces (see figure 1).

The centralization of the administration of the Manitoba Act (ultimately under the Minister of Justice) had a great deal to do with the way government in general was centralized in the early years of the Canadian federation;

FIGURE 1   Power links between the Canadian Department of Justice, and other Government Departments or Jurisdictions, 1870-1880.

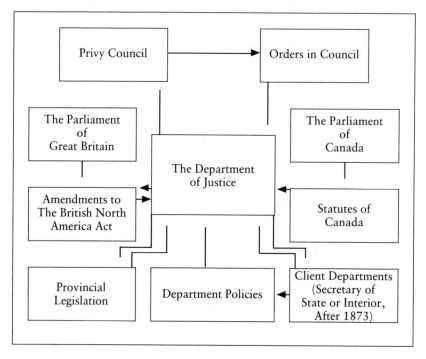

but this degree of centralism and bureaucratic control also had to do with the nature of the statute in question. The Manitoba Act was—and is—the constitution of a province which was to be a colony of Canada. In 1870, there was no doubt in Ottawa that this was desirable but some debate as to its legality. The Department of Justice solved the problem by writing an amendment to the BNA Act to legitimize the Manitoba Act, an amendment which would have had this effect and no other. The draft amendment left the Canadian Parliament free to alter the Manitoba Act at any time and in any way that it might wish.[13] But in England, as if to anticipate the issue of Hodge vs. the Queen, Canada's text was rewritten. The Imperial Statute known as the British North America Act of 1871 introduced a novel sixth section which declared that "it shall not be competent for the Parliament of Canada to alter the provisions" of the Manitoba Act or other such statutes to be passed in the future.[14]

The Department of Justice responded to this surprise by ignoring Section 6 insofar as it conflicted with the intention to revise what was inconvenient in Sections 31 and 32 of the Manitoba Act. As a result, the Department of Justice superintended revisions of Sections 31 and 32 on no fewer than nine occasions between 1872 and 1880.[15] Once, in 1875, Edward Blake and John A. Macdonald (future and former Ministers of Justice) expressed opinions on the questionable constitutionality of such amendments.[16] But this was in the House of Commons, not in the more important correspondence between Justice and its client departments. These opinions (copied in the Deputy Minister's Letter Books) were more forceful than the law itself because they were rulings on what to ignore or to grant, what policy to set and how it should be followed. In the case of Section 6 of the British North America Act of 1871 and its relation to the amendments of Sections 31 and 32 of the Manitoba Act, the Letter Books are completely silent.[17] But there are literally hundreds of references to Manitoba Act policy in general—the vestiges of the secret bureaucratic process of ruling and referral, order and amendment by force of Sections 31 and 32 were nullified in day to day administration.

Thus, the second point is that by the mid-1870s unconstitutional amendments to the Manitoba Act displaced the unalterable original law. Settlers might apply for recognition of land rights under Section 31 or 32; but the Department of the Interior—prompted by rulings from the Department of Justice—always disposed of these claims by their conformity to one or another of the *ultra vires* amendments.[18] Thus, the policy of dispersal triumphed. Having been worn down by a flood of paper and extra-legal complications, the Métis people were swamped by a tide of new settlers, the assurances of security in the Manitoba Act notwithstanding.

Consider first the redirection of Section 31 of the Manitoba Act. This portion of the original law promised allotments of vacant land to families of partially Indian ancestry "toward the extinguishment of the Indian Title." Archibald assumed that this meant an allotment to every member of the "mixed race . . . generally known as Half-breeds."[19] Also, he assumed that the allotments should be made as near as possible to the places at which people were already settled. At first the government repudiated only the location of the allotments. In April of 1872, they asserted that "the Half-breed lands could not be selected until the surveys were sufficiently advanced."[20] In other words, they decided to make the allotments from sections of bald prairie rather than near the settlement belt, to award lands where the Metis people never settled rather than from territory adjacent to the parishes in which they were already comfortably situated.

Then in 1873, the government repudiated Archibald's interpretation of eligibility. The Secretary of State informed Governor Morris that they were going to restrict allotments to persons who were children of partly Indian parentage and not themselves also heads of families. There was no explanation. In fact the Minister, then Joseph Howe, pretended to be ignorant of the previous policy.[21] But to prevent future confusion, the government proceeded to amend the Manitoba Act with "An act to remove doubts as to the construction of Section 31 . . ." (36 Vict. Chap. 38).

One part of the law declares that "The children meant and intended by the said thirty-first Section of the said Act shall be held to include those of mixed blood, partly white and partly Indian, and who are not heads of families." Another section repudiated "all proceedings except as are sanctioned by (Section 31) . . . as explained by this act." Thus, by one stroke of dubious constitutionality, the number of potential allottees was reduced by 40 per cent, from approximately 10,000 persons to about 6,000.[22]

Ironically, just as the heads of Métis families found themselves dealt out of allotments the two thousand descendants of original white settlers in the province found themselves dealt in to a special grant. On 14 May 1873, just two weeks after excluding the Half-breed heads of families from the bonus of Section 31, the government introduced resolutions to the House of Commons asserting that "Selkirk settlers . . . were as much pioneers and had suffered as many hardships as the Half-breeds." Since "Parliament had made a grant of 1.4 million acres to Half-breeds settlers . . . it was rather hard that they should not have the same advantages as those of mixed race." Accordingly, they proposed to give them 140 acres per head. "Hear, hear," said the opposition. The proposal was then put as a bill and received first, second and third reading all on the same day.[23] On grounds that the two populations should be treated equally, the descendants of original white settlers thus gained what the partly Indian heads of families had just lost.

As soon as Governor Morris learned of this irony he informed the government that such an injustice would lead to trouble in Manitoba. He therefore proposed "an issue of scrip . . . to the heads of families . . . ."[24] At first the Minister of the Interior was opposed to the idea. He promised nothing more than "consideration" of the recommendation.[25] But a new minister (and a new government) responded more favourably. In April of 1874, David Laird introduced a "bill to give the heads of families the rights which their children possessed"; and this measure to grant "each Half-breed head of family . . . scrip for one hundred and sixty dollars to be receivable in payment for the purchase of Dominion Lands" passed third reading in the middle of May.[26]

The history of the interpretation of Section 31 is thus tortuous since the government first included the heads of families among the persons to receive allotments, then excluded them but extended comparable benefits to original white settlers and finally offered the partly Indian heads of families the same bonus—scrip—but described the last action as a way to "give the heads of families the rights which their children possessed." The children's rights, the ones which should have been shared by the parents, were rights to an allotment of legally described land granted to a particular allottee. The parents' scrip, by contrast, was only paper, a kind of money to be used by whomever redeemed it.[27] In theory, the children's allotments were protected by complicated regulations governing the transfer of real property, thus more secure, especially since the children were almost all minors in the 1870s and therefore covered by the particularly stringent rules preventing the disposal of such estates by administrators. But in the actual process of appearing to comply with Section 31 (as amended), only the first prediction was confirmed in practice. The parents' scrip was treated as personal property and not protected; special laws were drafted to facilitate the transfer of the children's grants.[28]

The process began in 1875 as the Agent of Dominion Lands was ordered to compile three kinds of lists for every parish included in the census of 1870. Clerks in Winnipeg worked from the census rolls to enumerate all the "children of Halfbreed heads of families," all the "Half-breed heads" and the others called "old settlers." The lists were then posted in the twenty-four parishes with the notification that a commissioner would appear on a certain day to collect evidence regarding parentage, date and place of birth and residency in 1870. Every claimant was supposed to appear on that day and give his word corroborated by two neighbours that he was the listed person and that the information given to census enumerators had been true. Claimants gave their affirmations and secretaries filled out the various forms which had been printed for each kind of claim.[29] This survey occupied two commissioners and their secretaries working independently throughout the summer of 1875, during which time they interviewed nine thousand persons "to the satisfaction of all classes in the Province," according to the Minister of the Interior in his report for the year.[30]

But a group of about 500 speculators, usually from Ontario, operated from the same lists as the commissioners and worked just as systematically through every parish. Frequently, they told people that it was necessary to have an attorney now that the government was processing claims. Thus they secured powers of attorney. Sometimes they told claimants that the government was not to be trusted, no land would ever be granted but twenty-five dollars was offered for the claim on the chance some small portion would be granted. In this way they procured assignments of claims. Occasionally the powers of attorney or assignments were completely fraudulent; they were made up without contacting the claimant at all. But whether the document was a power of attorney or an assignment of claim (and there were thousands of both) nearly all have two attributes in common. These instruments of surrender were signed with a claimant's mark, an X, almost never a signature, and they were witnessed by two speculators rather than some disinterested third party.[31] The culpability of the government in this farce was two-fold. First, they failed to provide an institutional means for validating contracts between literate confidence men and illiterate claimants. Secondly, since the civil servants and elected officials who were closest to these proceedings knew well that it was almost impossible to prove fraud under the

TABLE 1   Partially Indian Heads of Family by Occupational
Classifications, Manitoba, 1875

Member of Parliament or the Legislative Assembly of Manitoba	12
Clergy or other Professional	4
Merchant	27
Farmer	984
Housewife	1610
Labourer or Voyageur	103
Hunter	37
no data	428
TOTAL	3205

SOURCE: Affidavits of Half-breed Heads of Families, P.A.C., R.G. 15, Volumes 996-1255.

accepted forms, they seized upon the opportunity and joined in the bonanza themselves.[32] As a result, virtually all of the money scrip which was supposed to have been awarded to Half-breed heads of families never reached the claimants. As soon as it arrived at the Dominion Lands Office in 1876, assignees and attorneys picked it up instead.

Similarly most of the allotments to children passed to third parties by power of attorney. In other words, heads of families and children never received the land they are supposed to have sold. The government issued scrip and allotments in the name of the individual Métis people, but delivered these awards to the persons who held assignments of rights or powers of attorney. To condone this questionable practice one would have to believe that the goal of dispossession was more important than scrupulously safeguarding the rights of illiterates. Alternatively, one could accept assignments and powers of attorney at their face value, with a racist shrug and a parenthetical assertion that the buffalo hunters of Manitoba had no use or interest in land in any case.

But the occupational profile of the heads of families interviewed by the commissioners in 1875 is a huge body of evidence which seriously inpugns the stereotype which suggests nearly all of the Métis people were nomadic buffalo hunters (see Table 1). In 1875, the vast majority of Métis people were farmers, thus interested in hanging on to all the land they could get, and not just for speculation. According to the surveyors, Métis people in the older parishes were cultivating their land as extensively as the original white settlers (see Table 2).

TABLE 2   Cultivated Acres by Ethnicity, Recognized Settlers, 1870-1873

Ethnicity	Acreage Under Cultivation				TOTAL
	5 or less	6-10	11-25	26 or more	
Person of Partially Indian Ancestry	112	53	65	179	409
Original White Settlers	20	10	1	25	56
TOTAL	132	63	66	204	465
chi square = 8.99 with 3 df p = .029					

SOURCE: Survey certificates in Parish Files, Land Records Office, Department of Mines Natural Resources and Environment, Government of Manitoba and survey certificates in Manitoba Act Files, P.A.C., R.G. 15, Volumes 140-169.

A second challenge to the assumption that Métis people were uninterested in land acquisition is the eagerness with which they sought to realize the land promises of Section 32. This was the section which covered the river lots on which people were already situated. It will be remembered that Archibald understood this section to mean that "possession should be assured as proof of right."[33] At first, the government did not bother to deny this interpretation. They differed primarily over the means of administering the statute. Archibald thought it could be done locally, in Manitoba; the government insisted on doing its own survey of the parishes first and then, having established an administrative apparatus in Ottawa, "report on the title of the claimants" from Ontario.[34] It took three years to complete these surveys and to establish the necessary administrative machinery. Then in 1873 a public notice began to appear in Manitoba newspapers inviting "all persons who claim titles under Section 32" to send applications "describing the situation and condition of the lot, and setting forth the particulars under which the patent thereto is claimed."[35] More than 2,000 claimants came forward at once.[36] A few produced applications written by the claimants themselves. Others sought the assistance of clergymen to fill out the form. Some were applications by assignees producing quit claim deeds alleging that 1870 occupants had sold out and moved on. But this last group was relatively small. As late as 1875, nine tenths of the 1870 population had not yet moved. They remained on their river-lot farms patiently awaiting the patents which Section 32 so clearly promised.

Many people waited in vain, not because their claims were invalid but because of differences in their relationship to the Hudson's Bay Company prior to 1870. Generally speaking, there were three classes of settlers in Manitoba before the transfer to Canada, three classes which reflected, as much as anything else, the role of the company as colonial proprietor. The first class consisted of recognized settlers; these were the persons who settled on lots which had been surveyed specifically for the purpose, and did so with company permission and recognition. Their names appeared in the company Land Register as having occupied a particular lot with a precise legal description. Normally each lot had at least six chains of river frontage, extended back from the river a distance of two miles and carried with it exclusive rights for cutting hay on the land of the same width extending back another two miles. Thus, each recognized settler normally had company permission for use of approximately two hundred acres of land (counting the outer as well as the inner river lot). Second-class settlers were squatters, people who moved onto vacant riverfront, built their houses, stables, barns, and began to cultivate the soil. If nobody objected, they developed their land in the same manner as the recognized settlers. The only difference between themselves and the recognized groups was that they lacked official, company sanction for taking up land. The third class could be called winterers. These were the people whose major occupation was in the production of plains provisions. Thus, they tended to be away from the Red River settlement in all seasons but the winter at which time they returned as squatters to river-lot shelters, ordinarily the same place on each return.

If Canada had dealt with these three groups in the manner that Archibald had first proposed, each person would have publicized that portion of river frontage which was his and also the depth of land that he claimed. Everybody probably would have claimed the portion of recognized settlers, and patents to this one-half million acres would have followed accordingly. But the government of Canada insisted after 1873 that "it would not do to give away the public property right and left."[37] Consequently, they distributed only a fraction of the land which was claimed; and that which they did distribute was granted in accordance with distinctions of class and race more than by principles of equity or the intention of Section 32.

Since the recognized settlers could bring forward third-party corroborative evidence in support of their clams, they were the most successful in securing the full extent of their acreage. But figure 2 shows that there was no uniformity to this process. In order to come close to gaining the full claim, a recognized settler had to be white and have at least twenty-six acres of his land under cultivation. Métis recognized settlers received about half as much as the whites, regardless of the number of acres they cultivated.

The next class, the squatters, gained only as much land as they had improved. Although their houses and cultivated acreage might be situated on a lot which measured almost two hundred acres in total area, since they were squatters the government insisted such persons were only entitled to that area which they had effectively occupied: they should receive a patent only for a portion of the lot "embracing the dwelling, etc. of the claimant, but not for any greater extent of the land."[38]

Not surprisingly, the government dealt even more harshly with the winterers. Correspondence between the Minister of the Interior and Governor

FIGURE 2   Breakdown of the Number of Acres Patented by Ethnicity and Extent of Cultivation

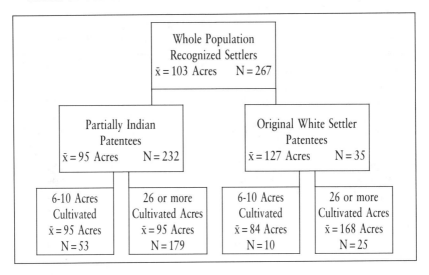

Morris, and also passages from the Minister's private papers, show that David Laird had utter contempt for persons of partly Indian ancestry who established a shelter on one of the rivers of Manitoba in the winter, planted a garden in the spring, spent the summers in pursuit of plains provisions, and returned in the fall to harvest the unattended garden. In Laird's words, they knew "something of farming" but he saw no place for them in a commercially agricultural Manitoba. He wanted to see them evicted from their river lots and encouraged to move north and west "around the different large lakes which abound with fine white fish." There, they would pose no obstacle to the development of commercial agriculture in the south. Also, they could be called upon as a labour force, from time to time, to work on "roads and bridges . . . as well as the freighting of stores and provisions."[39]

To make certain that such persons did not acquire patents to their lots, Section 32 was amended to make it more stringent. The new law, 38 V. Chap. 52, provided that a claimant would have to establish "occupancy rather than "peaceable possession" of his river lot. Thus, it did not exclude squatters, but it was used to bar anyone who had not made sufficient "improvements" of the land. Approximately 1,200 families lost all chance of obtaining patents due to the force of this amendment (see Table 3). In the district of Rat River, for example, 93 families had claims under subsection 4 of Section 32, the part of the Manitoba Act which 38 Vict. Chap. 52 repealed. Here was the result:

> 42 cases were disallowed on grounds that the occupants had nothing that qualified as a house or fenced and cultivated land; it was asserted that they had made 'no improvements whatever.'

TABLE 3   The Population of Métis Male Heads of Families* Enumerated by Various Government Officials, 1870-1875

Parish	1870 Census	1871-73 Land Survey	1875 HB Commissioners
St. Laurent and Oak Point	42	15	44
Baie St. Paul	47	29	413
St. François Xavier	295	115	19
St. Charles	66	24	53
St. Boniface	124	15	150
St. Vital	57	12	51
St. Norbert	173	78	158
Ste. Agathe	46	14	108
Ste. Anne	43	20	52
Portage La Prairie**	88	15	62
High Bluff	22	18	80
Poplar Point	96	35	4
Headingly	40	21	39
St. James	63	22	39
St. John	107	2	24
Kildonan	78	4	116
St. Paul	52	24	42
St. Andrews	243	83	189
St. Clement	94	48	66
St. Peter	157	0	27
TOTALS	1,933	594	1,726

*Includes only Métis males who were also parents with children; excludes solitaries and excludes cases whose ethnicity is not recorded.
**and White Mud
SOURCES: Manitoba Census, 1870, Public Archives of Canada; Parish Registers, Crown Lands Branch, Department of Mines Natural Resources and Environment, Province of Manitoba and Surveyors' Field Notes, Public Archives of Manitoba; Affidavits of Half-breed Heads of Families, Public Archives of Canada, RG 15, Volumes 1319-1324.

18 cases were disallowed on grounds that 'small patches of land' had been ploughed but there was no fencing or acceptable housing in sight.

24 cases were disallowed because their houses were 'in various stages of completion' and the cultivated land and fencing fell below a 5 acre minimum.

5 claimants were 'allowed to purchase 40 acres' because their 5 acres, fencing and houses were in order.

4 claimants were 'allowed to purchase 80 acres' because they had acceptable housing, fences and more than 10 acres under cultivation.[40]

Ninety-five percent of the acres at stake were thus held back as Dominion Lands, saved to be taken up later by newcomers.

By 1878, Manitoba Senators began to complain that "we hear of confiscation everywhere. The people are told they cannot remain any longer on the lands on which they have been settled for years." Girard and Sutherland asked "why so many improvements are requisite . . ."[41]

The government replied that no injustice had been done to "actual settlers." They said they had seriously considered even the "most remote claim." Later, in a similar debate, the government spokesmen held that the issue was "what occupancy gave possession?" This was not an issue for Parliament or the Courts. It was "a question which the Minister of Justice and the Minister of Interior should agree upon."[42] The deputies of these two officials—Z.A. Lash and J.S. Dennis—agreed that the winterers' claims were of a "very frail character" and could not be allowed. To entertain one would invite hundreds more. It "opened the door for the loss of very valuable portions of crown domain."[43]

There was more. Having whittled down the claims of the recognized settlers, reduced those of squatters to hardly more than the ground on which their houses stood, and having dispossessed the winterers altogether, one step remained. It was necessary to bring in one more amendment to give Dominion Land officers the power to disperse Métis who had failed in their applications for patents to parish lots or never applied in the first instance. This final amendment to the Manitoba Act, an "Act for the final settlement of claims to lands in Manitoba by occupancy,"[44] made patents mandatory rather than optional, declared that people had two years left to secure such recognition, and provided "for the removal of persons unlawfully occupying any of the said lands" in the future. Manitoba Senators protested that this latest amendment was completely illegal. But theirs were only two dissenting voices in a crowd of over three hundred. The measure passed Parliament and received Royal Assent in April of 1880.

By this date, amending the Manitoba Act had become a nearly annual exercise in the ongoing process of repudiating the promises of 1870. As early as 1873, some Manitobans were beginning to say that the "confederation of the province would never have take place" if the government had been honest about its intentions from the first.[45] Canada had disingenuously committed itself to distribute approximately two and one half million acres of land among the 1870 population as the price that the government would freely pay for peaceful annexation. Some patents and free grants were conceded, but a massive research project is still underway to determine the full story of the distribution of the 1870s.[46] On the basis of samples and impressions gained to date, a conservative estimate of the portion allotted to the Métis people by 1882 would be less than 600,000 acres. The rest of the land, perhaps as much as 2 million acres, was diverted to speculators leaving the original population land-poor in their home province.

But there was no rebellion—not until 1885, and then far away in the northwest territories. This was the place to which Métis people had drifted having been forced out of their homeland. By 1885, the remnant of the Métis in Manitoba was only 7 percent of Manitoba's total population. Ontario-born residents outnumbered them 5 to 1, and many of these newcomers were living on land which Métis people had occupied fifteen years before.[47] By insisting upon the distribution of parish lands in Manitoba as a matter of national policy rather than recognzing it as an issue of local control, the stronger province had defeated the weaker one; and this was not the last time that Ontario was able to fulfill a provincial interest in the name of Canadian nationalism.

NOTES

1. See the speeches of Mackenzie, Mills, Fergusan, Bowel, McDougall, Bodwell and Rymal, House of Commons *Debates,* 4, 5, 7, 9 and 10 May 1870.
2. House of Commons *Debates,* 9 May 1870.
3. *Ibid.*
4. P.A.C., Macdonald Papers, No. 74, p. 24, J.A. Macdonald to J. Rose, 23 February 1870.
5. Loyalists are listed in Sessional Papers (1872), No. 19. These persons also appear among the appointive officers in the first government, Sessional Papers (1871), No. 20.
6. P.A.C., R.G. 15, Vol 229, A.G. Archibald to Secretary of State, 27 December 1870.
7. P.A.M., Morris Papers (Ketcheson Collection, Correspondence), Taché to Morris, 14 January 1873.
8. P.A.C., R.G. 15, Vol. 229, A.G. Archibald to Secretary of State, 20 December 1870.
9. P.A.C., R.G. 15, Vol. 229, A.G. Archibald to Secretary of State, 9 April 1871.
10. Usually an accidental hand-shaking with Louis Riel is cited as the reason for Archibald's short term as governor of Manitoba. This view seems to be based on the opinion of Canada's Governor General in a letter dated 21 August 1873. See W.L. Morton, *The Critical Years: The Union of British North America* (Toronto, 1969), p. 260. But a dispatch from Joseph Howe to Archibald late in 1871 suggests that Archibald's administration of the land question was a more important cause for his loss of favour in Ottawa. Howe opened his letter with pleasantries about a recent holiday and then delivered a blistering criticism of Archibald's "giving countenance to the wholesale appropriation of large tracts of country by halfbreeds." Howe demanded that Archibald "leave the land department and the Dominion Government to carry out their policy without volunteering any interference." Only then did he go into "another question of some delicacy"—the Riel matter. PAC, C-1834, Vol. 9, pp. 729-45.
11. Example: William Kennedy, a Winnipeg lawyer, wrote the Justice Minister in June of 1881 regarding government policy with regard to scrip frauds and compensation to settlers for lands expropriated for railway purposes. He wrote Justice saying his letters to Interior had gone unanswered. "I therefore respectfully ask," Kennedy continued, "if your Department cannot apply its good services in

investigation of these things" (PAC, RG 13 A2, Vol. 50, file 1091). The Deputy Minister might have answered Kennedy's letter directly because both were matters on which Justice had issued many rulings, but this would mean breaking the confidentiality of the relationship between lawyer and client, Justice and Interior. Rather than breaking this secrecy, the Deputy Minister pretended to know nothing about scrip or land expropriation. The Deputy Minister replied that "the matters referred to do not come under the control of this Department. I am unable to take any action . . ." (PAC, RG 13, 43, Volume 603, p. 23). Secrecy in the name of client privilege to cover bureaucratic decision-making continues on the century-old matters even now. "As a general principle, files containing legal opinions furnished to other Government Departments are not disclosed without the consent of that Department. Sometimes, however, such files can be made available if there is no objection from the client department and the files are not otherwise of a confidential nature" (Roger Tassé, Deputy Minister of Justice, to B. Wood, Director of Research, Manitoba Metis Land Commission, and L. Heineman, Research Director, Association of Métis and Non-Status Indians of Saskatchewan, 27 September 1979).

12. The Department of Justice inadvertently violated its own policy of secrecy in the mid-1960s, however, by turning over to the Public Archives of Canada the Letter Books of past Deputy Ministers of Justice. At the same time, the annual index and registry of referrals was also sent to the same place. The documents which the Justice Department retained are the more interesting files from the client departments, the files which document the important questions on which Justice ruled. Obviously, these files should be in the Public Archives along with the Letter Books, Registers and Indexes. But systematic use of RG 13 A1 and RG 13 A3 is enough thoroughly to document the role of the Department of Justice in this all important process of bureaucratic policy formation and administration.

13. The Canadian draft of the British North America Act of 1871 had four sections. John A. Macdonald's letter submitting them to the Earl of Kimberly for submission to "the Imperial Parliament" summarized the four sections as follows:

"1. Confirming the Act of the Canadian Parliament 33rd Vict. Chap. 3 . . . and legalizing whatever may have been done under it according to its true intent.

2. Empowering the Dominion Parliament from time to time to establish other Provinces in the North Western Territory with such local government, Legislatures and Constitutions as it may think proper, provided that no such local government or Legislature shall have greater powers than those conferred on the local government and legislatures by the British North American Act of 1867 and also empowering it to grant such provinces representation in the Parliament of the Dominion.

3. Empowering the Dominion Parliament to increase or diminish, from time to time, the limits of the Province of Manitoba or of any other Province of the Dominion with the consent of the Government and Legislature of such Province.

4. Providing that the terms of the suggested Act be applicable to the Province of British Columbia whenever it may form part of the Dominion."

PAC, RG 13 A3, Volume 559, Macdonald to Kimberly, 29 December 1870, pp. 225-30.

14. Statutes of Great Britain, 34 and 35 Vict. Chap. 28.

15. Statutes of Canada, 36 Vict. Chap. 6, 38; 37 Vict. Chap. 20; 38 Vict. Chap. 52, 53; 39 Vict. Chap. 20; 41 Vict. Chap. 14; 42 Vict. Chap. 32; 43 Vict. Chap. 7. Obviously some were more important than others. Also, some of these amendments were more dubious in their constitutionality. The group which fit both criteria appear in the discussion which follows. A fuller discussion of Canada's defiance of Section 6 of the BNA Act (1871) appears in D.N. Sprague, "Government Lawlessness in the Administration of Manitoba Land Claims, 1870-1887," forthcoming in the *Manitoba Law Journal*, 10 (1980), pp. 65-92.

16. House of Commons *Debates,* 27 March 1875.

17. There are no references to the BNA Act of 1871 in any of the Letter Book indices covering the years between 1871 and 1882. PAC, RG 13 A3, Volumes 560-606.

18. For good examples, see PAC, RG 13 A3, Vol. 565, p. 882; Vol. 574, pp. 2, 3-4; and Vol. 593, p. 444.

19. P.A.C., R.G. 15, Vol. 229, A.G. Archibald to Secretary of State.

20. Senate Debates, 26 April 1872.

21. P.A.M., Morris Papers (Lieutenant Governor's Collection), Howe to Morris, 7 April 1873.

22. This is an estimate based on the ratio of adults to children in the 1870 census. See Sessional Papers (1871), No. 20, p.92.

23. House of Commons *Debates,* 14 May 1873.

24. P.A.C., R.G. 15, Vol. 230, File 478, Morris to Campbell, 13 September 1873.

25. P.A.M., Morris Papers (Lieutenant Governor's Collection), Campbell to Morris, 26 September 1873.

26. Statutes of Canada, 37 Vict. Chap 20.

27. As an interesting aspect of discriminatory law, the Department of Justice ruled that scrip awarded to whites was real estate but that of partly Indian persons was personal property. See RG 13 A2, Vol. 40, file 1372; and RG 13 A3, Vol. 580, p. 936; Vol. 588, pp. 119-20; Vol. 596, p. 526; Vol. 598, p. 662.

28. Ironically, the first was called a "Half-Breed Land Grant Protection Act," Statutes of Manitoba, 37 V. Chap. 44. In this original form it did afford some of the security suggested in the title. But the law was amended twice: 38 V. Chap 37 and 48 Vic. Chap. 30. The amendments inverted the original law.

29. Government of Canada, Order-in-Council, 26 April 1875 and letter of instruction from Surveyor General to Half-breed Commissioners, 11 May 1875. Both documents printed in N.O. Cote, *Orders in Council Respecting Claims of Half-breeds of Manitoba and the Northwest Territories . . . 1871 to 1911* (Department of the Interior, 1929), pp. 14-22.

30. Sessional Papers (1876), No. 9, p. xv.

31. Literally thousands of these documents have survived. See those in the P.A.C., R.G. 15, Vol. 1421-1423.

32. A high level example was John Lowe, the Deputy Minister of Agriculture. See P.A.C., R.G. M.G. 29, E 18, Vol. 25, Lowe Papers, Low to Tetu, 9 September 1878. Lower level officials may have been even more vicious in this regard. One clerk in the Dominion Lands office at Winnipeg extorted as well as speculated. Ultimately his actions became so flagrant he was investigated and fled to the United States to avoid prosecution. P.A.C., R.G. 15, Vol. 232, file 2447.

33. P.A.C., R.G. 15, Vol. 229, A.G. Archibald to Secretary of State, 20 December 1870.

34. N.O. Cote, *Grants of Land Under the Manitoba Act* (Department of the Interior, 1929), p.3.
35. *Manitoba Free Press,* 3 January 1874.
36. Report of J.S. Dennis, Surveyor General for 1874 in Sessional Papers (1875), No. 8.
37. Senate Debates, 11 April 1878.
38. P.A.C., R.G. 15, Vol. 235, File 5537, Laird to Privy Council, 17 April 1876.
39. P.A.C., M.G. 27, I.O. 10, David Laird Letter Book, 1874.
40. P.A.M., Morris Papers (Lieutenant Governor's Collection), Privy Council Memorandum on the Subject of the so called 'Staked Claims' in Manitoba, 20 December 1877.
41. Senate Debates, 8 March 1878.
42. *Ibid.*
43. *Ibid.,* 20 April, 1880.
44. Statutes of Canada, 43 Vict., Chap. 7.
45. House of Commons *Debates,* 30 October, 1873.
46. This is a million dollar project funded by the Government of Canada, Department of Indian Affairs and Northern Development for research by Métis associations such as the M.M.F. and A.M.N.S.I.S., cited in footnote 11.
47. Sessional Papers (1887), No. 12, Table III and Table IV.

GERHARD ENS

8 Dispossession or Adaptation?
Migration and Persistence of the Red River Metis, 1835-1890

The scholarly debate about the migration and dispersal of the Metis[1] of Red River has generally focussed on some concept of the immutable nature of "Metis society," and has concentrated on the period after 1870. Those who argue that the Metis were essentially a "primitive people" saw the Metis exodus from Manitoba as a self-imposed exile, a return to primitivism. More recently, scholars have rejected this civilization-savagery dichotomy and argued that the Metis of Red River were a settled people with strong attachments to the land. In this view the Metis dispersal was, in effect, a forced dispossession by the Canadian government and aggressive capitalism. While these views have some validity, both oversimplify the causes of Metis emigration from Red River, and do not examine the role of the changing nature of the Metis economy in Red River. Specifically they do not analyze the bases of migration and persistence of the Metis in Red River previous to 1870. An examination of this earlier period not only provides a more comprehensive explanation of the dispersal of the Metis, but accounts for the variability in the Metis experience at Red River.

Both G.F.G. Stanley and Marcel Giraud, whose works appeared in the 1930s and 1940s, saw the Metis as a primitive people doomed by the advance of the agricultural frontier. Unequipped to deal with the new economic order, they were submerged by the land rush after 1870.[2] G.F.G. Stanley's early work on the Metis was, in fact, much coloured by the increased impoverishment of the Metis in the 1930s, which he saw as leading inexorably to their eventual disappearance.[3] Stanley insisted that the troubles in the North-West (in both 1869 and 1885) were not primarily racial or religious, but normal frontier problems—the clash between primitive and civilized peoples. This view led Stanley to characterize Metis society as "static" and the Metis themselves as "indolent," "improvident," and unable to adjust.[4] Migration was the only alternative to racial absorption by an unfamiliar aggressive civilization that flowed into Manitoba after 1870. While Marcel Giraud's classic study of the Metis presented a much more comprehensive view of Metis society, it adopted Stanley's cultural-conflict thesis in which the Metis were doomed by the advance of agricultural settlement. Maltreated, pushed aside, and unable to adjust, the Metis left Red River for the north and west where they attempted to rebuild their traditional life.[5]

This view of Metis emigration from Red River has been disputed by D.N. Sprague, a historian retained by the Metis Federation of Manitoba to undertake research into Metis land claims. In a series of articles and in a published collection of quantitative data relating to the Red River Metis, Sprague has argued that the actions of the Canadian government, preceding and following the Resistance of 1869-70, and the promulgation of the Manitoba Act, represented a deliberate attempt on the part of Prime Minister Macdonald and Ontario to appropriate Red River from the Metis, legally or illegally.[6] Elsewhere, Sprague has argued that by 1870 the Metis of Red River were committed settlers, not primitive, nomadic hunters as Giraud and Stanley had claimed. Their subsequent migration to the North-West was to recover a livelihood denied them in Manitoba.[7]

Metis emigration from Red River, in fact, was tied very closely to the changes in their political economy from the 1830s to 1890. Metis persistence in, and migration from, Red River went through a number of stages of which the period after 1870 was only one, albeit the most dramatic. Until at least 1875, this emigration of Red River Metis was a response to attractive new economic activities that emerged in the fur trade after 1850. With the opening of new fur markets the Metis increasingly combined different types of economic activity in the same household: petty-commodity production, trading activities, and temporary wage labour. In effect, some Metis communities abandoned agriculture and increasingly specialized in the fur trade as new roles were opened to them. Migration was part of the relocation of labour consequent on this reorganization of the Metis family economy following the expansion of the capitalistic fur trade. Accordingly, the dispersal of the Red River Metis between 1850 and 1875 should not be seen primarily as the self-inflicted exile of a "primitive" people nor the forced dispossession by the Canadian government. Rather, it should be seen as an adaptive, innovative response to new economic opportunities. Only this broader economic view of the dispersal of the Red River Metis can make sense of the differential rate of migration, not only between the various Metis communities, but also within these communities at Red River. This is not to deny the fact that there were push factors involved in the Metis emigration after 1870—in particular the hostility of the incoming Ontario settlers.

The main sources for this study of persistence and migration were three sets of quantitative records: the Red River censuses of 1835, 1849, and 1870,[8] the North-West half breed scrip applications,[9] and the land records of the department of the Interior and Winnipeg Land Titles Office. The "Half-Breed Scrip" commissions of 1885-86 accepted claims from those Metis who had left Red River prior to 15 July 1870. These applications for claims thus provide an indication of emigration from Red River for the period previous to 1870. These applications, allowed by other scrip commissions up until 1906, gave the age and date of migration from Red River, home parish, and successive destinations. A more detailed analysis of persistence and migration has been carried out on the two Metis parishes of St. Andrew's and St. François Xavier, using the Red River censuses of 1835, 1849, 1870, and 1881. This has also been supplemented by a lot-by-lot analysis of the alienation of Metis land in these two parishes after 1870, along with a 10 per cent sample of the lots in the remaining parishes.[10]

To understand the transition that occurred in the economy of the Red River Metis in the period after the 1840s, and the effect this had on Metis emigration, some reference must be made to the Metis economy previous to the 1840s. By 1835 the various Metis communities of Red River had established a functioning way of life whose primary constituents were semi-autonomous village communities and cultures. Their subsistence household economy was based on the buffalo hunt, small-scale cultivation, and seasonal labour for the Hudson's Bay Company (HBC). It was, in effect, a "specialized" peasant economy whose primary aims were to secure the needs of the family rather than to make a profit. This society would have conformed to A.V. Chayanov's concept of a peasant society, which posits a balance between subsistence needs and a substantive distaste for manual labour determining the intensity of cultivation and size of the net product.[11] While produce from the buffalo hunt and farm was exchanged in Red River for other goods, and while the Metis were engaged in other activities such as occasional wage labour, the family remained the main unit of production in an essentially noncapitalistic mode of production. Given the level of local technology at the time and the absence of any real market, this was a rational course of action.[12]

In the period before 1849, these peasant communities exhibited a strong geographic stability or persistence. Of the ninety-four families in St. Andrew's in 1835, 80 per cent were still persistent in 1849.[13] In St. François Xavier 66 per cent of the ninety-seven families were still persistent in 1849. Those family heads who did migrate were generally younger and had smaller families and fewer resources. The limited qualitative evidence related to emigration from Red River before 1849 confirms this. In the 1830s and 1840s there was a small but steady trickle of emigrants to the USA from all communities in the settlement,[14] along with the movement of Hudson's Bay Company servants and officers to other posts in the northwest. The one large movement consisted of the trek of twenty families to Columbia under the direction of James Sinclair. This migration had been organized by the HBC to counteract the projected American movement of settlers into

Oregon.[15] The impact of these migrations on the colony was, however, minimal.

Instead it was changes in the political economy of the Red River Metis in the 1840s, changes that integrated the colony into the wider world, which produced large upheavals. These changes were tied to the increasing Metis involvement in a new capitalistic fur trade, especially the emerging buffalo-robe trade. This resurgence of Metis involvement in the fur trade did not signal a return to "primitivism" or "nomadism," but the penetration of an early form of capitalism into the Metis family economy—that is, the increasingly close association between household production of furs and robes based on the family economy on the one hand, and the capitalist organization of the trade and marketing of these products on the other. In the context of Red River these developments emerged with the breakup of the Hudson's Bay Company monopoly and the establishment of a new market for furs in the 1840s. Increasing Metis involvement in this new capitalistic fur trade, especially the emerging buffalo-robe trade, took place within the context of the Metis family economy. Involvement in this new "rural industry"[16] led to an abandonment of agriculture by a segment of Metis, and was an important impetus to emigration from Red River.

An important stimulus to this new capitalistic fur trade was the establishment in 1844 of a trading post at Pembina, seventy miles south of Red River in the American territory. This had the effect of bringing the American market to the front door of the Red River Colony.[17] Not only did this post create an alternative market, it became a source of supplies and capital that transformed the Metis economy of the region and precipitated an outburst of trading in furs throughout the Red River district. Especially important was the expansion of the buffalo-robe trade in the 1840s and 1850s. Buffalo robes had beeome an important and valuable trade item in the Upper Missouri in the late 1830s as the beaver trade waned[18] and, in the Red River Colony, the price received for buffalo robes increased in the 1840s and 1850s. Buffalo robes had long been used by traders and Indians as blankets and for packing furs, but their increasing value in the eastern market made them a prime trade item in the late 1830s and 1840s.[19]

An indication of the extent and expansion of this trade can be gleaned from the increase in the number of carts travelling annually to St. Paul. In 1844 only six carts are recorded as making the journey to St. Paul,[20] by 1855 four hundred carts,[21] by 1858, eight hundred carts,[22] and by 1869, twenty-five hundred carts were carrying furs and goods to St. Paul.[23] Fur sales in St. Paul, on the other hand, rose from $1,400 in 1844 to $40,000 in 1853, to $182,491 in 1857, and an average of over $215,000 annually in the following eight years.[24] The majority of these furs shipped to St. Paul from Red River were buffalo robes[25] and, by the late 1850s and early 1860s, St. Paul fur houses were sending "runners" to Red River to buy up buffalo robes in large quantities.[26] Norman Kittson, who had precipitated this new trade in the region by opening a post just south of the Canada/USA border at Pembina, was reported returning to Mendotta in 1857 with over four thousand buffalo robes.[27] In 1862 the settlement newspaper, the *Nor'wester*, commented that "the great business in this country is at present the trade in furs . . . Farming, shop-keeping, and all other vocations whatsoever, dwindle to the merest nothing when compared, in point of profits, with this vast business."[28] In 1865 alone close to twenty-five thousand robes had been shipped from Red River to St. Paul by Red River cart.[29]

Increasingly the Metis took advantage of these opportunities, and became involved in commodity production for market (furs, particularly buffalo robes) rather than for home consumption. Rather than being sold to the Hudson's Bay Company, their surplus was increasingly appropriated by merchant traders, many of whom were Metis themselves. Participation in this new trade cut across community and ethnic boundaries as both English and French Metis responded to the opportunities. The most important component of this new fur trade, and the greatest impetus to wintering on the plains and hence abandoning agriculture, was the growing Metis involvement in the buffalo-robe trade. With its intensive labour demands, and the imperative for hunters and their families to winter near the buffalo herds as they drew ever further away from the Red River settlement, this trade significantly altered the geographic mobility of those Metis families who participated in it. The demands this trade, or household industry, placed on Metis families would draw them away from Red River in increasing numbers. As the demands for robes increased and as the herds moved further from the settlement, the practice of Metis families wintering near the herds became increasingly common. By 1856 Governor Simpson reported that the phenomenon of wintering villages had become widespread.[30]

The point to be stressed here is that the buffalo-robe trade became a household industry for those Metis families involved in it. In securing the buffalo robes and hides hunting groups developed a considerable organization with a clearly defined division of labour. Some engaged only in riding and shooting, others in skinning, while still others followed up to stretch and tan the skins and robes.[31] There was, in fact, a good deal of intensive labour involved in producing a buffalo robe for market, and this had a significant effect on Metis family formation. The Metis family became, in effect, a household factory in the production of buffalo robes, necessitating long absences from the colony and thus making it impossible to continue cultivation of their family river lots.

A further stimulus to the transformation of the Metis economy in the 1840s was the succession of bad crop years, which failed to produce enough even for subsistence. In the five-year period 1844 to 1848, only 1845 produced a harvest sufficient to feed the colony.[32]

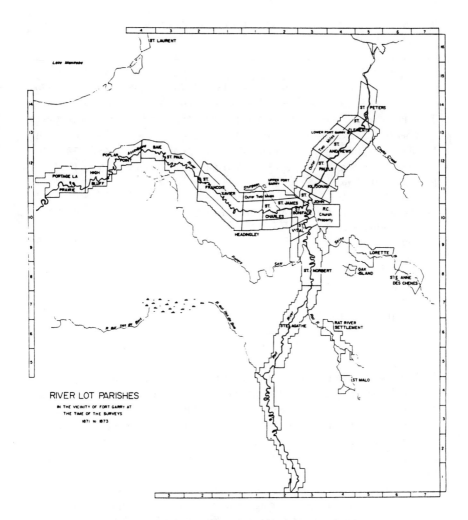

RIVER LOT PARISHES

IN THE VICINITY OF FORT GARRY AT
THE TIME OF THE SURVEYS
1871 to 1873

Parishes and Settlements of the Red River Settlement
At the time of the Surveys 1871-1873

TABLE 1   Population and Cultivation in St. Andrew's and St. François
Xavier 1835 to 1870[33]

	St. Andrew's				St. François Xavier			
	1835	1849	1856	1870	1835	1849	1856	1870
Total Population	547	1068	1207	1456	506	911	1101	1857
Number of Single Adults	3	10	—	44	5	4	—	24
Number of Families	94	187	214	287	97	165	178	334
Average Family Size	5.78	5.66	5.64	4.91	5.16	5.49	6.18	5.47
Percentage of Metis Family Heads	53.6	68	—	75.1	74.5	82	—	91.2
Total Cultivated Acres	566	1366	1646	2002	594	527	582	1335
Average Cultivation/ Family	6.02	7.3	7.7	6.97	6.12	3.19	3.26	3.99
Average Cultivation/ Person	1.03	1.28	1.4	1.37	1.17	0.58	0.53	0.72
Cultivation/European Family	4.04	10.6	—	10.35	4.62	5.1	—	18.8
Cultivation/Metis Family	7.93	5.2	—	8.8	9.34	2.6	—	3.8

Faced with a limited market for grain and a succession of bad crop years, it is small wonder that a large number of Metis abandoned agriculture and concentrated on the fur trade for which there was now an expanding market. Even without bad crop years, Governor Simpson commented, "the want of market (for wheat) . . . has prevented any agriculturalist from expanding their farms and increasing their livestock beyond the requisite quantity to meet the demands of the Company and their own absolute wants."[34]

By the time the 1849 census was taken in Red River, it was clear that some Metis families were abandoning agriculture completely. While the total area under cultivation increased, from 3504 acres in 1835 to 6392 acres in 1849, some communities showed a decrease in cultivated acres despite the fact that their population had almost doubled. The connection between the new trading opportunities and the decline of agriculture was observed by the *Nor'wester* in discussing the decline of sheep farming in the settlement. Introduced in 1830, the number of sheep in the colony rose to a peak of 4222 in 1846, declined to 3096 in 1849, and to 2245 in 1856, and totalled even less by 1860. The reason for this decline, the *Nor'wester* noted, had to do with the increase in dogs in the settlement and this, in turn, was related to the increase in plains trading. "About the year 1848 parties commenced their excursion out of the settlement to trade with the Indian, and were of course accompanied by dogs. As the traffic and the dogs increased the sheep diminished. They were attacked and destroyed by the dogs."[35]

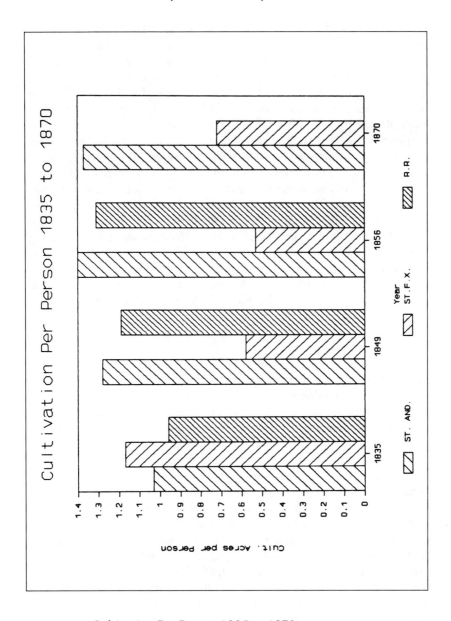

FIGURE 1   Cultivation Per Person 1835 to 1870

This brief sketch of the Metis economy between 1835 and 1870 makes it clear that by the 1830s the Metis communities in Red River combined subsistence agriculture and hunting to secure the needs of the family rather than to make a profit. Differences in cultivation between communities began to become apparent in the late 1840s as some Metis abandoned agriculture to pursue new economic opportunities in the emerging capitalistic fur trade, especially the buffalo-robe trade. This transition was more evident in St. François Xavier than in St. Andrew's, which continued to rely on peasant agriculture to a much greater degree. With the growing importance of the robe trade in the 1860s, Metis families in Red River were increasingly forced to make a decision between subsistence agriculture or the hivernement existence which went with the trade.[36] Hivernants (literally winterers) were those Metis who spent the winter on the plains to be nearer the buffalo herds. The best or "prime" buffalo robes were those taken from the animals in the winter when the hair was thickest. As the buffalo withdrew further from Red River it was thus necessary to winter on the plains. These Metis lived in temporary camps ranging from a few families to large encampments replete with a resident priest. Most Metis families did not have the capital required to remain in Red River and still continue in the buffalo-robe trade. The wealthier Metis, on the other hand, could outfit relatives or employees to visit these camps and trade for buffalo robes.

From the information given in the North-West scrip applications, it is possible to see that permanent emigration from Red River began to increase in the 1850s,[37] and that the parishes experiencing the greatest emigration were St. François Xavier, St. Andrew's, Portage la Prairie, and St. Boniface (see Table 2 and Figure 2). This timing corresponds very closely with reports of when hivernement camps were becoming more permanent.[38]

That these emigrants were responding to the exigencies of the buffalo-robe trade can be tested by examining the association between the number of migrants leaving Red River[39] and the rising buffalo-robe prices between 1847 and 1869 (see Figure 3). This scatterplot shows a positive linear relationship between the two variables, and the .67 correlation coefficient calculated from this data indicates a significant positive correlation between rising buffalo-robe prices and Metis emigration from Red River.[40] The destination of the individual migrants identified in the scrip applications further reinforces the association between the robe trade and Metis emigration. The majority of those leaving Portage went to Victoria, a settlement of English Metis buffalo hunters, while those from St. Andrew's left for both Victoria and the Saskatchewan Forks area. Those leaving St. François Xavier and St. Boniface, the two French Metis parishes which had the highest number of emigrants, left for the hivernement sites of Qu'Appelle, Wood Mountain, Saskatchewan Forks, Lac la Biche, Cypress Hills, and the Fort Edmonton area.[41] In 1864 the Nor'wester reported that twenty-five French Metis families were leaving Red River for Lac la Biche. While they were

TABLE 2   Metis Migration from Red River Before 1870

Parish	Number	Percentage
St. Peters	23	3.8
St. Andrew's	38	6.3
Portage	63	10.4
St. Pauls	7	1.1
St. Johns	5	0.8
Ft. Garry-Winnipeg	25	4.1
St. Boniface	76	12.5
St. Norbert	22	3.6
St. Vital	15	2.5
St. Charles	4	0.7
St. James	4	0.7
High Bluff	2	0.3
Poplar Point	3	0.5
St. François Xavier	187	30.9
Scratching River	1	0.2
Kildonan	3	0.5
Ste. Agathe	2	0.3
Baie St. Paul	20	3.3
Headingly	1	0.2
Unknown	105	17.3
Total	606	100.0

SOURCE: Scrip Records

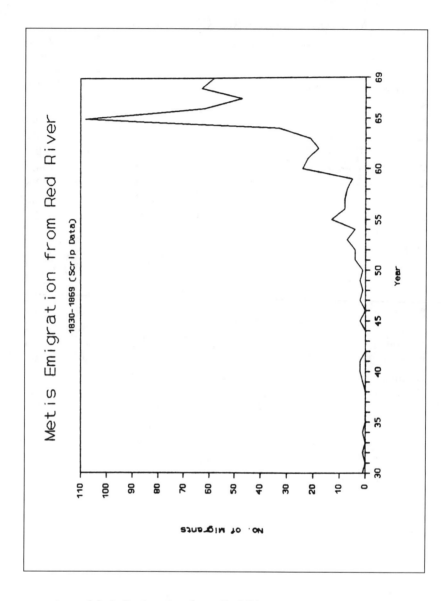

FIGURE 2   Metis Emigration from Red River

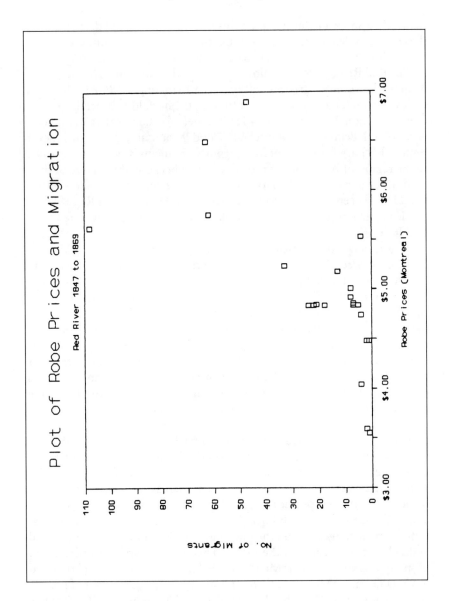

FIGURE 3   Plot of Robe Prices and Migration

taking their stock and farm implements, the main purpose of the migration, the correspondent noted, was to bring them near the buffalo, the pursuit of which would engross much more of their time than agriculture.[42]

The Red River-based buffalo hunt was by this time on its last legs with no more than one hundred and fifty carts participating in 1866.[43] The herds were now too far away, and to continue in the buffalo-robe trade necessitated migration. In the autumn of 1869 alone, forty families left St. François Xavier and Pembina to winter at Wood Mountain, and many never returned.[44] Large numbers of Metis from St. François Xavier also returned to the region of Battleford in the fall of 1869 because of the large buffalo herds there in past years.[45] In order to find large herds by the late 1860s it would have been necessary to travel five hundred miles from Red River.[46] While large hunts continued to take place, these no longer originated from Red River.

A more detailed statistical analysis of migrants, identified by linking the censuses between 1835 and 1870 in the parishes of St. François Xavier and St. Andrew's, shows the extent to which emigration affected all sectors of these communities.[47] Almost none of the 1849 census variables were significant when cross-tabulated with those heads of family who left the parish between 1849 and 1870. Those variables that had some degree of association with migration in the period 1835-49 had little or no relationship in the period 1849-70. It would appear that the economic attractions of the fur trade after 1849 affected even those who had substantial amounts of land under cultivation. Likewise, other indications of wealth, such as the number of buildings and livestock, had little predictive value with regard to who would or would not emigrate in the period 1849-70.

These trends continued in the period after 1870. However Confederation, along with the attendant land surveys and Dominion land regulations, which affected a change in the way property was viewed, added a new dimension to the movement out of Red River. The increasing importance of land ownership in the new political order can be seen clearly in both St. Andrew's and St. François Xavier. In both parishes there was a strong negative association between emigration on the one hand and the amount of land owned and cultivated acreage on the other. This new importance of land and property was not lost on the Metis. Even before the transfer of Rupert's Land to Canada, many Metis had their land surveyed to secure proof of possession.[48] The grants of land to Metis children and Metis heads of family were also main points in the negotiations leading up to the Manitoba Act. The Metis knew well that the land question involved nothing less than their stake in the new province.[49]

There was, however, a significant difference in the number of migrants leaving the two parishes in the period from 1870 to 1881. While the proportion of rather than percentage of 1870 residents who left St. Andrew's in the period 1870 to 1881 was 35 per cent, that of St. François Xavier jumped

TABLE 3   Cross-tabulation of Census Variables with Migrants:
St. Andrew's 1835-81

	1835-49	*1849-70*	*1870-81*
Race	.16*	.15*	.07
Age	.24	.22*	.20
Family Size	.16	.11	.17
Sons under 16	.14	.15	.05
Sons over 16	.13	.07	.07
Buildings	.24	.10	.39
Horses	.12	.04	—
Total Livestock	.27	.17	—
Carts	.13	.03	—
Cultivated Acres	.23	.13	.40
Total Acres	—	—	.34

NOTE: The measure of coefficience used here is "Cramer's V" which is derived from Chi-Squared. Cramer's V measures the independence between the variables cross-tabulated. A value of zero would indicate there was no relationship between the variables, while a value of 1.0 would indicate a perfect relationship between variables.
*Contingency coefficient used instead of Cramer's V. In a two-by-two table, however, it has the same value as Cramer's V.

TABLE 4   Cross-tabulation of Census Variables with Migrants:
St. François Xavier, 1835-81

	1835-49	*1849-70*	*1870-81*
Race	.18*	.06*	.16
Age	.30	.14	.12
Family Size	.28	.08	.09
Sons under 16	.13	.12	.09
Sons over 16	.12	.01	.09
Buildings	.33	.14	.43
Horses	.20	.20	—
Total Livestock	.25	.16	—
Carts	.32	.10	—
Cultivated Acres	.32	.10	.33
Total Acres	—	—	.38

to 60 per cent. This large differential was not due to any difference in land ownership, as the percentage of heads of family that owned land in the two parishes was almost equal.[50] Further, this large increase in emigration from St. François Xavier cannot fully be explained by the greater commitment of the French Metis to the buffalo-robe trade.[51] Rather, this difference in migration rates between St. Andrew's and St. François Xavier must be attributed to the linguistic and religious intolerance of the new settlers arriving from Canada.

Writing to John A. Macdonald in 1871 Lieutenant-Governor Archibald warned that the French Metis were very excited,

> not so much, I believe by the dread about their land allotment as by the persistent ill-usage of such of them as have ventured from time to time into Winnipeg from the disbanded volunteers and newcomers who fill the town. Many of them actually have been so beaten and outraged that they feel as if they were living in a state of slavery. They say that the bitter hatred of these people is a yoke so intolerable that they would gladly escape it by any sacrifice.[52]

In 1872 Father André reported that the French-speaking Metis wintering near Carlton held with an invincible repugnance any thought of settling in Red River again. Too many changes, at odds with their customs and morals, had taken place in both social and political realms.[53] The arrival of the Wolseley Expedition in 1870, in fact, instituted a reign of terror in the settlement. Intent on avenging the death of Thomas Scott, the Ontario volunteers acted in defiance of all law and authority and established virtual mob rule in Winnipeg in 1871-72. It was not safe for a French Metis to be seen near Fort Garry, the location of the land office, and those who did venture into Winnipeg risked life and limb.[54]

Father Kavanagh, the parish priest of St. François Xavier, who himself was almost killed by Protestant extremists on his way to Winnipeg, also complained that while the Metis of his parish had designated the lands promised them in the Manitoba Act, this had scarcely stopped the Orangemen from Ontario from occupying the same land. In the face of this infringement on what they took to be their land, Kavanagh reported that some Metis had begun to defend themselves, but most were abandoning the struggle and, in growing arrogance and resignation, were leaving for the plains. Many were, in fact, offering to sell their lands to the same Protestants: "Selon toute apparence nous sommes donc enveloppés et engloutis par le *protestantisme* et *l'orangisme*. C'est si visible maintenant, que ces personnes influentes dont j'ai parlé plus haut, en conviennent: mais il est bien tard!!!"[55] While these land issues were also problems for the English Metis of St. Andrew's,[56] the language and religion they shared with the newcomers made the issue of contiguous reserves less important, and the conflict over land less bitter.

An analysis of the alienation of river lots in the parishes of St. François Xavier and St. Andrew's, and a sample of the other parishes between 1870 and 1890 bears out the timing of this exodus. In both parishes and in Red River generally, the alienation of river lots[57] peaked in the periods 1872-75 and 1880-82 (see Figure 4). The first period coincided with the delays and frustrations over the granting of Metis lands, but it also represented a continuation of the exodus, which had begun previous to 1870, of those Metis involved in the buffalo-robe trade. This early glut of river-lot sales would seem to contradict Mailhot and Sprague's assertion that 90 per cent of those Metis found in the 1870 census were still in the settlement in 1875. According to Mailhot and Sprague this high percentage indicated that the Metis were indeed "persistent settlers," that their exodus after this time was due to government lawlessness, and that the land surveyors were part of a conspiracy to overlook most Metis while recording a few.[58] The evidence, however, does not support Sprague's argument.

A more detailed analysis of individual lot sales in St. François Xavier, St. Andrew's, or Red River generally shows a more rapid rate of alienation. In St. Andrew's, where there was a comparatively high rate of persistence (66 per cent from 1870 to 1881), 15 per cent of the 1870 land-owners had sold out by 1875.[59] In St. François Xavier, 27 per cent of the parish land-owners had sold their lots by 1875[60] and, in a 10 per cent sample of lots in the rest of the parishes, 29 per cent of the land-owners in 1870 had sold out by 1875.[61] Moreover these figures, which take only land-owners into account, underestimate the number of migrants by 1875.[62] While there is no doubt that government delays in dealing with Metis lands affected their migration from Red River, there is little evidence that land surveyors deliberately overlooked anyone. In St. Andrew's 86 per cent of those residents in possession of river lots in 1870 were recognized as occupants at the time of the survey. Of the remaining 14 per cent, where the surveyors listed a different occupant, 11 per cent had sold their lot between the census of 1870 and the survey, and the occupant recognized by the surveyor claimed the land through the 1870 resident. In only four lots—1 per cent of all lots—was there no legal explanation for the difference between occupation in 1870 and recognition by surveyor. This high percentage of recognition by the surveyors was also the case in St. François Xavier (see Table 5).[63]

The sample survey of the other parishes had a higher percentage of lots declared vacant by surveyors (10.58) despite the fact that someone subsequently claimed they had occupied the lots in 1870. It seems most likely that most of these cases occurred in the recently settled parishes of Ste. Agathe and Ste. Anne. Here, few improvements could have been made to the lots, making it difficult for surveyors to determine occupancy in the absence of someone on the lot at the time of the survey. This benign interpretation of this discrepancy is more than supported by the details of the individual cases. Of the twenty-two lots (10.58 per cent) judged to be vacant by surveyors

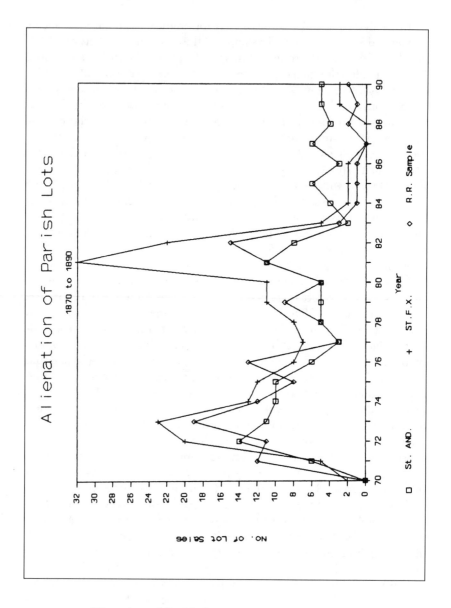

FIGURE 4   Alienation of Parish Lots

TABLE 5   Recognition of 1870 Occupants by Surveyors

Survey Recognition	St. Andrew's		St. François Xavier		Red River Sample	
	NO.	%	NO.	%	NO.	%
1870 Occupant	261	86.42	200	84.74	148	71.15
Metis	195		170		98	
Europeans	66		30		43	
Non-1870 Occupant but						
Intervening Transaction	33	10.92	23	9.75	36	17.31
Metis (1870 Occupants)	18		18		25	
Europeans (1870						
Occupants)	15		5		11	
Non-1870 Occupant						
Unexplained	4	1.33	9	3.82	2	.96
Metis (1870 Occupants)	2		9		1	
Europeans (1870						
Occupants)	2		0		1	
Vacant	4	1.33	4	1.69	22	10.58
Totals	302	100.00	236	100.00	208	100.00

despite later claims to the contrary, sixteen (7.69 per cent) were later awarded to the 1870 claimants anyway. Thus, in all, two hundred of the occupied 208 lots (96.15 percent) from the sample study of the other Red River parishes were eventually patented to persons deriving their claims from the original 1870 resident. This compares favorably to both St. François Xavier (94.49 per cent) and St. Andrew's (97.35 per cent). These findings also contradict Sprague's wider thesis that the Metis left Manitoba because they had trouble proving their claims to river lots.[64] In the two parishes studied in detail there were very few cases of nonrecognition by surveyors, and no evidence that claims were refused because of lack of evidence about occupancy. All that was necessary to prove occupancy in most cases was the sworn affidavit of a neighbour that the claimant had been the recognized owner of the lot previous to 1870.

Those Red River Metis who held onto their lots in this period generally did so until 1880, when the real-estate boom in Winnipeg and surrounding area made river lots prime real estate. Sales in this period might well be seen as taking advantage of a financial opportunity, allowing Metis a cash stake to reestablish themselves on larger farms elsewhere. The upsurge of emigration in this period also coincided with the loss of political power by the Metis in Manitoba. The connection between the loss of political power and emigration is perfectly illustrated in the person of Louis Schmidt. On losing his seat in the legislature in the 1878 election in St. François Xavier, Schmidt packed his bags and moved to Batoche.[65]

An examination of the destination of those who left after 1870 illustrates how the two peaks of emigrations (the early 1870s and the period around 1880) differed. While there is no consistent time-specific quantitative data that can be used to analyze the destination of migrants, individual references in parish files and other sources give some indication. Of those leaving in the early 1870s, many left for Metis wintering sites, in effect continuing their involvement in the buffalo trade. Pascal Breland, writing to Alexander Morris in 1873, noted that there were a great many Metis wintering at Wood Mountain. Of the four leaders he mentioned, two were St. Françis Xavier Metis who had been enumerated in 1870: Pierre Boyer, a landless Metis, and Pierre Poitras, who owned lot 41 and would sell it in 1874.[66] Similarly, François Swain left St. François Xavier with his parents in 1872 to move to Cypress Hills, while John Pritchard Mckay and his son sold lot 214 to the Catholic church in 1872 to winter on the plains.[67] Le Metis also reported that large numbers of Red River Metis had settled in the vicinity of Wood Mountain and near Carlton in the early 1870s.[68] This type of migration, while more impelled than before 1870, could still be characterized as adaptive to the trading economy of the early seventies.

Those who sold their lots later (1879-90) had already made the decision to farm. Their exodus after 1878 reflected the difficulty of commercial grain farming on narrow river lots. The problem was especially acute in cases where a head of family died without specifying a sole heir. In all cases encountered of this type, the heirs decided to sell the lot instead of subdividing it, moving elsewhere to farm.[69] Lists of claimants for "Halfbreed Scrip" in the settlements of St. Louis de Langevin, Batoche, and Duck Lake in the mid-1880s read like the parish rolls of St. François Xavier.[70] In 1882-83 alone twenty families, many of them from St. François Xavier, moved to Batoche from Red River.[71] Not all who left the parish lots in the late 1870s and 1880s went to the North-West, however. Many simply sold their lots to homestead and settled in areas of Manitoba where it was possible to live with kin and friends. Some from St. François Xavier moved to St. Eustache, St. Rose du Lac, or Ste. Anne, while a number of families from St. Andrew's moved sixty miles north to the community of Grand Marais on Lake Winnipeg.[72] A new settlement also arose ten miles east of St. Andrew's on Cook's Creek. According to James Settee this settlement was started in 1871 and comprised fifty adults by 1872.[73] Probably the largest offshoot community of St. François Xavier in Manitoba was the Metis settlement at Rivière aux Ilets de Bois, south of the Assiniboine. By the 1880s, Father Kavanagh was making regular trips to the mission (St. Daniel) to minister to the approximately thirty Metis families residing there.[74] Families such as the Emonds, Delormes, Lillies,

Prudens, and Gagnons sold their parish lots and bought larger farms here (the majority of Metis settled on township 7, range 5 W).[75]

A final determinant affecting the persistence and migration of the Metis of Red River, and one which explains, to some extent, the differential rates within communities after 1870, is that of class. While difficult to define and document in the social flux of Red River in the 1860s and 1870s, it was none the less observable. The one study that has dealt with this issue in the context of the Metis dispersal from Red River is Nicole St-Onge's work on the dissolution of the Red River Metis community of Pointe à Grouette (Ste. Agathe).[76] St-Onge sees the emergence of two distinct Metis groups separated by the late 1860s on economic and occupational lines: on the one hand were the trading and farming elite, and on the other the poorer bison hunters. In her analysis the richer traders and farmers were able to hold onto their land much longer than the poorer buffalo hunters, who had largely sold out and left the community by 1876. The fact that Metis speculators were involved in the buying out of their kinsmen suggests to St-Onge that the dispersal of the Metis was related to class rather than ethnicity.[77]

This pattern corresponds roughly to what occurred in St. François Xavier. Increasing involvement in the buffalo-robe trade after 1850 also fragmented Metis communities on socio-economic lines, and this explains a good deal of the differing rates of migration within communities. Those Metis families who were involved at the production end of the buffalo-robe trade had less land and fewer cultivated acres, and were generally the first to emigrate. The destination of these migrants was, in most cases, Metis wintering sites in the North-West. Continued involvement in the buffalo-robe trade for merchant traders, on the other hand, was not as dislocating. Not involved in the production end of the industry, this bourgeoisie could afford to stay in the settlement outfitting younger sons and relatives to undertake trading missions and, at the same time, maintain their river lot farms. Many of these wealthy Metis families remained in Manitoba through the 1880s, and became prominent in provincial politics.

J. Daignault, arriving in St. François Xavier in the 1870s from Quebec, observed that the parish was divided on socio-economic and geographic lines. While all got along with each other, there were distinct lines. Those Metis who lived in the Pigeon Lake community to the west of the church[78] were closely tied to the buffalo-robe trade as hunters, and held to traditional cultural practices. They were known as the "Purs." By contrast those Metis living to the east and south of the river and involved in the buffalo-robe trade as merchant traders and farmers were identified as living in "Petit Canada." These Metis made a show of imitating the French Canadians in their customs and dress.[79] The third group mentioned by Daignault was the emerging group of French Canadians from Quebec, who were starting to displace the Metis in the parish.

An analysis of the persistence of these two identifiable Metis classes corresponds to the pattern identified earlier, and the chronology of emigration identified by St-Onge. Of the nine landowning families resident at Pigeon Lake in 1870, only five retained their land after 1875, and only three past 1880. Those identified by Daignault as residing in "Petit Canada" all retained their land beyond 1881. My analysis differs from that of St-Onge in the emphasis placed on the actions of the federal government. Agreeing with Sprague, she argues that the poorer Metis hunters "left because of changes in the Manitoba Act which they were unable to circumvent." Incapable of establishing their improvements, and unable effectively to challenge adverse decisions related to their claims as the more affluent Metis were able to, "they sold, abandoned, or were swindled out of their claims for small amounts of money."[80] This theory, however, is not proven and little evidence is presented. St-Onge does show that the poorer Metis left first, but nowhere establishes that the motivation or the cause for their leaving was their inability to establish their claims. A closer examination of this charge, discussed earlier in this paper, in fact shows it cannot be supported.

In my analysis the decision to migrate was more a function of the changing Metis family economy and its involvement in the buffalo-robe trade. Increasing Metis involvement in this trade after 1850 necessitated an occupational specialization for those families involved and a consequent abandonment of agriculture. When the exigencies of the trade forced a permanent hivernement existence, emigration was the result. This emigration began well before Manitoba's entry into Confederation and continued to the mid-1870s when the buffalo-robe market collapsed. If there was an element of coercion in the Metis exodus from Red River, it was the intolerant actions and behaviour of the incoming Protestant settlers from Ontario.

Metis migration from Manitoba after the mid-1870s had other causes. Those who had retained their land to 1880 had, in fact, made the decision to farm rather than concentrate on the robe trade. The spate of river-lot sales, and the exodus from the Metis parishes in the early 1880s, were in response to high land prices during the real-estate boom of 1880-82. These sales gave the Metis a cash stake to reestablish larger farms elsewhere. By the late 1870s and early 1880s, there was a growing recognition of the limitations of the narrow river lots for commercial grain farming, and those Metis who wished to continue farming combined with occasional wage labour and freighting could best do this farther west. Those leaving in this period left to homestead in other areas of the province, or to join the growing Metis farming communities in the North-West.

NOTES

1. The term Metis, for the purposes of this paper, includes both the historical métis who arose in the St. Lawrence-Great Lakes trading system, who chose to see themselves in various collectivities distinct from their Indian neighbours and the "white" community, and those individuals of mixed Indian and European ancestry who arose in the Hudson Bay trading system who held similar views as to their relations with Indians and whites.

2. G.F.G. Stanley, *The Birth of Western Canada: A History of the Riel Rebellions* (Toronto, 1961). Marcel Giraud, *Le Métis Canadien: Son rôle dans l'histoire de provinces de l'Ouest,* 2 vols. (Paris, 1945).

3. G.F.G. Stanley, "The Métis and the Conflict of Culture in Western Canada," *Canadian Historical Review* 28 (1947).

4. Stanley, *The Birth of Western Canada,* 8, 18.

5. Giraud, *Le Métis Canadien,* 2:1154.

6. D.N. Sprague, "Government Lawlessness in the Administration of Manitoba Land Claims, 1870-1887," *Manitoba Law Journal* 10: 4 (1980); "The Manitoba Land Question 1870-1882," *Journal of Canadian Studies* 15: 3(1980): D.N. Sprague and R.P. Frye, *The Genealogy of the First Metis Nation: The Development and Dispersal of the Red River Settlement 1820-1900* (Winnipeg, 1983).

7. P.R. Mailhot and D.N. Sprague, "Persistent Settlers: The Dispersal and Re-settlement of the Red River Métis, 1870-1885," *Canadian Ethnic Studies* 17:2 (1985).

8. Manitoba, Public Archives (PAM), Nominal Censuses of the Red River Settlement.

9. Canada, National Archives (NA), RG 15, North-West Half Breed Scrip Applications.

10. The information for this lot-by-lot analysis comes from the Abstract Book of the Winnipeg Land Titles office which recorded the first sales of these parish lots after 1870. Also used were the parish lot files (PAM, RG17 D2), which were files kept by the department of Interior on each river lot, pertaining to the ownership and patenting of parish land. Some files are missing from the set found in the PAM. These were files retained by the department of the Interior when the records were transferred to Manitoba in 1930. These missing files are now located in the Manitoba Act Files, NA, RG15, vol. 140-68.

11. A.V. Chayanov, *The Theory of Peasant Society,* ed. Daniel Thorner, Basile Kerblay, and R.E.F. Smith (Homewood, Ill., 1966).

12. While the HBC purchased pemmican, dried meat, and agricultural produce from the settlers of Red River at an early date, the annual demand was fairly constant while the population in Red River increased rapidly. John Elgin Foster, "The Country-Born in the Red River Settlement, 1820-1850," PhD diss., University of Alberta, 1973, 219.

13. Censuses of this period listed only the head of the family along with the number of adults and children in the family. A family was considered persistent if the head of the family listed in the 1835 census reappeared in the 1849 census. In those cases where it could be shown that the head of family had died in the intervening years, and the family was present and listed under another name in the 1849 census, the family was still considered persistent. This required cross-referencing the census returns with the parish registers.

14. Foster, "The Country-Born," 219n.

15. George Gladman to James Hargrave (Fort Garry), 3 June 1843, as cited in *The Hargrave Correspondence, 1821-43,* ed. G.P. de T. Glazebrook (Toronto, 1938), 348.

16. As Irene Spry has written, the buffalo hunt "was, in fact, the basis of the first great industry in Western Canada." Irene Spry, "The Private Adventurers' of Rupert's Land," in *The Developing West: Essays on Canadian History in Honor of Lewis H. Thomas,* ed. John E. Foster (Edmonton, 1983), 54.

17. Alvin Charles Glueck, "The Struggle for the British Northwest: A Study in Canadian-American Relations," PhD diss., University of Minnesota, 1953, 27.

18. Erwin N. Thompson, *Fort Union Trading Post: Fur Trade Empire on the Upper Missouri* (Medora, N.D., 1986), 34-35.

19. These robes consisted of buffalo skins tanned on one side with hair on the other. In 1843 George Simpson, writing to the governors of the Hudson's Bay Company, commented that the Indians in the Saskatchewan District were paying more attention than usual to the preparation of buffalo robes, and that there was a large trade in these robes for which there was now a demand in both Canada and the United States. The Hudson's Bay Company, he added, intended to encourage this trade to the utmost extent of the company's ability to transport the robes. Hudson's Bay Company Archives (HBCA), D4/62, fo. 11-14, Simpson to governors, 21 June 1843.

20. Hattie Listenfeldt, "The Hudson's Bay Company and the Red River Trade," *Collections of the State Historical Society of North Dakota* 4 (1913).

21. HBCA, D4/75, George Simpson to governor and committee, 29 June 1855.

22. CMS Records, Incoming Correspondence, Letter Book VI, p. 368 (reel 6), Rev. Kirkby to the secretaries, 2 August 1858.

23. G.F.G. Stanley, *Louis Riel* (Toronto, 1963), 37.

24. *Nor'wester,* 31 January 1866: "To Red River and Beyond," *Harpers* (February 1861): 309-10.

25. *Nor'wester,* 14 May 1860, 15 June 1861, 31 January 1866.

26. *Norwester, 14* June 1860.

27. William John Peterson, *Steamboating on the Upper Mississippi* (Iowa City, 1968), 164.

28. *Nor'wester,* 1 September 1862.

29. *Nor'wester,* 31 January 1866.

30. HBCA, D4/76A, Simpson to governors and committee, 26 June 1856.

31. Merrill Burlingame, "The Buffalo in Trade and Commerce," *North Dakota Historical Quarterly* 3:4 (1929): 287.

32. CMS Records, Incoming Corrspondence, Letter Book IV, pp. 196-97, 213, 387, Smithurst to secretary, 18 November 1846; Wm. Cockran to secretary, 5 August 1847; Rev. James to secretary, 2 August 1848. PAM, Donald Ross Papers, MGI, D20, File 161, Alexander Ross to Donald Ross, 9 August 1847.

33. Except for 1856, this information has been reconstructed from the nominal censuses of the Red River settlement. The 1856 figures come from the tabulated census.

34. HBCA. D4/68, Simpson's report of 1847, p. 264.

35. "Sheep Farming in Red River," *Nor'wester,* 14 May 1860.

36. The literature on the hivernement experience is not large but is growing. The best contemporary description is found in the letters and writings of Father Decorby located in the Provincial Archives of Alberta. The best historical study to date is R.F. Beal, J.E. Foster, and Louise Zuk. "The Métis Hivernement Settlement at Buffalo Lake, 1872-77," report prepared for the Alberta Department of Culture, Historic Sites and Provincial Museums Division (April 1987).

37. These North-West scrip applications should not be regarded as a comprehensive record of all migration from Red River. For example, those Metis who migrated to the United States and never returned to Canada, would obviously never have applied for scrip. Further, since scrip claims were only made after 1885, over fifteen years after the event they recorded, migration from Red River was probably under-reported in all periods but probably more so in the 1830s and 1840s due to the death of Metis individuals. Despite these shortcomings, scrip records are useful in determining the general trends of emigration from Red River.

38. These hivernement camps, consisting of merchants and hunting families, ranged in size from a few families to upwards of two hundred. Some known hivernement sites included Turtle Mountain, Qu'Appelle River, Wood Mountain, Touchwood Hills, Cypress Hills, Souris River, Petite Ville, Buffalo Lake, Lac Ste. Anne, La Coulée Chapelle, Lac la Vieille, Coulées des Cheminées, St. Laurent, and Prairie Ronde.

39. Those are the individual migrants identified in the scrip applications.

40. To calculate this correlation coefficient using simple linear regression, robe prices at year N were paired with migrants in year N + 1 since price information cannot affect market behavior before it can become known. The coefficient may be said to measure how closely the correlation approaches a linear functional relationship. A coefficient value equivalent to unity denotes a perfect functional relationship and all the points representing paired values of x and y would fall on the regression line representing this relationship. Correlation coefficients are expressed in values ranging between -1 and + 1. The nearer a value is to either of these extremes, the better is the correlation between the two variables. If the value is positive then the correlation is direct: as the independent variable increases, so does the dependent variable. If the value is negative, the correlation is inverse.

41. North-West Half-Breed Scrip Applications.

42. *Nor'wester,* 21 June 1864.

44. *Henri Létourneau Raconte* (Winnipeg, 1980), 44.

45. Giraud, *Le Métis Canadien,* 821-22.

46. F.G. Roe, *The North American Buffalo* (Toronto, 1951), 396.

47. Migrants in this case consisted of heads of family as these were the only individuals identified in the censuses up to 1870. A head of family was considered a migrant if he / she was identified in one census and did not show up in the subsequent censuses. Those heads of family who had died in the intervening years and were recorded in the burial registers of the respective parishes were not recorded as migrants.

48. PAM, Parish Files. These files document numerous claims surveyed by Roger Goulet, between 1860-69.

49. *Le Métis,* 13 juillet 1871.

50. Fifty-six per cent of St. Andrew's families and 52 per cent of St. François Xavier families listed in the census of 1870 owned or were recognized as being in possession of river lots. These figures are deduced by cross-referencing the 1870 census, surveyor returns, parish files, and the land titles abstract book. The rest of the families in the parish were residing on lots owned by other members of the extended family (in effect patriarchal compounds), or squatting on others' land.

51. Previous to 1870, St. François Xavier experienced approximately 8 per cent to 14 per cent more emigration (between censuses) than St. Andrew's, but between 1870 and 1881 this differential jumped to 26 per cent.

52. A.G. Archibald to Macdonald, 9 October 1871, reprinted in *Journals of the House of Commons of the Dominion of Canada,* 37 Vic. (1874), vol. VIII, "Report of the Select Committee on the Causes of the Difficulties in the North-West Territories in 1869-70." Appendix (No. 6).

53. *Le Métis,* 3 avril 1872.

54. There were, in fact, a number of deaths and scores of attacks and beatings attributed to the soldiers in Winnipeg. This reign of terror has been painstakingly documented by Allen Ronaghan, "The Archibald Administration in Manitoba, 1870-72," PhD diss., University of Manitoba, 1987, 417-21, 500-05, 596-607.

55. Archives of the Archdiocese of Saint Boniface (AASB), Fonds Taché, T9222-9224, Kavanagh to Taché, 14 août 1871.

56. There were numerous articles and reports of meetings about the land question in the English Metis parishes in the *Manitoban* in the early 1870s.

57. For the purposes of this analysis of persistence and migration, the alienation of a lot was defined as the passage of the river lot out of the family. Thus a sale of a lot by an older parent to a son was not considered an alienation. Likewise a sale to a daughter, son-in-law, or wife was also not considered an alienation.

58. Mailhot and Sprague, "Persistent Settlers," 5.

59. Forty-eight lots of 297 were sold in this period. The figure of 297 lots, when there were only 288 numbered lots in the parish, was arrived at because different families often owned half lots. The HBC reserve was not included in the totals.

60. This represented seventy-one of 229 lots. Again the figure of 229 was arrived at in the same way as it was in St. Andrews.

61. This represented sixty-one of 208 lots. While 258 lots in total were examined in the sample survey of the other parishes, fifty-eight of these were vacant in 1870.

62. In 1877, only two years later, Father Kavanagh reported that the population of St. François Xavier was only 967 persons, almost nine hundred less than it had been in 1870. AASB, Fonds Taché, T18442, Kavanagh to Taché, 17 février 1877.

63. The sources for this reconstruction are the 1870 census, surveyors returns, parish files, and land titles abstract books.

64. D.N. Sprague, "Government Lawlessness," and D.N. Sprague and R.P. Frye, *The Genealogy of the First Metis Nation,* 27-28.

65. PAM, Louis Schmidt Memoirs.

66. PAM, Morris Paprs, Pascal Breland to Lt. Governor Morris, 10 May 1873.

67. PAM, St. François Xavier Parish Files; *Henri Létourneau Raconte,* 36.

68. *Le Métis,* letter of Father Lestanc, 23 janvier 1877; letter of Father André, 3 avril 1872.
69. This information is found in the parish files located in the PAM. These files recorded the alienation of these lots and often enclosed wills where they had a bearing on the transmission of the lot.
70. *Detailed Report upon All Claims to Land and Right to Participate in the North-West HalfBreed Grant by Settlers along the South Saskat-chewan and Vicinity West of Range 26 W 2nd Meridian* (Ottawa, 1886).
71. Diane Payment, *Batoche,* 1870-1910 (Saint Boniface, 1983), 24.
72. PAM. Parish Files; PAM, interview of Elsie Bear by Nicole St-Onge. 16 May 1985.
73. CMS Records, C.1/0, I.C. reel 26, J. Settee to CMS, 9 December 1872.
74. AASB, Fonds Taché, T23724-23725. Kavanagh to Taché, 22 avril 1880.
75. Crown Lands Branch, Patent Diagram; *The Rural Municipality of Dufferin, 1880-1980* (Rural Municipality of Dufferin, 1980).
76. Nicole J.M. St-Onge, "The Dissolution of a Métis Community: Pointe à Grouette, 1860-1885," *Studies in Political Economy* 18 (Autumn 1985).
77. Ibid., 157-62.
78. The body of water known as Pigeon Lake was situated on river lots 122 to 129. This was the former bed of the Assiniboine River, which through the natural process of erosion had relocated itself further south. Lots here were subdivided a good deal more than in the rest of the parish, and consequently had smaller acreages.
79. J. Daignault, "Mes Souvenirs," *Les Cloches de Saint-Boniface* (février 1945): 28.
80. St-Onge. "The Dissolution of a Métis Community," 162.

IV

THE WEST AND CONFEDERATION

In 1869, the newly-formed Canadian government, eager to fulfill its mandate to create a nation "from sea to sea," purchased Rupert's Land, that territory administered by the Hudson's Bay Company, for a sum of 300,000 pounds sterling plus one-twentieth of the fertile belt of the West. This transaction occurred without consulting the local Metis, Country-born, and the Amerindian. The Metis, under their leader, Louis Riel, resisted the Canadians. In "'Conspiracy and Treason': The Red River Resistance From an Expansionist Perspective," Doug Owram analyzes four phases of this expansionist perspective which resulted in the Red River resistance becoming not only a bitter local and regional controversy but also a national and cultural—English and French Canadian—crisis.

Louis Riel owes his mythic character in Canadian history to his involvement in the Red River resistance of 1869-70 and the subsequent North West Rebellion of 1885. Indeed Riel has gone from being seen as a "rebel" by English Canadian expansionists, and a "hero" by French Canadian nationalists at the time, to that of a frontier leader in the guise of an American Davey Crockett, an anti-imperialist guerilla fighter in the Che Guevera tradition, and a millenarian religious prophet. Yet all these interpretations have at least one thing in common: they focus on Riel in the tradition of the "Great Man" theory of history at the expense of his Metis followers. More recently historians have attempted to "go beyond" Riel by asking not why Riel led, but why the Metis followed. That shift in perspective has resulted in a proliferation of new historical works, within the genre of social history, on Metis women, families, and local communities. J.R. Miller analyzes this rich historiography in "From Riel to the Metis."

SELECTED BIBLIOGRAPHY

On the question of the West's place within Confederation, students should consult W.L. Morton's "The West and the Nation: 1870-1973," in A.W. Rasporich and H.C. Klassen, eds., *Prairie Perspectives* 2 (Toronto, 1970), pp. 8-24; and his pamphlet *The West and Confederation, 1857-1871.* Canadian Historical Association Booklet No. 9 (Ottawa, 1958); as well as Donald Swainson's "Canada Annexes the West: Colonial Status Confirmed," in Bruce Hodgins et al., *Federalism in Canada and Australia: The Early Years* (Waterloo, 1978), pp. 137-57.

Since Manitoba was the first new province to enter Confederation, and since it had a sizeable French-speaking population, the terms of agreement were a test case of the image of Canada as a unilingual or bilingual country and the constitutional rights of French Canadians outside Quebec as reflected in the minds of the Fathers of Confederation. This subject has generated considerable debate. See, for example, Donald Creighton, "Sir John A. Macdonald, Confederation and the Canadian West," originally published in the Historical and Scientific Society of Manitoba, *Transactions,* Series III, no. 23 (1966-67): 5-13 and reprinted in Donald Swainson, ed., *Historical Essays on the Prairie Provinces* (Toronto, 1970), pp. 60-70; Ralph Heintzman, "The Spirit of Confederation: Professor Creighton, Biculturalism, and the Use of History," *Canadian Historical Review* 52 (September, 1971): 245-75; and D.J. Hall, "'The Spirit of Confederation': Ralph Heintzman, Professor Creighton, and the Bicultural Compact Theory," *Journal of Canadian Studies* 9 (November, 1974): 24-43.

The question of limited French-Canadian migration into the West is discussed in Arthur Silver, "French Canada and the Prairie Frontier: 1870-1890," *Canadian Historical Review* 50 (March, 1969): 11-36. For a slightly revised view of the subject, see his *The French-Canadian Idea of Confederation, 1864-1900* (Toronto, 1982). For an alternate viewpoint see Robert Painchaud, "French-Canadian Historiography and Franco-Catholic Settlement in Western Canada, 1870-1915," *Canadian Historical Review* 59 (December, 1978): 447-66; and his *Le peuplement francophone dans les prairies de l'Ouest, 1870-1920* (Saint-Boniface, Manitoba, 1987). The first volume of Luc Dauphinais' history of the leading French-language community in western Canada has recently appeared, *Histoire de Saint-Boniface. Tome 1, A l'ombre des cathedrales, Des origines de la colonie jusqu'en 1870* (Saint Boniface, 1991).

Doug Owram has examined English-Canadian expansionist attitudes in the formative development of the prairies in greater depth in *The Promise of Eden: The Canadian Expansionist Movement and the Idea of the West, 1856-1900* (Toronto, 1980). An interesting article on the subject is J.E. Rea, "The Roots of Prairie Society," in D. Gagan, ed., *Prairie Perspectives* (Toronto, 1970), pp. 46-57.

The extensive literature on Louis Riel is reviewed in Doug Owram's "The Myth of Louis Riel," *Canadian Historical Review* 63 (September, 1982): 315-36. The most complete biography of Louis Riel remains G.F.G. Stanley's *Louis Riel* (Toronto, 1963). Hartwell Bowsfield has included a useful series of articles in his *Louis Riel: Selected Readings* (Toronto, 1988). All of Riel's writings have been edited by G.F.G. Stanley et al., *The Collected Writings of Louis Riel,* 5 vols. (Edmonton, 1985). An interesting biography of Riel's most important ally in 1885 is George Woodcock's *Gabriel Dumont* (Edmonton, 1975).

On the Metis in general at the time of the North-West resistance of 1885, see T.E. Flanagan, "Metis Land Claims at St. Laurent: Old Arguments and New Evidence," *Prairie Forum* 12 (1987): 245-55 and his larger study *Riel and the Rebellion: 1885 Reconsidered* (Saskatoon, 1983). In a new publication Flanagan also reviews the question of the Metis land grant in *Metis Lands in Manitoba* (Calgary, 1991). For a different interpretation of the Metis at the Red River and Batoche, see D.N. Sprague, *Canada and the Metis, 1869-1885* (Waterloo, 1988).

9 "Conspiracy and Treason"
The Red River Resistance from an Expansionist Perspective

In the autumn of 1869 a group of Métis under the leadership of Louis Riel forcibly prevented William McDougall from entering Red River. McDougall was Canada's governor designate for this territory, which was expected to soon become a part of the Dominion, and the Métis refusal to let him enter marked the beginning of what was to become known as the Red River resistance. It would take nearly nine months, the creation of a new province and the presence of a military force before the North West truly became a part of Canada. Through the intervening period the Métis continued by force of arms to assert their right to be consulted on their own future, while the Conservative government of John A. Macdonald sought to repair past carelessness and to find a compromise solution. Standing between these two parties and working to prevent any agreement was an informal coalition made up of expansionists and nationalists in Ontario and the pro-annexation "Canada Party" in Red River.

History has not been kind to these men who were most extreme in their opposition to the Métis. They have been assigned much of the blame both for the outbreak of the rebellion and for increasing the problems in the way of a solution.[1] Even more seriously, they have been accused of bringing unnecessary racial and religious prejudices to the surface, thereby undermining the understanding between French and English Canada that was essential to national unity.[2] Descriptions of their tragi-comic military efforts in Red River and their paranoid rhetoric in Ontario have ensured that the image presented to successive generations has been of a dangerous and slightly ludicrous group of fanatics.

Much of the criticism is justified. The economic designs of Canadians on the Red River settlement and their arrogance in assuming the right to impose these designs encouraged the Métis resistance to the transfer. Emotional meetings in the East and attempts to arrest delegates from Red

River aggravated an already tense situation and brought forth the spectre of racial conflict. Even if the main points of these traditional interpretations are accepted, however, two questions arise. First, what provoked these men to take such an extreme position? What distinguished the analysis of men like George Brown, Charles Mair and John Christian Schultz from that of other English Canadians, including John A. Macdonald, who saw the Métis action as a political problem and acted accordingly? Second, how was it that a rebellion on the banks of the Red River became a major threat to French-English relations in Canada? French Canadians had never closely identified the Métis with their own culture, and when the rebellion began the French-language press differed little in its reactions from its English counterpart.[3] Yet within a few months the resistance of the Métis became a symbol to many in both French and English Canada of their own position in the young Dominion.

In order to answer these questions, it is useful to view the Red River resistance through the eyes of those who most opposed it. In retrospect it is apparent that many of their attitudes were the result of misconceptions and prejudice. Nevertheless, given the assumption from which they operated, their actions were fairly consistent throughout. They were motivated not by a vindictive desire to obliterate a weaker culture in the West, but by a fear that others were manipulating these people for conspiratorial ends. They felt it their duty to unmask the true conspiracy that lay behind Métis actions. In attempting to do so, they transformed and aggravated the whole nature of the rebellion.

The reaction of those who took the hardest line during the rebellion was largely predetermined by their enthusiastic acceptance of the twelve-year campaign for annexation of the North West to Canada. Since 1857 groups in English Canada had been calling for the immediate transfer of the Hudson's Bay Territories, and those who figured prominently in the events of 1869-1870 were among the most ardent supporters of this movement.[4] From the beginning Canadian expansionism had been predicated on the assumption that the inhabitants of the Hudson's Bay Territories were unhappy with Company rule. The petitions presented to the Colonial Secretary by Alexander Isbister in the 1840s and the resistance of the Metis to Hudson's Bay Company rule in the Sayer trial had been factors in stirring Canadian interest.[5] By 1857, when the expansionist movement in Canada came into its own, the links between Canadian desires and supposed discontent in Red River had grown even stronger. The assumption had developed that there was a community of interest between Canada and Red River.[6] It was truly, if conveniently, believed that, as Isbister said, "the unanimous desire of the inhabitants of the Hudson's Bay Territories is to have the entire region annexed to Canada."[7]

During the expansionist campaign this belief was reinforced by numerous petitions from Red River. The pattern was set in the summer of 1857 when a petition with some 574 signatures was sent to Canada praying for the development of the region.[8] From then until 1869 numerous other petitions flowed eastward to Canadian and British authorities. Resolutions such as the one of January 1867 asking "to be united with the Grand Confederation of British North America" encouraged the idea that the extension of Canada's frontier was a two-way process.[9] Of course, a good many of these petitions were of a questionable nature, having the support of but a relatively small segment of Red River's population. Expansionists were not aware of this, however, and few in Red River who opposed the resolutions made their concerns known in the East. Canadian expansionists had neither reason nor the desire to doubt their authenticity, and the impression thus continued to grow that the settlers of Red River wanted annexation.

Actively encouraging this assumption were those expansionists who migrated west in the wake of the expansionist campaign and settled in Red River. They were to become known both by contemporaries and by history as the "Canada Party." This group's membership was succinctly defined in 1869 as being "those who favor annexation to Canada."[10] These individuals, centred around the young Dr. John Christian Schultz, had been the force behind many of the petitions that had originated in Red River. It is not surprising that these men, having made a material and personal commitment to the development of the North West, attempted to encourage annexation.

The Canada Party had an especially strong influence in shaping the Canadian image of Red River because it controlled the *Nor'Wester*, the only newspaper published in the North West. In 1859 two English-born journalists, William Buckingham and William Coldwell, arrived in Red River from Canada. Both had previously worked for George Brown at the *Globe*, and when they moved west they took not only their type and their practical experience in journalism but also a set of attitudes formed in Canadian expansionist circles. They founded Red River's first newspaper in order to further spread their expansionist views. Over the next several years the editorship of this paper would change hands many times, but it would remain a consistent advocate of the idea of Canadian expansion.

It is questionable whether the *Nor'Wester* did much to encourage support for Canada among the inhabitants of Red River. The *Nor'Wester*, like the Canada Party itself, proved a disruptive addition to the already unstable social structure of Red River in the 1860s and may have served to alienate rather than promote support for annexation to Canada.[11] Even if such was the case, the influence of the *Nor'Wester* on Canadian expansion cannot be discounted. As every editor of the paper sensed, as much could be accomplished in the name of Canadian expansion in the East as in the West. The real impact of the paper was not among its readers in Red River but in a constituency thousands of miles away. As John Schultz said, "by it we are not only influenced here but judged abroad." The *Nor'Wester* was "the lighthouse on our coast—the beacon that lets men know we are here."[12]

From Buckingham and Coldwell through James Ross, Schultz and W. R. Brown, the editors of the *Nor'Wester* realized that their paper could act as a spur to the eastern expansionists, and their style reflected that realization. As the only newspaper in the North West between 1859 and annexation, the *Nor'Wester* had a near monopoly on the interpretation of events in that region. Expansionists in the East, in turn, welcomed the information which the Nor'Wester provided as reliable and interesting. Editorials and opinions of the *Nor'Wester* were frequently printed in the Canadian papers and often served as the basis for their own editorial stance. Among Canadian expansionists a subscription to the *Nor' Wester* became a badge of membership in the campaign for annexation.[13] At times it even seemed as if the paper's real readers were not the inhabitants of Red River at all but the eastern expansionist community. When the *Nor'Wester* ran a special supplement on the formation of a Scientific Institute in Red River, none of the supplements reached the local populace for, as the paper unapologetically pointed out, "the whole impression [has] been mailed to foreigners."[14]

The *Nor' Wester* and the Canada Party worked consistently to convince their eastern audience not only of the potential of the land but of the urgent desire of the people to cast off the yoke of the Hudson's Bay Company. Attacks on Company rule were a consistent part of the paper's policy and, by at least the latter 1860s, it repeatedly argued that the best solution was annexation to Canada.[15] Further, many of the petitions which reached the East from Red River had their origins, and much of their support, in the group surrounding the paper. The petition presented by Sandford Fleming to the Canadian and British governments in 1863 was a case in point.[16] The meetings which led to this petition were headed by none other than the two current editors of the *Nor' Wester,* James Ross and William Coldwell.[17]

Thus, if the Canada Party was less than successful in its attempt to convert the people of Red River to annexation, the same cannot be said for its mission to convince Canadians that the settlement was ready and willing to join with them. The fictional and malicious character, Cool, in Alexander Begg's *Dot-It-Down* summed it up when he said that "Canada has had an eye to the North West for some years past, and is only too ready and willing to swallow anything that is said against the Honorable Company, whether true or not."[18] Expansionists had long believed that by bringing British progress and liberties to the North West they were a "ray of light" in a dark region, and when the *Nor'Wester* confirmed their opinions they found no reason to doubt it.[19] As the time for the transfer approached they confidently assumed, in the words of Charles Mair, that it was the unanimous desire of the people of Red River to possess "the unspeakable blessings of free Government and civilization."[20]

A second factor determining the expansionist attitude was the fact that the rebellion was primarily a movement of the French half-breed population. The men who had prevented McDougall's entry into the North West had all been French-speaking, Catholic, halfbreeds. Throughout the rebellion McDougall and those who shared his outlook saw the Métis as acting alone. It was believed, whether accurately or not, that the Canadians, English half-breeds and Europeans in the settlement were opposed to Riel. In other words the expansionists were convinced that the resistance had its origin and support in only one section of the population of Red River.

Until the rebellion, neither the Canadian government nor the expansionists had paid much attention to the Métis. The Sayer trial and the appearance of French names on various petitions had encouraged the assumption that their opinions were indistinguishable from those of the other segments of Red River's population. This is hardly surprising, given eastern reliance on the Canada Party and the *Nor'Wester* for information. Nevertheless, the failure to recognize this powerful and distinct community in Red River proved to be a costly blunder.

Contributing to the lack of understanding was the prevailing lack of knowledge concerning the Métis in Canada. Aside from the buffalo hunt, which drew general comment from tourists and writers before 1870, little was written on the Métis. Even in the case of the buffalo hunt, writers had consistently failed to follow the implication of such organization through to its logical conclusion. Those who wrote of the North West did not relate, or did not themselves perceive, the powerful sense of identity and ability to work in concert which was a part of the Métis tradition. Rather, when the Métis were mentioned at all, it was in a manner that portrayed them as rather quaint and undisciplined individuals whose habits and character were drawn from their wilderness environment.[21] It was a composite portrait that served to accentuate their Indian background rather than their French language or Catholic religion. Even among French Canadians, where the identity of religion and language produced some sympathy for the Métis, there was a general belief that these people were a poor semi-nomadic group whose only link to civilization was through the church.[22] English Canadians, while they noted the French language and Roman Catholic religion, saw the Métis character as distinct and separate from that of French Canada.

With such characteristics it was generally believed that the future of the Métis within a European framework was, at best, limited. The assumption was that they would only partly adapt to the onrushing civilization and would thus be relegated to the bottom end of the socio-economic scale. They "will be very useful here when the country gets filled up," Mair noted shortly before the transfer, for they are "easily dealt with and easily controlled."[23] The image of the Métis, and their role for the future, thus resembled that of peasant as much as it did Indian. Strong but manageable, able to cope with European civilization but unlikely to thrive on it, they were expected to passively accept their new lot.

Even such a limited prospect was regarded by expansionists as an improvement on the life which the Métis had led under the rule of the

Hudson's Bay Company. For both political and economic reasons Canadians expected to receive the gratitude of these people in the same way they expected the gratitude of all Red River. At the same time, it was hardly to be expected that the Métis, as either peasants or Indians, would be consulted in such a major transaction as the transfer of the North West. They were at best a "wretched half-starved people" whose comprehension of such matters would be feeble.[24] Even in the face of armed resistance, William McDougall could not understand that this image of the Métis was distorted and incomplete. "The Canadian Government," he maintained, had "done nothing to injure these people but everything to benefit them." There was thus no reason for the rebellion, except perhaps that "they—3 or 4000 semi-savages and serfs of yesterday—will not be trusted with the government and destiny of a third of the American continent."[25] With such an image of the Métis and such an underestimation of their sense of identity, it is not surprising that the expansionists were never able to comprehend the real reasons for the decisive resistance in Red River.

The first reaction of expansionists to this seemingly meaningless resistance was one of ridicule and contempt. McDougall initially predicted that the "insurrection will not last a week."[26] The *Globe*, on hearing of the activity, scornfully commented on November 17, 1869, that "it is altogether too much of a joke to think of a handful of people barring the way to the onward progress of British institutions and British people on the pretence that the whole wide continent is theirs." As autumn moved into winter, however, and Louis Riel's provisional government gained rather than lost strength, such offhand comments dwindled in number. Gradually expansionists were forced to take the whole issue more seriously.

In attempting to analyze the situation and thereby reach a possible solution, the expansionists were at a disadvantage. Their image of the Métis and their continued belief that the majority of Red River was in favour of annexation made them unable to accept the arguments of the rebels at face value. Only by portraying the Métis as puppets in the hands of artful manipulators, whose real purpose was not being revealed, were they able to find an explanation satisfactory to their own presuppositions. The *Nor'Wester*, in its last issue, maintained that the Métis had been "imposed upon" and led into rebellion.[27] McDougall concurred and wrote to Macdonald that "the half-breeds were ignorant and that parties behind were pushing them on."[28] The *Globe* referred vaguely but pointedly to "certain persons in their settlement, who are hostile to the Dominion" as the ones who "have made it their business to stir up discontent among the most foolish and ignorant of the population."[29] As expansionists, and those who agreed with them, developed this conspiratorial interpretation of the rebellion they began to focus on three individual but inter-related groups as the real instigators of the Métis resistance.

The conspirators who figured most prominently in expansionist thoughts came from south of the border. "It was well known at Fort Garry," McDougall commented in the fall of 1869, "that American citizens had come into the country." Ostensibly they were traders, but that was merely a mask for their plans to "create disaffection, and if possible, a movement for annexation to the United States." These men and their allies "had been actively engaged in circulating stories, absurd as they were unfounded, to alarm the fears of the half-breeds, and excite their hostility against the Canadian government."[30] It was not surprising that American designs on Red River should be seen as a force behind the Métis resistance. Canadian expansionists had long worried about American pretensions to the North West. The *Nor' Wester*, throughout its existence, had urged Canada to act quickly before Red River was forced into "annexation with the United States."[31] Also, as those interested in the North West were well aware, Canada was not the only home of expansionists. The effective monopoly which the State of Minnesota exerted over trade and transportation with Red River gave its own expansionists some hope that the North West would drift into the American political orbit.

The activities of American expansionists, such as Oscar Malmros, the U.S. Consul in Red River, Enos Stutsman and James Wickes Taylor, gave some reality to the charges, of American encouragement of the Red River resistance. What Canadians, and particularly expansionists, failed to realize, however, was that these annexationist forces were auxiliary rather than basic to the Métis resistance.[32] The presence of some annexationists in Riel's provisional government and the creation of the *New Nation* gave the American party some influence in Red River in December 1869 and January 1870. Thereafter, however, this influence rapidly declined. Ironically, these Americans were as unable to understand the purpose of the Métis as were Canadian expansionists. The Americans assumed that their dislike of Canada could be transformed into American annexationism, while the Canadians feared that such a goal was all too probable.

The second force which expansionists perceived behind the rebellion was the Hudson's Bay Company. When McDougall met resistance his first reaction, besides perplexed surprise, was to warn William McTavish, Governor of the Council of Assiniboia, that "you are the legal ruler of the country, and responsible for the preservation of the public peace."[33] It was, however, not as simple as that. As McTavish well knew, the Hudson's Bay Company had no force with which to assert its authority. This had been apparent as far back as the Sayer trial, and it would have been both impossible and dangerous for the Company to have attempted to face such a determined group as the Métis. Canadian expansionists, however, had a different explanation. "The Hudson's Bay Company are evidently with the rebels," Schultz wrote in November, 1869. "It is said the rebels will support the Government of the Hudson's Bay Company as it now exists."[34] The Member of Parliament for Brant North, J.Y. Bown, passing on the opinions of his brother, the deposed editor of the *Nor' Wester*, warned Macdonald that before the rebellion "certain parties then in the pay of the Company and holding office under it made threats of what they would do."[35] McDougall, perhaps because he was an official representative of Canada, was more circumspect but did point to "the complicity of some of his (Governor McTavish's) council with the insurrection."[36] However circumspect McDougall's letter, the message remained the same. The current government of the North West had actively encouraged opposition to the lawful transfer of the territory of Canada.

Though a few individuals in the Company showed some sympathy for the Métis, the expansionists had little evidence to support their charges. The expansionists had proclaimed for so long that the Company exerted an oppressive tyranny over the people of Red River that they could not now accept the fact that it was powerless. Those more detached from the expansionist perspective tended to have a more realistic analysis. John A. Macdonald sharply disagreed with McDougall's condemnation of McTavish, and at no time did the Canadian government accept the theory that there was any Hudson's Bay involvement in the rebellion.[37]

The third conspiratorial force perceived behind the rebellion was to prove the most dangerous in its implications for Canada. The Roman Catholic church, or at least its representatives in Red River, were also accused of aiding the Métis in their resistance. "The worst feature in this case," McDougall told Macdonald, "is the apparent complicity of the priests." Rather than support constituted authority they had openly supported rebellion. "It appears certain that at least one of them has openly preached sedition to his flock and has furnished aid and comfort to the parties in arms."[38] On December 9, 1869 the Toronto *Globe* singled out Father J. N. Richtot as the "head and front of the whole movement by the French half-breeds." The Catholic clergy joined the rapidly swelling ranks of those who were seen as the instigators of rebellion, having "worked upon the ignorance and fears of the French speaking portion of the people to such an extent as to lead them to armed resistance."[39]

Expansionist perceptions of the relationship between the Métis and the clergy made it natural for them to suspect the priests. The Métis were viewed as a superstitious and ignorant people and, as every good Ontario Protestant knew, the Roman Catholic church exercised totalitarian control over its membership. It followed that had the clergy wished to stop the rebellion they could have. Further, no individual priest would dare work in opposition to his own church hierarchy. Thus the ultimate conclusion had to be, as the *Globe* decided in the spring of 1870, "that Bishop Taché holds the whole threads of the affair in his hand."[40] At any time he could have commanded the Métis to cease resistance, but he consistently refrained from doing so. This was the best proof of all that the church was in league with the rebels. "A word from their Bishop," McDougall charged, "would have sent them all to their homes and re-established the lawful Government of Assiniboia, but that word was not spoken."[41]

These accusations against the clergy were an almost instinctive reaction to a body which was viewed with extreme suspicion. The expansionist movement and its nationalist allies consisted largely of English-speaking Protestants. French-Canadian Roman Catholics had played little part in the effort to acquire the North West and thus had no spokesmen within the ranks of the movement. Moreover, many expansionist leaders, such as William McDougall, had long viewed the Catholic church as some sort of hostile foe conspiring against Canada. The religious and political controversies of Canadian history had paved the way for the expansionist reaction to the clergy in 1869. Many English Canadians were all too ready to implicate the Catholic church in any activity directed against the Canadian nation or British Empire.

Such conspiratorial explanations enabled the expansionists and nationalists to reconcile the rebellion with their belief that the population of Red River favoured entry into Canada. The rebellion was not a popular uprising at all. The majority of the people opposed the resistance, but as Mair theorized "the Yankee, the Company and the Priests had a fair field; whilst the loyal English natives, comprising about two thirds of the population, without arms and ammunition, cursed their own helplessness and shrunk from the guns at Fort Garry."[42] The rebellion was the fault neither of Canada nor of the Canadian expansionists, and was not supported by the people of Red River. Foreign elements had manipulated an ignorant segment of the populace in order to gain their own nefarious ends.

The analysis of the rebellion had obvious implications for the policy to be pursued in bringing it to an end. For John A. Macdonald, who saw expansionist arrogance and Métis suspicions behind the outbreak, the best solution seemed to be "to behave in as patient and conciliatory a fashion as possible."[43] The rebellion was essentially a movement aiming at political guarantees; to Macdonald, that implied a political solution. Compromise with the Métis would allay their fears and allow the peaceful acquisition of the territory before American expansionists could exploit the situation. He even suggested bringing Riel into the police force which was planned for the region as "a most convincing proof that you are not going to leave the half-breeds out of the law."[44]

In contrast to Macdonald, those who saw the rebellion as a conspiracy felt it dangerous to assume that the matter could be resolved by conciliation. They perceived the ultimate goal of the rebellion to be the disruption of Canada and perhaps the whole British Empire. Attempts to reconcile the Métis were pointless, for they were not at the base of the rebellion. The problem went much deeper and had much more important consequences. Given these beliefs, the expansionists thus felt that the only possible response to continued rebellion was the use of force. Moreover, as the *Globe* concluded, the rebellion was not a popular uprising, and the use of troops would thus not put Canada "in the unpleasant position of oppressors forcing an unpopular government upon a protesting people." Military action would simply ensure the wishes of the majority of people of Red River were carried out while, at the same time, stopping those who "for merely selfish purposes" sought to overthrow "British authority and British freedom."[45] At a meeting of some five thousand citizens in April, 1870, the mayor of Toronto warned that the British Empire might employ troops to "put down that miserable creature . . . who attempts to usurp authority at Fort Garry."[46] As the months went by, the rhetoric of expansionism indicated a growing willingness, even enthusiasm, for the use of military force.

The official government approach remained much more conciliatory. Further, many government officials blamed leading expansionists, especially William McDougall, Charles Mair and John Schultz, for their provocative actions.[47] The expansionists replied with their own increasingly harsh criticisms. Macdonald was blamed for his abandonment of McDougall and his refusal to accept the transfer of the territory from Britain until peace was restored.[48] Joseph Howe, the Nova Scotian cabinet minister and former anti-confederationist, was suspected of secretly encouraging the rebellion during his visit to the settlement shortly before it began.[49] In this climate of bitterness and mutual recrimination, expansionists began to feel increasingly estranged from the government and to perceive themselves as an unjustly vilified minority within the nation. It seemed that only Ontario had enough national patriotism to create a forceful demand for the suppression of the rebellion. Other parts of the Dominion and the government itself delayed and hesitated while Canada's future remained in danger.

The charges that began to circulate in the spring of 1870 gave this sense of bitterness more concrete form. In the wake of the execution of Thomas Scott by Riel, the Canadian government reluctantly decided that a military expedition to the North West was necessary. From the expansionist perspective such an expedition was of the utmost importance. They had called for a show of force from the beginning, and Scott's death added a new emotionalism to these demands. Scott had been martyred for his loyalty and "humble though his position was—yet he was a Canadian; his mental gifts may have been few—yet he died for us."[50] As preparations were undertaken for the expedition, however, many individuals began to suspect that there was an element in the government working to hamper it. Singled out were prominent French-Canadian politicians, including George Cartier, Minister of Militia. Those who supported the use of force saw in Cartier and his allies a "party which opposed in every possible manner the departure of the expedition."[51]

Complicating matters was an increasing public opposition in French Canada to the use of such force. As attitudes in Ontario grew increasingly militant in the wake of Scott's death, many French Canadians became wary of the motivation which lay behind such vehemence. Naturally sensitive to the intolerance often exhibited by English-Canadian Protestantism, they had little difficulty in accepting the Métis rationale for the rebellion at face value. The Métis were, with good reason, simply seeking guarantees that their religious and linguistic rights would be protected under the new order. A military expedition seemed both unnecessary and oppressive, and many French Canadians protested against the decision to send one.

To the expansionists and to a good many other English Canadians, however, such a position was treasonable. More and more, the wrath of Ontario public opinion turned its attention from Fenians and foreign agents to those within Canada who would oppose their militant brand of expansion. French-Canadian opposition to the expedition, the *Globe* warned, contained within it an ominous principle:

> If British troops cannot go on British territory wherever the authorities desire to send them without being denounced as butchers and filibusters by fellow subjects, things must be in a poor way. If that can't be done in Red River, it can't in Quebec, and if the latter doctrine is held, by all means let it be advanced, but it is just as well to have it understood that a good many pounds will be spent, and a good many lives lost before it will be acquiesced in.[52]

Expansionists believed that Howe and others, for personal reasons, might have worked to thwart the interests of Canada. In the growing hostility of French Canada, however, they perceived a movement of much larger proportions and much greater significance.

The racial and religious implications of the Red River rebellion had never been far below the surface. The priests, accused of participation in the insurrection, had brought the issue of the Catholic religion into the question from the beginning. The Métis had often been rather loosely referred to as the "French party" and that term, in turn, used as a description of the rebellious elements in the settlement.[53] On the other hand, expansionists had tried to play down the popular support for the rebellion by portraying the rebels as a small segment of even the French half-breeds. John Schultz, for instance, made a point at the public rally in Toronto of distinguishing between the rebels and the loyal French half-breed elements in Red River.[54] Also, William McDougall had initially seen the clerical involvement in the rebellion as a result of the fact that most of them were foreign born.[55] Thus, if religious and racial undertones were present throughout the rebellion, they were muted.

The debate over the military expedition brought these undertones to the surface. The process was a dialectic one. French Canada objected to Ontario demands for the use of force against a people which it felt was, whether in a correct manner or not, simply trying to protect itself. Ontario expansionists, seeing the complaints of the Métis as a subterfuge for more malignant ends, took the French Canadian opposition to the expedition as a sign of disloyalty. The muted racial friction increased until it became a dominant ingredient of Canadian politics.

By July, 1870, it was being argued not only that French Canada opposed the expedition but that, unless loyalists acted quickly, the force would never reach Red River. Canada First members George Denison and R. G. Haliburton saw a devious plot on the part of Cartier and his cohorts to give Riel an amnesty and recall the force before it reached Red River. Warning was given by these "loyalists" that any such attempt would meet massive resistance from Toronto and that Cartier and Taché, scheduled to arrive in Toronto, would be confronted by hostile crowds. Shortly afterwards another huge rally was called, and there the honour of the Empire and the suppression of rebellion were again demanded.[56] Once again the cry of treason had been raised but in this case the traitors were identified as French Canadian cabinet members rather than the rebels themselves.

The slightly ludicrous hysterics of Denison and Haliburton indicate the change which had taken place in the analysis of the rebellion by the summer of 1870. Between March, when news of Scott's death first created widespread support for the use of force, and July the focus in the conspiratorial analysis of the rebellion shifted. Fenians and Hudson's Bay Company officials remained involved but it was the role of the priests that was assuming the greatest significance. Their role in the rebellion became much clearer once it was believed that French Canada was also involved. The two forces, linked through their common language and religion, were in league. Their joint goal was, as McDougall warned his constituents after his return to Canada, to have "the North-West made into a French Catholic Colony, with special restrictions on all their inhabitants."[57] The Toronto *Globe*, replying angrily to criticism of Ontario's militancy in the Quebec press, charged that "the fanatics are the French Canadians, who are striving to obtain for themselves peculiar and exclusive privileges."[58]

In a complex psychological process brought on by French-Canadian opposition to Ontario militancy, the conspiratorial figures of Red River were transferred from the North West to Canada. It was the story of the established church, clergy reserves and anti-democratic privileges for the minority all over again. French Canada had allied itself with the priests of Red River in order to prevent the natural development of British civilization and to preserve autocratic rule. And the expansionists argued that rule by the Catholic church, as surely as by the Hudson's Bay Company, would "lock up the splendid country under a more odious tyranny than that which has long ruled it."[59] French Canada had come to be considered as much of a danger as the Hudson's Bay Company to the sort of Protestant commercial culture which the expansionists envisaged for the North West.

The expansionists' fears concerning the West were reinforced by the government's proposed Manitoba Act, first introduced to Parliament on

May 2, 1870. The boundaries of the new province, the educational system and those clauses which set aside land for the Métis were seen as further evidence of a conspiracy to create a French Catholic province in the North West. The Act prompted McDougall to bring his view of the rebellion to the floor of the House of Commons. Over shouts of opposition he charged that "the rebellion in the North West originated with the Roman Catholic priesthood" and that "the priesthood desired to secure certain advantages for themselves, their Church or their people."[60] Captain G.L. Huyshe, a member of the Red River expedition, envisaged dire consequences were the Act to succeed and warned that if any land were given to the Métis "it is probable that a large portion of it will eventually fall into the hands of the Roman Catholic church." It would thus gain "an undue preponderance of wealth and power" in Manitoba.[61] To many the overall implications of the Manitoba Act were clear enough. Its designs threatened by Wolseley's advancing troops, French Canada had attempted one final time to gain what it had sought from the beginning. The Manitoba Act was nothing more than "a Bill to establish a French half-breed and foreign ecclesiastical supremacy in Manitoba."[62]

Two implications flowed from the shift of attention from conspiracies in Red River to those in Ottawa and Quebec. First, the French Catholic nature of the Métis was emphasized. Previously, as has been argued, the Métis tie to the wilderness was seen as the dominant factor in shaping their character. During the controversy surrounding the rebellion, however, this changed. As agents, whether wittingly or unwittingly, of French Canada and the Catholic church, the Métis' connection with French Canada began to be stressed. This shift was apparent in both French and English Canada. The continual references in the Ontario press to the "French party" had led French Canadians to identify with the Métis to an extent unknown before the resistance.[63] The year 1870 was only the beginning of a period which would see French Canadians increasingly associate the cause of the Métis and their leader, Louis Riel, with the rights of French Canadians.

The second implication for the expansionists was that only Ontario possessed the true spirit of Canadian nationalism. After all, they argued, only in Ontario had there been strong support for annexation of the North West and forceful suppression of the rebellion. If necessary, that province would have to abrogate to itself the development of the North West in the name of Canada, in the same way that Canada had claimed it in the name of the Empire. It was Ontario, as Schultz pointed out, from which "this movement to add Red River to the Dominion commenced; it was in Ontario this expression of indignation was expressed." It was therefore, he concluded, "to Ontario the Territory properly belonged."[64] The rebellion made explicit what had been implicit all along—the regional nature of Canadian expansionism.

While the arrival of the expeditionary force in Red River in August, 1870, ended the actual rebellion, its legacy was to be felt for many years to come. The soldiers of that force and those immigrants who followed them brought to Manitoba a set of suspicions which continually threatened to destroy the racial and religious balance which the Canadian government had recognized in Manitoba.[65] Contributing to this tension was the tendency of the Canadian volunteers stationed in Winnipeg to assume the right to mete out justice to those associated with the rebellion. The tragic climax of such vigilante action occurred when a former supporter of Riel drowned in the Red while attempting to flee pursuing militiamen. Thereafter violence declined, but there were sporadic outbreaks as religious and racial frictions prompted individuals to refight the rebellion of 1870.

Such individual violence was only a symptom of a general suspicion that French-Canadian attempts to turn Manitoba into a Catholic province had not ended with the collapse of the rebellion. Expansionists and nationalists continued to watch for signs of government or individual activity against English Canadians in Manitoba. Typical was Denison's warning to Schultz that the Ontario troops would be sent back east on some pretext rather than be allowed to disband in Manitoba and thus contribute to the permanent English population there.[66] Haliburton, not to be outdone, wrote Macdonald angrily when he heard that a French Canadian was to be appointed to the bench in Manitoba. Such an appointment, he argued, would simply aid Quebec in its attempts "at making Manitoba a New Quebec with French laws."[67] Suspicions of racial bias in Manitoba, distrust of the federal government and the question of amnesty for Riel perpetuated and deepened the attitude created by the rebellion itself. In the process eastern politics and prejudice were not only taken West but found there an ultimate test of the strength of the various factions:

> Manitoba has been to us on a small scale what Kansas was to the United States. It has been the battle-ground for our British and French elements with their respective religions, as Kansas was the battleground for Free Labour and Slavery. Ontario has played a part in the contests there analogous to New England, Quebec to that of the southern States.[68]

While the specific analogy may have been inappropriate, the comment was a perceptive one for it revealed how the resistance had been transformed by expansionist perceptions of it. The argument has been made that "the most persistent social theme of the Prairies has been the struggle for cultural dominance."[69] If so, then the events surrounding 1870 mark a decisive stage in the development of that theme. Expansionists saw in the resistance and its aftermath a contest between French and English in Canada for a dominant position in the West. Moreover, the events of the rebellion had proven to their satisfaction that French Canada had been willing to sacrifice or distort the development of the region for its own ends. It was thus impossible, expansionists believed, to entrust a heritage as important as the West to such a group. Not only was it necessary to have an eastern agricultural order dominant in Manitoba, but it also had to be English and Protestant. And as Kansas became a testing ground for dominance in the American West, so Manitoba became one for the Canadians. "Prairie culture," it has been noted, "developed from a Manitoba base."[70] Expansionists seem to have sensed this would be the case and they were thus determined to assert their dominance there in order to ensure their influence over the rest of the Prairies.

The racial strife which marked Manitoba's entry into Canada gradually subsided. The settlement of the question of amnesty for Riel, whether satisfactory or not, removed this contentious issue from the daily papers. In the same period legal and political institutions were firmly established under the governorship of Adams Archibald and his successor, Alexander Morris. Most importantly, the continuing inflow of population from Ontario gave assurance to English Canada that its culture would dominate in the new province and thus eased fears of a French-Canadian plot.[71] It was perhaps symbolic of the triumph of the Canada Party in old Red River that as early as 1872 Morris recommended that John Schultz, implacable enemy of the Métis, should be appointed a member of the North West Council.[72] The Manitoba "base" was, within a few years of 1870, increasingly English Canadian and Protestant.

The triumph of one order meant the collapse of the other. While the Province of Manitoba was able to incorporate many elements of old Red River into its social order, the French half-breed was not one of them. In increasing numbers the Métis sought refuge from the civilization of Red River and the intolerance of its new inhabitants. Moving to the still empty banks of the North Saskatchewan they remained separate representatives of the old order and of a French Catholic tradition. Their respite was to be temporary, however, for the agricultural frontier continued to spread westward and would soon threaten their distinct existence once again. Nor did either side seem to learn much from the experience of 1870. Alexander Morris's warning to Macdonald in 1873 that "the Saskatchewan will require prompt attention, or we will have the same game over again there" went unheeded in the same way as had the warnings of the 1860s.[73]

NOTES

1. G.F.G. Stanley, *The Birth of Western Canada* (Toronto, 1961), 44-143; W.L. Morton, *Manitoba, A History* (Toronto, 1957), 109-120, and *The Critical Years* (Toronto, 1968), 235-244; A.C. Gluek, *Minnesota and the Manifest Destiny of the Canadian Northwest* (Toronto, 1965), 254-261; Pierre Berton, *The National Dream* (Toronto, 1970), 29-30.
2. Morton, *The Critical Years,* 237; Mason Wade, *The French Canadians,* Vol. 1 (Toronto, 1968), 402.
3. Arthur Silver, "French Quebec and the Métis Question. 1869-1885," in Carl Berger & Ramsay Cook, eds., *The West and the Nation* (Toronto, 1976), 91-113, 92.

4. For a more complete description of the nature of Canadian expansion and the personnel behind it see D.R. Owram, "The Great North West: The Canadian Expansionist Movement and the Image of the West in the Nineteenth Century" (Ph.D. thesis, University of Toronto, 1976). For convenience the term expansionist will be used henceforth to describe members of the Canada Party, Canada First movement and individuals like Brown and McDougall who strongly opposed the rebellion.

5. A.K. Isbister, *A Few Words on the Hudson's Bay Company* (London, 1847). For an account of Isbister's efforts see E.E. Rich, *The Hudson's Bay Company, 1670, 1870,* Vol. 3 (Toronto, 1960), 545-547.

6. See, for instance, Toronto *Globe*, December 13, 1856; Montreal *Gazette*, June 6, 1857.

7. Toronto *Globe*, March 5, 1857. Letter from Isbister.

8. Great Britain, Parliament. *Select Committee on the Hudson's Bay Territories*, Appendix 15 (London, 1857), 439.

9. *British Parliamentary Papers*. Colonies. Canada. Vol. 27, 485. "Resolution Adopted at a Public Meeting of the Inhabitants of the Red River Settlement," dated January 17, 1867.

10. *Nor'Wester*, January 12, 1869.

11. Alexander Begg, *Dot-It-Down* (Toronto, 1871) portrays the *Nor'Wester* as the voice of a few self-interested men.

12. *Nor'Wester*, November 28, 1864.

13. Public Archives of Manitoba (P.A.M.), Schultz Papers, Box 16, Mair to Schultz, May 14, 1866; B. Chewitt and Co., to Schultz, December 30, 1867 (for a subscription for S.J. Dawson).

14. *Nor'Wester*, March 5, 1862.

15. *Ibid.*, September 22, 1865; December 1, 1866; July 13, 1867; August 4, 1868.

16. Sandford Fleming, *Memorial of the People of Red River to the British and Canadian Governments* (Quebec, 1863).

17. *Nor'Wester*, January 24, 1863.

18. Alexander Begg, *Dot-It-Down*, 107.

19. *Nor'Wester*, December 14, 1862.

20. Toronto *Globe*, May 28, 1869. Letter from Mair.

21. Paul Kane, *Wanderings of an Artist among the Indians of North America* (London, 1859), 51; Province of Canada. *Sessional Papers* (1859), Number 36; Daniel Wilson, "Displacement and Extinction Among the Primeval Races of Man," *Canadian Journal* (January, 1856), 12.

22. A.I. Silver, French-Canadian Attitudes Towards the North-West and North-West Settlement 1870-1890 (unpublished M.A. thesis, McGill University, 1966), 106.

23. Toronto *Globe*, December 4, 1868; February 16, 1869. Letters from Mair.

24. Queen's University Library, Mair Papers, Denison to Mair, March 29, 1869.

25. Public Archives of Canada (P.A.C.), Macdonald Papers, Vol. 102, McDougall to Macdonald, November 13, 1869.

26. *Ibid.*, McDougall to Macdonald, October 31, 1869.

27. *Nor'Wester*, November 23, 1869.

28. P.A.C., Macdonald Papers, Vol. 102, McDougall to Macdonald, October 31, 1869.

29. Toronto *Globe*, November 13, 1869.
30. Dominion of Canada, *Sessional Papers* (1870), Number 12, McDougall to Howe, November 5, 1869.
31. *Nor'Wester*, February 5, 1862. See also, July 28, 1860; September 28, 1860; May 28, 1862; July 13, 1867; January 12, 1869.
32. Gluek, *Minnesota and the Manifest Destiny of the Canadian Northwest*, 263-294, discusses American aims in Red River and the impact of these aims on the resistance.
33. P.A.C., Macdonald Papers, Vol. 102, McDougall to McTavish, November 2, 1869.
34. Dominion of Canada, *Sessional Papers* (1870), Number 12, Schultz to McDougall, November, 1869; see also Mair to McDougall, November 8, 1869.
35. P.A.C., Macdonald Papers, Vol. 102, J. Brown to Macdonald, November 26, 1869.
36. Dominion of Canada, *Sessional Papers* (1870), Number 12, McDougall to Joseph Howe, November 13, 1869.
37. P.A.C., Macdonald Papers, Vol. 516, Macdonald to McDougall, December 8, 1869.
38. *Ibid.*, Vol. 102, McDougall to Macdonald, October 31, 1869.
39. Toronto *Globe*, January 4, 1870.
40. *Ibid.*, April 15, 1870.
41. William McDougall, *The Red River Rebellion: Eight Letters to the Hon. Joseph Howe* (Toronto, 1870), 44.
42. G.T. Denison, *Reminiscences of the Red River Rebellion*. "Letter by Charles Mair" (Toronto, 1873), 6.
43. D.G. Creighton, *John A. Macdonald: The Old Chieftain* (Toronto, 1955), 47.
44. P.A.C., Macdonald Papers, Vol. 516, Macdonald to McDougall, November 20, 1869.
45. Toronto *Globe*, January 24, 1870.
46. *Ibid.*, April 7, 1870.
47. P.A.C., Macdonald Papers, Vol. 516, Macdonald to McDougall, December 8, 1869.
48. Toronto *Globe*, December 31, 1869.
49. *Debates*, 1st Parliament, 3rd Session, February 21, 1870, 111-116. Also, McDougall, *Red River Rebellion*, 5-6.
50. W.A. Foster, *Canada First, or, Our New Nationality* (Toronto, 1871), 33.
51. G.L. Huyshe, *The Red River Expedition* (London, 1871), 23.
52. Toronto *Globe*, May 2, 1870.
53. Dominion of Canada, *Sessional Papers* (1870), Number 12, "Proclamation by J.S. Dennis, December 9, 1869," 101.
54. Toronto *Globe*, April 7, 1870.
55. P.A.C., Macdonald Papers, Vol. 102, McDougall to Macdonald, October 31, 1869.
56. Norman Shrive, *Charles Mair Literary Nationalist* (Toronto, 1965), 112-115.
57. *Carleton Place Herald*, February 9, 1870.
58. Toronto *Globe*, April 14, 1870.
59. *Carleton Place Herald*, February 9, 1870. Speech by McDougall.
60. *Debates*, 1st Parliament, 3rd Session, May 2, 1870, 1302.

61. Huyshe, *The Red River Expedition*, 212. See also *Globe*, April 23, 1870.
62. McDougall, *The Red River Rebellion*, 46.
63. Stanley, *The Birth of Western Canada*, 157.
64. Toronto *Globe*, April 7, 1870.
65. W.L. Morton, *Manitoba*, 146-150.
66. P.A.M., Schultz Papers, Box 16, Denison to Schultz, January 28, 1871.
67. P.A.C., Macdonald Papers, Vol. 342, Haliburton to Macdonald, October 7, 1870. See also, *Ibid.*, Haliburton to Macdonald, October 6, 1870 and R.G. Haliburton, "The Queen and a United Empire," *St. James Magazine and United Empire Review*, January, 1874.
68. "Current Events," *Canadian Monthly and National Review*, September, 1874, 250.
69. J.E. Rea, "The Roots of Prairie Society," David Gagan, ed., *Prairie Perspectives* (Toronto, 1970), 46-55, 46.
70. *Ibid.*, 47.
71. W.L. Morton, *Manitoba*, 159.
72. P.A.C. Macdonald Papers, Vol. 252, Morris to Macdonald, October 1, 1872.
73. *Ibid.*, Morris to Macdonald, January 25, 1873.

J.R. MILLER

10 From Riel to the Métis

Although miscegenation must have been one of the earliest and most common effects of the expansion of Europe, its consequences have been relatively little studied by historians of Canada. Indeed, one of the few general histories of the western mixed-blood population suggests—only half-jokingly, one suspects—that the Métis people of Canada were founded nine months after the landing of the first European.[1] Perhaps because of traditional historiographical emphases, a limited methodological sophistication, or simply as a consequence of racist inhibitions on the part of Euro-Canadian historians who dominated the field until recently, the history of the Métis has not received much concerted and systematic attention from academic historians.

How have the limitations of our historiography, methodological backwardness, and prejudice accounted for this scanty treatment? The emphases of the first generations of Canadian historians on political themes, such as national consolidation and the achievement of autonomous status, or on economic development drew those investigators to documents that were confined to the elites of early Canadian society. The questions that Canadian historians first asked and the materials to which they put those interrogatories were not such as to lead investigators to an examination of the lives of mixed-blood peoples. So long as Canadian historical methodology was of the from-the-top-down variety, the Métis remained invisible unless they impinged on a Great Man, such as Sir George Simpson or Sir John Macdonald, or unless one of them was, like Louis Riel, a Great Man in his own right. Finally, the ethnocentric and racist prejudice and preferences of many historians made them reluctant, however unconsciously, to acknowledge the presence, much less the importance, of Canadians of mixed racial background. The Abbé Lionel Groulx, with his strenuous denials of miscegenation in New France, was only one example of this widespread, racially inspired blindness.[2]

So it was that early studies of the Métis treated that community within a Eurocentric and historiographically elitist framework. In general, the mixed-blood population only received serious attention when its activities intersected with European commercial companies or Canadian politicians. Perhaps owing to the legacy of Groulx, there was little attention to the Métis in the history of New France and the early colonial period of French Canada. Among economic historians, there was some notice of the role that the off-spring of unions between Hudson's Bay or North West Company men and Indian women played, especially in the nineteenth century. But even this perspective, as the later research of social historians would point out, was an extremely limited one. One would almost have thought, from reading Canadian history at least, that the Métis did not exist until they became enmeshed in the rivalries of Montreal and Bay traders, menaced Lord Selkirk's settlement plans, destroyed the Bay monopoly in 1849, or frustrated Macdonald and McDougall in the Red River district in 1869.

Early studies by George Stanley and Marcel Giraud that *did* attempt to examine the role of the Métis displayed many of these historiographical constrictions and methodological shortcomings. For G.F.G. Stanley the Métis, whether of Red River or Saskatchewan, were merely part of a 'frontier' of hunters and nomads that resisted before succumbing to an advancing frontier: 'Both the Manitoba insurrection and the Saskatchewan rebellion were the manifestation in Western Canada of the problem of the frontier, namely the clash between primitive and civilized peoples.'[3] The consequences of viewing the Métis through these Turnerian glasses were enormous. In the first place, Stanley tended to see all the people of mixed blood in the west as essentially the same. They were, after all, just part of the same frontier phenomenon. Consequently, *The Birth of Western Canada* discounted differences of denomination and levels of affluence that existed among the Métis, even within the Red River colony. Second, Stanley's perspective resulted in a blending of the stories of Indians and Métis in the insurrection of 1885. The Indian followers of Poundmaker and Big Bear who 'rose' in the spring of 1885 were portrayed as part of a concerted campaign of insurrection led by Riel. Why the southern Indians, who were even worse off than those in the Saskatchewan country, failed to take up arms; why so few of the more northerly Indians resorted to violence; why leaders such as Poundmaker and Big Bear appeared to have exerted themselves to minimize bloodshed; and why they ultimately surrendered—all these were discomfiting questions that were not addressed by a treatment of the events of 1885 as the clash of two frontiers. This distorted perception of what occurred at Red River in 1869 and in the Saskatchewan country unfortunately set the pattern for most later accounts of these clashes.[4]

Another pioneer in Métis studies, a contemporary of Stanley's, demonstrated a different type of deficiency in his view of the subject. Marcel Giraud's *Le métis canadien* (1945) is usually, and rightly, described as monumental, a paragon of painstaking research. Giraud's ethnographic study of the emergence of the mixed-blood communities in the west was based on field observations, vast researches in Hudson's Bay Company Archives in London, and exhaustive reading of every secondary source available to him. Its appearance at the end of the German occupation of France was testimony to the author's perseverance and energy. But, though the study was monumental and painstaking, it was not without its faults; and these shortcomings were attributable both to Giraud's own assumptions and prejudices and to some of his sources. George Woodcock's 'Translator's Introduction' to the handsome reissue of *Le métis canadien* brought out in two volumes under the title *The Métis in the Canadian West*[5] is at pains to stress that Giraud does not make ethnocentric judgments about the Métis. Says Woodcock: 'where judgments exist in *Le Métis canadien* they can be taken as relative to the changing situation of the West and not as absolute.'[6]

However, Giraud was very much in the grip of interpretations that attributed certain characteristics to particular nationalities or races, and he was unconsciously influenced by some of his sources. So one finds references to 'the inflexibility of the Anglo-Saxon temperament' and to the fact that Highlanders were 'frugal.'[7] The easy-going, convivial francophones got along with both Indians and mixed-blood peoples because of their temperament. Giraud also found that native societies tended to be 'less evolved' and European communities 'more evolved.' Whether a particular branch of the Métis community was more or less 'evolved' usually turned out to be a matter of the degree to which it accepted or spurned the clergy's urgings to give up nomadism and embrace sedentary agriculture.[8] The explanation of this bias resided in the methodology Giraud employed in his field research. As he recalled much later, 'The first stage of my work was mainly on-the-spot observation among people whom I had no difficulty approaching and questioning, thanks to the help of the missionaries of the various parishes which I visited.'[9]

The fact that Giraud's investigations were partially shaped by missionaries and those Métis of whom the clergy thought most highly, as well as by his own subscription to notions of ethnic or racial characteristics, imparted to *The Métis in the Canadian West* a number of disquieting features. Various groups were evaluated according to the degree to which they had 'evolved' towards a European or Euro-American standard of economic and social activity, rather than the extent to which they had adapted to their natural environment and economic opportunities. Furthermore, the Métis were portrayed as the malleable objects on which other, more 'evolved' groups worked. Accordingly, the sense of Métis nationalism that had begun to develop early in the nineteenth century was portrayed largely as the product of the machinations of the Nor'westers, rather than an understandable response to economic encroachment, commercial antipathies, and, later, increasing racism. Finally, in this version the events of 1869 and 1885, as well as the recriminations that followed the resistance and insurrection, led to 'The Disintegration of the Métis as a Group.'[10]

The accounts that George Stanley and Marcel Giraud produced in the 1930s and 1940s set the tone for Métis studies for a long time. In their different ways, and in spite of their quite distinctive approaches, they resembled one another in their refusal to treat the Métis as a people and a subject worthy of study in their own right. Stanley's interests may have been military and political while Giraud's were ethnographic, but in both cases the Métis were seen within a distinctively European framework of interpretation. Stanley's sources reinforced this Eurocentric tendency; Giraud's more innovative methods of investigation were offset by Eurocentric assumptions and 'filters.' For Stanley, the Métis were important as the principal constituent of the 'frontier' that unsuccessfully resisted the expansion of a more mature economy. Giraud purported to take the Métis more on their own terms, but he too saw them to a large extent as the product of European influences. Some 'evolved' and succeeded; most 'disintegrated' after Euro-Canadian society crushed them in 1885.

When scholars began to pay renewed attention to the Métis in the 1970s it was initially within the framework that earlier scholars had established. This meant that the Métis entered the ken of these scholars when their activities impinged on the doings and aspirations of European and Canadian society. More obviously, still, it was not so much the Métis as the Great Men of their community—especially Riel—that attracted attention. Indeed, Riel has always served as a mythic figure that a variety of groups have used to interpret, not the Métis, but themselves in the guise of history. Even before Riel was executed, French-Canadian nationalists had begun to transform him into a symbol of Quebec's political impotence and vulnerability within Confederation. The fact that Ontario critics of French Canada began in the summer of 1885 to attack Riel as a French, Catholic rebel made him into a symbol of Quebec militancy rather than native resistance, and drove French Canadians to embrace the Métis leader as a surrogate and champion of themselves.[11]

In the twentieth century Riel proved a useful rallying point for politicians of all sorts, including the leaders of native organizations that were beginning to find their political voice. This process reached a culmination of sorts in 1978 when the Association of Métis & Non-Status Indians of Saskatchewan (AMNSIS) petitioned the federal cabinet for 'a posthumous pardon for David Louis Riel.'[12] Western regional leaders joined in the process, Saskatchewan Liberal premier Ross Thatcher intoning that 'we of 1968 face a situation which is similar in some respects' to that of the 1880s. 'If Riel could walk the soil of Canada today, I am sure his sense of justice would be outraged as it was in 1885.'[13] Not to be outdone, Liberal prime minister Pierre Trudeau exploited Riel as a symbolic victim of nationalistic intolerance. Observed the champion of participatory democracy and multiculturalism: 'Riel and his followers were protesting against the Government's indifference to their problems and its refusal to consult them on matters of their vital interest . . . . Questions of minority rights have deep roots in our history . . . We must never forget that, in the long run, a democracy is judged by the way the majority treats the minority. Louis Riel's battle is not yet won.'[14] And, of course, Riel and his 'adjutant' Gabriel Dumont became Canadian versions of anti-imperialist guerilla fighters in the febrile orations of student radicals of the later 1960s and the 1970s.[15]

A refreshing gust of realism blew away much of this rhetoric when political scientists and sociologists turned to examine Riel in the 1970s. University of Calgary political scientist Thomas Flanagan foreshadowed his iconoclastic analysis in the 1974 article 'Louis "David" Riel: prophet, priest-king, infallible pontiff.'[16] Before Flanagan could loose his fully developed ideas on the Canadian academic world, a more traditional study of Gabriel Dumont by George Woodcock appeared.[17] Flanagan and Woodcock together represented the continuation of the traditional preoccupation with the Great Man approach, now with novel twists.

Woodcock, of course, came to Dumont from a background in which philosophical anarchism was at least as important as literary analysis. To Woodcock, Dumont and the Métis represented one of the last examples in North America of the liberated and self-regulating communities that he so much admired. The hunters in pursuit of the bison manifested an 'anarchic egoism, tempered by mutual respect among the strong and by generosity towards the weak. Bakunin, who stressed the virtues to be found in people not entirely absorbed into modern industrial society, would have loved, if he had known them, these free hunters who were his contemporaries.'[18] The 'Republic of St. Laurent' of the 1870s, and to a lesser extent Batoche of the 1880s, are a sort of anarchists' utopia in the Woodcock account. But Woodcock's approach by way of the inner dynamics of a pre-industrial, semi-tribal community did make a major contribution: it sketched a possible explanation for Dumont's willingness to follow Riel while disagreeing with his strategy in the spring of 1885. As Dumont put it, 'I yielded to Riel's judgment . . . although I was convinced that, from a humane standpoint, mine was the better plan; but I had confidence in his faith and his prayers, and that God would listen to him.' According to Woodcock, Dumont followed because of a combination of traditional loyalty to a leader, pious faith in a religious appeal, and the strong personal bonds that had been forged by Riel's earlier political success.[19]

Flanagan's initial interest was with why Riel led rather than why the Métis followed. In his important *Louis 'David' Riel: 'Prophet of the New World'*, Flanagan reinterpreted the Métis leader, not as a madman, but as a messianic prophet who stood in a long line of prophetic advocates in western history.[20] Reinterpreting the numerous writings Riel left behind, Flanagan stressed Riel's emphasis on the coming apocalypse and his radical ideas on religious reform to place the Métis leader in a lengthy tradition of millenarian leadership. Riel was, he claimed, 'more prophet and miracle worker than political leader,' the Northwest Rebellion was 'a politico-religious movement,' and Riel's actions were consistent with those of 'other millenarian leaders.'[21] The implications that could and would be drawn from Flanagan's reinterpretation were numerous and important.

First, Flanagan himself pursued his interest in the Métis Great Man within the confines of what was becoming known as 'The Riel Project.' A team headed by George F.G. Stanley was assembling an edited and annotated collection of everything Riel wrote that was still extant in time for the centenary of the Rebellion of 1885.[22] Flanagan's own work on the volume dealing with material written between Riel's acceptance of an invitation to return to Canada in 1884 and his execution in 1885 led him to produce another work that was decidedly not part of the centenary celebrations. In *Riel and the Rebellion: 1885 Reconsidered,* Flanagan argued against the position, championed by AMNSIS in 1978, that Louis Riel deserved a full, posthumous pardon. The Métis case was not that Riel deserved to be pardoned because of insanity, but because he had been driven to rebellion by an insensitive government. Flanagan argued that Riel should not be pardoned because he was, individually, responsible for the insurrection. The objective conditions that justified rebellion in liberal democratic theory did not exist in the Saskatchewan in 1884-5, and Riel was pursuing personal objectives as well as Métis claims. Needless to say, Flanagan's revision, which resembled no scholar's interpretation of 1885 so much as it did Donald Creighton's, caused a storm of controversy. There were calls for Flanagan's dismissal from his academic position and denunciations of him as a racist. The Métis of Saskatchewan now announced that they no longer sought a pardon for the simple reason that Riel had done nothing wrong. It was the government of Canada, not Louis Riel, that needed forgiveness.

The work of Woodcock and Flanagan on the politically climactic moment of 1885 served to focus attention on a crucial question that no one seemed able to answer. Why did the Métis follow Riel in the spring of 1885 as he departed from the agenda on which all had agreed in the summer of 1884? Woodcock had provided a provocative answer at the personal level of Dumont. But what of the Métis community as a whole? Two new answers emerged, significantly, from quite distinct areas of social history. That development, it would turn out, was an indicator of where studies on the Métis were headed in the 1980s.

The most ambitious attempt to explain why the Métis followed Riel came from a sociologist of religion. Gilles Martel of Université de Sherbrooke employed the model developed by Maria Isaura Pereira de Queiroz that explained that messianic leaders emerged at critical times in the development of peoples, especially groups that were being buffeted by social and economic change. His carefully constructed *Le messianisme de Louis Riel*[23] sought both to establish that the conditions of dislocation and marginalization prevailed among the Métis at Red River and Saskatchewan, and that Riel was the sort of messianic figure whose claims were accepted in such conditions. There were, however, difficulties with the model as Martel applied it in the Canadian west from the 1860s to the 1880s. First, it was by no means clear that the Métis in the Saskatchewan were experiencing the trauma that seemed necessary to prepare for upheaval. Second, there was almost no evidence that those who followed Riel understood any of the messianic ideas to which he subscribed. Finally, the theory conveniently ignored the very large numbers of mixed-blood residents in Red River and Saskatchewan who did not follow Riel. Frits Pannekoek had made a sustained, though controversial, argument about the earlier resistance that stressed that Red River was a divided community in which the English-speaking or 'country born' peoples were opposed to Riel.[24] (A number of scholars, most notably Irene Spry, have vigorously rejected this analysis.[25]) And the theory did not seem to explain how it was that of the mixed-blood community of thirteen hundred in the valley of the South Saskatchewan, only two hundred and fifty were at Batoche when it fell in May 1885.

The second attempt at explanation came from a different sort of social history, a community study of Batoche. Diane Payment's *Batoche (1870-1910)* was not only a significant example of the social history that was becoming increasingly important; it was also an instance of the work of a 'public historian.'[26] Payment's work cast doubt on Martel's sociological interpretation as applied to the 1880s by showing that the Métis of the Saskatchewan had been adjusting well to changing economic circumstances prior to the coming of the branch line railway in 1890-1. It also provided evidence for disunity in the Métis community in 1885, pointing out that probably one-third of those with Riel at Batoche had participated only under duress![27] But Payment also provided a tantalizing suggestion that might prove to be an important part of the explanation for whatever unity of mind and purpose existed between Riel and his followers. She suggested that the Métis had developed a syncretic religion from traditional Indian animism and Catholic Christianity.[28] Perhaps that religious amalgam had predisposed the Métis to recognize and follow a leader like Riel who spoke the language of religion in explaining political and military campaigns. If correct, Payment will have provided a link between the newer social history concerns and the older political and military preoccupations with the Great Man of the Métis.

Social history did not immediately have the field of Métis studies all to itself in the 1980s; several political and military histories continued to explore the field. Walter Hildebrandt, another Parks Canada Investigator, provided a valuable corrective to many of the generalizations about the climactic days of the 1885 campaign in *The Battle of Batoche*.[29] Don McLean, a sociologist who taught for several years at the Gabriel Dumont Institute, attempted to mount an answer to Flanagan. McLean constructed an argument that the federal government and local entrepreneurs fomented rebellion in 1885 to justify further appropriations for the foundering Canadian Pacific Railway in the one case, and to bring badly needed hard money into the Saskatchewan country on the other.[30] McLean's study must hold the record for the number of times such formulations as 'must have' or 'it is very likely' or 'it is difficult to find direct evidence' appear.[31]

Conspiracy theories aside, solid work was also being done in the traditional political history area of biography. Murray Dobbin's *The One-and-a-Half Men* was an interesting analysis of two Métis political organizers in the twentieth century, written from a Marxist perspective.[32] Dobbin was one of the first to dabble in the murky waters of provincial governments' relations with the native community, a stagnant pond that badly needs scholarly stirring up. Another fascinating study in Métis political leadership came from the pen of Hugh Dempsey of the Glenbow-Alberta Institute. One of the intriguing aspects of Dempsey's biography of his father-in-law, Senator James Gladstone, was that it was an analysis of a Métis who had chosen (and struggled hard) to become a status Indian, going on to play an important economic and political leadership role from the 1940s to the 1960s.[33] Like all of Dempsey's work, *Gentle Persuader* was a sensitive and sympathetic depiction of the native peoples in their interaction with the political apparatus dominated by Euro-Canadian society.

However, if some historians and social scientists continued to interest themselves in the military and political history of the Métis community, their more numerous colleagues were beginning to examine the natives from a variety of social history perspectives. Indeed, the most exciting development in the historiography of the Métis in the past generation has been the attention devoted to it by social historians. In this, perhaps, the study of the mixed-blood communities is historiographically similar to most areas of Canada's story. Like the history of labour, which moved away from a fascination with climactic events and powerful organizations to a concern with the every-day experience of working-class people, Métis history gradually forsook its obsession with Riel or fur-trading companies for an examination of life in the numerous mixed-blood communities. The types of social history that have been brought to bear during this evolution of the field were several. They included women's history, family and childhood history, and local history. Probably the most productive avenues of investigation thus far have been women's and family history, in particular the work of Sylvia Van Kirk of the University of Toronto and Jennifer S.H. Brown of the University of Winnipeg.[34]

Although the principal works by these two scholars were superficially similar, their approaches were in fact quite distinctive. Van Kirk's *'Many Tender Ties'* and Brown's *Strangers in Blood* were concerned with the social side of the fur trade in western and northern Canada from the beginning of the Hudson's Bay Company's contact, though both emphasized the later part of the eighteenth century and the nineteenth century because of the thinness of the documentary evidence from the earlier period. Both works drastically revised and substantially enriched our understanding of the fur trade and the distinctive western Canadian society that commerce had helped to create. A greater appreciation of the importance of Indian women and their native children of both genders to the trade was only one way in which these scholars deepened our understanding. Their insights into the shift of European men's taste in women from Indians to Métis to Caucasians helped to trace the onset and growth of racism in nineteenth-century western Canadian society, while simultaneously adding another dimension to our understanding of the emergence of Métis nationalism and resistance to Canadian imperialism. Brown and Van Kirk have added to our knowledge of the fur trade, western Canada, and the Métis through their new, social histories of what previously had been considered a well-developed area of Canadian history.

But there were also important differences between the approaches employed in *Strangers in Blood* and *'Many Tender Ties'* that were signalled in their subtitles. Brown's study had as its subtitle *Fur Trade Company Families in Indian Country;* Van Kirk was interested in *Women in Fur-Trade Society*. Of necessity, both paid considerable attention to the native and female side of the relationships, as well as to the offspring of those relations. But Van Kirk was especially interested in the women, and, although she did not ignore the fate of male offspring of country marriages, she understandably concentrated on the matrimonial and other fates of the daughters of these unions. Brown's interests were more extended, and to some degree their wide-ranging nature explained the fact that *Strangers in Blood* had less of a focus than did *'Many Tender Ties.'* Brown was interested in the formation of families and, to a lesser degree, social organizations, such as business partnerships, in which in the eighteenth and nineteenth centuries clan, kin, and friendship links had been very important. Consequently, she devoted more attention to family and business enterprise formation, to the evolving patterns of childhood among both anglophone and francophone fur trade families, and to the ways in which both these families and these commercial enterprises had related to their local, transcontinental, and transoceanic context.

Some measure of Brown's more extended interests could be found in the historiographical models that she employed. She placed particular reliance on Peter Laslett's *The World We Have Lost*[35] to explain both family formation and small business organization in fur-trade country. From this model she derived fascinating insights that went far to explain the relationship between economic and marital motives in seventeenth- and eighteenth-century families and the ease with which such a custom as 'placing' or 'turning off' native spouses had been adopted by European males. Similarly, her adoption of Japanese sociologist Chie Nakane's concept of 'the vertical society' to analyse the Hudson's Bay Company provided her with a useful explanatory tool that allowed her to dissect and display the inner operations and outer appearance of the business partnerships in which the Baymen had participated.[36]

But Brown's employment of these models from other disciplines and other fields of history also demonstrated some of the weaknesses of the social history approach. It was understandable that social historians reached for other models: those available were so sophisticated and the field to be reworked was so intimidating. However, the application of a model derived from an alien environment could cause difficulties. Van Kirk indirectly pointed out one problem about borrowing the interpretive scheme of someone such as Laslett when she insisted that the usual European distinctions between public and private spheres simply did not apply: 'Fur-trade society, as in both Indian and pre-industrial European societies, allowed women an integral socioeconomic role because there was little division between the "public" and "private" spheres.'[37] Given that difference, was it wise to apply concepts from British social history to family formation and business history in fur-trade country in the late eighteenth and nineteenth centuries?

In a somewhat parallel fashion, social historians such as Brown might have been more cautious in borrowing from sociologists, even ones as talented as Japan's Nakane. Nakane's 'vertical society' model was a fascinating interpretive searchlight turned on Japanese society. But did it work as well for links between British entrepreneurs? Were partnerships structured like Japanese families, even the extended families of the business and industrial world? Furthermore, Nakane's work was highly controversial and not universally accepted within Japanese academe. There was also a competing model in Takeo Doi's *The Anatomy of Dependence*, which emphasized *amae*—dependence, or the urge to be loved—as an interpretive tool to explain the group orientation of Japanese society and business.[38] There might well have been more clues to linkages within fur-trade enterprises in Doi than in Nakane.

The emphasis on women's and family studies pioneered so ably by Brown and Van Kirk has advanced Métis historiography by providing important new insights. By taking the viewpoint of the female partner in these *mariages à la façon du pays*, these scholars gained a new insight into what had previously been considered sexual exploitation at the hands of European men. Both pointed out the differing attitudes towards marriage, and towards dissolution of the matrimonial bond, that prevailed among many Indian peoples, and both argued convincingly that what Europeans took for amoral casualness had merely been a different attitude to sexual mores. Such insights enabled students of fur-trade social history to appreciate properly such things as 'serial polygamy' and 'turning off,' practices that had hitherto been referred to with barely suppressed sniggers by male scholars. The female-oriented approach has also helped students of the fur trade to understand fully the invaluable economic and diplomatic role of native women in exploration and commerce in early Canadian history. Since the work of Van Kirk and Brown, it has become almost ritualistic to refer to this important function.[39] A feminine emphasis has greatly expanded and deepened our understanding, not just of the emergence of a Métis community, but of the functioning of the western and northern fur trade as a whole.

Increasingly, family-oriented studies began to blend into another type of social history—the small community study. In some respects there was nothing new in this. John E. Foster had begun the process of scholarly investigation of a small, predominantly Métis community more than fifteen years ago in his doctoral thesis on the country-born of Red River.[40] More recently, a growing band of scholars has undertaken the systematic investigation of far-flung Métis communities, and in the process they have gone far to free Métis scholarship of what is sometimes referred to as 'Red River myopia.'[41]

The best example of this broader vision in Métis studies was *The New Peoples,* the papers of the 1981 Conference on the Métis in North America that was held at the Newberry Library in Chicago. The conference, which was addressed by Marcel Giraud, brought together many of the younger scholars at work on various aspects of Métis history and culture. Jacqueline Peterson of the University of Washington gave a useful overview of her work on the many mixed-blood communities of the Great Lakes area of the United States, while John S. Long discussed 'halfbreeds, Indians, petitioners and metis' in northern Ontario, and T. Nicks and K. Morgan dealt with the development of Grande Cache and the emergence of aboriginal identity among the mixed-blood people of that area.

These representative chapters from *The New Peoples* illustrated nicely the variety and richness of recent, community-oriented research. Peterson's careful scholarship should compel many people, including Marcel Giraud, to re-evaluate their generalizations about the Métis, because Peterson found that the communities she examined so thoroughly had evinced a sense of Métis nationalism long before the tensions between rival fur-trading companies in Rupert's Land supposedly engendered that feeling of ethnic pride and aspiration. Long's work was one of the few reminders one could find that the Métis, contrary to most of the historiography dealing with them, were not a purely western Canadian phenomenon. In fact, what was remarkable was the absence of studies of mixed-blood communities in Quebec and the Maritime provinces, to say nothing of British Columbia and the far north. If 'Red River myopia' is being cured, it is not being replaced by excellent peripheral vision.

But in many ways the most fascinating study in *The New Peoples* was the one by Nicks and Morgan on Grande Cache that combined the talents of an anthropologist and a geneticist. These scholars employed both traditional scholarly investigations of written sources with oral history and with family reconstruction and record linkage. Moreover, Grande Cache was not so much the product of fur-trade company penetration as it was of the migration of Iroquois-descended freemen. Finally, the Grande Cache Métis of northern Alberta behaved in divergent ways at the time of the coming of treaties and Ottawa directed policies aimed at Indians and mixed-blood peoples. The hunters and trappers of Grande Cache accepted Métis scrip, while others among their relatives—apparently the more sedentary and agriculturally inclined of them—entered Treaty 6. In the twentieth century the Métis of Grande Cache only slowly and belatedly developed a sense of aboriginal identity. It was not until 1972 that, 'with the assistance of white cultural brokers,' they put forward an aboriginal claim to land.[42] 'For the Grande Cache people, adopting a métis identity does not mean that they have lost sight of themselves as a distinct social group. Identifying themselves as métis achieves quite the opposite effect—it ensures their continued distinctiveness in a social, political and economic environment now dominated by Euro-Canadian immigrants.'[43] How many other unexplored mixed-blood communities does this pattern fit? It might well be that the model Nicks and Morgan have developed can be applied to other Métis communities with profit.

It seems highly likely that the short-term future of Métis studies lies in the sort of sophisticated analyses that Nicks/Morgan and Peterson have produced. At least one study, that of the Fort Vancouver native community in Washington, is being undertaken from the perspective of the history of children and of families.[44] Another examination is being made, along the lines of Peterson's work on the Great Lakes Métis and their diffusion, on the migration of Red River Métis to the Oregon territory in the 1840s.[45] What the intensive study of specific communities has shown thus far is that many of our generalizations are flimsy, and that the Métis experience is an extremely diverse one. Payment's excellent study of Batoche, for example, showed clearly that the traditional view that 1885 had been a devastating blow to the South Saskatchewan Métis simply will not hold up. They adjusted economically, socially, and politically, and continued to be a coherent and successful group until they were swamped by European immigrants in the first decade of the twentieth century. The more individual studies are multiplied, the more we are likely to find our restricted focus on one story widened to include the heterogeneity of mixed-blood experience in different topographic and economic zones of the continent.

However, in some ways Métis studies will probably become even more tightly focused and microscopic. For one thing, there should be increasing attention to Métis arts and crafts. 'In Search of Métis Art' by Ted Brasser, though it only scratched the surface of the artistic and artisanal production of the Métis, suggested strongly that there was a fascinating field to be developed.[46] The 1985 exhibition on 'The Métis' that was mounted at the Glenbow Museum, recorded by Julia D. Harrison in a well-illustrated work called simply *Métis*,[47] similarly suggested that handicrafts and artwork would repay further study. In addition, language and literature required more attention. The distinctive Métis language(s) known as Michif have received some attention.[48] More seems in order. At the same time, what of the bardic tradition whose existence, if nothing else, is known? What beyond Pierre Falcon constituted it? Does it survive?

Recent efforts have been made to recover the Métis literary and everyday voices. A powerful autobiographical statement by Maria Campbell, *Halfbreed*, touched many Métis deeply, while bringing home to the majority population in a direct way many of the problems of contemporary Métis society.[49] A more recent collection, gathered apparently in commemoration of the 1885 rising, was less successful. *No Feather, No Ink* contained many poems about Great Men such as Riel and Dumont, but little by Métis people themselves.[50] In marked contrast was Irene Poelzer's successful effort to record the views of a group of Métis women from northern Saskatchewan communities. *In Our Own Words* was noteworthy for the deliberately unstructured way in which the interviews were conducted and for the manner in which the results of the interviews were subjected to content analysis by trained social scientists.[51] The result was a poignant account of living the life of a Métis woman that had both the immediacy of first-hand testimony and analysis by scholars who did not obtrude on the subjects themselves. More such investigations would be most welcome.[52]

Métis studies would also benefit from zeroing in on the Métis in another sense. Though we know an increasing amount about specific Métis communities thanks to people such as Peterson, Payment, and the Nicks/ Morgan team, we do not know as much as we should about relations within those communities. There has been a fierce debate over internal relations in Red River in the 1850s and 1860s, with Pannakoek insisting that the community had been divided between francophone and anglophone, and Spry dismissing that argument and contending that the divisions that existed were along class lines. Payment's study of *Batoche* emphasized the differences between the Métis bourgeoisie, who had tended to cosy up to authority both in 1885 and afterwards, and the rest of the population that had been much more volatile politically. We need to know more about these divisions, if such they were.

We must, in short, study class as a factor among the Métis. There has been some fruitful analysis of the Hudson's Bay Company labour practices after the amalgamation of 1821.[53] And fur-trade historians have frequently commented in passing on relations between bourgeois and voyageurs, factors and servants. We need to know more about some of the Métis business success stories such as Letendre *dit* Batoche or Pascal Breland. If Spry was correct in her contention that the lines of cleavage in heterogeneous communities such as Red River had been along class or occupational group lines, such analysis will deepen our understanding of those communities.

If not, we will still know more about the economic history of the Métis than we do now.

However, while Métis scholarship needs in some ways to become more tightly focused, it also must simultaneously become more diffused. This is so in at least two senses: the artificial barrier between Métis and Indians should be obliterated; and Canadian Métis should be examined within a comparative, international framework. At the present time, students of Indian history and the history of mixed-blood communities barely communicate with each other. Those who are interested in the history of Indian-white relations systematically avoid, as though in some blind obedience to the dictates of the Indian Act of 1876, any consideration of the Métis. The most recent example of this approach was Brian Titley's study of Indian Affairs bureaucrat Duncan Campbell Scott.[54] In a note, Titley explained that once the Métis took scrip they 'no longer came under the jurisdiction of the federal government and therefore are not of immediate concern in this study.' But in discussing the making of Treaty 9 he was driven to mention them in passing.[55] And discussion of Indian education is misleading without some attention to the fact that mixed-blood, and even Euro-Canadian, children frequently attended the schools that Ottawa thought it was supporting solely for Indian children.

Other recent publications besides Titley's A Narrow Vision make clear the perils involved in sticking rigorously to the Indian group. Hugh Dempsey's biography of James Gladstone was in fact the story of a Métis who not only had become 'Indian,' but emerged as an important leader of the 'Indian' community. Jennifer Brown reminded us in Strangers in Blood that Mandelbaum some time ago explained that the 'Parkland People' who are regarded officially as Plains Cree were in fact descendants of mixed marriages.[56] Books by Yerbury, Thistle, and Francis and Morantz that supposedly dealt with 'Indians' in the fur trade in various parts of the country invariably had to mention the importance of mixed-blood people in the trade.[57] The most painful example of the folly of trying to ignore one community while studying the other was David Mulhall's biography of Father A.G. Morice. As Jacqueline Gresko has pointed out, Mulhall did not seem to recognize that the 'French of the Mountains' that Morice had used to communicate with the Babines of northern British Columbia was in fact Michif, the Métis tongue.[58] And, in the camp of the other solitude in native studies, Nicks and Morgan have shown in the case of the groups they studied how artificial was the distinction between Métis and Indian. Investigators of both Indian and Métis history topics really must ask themselves how much longer they are willing to allow obsolete statutory distinctions that were developed in Ottawa in pursuit of bureaucratic convenience and economy to shape their research strategies. All the evidence seems to be that the dead hand of the Department of Indian Affairs is exerting a pernicious influence.

It is also important that Canadian scholars in Métis and other native studies extend their horizon to include other countries where the interaction of aboriginal peoples and European newcomers produced miscegenation. Certainly comparisons with countries such as the United States, New Zealand, and Australia, in which British and other colonial expansion encountered indigenous peoples, seem potentially fruitful. To take but one of many possible examples, a recent study of Presbyterian missionaries in the United States in the nineteenth century suggested that *metissage* had had an impact on the internal relations of at least one Indian people. In this case, partially assimilated 'Choctaw halfbreeds' constituted a large part of the 'progressive' camp within the Choctaw nation that advocated acculturation and adaptation to the white people's ways.[59] Such comparative endeavours may be difficult among indigenous peoples who reject the notion of mixed-blood identity, but they seem worth pursuing for the light they might shed on developments in Canada.[60]

There are other obstacles, besides the inherent difficulties in studying similar experiences in a number of countries, to the successful pursuit of further studies of the Métis. One major hurdle that seems to be causing problems is politicization, which takes at least two forms: self-censorship and partisanship. Scholars who work with native communities frequently find themselves confronted with the question of whether or not to publish a scholarly opinion that might run counter to the current political objectives of the community they are studying. Examples abound. The introduction to *The New Peoples* agonized over whether or not to capitalize the word 'Métis' because of the political implications that either the upper or the lower case might carry.[61] Hugh Dempsey's Preface to his biography of James Gladstone concluded, 'As this book, in part, deals with the history of the Blood Reserve, I also submitted the manuscript to Roy Fox, the head chief, and his council, for their approval.'[62] Both academic and public historians need to think through carefully what their stance should be towards subject groups that have both moral claims and political agendas to pursue.

Partisanship is an equally serious potential danger. Among some native organizations there is a strongly held view that scholars are like politicians: those that are not with them are against them. The treatment to which Thomas Flanagan was subjected after the publication of *Riel and the Rebellion* was a particularly ugly example of that attitude. Some academics are predisposed to take a favourable, partisan position; others might be intimidated into doing so or remaining quiet. This, too, is a point of professional ethics that anyone working on subjects that might have a political interest to native groups ought to consider carefully.

Not completely unrelated to the corrupting influence of censorship and partisanship is the menace of venality. As Inuit, Indian, and Métis land claims proceed to the courts with increasing frequency, there are multiplying opportunities for historians, anthropologists, sociologists, and others to earn large fees as consultants and witnesses. Still more dangerous is the fact that it is usually the government that has the longer purse and therefore offers the greater pecuniary attraction. This is a problem with which the Canadian historical community is only beginning to grapple. Historians are going to have to think about if, and on what terms, they are going to participate in remunerative judicial jousting so as to maintain not only their own integrity, but also that of their discipline.

While problems are numerous in Métis history, there is every reason for optimism about its prospects. During the past fifteen years the study of mixed-blood communities has made rapid progress. It has broken free of its old fixation with the Great Man, and it has been partially cured of 'Red River myopia.' This field has become much more than the study of Louis Riel and his activities. To a considerable extent the field had moved 'From Riel to the Métis.' Thanks largely to the influences of other disciplines such as anthropology and sociology, as well as the powerful stimulus that has come from the expansion of social history, investigators have begun to examine carefully native women, childhood, and far-flung communities that had hitherto been ignored. Much remains to be done, both in attempting broader, comparative analyses and in examining individual communities more minutely. It promises to be a formidable task. However, if the students of the Métis show as much energy and imagination in the next generation as they have in the recent past, there is every reason to look forward eagerly to the results of their labours.

ACKNOWLEDGEMENT
I should like to thank my colleague W.A. Waiser for numerous helpful suggestions concerning this paper.

NOTES
1. D.B. Sealey and A.S. Lussier, *The Métis: Canada's Forgotten People* (Winnipeg 1975).
2. B.C. Trigger, *Natives and Newcomers: Canada's 'Heroic Age' Reconsidered* (Kingston and Montreal 1985), 34-5.
3. G.F.G. Stanley, *The Birth of Western Canada: A History of the Riel Rebellions,* 2nd ed. (Toronto 1960; first published 1936), vii.
4. A welcome exception is G. Friesen, *The Canadian Prairies: A History* (Toronto and London 1984), especially chapters 6-7 and 10.
5. Lincoln and London 1986.
6. Ibid., I, XIV.
7. Ibid., 287, 444.
8. For example, ibid., ii, 160-1.
9. J. Peterson and J.S.H. Brown, eds., *The New Peoples: Being and Becoming Métis in North America* (Winnipeg 1985), Foreword, xii.
10. Giraud, *Métis in the Canadian West,* 11, title of Part Six.

11. A.I. Silver, *The French-Canadian Idea of Confederation, 1864-1900* (Toronto 1982), chapter viii.
12. James Sinclair to P.E. Trudeau, 22 Sept. 1978, in *Louis Riel: Justice Must Be Done* (mimeograph 1978; since published by Pemmican Publications), frontispiece.
13. Quoted ibid., vi.
14. Ibid., iii.
15. D. Owram, 'The Myth of Louis Riel,' *Canadian Historical Review* [CHR] 63, 3 (Sept. 1982): 328, 335. See also ibid., 329-33.
16. *Journal of Canadian Studies* 9, 3 (Aug. 1974): 15-25.
17. G. Woodcock, *Gabriel Dumont: The Métis Chief and his Lost World* (Edmonton 1975). See also Woodcock's poem, 'On Completing a Life of Gabriel Dumont,' *Canadian Forum* 55 (Nov. 1975), 24.
18. Woodcock, *Dumont,* 36.
19. Ibid., 191-2.
20. T. Flanagan, *Louis 'David' Riel: 'Prophet of the New World'* (Toronto 1979).
21. Ibid., 141, 149, 186.
22. G.F.G. Stanley et al., *The Collected Writings of Louis Riel/Les Ecrits Complets de Louis Riel,* 4 vols. (Edmonton 1985).
23. G. Martel, *Le messianisme de Louis Riel* (Waterloo 1984), especially 1-8.
24. F. Pannakoek, 'The Anglican Church and the Disintegration of Red River Society, 1818-1870.' in C. Berger and R. Cook, eds., *The West and the Nation: Essays in Honor of W.L. Morton* (Toronto 1976), 72-90, and 'The Rev. Griffiths Owen Corbett and the Red River Civil War of 1869-70.' CHR 57, 2 (June 1976): 133-49.
25. I.M. Spry, 'The Métis and Mixed-bloods of Rupert's Land before 1870,' in Peterson and Brown, eds., *The New Peoples,* 95-118.
26. D. Payment, *Batoche (1870-1910)* (Saint-Boniface 1983). Payment has reiterated her basic arguments while extending the period analysed in 'Batoche After 1885: A Society in Transition,' in F.L. Barron and J.B. Waldram, eds., *1885 and After: Native Society in Transition* (Regina 1986), 173-87. Payment is a historian with Parks Canada.
27. Payment, *Batoche,* 67n77.
28. 'The Métis Homeland: Batoche in 1885,' *NeWest Review,* May 1985, 12.
29. W. Hildebrandt, *The Battle of Batoche: British Small Warfare and the Entrenched Métis* (Ottawa 1985).
30. D. McLean, *1885: Métis Rebellion or Government Conspiracy?* (Winnipeg 1985).
31. Ibid., 120-1. Undoubtedly more is to be expected from D.N. Sprague's *Canada and the Métis, 1869-1885,* which is forthcoming from Wilfrid Laurier University Press.
32. M. Dobbin, *The One-and-a-Half Men: The Story of Jim Brady & Malcolm Norris—Métis Patriots of the Twentieth Century* (Vancouver 1981).
33. H.A. Dempsey, *The Gentle Persuader: James Gladstone, Indian Senator* (Saskatoon 1986).
34. S. Van Kirk, *'Many Tender Ties': Women in Fur-Trade Society, 1670-1870* (Winnipeg nd); J.S.H. Brown, *Strangers in Blood: Fur Trade Company Families in Indian Country* (Vancouver 1980).

35. New York 1965.
36. Chie Nakane, *Japanese Society* (Berkeley and Los Angeles 1970).
37. Van Kirk, *'Many Tender Ties,'* 4.
38. T. Doi, *The Anatomy of Dependence* (Tokyo 1973).
39. See, for example, D. Francis and T. Morantz, *Partners in Furs: A History of the Fur Trade in Eastern James Bay 1600-1870* (Kingston and Montreal 1983), 84, 90-1; J.C. Yerbury, *The Subarctic Indians and the Fur Trade, 1680-1860* (Vancouver 1986), 91; Paul C. Thistle, *Indian-European Relations in the Lower Saskatchewan River Region to 1840* (Winnipeg 1986), 16.
40. J.E. Foster, 'The Country-born in the Red River Settlement: 1820-1850' (PhD thesis, University of Alberta, 1972).
41. Quoted by T. Nicks and K. Morgan, 'Grande Cache: The Historical Development of an Indigenous Alberta Métis Population,' in Peterson and Brown, eds., *The New Peoples,* 173.
42. Ibid., 'Grande Cache,' 172.
43. Ibid., 178.
44. J. Pollard, 'Growing Up Without the Means of Grace: Cultures and Children in the Pacific Northwest' (PhD thesis, University of British Columbia, in progress).
45. M. Patola, 'Red River Migration to Oregon, 1840-1856' (MA thesis, University of Saskatchewan, in progress).
46. In Peterson and Brown, eds., *The New Peoples,* 221-9.
47. J.D. Harrison, *Métis: People Between Two Worlds* (Vancouver/Toronto 1985).
48. For example, J.C. Crawford, 'What is Michif?' in Peterson and Brown, eds., *The New Peoples,* 231-41; 'Speaking Michif in Four Métis Communities,' *Canadian Journal of Native Studies* 3, 1 (1983): 47-55.
49. M. Campbell, *Halfbreed* (Toronto 1973). Concerning the authenticity and immediacy of this work for native peoples see Emma LaRoque, 'The Métis in English Language Literature,' *Canadian Journal of Native Studies* 3, 1 (1983): 91.
50. *No Feather, No Ink* (Saskatoon 1985).
51. D.T. Poelzer and I.A. Poelzer, eds., *In Our Own Words: Northern Saskatchewan Métis Women Speak Out* (Saskatoon 1986), especially xviii.
52. Although enough published accounts to provide a complete picture would be beyond the means of Canadian scholarship, recording of oral testimony on tape seems a feasible alternative. An excellent start has been made in many parts of Canada, most notably the Métis Oral History Project of the Provincial Archives of Manitoba.
53. P. Goldring, 'Papers on The Labour System of The Hudson's Bay Company, 1821-1900' (Parks Canada paper, 1979).
54. E.B. Titley, *A Narrow Vision: Duncan Campbell Scott and the Administration of Indian Affairs in Canada* (Vancouver 1986).
55. Ibid., 206n32, 212-13n35.
56. Brown, *Strangers,* 217.
57. For example, Thistle, *Indian-European Relations,* 81-2.
58. D. Mulhall, *Will to Power: The Missionary Career of Father Morice* (Vancouver 1986), 53. Mulhall has numerous references (39, 78, 81, 125) to Métis that appear potentially important, but he does not follow up. Gresko's critique is contained in a review of Mulhall that is soon to appear in *The NeWest Review.*

59. M.C. Coleman. *Presbyterian Missionary Attitudes Toward American Indians, 1837-1893* (Jackson, Mississippi, and London 1985), 58-9, 61.

60. Ron Bourgeault, assistant professor of native studies, University of Saskatchewan, learned that Maori leaders with whom he spoke while in New Zealand in 1986 rejected the notion of *metissage*. They told him that a person was either Maori or white.

61. Peterson and Brown, eds., *The New Peoples*, 6-7.

62. Dempsey, *Gentle Persuader*, viii.

V

INDIAN TREATIES AND THE ESTABLISHMENT OF CANADIAN LAW AND ORDER

With the acquisition of Rupert's Land in 1869/70, the Canadian government began preparations for large-scale settlement of the region.

First it negotiated Indian treaties. During the 1870s, the federal government signed seven treaties with the Plains and Woodland Indians. From the Indian perspective in several treaty areas, these treaties apparently allowed newcomers only the right to use their land, not to purchase it. In their minds, these arrangements were peace, not land settlement, treaties. From the Canadian government's perspective, however, these treaties were outright surrenders of title in return for annuities, reserves, and a trust relationship with the Canadian government. As well, in the treaty six area, Ottawa promised assistance in times of pestilence and famine. John Tobias outlines the Canadian government's Indian policy in "Protection, Civilization, Assimilation: An Outline History of Canada's Indian Policy."

Once the treaties had been signed, the government had to establish some form of Canadian law and order. In 1873, Parliament passed legislation establishing a North-West Mounted Police force for the West. Prime Minister John A. Macdonald saw this force as an integral part of his policy of western settlement. The Mounties were to ensure law and order by controlling conflict between Indians and whites, lessening the American influence in the area (especially American whisky trade), preventing feuds between ranchers and homesteaders, and ensuring the orderly construction of a transcontinental railway through the region. R.C. Macleod discusses the Mounted Police as part of the government's national policy in "Canadianizing the West: The North-West Mounted Police as Agents of the National Policy, 1873-1905."

SELECTED BIBLIOGRAPHY

Major scholarly books on the history of the North West Mounted Police are: Hugh Dempsey, ed., *Men in Scarlet* (Calgary, 1974); and R.C. Macleod, *The North West Mounted Police and Law Enforcement 1873-1905* (Toronto, 1975). Popular accounts include Ronald Aitkin, *Maintain the Right: The Early History of The North West Mounted Police* (Toronto, 1973); and S.W. Horrall, *The Pictorial History of the Royal Canadian Mounted Police* (Toronto, 1973).

For a suggestive account of the role of the Mounted Police in national symbolism, see Keith Walden, *Visions of Order: The Canadian Mounties in Symbol and Myth* (Toronto, 1980). Henry Klassen, "The Mounties and the Historians" in Hugh Dempsey, ed., *Men in Scarlet,* pp. 175-86, provides an overview of historical writing on the Mounted Police.

Two biographies of Blackfoot Indian leaders present a good overview of the life of the Blackfeet Confederacy in the mid-nineteenth century: Hugh Dempsey, *Crowfoot* (Edmonton, 1972) and by the same author, *Red Crow: Warrior Chief* (Saskatchewan, 1980). An excellent study of a Plains Cree leader is H. Dempsey, *Big Bear* (Vancouver, 1984). For background on the life of the Cree Indians, see D. Mandelbaum, *The Plains Cree* (Regina, 1979), previously published in 1940 by the American Museum of Natural History.

For an account of the impact of the whiskey trade on the Blackfeet, see Paul Sharp, *Whoop Up Country* (Norman, 1955).

For Indian points of view regarding the treaties, consult Richard Price, ed., *The Spirit of Alberta Indian Treaties* (Toronto, 1979 reprinted Edmonton, 1987); and John Snow, *These Mountains Are Our Sacred Places* (Toronto, 1977). For an overview of Canadian government policy toward native peoples, see J.L. Taylor, "The Development of Indian Policy for the Canadian North-West, 1869-79," unpublished Ph.D. thesis, Queen's University, 1975. John Tobias's "Canada's Subjugation of the Plains Cree, 1879-1885," *Canadian Historical Review* 64 (1983) : 519-48, and "The Origins of the Treaty Rights Movement in Saskatchewan," in F. Laurie Barron and James Waldram, *1885 and After: Native Society in Transition* (Regina, 1986), pp. 241-52, provide important insights into the role of the Cree in Canadian government policy in the 1870s and 1880s. This latter collection contains a wide range of useful articles on the North-West Rebellion and its aftermath, from both the government and native points of view. The best overview of the events of 1885 appears in Bob Beal and Rod Macleod, *Prairie Fire: The 1885 North-West Rebellion* (Edmonton, 1984). An excellent study of government policy and farming on the reserves is Sarah Carter, *Lost Harvests: Prairie Indian Reserve Farmers and Government Policy* (Montreal, 1990).

JOHN L. TOBIAS

11 Protection, Civilization, Assimilation
An Outline History of Canada's Indian Policy

Protection, civilization, and assimilation have always been the goals of Canada's Indian policy. These goals were established by Governments which believed that Indians were incapable of dealing with persons of European ancestry without being exploited. Therefore, the Government of Canada had to protect the person and property of the Indian from exploitation by the European, which meant that the Indian was to have a special status in the political and social structure of Canada. This distinction was made part of the constitutional structure of Canada through Section 91, Subsection 24 of the British North America Act of 1867, which gave the Government exclusive jurisdiction over "Indians and Indian land." However, the legislation by which the Governments of Canada sought to fulfill their responsibility always had as its ultimate purpose the elimination of the Indian's special status. The means to achieve this goal was by training, that is, "civilizing," the Indian in European values, to make him capable of looking after his own interests. Eventually, through this training the Indian identity and culture would be eradicated, and the Indian would be assimilable and no longer in need of special status. However, rather than furthering the ultimate goal of assimilation, such legislation has only served to thwart it. How and why this paradoxical situation arose is the subject of this paper.

COLONIAL ORIGINS OF CANADA'S INDIAN POLICY

The basic principles of Canada's Indian policy pre-date Confederation. They were a carry-over of policies developed by the Imperial Government during the century preceding Confederation. Protection of the Indian was the first principle of Imperial Indian policy, having its roots in the eighteenth century European struggle for empire in North America. It evolved from the exigencies of the French-British rivalry for dominion in mid-century and from the difficulties experienced by the British with the Indians when British colonials encroached on Indian lands. Realizing that the lack of a uniform system of dealing with the issue of Indian lands and Indian trade often led to the Indians allying with France, the Imperial Government decided to make relations with the Indians an imperial responsibility.

The British Government adopted the policy of protecting the Indians from European encroachment in the use of their lands and of preventing fraudulent trading practices that had been characteristic of much of the Indian-White economic dealings. Therefore, Indian superintendents were appointed and made responsible for these matters, as well as for making the Indians allies of the British through annual distribution of presents (Allan 1971:1-8; Alvord 1908:24-26; Scott 1913a; 698-699). Later, a boundary line was established between Indian lands and European settlement, which could be altered only by the Crown making treaties to take the surrender of Indian title to the land. Regulations for trade with the Indians were also made. These policies, adopted in the period 1745-1761, were made law when they were incorporated into the Royal Proclamation of October 7, 1763 (Alvord 1908:31-35, 51-52; Allan 1971:17-20).

Adherence to the principles of the Royal Proclamation of 1763 remained the basis of Britain's Indian policy for more than half a century, and explains the success of the British in maintaining the Indians as allies in Britain's wars in North America during that period. Even when Britain lost much of its North American territory after 1781, and its Indian allies lost their traditional lands as a result of their British alliance, the Crown purchased land from Indians living within British territory and gave it to their allies who moved north to remain under British protection. The British continued also to purchase Indian tide to any lands needed for European settlement and economic exploitation as the population of their North American colony expanded (Scott 1913a:700-719).[1] Such practices became the basis for later Canadian treaties with Indians living in the territories purchased from the Hudson's Bay Company.

It was after 1815 that the British adopted the policy of "civilizing" the Indian as an integral part of their relationship with the Indians. The policy evolved slowly, as a result of much propaganda in Britain and North America about the need to develop the Indian. Much of the propaganda in North America was made by Protestant sects which were in the throes of Evangelical and Revivalist movements stressing the need to Christianize all men. Many of these sects established missions among the Indians, similar to those the Jesuits and other Catholic orders had been carrying on for generations. Such missions were to teach the Indian not only a new religion, but also to encourage him to adopt European or American values. In Britain the "Humanitarians" who were responsible for the abolition of slavery in the empire and who supported such causes as the "Aborigines Protection Society" advocated the need to protect and "civilize" the Indian. Romantic writers on both sides of the Atlantic also joined the chorus which protested the British and American policy of pushing the Indian further into the wilderness, and tried to induce both Governments to instruct the Indian in European civilization (Surtees 1969:87-90; Allan 1971:207-211; Upton 1973:51-61).

These protests were effective, for in the 1830s the British initiated several experiments in civilization. Essentially, they entailed the establishment of Indian reserves in isolated areas. Indians were encouraged to gather and settle in large villages on these reserves, where they would be taught to farm, and receive religious instruction and an education. These endeavors became the basis of the reserve system in Canada (Surtees 1969).[2] The reserve system, which was to be the keystone of Canada's Indian Policy, was conceived as a social laboratory, where the Indian could be "civilized" and prepared for coping with the European.

Legislation was passed in the colonial assemblies to facilitate this purpose. In Upper Canada Indian lands, including the new reserves, were among the Crown lands upon which settlers were forbidden by a law in 1839 to encroach. By 1850, Indian lands were given special status by being protected from trespass by non-Indians and by being freed from seizure for non-payment of debt or taxes. In fact, Indian lands were designated as being held in trust by the Crown and freed from taxation. Finally, to protect the Indian from being debauched by certain accouterments of civilization, a ban on the sale of liquor to Indians was legislated (Statutes of the Prov. of Canada 1839, 1840, 1850a). All these protective measures were incorporated into Indian legislation of the Canadian Parliament and were later expanded.

Legislation for Lower Canada differed somewhat from that for Upper Canada. This difference was due primarily to the fact that there was much less political involvement in new efforts to "civilize" the Indian, since the Catholic Church had for more than a century been engaged in such work. Some protection was granted to these reserves and Indian lands when a commissioner was appointed to supervise them. What was most remarkable about legislation in Lower Canada was that it defined who was an Indian for the first time. It did so in very sweeping terms, for it included all persons of Indian ancestry, and all persons married to such persons, belonging to or recognized as belonging to an Indian band, and living with band (S.P.C. 1850b).[3] Subsequent legislation would modify this definition by requiring that ancestry and membership would have to be traced through the male line, and marriage would only grant such status if a non-Indian woman married an Indian. However, this act of 1850 established the precedent that non-Indians determined who was an Indian and that Indians would have no say in the matter.

Disenchantment with the efforts to "civilize" Indians on isolated reserves in Upper Canada became manifest by 1850. An evaluation of the program led to the conclusion that the reserve system as then constituted was impractical and a failure. However, rather than repudiate the ideal of the reserve as a school or laboratory for "civilizing" the Indian, blame for the failure was placed on the fact that such programs were carried out in isolation from centers of European civilization. American experience in Michigan was believed to have shown that where reserves were surrounded by settlement, Indians not only became "civilized," but also were being assimilated into the communities bordering on the reserves. Therefore the decision was made to try working with smaller reserves for individual bands located next to or near European-Canadian communities. With the change in location it was thought that the "civilization" policy would work (Hodgetts 1955:210), for the Euro-Canadian would serve as an example of what the Indian should become, and the existence of the town, it was thought, would attract the Indian from the reserve and into the non-Indian community where the Indians newly-learned values would supplant his old values and allow him to be fully assimilated.

This alteration in dealing with Indians and their reserves brought about a change in the ultimate goal of British Indian Policy. No longer was the end result simply to teach the Indian to cope with persons of European ancestry and to become "civilized," but he was to become European and to be fully assimilated into the colonial society. In order to achieve such a goal, it was thought necessary to give the Indian special legislative "status" in order that he could be "civilized"—indoctrinated with European values— and thereby made capable of being assimilated. This was the avowed purpose of the law, "an Act to encourage the gradual civilization of the Indians in this Province, and to amend the laws respecting Indians," passed in the legislature of the United Canadas in 1857 (S.P.C. 1857).

The paradox that was to become and remain a characteristic of Canada's Indian policy was given a firm foundation in this Act. After stipulating in the preamble that the measure was designed to encourage "civilization" of the Indian, remove all legal distinctions between Indians and other Canadians, and integrate them fully into Canadian Society, the legislation proceeded to define who was an Indian, and then to state that such a person could not be accorded the rights and privileges accorded to European Canadians until the Indian could prove that he could read and write either French or English language, was free of debt, and of good moral character. If he could meet such criteria, the Indian was then eligible to receive an allotment of fifty acres of reserve land, to be placed on one year probation to give further proof of his being "civilized," and then to be given the franchise (S.P.C. 1857). Thus, the legislation to remove all legal distinctions between Indians and Euro-Canadians actually established them. In fact, it set standards for acceptance that many, if not most, colonials could not meet, for few of them were literate, free of debt and of high moral character. The "civilized" Indian would have to be more "civilized" than the Euro-Canadian.

CANADA'S INDIAN POLICY

The principles of Canada's Indian policy were thus all established by the time of Confederation. What changed after Confederation was the emphasis placed on these principles. Until Confederation protection of the Indian and his land was the paramount goal. Civilization of the Indian was gaining in importance but was regarded as a gradual and long term process. Assimilation was the long range goal. These priorities were retained for a short period after 1867, for although the British North American Act in Section 91, Subsection 24, gave the Government of the Dominion of Canada exclusive jurisdiction over "Indians and lands reserved for Indians," the first legislation on this subject in 1868 merely incorporated the earlier colonial legislation concerning Indian lands. The only changes were the definition of who was an Indian and the penalties imposed for trespass on Indian lands (Statutes of Canada 1968).[4] In 1869 the goals of "civilization" and assimilation were added by the passage of "an Act for the gradual enfranchisement of Indians . . ." (S.C. 1869).

The title of this piece of legislation demonstrates a change in emphasis from that of the earlier acts to promote assimilation. Whereas the Colonial Legislation was "for the gradual civilization . . . ," this new Act was "for the gradual enfranchisement of the Indian." "Civilization," the prerequisite for assimilation or enfranchisement, was now to be the paramount goal. This shift is demonstrated by the power the Governor in Council was given to impose the Euro-Canadian political ideal of elected local government on an Indian Band and to remove from band office those considered unqualified or unfit to hold it. The elected band council was empowered to make by-laws on minor policy and public health matters, but before such regulations could be enforced, they had to be approved by the Superintendent General (The Minister) of Indian Affairs (S.C. 1869). This Act, designed for the Six Nations and other Indian people with long contact with Europeans and who were supposed to have received a rudimentary training in "civilization" under earlier legislation and missionaries, was to provide further training in Euro-Canadian values. This extensive education in what was regarded as the more sophisticated aspects of European civilization was to be provided by a paternalistic government which would lead the Indian away from his "inferior" political system. It thereby established another criterion of "civilization."

The new Dominion of Canada developed its Indian policy during the decade of the 1870s. It extended its authority over the Plains Indian through the treaty system. In doing so, the Canadian Government demonstrated its acceptance of the principles established by the old Imperial Government, for not only did the Dominion Governments purchase Indian title to the land, it also imposed the reserve system as a laboratory for cultural change on the Plains Indians by means of these treaties (Morris 1971).[5] In addition, through the "Act to amend and consolidate the laws respecting Indians" or, as it was short-titled, "The Indian Act" of 1876 (S.C. 1876; RG-10 Vol. 1923, file 3007),[6] the foundation for all Canada's future Indian Legislation was laid.

The new Legislation incorporated all the protective features of the earlier legislation, and established more stringent requirements for non-Indian use of Indian lands and for their alienation. It contained slight revisions of the mechanism for enfranchisement, which were thought would facilitate assimilation. Most of these changes, however, were related directly to furthering the process of "civilization" and permitting the Government to encourage and direct it. Thus the elective system was no longer to be imposed but was only to be applied if the band asked for it. To encourage this system of Government, band councils under the elective system were given increased authority. However, the Legislation set out the formula for the number of councillors and chiefs a band could have and who could vote in such elections (S.C. 1876; Debates of the Parliament of Canada March 2, 1876:342-343; Debates March 21, 1876:749-753).

The most important innovation of the new Indian Act, in the eyes of the Government, was the introduction of the location ticket. This was regarded as an essential feature of the "civilization" process and a necessity for enfranchisement. It was a means by which the Indian could demonstrate that he had adopted the European concept of private property, which was an additional test of whether he had become "civilized." The new policy stipulated that the Superintendent General have the reserve surveyed into individual lots. The band council could then assign these lots to individual band members. As a form of title the Superintendent General would then give the band member a location ticket. Before an individual received a ticket he had to prove he was "civilized" in the same manner as under the earlier legislation. On passing this first test, and receiving his location ticket, the Indian entered a three year probationary period during which he had to demonstrate that he would use the land as a Euro-Canadian might and that he was fully qualified for membership in Canadian society. If he passed these tests, he was enfranchised and given title to his land. If all band members wished, they could enfranchise in this way (S.C. 1876; Debates March 2, 1876:342-454; Debates March 21, 1876:749-753).

An alternative means of assimilation was also offered, which required less time and supervision than the one discussed above. An Indian who went to university and earned a professional degree as minister, lawyer, teacher, or doctor could be given a location ticket and enfranchised immediately without going through the probationary period (S.C. 1876). By earning such degrees, the Indian had demonstrated his acceptance of Euro-Canadian values, and his ability to function in Canadian society.

What becomes even clearer is the Government's determination to make the Indians into imitation Europeans and to eradicate the old Indian values through education, religion, new economic and political systems, and a new concept of property. Not only was the Indian as a distinct cultural group to disappear, but the laboratory where these changes were brought about also disappear, for as the Indian enfranchised, that is, became assimilated, he would take with him his share of the reserve. Therefore when all Indians were enfranchised, there would no longer be any Indian reserves. The first piece of comprehensive legislation by which the Government exercised its exclusive jurisdiction over Indians and Indian lands had as its purpose the eventual extirpation of this jurisdiction by doing away with those persons and lands that fell within the category of Indians and Indian lands.

The new Indian Act, as all previous legislation, was designed for the Indians living east of Lake Superior. The western Indians were excluded from the operation of most sections of the Indian Act until such time as the Superintendent General of Indian Affairs considered them advanced enough in civilization to take advantage of the Act. However to speed up their advance in "civilization," and under the guise of protecting them from exploitation, the 1876 Indian Act and subsequent amendments contained provisions which attacked traditional Indian sexual, marriage, and divorce mores and furthered the Christian-European values. Into this category fall the sections relating to illegitimate children, non-band members on the reserve after sundown, non-Indians on reserves and cohabiting with Indians, and Indian women in public houses (S.C. 1879, 1884a, 1887, 1898, 1894; RG-10 Vol. 2378, file 77,190; Vol. 2004, file 7728; Vol. 3947, file 123, 764-1; Vol. 1596; Vol. 6809, file 470-2-3, vol. 11, part 3. Many other examples could be given). In addition, Indian agents were given the powers of a Justice of the Peace to enforce sections of the Criminal Code relating to vagrancy, in order that the Western Indian could be kept on the reserve where he might be taught to farm and learn the value of work (S.C. 1890,1895; RG-10 Vol. 3832, file 64, 009; Vol. 2446, file 93, 503; Vol. 2497, file 102, 950; Vol. 3378, file 77, 020; Vol. 6809, file 470-2-3, vol. 11, part 4).

The Eastern Indians who were to be the beneficiaries of the Act rejected it, for they knew that if they adopted the elective system, the Superintendent General would not only have supervisory and veto power over band decisions, but according to other provisions of the Act, he could force the band council to concern itself with issues with which it did not wish to deal. Many eastern bands clearly stated that they would never request an elected band council because they did not wish to be governed and managed by the Government of Canada (S.C. 1876; RG-10 Vol. 2077, file 11, 432). Such protests were interpreted as demonstration of the fact that the Indian needed more direction and guidance, for subsequent amendments and later Indian Acts increased the authority of the Superintendent General to interfere in the band and personal affairs of the Indians.

The Indian Act of 1880 provided the means to manage Indian affairs. It created a new branch of the civil service that was to be called the Department of Indian Affairs. It once again empowered the Superintendent General to impose the elective system of band government whenever he thought a band ready for it. In addition, this new legislation allowed the Superintendent General to deprive the traditional leaders of recognition by stating that the only spokesmen of the band were those men elected according to the provisions of the Indian Act when the elective system was imposed. Otherwise the Indian Act of 1880 differed little from that of 1876 (S.C. 1880).[7]

The elected band council was regarded as the means to destroy the last vestige of the old "tribal system," the traditional political system. The reserve system, other sections of the Indian Act, and missionaries were thought to have effectively dealt with all other aspects of traditional Indian values. The only impediment to "civilization" and assimilation was lack of training in the Canadian political system. This evaluation was the reason for the stress on the elective system despite Indian opposition to it. It was also the reason for passage in 1884 of "An Act for conferring certain privileges on the more advanced bands of Indians of Canada with the view of training them for exercise of Municipal Affairs" (S.C. 1884). This bill came to be known as the Indian Advancement Act.

The Indian Advancement Act was an ideal tool for directed "civilization." It extended slightly the powers of the band council beyond those of the Indian Act by giving the band council the power to levy taxes on the real property of band members. It also expanded the council's powers over police and public health matters. At the same time it greatly increased the powers of the Superintendent General to direct the band's political affairs. Election regulation, size of the band council, and deposition of elected officials were all spelled out in the Act. Moreover, the Superintendent General or an agent delegated by him was empowered to call for the elections, supervise them, call band meetings, preside over them, record them, advise the band council, and participate in the meetings in every manner except to vote and adjourn the meetings. In effect, the agent directed the political affairs of the band (S.C. 1884).[8]

To further encourage the Indians to ask for this form of Government, for the application of this measure was only at the request of the band, Indians east of Lake Superior were granted the franchise in dominion elections by the Electoral Franchise Act of 1885. Thus they would be able to participate in the political process off the reserve as well as on it. However, few bands accepted either measure, and in 1896 the franchise was withdrawn from the Indians. Nevertheless, the Advancement Act was retained.

Despite most bands refusing to come under the Advancement Act, the elective system as provided for in the Indian Act was imposed on them. Because many bands merely elected their traditional leaders, who were often unsatisfactory to the Government, they were deposed as being incompetent, immoral, or intemperate, all grounds for dismissal under the Act. However, these men were usually re-elected, which thwarted the Government's intentions in deposing them. Therefore, in 1884, the Indian Act was amended to prohibit persons deposed from office from standing for immediate re-election (RG-10 Vol. 3947, file 123, 764-2; S.C. 1884). A decade later, an amendment was added to the Indian Act which allowed the Minister to depose chiefs and councillors where the elective system was not applicable. This amendment was included because the band leaders in the West were found to be resisting the innovations of the reserve system and the Government's efforts to discourage the practice of traditional Indian beliefs and values (RG-10, Vol. 6809, file 470-2-3, vol. 11, part 4; S.C. 1895).

Interference in and direction of a band's political affairs led to an increase in the Government's control of the band's resources. Because most bands opposed enfranchisement of their members and the alienation of reserve lands that this procedure entailed, they were able to thwart the goal by refusing to allot reserve lands to individual band members. Without a land allotment, no location ticket could be given, and without a location ticket, enfranchisement was impossible. Therefore in 1879, power to allot reserve lands was taken from the band and given to the Superintendent General (S.C. 1879, 1884; RG-10 Vol. 2378, file 77, 190). Because most bands refused to alienate their land, even for a limited period, persons who held location tickets and wanted to lease their land to non-Indians as a source of revenue could not do so, because the band refused to vote for the required surrender. Consequently, the Indian Act was amended in 1884 and 1894 to allow the Superintendent General to lease such lands for revenue purposes without taking a surrender. The first was for the purpose of revenue for those holding a location ticket and desiring to lease their land, while the 1894 amendment allowed the Superintendent General to lease the land of orphans or aged who held location tickets, but who did not specifically ask to have their land leased. The 1894 amendment was really a device for cutting the cost of government aid to various bands where the location ticket system was well established. By these means, the government thought it was preventing an "unenlightened" band council from holding a "civilized" band member in check (*ibid*. Also S.C. 1894, 1895; RG-10 Vol. 6809, file 470-2-3, vol. 11, part 4; Vol. 2378, file 77, 190). In 1898, as a result of bands refusing to exercise their police and public health powers and not expending their band funds for this purpose, the Superintendent General was empowered to make the necessary regulations and expend band funds for whatever expense was entailed in carrying out the regulations (S.C. 1898; RG-10 Vol. 6809, file 470-2-3, vol. 11, part 4).[9]

While the effort to direct "civilization" and assimilation of the Eastern Indian led to direct involvement in band affairs, legislation for the Western Indian was to further the initial process of the "civilization" program and was therefore geared much more to the individual. Because the Plains Indians and the Indians of British Columbia attempted to preserve their traditional religious and cultural values, despite pressure from missionaries and the Government to repudiate them for being contrary to Christian and European values, the Government decided to prohibit many of the traditional practices.

The "Sun Dance," "Potlatches," and all "Give Away" ceremonials were banned because they promoted Pagan beliefs and were an anathema to the development of a concept of private property (S.C. 1884a, 1895; RG-10 Vol. 6809, file 470-2-3, vol. 11, part 4). A similar purpose, to teach the Indian to husband his resources, was behind the legislated prohibition on the sale of produce and livestock from Indian reserves on the prairies (S.C. 1884a, 1890; RG-10 Vol. 2446, file 93, 503; Vol. 2497, file 102, 950).[10]

The ability of many Indians living in Manitoba and the old North-West Territories to pursue their old form of livelihood, hunting and fishing, was particularly irksome to the Government, for it was regarded as a drawback to the Indian's adopting more "civilized" economic base, farming. Besides, the hunting Indian was retarding the "civilization" of his children, because he took them with him into the bush, which meant they did not attend school. These children were regarded as being the first generation which would become "civilized" and to whom the full "benefits" of the Indian Act could be extended. However, if they were kept illiterate by their parent's economic pursuits, the Government's plans for them would be thwarted. Therefore in 1890, an amendment to the Indian Act was made empowering the Governor in Council to declare the game laws of Manitoba and the North-West Territories to be applicable to Indians (S.C. 1890; RG-10 Vol. 2378, file 70, 020; Vol. 3832, file 69, 009; Vol. 2446, file 93, 503; Vol. 2497, file 102, 950).

School attendance was of vital concern to the Government, for education of the Indian child was a key stone of the "civilizing" process the reserve system was to perform. Since schools on the reserve were not well attended by Indian children, they were regarded as ineffectual instruments of "civilization." Residential and industrial schools, which removed the child from the "detrimental" influence of "uncivilized" parents and Indian traditions, were regarded as better instruments of Government policy. Indian parents refused to send their children to such schools, because they were long distances from the reserve and alienated the child from his culture. Therefore, in 1894 amendments to the Indian Act were made authorizing the Governor in Council to make whatever regulations on the school question he thought necessary and empowering him to commit children to the boarding and industrial schools founded by the Government (S.C. 1894; RG-10 Vol. 3947, file 123, 764-3; Vol. 6908, file 470-2-3, vol. 11).

The program of directed and aggressive "civilization" that was a characteristic of Indian policy and legislation in the period after 1870 had spent its force by the turn of the century. By 1900, the reserve system was being questioned as a means to achieve assimilation. In fact, many had come to regard the reserve as preventing assimilation, and to believe that the existence of reserves was a check on the economic development and growth of areas where they were located. This attitude began to find expression in the new, or, rather, consolidated Indian Act of revised statutes of 1906 (S.C.

1906a).[11] Amendments to this Act in subsequent years reinforced this view, for most of them were designed to remove the protection the reserve seemed to provide the Indian, and to force the Indian people off the reserve. Assimilation was no longer regarded as a long term goal; it was one that could be attained immediately if the Indian were removed from the protective environment of the reserve.

The initial attack on the reserve began in the 1890s when the Superintendent General was given power to lease land for revenue purposes. Shortly thereafter amendments were made to ease the permanent alienation of reserve land, by allowing the Government to distribute in cash up to 50% of the value of the land as an inducement for a surrender for sale (*ibid*. Also S.C. 1898, 1906b; RG-10 Vol. 6809, file 470-2-3, vol. 11, parts 4 and 5). As was expected, much reserve land was made available for sale to non-Indians, particularly on the prairies. These measures were justified as promoting the economic growth of the country and removing a retarding influence on development of an area. Such arguments were also used when the Superintendent General was given the power to lease Indian land without taking a surrender for purpose of mineral exploration, to expropriate for right-of-ways for highways and provincially chartered railways, and to lease for revenue farm lands said not to be used by Indians. These powers were given because Indians had refused to make surrenders for these purposes in the past. Finally, a mechanism was established to deal with situations similar to those of Sarnia, Ontario, and Victoria, B.C., where reserves within the boundaries of a city could be abolished when it was found to be in the Indian and public interest (S.C. 1910a, 1910b, 1918; RG-10 Vol. 6809, file 470-2-3, Vol. II, Part 6; Vol. 6810, file 470-2-3, vol. 12, part 10).

Dissatisfaction with the reserve system was due principally to the fact that it only partially fulfilled its functions. It did "civilize" the Indian, but it did not complete the process as envisioned by encouraging them to enfranchise. In the period between 1857 when the enfranchisement process was first enacted and 1920, only slightly more than 250 persons enfranchised (RG-10 Vol. 6810, file 470-2-3, Vol. 12, Part 7; memo on enfranchisement). To remedy this situation the Government amended the Indian Act to permit Indians living off the reserve to be enfranchised without the required land. This change resulted in the enfranchisement of 500 people within two years after passage of the amendment (S.C. 1917; RG-10 Vol. 6809, file 470-23, vol. 11, part 6). Subsequent amendments reduced the number of Indians by making it easier for half-breeds who had taken treaty in the West to be enfranchised and for Indian women married to non-Indians to give up entirely their Indian status (S.C. 1914, 1920; RG-10 Vol. 6810, file 470-2-3, vol. 12, part 7).

The "civilized" Indian who preferred to live on the reserve was untouched by any of these amendments, but this was the individual the Government wanted off the reserve, for otherwise the reserve and the Indian would become permanent features of Canadian society. The Government found such a thought abhorrent, for it wanted to do away with the reserve and "make a final disposition of the individuals who have been civilized into the ordinary life of the country . . ." (RG-10 Vol. 6810, file 470-2-3, vol. 12, part 7; memo on enfranchisement). Therefore, assimilation was not to be a voluntary act on the part of the Indian. The Superintendent General, at his discretion, was given the power to establish boards of inquiry to examine the fitness of Indians for enfranchisement, without the persons making application, report on their fitness for enfranchisement, and the Superintendent General would then recommend to the Governor in Council that these persons be enfranchised. Such persons could then be given title to the reserve lands they occupied, receive their share of the band's monies, and be enfranchised (*ibid.*; S.C. 1920).

The outcry and protests that resulted from the operation of the procedures was so great that two years later the Government modified these sections of the Act to appoint such boards only after applications for enfranchisement were received. However, when this change failed to achieve the purpose established for the original amendments, power to create such boards was returned to the discretion of the Superintendent General, and compulsory enfranchisement was re-enacted (S.C. 1922, 1933; RG-10 Vol. 6810, file 470-2-3, vol. 12, parts 7-9).

Forced or compulsory enfranchisement was designed for the Indians east of Lake Superior. In the West, where the Indian peoples were thought to be less advanced, the policy of directed civilization was applied to hasten their development. Because the existing provisions of the Act were thought not strong enough to achieve this purpose, amendments were made to insure compulsory school attendance and to treat chronic non-attenders as juvenile delinquents (S.C. 1914, 1920, 1930; RG-10 Vol. 6809, file 470-2-3, vol. 11, parts 5 and 6; Vol. 6810, file 470-2-3, vol. 12, parts 7-8). Also, stronger efforts were made to put an end to Plains Indians' practice of old ceremonials, so that prohibitions against these Indians appearing in aboriginal garb and performing their traditional dances at fairs and stampedes under the guise of entertaining the non-Indian community were interpreted as being part of the Act. Later this section was amended to prohibit such dances in any type of dress, unless prior approval in writing was given by the Department of Indian Affairs (S.C. 1914, RG-10 Vol. 3825, file 60, 511, vol. 1 and 2). To promote farming on western reserves so that the Indians could become self-supporting land holders, the Superintendent General was authorized to use band funds to purchase farm machinery for individual Indians and to establish a fund from which loans might be made to allow Indians to purchase machinery or get started in small businesses (S.C. 1917, 1922, 1938; RG-10 Vol. 6809, file 470-2-3, vol. 11, part 6; Vol. 6810, file 470-2-3, vol. 12, parts 8, 10).

In an effort to reduce the distinctions between Indian and non-Indian communities, the Government also incorporated into the Indian Act authority for the Superintendent General to regulate the use and operation of amusement and recreational facilities on Indian reserves in accordance with provincial and local laws which forbade opening such facilities on Sundays. Moreover, provincial laws on general matters, such as on motor vehicles, could be declared to be applicable on reserves, and such laws would have the same effect as though they had been incorporated into the Indian Act (S.C. 1922, 1930, 1936; RG-10 Vol. 6810, file 470-2-3, vol. 12, parts 8, 10).

Enactment of compulsory enfranchisement and the breaking down of the barriers of the reserve boundaries both literally by lease and sale and figuratively by making provincial laws apply there, all were to promote more rapid assimilation. However, these acts had only limited success. With the economic crisis followed by a major war in the period 1933-1945, little attention was paid to Indian matters. In fact, in that period the Government and the civil servants in what became Indian Affairs Branch appear not to have had any policy. They left this whole area of Government-Indian relations in a state of flux and made only ad-hoc decisions. Perhaps this situation was a result of the realization that all previous policies had failed to attain the goal established for Canada's Indian administration. At any rate, there is an obvious lack of policy or policy goal in this period.

This apparent aimlessness changed after 1945, when public interest in Indian Affairs was awakened to an unprecedented degree. This interest was due largely to the strong Indian contribution to the war effort in the years 1940-1945. The public was generally concerned with what was regarded as the treatment of the Indian as a second class person and with the fact that the Indian did not have the same status as other Canadians—in fact, the Indian was not even a citizen. Veterans' organizations, churches, and citizen groups across the country called for a Royal Commission to investigate the administration of Indian Affairs and conditions prevailing on Indian reserves. All wanted a complete revision of the Indian Act and an end to discrimination against the Indian (RG-10 Vol. 6810, file 470-2-3, vol. 12, part 11).

No Royal Commission was appointed, but a Joint Committee of both the Senate and House of Commons was created in 1946 to study and make proposals on Canada's Indian Administration and the revision of the Indian Act. After two years, the Joint Committee recommended (Proceedings 1948:186-190):

1. The complete revision of every section of the Indian Act and the repeal of those sections which were outdated.
2. That the new Indian Act be designed to facilitate the gradual transition of the Indian from a position of wards up to full citizenship. Therefore the Act should provide:
   A. A political voice for Indian women in band affairs.
   B. Bands with more self-government and financial assistance.
   C. Equal treatment of Indians and non-Indians in the matter of intoxicants.

   D. That a band might incorporate as a municipality.

   E. That Indian Affairs officials were to have their duties and responsibilities designed to assist the Indian in the responsibilities of self-government and to attain the rights of full citizenship.

3. Guidelines for future Indian policy were to be:

   A. Easing of enfranchisement.

   B. Extension of the franchise to the Indian.

   C. Co-operation with the provinces in extending service to the Indian.

   D. Education of Indian children with non-Indians in order to prepare Indian children for assimilation.

In essence, the Joint Committee approved the goal of Canada's previous Indian policy—assimilation—but disapproved some of the earlier methods to achieve it. They assumed that most of the work of "civilization" was virtually complete, and that therefore many of the protective features of earlier Acts could be withdrawn and bands allowed more self-government as governmental interference. Moreover, since assimilation was soon attainable, the guidelines for the new Indian Policy and the new Indian Act stipulated that the Dominion Government should begin turning over responsibilities for providing services to the provinces. In this way barriers provided by the reserves and the Indians' special status under the constitution would be further broken down and assimilation made all the easier. Thus, the Indian and the Indian reserve were still regarded as a transitory feature of Canadian society.

In 1951 a new Indian Act was passed which met most of the criteria established by the Joint Committee. At first glance it appears to differ greatly from all previous Indian Acts back to 1876. Not since the 1876 Act had the Minister's powers been so limited, for under the new Act the Minister's "powers were reduced to a supervisory role" but with veto power. His authority to direct band and personal matters required band approval. The individual bands, if they desired, could now run their own reserves. As many as fifty sections and subsections were deleted from earlier Acts because they were antiquated or too restrictive on individuals or the band. Most of the provisions for aggressive civilization and compulsory enfranchisement were deleted (S.C. 1951).

A closer look at the 1951 Indian Act and a comparison with the Indian Act of 1876 shows that there are only minor differences between the two. In format, content, and intent they are quite similar. Both provide for a cooperative approach between Government and Indian towards the goal of assimilation, although enfranchisement is made easier in the 1951 Act by eliminating the testing period and the requirement for location tickets or certificates of possession. However, other provisions are virtually the same. The new Act definitely differs from the Indian Acts between 1880 and 1951, but only because it returned to the philosophy of the original Indian

Act: "civilization" was to be encouraged, but not directed or forced on the Indian people. Assimilation for all Indians was a goal that should be striven for without an abundance of tests or the compulsory aspects of the preceding Indian Acts. Through the 1951 Indian Act the Government managed to extricate itself from the "quicksand" that a desire to hurry assimilation had mired it in after passage of the 1876 Indian Act. Hence, the similarities between the 1876 and 1951 Indian Acts.

Speedy assimilation was not repudiated as the goal of Canada's Indian Policy—what was repudiated was the earlier means to achieve it. Therefore, when it became obvious that the 1951 Indian Act would not promote the purpose it was designed for any more than earlier Acts did, an alternative means to those tried between 1880 and 1950 was sought. This was provided in part by the recommendation by the Joint Committee to turn over responsibility for services to Indians to the provinces. Therefore this process was begun in the 1950s and continued in the decade of the 1960s. Then in 1969, when this transfer was nearing completion, the Government announced its intention to absolve itself from responsibility for Indian Affairs and the special status of Indians and to repeal special legislation relating to Indians; that is, the Indian Act.[12] By adoption of this policy and by repealing the Indian Act, the Indian would be assimilated by Government fiat, and what the Indian Act of 1876 had sought as a long term goal—the extirpation of the Indian and Indian lands—would be realized.

The announcement of this policy in the 1969 White Paper of Indian Affairs brought such a storm of protest from the Indian people, who had always rejected this goal, that the Government was forced to reconsider its policy, delay transfer of services, and in 1973 announce the withdrawal of the policy statement. However, this official withdrawal does not mean that the goal has been repudiated; at least there is no indication of such renunciation to date. It is simply that alternative means to achieve it are being considered. At the moment Canada's Indian Policy is in a state of flux, but unlike any earlier period, a more honest effort is being made to involve the Indian and Indian views in the determination of a new Indian Policy.[13]

NOTES

1. The best study of Britain's Indian Policy is that by Allan (1971). See also Surtees (1971:45-49), Scott (1913b:345-346), Wright (1943:40).
2. For a more detailed study of this policy see Surtees' unpublished M.A. thesis (1966) on which his article is based. See also Hodgetts (1955:209-210) and Upton (1973:51-61).
3. The Indian Reserves which existed in Lower Canada at this time were those that had been established by the various religious orders on lands granted to them during the French Regime. These reserves were therefore within or next to non-Indian communities. Thus, there was often inter-marriage or non-Indians living on the reserves, which were run by the religious orders and not by colonial

officials, as in Upper Canada. For this reason, it was necessary to define who was being protected by this legislation governing Indian lands. The special circumstances of Lower Canada made this definition necessary, for as was stated above, non-Indians were forbidden by law from living on Crown lands used for or regarded as being Indian lands, in Upper Canada.

4. Incorporated in this Act was a law not mentioned above, which dealt with surrender of Indian lands (S.P.C. 1860).

5. The last chapter of this book provides an excellent summary of the views of the man responsible for making many of the western treaties, and his reasons for including the various provisions of the Treaties.

6. The latter reference gives some background to this Act. From the RG-10 series, Vol. 1935, file 3589; Vol. 1928, file 3281; Vol. 3084, file 3608. All provide information as to reasons various provisions of the Act were made, but which cannot be discussed in detail in a paper of this nature.

7. Further amendments regarding the Minister's power in elections and band government were included in S.C. 1884a. See also RG-10 Vol. 2378, file 77, 190.

8. This amendment included provisions which gave band councils most of the powers, except taxation, provided in the Indian Advancement Act.

9. Barrier Acts, such as S.C. 1887, allowed leases for cutting hay and timber without a surrender.

10. The government had found that the Plains Indians disposed of all their agricultural and livestock produce each fall in order to get cash which was, in turn, expended for foodstuffs. However, since other purchases were also made, by mid-winter many of the Indians were destitute, having no food on hand and no means by which to procure it, for their money was completely expended. This situation meant that the government had to provide rations to keep these people alive. Rather than do this, the government thought that the Indian should be prevented from disposing of his crop all at once. It was assumed that the Indian, having seen that husbanding his crop would mean that he would be able to feed himself and have cash at intervals throughout the year, would then voluntarily limit himself to selling only a portion of his produce in the fall, and that he would have learned the efficacy of husbanding his resources.

11. See RG-10 Vol. 6810, file 470-2-3, vol. 12, part 7, for the correspondence concerning the new attitude towards the reserve.

12. See the *Statement of the Government of Canada on Indian Policy*, 1969, presented to the First Session of the 28th Parliament by The Honorable Jean Chretien, Minister of Indian Affairs and Northern Development (Ottawa, 1969).

13. Discussions concerning the development of a new Indian policy between government and Indian leaders have been going on since 1974. The chances of success for these discussions hinge to a large degree on whether the traditional dichotomy between Indian and government understanding of some basic concepts, such as reserves and treaties, can be resolved. This difference in views on the question of reserves and treaties is the subject of a paper that I have written entitled "Indian Reserves in Western Canada: Indian Homelands or Devices for Assimilation," which appeared in *Mercury: History Series* (National Museum of Man).

REFERENCES

Allan, Robert S.
  1971. A History of the British Indian Department in North America (1755-1830).
    National Historic Sites Manuscript Report No. 109. Ottawa: Department
    of Indian Affairs and Northern Development.
Alvord, Clarence W.
  1908. The genesis of the Proclamation of 1763. Michigan Pioneer and Histori-
    cal Society. Vol. XXXVl.
Debates of the Parliament of Canada
  March 2, 1876
  March 21, 1876
Hodgetts.
  1955. Pioneer Public Service, An Administrative History 1841-1867. Toronto.
Morris, Alexander.
  1971. The Treaties of Canada with the Indians of Manitoba and the North-West
    Territories. Toronto: Coles Publishing Company. (Orig. 1862)
Proceedings of the Joint Senate-House Committee on Indian Affairs
  1948.
Record Group 10 (RG-10)
  Indian Affairs Files. Public Archives of Canada - Ottawa. Volumes:
  1596
  1923, file 3007
  1928, file 3281
  1935, file 3584
  2004, file 7728
  2077, files 11, 432
  2378, files 77, 190
       files 70, 020
  2446, files 93, 503
  2497, files 102, 950
  3084, file 3508
  3378, files 77, 020
  3825, files 60, 511, parts 1 and 2
  3832, files 69, 009
  3947, file 123, 764-1
             123, 764-2
             123, 764-3
  6809, file 470-2-3, vol. 11, parts 3, 4, 5, 6
  6810, file 470-2-3, vol. 12, parts 7, 8, 9, 10, 11, 12

Statutes of Canada (S.C.)
  1860 23 Victoria, chapter 151.
  1868 31 Victoria, chapter 42.
  1869 32-33 Victoria, chapter 42.
  1876 39 Victoria, chapter 18.
  1879 42 Victoria, chapter 34.
  1880 43 Victoria, chapter 28.

1884 47 Victoria, chapter 27.
1884 47 Victoria, chapter 28.
1887 50-51 Victoria, chapter 33.
1890 53 Victoria, chapter 24.
1895 58-59 Victoria, chapter 35.
1898 61 Victoria, chapter 34.
1906 Revised Statutes, chapter 81.
1906 6 Edward VII, chapter 20.
1910 9-10 Edward VII, chapter 20.
1910 1-2 George V, chapter 14.
1914 4-5 George V, chapter 35.
1915 6-7 George V, chapter 56.
1917 8-9 George V, chapter
1918 9-10 George V, chapter 50.
1922 12-13 George V, chapter 26.
1930 20-21, chapter 25.
1934 23-24, chapter 42.
1936 1 Edward VIII, chapter 20.
1938 2 George VI, chapter 31.
1951 15 George VI, chapter 29.
Statutes of the Province of Canada (S.P.C.)
1839 2 Victoria, chapter 15.
1840 3 Victoria, chapter 13.
1850 13-14 Victoria, chapter 74.
1850 13-14 Victoria, chapter 42.
1857 20 Victoria, chapter 26.
Upton, L.F.S.
1973. The origins of Canadian Indian policy. The Journal of Canadian Studies.
Wright, Anna Margaret.
1943. The Canadian frontier, 1840-1867. Ph.D. dissertation, University of Toronto.

12 Canadianizing the West
The North-West Mounted Police as Agents of the National Policy, 1873-1905

It has become one of the commonplaces of Canadian history to see the experience of the prairie west in terms of protest. Those aspects of Western history which have received the lion's share of attention all fall into this category—the Riel rebellions, the responsible government issue, the Manitoba schools question, the Winnipeg general strike, the Progressive movement, and Social Credit. The National Policy has been perceived almost exclusively as an instrument of economic injustice. The C.P.R. with much justification, becomes the oppressor of the farmer as soon as the heroic saga of its construction is over. It is no coincidence that Pierre Berton stops with the last spike. In his definition of the National Policy, R.C. Brown noted that,

> . . . the spirit of the National Policy went much deeper than railways, immigrants and tariffs. Beneath these external manifestations was the will to build and maintain a separate Canadian nation on the North American continent.[1]

The fact that westerners have been deeply attached to the goals of the National Policy while being critical of specific policies has too often been overlooked by historians and others. Western protest certainly existed, but it existed in the context of efforts to reform the National Policy rather than to reject it. A letter to the editor of the Medicine Hat *Times* expressed the attitude very well:

> We would ask our Eastern friends to regard us as fellow Canadians who are prone to claim that they form a part of this great Dominion, and not as serfs . . . Do not look upon us as a selfish, unsatisfied people who want the world, but rather as a people who are struggling for those rights and liberties so dear to themselves.[2]

Eastern observers who know a little about Western Canadian history tend to give Western separatism much more attention than it deserves and are often baffled by indications that the West really is part of Canada.

Such misunderstandings can have serious consequences and it is time historians, without forgetting the history of protest, began redressing the balance by exploring those forces which have counteracted Western regionalism and prevented it from becoming separatism. The prairie west had its political origins as a colony of Eastern Canada. As with other colonies, the development of the West was shaped in part by utopianism, in the sense of a desire to improve upon the original model. The West was created by people who sought to reproduce there what they believed to be the best characteristics of Eastern Canadian life. Difficult as it is to think of Sir John A. Macdonald and his colleagues as utopians, their intention in Western Canada was, if not to create a new Jerusalem, at least to build a better Ontario. Many of their designs failed, of course, but not all did. The North-West Mounted Police succeeded so well in transplanting Eastern Canadian institutions and ideas to the West that they became a part of the fabric of Western identity.

John A. would no doubt have appreciated the irony inherent in the recent furore in the West over the government's proposal to replace the letters R.C.M.P. with the word POLICE in the insignia of the force. When this seemingly innocent change was announced the West rose as one to object to Eastern tampering with Western traditions. The *Edmonton Journal* for a period of months kept a daily watch on R.C.M.P. headquarters in the city to see if the offending sign had been removed. Huge petitions descended upon the Solicitor-General, who seemed totally unprepared for the reaction. The West had risen again but this time to protect a federal police force run from Ottawa. In the course of a century an organization that began as one of the federal government's most clearly imperialistic ventures in the West had become a symbol of regional identity; one which represented not only the uniqueness of the West, but its historical ties to the rest of the country.

The Mounted Police were successful in ensuring that the imperatives of the National Policy were carried out and they managed to do it in such a way that their popularity among the citizenry of Western Canada never faded. There can be no doubt that the primary reason for the establishment of the policy was to ensure a peaceful occupation and exploitation of the West. Long before Canada acquired the former domain of the Hudson's Bay Company, Sir John A. Macdonald had decided that the logic of the National Policy would require some means of exercising direct federal control in the area of law enforcement.[3] The only possible Canadian West was a peaceful and orderly one; a wild west would certainly have bankrupted the government in short order. Canadian authorities were only too well aware that the United States government by 1870 was spending approximately 20 million dollars a year to subdue the Indians, more than the total Canadian budget. Obviously, too, the transcontinental railway would be much cheaper if the project was not hampered by either opposition from the Indians or excessive labor unrest among the workers. Immigrants would be more easily attracted to a non-violent West.

The idea that law enforcement should be a function of local government was deeply rooted in the British legal tradition and had been enshrined in the B.N.A. Act which placed it unequivocally in the hands of the provinces. Difficult as it was to break with this tradition, the alternative of leaving law enforcement in local hands in the North-West Territories seemed an invitation to disaster. There was the obvious example of the American West to discredit this alternative and the Canadian experience was hardly more encouraging. In spite of the emphasis in Canadian mythology on peace, order, and good government, the country's law enforcement institutions at the time of Confederation were primitive and ineffective.[4] Political and religious violence occurred regularly and was regarded as normal, if not particularly desirable.[5] In the West itself the experience of the Hudson's Bay Company had demonstrated that local law enforcement institutions on the British model were even less effective on the frontier than in the settled regions of the East.[6] The uprising of 1869-70 merely confirmed their total ineffectiveness. Reluctantly therefore, because the traditional system had the great advantage of not costing the federal government any money, Macdonald created the Mounted Police in 1873.

The primary task of the new force was to effectively occupy the West for Canada until the growth of population established Canadian ownership beyond any doubt. This meant avoiding by whatever means possible, conflicts between white settlers and native peoples. In this respect the police were outstandingly successful. Firmness, fair dealing, and compassion for the plight of the Indians were their basic tactics, supplemented where necessary by bluff and histrionics. In maintaining peace with the Indians, the most significant victories of the police were over other government departments, whose zeal to civilize the Indians often outstripped their common sense. In 1881, for example, a group of Indians at Fort Walsh refused to accept their annual treaty payments until the government agreed to discuss some of their grievances with them. The Indian Agent in charge was infuriated and wanted to cut off their rations and starve them into submission. Fortunately for all concerned the Mounted Police refused to consider such action, negotiations were held, and the incident ended peacefully.[7] When an Indian named Standing Buffalo removed his sick child from a government Industrial School at Qu'Appelle in 1894, the principal asked the police to bring the boy back and arrest the father for stealing government property, namely the boy's clothes. Inspector Charles Constantine, in charge of the case, declined both requests and after citing some legal grounds for leaving the boy with his parents, reported:

Whether these reasons are good or not, it would have been an inhuman act to have taken the boy away, to say nothing of the criminality attached to it should the child have died after his having been taken out in such cold weather.[8]

This list of similar confrontations could be extended for pages.

The police also had to cope with a settler population, many of whom believed that the only good Indian was a dead one.[9] Every cow that strayed was assumed to have been killed by the Indians. Under these difficult circumstances the police managed to tread the narrow path between the interests of the two groups and avoid confrontations. Ranchers and farmers were given to understand that the Indians had first priority. The treaties gave them unrestricted hunting rights and there was no legal justification for ordering Indians away from farms and ranches.[10] The Police responded by trying, usually with success, to persuade the Indians to return to their reserves. On the other hand white squatters were kept strictly away from Indian lands."

After 1885 police dealings with the Indians began to shift gradually away from persuasion toward coercion.[12] From the point of view of the National Policy, and therefore the Mounted Police, the years between 1873 and 1885 were crucial. The treaties were negotiated in this period and relations with the Indians established on a firm enough basis that two great crises, Sitting Bull's sojourn in Canada and the 1885 rebellion, could be dealt with. Once the railway was complete, the Indians could safely be pushed to one side and forgotten, as indeed they were. The relationship based upon trust and mutual respect was never completely dissipated, however, and remained the dominant feature of the period up to the turn of the century.

The whole point of pacifying the Indians was to allow the unhampered construction of the C.P.R. The railway made more direct use of the police as well. Thousands of navvies had to be kept reasonably sober and on the job under working conditions that were frequently scandalous even for that unenlightened age. During the building of the C.P.R. main line, the Mounted Police allowed nothing to interfere with construction, even if it meant facing down angry mobs of strikers single-handed, as Sam Steele claims to have done in his memoirs, or strikebreaking by operating trains for the company.[13] Once again, however, 1885 marks an important change in police attitudes. After that date and during the construction of other railways less vital to the National Policy, such as the Crowsnest Pass Branch of the C.P.R., the Calgary and Edmonton Railway, and the two new transcontinental lines, the police were much less willing to give management a free hand. Construction was unquestionably aided by the strict enforcement of the Public Works Peace Preservation Act which prohibited the sale of liquor within 10 miles of the right of way. But in these later cases the police scrupulously avoided taking sides in labor disputes and in fact often went out of their way to ensure that the rights of the workers were protected. Police officers acted as mediators in countless disputes, persuaded construction bosses to make working and living conditions more tolerable, and assisted workers in extracting unpaid wages from reluctant contractors.[14] Relations between the police and labor were, on the whole, good between 1885 and 1905.

Settlement of the prairies was the indispensable corollary to the construction of railways. The police were as valuable to the government in carrying out this part of the National Policy as they had been in others. In the early years aid to settlers was direct. The police advised newcomers as to the most desirable locations, gave advice about crops and weather conditions, and even lent farm equipment. Such administrative services as there were prior to 1885 came largely from the police who in addition to their regular duties delivered mail, organized the fighting of prairie fires, and acted as health officers, to name only a few of their activities. Police officers gave conducted tours of the countryside to advance men for parties of prospective immigrants. Perhaps most important of all, police patrols attempted to visit every settler at regular intervals.[15] These patrols gave the isolated settler a sense of security and provided welcome relief from the loneliness of prairie life.

All these activities of the Mounted Police are well known and were of the greatest importance in the history of the Canadian West. Yet had police work been confined to supporting the institutional framework of the National Policy the force would long since have ceased to exist. What ensured the survival of the Mounted Police was the work done by the force in building and sustaining the informal National Policy in the West. There was little point in developing the West unless it became firmly a part of that independent North American nation the National Policy was intended to create. A west which existed only as an economic colony of Eastern Canada would be more trouble than it was worth. This meant, as far as the police were concerned, that the allegiance of Canadian settlers must be reinforced. Immigrants, of course, would have to be integrated. Many institutions participated in this process; the most important of those overtly involved in integrating the immigrant being the churches, the schools, and the Department of the Interior.[16] For a number of reasons the police were more influential than any of these. Not everyone went to church and only the children went to school. Many of the churches, in any case, were imported along with the immigrants and tended to perpetuate the traditions of the old country.[17] More important still was the fact that while clergymen and teachers might have rather hazy ideas about what Canadianism was, the police had very firm convictions on the subject. Their own area of concern coincided with one of the primary Canadian national myths: the conviction that Canadian society was more orderly and law-abiding than others. The Mounted Police had no doubts about what set Canadians apart from other men and their determination to impose what they considered proper standards of behavior imparted to their day-to-day activities an almost missionary zeal.

The background of the personnel of the Mounted Police, especially the officers, ensured not only that they would take the task of educating the settlers in the correct political attitudes very seriously but that they would be heard with respect. Although there is a tradition perpetuated in all early writings on the Mounted Police that many officers were British, most were Canadian. At least 80 percent of the officers of the force were Canadian-born throughout the period under discussion.[18] The percentage of British-born in the non-commissioned ranks was much higher, rising from 33 percent in 1888 to a peak of 61 percent in 1895 and dropping off sharply thereafter.[19] Significantly, however, in spite of the steady increase in the numbers of promotions from the ranks, the percentage of British-born officers remained the same.

That the leadership of the force was solidly Canadian was of the utmost importance. Since Canada's military establishment was almost non-existent, the Mounted Police provided an opportunity for talented young men with military ambitions. Public hostility to the granting of police commissions to British individuals was intense. On one of the rare occasions when the government dared to make such an appointment the *Canadian Military Gazette* commented, "We could have understood the appointment of a graduate of the Royal Military College or of an officer with a record in the militia; but for this appointment of a rank outsider there can be no excuse."[20] The Ottawa *Free Press* reacted savagely to a suggestion by W.R. Grahame, an immigration official at Winnipeg who acted as a recruiting agent for the Mounted Police, that the force recruit in England.

. . . one would imagine that Captain Grahame could find plenty of recruits in Canada without importing English dudes. If we are to have 'Canada for the Canadians' why send to England for troopers when Canadians can be obtained? The recruiting of the Mounted Police Force with strangers who have no sympathy with Canada, who know nothing of the country and who imagine that all their follies and vices should be condoned because 'they are English don't cher know' has been fruitful cause of trouble in the past, and if the management of the force is left to Captain Grahame and Mr. Herchmer the outlook for the future is not promising.[21]

By the late 1880s the pattern for recruiting officers was well established. Graduates of the Royal Military College at Kingston were considered the most desirable candidates and dominated the leadership of the force by the turn of the century.[22] Other officers came from the Active Militia and by promotions from within the force itself. The officers who emerged from this selection process were almost invariably upper-class, well educated, and well connected in Eastern Canadian society and politics. From the beginning they established themselves as social leaders in the growing settlements on the prairies and by the 1890s their status was taken for granted. Officers stationed at Calgary were entitled to membership in the exclusive Ranchmen's Club without having to pay the usual fees. Complaints were frequently heard that the officer without private means could not afford to do the entertaining expected of him.[23] Because the police associated with local opinion leaders on a basis of equality they were in an excellent position to influence the development of Western attitudes.

The origins of the other ranks in the Mounted Police were more diverse but they seem to have absorbed their officers' attitudes very thoroughly.[24] A large number of men from the force became settlers themselves and often leading figures in their community.[25] The opportunities for contact provided by the varied duties of the police and by their regular patrols were very great. For many settlers, the regular visits of the police were their most important source of information about the outside world. Rumors and neighborhood gossip could be verified and interpreted through such conversations. The police knew the importance of such contacts and used them in the short run to prevent any recourse to private justice and in the long run to encourage the 'correct' view of law and order.

While the police were constantly aware of the necessity to reinforce correct Canadian values concerning law and order, the arrival of substantial groups of non-Canadian immigrants brought forth a different response. The police considered it one of their primary functions to ensure the integration of these groups. Assimilation, it was assumed, would follow in due course. In a report of 1893 Commissioner Herchmer noted the problem as he saw it and outlined the steps necessary to deal with it.

> A very large immigration, as you are aware, took place last year into the Edmonton country, mostly from the Western States where law and order are not rigidly enforced, and I am credibly informed that the flow this year will greatly exceed all previous seasons, most of the immigrants being drawn from Oregon and Washington States, and it will be necessary to greatly increase our patrols in consequence, as the opinion these people form of our administration of the laws on their first arrival, has the greatest possible effect on their future conduct, and inability on our part to impress them with the necessity of strictly obeying our laws, will, in my opinion, be certain to lead to heavy expenses later on in the administration of justice, the cost of which would greatly exceed that of laying a good moral foundation at the start, through the activity and vigilance of the police.[26]

Where large concentrations of European immigrants were present the police endeavored to establish a detachment as soon as a settlement was founded. If possible the man selected for this duty would be one who spoke the language of the community; if not, an interpreter was hired.[27] Sometimes these detachments were set up as a result of pressure from other settlers in surrounding districts who harbored dire suspicions about all foreigners. If no such request was forthcoming, the police would establish a detachment anyway as a matter of principle.

Police outposts among colonies of European immigrants proved to have very little to do in the way of actual law enforcement. With the single exception of the Doukhobours, the police found European immigrants less prone to break the law than the general population. This was partly due to the close supervision exercised by the police and their concern to explain the law to the immigrants. It was also partly due to the fact that the police got along well with them and were able to act as a buffer against public and official nativism.

In one typical case a settler near Qu'Appelle by the name of D. Henry Starr wrote an angry letter to the Minister of the Interior, accusing some German colonists who lived nearby of stealing his hay. Warming to his task, he went on to say that the Germans,

> . . . have turned out to be the very worst and lowest class of people under the sun, who are considered quite a nuisance, and ought to be banished from the country otherwise they will be the means of driving every respectable settler out of the place.[28]

A corporal was despatched to investigate as soon as the charges reached the Mounted Police. He discovered that all Starr's ideas were based on hearsay; he had had no contact with the Germans since their arrival. By the time the corporal had finished his questioning, Starr was ready to admit that no shred of evidence existed to connect the Germans with the theft. In forwarding the report to Ottawa, the Superintendent in charge of the case appended his own views. "I might add that our experience of German settlers in different parts of the North West points to the fact that they are law-abiding and good citizens and cause the police little trouble."[29]

A similar incident at the Ukrainian settlement of Edna, near Edmonton, involved Frank Oliver, M.P. for the district and no friend of the non-Anglo-Saxon immigrant. In June of 1899, Oliver wrote to the police demanding that something be done to curb thievery by the Ukrainians, otherwise the English-speaking settlers would be forced to take the law into their own hands. He added that, in addition to the crime wave, filthy conditions in the settlement had caused a smallpox epidemic which threatened surrounding communities.[30] A police investigation began at once. The smallpox epidemic turned out to be two cases of measles. No one could be found who had experienced theft from any source, but rumors of the larcenous propensities of the Ukrainians abounded. Inspector J.O. Wilson, who investigated the complaints, reported that both English-speaking and Ukrainian settlers were strongly in favor of the establishment of a detachment in the community. He urged that this be done at once to prevent rumor from getting out of hand in the future. For the Ukrainian settlers, he had only praise as hard-working and law-abiding individuals.[31]

It might be thought that the police were interested only in anglicizing the immigrants and indeed their frequent references to British law and justice lend some credence to this view. But a closer examination reveals that the Mounted Police sought to assimilate the immigrant to specifically Canadian values. The Commissioner issued the following orders concerning a group of English settlers who arrived in 1903. "The police must be especially active in aiding the new settlers to overcome their difficulties. They must establish friendly relations, carefully explain the law without resorting to harsh measures, and give them general advice."[32] American settlers, who had no linguistic differences to set them apart, received even more attention from the police than the Europeans did. To the police, American settlers, so like Canadians in other ways, differed in that they carried with them American political attitudes; the seeds of anarchy, disorder, and violence. Commissioner A. Bowen Perry was merely expressing the view of the force as a whole when he wrote to Comptroller White in 1903, "I suppose the peace of the Territories may seem assured to those who are in the East, and even to the people of the Territories who are accustomed to it. They little know of the reckless class of American outlaws to the South of us."[33] Although there is no evidence in the police records to indicate that Americans were any less law-abiding than other groups, the Mounted Police continued to think of themselves as engaged in a desperate struggle to preserve Canadian civilization in the West.

The police arrived in the North-West with very definite ideas about Americans and American society. Early contacts were confined mainly to whisky traders and deserters from the U.S. Army; men who tended to reinforce the stereotype of the lawless American. The police were constant and interested observers of the American scene across the border. The only observations which registered permanently, however, were those which provided opportunities to compare the quality of American life unfavorably with that of Canada. The police records are filled with lurid accounts of lynchings, mob violence, and general lawlessness garnered from American newspapers, hearsay, and observation of border towns. Sergeant G.W. Byrne, travelling in Montana on the trail of some cattle stolen in Canada, reported that he had been forced to pass himself off as a merchant because the town to which he traced the cattle was controlled by a gang of thieves.

> I might state here that the town of Culbertson consists of two stores, two gambling saloons, one boarding house and a couple of houses of ill fame. There are about 20 cowboys or horse thieves and gamblers who take turns watching our every movement, and immediately one of us leaves the town scouts are sent out in all directions to give the alarm.[34]

Construction of a railway across the border provided an even better opportunity to contrast the two ways of life.

> The detachment stationed at Sterling, the new town on the Boundary on the Soo R'way did good service in keeping the peace. The track laying gang on the American side was accompanied by a number of whisky sellers, gamblers and prostitutes. S/Sgt. McGinnis' report, which I have forwarded you, relates that great disorder prevailed on the American side—serious rows, drunkenness and debauchery. On our side there was no trouble of any kind.[35]

It followed from these assumptions that if disorder existed in the Northwest Territories, it was probably attributable to Americans, indirectly if not directly. The police were not slow to draw this conclusion and on several occasions blamed disturbances on Americans on no better evidence than the mere presence of American settlers in the neighborhood. When an angry crowd of trial spectators at Carlyle voiced their disapproval of a liquor conviction by shouting, "To hell with the red coats!" Superintendent J.O. Wilson offered the following explanation.

> The settlers and residents of Carlyle and Arcola are chiefly Americans, a large proportion of them being single men, who are imbued with the American western idea of law and order, and consequently will have to be taught that they cannot do as they like on this side of the line.[36]

As Superintendent Wilson's remarks indicate, the remedy was as obvious to the police as the complaint. Reporting on a small American settlement on the Canadian side of the international boundary, Superintendent R.B. Deane wrote,

> They live in Canada but get everything from the United States and most likely they still believe they are American citizens and do not intend to abide by Canadian laws unless they are told to. No doubt a detachment of N.W.M. Police at that point will soon settle the matter.[37]

When Major-General Selby-Smyth, commanding the Canadian Militia, inspected the Mounted police in 1875, he noted that in spite of the exceedingly primitive conditions, the men of the force were generally contented. He believed that their satisfaction came from their future hopes for the region under their charge.

> . . . above all they have the conscious knowledge that they are pioneers in a rich and fertile territory, magnificently spacious though still strangely solitary and silent, which at no distant time will re-echo with the busy life, of a numerous and prosperous population . . .[38]

This was a very perceptive observation. To the Mounted Police the West represented an opportunity to create a new and better version of Eastern Canadian society; a chance to prove that Canadian institutions were fundamentally better than those of the United States. The society they envisaged was to be orderly and hierarchical; not a lawless frontier democracy but a place where powerful institutions and a responsible and paternalistic upper class would ensure true liberty and justice. Here was the Upper Canadian Tory tradition in its purest form. The corresponding Reform tradition was almost totally absent. This was hardly surprising since entry into the force, and especially into the commissioned ranks, was strictly controlled by patronage.[39] With the exception of a very few officers appointed during the Mackenzie regime, the leadership of the Mounted Police until the turn of the century was solidly Conservative.

It is very difficult to assess accurately the extent to which the Mounted Police were successful in imposing their concept of the West. Perhaps the best evidence of the strength and permanence of their contribution lies in the fact that the force was very popular among all citizens of the region and in its continuing symbolic significance. When the Liberal government of Wilfrid Laurier took office in 1896, it was decided to eliminate the Mounted Police.[40] The West was now safe for the National Policy and the Liberals were understandably anxious to rid themselves of what they correctly considered a nest of Conservatives. The Liberals, in any case, had an ideological commitment to local self-government. These plans encountered such a storm of protest, even from Liberal party workers in the West, that they had to be abandoned.[41] When Alberta and Saskatchewan received provincial status in 1905, the federal government made another half-hearted attempt to persuade the new provinces to set up their own police and abandon the N.W.M.P., but it proved easier to work out an evasion of the B.N.A. Act which allowed the force to continue to operate under provincial control, than to do away with it.[42] Westerners by this time found it almost impossible to conceive of the region without the Mounted Police. The North-West Mounted Police and all that it stood for had become an important part of the way in which the West defined itself.

NOTES
1. R.C. Brown, *Canada's National Policy, 1883-1900: A Study in Canadian-American Relations* (Princeton, 1964), p.12.
2. Medicine Hat *Times,* May 28, 1887, quoted in C.G. Edwards, "The National Policy as Seen by the Editors of the Medicine Hat Newspapers: A Western Opinion, 1885-1896" (unpublished M.A. thesis, University of Alberta, 1969), p.81.
3. S.W. Horrall, "Sir John A. Macdonald and the Mounted Police Force for the Northwest Territories," *Canadian Historical Review,* LIII, 1972, pp. 179-200. There are indications that Macdonald was thinking about the problems even

before Confederation. The following passage appears in a letter from Governor-General Monck in 1865: "I return Mr. McMicken's letter which appears satisfactory as regards the state of the West. I think the suggestion as to the appointment of Police as a good one." Public Archives of Canada, Macdonald Papers, Vol. 74, Monck to Macdonald, n.d. 1865.

4. Marjorie Freeman Campbell, *A Century of Crime: The Development of Crime Detection Methods in Canada* (Toronto, 1970) and Desmond Morton, "Aid to the Civil Power: The Canadian Militia in Support of Social Order, 1867-1914," *Canadian Historical Review,* LI, 1970, pp. 407-25.

5. When Lt.-Gov. A.G. Archibald reported serious election riots at Red River in 1872, Macdonald replied that they were regrettable but, ". . . not of a more serious character than we have seen in older communities . . ." Public Archives of Manitoba, Alexander Morris Papers, Macdonald to Archibald, October 7, 1872. See also Michael S. Cross, "The Shiner's War: Social Violence in the Ottawa Valley in the 1830s," *Canadian Historical Review,* LIV, 1973, pp. 1-26.

6. Dale and Lee Gibson, *Substantial Justice: Law and Lawyers in Manitoba, 1670-1970* (Winnipeg, 1972) and Roy St. George Stubbs, *Four Recorders of Rupert's Land* (Winnipeg, 1967).

7. P.A.C., Macdonald Papers, Vol. 210, Indian Agent T.P. Wadsworth to Indian Commissioner E.T. Galt, July 25, 1881.

8. P.A.C., R.C.M.P. Records (RG 18), Comptroller's Office Official Correspondence Series (A-1), Vol. 103, file No. 63, Father J. Hugonnard to Indian Commissioner, December 19, 1894 and Inspector Constantine to Superintendent A. Bowen Perry, January 8, 1895.

9. In 1888 a constable by the name of Simons was accused of giving some iodine to an Indian woman who drank it and died from the effects. Superintendent P.R. Neale reported, ". . . I do not think any western jury will convict him." P.A.C., RG 18, A-1, Vol. 24, No. 667, Neal to Commissioner L.W. Herchmer, July 17, 1888. See also Public Archives of Saskatchewan, Diary of William Wallace Clarke, 1875 and P.A.C., Diary of Constable R.N. Wilson.

10. P.A.C., RG 18, A-1, Vol. 26, No. 43, correspondence between the Commissioner and High River Branch, Alberta Stock Growers' Association, November 1888-January 1889.

11. P.A.C., RG 18, Commissioner's Office, Orders and Regulations, 1880-1954 (B-1), Vol. 8, General Order No. 901 (Old Series), 1883.

12. In the early days, for example, Commissioner Macleod had ruled that the Sun Dance was to be respected and no arrests were to be made during the ceremony, on the analogy of a church. By the 1890s the police were actively engaged in efforts to eradicate the Sun Dance as a relic of barbarism. P.A.C., RG 18, A-1, Vol. 36, No. 817, Superintendent S. Steele to Commissioner L.W. Herchmer, August 12, 1889 and Vol. 55, No. 586, Steele to Herchmer, June 23, 1891. See also Hugh A. Dempsey, *Crowfoot: Chief of the Blackfeet* (Edmonton, 1972).

13. S.B. Steele, *Forty Years in Canada* (Toronto, 1915), pp. 196-200. For the strikebreaking incident see P.A.C., Diary of Superintendent R. Burton Deane.

14. The best examples of this kind of police work are to be found in the reports of Inspector G.E. Sanders concerning his supervision of construction on the Crowsnest Pass Branch, P.A.C., RG 18, A-1, Vol. 145, No. 56.

15. See, for example, P.A.C., RG 18, A-1, Vol. 42, No. 495, Calgary Patrol Reports, April-June, 1890.
16. For the churches see G.N. Emery, "Methodism on the Canadian Prairies, 1896 to 1914: The Dynamics of an Institution in a New Environment" (unpublished Ph.D. thesis, University of British Columbia, 1970); for the schools see Neil Gerard McDonald, "The School as an Agent of Nationalism in the North-West Territories, 1884-1905" (unpublished M. Ed. thesis, University of Alberta, 1971).
17. This applied to such American immigrant groups as the Mormons as well as to Europeans.
18. P.A.C., RG 18, A-1, Vol. 96, No. 413 and Vol. 100, No. 886.
19. P.A.C., RG 18, A-1, Vol. 22, No. 413 and Vol. 117, No. 76.
20. *Canadian Military Gazette,* March 1, 1894.
21. Ottawa *Free Press,* February 16, 1888.
22. P.A.C., RG 18, A-1, Vol. 205, No. 110, and Vol. 269, No. 763.
23. P.A.C., RG 18, A-1, Vol. 134, No. 163, Commissioner L.W. Herchmer to Comptroller F. White, February 4, 1897 and Laurier Papers, Vol. 186, J.M. Skelton to Laurier, February 1, 1901.
24. See, for example, Glenbow-Alberta Institute Archives, Frederick A. Bagley Papers and Diary, A.C. Bury Diary and Reminiscences, Sergeant S. Hetherington Dairy; P.A.C., Constable James Finlayson Diary, Constable R.N. Wilson Diary.
25. Glenbow-Alberta Institute Archives, William John Redmond, "History of the Southwestern Saskatchewan Old-Timers' Association" (unpublished manuscript, 1932).
26. P.A.C., RG 18, A-1, Vol. 74, No. 68, Herchmer to White, January 13, 1893.
27. P.A.C., RG 18, A-1, Vol. 126, No. 6, Vol. 165, No. 193, Vol. 167, No. 224, and Vol. 257, No. 512.
28. P.A.C., RG 18, A-1, Vol. 97, No. 587, Starr to T.M. Daly, July 17, 1894.
29. *Ibid.,* Superintendent J.H. McIlree to White, August 16, 1894.
30. P.A.C., RG 18, A-1, Vol. 172, No. 438, Oliver to White, June 1 and 8, 1899.
31. *Ibid.,* Inspector Wilson to Superintendent Griesbach, June 21, 1899.
32. P.A.C., RG 18, A-1, Vol. 285, No. 24, Commissioner A. Bowen Perry to Superintendent Griesbach, May 11, 1903.
33. P.A.C., RG 18, A-1, Vol. 274, No. 353, Perry to White, October 17, 1903.
34. P.A.C., RG 18, A-1, Vol. 168, No. 241, Sergeant Byrne to Superintendent J. Howe, March 12, 1899.
35. P.A.C., RG 18, A-1, Vol. 76, No. 161, Regina Monthly Report for August 1893.
36. P.A.C., RG 18, A-1, Vol. 253, No. 304, Wilson to Assistant Commissioner McIlree, February 28, 1903.
37. P.A.C., RG 18, A-1, Vol. 250, No. 177, Lethbridge Monthly Report for October 1903.
38. P.A.C., RG 18, A-1, Vol. 8, No. 29, Major-General Selby-Smyth's report, p.8.
39. P.A.C., Macdonald Papers, Vol. 229, pp. 98707-8, Vol. 263, pp. 119719-20, Vol. 395, pp. 189133-5, Vol. 405, pp. 195420-1, Vol. 417, pp. 202381-3, 202511-13, 2022663-4, Vol. 430, pp. 210880-2, Vol. 442, pp. 219466-7. See also R. Burton Deane, *Mounted Police Life in Canada: A Record of Thirty-One Years' Service* (London, 1916), pp. 64-6.

40. P.A.C., Laurier Papers, Vol. 39, Memo by Comptroller White, March 5, 1897.
41. P.A.C., Laurier Papers, Vol. 45, Frank Oliver to Laurier, May 12, 1897; Vol. 65, Oliver to Laurier, February 5, 1898; Vol. 105, J.M. Douglas to Laurier, March 27, 1899. P.A.C., RG 18, A-1 Vol. 136, No. 268, T.O. David to White, March 31, 1897, and Vol. 168, No. 269, J.M. Douglas to White, January 28, 1899.
42. P.A.C., RG 18, A-1, Vol. 528, No. 108, Laurier to Premiers Walter Scott and A.C. Rutherford, February 7, 1906.

VI

THE ECONOMICS OF SETTLEMENT

Settlement of the Canadian prairies proceeded slowly prior to the late 1890s. Various interpretations have been offered to explain this delay. One explanation is the negative image of the grassland region for settlement. John Palliser's depiction of the region as a "desert" area in the report of his scientific expedition of 1857 no doubt discouraged settlement in this area. Large-scale ranchers in the North-West Territories encouraged this same negative view of agricultural settlement since they did not want farmers coming into the area to compete with their ranching interests.

Other explanations have been advanced. Some economic historians have argued that agricultural methods were insufficiently developed in the 1880s and 1890s to make agriculture viable in the harsh climate of western Canada. Still others blame the Hudson's Bay Company, the Canadian Pacific Railway, and colonization companies for withholding good land for purposes of speculation. Other economists point out that with good and cheap land still available south of the border, immigrants coming to North America preferred the more settled conditions of the American West.

Recently, economists have questioned the timing of prairie settlement. Previous scholars had simply assumed that settlement of the west had been the direct result of the federal government's national policy of land sales, railway building, and immigration promotion. But if so, why was there a decade-long delay after the completion of the transcontinental railway in 1885 before sizeable settlement began in 1896? Were there other factors besides the national policy which determined the timing of the massive settlement of the prairies? In his article, "The National Policy and the Rate of Prairie Settlement: A Review," Kenneth Norrie summarizes much of the recent discussion, and argues that the timing of western settlement was determined by the sudden unavailability of America sub-humid lands around 1900 along with the development and diffusion of dryland farming techniques.

Though economists may differ in their assessment of the success of the national policy, they agree that the wheat economy was the dominant fact of economic life on the prairies. It opened up tremendous economic opportunities for financial, marketing, and transportation companies in central Canada and for business interests in western towns and cities. But for western farmers wheat production had its challenges. Besides the hazards of the physical environment and the instability of wheat prices, farmers faced what they felt to be unfair and monopolistic freight rates from the CPR, monopolistic practices by grain companies in the marketing of grain, a government tariff which raised the cost of their farm machinery and other manufactured goods, and a banking system which seemed remote, uncaring, and exploitive. Ted Regehr analyzes one of these grievances—the resentment over the operation of a national transportation policy—in his article "Western Canada and the Burden of National Transportation Policies."

SELECTED BIBLIOGRAPHY

For an interpretive synthesis of the changes in the West's economy during the late nineteenth century, see Irene Spry, "The Transition from a Nomadic to a Settled Economy in Western Canada, 1856-1896," *Transactions* of the Royal Society of Canada, Vol. 6 (June, 1968): 187-201.

For an overview of Canadian agricultural policy see Vernon C. Fowke, *Canadian Agricultural Policy: The Historical Pattern* (Toronto, 1946). Early accounts of the wheat economy include G.E. Britnell, *The Wheat Economy* (Toronto, 1939) and Vernon C. Fowke, *The National Policy and the Wheat Economy* (Toronto, 1957).

For the major accounts of prairie settlement and dominion lands policy see A.S. Morton, *History of Prairie Settlement* (Toronto, 1938); and Chester Martin, *'Dominion Land's' Policy* (Toronto, 1938). W.A. Waiser's biography of the naturalist John Macoun, *The Field Naturalist* (Toronto, 1989), provides a good overview of the North-West in the late nineteenth century. For an overview of the history of agriculture on the prairies, including a discussion of farm technology, agricultural research, dryland and irrigated farming, animal husbandry and many other aspects of agricultural development see Grant MacEwan, *An Illustrated History of Western Canadian Agriculture* (Saskatoon, 1980).

On the Canadian grain trade, see D.A. MacGibbon, *The Canadian Grain Trade* (Toronto, 1932); D.A. MacGibbon, *The Canadian Grain Trade, 1931-52* (Toronto, 1952); and C.F. Wilson, *A Century of Canadian Grain: Government Policy to 1951* (Saskatoon, 1978). For an overview of the major problems facing the wheat economy, see W.T. Easterbrook and H.G. Aitken, *Canadian Economic History* (Toronto, 1956).

For an interesting debate on the cost of establishing and maintaining a farm in western Canada during the settlement period, see: Lyle Dick, "Estimates of Farm Machinery Costs in Saskatchewan, 1882-1914," *Prairie Forum* 6 (1981): 183-201. Irene Spry challenges Dick's analysis in "The Cost of Making a Farm on the Prairie," *Prairie Forum* 7 (1982): 95-99. Dick replies in "A Reply to Professor Spry's Critique," *Prairie Forum* 7 (1982): 101. Other relevant articles on the subject include William Carlyle, "The Changing Family Farm on the Prairies," *Prairie Forum* 8 (1983): 1-23; Ray Bollman and P. Ehrensaft, "Changing Farm Size Distribution on the Prairie Over the Past Hundred Years," *Prairie Forum* 13 (1988): 43-66; and Judith Wiesinger, "Modelling the Agricultural Settlement Process of Southern Manitoba, 1871-1891: Some Implications for Settlement Theory," *Prairie Forum* 10 (1985): 83-103.

On the history of ranching on the prairies see David Breen, *The Canadian Prairie West and the Ranching Frontier, 1874-1924* (Toronto, 1983); see as well two articles by Simon Evans, "The End of the Open Range Era in Western Canada," *Prairie Forum* 8 (1983): 71-89; and American Cattlemen on the Canadian Range, 1874-1914," *Prairie Forum* 4 (1979): 121-35; and Shelagh Jameson's "The Ranching Industry of Western Canada: Its Initial Epoch, 1873-1914," *Prairie Forum* 11 (1986): 229-42.

For popular accounts of the building of the CPR, see Pierre Berton, *The National Dream: The Great Railway, 1871-1881* (Toronto, 1970); and his *The Last Spike: The Great Railway, 1881-1885* (Toronto, 1971). See also John Eagle, *The Canadian Pacific Railway and the Development of Western Canada, 1896-1914* (Montreal, 1989). On the impact of the CPR on the west, see Hugh Dempsey, ed., *The CPR West: The Iron Road and the Making of a Nation* (Vancouver, 1984).

On the significance of the Canadian Northern Railway to the development of western Canada, see the two articles by T.D. Regehr, "The Canadian Northern Railway: The West's Own Product," *Canadian Historical Review* 51 (1970): 177-86, and "William Mackenzie, Donald Mann, and the Larger Canada" in A.W. Rasporich, ed., *Western Canada: Past and Present* (Calgary, 1975), pp. 69-83; and his book, *The Canadian Northern Railway: Pioneer Road of the Northern Prairies, 1895-1918* (Toronto, 1976). R.B. Fleming has completed a biography of Sir William Mackenzie (1849-1923) of the Canadian Northern Railway, *The Railway King of Canada* (Vancouver, 1991).

For an attempt to assess the significance of the freight rate issue for western Canada see Howard Darling, *The Politics of Freight Rates* (Toronto, 1980). Ken Norrie presents an opposing argument to Regehr's on the issue of discriminatory freight rates in "Some Comments on Prairie Economic Alienation," in *Canadian Public Policy/Analyses de Politiques* II, no. 2 (Spring, 1976), pp. 211-44.

Very interesting historical maps on western Canada from 1891 to 1961 are contained in Donald Kerr and Deryck W. Holdsworth, *Historical Atlas* of Canada, Vol. 3, *Addressing the Twentieth Century, 1891-1961* (Toronto, 1990). This volume should be consulted for this, and all the subsequent topics on Prairie Canada period maps from 1891 to 1961.

KENNETH H. NORRIE

13 The National Policy and the Rate of Prairie Settlement
A Review

1979 marks the official centenary of the National Policy, and the unofficial one of what has become known as the national policy. The former term refers to the broad-ranging structure of protective tariffs introduced by the Conservative government of Sir John A. Macdonald as promised in their 1878 election campaign. The latter, uncapitalized version is now taken to refer collectively to the combination of tariff, railway, land and immigration policies developed over the years after Confederation. Under most accounts, in fact, the national policy survived the electoral defeat of the Conservatives in 1896, with Sir Wilfrid Laurier and his government being perhaps even more vigorous (and successful) in pursuing this development strategy.

The form the national policy took is easily appreciated by noting the implicit "model" of economic development held by the politicians of the day. The clear intent, as Fowke has argued,[1] was to reproduce something akin to the commercial and industrial prosperity enjoyed during the agricultural development of Ontario in the first half of the century, or to the American boom that was so readily attributed to the continuous expansion of western settlement in that country. The Canadian West was to be the new agricultural frontier. Grain would be the export staple, requiring a host of linked commercial activities to gather it and market it in Europe. In turn, the derived demand of the agricultural population for goods and services would generate additional economic linkages.

In fact, of course, western Canada did soon thereafter become a major grain exporting region, and the country did experience significant industrial development. This naturally raises the question as to how large a role the federal government policies played in these developments. A longstanding historical view is that they were a major factor. The work of Innis, Creighton, Brebner and other leading historians, ". . . emphasized the positive role of the National Policy which by fostering secondary industry, transcontinental railways, and western settlement produced a national inter-dependent economy with one section of the country supplying the needs of the others."[2]

Some fifteen years ago John Dales launched an all-out attack on what he called this "historians' stereotype" of the national policy.[3] His message, in effect, is that these measures were neither necessary nor sufficient for the events that followed. In fact, he argued, they may have been even worse than irrelevant in that they acted to distort whatever economic development did occur. The tariffs promoted not industry, but rather inefficient industry. Giving away land at uneconomic prices led to much long-term harm to western Canada. Even the railway subsidies are criticized as having induced premature construction, and as perhaps even excessive.[4]

This challenge by Dales has led to a considerable revival of interest in the national policy and its impact on economic development. In this centenary year it seems particularly appropriate to attempt to survey what we have learned to date. This forms the primary motivation for the present paper. A second one is that a good deal of the recent work has been done by economists, using techniques that are not necessarily familiar to a broader audience of historians who might still be interested in the results. Thus there seems to be a need for some kind of general, non-technical overview of this material. Finally, for reasons that may not be unique to Canadian economic historians, much of the material has not yet been published and thus is not generally available to the non-specialist.

A comprehensive evaluation of the national policy divides naturally into three separate but related questions. Two deal with the efficiency aspects of the development strategy while the other concerns its income distributional consequences. First, in what manner if at all did the federal measures affect the timing, rate and extent of western agricultural expansion? Following this, what was the net social benefit of these promotional activities? The second topic would pose these same two questions about the relationship between industrial development and tariffs, railways and western settlement.[5,6] As regards the equity issue much of the concern has been over the regional implications of the policies,[7] but its effects on the personal and functional distributions of income are other interesting problems.

For reasons of length, this paper deals only with the first issue. Section II looks at Dales' critique in more detail, and examines his alternative explanation for the timing of Prairie settlement. The third section surveys several alternative hypotheses and the statistical evidence that has been marshalled for and against them. The intent in these two parts is to examine the literature to determine how, if at all, federal policies affected western agricultural expansion. Section IV then raises the question of what a socially optimal rate of settlement might have looked like, and uses this standard to evaluate the actual pattern. The final section makes some concluding comments.

FIGURE 1   Net Accumulated Homesteads in each year as a Percentage of
Total to 1930.

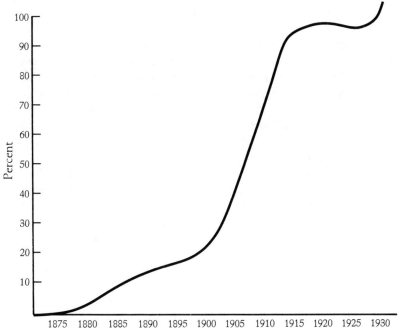

SOURCE: M.C. Urquhart & K.A.H. Buckey (eds.) *Historical Statistics of Canada*

II

Dales' main evidence against the national policy is that it failed to work for
some twenty or thirty years. Figure 1 shows the net accumulated free
homesteads in each year from 1872 as a percentage of the total to 1930.
As is evident from the figure, the vast majority of the entries were made after
1900. By 1885 only 8.8% of the eventual total net homestead entries had
been recorded, and by 1900 only 20%. By 1906, however, the proportion
had reached 51.4%, and by the outbreak of World War I nearly 89%. Yet
the CPR had reached the Prairies by 1882 or 1883, the Homestead Act had
assumed virtually its final form by 1882 and considerable efforts were being
made to advertise the region to potential migrants. Given this, it is difficult
to argue with Dales' contention that the efforts to promote western settlement were not sufficient in themselves.

He goes further though and asserts that they were not even necessary.

After 1900 the demand for western land was so brisk, and the C.P.R.
and various land companies so zealous in attracting settlers to the region,
that it is hard to believe that the homestead policy was in any sense necessary as a means of settling the West.[8]

An alternative explanation is proffered based on a rapid succession of
exogenous developments—the familiar favourable conjuncture of events—in
the mid 1890's that finally made Prairie settlement feasible on a large scale.
This list includes among other things a rise in wheat prices as a result of industrialization in Europe and the United States; falling transport costs on wheat
exports; the end of the American land frontier; the resumption of international capital flows and labour migration and technical breakthroughs in
the production, transportation and further processing of wheat.

The implication for the national policy of this interpretation of the timing of Prairie settlement is significant. None of the above factors relies in
any way on the federal initiatives. The inescapable conclusion is that settlement could not have proceeded any earlier than it did whatever promotional
efforts the government might have made. Equally, it would have occurred
when it did regardless of the national policy. The only article of faith required
here, it would seem, is that the necessary railway mileage would have been
available anyway, something not too difficult to accept given the motivation for rushing the CPR in the first place. At best then the national policy
was irrelevant and likely as not, Dales would argue, it was positively harmful.

Citing the favourable conjuncture of events in this manner does not provide a convincing alternative explanation, however. This can be seen by looking more closely at each of the items in the list. It is true, for example, that
world wheat prices rose more or less continuously after 1894, but this ignores
the fact that the levels after 1895 were significantly lower than those in the
1870's and 1880's.[9] The reference to falling ocean freight rates is equally
unconvincing since these charges had been falling continuously for many
years prior to 1900.

The figure of ultimate concern of course is the North American wheat
price—the world price less transport charges. The Chicago price of number
2 wheat increased from 1870 through to 1882 while the world price fell,
due to the decline in ocean freight rates noted above. It fell from 1883 to
1888, recovered slightly to 1891, fell to 1895 and then began a fluctuating
recovery to World War I. But again, the average level over the period
1896-1913 was 84.9¢, while that for the years 1879 to 1895 was 87.8¢.
What needs to be explained rather is why this range of wheat prices was
associated with an economic boom after 1897 but not earlier.

One obvious factor here is the further reduction in price from the export
point to the farm gate due to transport costs. Grain was hauled from the
local collection points to the central ones and then to the Lakehead by rail,
meaning that the availability of rail lines and the rates they charged need

to be taken into account in a proper analysis. Since the provision of railroad mileage was a central concern of the national policy this raises the possibility that it did play a part in stimulating Prairie settlement. Clearly the railroad issue needs to be dealt with in more detail, something that is done below.

The view that the resumption of international flows of capital and labour were responsible for the boom is equally difficult to accept. Figure 1 shows that the upturn in free homestead entries can be dated from 1897, and was well underway by 1900. Yet the major inflows of capital and labour only appeared later on in the decade. In the case of capital, for example, Meier notes,

> It is significant that the noticeable acceleration of growth in the Canadian economy after 1895 did not initially depend on the inflow of foreign capital. Not until 1905 did foreign borrowings reach significant proportions . . . .[10]

In his study of immigration, Corbett notes,

> But it can be urged, I think, that immigration was not as important an active causal factor in agricultural development as other factors . . . . The role of immigration in agricultural settlement was passive and responsive . . . .[11]

In both cases then the inflow of these factors must be viewed as responding to economic opportunity rather than initiating it.

The linking of the closing of the U.S. frontier to the beginning of Prairie settlement is commonplace.[12] But this overlooks the fact that the disposal of the public domain via homesteading in the U.S. took place at a greater rate after 1896 than before. Between 1881 and 1890 there were 497,083 homestead entries on 69,773,000 acres of land. In the 1890's these figures dropped to 456,943 and 62,857,000 respectively. But from 1901 to 1910 homestead entries rose dramatically to 832,140 and the acreage nearly doubled to 130,647,000.[13] In addition, as Hartland notes, the expansion of Australian and Argentinian wheat production and exports in the 1880's and 1890's suggests that the world market for food was expanding rapidly enough to absorb supplies in excess of the American output.[14]

Technical breakthroughs do not appear to provide the answer either. Marquis wheat was not even commercially available in the first decade of the century. Its earlier ripening features were instrumental in allowing the extension of settlement into the more northerly areas, and would not have been a factor in the regions that received the bulk of settlement between 1897 and 1911. Advances in the milling of wheat, the development of the steel-tipped plow, barbed wire and the like came out of the earlier American boom, and were thus available to Canadians at that time. It is rather their limited diffusion to 1895, and their rapid diffusion thereafter, that need to be explained.

In sum then, while Dales did succeed in raising serious doubts about an uncritical acceptance of the role of the national policy in promoting Prairie settlement, the alternative explanation based on a series of exogenous supply and demand shifts does not fare very well either. Until the major factor or factors responsible for delaying agricultural expansion can be identified, little can be said one way or another about the necessity of the government measures.

III

One alternative explanation for the timing of the Prairie wheat boom has been proposed by the present author.[15] In this interpretation the Canadian settlement is viewed as part of the larger North American agricultural expansion. A distinction is made between sub-humid and semi-arid lands, and between land generally free from the risk of frost and that not given the wheat strains available in the nineteenth century. In the U.S. the transitional zone from sub-humid to semi-arid land is generally put at the 98th to 100th meridians. In Canada the only sub-humid, frost-free area is the Red River area of south central Manitoba. The northern Park Belt region does not have the same aridity problems as further south, in part because of lower evaporation loss, but its growing season is significantly shorter. Thus until the development of earlier ripening varieties of wheat after 1900 this northern area was beyond the feasible margin of settlement.

The reason for emphasizing the aridity distinction lies in the fact that sub-humid land could support cropping with conventional (at the time) techniques, while semi-arid land could not. In the most arid parts of the Prairies—the Palliser Triangle section of southwestern Saskatchewan and southeastern Alberta—rainfall was simply inadequate to provide a crop except under unusually favourable circumstances. In other areas the problem was the extreme variability of yields rather than the long-term average. Continuous cropping in the transitional dark brown soil zone apparently would have given a long-run average yield equal to or even above that ultimately obtained under different techniques. But the average would have included both bumper crops and years with little or no return. Assuming that settlers were averse to risk, an asset with a given expected return but low variance would have been preferred to another with the same mean yield but with a higher dispersion of annual outcomes. In other words, the variability of yields *per se* from continuous cropping semi-arid land was an unattractive feature to most potential migrants.

With these considerations the pattern of the westward spread of settlement can be readily explained. Sub-humid land would always be chosen over semi-arid. After 1870 the only sub-humid land remaining was that east of the 98th to 100th meridians in the U.S., and the limited area in Canada around the Red River. In fact, or course, the settlement in the 1870's and 1880's was largely confined to these two areas. There were encroachments on the semi-arid lands in both countries in these years, but they lasted only as long as the attendant abnormal rainfall conditions did.[16] Since there was a much greater supply of sub-humid land in the U.S. it was inevitable that the American boom after 1879 would dwarf the Canadian one, and that many Canadians would be attracted to the U.S.

As settlement approached the feasible margin in both countries, however, there was an incentive to develop methods to overcome the obstacles to cultivating semi-arid land. Thus it is no accident that the apparently independent efforts of Angus Mackay at Indian Head and H.W. Campbell in South Dakota both date from the mid 1880's. Campbell's work came to emphasize deep plowing of the soil, subsurface packing and frequent surface cultivation.[17] Mackay on the other hand championed the practice of summerfallowing. By storing moisture in the subsurface of the soil from one year to be used for the next year's crop, this technique increased the average yield in those drier areas which otherwise could not support any cropping. In the transitional areas, summerfallowing reduced the variability of yields, thus making the land more attractive to individuals averse to risk.

The result of these technical changes was to open up an entire new area for settlement. Yields were higher, or more certain, meaning that for any given expected grain prices and operating costs settlement in the Canadian Prairies was now more profitable than it had been before. In technical terms the homestead response function, linking the number of settlers opting for the Canadian Prairies to the expected profitability of farming there, had shifted upwards. As wheat prices started rising again after 1896 this land was rapidly filled in, along with the semi-arid U.S. land. This also explains the large number of U.S. free homestead entries after a date when the frontier had supposedly closed.

This interpretation is essentially a modification and refinement of the old idea that settlement of the Canadian Prairies had to wait the filling in of the U.S. lands. As such, it points to the exhaustion of U.S. sub-humid lands, the development of appropriate dry farming techniques and the rise in world wheat prices after 1896 as the key factors explaining the wheat boom. By implication then, the national policy could have had little or no impact. Promotional efforts were unlikely to attract or even retain anyone as long as better land was available in the U.S. Even the extension of railroad mileage into unsettled areas was unable to promote anything much beyond some speculative ventures before 1896. Thereafter settlement proceeded rapidly and railroad construction was largely in response to it rather than inducing it.[18]

On the other hand, under this view the government cannot either be accused of delaying settlement to 1897 and later by not opening up the entire Prairies to free homesteads, as Studness has charged.[19] He calculated that the net revenue per acre from wheat farming in Canada was higher than that in the U.S. prior to 1900, and concludes that the relative lack of free homestead land in Canada must have been the impediment. If the Canadian government had located CPR lands in more remote areas, and had encouraged more extensive railroad construction through cost subsidies, ". . . there is little reason to believe that development before the turn of the century could not have been more extensive."[20] If the present argument is to be believed, however, the government could have thrown the entire semi-arid belt open to free homestead without changing much prior to 1897. The implication of this line of reasoning must be that the entire national policy was essentially irrelevant to the actual timing.[21]

Nevertheless the interpretation is only an assertion, and the question remains as to whether there is any empirical support for it. The original paper developing the hypothesis presented a regression model linking annual free homestead entries to Winnipeg wheat prices. A lagged adjustment settlement response was incorporated, and there was an attempt to distinguish among the three sub-periods 1879-1886, 1887-1896 and 1897-1911. These results were presented as being consistent with, but definitely not in any way proving, the hypothesis. There was no apparent change in structure over the years 1879 to 1896, which is consistent with the view that this was the period of settlement of sub-humid land. There was a sharp break around 1896, however, represented by the much longer time that it took for any given change in wheat prices to attract the settlement that was ultimately to be associated with it. This was interpreted as representing the uncertainties of venturing onto semi-arid land with an as yet untried technology, and the subsequent slow learning process.

The argument also requires that settlers be shown to be averse to risk, for otherwise settlement should have been attracted earlier by the comparably high long-term average yields obtainable in the transitional zone by means of continuous cropping. This was done subsequently[22] by showing that the net impact of summerfallowing in significant areas of the Prairies was to reduce long-run average yields below those attainable by continuous cropping, but that farmers employed the technique regardless. It is interesting to note, however, that only in rare cases did they plant all of their crop on fallow. More often they did so on only a portion of the land, the rest being planted on one or two year old stubble. Further, the proportion planted on stubble tended to vary inversely with the variability of the rainfall received. In technical terms, farmers were diversifying their holdings by simultaneously putting some of the seeded acreage on fallow land with its more secure return, and the rest on stubble with its less secure yield but zero opportunity cost. It was shown that the nature of this choice, and the pattern of cross-sectional variation in it, could be predicted by a model that uses risk aversion to explain the simultaneous holding of money and interest-bearing assets. The conclusion was thus drawn that homesteaders in this period were indeed averse to risk, that the variability of returns in parts of the Prairies as well as the outright aridity in others was a real impediment to settlement with traditional techniques, and that summerfallowing provided the key to opening up this large area to cultivation.

The regression analysis in the first paper has been criticized as being an inadequate formulation of the homesteading process. Grant[23] argues that the appropriate dependent variable is the stock of free homesteads at the end of any year rather than the flow during that year. Thus his model relates the change in the cumulated sum of free homestead entries during any year to the level of grain prices in the previous period, again allowing for a lagged adjustment. The same point was made by Marr and Percy.[24] In addition they introduced a new and apparently superior series for wheat prices attributable to Harley,[25] and deflated it by the wholesale price index to make changes in the stock of free homesteads a function of real rather than nominal prices. Both papers, however, conclude that the results they derive with these alternative formulations are consistent with the dry farming hypothesis.[26]

The Marr-Percy paper made a couple of important additions to the model of Prairie settlement of particular importance to this paper. First, the miles of completed railroad were entered as an additional explanatory variable on the grounds that for any given output price the greater the extent of the railway network the larger would be the stock of agricultural land within the feasible margin. In addition, they attempted to allow for the impact of government advertising expenditures on the rate of settlement. While the ultimate number of free homesteads would depend only on grain prices and railroad mileage, it was reasoned, the speed with which homesteaders reacted to changes in these variables would be affected by the government's promotional efforts. Thus the speed of adjustment co-efficient was itself made to be a function of the annual expenditures on immigration with a one year lag.

The results they obtain are interesting. The coefficient on the railroad mileage variable is significantly larger for the period 1887-1896 than for 1879-1886. In other words, any given extension of the railroad network in the latter period was associated with a larger addition to the stock of free homesteads than in the earlier years. Since the major part of railway construction to 1886 was connected with completing the main line, while that for the next ten years was with developing a system of branch lines, this result makes intuitive sense. The period 1897 to 1911 differs from the earlier ones in one of two respects. Either the response of settlement to additions to the railway network was even greater, or the value of the intercept was greater. These separate results were obtained from two different regression equations, and since there is no logically correct specification for the relationship it is impossible to choose one over the other. Either result, however, is consistent with the dry farming hypothesis.

They obtained mixed results with the advertising variable. It was statistically significant in all three periods, yet bore a negative relationship to the stock of free homesteads from 1879 to 1896, and a small positive one thereafter. Literally interpreted, the findings for the early period imply that an increase in advertising efforts in a year led to a smaller change in free homestead entries the following year. These seemingly perverse results can perhaps be explained, as the authors note, by recognizing that the direction of causality runs as much from homestead entries to advertising expenditures. Thus the disappointing results before 1896 may have led to a redoubled effort by the authorities. If immigration expenditures are correlated over time, even entering them as an explanatory variable with a one year lag would generate the negative sign. Given this ambiguity as to the effect of these expenditures though, one wonders why the authors conclude so unequivocally that the positive relationship obtained after 1897 confirms the hypothesis.

The Marr-Percy results provide a possible avenue for those wishing to defend the efficacy of the national policy in this period. For if railroad mileage was an important determinant of the size of the homestead response, and if it could be shown that the government's railroad policy actually promoted rail lines where none would have been otherwise,[27] then the policy must have had some positive effect. In addition, if the net addition to output as a result exceeded the opportunity costs of the resources utilized to construct the railroad, then it could be concluded that the efforts were socially beneficial. Much the same argument applies to immigration expenditures, except that the net positive effect results from homesteaders cultivating the same land earlier than they otherwise would have, rather than that there was an actual permanent expansion of the total cultivated acreage. This net addition to output, compounded at an appropriate interest rate, would then have to be compared to the social costs of the advertising expenditures to judge their net impact. While none of this has been done, the point of interest here is simply that the Marr-Percy paper does at least open up the possibility that the promotional efforts did play some role.

Neither version of the stock adjustment formulation, however, is really an appropriate test of the dry farming hypothesis. The argument in the original paper was essentially that the establishment of rail connections to export points in 1879 meant a large, irrevocable shift in the area of sub-humid land available for cultivation. The experience of subsequent years involved the rate at which this intramarginal land was filled in. The same is true for the period after 1896. The end of the sub-humid land in Canada and the U.S. and the availability of suitable dry farming techniques meant another once-and-for-all shift in the extensive margin of cultivation, this time a much larger one. Again, the following period witnessed the progress by which the actual margin of cultivation was extended to meet the potentially feasible one. Price changes would affect the exact delineation of this latter frontier of course, but this effect would not necessarily be noticed in the early disequilibrium years.[28] The stock adjustment model really only becomes a valid representation of the adjustment process once an initial equilibrium is reached where the actual settlement frontier is concomitant with the feasible one. It would not seem to have much relevance to a period when only intra-marginal land was being settled.

These considerations suggest that a more realistic model of the settlement process would need to specify the determinants of both the long-run equilibrium stock of homesteads as well as the rate at which the intramarginal units were occupied. Sandford Borins has provided a preliminary and partial model along these lines.[29] He notes that an econometric model should explain both the settlement flows and levels over time and space. The dependent variable is the number of homesteads settled in each of several land districts by year as a proportion of those ultimately taken up. This ratio takes on values between 0 and 1, although he also estimates it with all values below 0.03 and 0.97 truncated. The explanatory variables are real wheat prices and real per capita GNP's in Canada, the U.S. and the U.K., which vary over time; proxies for moisture and frost danger which vary over space; and railroad mileage which varies over both.

In terms of the above discussion, Borins attempts to explain the adjustment from one equilibrium to another. The speed with which the Prairie farm land was filled up is related to the expected profitability of each subregion at any point in time. Interestingly, grain prices were never significant with the pre-dicted sign, which is consistent with the view that the process was largely a dis-equilibrium one. The relative real income variables give mixed results, with the ratio of the Canadian to British one being significantly positive while the Cana-dian to American one was often negatively correlated. In light of the certain simultaneity between agricultural expansion and Canadian GNP, however, such perverse results are perhaps not unexpected. The climatic variables turn out as expected. On a cross-sectional basis those lands with greater average moisture and longer frost-free growing periods were settled first, which is con-sistent with the dry farming hypothesis. Finally, the railroad mileage variable is highly significant, confirming the Marr-Percy results and suggesting again a need to take the factor into account when evaluating the national policy.

The most recent attempt to model the determinants of Prairie settlement, and to test a variety of hypotheses in the process, is contained in a paper by Percy and Woroby.[30] They take a totally different approach in that they examine the cross-sectional variation in the observed American migration to Canadian free homesteads. In addition, they begin with a formal, human capital model of migration rather than an ad hoc specification. The observed migration to Canada from each of the states, as a proportion of the total poten-tial flow, is related to distance, advertising expenditures by the federal govern-ment, state farm tenancy ratios,[31] the ratio of U.S. to Canadian real wages, and a dummy variable for states where dry farming techniques were commonly employed. The latter term represents an explicit attempt to test whether a previous association with dry farming increased the probability of migration to the Canadian Prairies. If it did, this could be taken to imply that acquiring these skills was an important prerequisite to successful settlement.

For their test of the dry farming hypothesis, the conclusion is that ". . . a statistically significant difference existed between dry farming and non-dry farming states in the determinants of rates of migration to the Canadian Prairies."[32] Bicha's agricultural ladder hypothesis does not receive the same support though. The paper demonstrates that there was a remarkable synchronization of free homestead entries from the U.S., U.K. and Canada over the period 1894-1913, suggesting that it is incorrect to focus on factors specific to one sending country only. Finally, and in support of earlier work by one of the authors cited above, the level of advertising expenditures was found to be a significant factor in 1909 but not in 1899.

Thus far the discussion of the relationship of railroads to the timing of prairie settlement has been limited to the mere presence of the lines themselves. But the rates charged on both incoming and outcoming goods might be expected to play some role. There has long been concern in the west over the allegedly adverse effects of freight rate levels. On the other hand, however, there is also a firmly held conviction that the Crow's Nest Pass rate reductions of 1897 were instrumental in opening up the region to settlement. The implication of this view is that earlier rate reductions would have speeded up settlement or, alternatively, that in the absence of the agreement the wheat boom would have occurred later or have been significantly circumscribed in extent.

It seems unlikely that this conclusion would receive much empirical support however. The 1897 agreement reduced rates by 3¢/cwt, or about 1.8¢/bushel. The price of #1 Northern wheat at Winnipeg in 1897 was 79¢/bushel, so the rate reductions would have amounted to a percentage increase in farm gate price of 2.3 assuming that producers bore all the transport costs. If any of the reductions were shifted forward the effect would be even less. In addition, since wheat prices rose generally after 1897, the percentage impact would have been even less subsequently. A recent study of the U.S. wheat producing states for the period 1872-1913 found that the area in crops in any year as a proportion of the eventual area in 1913 was responsive to changes in the real price of wheat, but with an elasticity below 1.0.[33] If these results are applicable to Canada, the increase in land area in any year as a result of the Crow's Nest reduction amounted to at most 1.6%. Even this has to be modified to account for the fact that the actual rates changed were below the maximum areas from 1903 to 1918 as a result of increased competition. Thus any impact they did have, slight as it was, was also restricted to the years 1899 (allowing for the two year transitional period) to 1902.

Focusing on the impact of the Crow's Nest Pass Agreement on rate levels and hence on wheat prices may seriously underestimate the impact of the agreement however. Gillian Wogin has recently introduced a new and potentially very important perspective on this debate.[34] She begins by asking why the CPR would ever have agreed to a rate reduction "in perpetuity," in exchange for a cash subsidy to build one branch line. The answer she provides is that by agreeing to regulation the CPR was effectively demonstrating to farmers that the rates they anticipated charging in the medium term future were no higher, and probably even less, than the current ones. A mere assertion of this by the company would not have been credible. Potential settlers still might have believed that the railroad would begin to exploit its monopoly position once they had made the necessary investments in a farm. By agreeing to be held to a maximum rate though, the CPR alleviated this fear.

With this uncertainty removed, the price that the homesteader would be willing to pay for land ought to increase. If the CPR felt that this appreciation in the sales value of its land exceeded any anticipated losses from freight rate limitations, it would thus have been economically rational for it to enter into this agreement. In effect, they were trading a potential future loss from constraining their ability to set freight rates for an immediate capital gain from their land holdings. Since they had good reason to believe that they would ultimately be subject to regulation anyway,[35] they were probably not giving up much. They could also be reasonably certain that the anticipated increase in settlement would generate additional traffic, allowing them to move down along a declining long-run average cost curve. The lower rates, in other words, would still be remunerative ones.

If this argument is accepted, and it has yet to be tested, it has significant implications for an evaluation of the national policy. The removal of the uncertainty surrounding future rate increases would increase the attractiveness of free homestead land as well. If the uncertainty discount were sufficiently large, its removal could have meant a significant once-and-for-all shift in the feasible margin of settlement. Thus by striking this deal with the CPR, the government would have removed a major obstacle to the settlement of the region.

The force of this argument depends on the degree to which it can be established that farmers did fear an ultimate exercise of monopoly power by the CPR, and felt there was no alternative recourse. Freight rates had been falling prior to 1897, and this is usually ascribed to increasing competition. Thus one would have to show why people were not building expectations of even greater competition into their predictions. It was mentioned above that the CPR might not have felt it was giving up much by agreeing to rate regulation since it was going to face at least the threat of it sooner or later anyway. But if the CPR could reason in this way, so could potential settlers. Alternatively, it could be argued that the CPR agreed to the limitation because it felt it had the political power to have it revoked whenever necessary. But again, the would-be immigrant had at least as good grounds for believing this as the CPR, and thus the agreement really would not have had any effect. In sum then, the hypothesis needs to be subjected to careful testing before it can be used to explain the timing of the wheat boom.

The literature on the timing of prairie settlement can be summarized very briefly then. The link between the occurrence of the wheat boom and the national policy, made often and casually in the past, seems to have been rejected, but so has the rote recitation of a series of external disturbances.

The emphasis has shifted instead to a more carefully specified series of exogenous factors, specifically the end of the U.S. frontier of sub-humid land, the development and diffusion of appropriate dry farming techniques, and the movements in relative real wages in Canada, the U.S. and the U.K. Within this view the federal government's promotional efforts played a role only insofar as they aided in the development and diffusion of dry farming technology, increased the speed by which settlers reacted to the emergent profit possibilities through advertising expenditures, and aided in the development of branch lines. In all these cases though, it still needs to be established that the national policy did not simply substitute for developments that would have occurred anyway. In addition, for the policy to be judged a success in even these modest dimensions, it must be true that the resulting additions to total output exceeded the opportunity costs of the resources used in promoting them.

IV

To this point the analysis has been conducted within the broad framework of a standard human capital model of migration. Homesteaders are viewed as beginning to come to the prairies as the expected net present value of investing in a farm, inclusive of opportunity costs, turned positive. The national policy was accordingly evaluated as to whether or to what extent it shifted either the expected gross returns or the costs to farming. The net worth of the policy, it was then suggested, would be the additions to output less the opportunity costs of the resources used in effecting the changes.

Two recent contributions on federal lands policies, however, one for Canada[36] and one for the U.S.,[37] have questioned whether even this is a sufficient evaluation of these development strategies. They argue instead that the very institutional structures of the free homestead and railway land grant systems probably induced agricultural settlement and rail line construction before it was socially profitable. In other words, far from being beneficially stimulative or even largely irrelevant, the policies actually led to a significant misallocation of scarce resources. Since this argument implies a potentially strong condemnation of policies that have generally been considered above reproach, it is worth looking at in some detail.

In this approach, the settlement of agricultural land is treated as a dynamic problem involving investment alternatives over time. The object is to determine the optimal time to clear and bring into production any potential acreage. At any moment in time a would-be investor is assumed to be able to predict an annual stream of net returns from farming the land inclusive of opportunity costs, and to capitalize these to arrive at a present value figure. Against these he has to set the costs of clearing and preparing the land, assumed to be a once-and-for-all outlay. The socially optimal point at which to prepare the land for cultivation, then, is that which maximizes the difference between the present value of the rental stream and the figure for the set up costs. In this way the homesteader captures the greatest possible economic rent from the land, and society as a whole benefits from a proper allocation of scarce resources among competing uses.

Mathematically the solution to the above problem turns out to be the requirement that clearing and cultivation commence when the annual net rental flow just equals the annual interest charges on the set up costs. Any settlement before this date is premature in the sense that the annual net revenue, though positive, is less than the opportunity costs of the funds sunk into preparing the land. In this case society would have been better off if the homesteader had delayed clearing the land and instead invested the resources in the alternate uses for which the return was higher. On the other hand, delaying settlement past this point is also wasteful since there is foregone production which can never be recouped. In this case, the returns to producing agricultural products would have exceeded those obtained from whatever alternative use the resources were put to.

These results can be depicted graphically as in Figure 2. Net annual returns $v(t)$ are shown as initially negative but rising over time, due to increasing grain prices or technological progress to name two factors. For any given interest rate r the opportunity cost of the set up costs, C, will be a constant equal to rC, and is thus shown as an horizontal line. In the diagram the socially optimal settlement date is t^*. Farming operations will commence on that date, and in each subsequent period the farmer will garner the difference between $v(t)$ and rC. It is the opportunity to appropriate this economic rent which is assumed to attract settlers to the region.

The discussion in Section III was essentially about how the national policy might have affected the date at which these curves intersected. The development and diffusion of dry farming technology, for example, would have shifted the $v(t)$ curve upwards relative to the rC one, thereby moving the optimal settlement date ahead in time. More rail lines or lower rates would have had the same effect, while the tariffs on agricultural implements would have reduced net returns and delayed the agricultural expansion. The essential point to note for purposes of distinguishing this literature from that to be discussed below is that Section III assumed, implicitly at least, that the optimal date t^* was the one actually chosen, and thus that the private investment decisions made in the period generated a social optimum as well.

It is easier to understand why the land disposition system actually employed may have led to a socially inefficient allocation of resources if an hypothetical alternative one that would have necessarily generated the optimally timed response is described. Suppose that all of the prairie land held by the government is periodically put up for auction. The price that any individual would pay for a specific acreage is the capitalized value of the annual economic rents he expects to earn from the land. As was seen above, this figure is at a maximum only if the land is cleared and cultivation commences exactly at t^*. Any other initiation date will yield a lower present value and thus a lower maximum

FIGURE 2

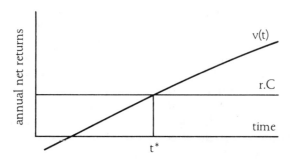

bid for the ownership of the land. If the auction is competitive the would-be owner is forced to bid up to the maximum, with the result that the government would have appropriated all of the anticipated economic rent. For the purchaser to make even a normal rate of return, then, he will have to actually produce this maximum set of future rents, which means that he will of necessity commence farming operations at t^*. If he deviates to either side of this point, he will lose out by having paid too much for the land. Thus the competitive bidding system ensures that the maximum possible price will be paid for the land, and the fact that this is the price that must be paid guarantees that the socially best starting date will be chosen.

Suppose now, however, that the land is given away rather than sold, and that eventual title depends on the investor initiating clearing and cultivation at once. In this event, the historically relevant one for about one-half of prairie land, whoever lays claim to the land will capture any of the economic rent accruing to it. Claiming the acreage and commencing agricultural operations at time t^* will still yield the maximum ultimate return. But now the competition for this takes the form not of willingness to pay but rather whoever gets there first to lay claim to the land. Thus it would pay someone to lay claim to the land, and begin clearing as required, one period before t^*. The overall economic rent he will thereby appropriate is lower than if he had waited another year, since he will not cover his opportunity costs of clearing the land in the first year of operation, but it is still positive. If this is true, however, then it pays yet another individual to claim the same piece of land and commence farming two periods before t^*. He does not earn enough to cover rC for the first two periods now, but is still ahead overall.

Extending this reasoning to its logical conclusion yields the following observation. With competition for the homestead, the date at which it actually is claimed will be pushed back to where the value of the economic rent expected from it is exactly offset by the opportunity costs incurred from too early settlement. As long as any economic rent is left, someone will lay claim to the land even earlier. The one finally obtaining it will be that individual for whom investing the sum for clearing costs C at interest rate r will give him as large a lifetime return as farming the land would have. In technical terms, all of the economic rent has been dissipated by too early settlement.[38]

This same type of argument has been applied by Southey to the case of railroad charters as well. As part of the subsidy, the government granted land to the railroad companies, but it was generally tied to a commitment to begin construction immediately. In these respects this is exactly analogous to the granting of a homestead to an individual. In the competition to gain access to these land grants, and the expected economic rent to be derived from them, the railroads would promise to begin construction earlier and earlier. In the limit, as above, the line would be initiated enough in advance of the "best" date that all the eventual economic rents ultimately absorbed would just be sufficient to offset the below opportunity costs returns of the early years. The economic rents would again be dissipated through premature investment, something that has long been suspected in the Canadian case.

While these points are intuitively appealing, it is not immediately clear how relevant they are to the Canadian case. As with the Wogin hypothesis regarding the Crow's Nest Pass Agreement discussed above, much empirical work remains to be done. Consider first the fact that a large proportion of those settling on the prairies came from the U.S. and Europe. It is unlikely that they would have come to Canada in the absence of the wheat boom. Any funds they sunk into premature homesteading—at least those the immigrants brought with them—would not have been available to the Canadian economy otherwise. Thus Canada as a whole did not incur an opportunity cost in the early years of the magnitude implied by the model. The economic rent would still have been dissipated when viewed on an international scale, but Canada would have gained by the net addition to output while the opportunity costs are borne by the sending nations.

Another consideration is that the model might never have been empirically relevant in the Canadian case. This can be illustrated as in Figure 3. The socially optimal settlement date is again t^*, while t_1 is that date at which the opportunity costs will just exhaust the eventual economic rent generated over the lifetime of the farm. Suppose now that the actual historical date is t_2 to the left of t_1. Here even giving away the land cannot induce any settlement. In historical terms, t^* might be 1910, t_1 equal to 1902 or 1903 and t_2 set somewhere in the early 1890's. If over the next few years there are one or more technical or policy changes which increase the profitability of growing wheat, the $v(t)$ curve will shift upwards. If the changes are dramatic enough t^* will move leftwards to t^{**}, equal to or even to the left of the actual date. Now it is socially optimal to cultivate the land as quickly as possible, or at least until the net additions equal the social costs of providing for rapid expansion if the latter are thought to be rising.

In this case, of course, there is no premature settlement and thus no rent

FIGURE 3

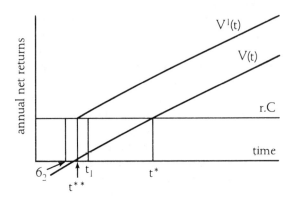

dissipation. The homestead act would be largely irrelevant to the act or timing of settlement. Its only effect would be to direct whatever economic rents there ultimately are to the settler rather than to the government[39]—since the land could have been sold—and perhaps to affect the order in which homestead and land ultimately sold were occupied.[40] Thus in the event that any of the Section III hypotheses purporting to explain a structural change in the profitability of wheat growing could be established with any conviction, the Southey conjectures about the possible impacts of the free homestead policy would be unfounded.[41]

V

This paper has attempted to survey in a reasonably non-technical manner the economic history of the last decade that has dealt with the national policy and the rate of prairie settlement. As was evident throughout, a consensus has not been established. Nevertheless many issues have been clarified, several sophisticated attempts at empirical verification have been made, and a host of interesting new insights have emerged about what remains to be done. Thus the only safe prediction to be made at this time is that the literature in the area will continue to grow. Indeed as Jack Madden has said, the production of papers on the wheat boom will probably exhaust in the end all the surplus that the event itself ever created.[42]

ACKNOWLEDGEMENTS

This paper was presented to the Annual Meeting of the Canadian Historical Association at the University of Saskatchewan, Saskatoon, June 4, 1979. I would like to thank, without implicating in any way, Doug Owram, Mike Percy and Paul Phillips for their useful comments and suggestions.

NOTES
1. V.C. Fowke "The National Policy—Old and New" *Canadian Journal of Economics and Political Science* Vol. 18, no. 3 (August, 1952) 271-286.
2. Introduction to J.H. Dales "Some Historical and Theoretical Comment on Canada's National Policies" reproduced in B. Hodgins and R. Page (eds) *Canadian History Since Confederation* (Georgetown, 1972) 141.
3. J.H. Dales "Some Historical and Theoretical Comment . . ." The article first appeared in *Queen's Quarterly* Vol. 71 (1964) 297-316.
4. This was subsequently confirmed by P.J. George "Rates of Return in Railway Investment and Implications for Government Subsidization of the CPR: Some Preliminary Results" *Canadian Journal of Economics* Vol. 1, no. 4 (November, 1968) 740-762; see also L.J. Mercer "Rates of Return and Government Subsidization of the Canadian Pacific Railway: An Alternate View" *Canadian Journal of Economics* Vol. 6, no. 3 (August, 1973) 428-437; P.J. George "Rates of Return and Government Subsidization of the Canadian Pacific Railway: Some Further Remarks" *Canadian Journal of Economics* Vol. 8, no. 4 (November, 1975) 591-600; E.F. Haites "Government Subsidization of the Canadian Pacific Railway: A Review of the Issues" (Mimeographed, 1976).
5. The role of the tariffs in promoting industrial development has not been rigorously studied yet. Dales repeats Mackintosh's assertion that Canadian manufacturing was developing well before 1879. He also notes that this sector developed more slowly than its American counterpart both before and immediately after imposition of the duties, but more rapidly during the wheat boom years after 1900. The alternative to tariffs in other words was not necessarily no industry, but rather a somewhat different and more efficient manufacturing sector. An attempt by McDougall to test for the impact of the tariffs proved inconclusive ("The Domestic Availability of Manufactured Commodity Output, Canada 1870-1915" *Canadian Journal of Economics* VI, no. 2 (May, 1973) 189-206). D.F. Barnett demonstrates that the 1859 Galt tariffs did increase manufacturing output however ("The Galt Tariff: Incidental or Effective Protection?" *Canadian Journal of Economics* IX no. 3 (August, 1976) 389-407), so a similar methodology might prove useful for the later changes as well.
6. The welfare effects of the Canadian tariffs have been studied in great depth of curve. Dales' monograph was a pioneering effort in this regard. For a comprehensive and up-to-date account of the literature that has followed the reader is referred to Economic Council of Canada *Looking Outward: A New Trade Strategy for Canada* 1975 and the various background studies to the report.
7. The classic reference here is the Rowell-Sirois Commission of course. For an attempt to evaluate some of the western claims see K.H. Norrie "The National Policy and Prairie Economic Discrimination, 1870-1930" in D.H. Akenson (ed) *Canadian Papers in Rural History* Vol. 1, 1978, 13-32. For a Maritime perspective see Barry Lesser "The Maritimes and Confederation: A View of the Regional Impact of the National Tariff Policy of 1879" (Paper presented to the Ninth

Conference on Quantitative Methods in Canadian Economic History, University of Western Ontario, March 17-18, 1978).

8. Dales "Some Historical and Theoretical Comments . . ." 302.

9. C. Knick Harley "Transportation, the World Wheat Trade and the Kuznets Cycle." Paper presented at the MSSB Conference on Exports and National Economic Growth, 1975 (Princeton, forthcoming).

10. G.M. Meier "Economic Development and the Transfer Mechanism: Canada, 1895-1913" *Canadian Journal of Economics and Political Science* Vol. 19, no. 1 (February, 1953) 3.

11. D.C. Corbett "Immigration and Economic Development" *Canadian Journal of Economics and Political Science* Vol. 17, no. 3 (August, 1951) 364.

12. See K.A.H. Buckley *Capital Formation in Canada* (Toronto, 1955) 15.

13. *Historical Statistics of the US, Colonial Times to 1957* (Washington, 1960) 237.

14. P. Hartland "Factors in Economic Growth in Canada" *Journal of Economic History* Vol. 15 (March, 1955) 13-22.

15. K.H. Norrie "The Rate of Settlement of the Canadian Prairies, 1870-1911" *Journal of Economic History* Vol. 35, no. 2 (June, 1975) 410-427.

16. Norrie "The Rate of Settlement . . ." 420-424.

17. M.W.M. Hargreaves *Dry Farming in the Northern Great Plains, 1900-1925* (Cambridge, 1957).

18. See W.A. Mackintosh *Prairie Settlement: The Geographical Setting* (Toronto, 1934) Ch. 3.

19. C.M. Studness "Economics Opportunity and the Westward Migration of Canadians During the Late Nineteenth Century" *Canadian Journal of Economics and Political Science* Vol. 30, no. 4 (November, 1964) 570-584.

20. Studness "Economic Opportunity . . ." 583, ff. 21.

21. Except perhaps insofar as the government funding of the research and its diffusion made the technique more widespread and easily available than it might otherwise have been.

22. K.H. Norrie "Dry Farming and the Economics of Risk Bearing: The Canadian Prairies, 1870-1930" *Agricultural History* Vol. 51, no. 1 (January, 1977) 134-148; "Cultivation Techniques as a Response to Risk in Early Canadian Prairie Agriculture" (University of Alberta, Department of Economics Research Paper #78-23, 1978).

23. K. Gary Grant "The rate of Settlement of the Canadian Prairies, 1870-1911: A Comment" *Journal of Economic History* Vol. 38, no. 2 (June, 1978 471-473.

24. W. Marr and M. Percy "The Government and the Rate of Prairie Settlement" *Canadian Journal of Economics* Vol. 11, no. 4 (November, 1978) 757-767.

25. Harley "Transportation, the World Wheat Trade . . ."

26. For a comment on Grants' conclusion in this respect see K.H. Norrie "The Rate of Settlement of the Canadian Prairies, 1870-1911: A Reply" *Journal of Economic History* Vol. 38, no. 2 (June, 1978) 474-475.

27. Alternatively they might only have speeded up their construction. In this event they would need to be evaluated as to their net contribution in the same manner as the promotional efforts.

28. Thus one would not necessarily get statistically significant coefficients for a price elasticity if the equation is only estimated over the transitional period. Marr and

Percy, for example, do not find any of these estimates significant in the regressions they report.

29. S.F. Borins "An Econometric Model of Western Canadian Settlement, 1882-1918" (Mimeographed, 1975).

30. M. Percy and T. Woroby "The Determinants of American Migration By State to the Canadian Prairies: 1899 and 1909" (Mimeographed, 1978).

31. To test the so-called agricultural ladder hypothesis advanced by K. Bicha "The Plains Farmer and the Prairie Provinces Frontier 1897-1914" *Proceedings of the American Philosophical Society* Vol. 109, 1965, 398-440.

32. Percy and Woroby "The Determinants . . ." 20.

33. C. Knick Harley "Western Settlement and the Price of Wheat 1872-1913" *Journal of Economic History* Vol. 38, no. 4 (December, 1978) 865-878.

34. This is work connected with her Ph. D. thesis for Carleton Univeristy. I am grateful to Ms. Wogin for taking the time to discuss her work with me.

35. The original charter had specified that the CPR would be exempt from rate regulation only until profits exceeded 10% on investment.

36. C. Southey "The Staples Thesis, Common Property, and Homesteading" *Canadian Journal of Economics* Vol. 11, no. 3 (August, 1978) 547-559.

37. R.T. Dennen "Some Efficiency Effects of Nineteenth Century Federal Land Policy: A Dynamic Analysis" *Agricultural History* Vol. 51, no. 4 (October, 1977) 718-736.

38. Note that the settler comes out earning exactly a normal return in either case. In the first instance the economic rent is fully appropriated by the government while in the second it just covers the loss due to failure to cover opportunity costs in periods. He could conceivably be better off in the former case though if the government used this revenue to increase the supply of public goods or to reduce taxes.

39. There could be some additional resource waste due to individuals queuing to earn the chance to appropriate these rents. See Dennen "Some Efficiency Effects . . ." 729-730.

40. Southey has suggested that a test of his model would be to see whether farming began first on homestead land, then on railway land and finally on free land ("The Staples Thesis . . ." 557, 8ff). But given that the settlers could appropriate the economic rent in the first case, while the land companies would through the purchase price in the others, this would be the predicted order here as well. Thus establishing that this in fact occurred would not necessarily imply that his thesis was valid.

41. It still might be valid as regards the construction of the CPR though. As the literature cited in footnote 4 shows, the company was earning a rate of return below its opportunity costs to at least 1895. This is a necessary condition for the explanation to hold. But given that no other companies were seriously considered by the Macdonald government when it came to issuing the charter in 1880, it is more reasonable to conclude that the government wanted the railroad built prematurely if necessary for political reasons, and that it subsidized the company accordingly. The later railway projects come largely after 1896, so if the reasons given for dismissing the thesis for free homesteads applies it must to these projects as well.

42. J.J. Madden "Quantitative Economic History—Ten Years On" (Mimeographed, 1975).

T.D. REGEHR

14 Western Canada and the Burden of National Transportation Policies

Transportation and transportation costs are of vital concern in a country as large as Canada. They are of particular importance to the more isolated areas such as the western interior of the continent. These areas generally pay more for transportation, simply because of the distances involved. In western Canada, however, transportation costs are further increased by a discriminatory rate structure which has been built into all Canadian transcontinental transportation policies.

No single issue has contributed more to western Canadian discontent within Confederation than the so-called national transportation policies. Since 1883, when the first freight-rate schedule of the Canadian Pacific Railway was published, there has been deliberate and admitted freight-rate discrimination against the West. This discrimination was ameliorated, but not removed, when western governments and politicians resorted to unilateral action in defiance of national policies and secured freight rate reductions. Such unilateral action was loudly denounced as very dangerous to Confederation, to national unity, and to national policies. In fact it simply proved that the less populous and therefore politically less powerful regions cannot look to national policies to meet their requirements unless, in times of particular stress, they have the power, the means, and the will, to assert their demands and thus forcibly restructure unacceptable aspects of national policies.

"FAIR DISCRIMINATION" AGAINST THE WEST

At the Western Economic Opportunities Conference held in Calgary, in July 1973, the background paper prepared by the federal government expressed sympathy for western problems and offered a few minor short-term concessions. The writers of the federal background paper insisted, however, that nothing must be done to shift any portion of the western freight rate burden to other parts of the country. The federal writers argued that "the railways have to achieve a balance between their costs and revenues, taking into account the total spread of their operations and differing degrees of competition."[1]

The logic of the federal statement seems unassailable; yet it presents the core of the western transportation and freight-rate problem. The difficulty arises because of differing degrees of competition in the various regions of Canada. In one region the railways must meet very vigorous competition, both from rival American railroads and from water transport on the great Lakes and St. Lawrence River system. In another region the railways have a virtual monopoly. National policies specifically permit and, indeed, require the railways to charge whatever the traffic of a particular region can be made to pay, subject only to fixed maximums set by the Board of Transportation Commissioners which are much higher in non-competitive than in competitive areas.[2] The railways set low rates, or reduce their rates, wherever competition from other railways or from other forms of transport compel them to do so, even if those reduced rates lead to operations losses in the affected region. In areas where no effective competition exists the railways set their rates at much higher levels. If the railways are forced to operate uneconomical sections, or if there are operational losses in highly competitive areas, they recoup their losses by charging higher rates in non-competitive areas. The federal regulatory agencies have repeatedly described the resulting rate differentials between the competitive St. Lawrence region and the non-competitive prairie region as discriminatory, but the agencies have also consistently ruled that these differentials constitute "fair discrimination."[3]

The policy of "fair discrimination" is rooted in the National Policy first enunciated in 1878 and, more specifically, in the 1881 contract signed by the Canadian Pacific Railway syndicate on the one hand, and the federal government on the other. Both parties to that agreement were well aware of the magnitude of the task in hand. Building a transcontinental railway along an all-Canadian route was very difficult and very expensive. Massive government subsidies were provided to assist in the construction. Once built, however, the new railway faced additional and very serious operational problems. Fully one-half of the new line passed through areas where little or no local traffic could be expected. There would certainly be operational deficits on such mileage, the longest "unproductive" stretches being north of Lake Superior and through the British Columbia interior.

Much of the remaining mileage served the St. Lawrence region where very stiff competition from rival railways and from water transport was certain. Water transport in particular posed problems, since most of the canals and harbour facilities throughout the St. Lawrence and Great Lakes shipping system had been built as public undertakings and were made available to shippers free of charge or upon payment of only nominal tolls. The railways had to maintain their own rights of way and station facilities, while holding at least their summer rates at the low competitive levels set by water carriers. It was therefore very unlikely that the Canadian Pacific Railway would earn sufficient operational surpluses in Ontario and Quebec to offset the anticipated deficits north of Lake Superior and in British Columbia.

The prairie region was still largely unsettled and was not expected to generate large volumes of traffic for many years. It nevertheless offered the Canadian Pacific Railway the prospect of sufficient surpluses to permit a balancing of its national accounts. Water transport at reasonable cost was not a factor on the prairies and, from the beginning, the syndicate insisted that all American railway competition be kept out of the region.[4] Without any competition to contend with, the syndicate intended to set its western rates at a sufficiently high level to offset the anticipated losses north of Lake Superior. George Stephen, the first president of the Canadian Pacific Railway, was convinced that his company would not be viable unless it held a western monopoly which would force all traffic to and from the prairies onto its lines at high rates. Without a monopoly west of Winnipeg he believed "the whole line from Winnipeg to Ottawa would be rendered all but useless, and the large sums of money spent, and to be spent thereon, might as well have been thrown in the lake."[5] He believed that "no sane man would give one dollar for the whole line east of Winnipeg," if the West enjoyed the same competitive conditions as prevailed in the East. The loss of prairie traffic to American roads, or western rate reductions sufficient to hold that traffic by competitive means, would, in George Stephen's opinion, "in a very short time make it impossible to operate the C.P.R. east of Winnipeg."[6]

The only alternative to discriminatory western rates in 1881 was a federal operating subsidy for the Lake Superior and British Columbia sections. Both of Canada's major political parties, however, were fiercely determined that no public funds be used to subsidize C.P.R. operations.[7] Both considered construction subsidies entirely proper, but never seriously considered lightening the western rate burden by offering the company operational subsidies. The western monopoly and the freight-rate discrimination it facilitated were therefore approved, and the basis of a troublesome national transportation policy was laid. Rates on traffic east of Thunder Bay were set to meet American railway and heavily subsidized Great Lakes and St. Lawrence water transport competition. Rates west of Thunder Bay, on the other hand, were protected by monopoly and set in a manner which would allow the railway to balance its total costs and revenues. Competition was the criterion in the East, while the railway's total needs were the determining factor in monopoly-protected western rate-making.[8]

The results were predictable. The first western rate schedule published by the C.P.R. appeared in 1883. It set a rate for wheat which was almost three times that for comparable distances in competitive eastern areas. The rate was 21.6 cents per bushel from Winnipeg to Thunder Bay. Wheat shipped from Moose Jaw to Thunder Bay was carried at 30.6 cents per bushel.[9] The rate from Thunder Bay to the seaboard, covering a distance about twice that from Winnipeg to Thunder Bay but subject to water competition, was 15 cents per bushel. The summer rate for grain on the Grand Trunk Railway and later on the C.P.R. between Toronto and Montreal, a distance nearly as great as that from Winnipeg to Thunder Bay, was well below 10 cents per bushel.

The price of wheat at Thunder Bay in the 1880s was approximately 65 cents per bushel. The freight rates therefore threatened to consume half of the farmer's gross income from his grain crop and placed an intolerable burden on the struggling pioneer homesteaders. When, as was the case in 1883, the wheat crop suffered serious frost damage, there was little, if anything, left after the farmer paid the freight charges and his immediate operating costs.[10]

The C.P.R. certainly did not earn exorbitant profits in the early years. High operating costs and sparse traffic on the long mileage north of Lake Superior, and difficult operating conditions in the Rockies, took care of any surpluses generated by traffic going to or coming from the prairies.[11] The defenders of the National Policy did not think this an unfair arrangement. After all, the entire line from Ottawa west had been built to open up and develop the West. There was therefore no reason why western traffic should not meet the operating costs of the entire line. This argument failed to acknowledge that, as far as the West was concerned, a cheap and direct line running south of Lake Superior might have carried their products to export markets at much lower rates. The "national" Lake Superior section was not built merely as a service to the West. It was accepted as the instrument which would tie the western traffic to the Canadian metropolitan centres in the St. Lawrence lowlands. Far from being simply a generous and magnanimous gesture to the West, the Lake Superior line was also an instrument of Canadian nationalism and eastern Canadian economic imperialism.[12] It was built because of fears that western traffic shipped along a railway south of Lake Superior would not find its way to Toronto and Montreal, but would pass instead through New York on its way to world markets. Westerners have never understood why they and they alone should be charged with the operating deficits on that "national" mileage.

Canadian railway officials and the federal regulatory agencies sometimes allude to the fact that American transportation policies also permit discriminatory rates against non-competitive regions.[13] Farmers in the American Midwest, of course, find it as difficult as their Canadian counterparts to understand and accept the concept of "fair discrimination," and they have successfully demanded huge government grants and subsidies to build a highway system on which trucks can offer effective competition, thus bringing their western rates down. The substantially greater transcontinental distances in Canada make that solution less practical and certainly much more expensive.

Sometimes the railways and federal agencies also maintain that operating costs on the Canadian prairies are higher than in eastern Canada.[14] A harsher climate, the seasonal nature of much of the agricultural traffic, and the fact that the bulky grain trade is all one way (thus necessitating extensive deadheading of empty grain cars), all add to western operating costs. Higher rates in the West, it is alleged, are therefore justified, although some very similar operating disadvantages for many eastern commodities are seldom mentioned.

It is important to point out that the railways do not calculate, or at least refuse to reveal, regional operating costs. Such costs, in any case, have never been the basis for regional rate-making. Western Canadians have long, but entirely unsuccessfully, demanded effective regional cost accounting and cost disclosures by the railways, and the implementation of regional rates commensurate with regional costs. The railways and the federal agencies have never agreed to do this. They believe "fair discrimination" is absolutely essential if they are to "balance their costs and revenues, taking into account the total spread of their operations and differing degrees of competition."[15]

The national policy of permitting "fair discrimination" against non-competitive regions created enormous economic, political, and constitutional problems in Western Canada. In the 1880s Premier John Norquay of Manitoba and many of his supporters believed the problem of high freight rates would be resolved if and when the prairie region was opened up to American railroad competition. Norquay was not particularly concerned about the problems of the C.P.R. elsewhere, and he chartered local railway companies which were expected to make connections at the international boundary with American railroads.

The province of Manitoba apparently had the power to charter local railway lines, including those running to the border, but the federal government decided to disallow such provincial charters on grounds that they were not in the interests of the Dominion. This disallowance policy, exercised repeatedly as Manitoba continued to pass railway charters which Ottawa found objectionable, transformed the economic problem into a political and constitutional dispute. The interests and policies of one region of the country had come into sharp conflict with a basic aspect of national policy, and Sir Charles Tupper, the federal minister of railways, summed up the situation when he said in the House of Commons, "Are the interests of Manitoba and the North-west to be sacrificed to the policy of Canada? I say, if it is necessary—yes."[16]

An effective federal system should provide the means whereby a province or region whose interests are blatantly flouted can have effective political and constitutional recourse. In the years after 1883 Premier Norquay tried all the political and constitutional procedures available to him in his efforts to resolve the railway problem. He travelled repeatedly to Ottawa to explain the problem, to present petitions, and to seek assistance. He certainly was willing to consider compromises, provided Manitoba's basic transportation needs were met. In Ottawa he did receive a number of minor concessions, but Sir John A. Macdonald was determined that the basic provisions of his railway policy remain unchanged. Letters, petitions, and warnings from western members of Parliament, from western boards of trade, from the press, and from local party officials and workers all failed to move the prime minister. When warned that violence and an agitation for Manitoba's secession from Confederation were imminent, he attributed the difficulty to discontented Liberals and broken land speculators,[17] and inquired of the Colonial Office if imperial troops would be available if the national policies led to armed confrontations between federal authorities and western farmers.[18]

By 1887 the magnitude of the problem had become clear. A national policy entirely unacceptable to one region of the country had been implemented, and all proper political and constitutional devices open to the aggrieved region had been exhausted. W.B. Scarth, a Conservative member of Parliament representing a Manitoba constituency, clearly recognized the problem. He wrote to the prime minister: "I remember my dear Sir John that when I was a resident of Ontario you used sometimes to say when Manitoba was kicking that it only had five votes. Five votes are not many now, but if your majority were only fifteen instead of what it is five votes would count."[19] The five Manitoba votes, of course, counted for very much less with Macdonald than did the ninety-two from Ontario and the sixty-five from Quebec, and most of the Ontario and Quebec members were pleased with the national transportation policy. The federal Liberals, despite considerable huffing and puffing against the C.P.R. monopoly, were as adamant as the Conservatives in opposing government operating subsidies or eastern rate increases. Yet, in order to remain viable in the early years, the Canadian Pacific either had to retain its high western rates or had to obtain government subsidies to operate the Lake Superior and British Columbia sections. Both national parties were in basic agreement regarding the choice between those two alternatives.

Macdonald was so sure of eastern support for his transportation policy that he even authorized Scarth to promise his constituents in the 1887 election that he, Scarth, would introduce in the House of Commons a motion of want of confidence in his own party's transportation policy. Scarth thought this was the only way to save his Conservative seat in Manitoba.[20] The transportation policy certainly would not have been endangered, even if Scarth had actually introduced his promised motion. Within the Canadian federal structure a region with only 5 votes out of 242 had virtually no chance of altering fixed national policies, no matter how determined the region's representative might be.

MANITOBA'S UNILATERAL ACTION TO REMOVE "FAIR DISCRIMINATION"

The railway problems of Western Canada were not ameliorated until the provincial government of Manitoba resorted to unilateral action, the threat of violence, and open defiance of the federal government and its policies. Norquay's moderate policies of negotiations, conferences, petitions, and accommodation led only to his removal from office. In 1888 he was replaced by Thomas Greenway, a Liberal who promised to build a railway from Winnipeg to Emerson and bring in American competition, even if such a policy led to armed confrontations between federal and provincial authorities. After a final and seemingly fruitless visit to Ottawa, Greenway went to Chicago and St. Paul to enlist American financial and political support for his program.[21] There were even rumours that the premier was also looking for American military support.

Greenway's show of determination accomplished within a matter of weeks what all the politics of federalism during the previous seven years had failed to accomplish. The federal government abandoned its policy of disallowance, bought out the C.P.R. monopoly, and granted that company sufficient financial assistance to allow it to withstand American competition.[22] The provincial railway to Emerson was immediately built and a running rights agreement with the Northern Pacific Railroad negotiated.

One of the conditions under which the American Company entered Canada on the provincially built railway was that it would set its initial rates at 85 per cent of the then prevailing C.P.R. rates. The C.P.R. immediately responded with a 15 per cent rate reduction of its own. Competition had arrived in Western Canada. Premier Greenway and his cohorts were convinced that the initial 15 per cent reduction would mark only the beginning of a competitive battle between the C.P.R. and the Northern Pacific Railroad which would drive western rates down to the levels prevalent in the East. In this the Manitobans were sorely disappointed. The truth of the matter was that the American railways, like their Canadian counterparts, were far more interested in maximizing profits than in competing with one another just for the sake of competition. Both roads operated under rate structures which were higher in the West where the railways enjoyed a natural monopoly than in the East where they had to face competition from water transport. Neither was eager to see drastic reductions in western rates, and the C.P.R. and the Northern Pacific soon reached an informal agreement under which the Northern Pacific agreed to refrain from competitive raids and rate-cutting in Manitoba. In return the C.P.R. promised to discontinue its attempt to attract American traffic at Puget Sound to its lines. For the Northern Pacific the new Manitoba connection was simply a device to force the C.P.R. to "play fair" in Washington.[23] No really effective competition developed in Manitoba.

The crucial factor leading to lower rates in Central and Eastern Canada was competition from water transport, not competition from rival American roads. Lack of similar competition in Western Canada blunted and nearly nullified Manitoba's first assault on the national transportation policies. Further significant western rate reductions were only achieved in 1897 and 1901 when once again westerners threatened open defiance of national policies in their determination to create a competitive transportation system in the West. Only then was the burden of national transportation policies significantly reduced and the ratio between eastern and western rates substantially altered.

In 1897 the Canadian Pacific Railway, which had always been determined to keep Western Canada as its economic preserve, found itself vulnerable when rich mineral deposits were discovered in the Kootenay District of southeastern British Columbia. The C.P.R. mainline through Rogers' Pass was too far away to serve this region adequately, and American railways began to move in. Officials of the C.P.R. sought federal assistance to build their own line from Lethbridge, Alberta, to Nelson, British Columbia, via the Crow's Nest Pass. The federal government knew that such assistance would be opposed by many eastern politicians who could foresee no immediate benefit for their region. It would also be very unpopular in Western Canada unless some major concessions were offered on the most serious western transportation grievances. Federal assistance for a new C.P.R. line would obviously enhance the practical monopoly that company still enjoyed in Western Canada.[24] There were, moreover, other railway contractors and promoters eager and willing to take on the Crow's Nest Pass project. Foremost among these were William Mackenzie and Donald Mann, both former C.P.R. contractors who, in 1896, became promoters of a new western Canadian and later transcontinental Canadian Northern Railway system. They were very eager to secure the federal contract to build the Crow's Nest Pass Railway in 1897.

It is not clear what concessions Mackenzie and Mann offered in 1897. They did negotiate with the federal government and with the provincial governments of British Columbia and Manitoba, offering to build across southern British Columbia all the way to Vancouver if offered sufficient aid. They presented their railway as the only one which might eventually compete effectively with the C.P.R. American competition had failed, but a new hope was rising.

Premier Turner of British Columbia found the Mackenzie and Mann proposals sufficiently attractive to vote them substantial subsidies. These, however, were not sufficient to get the railway across southern British Columbia built and connected with the Manitoba mileage controlled by Mackenzie and Mann. The two promoters had to go to Ottawa to seek federal aid for their project. The promise of independent action in British Columbia certainly complicated the negotiations in Ottawa. The federal government was inclined to deal with the C.P.R., but for a time President

Van Horne and Vice-President Shaughnessy were not willing to match the concessions offered by Mackenzie and Mann. At one point the C.P.R. men were prepared to see the entire Crow's Nest Pass contract go to Mackenzie and Mann.[25]

Mackenzie and Mann, despite their ambitious and visionary proposals, were weak contenders in 1897. They controlled many railway charters, but only 125 miles of track in actual operation, and that was 800 miles from the proposed Crow's Nest Pass line. They depended on the C.P.R. and the Northern Pacific Railroad for all rail connections to points outside Manitoba, and any rate concessions they could make in 1897 depended on the kind of rate divisions they could get from the transcontinentals on through traffic. The federal government therefore continued its negotiations with the C.P.R.[26]

The offer made by Mackenzie and Mann in 1897 did not get them the Crow's Nest Pass contract, but it significantly increased the likelihood of provincial action in opposition to the federal program unless the federal plan included significant rate reductions. The C.P.R. was very reluctant to make such reductions, but in the end President Van Horne decided his company should make sufficient concessions to obtain the Crow's Nest Pass contract. The mere presence of potential competitors in 1897 paid handsome dividends for western shippers.

The terms of the Crow's Nest Pass contract provided a federal subsidy of $11,000 per mile for the proposed 330-mile line. This was expected to cover approximately two-thirds of the estimated construction costs. In return for this subsidy the C.P.R. agreed to reduce its western freight rates on a wide range of products by approximately 20 per cent. The crucial rate on grain was reduced from 17 cents to 14 cents per hundredweight from Winnipeg to Thunder Bay. These reductions were only obtained because western politicians were determined to resist and oppose any federal subsidies for the C.P.R. unless these were coupled with rate reductions, and because rival promoters were available and made plausible the threat of independent provincial action.

The Crow's Nest Pass rates did not bring western rates down to the same levels as prevailed in Central Canada, and many western farmers and the provincial government of Manitoba continued to demand further reductions. Increases in the volume of western traffic carried by the C.P.R. made it possible for the company to absorb the 1897 rate reductions without serious difficulty, but neither the C.P.R. nor the federal government thought any further reductions could be justified. A new threat, or perhaps the reality of railway competition, was needed before rates would be further reduced.

In 1901 Mackenzie and Mann offered Manitobans an opportunity to provide the necessary competitive pressure which would result in further reductions of western freight rates. Their failure to obtain the Crow's Nest Pass contract had slowed and altered but not halted the railway schemes of

Mackenzie and Mann. By 1901 they were busily at work extending their small Manitoba system eastward to Port Arthur and westward towards Prince Alberta and Edmonton. Operationally their railway differed markedly from the C.P.R. The Canadian Northern at that time was simply a prairie system, and Mackenzie and Mann were quite willing to set their rates, according to operating and capital costs actually incurred. They did not have to take into account any operating deficits north of Lake Superior, although they could send all the traffic originating on or destined for their prairie lines east over the lines of the established railroads at rates determined by Great Lakes water transport. Mackenzie and Mann could afford to make further rate reductions and still operate at a profit. In 1901 they agreed to do so in return for substantial government assistance.[27]

The construction of the line from Winnipeg to Port Arthur was well advanced in 1901, but it created serious financing problems for Mackenzie and Mann. At the same time, the Northern Pacific Railroad, which had been brought into Manitoba with such enthusiasm in 1888, indicated that it intended to sell its Manitoba lines, preferably to the C.P.R. There was consequently great fear that the C.P.R. might take over both the tired Northern Pacific and the financially embarrassed Canadian Northern Railway, thus re-establishing a complete monopoly in Western Canada.

Mackenzie and Mann were convinced that their system could and would become a very effective competitor of the C.P.R., if it could obtain the funds to complete the line to Port Arthur, and if it could acquire the Northern Pacific mileage. Premier Roblin of Manitoba did not like the prospect of a re-established C.P.R. monopoly and was willing to help the Canadian Northern. He insisted, however, that the anticipated competitive benefits promised by Mackenzie and Mann be written into the agreement he would sign with them. The result was an agreement whereby the Manitoba government guaranteed Canadian Northern construction bonds for the entire mileage from Winnipeg to Port Arthur. The Manitoba government also leased the Northern Pacific lines and then reassigned the lease to the Canadian Northern. In return, the Canadian Northern agreed to further substantial western freight-rate reductions. The rate for grain, which was considered of the greatest importance, was to be cut from 14 cents to 10 cents per hundredweight, Winnipeg to Port Arthur.[28]

On the strength of the assistance thus granted, the Canadian Northern Railway became a regional railway of Western Canada which set its freight rates as only a regional railway could. The C.P.R., of course, had to lower its western rates to remain competitive. At first only rates at C.P.R. points which also had Canadian Northern connections were reduced, but eventually the reductions were applied across Manitoba. Similar but somewhat smaller reductions were granted on traffic in the Northwest Territories. Only increased traffic volumes and a very cautious developmental policy enabled the C.P.R. to continue effective competition with its new regional rival, which quickly built numerous developmental prairie lines that were initially not very profitable.

The action of the Manitoba government in dealing directly with a regional railway and unilaterally reducing regional rates without regard to national considerations was severely criticized by a number of Ontario and Quebec politicians. There was great concern that the stability of the national transportation policies would be upset. The federal politicians feared that Manitoba was disregarding the interests of other regions in the attempt to obtain lower prairie freight rates. Henri Bourassa expressed the apprehensions of many when he complained that the 1901 agreement "put in the hands of a provincial government a power that may be used at any time against the general interests of Canada."[29] Who would pay the operational deficits on the Lake Superior section if the Manitoba government, working in cooperation with a regional railway system, created a genuinely competitive rail system on the prairies?

No federal government was willing to initiate the kind of railway policies pursued by the Manitoba government in 1901. Yet, thanks to the determined action of the provincial government, western rates were significantly reduced and a new balance established between central, and western rates. It seems clear that the relief from the burdens imposed on Western Canada by the national transportation policies would not have come in 1901 without the unilateral action taken by Manitoba.

Premier Roblin was convinced that effective railway competition had become a reality in 1901. In his capacity as railways commissioner he proudly announced that his government resolved, for all time to come, Manitoba's railway freight-rates problem. Unfortunately Roblin was quite mistaken. The western freight rates had certainly been reduced. Manitoba had established regional railway competition, but that competition proved of short duration, and western rates were substantially increased again.

Less than two years after Manitoba signed its agreement with the Canadian Northern Railway, the federal government introduced railway policies which eventually destroyed the advantages gained by Manitoba. In 1903 the federal government introduced legislation which provided enormous subsidies for the construction of a new transcontinental system—the National Transcontinental—Grand Trunk Pacific railways which were to link up with the eastern Grand Trunk Railway. This action by the federal government threatened to cut off many of the Canadian Northern Railway's connections in the East with the Grand Trunk. Consequently the Canadian Northern managers felt that under the circumstances they had no alternative but to expand their regional railway into a transcontinental system. They sought federal aid and by 1911 two new lines were being built across the bush and rock of the Canadian Shield north of Lake Superior. The long-term operational prospects of the two new lines north of Lake Superior were certainly no better than those of the C.P.R. had been in 1881. With the construction of their own line north of Lake Superior, Mackenzie and Mann expanded their profitable regional railway into an unprofitable transcontinental service. The rates charged by the Canadian Northern in Western Canada were soon affected.

The financing of the new transcontinental mileage, coupled with wartime inflation and financial stringencies, ruined both the Canadian Northern Railway and the National Transcontinental—Grand Trunk Pacific systems.[30] The two still incomplete transcontinentals were taken over by the federal government, and in 1918 the federal Board of Railway Commissioners authorized the railways to raise their western rates above the levels set in the 1901 Manitoba agreement. The federal board ruled that that agreement, although in force for many years, was beyond the constitutional power of a province to enact. The board believed the regulation of all interprovincial traffic was a federal responsibility.[31] This ruling was immediately appealed, but ultimately upheld in the courts, and the rates set by the 1901 agreement were a thing of the past, although the more favourable ratio between central and western rates established by the 1901 agreement was maintained since both central and western rates rose by approximately the same percentage. In Western Canada the increases up to the levels set by the Crow's Nest Pass Agreement were authorized. The Board of Railway Commissioners held that it did not have power to authorize increases beyond that level since the Crow's Nest Pass Agreement was incorporated in federal rather than provincial legislation.

Two years later inflation, and particularly a labour agitation for wage parity between Canadian and American railway workers, induced the federal government to authorize further rate increases. This time, under authority of the War Measures Act, the provisions of the Crow's Nest Pass Agreement were set aside, although again central and western rates were raised by approximately the same percentage.

The setting aside of the Manitoba agreement and the Crow's Nest Pass rates created very much dissatisfaction in Western Canada. It was one of the most important factors in the political success of the Progressive party in the federal election of 1921. The restoration of the Crow's Nest Pass rates and significant tariff reductions were the two issues on which the frequently divided Progressives all agreed. The government that had set aside the Manitoba and Crow's Nest Pass rates was very decisively defeated in 1921, and Canada's first minority government was elected to office.

In this situation, and with the conciliatory William Lyon Mackenzie King as prime minister, the Progressives were able to obtain a partial restoration of the old rates. After some irritating delays, the Crow's Nest Pass rates for unprocessed cereal grains were restored, and they have remained in effect ever since. This restoration of the Crow's Nest Pass rates for cereal grains met the most important demands of western export-oriented agricultural producers. They wanted low rates to send their staple commodities to world markets, and the compromise of a partial restoration of the Crow's Nest Pass rates was accepted, if not cheered, in Western Canada.[32]

In 1923, after forty years of agitation and determined initiatives by the province of Manitoba, the freight-rate problems of western grain farmers had been significantly improved, but they had not been solved. The ratio between central and western rates had been altered in 1888, 1897, and 1901, and the altered ratios, if not the absolute rates, have remained fairly constant since 1923. Further, on those commodities of greatest importance to western grain farmers, the maximum rates set under the Crow's Nest Pass Agreement were re-established in 1923 and have not been altered since then. Both the altered ratios and the fixed rates on unprocessed grains are at least in part attributable to the direct action taken by the Manitoba government.

INDUSTRIALIZATION AND NEW TRANSPORTATION POLICIES

Western Canada and the economic aspirations of Western Canadians have changed significantly since 1923. The freight-rate arrangements which were tolerated in 1923 are no longer acceptable. Three main reasons can be given for the renewed demands in Western Canada for an end to freight rates which discriminate against Western Canada on everything except unprocessed grain products. The first of these reasons is the effect of the so-called horizontal rate increases of the last thirty years; the second is the diversification and increased industrialization of the Western Canadian economy; and the third is the technological obsolescence of much of Western Canada's transportation and grain-handling system.

Since 1923 costs and prices of all goods and services have increased very substantially; particularly after 1945. The normal response to increased railway costs has been an application for rate increases. All the major rate increases since 1945, subject only to some comparatively minor and technical exceptions and to the provisions of the Crow's Nest Pass Agreement, have respected the ratio between central and western rates established by the Manitoba government in 1901. The railways have been authorized to increase their rates from time to time, but always by fixed percentages which were applied more or less equally to eastern, central, and western rates. Such fixed percentage increases, across the board, are referred to as horizontal increases.

Horizontal increases may sound fair, but they have been frequently denounced in Western Canada. They maintain and often exacerbate the discrimination built into the national rate structures. The western problem is best illustrated by a simple example. Let us assume a 30-per-cent increase is applied against a commodity rate which stood at 10 cents per hundredweight in Central Canada and at 20 cents per hundredweight in the West. Applying a 30-per-cent increase to both will make the new rates 13 and 26 cents per hundredweight respectively. The percentage increase is the same, but the net difference between the rates has increased from 10 to 13 cents. Firms and industries which were competitive in the less-favoured region when their rate was only 10 cents per hundredweight higher than that of their central rivals, might be unable to compete when that difference rises to 13 cents per hundredweight. As a result, each horizontal rate increase makes it more difficult for western businesses to compete with their more central counterparts.[33]

The Crow's Nest Pass rates have been consistently exempted from successive horizontal rate increases and have in fact become the best transportation bargain on the continent. It is this fact which makes the rate structure tolerable to many western grain farmers. Western Canada, however, is no longer the exclusive domain of the grain farmer. As technology and mechanization reduce the numbers of people needed to tend to the grain fields, there are more and more demands that western raw materials be processed in Western Canada, and that more new primary and secondary industries locate in the region. Unfortunately the discriminatory rate structure is a major obstacle to such economic diversification.

It is almost impossible for many western businesses and industries to compete with eastern rivals if the freight rates for everything they bring into the region and everything they send out are significantly higher than the comparable rates paid by their competitors. A few examples, shown in Table 1, illustrate the degree of discrimination between competitive and non-competitive regions still prevalent in our national railway rates structures, and clearly indicate the magnitude of the problem. In the examples given, Vancouver is considered a "competitive" point because of water transport available there. The prairie centers are not considered "competitive" points.[34]

Officially the Vancouver rates are justified as so-called long-haul rates, while the prairie rates are classed as short-haul rates. It has been demonstrated repeatedly, however, that the so-called long-haul rates have little or nothing to do with the distance the goods are hauled, and a good deal to do with the degree and extent of transportation competition at particular points. Vancouver long-haul rates, for example, were very significantly reduced when the Panama Canal was opened, thus making cities on the Pacific Coast truly competitive. The basic concept underlying all rate-making in Canada is competition, or the lack of it. Such rate-making is a very serious obstacle to any economic diversification or industrialization in regions which lack effective transportation competition and therefore suffer from high and discriminatory freight rates.

Even the discrimination inherent in the Crow's Nest Pass rates and generally considered very favourable to the West has become an obstacle to western economic diversification and development. The Crow's Nest rates apply only to unprocessed grain, while the "fair discrimination" rates are applied to processed or milled products. Thus grain is carried from Saskatoon

TABLE 1   Examples of Freight Rates

From	To	Commodity	Rate/cwt.
Toronto	Vancouver	Canned goods	212
Morden	Vancouver	Canned goods	190
Toronto	Vancouver	Iron and steel products	168
Toronto	Saskatoon	Iron and steel products	247
Hamilton	Vancouver	Skelp	135
Hamilton	Edmonton	Skelp	211
Hamilton	Calgary	Structural steel	246
Hamilton	Vancouver	Structural steel	164

to Moncton at 92 cents per hundredweight, but millfeed at 162 cents.[35] It was this rate structure which made it cheaper for the Quaker Oats Company to close down it large rolling mills and elevators in Saskatoon, next door to the fields where the oats are grown, and to expand and modernize their mills in Peterborough, Ontario.[36] The attempts to obtain a crushing plant to process the rapeseed grown in Saskatchewan have encountered similar problems. The fixed Crow's Nest Pass rates are too low, at least when compared with the high rates on processed grain products, to allow the establishment of extensive agricultural processing plants in Western Canada. Yet many prairie grain farmers are determined to resist any tampering with the Crow's Nest Pass rates, and a rural-urban, agricultural-industrial cleavage on this issue seems inevitable.

A third western transportation problem concerns the technological obsolescence of much of Western Canada's rail transportation and grain-handling systems. These systems were built in the late nineteenth and early twentieth centuries and have remained basically unchanged since that time. It is important to remember that the system was built at a time when few roads or highways were available. Consequently it was widely believed that every farmer must be within ten, or at most twenty, miles of a rural grain delivery point. The time and cost involved in hauling grain by sleigh over the open prairie in winter for more than ten miles were considered prohibitive. As a result numerous branch lines were built. With the development of excellent grid and main roads and the widespread use of motor trucks it is possible to haul grain much further with comparative ease. Many of the rural branch lines, moreover, were not high standard roads at any time. Some have not been properly maintained since they were built. As a result most branch and feeder rail lines cannot handle the new, heavier, and faster rolling stock now used by the companies. Many of the local delivery points are also too small to justify the employment of local agents, or to introduce new and more modern but often very expensive equipment. The economies of scale through the effective use of equipment and the volume necessary to justify new developments like large-unit-trains are simply not suited to the smaller delivery points on inadequate branch lines. Put simply, the grain-handling and transportation system is technologically obsolete and in need of modernization. Modernization, however, requires the abandonment of uneconomic branch lines and delivery points and the upgrading and improving of the larger centres. Such modernization is often bitterly resisted in rural areas. It is widely regarded as a threat to the survival of the much-vaunted family farm and the small prairie communities. Recognition and acceptance of the need for change is a prerequisite for any drastic overhaul and improvement of the western rail system. At present the inefficiencies of western operations increase rail costs and threaten to provide the railways with a better justification for their discriminatory rates than they have had at any time in the past.[37]

The survival of rural life in Western Canada is directly affected by transportation costs. Clinging grimly to the remnants of the statutory Crow's Nest Pass rates and to inadequately maintained branch lines is no longer sufficient. Future farming costs will depend to a very large extent on the modernization and improvement of the existing grain-handling and transportation systems. The first requirement in any such overhaul should be an abandonment by the railways and by the Board of Railway Commissioners of the policy of "fair discrimination"—the policy of setting rates at low levels where competition exists and at much higher levels where water carriers cannot meet the needs of shippers.

Economic diversification and industrialization has become the objective of increasing numbers of Western Canadians. In order to facilitate this the discriminatory national freight-rate structure must be dismantled. The policy of "fair discrimination," modified by a few concessions to western grain farmers, is no longer adequate. What is needed is a genuine national transportation policy. Such a policy must encompass inter-regional rates which reflect equalization of rail service in much the same way that federal officials have found ways and means of equalizing fiscal resources, health services, education, unemployment insurance, pension schemes, and many other things between various regions. It should not, however, encompass transportation matters which are essentially matters of local or regional concern only. The subsidization of uneconomic local branch lines and the support of specific local industries or shippers are not proper concerns of the federal government. The responsibility of the federal government should be restricted to the provision of adequate, non-discriminatory main-line transportation facilities, suffciently flexible to permit individual provinces to provide local subsidies if these are considered desirable locally or regionally. Almost all the prairie branch lines were originally incorporated and subsidized by provincial governments, not by the federal government. The relatively clear definition between national (i.e., main line) and provincial (i.e., local branch lines) which was worked out by the Laurier government between 1906 and 1910 needs to be re-established.[38]

The need for a non-discriminatory national transportation policy is obvious to Western Canadians. Unfortunately the federal position paper at the Western Economic Opportunities Conference indicates clearly that the old national rate-making philosophy based on competition or the lack of it is still alive and well in Ottawa. In the past, as has been shown, alterations in the national freight-rate structure which were regarded as indispensable to the development of Western Canada were achieved only when Western Canadians resorted to actions of their own, in defiance of national policies and of the rulings of the Board of Railway Commissioners. Manitoba created new and more competitive conditions by subsidizing and supporting new regional railways, thus forcing changes in national freight rates. Manitoba successfully meddled in national transportation policies, doing by indirect means what the federal government could have done by direct means. The problem was that the federal government would not act on its own. The real and permanent benefits obtained were obtained only because of Manitoba's actions.

The apparent federal reluctance to abandon the old rate-making philosophy makes it necessary for Western Canadians to once again consider aggressive action on their own. New and competitive regional railways would, of course, be inappropriate in an era of excessive regional rail capacity. Subsidization of alternate forms of transport, such as regional air lines and trucking systems, probably would prove far more effective. The railways and the Board of Transport Commissioners have great difficulty in understanding complaints about obvious discrimination, but they understand competition very well, whether that competition be real or artificial (i.e., from water carriers using government built and operated harbour and canal facilities).

There can be little doubt that subsidization of artificial competition is wasteful in most cases. It is nonetheless a very useful weapon in forcing changes in federal policies which are unacceptable to one region of the country, but which seem insoluble through the usual channels of the federal system. Certainly western governments today could argue as forcefully as their predecessors did decades ago that the savings in reduced regional transportation costs would more than offset the provincial costs of subsidizing competition for the railways. The basic objective, of course, would be to create competition and reduce rates, not necessarily to transfer traffic from one carrier to another.

An alternative certainly open to wealthy provinces like Alberta would be to subsidize western shippers to the extent that the government believes the national railway rates discriminate against such shippers. Demands that money thus expended be taken into any calculations relating to federal-provincial finances or to equalization payments might well create a serious federal financial and constitutional problem. Federal-provincial financing arrangements and calculations would suffer for a time, but clearly greater regional pressure is needed to end nearly one hundred years of freight-rate discrimination.

Certainly unilateral action by one or more western governments to eliminate freight-rate discrimination is fraught with dangers. Not the least of these dangers is the disunity that might be created in Western Canada if freight-rate discrimination were eliminated. Western grain farmers now enjoy very considerable favourable discrimination under the Crow's Nest Pass Agreement and under the federal subsidization of rail operations on uneconomic branch lines. It is inconsistent and has often greatly weakened the western case when Westerners vehemently defend the Crow's Nest Pass rates or obsolete branch lines. On balance Western Canada has certainly suffered far more than it has gained from discriminatory freight rates, but a logical and united western position has often been difficult to achieve because of specific statutory concessions such as the Crow's Nest Pass rates.

Any coherent, logical, and determined action by one or more western provinces to eliminate freight-rate discrimination is likely to encounter legal, financial, and constitutional problems. The federal government probably has the power and the resources to defeat the policies of any province if it is willing to risk a complete rupture in its relations with that province and perhaps with an entire region. The experience of the past indicates that no federal government is likely, on its own initiative, to ameliorate or remove unpopular features of a policy which receives strong support in Central Canada, but is opposed in one or more minority regions. On the other hand, no federal government has been willing to thwart and nullify determined, well thought out, and sustained action by provincial governments in a minority region to remove major grievances. The challenge for Western Canadians is to devise a rational transportation policy and to take whatever action is necessary to achieve that policy. The Western Economic Opportunities Conference in July of 1973 demonstrated that the federal government can speak very sympathetically about western transportation problems, but has not yet abandoned the practice of setting rates according to differing degrees of competition.

CONCLUSION

National transportation policies certainly have been unduly burdensome to Western Canadians in the past. Those burdens have been ameliorated but not removed by the unilateral action of the province of Manitoba in the three decades after the incorporation of the Canadian Pacific Railway. The burden will only be further lightened if western politicians and spokesmen develop rational and more equitable alternative policies and insist on their implementation, through the federal process if possible, but through unilateral action if the parliament of Canada and the Canadian Transport Commission prove intransigent. Contradictory and carping criticism and complaints, or mendicant requests for make-shift subsidies, are no longer adequate. A well-defined and rational western transportation policy, backed by provincial government willing and able to act on their own if necessary, offers the best and perhaps the only prospect for the easing of the burdens that national transportation policies have imposed on Western Canada.

NOTES

1. Western Economic Opportunities Conference, 24 to 26 July, 1973, Calgary, Alberta (hereafter referred to as W.E.O.C.), Background Paper on Transportation prepared by the Federal Government.

2. D.A. MacGibbon, *Railway Rates and the Canadian Railway Commission* (Boston, 1917), chap. III; R.A.C. Henry et al., *Railway Freight Rates in Canada: A Study Prepared for the Royal Commission on Dominion-Provincial Relations* (Ottawa, 1939). No reference will be made in this study to freight rates in the Maritime provinces. Those rates are the subject of a separate study in *Canada and the Burden of Unity*, edited by D.J. Bercuson (Toronto, 1977).

3. For an elaborate discussion and justification of western rates and the concept of "fair discrimination" see *Canadian Railway Cases*, Vol. 17, pp. 123-230, Western Tolls Case, Board of Railway Commissioners File No. 18755. The Board of Railway Commissioners in its judgment in the Western Tolls case acknowledged that "Prima facie discrimination in such tolls exists," but argued that this discrimination "is justified by effective water competition, and by the competition of U.S. railways throughout eastern Canada." Ibid., pp. 123-25.

4. Stephen to Macdonald, 27 August 1881, Macdonald Paper, Vol. 288, p. 121884, P.A.C.

5. Stephen to Macdonald, 13 November 1880, ibid., Vol. 268, p. 121844.

6. Stephen to Macdonald, 18 October 1880, ibid., p. 121836-37.

7. Chester Martin, *"Dominion Lands" Policy* (Toronto, 1973, reprint ed.), chap. II, "The Purposes of the Dominion."

8. MacGibbon, *Railway Rates*, chap. IV, "Results of the Canadian Transportation Policy."

9. Van Horne to E.B. Osler, 27 January 1883, Van Horne Letterbook No. 1, p. 211-12, P.A.C.

10. Aikins to Mcdonald, 30 November 1883, Macdonald Paper, Vol. 186, pp. 77427-28; P.A.C. Van Horne to the Editor of the *Manitoba Free Press*, 24 December 1883, Van Horne Letterbook No. 4, pp. 12-13, P.A.C.

11. H.A.Innis, *History of the Canadian Pacific Railway* (Toronto, 1971, reprint ed.). Detailed operating statistics are given in chapters 7, 8, and 9.

12. *Canadian Railway Cases*, Vol. 17, p. 128.

13. William J. Wilgus, *The Railway Interrelationships of the United States and Canada* (New Haven, 1937).

14. *Canadian Railway Cases*, Vol. 17, p. 124, point 9.

15. W.E.O.C., Background Paper on Transportation prepared by the Federal Government.

16. Canada, *Debates of the House of Commons, 1883*, p. 971, Sir Charles Tupper on 4 May 1883. A more detailed discussion of this allowance of Manitoba railway legislation is contained in J.A. Jackson, "Disallowance of Manitoba Railway Legislation in the 1880's; Railway Policy as a Factor in the Relations of Manitoba with the Dominion" (MA thesis, University of Manitoba, 1945); and T.D. Regehr, "The National Policy and Manitoba Railway Legislation, 1879-1888" (MA thesis, Carleton University, 1963).

17. Macdonald to McDougall, 30 July 1884, Macdonald Papers, Vol. 526, pp. 42-43, P.A.C.

18. Records of the Governor General's Office, Series G. 21, File 191, P.A.C.

19. W.B. Scarth to Macdonald, 5 May 1886, Macdonald Papers, Vol. 261, p. 119026-39. P.A.C.

20. Scarth to Macdonald and Macdonald to Scarth, 18 January 1887, and Scarth to Macdonald and Macdonald to Scarth, 2 February 1887, ibid., Vol. 262, pp. 119172, 119176, 119215.

21. Canada, *P.C. 577 of 1888* (Dormants), Final Memorandum respecting the visit of the delegation of the Manitoba government in reference to the disallowance of provincial legislation.

22. Lt. Col. Scoble to Greenway, 20 March 1888, Greenway Papers, Folio No. 283, Public Archives of Manitoba; Macdonald to Greenway, 30 March 1888, Macdonald Papers, Vol. 527, p. 458, P.A.C.

23. Villard Papers, Folder entitled "Northern Pacific and Manitoba Railway Company Testimony," Baker Library, Harvard Business School; Minnesota State Historical Society, *Northern Pacific Railroad Company Records*, Office of the Secretary, File 26, entitled "Northern Pacific and Manitoba Railway Company, 1888-1899." Both of these sources contain extensive evidence relating to the railway situation in Manitoba and the arrangement between the Northern Pacific Railroad and the Canadian Pacific Railway to avoid real competition.

24. A good discussion of the general background of the Crow's Nest Pass Agreement can be found in D.J. Hall, "The Political Career of Clifford Sifton, 1896-1905" (Ph.D. thesis, University of Toronto, 1974).

25. Porteous to James Ross, 15 June 1897, Porteous Papers, Vol. 26, Letterbook, 1897-1898, p. 102; Porteous to Mackenzie, 29 July 1897, ibid., p. 119, P.A.C.

26. T.D. Regehr, *The Canadian Northern Railway: Pioneer Road of the Northern Prairies, 1895-1918* (Toronto, 1976), chap. 3.

27. T.D. Regehr, "The Canadian Northern Railway: The West's Own Product," *Canadian Historical Review* (June 1970), p. 177-87.

28. Manitoba, *1 Edw. VII, Cap. 39.*

29. Canada, *House of Commons Debates, 1901*, p. 5206.

30. *Canadian Railway Cases*, Vol. 22, pp. 4-49; Eastern Tolls Case, Board of Railway Commissioners File 25347. The difficulties of the new transcontinentals in operating their new lines north of Lake Superior are discussed in some detail in this case.

31. *Canadian Railway Cases*, Vol. 22, pp. 49-84; Increase in Passenger and Freight Tolls Case, Board of Railway Commissioners File 27840.

32. A.W. Currie, "Freight Rates on Grain in Western Canada," *Canadian Historical Review* (March 1940), pp. 40-55.

33. W.E.O.C., "Transportation" (position paper jointly submitted by Premiers Allan Blakeney, David Barrett, Edward Schreyer, and Peter Lougheed).

34. W.E.O.C., Document, Jean Marchand to Hon. E.J. Benson, President, Canadian Transportation Commission, 19 July 1973.

35. Ibid.

36. John Channon, Section Three, Paper five, in *Grain Handling and Transportation Seminar*, held 8 and 9 March 1973, Saskatoon, Saskatchewan. Proceedings published by the Canada Grains Council and the University of Saskatchewan.

37. All these issues and problems have been discussed repeatedly. The Grain Handling and Transportation Seminar focused on many of these issues.

38. For an interesting and thoughtful approach to the problem see J. Donald Howe, "The Possible Railroad: Towards a New Transport Policy," *Canadian Forum* (February 1974), pp. 4-10.

VII

ETHNIC GROUPS AND PRAIRIE SOCIETY

From the time of its acquisition in 1870, the Canadian government attempted to attract settlers to the North-West. Up until 1890, the largest number
came from eastern Canada and Britain, with only a few ethnic groups coming: a group of Icelanders settled in Manitoba in 1874, some Russian
Mennonites in 1874, as well as small numbers of Americans, Russians, Jews,
Hungarians, and Germans. But beyond these small numbers few came
prior to the late 1890s.

After 1896, the situation changed dramatically. Between 1896 and 1914
over a million and a half new immigrants came to Canada, the majority
to the Prairie West. Economists have emphasized economic factors in
explaining the upsurge of immigration at the end of the 1890s (as noted
in Topic VI). Historians have stressed the human element as well, especially
the efforts of Clifford Sifton, Minister of the Interior in the newly-elected
Liberal government of 1896. Sifton tightened the regulations in the Department of the Interior to prevent speculators from withholding large amounts
of land from settlement. He made it easier for immigrants to acquire
homesteads, and undertook an extensive immigration propaganda campaign. In Britain, continental Europe and the United States, he established
organizations to promote immigration.

Sifton wanted farmers, regardless of nationality. But most Canadians
preferred immigrants from the United States, Britain or northern Europe
only. When these more popular sources of potential immigrants proved to
be insufficient, Sifton looked to central and eastern Europe. The Ukrainians
were one of the largest eastern European groups to come to the prairie West.
Their determination to maintain their language and their distinctive culture
led to conflict with educational authorities who wanted to assimilate them
into Anglo-Canadian society. In a study which combines ethnic and educa-

tional history, Stella Hryniuk and Neil McDonald discuss "The Schooling Experience of Ukrainians in Manitoba from 1896-1916."

With the influx of numerous diverse ethnic groups, a debate arose over the nature of prairie society. Some western Canadian leaders favoured a British culture, similar to that established in Ontario, to which other ethnic groups would conform. Others argued for a unique prairie culture which would combine the best qualities of the various ethnic groups but would still be predominantly the old English-speaking Canadian culture. Howard Palmer discusses these differing perspectives in "Strangers and Stereotypes: the Rise of Nativism," a revised excerpt from his book, *Patterns of Prejudice.* Although he limits his analysis to Alberta, the attitudes he discusses were shared across the Prairies in the period from 1880 to 1920.

SELECTED BIBLIOGRAPHY

Much of the early writing on immigration and ethnic groups in western Canada dealt with the issue as a social problem. For an overview of the literature on the subject to the early 1970s see Howard Palmer, "History and Present State of Ethnic Studies in Canada" in W. Isajiw, ed., *Identities: The Impact of Ethnicity on Canadian Society* (Toronto, 1977), pp. 167-83. The 1970s and 1980s witnessed a significant upsurge in academic research on the impact of immigration and ethnicity on the Prairies. For an overview of this research, see Howard Palmer "Canadian Immigration and Ethnic History in the 1970's and 1980's," *Journal of Canadian Studies* 17, no. 1 (Spring,1982): 35-50. See as well, Alan Anderson's, "Prairie Ethnic Studies and Research: Review and Assessment," *Prairie Forum* 7 (1982): 155-69 This latter article forms part of a "Special Issue" on Ethnic Studies. The bibliography of Chapter Four in Howard Palmer, with Tamara Palmer, *Alberta: A New History* (Edmonton, 1990), pp. 381-83, provides a group by group bibliography on immigration in Alberta.

The Canadian Ethnic Studies journal regularly contains articles on the prairie experience of various ethnic groups. Special issues on Education (1976), Ethnic Radicals (1978), Geography and Ethnic Groups in Western Canada (1977), Ukrainians (1980), Femininity (1981), Ethnic Literature (1982), and Ethnic Art and Architecture (1984) contain many important articles and bibliographical surveys. The journal also contains an annual bibliography of new material in the area of ethnic studies.

For short overviews of the history of ethnic groups across the country see the entries in *The Canadian Encyclopedia,* 2nd edition (Edmonton, 1988). The Department of the Secretary of State and McClelland and Stewart have cooperated to publish a series of histories entitled *Generations* dealing with many different ethnic groups across the country. Among the books published so far have been studies of the Arabs, Dutch, Japanese, Scots,

Greeks, Portuguese, Poles, Norwegians, Croatians, Hungarians, Chinese, and Ukrainians. The Canadian Historical Association has also published a series of 11 booklets on Scots, Portuguese, Japanese, Poles, East Indians, West Indians, Jews, Finns, Chinese, Ukrainians and Germans most of which have information relevant to the histories of these groups on the prairies. The Ukrainian volume, in the Generations series, Manoly Lupul, ed., *A Heritage in Transition: Essays in the History of Ukrainians in Canada* (Toronto, 1982) discusses one of the largest ethnic groups on the prairies.

For more detail on Canadian immigration policy and immigration during the settlement period see Pierre Berton, *The Promised Land: Settling the West, 1896-1914* (Toronto, 1984). Howard and Tamara Palmer, ed., *Peoples of Alberta* (Saskatoon, 1985) surveys the history of immigration and ethnicity in Alberta and includes specialized studies of nineteen ethnic and ethno-religious groups. Donald Avery's *Dangerous Foreigners: European Immigrant Workers and Labour Radicalism in Canada, 1896-1932* (Toronto, 1979) discusses immigration policy, ethnic relations, and ethnic labour radicalism.

D.J. Hall, *Clifford Sifton, Vol.1, The Young Napoleon, 1861-1900* (Vancouver, 1981) discusses the first stages of Sifton's federal role as Minister of the Interior, while his article "Clifford Sifton: Immigration and Settlement Policy, 1896-1905," in H.D. Palmer, ed. *The Settlement of the West* (Calgary, 1977), pp. 60-85, 243-51, discusses the origins, nature, and underlying assumptions of Sifton's immigration and settlement policies.

Other recent studies with a good deal of information on ethnicity on the prairies include Jean Burnet, with Howard Palmer, *'Coming Canadians': An Introduction to the History of Canada's Peoples* (Toronto, 1988); Herman Ganzevoort, *A Bittersweet Land: The Dutch Experience in Canada, 1890-1980* (Toronto, 1988); Norman Hillmer, et al., *On Guard for Thee: War, Ethnicity, and the Canadian State, 1939-45* (Ottawa, 1989); John C. Lehr, "Government Perceptions of Ukrainian Immigrants to Western Canada, 1896-1902," *Canadian Ethnic Studies* 19 (1987): 1-12; and Frances Swyripa, "Baba and the Community Heroine: The Two Images of the Ukrainian Pioneer Woman," *Alberta* 2, no. 1 (1989): 59-80.

STELLA M. HRYNIUK and

NEIL G. MCDONALD

15 The Schooling Experience of Ukrainians in Manitoba, 1896-1916

The schooling of the immigrant child in western Canada has usually been interpreted from the perspective of the assimilationists, whether bureaucrat, inspector, or teacher.[1] Rarely has it been examined from the viewpoint of the immigrants themselves. Moreover, consideration has seldom been given to their educational experiences in their native lands or the aspirations they held for their children. This chapter describes and interprets the Ukrainian schooling experience in Manitoba during the first twenty years of Ukrainian settlement in this province, mainly from the immigrants' perspective.

Ukrainians are a Slavic people who inhabit extensive territories in Eastern and East-Central Europe. At the time of their mass migration to western Canada at the end of the nineteenth and beginning of the twentieth centuries, their lands were divided between the Austro-Hungarian Monarchy and the Russian Empire. The total number of Ukrainians at that time was around twenty million, of whom about four million lived in Austria-Hungary. The Ukrainians who came to Canada were from two Austrian provinces, Galicia and Bukovyna.[2]

Although they formed a majority of the population in eastern Galicia and in Bukovyna, in neither province did the Ukrainians enjoy much political influence. Mostly they were peasant agriculturalists working small land-holdings of 1-5 hectares; many of them also worked for large landowners, especially at seeding and harvest time. Productivity was low, but significant improvements were evident in the last two decades of the nineteenth century: crop yields increased, as did the number and quality of the animals that were raised. The Ukrainians lived mainly in the small towns and villages of the two provinces, going out daily to work their intensively cultivated plots. Villages could be clusters of houses of two or three hundred inhabitants or larger conglomerations of two thousand people or more.[3]

From the 1880s onwards, the Ukrainian rural population began to free itself from the influence of Polish and Rumanian landlords. They participated in movements for promoting popular education and producer and consumer co-operatives, and they strove to acquire greater control of local government. Ukrainians in Galicia were Ukrainian-rite Catholics, while those in Bukovyria belonged predominantly to the Ukrainian Orthodox church. Village priests, particularly in Galicia, played a leading role in furthering popular enlightenment and economic improvements in the countryside, though schoolteachers and a handful of lawyers and doctors also played a part.[4]

At the provincial level, school authorities in Galicia were controlled by the politically-dominant Polish element, those in Bukovyna by Germans and Rumanians. School curricula were set by the Austrian (federal) government, but it was the province that determined the language or languages of instruction. Until the 1870s there had been very few village schools in eastern Galicia and Bukovyna, and their rural populations were almost entirely illiterate. Compulsory education was then introduced by law, but it was a long time before it could become a reality.[5]

The building of a school was the responsibility of a local school district. Over the years Ukrainian villagers organized themselves, and taxed themselves in order to construct and maintain schools, and frequently provided manual labour and materials. Transfer payments from local school taxes also contributed toward teachers' salaries and pensions, though these were in fact paid by the next highest level of educational authority, the county education councils. The latter might on occasion also provide loans or subsidies for local education purposes. During the 1880s and 1890s many new schools were built in the villages. In the Southern Podillia region of eastern Galicia, from which a great number of Manitoba's early Ukrainian immigrants came, the number of elementary schools in Borshchiv county (seventy-five small towns and villages, population about 100,000) rose from 27 in 1880 to 57 in 1900, and the number of those in Chortkiv county (44 small towns and villages, population about 67,000) increased from 23 to 39 in the same two decades. Moreover, by 1900 many of the schools were no longer one-room schools.[6]

School attendance also rose quite dramatically, though it is clear that not every child attended, or attended for the period prescribed by law. By 1900, however, an ample majority of the children of school age were attending school.[7] In first and second grades they learned reading and writing, arithmetic, and singing; religious instruction was also given, not by the teachers but by priests. The teaching of a second language was introduced in grade two. In grades three and four the natural sciences, geography and history, drawing and geometry, and domestic science for girls and physical education for boys were added. By 1900 a few more technical or practical subjects had also entered the curriculum: physics and chemistry in the towns, horticulture and agriculture in the villages. Despite systematic attempts by the provincial authorities to ensure that villagers should not receive an education "above their station in life," some village children—usually encouraged by their priests and / or teachers — went on to higher education.[8]

With the increased emphasis on schooling, there was also a significant increase in the literacy rate. Literacy rates, here expressed as a percentage of the *total* population, varied from one county to another, depending on local circumstances. In Borshchiv county, in 1880, only 8.4 percent of the male population and only 4.8 percent of the female population could read; in nearby Terebovlia county the percentages were 20 and 11.9 respectively. By 1900 there had been considerable improvements: 20.8 percent of males and 13.4 percent of females in Borshchiv county were now literate, while in Terebovlia county the percentages were now 45.2 and 33.1 respectively.[9] It is interesting to note that Paul Wood, immigration agent in Dauphin, Manitoba, estimated in 1900 that,

> . . . fully 35 percent of the male adult Galicians can read and write in their own language, and many of these can also read and write Polish. Of the children who were attending school any length at home in the old country before leaving for Canada, nearly all can read and write.[10]

Wood's reference to "their own language" (i.e. Ukrainian) and to Polish is instructive. Bilingual schooling was not at all unusual for Ukrainian villagers. Their children attended schools in which Ukrainian was generally the language of instruction in the first grade. In Galicia, Polish was added in the second grade, and normally as a second language of instruction.[11] For villagers living in mixed-language areas, the learning and use of two languages was part of their daily experience.

The Ukrainian immigrants to Manitoba, therefore, came from regions in which there had been recent and significant improvements, including those in the realm of public education. Important also was the work of voluntary societies which published simple reading materials and to which the reading clubs that were established in many villages were loosely affiliated. A tradition of schooling had been painstakingly established over the years, and many villagers were proud of their schools and what they had accomplished: as the village of Kolodribka reported in 1890, "we have educated people now."[12]

It has been estimated that about 100,000 Ukrainians migrated to Canada between 1896 and 1914. With natural increase, there were probably about 128,000 people of Ukrainian origin in Canada in 1911 and around 220,000 in 1921, mostly in the three prairie provinces. It appears that over one-third lived in Manitoba.[13] Their initial arrival, however, followed one of the most unsettling social and political periods in the post-Confederation era. The immediate cause of the friction was located in Manitoba and became known as the Manitoba School Question. This issue preoccupied Canadian political life from 1890 to 1897, and the negotiated compromise solution, however unanticipated, directly influenced the schooling experience of the early Ukrainian immigrants.

Although Manitoba came into Confederation in 1870 as a bilingual province and with a dual (Catholic and Protestant) school system, these arrangements were not to last.[14] Within twenty years, under the impact of a population growth that altered the early French/English balance, the fledgling province began to reflect the social and cultural image of its new majority —Anglophone, Protestant, and largely Ontario-born.

Consequently in 1890, a Liberal government, led by Premier Thomas Greenway, abolished the official use of the French language and the dual system of denominational schools. This heavy-handed legislation resulted in a long campaign of litigation and political agitation. The dispute engaged French and English, Catholic and Protestant, Quebec and Ontario, and Conservative and Liberal in a national debate that challenged the very basis of Confederation. So serious was the controversy that it became a major issue of the federal election of 1896, and was a significant factor in the defeat of the governing Conservative party. In 1897 a newly-elected Liberal government, under Wilfrid Laurier, negotiated a compromise that led to an amendment to the Manitoba Public Schools Act of 1890. It read:

> When 10 of the pupils in any school speaks the French language or any language other than English as their native language, the teaching of such pupils shall be conducted in French or such other language, and English upon the bilingual system.[15]

The wording in this clause that allowed pupils to be taught in "any language other than English" was an attempt to avoid charges from Ontario that the French language had been made equal to English.[16] In Manitoba, however, the practical application of the legislation gave great comfort to the new immigrants. They soon realized that the amended School Act was permissive and allowed their children to be schooled partially in their own language. This "loophole" in the act helped solve two of the most pressing and closely-related schooling problems that worried Ukrainian parents. There was the real concern first about linguistic assimilation; and second, about the supply of Ukrainian/English-speaking teachers. Although parents acknowledged the need for their children to learn English, they were not willing to let this happen at the risk of losing their first language. The obvious solution was a reliable supply of certified bilingual teachers. As the first organizer of Ukrainian schools, John Baderski, observed, the new settlers did not wish "to go to the expense of building a school if they must afterwards see the school stand idle for want of a teacher."[17] Moreover, from a practical perspective it was important that bilingual teachers be found because the immigrant children could not speak English.[18]

Interestingly, the anxiety of the immigrant parents neatly complemented that of other Manitobans who worried about the possible social costs arising from this heavy influx of culturally distinct peoples. The latter group regularly expressed two distinct but related concerns, namely assimilation and illiteracy. To many among the latter group the best answer was a more selective immigration policy; to others, the public school could become an effective solution. Arguments for the two positions often found public expression. For example, in 1901, W. Sanford Evans, a recent Ontario-born arrival and newly-appointed editor of the *Winnipeg Telegram*, wrote in reference to "Slavonic immigrants":

> Those whose ignorance is impenetrable, whose customs are repulsive, whose civilization is primitive, and whose character and morals are justly condemned are surely not the class of immigrants which the country's paid immigration agents should seek to attract. Better by far to keep our land for children, and for the children's children of Canadians, than to fill up the country with the scum of Europe.[19]

Another less strident but equally concerned voice was represented by prominent clergy in the province, especially among those Presbyterians, Catholics and Anglicans who helped organize the Galician Education Committee.[20] Their view was perhaps best expressed by the Presbyterian Reverend Thomas Hart, a professor at Manitoba College. In an article on schools in Manitoba, he wrote:

> The education problem of Manitoba is both difficult and important . . . when we consider that . . . almost one third of the whole population is of other than British origin we can easily see that the task of unifying these diverse races, and making them intelligent citizens, English in speech, Canadian in sentiment, and British in loyalty to the empire, is one of no ordinary magnitude.[21]

The appraisal of the situation by Hart, his implied resignation to the task, and the "other language" clause in the School Act combined with the expressed wishes of the Ukrainians to modify the school experience of some children in those first years of settlement. These factors, however, did not always ensure satisfactory relationships with the school system.

The Ukrainians were lured to Canada by cheap land and the opportunity to create a better life, politically and materially, than appeared possible in Galicia and Bukovyna. They settled for the most part in areas still undeveloped — in the Dauphin, Riding Mountain, and Stuartburn areas, the Interlake, and the Cook's Creek-Brokenhead region.[22] Initially, the energies of the settlers were almost entirely taken up with clearing the land, planting their first crops, and erecting a dwelling. Males often left their homesteads to work for wages elsewhere, leaving much of the farm work to their wives and children.

The pattern of life on the homesteads with their widely-dispersed houses was very different from that of the villages of the homeland with their clusters of houses and better means of communication. Some settlers, misled by statements about Canada's excellent schools, appear to have expected to find schools in the rural areas to which they came.[23] Occasionally, this was indeed the case, as in Winnipeg and for some settlers in the Stuartburn area,[24] but in such instances the Ukrainian children at times encountered discrimination which led parents to keep their children at home.[25]

The schooling experience of Ukrainians in Winnipeg differed from that elsewhere in the province. According to the census data, there were 3,599 Ukrainians in Winnipeg's metropolitan area in 1911 and 7,001 in 1921;[26] these figures were probably understated. The Ukrainians lived mainly in the city's north end, and the children attended schools such as Strathcona, Aberdeen, Lord Selkirk, Norquay and Somerset. Daniel McIntyre, the long-term, influential superintendent of Winnipeg's public schools, was an adamant advocate of a unitary school system and of unilingual English instruction.[27] Although obligated by law to provide bilingual instruction when there was sufficient demand, McIntyre and the school board ignored petitions from Ukrainians for its introduction into the division's schools.[28] Notwithstanding the school board's failure to live up to its obligations, some Ukrainians looked back with appreciation to the education they received at Strathcona school where W.J. Sisler, another outspoken opponent of bilingual education, was principal.[29]

The Ukrainian press of Winnipeg regularly paid attention to educational matters. It encouraged the attendance of children at school and of adults at evening classes (some of which were organized by the city council and others by Ukrainian associations), and it stressed the importance of learning both English and a trade.[30] How many of Winnipeg's children of Ukrainian extraction attended school regularly cannot be established; clearly quite a number did not.[31]

It is scarcely surprising that the Ukrainian community in Manitoba, as most other communities, was factious. In the winter of 1915-16, for example, one grouping ultimately set up its own socialist Sunday schools "to counter the influence of the capitalistic schools on our young generation."[32] But the absence of bilingual elementary education in Winnipeg's schools seems to have been accepted by the Ukrainian community with a fair amount of equanimity. Evening and Sunday schools served to some extent to educate children in their mother tongue. One private bilingual elementary school was established, however, in 1905: St. Nicholas School, run by the Sisters Servants of Mary Immaculate (a Ukrainian-rite Catholic religious order). Numbers quickly increased from fifty students in 1905 to 160 in 1906 and even more in subsequent years; when health inspectors wanted to close the school, the Roman Catholic Archbishop of St. Boniface raised money for the building of a new one.[33]

The experiences of Ukrainian settlers and their children in the rural areas of Manitoba were very different. Predominantly, they came into empty lands. Where there were already some settlements, as in the Stuartburn area, they tried to work within the established school system at least for a time, but by 1915 they had set up a large number of school districts.[34] In some instances, the Ukrainian settlers took over some already-existing school districts, but in most cases it was they who formed the district and built the schools. In January 1916, two months before the Manitoba Legislature voted to repeal the section of the Public Schools Act that permitted the bilingual schools, Charles K. Newcombe, superintendent of schools, reported on the state of these schools: "One hundred and eleven districts operate Ruthenian, or Polish, bilingual schools, employing 114 teachers, with an enrolment of 6,513 pupils and an average attendance of 3,884."[35]

Interest in schooling, therefore, was evident from the outset, and by and large the settlers were well aware of the advantages that education and a knowledge of English would provide for their children. Thus, A.L. Young reported from the Stuartburn area in 1901: "The Galician settlers take an active interest in all school meetings and are evidently quite alive to the necessity of giving their children all the advantages of a good school education."[36]

There were instances when Ukrainian settlers organized informal classes for their children or where parents taught their children to read and write in Ukrainian.[37] Quite early, however, some of the settlers, following normal Manitoba practice, were able to organize their own school districts. The first public school district established by Ukrainians in Manitoba appears to have been the "Galicia" district in the Interlake in 1898.[38] The Presbyterian and Roman Catholic churches helped establish a handful of early Ukrainian schools: Trembowla, Kosiw, Willow Creek and St. John Cantius.[39] The immigration agent in Sifton was for a time authorized by his superiors to teach the Ukrainian children there, and lessons were held in a makeshift schoolhouse — the station of the Lake Manitoba Railway Canal company.[40]

Some Ukrainian areas organized their own schools without any outside help. As early as 1901-02, for example, schools appeared at Mink River, Ukraina, Lukowce, Wolodimir, Kolomyja and Olha.[41] Among the early immigrants were three qualified teachers who taught school in Manitoba: Ivan Negrych, Ivan Bodrug, and Vasyl Cichocky. The last-named, at least initially, taught only in Ukrainian.[42] Other teachers were unilingually English, and settlers' children who had acquired some English acted on occasion as interpreters for those who had not learned English. Occasionally, an English settler's child learned Ukrainian and could also act as translator. And "Eaton's catalogue was also very useful" as a tool in the classroom.[43] Some schools, for the first two or three years, were held in private homes until a schoolhouse was built.

By no means could all the Ukrainian settlers during the first decade of the century afford to tax themselves sufficiently to support a school. Most of them had come to Canada with relatively little capital. Inspector E.H. Walker noted in 1905 that:

> Not one of the six Galician districts in Rossburn Municipality has a school. This failure is explained partly by the fact that they have been in the country such a comparatively short time that they do not feel able to support schools.[44]

The school at McMillan—"The building was a shabby job, cold and drafty, with rough seats and an oil-drum heater" cost around $500 to build.[45] Later, schools cost more: $850 for Budka school, $1,355 for that at Malonton. The potential tax base was reduced where adjacent lands were owned by non-resident speculators, who were exempt from paying taxes. "This state of affairs is not only a hardship and a grave injustice to the settlers," wrote Inspector Best, "but also a formidable hindrance to education work."[46]

Frequent alterations of district boundaries, caused by changes in land ownership, for example, from private to public and vice versa, also affected the potential funding base.[47] Established municipalities were at times most unsympathetic to the educational needs of the new settlers' children and refused to help them. In consequence, the Ukrainians formed their own municipalities, as in the case of Stuartburn:

> When they applied to Franklin council for financial help to build schools, they were turned down. Franklin said they were too new a community to receive financial assistance. Their only option was to break away from Franklin and form their own municipality. And thus the Stuartburn municiplity came to be formed.[48]

As the settlers became better established, more schools were founded. In 1903 the Department of Education appointed a School Organizer and Inspector for Schools Among the Galicians, and although the appointee, John Baderski, was not much liked among Ukrainians on account of his pro-Polish sympathies, he, and later Theodore Stefanyk and Paul Gigeychuk, did help settlers organize school districts.[49] Also helpful in this respect were articles in the Ukrainian language press explaining how settlers might approach the task of establishing school districts.[50] Undoubtedly, there were also Ukrainian settlers who were not much interested in education.

In his 1904 report, Baderski noted that school attendance in Ukrainian areas had improved under bilingual teachers. He recommended that there be established a "special preparatory school" for bilingual teachers, and in February 1905, the Manitoba government opened the Ruthenian Training

School in Winnipeg to prepare Ukrainian/English and Polish/English teachers. It was so successful that in 1907 it was divided into two sections and the Ukrainian section was moved to Brandon, where it functioned until the abolition of bilingual education in Manitoba in 1916.[51] Some prospective teachers took a three-year course there, others attended for shorter periods. "Some knew much English; others very little." It is difficult to establish their competence as teachers, though it is clear that some came to be greatly respected.[52]

Once there was a steady supply of bilingual teachers, the number of school districts began to rise quickly. Ukrainians became school trustees in greater numbers, formed school districts, and undertook the responsibility of building and maintaining schoolhouses and sometimes teachers' residences too. Due to their lack of knowledge of the English language, the Ukrainians kept school district records at times in various combinations of Ukrainian, Polish and English, but a steady and lively interest in their schools is revealed in the minutes of meetings and the ledgers.[53] Not atypically, in Lukowce school district in 1904, the parents did carpentry, hauled lumber and repaired the chimney for a minimal fee, and later maintained the school building and grounds and the school equipment.[54]

The rate of establishment of schools varied from one settlement to another, but public schooling clearly became a regular feature in the Ukrainian settlements of Manitoba. As of the middle of 1915, the official list of "Ruthenian" schools kept by the Department of Education, contains the names of ninety-one school districts that offered bilingual instruction in English and Ukrainian[55] a handful of which also offered instruction in Polish. In addition, there were school districts in areas of mixed settlements, for example around Beausejour, where Poles and Ukrainians, and sometimes Germans too, could not agree on what language other than English should be used, and decided that the Ruthenian-English teacher should teach only in English[56] Often, extraordinary efforts were made to provide schooling opportunities for the children. Thus, Inspector Best, reporting on the Gimli district, wrote in 1913:

On the completion of the new schools at McMillan, Komarno, Kreuzberg, Malonton and Rembrandt, there will be more than twenty schools in this settlement erected within the last few years, a fact that speaks well for the enterprise and self-sacrificing spirit of these people . . . . The efforts of these Northern colonies can be better appreciated when it is known that to obtain the most meagre education for their children they tax themselves sometimes as high as forty mills on the dollar: they pay higher salaries than most places and provide accommodation that would put to shame many of our old and wealthy districts.[57]

Likewise, Inspector Fallis wrote as follows about one new school district in what had been just a short time before the virgin lands south of Riding Mountain:

In the Galician settlement north east of Erickson, the new district of Round Lake has been formed. The anxiety of these people to have a school is shown by the fact that the district comprises only eight sections, of which only about six and one-half sections are assessed at a valuation of about fifteen thousand dollars and not over twelve hundred acres of land are cultivated in the district. I venture to say that many of our Canadian people might hesitate before assuming the responsibility of operating a school under such conditions and yet these people have called for tender for the erection of a new school, to be completed as soon as possible.[58]

Clearly, education for their children was important for many of the settlers. In the early days of settlement, some parents even taught their own children at home, "Of course, when we did not go to school, my father taught us at home. However, he did not know English so he taught my brother and sister other languages: Ukrainian, German and Polish."[59]

Some parents, even though illiterate themselves, gave every encouragement to their children to learn. F.T. Hawryluk, who had completed grade three in Galicia and was later a teacher in the Gimli area, recalled that he had to study on his own for two or three years before a school was opened in his neighbourhood. He said: "My father, though he himself was illiterate, always encouraged me to study and would carefully observe me as I wrote and listened attentively as I read."[60]

Some parents were indifferent to schooling: W. Kostiuk's father did not mind his going to school when he was not needed for farm work.[61] Others were no doubt hostile, afraid perhaps that their children would be alienated from them in the strange Canadian environment if they acquired an education and a knowledge of English. Like Kostiuk, they also felt themselves in need of all the family's work potential.[62] Some, however, clearly went to great lengths to ensure that their children got education, even when it entailed a financial sacrifice. One example was that of a child whose parents were themselves illiterate, but sent him to attend grades three to eight in Dauphin. There he boarded with a family who were paid for his keep in produce and in money.[63] Often, great physical exertion and discomfort were experienced. One mother recalled that:

We belonged to Senkiw School District, but were on the other side of the Roseau River. In spring when the children were small, they could not cross the river — there was no bridge, so I had to go with them. I would hitch up my skirt and carry them across on my back. I also had to meet them again in the evening — but the children had to get an education.[64]

While the desire for education for their children can be well documented, it is not always clear why this should have been so. In some instances, one may assume that respect for schooling, inculcated in the homeland, was carried over into the new land: attendance at school had thus become part of everyday life. Many settlers had migrated primarily to secure a better life for their children,[65] and no doubt recognized that education was one way towards achieving that better life. One person interviewed recalled that his parents wanted him to learn agriculture, reading and writing, and the English language, so that he should be able to communicate and to get work.[66] A striving for greater security for their children thus appears to have been a motivating factor. So too, it seems, was a concern that their children might be able to avoid the hardships which the parents had faced, possibly in Galicia and Bukovyna, but probably more so during the initial years in Manitoba; as one son was told: "Go to school, learn, so you don't have to work hard like us."[67]

Newspaper articles and letters to editors noted other reasons for education: public schooling was the first step towards the training of teachers, government officials, lawyers, doctors and priests.[68] Education would put Ukrainians "on an equal footing with other nationalities";[69] it was the road to success and everybody would then live together in harmony;[70] arithmetic was important so that "everyone should know the income and expense from his husbandry."[71]

The Ukrainian settlers also knew that ability in English was vital for their children—"One cannot exist in Canada without English."[72] This necessary knowledge could normally be best provided by the schools. But parents also wanted their children to retain their knowledge of Ukrainian and of their Ukrainian culture; here too the fear of their children becoming culturally separated from them played a major part.[73] Bilingual education thus seemed best to answer their needs. The children would grow up literate in both languages; learn what was useful to them in their Canadian context, and yet not forget their Ukrainian heritage. Furthermore, attendance was likely to be better at schools in which children had no difficulty communicating with their teacher and vice versa,[74] and it was thought that children learned more when they received instruction in Ukrainian as well as in English.[75] Moreover, bilingual education was a right. As *Kanadyiskyi Farmer* stated in 1909:

> We need to know the English language but we have the right to learn the Ruthenian language in schools. We should see to it that in all Ruthenian colonies school should be taught in both languages . . . . Because our people pay for the schools and teachers, we should have Ruthenian instruction too.[76]

Settlers, and children too, wrote to the newspapers about their satisfaction with bilingual schools and bilingual teachers.[77] Initially, however, they were in very short supply, and even later there were never enough. Salaries were sometimes low, and teachers' accommodation was often not satisfactory. Isolation and poor communications were other impediments.[78] Even officially bilingual schools, on occasion, had to hire unilingual English teachers.[79] At times, too, parents and school trustees did not appear to some members of the Manitoba-Ukrainian community to be concerned sufficiently about the need for a bilingual teacher.[80] The number of advertisements for bilingual teachers in the Ukrainian language press in Manitoba, however, plainly shows the general demand.[81] The clearest evidence of the desire for bilingual teaching was provided by the united opposition among Ukrainians of all political persuasions to the abolition of the bilingual system in 1916.[82]

Bilingual teachers, and sometimes unilingual English-speaking ones, were highly respected in their communities.[83] They not only taught the children but also promoted choral and musical groups, drama clubs, and organized evening classes to provide opportunities to those who had grown up before schools had been organized in outlying districts."[84]

The Ukrainian language press, the Ukrainian Teachers' Association, and individuals also called for the introduction in Manitoba of compulsory education, to which they were accustomed in their original homeland.[85] The Ukrainian socialist press also called for compulsory education,[86] while at the same time demanding a different type of education. It was this faction of the community which railed most insistently against the shortcomings of the school curriculum. They objected, for example, to the monarchist, imperialist and capitalist content of the stories used in the children's primers.[87] Other Ukrainians merely asked that Ukrainian books be used even if they had to be obtained from the homeland.[88] Bilingual readers were eventually published for Manitoba schools in 1913, but their usage was not altogether favoured by the school inspectors.[89]

Some Ukrainians resented portions of the curriculum because they believed that the children were deliberately being anglicized.[90] Others thought it very proper that the children should be taught knowledge appropriate to living in one of the Dominions of the British Empire, including Anglo-Saxon principles of democracy.[91] Ukrainian language primers were evidently used by bilingual teachers, often at the request or instruction of the school trustees.[92] Following the formal abolition of the bilingual system in 1916, a few continued to be used, though more secretively because communities risked the wrath of the school inspectors.[93]

School attendance was an ongoing problem, and one that was not resolved by the decreeing of compulsory education in Manitoba. In the early years of Ukrainian settlement in Manitoba, when many heads of families worked away from their homesteads for months at a time, children were especially needed for farm work.[94] Sometimes an individual was not suited for a teaching position and "antagonize[d] both parents and pupils."[95] Another inspector reported that, "In many cases when the teacher is not experienced and probably not too well educated and does not speak the Galician language, parents come to think that their children are not making progress and they take them from the school altogether."[96] In some instances the trustees were unable to hire teachers, and schools remained closed for months at a time.[97] Seasonal farm work also caused many parents to keep their children at home —the Kosiw School Register consistently showed low attendance in September[98] — and this problem was certainly not resolved by the introduction of compulsory education or by placing allegedly recalcitrant Ukrainian school districts under official trusteeship, as is evidenced by the report from Pine Ridge school which explained low attendance in September 1921, by reference to Jewish holidays and delayed work on the farms: "everybody seems busy digging potatoes just now."[99] The biggest obstacle to school attendance, however, was the distance that often had to be covered by small children, in all sorts of conditions and over various types of terrain. One vivid example from a memoir, not atypical, stated:

> The children walked as far as five miles to school. In the beginning the roads were very poor. Many used only trails, crossing creeks and grades made of young white poplar or willow covered with manure. If the winter were heavy, the grades would get so mucky in the spring that the children had to walk through the fields to get to school. For years those coming from the south had to cross a ravine gushing with water every spring. One of the bigger boys would have hip-waders and would take the young children across one by one. In the winter months most children came with a horse and buggy.[100]

It was not until more schools and better roads were constructed that the dream of schooling for all Ukrainian settlers' children could be realized. Meanwhile some, to their regret, were unable to go to high school.[101] Quite a number did manage to go on to higher education, including university, and became teachers, lawyers and so on.[102] Others, with their grade school education, became the backbone of the communities in which they resided.[103]

The schooling experience of Ukrainians in Manitoba up to 1916 was in many ways not dissimilar to that of other non-English-speaking immigrant groups. They did not find in their new homeland an established school system in the rural areas, as many of them had expected. Some regressed from educational standards which they had achieved in Galicia and Bukovyna.[104] They had to contend with the bigotry of people like Sisler, who in an article published in 1906 wrote that Ukrainians were "inferior in every department both of mental and physical activity, excepting where only slow mechanical movements are required."[105] Although some of the school inspectors recognized both the difficulties they encountered and their achievements, city-bound administrators, politicians and editors knew and cared all too little about the long distances, bad roads and inadequate tax bases which the Ukrainian settlers and their children confronted in their quest for schooling.

Yet clearly there was this quest, and by 1916 an extensive network of "Ruthenian" schools covered the areas where the Ukrainian settlers lived. They had shown themselves to be seriously concerned about their children's education, and according to their means (and sometimes beyond) they had built schools and hired teachers, and thus provided for their children's elementary education. The children themselves were frequently recognized by their teachers to be intelligent and eager to learn, and they often made quite extraordinary efforts under the most difficult circumstances to attend the schools in their scattered settlements. Contemporary Anglo-Canadian literature, however, often portrayed these Ukrainian settlers and their children as ignorant and backward. The evidence suggests that this characterization was grossly unfair.

NOTES
1. See, for example: Alan F.J. Artibise, *Winnipeg: A Social History of Urban Growth, 1874-1914* (Montreal: McGill-Queen's University Press, 1975), pp. 195-206; Cornelius J. Jaenen, "Ruthenian Schools in Western Canada, 1897-1919", in David C. Jones, Nancy M. Sheehan, and Robert M. Stamp, eds., *Shaping the Schools of the Canadian West* (Calgary: Detselig, 1979), pp. 39-58; and J.E. Rea, "'My Main Line is the Kiddies . . . Make Them Good Christians and Good Canadians, Which is the Same Thing,'" in Wsevolod Isajiw, ed., *Identities: The Impact of Ethnicity on Canadian Society* (Toronto: Peter Martin Associates, 1977), pp. 3-11.
2. Hence the earlier description of the Ukrainians as Galicians and Bukovynians.
3. See S.M. Hryniuk, "Peasant Agriculture in East Galicia in the Late Nineteenth Century", *Slavonic and East European Review*, 63 (Apr. 1985): 328-243; also S.M. Hryniuk, "A Peasant Society in Transition: Ukrainian Peasants in Five East Galician Counties, 1880-1900" (Ph.D. thesis, University of Manitoba, 1984), pp. 47-49 and 52-54.
4. Hryniuk, "A Peasant Society," esp. pp. 414-418.
5. S.H. Badeni, "Schulpflicht und Schulbesuch in Oesterreich," *Statistische Monatschrift*, XXVI (1900): 281; A. Sirka, *The Nationality Question in Austrian Education: The Case of the Ukrainians 1867-1914* (Frankfurt: Lang, 1980), pp. 35-50; Hryniuk, "A Peasant Society," pp. 115-122.
6. Hryniuk, "A Peasant Society," pp. 124-126, 131-133; Sirka, *The Nationality Question* pp. 76-78.
7. Relevant data are in *Oesterreichische Statistik*, LXII, no. 2. Education was compulsory for children aged 7 to 12; those aged 13 to 15 were to attend "continuation classes" in the elementary school for four to six hours per week.
8. Hryniuk, "A Peasant Society," pp. 122 and 133-135; on education in Bukovyna see V. Kubijovyc, ed., *Encyclopedia of Ukraine*, vol. 1 (Toronto: University of Toronto Press, 1984), p. 798.
9. Hryniuk, "A Peasant Society," p.153.

10. Cited, from *Dauphin Weekly Herald,* in V.J. Kaye-Kysilevskyi, "The Descendants of the Boyars of Halych on the Prairies of the Canadian West," in A. Baran *et. al.,* eds., *The Jubilee Collection of the Ukrainian Free Academy of Sciences* (Winnipeg, 1976), p. 363.

11. In Bukovyna, the second language was normally German or Rumanian.

12. *Batkivshchyna,* Mar. 28, 1890; Kolodribka's school was older than most, having been established in 1865.

13. Kubijovyc, *Encyclopedia,* p. 821; Canadian census data are not reliable sources for the numbers of Ukrainians in Canada, see W. Darcovich, "The 'Statistical Compendium': An Overview of Trends," in W.R. Petryshyn, ed., *Changing Realities: Social Trends Among Ukrainian Canadians* (Edmonton: Canadian Institute of Ukrainian Studies, 1980), esp. p. 8.

14. For a discussion of these developments in Manitoba, see W.L. Morton, *Manitoba: A History,* 2nd edition (Toronto: University of Toronto Press, 1967), pp. 199-250; also Gerald Friesen, *The Canadian Prairies: A History* (Toronto: University of Toronto Press, 1984), pp. 195-219 and pp. 242-273; and Cornelius Jaenen, "The Manitoba School Question: An Ethnic Interpretation," in Martin Kovacs, ed., *Ethnic Canadians: Culture and Education* (Regina, Canadian Plains Research Centre, 1978), pp. 317-331.

15. *Canada: Sessional Papers,* Vol. XXXI, No. 13, 1897, p. 2, Clause 258.

16. J.W. Dafoe, *Clifford Sifton in Relation to his Times* (Toronto: MacMillan company, 1931), p. 98.

17. Manitoba, Department of Education, *Annual Report,* 1904, p.351.

18. See, for example, Peter Humeniuk, *Harships and Progress of Ukrainian Pioneers* (Winnipeg: Author, 1977), p. 103; and M.H. Marunchak, *The Ukrainian Canadians: A History* (Winnipeg; Ukrainian Free Academy of Sciences, 1982), p.115-120.

19. *Winnipeg Tribune,* May 13, 1901.

20. *Winnipeg Tribune,* Jan. 17, 1902; Marunchak, *The Ukrainian Canadians,* p. 116.

21. Thomas Hart, "The Educational System of Manitoba," *Queens Quarterly,* XII, (1905): 240.

22. P. Yuzyk, *The Ukrainians in Manitoba: A Social History* (Toronto: University of Toronto Press, 1953), pp. 33-35.

23. V.J. Kaye, *Early Ukrainian Settlers in Canada, 1895-1900* (Toronto: University of Toronto Press, 1964), pp. 15, 173; M. Ewanchuk, *Spruce, Swamp and Stone: A History of the Pioneer Ukrainian Settlements in the Gimli Area* (Winnipeg: the author, 1977), p.77; the CPR's propaganda as early as 1890 stated that "railways, schools, churches, and thriving towns are now scattered all over the country" (*Free Homes and Cheap Railway Land,* CPR pamphlet, n.d., p.5).

24. Ukrainian children "are bright, intelligent, and most anxious to acquire a knowledge of the English language. They are well behaved in school and easily managed," Public Archives of Manitoba (hereafter PAM), Department of Education, *Annual Report.* 1897, p. 35. See also Kaye, *Early Ukrainian Settlers,* p. 165.

25. P. Humeniuk, as quoted in M. Ewanchuk, *Pioneer Profiles: Ukrainian Settlers in Manitoba* (Winnipeg: the author, 1981), p. 196; see also Ibid, p. 213; for a different, pleasant experience, see p. 26.

26. L. Driedger, "The Urbanization of Ukrainians in Canada," in Petryshyn, ed., *Changing Realities,* p. 114.

27. W.J. Wilson, "Daniel McIntyre and Education in Winnipeg" (M.Ed. thesis, University of Manitoba, 1978), esp. p. 142.

28. *Kanadyiskyi Farmer,* May 24 and June 7 and 14, 1907; J. Pampallis, "An Analysis of the Winnipeg Public School System and the Social Forces that Shaped it, 1897-1920" (M.Ed. thesis, University of Manitoba, 1979), p. 76; O. Woycenko, *Litopys ukrainskoho zhyttia v Kanadi, I, 1874-1918* (Winnipeg: Trident Press, 1961), p. 16. Ukrainians, of course, were not the only immigrant group to have a request for bilingual instruction turned down: for example, a German petition was declined in 1899 (School District of Winnipeg No. 1, Board Minute Book 1897-1900, no. 4, p. 292).

29. For Sisler's early views on Ukrainians see "The Immigrant Child," *The Western School Journal,* 1 (Apr. 1906): 3-6, and his 1912 address to the Council for Character Education, "The School and the Newer Citizens of Canada" (PAM, W.J. Sisler Papers, Box 66); for a later and more positive view see Sisler's letter of May 1, 1919, to R.L. Richardson, MPP (Ibid, box 5). We are indebted to Mrs. G. Russin for much of the above information.

30. *Kanadyiskyi Farmer,* Oct. 11, 1906; Jan. 10, Apr. 26, Oct. 11 and 25, 1907; Feb. 12, June 11, Oct. 15 and 22, and Dec. 15, 1909, etc.; *Ukrainskyi holos,* Jan. 18 and 25, and Feb. 11, 1911, etc.

31. According to Sisler's calculations, in April 1910, 19 out of Strathoona school's 618 students were "Galician or Ruthenian": in 1915 the total was 147 out of 1254 (11.7 percent) (PAM, Sisler Papers, Box 6).

32. *Robochyi narod,* Oct. 17, 1916, Jan. 26 and Sept. 26, 1917.

33. F. Swyripa, "The Ukrainians and Private Education," in M.R. Lupul, ed., *A Heritage in Transition: Essays in the History of Ukrainians in Canada* (Toronto: McClelland and Stewart, 1982), p. 248; Marunchak, *The Ukrainian Canadians,* p. 152.

34. A listing of the "Ruthenian" school districts with bilingual instruction together with dates of their establishment is given at the end of this chapter. The list goes to 1915: PAM, Department of Education, Inspectors' Reports, 1915, "Ruthenian Group." See also note 55.

35. Manitoba, Depertment of Education, *Special Report on Bilingual Schools in Manitoba,* 1915.

36. PAM, Department of Education Annual Reports, 1901.

37. See for example, "Had Mother not taught me Ukrainian, I would have been illiterate," Ewanchuk, *Pioneer Profiles,* pp. 101 and 194.

38. Ewanchuk, Spruce, *Swamp and Stone,* p. 79.

39. Ibid.; Kaye, *Early Ukrainian Settlements,* pp. 220-222; Swyripa, "Ukrainians and Private Education," pp. 245-246. Later, the Roman Catholic church also funded for the Ukrainian Catholics a minor seminary in Sifton (1912-16), which subsequently became a school for girls.

40. Kaye, *Early Ukrainian Settlements,* p. 223.

41. On the founding of the schools at Kolomyja and Olha see Ewanchuk, *Pioneer Profiles,* pp. 27 and 49.

42. Marunchak, *The Ukrainian Canadians,* p. 115; Ewanchuk, Spruce, *Swamp and Stone,* p. 78. On the other hand, Olha's first teacher, Mr. Drabyniasty,

"followed the bilingual approach and taught using the Ukrainian and the English languages." (Ewanchuk, *Pioneer Profiles,* p. 49.)

43. Ewanchuk, *Pioneer Profiles,* p. 27; Ewanchuk, *Spruce, Swamp and Stone,* p. 80; on Eaton's Catalogue see also *Canadian Heritage,* 11 (Feb./Mar., 1985): 21.

44. Inspector E.H. Walker, PAM, Department of Education, *Annual Report,* 1905, p. 50. See also Inspector Young in same, 1906, p. 34.

45. Ewanchuk, *Spruce, Swamp and Stone,* p. 80.

46. Inspector E.E. Best, PAM, Department of Education, *Annual Report,* 1905, pp. 28-30.

47. Inspector T.M. Maguire, PAM, Department of Education, *Annual Report,* 1897, pp. 31-32.

48. M. Paximadis, *Look Who's Coming: The Wachna Story* (Oshawa: Maracle Press, n.d.), p. 32; see also Ewanchuk, *Spruce, Swamp and Stone,* pp. 81 and 142.

49. PAM, Department of Education, *Annual Report,* 1903, esp. pp. 50-51; Marunchak, *The Ukrainian Canadians,* pp. 118 and 121; M.R. Lupul, "Ukrainian Language Education in Canada's Public Schools," in Lupul, M.R., ed., *A Heritage in Transition,* pp. 216-217. (We have made a conscious effort here to avoid a discussion of Manitoba party politics, but it has to be noted that all the Department's organizers of schools for Ukrainians and Poles were Conservative party activists.)

50. *Kanadyiskyi farmer,* July 12, 1907, Feb. 14, 1908, July 13, 1910.

51. PAM, Department of Education, *Annual Report,* 1904, p. 46; *Kanadyiskyi farmer, July 12, 1907, Feb. 14, 1908, July 13, 1910.*

52. *Kanadyiskyi farmer,* July 12, 1907, Feb. 14, 1908, July 13, 1910.

53. PAM, School district Records, Bradbury S.D. no. 1481, Record Book and Ledger; Budka S.D. no. 1717 Ledger; Kupezanko S.D. no. 1434 Record Book 1909-1921 and Ledger; Lukowce S.D. no. 1202 Record Book 1904-1919.

54. PAM, Lukowce Record Book.

55. PAM, Department of Education, Education Inspectors Report, 1915, "Ruthenian Group," lists 87 English-Ukrainian school districts, 4 school districts with English-Ukrainian-Polish instruction, and one each with English-Polish and English-Russian. Other authorities give different totals, e.g. 132 in 1914 (Marunchak, *Ukrainian Canadians,* p. 148); and 111 in 1915/16 (Marunchak, *Ukrainian Canadians,* p. 148; and Lupul, "Ukrainian-Language Education," p. 218. For the dates of establishment of school districts see M.B. Perfect," One Hundred Years in the History of the Rural Schools of Manitoba: Their Formation, Reorganization, and Dissolution (1871-1971)" (M.Ed. thesis, University of Manitoba, 1978), pp. 95-147.

56. *Kanadyiskyi farmer,* Jan. 8, 1909; see also the recollections of probably the first graduate of the Ruthenian Training School of how he obtained his first job, in the Beausejour area, W.A. Czumer, *Recollections About the Life of the First Ukrainian Settlers in Canada* (Edmonton: Canadian Institute of Ukrainian Studies, 1981), pp. 65-67.

57. PAM, Department of Education, *Annual Report* 1912-13, p. 63.

58. *Annual Report,* 1912-13, p.78.

59. Ewanchuk, *Pioneer Profiles,* p. 194.

60. Ewanchuk, *Spruce, Swamp and Stone*, p. 85.
61. Interview with Mr. W. Kostiuk, 1984 Oral History Project, Tapes 16/17.
62. The family structure of the regions from which the Ukrainians came to Canada was in a transitional state at the turn of the century, moving from "extended" to "nuclear." However, the eldest son was still expected to look after his parents until their death; see O. Kravets, *Simeinyi pobut i zvychai ukrainskoho narodu* (Kiev, 1966), p. 19, and H. Muchin, "The Evolution of the Ukrainian Family and its Portrayal in Illya Kiriak's novel *Sons of the Soil*" (M.A. thesis (in Ukrainian), University of Manitoba, 1978), esp. p. 6.
63. Interview with Mr. J. Melosky, 1984 Oral History Project, Tapes 12/13/.
64. Ewanchuk, *Pioneer Profiles*, p. 70.
65. This was an often-heard theme; see for example Kaye, *Early Ukrainian Settlers*, p. 165; Ewanchuk, *Pioneer Profiles*, pp. 58 and 191; and *Kanadyiskyi farmer* Mar. 6, 1908.
66. Interview with Mr. V. Chopek, 1984 Oral History Project, Tape 1.
67. Interview with Mr. W. Kostiuk, 1984 Oral History Project, Tapes 16/17.
68. *Kanadyiskyi farmer*, May 24, 1906, and May 21, 1909.
69. *Kanadyiskyi farmer*, Jan. 24, 1907, also June 25, 1909.
70. These sentiments were contained in an 88 line poem by H. Burak in *Kanadyiskyi farmer*; Mar. 5, 1909.
71. *Kanadyiskyi farmer*, Jan. 10, 1908.
72. *Kanadyiskyi farmer*, May 10, 1907.
73. *Kanadyiskyi farmer*, Mar. 6, 1908 and Sept. 10, 1909.
74. J. Baderski's report in PAM, Department of Education, *Annual Report*, 1905, p. 53.
75. *Kanadyiskyi farmer*, July 12, 1907.
76. *Kanadyiskyi farmer*, Jan. 29, 1909.
77. *Kanadyiskyi farmer*, July 10, 1908, June 25, July 9, Oct. 1, and Nov. 19, 1909.
78. PAM, Department of Education, *Annual Report*, 1906, p. 51, 1910, p. 67 and 1911, p. 41; *Kanadyiskyi farmer*, Nov. 15, 1907; *Ukrainskyi holos*, May 10, 1911.
79. B. Bilash, "Bilingual Public Schools in Manitoba, 1897-1916" (M.Ed. thesis, University of Manitoba, 1960), pp. 66, 72. Interview with Mrs. K. Michal-chyshyn, Mar. 8, 1985.
80. Complaints from "Ukrainets," Sifton, *Kanadyiskyi farmer*, Dec. 29, 1909.
81. *Kanadyiskyi farmer*, Jan. 18, 1906, Mar. 15 and 22, and Apr. 5, 1907, Jan. 17, Feb. 14 and 21, Mar. 6 and 13, 1908, etc.; *Ukrainskyi holos*, Jan. 4 and Feb. 15, 1911, etc. The trustees of Wheathill decided in 1914 that they wanted a certificated teacher who would "be moral, sober, Greek Catholic"; PAM, Wheat Hill S.D. no. 1650, Minute Book, Dec. 14, 1914.
82. Lupul, "Ukrainian Language education," p. 219-221; *Ukrainskyi holos*, Dec. 29, 1915, Jan. 112, 19, and 26, 1916, etc.
83. Interviews with W. Kostiuk and J. Melosky, 1984 Oral History Project; Ewanchuk, *Pioneer Profiles*, pp. 192-194.
84. Ewanchuk, *Pioneer Profiles*, p. 39; E. Preston, ed., *Pioneers of the Grandview and District* (Grandview: Pioneer Book Committee, 1976), p. 240. Marunchak, *Ukrainian Canadians*, p. 120, notes that some schools had libraries for the general public.

85. *Kanadyiskyi farmer,* July 17, 1907, July 10, 1908, Jan. 8, 1909.

86. *Robochyi narod,* Oct. 23, 1912, and Feb. 26, 1913.

87. *Robochyi narod,* Oct. 30, 1912.

88. PAM, Department of Education, *Annual Report,* 1908, p. 108; *Kanadyiskyi farmer,* July 17, 1908; *Ukrainskyi holos,* Apr. 19, 1911 (which also reported that the Department of Education had forbidden the use of old-country books).

89. Interview with Mr. P. Humeniuk, Aug. 11, 1983; see also Marunchak, *Ukrainian Canadians,* p. 144. The Manitoba Department of Education evidently ordered the withdrawal of bilingual primers, at least from some schools, before the ending of bilingualism in 1916, see PAM, RG 19 G1, Education Inspectors Report, 1915, reports by Inspector Peach on Borden school, Inspector Van Dusen on Lakedale school, and Inspector Jones on Franko school. For the introduction of the bilingual primers see *Ukrainskyi holos,* July 30, 1913.

90. *Kanadyiskyi farmer,* Feb. 14, 1908; *Ukrainskyi holos,* Jan. 25 and Mar. 22, 1911.

91. P. Gigejczuk in PAM, Department of Education, *Annual Report,* 1910; interview with W. Kostiuk; Marunchak, *Ukrainian Canadians,* p. 122.

92. PAM, Education Inspectors Report, 1915, reports by Inspectors Peach on Borden school and by Inspector Poulain on Oukraina school.

93. Interview with P. Humeniuk, Aug. 11, 1983.

94. PAM, Department of Education, Annual Report, 1904, pp. 34 and 46.

95. *Annual Report,* 1901, p. 34; Ewanchuk, *Pioneer Profiles,* p. 173.

96. PAM, Department of Education, *Annual Report,* 1904, p. 46.

97. *Annual Report,* 1910, p. 67, and 1911, p. 41.

98. Dauphin-Ochre School Area No. 1 Archives, Dauphin, Kosiw School District no. 1245, School Register.

99. PAM, Pine Ridge S.D. no. 608, unsigned letter of Oct. 4, 1921, to I. Stratton, official trustee of schools. On the placing of school districts under official trusteeship in 1916 and subsequently, and the resentment this caused in the Ukrainian areas of settlement see M. Ewanchuk, "Development of Education Among the Early Ukrainian Settlers in Manitoba: 1896-1924," in Baran *et al.,* eds., *Jubilee Collection,* pp. 399-400; and Ewanchuk, *Spruce, Swamp and Stone,* pp. 237-238.

100. *Echoes — Oakburn, Manitoba, 1870-1970* (Oakburn: Centennial Committee, n.d.), p. 54. Poor communications were mentioned often by the school inspectors; see for example PAM, Department of Education Annual Reports, 1906, p. 62 and 1908, p. 108. See also Ewanchuk, *Pioneer Profiles,* p. 108, etc.

101. Ibid, pp. 52, 58, 70, and 155.

102. See, for example, ibid, pp. 52, 77, and 96, Ewanchuk, *Spruce, Swamp and Stone,* p. 81 and *passim.*

103. Ewanchuk, *Pioneer Profiles, passim:* Marunchak, *Ukrainian Canadians,* pp. 223, 233-237, and *passim.*

104. The Mennonites likewise did not find the schooling arrangements in Manitoba that they had been led to believe; see in particular the bitter remarks of G. Bryce, "Yes, British Manitoba has been a better foster mother of ignorance than half-civilized Russia had been," cited in J.S. Ewart, ed., *The Manitoba School Question* (Winnipeg, n.p., 1894).

105. W.J. Sisler, "The immigrant Child," *Western School Journal,* I (Apr. 1906): 5.

HOWARD PALMER

16 Strangers and Stereotypes
The Rise of Nativism, 1880-1920

INTRODUCTION

Most of the basic assumptions concerning immigration and ethnic groups which shaped Albertan's attitudes throughout the first half of the twentieth century emerged during the province's era of early settlement. Following a period of slow economic and population growth, Alberta emerged from the late 1890s until the outbreak of World War I as one of North America's major new agricultural frontiers.

Out of the major immigration boom from 1896 to 1913 emerged the basic settlement patterns, ethnic composition, and class structure which would shape ethnic relations in Alberta for decades. In a society which was made up overwhelmingly of new immigrants, some newcomers— particularly those from English-speaking countries—felt almost immediately at home. Others, notably those from central and Eastern Europe and the Orient, would find acceptance an uphill struggle. Despite the relative prosperity and optimism of these boom years, ethnic conflict was at times intense and stereotypes abounded as people from diverse backgrounds attempted to make sense of one another and establish relationships in a new society.

The pattern of ethnic relations was certainly not uniform across the province. Urban centres provided more fertile ground for the development of nativism than rural areas. In the rural communities, where people were scattered across an immense area, where farmers faced the common tasks of pioneering and where almost everyone was a newcomer, indifference or tolerance rather than prejudice was usually the prevailing mood. In the urban areas, universally dominated by Anglo-Saxon Protestants, a middle class developed which concerned itself with social issues. With their ideal of a society based on "British" Protestant principles, many became uneasy over the type of social "vices" and problems which seemed to be associated with the new frontier. For reform minded citizens in Alberta's emerging urban centres, prostitution, crime, the use of alcohol, and non-Anglo-Saxon immigration were seen as interrelated social problems which needed to be met if Alberta and Canada were to become the societies they envisaged.[1]

By the time of the 1911 census, forty per-cent of the population was of non-British origin, with sizeable German, Scandinavian, and central and eastern European minorities. Thus, those Albertans who concerned themselves with the future of the province—whether in their roles as politicians, journalists, educators, clergymen, or community leaders—had to come to grips with the obvious fact of ethno-cultural diversity. Immigration was an important political issue of the day, often surfacing as a feature of the intense partisan struggle between the Conservatives and the Liberals. Immigration was also often linked with another event of growing political significance— the emergence of the labour movement. Particularly in the province's coal mining areas, organized labour relied heavily on the support of non-Anglo-Saxons. A number of violent strikes in which non-Anglo-Saxons appeared to play a prominent part, served to solidify the image held by many Albertans of the unruly, conflict-prone immigrant whose presence seemed to precipitate class conflict.

With the outbreak of World War I in 1914, the immigration boom ended abruptly. Because many central and eastern European immigrants came from the Austro-Hungarian Empire, one of Canada's adversaries, the war crystallized the fears and anxieties about non-British immigrants which had been developing among sectors of Alberta's society since the 1880s.

THE BEGINNINGS OF SETTLEMENT

Until the 1890s, the Northwest Territories, of which Alberta formed a part, were sparsely populated. Immigration remained small until after 1896. Central Canadians and British immigrants formed the overwhelming majority of newcomers during the 1870s and 1880s and they gradually overtook in numbers the native Indians and the Metis. These newcomers had neither the time nor the inclination to spend much energy assessing and debating the desirability of the few non-British or non-French people who arrived sporadically to join them in carving farms and settlements out of the western wilderness. Most people of British background were eager to see their settlements grow and they urged the government to promote immigration.

In 1892, the *Calgary Herald* told its readers that the Calgary district should ask only one question of its prospective immigrants: "Are they healthy, industrious and moral living?" If immigrants could answer yes to these questions, they should be met with "open hearts."[2] However, not all immigrants who arrived during the 1880s or early 1890s were in fact met with "open hearts." A heated press and political debate developed in southern Alberta over the desirability of polygamous Mormon farmers who had come from Utah to southwestern Alberta beginning in 1887. Police and local citizens in Lethbridge, the earliest coal mining community in the province, also worried about the "unruliness" of Hungarian and Slavic miners who had come to work there during the 1880s. Calgarians' hostility toward Chinese laundrymen culminated in an anti-Chinese riot in Calgary in 1892 at a time when the town had a population of approximately 4,000.[3]

Although prior to the 1890s nativist traditions were not yet firmly ensconced, a set of negative stereotypes had developed toward each of these three groups—Mormons, central and eastern Europeans, and the Chinese—which would be used in the late 1890s when larger numbers of each of them came to Alberta. For most of the 1880s and 1890s however, nativism was limited.[4]

The years from 1896 to 1914 marked the first boom period of growth in Alberta history. Alberta's population increased by five and one-half times between 1901 and 1911, surging from just over 73,000 in 1901 to almost 375,000 in 1911. A variety of economic, political and technological factors combined to transform the prairie provinces into the centre of attraction for immigrants from around the world. With the American frontier largely settled by the mid-1890s, farm-bound immigrants to North America, headed for the Canadian prairies; the "Last, Best, West."[5]

IMMIGRATION POLICY, "PROMISCUOUS FOREIGN IMMIGRATION" AND THE ETHNIC PECKING ORDER

The arrival of hundreds of thousands of newcomers from around the globe touched off a debate over immigration policy which would continue until the outbreak of the First World War, when the debate assumed a new focus and urgency. The framework within which this took place was established by Sifton's immigration policy. Sifton was dedicated to the task of peopling the Canadian West. His policy was guided by the same economic and nationalistic motives which had inspired John A. Macdonald's National Policy: immigration to western Canada would be encouraged to establish a market for eastern manufactured goods, to provide freight and traffic for the railways, and to secure the West for Canada.

Sifton's immigration policy was clearly that of attracting farmers, whatever their nationality. This preference for farmers would long continue as a feature of Canadian immigration policy, even (for a brief period) after the Second World War.[6]

Anglo-Saxon Protestants, mostly from Ontario and Britain, had established almost exclusive control of the political, legal, cultural, and educational institutions in Alberta as well as in the other prairie provinces. They set the parameters and conducted the public debate over immigration. This Anglo-Canadian elite was not homogeneous, differing in national origin and religious affiliation. The Ontario influence was stronger in Medicine Hat and Red Deer while due to the influence of the ranching elite, the British influence was stronger in Calgary. But despite these variations, the elite, whatever their ethnic origin, birthplace, or religion, had been taught to believe that the Anglo-Saxon peoples and British principles of government were the apex of both biological evolution and human achievement and they believed that Canada's greatness was due in large part to its Anglo-Saxon heritage. The 1906 *Edmonton Bulletin* expressed this widely held view concerning the model society: "The ideal of the west is not only greatness, but greatness achieved under the British Flag and stamped and moulded by the genius of race."[7]

Given these assumptions, there was a high degree of consensus among opinion leaders about the type of society they wanted and consequently the relative desirability of different ethnic groups. The desirability to Canada of particular immigrant groups varied almost directly with their physical and cultural distance from London, England and the degree to which their skin pigmentation conformed to Anglo-Saxon white. While this hierarchy was seldom spelled out so baldly, it became evident in the initial reaction of Albertans to individual ethnic groups and in the patterns of social and economic interaction and discrimination which subsequently developed.

In assessing the reaction of Albertans to new groups of immigrants, it is virtually impossible to disentangle the initially negative ethno-centric reaction of different peoples from negative reactions based on formal racist thinking. Certainly racism was on the rise in the late nineteenth century as Darwinism combined with anthropology to produce an array of schemas about the biological and social evolution of man. In their judgments of different groups, some Albertans drew upon the writings of the English intellectual and close associate of Darwin, Herbert Spencer on racial characteristics and upon notions of the superiority of Anglo-Saxons to judge potential immigrants on the basis of their "racial" background. But their ideas on these questions were seldom clearly developed. Notions of racial superiority and cultural superiority were hopelessly confused.[8]

The Alberta elite, as elsewhere on the Prairies, regarded British and American immigrants as the most desirable settlers. The British, who comprised the largest group of immigrants to Canada at this time, were usually considered the most desirable because of their similar cultural background. They obviously fit in with the prevailing conception of what type of society ought to emerge in Alberta. British immigrants came from virtually every stratum of British society and found their way into almost all fields of endeavour in Alberta; however, most were concentrated in the urban areas. Because of the similarity of their cultural background to that of other Canadians, they hardly seemed to be "immigrants" in the usual sense. They were rarely tagged with opprobrious names and there was little pressure on them to conform to a Canadian norm.[9] In fact, the more wealthy British were often regarded as models for upper-middle class Canadians who were proud of British traditions and looked to England for standards of taste.[10]

Americans were also regarded as highly desirable immigrants though for somewhat different reasons. Nearly all sections of the population, including journalists, government officials, businessmen, and farmers, welcomed the influx of over one-half million Americans (mostly farmers from the mid-western states) who came to the prairie provinces between 1898 and 1914. Almost all of those who came to Alberta began farming in central and southern Alberta where, in many communities, they formed the largest single group of newcomers. By 1911, 21 per cent of Alberta's population was American born. Government officials regarded these settlers as ideal since they brought farm skills, capital, and machinery which would enable them to farm successfully in western Canada. The province's opinion leaders were not only pleased by the boost which these settlers gave to the economic development of the country but also realized that the Americans could help them establish common schools, churches, community, and political institutions which they both regarded as essential to "civilized" life.[11]

Despite the enthusiasm about American immigration in general, some opposition developed to a second wave of Mormons who came to south-western Alberta from the western United States between 1898 and 1908. For some conservatives, the Mormon religion was the prime example of the undesirable outcome of American republicanism and democracy, and Protestant clergymen objected both to their religious beliefs, and to their proselytizing activities. However, the official discontinuance of polygamy in 1890 and the contribution that Mormons made to the establishment of an irrigation system which greatly facilitated southern Alberta's settlement, helped allay hostility. Despite a concerted anti-Mormon crusade in the national and religious press by the major Protestant denominations, by 1905 western newspapers, C.P.R. officials, and politicians of both major parties defended the Mormons as desirable citizens. The 10,000 Mormons in southern Alberta began to win gradual acceptance through their rapid adjustment to the economic, educational, and political institutions of the area. As writer and women's activist Emily Murphy reminded her readers in a 1911 article defending the Mormons, "they are Anglo-Saxons . . . who in the end will swing into true balance because of the sanity and finer sense of justice that go to make up the bed-rock principles of the race."[12]

Immigrants of German and Scandinavian origin who came to Alberta in increasing numbers after 1896 were considered to be among Canada's best citizens since they were thought to be industrious and culturally and racially similar and thus readily assimilable. With the exception of some cohesive German-speaking religious minorities, assimilation of Germans and Scandinavians was facilitated by the great diversity within each group and by their wide dispersal across the Province. The majority of immigrants of German origin were part of the German-speaking minorities of eastern Europe who were seeking escape from the problems of scarce land and rising eastern European nationalism. Germans from Germany itself were a distinct minority in western Canada. Many Germans and Scandinavians came to Canada via the mid-western United States, where they had acquired agricultural skills which helped them adapt to the Canadian prairie. In large sections of central Alberta, Scandinavian-Americans made up the founding and largest group. Although people of German and Scandinavian origin eventually formed the largest non-British minorities in Alberta, with the Germans comprising 11 per cent of the population of 374,000 and the Scandinavians eight per cent by 1911, there was virtually no negative public comment on either group before the Great War. According to the editor of the *Edmonton Bulletin*, Frank Oliver, the German immigrant was "a man of dominant race, of untiring energy, of great foresight; he is a man of sterling honesty and reliability . . . of the highest character."[13]

The Germans and Scandinavians were followed in the ethnic pecking order by central and eastern Europeans. In the eyes of Clifford Sifton, immigration agents and some members of the public, the Slavs had a slight edge on Jews, Italians and Greeks because they were more inclined to choose farm life. Central and eastern European immigrants comprised nearly one-third of Canada's immigration between 1897 and 1900 and by 1911 they formed approximately 15 per cent of the prairie population and 12 per cent of Alberta's population. Although opposition to them from Albertans and other prairie dwellers never reached the point that the federal government thought it necessary to severely restrict their immigration, as it did with Asian immigration, the concern over what role they should play in prairie society attracted the attention of nearly all the major opinion leaders in the province—newspaper editors, educators, clergymen, and politicians.[14]

The central and eastern European groups most often singled out for hostility on the prairies were two groups of peasants from eastern Europe—the Ukrainians and the Doukhobors. The Ukrainians were the most conspicuous and numerous eastern European group to arrive in western Canada after 1896. Through the promotion of various steamship companies and Dr. Josef Oleskiw, a Ukrainian intellectual, about 170,000 land-starved Ukrainian peasants came to Canada between 1896 and 1914. They settled primarily in blocs in the parkland area of Manitoba, Saskatchewan, and Alberta, although some remained in urban centres like Edmonton, where due to lack of skills and negative public stereotypes they were forced to take the lowest paying jobs. Those who came to Alberta were concentrated primarily in a bloc east and north-east of Edmonton along the North Saskatchewan River, though there were scattered settlements in other parts of the Province.[15]

At the time they arrived, the Ukrainians were referred to as "Galicians" since a majority came from the province of Austria-Hungary known as Galicia. But the term "Galician" acquired more general connotations and was used to refer to all immigrants from central and eastern Europe.[16]

Initial public reaction across the prairies to the arrival of the Ukrainians was generally negative. While dislike of the "Galicians' " cultural characteristics caused some prejudice, ethnocentrism was not the only basis for the opposition which developed. The poverty of the immigrants aroused concern that they would become dependent on charity and reports of small-pox among them brought the threat of "Galician" immigration to an intensely personal level. The bloc settlement of the Ukrainians caused further anxiety. While immigration officials saw the bloc settlement pattern as a way of attracting immigrants to western Canada, as a means of keeping them there, and as a convenient method of confining them to facilitate both close supervision and assistance, other western Canadians feared that the bloc settlement pattern would postpone assimilation indefinitely.[17]

From 1898 till at least 1905, opposition to the "Galicians" also became a partisan issue. The Conservative press and politicians, who were strongly convinced of the importance of preserving British institutions and were also seeking campaign issues, expressed the most intense anti-"Galician" sentiment and began a campaign for immigration restriction. A flood of editorials in Alberta's Conservative papers, including the *Macleod Gazette* and the *Calgary Herald* condemned the Galicians as dirty, poor, sickly, rebellious, and immoral.[18]

While the opposition to the "Galicians" was partly partisan, it also reflected basic Anglo-Saxon nativist fears. Since so few books were written by Albertans prior to 1920, it is significant that one of the few was on immigration and was authored by C.A. Magrath, a prominent Alberta Conservative who attacked the Liberal government's immigration policy and expressed Anglo-Saxon nativist fears. The Ontario-born Magrath was a well-known pioneer southern Albertan, a former manager of the Northwest Coal and Navigation Company (which dominated Lethbridge's economy) and a Conservative Member of Parliament from the Lethbridge area from 1908 to 1911. In his book, *Canada's Growth and Problems Affecting It*, which was published in 1909, Magrath demanded restrictions on central and eastern European immigrants because of the alleged threat they posed to "Anglo-Saxon" institutions. Magrath argued that many sections of southern and eastern Europe had been oppressed for years and as a result-were "behind in the march of civilization . . . many of who cannot understand the meaning of liberty, which to them is licence, and who evidently have an intense hatred for the majesty of the law." While the problem could be solved through assimilation, the process would be slow: "it will take many years under the British constitution with our free institutions to translate such people into good, intelligent citizens."[19]

The arrival in 1899 of 7,000 Russian peasants who belonged to a nonconformist Russian pacifist sect known as the Doukhobors further aroused the anxieties of many Anglo-Canadians on the prairies who were already troubled by "Galician" immigration. Although there were a number of central Canadian academics who looked sympathetically on the Doukhobor experiment and the eastern press and immigration agents welcomed the Doukhobors as desirable settlers, public opinion towards them in western Canada was not friendly. Immigration officials who were contemplating locating Doukhobors in the Edmonton area decided to settle them in Saskatchewan after a cry of protest from Edmontonians who complained that there were already too many "Galicians" in the area. Ontario-born Frank Oliver, the fiery and influential editor of the *Edmonton Bulletin* who later succeeded Clifford Sifton as Minister of the Interior, objected strenuously to the Doukhobors, arguing that they were being given preferential treatment and were pushing aside British subjects and "native sons." He stated bluntly, "This may be Christianity, philanthropy, charity or any other of the virtues, but it is not immigration."[20]

Central and eastern European immigrants were the focal point of public debate over immigration across the prairies prior to the First World War. However, they were the major cause of nativist anxiety simply because of their large numbers, not because they were considered the least desirable immigrants. Public debate over Slavs focused more and more on how they could be assimilated rather than on whether they should be allowed to enter Canada. But the debate over Blacks, Chinese, and Japanese focused on whether they should be allowed to come to Canada at all. Controversy over non-whites already in Canada was not primarily over how they could be assimilated, since this was seen by most people as both impossible and undesirable, but whether or not they deserved the same voting, residential, and occupational rights as other citizens—whether the vote should be kept from them, whether they should be restricted residentially, and whether, in the case of the Chinese, special business licenses should be required to restrict their ability to compete.

The Chinese bore the brunt of the resentment against non-whites, but opposition to them was diffuse and sporadic. Throughout the late 1890s and early 1900s they continued to move into Alberta from B.C. and by 1911 there were 1,787 Chinese in Alberta. In a frontier society where women were always a distinct minority, the Chinese engaged in various types of domestic service, principally cooking and washing, as well as working as hotel workers and market gardeners. They were forced to take up work that Caucasians were unwilling to do since lack of skills and capital prevented them from farming or ranching, while discrimination and lack of language skills confined them to the lowest ranks of the working class in the cities. Since they came mostly as "sojourners," intending to return to their families in China, few had originally brought their wives with them. After 1904, the $500 head tax imposed by the Federal government on new Chinese immigrants prohibited all but the most well-to-do Chinese from bringing wives and children to Canada. By 1911, only 20 of the Chinese in Alberta were women.[21]

Despite their relatively small numbers and their lack of direct competition with white workers, a good deal of hostility towards Chinese developed in Alberta. It certainly was not as great as it was in British Columbia where the Chinese were a major political issue for 60 years, but nevertheless they encountered more intense hostility than any other group in Alberta. The Chinese were culturally and "racially" remote, and some behavior patterns—particularly gambling and the use of opium—violated middle-class values. Many felt their coming might compromise Christian religion, ethics and progress because of their alleged illiteracy, lack of experience with self-government and moral turpitude. Following the September 1907, anti-Asian riot in Vancouver, *The Lethbridge Herald* summarized some of these arguments in an editorial advocating that Alberta follow the lead of British Columbia and disfranchise the Chinese and Japanese. According to the *Herald* "Orientals" had no right to compete with either white labour or white votes: "We do not want people without our ideas of civilization, without our ideals of government, without our aspirations as a province and a nation to bear any part in the election of our representatives. We have enough poor stuff in the voting class now."[22]

The "Oriental question" had become one of the major preoccupations of organized labour in British Columbia and some of this sentiment spilled over into Alberta. British and Canadian workers regarded most East Asians with condescension, contempt, or hostility and organized labour was the most consistently and emphatically anti-East Asian of any group in the Province; indeed, it was much more concerned with the threat of "Oriental" labour in Alberta than it was about the more numerous central and eastern Europeans. Anglo-Albertans expressed hostility toward the Chinese by attempting to disfranchise them, by segregating them residentially (in Lethbridge and Calgary), by attempting to prevent the employment of white girls in Chinese stores, by forcing them to leave town through boycotts or taxes on Chinese laundries, and by petty physical harassment.[23]

The Japanese in Alberta fared better than the Chinese. In British Columbia, anti-Japanese sentiment during the early 1900s eventually surpassed anti-Chinese sentiment, as Japanese immigration increased significantly in the late 1890s and early part of the century and Japanese miners, loggers and fishermen came into conflict with white workers. In Alberta, however, anti-Japanese sentiment prior to 1920 did not approach the intensity of anti-Chinese sentiment. Nonetheless, the Japanese who did come, mostly as farmers or miners, faced many of the same criticisms which the Chinese had encountered. Like the Chinese, the Japanese were thought to be racially inferior, unassimilable and a threat to organized labour. Outbursts of anti-Japanese sentiment included opposition in 1908 to a plan for establishing a large community of Japanese farmers on C.P.R. irrigated land east of

Calgary and labour antagonism to the use of Japanese strike breakers during the C.P.R. mechanics' strike in Lethbridge in 1909. The Alberta press also generally supported the "Gentlemans' Agreement" which the federal government introduced in 1908 (after the anti-Oriental riots in Vancouver in 1907), to reduce the influx of Japanese immigrants.[24]

But anti-Japanese sentiment in Alberta had little to nourish it. In British Columbia, hostility was stimulated by the rapid influx of Japanese immigrants and by their high birth rate. But in Alberta in 1911, there were only 244 Japanese and they were concentrated in relatively isolated sugar beet and coal mining areas of southern Alberta where their labour was needed. Nor did concerns about the moral and sanitary practices of the Japanese arise as they did with the Chinese. Although there was definitely a predominance of men among the Japanese in Alberta, there was still a much greater proportion of women than among the Chinese: the male-female ratio in 1921 was 19:1 among the Chinese and 3:1 among the Japanese. Many more Japanese than Chinese established families and were residentially scattered whereas the almost exclusively single male Chinese population congregated in urban Chinatowns. This urban concentration along with traditional cultural differences between the Chinese and Japanese, helps explain why the moral issues of gambling, opium use, and "white slavery" did not arise with the Japanese as they did with the Chinese.[25]

The issues of Chinese and Japanese immigration were tied together in the public mind. Black immigration was a separate issue, but the intense opposition which Albertans expressed to the entry of Black farmers from the United States in 1910 and 1911 revealed many of the same basic assumptions about the inferiority of non-whites and the economic, sexual, and cultural "threats" which they allegedly posed. There had been controversy over the entry of a few hundred Black farmers to the Edmonton area in 1908 and 1909, but the question of Black immigration to Alberta only became a major public issue in 1910 and 1911 with the proposed immigration of approximately 1,000 blacks (primarily from Oklahoma) who were fleeing a wave of discrimination which developed as whites began to settle Oklahoma. The decision by the Liberal government to keep out as many of these immigrants as possible, within the framework of existing regulations, was based on the combined prejudices of immigration officials, the public and politicians, together with an assessment by the latter of the probable political consequences of allowing Blacks to enter. Frank Oliver, Minister of the Interior, was particularly susceptible to public pressure on this question since many of the Blacks had taken or intended to take up farms in his home riding of Edmonton. Not surprisingly, the most vociferous expression of anti-Black sentiment came from groups in the Edmonton area.[26]

Oliver and his officials considered several responses to the public outcry against the influx of Blacks, which came not only from Alberta and other urban centres in western Canada, but also from newspapers and politicians in eastern Canada. At first they adopted an informal exclusionary policy to discourage Blacks who requested information on Canada and applied rigorous financial and medical examinations at the border for those who did try to come. In the spring of 1911, when the public outcry became most intense, Oliver drafted an Order-in-Council to bar Blacks from Canada for one year. But concern about Canadian-American relations and about Canada's public image eventually led the government to continue its reliance on informal exclusionary policies. The Canadian government hired agents, including a Black medical doctor, to go to Oklahoma for the purpose of discouraging Black immigration, telling prospective Black emigrants that in Canada they would either starve or freeze to death, that the soil was poor and that in any case, they would have trouble getting across the border. The informal policy was effective: by 1912 Black immigration to Canada virtually ceased.[27]

Black immigration became a public issue only once in Alberta because of the swiftness with which government officials cut off the potential flow of settlers. But the public controversy starkly revealed the basic racist assumptions which permeated both rural and urban Alberta. The immigration restrictions on Chinese, Japanese, and Black immigrants to Canada kept their numbers in Alberta to a minimum. This played an important role in keeping the amount of legal discrimination and public agitation demanding such discrimination, at a minimum.

THE IMMIGRANT AND THE REFORMER

The immigration boom of the pre-war period coincided with the rise in western Canada of three closely related reform movements which were determined to shape the region into a new and cohesive society. Partly as a response to local frontier conditions and partly as a result of the influence of the American progressive movement and British reform ideas, a reform movement emerged in western Canada in the years just prior to the First World War, dedicated to the task of righting the social ills and building a truly Christian Canada. Some reformers hoped for a replica of Britain or Ontario, others for a new and even better society. Most of the reformers hoped for a more egalitarian system than that envisioned by the more conservative members of the province's elite, but they nonetheless shared the ideal of a homogeneous social order based on British ideals of government and Protestantism. Three of the major social reform movements—the social gospel, prohibition, and women's rights—found particular reason to be concerned about the "threat" the new immigrants posed to the type of "progressive" society which they envisioned. To the urban middle-class Anglo-Canadian reformers who led these movements, the new immigrants possessed an array of moral and social defects. Central and eastern Europeans were not Protestants, they were not sympathetic to either prohibition or feminism and they were viewed as among the principal offenders in the abuse of both alcohol and women.

In western Canadian cities, the predominantly European immigrant working class neighbourhoods which grew up at the turn of the century were seen as urban slums and the immigrants were alleged to be more prone to crime, violence, prostitution, family breakdown and political corruption than the rest of the population. Some reformers saw social problems in the immigrant neighborhoods resulting from poverty and illiteracy, which could be corrected through education and assimilation programs; a few believed they were biologically determined and sought a solution to the problem in exclusionary immigration laws. Whatever their solutions, the reformers were united in viewing the central and eastern European and non-white immigrants as a threat to the type of society they wanted to create.[28]

The prohibition movement in western Canada focused on central and eastern European immigrants as a major stumbling block to their goals. In 1910 the president of the combined Alberta and Saskatchewan Women's Christian Temperance Union lamented the problems posed by the "foreign population. These people are coming to us in vast numbers and are bringing with them, not only their European drinking customs but their low ideal of morals and citizenship." According to the prohibitionists, the drinking habits of the immigrants were undesirable, not only because of their relationship to crime, violence, family breakdown, and every other social problem, but also because their taste for alcohol made the immigrants more vulnerable to election bribery. Prohibitionists across the prairies perceived a tightly knit web of corruption involving immigrants, liquor dealers, and politicians.[29]

Since the feminist and prohibition movements were closely linked, it is hardly surprising that anti-immigrant sentiment was also expressed by advocates of women's rights. One of the reasons women believed that they needed the vote was to help offset the detrimental effect which they claimed immigrants were having on prairie society. Women's groups pushing for the vote argued that certainly they deserved the vote if "ignorant foreigners" had it. Some women's groups even suggested that it was more important that the franchise be restricted among immigrant men than that women receive the vote.[30]

The social gospel was the underlying ideology which sustained the other social reform movements on the prairies. Many of the prohibitionists and advocates of women's rights had been deeply influenced by this religious movement, which had considerable impact on the prairies prior to 1920. It attempted to imbue Protestantism with a concern for the salvation of society as well as for the salvation of the individual soul.

As they set about their goal of attempting to build a truly Christian society on the prairies, social gospel clergymen and lay people saw "the immigrant" as one of their main stumbling blocks. The immigrants who were singled out for attention were southern and eastern Europeans and Asians since they were seen as inferior to other immigrants. As historian Marilyn Barber has shown, "the Protestant churches accepted without question the common racial division made between immigrants from northwestern Europe and those from eastern and southern Europe . . . North was superior to south; the northern race was inherently superior to the southern race." Thus, the major Protestant churches, the Presbyterian and Methodist, did not concern themselves with the predominantly Protestant immigrants from northern Europe, but focused on immigrants from other parts of the world, who were not Protestant and "lacked the desirable Anglo-Saxon qualities."[31]

As missionary work proceeded, however, proselytizing to Protestantism came increasingly to be seen as secondary to the task of assimilating the immigrants to the standards of Canada's English-speaking majority. As the Methodist Missionary Society explained in 1910, "Our objective on behalf of European foreigners should be to assist in making them English-speaking Christian citizens who are clean, educated, and loyal to the Dominion and to Greater Britain." Missionaries believed that Protestantism could save Galicians from the "vices" of card playing, Sabbath breaking, drinking, and "religious superstition." Assimilation would both alleviate the social problems facing immigrants and prevent the deterioration of "Canadian" or "British" institutions, which were regarded as synonymous.[32]

The response of the Protestant churches to the new immigrants must be seen, then, within the context of the relationship between Protestant religious values and nationalism. One of the main goals of the Protestant churches was to create a Christian nation. Describing the importance of this religious vision and its relationship to immigration, historian N.K. Clifford contends that,

> The inner dynamic of Protestantism in Canada during the first two thirds of the century following Confederation was provided by a vision of the nation as "His Dominion." This Canadian version of the Kingdom of God had significant nationalistic and millenial overtones, and sufficient symbolic power to provide the basis for the formation of a broad Protestant consensus and coalition. Not only the major Protestant denominations but also a host of Protestant-oriented organizations such as temperance societies, missionary societies, Bible societies, the Lord's Day Alliance, the YMCA's and YWCA's utilized this vision as a framework for defining their task within the nation, for shaping their conceptions of the ideal society, and for determining those elements which posed a threat to the realization of their purposes . . . Amongst the threats to this vision was the massive immigration to Canada, between 1880 and World War II, of people who did not share it . . .

This nationalistic religious vision of "His Dominion," with its implicit assumption of "a homogeneous population which shared a heritage of political democracy and evangelical Protestant Christianity," was clearly at odds with the concept of a pluralistic society; the reform movements, deeply imbued with this vision, responded to new immigrants—the agents of pluralism—with alarm, "demanding either that these newcomers conform to their way of life or that their entry into Canada be severely restricted."[33]

SOLUTIONS TO THE IMMIGRATION "PROBLEM"

Despite widespread concern among Conservatives and reformers about the impact of the new immigrants, as long as Sifton was Minister of the Interior, the Liberals basically ignored demands for tighter controls on immigration because of their continuing belief in the relationship between immigration and economic growth and in the necessity of immigrant labour for railway construction. However once Frank Oliver, Edmonton's Liberal Member of Parliament, became Minister of the Interior in 1905 following Sifton's resignation, some concessions were made to nativists in the form of tightened immigration regulations governing central and eastern Europeans. Oliver, the editor of the *Edmonton Bulletin*, was the most influential federal politician in Alberta prior to 1920. As editor and politician he had originally opposed Mormon, Chinese, "Galician," and Doukhobor immigration since none of these groups fitted into the picture of the new Ontario which Oliver hoped would develop on the prairies. He felt that these groups "who know nothing of free institutions" would "be a drag on our civilization and progress."[34]

Immigration restriction could not however "solve" the immigration problem—it could only prevent its further aggravation. Although Frank Oliver wished it otherwise, the Sifton immigration boom had made western Canada's multicultural composition a *fait accompli*. Tighter naturalization laws would only postpone the immigrants' impact on society. But assimilation of the immigrant—or if that proved impossible, assimilation of his children—still held out hope. As a result, immigrant assimilation became the most important and the most widely advocated of the three standard remedies—immigration restriction, tighter naturalization, and assimilation—proposed to the immigration "problem."[35]

The reactions of various opinion leaders in Alberta to the new immigrants reveal that they shared a common set of assumptions about the future role that non-Anglo-Saxon immigrants should play in prairie society. Virtually all subscribed to the tenets of Anglo-conformity, or the belief that it was the obligation of newcomers to conform to the already fixed values and institutions of Canadian society. Most Anglo-Albertans judged minority groups on the basis of how quickly they could be assimilated and European immigrants who were not assimilated were thought to be in need of an intensive "Canadianization" campaign. Liberals like Sifton who favored an open door policy on European immigration were confident that assimilation was possible. They did not question the assumption of the desirability of assimilation. Since non-whites could not be assimilated, they would either have to be excluded or their numbers kept at a minimum.[36]

The focal point for the assimilationist sentiment of Protestant clergymen, patriotic organizations, women's organizations, politicians—indeed everyone concerned with the immigration question—was the school system. These groups saw assimilation through education as the eventual answer to all the social problems of the immigrants and as necessary for both social integration and the preservation of a democracy which presupposed a literate electorate. The predominant goal of the Alberta school system was Anglo-conformity. The values which were to be inculcated by the schools were those of British-Canadian nationalism, citizenship, individualism and the Protestant work ethic. Assumptions of Anglo-conformity were evident not only in the school curriculum, but also in the virtual exclusion of languages other than English and the strong resistance which the provincial department of education showed toward attempts to introduce other languages such as Ukrainian or German into the school system.[37]

THE WAR PERIOD AND THE THREAT OF THE ENEMY ALIEN

Although the growing integration of Ukrainians and other central and eastern Europeans in the years immediately prior to the Great War led to a gradual decrease in hostility from the peak periods at the turn of the century, the advent of World War I precipitated the most strenuous nationalism and the most pervasive nativism in Alberta's history. Wartime propaganda dramatized the image of Germans as barbarous "Huns" and the frustration, deprivation, and bitterness which the wartime experience engendered found a convenient scapegoat in the "enemy alien." The Germans, who formerly had been counted among western Canada's most desirable citizens, now became the most undesirable. Immigrants from the Austro-Hungarian empire, including Austrians, Croats, Poles, Hungarians, Czechs, Slovaks, and Ukrainians, also found themselves under intense suspicion even though few had any loyalty to the empire. Indeed, many had come to Canada to escape military service demanded by Austrian imperial authorities. There were approximately 37,000 unnaturalized Germans and unnaturalized immigrants from the Austro-Hungarian empire in Alberta at the outbreak of the war. These "enemy aliens," as all immigrants from "enemy" countries were called, became the objects of persecution and hostility and the fires of Anglo-conformity were stoked to demand unswerving loyalty and an end to "hyphenated Canadianism."[38]

The "enemy alien" faced a barrage of official and unofficial restrictions. Across the Province as in other parts of the country, German, Austrian, Ukrainian, and other eastern European workers were dismissed from their jobs and placed under police surveillance, their language schools and many of their churches were closed, their newspapers were first censored and then gradually suppressed, their imported newspapers were banned, and some of the immigrants, particularly those in cities and in mining towns, were placed in internment camps. Naturalization was suspended for the duration of the war. It was little consolation to interned immigrants that their internment was not simply because of suspect loyalty, but also because relief authorities in cities where immigrant unemployment had reached high proportions, in the aftermath of wartime dismissal from jobs, wanted to remove part of their case load. The majority of immigrants from "enemy" countries, particularly those on farms, were not interned but were required to turn in their firearms and register and report monthly to the police. Although many of those who had been interned earlier were released in the spring and summer of 1916 in order to help fill the manpower shortage which developed during the war, pressure mounted at the end of the war from veterans' groups and patriotic organizations to again have "enemy aliens" dismissed from their jobs to make way for returning veterans.[39]

For many western Canadians during the war, loyalty and cultural and linguistic uniformity were synonymous. Both the federal and provincial governments enacted measures to ensure homogeneity. At the federal level, the formation in 1917 of the Union Government composed of Conservatives and some Liberals, can be seen in part as an attempt to create an Anglo-Canadian party, dedicated to "unhyphenated Canadianism" and the winning of the war even if this meant trampling the rights of immigrants. The Conservative leader of the opposition in Alberta, E.A. Michener, reported to Conservative Prime Minister Robert Borden that the "foreign population" had voted against the Alberta Conservatives in the 1917 provincial election because of the untimely announcement by the federal government of its plan for conscription. Michener urged disfranchisement:

> Before the election I was not in favor of the disfranchisement of the alien enemy born, but seeing the result of the present campaign and the pro-German appeal that the government has made, I am satisfied that if you decided to appeal to the country, unless you decide to disfranchise all the enemy alien born they will have the balance of power to defeat most of our candidates in the Province.[40]

Faced with similar pressures from across western Canada, Borden's reply came in the form of the Wartime Elections Act which disfranchised "enemy aliens" who were born in an enemy country, whose mother tongue was the language of an enemy country and who had been naturalized after March 31,

1902. Unlike the provisions for registration and internment, which were directed to unnaturalized immigrants, the Wartime Elections Act was directed at naturalized Canadian citizens. The only exceptions which were made were for men who had volunteered and been accepted into the armed forces. Although some Liberal politicians and the Liberal press in Alberta felt that taking the vote away from some Canadian citizens was unfair and "un-British," the measure had been insistently demanded not only by Conservative newspapers and politicians in Alberta but also by an array of patriotic and women's organizations.

WARTIME NATIVISM AND THE PACIFIST GROUPS

The restrictive measures enacted under the authority of the War Measures Act reflected a growing anxiety about the loyalty and assimilability of new immigrant groups. Concern was not, however, simply limited to immigrants from "enemy" countries, but also included three pacifist religious sects—Doukhobors, Mennonites and Hutterites—each of whom came to Canada under specific guarantees from the federal government that they would be able to maintain their autonomy, educational freedom and exemption from military service.[41]

Resentment toward both Mennonites and Doukhobors had built up in western Canada during the war because of their separatism, pacifism and resistance to compulsory schooling. Many western Canadians felt that their exemption from military service was allowing them to prosper while other Canadians were making the ultimate sacrifice in the war effort. Returning veterans were particularly hostile to pacifist groups. Animosity toward Mennonites and Doukhobors in Alberta was not as great as in Manitoba or Saskatchewan because their numbers were fewer (their total number amounted to only 0.5 per cent of the population) but controversy surrounding them was brewing.

The First World War focused attention on Alberta's Mennonites. Resentment began to build in a few communities over Mennonite pacifism. They were also among those groups who were disfranchised by the federal government under the War Time Elections Act. Ironically, however, anti-Mennonite sentiment in Alberta was not directed primarily against Mennonites. When Hutterites began coming to southern Alberta from South Dakota in 1918, they were mistakenly thought to be Mennonites and the press and politicians continually referred to them as Mennonites. (Though emerging out of the same Anabaptist roots as the Mennonites, the Hutterites trace their origins to Jacob Hutter rather than to Mehno Simmons, and the Hutterites live communally while the Mennonites do not.) The hostility which was expressed toward these "Mennonites" was conditioned primarily by the controversial Manitoba experience rather than the Alberta one. The storm of protest over "Mennonite" immigration may have been mistaken in several ways, but it did reveal prevailing conceptions which Albertans had about Mennonites. Whether they liked it or not and despite their minimal ties, Mennonites and Hutterites would almost always be fused in the Alberta public mind.[42]

With resentment toward Germans, "enemy aliens" and pacifists at peak levels, the arrival in October 1918, of a group of Hutterites to southern Alberta was most untimely. The Hutterites came to Canada from South Dakota to escape wartime persecution in the United States. They arrived with the assurance of immigration officials that the privileges which had been extended to them by Order-in-Council in 1899 when they had first looked into the possibilities of coming to Manitoba (giving them military exemption, the right to their own schools and permission to live communally) were still intact. By the end of 1918, there were ten Hutterite colonies in Alberta with approximately one hundred Hutterites in each colony.

Opposition to the Hutterites was immediate. It came not only from veterans' groups but service clubs, politicians, temperance groups and church groups. The group had everything against it. They were German-speaking, they were pacifists and they were determined to maintain their way of life through segregated communal living. Press reaction in Alberta was vitriolic. The *Edmonton Bulletin,* one of the few strong critics in western Canada of the federal Union government thundered: "It was not for the purpose of making Canada an asylum for slackers and a paradise for semi-citizens that Canadians enlisted to fight for the overthrow of autocracy." There was little humour in the reaction of Bob Edwards, the colourful editor of the usually witty *Calgary Eye Opener:* "Calder (Minister of the Interior) may be permitted to keep the Mennonite colonies to himself in Saskatchewan; they can't get away with that stuff over here. It's too bum. BUT WHY SHOULD THEY WANT TO IMPOSE SUCH A BUNCH OF GERMAN CATTLE ON US? That gets our goat. WHY?"[43]

By 1919, the Mennonites, Doukhobors, and Hutterites—despite significant religious and cultural differences among them—were locked together in the public mind as being undesirable and unassimilable. Agitation against them by "patriotic" and veterans' groups across western Canada finally resulted in the passage by the federal cabinet of an Order-in-Council in June 1919 which specifically barred the entry of members of these groups into the country.[44]

ANTI-RADICAL SENTIMENT AND THE APEX OF NATIVISM

The return of the veterans at the end of the war and the post-war economic depression not only brought to a peak the hostility towards the three pacifist sects in late 1918 and early 1919 but also contributed to the full flowering of a relatively new and virulent form of anti-immigrant sentiment—anti-radical nativism. The earlier image of the Slavic immigrant as being easy prey to political corruption had, on occasion, given way to an image of the immigrant as dangerous revolutionary. This was particularly true in the coal fields of southern Alberta where over 50 per cent of the workers were from southern, central and eastern Europe. Anti-radical nativism had been intense in Lethbridge and the Crow's Nest Pass in 1906 and 1907 during a period of pronounced labour conflict and unrest. During the war, businessmen and community leaders saw radical activity on the part of organized labour as being connected with pro-German feeling because radicals also led the opposition to the war in western Canada.[45]

The anti-radical sentiment which developed in 1918 and 1919, a period of profound labour unrest, tended to assume a nationalistic form because a large proportion of the radicals were Slavic immigrants. Some immigrants brought ideas of class consciousness with them from Europe and the majority of workers in the coal mining industries where radicalism flourished were immigrants. Discrimination, wartime regimentation and repression, inflation and deaths due to unsafe working conditions in the mines combined to produce a situation in which a number of central and eastern European immigrants were attracted to radical organizations. In mining camps and cities across western Canada, Slavic immigrants formed a large proportion of leftist union membership (though not the leadership) and left-wing organizers formed groups in western Canada among Russians, Finns, Jews, Lithuanians and Ukrainians. With the growing connection in the public mind between immigrants and radical activity, many Canadians began to wonder what right "foreigners" had to disrupt the harmony of national life and reasoned that class conflict was an alien and imported phenomenon unnecessary in Canada where there was ample opportunity for all.[46]

The "Red Scare" of 1919 brought to a culmination all of the fears and anxieties which had developed concerning central and eastern European immigrants. Veterans and immigrants clashed openly and violently in Alberta at Drumheller, Brule, Calgary, and Medicine Hat. Police rounded up immigrant radicals in Alberta who possessed "subversive" newspapers or literature. Veterans' organizations across western Canada bombarded the government with resolutions demanding that all property of enemy aliens be confiscated, that immigrant radicals be arrested or deported, and that "enemy aliens" be prevented from voting for at least twenty years. They also pressed employers and governments to replace immigrant workers with veterans. Some mine managers in Alberta, who also feared immigrant radicals, began dismissing allegedly radical immigrants while the federal government responded to this public indignation with new laws preventing the entry of immigrant radicals, as well as making possible the deportation of immigrant radicals in Canada. Major Stafford of the Alberta Great War Veterans Association put the issue simply to rank and file of his organization: "There is no room in Canada for the enemy alien and the Great War Veterans Association. One of them has got to go and that one will not be the returned soldier."[47]

CONCLUSION

The period from 1896 to 1920 had witnessed a gradual shift in the form and intensity of anti-immigrant sentiment. Although public opinion was divided on the desirability of central and eastern European immigrants, assumptions about the link between immigration and economic growth enabled the federal government to largely ignore nativist rumblings prior to the war. The federal government did eventually make some concessions to nativists in the form of tightened immigration regulations; but it did not give in completely to the demands of patriotic organizations and reformers.

World War I precipitated important shifts in public opinion toward immigrants. The old notions about Anglo-Saxon superiority and about the threat posed by immigrants to Anglo-Saxon institutions were, in the climate of war, enacted into public policy. Many people thought that immigrants from "enemy" countries could not be trusted; they had to be controlled and their franchise restricted. The optimistic assumption that the assimilation of European immigrants would simply occur in the course of time became suspect. Assimilation would have to be enforced through the school system. Agrarian-based religious minorities, such as Hutterites, Doukhobors, and Mennonites, previously encouraged by the federal government to come to western Canada, were now thought incapable of assimilation—they would have to be excluded. Central and eastern Europeans, whose major defects had previously seemed to be their lack of education and their susceptibility to what were viewed as moral vices by middle class Anglo-Saxons, were now seen more and more as dangerous revolutionaries. By 1919, notions of ethnic, cultural and political acceptability had triumphed over economic considerations in the formation of national immigration policy.[48]

Underlying all the various coercive and restrictive measures which governments enacted during wartime in response to public pressure, was an anxiety about the need to control immigrants. Along with internment, registration, censorship, immigration restriction, deportation, and forced assimilation one must add prohibition and the enfranchisement of women to the list of wartime measures which attempted to provide this constraint. The reform spirit which the war engendered was central to the wartime success in all three prairie provinces of prohibition and votes for women; but prohibition was also another way of controlling the behaviour of German and central and eastern European immigrants and enfranchising women was a way of assuring that the old Protestant middle class virtues could be better protected against the "enemy aliens."[49]

The wartime experience revealed how powerless immigrant minorities were in the face of hostile public opinion and a federal government which distrusted them. The government had armed itself with the War Measures Act which enabled it to take any measure it deemed necessary and these measures it enacted were largely responses to public pressure, rather than to any real threat "enemy aliens" posed. Most of the immigrants from the Austro-Hungarian Empire had come fleeing social and economic problems and either had little or no sense of loyalty to the Empire or were actively hostile towards it. The vast majority of German-speaking immigrants to Canada came from German-speaking enclaves in eastern Europe or the United States and their loyalties focused on their religious and cultural heritage rather than on the German nation. Neither the federal government nor the general public had much awareness of these facts, however and there was little reluctance to trample on the rights of these minorities and little willingness to take their views into account.

Nor could the Germans and central and eastern Europeans mount any effective protest against their treatment. The German-speaking community in Alberta, though fairly numerous, was geographically dispersed and highly heterogeneous—divided both by area of origin and religion. The group, com-posed primarily of pioneer farmers, was not highly politicized and some of the most educated among them, the German army officers and reservists, had either been arrested at the outbreak of the war, or had left Canada. Although the Ukrainians were more geographically concentrated and more homogeneous, they were composed predominantly of farmers and labourers who had little education or political experience. The most highly educated among them—clergymen, teachers and newspaper editors—had all been dis-credited in the eyes of public officials and the press.[50]

The assimilation campaign and the drive to restrict Slavic immigration were primarily the concern of middle class Anglo-Albertans, but nativism was certainly not limited to the middle and upper middle class. Dislike for "foreigners" among working class people did not find much expression in the newspapers, but it was revealed in the widespread use of opprobrious names like "Bohunks" or "Chinks" and the use by the native-born and British workers of the term "white men" to distinguish themselves from the southern, central, and eastern Europeans and Asians with whom they worked. The opposition which labour unions expressed to immigration was based partly on concern about economic competition, but was also based on assumptions about the inferiority of central and eastern Europeans and Asians, and ethnic prejudice sometimes impeded the work of unionization. Much of the hostility which was expressed toward "alien" workers both, at the outset of the war and at the end of the war, came from English-speaking workers. The syndicalist One Big Union might declare in 1919 that "there was no alien but the capitalist," but most veterans' organizations across the prairies were staunchly anti-"alien" and they certainly had more support among the English-speaking working men than did the O.B.U.[51]

By 1920 almost all the major nativist webs of thought and feeling which were to be expressed in Alberta had been established. Anglo-Saxon and anti-radical nativism had each coalesced, though Anglo-Saxon nativism emerged earlier and seemed to be the major touchstone for the various rationalizations of prejudice toward ethnic minorities. The basic ethnic "pecking order" or "hierarchy of desirability" which was, in its broad contours, widely accepted throughout the English-speaking world, had been articulated. These assumptions would continue to be expressed in immigration policy and in patterns of ethnic discrimination and class stratification until after the Second World War. The attitudes of a whole generation of opinion leaders, including politicians, had been formed by their experience during the immigration boom.[52]

NOTES

* This is an abbreviated version of Chapter 1, from H. Palmer, *Patterns of Prejudice* (Toronto: McClelland and Stewart, 1982).

1. For discussion of the concerns of reformers with alcohol and prostitution see James Gray, *Booze: The Impact of Whiskey on the Prairies* (Toronto, 1972); and *Red Lights on the Prairies* (Toronto, 1971); for discussion of general developments in Alberta see J.G. MacGregor, *A History of Alberta* (Edmonton, 1972), Chapters 9-15, and L.G. Thomas, *The Liberal Party in Alberta: A History of Politics in the Province of Alberta, 1905-1921* (Toronto, 1959).

2. *The Calgary Herald* (hereinafter cited C.H.), January 27, 1892.

3. Howard Palmer, "Nativism and Ethnic Tolerance in Alberta, 1880-1920," (M.A. thesis, University of Alberta, 1971), Chap. 1. Lawrence B. Lee, "The Mormons Come to Canada, 1887-1902," *Pacific Northwest Quarterly*, 59 (1968), pp. 11-22; Brian Dawson, "The Chinese Experience in Frontier Calgary," in A.W. Rasporich and Henry Klassen (eds.), *Frontier Calgary 1875-1914* (Calgary, 1975), p. 127-132; William Beahen, "Mob Law Could Not Prevail," *Alberta History* 29, 3 (1981), pp. 1-7.

4. Palmer, *Patients of Prejudice* p. 21.

5. J.B. Hedges, *Building the Canadian West* (New York, 1939), p. 126.

6. D.J. Hall, "Clifford Sifton: Immigration and Settlement Policy: 1896-1905" in H. Palmer (ed.), *The Settlement of the West* (Calgary, 1977), pp. 60.85; Mabel Timlin, "Canada's Immigration Policy 1896-1910," *Canadian Journal of Economics and Political Science* (hereinafter cited as C.J.E.P.S.), (1960), p. 517-532; J.W. Dafoe, *Clifford Sifton in Relation to His Times* (Toronto, 1931), p. 141.

7. For discussion of the vision of western Canada as the "Britain of the West," see L.G. Thomas, "Alberta Perspectives, 1905," *Alberta History* (hereinafter cited as *A.H.*) 28 (1980), pp. 23; and Douglas Owram, *Promise of Eden: The Canadian Expansionist Movement and the Idea of the West 1856-1900* (Toronto, 1980), Chap. 7. Although the term Anglo-Celts is more accurate for the group which I am describing (since it included peoples of Scots, Welsh, and Irish backgrounds), I have used the term Anglo-Saxon since it was historically more widely

used. The elite was not exclusively Protestant. A few Catholics, such as Patrick Burns, penetrated the Calgary elite. A handful of French-Canadian business and professional men in Edmonton achieved economic, social and political prominence prior to the 1920s, but prominent Catholics and non-Britishers were few and far between. For detailed evidence on Anglo-Saxon Protestant domination see H.L. Malliah, "A Socio-Historical Study of Legislators of Alberta, 1905-1967" (Ph.D., University of Alberta, 1970); James Gray, *Booze* (Toronto, 1972), p. 36; Suzanne Nagy, "A Statistical Analysis of John Blue's Alberta Past & Present" (unpublished seminar paper, History 532, University of Calgary, 1979); P.L. Voisey, "In Search of Wealth and Status: An Economic and Social Study of Entrepreneurs in Early Calgary," in A.W. Rasporich and H.C. Klassen (eds.), *Frontier Calgary* (Calgary, 1975), pp. 221-241. For discussion of British and eastern Canadian dominance in the ranching industry, see David Breen, "The Turner Thesis and the Canadian West: A Closer Look at the Ranching Frontier," in L.H. Thomas (ed.), *Essays on Western History* (Edmonton, 1976), p. 153; on Anglo-Saxon ideology see Carl Berger, *Sense of Power* (Toronto, 1970), p. 186 and Palmer, "Nativism," p. 134. Quote from *Edmonton Bulletin* (hereinafter cited as *E.B.*), January 10, 1906.

8. John Higham, *Strangers in the Land* (New York, 1955), Chap. 6; Thomas F. Gossert, *Race: The History of an Idea in America* (Dallas, 1963), Chap. 13. For further discussion of this confusion between notions of cultural and racial superiority see Marilyn Barber, "The Assimilation of Immigrants in the Canadian Prairie Provinces, 1886-1918: Canadian Perspective and Canadian Policies," (Ph.D. University of London, 1975); and Christine Bolt, *Victorian Attitudes to Race* (London, 1971), p. 206-208.

9. Henry Klassen, "Life in Frontier Calgary," in A.W. Rasporich, (ed.), *Western Canada: Past and Present* (Calgary, 1975), pp. 42-57. For discussion of the exceptions to the rule of acceptance of the British, see Palmer, *Patterns of Prejudice* p. 24-25.

10. On critical attitudes toward remittance men, see Patrick A. Dunae, "Tom Brown on the Prairies: Public Schoolboys and Remittance Men in the Canadian West, 1870-1914" (paper presented to the CHA meetings, Saskatoon, Sask., 1979).

11. Robert Sloan, "The Canadian West: Americanization or Canadianization?" *A.H.*, 16, 1 (1968), pp. 1-7; H. Troper, *Only Farmers Need Apply* (Toronto, 1972); Palmer, "Nativism," pp. 5869; *E.B.*, June 26, 1906; CAR (1919), p. 589; Department of Interior Reports, 1900-1914; R.N.W.M.P. Report, 1907, p. 766; *Lethbridge News*, September 11, 1908; *Lethbridge Herald* (hereinafter cited as *L.H.*) November 15, 1905; CAR 1903, p. 395; Adam Shortt, "Some Observations on the Great North-west," *Queen's Quarterly*, 2 (1894), p. 194; *L.H.*, March 12, 1912.

12. Palmer, "Nativism," pp. 76-93; Howard Palmer, *Land of the Second Chance: A History of Ethnic Groups in Southern Alberta* (Lethbridge, 1972), Chapter 10. On the conception of Mormonism in conservative Canadian thought, see Carl Berger *Sense of Power* pp. 155, 158; Emily Murphy, "Till Death Do Us Part," *Canada Monthly,* December, 1911, pp. 83-90.

13. Palmer, "Nativism," pp. 69-76; Palmer, *Land of the Second Chance* Chaps. 11 and 13; speech by Oliver in *Debates* House of Commons, April 12, 1901, p. 2934.

14. For ethnic proportions see Table 1.
15. Palmer, *Land of the Second Chance* pp. 77-78; Alexander Royick, "Ukrainian Settlements in Alberta," *Canadian Slavonic Papers*, V, 3 (1968), p. 278-297.
16. For a discussion of attitudes toward other central and eastern European groups, see Palmer, "Nativism," pp. 119-39.
17. John Lehr, "The Government and the Immigrant; Perspectives on Bloc Settlement in the Canadian West," *Canadian Ethnic Studies*, IX, 2 (1977), pp. 44-45. On public attitudes toward Ukrainians see Palmer, "Nativism," pp. 97-111; Donald Avery "Canadian Immigration Policy, the Anglo-Canadian Perspective" (Ph.D., University of Western Ontario, 1973), p. 151; Helen Potrebenko, *No Streets of Cold: a Social History of Ukrainians in Alberta* (Vancouver, 1977), pp. 36-41; *E.B.*, October 24, 1898.
18. Palmer, "Nativism," pp. 102-103; *C.H.*, January 19, 1899, July 19, 1900; *Macleod Gazette* November 23, 1900.
19. C.A. Magrath, *Canada's Growth and Problems Affecting It* (Ottawa, 1910) p. 54; Palmer, "Nativism," p. 131; *Macleod Gazette* November 19, 1910. *E.B.*, Dec. 22, 1898.
20. *E.B.*, Dec. 22, 1898; On Oliver's views toward "Galicians" and Doukhobors, see Palmer, "Nativism," pp. 17-18, 108-110, 117-118.
21. *C.H.*, June 6, 1888; Brian Dawson, "The Chinese Experience in Frontier Calgary—1885-1910," pp. 124-140.
22. For a listing of the extensive literature dealing with attitudes toward Asians in British Columbia see Alan Artibise, *Western Canadian Since 1870* (Vancouver, 1978), pp. 197-209. For a detailed discussion of attitudes toward Chinese and Japanese in Alberta see H. Palmer, "Anti-Oriental Sentiment in Alberta; 1880-1920," *Canadian Ethnic Studies, 2*, 2 (1970), pp. 31-58; Quote from *L.H.*, October 24, 1907.
23. Palmer, "Anti-Oriental Sentiment"; Gunter Baureiss, "The Chinese Community in Calgary," *A.H.*, 22, 2 (1978), p. 1-8.
24. Ken Adachi, *The Enemy That Never Was* (Toronto, 1976); Palmer, "Anti-Oriental Sentiment," pp. 42-46.
25. On the early history of the Japanese in southern Alberta see H. Palmer, *Land of the Second Chance*, Chap. 6 and David Iwaasa, "Canadian Japanese in Southern Alberta," Research Paper, University of Lethbridge, 1974, published in Roger Daniels (ed.), *Two Monographs on Japanese-Canadians* (New York, 1979). In 1921, there were 3,399 male Chinese and 182 females, while there were 360 male Japanese and 113 females. *Census of Canada*, 1921, I Table 25.
26. Palmer, "Nativism," pp. 182-87; Robin Winks, *Blacks in Canada* (New Haven, 1971), pp. 305-313; Harold Troper, "The Creek Negroes of Oklahoma and Canadian Immigration, 1901-1911," *Canadian Historical Review* (hereinafter cited as *C.H.R.*) 53, 3 (1972), pp. 272-88; Colin Thomson, "Dark Spots in Alberta," *A.H.*, 25, 4 (1977), pp. 30-36; R. Bruce Shepard, "Black Migration as a Response to Repression: The Background Factors and Emigration of Oklahoma Negroes to Western Canada, 1905-1912" (M.A., University of Saskatchewan 1974), Chap. 4.
27. Winks, *Blacks,* p. 305-313; Troper, "The Creek Negroes"; Shepard "Black Migration." Chap. 4.
28. Avery, "Canadian Immigration Policy," p. 306.

29. James Gray, *Booze*, pp. 42-43; Barbara Nicholson, "Feminism in the Prairie Provinces (M.A., University of Calgary, 1974), p. 70; J.H. Thompson, "The Liquor Question in Manitoba, 1892-1926" (M.A., University of Manitoba, 1969); Tom Peterson, "Ethnic and Class Politics in Manitoba," in Martin Robin (ed.), *Canadian Provincial Politics* (Scarborough, 1972), p. 75.

30. Nicholson, "Feminism," pp. 83-85, 114, 121, 165, 166, 169, 186-87; Carol Lee Bacchi-Ferraro, "The Ideas of Canadian Suffragists, 1890-1920" (M.A., McGill University, 1970), p. 48. *C.H.*, November 30, 1905; Nicholson, "Feminism," p. 84. For a detailed account of WCTU attitudes toward immigrants and efforts to promote prohibition among them see Nancy Sheehan, "Temperance, the WCTU and Education in Alberta, 1905-1930" (Ph.D. thesis, University of Alberta, 1980), pp. 138-142, 219-223, 262-263.

31. See Richard Allen, *The Social Passion: Religion and Social Reform in Canada, 1914-1928* (Toronto, 1971) for a discussion of the background and impact of the social gospel movement. Quotes from Marilyn Barber, "Nationalism, Nativism and the Social Gospel: The Protestant Church Response to Foreign Immigrants in Western Canada, 1897-1914," in Richard Allen (ed.), *The Social Gospel in Canada* (Ottawa, 1975), pp. 208, 209; George Emergy, "Methodist Mission among the Ukrainians," *A.H.*, 19, 1 (1971).

32. Marilyn Barber, "Nationalism, Nativism and the Social Gospel," pp. 186-226; Amy Peyton, *The Friendly Door: A History of Bissell Centre* (Edmonton, 1979); Palmer, "Nativism," pp. 82-89; 158-64; 206-207.

33. N.K. Clifford, "His Dominion: a vision in crisis," *Studies in Religion* 2, 4 (1973), pp. 314-326. Quotes from p. 314.

34. House of Commons, *Debates*, April 12, 1901, c. 2934.

35. Palmer, "Nativism," pp. 139-65.

36. D.J. Hall, "Clifford Sifton," p. 84.

37. Myrna Kostash, *All of Baba's Children* (Edmonton, 1977), Chap. 6; Palmer, "Nativism," Chap. 2. For an excellent overview of assimilationist pressures in educational attitudes and policy, see Neil McDonald, "Canadian Nationalism and North-West Schools, 1884-1905," in Alf Chaiton and Neil McDonald (eds), *Canadian Schools and Canadian Identity* (Toronto, 1977).

38. Palmer, "Nativism," pp. 216-29; Thompson, *Harvests of War* (Toronto, 1978), pp. 75-77.

39. Palmer, "Nativism," Chap. 3; J.A. Boudreau, "Western Canada's Enemy Aliens in World War One," *A.H.*, 12, 1 (1964), pp. 1-9; Desmond Morton, "W.D. Otter and Internment Operations in World War I," *C.H.R.*, LV, 1 (1974), pp. 1-9; Donald Avery, "The Immigrant Industrial Worker in Canada, 1896-1930: The Vertical Mosaic as an Historical Reality," in W. Isajiw (ed.), *Identities* (Toronto, 1977), pp. 15-29; W. Entz, "The Suppression of the German Language Press in September, 1918," *Canadian Ethnic Studies*, 8, 2 (1976), pp. 56-70; Joseph Boudreau, "Interning Canada's 'Enemy Aliens,' 1914-19," *Canada* 2, 1 (1974), p. 17. For evidence that discrimination against Germans affected the well to do and the influential as well as farmers and labourers, see the memoirs of German immigrant Martin Nordegg in T.D. Regehr (ed.), *The Possibilities of Canada are Truly Great: Memories, 1906-1924* (Toronto, 1971), pp. 201-222. For examples of discrimination as reported by the German

language press, see *Der Deutsch-Canadier,* September 3, 1914, p. 4; *Alberta Herald,* January 16, 1915, p. 2; May 13, 1915, p. 4; April 15, 1915, p. 4.

40. Cornelius J. Jaenen, "Ruthenian Schools in Western Canada 1897-1919," *Paedagogica Historica, International Journal of the History of Education* X, 3 (1970) pp. 517-41; Donald Avery, "Canadian Immigration Policy," pp. 374-420; Palmer, "Nativism," pp. 244-54; PAC, R.L. Borden Papers, Michener to Borden, June 11, 1917. For Borden's reply see *ibid.,* Borden to Michener. For further background on the wartime Elections Act see Roger Graham, *Arthur Meighen, I* (Toronto, 1960), p. 163-170.

41. George Woodcock and Ivan Avakumovic, *The Doukhobors* (Toronto, 1968), p. 133; Victor Peters, *All Things Common* (Minneapolis, 1965), p. 47; Frank Epp, *Mennonites in Canada: The History of a Separate People* 1786-1920 (Toronto, 1974), p. 192.

42. Palmer, "Nativism, 1880-1920," p. 234.

43. Victor Peters, *All Things Common,* pp. 48-50; Palmer, "Nativism," pp. 254-60; *E.B.,* September 30, 1918; *Calgary Eye Opener,* October 5, 1918.

44. Order-in-Council, P.C., #1204, *Canada Gazette,* June 14, 1919.

45. Palmer, "Nativism," pp. 124-25; Donald Avery, "Immigrant Workers and Labour Radicalism in Canada, 1900-1920, A Case Study of the Rocky Mountain Coal Mining Industry," unpublished paper, University of Western Ontario, 1975. Donald Avery, *Dangerous Foreigners: European Immigrant Workers and Labour Radicalism in Canada,* 1896-1932 (Toronto, 1979), Chapter 2.

46. Palmer, "Nativism," pp. 264-76; David Bercuson, *Fools and Wise Men: The Rise and Fall of the One Big Union* (Toronto, 1978), Chap. 4; David Bercuson (ed.), *Alberta's Coal Industry,* 1919 (Calgary, 1978), p. 39.

47. *R.N.W.M.P. Reports,* 1919, p. 14. For details of the violence at Drumheller, see Ann Woywitka, "Drumheller Strike of 1919," *A.H.,* 20, 4 (1972), pp. 1-5, and Bercuson, *Fools and Wise Men,* p. 197-200; Potrebenko, *No Streets of Gold,* pp. 144-47. On anti-radical sentiment in general, see Avery, "The Industrial Worker," p. 23; David Smith, *Prairie Liberalism: The Liberal Party in Saskatchewan,* 1905-1971 (Toronto, 1975), p. 125; *E.B.,* February 7, 1919; Palmer, "Nativism," pp. 271, 274-75.

48. Palmer, "Nativism," pp. 229-31; Avery, "Canadian Immigration Policy," p. 20.

49. Nicholson, "Feminism," p. 187; Thompson, *Harvests,* p. 109.

50. At the outset of the war, the pastoral letter issued by the Greek Catholic Bishop Budka in Winnipeg, in which he counselled Ukrainians to return to Austria and fight for the Emperor, had effectively discedited the clergy. Both the teachers and the newspaper editors were generally thought to be dangerous proponents of Ukrainian nationalism. Paul Yuzyk, *The Ukrainians in Manitoba* (Toronto, 1953), Chap. 13; Palmer, "Nativism," p. 241. PAC, R.L. Borden Papers, J.T. Ferguson to R.B. Bennett, January 5, 1917; R.B. Bennett to Borden, January 22, 1917.

51. Palmer, "Nativism," p. 120; A.R. McCormack, *Reformers, Rebels and Revolutionaries* (Toronto, 1977), p. 10; Robert Babcock, *Gompers in Canada* (Toronto, 1974), p. 116; Bercuson, *Fools and Wise Men,* p. 23, 31.

52. The "ethnic pecking order" which emerged in Alberta was very similar to that in other parts of English-speaking Canada and the United States. It emerges very clearly for example in J.S. Woodsworth's *Strangers Within our Gates* as well as in many other books and articles in magazines and journals of the day. Basically the same pecking order emerged in the United States, with variations depending primarily on the presence of differing ethnic minorities. See John Higham, *Strangers in the Land*.

VIII

THE SETTLEMENT EXPERIENCE AND THE CREATION OF PRAIRIE INSTITUTIONS

In addition to their common hopes which had brought them to western Canada, the newcomers shared a common set of problems. The weather was unpredictable. The crops were uncertain. Transportation at points away from the rail lines was slow and difficult. Farmers did not have telephones until the end of the pioneer period, and they did not have radios to bring them into contact with the outside world. Farm machinery was still fairly simple, and much of the farm work had to be done through the labour of people and their animals. Money was scarce, and farm families could afford very few things beyond basic necessities.

Such hardships and common economic problems fostered cooperation in rural areas. Usually the building of churches and schools first brought the settlers together. But newcomers also established other types of cultural, social, and economic organizations. Wilfrid Eggleston, who came to southern Alberta from England as a boy with his family to homestead in 1909 (before going on to a distinguished career as a national journalist), gives a personal account of his family's homesteading experience in the drybelt of southeastern Alberta in "The Old Homestead: Romance and Reality." His account gives us insight into some of the factors involved in settlers' choosing land, into the nature of rural life, and into the difficulties facing prairie farmers in a harsh environment.

The government's relatively open immigration policy and the lure of the frontier attracted many groups who wanted to establish utopian settlements on the prairies. In his article "Utopian Ideals and Community Settlements in Western Canada, 1880-1914," Anthony Rasporich describes a number of utopian settlements in western Canada in the period prior to the First World War and explains why some were successful and others unsuccessful. Though utopian settlements were the exception rather than the rule, they exemplified the underlying utopian ideal (discussed by Morton in Chapter 2) of a new and better society in western Canada.

The massive population growth at the turn of the century led to growing public demands that the North-West Territories be given greater autonomy. Many people felt that provincial status would give the region more political clout, more public revenues, and more opportunity to control its own destiny. But first of all, a number of controversial issues had to be resolved. Would there be one or two new provinces? Would the federal or provincial government own the natural resources? What guarantees would be given for separate schools? Who would be chosen as interim premier to set in motion the mechanisms for the first provincial elections? Where would the capitals be located? These questions generated a great deal of public debate, and their eventual resolution had permanent effects on the shape of the region. In "The 'Autonomy Question' and the Creation of Alberta and Saskatchewan, 1905," William Brennan analyzes scholars' attempts to provide explanations for the ways in which these controversial questions were resolved when Alberta and Saskatchewan became provinces in 1905.

SELECTED BIBLIOGRAPHY

For an overview of the main social changes during the settlement period, see James Gray, *Boomtime* (Saskatoon, 1979). Interesting interpretative accounts of the settlement process include L.G. Thomas, "Associations and Communications," Canadian Historical Association *Historical Papers* (1973): 1-12; and Lyle Dick, "Factors Affecting Prairie Settlement: A Case Study of Abernethy, Saskatchewan in the 1880s," Canadian Historical Association *Historical Papers* (1985): 11-26. A valuable collection of articles on topics in social history of the West is David Jones and Ian Macpherson, eds., *Building Beyond the Homestead* (Calgary, 1988).

There are many useful first person accounts of pioneer life on the prairies. These include Barry Broadfoot, *The Pioneer Years, 1895-1914* (Toronto, 1976), an oral history collection; Linda Rasmussen et al., *A Harvest Yet to Reap: A History of Prairie Women* (Toronto, 1976), and Heather Robertson, *Salt of the Earth* (Toronto, 1974). For more scholarly accounts of pioneer life and rural society consult C.A. Dawson and Eva Younge, *Pioneering in the Prairie Provinces: The Social Side of the Settlement Process* (Toronto, 1940); and Jean Burnet, *Next Year Country* (Toronto, 1951). While there are numerous autobiographical and family accounts of pioneering experience some of the best are J.G. McGregor, *Northwest of Sixteen* (Toronto, 1958); and James M. Minifie, *Homesteader: A Prairie Boyhood Recalled* (Toronto, 1972). David Jones discusses the impact of country fairs in the Prairie West in his illustrated history, *Midways, Judges, and Smooth-tongued Fakers* (Saskatoon, 1983). On the characteristics of early pioneers, see J.W. Bennett and Seena B. Kohl, "Characterological, Strategic and

Institutional Interpretations of Prairie Settlement," in A.W. Rasporich, ed., *Western Canada: Past and Present* (Calgary, 1975), pp. 14-28. An interesting study of adaptation and settlement is Greg Thomas and Ian Clarke, "The Garrison Mentality and the Canadian West," *Prairie Forum* 4 (1979): 83-104. An excellent scholarly study of settlement in one area of Alberta is Paul Voisey's *Vulcan* (Toronto, 1988).

An important dimension of social and political life on the Prairies not discussed directly in this Reader is education. For an overview of research on prairie education see the special issue of "Schools, Reform and Society in Western Canada," *Journal of Educational Thought* 15 (August, 1980): 60-159.

For discussions of political developments in the North-West, students should consult the works cited by Brennan in his article, and in addition the collected documents edited by L.H. Thomas, ed., *The Prairie West to 1905* (Toronto, 1975). Doug Owram has collected primary source material related to the birth of Alberta as a province in *The Formation of Alberta* (Edmonton, 1979).

For political developments in Manitoba, see W.L. Morton, *Manitoba: A History* (Toronto, 1967); for Saskatchewan, see David Smith, *Prairie Liberalism: The Liberal Party in Saskatchewan, 1905-1971* (Toronto, 1975); and for Alberta, see L.G. Thomas, *The Liberal Party in Alberta* (Toronto, 1959), and Howard Palmer with Tamara Palmer, *Alberta: A New History* (Edmonton, 1990).

WILFRID EGGLESTON

---

17 The Old Homestead
Romance and Reality

The homesteading era in southeastern Alberta ended long ago. There are very few "originals" left. My father, who is the central figure of this account, died twenty years ago at the age of eighty-nine. The last of the homesteaders in our immediate neighbourhood died in 1969 at the age of ninety-one. Since an applicant had to be at least eighteen years of age to file on a homestead, the youngest of the survivors of the land-rush of 1909 would now be in his middle eighties.

I was only eight years old when the last big tract of homestead country was opened up in southern Alberta. As the son of a homesteader I enjoyed all the romantic aspects of homesteading without much of the burden of work and anxiety assumed by my parents and their fellow settlers.

My father filed blind on a quarter section of short grass prairie fifty miles south of Medicine Hat in the month of February, 1910. We were living at the time in a draughty two-storey frame farmhouse about eleven miles east of Nanton, fifty miles south of Calgary, heated only by a small kitchen range.

We were a family of five, English immigrants who had landed in southern Alberta the previous May. My father was what the English would call a small tradesman: he had been a warehouse hand, an insurance agent, and a shopkeeper after a boyhood spent on a Nottinghamshire farm. My mother was the daughter of a Lincolnshire shoemaker, who had been apprenticed to a milliner before her marriage. The family had not prospered; illness had plagued us for a time; emigration was in the air. My parents had decided to start life anew in another part of the world. New Zealand, Australia, and the United States were all contemplated; but southern Alberta was the final choice, made early in 1909. The deciding factor was one well known in immigrant literature—the testimony of a friend who had gone out earlier. In Nottingham the Eggleston family had known a girl named Alice Stokes, who now, many years later, was Mrs. J.B. Dew, wife of an Alberta rancher living east of Nanton: her enthusiastic letters about sunny southern Alberta finally convinced the Egglestons that they would make no mistake in choosing Alberta for their new home.

"Free Land" was, of course, the magnet which drew hundreds of thousands of immigrants to western Canada in the early years of this century. When my parents arrived at the J.B. Dew ranch in mid-May of 1909, they immediately began to inquire about locating on one of the free homesteads which had been made so alluring in all of the immigrant literature. It was a shock to learn that the last of the free land in the Nanton country had been taken up four or five years earlier. There were still a few homesteads many miles further east, but the area was not yet served by a railroad. The Peace River country was being talked up that summer, but my mother quailed at the idea of trekking another three or four hundred miles away from "home", and toward the North Pole. So for several months our dream of "Free Land" remained a dream. We rented the two-storey farmhouse and my father looked about for casual farm work.

Then, the following February, there came what seemed to be a lucky break. Our nearest neighbours were two bachelors, who raised grain and ran a threshing outfit in the fall. One of these, Tom Chambers by name, who had given my father work as a spike pitcher on his outfit the previous autumn, turned up late in February, 1910, with the exciting news that he had found himself a homestead after the threshing season was over, and that there was a vacant quarter only a mile away. If my father was interested Tom would meet him in Nanton to help him fill out the necessary papers for an application.

By now my parents were growing disillusioned about the rosy promises of the railway and steamship propaganda, and were ready to jump at the first attractive opening. They quizzed Tom Chambers at length on the nature of the countryside, the prospects for a living, the distance from a railway, the distance to the nearest school, and similar essentials. There were difficulties. For one thing, there were no schools built yet. The homestead location was thirty-five miles from the nearest railway station. There were still wild range cattle rambling across unfenced land. But a village named Manyberries was already growing up only eight or nine miles away, and there was a surveyed branch line of the Canadian Pacific which would strike, when built, right through the heart of the new homestead country. Tom Chambers was able to reassure them on most of their doubts. And the fact that he, as a native Canadian and a resident of Alberta for several years, had enough faith in it to go down and pick out a quarter section, build a shack on it, live there for several months; and that he was preparing to move from Nanton and settle down there for good, was bound to make an impression on my parents. It is relevant to remember, too, that in 1909 Alberta had enjoyed the best grain crop in its history, and that southwest Alberta had reported the highest per-acre wheat yields in western Canada.

It ended with my father agreeing to meet Tom at the Nanton Land Office at a specified date and time. We were eleven miles from town and as we had not yet acquired a suitable rig for winter travel my father arranged with another neighbour to drive him in. That morning coincided with one of the worst blizzards of the winter and the neighbour decided it was not a fit day for man nor beast. He did not show up. My father, being a "green" Englishman and stubborn as well, elected to set out on foot. He was fortunate to get to Nanton alive.

As a result of that February struggle through a wild blizzard and the confirmation a few days later that my father's application had been successful, I was personally destined to spend some of the most impressionable years of my boyhood on those high undulating plains, a few miles north of the Montana border. To locate our homestead I can say that it was about thirty-five miles south of Seven Persons, twenty-five miles southwest of the Cypress Hills, six or seven miles northeast of Lake Pakowki, and nine miles northwest of the newly created community of Manyberries. The figures on my father's homestead application recite: *the SE ¼ of Section 18, Township Six, Range Six, West of the Fourth Meridian,* and these details still locate our homestead precisely.

When I think back to those faraway homestead days I cannot escape a sort of bi-focal image. I made my acquaintance with the old homestead first through the imagination and later on through the eyes of a sensitive boy. And after sixty-five years those early impressions still dominate. So I see the experience through a romantic veil. There is still an element of dream or fantasy in my memories. I was a precocious reader and had been raised on such fare as *King Arthur and his Knights of the Round Table, Robin Hood and his Merry Men,* on *Swiss Family Robinson,* on the novels of Henty and Ballantyne, on *Coral Island* and *Treasure Island* and *Lorna Doone* and all the rest. It was more than two years after my father's struggle through the blizzard before we children actually saw the homestead, and this period of delay only heightened the suspense and enhanced the glamour. It became a sort of Promised land, the Garden of Eden, or Shangri-La.

The grimmer realities of course had to be faced by my father from the beginning. In order to keep his claim alive he had to get down there within a few weeks to begin occupation, to build a residence, to fence it off, and make plans for cultivating part of it.

The simplest procedure would have been for the whole family to settle on the homestead immediately. Many pioneer families did. But the absence of a school was decisive, in our own case. My mother was almost a fanatic in her zeal for education for her children. It is true that even when a "little white school house" did come into being it would only operate in the summer months; and it looked as though it would be another two years before even that would be available. Never mind, she would stay on in the Nanton country with us three children, and when a school was in prospect in the homestead country we would move down. In the meantime my father would have to rough it and "batch it" on his own.

And that is what happened. My father went down in the spring of 1910 with Tom Chambers as partner. They travelled by train to Seven Persons, where, by previous arrangement, they were met by two neighbours of Tom's, earlier homesteaders, who had driven in the thirty-five miles with their wagon gear ready to load up with lumber and other building materials for the Eggleston cabin, as well as a summer's supplies for Tom himself.

It was a long day's drive from Seven Persons but on the evening of May 26, 1910, the two heavily loaded wagons drove along the southern boundary of our new homestead—located with the aid of the surveyor's four earth pits and inscribed iron stake. Then, at once, a decision had to be made in a quarter of an hour or so where to unload the lumber, and, as a consequence, where our homestead cabin was to be built.

Then they went on to Tom's shack, where Tom and my father spent the night. The following day my father started digging a cellar and in the following two or three weeks our modest dwelling, fourteen by twenty feet, pine siding with a shingle roof, gradually took shape.

The spring and summer of 1910 began ominously dry—one of the worst in the history of Alberta. Prairie fires were raging in many areas. One started mysteriously near Tom's shack, and nearly burned up our future home before it was half-finished. Fortunately my father was able to fight off the flames.

He put in a few weeks' residence that summer. Tom had promised him a job again on the threshing outfit, but the crop failure of 1910 was widespread and it gradually became clear there would be precious little grain to thresh that fall. My father badly needed a few dollars in cash for winter's fuel and groceries, so it was a lucky turn when he heard of a chance to do some haying up in the Cypress Hills for an old timer named Charlie Mudie. This was a happy circumstance which led to many trips and visits in the years ahead. My father and later on my brother and myself got to know the Cypress Hills country very well as a result.

In August 1910 my father came back by train from Seven Persons to Parkland, near Nanton, and regaled the family with all the latest homestead news. With no wages from threshing outfits in sight my father found work of a sort, doing daily chores for one of the neighbours, such as looking after his livestock and driving them down to the Little Bow River and chopping ice so they could drink.

His next foray into the homestead country was a bit more ambitious. By the spring of 1911 he had been able to assemble a modest outfit to begin the next stage of his homestead duties. By now we owned three nondescript horses—bought at bargain prices, I am sure—a wagon gear, a hay rack, a walking plow, a disc, and some hand tools. Thus equipped, he set off from the Tom Chambers country east of Nanton in May, 1911, to drive the long trail to the homestead cabin, 150 miles or more across country, without a map and, in many areas, with very sketchy trails to follow. It took him a week. Most nights he slept in the wagon. His biggest problem, aside from losing his way, was to make sure of water and feed for his horses. Judging from the scribbled accounts he turned over to me, his own food consisted of bread, crackers and cheese, with an occasional orange as a treat.

Once on the homestead site he spent a busy two months. He hauled logs for fenceposts from the Cypress Hills. He plowed a small patch for potatoes and a ten-acre strip which some day would be sown to wheat. When August arrived he started back for the Nanton country. Again he spent a full week on the trail. This time he returned to a region blessed with a bumper crop once more. He and my mother teamed up to work for a big grain farmer as hired man and housekeeper. We lived with the grain farmer in his commodious house. School was two and a half miles away and on some bitter winter days it was an ordeal to get there on foot. But we emerged from the winter with a few dollars to the good to invest in homestead supplies.

At long last, in May of 1912, the Eggleston family was ready to begin the last trek. We had to load up a railway box car at Nanton station with our livestock, implements, and household effects. My father rode in the car and looked after the animals. My mother and we three children were passengers on the train from Nanton to Seven Persons. Our trips were arranged so that we would all arrive in Seven Persons at about the same time. We unloaded our box car and set up temporary camp on the banks of the Seven Persons Creek, south of the railway line, until we could get our modest cavalcade organized for the last leg of our journey, the thirty-five mile drive south to the homestead.

Since our hay rack had no cover, I could call this the "Uncovered Wagon" part of our journey. I suspect it was not an impressive outfit but to an impressionable boy it marked the dramatic peak of an adventure story which had already been running for over two years, and it made such a deep impression that many details are still alive in my memory, over sixty years later. (I even remember the number of our CPR box car—it was 39102!) One of the three horses of 1911 had died in the winter, but we had two lively colts, who were tied to the back of the hay rack. Implements, furniture, clothes, and supplies added up to a heavy load, and the two horses pulling the load were in poor shape. So we had to wind along the Milk River trail southward at a leisurely pace. The route south from Seven Persons runs at first along the flat bed of an old post-glacial lake. Then comes the "Big Hill", where in those days a winding trail up a coulee bank lifted one to a ridge or benchland about six hundred feet above Seven Persons Flats. That hill took some negotiating; in bad weather, teams had to double up, but by slow stages we got to the top.

By sunset we were still only about half way, so we camped in a homesteader's yard and slept in the wagon, under the stars. What a picnic for the kids! (I doubt if my mother shared our childish enthusiasm!) The next morning we continued our journey along the level benchland, which, for ten or twelve miles offered nothing more in the way of a view than the hard skyline a couple of miles distant. But we were approaching the Continental Divide, which separates the South Saskatchewan Basin from the Missouri, and in those days the trail south lay almost over the summit of Bullshead Butte. There, of a sudden, we had a magnificent view of the whole Lake Pakowki country, with the steep bluffs of Milk River behind the Lake and the Sweet Grass Hills of Montana filling the southwestern horizon. (The name suggests pastoral elevations. But they are true mountains—volcanic plugs or laccoliths—and West Butte rises as high as Mount Washington, the highest elevation in New England.)

Descending from Bullshead Butte we had to negotiate a series of deep coulees: Deer Creek, the Little Piegan, the Big Piegan, Wolf Creek. This took time and careful driving, so that it was well into the afternoon of our second day that we came to the corner of our own land, crossed the new wooden bridge that spanned our own coulee, and drew up triumphantly, if in great fatigue, before the door of our homestead cabin.

First impressions were favourable. It was late in May, when the Great Plains enjoy a brief season of ecstasy. The range was lush with knee-high grass after the wet summer of 1911. The pasture was unusually healthy because the range cattle of Hooper and Huckvale, the ranchers dispossessed by the settlers, had been driven south in 1910.

As soon as our wagon had come to a halt in front of the cabin I retrieved an empty bucket from the loaded hayrack and sped off to the coulee to fetch water for my mother's tea. I failed to find our spring, to which I had been directed, but I came upon a limpid pool of pure water, surrounded by gooseberry bushes. The sun was breaking through thin clouds, the air was soft and sweet, the birds were singing, the gophers whistling, and I was in Paradise.

The next few weeks still stand out in my memory as the Golden Age of my boyhood. We had entered The Promised Land. On every side there were magical regions to explore. No fences barred young adventurers. The little white schoolhouse was only partly built. A long spring and summer holiday stretched out ahead. There were immigrant children in nearby homesteads to meet, to mingle with and go berry-picking with, to share lunches with and go gopher-hunting with and perhaps fall in love with. Everyone was friendly and helpful. Barriers of race and sect had not yet emerged. The homestead community had been assembled by pure chance: we were diverse peoples but shared a common challenge. At first everyone of appropriate inclinations was free to attend divine service as offered in a half-finished schoolhouse or homesteader's cabin. We would all attend the same classrooms, the same socials and dances. There was lending and borrowing and pooling of useful information.

By September the little white schoolhouse was finished. Some unimaginative trustee gave it the name of "Six Six School", No. 2541, and such it remained. Winter school was ruled out by the cost of fuel and the scarcity of winter clothing. But a three-month fall term began in September. It was formally opened with a dance. My mother, my sister, and I attended, in spite of my mother's Wesleyan Methodist objection to such a frivolous activity. We walked home as the dawn was breaking, the following morning.

On the first day of school term the teacher at the front of the tiny classroom turned out to be the daughter of our neighbour to the south. She was sixteen and had Grade Ten standing from Ontario. Most of the motley collection of farm children were Scandinavians; most of these had little or no English. The teacher's first task was to teach the Swedish boys and girls their ABC's. While they struggled with the elements of language, my sister and I were left to our own devices for long periods. My sister soon reached the school-leaving age of fourteen and then I was left alone in Grade VIII. Nothing higher was attempted. I devoured the limited school library and investigated the unabridged Webster. At recess and noon hour we played all the familiar games of the Alberta school yard—Duck on a Rock, Dare Base, Anti-I-Over, and especially baseball was a passion with them, and it soon became so with me. As one of the older boys and a senior scholar I found my status much improved over the schooldays near Nanton. The whole family had risen in the social scale. There we had been latecomers, outsiders, immigrants, a green Englishman and his brood, my father a hired hand, a renter, doing chores, my mother helping in others' kitchens. Now, suddenly, we were charter members of a pioneer community, landowners, originals, in some respects even leaders in the community activity.

In those early months on the homestead I was as free as a bird to rove far and wide. There was our own homestead, to begin with, coulees and draws and Indian rings and mosaics. Between us and the new schoolhouse there was an open Hudson's Bay section, 640 acres, never occupied while I was a boy. Our coulee could be followed upstream and down, with no sense of trespass. There was another coulee running through Tom Chambers' quarter and below it, with a wealth of rock exposures. Fossils and petrified wood and an occasional flint arrowhead were there for the finding. I made maps, gave names to all the prominent features of our coulee, borrowed Tom Chambers' spy glass to study the heavens. My brother and I dug a cave in the coulee and cleared out sylvan "houses" from among the berry bushes at North Hill. The sky was an endless spectacle by day or night, the panorama was fascinating, the air was bracing and the spirit of the frontier permeated the neighbourhood. It may have troubled our parents that our house was little more than a shack, that our food was plain and frugal, that our clothes were often shabby, and that ready cash was very hard to come by. I don't remember giving these things much thought. We were pioneers and nobody in the district had much more.

The mood of my narrative darkens at this point. I have been looking at the old homestead through the romantic eyes of an uninformed boy. The whole homestead enterprise looked very different to a dispossessed rancher. And it would have seemed even more dubious to an economic historian of 1910, familiar with the American settlement of the Great Plains—a Walter P. Webb, for example.

No one had bothered to inform my father—and he had not found out on his own—that our homestead was close to the geographical centre of "Palliser's Triangle", which Palliser himself regarded as the northern tip of "The Great American Desert". If my father had heard Palliser's name at all it would be as the person whose name had been preserved in a Calgary hotel. My father had never seen Palliser's 1859 map of our region, with the ominous legend inscribed across it: *Arid rolling prairie traversed by coulees*. Not semi-arid, but *arid*. No one had read to my father Palliser's praise of the Cypress Hills as "a perfect oasis *in the desert* we have travelled." Nor his appraisal of his Triangle in the same report: "This district can never be of much advantage to us as a possession . . . . The true arid district . . . has even early in the season a dry parched look. The grass is very short on these plains and forms no turf, merely consisting of little wiry tufts."

I don't know, either, whether my father faced up to the fact that even in this marginal area our own homestead had to be regarded as one passed up in the early land rush in that region. Otherwise how did it happen that it was still open for his entry five months after the first claims were filed?

A historian would have known that even the ranchers had stayed away from those arid townships until all the more attractive ranch sites in southern Alberta had been occupied. The range was thin and the water sources limited. There were, from the beginning, a few choice locations on the slopes of the Cypress Hills, on Milk River, and in some of the larger coulees, but there were also great expanses where grass and water were scanty. If range animals have to travel more than a couple of miles daily to find forage and water they "walk off" all the profits. Yet even some of the inferior rangeland had been included in the land opened up for homestead entry in 1909.

My father did not know, either, that a year before we left England there had been an earnest debate in the House of Commons in Ottawa in which old timers in the North-West Territories (Alberta and Saskatchewan had been created as provinces only three years before) had warned against the folly of taking such regions away from the rancher and inviting settlers to engage in small-scale grain growing. The Canadian prairie experience was supplemented by reports of American geographers and meteorologists concerning similar country south of the border. As far back as 1878 Major John Wesley Powell had issued his famous U.S. report on the *Lands of the Arid Region*, in which he had declared, categorically: "The grasses of the pasturage lands are scant, and the lands are of value only in large quantities . . . . The farm unit should not be less than 2560 acres." This, it might be stressed, is sixteen times the acreage chosen for the family homestead, the basic unit of the Canadian land settlement scheme. There were preemptions and purchased homesteads which could be acquired for three dollars an acre, of course, but thousands of immigrants came to southern Alberta believing that a homestead of 160 acres was an adequate unit for a family farm.

The debate in the House of Commons did not sway the government. It went ahead with the cancellation of ranch leases. Perhaps the thinking was that the area in dispute was superior in soil fertility, perhaps in annual precipitation, to the lands Powell had in mind in the United States. Perhaps it was affected by the improvements in dryland farming since 1878. Actually there was no reliable data about the aridity of the land south of Medicine Hat. It was known that there had been dry cycles and somewhat wetter cycles. But one member of parliament on long experience in the West quoted an authority as contending that in any area where the annual precipitation averaged less than twenty inches, grain farming became precarious, and some irrigation was desirable if not essential.

The homesteaders who trekked in with my father had no official data to instruct them. They soon learned that wide swings could occur from year to year. The excessively dry summer of 1910, for example, had been followed by a wet June and July in 1911. There were also much longer cycles. It now seems evident that Palliser saw the region in the midst of an extremely dry cycle. John Macoun, Dominion botanist, came along a decade or so later and found far more favourable evidence. He dismissed Palliser's theory of a northern tip of an American desert and even claimed that the so-called arid country was "one of unsurpassed fertility."

The debate in the Commons made reference to a number of wetter summers early in the century, which should not be taken as evidence that the climate was changing, prairie members contended. The dry cycles would return.

Not to leave the vital matter of annual precipitation in our homestead region in the air, I should add that official recording began when a range station was set up near Manyberries in 1927. When I was there in the 1950's the average annual precipitation was levelling off at between twelve and thirteen inches a year. When you combine this with the high figures for insulation and evaporation because of sunny skies and hot winds, you identify the Manyberries country as being close to the driest spot in the three prairie provinces.

They discovered another disturbing fact at the Manyberries station. Ranchers had known it of course for many years. The carrying capacity of the range as pasture for horses and cattle was surprisingly low. Most of the range was such that from thirty to fifty acres per animal were required if you were to avoid over-pasturing and gradual destruction of the forage plants. (With over-pasturing the inedible weeds like sagebrush and greasewood soon invaded and impaired the pasture.)

Taking forty acres per animal as a fair average allowance, these figures made a mockery of the whole 160 acre homestead policy, even before the settlers arrived. A well-informed rancher could have thus addressed my father, on his arrival at the homestead site in 1910:

"Look, Sam, you are beaten before you start. To run any sort of a grain farm you'll need four work horses. To keep up your team you ought to have a colt or two coming along. You'll need at least one cow for milk and butter and that means pasturing a calf most of the time. So you need pasture for six or seven animals to start with.

"That alone would overtax your whole homestead, if you kept it all in pasture. But you need wheat or flax for a cash crop. Let's say you fence off sixty acres to put under the plow, and keep a hundred acres for pasture. You're going to overgraze that hundred acres, and in time you'll probably destroy it, but you can ease that problem a bit by raising oats or alfalfa—if you can get it or some other forage crop to grow. Anyway, let's look at your sixty acres under the plow. In this dry climate you have to keep part of it fallow every year. I think you'll do well to plant thirty acres of wheat a year, on the average; if you harvest fifteen bushels an acre you'll be lucky. By the time you've paid for threshing and taken out the wheat you need for seed next spring you'll have perhaps six wagon loads of wheat to haul thirty-five miles to Seven Persons in the fall. At less than a dollar a bushel, you may gross 350 to 375 dollars in a good average year. That has to finance your year's farm operations, pay for machinery, harness, supplies, formaldehyde, binder twine and the rest. You'll be a good manager if you have 200 dollars a year left. Can you raise a family of five on 200 dollars? And don't forget there will be dry summers when you'll do well to get five bushels to the acre instead of fifteen."

(If these figures sound "cooked" on the low side, I should add that my father kept accurate records of farm receipts in 1921-24, and his average gross cash receipts from the homestead ran just over 160 dollars a year. It included returns for cream and eggs. That was during one of the long dry cycles).

An optimist might have hoped that there would be years when bumper crops would coincide with high prices. But the reverse would also be true. As it turned out, that region saw both extremes and everything in between before many years had gone by. But the inexorable logic of the rancher would prevail in the end.

The logic implied that the area was grossly overpopulated from the very beginning and that the 160-acre homesteader would soon be defeated. What actually happened?

Most of the settlers arrived in 1910 and 1911. As we have seen, 1910 was excessively dry. The following summer was unusually wet, but there was little land yet in cultivation. The harvest in 1912 was average; 1913 was a bit drier. Then came a crusher. The spring of 1914 was excessively dry again and things got worse. Many homesteaders, including my father, did not thresh a single bushel of grain. We ran the hay mower over the field to pick up some fodder and chicken feed. By now most of the homesteaders were flat broke. There would have been widespread malnutrition, if not starvation, if federal and provincial authorities had not mounted a relief operation. There was some abandonment, but most settlers had nowhere else to go and no capital to use in starting again.

Then a sort of miracle occurred. The "bumper" crop of 1915 made agricultural history. Rains fell at the right time; there were no hot winds; yields of sixty bushels per acre and more of No. 1 hard wheat were harvested even in the heart of Palliser's Triangle. The following summer, 1916, was almost as favourable. Meantime the war was driving up the price of farm produce. The Canadian Pacific Railway's faith in the region was restored to the point where it pushed its branch line from Lethbridge another thirty miles east to Manyberries. Ended were the three-day journeys to and from Seven Persons. Now, in the late summer of 1916, the village of Orion appeared almost overnight, only a mile from the Eggleston homestead.

In the late fall of 1916 it could have been argued that Palliser had been wrong. The heart of his Triangle was enjoying an unmistakable boom. But the mirage did not last. In early summer of the following year the drought cycle returned and settled down with a vengeance. There were seven crop failures in the next nine years and the other two seasons only yielded a half-crop. By the autumn of 1924 perhaps ninety percent of the original homesteaders had given up. My parents and my brother had been among the stubborn ones but now they too began to look for a place to begin again. By now the two governments concerned and the Canadian Pacific Railway had agreed to help the settlers move out and make a new start. After a long search my folks found a small irrigated tract south of Coaldale available on easy terms and with a small cash deposit. In March and April of 1925 they stripped the old homestead of every board, every fencepost, every bent nail, and, with the generous assistance of a few remaining neighbours they loaded up a railway box car similar to the one that had brought them down from Nanton to Seven Persons thirteen years before. They left their quarter section as open range, the way they had found it, except that the pasture had been cropped down to the bare soil. The gopher, the coyote, the horned lark, and the grasshopper again reigned supreme.

That was half a century ago. What happened to these abandoned homesteads? And the communities created by the pioneers?

Not everybody left. A few seemed to have what it took to survive. Perhaps they had found a way to lick the problem. Perhaps their sites were superior, or they had come in with more capital, or they had substantial cash reserves. Some were too stubborn to quit, too old, too poor, too discouraged, to think of beginning all over again on some newer frontier.

The departure of their neighbours made the countryside more lonely but it also eased their economic problems. Now there were many abandoned fenceless homesteads which turned into free community pastures. In effect their own holdings were greatly increased as the pasture problem eased. Hard times had brought a moratorium on debt, and taxes fell as community services were no longer needed. Overhead costs fell.

What happened to my father's quarter section tells a typical story. The year he abandoned it was once again dry, and 1926 was even drier. Then the rains returned and there were two big crops, in 1927 and 1928, in the fields of those who had hung on. My father, to his great surprise, had a letter from Axel Mattson, a fellow-homesteader of 1910 (his son Arvid had been a school chum of mine), offering to buy our abandoned quarter section. My father still held title to it, though it was encumbered with relief liens and unpaid taxes. Axel offered a thousand bushels of wheat, to be delivered as and when the harvests permitted. There was no time limit. Counting on an occasional good crop, Axel could in this way make the homestead itself provide the payments. At the time wheat was selling for a dollar or so a bushel. My father agreed. It took Axel eight or nine years to squeeze out the thousand bushels from the sketchy harvests; and before the deal was concluded wheat had fallen to twenty cents a bushel at the Orion elevator.

My guess would be that Axel acquired our quarter section for the grain equivalent of not more than five hundred dollars. He made similar deals with other old neighbours and in the end picked up several sections of land. I ran across him many years later and he told me he had become a wealthy man by the standards of that district. In 1969, when I last visited the old homestead country, I found out that two younger sons of our old neighbour, Olaf Brodin, had also picked up abandoned quarters and each of them was farming about four sections. I couldn't help recalling Major John Wesley Powell's recommendation of 1878 that a farm unit in the arid lands should not be less than 2,560 acres. It has been amply proved that even the sparsely grassed range can support such farm-ranch units. In the main the soil is fertile and the limiting factor is moisture. The truck, the tractor and the automobile reduced dependency on pasture and released the land earlier sown to feed grains. Water conservation and local irrigation projects, generally higher prices for grain and beef, better land use, and new cultivation techniques have enabled adequate farm-ranch units to survive, even to prosper. That country could not support the excess population of the homestead era, but when it had gone through the economic wringer and the population had fallen by about ninety percent the rest could make things go.

Of course this depopulation spelled the end of the homestead communities I had known as a boy. In our immediate area the coming of the railway and the emergence of the village of Orion distorted the development. Elsewhere one could witness the decline of the rural community as the settlers left. The community store went, the post office closed up, the little white schoolhouse was no longer needed for three or four scattered children. In time, buses carried children as far as twenty or thirty miles into Manyberries.

(Those old country schoolhouses ended up in some odd places. Our Six Six Schoolhouse, which we had watched them building in the summer of 1912, was sold in the thirties to a German Evangelical congregation and hauled fifteen miles north over Bullshead Butte to serve as part of a country church. The school at the Butte where I later taught my first classes ended up in a nearby farmer's corral as a grain bin).

Those early pioneer communities had a short life. What is left is the memory of the old timer. Such novices as my parents contributed almost nothing to the *economic* conquest of the semi-arid country. But they had taken part in the pioneering. My mother played the reed organ for Sunday services or sang in the little choir. My father, who had a good bass voice, taught a Bible Class, and served for a while as Sunday School Superintendent; he was secretary-treasurer of the school district, Justice of the Peace, and then Police Magistrate; he provided local news to the Medicine Hat and Lethbridge papers; and he and my brother were active members of the United Farmers of Alberta.

When hard times set in a certain amount of bitterness and recrimination could have been expected. Apart from the hopeless struggle against drought and hot winds, hail, grasshoppers, frost, and cutworms, there were economic grievances galore: the high cost of farm machinery, of warm clothing, of harness, the high freight rates, high interest rates, tight credit, high taxes, ruinously low returns at times for farm products . . . . The editorials in the *Grain Growers Guide* (on which I was nurtured) singled out the villains of the piece.

But what surprised me, when I talked over those days with my parents and other old timers, was the absence, in the main, of such bitter notes. The originals tended to look back with mellow nostalgia. It was a wonderful country, they said—*when it rained*.

It is now more than half a century since I left the old homestead and the memories which survive are, on balance, still enchanting. I shall never forget the meadowlark's haunting flute-like melody, the windborne fragrance of the wolf willow on the coulee banks, the shimmering mirage on the distant horizon, the vast cumulus clouds filling the southern sky, the infinite patterns of the ripening wheat in the morning breeze. I recall with affection the motley band of pioneers who shared with us the struggles on a rude frontier. I can still remember a bank of wild roses in June and the moment of magic when the sun has set after a torrid July day and the Sweet Grass Hills are beginning to fade in the cool night air. No doubt we chose a location too close to the northern rim of the Great American Desert, but desert landscapes have their own peculiar fascination. Old timers like myself fell in love with that country and our affection endures to the end.

A.W. RASPORICH

18 Utopian Ideals and Community Settlements in Western Canada, 1880-1914

Utopia is a term of many definitions and dimensions. Broadly considered, the utopian tradition is based upon the optimistic assumption that harmony, co-operation and mutual trust are more natural to humanity than competition, exploitation, and social alienation. Spiritually, utopia also represents refuge or escape from the existing evils of society, and projects a new social order based upon communitarian ideals. The literary expression of these ideals may be expressed in extraordinary voyages to lost islands, planets, or cities out of time, or more practically in platonic speculations upon ideal constitutions in social reorganization of family relationships or a radical re-ordering of economic production and work. The social forms which utopian ideals take have also varied widely, from static to dynamic, from aristocratic to democratic, and from collectivist to individualist in their aims and structure.[1]

But, despite its elasticity and universality, utopia is still not a term which has been treated widely in Canadian or western Canadian historical literature. Suggestive allusions have been made by W.L. Morton to the utopian element in the ideology of Henry Wise Wood, and later in the Social Credit movement. Direct examination of the utopian concepts expressed in E.A. Patridge's "co-operative commonwealth" has been made in a brief but penetrating essay by Carl Berger. And George Woodcock, among others, has examined the imperfect realization of utopianism in the radical Finnish social experiment at Sojntula (Harmony) on Malcolm Island in British Columbia.[2]

Such studies, including modern sociological analyses of communal societies in western Canada, tend however to ignore the broader role which utopian and quasi-utopian idealism played in the social and intellectual development of the West prior to the First World War. At Confederation, the prairies were in essence little more than a literary projection, a garden (or a desert) in the eyes of eastern beholders such as Palliser, Hind, or Dawson.[3] But, shortly after the completion of the railway, the image of the West in central Canada and Great Britain progressed rapidly from the *outopia*, "nowhere" or *terra incognita*, to *eutopia*, a "somewhere" or "good place" of unlimited progress, enterprise, and development.[4] Indeed, not only the garden West of the farm, but also the city, became the literary paradise of the boosters and pamphleteers who conjured mirages of industrial and commercial progress in the West.

The colonization land company and community settlement were the vehicle by which the prairies were to be settled. The central Canadian government in fact extended a familiar technique of land settlement derived from the romantic schemes of systematic colonization such as the Canada Land company, which had peopled the western peninsula of Upper Canada. The central difference was that most of the colonization companies of the 1880's were in fact paper schemes generated in the capital markets of England and the United States, and calculated to reap short-term gains.[5] Very few of these Empire settlement schemes actually placed settlers on the land, with their mixture of motives, which lingered in Stephen Leacock's satire *My Discovery of the West*, half-way between "philanthropy and rapacity."[6]

The ideology of the English land settlement schemes was, however, a persuasive one, as Leacock himself suggests in his inverted utopian satire of the company's operations. As he describes it, the appeal to the prospective settler was both "patriotic as well as pecuniary," since the company was pledged to all-British settlement, to an annual dividend, and to the eventual prospect of land-ownership in "The Valley of Hope." The English village system which was promised by many of these co-operative land schemes was the central focus of their inspiration. Its appeal was recaptured in another literary reconstruction of the land company utopia rendered later in 1920 by the CPR colonization agent Robert Stead, in his novel *Dennison Grant*. His central character's "Big Idea" was a carefully planned co-operative venture which substituted group settlement in villages for the rectangular survey. Such a large joint-stock venture would, in Grant's view, provide centralized urban services in a rural context, and allow centralized direction of all economic and social activity "to the betterment of humanity."[7]

The point of these literary digressions is simply to establish that group settlement ideology combined with a moral projection of a new order was a continuing theme in early western Canada. Indeed, if some of the early examples of actual settlements were to be examined closely for their social ideals and aspirations, and in their economic and social organization, there are parallels to the late nineteenth-century utopian visions of Ruskin, Bellamy, Hudson, and Morris. Either as social experiments or as arcadian refuges, they generally failed within a generation to achieve either the intrinsic perfection of their ideals, or the anticipated benefits of social escape from the industrial ills of urban England, continental Europe, and central Canada.

Most resulted in settlement abandonment within a generation, as had their counterparts in England and America, but they reveal at least something of the idealistic roots of prairie society prior to the First World War.

I

The Qu'Appelle Valley of Saskatchewan was the focus of several such community experiments in the 1880's, and became a promised land to a wide variety of social classes and ethnic groups. These ranged from the Scottish crofter colony at Benbecula and the East London Artisan's Colony near Moosomin to a welter of ethnic colonies such as Esterhazy, New Sweden, and Thingvalla.[8] Perhaps the two most obvious utopian projections from among the English-speaking settlements were the aristocratic society at Cannington Manor south of Moosomin, and the democratic social experiment at Harmony, near Tantallon, on the Qu'Appelle River. They were bipolar opposites as expressions of the utopist outlook, the first emanating from the urban middle-classes of England, and the latter from the western Ontario agrarian tradition, and briefly co-existed less than seventy-five miles apart before their common failure at the turn of the century.

Cannington Manor anticipates in ideal terms what Lewis Munford describes as the utopia of the "Country House," or in literary terms is expressed in the medieval visions of William Morris's *News from Nowhere* (1891) and W.H. Hudson's *Crystal Age* (1905). Past, present, and future are fused in the latter about a self-sufficient little feudal community centered around a magnificent country house, peopled by beautiful, cultured inhabitants. Life in nature is idealized, and the inhabitants happily engage themselves in agriculture, in artisan handicrafts, or in the leisure activities of art, music, and cultured conversation.[9]

The real Cannington Manor was established in 1882 by Captain Edward Mitchell Pierce, a British "gentleman and soldier" ruined by a London bank failure. The Canadian Northwest and the prospect of homesteads for himself and his four sons represented a social escape, as it apparently did also for those who followed. Shortly after his arrival, Pierce wrote a letter to an English newspaper offering to take on "young men of good birth and education" under his superintendence for $500-$1000 per year, and instruct them in the art of farming. The collection of remittance men who were attracted by the advertisement is described in the colourful prose of one of Cannington's early founders:

It is well known that oft times a wild son was shipped off to Canada and allowed enough to live on so long as he stayed there; there were and still are others who have left their native shores because they deemed it expedient to beat a hasty retreat; then there are the failures, the misfits, the men who fail in some examination for the Army, Navy, Civil Service, for the Bar, for the Church, or other calls in life; the colonies as they were once called, now the Dominions, offer a home and a fresh start to all of those who wish to embrace it; as a rule this class of Englishman has been well educated, he has been taught how to comport himself as a gentleman, he has been taught how to idle, how to spend money, and how to get amusement out of life. As a rule he is sport and natural, devil-me-care, and often loveable, but he has never been taught how to work, that important part of a modern education has been omitted.[10]

The village society which was reconstructed at Cannington consciously defied the individualistic precepts of homestead farming and the rectangular survey. Its co-operative economic nexus was the Moose Mountain Trading Company centrally placed on the Pierce land by its several trading partners. The company planned, built, and owned the community services which included a grist-mill, blacksmith's and woodworker's shop, co-operative cheese factory, hotel and post-office. In addition it built a village church and a community Assembly Hall which operated as a school, and co-operatively hired the services of a doctor from England.[11]

Community life for the English group at Cannington revolved about two poles: work and leisure. James Humphrys, a marine engineer from Barrow-in-Furness, was the leader of the "worker" or artisan faction in the colony, and marshalled pork production for export back to the mother country. His spacious home, built in 1888, was an impressive reflection of his utilitarian personality—its capacious attic was built large enough to quarter two hundred troops in anticipation of another uprising such as the recent Northwest Rebellion. In direct contrast was the domicile of the sporting faction represented by the Beckton brothers, who inherited their wealth from Sir John Curtis, the ex-Lord Mayor of Manchester. Their palatial manor house, "Didsbury," completed in 1889, contained twenty rooms, a bachelor wing of another five rooms, and a large billiard parlour. Even the livestock quarters were an elaborate complex of stone barns, kennels, and sheds designed to segregate species as well as the sexes.

The community of leisure which played in and around the Beckton establishment was the preserve of the "drones," who occupied themselves with an elaborate ritual of indoor and outdoor pastimes. The former were comprised of equally refined parlour activities, from choral music and painting to poetry readings and "scientific" discussions of agriculture and politics. The latter included the outdoor class sports of the English aristocracy, from cricket and tennis to sailing and fox-hunting. A typical summer day in the life of Canningtonians is described by one of the residents, who first explained that during the winter they would often return home overseas or to other warmer climes in the tropics:

Tea was served on the Tennis Courts by the Ladies, and indeed it was a bright and happy scene intermingling with the pretty summer frocks of the ladies could be seen young men in flannels wearing the blazers and colours of all the best known English and Scottish public schools and even varsity blues. Eton, Harrow, Fettes, Loretto, Cheltenham, Clifton, Rugby, Marl-borough, Wellington, Shrewsbury were all represented, to mention only a few of the best known schools. Then back usually in a buckboard home to dress for dinner, to dine with friends or attend some public or private dance, card party, midnight frolic, drive or ride to the lake.[12]

Political enthusiasm also ran high, and imperial events such as the relief of Mafeking during the South African War occasioned the entire settlement to take to their "ponies" and to ride to Cannington Hall, where one of the bluebloods, Cecil LeMesurier, impersonated Queen Victoria presenting medals to the returned soliders.[13]

Ultimately this sporting culture declined, notably because of its failure to establish a sustained economic base beyond its elaborate first phase of construction. The bachelor society gradually disbanded, some by the gentle attrition of intermarriage with the Ontario and English women on the nearby homesteads, and others by the sudden patriotic fever engendered by the Boer War and the speculative excitement of the Klondike gold rush. Certain economic decline was ensured to Cannington when the CPR built its spur line ten miles to the south in 1900, and the village store was forced to relo-cate in the new village of Manor. Only a few of the original English settlers remained in old Cannington, clustered about their tennis courts, village church, and manor house.[14]

A sobering Calvinist contrast was offered by the radical utopian experi-ment entitled the Harmony Industrial Association located at the centre of a bloc of free homesteads near Tantallon. In 1895 a group of western Manitoba farmers of radical Protestant denominational roots in western Ontario met at Beulah, Manitoba, to project a new social order of "Hamona" further to the west. Directly inspired by the writings of John Ruskin, William Morris, and Edward Bellamy, they drafted a constitution and by-laws for a co-operative community based upon the ideal of brotherhood.[15] The preamble to the constitution fused evangelical and universalist precepts with co-operative economic ideals and common ownership:

> Feeling that the present competitive social system is one of injustice and fraud directly opposed to the precepts laid down by "Our Saviour" for the guidance of mankind in subduing all the forces of nature and evils springing from selfishness in the human heart, we do write under the name of the "Harmony Industrial Association" for the purpose of acquiring land to build homes for its members, to produce from nature sufficient to insure its members against want or fear of want.

To own and operate factories, mills, stores, etc. To provide educational and recreative facilities of the highest order and to promote and maintain harmonious social relations on the basis of co-operation for the benefit of its members and mankind in general.[16]

The economic organization of Hamona followed the joint-stock formula, established upon a common stock of $100,000 divided into 500 shares of $200 each. To ensure social equality, the constitution provided that each member could hold no more than five shares and that profits be divided annually upon the basis of the number of days of labour given in work to the colony. Economic activity would be closely prescribed and regulated, despite legal guarantees that individuals could be fully employed at whatever activity they performed best. Day labour would be limited to ten hours, and rates of hourly or daily compensation were to be equal. But the problem of productivity was clearly one which concerned the founders, who also provided for penalties to those of greater ability who under-produced and required that work foremen be obeyed at all times. On the other hand, they feared that enterprise might be under-rewarded, and provided for special incentives "to call out the best endeavour of employees" and "a system of preferment subject to the approval of a majority of the membership and designed to best promote the interests of the Commonwealth."

Its puritanical and totalitarian control of its membership was further apparent in the rigorous qualifications for entry and for expulsion beyond its pale. Applicants were strictly enjoined to possess "good moral character," and also to pass an examination in the principles of social co-operation. After receiving two-thirds of the colony's support for entry, the novice was reminded upon entry that he surrendered his natural freedom for the freedoms of right and justice conferred by the civil or social contract. And despite disclaimers protecting the free exercise of individual rights, majority rule obtained in matters of public discipline. Arraignment would be determined after inquisition, and the question of innocence or guilt voted in public meeting, with the offending member being expelled from the association payroll.

Despite the considerable number of social services in the way of health care, education, and child allowances which the Harmony Industrial Association offered, the colony did not attract widespread interest. At most, fifty persons joined the village settlement. Economic failure soon overtook the community, which, like Cannington, failed to develop a stable export base to sustain the expensive services it offered to its members. The anticipated railway link failed to revive its economic fortunes, and by 1900 the association disbanded after less than two full years of operation.[17]

Hamona came closest then in conception and actuality to the literary utopias later articulated by Robert Stead in *Dennison Grant* and E.A. Partridge's *War on Poverty*.[18] The autocratic methods of social control which Stead's protagonist places in the hands of the board of directors are clearly intended to substitute community control for the State. Equally, the thought-control and government by experts in Partridge's co-operative common-wealth of virtue are anticipated in miniature by the Harmony Industrial Association a generation earlier, and only a few miles to the east of Partridge's Sintaluta. While Partridge's High Court of Control may have owed more intellectually to H.G. Well's *A Modern Utopia* than to Hamona, its totali-tarian and plebiscitarian paradoxes are probably explained better by the agrarian populism of eastern Saskatchewan and its grass-root adaptations of nineteenth-century English utopianism.

II

Significantly, it was to be the utopia of calm, pastoral felicity which was to hold greater attraction for later British experiments in the developing Northwest. While none would match Cannington Manor in the refinements of leisure, they would nevertheless attempt a more modest recreation of British society and ideals on the prairies. Among such group settlements com-munitarian ideology was poorly developed or absent, and depended in the main upon the shared assumptions of Anglo-Saxon race and imperial ideals. Their economic objectives were more individualistic than collective, and a group identity and community focus served only as a transitional vehicle to individual survival. In this sense, the pastoral vision is the primary object of the quest for self-fulfillment in nature, much as in Thoreau's *Walden*, or in the English romantic poets, and the secondary objective the survival of communitarian values.[19]

The Edenic quest for paradise is clearly evident in the story of the Parry Sound colonists, who travelled from their homesteads near Georgian Bay to Fort Saskatchewan in 1894. At least insofar as related by their main chronicler, W.C. Pollard, in *Life on the Frontier,* the opening of the West by the CPR excited the romantic imaginations of the predominantly Anglican farming village of Magnetawan, who sensed that their present lives were "erring and aimless."[20] From Pollard's perspective, two main ideals spurred them on to the West: the prospect of entering "the Promised Land," and the realization of the landed heritage of the British people on the 160-acre homestead. And, despite the considerable hardships endured in the process of settlement along the North Saskatchewan, he could relate in retrospect at least his enthusiasm for the pioneering experience in lyrical poems addressed to the "Prince of Nature," and ecstatic pastoral prose upon his early years in the Northwest:

> Did humanity ever set for itself a nobler task than that of pioneering in a new and virgin country, there the work of Nature can be seen on every side, and there avarice and selfishness are unknown, and all are engaged in Man's primitive occupations: tilling the soil, guarding the flocks and

herds, fishing in the waters, hunting in the wilderness and mining under the ground.

There the brotherhood of man is amplified and common interest cement together social ties and friendships and there the works of the Creator are seen before man makes any contributions or contaminations.[21]

Not untypically, "the building of Jerusalem in this pleasant land" proved more an individual than a collective enterprise, and the Parry Sound Colony prospered and gradually moved on. Pollard himself studied law with the prominent Calgary firm of Lougheed and Bennett and then at Osgoode Hall, and moved back to Uxbridge, Ontario, after the First World War.

A rather more familiar form of British Israelitism and pastoral capitalism in the Northwest was the Barr Colony in western Saskatchewan. Its founder, the Anglican curate of Tollington Park, Rev. Isaac M. Barr, drafted a prospectus for the Canadian Northwest designed to appeal to urban clerks, artisans, and professional men intent on seeking a rural life in the New World. In common with a vast amount of literature then being generated to popularize the Canadian Northwest among British youth,[22] Barr rang the imperial changes with such masculine appeals as "Britons have ever been the great colonizers. Let it not be said that we are the degenerate sons of brave and masterful sires." His second prospectus to intending members of the colony in 1903 was even more explicit in its clarion call: "Let us take possession of Canada. Let our cry be 'CANADA FOR THE BRITISH'."[23]

The projected settlement was either a naive rendering or a calculating exploitation of English middle-class perceptions of prairie life. Barr assured the prospective settler that "this is to be no village or communistic settlement. Everyone will live on his own land; that is, it will be a settlement of the ordinary kind." Companionship, social co-operation, and mutual help would naturally spring forth from the community values of the British population. Indeed, prospective settlers were urged to leave behind all but the basic household items and a few garden seeds, and perhaps bring along a gun or an English saddle if they possessed one. Since any form of labour could be reasonably bought in this land of felicity, no implements or horses were required of the small homesteader. But everyone should "own a cow or two, and perhaps a pony with a light waggon, and some hens and pigs." This pastoral vision of happy farm life was completed with a recitation of the great natural benefits which the land possessed, from temperate climate, abundant fuel, and accessible transportation, to good markets for everything that the farmer would want to produce. Vague mention was even made of a product for export, since British Columbia was "a good and growing market" for the total production of a community creamery.[24]

Despite the understandable failure of Barr's enterprise, the British ideals which inspired community life were sustained after his replacement by Rev.

George Exton Lloyd. According to the latter, the British colony was very much alive, although the Barr Colony was dead; he officially renamed it "Britannia," and the first town he modestly named after himself, Lloydminster. The sense of British election among the survivors of the Barr disaster increased as communitarianism dissolved into the community of the surviving elect. One Cockney took pride in his ability to clear up his debts and win a prize for his wheat in 1911, despite his complete lack of experience in farming before coming to Canada. And another fantastic success story followed Jimmy Bruce, who inherited a fortune from a rich aunt in Manchester, thus enabling him to build a $150,000 mansion in nearby Lashburn, which contained thirty-five rooms, including reception rooms, conservatory, and a billiard room.[25] Such was the stuff that pioneers were made of in North America, and the sight of Lord Jimmy parading with coach and livery down the streets of Lashburn confirmed the great myth of progress which other immigrant bachelor societies depicted in the symbolic return to "The Mountain of Gold."[26] But in the case of the Britannia colonists, the pioneering myth was more ideally cast in the brave new world of Walt Whitman's *Pioneers* (as quoted by one of the colonists, J. Hanna McCormick):

All the past we leave behind:
We debouch upon a newer mightier world, varied world,
Fresh and strong the world we seize, world of labour and the march,
Pioneers, O Pioneers.[27]

Nowhere was the pastoral theme of economic self-realization in nature so eloquently stated as in the promotional literature for the fruit lands of British Columbia intended for the overcrowded urbanites of Great Britain. Following closely upon the late nineteenth-century promotion of the ranchlands of Alberta, this literature, which circulated in the decade prior to the First World War, was calculated to persuade the scions of wealthy British families to settle in the interior valleys of southern British Columbia. The Canadian Pacific Railway, various trust companies, and government agencies in British Columbia assiduously peddled the theme of the fruit farmer as "nature's gentleman," toiling in the idyllic climate of the dry interior. Three themes stand out strongly in the promotional advertising of B.C. "fruit ranching": the myth of the garden and a neo-Rousseauistic idyll of natural man at work and play in a paradise; the racial nostrums of Anglo-Saxon imperialism in the late nineteenth century; and the idea of social and economic co-operation as an evolved characteristic of the British upper class.[28]

A typical piece of "booster" literature of this genre was that produced by the British American Trust Company in 1907, entitled "The Potential Riches of British Columbia."[29] Contained within its frothy contents was an article by the Anglo-American traveller and journalist Agnes Deans Cameron, entitled "England's Last Vedette: The New British Columbia." The garden myth was amply orchestrated in such hollow clichés as: "Great is the power of environment. In her giant mountains, lone lakes, deep rushing rivers and lush valleys, Nature intended this Pacific province to cradle a people big, broad and unselfish." More specifically, Cameron hoped that the British immigrants' children would be counselled in the natural beauties of British Columbia. This birthright of nature was of course the natural right of Englishmen, and Canada was unequivocally declared the outpost of the Anglo-Saxon race and its historic traditions. More important to Cameron than the citation of those paradigms of English values from King Alfred to Florence Nightingale, was the emphasis upon co-operative ideals among the refined classes, who should be encouraged to take up their birthright in western Canada. To this purpose, she cited a poem exemplifying a Ruskinian spirit of brotherhood which was in the air of the far West:

There shall come from out this noise of strife and groaning
A broader and a juster brotherhood
A deep equality of aim postponing
All selfish seeking to the general good
There shall come a time when knowledge wide extended
Sinks each man's pleasure in the general health
And all shall hold irrevocably blended
The individual and the commonwealth.

More detailed brochures and personal testimonials spelled out the practical applications of these social ideals to "fruit ranching" in the interior. J.S. Redmayne's *Fruit Farming in the "Dry Belt"* and J.T. Bealby's *Fruit Ranching in B.C.* were both published in London in 1909 to encourage both young people and families to emigrate from English cities.[30] Public school boys were enticed to leave their school desks and to continue their schoolties in British Columbia, "with joint sporting expeditions as happy interludes to lucrative fruit-farming operations." Further to this, they were cautioned to beware of "land sharks" (usually Americans), but to trust in the larger "Land Development Corporations" for sale and counsel in the science of fruit culture in arid regions. Intending farmers were also advised to join the fruit-growers' associations, since these were practical expressions of the principle of social co-operation. Through co-operative distribution and marketing techniques, the individual member would be secured the best prices for the least possible costs in transport. In fact, the destination of the apples themselves had an imperial mission, for this western "Orchard of the Empire" would provide apples for the hungry consumers in British cities and thus contribute to the dual benefit of colony and empire.

The most conspicuous of the community experiments which was inspired by this spate of imperial boosterism was the settlement of Walhachin, established between Kamloops and Lytton in 1910. The excellent research article by Nelson A. Riis, "The Walhachin Myth: A Study in Settlement Abandonment," has described in detail the nature and duration of this precarious experiment in irrigated apple-growing.[31] In brief, his research demonstratres the same intellectual and social factors at play as were previously revealed in the Cannington experiment twenty years earlier. A similar bachelor society of remittance men made up of the graduates of English public schools and the Army Service formed the core of this community of nearly two hundred. Their passion for sumptuous residences and an endless round of games and activities was the equal of those at Cannington. And the ultimate abandonment of the settlement followed the prescribed formulae of earlier abortive experiments. The outbreak of war in 1914 attracted many of the army men back to their regiments, and careers in the imperial civil service beckoned for others. Also, the negative attitude of Oliver's Liberal government in British Columbia destroyed the conservative ties which had linked the community's largest landowner, the Marquis of Anglesey, to the previous administration of Sir Richard McBride. And in common with other similar ventures in British idealism there was the fatal economic flaw, an export-oriented mentality which sought the magic commodity, whether apples or tobacco, but which failed to develop a sufficiently diversified agricultural base. Walhachin probably outdid all others, however, for the sheer magnitude of its capital debt structure, for it bequeathed a costly irrigation system of wooden water flumes which would require a quarter of a million dollars to be made operable if the orchards were to be revived after the Great War.

III

The aristocratic and democratic utopias of social escape and the pastoral ideal were not confined solely to English-speaking groups. A high degree of fragmentation along ideological and class lines occurred among French settlers in western Canada at *fin de siècle*. Increasing cleavages in old-world French society created similar social fragments which sought refuge in an idealistic re-creation of a declining class-order, or in the projection of a democratic social order in the new world. Increasingly, the impulse to establish community settlements on the Canadian prairies devolved from optimistic adventures on the part of the French aristocracy resembling the utopias of commerce and leisure at Cannington manor, to negatively-inspired political life in the Third French Republic.

The French settlement at Whitewood, near Moose Mountain, Assiniboia, was a replica of the Cannington experiment some forty miles away. A community of French counts and noblemen took up several homesteads in 1885 and concentrated their settlement about the chateau of *La Rolanderie*, which became the focal point of the ranching venture later headed by the Comte de Roffignac. Other noblemen established homes in the valley, importing various types of livestock for breeding, a labour force to do their menial work, and the accoutrements necessary for the fine life to which they were accustomed. Their "Race Days" rivalled and often surpassed the horse races of Cannington for their opulent parade of wealth and Parisian fashions. And the "Frenchmen's Ball" held in the Commercial Hotel in Whitewood was the outstanding social event of the Pipestone Valley in the late 1880's, complete with white shirt fronts, white kid gloves, and the *politesse* of French aristocratic society.[32]

The co-operative economic ventures of the French counts suffered the common fate of nearly every other trading company established in the Qu'Appelle region. Cattle and sheep ranching were tried, and the Rolanderie Stock Society underwent two reorganizations of capital funding by 1890. Several ventures were then launched by the Society to process agricultural products for export, ranging from Gruyère cheese to chicory and sugar beets. The Gruyère cheese failed because of dry prairie pastures; the chicory scheme flourished all too well and glutted for years to come markets in the Northwest; and the sugar beets were frustrated by the government's ban on the sale of alcoholic by-products, thus precluding the manufacture of rum. The French noblemen also proved singularly cavalier in approaching their losses in livestock, for they occasionally abandoned their sheep to prairie blizzards or threw their excess Berkshire hogs into Pipestone Creek. The community soon lost its social cohesion as economic failure dogged its capital ventures, and the noblemen gradually returned to France. Occasionally their journey was punctuated by a diversion to the Klondike or to the South African War, and sometimes even a return to the Northwest.[33] The quixotic spirit of the colony was summed up by the return of the Comte Henri de Soras who returned after the turn of the century to the village of Whitewood in the middle of winter because he preferred prairie snowstorms to the perpetual rain in Paris!

An element of continuity was established between the Whitewood experiment and one further to the West in Alberta at Trochu by the Comte Paul de Beaudrap. Originally a secondary member in the first community, he emerged with Armand Trochu as one of the founders of the French ranching company at Trochu in 1905.[34] Composed partially of army officers disillusioned by the Dreyfus affair and the consequent expulsion of the Catholic religious orders, and of urban *bourgeois* seeking economic opportunity in Canada, the group formed the St. Ann Ranch Trading Company and the Jeanne d'Arc Ranch. Its pastoral vision was pre-eminently stated by its major stockholder, Joseph Devilder, the son of a banker in Lille, who noted that the group "devient un modèle d'installation pratique qui va nous permettre de nous livrer tranquillement à l'élevage des chevaux et à l'engraissement du bétail—par conséquent de gagner de l'argent, but de nos efforts."[35]

The bachelor communal society which briefly flowered on the St. Ann Ranch from 1905 to 1907 was a romantic exercise in co-operative capitalism and urban customs transferred to a rural context. The men rose with military precision to their tasks at 5 AM from May 1 to November 1, and at a more indulgent 5:30 in the winter months. Bookkeeping and accounting was a passion; meticulous records were kept of livestock and poultry production, and egg counts were documented with some excitement in the personal diaries of Paul de Beaudrap: "(Jan. 8, 1906) aujourd'hui deux oeufs!!! (Jan. 11, 1906) aujourd'hui, trois oeufs! (Feb. 25, 1906) Huit oeufs!!"[36] Other ventures such as a co-operative creamery which was established in 1907 for export also gave the company a common element of failure which united it with the previous French business experiments in Saskatchewan. On the other hand, its success as a social experiment was equally resounding. The camaraderie of social life in "Bachelor's Hall," the merrymaking which followed monthly mass, and the passionate pursuit of leisure activities such as rabbit-hunting, swimming, and horse-racing established Trochu Valley as a masculine refuge *par excellence* in the Far West.

Ironically, the coming of the railway disrupted the tranquillity of this pastoral idyll, for it brought a new townsite and all of the other trappings of civilization common to the urban frontier. Women arrived from France to join their husbands; general stores and other essential services, such as schools and churches, were established at Trochu; and even sports became institutionalized in the Sports Days after 1907. The community ultimately lost its French homogeneity as it was opened to the outer world with the arrival of the Grand Trunk Pacific in 1911, which resulted in the gradual departure of the French settlers. The coming of the First World War in 1914 spelled the final end to the officer class which had formed the backbone of the Trochu colony, for most returned to serve in their former regiments, and their sons often enlisted in the British or American armed services.

A contrast in abortive French communities prior to 1914 was the democratic-socialist experiment attempted not far from Red Deer, at Sylvan Lake, in 1906. Although little is known of this community, it was apparently inspired by the abortive coal miners' strikes in the Lille-Vieux Condé regions of northern France in 1905. Routed by Belgian strike-breakers and French regiments of *cuirassiers*, several of these miners and other townspeople banded together under the direction of one Dr. Tanche of Lille to project a socialist colony in the new world. Attracted by the ubiquitous advertising of the CPR land prospectuses and the possibility of coalescing a few homesteads into a village settlement, they set out in the winter of 1906-07 to establish a model community which would consist initially of machinists, carpenters, a blacksmith, baker, butcher, seamstress, cook, musician, poet, doctor and druggist.[37]

Economic difficulties beset the colony almost as soon as it began. The intermediary sent to secure homesteads failed in his mission, and the cattle which he purchased froze to death in the winter of 1907. Farming on a collective basis proved impossible on the marshy land of Burnt Lake, and gradually its members began to desert to homesteads of their own, or to return gradually to France. Co-operative business ventures such as the saw-mill proved unworkable when the Sylvan colony failed to secure a stable external market and lost much of its stockpile in floods along the Red Deer River. Finally the leader of the colony, Dr. Tanche, suffered a stroke in 1911 while trying to break the unyielding prairie sod, and died back in France while visiting his brother in 1917. The query which his son, the chronicler of the colony raised concerning the lack of communitarian ideals by the membership of the colony speaks volumes for the curious admixture of motives which destroyed this socialist commonwealth: "It seems rather than trying to develop a socialist colony, they tried to become rich overnight, the riches of communal lives, of getting along together, of understanding one another as a steppingstone to future greater endeavours, seemed to have been marked by an insane desire to get rich quick, something alien to the country. Does an intellectual produce the best leadership?"[38]

IV

Another common social impulse to nineteenth-century reform utopias was alcoholic temperance, which inspired at least one industrial utopia in England founded in the 1850's by Titus Salt near Leeds. The model community of "Saltaire" warned at its boundary that "ALL BEER ABANDON YE THAT ENTER HERE," since its founders believed that drink and lust were at the root of all urban social evil. And others such as the "Cosme" colony of English workingmen in Paraguay were clearly founded in the early 1890's by William Lane in the anticipation that it would be a dry workingman's paradise in the new world.[39] American frontier utopianism was similarly inspired by the prospect of a temperate haven in the wilderness for the degraded masses of the industrial city. Part of Horace Greeley's fascination for Fourier's socialist phalansteries was inspired by his strong teetotalling convictions, and the prohibition of alcoholic beverages became a central feature of many American frontier communes.

It is in this context that the short-lived Temperance Colony of Saskatoon can be seen as a form of frontier social escape prompted by the temperance movement of late nineteenth-century Toronto. As Bruce Peel has noted in *Saskatoon Story*, "The idea of a colony founded for moral or religious reasons was not unique in the history of the North American frontier: cheap land and isolation had always beckoned reformers seeking sites for their utopias. However, Saskatoon was probably the only frontier colony founded on temperance principles alone."[40] Spurred by a massive publicity campaign endorsed by Toronto merchants, the Sons of Temperance, the Odd Fellows, and the Methodist Church, the organizers attracted Principal Grant of

Queen's University as their speaker at the Toronto Exhibition and Stampede in September, 1881. The Temperance Colonization Society subsequently received over three thousand signatures in support of their application for nearly two million acres of prairie land. The inevitable joint-stock company was formed with a grandiose capitalization of two million dollars, divided into twenty thousand shares valued at one hundred dollars each, to take advantage of the recent order-in-council permitting large land sales to such colonization companies.

A classic pioneer trek to the promised land was in the making, complete with the trying prelude of a wagon-journey of 150 miles out of Moose Jaw, which was the end of steel in the fall of 1883. The founding of a village of virtue in the wilderness was enshrined in the constitutional of the Temperance Colony Pioneer Society, the preamble of which declared its communal purpose as "the discussion of matters pertaining to the welfare of settlers, mutual counsel, the dissemination of useful knowledge, and social intercourse." Among some of its first discussions were the establishment of essential services, but also included were some cosmopolitan digressions into climate, tariffs, socialism, and physiology. Indicative of the community penetration of decision-making was the successful passage of a resolution in March on 1885 that the settlers should not flee to Moose Jaw because of the impending Métis rebellion but should calmly attend to their "usual avocations." It appeared to win popular favour, for sporting diversions planned for Dominion Day appeared more important than either agriculture or the rebellion, and one veteran of Middleton's army later reminisced that the last time he had seen cricket played was in July, 1885 in Saskatoon!

Ultimate abandonment of the settlement did not follow as was the norm with many similar utopian experiments but only because the Temperance Colony was saved from extinction by the Qu'Appelle Long Lake and Saskatchewan Railway, completed in 1890. All told it had only attracted 101 settlers, for which the society received 100,000 acres from the Dominion government. In common with most other communitarian joint-stock ventures, its successes were in community and cultural services such as schools and recreation or the community-owned ferry and telephone service, and its failures were in such business ventures as the steamboat and sawmill enterprises. Even its efforts at community social discipline proved less viable on the frontier than in urban Toronto, for internal factional disputes soon wracked the colony and called the enforcement of the temperance pledges by the society into question. The prospect of moral compulsion even upon an issue which united most of the colonists proved impossible of success with the availability of economic and social opportunity in the nearby frontier.

Other efforts at establishing temperance-oriented co-operatives among the Scandinavian groups in the West were more successful initially, although they too eventually suffered a similar fate. British Columbia appeared to attract a wide variety of such temperance-inspired experiments, particularly

among the Norwegians and the Finns, although several co-operative Scan-
dinivian settlements such as New Finland and Thingvalla (Icelandic) sprang
up in the late 1880's in the Qu'Appelle Valley of Saskatchewan.[41] As a recent
study of the Scandinavians in British Columbia has indicated, the banning
of spirituous liquor was "a theme which was to be perpetuated in the temperance societies which were an important feature of the community life of
all Scandinavian groups."[42] The membership of the Bella Coola colony of
Norwegians, founded in the 1890's by Reverend Christian Saugstad,
demanded that its members give evidence of "good moral character and
working ability." The prospect of a dry haven in the wilderness seemed particularly appealing to a group of well-to-do Norwegians of Minneapolis,
as indeed it seemed to many other Scandinavian groups, who were being
evangelized against the demon drink throughout the urban frontiers of Wisconsin and Minnesota.[43] Another group of Norwegians from Minneapolis
was attracted to nearby Quatsino Narrows with the prospect of establishing a logging co-operative, but it grew to only 125 settlers, and gradually
declined after the turn of the century. The Bella Coola settlement proved
more self-sufficient and economically successful, probably because it had
more capital to begin with, but the co-operative ideal dissipated there as well,
and it soon hived off into other colonies. Their main distinguishing feature
was their Norwegian ancestry and success at free-enterprise occupations such
as fishing, construction , the skilled trades, and professions.

The much discussed radical-socialist features of the Finnish utopia
"Sojntula" on Malcolm Island need only be discussed in general here. As
J. Donald Wilson has noted, Sojntula, in common with other Scandinavian
settlements "was characterized by virtual isolation, a homogeneous ethnic
population, a desire to escape from 'civilization' and government supervision, and a determination to control the education of their children."[44] Thus
social escape, particularly from the precarious existence in the mines of
Vancouver Island, operated as a primary impulse to this Finnish island com-
mune. The founders invited the Finnish socialist intellectual Matti Kurikka
from Australia where he had founded a similar utopian colony in Queensland. Convinced that drunkenness had ruined the Queensland experiment,
he married temperance to his radical anti-clericalism as the twin ideals of
the British Columbia colony. Thus, neither churches nor liquor were to be
allowed in Sojntula. Otherwise the colony was organized along similar lines
to other co-operative colonization companies, with common shares, and
communal business undertakings based upon a common wage-labour rate
of a dollar a day plus board.[45]

In brief, the company collapsed within four years of its inception in 1901.
In common with other utopian ventures, the Kalevan Kansan Colonization
Association proved highly successful as a cultural arm but uncommonly poor
in pursuing its business undertakings. Its initial lumbering and fishing operations yielded little revenue, and the colony experienced several subsequent

disasters such as the fire of 1903 which caused $10,000 in damages. As a result, the colony declined rapidly in numbers, approaching 250 in 1903 when Kurikka himself departed, and fought desperately to liquidate its mounting debts, which were finally too great to overcome when a $3,000 bridge-building contract in 1904 failed to recoup even its equipment costs. There were also strong challenges within the community to Kurikka's peculiar views on marriage and free love, much as there had been in 1879 with John Humphrey Noyes, the leader of the utopian colony at Oneida, New York. No doubt Kurikka's premature departure had as much to do with suspicion of his mismanagement of the colony's funds as with the moral outrage he had created by challenging traditional Victorian shibboleths surrounding monogamy. Intellectual schism also emerged from the Marxian left-wing elements in the colony, led by A.B. Makela, which regarded Kurikka and his faction as hopelessly utopian "windbags and fanatics" incapable of realizing their ideals. Ultimately the schismatics left to establish their own colony in the Fraser Valley, which also ended, as the Island colony did, in settlement dispersal and reversion to a series of individual family farms.

V

Elements of utopianism may also be seen in the early history of sectarian religious groups which established community experiments designed to achieve social perfection. In this respect, the early history of the Mormon experiment in southern Alberta, and the early Doukhobor settlements in eastern Saskatchewan were atypical to those abortive utopias described above in that they ultimately survived, although in somewhat altered forms of social and economic organization. Their survival was, however, connected more to the commitment mechanisms usually found in the communitarian religious sects, the most successful of which in western Canada were the Hutterites and Mennonites. Strong restrictions on membership, powerful ideological commitment, asceticism, and charismatic leadership were all characteristic of such sectarian movements. Indeed, their pre-adaptation to rural life and agriculture made them distinctly unlike their urban utopian counterparts in their capacity to survive economically as well as culturally. Yet despite their ultimate success at group survival, early elements in their economic and social organization and group ideology had certain overtones of utopian idealism which were subsequently altered by the successful adaptation of the sect to frontier life.

The Mormon experience in the western United States has in fact been described by Leonard J. Arrington as inspired by communitarian ideals and a pragmatic and open concept of membership. As he explains: "Group economic self-sufficiency was the hallmark of Mormon policy on the Great Basin frontier. Above all, co-operative economic endeavour, which played such an important role through the history of the church, was to a large extent an outgrowth of this ideal economic system, or of the same ethic which produced it."[46] What is perhaps doubly important from the point of view of the Canadian Mormon experience was that it became a social fragment of the American experience during a phase of conscious de-theocratization occasioned by the Edmunds Act of 1882, which established heavy penalties against polygamy.[47] That year also conformed with the end of the Mormon boycott of Gentile stores, thus creating a boom period of business formation outside of ecclesiastically sponsored co-operatives. The diaspora to Canada thus occurred in a period of forceful assimilation of American economic and social values, and the flight northward may be seen as a form of conservative social escape to preserve the integral socio-economic features of their culture.

Several distinctive aspects of early community settlement in the Cardston area mark the Mormon settlements as an attempt to restore a past state of social perfection. First was the appeal in 1887 to Edgar Dewdney, Minister of the Interior, by Francis Lyman, John Taylor and Charles Ora Card to recognize polygamous marriages to that point.[48] Failing this, polygamous practices were defended by the Mormon convert from British Columbia, A. Maitland Stenhouse, when he came to Cardston in 1888. Urging the citizens of Lethbridge and Fort Macleod to adopt polygamy, he noted with sociological precision that, "Polygamy secures a husband for every woman that wants one, giving her a large stock to select from, and by division of labour, it also ensures better supervision and kinder treatment for the rising generation."[49] Other aspects of conscious ideological design on social organization were more visible than the clandestine polygamy which followed in the nineties. The nuclear farming village modelled roughly on the millennialist Plat of Zion with centrally located public buildings, temple, and storehouses was consciously favoured by C.O. Card and John Taylor. The square-grid pattern of block settlement became the standard form of community plan in the first ten years of Morman settlement, thus imposing the town plan of settlement used in eighteenth-century New England.

The co-operative economic organizations sponsored by the Cardston Company which applied for a charter from the Governor of the North-West Territories in 1890 was a central economic feature of early Mormon settlement in southern Alberta.[50] A number of successful economic institutions in Cardston were financed by the Cardston Company and organized and supervised by the leaders of the Church. The degree of their commitment in this early co-operative phase was apparent in times of depression and monetary scarcity in the early nineties, when C.O. Card signed his name to paper scrip which circulated freely among the Saints. And, when prosperity returned in 1895, the Cardston Company paid a forty-percent dividend, half in cash and half in goods.[51]

It was only after 1895 and the organization of the Alberta Stake and the sale of 600,000 acres of land by Card and Taylor to the Church in Salt Lake City that the economic self-sufficiency of this pioneer co-operative enterprise began to break down. Further signs of economic and institutional integration appeared with the first issue of the Cardston *Record* in 1898, and the creation of the first branch of the Bank of Montreal in the same year. With the inception of the large-scale irrigation project in 1898, the community became even more dependent upon its larger economic connections with Salt Lake City which sponsored the labor costs in building the St. Mary's canal and found capital in England to back the large-scale project. Further capital penetration followed in 1901 with the investments of Jesse Knight, a wealthy Utah industrialist who began sugar-beet production and invested widely in milling and elevator companies near Raymond and Lethbridge. Whether coincidental or not, community plans for the new farming villages after 1898 also reflected greater deviation from the square-grid Plat of Zion, reaching their most unorthodox with Apostle John Taylor's radial street plan for the town of Raymond, which he reputedly borrowed from Paris![52] Taylor's openly avowed practice of polygamy and his excommunication by Salt Lake City in 1904 was also an index of the increased direct control exercised by orthodox elements in the American church over this small Canadian fragment of Mormonism. The community itself was submerged demographically with the wave of American migration into southern Alberta after 1898, and the small community of Cardston which numbered about a thousand was rapidly absorbed by the new farming villages such as Caldwell, Stirling, Raymond, and Taber which mushroomed around it.[53] A common Canadian-American frontier had by 1905 absorbed this small pocket of sectarian utopianism and its brief attempt to establish a self-sufficient community of Saints in southern Alberta.

Several sects and cults would follow into southern Alberta in the next decade, such as the Dreamers, the latter of which visited their peculiar notions of charismatic occultism, inspirational dreams, and occasional pyromania upon the farmers of the Medicine Hat region in 1907-08. The American "Sharpites" or "Adamites" who followed next in the summer of 1908 were subsequently denied entry to Alberta by immigration agents. They must have wondered at the claim of their leader James Sharpe, who claimed to be Christ and had personally led his band of twelve on a special mission to the Saskatchewan Doukhobors only to be rejected by Peter Verigin, who had his own claims in that direction. Subsequent vigilance at Alberta border crossings miliated against further incursions of any other charismatic sects of the kind which might disturb the fragile social peace of southern Alberta.[54]

The Doukhobors themselves present a fascinating case study in sectarian utopianism. While their movement has attracted much historical interest and voluminous scholarship, several salient utopian features in their group ideology might be mentioned. In the first instance, the communitarian outlook of the Doukhobors was the extrinsic object of admiration among late nineteenth-century British idealists, utopians, and anarchists who came to sponsor their migration to Canada. The role of J.C. Kenworthy and the anarchist colony at Purleigh is occasionally neglected in the Doukhobor chronicle. Kenworthy was a conscious disciple of Carlyle, Ruskin, and Henry George (and critic of Marxian socialism), and a strong exponent of the utopian rural communes which had been established in nineteenth-century America. He promoted similar ventures in England such as the English Land Colonization Society in 1893 for middle and lower-class people seeking escape from the city. In 1894 he formed a Brotherhood Church in Croydon which was economically based on fruit-growing, and socially centred about five o'clock tea. Kenworthy's magazine, the *New Order*, printed by the Brotherhood Publishing Company, soon reported on communitarian experiments across the world, and it was this venture which brought him in 1896 to Russia and into contact with Leo Tolstoy and the Doukhobors.[55] In fact, it was from Kenworthy's visit that Peter Verigin, the Doukhobor teacher, borrowed the concept of the "Brotherhood Church" for his own putative sect "The Christian Community of Universal Brotherhood."[56] And it was Kenworthy and other Tolstoyans such as J. Bruce Wallace, Aylmer Maude, Vladimir Tchertkoff (Chertkov), and Prince D.A. Hilkoff who lent the moral and material support of the Purleigh garden colony in Essex to the migration of the Doukhobors to Cyprus and to Canada in 1899. Over one thousand pounds was raised for their transportation to western Canada, and a young Tolstoyan teacher from the Purleigh colony, Herbert Archer, was sent to instruct the Doukhobor colony at Swan River in Saskatchewan.

Once in Canada, the Doukhobors established highly successful communal colonies in eastern Saskatchewan, which have been described at length in the rich historical literature on such settlements at Thunder Hill, Swan River, and Yorkton. Perhaps these village communities on the prairies which were broadly based and ideologically pluralistic, might be considered less consciously utopian in character than the communities established by Verigin and the CCUB in southern British Columbia from 1908 to 1917. An analysis of the spatial structure of Doukhobor communal architecture by F.M. Mealing at Brilliant demonstrates a sharp departure from the traditional Russian *mir* characteristic of the Saskatchewan colonies and the appearance "of a wholly novel material expression of the social ideal of Communalism . . . drawing equally upon Russian and North American traditions, and upon an innovative complex, the Community Village."[57] More insular and tightly organized, they combined large dormitories with industrial and administrative buildings such as saw mills, canning works, office and warehouse buildings, and a community meeting hall. It is this unique village life-style which Woodcock and Avakumovic also describe as a utopian spatial organization and material culture most consciously resembling the Phalansterian and Icarian colonies of mid-nineteenth-century America.[58]

But the Doukhobor experiments probably succeeded more because of their social character as charismatic millenarian movements and less because of their utopian-anarchist ideology, and because they were rural not city people. Classic resistance mechanisms of the sect also made them ultimately impervious to social leadership from the outside, as is indicated by the failure of Herbert Archer and the persistent Quaker teachers to penetrate the communities in Saskatchewan. Verigin himself conformed more to the ideal type of messianic-charismatic leader typical of millenarian movements—at least in Saskatchewan—although he appeared to mute somewhat the oriental deference he demanded in the Second Community. But his claims to miraculous birth and near divinity separated Verigin's universal Christianity from the utopian tradition which usually outlines a plan of what is possible through human effort rather than dependence on divine plan and revelation.[59]

VI

The abortive utopia was thus a common mirage in the vanishing landscape of the pioneering West. This first generation of early western settlement was inspired by a common desire to escape the social confines of the late nineteenth-century city and the broader national and imperial controls which characterized European and North American polity. In classical utopian terms, their common urge appeared to be rooted in a desire for a pastoral social condition in which work and leisure would be equally complemented in nature. The term "pastoral capitalism" which Soviet historians pejoratively applied to the Doukhobor experiment in universal brotherhood might profitably be applied to the abortive utopias above, for their ideological derivation was more often in liberal-anarchism than in utopian socialism.[60] The persistent acknowledgement of their intellectual debt to the pastoral ideals of Ruskin, Carlyle, and Morris reveal common roots in nineteenth-century British idealism. The ideals of social co-operation and of work as a creative act of self-fulfilment, and the concept of the garden city were all essential components of these strains of late-century liberal-imperial thought which shaped the Anglo-Canadian mentality of the early Northwest before the First World War.

Northrop Frye's interesting analysis of literary utopias makes an observation which also helps explain the significant role of the Scandinavians as perhaps the most prominent of the ethnic groups to establish utopian community experiments. He notes that William Morris's concept of artisan manufacture came close to a Scandinavian ideal of craftsmanship and the simplification of human wants.[61] Indeed, it appears that the short-lived utopias established on the Pacific coast were attempts by the Danes, Norwegians, and Finns to recapture that simplified rural life as a response to the first contacts with North American cities in the mid-western United States. In this respect, the company designation of the Finnish settlement as Sojntula as the Kalevan Kansan Association literally translates, the "People of Kaleva," or the ancient Finns as described in the national epic poem the *Kalevala*. Archaism as a central theme in recapturing a pastoral innocence thus played as central a role in the utopian literature of Scandinavian as well as Anglo-Saxon folklore. Indeed the common rooting of the co-operative idea in both the political culture of Britain and the Scandinavian countries, particularly Denmark, was to have a profound impact on the later development of the Canadian West in the 1920's and 1930's.

It might be ventured as a closing hypothesis that pastoral utopianism and the theme of economic failure and settlement abandonment was a dominant aspect of the first phase of western settlement. Whether aristocratic or democratic, liberal-anarchist, communist or socialist, the utopian experiments were a necessary pastoral phase in the pioneer development of the West. For if nothing else, the frontier phase of development provided ample mistakes from its misplaced dreams and aspirations of unknown space and indeterminate time. The second generation of settlement which followed the war would develop a collective agrarian ideology which was more comprehensive and totalitarian in its organization of co-operative production and consumption. Ironically, the militaristic social commonwealth which E.A. Partridge would conjure in his *War on Poverty* in 1925 was a far cry from the fervent Ruskinian ethics and co-operative brotherhood which inspired his attacks on the corporate giants in 1905.[62] Perhaps even Partridge would have admitted that the naive experiments and lost causes of the generation contributed to the realities of economic co-operation in the second, and may even have been more humane.

ACKNOWLEDGEMENTS

The author would like to thank several individuals who have helped me with bibliographic references to western utopias, or have assisted in the development of the ideas presented in this paper: Sheilagh Jameson and Hugh Dempsey of the Glenbow Archives; Henry Klassen, Howard Palmer, and John Ennis of the Department of History, The University of Calgary; and to Beverly Rasporich and Colleen Knudtson of the Department of English, The University of Calgary.

NOTES
1. Frank Manuel, ed., *Utopias and Utopian Thought* (Cambridge: Riverside Press, 1966), introduction; Rosabeth Moss Kanter, *Commitment and Community: Communes and Utopias in a Sociological Perspective* (Cambridge, Massachusetts: Harvard, 1972).

2. See for example: W.L. Morton, "A Century of Plain and Parkland," *Alberta Historical Review*, vol. 17, no. 2 (Spring, 1969), p. 6; "The Social Philosophy of Henry Wise Wood, The Canadian Agrarian Leader," *Agricultural History*, vol. 22, 114-23 (April, 1948); Carl Berger, "A Canadian Utopia: The Cooperative Commonwealth of Edward Partridge," in Stephen Clarkson, ed., *Visions 2020* (Edmonton: Hurtig, 1970), pp. 257-62; George Woodcock, "Harmony Island: A Canadian Utopia," in R.E. Watters, *British Columbia: A Centennial Anthology* (Toronto: McClelland and Stewart, 1958), pp. 206-13.

3. See J. Warkentin, "Steppe, Desert and Empire," in A.W. Rasporich & Henry C. Klassen, *Prairie Perspectives 2* (Toronto: Holt Rinehart and Winston, 1973), 102-36; and for the American West in literature, Henry Nash Smith, *The Virgin Land, The American West as Symbol and Myth* (New York: Vintage Books, 1950).

4. These terms commonly employed in descriptions of the utopian genre in literature are contained specifically in E.A. Partridge's *War on Poverty: The One War That Can End War* (Winnipeg: Wallingford Press, 1925), p. 130.

5. Norman Macdonald, *Canada, Immigration and Colonization, 1841-1903* (Toronto: Macmillan, 1970), ch. 5, pp. 235-57; W.A. Carrothers, *Emigration from the British Isles* (London, 1929); Stanley C. Johnson, *A History of Emigration from the United Kingdom to North America, 1763-1912* (London, 1913).

6. Stephen Leacock, *My Discovery of the West* (London: John Lane, 1937), pp. 278-304.

7. Robert Stead, *Dennison Grant: A Novel of To-day* (Toronto: Musson, 1920), pp. 270-77.

8. See J.R.A. Pollard, "Railways and Land Settlement, 1881-91," *Saskatchewan History*, vol. 1, no. 2 (May, 1948) pp. 16-19.

9. Frederik L. Polak, *The Image of the Future* (Leyden: A.W. Seythoff, 1961), vol. 1, pp. 357-68.

10. University of Saskatchewan Archives, Cannington Manor, MSS, C555/2/14.11, no. 20; "Old Cannington Manor," by Irr. W. LXXIII, May 22, 1927, written by Fred Kidd, p. 2, typescript.

11. A.E.M. Hewlett, "The Manorless Manor of Cannington," *The Producing News*, 1960, pp. 15-22; from clippings file, University of Saskatchewan Archives, MSS, C555/2/14.14.

12. Fred Kidd reminiscence, *op cit.*, ff. 10. See also C. Evelyn Sheldon-Williams, "Chronicles of Cannington Manor" (Regina, ept. 15, 1938), ms. copy for A.S. Morton, 7 pp., University of Saskatchewan Archives, MSS, C555/2/14/11, no. 16.

13. University of Saskatchewan Archives, A.E.M. Hewlett Collection, MSS, C555/2/14.15, no. 7, "Life of Old Cannington Village," p. 3.

14. *Ibid.*, A.E.M. Hewlett, "Old Cannington Manor, N.W.T., An Experiment in English Colonization," MSS, C555/2/14.15, no. 15 (b).

15. Gilbert Johnson, "The Harmony Industrial Association: A Pioneer Co-operative," *Saskatchewan History*, IV, no. 1 (Winter, 1951), pp. 11-21. See also D.S. Spafford, "Independent Politics in Saskatchewan Before the Nonpartisan League," *Saskatchewan History*, XVIII, no. 1 (winter, 1965), pp. 4-6.

16. Saskatchewn Archives, University of Regina, "Prospectus of the Harmony Industrial Association (Co-operative System)" (Birtle Printing Co., Beulah, Manitoba (1895)), p. 4.

17. Gilbert Johnson, "The Harmony Industrial Association," p. 15.

18. E.A. Partridge, *A War on Poverty* (Winnipeg: Wallingford Press, 1925).

19. Northrop Frye, "Varieties of Literary Utopias," in F. Manuel, *Utopias and Utopian Thought*, 48-50.

20. W.C. Pollard, *Pioneering in the Prairie West: A Sketch of the Parry Sound Colonies* (Toronto: Thomas Nelson, 1926), p. 7.

21. W.C. Pollard, *Life on the Frontier: A Sketch of the Parry Sound Colonies That Settled near Edmonton N. W. T. in the Early Nineties* (London: Arthur Stockwell, 1931).

22. Patrick Dunae, "The Popularisation of the Canadian West Among British Youth: 1890-1914," unpublished paper delivered to the Canadian Historical Association, Edmonton, June 1975.

23. Eric J. Holmgren, "Isaac M. Barr and the Britannia Colony," unpublished M.A. thesis, University of Alberta, 1964, p. 52. Citation from I. Barr, *British Settlements in Northwestern Canada on Free Grant Lands* (London, 1902).

24. Isaac Barr, *British Settlements . . .*, p. 18.

25. C. Wetton, *The Promised Land: The Story of the Barr Colonists* (Lloydminster Times, 1953), pp. 48-49.

26. See Betty L. Sung, *Mountain of Gold: The Story of the Chinese in America* (New York: Macmillan, 1967); Kenneth O. Bjork, *West of the Great Divide: Norwegian Migration to the Pacific Coast, 1847-93* (Northfield, Minn., 1958), ch. 2, "Argonauts in California," pp. 22-73.

27. J. Hanna McCormick, *Lloydminster, or 5,000 Miles with the Barr Colonists* (London: Drane's, 1924), pp. 248-29.

28. Typical early examples would include, E. Hepple-Hall, *Lands of Plenty: British North America for Health, Sport and Profit* (London: W.H. Allen, 1879); *British Columbia: Its Position, Advantages, Resources and Climate* (C.P.R. pamphlet, 1904).

29. *Potential Riches of British Columbia* (British American Trust, 1907), pp. 11-19.

30. J.T. Redmayne, *Fruit Farming on the "Dry Belt" of British Columbia* (London: The Times Book Club, 1909); J.T. Bealby, *Fruit Ranching in B.C.* (London: A. & C. Black, 1909), pp. 2-196.

31. Nelson A. Riis, "The Walhachin Myth: A Study in Settlement Abandonment," *B.C. Studies*, pp. 3-25; "Settlement Abandonment: A Case Study of Walhachin, B.C.," *Urban History Review*, no. 2 (June, 1972), pp. 19-24. See also, Kathleen Munro, "The Tragedy of Walhachin," *Canadian Cattleman*, vol. 18, no. 1 (May, 1955), pp. 7-31.

32. A.E.M. Hewlett, "France on the Prairies," *The Beaver* (March, 1954), pp. 3-8.

33. John Hawkes, *The Story of Saskatchewan and its People* (Chicago: S.J. Clark, 1924), vol. 2, pp. 937-46.

34. Sheilagh S. Jameson, "The Story of Trochu," *Alberta Historical Review*, vol. 9, no. 4 (Autumn, 1961), pp. 1-10.

35. P.A. Shandro, "The French Settlers at Trochu, 1903-14," unpublished thesis, McGill University, 1974, p. 30.

36. Glenbow-Alberta Archives, Paul de Beaudrap Diary (micro-film), entries for January, February, 1906.
37. Glenbow-Alberta Archives, John Tanche, "Reminiscences and Biography of Tanche Family, Sylvan Lake, Alberta, 1906-16," pp. 1-2.
38. *Ibid.*, p. 6.
39. W.H.G. Armytage, *Heavens Below: Utopian Experiments in England, 1560-1960* (University of Toronto Press, 1961), 252-54, 359-69.
40. Bruce Peel, *The Saskatoon Story, 1882-1952* (Saskatoon, 1952), p. 9.
41. See e.g. W.J. Lindal, *The Saskatchewan Icelanders* (Winnipeg: Columbia Press, 1955), pp. 82-88; Gilbert Johnson, "The New Finland Colony," *Saskatchewan History*, XV, no. 2 (Spring, 1962), pp. 69-72.
42. John Norris, *Strangers Entertained: A History of the Ethnic Groups of British Columbia* (Vancouver: Evergreen Press, 1971), p. 127.
43. John Kolehmainen and George Hill, *Haven in the Woods: The Story of the Finns in Wisconsin* (Madison, 1965), 113-18, 156-60.
44. J.D. Wilson, "Matti Kurikka: Finnish-Canadian Intellectual," *B.C. Studies*, no. 20 (Winter, 1973-74), p. 65.
45. John Kolehmainen, "Harmony Island: A Finnish Utopian Venture in British Columbia," *B.C. Historical Quarterly*, V, no. 2 (1941), p. 114.
46. Leonard J. Arrington, "Early Mormon Communitarianism," *Western Humanities Review*, VII (Autumn, 1953), pp. 341-69.
47. Leonard J. Arrington, "Crisis in Identity: Mormon Responses in the Nineteenth and Twentieth Centuries," in Marvin S. Hill, *Mormonism and American Culture* (New York: Harper and Row, 1972), p. 171.
48. Cited in Carlana Bartlett, "Early Mormon Settlement in Alberta," unpublished Honours thesis, Lakehead University, 1973, p. 43.
49. *Ibid.*, pp. 46-47. Citation of *Macleod Gazette*, Dec. 26, 1888.
50. *Ibid.*, p. 58.
51. *A History of the Mormon Church in Canada* (Lethbridge Stake, 1968), p. 57.
52. J. Lehr, "Mormon Settlement Morphology in Southern Alberta," *Albertan Geographer*, 1972, pp.
53. See C.A. Dawson, *Group Settlement: Ethnic Communities in Western Canada*, vol. VII (Toronto: Macmillan, 1936), "Mormon Settlement Process," pp. 205-13.
54. See Howard Palmer, "Responses to Foreign Immigration: Nativism and Ethnic Tolerance, 1880-1920," M.A. thesis, University of Alberta, 1971.
55. W.H.G. Armytage, *Heavens Below: Utopian Experiments in England*, ch. 5, "The Tolstoyan Communities," pp. 342-58.
56. George Woodcock and Ivan Avakumovic, *The Doukhobors* (London: Faber and Faber, 1968), p. 96.
57. F.M. Mealing, "Canadian Doukhobor Architecture: A Conspectus," unpublished ms., paper presented to the Canadian Society for the Study of Architecture, June 1975, Edmonton, p. 14.
58. G. Woodcock and I. Avakumovic, *The Doukhobors*, pp. 234-36.
59. F. Manuel, ed., *Utopias and Utopian Thought*, p. 70; Frederik L. Polak, *Image of the Future*, pp. 407, 437; Michael Barkun, "Law and Social Revolution: Millenarianism and the Legal System," paper delivered to the American Political Science Association, Los Angeles, 1970.

60. G. Woodcock and I. Avakumovic, *op. cit.*, p. 275.
61. Northrop Frye, "Varieties of Literary Utopias," in F. Manuel, ed., *Utopias*, pp. 25-50.
62. See W.A. Mackintosh, *Agricultural Co-operation in Western Canada* (Queen's University: Ryerson Press, 1924), pp. 18-21.

19 The "Autonomy Question" and the Creation of Alberta and Saskatchewan, 1905

Canada's eighth and ninth provinces were born in controversy. The terms of the Alberta and Saskatchewan Acts, particularly the clauses guaranteeing the right of the minority to separate schools, and reserving control of the public domain to the federal government, were hotly debated in Parliament, in the press and in the first elections which took place in the new provinces before the end of 1905. The "autonomy question" has not escaped the attention of Canadian historians either. The earliest histories of the new provinces, appearing only a few years after Alberta and Saskatchewan entered Confederation, touched upon it,[1] as did O.D. Skelton's biography of Sir Wilfrid Laurier, which was published in 1921.[2] The first full-length study appeared in 1946, with the publication of C. Cecil Lingard's *Territorial Government in Canada: The Autonomy Question in the Old North-West Territories*.[3] Ten years later L.H. Thomas described the evolution of self-government in the North-West Territories, culminating with the achievement of responsible government in 1897.[4] During the past three decades other works have appeared, written largely though not exclusively by historians, and to some degree these have modified or contradicted the conclusions found in Lingard's pioneering study. The purpose of this essay is not simply to recount what is admittedly a more than twice-told tale, but to offer some assessment of the literature dealing with the founding of Alberta and Saskatchewan in 1905.

The fullest and still the best account of the evolution of self-government in the North-West Territories remains L.H. Thomas's *The Struggle for Responsible Government in the North-West Territories*. The acquisition of the west, Thomas noted by way of introduction, was an important objective of the Fathers of Confederation, and the transfer of Rupert's Land from the Hudson's Bay Company one of the first accomplishments of the new Dominion. From the outset, the federal government intended that its authority and policies should be paramount in the new territory, which was to be administered, temporarily at least, through a Lieutenant-Governor who would receive his appointment and instructions from Ottawa. The diminutive province of Manitoba was created in 1870, but the remainder of the North-West continued to be governed as a territory. In this regard he has drawn attention to the striking similarity between the cautious approach to colonial self-government displayed by the British authorities before 1846 and the policy of successive administrations at Ottawa after 1870. The American example, on the other hand, was far less important in the field of territorial policy than in other aspects of western administration; it did not extend beyond accepting the principle of ultimate provincial status for the North-West. Having satisfied the demand for provincehood in the largest settlement on the prairies, Ottawa found itself under no immediate pressure to formulate a policy for the creation of additional provinces. The remainder of the region was still a vast, empty land with a scattered white population for which a primitive form of government would suffice.[5]

There was to be no Ordinance of 1787 in Canada.[6] Not until 1881, when the boundaries of Manitoba were extended, was a detailed scheme for the future subdivision of the Territories drawn up. According to this plan, which was prepared by J.S. Dennis, the Deputy Minister of the Interior, there were to be four provinces, ranging in size from 95,000 to 122,000 square miles. On the basis of this plan, the Macdonald government established the four provisional districts of Alberta, Assiniboia, Athabasca and Saskatchewan the following year. Macdonald intimated at the time that these districts might later become provinces in their own right, though he refused to make any definite commitment. In fact, these provisional districts never became independent jurisdictions, though they did provide the focus for a sense of "district consciousness" among Territorial residents.[7]

The principal focus of *the Struggle for Responsible Government* was, of course, the lively struggle for full local self-government which dominated Territorial politics during the 1880s and 1890s. The Legislative assembly of the North-West Territories, like the appointed council which it supplanted in 1888, possessed some but not all of the legislative powers of a province. It could raise revenue by direct taxation, issue licences of various sorts, establish municipal institutions and courts and incorporate local companies. The bill establishing the Legislative Assembly made no provision for a cabinet, though there was to be an "advisory council in matters of finance," presided over by the Lieutenant-Governor. It was to have control of the spending of local revenues, but the annual parliamentary appropriation, which constituted the largest single source of revenue, remained under the exclusive control of the Lieutenant-Governor.

It was not to be expected that this arrangement would long satisfy a Territorial population whose numbers were steadily being augmented by new arrivals from Ontario and Great Britian. One such newcomer was

Frederick William Gordon Haultain, who came west from Ontario to begin the practice of law at Fort Macleod in 1884. He was early attracted to politics, representing the district at Regina from 1887 on, and was one of four members selected to serve on the Advisory Council in 1888. It was Haultain who quickly assumed the leadership of struggle to extend the jurisdiction of that body to include the whole field of Territorial administration, and to secure popular control of the annual federal grant. In 1891 the North-West Territories Act was amended to increase the powers of the Assembly, and to provide for the first time that local revenues and the federal appropriation could be expended by the Lieutenant-Governor on the advice of the Assembly or a committee of that body. Such a committee was duly established later in the year. It closely resembled a cabinet, for its members were to receive salaries and take an oath of office and the Lieutenant-Governor was to be exluded from membership, but Ottawa proved unwilling to extend the principle of responsible government in full.

With one brief interruption, Haultain headed this Executive Committee of the North-West Territories, as it was called, from 1891 to 1897. He proved to be an efficient and honest administrator, and his considerable intellectual and oratorical powers made him a master of debate in the Assembly. Thomas's sympathies lay with Haultain, the vigorous and outspoken champion of the interests of the North-West, constantly pressing reluctant federal politicians to concede full responsible cabinet government to the Territories, and finally succeeding in 1897. Successive federal governments Thomas justly criticized, not only because they opposed responsible government (indeed on occasion confused it with provincial status which was regarded in the Territories as being premature[8]), but also because they consistently failed to understand and come to grips with western problems and aspirations.

F.W.G. Haultain also became closely identified with the non-partisan political tradition which took root in the Territories during these years. To be sure, as L.H. Thomas has pointed out, "partyism" early triumphed in federal politics in the Territories. The influence of the press, the patronage of the federal government, traditional party loyalties and the power of the party organizations all tended to prepare the ground "for a contest along traditional party lines when the first election of members for the House of Commons took place in 1887."[9] However, federal party distinctions were scrupulously avoided in local politics. *The Struggle for Responsible Government* touched only lightly upon this non-partisan tradition, but it has received a good deal more attention from other scholars. Generally they have agreed that it derived not from any philosophical principle, but from an assessment of the hard realities of the moment. Thus it was widely believed that federal party divisions were largely irrelevant to a consideration of the problems of schools, roads and public works which occupied the attention of the Assembly in Regina. Furthermore, the financial and constitutional position of the Territories was too precarious to risk the opposition of a rival party in power at Ottawa, or to withstand the pressures and claims of federal party considerations if the two governments were controlled by the same party. After 1900, of course, these two pragmatic considerations were reinforced by a third: the desire to maintain a united front in the negotiations with Ottawa to secure provincial autonomy.[10]

That final stage in the constitutional evolution of the Territories has been described in greatest detail by Cecil Lingard. The agitation for provincial statutes, he emphasized, was directly related to the success of the aggressive immigration campaign launched by the Liberals after 1896. Regina was expected to provide the schools, local public works and other services required by an expanding population. For a government which by now possessed most of the powers and responsibilities of a province but still lacked the commensurate financial resources, this became an increasingly difficult task. The territorial government could not borrow money, could not secure revenue from the public lands which were controlled by Ottawa, and could not tax the Canadian Pacific Railway, since its federal charter had exempted the railway from any form of taxation on its property and capital stock. To supplement meagre local revenues, the Haultain government continued to receive an annual grant from Ottawa, but until 1904 this grant proved insufficient to meet Territorial requirements. Better railway facilities were a matter of pressing concern to struggling pioneers who were often located many miles from the nearest line, yet the Territorial government also lacked the power to charter railways or grant them financial assistance.

Provincial status seemed to offer a solution, and in October 1901 Haultain met with Prime Minister Laurier and his cabinet in Ottawa to discuss terms. Subsequent to that meeting the Territorial Premier prepared a draft bill creating a single province which would comprise all territory between Manitoba and British Columbia and between the forty-ninth and fifty-seventh parallels of north latitude. This province was to have full provincial rights, including control of all public lands and natural resources. Laurier and his colleagues rejected these proposals in March 1902, claiming that the demand for provincial autonomy was premature and that there was no general agreement in the Territories or elsewhere on the number of provinces to be created. Haultain promptly called an election on the issue, and was returned with a large majority.[11]

It was at this point that provincial autonomy became, as Lingard put it, "a shuttlecock in the field of national policies."[12] During a speaking tour of the west in 1902 and later in the House of Commons the leader of the Conservative party, R.L. Borden, declared his support for immediate provincial status for the North-West Territories and full provincial powers, including control of all lands and natural resources. This had the effect of further chilling the enthusiasm of federal Liberals for immediate provincial autonomy. Not until the eve of the 1904 election did Laurier finally promise to deal with the autonomy question if his government was sustained at the polls. Haultain campaigned vigorously for the Conservative party and attempted to use his personal prestige to make autonomy the main issue in the Territories. The Conservatives took three seats there and the Liberals seven, but even Lingard, ever sympathetic to Haultain, concluded that the question of provincial status "exercised comparatively little influence on the public mind."[13]

With the election over, the way was clear to end the subordinate status of the North-West Territories. Early in January 1905 Haultain and his senior cabinet colleague, G.H.V. Bulyea, arrived in Ottawa to begin negotiations with the Laurier government. These discussions continued over a period of several weeks. During this time Laurier also consulted with Territorial Liberals in the House of Commons and the Senate, as did Haultain and Bulyea. Following these meetings a committee of the cabinet prepared the draft legislation, which Laurier himself presented to the House of Commons.

In three important respects the terms of this legislation differed greatly from Haultain's draft bill of 1901. The draft bill would have created a single province; Laurier proposed establish two, Alberta and Saskatchewan. Edmonton and Regina were named as their respective provisional capitals, subject to alteration later by the local legislatures. Haultain had wanted provincial control of the public domain; the federal government intended to retain control of the public lands and natural resources of the new provinces and provide financial compensation in the form of an annual subsidy. The territorial Premier had wanted complete provincial control of education; the Liberals inserted a clause in the autonomy bills which would, in Laurier's words, ensure "that the minority shall have the power to establish their own schools and that they shall have the right to share in the public moneys."[14]

The decision to create two provinces has long fascinated historians. Premier Haultain, of course, was publicly committed to the concept of a single province, but even he was aware that his views were not shared by all residents of the Territories.[15] As early as 1896 the creation of a separate province of Alberta (embracing the boundaries of the provisional districts of Alberta and Athabasca) had been mooted in the Assembly.[16] The idea of establishing two provinces, on an east-west or a north-south basis, became more popular as the years passed and the ambition of rival communities to be elevated to the status of provincial capitals grew more intense. For a time the idea of creating a single smaller province and adding the eastern portion of the existing districts of Assiniboia and Saskatchewan to Manitoba also attracted some interest, particularly among Manitobans. It formed the subject of a public debate at Indian Head in December 1901 between Premier Haultain and his eastern counterpart, R.P. Roblin, but the response of the local residents made it clear that they did not favour annexation to Manitoba.[17]

Whatever the merits of creating a single large province, or a smaller province with a portion of the Territories added to Manitoba, all available sources suggest that Laurier's cabinet was agreed that the Territories should be divided into two provinces.[18] Laurier explained to the House of Commons that his government believed the immense area of the Territories was too large for a single province. He made a point of rejecting Manitoba's claim for a westward extension of its boundary on the grounds that it would be contrary to the wishes of Territorial residents. Instead two provinces of approximately equal size were to be established, with the fourth meridian serving as the dividing line. Laurier offered no special reasons for the choice of the fourth meridian, save to declare that it would give roughly the same area and population to each of the new provinces.[19]

Lingard, of course, found little merit in these arguments:

> The year 1905 . . . was an occasion for a broad statesmanlike policy with respect to the Territories . . . Many public men realized that the Dominion was already suffering from multiplicity of governments. The North-West was in possession of a single legislature, which had served the people for nearly thirty years. It had an administrative machinery and a body of law, and was in every sense a single political entity, ready to assume provincial status . . .
>
> That the territories were divided may be attributed to the unfortunate development of local and personal ambitions centred in two or three communities, the willingness of the federal authorities to give more weight to the representations of the north-west Liberal members than to those of the Territorial government, who alone were elected on the autonomy platform, and the fear in the older provinces that one large province would assert a preponderant influence in the Dominion Parliament.[20]

Others have taken a somewhat different view of the decision to create two provinces. L.H. Thomas, for example, has concluded that by 1905

> a sufficiently strong 'district consciousness' . . . had developed in Alberta that any attempt to create one large province between Manitoba and the Rockies was foredoomed to failure. The Regina bureaucracy, headed by Premier Haultain, was unresponsive to the metropolitan ambitions of Calgary and Edmonton. This played into the hands of the federal government, which had no wish to create another large, strong province which might well challenge its policies.[21]

In his study of early Alberta politics L.G. Thomas has noted that those who favoured two provinces were very much better organized for the purpose of exerting pressure and that "the western press generally, which began by advocating a single province, gave the idea no vigorous support during the critical negotiations preceding the introduction of the autonomy bills."[22]

More significantly, L.G. Thomas has suggested that Haultain's proposal for a single province was also unattractive for political reasons, on account of the gradual erosion of trust between the Premier and Territorial and federal Liberals. This interpretation has been given added force by subsequent research on Territorial politics, notably by Evelyn Eager and D.H. Bocking. The rift between Haultain and the Liberals had its origins in that non-partisan approach to Territorial politics with which Haultain had become so closely identified. While Haultain was a Conservative in federal politics, this had not prevented such prominent Territorial Liberals as James H. Ross, Arthur Sifton and G.H.V. Bulyea from serving under him. The cabinet was not regarded as a coalition, for such an arrangement would have been a recognition of the existence of federal party distinctions.

This method of administering Territorial affairs drew criticism from a group of Conservatives who wished to see the local Assembly divide on federal party lines. At a convention in Moose Jaw in March 1903 delegates passed a resolution in favour of contesting the next Territorial election as Conservatives. Although Haultain opposed this resolution, he remained in the convention after it was approved, and accepted the position of honorary president in the newly formed Territorial Conservative Association. He subsequently declared in a newspaper interview that he remained convinced that there should not be a party division in the Assembly and that he was not bound by the convention resolution. Haultain's public statement and further private assurances satisfied his Liberal colleague, Bulyea, who had offered his resignation immediately after the convention. In spite of these assurances, Territorial Liberals came increasingly to believe that Haultain's actions were motivated principally by a desire to embarrass the Laurier government and assist the Conservatives. His refusal of a loan for capital construction or "capital advance" offered by the federal government in 1903 strengthened this conviction, as did his subsequent rejection of an appointment to the bench after it had been arranged by Territorial Liberals at his request. Haultain's vigorous denunciation of the federal Liberal government during the 1904 election only widened the breach still further.[23]

The Premier was later to claim that the members of his cabinet had always been free to take part in federal campaigns and that, in supporting the Conservative party in the 1904 election, he had simply exercised the freedom accorded to his Liberal colleagues in the past.[24] Lingard advanced the same argument, but others have questioned whether Haultain acted primarily in the interests of the North-West Territories or the Conservative party. In any case his actions did little to strengthen his position in the negotiations with the Laurier government after the election, for Liberals in the Territory and at Ottawa had come to regard Haultain as a political opponent. Haultain's support in the Territories and in the Territorial Assembly had become artificial and precarious. A division of the Assembly on federal party lines,

Evelyn Eager has concluded, was prevented only by the pressure of political necessity upon its Liberal members.[25] In a single province Haultain's claims for the premiership would have been difficult to disregard, and in the event that the provincial legislature did divide on federal party lines the Liberals would have found him a formidable opponent. From the point of view of party advantage the creation of two provinces, with two governments and two sources of patronage, was far more attractive.[26]

No less controversial was Ottawa's decision to retain control of the public lands and natural resources of the new provinces. It preoccupied the attention of Parliament and the press for a time in 1905, but has largely escaped the notice of Canadian historians. Chester Martin's *"Dominion Lands" Policy*, first published in 1936 and still the most exhaustive study of federal land policy, devoted only scant attention to it. To Martin the motives of the federal government were clear: the encouragement of western settlement was considered to be a matter of national concern, too important to be entrusted to uncertain and parochial local administrations.[27] Cecil Lingard examined the issue in greater detail. His assessment of the Liberals' motives was little different,[28] but he was more critical of the logic of it all. It was hardly likely, given the keen interest in immigration in the Territorial Assembly and the realization of its importance for the development of the west, "that the new provinces would have changed the principle of cheap lands for the immigrant, had they received control of their resources in 1905," Lingard has argued. "One wonders whether the federal government was not, after all, ill-fitted to cope with the many problems of immigration, especially those of homestead selection and supervision, and whether the homesteading of semi-arid tracts, necessitating the untold hardships and sacrifices of recent years, could have taken place under local administration."[29] That question has yet to be answered by Canadian historians.

The political repercussions of the decision to continue federal control of public lands were mild, however, compared to the storm which erupted over Laurier's attempt to safeguard the educational rights of Roman Catholics in Alberta and Saskatchewan. It raised again the controversial question of separate schools, caused the resignation of a cabinet minister and precipitated a serious government crisis at Ottawa. No other aspect of the autonomy bills has sparked more interest among Canadian historians either, and on no other has there been as much disagreement. An essential preliminary to any discussion of the historiography of this school controversy must be a brief review of the development of the Territorial school system and the events leading up to the 1905 cabinet crisis.

Federal legislation, the North-West Territories Act of 1875, had made provision for the creation of a system of separate schools, and the ordinance of 1884, which established an educational system for the Territories under the control of a Board of Education, permitted the minority in any district to establish a separate school and assess themselves for its support. The Board functioned in two sections and each, Roman Catholic and Protestant, exercised exclusive supervision over such matters as the management and inspection of schools, examination and licensing of teachers, and selection of textbooks. Subsequent ordinances gradually diminished the powers of the separate sections of the Board and provided instead for joint supervision of all schools. The final step in this process was taken in 1892 when the Board of Education was replaced by a Council of Public Instruction, consisting of members of the government and representatives of each of the two religious groups, but with the latter having no vote. The government now exercised effective control over the separate and public systems in all important matters. A further ordinance of 1901 replaced the Council of Public Instruction with a Department of Education headed by a member of the government.[30]

Thus while the original Territorial ordinance of 1884 had made possible the establishment of a system of schools under clerical influence and control, the eleven "separate" schools in operation in 1905[31] were in fact "national" schools in all but name. The Minister of the Interior, Clifford Sifton, and the other western Liberal members agreed to include in the draft of the autonomy legislation a clause perpetuating the educational system in its existing form, but the school clause in the legislation presented to the House seemed designed to restore the privileges which the Roman Catholics had lost in successive amendments of the Territorial school law. This Sifton could not accept, and he resigned from the cabinet in protest.[32]

The school clause was also subjected to a torrent of public criticism, particularly in Ontario.[33] In the North-West Territories, on the other hand, a Toronto *Globe* correspondent found

> that the school question really excites but a languid interest . . . I can quite
> believe that if we hunted up all the fiery Methodist or Presbyterian clergy
> that strong expressions of opinion might be obtained, but the average
> Western man is not much worked up about it.[34]

One significant exception of course was the Territorial Premier. In an open letter to Laurier he declared his opposition to the creation of two provinces, to the retention of the public lands by the federal government and to the school clause which, he complained, had not been shown to the representatives of the Territorial government until noon of the day on which the legislation was introduced. Haultain vigorously defended the right of the new provinces to deal with the subject of education according to the provisions of the British North America Act. It was strictly a constitutional matter, involving the question of provincial rights, and not the rights of a religious minority "which must be properly and may be safely left to the Provincial Legislatures to deal with subject to the general constitutional provisions in that regard." What Haultain demanded for Alberta and Saskatchewan, in other words, were the same rights and powers as the older provinces of Canada enjoyed.[35]

In the midst of this public uproar, steps were being taken within the Liberal caucus to prepare a more acceptable version of the school clause. Sifton and his western colleagues submitted a new draft early in March, and the amended clause was presented by Laurier in moving second reading of the autonomy bills. It secured exactly what the western members had originally agreed to, a continuation of the existing system, by specifically limiting the right of the minority to separate schools as they existed under the provisions of the Territorial ordinance of 1901.[36]

Laurier's motives in introducing the original draft of the school clause, and Sifton's in resigning from the cabinet, have long intrigued historians. A variety of explanations have been offered, the first by O.D. Skelton in his biography of the Liberal leader published sixteen years after the event. Skelton concluded that Laurier had had no idea that the original clause, drafted by the Minister of Justice, Charles Fitzpatrick, restored the clerical control which successive amendments to the school ordinance had removed. It was "undoubtedly a mistake" not to have consulted Sifton about the clause before the autonomy bills were presented to Parliament, but the "undesirable ambiguity" in its working Laurier at once offered to clear up. Sifton, however, was determined to resign for other reasons, including growing personal antagonism between himself and Fitzpatrick and "the personal attacks which were being made or prepared against (him) from other quarters," and refused to be pacified. The autonomy bills, or rather the school clause in them, "gave an opportunity to withdraw with kudos."[37]

This explanation was directly contradicted in J.W. Dafoe's biography of Clifford Sifton a decade later. "Laurier's course was not a blunder," Dafoe wrote, "it was a carefully thought out bit of strategy which misfired because intangible elements entered into the operation which he did not accurately appraise." Laurier knew very well the meaning of the clause, and the strength of Sifton's views on the matter, but hoped to confront the Minister of the Interior with a *fait accompli*.[38] This interpretation found favour with Cecil Lingard as well, since it offered an explanation as to why Haultain and Bulyea had been given no opportunity to discuss the proposed school clause in the weeks before the autonomy bills were brought down.[39] Much recent scholarship on the cabinet crisis of 1905 has also accepted Dafoe's interpretation. Thus Robert Craig Brown and Ramsay Cook have observed:

> Laurier could set as his life's work the cementing of national unity but his own tactics in the 1905 crisis . . . contributed to division. His attempt to muffle the problem of separate schools in the west was understandable, given its explosive nature . . . But his apparent attempt to circumvent Sifton's well-known views could hardly have been expected to pave the way to a harmonious settlement. In the end he lost Sifton without gaining much for the minority.[40]

A fuller and more sympathetic analysis of the Prime Minister's part in the controversy can be found in Blair Neatby's *Laurier and a Liberal Quebec*. From 1904 on, Laurier found himself under increasing pressure from some members of the Quebec Roman Catholic hierarchy and more especially the Papal Delegate, Mgr. Sbaretti, to secure more comprehensive constitutional guarantees for their co-religionists in the Territories. With this objective Laurier was in complete sympathy, Neatby asserted, and it was he who played the major role in the drafting of the original school clause. Laurier had no intention of creating a dual administrative system modelled on that of Quebec, or of creating any other form of denominational school system. The draft of the school clause simply reflected Laurier's assumption "that the minority were entitled to some form of separate school system, that the system as it existed in the Territories was satisfactory, and that the only problem was to secure this system against the encroachments of future provincial enactments."[41] Nevertheless the wording of the clause prompted Sifton to resign. The point of disagreement between the two men lay

> not in the immediate effect that the Bills would have upon the educational system as it existed in the Territories, but in the possible effect in the future. Laurier's intention was to transform the educational privileges of the minority as they existed, into educational rights guaranteed by the constitution, and thus to give the minority a legal security which the Manitoba Act had failed to give. Sifton was interested in maintaining the legal as well as the educational conditions as they existed in 1905 . . . Sifton seems to have exaggerated the possible misinterpretation of the original (clause), but Laurier seems to have minimized its implications. There can be no positive conclusion as to what the clause actually meant since it was never tested in the courts.[42]

What Neatby did for Sir Wilfrid Laurier David Hall has more recently done for Clifford Sifton. The Minister of the Interior took his ground in 1905 on the basis of what he conceived to be national interest, just as much as Laurier did, Hall has argued in a more sympathetic treatment of Sifton's part in the affair. Each represented a very different view of the nature of Canada. Laurier embodied the traditional view of his native province in his vision of a broad Canadian culture encompassing equitably both French and English, while Sifton's perspective was that of Anglo-Saxon Protestant western Ontario and Manitoba and the Clear Grit Reformism of George Brown. Sifton had a widespread dislike and suspicion of French Canadians, both as an ethnic group and as Catholics; accepted the idea that Canada was mainly a British country and believed that it was essential that all Canadians, regardless of their origin, be inculcated with a common set of British values. He was representative of western Canadian sentiment in his refusal to recognize any special status for French Canadians because this would impair the efficiency of the "national" schools that were necessary if the state was to realize the objective of bringing unity out of diversity.

Hall has also made a point of debunking the notion, first advanced by O.D. Skelton, that jealousy over Fitzpatrick's appointment as Minister of Justice, a portfolio which Sifton himself had coveted, or a desire to escape public life before embarrassing scandals came to light, were the real cause of Sifton's resignation. While Sifton was probably ready to retire or to demand a change of portfolio by 1905 (since the Department of the Interior held no more challenge and he had been passed over for both the justice and railways portfolios) it was the school clause which precipitated his departure from the government.[43]

Hall's work reflects the continuing vitality of the view first propounded by that earlier biographer of Clifford Sifton, namely that Laurier knew exactly what he was doing in 1905. Through five decades this interpretation has remained the dominant one in Canadian historiography, but its acceptance has by no means been universal. C.B. Sissons, for example, was more guarded in his interpretation of the controversy, asserting only that the Prime Minister could be accused of "want of care, or want of acumen, one or the other, in (his) interpretation of the clause drafted by Fitzpatrick" if, as Laurier claimed, the government had no other intention than to preserve the *status quo* so far as the educational rights of Roman Catholics in the new province were concerned.[44] Evelyn Eager has concluded that Laurier was unclear as to the meaning of the original clause, and implied that his clumsy handling of the whole affair reflected the fact that he was too much influenced by Fitzpatrick and R.W. Scott, the government leader in the Senate, both of whom were Roman Catholics and knew very well what was intended.[45] In M.R. Lupul's *The Roman Catholic Church and the North-West School Question*, which makes extensive use of ecclesiastical correspondence in Catholic archives, the wheel seems to have come full circle. Like O.D. Skelton, Lupul too concluded that the full implications of the original school clause were not clear to Laurier, who only wished to "secure the educational status quo."[46] Given such diversity of opinion it is unlikely that the last word has been heard from Canadian historians on this contentious subject.

The Alberta and Saskatchewan Acts received final approval in July, with the new provinces officially coming into existence on September 1. During that interval the attention of politicians in Ottawa, Regina and Edmonton turned from the controversial questions of schools and public lands to more congenial matters: the choice of a Premier in each of the new provinces, and preparations for the first provincial elections. It seemed at the outset to be a virtual certainty that F.W.G. Haultain would be offered the premiership of one of the new provinces. His claim for consideration was a strong one, for he had spent a long and active career in Territorial public life. In the end, though, Haultain was not called in either province, and his exclusion has not gone unnoticed or unexplained.

O.D. Skelton and Cecil Lingard have suggested that the Territorial Premier was passed over because of his outspoken opposition to the terms of the autonomy bills.[47] This explanation is not entirely satisfactory, others have concluded, since it does not take into account the accumulation of irritations which had strained relations between Hautlain and the Liberals even before the bills were introduced in Parliament. Haultain's public criticism of the terms of the autonomy bills in his open letter to Laurier and his participation in two federal by-elections in Ontario in June 1905 certainly lost for him whatever support he might still have enjoyed among Liberals in the Territories and at Ottawa. Laurier himself seems to have been reluctant to abandon the Territorial Premier, but by late July even Sir Wilfrid agreed that Haultain's claims should be ignored.[48]

Lingard has also asserted that the passing over of Haultain in 1905 was as constitutionally unjustified as would have been the passing over of John A. Macdonald in 1867, but this argument ignores the fact that Macdonald was a staunch supporter of the settlement which brought Canada into being while Haultain was a determined opponent of the settlement of 1905. There is little reason to quarrel with Lingard's claim that "the Lieutenant-Governor deprived Mr. Haultain of the opportunity of forming the first Saskatchewan administration through His Honour's acceptance of advice tendered him by the Laurier government," but it does not necessarily follow that the choice of Walter Scott rather than Haultain was improper. The Lieutenant-Governor might have been expected to select as Premier the leader of the party which had the support of the people, John Saywell has argued, and two factors, imprecise though they might be, suggest that Haultain no longer commanded a majority of such support by 1905. The federal political affiliation of the majority in the Territorial Assembly at the time of its dissolution was Liberal, and seven of the ten Territorial members returned to the House of Commons in the election of 1904, which was fought partly on local issues, were also Liberals.[49]

Of the first elections in the new provinces little need be said, since only one detailed account of the Alberta contest, and two of the Saskatchewan election, have appeared to date. The 1905 elections were fought on party lines, and there is general agreement that in both provinces the Liberals possessed several considerable advantages over their opponents. Among these were control of provincial and federal patronage, the assistance of the Department of the Interior and its army of homestead inspectors who doubled as party workers and a buoyant prosperity which reflected well upon the Liberals. Furthermore, at a time when a growing diversity of ethnicity and language was challenging the ingenuity of educators and political organizers, it was the Liberals who proved more successful in capturing the "foreign vote." In Alberta, L.G. Thomas has noted, Liberal fortunes were dimmed only by the lingering resentment among southern Alberta Liberals, and those in Calgary in particular, over the way in which the north had been favoured in the selection of Edmonton as provisional capital and in the establishment of the constituencies for the first election.

It was also to the advantage of the Liberals in 1905 that they faced weak and irresolute opponents. This was particularly so in Alberta, where the Conservatives entered the campaign with all the liabilities of an opposition party and none of its advantages: they could not attack the record of the Rutherford government because there was as yet no record to attack. The Conservatives were handicapped, too, by the personality of their leader, R.B. Bennett, and his close ties to the C.P.R. which Liberals never ceased to insist were not in Alberta's best interests.[50] In Saskatchewan, the Liberals faced a more formidable opponent. F.W.G. Haultain had been for eighteen years the almost undisputed leader of the Territories, and his reputation as an able administrator stood high. It was Haultain who was the moving force behind the organization of a Provincial Rights party to contest the first election there. Liberals at the time and scholars since have conceded that his appeal for support irrespective of federal party distinctions was a shrewd one. However, Haultain's position was far from impregnable, for the school clause to which he took most exception was generally considered satisfactory. As David Smith has noted, "the Provincial Rights party would have to keep the issue hot to secure advantage from it, and that in itself might alienate voters."[51]

Students of Saskatchewan's first provincial election have concluded that in fact Haultain played his cards badly, and point to an episode late in the campaign as proof. Three weeks before polling Conservative newspapers across the province published what was alleged to be a pastoral letter from Archbishop Langevin of St. Boniface which had been read in many churches in Saskatchewan. This document criticized Haultain for his position on separate schools and urged Roman Catholics to "unite and vote for those who are in favor of the actual system of separate schools though these schools are neutral because it is a partial recognition of their rights as free citizens of this country."[52] Haultain might have relied on Langevin's "pastoral letter" alone to discredit the government, but he chose to add the charge that a compact existed between the Liberals and the Roman Catholic hierarchy. The Liberals were unable to say anything about the Archbishop's instructions to Catholics except to protest that the document was in fact not a pastoral letter and had not been read in any churches, but they could and did deny that any agreement had been made to restore denominational separate schools in return for political support. Scott challenged Haultain to meet him in public debate and prove these charges. Haultain's reply was evasive, and when the two leaders did meet late in the campaign he was forced to admit that he had no proof to support his compact charge.[53]

One issue still remained to be decided after the ballots had been counted—the selection of a permanent capital in each of the new provinces. This subject has engaged the attention of a host of urban histories, both popular and scholarly. For the most part these accounts have tended to approach the issue only from the perspective of a particular community,[54] but two published studies, by Jean Murray and A.B. Kilpatrick, are more wide-ranging in their approach. A detailed examination of the provincial capital controversy in Alberta has prompted the latter to conclude that Edmonton's triumph was due in almost equal measure to the persistent and aggressive actions of its "boosters," not the least of whom was Frank Oliver, and to the inadequacy or failure of its rivals' (notably Calgary's) promotional efforts.[55] The contest in Saskatchewan was never as spirited, Murray has shown, because Regina had the advantage of a prior claim, "it was the largest city in the eastern half of the Territories and once the Laurier Government had decided on two provinces with the dividing line at the fourth meridian, there was not much doubt about Regina being the capital of Saskatchewan."[56]

It is fitting that this survey end with some further comment on F.W.G. Haultain's place in the history of western Canada. Haultain has been remembered, and rightly so, for his leadership in the struggle to secure responsible government and later provincial autonomy for the North-West Territories, but he was in many ways an enigmatic and even a tragic figure. "F.W.G. Haultain accomplished for the further west what Louis Riel and Adams G. Archibald did for Manitoba," L.G. Thomas has written,

> and the territorial premier was almost as much of an embarrassment to Laurier and his cabinet as the Métis leader to Macdonald and the Conservatives. And Haultain was perhaps also a martyr of the North-West, even though his life ended, not upon the scaffold, but upon the bench of the Saskatchewan Supreme Court.[57]

Haultain dominated Territorial politics, partly perhaps because many potential rivals were early attracted to the larger stage at Ottawa, but he did not enjoy the same success in a more competitive political arena in 1905. A recent study of politics in the provisional district of Alberta has concluded that Haultain was to a large extent himself responsible for the swift decline of his political fortunes:

> . . . his non-partisan stance in the Territorial Assembly and his staunch Conservatism in federal elections made him an enigmatic figure to both Conservatives and Liberals alike . . . Haultain, through his conduct in 1903 at the Moose Jaw convention, and because of his active campaign for the Conservatives in the 1904 election and subsequent by-elections in Ontario in 1905, was left standing forlornly in the ruins of the house he had created, by-passed by those Territorial Conservatives who had opted for party lines in the west on the one hand, yet condemned for abandoning non-partisan politics by the Liberals on the other.[58]

There remains a need for a fuller study of the career of F.W.G. Haultain in Territorial and Saskatchewan politics, and his troubled personal life,[59] if his true contribution to the development of the west is to be measured.

More than three decades have passed now since the publication of Cecil Lingard's *Territorial Government in Canada.* Subsequent research has shown it to be too favourable to Premier Haultain in some respects, but it remains the fullest account of the "autonomy question." The substantial body of literature which has appeared since 1946 might suggest that there are no avenues left to explore. Such, of course, is not the case. The need for a fuller biography of Haultain has already been noted; a detailed study of Territorial politics would be no less valuable, since more than one student of the "autonomy question" has noted that "by the time the provinces of Saskatchewan and Alberta were created in 1905, party alignments and political issues had so evolved that their imprint on the new provinces' political systems lasted for several decades."[60] L.H. Thomas has drawn attention to a sense of "district consciousness" among Territorial residents, and it would be interesting to explore the emergence of that sense of "provincial consciousness" which now exists in Alberta and Saskatchewan. A detailed account of the "natural resources question," culminating with the transfer of what remained of the public domain to the new provinces in 1930, has yet to be written. These few suggestions do not exhaust the possibilities for future research, but each in its own way would contribute to a fuller understanding of the creation of Alberta and Saskatchewan, and of the history of the two provinces during the past seventy-five years.

NOTES

1. A.O. MacRae, *History of the Province of Alberta*, Vol. 1 (Western Canada History Company, 1912), pp. 446-58; N.F. Black, *History of Saskatchewan and the Old North West* (Regina: North West Historical Company, 1913), pp. 453-79. There was little interest of analysis or interpretation in these accounts of course, and the same can be said of J. Hawkes, *The Story of Saskatchewan and Its People* (Chicago: S.J. Clarke Publishing Company, 1924); J. Blue, *Alberta, Past and Present, Historical and Biographical* (Chicago: Pioneer Historical Publishing Company, 1924); and C.M. MacInnes, *In the Shadow of the Rockies* (London: Rivingtons, 1930). The two most recent histories of the provinces, J.F.C. Wright's *Saskatchewan: The History of a Province* (Toronto: McClelland and Stewart Limited, 1955) and J.G. MacGregor's *A History of Alberta* (Edmonton: Hurtig Publishers, 1972) similarly offered little detail and few insights on the "autonomy question."

2. O.D. Skelton, *Life and Letters of Sir Wilfrid Laurier*, Vol. II: *1886-1919* (Toronto: Oxford University Press, 1921), pp. 223-47.

3. C.C. Lingard, *Territorial Government in Canada: The Autonomy Question in the Old North-West Territories* (Toronto: University of Toronto Press, 1946).

4. L.H. Thomas, *The Struggle for Responsible Government in the North-West*

Territories, 1870-1897 (Toronto: University of Toronto Press, 1956; 2nd ed., 1978). All references are from the second edition.

5. *Ibid.*, pp. 5, 261-64.

6. This ordinance, approved by the Congress of the Confederation in July 1787, provided for the gradual introduction of territorial government, and eventual statehood, for the area between the Ohio and Mississippi Rivers. Initially this territory was to be governed by a governor, a secretary and three judges appointed by Congress, and a bicameral legislature was to be established when the free adult male population reached 5,000. Statehood would come when the free population reached 60,000, and the Northwest Ordinance, as it was popularly called provided that all new states were to be on an equal footing with the original thirteen. This same principle was later applied to the Louisiana Purchase and the Mexican cession. By 1870 the Northwest Ordinance, or modifications of it, had formed the basis of the constitutions of twenty-eight territories, and eighteen of these had by that time acquired statehood. (*Ibid.*, pp. 4-5.) For a more detailed treatment of the genesis of the Ordinance of 1787 see J.E. Eblen, *The First and Second United States Empires: Governors and Territorial Government, 1784-1912* (Pittsburg: University of Pittsburg Press, 1968), pp. 17-51.

7. L.H. Thomas, pp. 97-98.

8. *Ibid.*, pp. 241-42.

9. *Ibid.*, p. 106.

10. E.L. Eager, "The Government of Saskatchewan" (Ph.D. Dissertation, University of Toronto, 1957), pp. 41-45; L.G. Thomas, *The Liberal Party in Alberta; A History of Politics in the Province of Alberta, 1905-1921* (Toronto: University of Toronto Press, 1959), pp. 3-4; C.B. Koester, "Nicholas Flood Davin: A Biography" (Ph.D. dissertation, University of Alberta, 1971), pp. 146-52.

11. Lingard, pp. 8-54, 114. Haultain's draft bill, and much of the correspondence exchanged between the Territorial and federal governments, are reproduced in D.R. Owram, ed., *The Formation of Alberta: A Documentary History* (Calgary: Historical Society of Alberta, 1979). As its title suggests, this volume draws together a wealth of documentary material illustrating the constitutional evolution of the North-West Territories and the controversy surrounding the granting of provincial statues in 1905.

12. Lingard, p. 58.

13. *Ibid.*, p. 111.

14. Canada, *House of Commons Debates*, 1905, col. 1457.

15. University of Alberta Archives, A.C. Rutherford Papers, File 2/3/7/2-13, F.W.G. Haultain to Rutherford, April 26, 1902.

16. *Regina Leader*, November 12, 1896; November 19, 1896.

17. *Regina Standard*, December 25, 1901.

18. Skelton, p. 226; J.W. Dafoe, *Clifford Sifton in Relation to His Times* (Toronto: Macmillan Company of Canada, 1931), p. 280.

19. Canada, *House of Commons Debates*, 1905, cols.1426-31. The choice of the fourth meridian has not escaped criticism from historians and geographers. See, for example, D.H. Breen, "The Canadian West and the Ranching Frontier, 1875-1822" (Ph.D. dissertation, University of Alberta, 1972), pp. 296-98; N.L. Nicholson, *The Boundaries of the Canadian Confederation* (Toronto: Macmillan Company of Canada, 1979), pp. 129-38.

20. Lingard, pp. 204-205.
21. L.H. Thomas, p. 265.
22. L.G. Thomas, p. 14. Once the autonomy bills were brought down even one of Haultain's staunchest supporters in the eastern portion of the Territories was quick to advise the Premier to abandon his " 'one-province' fad" on account of the near-unanimous public approval of the decision to create two provinces. (*Daily Standard* (Regina), March 13, 1905.)
23. L.G. Thomas, pp. 3-6, pp. 41-42, 68-69; D.H. Bocking, "Political Ambitions and Territorial Affairs, 1900-04," *Saskatchewan History*, Vol. XVIII, No. 2 (Spring 1965), pp. 63-75.
24. *Daily Standard* (Regina), August 9, 1905.
25. Lingard, pp. 117-23; Eager, pp. 73-74, 83-84; Bocking, p. 74.
26. L.G. Thomas, pp. 7-8, 14-15, 19.
27. C. Martin, *"Dominion Lands" Policy*, edited and with an introduction by L.H. Thomas (Toronto: McClelland and Stewart Limited, 1973), pp. 210-11.
28. Lingard, p. 218. A similar view can be found in R.C. Brown and R. Cook, *Canada, 1896-1921: A Nation Transformed* (Toronto: McClelland and Stewart Limited, 1974), p. 75.
29. Lingard, p. 221.
30. Canada, *Statutes*, 38 Vic., Chapter 49, sec. 11; North-West Territories, *ordinances*, 1884, no. 5; 1892, No. 22; 1901, Chapter 29.
31. J.C. Hopkins, ed., *The Canadian Annual Review of Public Affairs, 1905* (Toronto: Annual Review Publishing Company, 1906), p. 47.
32. Public Archives of Canada (PAC), Clifford Sifton Papers, Letterbook, Sifton to J.W. Dafoe, February 25, 1905; Sifton to W. Laurier, February 26, 1905; same to same, February 27, 1905.
33. E. McCartney, "The Interest of the Central Canadian Press, Particularly the Toronto Press, in the Autonomy Bills, 1905," *Canadian History Since Confederation: Essays and Interpretations*, eds. B. Hodgins and R. Page (Georgetown, Ontario: Irwin-Dorsey Limited, 1972), pp. 317-33.
34. PAC, Wilfrid Laurier Papers, J.A. Ewan to Laurier, March 1, 1905, pp. 208833-34.
35. *Ibid.*, F.W.G. Haultain to Laurier, March 11, 1905, pp. 95679-91.
36. PAC, Clifford Sifton Papers, Letterbook, Sifton to W. Laurier, March 3, 1905; Sifton to J.W. Dafoe, March 11, 1905; Canada, *Statues*, 4-5 Edw. VII, Chatpers 3, 42, sec. 17.
37. Skelton, pp. 234-37.
38. Dafoe, pp. 278-95.
39. Lingard, pp. 177-80.
40. Cook and Brown, pp. 78-79. Joseph Schull also adopted much the same view as Dafoe in *Laurier: The First Canadian* (Toronto: Macmillan Company of Canada, 1965), pp. 444-53.
41. H.B. Neatby, *Laurier and a Liberal Quebec: A Study in Political Management* (Toronto: McClelland and Stewart Limited, 1973), p. 153.
42. *Ibid.*, pp. 155-56.
43. D.J. Hall, "A Divergence of Principle: Clifford Sifton, Sir Wilfrid Laurier and the North-West Autonomy Bills, 1905," *Laurentian University Review*, Vol. VII, No. 1 (November 1974), pp. 3-24.

44. C.B. Sissons, *Church and State in Canadian Education* (Toronto: Ryerson Press, 1959), p. 268.

45. E. Eager, "Separate Schools and the Cabinet Crisis of 1905," *The Lakehead University Review*, Vol. 2, No. 2 (Fall 1969), pp. 107-109.

46. M.R. Lupul, *The Roman Catholic Church and the North-West School Question: A Study in Church-State Relations in Western Canada, 1875-1905* (Toronto: University of Toronto Press, 1974), p. 178.

47. Skelton, p. 24; Lingard, pp. 248-49.

48. L.G. Thomas, pp. 15-20; D.H. Bocking, "Premier Walter Scott: A Study of His Rise to Political Power" (M.A. thesis, University of Saskatchewan, 1959), pp. 89-113.

49. Lingard, pp. 249-50; J.T. Saywell, "Liberal Politics, Federal Policies, and the Lieutenant-Governor: Saskatchewan and Alberta, 1905," *Saskatchewan History*, Vol. VIII, No. 3 (Autumn 1955), pp. 87-88.

50. L.G. Thomas, pp. 21, 23-27. Dr. Thomas has described the infectious optimism of the 1905 period in greater detail in "Alberta Perspectives, 1905," *Alberta History*, Vol. 28, No. 1 (Winter 1980), pp. 1-5.

51. Archives of Saskatchewan, Walter Scott Papers, Scott to T.A. Burrows, August 23, 1905, p. 5351; D.H. Bocking, "Saskatchewan's First Provincial Election," *Saskatchewan History*, Vol. XVII, No. 2 (Spring 1964), p. 42; D.E. Smith, *Prairies Liberalism: The Liberal Party in Saskatchewan, 1905-71* (Toronto: University of Toronto Press, 1975), p. 20.

52. *Daily Standard* (Regina), November 22, 1905; *Vidette* (Indian Head), November 29, 1905.

53. Bocking, "First Provincial Election," pp. 46-48; Smith, p. 23.

54. See, for example, G.W.D. Abrams, *Prince Albert The First Century, 1866-1966* (Saskatoon: Modern Press, 1966), pp. 152-53; E.G. Drake, *Regina: The Queen City* (Toronto: McClelland and Stewart Limited, 1955), pp. 128-30; M. Foran, *Calgary: An Illustrated History* (Toronto: James Lorimer and Company, 1978), pp. 60-64; J.G. MacGregor, *Edmonton: A History* (Edmonton: Hurtig Publishers, 1967), pp. 134-54, *passim*.

55. A.B. Kilpatrick, "A Lesson in Boosterism: The Contest for the Alberta Provincial Capital, 1904-1906," *Urban History Review*, Vol. VIII, No. 3 (February 1980), pp. 47-109.

56. J.E. Murray, "The Provincial Capital Controversy in Saskatchewn," *Saskatchewan History*, Vol. V, No. 3 (Autumn 1952), p. 81.

57. L.G. Thomas, *Liberal Party*, p. 3.

58. G.H.W. Richardson, "The Conservative Party in the Provisional District of Alberta, 1887-1905" (M.A. thesis, University of Alberta, 1977), p. 184.

59. The fullest biographical sketch of Haultain to date has been L.H. Thomas, "The Political and Private Life of F.W.G. Haultain," *Saskatchewan History*, Vol. XXIII, No. 2 (Spring 1970), pp. 50-58.

60. Smith, p. 3. A similar view may be found in L.G. Thomas, *Liberal Party*, p. 3.

IX

PRAIRIE WOMEN

Women have always played a prominent role in prairie society. Traditionally, their involvement was in the household, performing domestic duties (often including outside work), and rearing children. Only occasionally did prairie women have the opportunity to participate in business, politics, or union activities. Until recently, women's history concentrated on these "exceptional" women. In particular, the emphasis was on the suffrage movement as an example of prairie women's accomplishments. Yet this approach overlooks the important role of women in their own day-to-day lives, and tends to apply male values—political over apolitical, public over private, and male over female—to the study of women's history. It also diminishes the importance of the post-suffrage era when issues other than the vote preoccupied women. In this period, activists tried to find ways to improve the lot of women in the home. As Veronica Strong-Boag notes: "Theirs was the feminism of the workplace, of day-to-day life." In "Pulling in Double Harness or Hauling a Double Load: Women, Work and Feminism on the Canadian Prairie," she chronicles the efforts of rural prairie women in the interwar years to improve their daily lives.

Recent research suggests that some women turned to radical politics and the labour movement to advance the feminist cause. One such woman was Amelia Turner of Calgary. In the interwar years, she participated in the birth of the Women's Section of the Dominion Labour Party, was active in the Women's Labor League, and supported the CCF, running as a candidate for the provincial party in Alberta. Through these organizations, she worked for women's causes in terms of her feminist and socialist vision. Patricia Roome discusses the life and activities of Amelia Turner and those of other Calgary labour women in "Amelia Turner and Calgary Labour Women, 1919-1935."

To what extent was Amelia Turner characteristic of prairie urban women? And how were the lives of prairie women different from those of women in other regions of the country? Did prairie women identify more with Canadian women or with regional interest groups, such as prairie farmers, even if such regional concerns went against their feminist interests? To what extent did "first wave feminists" concern themselves with women's issues as opposed to generic social issues? What was distinctive about the prairie women's movement? These are the kinds of questions that historians of prairie women are asking of their sources. Their research is opening up a new and important field of history.

SELECTED BIBLIOGRAPHY

On prairie women's history in general see the relevant sections in Alison Prentice et al., *Canadian Women: A History* (Toronto, 1988); footnote references and bibliographic entries are extensive. See as well Linda Rasmussen et al., eds., *A Harvest Yet to Reap: A History of Prairie Women* (Toronto, 1976), and for Manitoba, Mary Kinnear, ed., *First Days, Fighting Days: Women in Manitoba History* (Regina, 1987).

Rural prairie women are discussed in Eliane Silverman, *The Last Best West: Women on the Alberta Frontier, 1880-1920* (Montreal, 1984); Susan Jackel, ed., *A Flannel Shirt and Liberty: British Emigrant Gentlewomen in the Canadian West, 1880-1914* (Vancouver, 1982); Ann Leger Anderson, "Saskatchewan Women, 1880-1920: A Field Study" in H. Palmer and D. Smith, eds., *The New Prairie Provinces: Alberta and Saskatchewan* (Vancouver, 1980), pp. 65-90; Mary Kinnear, "Do You Want Your Daughter to Marry a Farmer?: Women's Work on the Farm, 1922," in Donald H. Akenson, ed., *Canadian Papers in Rural History*, Vol. VI (Gananoque, Ont., 1988): 137-53; and Georgina M. Taylor, "Should I Drown Myself Now or Later?: The Isolation of Rural Women in Saskatchewan and Their Participation in the Homemakers' Clubs, the Farm Movement and the Co-operative Commonwealth Federation, 1910-1967" in Kathleen Storrie, ed., *Women, Isolation and Bonding: The Ecology of Gender* (Toronto, 1987), pp. 79-100.

On women in the ranching community see Sheilagh Jameson, "Women in the Southern Alberta Ranching Community, 1881-1914" in Henry Klassen, ed., *The Canadian West* (Calgary, 1977), pp. 63-78. Veronica Strong-Boag places prairie women of the interwar years into a wider context in her *The New Day Recalled: Lives of Girls and Women in English Canada, 1919-1939* (Toronto, 1988).

Students wishing to pursue further the topic of women's suffrage in the West should consult: Carol Bacchi, "Divided Allegiance: The Response of Farm and Labour Women to Suffrage," in L. Kealey, ed., *A Not Unreasonable Claim: Women and Reform in Canada 1880s-1920s* (Toronto, 1979), pp. 89-108; Ramsay Cook, "Francis Marion Beynon and the Crisis of Christian Reformism," in C. Berger and R. Cook, eds., *The West and the Nation* (Toronto, 1976), pp. 187-208; Barbara Jean Nicholson, "Feminism in the Prairie Provinces to 1916" (M.A. thesis, University of Calgary, 1974); Christine Macdonald, "How Saskatchewan Women Got the Vote," *Saskatchewan History* (October 1948): 1-8; June Menzies, "Votes for Saskatchewan's Women" in N. Ward and D. Spafford, eds., *Politics in Saskatchewan* (Toronto, 1968), pp. 78-92; Paul Voisey, "The 'Votes for Women' Movement," *Alberta History* 23 (1975): 10-23; and the relevant section of Catherine Cleverdon, *The Woman Suffrage Movement in Canada* (Toronto, 1950).

On Nellie McClung and women's suffrage, students are encouraged to read her tract *In Times Like These* (1915) (Reprinted Toronto, 1972). Also see V. Strong-Boag " 'Ever a Crusader' : Nellie McClung, First-Wave Feminist," in V. Strong-Boag and A. Fellman, eds., *Rethinking Canada: The Promise of Women's History* (Toronto, 1986), pp. 178-90; as well as Candace Savage, *Our Nell: A Scrapbook of Nellie McClung* (Saskatoon, 1979).

On women in politics in the post-suffrage era see the relevant articles in L. Kealey and J. Sangster, eds., *Beyond the Vote: Canadian Women and Politics* (Toronto, 1989). On women and the Winnipeg General Strike see Mary Horodyski, "Women and the Winnipeg General Strike of 1919," *Manitoba History* 11 (1986): 28-37. Mary Kinnear's *Margaret McWilliams: An Interwar Feminist* (Montreal, 1991) chronicles the life of the first president of the Canadian Federation of University Women and a Winnipeg city councillor.

Good bibliographic essays are Susan Jackel, "Canadian Prairie Women's History: a Bibliographic Survey," *CRIAW Paper* No. 14 (April, 1987): 1-22; and E.L. Silverman, "Writing Canadian Women's History, 1970-82: An Historiographical Analysis," *Canadian Historical Review* 63 (1982): 513-33.

VERONICA STRONG-BOAG

20 Pulling in Double Harness or Hauling a Double Load
Women, Work and Feminism on the Canadian Prairie

What happened to first wave feminism, the feminism of the suffrage generation? This question has occasionally concerned historians and more regularly troubled feminists. To date in Canada there have been a number of
answers. Some of the earliest commentators, focusing on the vote, seemed
to conclude that the agenda was complete. There was no need for feminism
in a nation where equality was a fact of life; it died of benign neglect.[1] In
The Woman Suffrage Movement in Canada (1950), the first major treatment of the suffrage cause, Catherine Cleverdon was much less sanguine,
seeing much to be done and "the political performance of the dominion's
women . . . a disappointment." Her interviews with some prominent
figures, notably Charlotte Whitton, suggested that Canadian women didn't
value the vote because they hadn't fought hard enough and in some crucial
way didn't deserve it.[2] While Cleverdon was sympathetic to the suffrage
generation, later scholars influenced by American debunking studies and
especially by a recognition of the class-based nature of reform were much
less positive. The most recent monograph on suffrage, Carol Bacchi's *Liberation Deferred? The Ideas of the English-Canadian Suffragists, 1877-1918*
(1983) castigates suffragists for betraying the promise of a feminist revolution. Indeed, in her view they were not so much radical critics as conservative defenders of privilege. Bacchi implies that this middle-class feminism
didn't survive because it didn't deserve to. She leaves the distinct impression that activists in Canadian feminism, or at least its suffragists, were
a pretty poor lot, hardly proper foremothers for "better" feminists today.
My own early work on female doctors is in much the same vein with its
observation that an essentially male code of professionalism tamed much
of the feminist spirit that armed women for entry into medicine.[3] The newest
history of Canada during the interwar years, John Thompson and Allen
Seager's *Canada 1922-1939: Decades of Discord* (1985), plots a somewhat

middle course in these debates, concluding that suffrage was necessary and that its advocates were decent enough people but that it and feminism in general were oversold and died of an acute case of disillusionment.[4] Finally, another interpretation surfacing in important new work on radical politics, notably by Linda Kealey and Joan Sangster, suggests that "advanced women," that is, "radical women," found feminism too conservative for their tastes and opted for "real" change in the politics of the left. In the Communist Party and the Cooperative Commonwealth Federation what might otherwise have been feminist energies were subordinated for the most part to the more hard-nosed—that is, male-defined—politics of class.[5]

Although, as Joan Sangster notes, radical groups like the Women's Labor Leagues were extremely conscious of the reality of politics in the private sphere, historians have, for the most part, tended to reduce feminism to the struggle for power in the public realm. Any approach focusing so heavily on the public political arena must of necessity emphasize the discontinuity in the feminist identity in Canada's past. Indeed, none of the groups admitted late to the preserve of elite male power—women, the working class, various racial groups—have appeared as more than intermittent and isolated voices when you count up MPs, MLAs, beneficial legislation, and the like. That preserve has been well and truly guarded.[6] The few women who overcame man-made hurdles were effectively marginalized in institutions which considered them and their concerns interlopers on essentially male terrain.[7] No wonder then that they had great difficulty in translating their individual successes into a transformation of the political agenda of the public realm to reflect more fairly women's needs and experience.

Yet just as feminism before female enfranchisement was a good deal more than a debate about the vote, it survived into the 1920s and 1930s as much more than what could be found in the stubbornly male world of elite politics. The insight of some Women's Labor League members into the significance of domestic politics was central as well to the feminism that survived the Communist Party and the CCF. Barred from the inner circles of power in their society and lacking any strong tradition of looking to public politics for a resolution of their dilemmas, indeed taught to find solutions in personal ways, most women have carried on a discourse independent of the public world of male politics. This "woman's talk," as Susan Mann Trofimenkoff suggested in her 1985 presidential address to the Canadian Historical Association, is frequently dismissed as personal or private, as not political or substantive in the way that men's high-flying debates over international affairs or post office patronage or German night club life might be said to be. This dismissal is part of what feminist critics are arguing is "an illegitimate superimposition of three dichotomies: political/apolitical, public/private, and male/female,"[8] In other words, we must reexamine our understanding of what is political, where it occurs and who is involved. Private life can be very political indeed, involving important struggles over power and authority which engage both women and men. The outcome of these struggles is often played out in turn in publicly political ways, of which the recent case of an MP criticized for beating his wife is only an extreme example.

In the 1920s and 1930s women continued to talk about and act on the politics of the private sphere. Theirs was the feminism of the workplace, of day-to-day life. It was not for the most part an organized movement as the campaign for enfranchisement had been, but it flowed from a similar awareness of women's oppression and a desire to end it. A few women were prominent feminist advocates of workplace politics. Many more spent their hours preoccupied with working out in their own lives the consequences of gender. Their often inchoate feminism has been hidden from history because it found expression largely in the private realm. To a considerable degree the concerns of feminist leaders and this grassroots constituency coincided in these two decades. The result was a continuation of a feminist politics directed to the amelioration of women's situation in the private sphere.

The sexual division of labour has always preoccupied feminists. Responsibility for work, whether in the private or public sphere, but especially the former, has been consistently identified as crucial to the oppression of women.[9] In the post-suffrage years the issue of women's work was the example *par excellence* of Canadian women's understanding of gender as a crucial political issue. Even if they developed no coherent body of theory about women's work, many women shared a common-sense understanding that the possibilities for their sex in the public sphere would continue to be severely limited until the issues of their labour in the private sphere had been resolved. Individual causes as varied as access to higher education, equal homestead rights and married women's property acts shared a crucial concern with the implications of female labour. Feminists differed, sometimes sharply, on the precise solutions but almost without exception they identified work as lying at the heart of women's oppression.

A good example of this understanding is provided by prairie rural women in the 1920s and 1930s. The feminism of western farm activists has been largely dismissed by Carol Bacchi, who credited them with feeling "no more oppressed than their husbands, with whom they faced a common oppressor, the Eastern interests."[10] This is typical of a recurring tendency on the part of historians to see female activists as differing in little more than gender from male activists of the same economic class. The result ignores the strong, even passionate, sense of same sex identification which moved Canadian women to sign temperance petitions, to contribute their mite to women's missionary societies, to agitate for the vote, and to demand recognition of women's right to employment and the value of their domestic labour. Argue as they did about precise solutions, profitable tactics and suitable allies, prairie activists were highly sensitive to the particular situation of their sex.

The feminist cause on the prairies was first carried in town and country by the Women's Christian Temperance Union. The Union was considerably more than the conservative agent of social control as it has sometimes been portrayed.[11] It represented the organized might of women opposed to violence against women. Even when separate farm organizations had been created, the temperance society's sober, feminist spirit gave direct and continual inspiration to rural women. WCTU activists like Louise McKinney, elected for the Non-Partisan League to the Alberta house in 1917, and Nellie McClung, elected to the same house in 1921 under the Liberal banner, shared an awareness of the dangers of domestic or workplace violence that has long been central to feminist politics. Individuals so inspired did not easily forget women's predicament in the private sphere once they entered public politics. Their agenda was far from complete.[12]

This is not to suggest that prairie women did not exhibit class and regional loyalties as well. Rural women frequently rejected the pretensions of urban suffragists.[13] Brought to political consciousness during the flood tide of agrarian protest, they owed powerful loyalties to the organized farm movement. This after all was the source of much of their strength. Like the Maritimers discussed by Ernest Forbes in a recent article in *Atlantis,*[14] pragmatic feminists in Manitoba, Saskatchewan and Alberta knew full well the terms on which success could be won in their region. Unlike their eastern counterparts, however, they had less history of failure and more reason for optimism. While some had fought feminist battles before they moved to prairie Canada,[15] the movement in the rural west dated in general only from the years immediately preceding the Great War. The Women's Section of the United Farmers of Manitoba, the Women's Section of the Saskatchewan Grain Growers, the first women's local of the United Farmers of Alberta, the UFWA itself, and the Interprovincial Council of Farm Women all emerged between 1913 and 1919. Their creation heralded the appearance of a collective consciousness for which circumstances at last permitted expression.

Like those elsewhere, organized rural women shared many grievances with their menfolk, but their enthusiasm for male farmers was tempered by a feminism rooted in an awareness of the very different realities faced by the sexes and a recurring lack of consideration by the male farm movement.[16] For example, Violet McNaughton, founder of the Saskatchewan Women Grain Growers and women's editor of the *Western Producer* from 1925 to 1951, a woman whom Bacchi designates as "a good barometer of farm sentiment" and who, just as importantly, identified herself as a feminist,[17] was quick to distinguish the situation of the sexes. In a typical address she observed: "Prairie men *may* work hard, there may be chores early and late, but never later than the woman, besides there is eight hours rest per day on many of the implements. I would rather disc than bake any day." Nor, she continued, do farmers always acknowledge women's contribution, "Do men believe that women are just a domestic machine for keeping the wheels of life going[?]," she asked.[18] Nellie McClung made much the same point still more dramatically:

> On the farms before electricity and labor-saving devices lightened their loads, women's work obsessed them. Their hours were endless, their duties imperative. Many broke under the strain and died, and their places were filled without undue delay. Some man's sister or sister-in-law came from Ontario to take the dead woman's place. Country cemeteries bear grim witness to the high mortality rate in young women.[19]

Another westerner, Emily Murphy, summed up the situation pithily in her observation that female Canadians were to "be a combination of Mary, Martha, Magdalen, Bridget and the Queen of Sheba."[20]

It was readily observable that women, for all their efforts, were only infrequently recognized and rewarded. Irene Parlby, as a UFA member of Alberta's legislature, criticized the province's Dower Act, which gave only limited property rights to wives for just this failure:

> Because the work of the married woman, in caring for her household, was supposed to be a labor of love, and of no economic value . . . women were at first content to sell their work at far below its real value . . . . Perhaps no group of women has suffered more from this condition of affairs than Farm women. Certainly no group of women has labored so hard[,] so ungrudgingly and so unselfishly. And yet we know for a fact that in many instances, not even the produce that they raise by their own labor, can be sold and claimed as their own.[21]

Such insight into women's situation was not limited to the elite of prairie women. Letters by female readers to the *Grain Growers' Guide*, the *Western Producer* and the *Free Press Prairie Farmer* during the interwar years confirm the widespread recognition that women did not so much work in double harness as carry a double load.

Until most discussion of sexual politics was pre-empted by debates over solutions to the collapse of the economy and the international order, much of the 1920s and the early 1930s was taken up by essentially feminist attempts to win acknowledgement of women's labour and, with this, a greater degree of female autonomy. This campaign was waged over a wide front, involving at one time or another most women who could find a public voice. Diffuse as their efforts were, lacking a focus comparable to the vote, they can be generally identified as of two types. The first concentrated on charting the extent of women's labour in order to raise female and public consciousness. The second, which often came hard on the heels of the former, proposed ways of lightening the heavy weight of toil. In the minds of their champions women's freedom of action was inextricably tied to their situation as workers.

Given the rural nature of much of the prairies, most attention focused on farm homes, and that is the particular concern of the discussion which follows, but feminists were also determined to defend married women's right to paid employment which spoke more particularly to conditions existing in the cities.[22] Interest in the farm home formed an important part of the country life movement, as it was known after World War I. Hoping to counter the drift to the cities, farm advocates endeavoured to revitalize rural living.[23] As far as many women were concerned, this required a major rethinking of women's role.

Women's arguments were marshalled carefully. Like other feminists in a later day, prairie dwellers were conscious of the need to document unambiguously the extent of women's contribution in and outside the home. In particular, they sought home-grown evidence to convince the sceptical of the merits of their cause. In 1920 the Women's Section of the United Farmers of Manitoba acted on this by conducting an initial survey of conditions in 48 farm homes; two years later 307 were investigated. In 1923 the Women Grain Growers of Saskatchewan sent out a questionnaire to document the problems of the rural housewife.[24] The resources of provincial universities were also tapped. In December 1927, for instance, a Research Committee was established by a conference on women's work held at the University of Saskatchewan. Violet McNaughton joined faculty from the agricultural college in directing the committee to the study of labour-saving devices, water supplies, waste disposal, ventilation, humidification, insulation, electrification and power. Better documentation was pursued as the surest way to arouse "thought, intelligent discussion and action that will lead toward the improvement of farm homes" and thus the alleviation of women's lot in the private sphere. Such a strategy would, it was hoped, counter the almost invariable practice of spending money first and almost exclusively on making the male farmer's work more productive while ignoring the conditions of female farm labour.[25]

Certainly the picture was grim enough. Formal investigations conducted during the 1920s combined with the personal observation and experience of female activists to reveal grueling, almost constant, labour. The rural survey conducted by the United Farm Women of Manitoba in 1922, for instance, showed that 176 of 307 farm homes lacked a kitchen water system. Only 37 had baths. Fewer still benefited from labour-saving technology: only five gasoline irons, five electric irons, one mangle, two bread mixers, and two vacuum cleaners were reported. Two-thirds of the correspondents cleaned stoves, carried in wood, and took out ashes, only one-third had furnaces. Lighting was also far from optimal: 21 farms were lit by electricity but 243 made do with coal oil lamps. In addition, farm homes were usually equipped with cellars rather than basements, making access to storage difficult: "Usually we see a chair dropped down and the woman swings herself down, and strains herself up."[26] In these primitive conditions women took on a multitude of tasks. Only 15 women, for example, did not sew; the majority sewed for the entire family. Although 25 percent performed no outside chores, 50 percent milked and 45 percent assumed responsibility for gardens, poultry, and outside jobs in general. The majority also laundered, and sometimes mended, for hired men. Yet, with all these duties, only 15 women employed domestic help year-round. Nor, as Frederick Philip Grove depicted so well in *Settlers of the Marsh* (1925) and *Fruits of the Earth* (1933), did large holdings guarantee comfort. One farm of 960 acres, for example, reported

> . . . no water in kitchen; no sink; no bath; the use of lamps for lighting; no power in house for even washing; no labor savers beyond cream separator; the well one-eighth of a mile from the house; the woman does all the sewing; she helps stook and haul grain; gets no spending money; takes only one paper to instil into her mind all the finer things of life; no telephone; house heated by stoves; woman cans all she can afford to; keeps no domestic help.[27]

Formal surveys were only one of the means by which female labour was brought to the attention of the public. The western press, especially its "women's pages," regularly addressed women's distinctive work experience. In the long-running women's section of the *Free Press Prairie Farmer*, "Home Loving Hearts" (from the 1890s at least through the 1930s), and its counterparts in other prairie newspapers and farm journals, thousands of female correspondents and readers discovered their own voice. Debates on issues like child care, birth control, abusive husbands, and housework help bring to light the cares of grassroot women and provide one measure of the degree to which feminist concerns have engaged the minds as well as the hearts of women normally far from the public limelight.[28] Even a quick inspection confirms the deep preoccupation with all aspects of women's work, a reality in which women engaged in housework, care of children and adults, paid work within the home, and, not infrequently, extensive outside work both on and off the farm. The press's presentation of these activities between the wars documents both the persistent, if often unself-conscious, feminism of its readership and the magnitude of the problem confronting those who wished to lessen female burdens.

Housework had many elements but, as the extensive coverage of recipes and tips on greater household efficiency suggested, food preparation, including preserving and cleaning, was the most time-consuming and inescapable. Even in the 1920s substantial numbers of prairie women, especially those living in newly settled areas and the dry belt, "made do" in near-primitive conditions. Nevertheless, advertisements and columns aimed at female readers conveyed a strong sense of optimism about the improvements increasingly available in the form of new products, menus and technologies.

Nor was hope for a transformed life-style confined to developments in the kitchen. Especially dramatic was the effect attributed to the purchase of the combine. One Saskatchewan farm wife enthused:

> The combine is surely a great invention. No more big supplies of food to be stored up for hungry threshers. No more getting up at half past three in the morning to prepare breakfast for fifteen or twenty hungry men and perhaps be awake for an hour before getting up time, for fear you'd over-sleep. Now I get up at half past five, have breakfast at six, the men go to the field and you hear the hum of the combine at half past six . . . . With the old method of threshing, there came wet weather, you had a crew on hand for perhaps several days . . . . You were supposed to feed them and be very pleasant as well . . . . With the combine that all changed.[29]

In the 1930s hopes, along with machinery and homes, ran downhill, and women's pages reflected women's efforts to substitute where possible their own labour for purchased goods and services. Many contributors took considerable pride in their accomplishments:

> If you drink your own water and milk, let the grocer keep his tea, coffee and cocoa. Take your own wheat to the mill. Get your flour and cracked wheat for porridge. Buy your own cloth and make dresses. You can make three for the price of one, and better goods in it. Make your own bread, cake, pie, pickles. Can your vegetables and fruit. Make your own cheese and sauerkraut. These are all easy to do, if you have the will to try.[30]

The ability to curtail cash purchases in bad times and good contributed to housewives' strong belief that they were doing their share and more and that they had no reason to be defensive before anti-feminist and misogynist critics.[31]

Like other women across the Dominion, prairie mothers in the inter-war years were subjected to a barrage of well-intentioned advice from child-care specialists, whose attempts to raise standards made women increasingly self-conscious about measuring up as parents.[32] Not all succumbed. A writer in *Western Home Monthly* in 1932 protested that "Child Psychology Does Not Always Work."[33] Even if persuaded, however, many farm women were in no position to implement the experts' advice. Houses were often small, amusements few; when inclement weather kept families indoors for days or weeks at a time, the trials of child-raising must often have obscured the rewards. Discussion about children among women in prairie publications was rarely sentimental. Yet, given the isolation of many homesteads and the absence of husbands, or the absence of good marital relationships, women often placed much emotional energy into the "wee ones" or my "dear little one." In face of many other disappointments children could make life bearable. No wonder then that women took childrearing seriously, according to it an important place in the hierarchy of the world's tasks.

The prairie press's promotion of modern childrearing methods, with their emphasis on discipline, a variety of up-to-date purchases and one-to-one care, also helped prepare the climate for a public discussion of birth control. When the number and spacing of births could not be rigorously controlled, farm mothers could not easily live up to their own high standards. The unlucky, like one wife searching for contraceptive advice, went "through it [pregnancy] regularly every year since I was married . . . ."[34] Observing as they could all around them the consequences of unchecked fertility, many women confronted the prospect of pregnancy with hard-headed realism. There is ample evidence of women who were knowledgeable or optimistic, whose menstruation was regular and husbands amenable, trying to accommodate pregnancy to seasonal work schedules and personal ambitions.[35] Such aspirations for greater individual autonomy transcended economic cycles but became especially urgent during the Great Depression when mothers' desperate plight echoed through many pages in the rural press.

Childbearing and childrearing lay at the heart of many women's lives but the management and care of adults also required considerable attention if the farm and the family were to function effectively. Relationships with hired help, aged parents and, especially, spouses helped set the extent and nature of female labour. Mothers and daughters might work as a team to feed and clothe the household. Housewives might find the water-carrying and wood-splitting contributions of a hired man invaluable. Perhaps most prized of all were the husbands who were good helpmates. As one correspondent suggested, cooperation often rested on mutual flexibility: "My husband often helps me in the house, but when spring comes I will not mind one bit if I do have to help with the chores." Not all wives were so fortunate. One stated bluntly, "About good husbands, the only good ones . . . are the dead ones."[36] Frequent accounts in the prairie press of wife battering, and even murder, illustrated, for any who cared to see, the unequal relationship of the sexes.[37] Bad marriages with their violence and distress elicited, as they had in the past and would in the future, special attention from those concerned to improve women's lot. Given the difficulties of obtaining a divorce with any reasonable financial settlement, however, the first advice an abused wife frequently received was to make the best of matters and find her comforts in her children.[38] Bad times sometimes increased intimacy in a marriage but they often required relationships to be managed carefully. This could be all the more true when the collapse of markets and cash crops made women's contributions the mainstay of the domestic economy and undermined the male bread-winner role and thus, for some men at least, the basis of male identity.[39]

The incorporation of paid work into domestic routines appeared relatively commonplace in both decades, a good index both of how "tough times" were not restricted to the depths of the Great Depression and how a woman's choices might include not only substituting her labour for cash purchases but also switching to paid home-based production. Certainly, if women's pages are any indication, money-making was never far from readers' minds. Advertisements for the Auto Knitter whose Toronto hosiery company promised to buy a purchaser's entire output of socks, stockings, toques, and sweaters appeared regularly in the prairie press. One Saskatchewan homemaker was depicted as earning the magnificent sum of $65.00 a month "when things looked black." The *Farm and Ranch Review* addressed the same concern in "Making Farm Hobbies Pay" which assessed the prospects for producing flowers, livestock, poultry, rabbits and foxes.[40] The value of women's cash-producing efforts was acknowledged matter-of-factly by Moose Jaw's Saskatchewan Creamery Company which referred to

> The Woman in Charge . . . of the farm home . . . [as] the one who says whether or not they receive the highest grade for their cream. She is the one who checks up on the proper washing of milk pails, strainer, cream separator, cans and other utensils used around the milk house. It is necessary that she know many things about the proper milking and handling of the milk from the time it goes into the pail until the cream is ready to ship to the creamery.[41]

Detailed exchanges of information among female correspondents on breeds, breeding and care of poultry in the *Free Press Prairie Farmer*, like the creation in 1923 of an Egg and Poultry Pool by the United Farm Women of Alberta and the appointment of a member of the Women's Section of the Grain Growers as President of the Saskatchewan Egg and Poultry Pool,[42] reflected women's major role in yet another income-producing endeavour.

In face of the great need for additional cash, debates about the appropriateness of outside work for women that filled newspaper pages from time to time were largely theoretical. Indeed, some women householders and their daughters, despite admonitions to the contrary, proclaimed their preference for outside chores.[43] The fact that the costs of replacing their low-priced domestic labour, if that were possible, were significantly less than employing a hired man made such solutions to the demands of farm life all the more attractive.

Some women also assumed additional tasks off the farm. Their earnings could be critical to the family's survival as one "Farmer John" attested in his heartfelt salute to his wife's initiative in taking employment as a teacher. Although he felt it "a disgrace to let my wife work out," he bowed to her cheerful willingness to add to his insufficient earnings. In a still more unusual response he took up the slack at home where "that winter's experience opened my eyes to women's work."[44] That story had a happy ending. Other stories involving women with children who sought housekeeping jobs during the winter months when they could not afford to remain at home were sometimes tragic. Such was the case with one mother of a large family who planned to take her two youngest—two years and five months old—with her when she worked from April to December. This was the only way she could hope to "pay the debts" that crippled her and her husband.[45] As conditions worsened on the prairies, especially in the dried out and "hoppered out" regions, paid off-farm employment became more difficult to find. Teaching in particular was problematic for married women who were often blamed for snatching wages from men and single women. Prejudices of this kind did not reduce the desperation of wives but they undoubtedly made them sell their services more cheaply.

The increase in the relative worth of female labour on the farm during the 1930s highlighted, sometimes dramatically, the importance of wives, daughters, and sisters. Although women's pages acknowledged that hardship was widespread and war a reality, they insisted on, even during the worst of the Depression, the value of women's contributions. Their ability to "make do," the produce of their gardens, cows and chickens, and their earnings from outside sources helped sustain women's demands for recognition and respect. Letters to the prairie press requesting information about the legal rights of homemakers to egg or milk money or to children and family property upon the death or desertion of husbands, like the enduring interest in homesteads,[46] revealed consciousness not only of women's vulnerability but of their claim to justice. The anger that accompanied observations that "Police [were] No Protection" against an abusive husband[47] signalled that wives and mothers far from the public spotlight were not immune to demands for substantial improvements in the situation of their sex.

Only rarely did such women have the optimism or the energy or the experience to demand the solutions we have traditionally come to define as political. This did not, however, mean passivity or indifference or the absence of feminist sentiments. Women turned to age-old customs of mutual encouragement and support. One representative letter-writer to a women's page, for example, addressed a previous contributor with a bad husband: "He has a very queer way of showing his love by abusing you. I wish you were closer tonight so I could throw a scarfe over my shoulders and run in and have a chat with you. Possibly you would drop me a line some time . . . ." Another woman advised "Splash," who had eight children under twelve, milked eight cows daily, cleaned the barn, fed the pigs and chickens and did all her own housework as well, to drop the outside work; her husband would be forced to take up the slack. Solutions could be drastic. One reader proposed a "Baby Moratorium" until women's contribution was recognized by better maternity and obstetrical care. One equally angry observer spoke on behalf of overworked farm wives: "We Women Should

Go On Strike."[48] Another thirty-three year old contributor favoured a still more radical proposition, bragging:

> Today . . . I own my own home, cattle, chickens, and operate a small farm without the help of any man. When I need help I get a girl. I handle horses in real western style, including hauling grain. I would not have a man on the place. I always have a big garden and make quite a lot of cash from it.[49]

In just such pragmatic ways grassroots women expressed their irrepressible sense of solidarity and competence.

Even prominent representatives of women's cause could rarely escape the domestic cares which worried and energized the less fortunate: the practical realities of life helped bind together grassroots and elite women, Violet McNaughton's responsibility or the maintenance of an aged and difficult father made her especially sympathetic to similar dilemmas reported by her readers and correspondents. Another leading Saskatchewan activist had to put up with a hostile husband, a problem which may help explain her enthusiasm for women's cause. Dorise Nielsen's experiences on relief in the Peace River country in the 1930s fed her political radicalism and her insights into women's situation.[50] And as Nellie McClung's frequent acknowledgement of the value of her hired girls also indicated, even those with some exemption from women's labour were not necessarily indifferent to its implications.[51] Sensitized as they were to the extent of women's work, female activists like their humbler counterparts remembered in prairie papers sought remedies. For the more radical only the overthrow of the capitalist system would suffice. Most high-profile women, however, continued to favour reforms which, while more encompassing than the individual remedies turned to by the rank-and-file, were essentially reformist and piecemeal. At one time or another many placed their hopes on domestic servants, assistance from husbands, household science, cooperation, technology, and legislation covering married women's property rights, homestead acts, divorce reform, and mothers' pensions acts. Such options with their emphasis on redressing the inequities of the private sphere showed feminism at its most pragmatic.

The search for more and better household help has long preoccupied better-off women. It is easy enough to deplore their enthusiasm with all its class biases.[52] Yet, well as the self-interest of a potential mistress might be served, the campaign for servants could sometimes contain the seeds of feminist insight into the nature of domestic labour. The special difficulties prairie rural women had in attracting domestic help—better pay and more comfortable situations were usually available in cities[53]—together with the fact that social distance was difficult to maintain while doing much the same work in a shared setting, could raise consciousness. By reminding housewives that servants might well marry sons and neighbours and thus were much like themselves western feminists effectively acknowledged that the key problem was in fact the lack of value attached to women's work in general. As Nellie McClung recognized, "if women took themselves seriously, they would think well of those who did 'women's work.' " This altered vision was, however, far from universal. Working too hard themselves, farm women expected the same sacrifices of those they employed. Not surprisingly, Mary McCallum, women's editor of the *Grain Growers' Guide*, concluded, "it is necessary for farm women to be educated as to the relationship between the farm housekeeper and her hired help."[54] That education would require admission of their common predicament as women.

A radical alternative to the search for domestic servants was the effort to get other family members, especially the husband, to take up home responsibilities. If women's pages in newspapers were any guide, one sign of a good husband was his willingness to pitch in. Many women would have agreed that "If a man wants his home perfect, let him help to make it so. Let him remember when he comes in tired from his work his wife . . . will be equally tired . . . ."[55] Men who were committed to a more egalitarian marriage were probably most likely to "help out" but there is little evidence that many questioned the traditional division of labour. The problem of course, as modern commentators have also appreciated, is how to encourage more flexibility about acceptable behaviour. An article entitled "Dolls for Small Boys" in the *Farm and Ranch Review* in 1919 had a familiar ring. Contending that male helplessness in domestic matters was largely a product of conditioning, the writer argued that it would be much better to "allow our children to grow up naturally. If the small boy wishes to play with dolls, let him, he won't then be so useless when he is a father . . . ."[56] Such advice was in keeping with the view of history held by many feminists. This argued that during an earlier stage of human development men had shared domestic responsibilities, only later relegating to women the duty of maintaining the home.[57] Such a view did not deny women a special role in the family; it did, however, insist that men like women had obligations in both spheres. Perhaps, subconsciously, feminists knew that once men took even a modest share of domestic labour it would acquire the importance women had always claimed for it.

Looking to men for help had to be something of a long shot and women turned as they had in the past to campaigns for domestic science instruction which directly addressed the question of female labour. One activist opposed the discontinuation of a director of home economics in Saskatchewan's Department of Education, typically arguing that "homebuilding, if it is to remain the *dominant concern of civilization, must receive proper consideration*."[58] In 1928 a conference on home economics at the University of Saskatchewan brought together rural and urban women's groups led by the president of the women's section of Saskatchewan's United Farmers. Arguing "on behalf of *all women of the province*," she explained to government representatives that "while large sums of money had been devoted to the development of agriculture . . . comparatively little had been done to better conditions in the home itself." She was supported by speakers who pointed out that women had helped to earn the homes as much as the men had, but in the matter of equipment, while most farms were being conducted by means of modern machinery and methods of procedure, that the inside of the home was 50 or 75 years behind the times in a great many instances, simply because they had never had a chance. They proposed a well-organized and far-reaching Home Economics Extension Department sufficiently staffed and equipped to do research . . . to render efficient service . . . and to carry on propaganda and educational work . . . [and] that 'Home Economics be made a compulsory, or required subject for the issuance of teachers certificates.' " Once the study of domestic life was taken seriously, it would revolutionize the running of the home. As Violet McNaughton put it, "A practical home economics program must contain very definite teaching as to what constitutes productive and unproductive labor in the home . . . ."[59] In critical ways home economics was to have some of the same consciousness raising and research goals of the modern women's studies programmes. Above all it was to make women and their work a subject for serious study. Remedies for domestic difficulties would, it was hoped, soon follow.

If knowledge of modern home economics potentially allowed women to do without additional help, so too did the promise of cooperation. Like feminists elsewhere in the Dominion, prairie thinkers considered the possibility of common remedies. This was hardly surprising given their fascination with various producer cooperatives, notably in the wheat, dairy and poultry pools. Feminists like Irene Parlby believed that cooperation was learned best in the home and women were its most natural practitioners.[60] Women could end much of the drudgery that beset them by exercising this talent in the community at large. Cooperative laundries and bakeries found special favour, offsetting as they might the heavy weight of daily labour. The WGGA, for example, passed a number of resolutions in the interwar years advocating just such initiatives.[61] Yet prospects for cooperation floundered even in the more optimistic 1920s. Finally, a conservative individualism centred on the family, a rival ideology emanating from modern capitalist producers, and the physical reality of women's isolation in the home, undermined every effort to find a cooperative solution to women's difficulties.

Closely related to the enthusiasm for both home economics and cooperation and in keeping with economic trends favouring consumption was the interest in technology. Feminists made invidious comparisons between the "high tech" solutions to the labour problems of male farmers and the primitive conditions facing housewives.[62] Awareness was sharpened by the hard sell that advertisers adopted in the years after the First Great War. Canadian General Electric, for example, first became "jobbers of household appliances" as "part of the plan to increase power consumption." By 1930 it had adopted the "line" approach to the sale of its appliances and in the depths of the Depression was taking the "General Electric Kitchen" on wheels across Canada and building "GE" electric homes in an aggressive sales campaign.[63]

Marketing tactics were especially important since women's unfamiliarity with domestic hardware meant, according to feminist observers as well as advertisers themselves, that "many were afraid of machines."[64] Such timidity combined with the late electrification of rural areas and the usual cash shortages of farmers to encourage the promotion of the simplest kind of technology. Advocating the cement cistern, the female Grain Growers pointed out that "Running water is just as essential . . . as up to date machinery is on the efficiently equipped farm. Up to date machinery has made the hard work of tillage, seeding and harvesting lighter for the men; running water in the home lightens the load for the women . . . ."[65] Although feminists tended to be realistically frugal in their advocacy of improvements, they did challenge priority given to the relief of male workers. They also recognized that women as well as their husbands had to discard the notion that female labour was less valuable and less worthy of assistance. Advice about "Reducing Kitchen Mileage," "A Kitchen Remodelled," and "Being A 'Speed Artist' " was seemingly innocuous but it helped raise consciousness about the extent of women's work and the possibilities of remedy.[66] In 1934 the UFWA Home Economics Convenor summed up hopes:

> Take heed to ways of doing things easier and better and in a shorter time. Avail ourselves of all labor-saving devices within our reach. That is why I wonder if we are wise in undertaking so much canning, etc., when . . . most housewives are already heavily burdened with more than they can do, and keep strong and healthy, companions to their husbands and families, friends to neighbors and those in sorrow and want, and keep up a place in the country's affairs.[67]

Technology, old as well as new, also supplied one of the most controversial means for reducing women's heavy workload: birth control. Feminists handled this issue gingerly but they recognized its significance. Indeed, the question of "Keeping the Stork in his Place" could hardly be avoided since it went right to the heart of much of the politics of the private sphere.[68] As letters to women's pages revealed, the Great Depression made the problem of unwanted children all the more acute. It could also undermine the search for a solution. This happened in 1931 at the Saskatchewan farm women's convention when, as McNaughton explained to one critic, "Everyone was feeling the need for united action on the economic question of what is to be done with our wheat so seriously that it was decided to withdraw the resolution [on birth control]" since it would prove so divisive.[69] For all such setbacks, birth control continued to find champions. Violet McNaughton herself, for instance, served as a clearing house for Margaret Sanger's *Birth Control Review* and as a forceful advocate of women's right to control conception. The UFWA had a ready audience in asking "What misery and suffering would be spared to women and children if all laws against birth control were annulled and its practice under medical supervision considered a public utility . . . "[70] Like Alberta's IODE and its Provincial Executive in the National Council of Women, the farm organization accepted birth control clinics as a logical solution to a long-standing dilemma.

Women looked first to their own ingenuity and then to each other for dealing with the problems of the private sphere. The possibility of legislative remedies seemed very remote to the great majority. Yet they had numerous occasions to recognize that, like Irene Murdoch some four or five decades later, they had little legal recourse.[71] One prairie wife wrote on behalf of herself and many others: "My husband takes off pretty good crops every year, but he will never give me anything in the fall, or any other time . . . . and I have worked so hard to help to earn the farm. It is not fair."[72] Campaigns for improved property rights for married women, equality in divorce, homesteads on the same terms as men, and mothers' pensions were powered by a strong sense of injustice. It was just this unfairness which caused Irene Parlby to support Alberta's 1925 Community Property Act. Assets acquired by either spouse during the marriage were to become community property. Even this act, as she acknowledged, was only the "embryo from which some satisfactory legislation may result," Although it gave the husband "absolute power of disposition, other than testamentary," he could not "sell, convey or encumber the community real estate unless the wife joins with him in executing the instrument of conveyance . . . ."[73] Unfortunately, as with many proposals benefiting women, this never became law. A reformed homestead act was another such case. Provisions in the Dominion Lands Act of 1872 were the "target of the homesteads-for-women movement carried on . . . most intensively between 1909 and 1913, and then sporadically thereafter right up to 1930, when the three prairie provinces inherited control of public lands."[74] Thereafter remaining public lands were sold and women became, theoretically, men's equals as purchasers. Some sixty years of refusal, however, had handicapped numerous women in their efforts to win a living from the land.

Divorce legislation that gave men preference in proceedings was also a source of continuing protest. The United Farm Women of Manitoba voiced widespread dissatisfaction in contending that "There is no argument which is not an insult at once to Canadian womanhood and Canadian manhood against equality in divorce laws."[75] Without equality women's marital "job" could easily become intolerable but unremediable. The campaign to win financial support for destitute widows and deserted wives was part and parcel of the same effort to gain proper recognition of women's contribution. In the case of mothers' pensions or allowances the state would substitute for the absent husband.[76] "Wages for housework" seemed only fair to women who in the 1920s and 1930s concentrated on the problems of domestic labour. Such legislative successes as mothers' allowances did not, however, typify the post-suffrage period. Even funding for these was regularly in jeopardy. Appeals to the legislative process most frequently met with failure, as was the case with the "homesteads-for-women movement."

Prairie women knew, often only too well, the special nature of their situation. Loyal as they were to their region's interests, they could not ignore the claims of their sex. Their own surveys, the region's papers, and their own experience demonstrated that the crux of women's oppression lay in their heavy responsibilities for work in the private sphere. This essential insight nourished both elite and grassroots feminism. Like male farmers who in the 1920s turned away from politics to such practical remedies as the wheat pools, women, too, generally looked elsewhere for relief. Above all prairie feminism in the postsuffrage decades concentrated on assistance to women in the private sphere. Yet, while not without individual successes, especially in the 1920s, farm women for the most part found their labours neither lessened nor more fairly rewarded in these years. Feminism could make only small gains in face of recurring economic crisis on the farm and deep-running anti-feminism in the country at large. Better times would be a long time coming. In 1952 a Saskatchewan Royal Commission on Agriculture and Rural life confirmed that drudgery remained a fact of life for most farm women. Today farm women organize to protest conditions remarkably similar to those reported a half century ago.[77]

The costs of women's inequitable load have been heavy. So long as women laboured so hard without proper relief or recompense they could not enlarge their contribution to society. As Violet McNaughton concluded, "Long, laborious days chiefly taken up with over-expenditure of 'woman power' do not leave much energy or inclination for interest in participation in the finer things of life . . . ." Here was a major explanation for women's failure to seize the promise of the vote. They were already too hard pressed, as McClung lamented, as "the unpaid servants of men."[78] This dilemma did not disappear in the two decades between the wars. The Great Depression drained still further women's reserves of strength and confidence. Attacked by misogynists and anti-feminists when they worked outside the home, except in the most servile of posts, they were urged to make the best of their home duties. Too often the result for a woman was, as the *Western Producer* recognized, that her

> . . . working day is the length of time she can manage to stand upon her legs. Her reward is desertion by her children when they are old enough to take care of themselves. Poverty and isolation make her function of

motherhood a real hardship and burden, and self-neglect makes her old before her years.[79]

In the general disaster engulfing prairie residents in the 1930s remedies for women's domestic situation appeared further away than ever. Despite the best hopes of feminists, for most women life continued to consist of hauling a double load, or, as today's feminists would have it, working a double shift. Yet, more positively, the insight of prairie women into the nature of their sex's oppression contributed to the persistence of that hardy survivor, the counter to a male centred view of human experience, the feminist voice in Canadian history. Feminism survived the suffrage campaigns. It continued, as always, to be far more than a debate about a share in public spoils, its arguments went to the heart of human relationships, in the home and the family.

NOTES
*   My thanks to Kathryn McPherson and Heather McLeod for their research assistance and Anita Clair Fellman, Susan Jackel, Kathryn McPherson, Angus McLaren and Arlene Tigar McLaren for their comments on earlier drafts. I would also like to thank Trent University and its Canadian Studies Programme, especially its chairman, John Wadland, for the opportunity to give the 1985 W.L. Morton Lecture from which this article is substantially derived.

1. See, for example, W.L. Morton, "The Extension of the Franchise in Canada," Canadian Historical Association, *Annual Report*, 1943, pp. 72-81.
2. C.L. Cleverdon, *The Woman Suffrage Movement in Canada* (Toronto: University of Toronto Press, 1974), pp. 272, 273.
3. V. Strong-Boag, Canada's Women Doctors: Feminism Constrained," in *A Not Unreasonable Claim. Women and Reform in Canada, 1880s-1920s*, ed. L. Kealey (Toronto: The Women's Press, 1979).
4. See J.H. Thompson with Allen Seager, Canada 1922-1939: *Decades of Discord* (Toronto: McClelland and Stewart, 1985), pp. 69-75.
5. See Linda Kealey, "Canadian Socialism and the Woman Question, 1900-1914." *Labour/Le Travail* 13 (Spring 1984), pp. 77-100; and Joan Sangster, "Canadian Women in Radical Politics and Labour, 1920-1950," Ph.D. Thesis, McMaster University, 1984.
6. See John Porter, *The Vertical Mosaic* (Toronto: University of Toronto Press, 1965); and Wallace Clement, *The Canadian Corporate Elite* (Toronto: McClelland and Stewart, 1975).
7. See, for example, the careers of Agnes Macphail and Judy LaMarsh: Margaret Stewart and Doris French, *Ask No Quarter: A Biography of Agnes Macphail* (Toronto: Longmans, Green, 1959); and Judy LaMarsh, *Memoirs of a Bird in a Gilded Cage* (Toronto: McClelland and Stewart, 1969).

8. Susan Mann Trofimenkoff, "Presidential Address," Canadian Historical Association, *Report*, 1985; Janet Siltanen and Michelle Stanworth, "The Politics of Private Woman and Public Man," *Theory and Society* 13 (1984), p. 101.

9. See *inter alia*, Pat Armstrong and Hugh Armstrong, *The Double Ghetto* (Toronto: McClelland and Stewart, 1978): and P. Armstrong and H. Armstrong, *A Working Majority* (Ottawa: Canadian Advisory Council on the Status of Women, 1983).

10. Carol Bacchi, *Liberation Deferred? The Ideas of the English Canadian Suffragists, 1877-1918* (Toronto: University of Toronto Press, 1983), p. 127.

11. See, for instance, James G. Snell, " 'The White Life for Two': The Defense of Marriage and Sexual Morality in Canada, 1890-1914," *Histoire sociale/Social History* 16:31 (May 1983), pp. 111-28: and Michael Bliss, "Neglected Radicals: A Sober Second Look," *Canadian Forum* 50 (April/May 1970), pp. 16-17. See also Nancy Sheehan, "The WCTU on the Prairies, 1886-1930: An Alberta-Saskatchewan Comparison," *Prairie Forum* (Spring 1981), pp. 17-33.

12. See Veronica Strong-Boag, " 'Ever a Crusader': Nellie McClung, First-Wave Feminist," in *Rethinking Canada: the Promise of Women's History*, ed. V. Strong-Boag and Anita Clair Fellman (Toronto: Copp Clark Pitman, 1986).

13. Bacchi, *Liberation*, chapter 8.

14. Ernest Forbes, "The Ideas of Carol Bacchi and The Suffragists of Halifax: A Review Essay on *Liberation Deferred? The Ideas of the English Canadian Suffragists, 1877-1918.*" *Atlantis* 10:2 (Spring/printemps 1985), pp. 119-26.

15. See, for example, the case of Mrs. G. Hollis, president of the Women Grain Growers in 1926 and former member of England's Women's Social and Political Union, "The Lady Who Presides," *Grain Growers' Guide* (henceforth *GGG*), March 17, 1926, p. 25.

16. See, for example, Saskatchewan Archives Board (henceforth SAB), Voilet McNaughton Papers (henceforth VMP), folder 92(6), A.L. Hollis to McNaughton, Sept. 11, 1921 where this feminist complains about the attitude of the male *Grain Growers* to woman suffrage; another supporter of the women complained that "our men, while they profess to believe in equal rights for women, seem to have might little appreciation of what the woman vote means and have made no effort to secure woman speakers . . . ." SAB, VMP, Folder 92(6), M.L. Burbank to McNaughton, Nov. 23, 1923.

17. Bacchi, *Liberation*, p. 127. See SAB, VMP, v. 28, folder 33, McNaughton to Andrew Sibbald, Sept. 27, 1934, "I am a feminist," and folder A1, D, 2, 1, McNaughton to Mary Crozier, Oct. 1, 1931, in which she tells of being asked why she called herself "Mrs. Violet McNaughton instead of Mrs. John. I said because my husband did not regard me as a chattel and for the same reason I didn't wear a wedding ring."

18. SAB, VMP, v. 28, folder 33, McNaughton, "The Prairie Woman," handwritten, n.d.

19. Nellie McClung, *The Steam Runs Fast*, cited in Linda Rasmussen *et al.*, *A Harvest Yet to Reap. A History of Prairie Women* (Toronto: The Women's Press, 1976), p. 82.

20. Emily Ferguson, *Janey Canuck In The West*, cited in Rasmussen *et al.*, *A Harvest Yet to Reap*, p. 56.

21. Irene Parlby, *Alberta Labor Annual*, Sept. 5, 1925, cited in Rasmussen *et. al.*, *A Harvest Yet to Reap*, p. 170.

22. See, for example, Emily F. Murphy, "Married Women and School Teachers," *Western Home Monthly* (henceforth *WHM*) Sept. 1925, pp. 25, 49, 50; Murphy, "Matrimony and the Matter of Money," *National Home Monthly*, April 1932, pp. 12-13, 54, 58; and Cora Hind, "The Woman's Quiet Hour," *WHM*, Jan. 1922, pp. 31, 36.

23. For some discussion of the country life movement in Saskatchewan see David Jones, "Better Schools Day in Saskatchewan and the Perils of Educational Reform," in *Schools, Reform and Society in Western Canada, The Journal of Educational Thought* 14 (Aug. 1980), pp. 125-37.

24. Provincial Archives of Manitoba (henceforth PAM), MMG 10, E1, Box 20, United Farm Women of Manitoba (henceforth UFWM), "Rural Survey Report," c. 1923; Marilyn Barber, "Help for Farm Homes: The Campaign to End Housework Drudgery in Rural Saskatchewan in the 1920s," typescript, p. 32.

25. SAB, VMP, v. 27, folder 26, "Report of a Meeting of the Research Committee . . . 1927," typescript; PAM, MMG 10, E1, Box 20, UFWM, "Rural Survey Report," p. 6. This allocation of resources overwhelmingly to the improvement of men's work seems the practice in farming. See, for example, Marjorie Griffin Cohen, "The Decline of Women in Canadian Dairying," in *The Neglected Majority*, v. 2, ed. Alison Prentice and Susan Mann Trofimenkoff (Toronto: McClelland and Stewart, 1985).

26. PAM, MMG 10, E1, Box 20, UFWM, "Rural Survey Report," p. 4.

27. *Ibid.*, p. 5.

28. Correspondents to Ann Landers seem to be the modern day equivalent.

29. "Farm Women Praise the Combine," *GGG*, April 15, 1930, p. 19.

30. "All Kinds of Geese," *Free Press Prairie Farmer* (henceforth *FPPF*), Sept. 18, 1935, p. 4.

31. See especially the spirited defence of women by 'Celia II' in "Here You Are R-100," *FPPF*, Aug. 10, 1932. See also "Women Worked Then," *FPPF*, July 6, 1932, p. 4; "New to Farm," *FPPF*, July 13, 1932, p. 4; and "General Advice," *FPPF*, Aug. 3, 1932.

32. See, for instance, Margaret Bartlett, "'The Girl Who Didn't Love Babies," *WHM*, March 1920, pp. 38-39; Beulah France, "Cultivating Habits," *WHM*, Oct. 1934, p. 22; "Is Your Child Normal," *FPPF*, Jan. 21, 1925, p. 24: and "Reward in Praise," *FPPF*, Jan. 1, 1930, p. 105. See also Strong-Boag, "Intruders in the Nursery: Childcare Professionals Reshape the Years One to Five, 1920-1940," in *Childhood and Family in Canadian History*, ed. Joy Parr (Toronto: McClelland and Stewart, 1982).

33. "An Average Mother," "Child Psychology Does Not Always Work," *WHM*, Dec. 1932, p. 54.

34. "Child Cheated," *FPPF*, Jan. 25, 1933, p. 4.

35. See, for example, "Pay Twenty Games," *FPPF*, Dec. 28, 1932, p. 5: on the consequences of a failure in planning see also "Hard on Husband," *FPPF*, Feb. 22, 1933, pp. 4-5.

36. "Glad to Help," *FPPF*, Jan. 1, 1930, p. 5; "Strawberry Tea," *FPPF*, June 28, 1933, p. 5.

37. See, for example, "Farmer Kills Wife and Ends Own Life," *FPPF*, March 10, 1937, p. 10; "Wife Beater Gets Two-Month Term," *FPPF*, Aug. 17, 1932, p. 25; "Kills Housekeeper, Then Ends Own Life," *FPPF*, Oct. 19, 1932, p. 3; "Sentenced to Death for Murdering Wife," *FPPF*, Nov. 30, 1932, p. 4; "Held on Charge of Killing Wife," *FPPF*, July 12, 1933, p. 1; "Alberta Farmer Kills Wife, Son and Self," *FPPF*, June 26, 1935.

38. "What Should I Do?," *FPPF*, March 22, 1933, p. 15 and July 13, 1932, p. 15.

39. See the importance of the cream cheque in "Advice," *FPPF*, Feb. 4, 1920, p. 15. See also Winifred D. Wandersee, *Women's Work and Family Values 1920-1940* (Cambridge/London: Harvard University Press, 1981), chapter six, for its sensitive discussion of the impact of male unemployment on marital relations.

40. "This Woman Earned $65.00 a Month—Right at Home," *WHM*, Jan. 1927, p. 1; Doris S. Milligan, "Making Farm Hobbies Pay," *Farm and Ranch Review* (henceforth *FRR*), May 1931, pp. 26-27, 35.

41. "The Woman in Charge," *The Western Woman and Rural Home*, June 1924, p. 25.

42. Amy J. Roe, "Interesting Farm Women," *GGG*, Oct. 1, 1926, p. 31.

43. See "Helps in Fields," *FPPF*, June 27, 1934. See also "Should Women Do Outside Work?," *GGG*, April 1, 1926, pp. 6, 30-31 and April 15, 1926, pp. 6, 37.

44. "A Wife's Partnership in Success," *GGG*, Aug. 1930, p. 30.

45. "Making Ends Meet," *FPPF*, Jan. 28, 1920, p. 26. See also "Mountain" 's letter in *FPPF*, Oct. 22, 1919, p. 14.

46. See Susan Jackel, "Introduction" to Georgina Binnie-Clark, *Wheat & Woman* (Toronto: University of Toronto Press, 1979), pp. xx-xxxii.

47. "Police No Protection," *FPPF*, May 29, 1935.

48. "Wish She Could Call," *FPPF*, Jan. 28, 1925, p. 17; "Let Chores Stand, *FPPF*, Feb. 6, 1935, p. 5; "Baby Moratorium," *FPPF*, May 21. 1934, p. 5; "We Women Should Go on Strike," *FPPF*, Jan. 1, 1936, p. 4.

49. "Manless Farm," *FPPF*, May 17, 1933, p. 4.

50. SAB, VMP, Box 1, folder 5, McNaughton to John McNaughton, June 15, 1936; SAB, VMP, v. 37, folder 92(5) (the case is Mrs. Flett of the Women Grain Growers); comments of McNaughton on Nielsen in SAB, VMP, v. 22, folder 69, McNaughton to Charlotte Whitton, April 4, 1940.

51. See, for example, McClung, "Can A Woman Raise a Family and Have a Career?," *Macleans*, Feb. 15, 1928. Nor did McClung have household help for the first years of her marriage before she moved to Winnipeg.

52. See Genevieve Leslie, "Domestic Service in Canada, 1880-1920," in *Women at Work, Ontario 1850-1930*, comp. Janice Acton (Toronto: Canadian Women", Educational Press, 1974).

53. See Mrs. G. Cran, *A Woman in Canada* (London: W.J. Ham-Smith, 1911).

54. See SAB, VMP, E27, McNaughton to Mrs. Jean Robson, April 30, 1919, cited in Barber, "Help for Farm Homes," p. 20; Provincial Archives of B.C., McClung Papers, McClung, "The Domestic Help Problem," undated manuscript cited in Candace Savage, *Our Nell: A Scrapbook Biography of Nellie L. McClung* (Saskatoon: Western Producer Prairie Books, 1979), p. 170; SAB, VMP, Mary P. McCallum to McNaughton, April 10, 1918, cited in Barber, "Help for Farm Homes," p. 19.

55. See letters in "Should Men Help with Housework," *GGG*, July 1, 1927; Rose Paynter, "Man—the Home Maker," *WHM*, Feb. 1923, p. 43.

56. See Penney Kome, *Somebody has to do it. Whose Work is Housework?* (Toronto: McClelland and Stewart, 1982); 'Mater,' "Dolls for Small Boys," *FRR*, Oct. 20, 1919. See also "New Fashioned Chores," *GGG*, March 21, 1923, p. 24.

57. See, for example, SAB, VMP, v. 27, folder 26, Mrs. T.L. Guild, "What the Farm Woman Can Contribute to Home Economics."

58. *Ibid.*, p. 4.

59. *Ibid.*, pp. 6-7: SAB, VMP, v. 27, folder 26, McNaughton, "Economy of Labour in the Home," typescript, p. 5.

60. Irene Parlby, "Co-operation in the Rural Home," *Annual Report of the U.F.W.A.*, 1927, pp. 6-9. See also Parlby, "The Great Adventure," *GGG*, April 1, 1927, p. 5.

61. Barber, "Help for Farm Homes," p. 21. See also "Cooperative Laundries," *WHM*, May 1925, p. 55.

62. See, for example, "Old Dames Cheer," *FPPF*, Oct. 3, 1934, p. 5. See also "In a Modern Farm Kitchen," *FPPF*, July 6, 1932, p. 14.

63. "G.E. Electric Home Featured in 1936 Advertising Campaign," *Marketing*, Feb. 22, 1936, p. 1. See also the efforts of Saskatchewan's Dominion Electric Power Ltd., in SAB, Saskatchewan Power Corporation, File Po. 1 88, Walter H. Schlosser, General Manager, Dominion Electric Power Ltd., to Miss Dorothy Ross, July 10, 1936. She was demonstrating new appliances in Winnipegosis in order to create "a desire among the new customers . . . for electrical equipment . . . ." On rural marketing in particular see "Improved Living Conditions Create a New Field for Business," *General Merchant of Canada*, June 5, 1928, p. 4.

64. See SAB, Saskatchewan Grain Growers, B2, 11, 1. Minutes 1919-25, Minutes of WGG Meetings . . . Feb. 2, 1921, comments by Mrs. Haight. See also L. Fife, "Educational Copy Sells Electric Ranges," *Marketing*, June 30, 1923, pp. 428, 430, 432.

65. SAB, VMP, v. 27. folder 26, "Running Water on the Farm," c. 1928, typescript.

66. See, Barber, "Help for Farm Homes," espccially pp. 25-27; M. Speechly, "Reducing Kitchen Mileage," *GGG*, May 14, 1924, pp. 12-13; M.R. Whitmore, "A Kitchen Remodelled," *GGG*, Nov. 4, 1925, p. 18; and Speechly, "Being a 'Speed Artist,' " *GGG*, July 9, 1928, p. 15.

67. Mrs. Agnes E. Postans, "Home Economics," *Annual Report of the U.F.W.A.*, 1934, pp. 75-76.

68. "Keeping the Stork in his Place," *FPPF*, March 3, 1920, p. 11.

69. SAB, VMP, McNaughton to Mrs. L. Shoebridge, April 1931.

70. U.F.W.A. Executive and the Convenor of Health, "Report of Birth Control," *Annual Report of the U.F.W.A.*, 1933, p. 41.

71. See Susanne Zwarun, "Farm Wives 10 Years After Irene Murdoch," *Chatelaine*, March 1983, pp. 59, 176, 178-80, 182.

72. Mrs. F. Stewart to Miss Stocking, July 1, 1918, quoted in Rasmussen *et al.*, *A Harvest Yet to Reap*, p. 168.

73. Parlby, *Alberta Labor Annual*, Sept. 5, 1925, quoted in *ibid.*, p. 170; "Bill No. 54 of 1925," quoted in *ibid.*

74. Jackel, "Introduction," *Wheat & Woman*, p. xxi.

75. "United Farm Women of Manitoba," *FPPF*, Feb. 18, 1920, p. 11.

76. On the campaigns for mothers' allowances see Strong-Boag, " 'Wages for House-work': Mothers' Allowances and the Beginnings of Social Security in Canada." *Journal of Canadian Studies,* 14:1 (Spring 1979), 24-34.

77. See Gisele Ireland, *The Farmer Takes a Wife: A Study by Concerned Farm Women* (Concerned Farm Women, 1983).

78. SAB, VMP, v. 27, folder 26, McNaughton, "Economy of Labour in the Home," p. 2; McClung, Manuscript, personal papers quoted in Rasmussen *et al.*, *A Harvest Yet to Reap*, p. 150.

79. *The Western Producer*, Oct. 23, 1924, quoted in Rasmussen *et al.*, p. 150.

PATRICIA ROOME

---

21 Amelia Turner and Calgary Labour Women, 1919-1935

I think, on every occasion, that you appeared before the public, whether on the radio or on the platform, that you made friends. And not merely because of your fine presentation of socialist theories, but because of your dignity and modesty. One of the Stanley Jones teachers said of you, after the Sunday meeting, she looked so sweet and modest. We all owe you a great debt and we will surely try to repay it in loyalty and greater appreciation.[1]

When Edith Patterson wrote this note to Amelia Turner on the evening of her defeat in a Calgary provincial by-election (20 January 1933), she was articulating the widely held expectation that women politicians must be 'sweet and modest' both in their style and their politics. Consistent with the maternal feminism and ethical socialism that the Calgary Dominion Labor party (DLP) espoused, it was also a confining ideal under which many labour women chafed, but only a few, like Jean McWilliam of the Women's Labor League (WLL) and Communist Sophie McClusky, rejected. As a Calgary School Board trustee from 1926-36 and as a Cooperative Commonwealth Federation (CCF) candidate in the 1933 and 1934 by-elections, Amelia Turner fulfilled these expectations of feminine respectability; at the same time, her career symbolized the ambitious, committed, and important work of socialist women who built the Women's action of the Dominion Labor party.

Influenced by William Irvine and the experiences of the British Labour party, Turner believed that women's socialist and feminist agenda could best be achieved through political action and success at the polls; however, from 1919 to 1925, Calgary labour women sought greater involvement in the labour movement beyond their traditional participation in union auxiliaries; they created the Women's Labor League to achieve these goals.

Throughout this period a fruitful partnership flourished between women in the DLP and WLL; but, as this essay will demonstrate, the mid 1920s witnessed an erosion of this co-operation as the Alberta section of the Canadian Labor party moved to end alliances with communists and encouraged women to achieve their goals within the confines of the Women's Section of the Labor party. As a result, the later period from 1925 to 1935 became a more partisan era of consolidation for women.

A study of Amelia Turner's career and relationship with Calgary labour women challenges the assumption made by standard historical accounts of the period that the women's movement collapsed and post-war feminists retreated into their private lives after winning the vote.[2] That labour women rejected private domesticity for socialist politics is easily demonstrated: more difficult to answer are questions regarding their effectiveness within the labour political movement. Were they marginalised within this movement; or, despite tacit acceptance of the image of sweet, modest, and dignified woman, were women able to effect change consistent with their vision of socialist feminism?

I

Amelia Turner's passion for social justice was rooted in her family milieu and their experiences.[3] Born on 11 February 1891, she was the eldest of ten children born to Letitia Keefer Turner, a physician's daughter and United Empire Loyalist descendant, and Henry James Turner, the only child of a British tailor and his wife who immigrated to Canada in the 1860s.[4] Grandfather Thomas Turner and Amelia's father owned a store in Tottenham, Ontario, where Amelia spent a comfortable childhood. In 1898 the Turner families travelled west to the booming mining town of Fernie, British Columbia, where Henry Turner bought and managed a hotel, the Victoria. In Fernie, Amelia attended school, studied music, and enjoyed the excitement of a frontier town until her father became disenchanted with the saloon business, sold his hotel, and moved the family onto a southern Alberta homestead.[5]

During these financially troubled farming years, Amelia continued her education, tutored by her grandfather and father ('an intellectual snob'). Although isolated, their pioneer homestead provided Amelia with a stimulating environment through its extensive library, many newspapers, and visitors.[6] Eventually the Turner home became the centre for education in the Ewelme community, with Amelia acting as the teacher. Between teaching and domestic duties, Amelia wrote, published a bulletin for her family, and took correspondence courses in shorthand, bookkeeping, and typing, which qualified her for a job in Fort Macleod with the *Macleod Advertiser* in 1911.[7]

Her working experiences over the next five years in a variety of newspaper offices paralleled those of many Canadian girls, but Amelia was not typical.

Even before she moved to Fort Macleod she proudly called herself an agnostic, suffragist, and socialist. After reading Robert Blatchford's *Merrie England* at the age of twelve, Amelia became a devoted socialist, as did her brother Hereward. Initially, the immediate homesteading experiences of economic discrimination were the focus of numerous family discussions.[8] But socialism also exerted a lifetime influence on Letitia Turner and the eldest Turner children, especially Amelia, who emerged as the leader determined to become a journalist, a newspaper publisher, and an activist.[9]

Amelia moved to Calgary in 1913 and worked at a series of 'dull office jobs' while she assisted her sister Donata through high school and normal school. She spent her leisure time in the stimulating company of members of Calgary's 'labor group,' which coalesced around William Irvine, pastor of the Unitarian church in 1916.[10] Involved in this closely knit labour group were most of the future leaders of the Dominion Labor party and Women's Labor League, whose political lessons were learned through participation in the People's Forum, the Unity Club, the Non-Partisan league, and the Labor Representation League (LRL). In the June 1917 election, the LRL entered provincial politics and candidates William Irvine and Alex Ross contested two seats.[11] Amelia was invited by Edith Patterson to hear Irvine speak at Unity Hall in 1916 and identified immediately with his Fabian socialism.[12] Within months, Amelia and her sister were boarding with the Irvine family, marking the beginning of a lifelong and intimate friendship.[13]

The Irvine family provided congenial companionship for Amelia, and, perhaps more important, William Irvine encouraged her intellectual development and supervised her political apprenticeship. Throughout the years 1916-20, Amelia attended the Unitarian church and the People's Forum, joined the LRL, and campaigned for Irvine. Employed as his secretary at the Non-Partisan League's office, she later moved with Irvine to the *Western Independent* newspaper.[14] Amelia's apprenticeship deepened her knowledge and commitment to the farmers' movement, building on strong sympathies developed on her father's homestead before the war. When the United Farmers of Alberta (UFA) decided to enter politics and the Non-Partisan League was dissolved, Turner naturally progressed to the UFA office in 1910 and joined the staff of the UFA magazine in 1922.[15]

Amelia was deeply convinced by Irvine's argument articulated in *Farmers in Politics* (1920) that organized workers and farmers must enter politics and co-operate to revise the democratic structures of government in order to facilitate the creation of a new egalitarian social order with radically altered economic and social structures. Co-operation and evolution were key elements in the Fabian-like philosophy espoused by Irvine and explained to Calgary audiences like the members of the new Labor church, who heard Irvine label the One Big Union tactics as anti-democratic, destructive, and counterproductive. For him, the new social order would 'be an equilibrium of all conflicting forces . . . a society in which every class will have expression and be allowed to function.'[16] To realize this co-operative commonwealth, Irvine and Alberta UFA MPs entered into an uneasy alliance with provincial UFA leaders like Henry Wise Wood. Although Amelia's association with the UFA was closer than Irvine's, she also built strong friendships in the Calgary labour community, the 'Ginger Group' of the federal Progressives, and the CCF. Though attempts at group government in the 1920s ultimately failed, both Irvine and Turner remained firm in their commitment to a co-operative commonwealth.[17]

Amelia was drawn initially to socialism by the ideas of Robert Blatchford and Keir Hardie, but the ideas and style of middle-class intellectuals like Sydney and Beatrice Webb and George Bernard Shaw deeply influenced her. Later in life she wrote: 'I was, I think a congenital Fabian.'[18] Turner's optimism sprung from her belief in the inevitability of socialism, the necessity of moral reform, education for citizenship, and the civilizing role of the middle class. Far more than Irvine, who was a popular agitator, Turner was the genteel idealist armed with a cheerful practicality reminiscent of Beatrice Webb though, in contrast to Webb, both Irvine and Turner were concerned with feminist issues.[19]

Bourgeois respectability with its ideal of gracious womanhood was Amelia's family legacy, as much as was socialism. Although few of the labour women leaders she met in Calgary during the First World War became socialists as early in life as did Amelia, they came from similarly cultured and politically literate middle-class families that encouraged women's involvement in social reform and politics. Sisters Marion Carson and Rachael Coutts, who were Amelia's elders, were from a comfortable Ontario family; influenced by the social-gospel movement, they were led to socialism by their pacifism and experiences in the Alberta Temperance and Moral Reform League. For these two women, political literacy had developed gradually, influenced by the experience of Marion Carson's husband, who was a Calgary alderman in 1905.[20] Edith Patterson's Nova Scotia father, a long-time school trustee and Conservative MP, gave her a model of community service, but her commitment to social justice came through her own experience of poverty when teaching miners' children in Glace Bay, Nova Scotia. Conversion to socialism and political action initially precipitated a personal crisis for Patterson, who had to make a decisive choice 'for or against a new political party, in harmony with the social gospel' as preached by Irvine.[21]

II

What role did the young and ambitious Amelia Turner play in the Calgary labour community between 1919 and 1925? Involved in the birth of the Dominion Labor party and influenced profoundly by William Irvine, Amelia believed partisan political action was integral to achieving socialism. Nor did her experiences during these formative years alter her stand, even though most of her more experienced female colleagues believed in co-operation among women and held joint memberships in the non-partisan Women's Labor League and the DLP. This section focuses on the organizational work of senior activists who were Turner's mentors. Through the independent WLL and the Dominion Labor party, these Calgary women laid the foundation for women's political action and determined its direction in the later decade, when Amelia easily dominated electoral politics. This section also examines the relationship between these two organizations. Was the WLL, with its political independence, more outspoken on gender and class questions and able to steer a more radical course than the DLP?

The genesis and early years of the Calgary Labor party are a story of coalition politics, left-wing factionalism, and idiosyncrasies. In Calgary, LRL activists formed the nucleus of a labor-party local in April 1919 and called it the Dominion Labor party (DLP). Although the DLP local eventually affiliated with the Alberta section of the Canadian Labor party (CLP) and joined the Calgary Central Council of the CLP, labourites refused to change their name partially because they disliked the influence communists held in the CLP. Until the expulsion of the communists in 1928, Calgary members insisted they were 'The Dominion Labor party.' After 1928, usage of the name Canadian Labor party gradually gained acceptance. Trivial as it may appear, the Calgary conflict over labels was symbolic of deeper tensions within the labour political movement.

In 1917 the Alberta Federation of Labor Convention endorsed the principle of establishing a labour party, and the trade unions played a major role at the founding convention, in January 1919, of the Alberta branch of the CLP. Alvin Finkel argues union support was crucial to the CLP success and signified a departure from 'pure labourism to ethical socialism as the official ideology of the labour movement.' In contrast to working-class Marxists with whom they formed an 'unholy' alliance through the central councils of the CLP, ethical socialists accepted change at ballot boxes. 'Rather than speaking of the inevitable hostility between an exploiting class and an exploited class, they stressed moral superiority of socialism with its emphasis on production for use over capitalism with its emphasis on production for profit.' Although the Alberta party formally adopted the British Labour party's post-war program, implementation proved impossible: the CLP gradually sacrificed these socialist principles to accommodate the more conservative and strictly labourite demands of its craft-union membership.[22]

Women played an important role in this debate and also within the structures of the Calgary DLP, where they formed over 50 per cent of the membership, joined the executive, contested elections, and worked as politicians on both city council and the school-board. Throughout the 1920s, the Dominion Labor party maintained a core of fifty to seventy-five active women who were primarily of two types: single working women, usually teachers or journalists, and married women, often union auxiliary members (such as Mary Corse). Not all these labour women maintained as high a profile as did Marion Carson; instead, many, like Adelia Irvine herself, supported socialism but centered their lives on their families and thus were 'not the type' for leadership. Women labour leaders were usually ambitious, experienced, and older, with both freedom and finances to pursue a political career.[23]

As a young woman of 28 years, few of these characteristics described Amelia's situation. Despite a strong commitment to ethical socialism, gender, inexperience and youth prevented Amelia from rapidly assuming a leadership role. 'It was an ordeal,' she remembered, 'for me to say "present" at a study group.' Ironically many progressive and socialist women found that, despite their shared goals, socialist politics remained a male world. Amelia's political education in the DLP took place among senior female activists, who encouraged Canadian and British labour women to visit Calgary and share their experiences. Important as these links were, Amelia firmly believed that separate women's organizations were essential also for training women who lacked a tradition of political participation. Equally confining for Amelia were family and career pressures, for in the small office of *The UFA* magazine, she worked long hours learning a variety of jobs. When her father died in 1921, Amelia's mother, with her younger sons, moved to Calgary, re-established the family home, and relied upon Amelia's salary for support.[24]

Although Amelia concentrated on the Dominion Labor party and municipal election campaigns, her female colleagues created organizations like the Women's Labor League, which was born in April and May 1919, the child of experienced activists Mary Corse and Jean McWilliam. As Linda Kealey has demonstrated, the First World War's differential impact on Canadian women radicalized progressive women, who formed organizations devoted to advancing the cause of social justice for working-class women. In Calgary, for example, the Next of Kin organization founded by outspoken Scots immigrant Jean McWilliam advocated increased mothers' pensions and pensions for soldiers' dependants.[25] Inflation, wartime profiteering, and conscription of labour further radicalized these women, whose reform agenda was echoed in other organizations like the Local Council of Women.[26] When Calgary experienced a wave of strikes between 1918 and 1919, labour women found themselves directly involved, supporting women restaurant and hotel workers on the picket line, assisting striking husbands, joining union auxiliaries, and sitting as delegates on the Trades and Labor Council.[27]

Mary Corse's advocacy of both industrial unionism and political action made her one of Calgary's more radical socialist women. By 1919 she was the labour trustee on the Calgary School Board, a voting delegate for the Typographical Women's Auxiliary on the Calgary Trades and Labor Council (TLC), and their delegate to the Western Canadian Labor Conference held in Calgary 13-15 March 1919. Here she met and heard Winnipeg Labor League women Helen Logan and Helen Armstrong assert to the male, delegates that neglect of their wives' political education and working women's issues had weakened the labour movement. Following the conference, Mary Corse joined the Alberta executive committee of the One Big Union. As the Calgary General Strike developed, she encouraged McWilliam, who was her frequent partner on TLC committees, to help develop a WLL, similar to the Manitoba model. While the league's primary aim was to support the families of striking workers, they also endorsed collective-bargaining strategies and strike action for all workers, especially working women.[28]

Born in crisis and independent of political affiliation, the Calgary WLL differed substantially from the WLLs that the British Labour party created from 1906 to 1918 to encourage women's participation in the Labour party.[29] Most labour women who joined the Calgary League had worked in the movement since 1916, attended Irvine's Unitarian and Labor churches, and developed high hopes for the creation of a new, but vaguely defined, social order. This social-gospel tradition carried over into the WLL, whose motto was 'Deut. 3:16. Be strong and of good courage, fear not nor be afraid of them, for the Lord thy God He will go with thee. He will not fail thee nor forsake thee.'[30] Although not always consonant with the image of sweet and modest womanhood, this motto still promoted a religious perception of socialism.[31] When Mary Corse was president of the WLL and active in the Dominion Labor party, the WLL executive included DLP women. Although some league women remained aloof from affiliation and some DLP members did not join the WLL, throughout this period the two organizations complemented each other and allowed labour women to be articulate on gender and class issues.[32] In contrast to the league's independence and commitment to support industrial action, the DLP worked on annual civic elections, groomed women politicians like Amelia Turner, and supported a platform in which women's issues were secondary.[33]

Conscious of working-class women's grievances, Corse and McWilliam gave testimony at the Calgary hearings, 3-5 May 1919, before Justice T.G. Mathers's Royal Commission on Industrial Relations. As the women's representative from the TLC, in her speech Corse outlined problems of high rent, low pay, and poor working conditions. Her case rested on evidence she had gathered during the April 1918 strike of waitresses and hotel employees. Bourgeois indifference and class inequalities, she said, were a source of unrest that encouraged women 'to join the socialist parties.'[34] While assuring the commission that she was a reformist, Corse emphasized Calgary women's growing radicalism and resentment at not 'getting a square deal' and at being 'kept in the background,' even though 'women have been the backbone of the labour movement.'[35] She explained that her viewpoint had 'utterly changed' since 1917, when her union-organizing activities exposed her to prostitution, poverty, and exploitation of working girls.[36]

A 'living wage,' not merely a minimum wage paid to young girls, was her solution to female labour unrest.

Jean McWilliam's fiery testimony presented additional information that she had gathered while organizing laundry workers and investigating conditions of hotel and restaurant employees.[37] Unionization of women and a fair minimum wage were McWilliam's solution to the crisis. Exploitation by capitalists and government, along with the callousness and bourgeois apathy of the Local Council of Women, represented for her examples of liberalism's failure. She broadened her analysis of women's problems to include hardships experienced by soldiers' wives and widows, advocating generous widow's and mother's pensions as a partial solution in the redistribution of income.

Neither McWilliam nor Corse presented a critique of the family and the problems of working-class wives; instead, they opposed the right of married women with employed husbands to work. Corse felt obliged to use maternal feminist arguments to justify her volunteer political work, explaining that 'it is the duty of every mother who has girls to find just how employers . . . are keeping house for our children.'[38] For her, political work was a logical expression of womanhood, 'militant mothering' as Joan Sangster defines it.[39] Guided by Corse and McWilliam, the Women's Labor League infused maternal feminism with a strong class consciousness. Within the first year they organized the Calgary Defence Committee with McWilliam as president, raised $1200 for strikers, sent protests to Ottawa regarding deportation of strikers through amendments to the Immigration Act, and organized a petition demanding that the federal government reinstate the postal workers. Convinced that women's organization and education assisted the struggle, McWilliam travelled widely in southern Alberta encouraging women to form leagues.[40]

Throughout the immediate post-war period, the WLL defended the general strike weapon and OBU supporter Alderman Broatch.[41] Later, McWilliam encountered stiff opposition to the WLL's position when she requested that the May 1920 United Mineworkers of America Convention pledge support for the jailed Winnipeg strikers. When a struggle ensued, *The Searchlight* claimed that McWilliam discovered 'her mistake in thinking she had got into a bunch of labor men' and as she departed accused them of being 'just like a bunch of old women.'[42] While such naivety and pugnaciousness won McWilliam paternalist amusement and notoriety, the incident also illustrates her disregard for the complexities of union politics when issues of social justice were involved. Likewise, despite Mary Corse's position on the OBU, she maintained an amiable relationship with the Calgary Labor Council, which tolerated her politics because, like McWilliam, she lacked membership in a powerful union, and therefore could exercise marginal influence.[43]

By 1922, the WLL had politicized many women voters and awakened some to 'a realization that organization is necessary to remove the economic shackles now bearing so heavily upon them.'[44] But in the adverse labour climate of 1921-4, the WLL relied more heavily on protection of working women through adequate minimum-wage legislation than on union organizing. In 1919 it proposed an amendment to the Alberta Factory Act creating a Minimum Wage Board with a woman representative from the 'labouring classes'—subsequently Edmontonian Harriet J. Ingam, president of the Garment Workers' Union. The league successfully pressured the Calgary Labour MLA and Minister of Labour Alex Ross to create a Women's Bureau and campaigned for a board of women to assist Margaret Lewis, the factory inspector, in enforcing the Factory Act. Despite some successes, the league's strategy was a failure, as demonstrated by the experience of three league women who represented domestic workers of the Housekeeper's Association in 1920 before the Minimum Wage Commission hearings. Regardless of their protest, domestic workers were not granted an eight-hour day and wages of $25 monthly, nor were they likely to be covered by future legislation. Although in 1922 some women won a new minimum wage of $14 and a maximum work week of 48 hours, the UFA government even delayed its implementation of these changes for several years.[45]

Focusing on the needs of working-class families, the WLL created task forces and accumulated data to demonstrate that ill health, prostitution, and malnutrition were rooted in economic inequality. Reflecting Marion Carson's involvement in the campaign for free hospital treatment for tuberculosis patients, the league championed this cause as part of state-funded medical services.[46] Eager to challenge the establishment, Jean McWilliam 'crossed swords' with a Presbyterian minister, the Reverend McRae, over malnutrition among children. Publicly she ridiculed both his characterization of working class fathers as 'scalliwags' and his belief that charity was a substitute for economic justice. The WLL assigned delegates to attend meetings of the hospital board, city council, and school-board as watchdogs on labour women's behalf.[47]

Between the Women's Labor League's goal of 'principles before party — measures before men' and the Dominion Labor party's need for party discipline, a chasm existed that women bridged by fragile alliances. McWilliam opposed women joining political parties; rather, she believed the best strategy was lobbying, support of collective bargaining, and union organizing. In sharp disagreement with McWilliam's philosophy, Mary Corse (like Amelia Turner) argued that elected representatives meant power for the labour movement.[48] Although DLP women played an active role in the party, they were rarely as free as the WLL women to concentrate on gender issues; party commitments meant they served on the DLP executive, organized the women's vote — especially in 1921-4 elections — supported women candidates, and encouraged ladies' auxiliaries to support the DLP. When the Calgary TLC finally voted to affiliate with the Canadian Labor party and to create a central council in 1924, DLP women created a Women's Section that joined CLP. If Mary Corse had remained in Calgary, the WLL might have dissolved and encouraged its members to work through the Women's Section, but McWilliam's leadership meant labour women were forced to choose. Most opted for membership in the DLP Women's Section, where many were already active on the DLP, filling every position but president.[49]

Although the need to achieve workplace equality was high on labour women's agenda, there was disagreement within the labour movement on this issue. Some male DLP colleagues, like school trustee Harry Pryde, did not endorse the Calgary TLC's 1921 decision to oppose the employment of married women with working husbands and argued that 'self-determination for women is the slogan being used in the women's forward movement and they take the stand that a woman has as much right to hold down a job as a man.'[50] Ironically, the WLL in 1923 petitioned the Calgary School Board to reduce married women on staff, supporting instead the concept of a family wage and married women's duty to raise a family.[51] Throughout this period, a married woman's right to work was a contentious issue for labour women, who usually avoided public debate. Generally, the league advocated measures like the 1919 Mother's Allowance Act as a solution to female poverty, subsequently sponsoring several amendments requesting inclusion of women whose husbands were invalids, in mental asylums, or had deserted the family. In 1922 a WLL delegation appeared before Premier Brownlee to address these changes.[52] Whereas most of the younger generation tacitly shared Amelia Turner's view that married women's rights included the opportunity to employment, equal pay, and access to birth control, elder leaders like Marion Carson strongly opposed married women working and refused to place birth control on the agenda of the DLP Women's Section meetings.[53]

In contrast to the WLL, the Dominion Labor party worked closely with teachers supporting the new Alberta Teacher Alliance's (ATA) attempt to achieve collective bargaining and representation on the school-board. In 1920, the DLP adopted a labour educational policy, which supported ATA wage demands, recognized experience, required representation from the ATA in dismissal cases, ensured more independence for principals, extended part-time classes, set a pupil maximum of thirty-five, supported the principle of free school supplies, and argued for the extension of school clinics. Later, the DLP supported the Public School Ladies Association and endorsed the feminist principles of equal pay and advancement to principal's position. Radicalized by the organizing work of the ATA and the 1921 strike, many women teachers joined the DLP.[54] As a young activist, Amelia Turner identified primarily with this group, which included her sister Dorothy. Initially she received emotional support and intellectual stimulation from female teachers, and later, as a trustee, she championed their cause for a decade. Thus, while the WLL could afford to ignore the issue of equality for teachers, the Dominion Labor party could not and on this issue demonstrated greater consciousness of discrimination.

A characteristic of both DLP women and the WLL was their contribution to labour's cultural cohesiveness through fund-raising tag days, whist drives, and family events like Christmas concerts and May Day picnics. The WLL and DLP women (and often it was the same women serving in different capacities) sponsored speakers whom they entertained royally. Through the 'Women's Page' of the *Alberta Labor News* (ALN), labour women in Alberta maintained a lively forum for discussion of local and international events. Considerable solidarity with women involved in the United Farm Women of Alberta (UFWA) and networking developed, mirroring the alliance of the Dominion Labor party with UFA government.[55]

In her study of Canadian women's political involvement, Bashevkin argues that 'early women's groups were attracted toward a position of political independence, which would guarantee both organizational autonomy and purity: on the other hand, they were drawn toward conventional partisanship, which might better ensure their political influence and legislative success.' The British Columbia example of combining partisan alliances, 'including the election and cabinet appointment of an active feminist woman, with politically independent and effective women's organizations,' she argues, 'became the exception rather than the rule for many years following 1918.[56] However, the experience of Calgary labour women in the WLL and DLP until 1924 provides another example of successful co-operation. These women shared a similar commitment to elements of maternal feminism, regarded the vote as a democratic right, and wanted to increase labour's political power. While neither group viewed women as its exclusive constituency, both were articulate about gender and class issues — though each group was sometimes cautious, even contradictory in its perspective. The WLL championed the working girl but rejected the right of married women to work, while Dominion Labor party women, despite their labour loyalties, focused on professional women's issues like equal pay and promotions.

Two significant case studies from the early 1920s demonstrate the fragile nature and limitations of co-operation. The first revolves around the WLL and DLP women's role in the unemployment struggles of the early 1920s; the second concerns the controversy over rehiring part-time teacher Sophie McClusky, a well-known communist, active in organizing the unemployed. These two struggles are important because they marked a turning point for Amelia Turner and Calgary labour women. After 1924, labour women increasingly chose partisanship over independence as the latter became synonymous with a communist alliance. By the mid 1920s, the communist presence on the Calgary Central Council of the CLP had become barely tolerable to the moderate elements of Calgary's labour community.

The link between the Women's Labor League, the DLP, and the Committee for the Unemployed occurred at two levels. Many of the committee's organizers lived at Jean McWilliam's boarding-house, where radicals were welcome and able to enlist her support. Through the Central Council of the Unemployed (CCU), which was communist-dominated, other labour women became directly involved. Over the tough winter of 1921-2, the CCU lobbied the Calgary City Council to centralize the administration of relief by placing it under the management of a city council committee composed of aldermen and representatives of labour and of the unemployed. After the December elections, the presence on the Calgary City Council of five DLP aldermen provided the Council of the Unemployed with allies. Militancy grew among the unemployed, who were housed over the winter at Calgary Fair Grounds, and culminated in a march to occupy city hall on 7 April 1922.[57]

Since November 1921, the WLL had pressured city council to accept greater responsibility for unemployment. During the demonstration, the WLL's involvement increased beyond fund-raising drives, when the president Alice Corless interceded with the mayor following the police dispersal of the marchers. An earlier emergency meeting at the Labour Temple revealed many labour women assembled to prepare resolutions for city council, but with a Dominion Conference on Unemployment planned for 3-4 August 1922, the city administration remained intransigent and, even in August, the municipalities failed to persuade the federal government to finance relief.[58] The WLL and another organization called Women of Unemployed Committee, which McWilliam founded, contributed two unsuccessful resolutions to the conference demanding the dismissal of the city relief officer for 'offensive treatment' to wives of the unemployed and reallocation of monies from the Canadian Patriotic Fund to families of disabled soldiers.[59]

During the spring of 1922, solidarity on the unemployment problem crumbled when conservative trade unionists withdrew their delegate from the CCU and told the unemployed to affiliate with craft unions. While the presence of One Big Union and Workers' party organizers alienated conservative trade unionists, the WLL continued to 'vigorously protest the present administration of relief,' requesting the firing of board of welfare officer McKillop.[60] Although Dominion Labor party women held five executive positions in the WLL, they maintained support for the CCU and championed other politically explosive causes, despite pressure from craft unionists. Through McWilliam's influence and connections with Drumheller miners, who often came to Calgary to work during the turbulent years before 1925, the WLL had successfully petitioned for a retrial for miner Gallagher who was first found guilty of murdering a mine manager but acquitted in 1922.[61]

One of the CCU organizers objected to by the conservative trade unionists of the TLC was Sophie McClusky, who applied to the Calgary School Board to teach English to immigrants in 1921, but was refused employment because of her political activities. McClusky vigorously protested her treatment in the press, arguing that her socialist ideas were not relevant to her teaching credentials. According to McClusky, Marion Carson, the only trustee who accepted her invitation to observe her teaching, 'did not hear me teach Bolshevism or socialism. I taught English to a class of anxious Ukrainians who were bright and willing to learn but unable to pay rent and a teacher's salary.'[62] Superintendent Melville Scott of the Calgary School Board wrote that opposition to her politics was 'shared by all members of the Board but one and is especially strong, apparently among the Labour members on the Board.' Was Marion Carson the one sympathetic supporter of McClusky? Although it is difficult to answer this question with certainty, Carson was the only trustee involved in the Council of the Unemployed. Regardless of McClusky's protest and reapplication in later years, the blacklisting was effective.[63]

Despite common interest in the unemployed, McClusky never identified with women's issues or joined the Calgary WLL. Instead, McClusky organized unemployed single men, headed a delegation to the mayor and commissioner in 1925, and requested work at union wages and accommodation instead of charity. For spreading communist ideas among the unemployed, she earned the wrath of police magistrate Colonel Sanders, before whom she appeared over a dispute with her husband. Accusing her of leading single men astray, Sanders recommended McClusky be taken down to the river and given 'a good ducking.' Colonel Sanders's treatment drew a formal protest from the Calgary Trades and Labor Council to the Attorney General's department in 1925, but a surprising silence from labour women who obviously knew her well. This lack of response foreshadowed future problems in the late 1920s.[64]

By 1925 the heyday of co-operation among labour women had ended. Following Margaret Bondfield's visit in 1924, the DLP women created a 'ladies section,' withdrawing support from the WLL, which affiliated with the eastern-based Federation of Women's Labor Leagues. Remaining in the WLL were women whose husbands opposed the Dominion Labor party or those whose views, like McWilliam's, favoured nonpartisanship.[65] In later years Amelia Turner expressed her contempt for Jean McWilliam and the league, with its 'Communist connections.' Increasingly, DLP women bowed to party discipline, though many abandoned their other alliances with reluctance. In an address to the 'wives of labour men' at Marion Carson's home on Elbow Drive, British Labour party representative Ethel Snowden counselled: 'The best type of Labor woman . . . was the one who was able to keep her ideals and yet to find in others of different views, some point of contact and always to be kind.'[66] Although it described Amelia Turner and Dominion Labor party women and was compatible with their ethical socialism, this conservative version of womanhood certainly excluded women like McWilliam and McClusky, who found that bourgeois respectability contradicted and compromised socialist goals.

III

Political maturity for Amelia Turner and Calgary labour women characterized the 1925-35 era as the DLP Women's Section developed a common analysis of women's role in politics and a strategy to accomplish socialist goals. Through study groups, networking within other labour parties, participation in the peace movement, and political action, these women sought to develop the co-operative commonwealth. Within the world of politics, however, they found 'male elite power' to be 'well and truly guarded.' Although many labour women challenged these barriers, as Veronica Strong-Boag explains, often they 'were effectively marginalized' and experienced 'great difficulty in translating their individual successes into a transformation of the political agenda of the public realm to reflect more fairly women's needs and experience.'[67] Amelia Turner and Edith Patterson were exceptional women; significantly, their success came because they had developed a partnership with a committed women's network, which was a product of women's separate culture.

Amelia Turner and other DLP women shared a vision of women's role in the socialist movement and accepted Agnes Macphail's challenge that 'a woman's place is any place she wants it to be,' but few Calgary labour women questioned the supremacy of motherhood. Instead, they expected women to make marriage and children their primary commitment. According to this view, the barriers to women's participation in labour politics were simply a lack of education and the absence of leisure time. Labour women accepted that political activism would be primarily the responsibility of single, career, and elder married women, who would be backed up by the women whose domestic work limited their involvement.[68] Although Amelia Turner managed to combine marriage and a career, even her case demonstrates this accepted division of labour: she married W. Norman Smith at the age of 45, when her political and advertising careers were secure; motherhood was not an option. Accepting these familial limitations on women's activism as 'natural,' labour women often confused their party's success at the polls and the achievement of social reforms with gender equality and access to power within their own movement.[69]

After the DLP women withdrew from the Women's Labor League, the league continued to have a strong focus on the problems of the working girl and solidarity with labour struggles, but by 1926 its activism seemed spent and its membership was confined to a few faithful crusaders.[70] By contrast, the DLP Women's Section became a vigorous group with an expanding membership. Its unchallenged president, Marion Carson, shepherded the group over the next decade of educational inquiry, networking, lobbying, and political victory. Established in 1926, the Women's Section's study group was often led by one of the studious Turner family and included articulate teachers like Rachael Coutts and Annie Campbell, who gave formal papers like 'The Birth of the Labour Movement' and 'The Causes of War.'[71]

As DLP's participation in the peace movement reveals, the purpose of education was to inform activism. After Laura E. Jamieson addressed their group in October 1927, DLP women affiliated with the Canadian branch of the Women's International League for Peace and Freedom. Over the next decade their participation was based on the assumption that although 'peace would not come under the present economic system,' nevertheless peace campaigns were essential to political change.[72] 'The maintenance of world peace is eminently women's work,' Carson argued, and 'the maternal instinct, which is strongest in women who are not mothers, finds outlet in extending protection . . . and preventing suffering.'[73] This concept of womanhood was a great unifying force and the 'intellectually rigorous, rational discourse' of women peace activists influenced members of the inter-war generation and 'conditioned the way they approached their careers.'[74] As illustrated by Amelia Turner's political work and Rachael Coutts's teaching career, which focused on promoting internationalism and pacifism, DLP women promoted a peace agenda that unified much of their thought and work.

To achieve these goals and break their isolation from male structures, the DLP Women's Section became adept at networking, linking up with both a national and international support groups such as the Women's International League for Peace and Freedom. Although birth control advocates like Emma Goldman and Margaret Sanger also spoke in Calgary, it was the tours of the more 'respectable' British Labour party women that most influenced labour women. They were avid readers of the British *Labour Woman*, later the model for Patterson's column named 'The Alberta Labor Woman.' On the national level, Calgary DLP women affiliated in 1927 with the Western Labor Women's Social and Economic Conference (LWSE Conference) when it held the fourth annual conference in Calgary.[75] While the Calgary WLL organized the meetings, Dominion Labor party women actively participated also in debating resolutions.[76] On the provincial level, when the Alberta CLP met in Calgary in 1928, Calgary DLP women organized a luncheon for women delegates featuring J.S. Woodsworth as speaker.[77] Invited to attend were executive members of the United Farm Women of Alberta, a connection the Calgary women carefully nurtured by inviting Cabinet Minister Irene Parlby to address their members on a regular basis. When the UFA government created a Woman's Bureau under the Department of Agriculture, president Carson attended the convention as a delegate.[78]

Because winning yearly elections was a formidable challenge for the DLP, the Women's Section provided its share of organizers and candidates. Prior to 1925, Mary Corse and Marion Carson had represented DLP women on the Calgary School Board. When Carson resigned, she recruited Turner, who had expressed confidence in handling the difficult board chairman. Although she was unsuccessful in the December 1925 municipal election, when the new school-board met in January 1926 and voted to discontinue supplying free textbooks, Turner received another chance. The Dominion Labor party organized a mass meeting to protest the move and passed a resolution requesting the school-board at its January meeting to call for a plebiscite within twenty days or face recall proceedings against the mover and seconder of the motion. When the board refused to hold a plebiscite on the issue, the DLP swung into action. On 31 March 1926 a recall election resulted in the defeat of both men by DLP candidates Amelia Turner and W.E. Turner.[79]

This famous recall election established Amelia's reputation for independence and provided the opportunity for her to advance the Dominion Labor party's education agenda, which involved providing free milk, dental and medical services, classes for the handicapped, greater access to technical education, and the abolition of cadet training from schools. From 1918 until 1936, at least one woman labour trustee sat on the Calgary School Board and supported collective-bargaining rights for the ATA and equality for female teachers. Both these issues earned strong support and recruits for the DLP.[80] Over the next decade, Amelia Turner and other labour trustees, who hammered away at Citizens Government Association trustees' opposition to their agenda, often controlled the vote and succeeded in implementing much of their program. A popular and respected politician, Turner was also an able administrator and financial manager: she demonstrated strength and independence when serving as board vice chairman with F.S. Spooner, who openly opposed her politics and disliked her partnership with the DLP Women's Section and the Ladies Public School Local of the ATA. Despite such opposition from within the board, Turner chaired the school-board for two terms and the school management and health committees many times.[81]

Dominion Labor party women scored another success in the election to the Calgary City Council of alderman Edith Patterson, Amelia Turner's closest friend. Although a colleague predicted Patterson would 'take great interest in those things which come closer to the scope of the female part of the community . . . hospitals, clinics, unemployment and all social legislation,' Patterson also showed an interest in issues of public ownership and taxation. During her aldermanic term, 1927-32, and in her newspaper column 'The Alberta Labor Woman,' Patterson championed feminist networking; but, she also challenged women to oppose both privatization of garbage collection in Calgary and taxation on publicly owned utilities. Although anxious for increased female participation on city council, she wrote: 'Though we greatly desire representation of women on the governing bodies, more fervently do we desire greater representation of labor.'[82] Though sensitive to gender inequality, Patterson none the less approached divisive gender issues (including birth control) by cautiously urging working-class unity above all else.

As models of bourgeois respectability, Amelia Turner and Edith Patterson knew the rules, kept their frustrations private, and never challenged the CLP or the newly formed CCF on feminist issues. Reporting on the women's luncheon at the 1933 Regina Conference, Turner conceded there was 'a suggestion of "feminism" here and there, since many of the women had been "keen feminists"'; however, she concluded, 'talk of fair play for women was quite unnecessary . . . all are working together for great ideals.'[83] Although Amelia wanted to downplay conflict, not all CCF women were prepared to overlook gender inequality in politics.[84] In Calgary conflict was muted: women who served on the DLP executive during the 1920s assumed a supporting role, reproducing the societal sexual division of labour in politics. As activists and candidates, women represented women's concerns and won their votes, but few Dominion Labor party members expected women to direct the future of the movement. Neither Amelia Turner nor Edith Patterson was consulted on questions of policy or strategy in these years.

What, then, did Amelia Turner's candidacy in the provincial by-election campaigns of January 1933 and January 1934 mean? Following the 1932 Western Conference of Labour Political Parties, the CLP selected Amelia to run as a joint CLP/CCF candidate. Not only popular and able, she was also trusted by the new CCF party establishment, who knew of her longstanding connections to radical Progressives through Irvine and W. Norman Smith, *The UFA* magazine's editor. Amelia's ideological identification with this group rather than with the conservative and discredited UFA government of Premier Brownlee meant she would challenge the Alberta UFA and support attempts to force its program leftward.[85]

Between 1933 and 1935, Turner contested two provincial by-elections and Patterson a federal election. These elections are significant because Turner was the first CCF candidate in Canada and polled the largest percentage of votes ever received by a Calgary labour candidate. Furthermore, both by-elections featured a high turn-out of women voters, demonstrating the activist and party-building role that Calgary women had played over the last decade. Finally, the elections revealed serious problems within the alliance of labourites and the UFA, as well as labour's vulnerability to the Social Credit movement. When Edith Patterson contested the 1935 election, a new era had arrived: it was characterized by the disorganization and demoralization of the former Dominion Labor party and its new CCF ally. In 1935, Amelia refused to 'carry the banner in some hopeless ridings,' sensing the exploitation of women candidates as 'sacrificial lambs.'

In the January 1933 election, Amelia Turner polled 12,301 votes to her opponent Norman Hindsley's 14,128. She was billed as the people's favourite, and an impressive team waged a tough fight on her behalf. But Turner battled with party fragmentation, and her defeat foreshadowed the future problems of the Alberta CLP and the CCF. When long-time Calgary labour alderman and MLA R.H. Parkyn entered the race as an Independent Labour candidate, the Calgary CLP group refused to endorse him and instead nominated Turner; however, Parkyn's candidacy spoiled labour's chance of a victory and communist John O'Sullivan's candidacy completed the defeat.[86] Both candidates viewed with hostility Turner, the new CCF, and the CLP's partnership with the UFA government. Former political enemies like school-board chairman F.E. Spooner, now Hindsley's campaign manager, tried to damage Turner's credibility. Although these problems cost her the election, they did not prevent working-class women from turning out in record numbers to vote for her.[87]

Analysing the demise of the CLP in 1935, Finkel argues that by the depression era the party had become the preserve of a small group of union bureaucrats who commanded little public support. What then is the explanation for Turner's electoral support? In the 15 January 1934 by-election, she gave a repeat performance in a closer contest, winning 44.9 per cent of the popular vote, but losing to W. Harry Ross who received 10,968 votes to Turner's 9065. Again, a former DLP member and school trustee, E. H. Starr, who resigned from the party to run as an independent Progressive-Labor candidate, opposed Turner. Some dissatisfied party members argued that the Labor party MLAs had become apologists for the reactionary UFA government and pushed for an 'independent' labour party.[88] Brownlee's suppression of the 1933 Hunger March in Edmonton with support of a Canadian Labor party mayor and labour councillors made it difficult for the party to maintain discipline, and confusion over the nature of the CCF affiliation also compounded the problem.

Yet Amelia Turner's supporters did not seem alarmed by her UFA connections, nor did they appear troubled by relief strikes in Calgary during 1933. Audiences were impressed with her explanation of the 1933 Regina Manifesto's support for a planned economy, banking reform, public ownership of essential services, socialization of health services, and free education.[89] An astute politician, Turner viewed with alarm the Social Credit movement with its brilliant organizing tactics and growing following of working-class voters. To please her audience she presented social credit positively by supporting its creation at the federal level and promising to prod the UFA government to fully investigate social credit.[90] Without fragmentation from CLP members, Amelia could have won both elections, but such a victory would have been bittersweet.

After 1934 the Canadian Labor party and the CCF followed a disastrous course, unable to undermine the appeal of the Social Credit movement by adopting a 'populist discourse as well as class discourse.' Voters reacted swiftly to the populism of Social Credit, for by the 1935 federal election the CLP's vote went from 44.9 per cent for Amelia Turner to 4.5 per cent for Edith Patterson.[91] Between 1934 and 1935, Social Credit rapidly captured the CLP's Calgary working-class base, striking hard at the ageing labour group. Under siege from unemployment and declining union membership, the CLP/CCF collapsed. Women felt the political chaos keenly: many, like

Amelia, could not adjust to political failure and retired from active politics. Nor did Calgary develop such a cohesive group of socialist women until the 1970s.[92]

IV

Yet from 1919 to 1935, Calgary labour women had politicized women to support a socialist and feminist agenda. From radical roots laid in the First World War, the labour women's groups blossomed and matured into the Women's Labor League and the DLP Women's Section. The WLL maintained a consistent emphasis on gender inequality; in the DLP Women's Section, class issues dominated over incipient interest in women's equality. Ultimately, non-partisan alliances were forsaken by Dominion Labor party women for power and influence within their own organization, where women's presence helped prevent the party from being solely the expression of craft-union leaders.

Because female activists were primarily either single professional women or married women with grown families, who volunteered time for a 'second' career, they did not encounter the contradictions of 'hauling a double load,' nor did they advance a feminist analysis of women, work, and the family. Even for labour women, married women with small children could hope for neither a political career nor paid employment. Married women in the labour political movement began to 'mother the world' when they had the energy, leisure time, and support from their husbands. Problems of rivalry were avoided because many politically active wives were widows or had a husband indifferent to politics, as Mary Corse and Jean McWilliam's careers illustrate.

Successful female politicians were rare in Alberta as elsewhere in Canada, so Amelia Turner occupies a unique place in provincial politics. Along with Liberal MLA Nellie McClung and UFA cabinet minister Irene Parlby, she experienced gender discrimination. Although personally successful, her career represents neither a transformation of political structures to include women nor a significant broadening of the agenda in a feminist direction. At the same time, her municipal and provincial campaigns were grounded in the DLP women's own agenda of international co-operation and peace, democratization of education, availability of free medical and dental service, unemployment insurance, fair minimum wage, mother's allowances, and pensions for women. These 'mothering issues' formed the nucleus of the Canadian Labor party's program, but movement on these issues was equally the goal of Dominion Labor party women, who organized and promoted women politicians specifically to implement this agenda. Amelia Turner spoke clearly for her constituency and received their full support. Her career demonstrates that women failed to penetrate the inner sanctum of labour politics, but it also illustrates that women were a significant political force.

Calgary labour women rejected the image of passive apolitical women, and utilized their new political power to effect change consistent with their earlier maternal feminist and socialist vision. A continued focus on male elites keeps hidden from analysis the structural barriers and contradictions that women faced, and precludes an understanding of the solutions they developed.

NOTES
The author wishes to acknowledge the critical reading and useful comments of Linda Kealey and Joan Sangster on an earlier draft of this paper.

1. Edith Patterson to Amelia Turner, 20 January 1933, Norman Smith Papers (NS Papers) AS5663 f. 215, Glenbow-Alberta Institute (GAI).
2. See, for example, John Herd Thompson with Allen Seager, *Canada 1922–1939* (Toronto 1985), 69–75; and Alvin Finkel, 'The Rise and Fall of the Labour Party in Alberta 1917–42,' *Labour/Le Travail* 16 (Fall 1985), 61–96. For an insightful discussion of feminism in 1920s, see V. Strong-Boag, 'Pulling in Double Harness or Hauling a Double Load: Women, Work and Feminism on the Canadian Prairie,' *Journal of Canadian Studies* 21:3 (Fall 1986), 32–52; and Sylvia B. Bashevkin, *Toeing the Lines: Women and Party Politics in English Canada* (Toronto 1985), ch. 1.
3. For a more detailed biographical sketch, see P. Roome, 'Amelia Turner: Alberta Socialist,' in Max Foran and Sheilagh Jameson, eds, *Citymakers: Calgarians after the Frontier* (Calgary 1987).
4. Frederick Turner to P. Roome, 2 August 1985, and photocopy 'Turner Family Tree,' 17 July 1969, at family reunion, Calgary, Alberta; wedding certificate of James Turner and Amelia Dyke, GAI.
5. E. Silverman interview with Amelia Turner Smith, 10 December 1975, typescript 1–9, Provincial Archives of Alberta (PAA). On financial problems see Henry J. Turner, file 10 May 1902–1 June 1921, Homestead Records, PAA.
6. Silverman interview, 1975, 5–9.
7. Ibid., 12.
8. Ibid., 12–14. Letter, A.T. Smith to Isa Grindlay Jackson, 14 January 1966, NS Papers, AS5663, file 27, GAI.
9. Hereward Turner farmed at Alliance, Alberta, and was active in UFA/CCF. Donata married Frank Irvine; both were active in UFA/CCF. Dorothy, Amelia, and Mrs L. Turner lived together in Calgary, working in the DLP. See *Alberta Labor News* (ALN), 28 April 1928, for notes on Mrs L. Turner's leadership of a study group; Elise Corbet interview with Amelia Turner Smith and Dorothy Smith, n.d., RCT-475, GAI. Amelia described herself as different from other girls, with more drive, knowledge of the world, and desire for a different life.
10. For insight into this period see Diary 1913–1917, Amelia Turner Smith Papers (ATS Papers) AS5663, file 12, GAI. See also G. Lowe, 'Women, Work and the Office: The Feminization of Clerical Occupations in Canada 1901–1931, *Canadian Journal of Sociology* 5:4 (1980), 376–8; and 'Class, Job and Gender in the Canadian Office,' *Labour/Le Travail* 10 (Autumn 1982), 1–37.
11. Anthony Mardiros, *The Life of a Prairie Radical: William Irvine* (Toronto 1979), ch 3. See also J.E. Cook and F.A. Johnston interview with Amelia Turner Smith,

28 May 1973, PAA; J.E. Cook interview with Dr A. Calhoun, 28 May 1972, PAA. On the Unity Club, see Rachael Coutts, *Voice*, 7 September 1917 and 27 July 1917. There was also a Women's Alliance of the Unitarian church affiliated with the Local Council of Women for 1919–20. Minute Book 1919–1921, Local Council of Women, M5841, file 24, p. 192, GAI.

12. P. Roome interview with Amelia Turner Smith, 21 July 1982, typescript 1. See also Edith Patterson, 'Memories of William Irvine,' *The Commonwealth*, 27 February 1963.

13. Roome interview, 1–2. Often Nattie Turner baby-sat the Irvine children while Amelia and Mrs Irvine attended movies or played cards with friends like Kate Clark or Edith Patterson.

14. Silverman interview, 1975, 16; Cook and Johnson interview, 1973.

15. Silverman interview, 1975, 15.

16. ALN. 25 September 1920.

17. See Allen Mills, 'Cooperation and Community in the Thought of J.S. Woodsworth,' *Labour/Le Travail* 14 (Fall 1984), 103–20.

18. Amelia Turner Smith, autobiographical notes, n.d. GAI.

19. See Norman and Jeanne Mackenzie, The *Fabians* (New York 1977).

20. Mr and Mrs William Carson clipping file, GAI. Marion Carson (1861–1947?) came to Calgary in 1898 with husband William (d. 1924), who became the successful owner and manager first of Calgary Milling Co. and then of Western Milling Co. During the First World War, he was in the grain-commission business. Marion, mother of six children, co-founder with Rachael of the Tuberculosis Society, joined the Unitarian church in 1913 and became a pacifist, strongly active after the death of her son overseas in 1917. She was the most socially prominent labour woman, able to bridge the gap between women on Local Council of Women and labour women in DLP, as demonstrated by her position as Convenor of Peace and Arbitration (renamed many times) for the LCW for more than a decade, president of DLP Women's Section, and trustee 1920–4; Rachael Coutts clipping file, GAI. Rachael Coutts was teacher, charter member of ATA, active on ICW, the Unitarian church, and executives of WLL and DLP, League of Nations clubs, and WILPF.

21. Edith Patterson to Mr Cook, William Irvine Papers (WI Papers), 83, 115/15, PAA; Edith Patterson clipping file, GAI; 'East Calgary Nominates Former Labor Alderman,' ALN 5 October 1935. E. Patterson (1876–1967) taught in Calgary 1913–40, served on the executives of WLL and DLP and became DLP president after Carson in the 1930s. Patterson was an alderman (1928–32, 1937–8) and CCF candidate in 1935, president of the Alberta Education Association, and, in 1934, president of ATA. She edited the column 'Alberta Labor Woman' in ALN between 1927 and 1935. Some of Edith Patterson's brothers, sisters, and their children — all Conservative party supporters — lived in Calgary. One nephew was Judge H.S. Patterson.

22. Finkel, 'The Rise and Fall,' 67–8. While the Canadian Labor party was formed in Alberta in 1921, factionalism prevented Calgary from setting up a central council until 1924.

23. 'Alberta Labor Woman,' ALN, 17 September 1927 and 3 March 1928; see notes 20, 21 above. Lte Clark was a teacher who lived with Patterson for over twenty years and served on WLL and DLP executives in the 1920s. Mary Corse was

a mother of six, resident in Calgary sporadically from 1916–24, member of Women's Auxiliary Typographical Union No. 449, a DLP school trustee 1918–20, on the executive of DLP, president of WLL. Her husband was a linotype machinist on the *Morning Albertan*. Elizabeth Broatch (d. 1944) was a mother of seven, on the executive of WLL, member of the Women's Auxiliary of Machinists (with a husband who was a machinist), OBU member, and alderman. Mrs M.L. Parkyn was a mother, active on the executive of WLL, Sunnyside PTA, Sunnyside Community Club, and wife of carpenter and activist R.H. Parkyn — DLP member, alderman, MLA. On types of women, see Roome interview with Amelia Turner, 21 July 1982. Marion Carson's upper-middle-class position set her aside from most of these women and gave her an unquestioned position of power.

24. Roome interview with Amelia Turner, 21 July 1982; Frederick Turner to P. Roome, 2 August 1985.
25. Linda Kealey, 'Prairie Socialist Women and WWI: The Urban West,' unpublished paper 1986, 15–16.
26. Minute Book 1919–1921, Local Council of Women; Jean (McWilliam) McDonald Papers, A.M135B, file 1, 2, GAI. Jean McWilliam (1877–1969) came from Scotland to homestead near Calgary in 1907, with husband William McWilliam. She ran a boarding-house from 1912 to the 1930s, and supported radical socialists and communists like John Reid and John O'Sullivan. She was president of WLL, president of Local Council of Women 1927–8, and active on LCW throughout the 1920s and 1930s. In the 1940s she formed the National Social Security Association. Mrs F.W. Grevett was later president of WLL, active on LCW from 1919 onward, becoming second vice-president in 1929 and Convenor of Immigration 1927–32. Her husband was a clerk at CPR in 1920.
27. Elizabeth Ann Taraska, 'The Calgary Craft Union Movement,' MA thesis, University of Calgary 1972: Calgary TLC Minutes (CTLC Minutes), 27 April 1918, M4743 file 6, GAI. Mrs J. McWilliam is recorded as a voting delegate for Federated Workers Union and Mrs George Corse for Typographical Auxiliary, 5 July 1918.
28. Western Convention Report, Western Canada Labor Conference, Calgary, 13–15 March 1919, Alfred W. Farmilo collection, 72.159, PAA. For Corse/McWilliam roles on the TLC, see CTLC Minutes, 5 July 1918, 19 July 1918, 2 August 1918, 30 August 1918, 22 November 1918, GAI.
29. On the British WLLs see Lucy Middleton, ed., *Women in the Labour Movement* (London 1977) 25–35; Caroline Rowan, 'Women in the Labour Party 1906–1920,' *Feminist Review* 12 (October 1982), 74–91.
30. 'People's Church in Calgary,' *Searchlight*, 9 April 1920. 'Work of the Women's Labor League in Calgary,' *Searchlight*, 3 September 1920.
31. 'Women's Labor League of Calgary,' *Searchlight*, 28 November 1919.
32. E.g. Elizabeth Broatch, Alice Corless, Kate Clark, Rachael Coutts, and Edith Patterson.
33. See note 23 above. Mrs A. Corless (d. 1942), mother of a large family, husband a janitor at Earle Grey School, both active in Unitarian church, later Labor church, until about 1925 when they moved to the United States (A. Corless to William Irvine, January 1945, WI Papers 83.115/2, PAA). Other WLL executive members: Mrs Elizabeth Petrie, secretary of Bridgeland PTA 1928,

husband a lawyer; Mrs J.H. Sprague, mother, husband a traveller for Drumheller Coal; Mrs G.H. Gerrad, WLL's vice-president 1922, president 1923–7, treasurer of Canadian Council of Child Welfare 1926; Mrs R.H. Parkyn; Mrs E.E. Antis, husband a carpenter, active in Machinists, Women's Auxiliary.

34. 'Mrs. George Corse, Representative of Trades and Labor Council,' *Royal Commission on Industrial Relations, 1919 Testimony*, Calgary 3 and 5 May 1919, Department of Labour Library, 35.

35. Ibid., 41. For a more rigorous critique, see Florence Custance, 'Why the Women's Labor League Movement?' *Woman Worker* 1:2 (August 1926).

36. 'Corse,' *Royal Commission, 279.*

37. 'Mrs. Jean McWilliam, representing no organization but appearing as a citizen,' *Royal Commission, 182–6.*

38. 'Corse,' *Royal Commusion, 279.*

39. Joan Sangster, 'Canadian Women in Radical Politics and Labour, 1920–1950,' PhD diss., McMaster University 1984.

40. 'Work of the Women's Labor League,' *Searchlight*, 3 September 1920; Georgia Baird and Karl Kaesekamp interview with Molly (McWilliam) La France, 3 May 1972, PAA. See also Royal North West Mounted Police Report, re: One Big Union, Strike in Calgary, dated Calgary 27 May 1919, signed S.R. Waugh, Det.-Corpl, copy in Warren Carragata Collection, BO 218, box B, PAA. Waugh falsely accuses McWilliam of being a member of SPC because she supported OBU and was on the Central Strike Committee with R.H. Parkyn; also, Waugh reports, a member of the SPC.

41. 'An Appreciation of Alderman Broatch,' *Searchlight*, 2 January 1920.

42. 'Speaker Called Them Bunch of Old Women,' *Searchlight*, 28 May 1920.

43. CTLC Minutes, 2 July 1920, GAI. Mrs G.S. Corse was presented with a purse of money by the council and its locals on behalf of her 'able services as a delegate and representative of Council.' She was leaving for Vancouver but returned, 1922–4.

44. 'The Woman's Vote in Calgary,' *ALN*, 4 November 1922.

45. 'Women's Labor League Active,' *Searchlight*, 23 January 1920. '$25 Per Month Minimum for House Workers,' *ALN*, 25 September 1920. 'Mrs. McWilliam Asks Minimum Wage of $21.48,' *ALN*, 9 October 1920. See also *ALN*, 10 September 1921 and 11 November 1922. 'Women's Labor League 40 Protests Delay in Minimum Wage Law,' *ALN*, 1 December 1923. Alice Corless to His Worship the Mayor and Councillors, 2 July 1919, Calgary City Clerk Papers (CCC Papers) box 161, file 971, GAI. Bessie Petrie to J.M. Miller, 23 August 1920, CCC Papers, box 176, f. 1036. Elise Corbet, 'Alberta Women in the 1920s: An Inquiry into Four Aspects of Their Lives,' MA diss., University of Calgary 1979, ch. 1. See also Linda Kealey, 'Women and Labour during World War I: Women Workers and the Minimum Wage in Manitoba,' in Mary Kinnear, ed., *First Days, Fighting Days* (Regina 1987), 76–99. Margaret E. McCallum, 'Keeping Women in Their Place: The Minimum Wage in Canada 1910–1924,' *Labour/Le Travail* 17 (Spring 1986), 29–56.

46. 'Women's Labor League Active,' *Searchlight*, 23 January 1920. Mrs George Corse argued for socialized medicine during her testimony in 1919, *Royal Commission*, 281: 'During the war the Government has proven that the nationalization of one medical profession is a possibility.'

47. 'Children Starve in This City,' *Searchlight*, 20 February 1920.
48. 'The Woman's Vote in Calgary,' ALN, 4 November 1922. See also P. Roome interview with Amelia Turner. Autobiographical notes by Annie Gale, 9 July 1919, Annie Gale collection, M402, GAI. Annie Gale (1867–1970) was an English woman who organized the Calgary Women's Consumers League, became president of the Women Rate Payers Association, alderman 1918–24, school trustee 1924–5. As an independent, she supported labour's goals, serving for two years as treasurer of People's Forum.
49. Although Lethbridge did affiliate with the Central Council of CLP, there is no existing evidence that the Calgary WLL did. Because Mary Corse was absent from Calgary from 1920 to 1922, returned 1922–4, then left permanently, Jean McWilliam was able to dominate the league and oppose affiliation with CLP ALN, 14 April 1923 and 20 September 1924.
50. ALN, 26 March 1921.
51. Calgary School Board Minutes, 10 April 1923, Calgary Board of Education (CBE). Bessie Petrie to Mr D. Bayne, secretary school board, 19 September 1924, CCC Papers, file 9E, box 356, GAI.
52. Corbet, 'Alberta Women in the 1920s,' 18.
53. Corbet, interview with Amelia Turner.
54. ALN, 20 November 1920, 2 April 1921, 16 April 1921, and 30 April 1921.
55. Ibid., 11 June 1921: 'I like the idea of all women's organizations getting together on a plane of usefulness.' On behalf of WLL, Mrs A. Corless argued this view at a tea given by Calgary women for Mrs Sears, president UFWA.
56. Sylvia Bashevkin, 'Independence vs. Partisanship: Dilemmas in the Political History of Women in English Canada,' in Veronica Strong-Boag and Anita Clair Fellman, eds, *Rethinking Canada: The Promise of Women's History* (Toronto 1986), 248.
57. E.R. Fay to the mayor and alderman, 23 December 1921; E.R. Fay to Mr Miller, 2 January 1922, CCC Papers, box 217, file 1228, GAI. Special committee membership: Mrs Sprague, Mrs McWilliam, E. Croft, A. Davidson, Mrs Carson, A. Allison; see also interview with Molly La France.
58. E.R. Fay to J.M. Miller, 3 April 1922, CCC Papers, box 217, file 1228, GAI. Central Council of Unemployed Petitions and Resolutions, CCC Papers, box 211, file 1192, GAI; 'Calgary Unemployed Occupy City Hall,' ALN, 8 April 1922. See also Judith B. Bedford, 'Social Justice in Calgary: A Study of Urban Poverty and Welfare Development in 1920s,' MA thesis, University of Calgary 1981.
59. Resolutions no. 12 and no. 13, CCC Papers, box 202, file 1145; report of Unemployment Conference held in Calgary, 4 and 5 August 1922, CCC Papers, box 207, file 1175, GAI.
60. 'Trades Council Will Organise Workers,' ALN, 10 June 1922; E.R. Fay to J.M. Miller, 3 April 1922, CCC Papers, box 217, file 1228. Mr Cassidy and Mr Lessey were OBU organizers whom TLC opposed. On Cassidy, see David J. Bercuson, *Fools and Wise Men* (Toronto 1978), 227–33. A.J. Boulter was the Worker's party organizer on CCU. Boulter, a miner from Drumheller who worked as labourer at CPR yards, was very hostile to craft unions. In 1927 he secured CLP nomination for alderman and was supported by the General Worker's Union. Calgary organized this first local of ACCUL with Boulter as a key person.

The Boulter family were friends of McWilliam, who supported other miners. Resolution re case of P.T. Thompson, Jean McWilliam to city clerk, 22 May 1922, CCC Papers, box 203, file 1151. WLL protested police harassment of Thompson, who was an unemployed Drumheller miner active in CCU.

61. 'The Women's Vote in Calgary,' ALN, 4 November 1922.

62. Sophie McClusky was a Russian immigrant, SPC organizer, and provincial Secretary for Alberta, known in 1913–14 in Calgary as Sophie Mushkat. She taught English to immigrants at Riverside School and was active in the Unemployed Committee (Calgary Protestant Public School Board Minutes, 20 January 1913, 13 January 1914, CBE); Warren Carragata collection, 80.218, box A, PAA; See Kealey, 'Prairie Socialist Women,' 8–9.

63. Dr Scott to Mr G.F. McNally, 3 November 1921, Calgary School Board Papers, box 40B, file 1921 L-Z, GAI. On reapplication, see Calgary School Board Minutes, 19 September 1925.

64. Sophie McClusky file, GAI; ALN, 14 February 1925. See also T. Thorner and N. Watson, 'Keeper of the King's Peace: Colonel G.E. Saunders and the Calgary Police Magistrate's Court 1911–1932,' Urban History Review 12 (February 1984), 45–55.

65. For example Mrs M. Parkyn, Mrs G.H. Garrad, and Mrs F.W. Grevett.

66. ALN, 24 January 1925.

67. Strong-Boag, 'Pulling in Double Harness,' 33.

68. 'Reply to Address of Welcome, Mrs. M. Lowe,' ALN, 6 April 1929 and 'By the Way,' ibid., 1 December 1928.

69. 'Alberta Labor Women,' ALN, 17 December 1927, 26 January 1928, 3 March 1928.

70. A full discussion of the demise of the Calgary WLL lies beyond the scope of this paper. McWilliam, Parkyn, Hunt, and Grevett continued to be involved. The WLL hosted the 1927 Women's Social and Economic Conference in Calgary and Mrs D. Hunt joined the executive. In 1928 it helped A.E. Smith raise money for the Canadian Labor Defence League. By 1930, the WLL was affiliated with the Local Council of Women, because of McWilliam's and Grevett's participation from 1919 onward. They both served on the executive with McWilliam as president (1926–8) giving lectures on Russia (February 1927) at Central United Church (see Minutes of Local Council of Women, 21 January 1927, M5 841, file 24, GAI; Alberta Labor News, 28 March 1927, 2 April 1927, 9 April 1927, 28 April 1927, 28 February 1928).

71. 'Alberta Labor Woman,' ALN, 17 September 1927, 15 February 1928, 28 April 1928, 26 May 1928, 20 October 1928.

72. Ibid., 17 September 1927; 'Mrs. Jamieson Has Message for Calgary Women,' ALN, 22 October 1927.

73. 'Internationalism Means Loyalty to Human Race,' ALN, 17 September 1927. Marion Carson, 'Some Peace Movements Other than League of Nations,' Alberta Labor Annual, September 1921; Carson, 'The Growing Revulsion toward War,' Alberta Labor Annual, September 1928; Carson, 'Women and the Peace Movement,' ALN, 20 October 1928.

74. Francis Early, 'The Historic Roots of the Women's Peace Movement in North America,' Canadian Women Studies/Les cahiers de la femme 7:4 (Winter 1986), 47; Thomas P. Socknat, 'The Pacifist Background of the Early CCP,' in J.

William Brennan, ed., *Building the Co-operative Commonwealth: Essays on the Democratic Socialist Tradition in Canada* (Regina 1984), 57–68.

75. 'Our Labor Leagues at Work,' *Woman Worker,* May 1927; 'Mrs. McArthur Heads Labor Conference,' ALN, 2 April 1927; 'Agnes MacPhail,' *Alberta Labor News,* 9 April 1927 and 'Labor Women Discuss Many Vital Matters,' ALN, 9 April 1927. On LWSE Conference, see Joan Sangster, 'Communist Party and the Woman Question 1922–29,' *Labour/Le Travail* 15 (Spring 1985), 31. On founder of LWSE Conference, see B. Brigden, 'One Woman's Campaign for Social Purity and Social Reform,' in Richard Allen, ed., *The Social Gospel in Canada* (Ottawa 1975), 36–62.

76. 'Alberta Labor Woman,' ALN, 10 March 1928, 21 April 1928, 5 May 1928, 17 November 1928, 16 March 1929, 23 March 1929, 30 March 1929, 6 April 1929.

77. Ibid., 10 November 1928, 17 November 1928.

78. 'Fine Spirit Prevailed at Conference,' ALN, 12 May 1928.

79. Calgary School Board Minutes, 25 January 1926 and 13 February 1926, *Calgary Herald*, 30 March 1926, 31 March 1926. For a more detailed analysis, see P. Roome, 'Amelia Turner: Alberta Socialist.'

80. Annual reports, Calgary School Board 1927–1936, CBE.

81. Calgary School Board Minutes, 8 June 1926, 25 June 1926, CBE.

82. 'Alberta Labor Women,' ALN, 29 October 1927, 5 November 1927, 12 November 1927, 19 November 1927, 10 December 1927, 17 December 1927, 26 January 1928, July 1928.

83. *The UFA*, 1 August 1933.

84. For example, the Women's Joint Committee; see John Manley, 'Women and the Left in the 1930s: The Case of the Toronto CCF Women's Joint Committee,' *Atlantis* 5:2 (Spring 1980); 100–19; Joan Sangster, 'Women of the "New Era": Women in the Early CCF,' in Brennan, ed., *Building the Co-operative Commonwealth*, 69–98.

85. Irvine/Smith correspondence, 1933–4, WI Papers, 83.115/199, PAA; also Irvine/Smith correspondence, NS Papers, box 2, file 22, GAI. DLP and its Women's Section formally adopted the Canadian Labor party label in 1930.

86. *Calgary Herald*, 13 January 1933. For detailed analysis of 1933, 1934 by-elections, see P. Roome, 'Amelia Turner.'

87. Robert M. Stamp, *School Days: A Century of Memories* (Calgary 1975), 59–63.

88. *Calgary Albertan*, 5 January 1934, 9 January 1934, 11 January 1934.

89. Ibid., 11 January 1934, 12 January 1934, 13 January 1934.

90. Ibid., 15 January 1934.

91. Larry Hannant, 'The Calgary Working Class and the Social Credit Movement in Alberta 1932–1935,' *Labour/Le Travail* 16 (Fall 1985), 97–116; Alvin Finkel, 'The Obscure Origins: The Confused Early History of the Alberta CCF,' in Brennan, ed., *Building the Co-operative Commonwealth*, 99–122.

92. Alvin Finkel, 'Populism and the Proletariat: Social Credit and the Alberta Working Class,' *Studies in Political Economy* 13 (Spring 1984), 109–35.

X

RURAL AND AGRICULTURAL SOCIETY OF PRAIRIE CANADA

By the 1890s, farming, particularly wheat production, had become the major economic occupation of the North-West. Rural newspapers and periodicals in the North-West, sometimes consciously (but often unconsciously) extolled the virtues and strengths of this rural and agrarian life. Their "country life ideology" depicted the land as the natural source of mankind and the mainspring of health, happiness, peace and virtue. Farmers were seen as being close to Nature and nearer to God than urban man. This belief was best captured in the slogan of the agrarian reform movement—"God Made the Country; Man Made the City." This ideology shaped the agrarian reform movements of the early twentieth century and inspired a generation of prairie writers. David Jones analyzes the nature of this country life ideology and evaluates its significance for both a regional and national identity in his article, "'There Is Some Power About the Land'—The Western Agrarian Press and Country Life Ideology."

While prairie farmers perpetuated a rural agrarian myth and struggled to preserve farming against the onslaught of urbanization, they also adopted modern and efficient business methods such as scientific agriculture, better machinery, technological advancements in production, and increased capital investment. In short a number of small farmers became agricultural businessmen, and their operations, agribusiness. Historians have traditionally seen this shift as a moving away from the rural agrarian values that underlay their country life ideology in favour of urban and commercial values. In "The Business of Agriculture: Prairie Farmers and the Adoption of 'Business Methods', 1880-1950," Ian Macpherson and John Thompson challenge this assumption. They argue that the simple and obvious antithesis of farming as a way of life and farming as a business is a modern perspective which had no meaning for earlier generations of prairie farmers. As these historians remind us: "Rural people did not adopt business methods to become mere imitations of urban business culture; rather they searched for the best way to guarantee an economic return for their work—a return which would build rural communities and which could assure the survival of their families upon the land." Business practices were, then, yet another way that prairie farmers attempted to perpetuate—not negate—the rural and agricultural society of prairie Canada, according to Macpherson and Thompson.

Along with a resurgence in rural and agricultural history has been a renewed interest in local history. Historians are discovering the need to test the validity of general historical theories by their application to specific local areas. In "Rural Local History and the Prairie West," Paul Voisey argues for the importance of good local history by professional historians.

Western Canadian historians interested in rural and agricultural history have recently shifted the focus of their analysis from institutions, the wheat economy, and regional-dominion concerns to topics of everyday life on prairie farms. New questions are being asked of the sources. For example, how did the prairie homestead function economically? What factors contributed to financial success or conversely to financial failure for prairie homesteaders? What was life like for the various members of prairie farmsteads—women, children, hired hands, and male owners? What cultural life existed in rural prairie society? Did social and class distinctions exist, and if so, did they form only at certain stages in the settlement process? Was rural life independent and self reliant, or did prairie farmers depend on metropolitan centres for their survival? Were there tensions between towns or cities and the surrounding rural society they served and often dominated? These questions have moved the debate into the realm of social history and thus enriched our understanding of everyday life on the prairies.

SELECTED BIBLIOGRAPHY

A number of useful articles on aspects of rural and agricultural society in prairie Canada are available in volumes of the series *Canadian Papers in Rural History* (Gananoque, Ontario: Langdale Press), of which seven volumes have been published to date. A valuable single collection of essays is D.C. Jones and Ian Macpherson, eds., *Building Beyond the Homestead: Rural History on the Prairies* (Calgary, 1985). The best detailed study of rural and agricultural life in a single prairie town is Paul Voisey's *Vulcan: The Making of Prairie Community* (Toronto, 1988). An earlier sociological study of the town of Hanna, Alberta is Jean Burnet's *Next-Year Country: A Study of Rural Social Organization in Alberta* (Toronto, 1951). David Jones provides a moving account of rural life in the dry belt area of southeastern Alberta during the 1920s in *Empire of Dust: Settling and Abandoning the Prairie Dry Belt* (Edmonton, 1987). A documentary study of the subject is available in David C. Jones, *"We'll All Be Buried Down Here":* *The Prairie Dryland Disaster 1917-1926* (Edmonton, 1986). For personal accounts of growing up in rural prairie Canada, see Wilfrid Eggleston's "The Old Homestead: Romance and Reality," in Chapter 17 and James M. Minifie, *Homesteader: A Prairie Boyhood Recalled* (Toronto, 1972).

John Thompson has written extensively on the subject of prairie agriculture. Besides his article with Ian Macpherson included here as Chapter 23, see "Bringing in the Sheaves: The Harvest Excursionists, 1890-1920, *Canadian Historical Review* 54 (1978): 467-89; "Permanently Wasteful But Immediately Profitable: Prairie Agriculture and the Great War," Canadian Historical Association *Historical Papers* (1976): 193-206; and with Ian Macpherson, "An Orderly Reconstruction: Prairie Agriculture in World War II," *Canadian Papers in Rural History,* Vol. IV (Gananoque, Ont., 1984), pp. 11-32. Ian Macpherson's *Each For All: A History of the Co-operative Movement in English Canada, 1900-1945* (Toronto, 1979) is a good study of this important institution in rural and agricultural prairie Canada.

For information on the Amerindians' rural world in the late nineteenth century, see Sarah Carter's *Lost Harvests: Prairie Indian Reserve Farmers and Government Policy* (Montreal, 1990). This can be supplemented for the later period by Stan Cutland's "The Native Peoples of the Prairie Provinces in the 1920s and 1930s," in *One Century Later: Western Canadian Reserve Indians Since Treaty 7,* edited by Ian Getty and Donald B. Smith (Vancouver, 1978), pp. 31-42. A good biography of a Plains Indian leader in the twentieth century is Hugh A. Dempsey's *The Gentle Persuader: A Biography of James Gladstone, Indian Senator* (Saskatoon, 1986). For a comparison of Amerindian agriculture on the Canadian and the American Plains, see Hana Samek, *The Blackfoot Confederacy 1880-1920: A Comparative Study of Canadian and U.S. Indian Policy* (Albuquerque, 1987).

DAVID C. JONES

---

22 "There Is Some Power About the Land"
The Western Agrarian Press and
Country Life Ideology

It is the nature of societies to attempt to identify and define themselves. While this process often occurs more than once in the life of a social system, it frequently begins in the formative stages of societal development. At such times there is often a sense that the emerging way of life can or should be directed toward certain models or ideals. If contrary ideals are perceived as threats, it is not unusual for spokespersons of the emerging culture to construct an elaborate ideology which justifies the preferred ideals. Such ideology of course is simultaneously defensive and highly positive. It is likely to be optimistic as well. What typically happens is that the developing order creates a morality which underscores certain of its values or attitudes, especially those which seem to contrast most sharply with the values of any force or culture which may directly threaten it. As those concerned in the new order survey the significance of the clash between models or ideals, they determine facets of their life most worth perpetuating and they begin to justify and crystallize the meaning of their existence through a celebration of those facets.

The Canadian prairie west underwent such a process during the first two decades of this century when its population jumped from 419,512 in 1901 to 1,328,121 in 1911 and 1,956,082 in 1921.[1] In those years the social and economic destiny of the west was established for the foreseeable future. That destiny was to be fundamentally rural and agrarian. At the same time, particularly in the first decade, a waxing urban civilization grew more and more menacing. Reflecting trends in other countries and in Canada as a whole, between 1901 and 1911 the percentage of urban population in the prairie west rose from 19.3 percent to 28.8 percent. Over the longer span between 1901 and 1926 the rural portion in Alberta dropped from 74.6 percent to 61.5 percent and that in Saskatchewan declined from 84.4 percent to 70.5 percent. In Manitoba it slipped from 72.4 percent to 56.4 percent.[2]

In establishing simultaneously its essence and its antithesis the west also established, in concert with the cultural baggage of its inhabitants and the philosophy of rural contemporaries and precursors elsewhere, what I have identified earlier as the *Zeitgeist* of western Canadian settlement, a spirit of the times akin to a *Weltansicht*, or world view.[3] In that work I tried to demonstrate that there were several aspects of life on the land in the western settlement period which combined to produce a rural myth, or a way of seeing the world. This myth was essentially positive and optimistic; those who believed felt generally that the land being occupied was livable, that man with the aid of science could subdue nature and pave the way for an era of agrarian splendour. In that era the elemental industry, agriculture, would be seen for what it was—the mainspring of national greatness and the moulder of national and personal character.

While I focussed in that paper on the role of the schools in propagating the myth, it was clear that there were many other factors, including local newspaper boosterism, the general nature of advertising, railway promotion, land speculation, conservation societies, wildlife societies, and other voluntary associations, art, literature, and agrarian periodicals—in other words, all those educational agencies which combined to create and reflect an outlook of systematically related ideas, an ideology.

This paper singles out one of those elements, the agrarian periodical. My purpose is quite circumscribed. I propose to identify and assess the ideology of country living as it appeared in representative farm journals in the period 1900-1920.

By 1920 four major western Canadian farm periodicals and their circulations were: *The Nor'-West Farmer* (67,401), *The Farmer's Advocate and Home Journal* (40,917), *The Grain Growers' Guide* (74,606), and the *Farm and Ranch Review* (48,844).[4] The first three were printed in Winnipeg, the second was published in London, Ontario, as well, and the fourth was printed in Calgary. *The Nor'-West Farmer* was established in 1882; the *Advocate* (Western edition) in 1890; the *Guide* in 1908; and the *Review* in 1905.

In these papers there were many manifestations of the ideology of rural life. Combined, the four periodicals provided an enormous repository of social information averaging, in the period under study, five to seven thousand pages a year. Every aspect of rural existence was reflected and the coverage overlapped most other sources in the period, with commentaries, articles, speeches, and letters from those who wrote books, those who preached the social gospel, who represented federal and provincial departments of agriculture, women's institutes, homemakers' clubs, agricultural societies and other farm organizations, and those who attended important agrarian conventions, or who were simply farmers and farm wives. That is, the source by its very nature was multifaceted. It also represented the whole region. Despite the location of three of the papers in Winnipeg, correspondents travelled extensively and articles and letters issued from all corners of the prairies. To the extent that Alberta and Saskatchewan were sometimes underrepresented, the *Review* sought to fill that void. The farm press, in sum, was something of a catchall, not sufficient in itself as a means of understanding the time, but probably the single source most likely to address most themes which agricultural historians deem significant.

In that source the ideology of rural life appeared as a cluster of notions about the nature and worth of country living, which tended to be equated with its basic western manifestation—farming. Indeed, before 1910 farming had largely forced the related ranching from its natural habitat in southern Alberta and southwestern Saskatchewan.

Country life advocates identified the city as the counter culture, the source of many of their basic problems. In Canada this meant the metropoles of Toronto and Montreal and, to a lesser though still significant extent, Winnipeg. More ominous for many Canadians were American centres like Chicago, Detroit and New York. In fact, the Canadian country life movement was intimately tied to the analogous campaign in the United States— a point to which I shall return.

It was perhaps inevitable that the creation of a vast agrarian empire in the west should have resurrected certain ancient idealizations of agricultural life. Early issues of the *Farm and Ranch Review* carried on the title page the wisdom of Socrates:

> Agriculture is an employment most worthy of the application of man, the most ancient and most suitable to his nature; it is the common nurse of all persons in every age and condition of life; it is the source of health, strength, plenty and riches and of a thousand sober delights and honest pleasures. It is the mistress and school of sobriety, temperance, justice, religion and, in short, of all virtues.[5]

Throughout the period before 1920 agricultural periodicals reminded readers of Cicero's opinion that "Nothing can be more profitable, nothing more beautiful than a well-cultivated farm."[6] "The agricultural population," wrote Cato, "produces the bravest men, the most valiant soldiers and a class of citizens least given of all to evil design."[7] Even the moderns were often delighted with agriculture or the allied virtues of hard work—for, said Thomas Carlyle, "there is perennial nobleness, and even sacredness in work. Were he never so benighted, forgetful of his high calling, there is always hope in a man that actually and earnestly works; in idleness alone there is perpetual despair."[8]

These views the agrarian press promulgated, noting in 1903 that the King of England himself was "an enthusiastic farmer" and that "the nobility of England do not consider it a compliment to be classed with the doctors and lawyers, but are proud to be called agriculturists."[9] The American "nobility" too were regarded respectfully and cited opportunely. "The time of [Great Britain's] greatness," railroad baron J.J. Hill said, "was the era of prosperous agriculture, with other industries proportioned to it duly. Long after that balance was disturbed she maintained herself because the growth of her colonies was equivalent to added farms in England." In whatever country at whatever time, national well-being hung on farm prosperity. "It is not, as in the old mythology, Atlas whom we see groaning beneath the weight of the world," Hill concluded, "but the homelier and humbler figure of the cultivator of the soil."[10]

This theme of the centrality of the farmer was also promoted by those of humbler origins and accomplishments. In May 1908 M.D. Geddes, Calgary stock judge and editor of the *Farm and Ranch Review*, drew attention to an article in *Scientific American* which called for "a recognition of the fact once so well understood, that the soil is the foundation of all wealth and prosperity."[11] "Bankers may handle money and store it; tradesmen may handle goods and make a profit," an article in *The Farmer's Advocate* stated, "but the man who creates a new dollar is the farmer."[12] In 1915 *The Grain Growers' Guide* carried Charles G. Leland's poem, "The Farmer Feedeth All":

> Man builds his castles, fair and high,
> Wherever river runneth by;
> Great cities rise in every land,
> Great churches show the builder's hand;
> Great arches, monuments and towers,
> Fair palaces and pleasing bowers;
> Great work is done, be it here or there,
> And well man worketh everywhere.
>   But work or rest, whate'er befall,
>   The farmer he must feed them all.[13]

This point the war made all the clearer. As one Ontario Agricultural College graduate said, it "had shown the man on the land to be the first essential of the race."[14]

In sustaining the world the farmer worked in a state of nature. He "lives under clearer skies and breathes purer air than the dweller of the city," wrote W.J. Way. "His work and mode of life are more natural, and, therefore more healthful."[15] "The Country Girl" in the *Guide* elaborated, comparing her own city existence in Winnipeg to a life she once knew: "When your day's work is done you sit on your doorstep and listen to the murmur of night life—frogs croaking, night birds calling, which sounds only serve to emphasize the stillness." In the city there was never rest. "All day long and all evening there is the rumble of street cars, the hum of automobiles, the sounds of people talking on the porches all about us. We never get away from people."[16] In the country Bert Huffman, a Langdon, Alberta rancher, concluded, "there is no room for the crushing conflict of your soulless, narrow street."[17]

There was, of course, more than calmness and peace to the country. As *The Nor'-West Farmer* editorialized in 1915: "It is one of the seldom appreciated advantages of country life that a rural environment conduces to better morals than are so frequently the rule in our cities and towns."[18] There were a hundred thousand children in Chicago, said well-known American divine W.H. Hicks, "who cannot tell a rose from a dandelion, but who can give the names of popular pugilists, gamblers and thugs."[19] Farm children, fortunately, were undefiled by such worthless and degrading interests. Indeed, G. Abbott, director of the U.S. League for the Protection of Emigrant Children, reported that children from rural areas where there was abundant exercise or from German states with supervised play were free from "criminal taint." Only after an apprenticeship in America's tenement districts did they "fall from grace."[20]

The fact was, said the *Advocate*, that "there is some power about the 'land' that elevates, morally and emotionally, if not intellectually." Even penitentiary wardens had seen this truth whenever they took their inmates to farm prisons. As one warden said, "once I get them on to the land they begin to improve." The paper concluded: "If then, the very fact of working on a farm, though it be a prison farm, flanked by the rifles of ever watching guards, can suffice to soften and raise men, the lowest or weakest of their kind, what must the glorious freedom of land, and woods, and sky, do for youth who comes clean-handed, clean-souled, to his heritage of Lord of the Soil."[21]

Years later the same journal explained the deeper meaning of country life. The land was a permanent, ever-renewing source of sustenance; it was "the endowment of the race." And there was more to the meaning of endowment than the production of food, for its long purpose, the journal said, "surely must be the nurture of men and women who are destined to carry forward the best ideals of the race in religion, conduct, industry, recreation, education and cooperation."[22]

Religious leaders whose sermons enlightened farm readers amplified this theme. Reverend J.A. Clark of Knox Church, Calgary, who wrote for years in the *Review*, reminded readers that Christ's ministry had been under clear skies. "A great deal of our worship and teaching," Clark said, "is greatly vitiated in these northern lands of ours because it is indoors. Our worship and our teaching are like the buildings we meet in, man-made, limited, unnatural, artificial."[23] The purpose of the country was seen as the revitalization of man's spiritual powers.[24] "God's open air" guaranteed sanity, affirmed social gospeller Salem Bland in the *Guide* in 1918, and after four years of war the need for mental stability was paramount. "It is one of the blessings that are so strangely interwoven with the unspeakable evils of this war that multitudes of people who had never known, or had forgotten, how good is the smell of newly-turned earth, how wonderful is the unfolding life of leaf or bud, have gone back to nature, even if only in a backyard or vacant lot."[25] The peace and the quiet power of war gardens and school gardens, Bland reckoned, would set man's mind right.

The gardens and youth agricultural clubs which mushroomed during the war were symbols of the farm, fount of so many virtues. Echoing Liberty Hyde Bailey, American nature-study enthusiast and author of *The Outlook to Nature* (1905), the *Advocate's* editor, J. Albert Hand, agricultural graduate and former Ontario farmer and school teacher, showed how the farm taught resourcefulness, improvisation, and industriousness. The farmer was "not depending on some storekeeper friend or ward politician to float him into a job where he can 'sojer' for eight hours, like the 'laborers' who roost about the employment bureaus waiting for a job with the least work in it." The farm taught perseverance and frugality. It provided honest work and genuine satisfaction, two elements often missing in city work. It instilled independence and freedom from social snobbery. It made each lad "a home boy rather than a street boy." It offered its sons a carefully paced growth, for "the country boy comes to maturity more slowly and naturally, like a tree, rather than a hothouse plant." And finally, the farm gave balance and equilibrium, a freedom from anxiety and perverted tastes. The farm boy could "eat eggs without a string-band accompaniment, and, if the home cooking is up to the mark, does not need to go round with a box of 'little digesters' in his vest pocket."[26]

The problem with the city was the way "it dissipates energy, weakens the moral fibre, distracts with too many frivolous side interests, until the youth feels that he must be forever entertained with the 'gew gaws' and 'attractions' and 'freaks.' " It was replete with entertainers for those who could not entertain themselves and with flimflammers who knew nothing but con games and fleecing.[27] The world was "full of shams," warned Ginger in *The Nor'-West Farmer*, and as a result so many city folks were "dazzled by the vanities and baubles" of superficiality.

> We live in an age of imitations and veneers—imitation draperies, veneer furniture, shoddy fabrics, paste jewellery; even the very hair on the heads of many of the city women is false. Modern city life has developed in many of the young people a craze for excitement, a love for false show and a weakness for tinsel that is extremely enervating to the character and mis-directing to the life.[28]

There was also a certain barbarity to city life. When effort was made in 1913 to transform the Winnipeg Exhibition into a stampede, J. Albert Hand of the *Advocate* editorialized: "Such is the judgment of some city men in regard to exhibitions—they prefer some silly entertainment or blood-curdling stunt that should not be considered in a civilized country."[29] Later that year the *Guide* said the steer roping at the stampede was "rather rough on the steers. A certain amount of roughness is necessary in handling steers on the range but our civilization seems slightly out of joint when the chief attraction at our holiday celebration is the murdering or maiming of defenceless lower animals."[30] Likening the scene to a relic of bygone times or a Spanish bullfight, one correspondent urged the immediate elimination of both steer roping and bucking horse contests. Moved by the lack of practical application and the irrelevance to the progress of the west, especially of bucking, the writer snapped: "We have improved our horses out of those habits, and we should be ashamed of them."[31]

Urban barbarity extended beyond the tasteless transformation of legitimate agricultural exhibitions into senseless spectacles. The city was a malignant force, an evil breeding ground. "With its great white ways and . . . its snares of pain," the city was replete with vulgarians of every stripe.[32] It sheltered the lollers, the indolent and the debauched prostitutes, gamesters, loafers and speculators.

Concerning the last, as the pre-war wheeling and dealing climaxed, the *Guide* regarded it "as one of the greatest evils at present rampant in Western Canada."[33] Peace River agricultural scientist W.D. Albright wrote:

> Real estate speculation is a curse . . . . It plants subdivision stakes in good farm land and interferes with its cultivation. It spreads town and city out over excessive areas, compelling builders to go out further than they would like in order to escape extortion. The cost of every civic service . . . is enhanced. A small army of drones and parasites are supported in the person of landlords, real estate agents, speculators, lawyers, conveyancers, etc.

Albright believed that real estate speculation was a moral menace providing "potent temptation to graft, deception, fraud and political wire pulling." The term "real estate agent" indeed had become "synonymous with chicanery."[34] The cities reeking with such scum, it was little wonder that Herbert Quick, American educator and author, claimed the overexpansion of urban areas to be "like pulsating tumors on the body politic."[35]

A persistent question of many articles was the fate of the poor country waif who wandered into the city. The agrarian papers of the period offered, according to their particular purpose, two largely incompatible answers. The first and probably less used response was that those who went to the city became community leaders and worthy citizens. One article in the *Guide* in 1909 tallied the number of presidents, governors, and cabinet officers in the United States that had been furnished by the city and the country. Regarding presidents, the city had provided two compared with the country's twenty-three; regarding governors, four, compared to the country's forty-one; and regarding cabinet officers, fifteen, compared to the country's eleven.[36]

These and similar tales of success were dwarfed by the dominant response that a large percentage of farm girls and boys would "jump into the great city maelstrom to take that one chance of a hundred of coming up from that undercurrent and making a livelihood among the middle classes."[37] The freedom-loving country spirit would choke in the foul factories of limited opportunities.[38] Professional life was often viewed as having "many drawbacks and heartaches."[39] During the 1914-1916 hard times in Canadian cities, potential migrants were warned by W.W. Gamble that "the town foundation is a foundation of sand that often shifts to the discomfort and inconvenience of the occupant of the edifice."[40]

At the height of the postsettlement depression, the *Guide* went so far as to commandeer J.S. Woodsworth, secretary of the Canadian Welfare League, to write a series of articles on the problems of city life. Greatly moved by the squalor of urban America, Woodsworth also understood the shortcomings of Canadian cities, particularly Winnipeg. The expense of living in the city, wrote Woodsworth, was enormous. While wood cost a farmer nothing, the city dweller had to pay. A man could not dig a well in a city. In fact, there he could not act independently.[41] The city worker was "simply 'the hired man' with little chance of ever owning anything of his own." Even his time was not really his.[42] "The city boy, rich or poor, has no millpond, no fields or woods, no country lanes, no old barn loft, no unused attic for [r]ainy days." He had only tenement congestion.

As well, rural folk would find a different psychology in the city. "The farmer, after all," said Woodsworth, "is a Canadian, the mechanic an old countryman."[43] While he did not elaborate Woodsworth seemed to refer to the numerous English skilled labourers and machinists recently drawn to Canadian cities. Clearly, however, many farmers were also old countrymen. Thus he may have been alluding to the fact that English farmers often came from the gentry whereas the machinist typically hailed from the working classes. The latter to some extent had just arrived in Canada, while the former had been around for some time—on cattle ranches in Alberta, for example, or orchards in British Columbia. Possibly this longer exposure to Canadian conditions qualified "the old country farmer" in Woodsworth's mind as somewhat more Canadian.

At any rate, if Woodsworth were right, farm boys and girls could expect to experience economic and social dislocation in the city. They could also expect to undergo moral degeneration. As T.L. Masson wrote in the *Guide* in 1909:

Cities pass their time in loafing and drinking, and in consuming the things that are grown for them. No self respecting city would deign to earn its own living. It insists on being supported in luxury and in return furnishes the styles and standard of bad manners for the outlying districts . . . .

Hayseeds have to be continually grafted on to cities, in order to keep [cities] alive. If left to themselves they would decay.

For Masson the city was some creeping colossus, alive and vile, for even the cobblestones, he said, "are constantly moving from street to street, like corpuscles."[44]

In view of the danger, Edgar L. Vincent's revelation in the *Advocate* was perhaps understandable. Vincent quoted a First World War general who complained: "We cannot enroll young men of as good fiber, physically, morally and otherwise as we could 15 years ago." The general blamed the many divertisements including picture shows for enticing the young to deflect their energies into frivolity rather than substance.[45]

The false glow of urbanism was most apt to ensnare youth of an impressionable age. Vincent told of one young man's father who had moved off the farm about 1915. "It is always a dangerous thing to do," Vincent argued, "especially when there are young folks, unless they have their feet well grounded." It made him "fairly tremble" when he contemplated the family's removal "from the old farm with its calm, its quiet and its things to make us think of the best there is." Vincent was "afraid that something would happen to the boy." He recalled the warm send off the country paper had given George, "one of our most popular young men." Short months later, a city newspaper revealed the lad's fate:

Locked in his cell at the station house last night young [George], who snatched a lady's pocketbook and was captured by the crowd in pursuit, was the picture of misery. He stated that he belonged to a respectable family in the country. It appears that he lost his position as shipping clerk because of dissipation. Yesterday morning he found himself out of money and friends, with no work and hungry. He grew desperate and committed the crime. 'I just got in with the wrong crowd when I came here,' he said.[46]

Regarding the fate of country girls, "Margaret" who conducted the "Sunshine Guild" for the *Guide* advised young females that "the life of an unprotected girl in a great city is full of torturing temptations."[47] As in the case of young George, there was a tendency for adolescent girls to be led astray by their peers. Margaret Freeston reported in *The Nor'-West Farmer* in 1920 that she had often heard employers say, "Give me the country girl for the first year or so she is in the city, before she has made too many friends." But, Freeston continued: "As time goes on, and she gathers friends and interests, she begins to go out more in the evenings, stays up late, and no employer has to be told that she has changed her way of spending her spare time, for the change is plainly discernible in the work she does."[48]

The tainting might also come through agents more sinister than "friends." A mere *visit* to the city might suffice. Casting a watchful eye on the "white slavers," the Young Women's Christian Association warned country girls who visited western cities never to ask direction of any but recognized officials. "Girls should never stay to help a woman who apparently faints at their feet, but should immediately call a policeman to her aid," the Y said in the *Review*. Nor should they go with a stranger, even one "dressed as a hospital nurse, or believe stories of their relatives having suffered accident or having been taken ill suddenly," as these were "common device[s] of kidnappers."[49]

Such was the agrarian press's sense of the certain destiny facing so many country boys and girls who entered the city. "The young people are gradually drawn into a life full of viciousness," wrote an Albertan identified only as H.S., "till they are absolutely lazy, irresponsible, shallow in mind, and shattered in health. We have these conditions in Canada right now."[50] Comparatively few would succeed, said Henry Wallace, member of the U.S. Country Life Commission, editor of the Iowa farm paper, *Wallace's Farmer*, and Chairman of the Conservation Congress for "the city uses men and families as it uses up horses . . . . The children of these few become wealthy; their grandchildren usually spend gaily the fortunes they never earned; and naturally the family dies out."[51]

With these pronouncements it was little wonder that a letter in the *Guide* concluded, "Every city has a soul—of dishonor."[52] And it was even less wonder that "The Country Girl" column reiterated the opinion of "scientists" that "it is necessary for the mental and moral health of a people that they return to the land with every third generation."[53]

While the press abounded with such sentiments, it was Nellie McClung's colourful and persuasive prose which best captured the ideology of city and country:

The city offers so may dazzling, easy ways to wealth. It is so rich in promise, so treacherous in fulfilment. The city is a lenient, unfaithful nurse, pampering and pandering the child in her care, not for his own good, but for her gain, soothing him with promises she never means to keep, a waster of time, a destroyer of ambition, a creator of envy, but dazzling gay with tinsel and redolent with perfume, covering poverty with cheap lace and showy ribbons, a hole in her stocking but a rose in her hair!

The country is a stern nurse, hard but just, making large demands on the child in her care, but giving great rewards. She tells the truth, demands obedience, and does better than she promises. Though she sends her child on long cold journeys, and makes him face the bitter winds of winter, she rewards him with ruddy health, high purpose and clear vision. Though she makes him work till every muscle aches she rewards him with a contented mind, an appetite that makes his life a joy, and though the midday sun may blaze on him with burning heat, at evening time comes shade, and in the night comes rosy slumber. And always there are the sun and the moon and the stars and the miracle of growing things.[54]

The imagery doubtless seemed both apt and powerful. It was rooted in an extended discussion in the farm press involving the terms "agriculture," "the country" and "the land." These words the press used interchangeably—especially when personifying them in order to capture their significance and mystical power. The predominant personification of each was that of mankind's nurse, a gentle governess and mentor, worthy and right-minded, ministering to the growth of the nursling, man. It was not quite the image of Eden or of the garden which so characterized the west in the promotional and immigration tracts of the late nineteenth century.[55]

The difference in the metaphors was subtle. In the promotional literature, the image was more a given state of affairs; in the agricultural press, it was more an object to be sought, an ideal state that was merely possible. The settlement period image was in a sense the sequel to the image of the garden after man had entered and failed to reap the bounty. The new symbol was partially the product of the outcry against man's apparent perversity. That is, it issued partly from the reformist mentality of virtually all agrarian editors. Time and again the editors and their staffs worried that westerners did not understand the full meaning of country life, that farmers were not achieving their potential, that improvements were languishing.

There were, indeed, many signs that despite its manifold advantages, country life was not as it should have been. Numerous articles complained about the drudgery, monotony, long hours and low wages of farm life, the lack of amenities, of labour-saving devices, of adequate school and church facilities. They regretted that the national policy served primarily the east and that agrarian unity undermined the west. Genius on the farm went unrecognized, and both rural and urban folk held the small town in contempt. Tilling the soil, some said, offered neither the social prominence nor the air of gentility enjoyed by the city's learned professions. There were many things wrong with rural life, and the agrarian press, bent on amelioration, depicted them.[56] Occasionally when the weight of criticism seemed to overpower the image of the faithful nurse, elements within the press questioned the role the press itself was playing. Thus, while fully cognizant of the difficulties of farm life, *The Nor'-West Farmer* once suggested that the agricultural journals themselves were contributing to the rural exodus "by always picturing the farmer as the victim of constant conspiracy."[57]

Significantly the litany of farm problems was not considered inconsistent with the country life ideology. The problems were part of what many called rural *degeneration*; the essential goodness of rural life was seldom doubted. The problem lay with man, the way he had let the fields go to seed and the offer of country godliness and abundance go by default. Thus a theme as powerful as man's backsliding was the promise of his redemption.

Of all the agencies of uplift which preached this text of redemption—from the university extension departments, to women's farm organizations, provincial and federal departments of agriculture, farm youth organizations, and the farm press—few did so as long, as dynamically and observably as the last. Most farm editors were highly informed boosters of organized agriculture and advanced country living. All had farm backgrounds and all were now operating from cities. Consistently their writing betrayed their discomfort in an alien environment, their longing for the fields and their own roots. Sometimes, as in the case of Charles W. Peterson, a founder and long-time editor of the *Review*, they had previous connections with government agriculture departments. As deputy commissioner of agriculture for the Territories, Peterson displayed the strong reformist impulse so characteristic of the early department staffs which sought in the absence of established patterns to launch the new society in the right direction.[58] Peterson's novel, *The Fruits of the Earth* (1928), understandably exhibited the same country life spirit which so animated the *Review*.

Several agrarian editors were formally tied to the farm movement, as in the case of Roderick McKenzie, early editor of the *Guide*, secretary of the paper's founding body, the Manitoba Grain Growers' Association, and later secretary of the Canadian Council of Agriculture.[59] McKenzie's successor, George Chipman, was linked with the movement through his father who had been a leader in every Nova Scotian farm organization for two decades.[60]

Often the staffs of the agrarian press had been professionally trained at Ontario Agricultural College (OAC), the great national propaganda mill of the country life ideology. One example was Frank S. Jacobs. After graduating from OAC in 1902, he became associate editor of *The Farmer's Advocate*, London. Two years later he took the same position with the *Advocate* of Winnipeg before becoming editor-in-chief in 1907. From 1909 until late 1915 he was editor of the *Review*, then was appointed professor of animal husbandry at Manitoba Agricultural College.[61] His transition into the College revealed the alliance of the colleges, extension divisions and farm press in generating the "proper" rural outlook and in ameliorating conditions so that land might do its work of nurturing man.

When one assesses the context which influenced such editors, the tone of alarm so notable in the farm press is more readily comprehensible. Reaching a crescendo in the war years and just after, this tone was a curious mix of runaway enthusiasm and impatience. The war played a great part in destroying old orders, in "spiritualizing" humanity, in raising the ideal of service and of universal improvement. All these factors generated expectations of constructive change in the west concerning railway rates, implement costs, wheat prices, consolidated schools, household conveniences, farm political representation, and the general quality of farm life. The more farm writers advanced these themes the more distant the realization of some seemed to be.

Another explanation of the alarmist tone lay in the heterogeneous nature of the population, in the pools of foreigners which so affected the prairie west. These pools interfered with the country life movement by hindering community effort and by resisting the lessons of enlightened country living, of new techniques in health and nutrition, and of better methods of animal breeding. The influx of immigrants worried many about the future of country life and the glum prospects of ever fashioning a regenerated English-speaking rural commonwealth.[62] In a period when purity of breeding was heavily advocated, farm papers pointed to the incidence of scrub, or inferior stock, among foreigners. One settler in the territories, dutifully improving his herd, complained bitterly to *The Nor'-West Farmer* of the Russians and Hungarians in his neighbourhood who kept "the very worst of scrubs" and allowed the bulls to run among his high class stock. "A good grade bull is not so bad," he told a concurring editor, "but these long-legged runts are hardly fit to eat, except by Indians."[63]

At the height of the settlement boom Reverend J.A. Clark of Calgary exhibited the reformers' impatience with immigrants. Wondering why progress came so slowly and why evils persisted, he concluded that people did not take time to understand the state of affairs in which they lived, much less to improve that state. "It is notorious that in new countries many unfortunate conditions always exist," he wrote. "There is usually much financial waste and extravagance and much moral looseness and open evil and one chief explanation for this is that the average immigrant is indifferent to the politics of his adopted country."[64]

A third explanation of the uneasy mood pointed to the meteoric rise and decline of the prairie west. In 1900 settlement had hardly begun, and by 1920 it had not only ended but the social and economic disintegration of the large dry belt regions of Saskatchewan and Alberta was already underway. And from that disaster, for thousands of settlers, the only escape would be outright abandonment. After 1916 some of the misgivings of farm editors, especially of C.W. Peterson of the *Review*, were closely related to the tragedy in the drylands. After the monumental renunciation of the land in the early and mid-twenties, the country life message was never again preached with the same persistence or authority.[65]

Given the preoccupation of the country press with the city, one must inevitably ask why the city was depicted so negatively. The most obvious reason seems to have been the genuine menace cities posed to the country, both economically and socially. They threatened to take over the services provided by small-town businesses. They conspired to reverse the early agricultural priorities of the west, and they swept away farmland in their expansion. Luring youth from the land, cities fractured the solidarity of the farm family. Living so apart from the work of the soil, city-dwellers became a class apart. Repeatedly farmers were told that they were the producers; cities, the consumers. Farmers were the exploited; city folk, the exploiters. In the dichotomizing of rural and urban existence, the derision of the latter and the exhaltation of the former were constantly embellished. Even the local boosterism, so intrinsic to the period, naturally pitted the little towns against the larger centres, and when there was no contest in the race for amenities the small-town mind still rationalized, and magnified the shortcomings of the city. In some rural quarters too, a fear of Catholic and especially Slavic immigration to the cities seems to have contributed to a lowering of the popular estimate of centres like Winnipeg. Finally, as farmer discontent mounted in the 1910s, eastern corporate interests, ensconced in eastern metropoles, were increasingly assailed. And the dens of iniquity, the cities, became more or less synonymous with the financial blackguards in them.

As for the significance of the commentary in the journals, consider first its uncertain effect on demography. Over the period in this study the rural portion of prairie population dropped from 75 percent in 1901 to 65 percent in 1911. Thereafter it leveled off at 64 percent in both 1916 and 1921 before a slip to 63.5 percent in 1926.[66] This stabilization suggests that those agencies, including the agrarian press, designed to keep the population on the land, may have helped to do just that. More important probably were the women's clubs, junior branches, various university extension measures and schools of agriculture—to say nothing of economic factors during the war. The press itself, however, likely did as much to move people *off* the land by constant reference to the farmers' plight. Its value lay less in its impact on demographic trends than in its revelation of popular attitudes and their relationship to national consciousness and social reform.

Regarding the former, there is an aspect already begging comment: that is, the way that American material was "mixed" indiscriminately with Canadian. I have tried to replicate as faithfully as possible the general manner in which this mixing occurred in the journals. The fact was that the country life movement in the United States was deemed to be very nearly identical to that in Canada. The core notion, or imperative, that people born on the land should stay on the land, and the supporting claims of not only the benefits of following the imperative but the consequences of ignoring it, were fundamentally the same in both countries. American examples abounded in the Canadian rural press, and not just to interest thousands of expatriate Americans. Virtually everyone interested *assumed* that the matter of country life transcended boundaries. Often this assumption was made explicit. When, for example, *The Nor'-West Farmer* printed extracts of Henry Wallace's address before the U.S. Conservation Congress in 1911, the speech, the paper said, "voices sentiments that are applicable to Canadian as well as American life."[67] American pronouncements regarding the iniquity of cities, the worth of country living, and the solutions to rural difficulties, were always viewed favourably. In these important matters, the sense that there was something distinctive about either nation's experience was never apparent.

A significant outcome was that this transnational ideology of country life seems to have been an important obstruction in the long enduring Canadian attempt to crystallize a national identity. Distinctiveness was just that—difference—and here there was none. The revelations of the western agrarian press in this regard were but a small part of the enormous Yankee impact on Canadian consciousness in the period. Contemporary immigration literature, for example, often sought expressly to inculcate the notion that, as one release said, American emigrants would find no difference in Canada and that, as another said, the developing prairie personality to the north would be closely akin to the midwestern composite in the south.[68] Even the American cinema, which grew important later in the period, was released in Canada partly on the assumption that the lives and interests of Uncle Sam were similar to those of Jack Canuck.[69] A problem arising for Canadians from this bombardment of what might be termed the consanguinity theme has been to delineate precisely the point at which exaggeration occurs. At times, as in the country life issue, the assumptions, hopes and fears of Canadians have indeed been little different from those of Americans. It is exactly the element of truth in the theme which Canadian nationalists have sometimes found so perplexing.

A second broad significance of the country life ideology was the way it related to so many reform movements of the period. The "purity" of country living was an important and underemphasized feature of the prohibition crusade since intemperance and dissolution were so intrinsic to the country view of the debilitating city and so incompatible with the alleged character attributes nurtured by the soil. The ideology of country living was fundamental to the entire agrarian revolt of the period, to the pure food and health drives, and to western homemakers' clubs and women's institutes sworn to enhance rural life. The ideology also touched "city beautiful" campaigns and school reform involving nature study, gardening and agricultural clubs. Without the ruling set of ideas about rural life, moreover, it is impossible to understand the motivating force behind virtually every single educational strategy designed in the era to elevate life on the farm. And it is impossible to understand fully the literature of the time, the work, for example, of Stead or Grove, whose characters were steeped in the rural tradition and contaminated by urban contacts.

Generally historians have not recognized the explanatory power of the country life ideology. In Grove's case, for example, a fuller acknowledgement of the context which surrounded his life as a Manitoba teacher would probably redirect attention from his European roots to the Canadian milieu, which obviously influenced him more than is generally believed. During Grove's tenure as a teacher and principal, Manitoba was at the forefront of the school gardening movement, boys' and girls' club work, and school and club fairs. School reformers throughout the department of education constantly preached the importance of fostering a genuine interest in country life and in relating the curriculum more to the fundamental agricultural reality of the land. Manitoba was the first western province to appoint a director of elementary agriculture and nature study in the schools. During this period the Manitoba Summer School for teachers was held at the Agricultural College. Enthused by the prospects of demonstrating the virtues of the work of the soil, a powerful outreach was launched from the college. Its president, J.B. Reynolds, another Ontario Agricultural College graduate and a future president of OAC, was one of the most insistent advocates of the country life ideology in Canada.

Grove was very much linked to this movement. Manitoba school reports showed the enormous effervescence in the very districts in which he taught.[70] He personally opposed mere book learning and he promoted manual training and first-hand observation of nature. The Stobie collection at the University of Manitoba is filled with reminiscences of his students which set him centrally into the indigenous context of the rural movement as a lover of country life, of nature and of school agriculture. Grove even judged at club fairs. He constructed mounted collections of insects, of weed seeds and of dried plants—typical pursuits of school reformers of the time.[71] He knew first hand the tragedy of youth leaving the farms, stories of which abounded not only in the big presses, but also in the local papers, like the *Gladstone Age* which he read. He knew what the *Canadian* city meant to so many farm folk. With these influences in mind, the need to redirect his motivation from an excessive preoccupation with his European background should be apparent.[72]

What influenced Grove impressed others too. When Anna M. Archibald, provincial secretary of the Alberta United Farm Women, urged the ladies to "keep high our ideals of a purified public administration, of a high type of rural life, economically, socially, educationally, and a general uplifting of humanity"—she was revealing part of the grip of the country life ideology on her mind and soul.[73] The truth was that many of an entire generation felt the same way.

The settlement period accentuated the values of frugality, hard work, industriousness, improvisation, cleanliness, forebearance and perseverance. These were very much the mores of a new life. In leaving the past and starting afresh, settlers in a sense had already pre-selected them, for they were the values, it was believed, by which persons of substance were forged. Homesteaders and their spokespersons hoped that the start in the new land would be free from moral contaminants which could divert their purpose and flag their energy. The period was one of promise; its thinkers recognized above all the need for restraint, thrift and patient enterprise while putting the land in shape and rendering it the endowment of the race. It was a time of self-sacrifice before the future could be made. In this milieu evil was defined as those forces which undermined the thesis that hard work produced self realization, goodness and earthly contentment. The epitome of evil was thus the city with its veneers and its laxity, its frivolity and its dissipation.

All this is not to argue that the values of the country life movement were actually new. Yet there was something unique about the way they were invested with a sense of legitimacy by the circumstances and demands of western settlement. And there was something unusual about the place so many contemporaries identified as the source of the Spirit. It was the singular fate of many during the settlement period of the Canadian west that the mystical power each era seeks so possessively was to be found in the land itself.

NOTES

I thank R.L. Schnell, N.M. Sheehan and John McNeill for their constructive comments on an earlier version of this paper.

1. *Census of the Prairie Provinces*, 1936, Vol. 1, p. xiii.
2. Alan F.J. Artibise, "The Urban West: The Evolution of Prairie Towns and Cities to 1930," *Prairie Forum*, 4 (1979): 240. *Census of the Prairie Provinces*, 1936, pp. 4, 359, 832.
3. David C. Jones, "The Zeitgeist of Western Settlement: Education and the Myth of the Land," in J. Donald Wilson and David C. Jones, eds., *Schooling and Society in Twentieth Century British Columbia* (Calgary: Detselig, 1980), pp. 71-89. See also Henry Nash Smith, *Virgin Land: The American West as Symbol and Myth* (Cambridge: Harvard University Press, 1950); Patricia Anne Roome, "Images of the West: Social Themes in Prairie Literature: 1898-1930," M.A. Thesis, The University of Calgary, 1976; Cole Harris, "The Myth of the Land in Canadian Nationalism," in Peter Russell, ed., *Nationalism in Canada* (Toronto: McGraw-Hill, 1966), pp. 27-36; George Altmeyer, "Three Ideas of Nature in Canada, 1893-1914," *Journal of Canadian Studies*, 11 (Aug. 1976): 21-36; Gerald Friesen, "Studies in the Development of Western Canadian Regional Consciousness, 1870-1925," Ph.D. Thesis, University of Toronto, 1973; Patrick A. Dunae, " 'Making Good': The Canadian West in British Boys' Literature, 1890-1914," *Prairie Forum*, 4 (Fall 1979): 165-81; Doug Owram, *Promise of Eden* (Toronto: University of Toronto Press, 1980).
4. *The Canadian Newspaper Directory 1921* (Montreal: A. McKim, 1922), pp. 188, 191, 238.
5. *Farm and Ranch Review*, Feb. 1905, hereafter *Review*.
6. W.J. Way, letter to editor, "Keep the Boys on the Farm," *Farmer's Advocate*, Dec. 5, 1903, p. 1163, hereafter *Advocate*.
7. Filler, *Review*, May 20, 1920, p. 48.
8. Editorial, "The Care for Discontent," *Advocate*, May 12, 1920, p. 827.
9. Way, "Keep the Boys," *Advocate*, Dec. 5, 1903, p. 1163; Rusticus, "Agricultural Knowledge," *Advocate*, May 20, 1903, p. 501. Rusticus is unidentified, but likely was part of the *Advocate's* editorial staff.

10. "Farmers are Nation's Backbone," *Grain Growers' Guide*, Sept. 22, 1909, p. 6, hereafter *Guide*. See also "Back to the Farm," *Review*, Apr. 1908, p. 4 and "Pres. Roosevelt's Country," *Review*, Mar. 1909, pp. 103-04.

11. Editorial, "Agriculture the True Source of Our Wealth," *Review*, May 1908, p. 7.

12. Max McD., "Good Rural Homes Keep Boys on the Farm," *Advocate*, Dec. 10, 1913, p. 1809. Max McD. is unidentified.

13. *Guide*, Dec. 1, 1915, p. 43, stanza 3. Leland is not identified but may have been an amateur poet.

14. BSA, "The Story of a Farm Boy," Part 4, *Advocate*, Dec. 25, 1918, p. 2063. BSA is not otherwise identified.

15. Way, "Keep the Boys," *Advocate*, Dec. 5, 1903, p. 1163.

16. "Country Girl's Ideas," *Guide*, May 7, 1913, p. 18. The regular country girl column was aimed at adolescent and preadolescent farm girls. The author was not identified by name.

17. Bert Huffman, "The Creed of the Open Plain," *Review*, Apr. 5, 1910, p. 239.

18. Editorial (Geo. Batho), "The Value of Environment," *The Nor'-West Farmer*, Jan. 20, 1915, p. 48, hereafter *NWF*.

19. " 'Best Things' in Country Life," *Advocate*, Nov. 30, 1904, p. 1728.

20. "Play the Cure of Crime," *Review*, Aug. 5, 1911, p. 510.

21. " 'Best Things' in Country Life," *Advocate*, Nov. 30, 1904, p. 1728.

22. "What Does Country Life Mean," *Advocate*, May 21, 1919, p. 877.

23. J.A. Clark, "Nature and Revelation," *Review*, May 5, 1910, p. 313.

24. See Clark, "The Country Church: The Gospel of the Out-of-Doors," *Review*, Sept. 5, 1916, p. 673; Clark, "The Spiritual Significance of The Earth and Her Seasons," *Review*, Mar. 20, 1911, p. 190.

25. S.G. Bland, "The Deeper Life—the Divinely Ordained Occupation of Farming," *Guide*, Nov. 20, 1918, p. 39.

26. Editorial, "Farm Life the Ideal," *Advocate*, June 14, 1911, p. 841.

27. *Ibid*.

28. Ginger, The Weakness of City-Bred Character," *NWF*, Jan. 5, 1916, p. 12. Ginger is unidentified but was likely part of *The Nor'-West Farmer* editorial staff.

29. Editorial, "Exhibition Versus Stampede," *Advocate*, Mar. 6, 1913, pp. 330-331.

30. Editorial, no title, *Guide*, Aug. 20, 1913, p. 6.

31. N.a. letter to editor, *Guide*, Sept. 17, 1913, p. 10.

32. "Back to the Farm," *Review*, Apr. 1908, p. 4.

33. Editorial (Geo. Chipman), "Land Speculation," *Guide*, Mar. 7, 1913, p. 6.

34. W.D. Albright, letter to editor, "The Root of Real Estate Speculation," *Advocate*, May 14, 1919, p. 842.

35. "The Countrywoman," *Guide*, June 14, 1922, p. 24, quoting an issue of the *Ladies' Home Journal* in 1919.

36. "Country vs. City Boys," *Guide*, Oct. 20, 1909, p. 23.

37. Editorial, "The Boy that Leaves," *Advocate*, May 6, 1914, p. 625.

38. BSA, "The Story of a Farm Boy," Part 2, *Advocate*, Dec. 4, 1918, p. 1888.

39. Editorial, "Farm Girls and Farm Houses," *Advocate*, Nov. 3, 1920, p. 1761.

40. W.W. Gamble, "The Girl and the Farm," *Advocate*, Jan. 12, 1916, p. 42. Gamble is unidentified but appears to have been a western Canadian.

41. J.S. Woodsworth, "Some Problems of City Life," Part 1, *Guide*, Apr. 8, 1914, p. 7. Woodsworth also wrote a series of sermons for the *Guide* later during the war.

42. Woodsworth, "Some City Problems," Part II, *Guide*, Apr. 22, 1914, p. 7.

43. Woodsworth, "Some City Problems," Part III, *Guide*, May 6, 1914, pp. 7, 27.

44. T.L. Masson, "Our National Products," *Guide*, Aug. 7, 1909, p. 10. Masson is not identified.

45. Edgar L. Vincent, "The Boy Industry on the Farm," *Advocate*, Feb. 3, 1915, p. 118. Vincent, who contributed fairly often to the *Advocate*, was not otherwise identified, though he was very likely Canadian.

46. Vincent, "In with the Right Crowd," *Advocate*, June 9, 1915, p. 694.

47. "Margaret's Special Message," *Guide*, Sept. 20, 1911, p. 26, quoting the Chicago Vice Commission for the protection of young girls.

48. Margaret Freeston, "The Country Girls' Chances in the City," *NWF*, Dec. 6, 1920, p. 657. Freeston may have been "The Country Girl" in the rival *Guide*, or perhaps the "Margaret" in charge of the *Guide's* "Sunshine Guild," aimed at farm children. She appears to have lived in Winnipeg.

49. "Advice to Country Girls," *Review*, July 5, 1913, p. 642.

50. H.S. letter to editor, "The Future of the Country Boy," *Advocate*, Sept. 22, 1920, p. 1546.

51. "Back to the Land," *NWF*, Dec. 20, 1911, p. 1511.

52. Masson, "Our National Products," *Guide*, Aug. 7, 1909, p. 10.

53. "The Country Girl," *Guide*, May 7, 1919, p. 18.

54. Nellie L. McClung, "Why Boys and Girls Leave the Farm," *NWF*, Sept. 5, 1913, p. 1105, from an address to the annual convention of Manitoba Home Economics Societies. The quotation originally appeared in a single paragraph and is divided here for emphasis.

55. See Owram, *Promise of Eden,* ch. 7.

56. For a sampling, see n.a., "Why We Left the Farm," *Guide*, May 7, 1913, pp. 7, 18, 19; BSA, "The Story of a Farm Boy: Part I—Why the Boy Left the Farm," *Advocate*, Nov. 20, 1918, pp. 1815, 1838; Nellie McClung, "Why Boys and Girls Leave the Farm," *NWF*, Sept. 5, 1913, p. 1106.

57. Editorial, "Farmers and Rural Depopulation," *NWF*, Nov. 20, 1914, p. 1138.

58. See for example, North West Territories, *Annual Report* Agriculture, 1902, p. 123.

59. Hopkins Moorhouse, *Deep Furrows* (Toronto: George J. McLeod, 1918), pp. 134-36, 295.

60. *Ibid.*, p. 163.

61. "Prof. F.S. Jacobs," *Advocate*, Dec. 15, 1915, p. 1554.

62. For an elaboration of this theme and of the relationship between the country life enthusiasts and the forces of unilingualism see Jones, "Better Schools Day in Saskatchewan and the Perils of Educational Reform," in *Schools, Reform and Society in Western Canada*, eds. R.L. Schnell, D.C. Jones and N.M. Sheehan, *Journal of Educational Thought*, 14 (Aug. 1980): 125-37.

63. "Scrub Immigrants and Their Cattle," *NWF*, July 5, 1899, p. 467.

64. J.A. Clark, "The Emigrant and his Political Conflicts," *Review*, Jan. 6, 1913, p. 27.

65. See Jones, "Schools and Social Disintegration in the Alberta Dry Belt of the Twenties," *Prairie Forum*, 3 (1978): 1-19; Jones, "We'll All Be Buried Down Here In This Dry Belt . . . ," *Saskatchewan History* (Spring 1982): 41-54. This disaster has unaccountably been virtually ignored by historians to date.

66. *Census of the Prairie Provinces*, 1936, Vol. 1, pp. xiii, Liii.

67. Wallace, "Back to the Land," *NWF*, Dec. 20, 1911, p. 1411. See also the Canadian women wishing to emulate town beautification conducted by an American society in "Cleaning up the Small Town," *Review*, May 5, 1911, p. 294.

68. Western Canadian Immigration Association, *What Famous Correspondents Say About Western Canada* (Minneapolis: 1905c), n.p.; Canada, *Canada, the Granary of the World* (Ottawa: Department of the Interior, 1903), n.p.

69. See D.C. Jones, "Movies, Censorship and Progressive Education: The Prairies Between the Wars," paper presented to the Second Conference of the Canadian History of Education Association, Toronto, Feb. 1982.

70. See for example Manitoba, *Annual Report* Education 1917, p. 250.

71. See interviews conducted by Margaret Stobie for her book *Frederick Phillip Grove* (New York: Twayne, 1973), Stobie Collection, University of Manitoba Archives.

72. This preoccupation is present for obvious reasons in Douglas Spettigue's *Frederick Phillip Grove: The European Years* (Ottawa: Oberon, 1973). See also Stobie, *Frederick Phillip Grove*.

73. Anna M. Archibald, "A Cure for the Blues," *Review*, Jan. 5, 1920, p. 34.

IAN MACPHERSON and

JOHN HERD THOMPSON

23 The Business of Agriculture
*Prairie Farmers and the Adoption of
"Business Methods," 1880-1950*

In the introduction to his massive survey *Northern Enterprise*, Michael Bliss
apologizes for leaving out what was Canada's most widespread business
activity: agriculture. Need Professor Bliss have excused himself? Were farm
families "entrepreneurs" managing "enterprises" which can be studied within
the paradigms of the business historian? An advertisement inside the front
cover of the February, 1988, *Country Guide* suggests an ambiguous answer.
"How can you put a price on a way of life?," asks the Century 21 real estate
chain as it urges farmers to list with their agents:

> When you buy or sell a farm . . . , you're not just talking about the mone-
> tary value of the land, buildings and machinery. You're talking about
> values with a deeper meaning—the feel of the earth between your fingers
> and the warm sun on your face, the tiny creek that swells to a pond in
> the spring and the barn that looks like it should fall down, but never does.[1]

This idea that farming is a "way of life" which perpetuates a value system
superior to the vulgar dollars and cents ethic of urban business runs back
through W.R. Motherwell, Egerton Ryerson, William Lyon Mackenzie,
Thomas Jefferson, and the eighteenth-century *philosophes*. "Rural life,"
wrote W.C. Good in 1919:

> is the permanent source from which all life springs . . . . No one who
> does not know intimately the possibilities of farm life can appreciate the
> tremendous advantages which agriculture possesses over other occupa-
> tions in the education of children and in the development of some of the
> most important virtues . . . .[2]

American historians have not been kind to this "agrarian myth." In *The*

Age of Reform Richard Hofstadter lampooned the notion of the virtuous self-sufficient yeoman and his family, and pointed instead to the "commercial realities" of the countryside as evidence that farming was a business like any other. "Commercial goals made their way among [America's] agricultural classes" just as they did among urbanites, Hofstadter maintained, and rural America was populated with individualistic agrarian capitalists "whose real attachment was not to land but to land values."[3] William N. Parker went so far as to argue that "an agro-business culture" dominated even colonial America:

> Rural families [showed a] driving zeal in joining the American pursuit of wealth . . . . That farming should be a business, an undertaking to make a financial profit, was an idea that only gradually took root in Europe. In America it had been present from the beginning.[4]

James Henretta best represents those who have challenged this image of the business farmer. In his oft-cited "Families and Farms: *Mentalité* in Pre-Industrial America," Henretta rejects this "entrepreneurial interpretation" which sees in the farmer "the embryo John D. Rockefeller." Instead, he describes a community-oriented rural society in which "decisions were not made for narrowly economic or strictly utilitarian reasons," but to fulfil "a much wider range of social and cultural goals." Family security and a decent standard of living were more important than any expectation of profit.[5]

The two schools confront each other most violently in their interpretations of agrarian insurgency. Those who accept the farmer-as-entrepreneur model see rural protest as the outcry of cranky small businessmen unable to compete, and farm organizations as industrial lobby groups. Those who understand farming as "a way of life" (David P. Szatmary, Robert McMath and Lawrence Goodwyn are the best examples) explain the same protest as resistance by rural communities to the advance of corporate industrial capitalism.[6]

Historians of rural Canada have given little attention to this debate. Their almost-universal[7] assumption has been that the farmer was a rural businessman. Canada's pre-eminent historian of agriculture has heaped scorn on "the myth of the self-sufficient Canadian pioneer . . . . The typical frontier farmer could never be regarded as indifferent to conditions in the market place", wrote V.C. Fowke, because he produced crops for market, bought, sold, and borrowed.[8] That the prairie farmer was a businessman is considered so self-evident as to need no explanation. The opening of the Prairie West to extensive agricultural development coincided with the advent of commercial agriculture in the longer-settled regions of Canada. There has been as yet no Canadian equivalent to Clarence Danhof's *Change in Agriculture*,[9] but the contours of this "great transformation" (the phrase is appropriated from Karl Polanyi) were essentially the same in British North America as in the Northern United States: a tendency towards specialization in one or two agricultural activities, an increase in the amount of hired labour, the adoption of machinery like the horse-drawn hay rake and mowers or mechanical reapers.

Prairie settlement took place amidst and because of these changes. But to see all prairie farms as purely commercial enterprises, and to explain the behaviour of farm families in the calculus of the market is to lose sight of many of the farm families who populated prairie rural history. Although most of the newcomers to Manitoba, Saskatchewan, and Alberta intended to become commercial farmers, the rural society they fashioned between the 1880s and the 1920s became another sort of "traditional" society, made up of some two thousand isolated, relatively self-sufficient farm communities spread across the Prairie West. All of these communities within the region shared the settlement experience, similar economic interests, and the rituals of similar local associational activities, even though ethnicity, religion, time of settlement, and the differing economic opportunities offered by local environments meant that prairie rural society was not homogeneous.

At one end of a broad agricultural continuum were communities of peasants who can be interpreted in terms of A.V. Chayanov's *Theory of Peasant Economy*;[10] at the other were a handful of multi-section capitalist farms best analyzed in the language of Alfred Chandler. Although no farm family depended entirely on its own efforts to meet all its needs, there continued until the 1940s to be a "pioneer fringe" of farm families which practiced near self-sufficient agriculture.[11] Like the Ukrainian settlers of southeastern Manitoba described in the work of John C. Lehr,[12] they produced as much of what they consumed as was possible and participated in local markets, in kind as well as for cash, to provide the rest. In the middle of the continuum were those farmers who attempted to achieve the much-discussed concept of "diversified farming" through mixed farms;[13] as portrayed in Donald Loveridge's study of the Rock Lake district of Manitoba, they were commercially-oriented but strategically flexible.[14] Closer to the other end of the continuum was "the more aggressive frontier of the grain farmer,"[15] which has been characterized so well in Paul Voisey's study of Vulcan, Alberta.[16] Grain growing meant participating in a complex marketing and delivery system involving large railway and shipping companies, and the apparently mysterious operations of grain exchanges. But even the families among this group satisfied many of their consumption needs from their own farms. There was only a tiny number of mega-farmers like W.J. Blair of Provost, Alberta, who operated his seven sections with a foreman, hired labour, and a manager to oversee operations, which could be categorized as entirely commercial enterprises.[17]

This variegated society expanded until the drought and depression of the 1930s, and then during the 1940s entered what John Shover has termed for the United States "the great disjuncture," the exodus from the farm which shattered traditional patterns of rural life.[18] Shover's concept of a "great disjuncture" has relevance for the prairie West, but there were important differences in the process of modernization as it took place in the Prairie West and in the parts of the American Plains region most like it. Canadian prairie farmers, through their own community institutions, developed their own strategies for influencing the pace and mitigating the effects of modernization.

Between the first period of extensive settlement in the 1880s and the "great disjuncture" which followed World War II, one such strategy was the adoption of "business methods." The combination of scientific agriculture, technological changes in tillage, harvesting, and transportation equipment, and the enormous increases in capital investment that they required were part of the process which turned farming communities into individualistic, entrepreneurial societies in many ways indistinguishable from mainstream North American urban culture. That was not the end the advocates of a more "businesslike" agriculture envisaged, however. They did not see farming as a way of life and farming as a business as antithetical, as the Hofstadter-Henretta debate would have it: instead the latter was seen by many farmers as the only means by which the former could be preserved; indeed for generations farm families had made hard-headed economic decisions that had profoundly affected rural life.

By the early twentieth century, however, the application of business methods to family farming had become a panacea. The way to maintain "*Better Living*" on the farm, as W.C. Good explained it, was through:

> *Better Business*, which consists of good farm management so far as the individual farmer is concerned, and . . . [the] application of modern commercial methods to the business side of the farming industry . . . . Every farmer should aim to utilize as much as he can all technical information pertaining to the business of farming. He should study soils, plant life, live stock and all the other mutifarious things with which the farmer has to deal. He should keep in touch with the best farm practice, and he should inform himself of the latest results of scientific investigation.[19]

This paper explores the ways in which many farm families attempted to follow such advice. It seeks to understand the limits within which farm people had to work, and to explore the complexity of the decisions they had to make. Some of these choices were based on sophisticated analysis; others were made from tradition and habit, and their implications understood only in retrospect. The complexity of their business can be seen by considering the decisions they had to make in utilizing their basic resource, the soil; in choosing and purchasing equipment; in selecting sources of credit; and in the development of their farmer-owned cooperative marketing businesses.

The limited evidence which is available on individual farmers' decision-making suggests that virtually no prairie farm was managed according to a systematic business strategy. Every major prairie repository—the three Provincial Archives and those of the Glenbow-Alberta Institute—holds several dozen farm familys' account books. On examination, however, almost none of these could be considered serious business records. The introduction of income tax in 1917 theoretically required more careful accounting, but the harvest of documentation remains disappointingly meagre. When financial records do exist, the historian must ask how typical even these limited sources are of the elusive "ordinary" farm families' activities.[20]

But the ready adoption of new techniques and technologies, and the frequent discussions of production costs in farm journals and the ubiquitous manuals of farming advice suggests that farmers felt considerable concern about the efficiency of their farm operations. It is important that we understand, however, that the drive for efficiency was not seen as inimicable to rural culture and rural values established in pre-commercial communities. For all but the handful of large-scale agro-businessmen, the goal which guided these decisions throughout was not unalloyed profit but the improvement of rural family life. What prairie farmers hoped to create were profitable farm enterprises for themselves and for their children. Rural people did not adopt "business methods" to become mere imitations of urban business culture; rather they searched for the best way to guarantee an economic return for their work—a return which would build rural communities and which could assure the survival of their families upon the land.[21]

I

The basic element of the farm business was land—the common currency of Prairie settlement. Between 1891 and 1941 over 100 million acres were opened for development, an irresistible invitation to a speculative binge. The manipulations of the corporate speculators—the C.P.R., the Hudson's Bay Company, and the smaller land companies—are part of the folk wisdom of the region. Less frequently acknowledged are the speculative instincts of Prairie farm people themselves. The farm families who moved west at the end of the nineteenth century could be remarkably unemotional and detached in assessing the values of their land, and many were willing to sell and move on if prospects seemed better elsewhere. The textbook model of prairie settlement is the homestead secured by a "ten dollar bet" with the Dominion government, but at least 40% of the half million who claimed public land never "proved up" by meeting the minimal obligations of residency and cultivation necessary to gain title. More land was in fact purchased than homesteaded, and the C.P.R.'s foreclosure rate of 33% of total sales suggests that there was considerable movement among farm people, during both good and bad times.[22]

This continual movement has sometimes been used to portray Prairie farmers as aggressive speculators rather than founders of rural dynasties. It is important to emphasize that one of the strongest motivations for migrants to move to the region was to find homes nearby for their children. When the C.P.R. questioned 342 farm women in 1885, the most frequent explanation offered of their move westward was summarized by one woman as having "the pleasure of seeing my sons settled on farms and doing well."[23] In 1898 Manitoba's "wheat king", A.J. Cotton, left a successful farm in southern Manitoba and moved north to the Swan River Valley "to provide contiguous farms for his sons."[24]

The dilemma of land scarcity which appeared after 1920 was created in part by the fact that there were fewer new districts available, in part by the pressure to expand farm size to adopt new technologies and in part by damage to soil caused by cultivation. Only the last of these could be addressed by farmers' individual and collective action. The most obvious area in which soil was abused was the Palliser triangle, the dry belt of southeastern Alberta and southern Saskatchewan, where, in many districts, grain growing should never have been attempted.[25] But even areas with adequate moisture confronted serious problems as early as the 1920s. Southwestern Manitoba, once called "The Garden of the West," had been so overworked that humus had been depleted, weeds had become an extensive problem, and farmers were moving out. Thus it was that in 1924 a few farmers near Deloraine began to meet together to see what they could do to reclaim their soils. The "District Builders Association" they formed was one of many similar organizations established in the three provinces during the decade, as farmers began to study their soils more closely, using information and assistance from the Departments of Agriculture and the universities.[26] The interest in agricultural improvement through a more 'scientific' approach to the soil demonstrated the region-wide determination to pursue any new approach that might reduce costs or increase production, but it also demonstrated the understanding that stable farms depended upon careful husbandry of their most fundamental resource, the land itself.

Despite the impression of uniformity created by the term "prairie provinces," the prairie West possesses a bewildering diversity of soil types. Learning to farm them came as the result of a long-time partnership between farmers and soil scientists. In the early 1920s Alberta and Saskatchewan began rudimentary surveys to classify soil textures; by 1940 the three provincial Departments of Agriculture shared a common terminology and a coordinated approach with their federal counterpart and were united through the National Soil Survey Committee in a comprehensive survey of the region's soil resources. The information which resulted enabled farmers to use their soils more effectively; it also revealed how poorly prairie soils had been treated since the beginning of the settlement period.[27]

As the droughts of the 1930s made problems with land more evident, farmers adopted new strategies to protect their declining resource base. Summerfallowing to conserve moisture was practiced more extensively,[28] but the traditional dry farming techniques which had contributed to wind erosion gave way to experiments with strip farming and later to 'trash farming' (leaving a 'trash' cover on summerfallow instead of cultivating it.) New techniques went hand in hand with new tools: the Noble blade cultivator and the discer replaced the venerable moldboard plough.[29] The work of the Prairie Farm Rehabilitation Administration in rehabilitating the dry belt has been appropriately lauded, but most of these changes were initiated by rural people themselves. As Thomas Isern and Paul Voisey have independently demonstrated, "folk technology was a powerful force in agricultural practice"; farmers themselves "actually developed most of the new techniques to control soil drifting . . . ."[30]

Attempts to use the soil resources more effectively were evidence of a more general willingness to employ 'scientific' methods. In the late 1930s individual farmers began to follow the lead of municipalities in using sodium chlorate to control weeds. "Chemurgy," as the application of chemistry to agriculture came to be called, expanded rapidly. Sinox was imported from the United States and followed by 2,4-D in 1945. By 1949, this latter herbicide was spread over 20 million acres of grain—more than half the prairie crop—and 4 million acres of pasture.[31] In this same period commercial fertilizers made their appearance. Between 1929 and 1931, the Canadian Pacific Railway's Cominco subsidiary provided superphosphate fertilizer to the Manitoba Department of Agriculture to conduct trials on individual farms in grain-growing districts of southwestern Manitoba. The tests demonstrated yield increases of up to 30 percent, and by the early 1940s, drilling in phosphate pellets while seeding grain became such a routine practice that fertilizer had to be placed under wartime controls.[32] Initially application rates and costs were relatively low and returns relatively high. But unlike changes in tillage, over which farmers had a considerable degree of control, fertilizers and herbicides required constant cash outlays. They also created a sort of "chemical dependence," as farmers perceived no alternatives to their use.

By 1950, then, prairie farmers no longer perceived their soil as inexhaustible. Those who were still in "business" had reconsidered their relationship to their most fundamental resource. Even more than in the past, managing the farm business was now in part "scientific", and, like other businesspeople, the farmer had to balance the cost of change against potential income, with failure the price of miscalculation.

II

New crops, better care of the soil, and the application of fertilizers and herbicides were innovations which made the farm enterprise more efficient— at least in the short term—by increasing its output. A second approach to more businesslike farming was the employment of cost-reducing technology, the substitution of machinery for human and animal muscle. The large-scale opening of the prairies to commercial agriculture was made possible by improved grain harvesting technology: the self-binding reaper, called simply a 'binder', took the place of the cradle in cutting grain, and the threshing machine, powered by a steam engine, replaced the flail and the horse-powered sweep.[33] In the Red River settlement, "implements and instruments of various kinds . . . [had been] handed round from one to the other amongst the neighbours as if they were common property."[34] In the post-1880 west, the farmer's goal was to own individually as much of his equipment as possible, in particular his binder. As one homesteader remembered it, 'time was the great deciding factor' in a region where frost and hail threatened every crop; "very often when we needed these new implements, we needed them in a hurry."[35] Buying them, however, was an investment decision fraught with peril. Contemporary accounts describe failures brought on because a farmer succumbed to "the persuasive powers of the local machinery agent."[36] A Saskatchewan Commission which investigated the farm machinery industry in 1915 reported that "companies sold machinery to farmers (often homesteaders) [note the distinction] who were not of the experience or business ability necessary to make a success of its operation . . . . When he failed to pay they sold him out."[37]

Sharing equipment, particularly harvesting machinery, provided a means to avoid the capital expense and the dangers of foreclosure. "During the days of early settlement in every part of Western Canada, the co-operative use of farm machinery was as essential to success as possession of suitable seed," noted a Dominion agriculturalist in 1942. This took place not only in ethnic bloc settlements and within extended families, but was sufficiently common that "no comment is necessary on this as everyone is familiar with first hand examples."[38]

Because steam engines were too heavy, cumbersome, and expensive to be used for field work,[39] draught animals were the basic source of power for tillage and transportation before the application of the internal combustion engine. The persistance of the horse after the development of the gasoline tractor in the prairie West (not until 1946 did one-half of prairie farms own tractors) frustrated experts whose tests showed that tractors outperformed horses, and has led some historians to conclude that prairie farmers were unable to recognize that "the new methods were more efficient than the old.[40] But the farmers' caution demonstrated their understanding that resisting technological change could make as much sense as adopting it. Buying a tractor was a complicated investment decision which demanded additional capital outlays for tractor-drawn machinery and a truck to replace the horse-drawn wagon. Interest charges on loans to buy these things did not stop when crops were thin, and tractors could not be fueled with farm-grown oats.[41] A letter in *The Western Producer* in 1928 summed up the case against the tractor and urged farmers not:

to sacrifice our own means of power and buy our power from machine companies . . . . I remember how the first tractor in our district made its owner quit farming, and could name dozens of cases where farmers bought tractors to get rich quick and lost both farm and tractor.[42]

As the pace of technological change increased with the introduction of the combine, the crucial importance of each decision increased along with it. Making farming a modern business dictated individual expenditures on more modern machinery and a reduction in co-operative use of implements. Thus, in 1927, Professor William Allen commented—reflecting the coming conventional wisdom—that when machinery was shared, "family contracts and agreements between neighbors are not usually based on sound business principles."[43] Indeed, so strong was the drive toward technological self-sufficiency on each farm that in 1930 an agricultural engineer from the Swift Current area reported that the "swing from the interdependency of the early days . . . [had] rapidly reach[ed] the point [of] going beyond reason in many districts." After a twenty-year survey of machinery use, he concluded that:

practically every farm is from 50 to 200 percent overequipped . . . . Every farmer . . . purchase[s] whatever piece of equipment he considers suited to his own needs, but that very independence of thought and action has too frequently resulted in a major investment which later proved to be disastrous because of its misapplication.

The "disaster" was "serious difficulties of farm credit . . . [which] frequently resulted in hardship to many innocent parties"—an indirect description of farm failure.[44]

III

There has been surprisingly little study of how prairie farm people financed their operations. Farm families used a wide variety of sources of credit: banks, insurance companies, trust companies, local merchants, private foreign investors and relatives were all potential creditors. Farmers complained about credit, regardless of its source: loans smaller than requested, high interest rates, short loan periods and unfair collection and foreclosure techniques were typical themes.[45] These very real problems made prairie farm people advocates of cheap money, and help explain why co-operative forms of credit and government-sponsored rural credit schemes became so popular in the region.

Attempts to expand to take advantage of grain prices inflated by the Great War sharply increased farm indebtedness in 1915 and 1916. In 1917 prairie provincial governments responded to the credit crisis by creating farm loan boards as alternate lending sources. With limited capital provided to them, however, the boards made little difference to the hardest-pressed debtors, and were unable to cope with major problems like those of the dry belt.[46] Despite the efforts of farm organizations to change things, credit remained a function of the market place, and the market place was neither generous nor understanding.

Making the right decision about borrowing was as much good luck as good management, but gaining access to credit demanded the adoption of rudimentary business procedures among farmers. When the agrarian press offered advice on applying for a loan, they stressed the necessity of making a good business case, which required records of expenses and revenues, understanding the true "labour income" from their efforts, and maintaining a reasonable equity in their farms.[47] There is other evidence of the dissemination of a business approach. A book of advice to prairie farmers published in 1920 was entitled *The Farmers' Manual, Legal Advisor and Veterinary Guide*; a successor ten years later was entitled *Farm Management*.[48] During that same decade, the three Departments of Agriculture, the university extension departments, and private educational institutions, most of them in the United States, all began to offer courses in farm management. The University of Saskatchewan's College of Agriculture, for example, created a Department of Farm Management under the direction of Professor William Allen. But this new business science was linked with older values before it was presented to farmers. In *The Farm Business in Saskatchewan* Allen explained that:

> The real success of the farmer cannot be measured solely by financial returns for there are many satisfactions other than financial ones . . . . The successful farm is the basis of the success of the rural community . . . . Where there are many successful farmers, the contributions made to community life will be materially greater than where farming is generally unrenumerative. It is to the interest of all to build up agriculture on a profitable and permanent basis.[49]

IV

One of the variables over which farm people had considerable control was the nature and amount of work that went into their enterprise. The decisions they had to make about labour and controlling labour costs were, however, among the most difficult and—because they involved family members—the most agonizing. During the settlement phase of any district almost all labour came from within the family unit, and families who remained near the self-sufficiency end of the agricultural continuum continued to rely heavily on family workers. The ubiquity of binders and steam threshers did not at first reduce the need for labour; farmers who grew commercial quantities of grain needed hired labour at harvest-time, and employed other local people "working out" or excursionists from central and Atlantic Canada. As the combine replaced the threshing machine, a process which took place gradually from the mid-twenties into the 1950s, there was a precipitous decline in the demand for labour; two people could do the work that a gang of twenty had done at the beginning of the century. The move toward mechanized commercial agriculture, had an effect on both labour needs and labour supply. Not only were fewer hands necessary to produce a crop; at the same time increasing scarcity of land and the increased costs of starting a farm imposed by mechanization discouraged those young men who had at one time believed they might work their way up the "agricultural ladder" from hired man to operator. Between the early settlement period and the 1930s, in the words of Cecilia Danysk, the prairie farmworker saw his place in society transformed from that of "apprentice farmer" to "agricultural proletarian."[50] Young prairie people, like their contemporaries in the older rural areas to the East, looked outside agriculture for their opportunities.

The revolution in the farm workplace wrought by the combine was obvious, but no less profound for being more subtle were the changes which took place in women's work. In the settlement phase there was a strong, mutual and hard-headed dependency between husbands and wives, as "men and women worked together to meet and solve the . . . challenges posed by wilderness living."[51] The closer a family was to self-sufficiency (or the farther it was from a commercial farm enterprise) the more important was the farm wife's role in the production process. When a garden was critical to the settlers' food supply, hens provided meat and eggs for home consumption and a small cash income and a dairy cow did the same, women's traditional tasks had more importance than they did on a specialized grain farm.[52] A Manitoba farm wife wrote about the importance of her activities to the family's livelihood in 1885: "they are about the most profitable thing we have and thrive very well."[53] Only as a farm became more specialized, more committed to commercial agriculture, did some women gain enough time to embrace the ideology of domesticity which has been called "the cult of true womanhood." Only then did some women carve out separate spheres within the family, in social institutions, and in the great causes like suffrage and prohibition.

As grain farms became more commercialized the role of women in the direct production activities tended to decline, at least on more successful farms. Judging from the agrarian press, however, they assumed a greater role in maintaining accounts and in the basic off-farm but initially important rural issues of education, health and social services. In the egg and poultry business, women played crucial roles in the development of local marketing organizations and in the improvement of product; as these industries became more established, more renumerative and more like full-time

jobs, positions within them tended—as in the case of the dairy industry—
to be taken over by men. All of these tendencies, however, were abruptly
negated in difficult times and were far less common on poor farms; when
profits were low, women's work extended more frequently and for longer
periods out into the fields.

Similarly, the work of children could be a necessity. In the earlier days
of settlement and before the widespread use of the combine, the labour of
children between the ages of eight and sixteen was a valuable commodity.
Thus families were, on average, large; schooling was structured (and often
barely tolerated) in the periods of lull between planting and harvesting; children undertook chores at an early age; and the participation rate in secondary education was low. As prosperity and the new technology appeared,
the labour of children was less crucial, and large families faced difficult decisions as farms grew larger and labour needs decreased: the harsh truth was
that many families could not support all their children on their farms as they
grew older, and a difficult choice had usually to be made. A.J. Cotton's dream
of watching his children mature on contiguous farms was an illusion for most
prairie farm families in this century.

Inevitably, therefore, farm people were forced to change their view of work.
Instead of being part of an open-ended commitment to a multi-faceted family
endeavor, it became steadily—as indeed it had been becoming since the eighteenth century—a question of cost-benefit analysis. Professors, "experts," and
journalistic advocates of "business farming" urged the farmer to measure his
labour income, "what [he] received in the year from his farm in return for his
labour and management," and advised him to be ruthless in determining that
"point in the cultivation of a field beyond which the increased yields secured
[did] not pay for the labour expended."[54] Changing attitudes towards work
are difficult to evaluate, however, and it is impossible to estimate how many
farmers adjusted their working habits after serious analysis of the cost-benefits
of their labour. The comments of an economist who studied prairie agriculture
suggest the difficulty of effecting such a change. After three years of depressed
agricultural prices, C.R. Fay observed in 1924 that "if the average farmer
had charged against his product a wage at the rate of that paid to unskilled
town labour, he would have been put out of business."[55]

V

Attempts to make farming a better-paying "business proposition" simply
by increasing the efficiency of production offered limited long term prospects
of success. The scientific advances and new technologies which made one
farmer more efficient were available to all farmers on similar terms. An
expanding number of more efficient farmers produced more grain and the
increased supply drove down the price they received for each bushel. V.C.
Fowke summarized this effect succinctly:

Improvements in cultural practices, in methods of controlling pests or obtaining a greater variety of seeds or animals . . . will consequently tend to reduce the costs of production and selling prices in equal measure."[56]

Thus farmers supplemented efforts to reduce costs by attempting to gain some control of the prices they received for their products. If those prices were determined by distant commodity exchanges, farmers would organize their own companies to represent themselves. As a Saskatchewan farmer wrote to *The Grain Growers' Guide*, "We have learned that to be good farmers means more than to raise wheat and other farm produce—we must also market these products to the best advantage."[57] "The Patrons of Husbandry, the Patrons of Industry, and some thirty local farmer-owned elevator companies organized in the late nineteenth century were the first businesses organized by prairie farmers. Larger-scale marketing enterprises followed: the Grain Growers' Grain Company in 1906, the Saskatchewan Co-operative Elevator Company in 1911, and the Alberta Co-operative Farmers' Elevator Company in 1913. During the 1920s the wheat pool movement swept the countryside, enrolling more than half the region's grain growers. Dairy producers, poultry raisers, and stock growers also created companies in response to their marketing needs.

These farmer-owned enterprises were partly elaborations on traditional community strategies to deal with adversity and protect farmers' interests; they were also partly combinations in restraint of trade on behalf of rural interests. Farm families were striving to maintain control over the things that determined the quality of their lives. Like the Populists of Lawrence Goodwyn's *Democratic Promise*, these prairie co-operators built on feelings of community and yeoman self-reliance which were part of traditional rural culture. They also built organizations that could help more vulnerable farm families to survive: as one implement salesman noted, the Wheat Pools allowed "the marginal farmer . . . to reap the benefits which usually come only to those farmers who have a business head on their shoulders.[58]

The institutions Prairie farmers created differed significantly from conventional businesses. Farmer-owned companies not only marketed their members' products; they also sold them binder twine and lubricating oil, helped them improve the quality and volume of what they produced, and represented them in Edmonton, Regina, Winnipeg and Ottawa. Most of the farmer-owned companies reflected an agrarian critique of corporate capitalism. But although some school boards refused to rent their buildings to Wheat Pool organizers because trustees felt they were "linked with the Bolshevik movement,"[59] the farmer-owned companies did not, in the words of an Alberta member, "mean a socialistic system nor doing away with the capitalist system." Instead, for many pool members, their objective was "to save the best of the capitalist system, not to do away with it."[60] For still others, the aim was to create a new form of enterprise which blended economic viability with social purpose. "They tried to do this by adapting co-operative methods of organization to their businesses, and by attempting to address the social needs of rural families. In all cases until the 1940s, and in some instances to the present day, their lengthy annual meetings discussed a broad range of non-business issues.

They were thus a distinct type of business enterprise which followed neither the capitalist nor state-capitalist model (such as the crown corporations which became common in the CCF era in Saskatchewan.) Many farmer-owned companies experimented with basic economic power relationships. Giving ultimate power to the farmer through democratic structures, they sought to minimize the role of capital and to control the power of management. By emphasizing communication among farmer-owners, they sought to lessen the secrecy rural people saw enveloping the operation of traditional corporations with their head offices located far away on Bay and St. James Streets. By vesting real power in democratically-elected boards of directors, they hoped to serve community interests rather than those of privileged minorities.

Because of the size their businesses rapidly achieved and because of the lack of appropriate management models, their experiment achieved mixed success. The first large farmer-owned enterprise—the Grain Growers' Grain Company—went on to outstanding commercial success as the United Grain Growers, but did so at the cost of its co-operative structure. The smaller dairy, livestock, poultry, and sugar beet marketing co-ops also evolved into minor images of conventional businesses, with the "cooperative" in their names as vestigial reminders of the vision of an alternative to corporate capitalism. The Wheat Pools, however, reflected the light of the original vision for much longer; some argue that it glows on even today. Similarly, the several hundred local co-operative stores retained for several decades a commitment to an alternative control structure and a belief in community-based economic development. In one important respect, labour-management relations, farmer-owned owned businesses functioned squarely within the framework of the capitalism they criticized. Respectful of the rights of member/patrons, many of the cooperatives treated their employees as poorly as any conventional business boss could have. Managers and staff worked long hours for low wages, and were expected to take part of their reward from the opportunity for service to the cause.[61] As a result, by the 1950s both the grain companies and the local consumer co-ops experienced bitter confrontations with their workers.[62]

Despite these failures, the success of farmer-owned enterprises in the prairie West have been impressive. They did much more than effectively market the commodities for which they were originally created. They helped launch the prairie credit union system, a trust company, and a large insurance company, and established flour mills and abbatoirs, an oil refinery and a farm implement company.[63] At the same time, they took part in the earliest co-op housing projects and built co-operative health care facilities. All of these organizations were essentially controlled by farmers. Farm leaders, and the rank and file members who elected them, repeatedly proved themselves able to make the difficult business decisions necessary to run what are today multi-million dollar operations.

VI

The success of the managerial initiative within farmer-owned marketing organizations carried over into the relationship between farm organizations and governments. The confrontational politics of the formative period, typified by marches on Ottawa in 1910 and 1918, the Progressive party, and the "100% Pool" campaigns, was gradually supplanted by a lobbying and consultative relationship more like that of other business groups. The change was symbolized in the choice of a name for a new national farm organization formed in 1935 which had its beginnings in the West: the Canadian *Chamber* of Agriculture. Prairie farmers were beginning to adopt "the solutions of modern enterprise—pressure politicking, trade organization, government subsidies" to achieve their commercial goals.[64]

But a significant difference remained between most farmers and most businessmen in their attitudes to government intervention in their respective businesses. Historians of the relationship between the state and business have divided government intervention into "promotional" and "managerial" categories.[65] Promotional intervention, such as bonuses, tariff protection or subsidies, which "conferr[ed] needed aid without imposing conditions or obligations that would infringe on the customary right of businessmen to operate their enterprises as they saw fit", was accepted and applauded by business. Managerial intervention, such as the regulation of prices or working conditions, was more often resisted as "an impudent challenge to long-held prerogatives." With the exception of the World War One period, up to the 1930s most government intervention into the prairie agricultural economy had been promotional: the operation of experimental farms and the sponsorship of inter-regional harvest labour excursions, are two examples of such intervention.[66] The social calamity of the Dirty Thirties and the exigencies of the Second World War forced the federal government to attempt to "manage" prairie agriculture through the Wheat Acreage Reduction Act of 1941, the imposition of acreage quotas for wheat, and the decision in September, 1943, to make the Canadian Wheat Board the sole and compulsory marketing agency for the largest prairie crop.[67] But whereas most Canadian businessmen resisted this sort of "managerial" intervention, most Prairie farmers actively sought and eagerly embraced the idea of regulating production in the hope of better returns. Throughout the war, leaders of the major western farm organizations collaborated with the federal government in the creation and implementation of these management schemes.[68]

Government policies were not just the projects of "Ottawa Men" or examples of Jimmy Gardiner's effectiveness in winning cabinet support for programs for the prairie West; they were the reflections of the wishes of dominant forces within the prairie farm movement. By the 1940s, however, much of the unity of the Wheat Pool campaigns of two decades earlier had been lost. Within the mainstream farm organizations—the Pools, the United Farmers of Alberta and of Manitoba—the more successful "business" farmers had come to dominate policies and to set direction. If they were not simply motivated by the "bottom line," and adopted "business methods" so as to mitigate the effects of change in order to ensure the survival of farming as a "way of life," neither were they Luddites or socialist utopians. If they were anti-corporate and anti-monopoly, they were not anti-capitalist. If they rejected the absolute right of private property, they were all property owners to whom the concept of private property was a cornerstone of their rural world. They tried to regulate the marketplace so as to facilitate a reasonable return for farmers operating medium-sized farms on sound business principles, not to guarantee a minimum standard of living that would allow every farm family to survive on the land.

The economic benefits of higher wartime agricultural prices were felt on both small and larger farms, but government policies directed a disproportionate share to the latter. The Wheat Acreage Reduction program, for example, provided little to the farmer with a quarter or a half-section who could not increase his coarse grains or summerfallow to qualify for a government cheque. Subsidies to more efficient, larger dairymen drove those who used a tiny dairy herd as part of a mixed-farm strategy out of business. Government labour policy appealed to the large-scale farmer who was anxious to see both labour costs and the workers themselves brought under control; it provided few benefits to the smaller farmer and by lowering farm wages perhaps deprived him of higher income if he occasionally "worked out" on a larger farm. Federal wheat policy held out little to the smaller, non-mechanized, and thus less efficient producer. The Wheat Board's maximum price of $1.25 a bushel left him little return after costs of production, and the Board's delivery quotas—restrictions on the number of bushels a farmer could sell from each acre planted to wheat—also disadvantaged smaller farmers.

The ultimate result of wartime agricultural changes was to hasten the demise of more radical farm organizations like the United Farmers of Canada, and of the quarter- and half-section farmers who were disproportionately represented in their ranks. The failure of the 1946 Alberta and Saskatchewan delivery strikes that the radicals used in their drive for parity was a sign of their growing impotence, and solidified the claim of the farmer-businessmen of the Canadian Chamber of Agriculture (renamed in 1940 the Canadian *Federation* of Agriculture) that they alone spoke for the prairie farm community.[69]

VII

Between the 1880s and the 1950s, farm life on the prairies changed dramatically. Business methods had seemed to offer the only way in which farm people could harness the changes that swept the countryside to protect their family enterprises and preserve their rural communities. The harsh truth is that many farm families were unable to adapt, hence the continual movement within the countryside and the widespread exodus from the farms which began during the Second World War and accelerated thereafter. The 1951 census revealed that in the previous fifteen years, the total number of farms in Manitoba, Saskatchewan and Alberta had decreased by 17 percent. Small farms, those of a half-section or less, disappeared at twice this rate. More than one in five of the region's farm population left the land between 1936 and 1951.[70] These figures foretold the future of the rural prairie West.

For farm families, the dream had been to provide a relatively secure income to enable a stable way of life over the generations. Becoming more "businesslike" was seen as a means by which this end could be achieved, and for some families this strategy worked and allowed for the successful transfer of the patrimony from one generation to another. For many others it did not: either they applied business methods badly and tired of a low return, or they were forced to leave the land by the bad weather and by the low international prices over which they had no control.

In understanding the departure of so many families from their farms, it is necessary to take into account the complexity of farm businesses—even in the wheat economy which can appear to be simplistic to outside observers. All of the basic elements of that business—land, equipment, labour, credit, and marketing—involved complex decisions within rapidly changing contexts. Many of those decisions had to be made on the basis of limited, contradictory, or inaccurate information and, for family farm businesses facing calamity, they were life or death decisions made annually. It was a difficult business which, despite the resiliency permitted by families absorbing losses or low profits in bad years, made prosperous survival problematic.

On another level, the widespread application of business practices raises the question of the original strength and the survival capacity of rural values; it questions W.C. Good's faith that better business would preserve rural life. Those families who developed their farms according to the strictest "business" principles overtly or subconsciously rejected the concept of rural distinctions. Those who sought to place their farm enterprise within the concerns of rural life and to create agricultural businesses based on value systems different from the norms of industrial capitalism found their task even more complex. The advent of business methods was essential to survival; the question is whether those methods rendered impossible the survival of a culture that was once vibrant, innovative, and reflective.

Yet, while these historical trends are clear, some farm families persist in believing in the value and uniqueness of rural life. Many of them accept a much lower return on their capital than they would receive from the most conservative investments. The fact that more than one-third of them do off-farm work to enable the farm enterprise to survive further demonstrates the continued importance they attach to their "way of life." And what other business defines "survival" as success? For many involved in large-scale "agribusiness", however, the relationship between the "way of life" and "business" faces of farming has been reversed. Whereas once the "business" side was looked to as the savior of the "way of life," the special pleading of some lobbyists and bucolic advertisements such as those cited in the first paragraph of this paper suggest that "way of life" rhetoric is often used today to buttress their business interests!

NOTES

1. Century 21 advertisement in *Country Guide* (February 1988). Century 21's pitch is not unusual; the Bank of Commerce's full-page ad in the January number of the same journal exploits the same theme under the headline "Farming is special."

2. W.C. Good, *Production and Taxation in Canada from the Farmer's Standpoint* (Toronto, 1919).

3. Richard Hofstadter, *The Age of Reform: From Bryan to FDR* (New York 1955) chapter I *passim*, with direct quotations from pp 24, 29 and 41.

4. The quotations are from Parker's chapter "The American Farmer" in Jerome Blum's coffee-table book *Our Forgotten Past* (New York 1982), 193-6. By far the most thoughtful of the studies which portray American agriculture as entrepreneurial and individualistic is James T. Lemon's *The Best Poor Man's Country: A Geographical Study of Early Southeastern Pennsylvania* (New York 1976).

5. James A. Henretta, "Families and Farms: *Mentalité* in Pre-Industrial America," *William and Mary Quarterly*, 35 (1978), 3-32.

6. David P. Szatmary, *Shay's Rebellion: The Making of An Agrarian Insurrection* (Amherst, Mass. 1980); Rohert C. McMath Jr, *Populist Vanguard: A History of the Southern Farmers' Alliance* (Chapel Hill, N.C. 1975); Lawrence Goodwyn, *Democratic Promise: The Populist Movement in America* (New York 1976). The best recent examples of this literature are several articles in the collection edited by Steven Hahn and Jonathan Prude, *The Countryside in the Age of Capitalist Transformation* (Chapel Hill 1985). See also the insightful review essay by Allan Kulikoff, "The Transition to Capitalism in Rural America," *William and Mary Quarterly* (1988), 120-144.

7. There are several French-language exceptions which take their inspiration from Louise Dechene's *Habitants et Marchands de Montreal au XVIIieme siecle* (Paris and Montreal 1974). The only English-language exception is Allan Greer's *Peasant, Lord and Merchant: Rural Society in three Quebec Parishes, 1740-1840* (Toronto 1985) which concludes unequivocally that "the rural economy of the

region remained one essentially of household self-sufficiency" into the mid-nineteenth century. "Peasant families continued to satisfy their material needs primarily through their own efforts . . . ." (pp 202-231, quotations from 203 and 230).

8. His most vigorous presentation of this case is in Fowke, "The Myth of the Self-sufficient Pioneer," *Transactions of the Royal Society of Canada*, section II, LVI (1962), 23-37; but he makes the same argument in "Agriculture and the Investment Frontier Before Confederation," chapter II of *The Wheat Economy* (Toronto 1957), 12-21.

9. C. Danhof, *Change in Agriculture: The Northern United States, 1820-1870* (Cambridge, Mass. 1969).

10. For a summary of Chayanov and a useful synopsis of the literature on the European transition to capitalist agriculture, see William W. Hagen's review article "Capitalism and Countryside in Modern Europe: Interpretations, Models, Debates," *Agricultural History*, 62 (1988), 13-47.

11. New near self-sufficient homesteads were being created in the northern-most fringes of the parkbelt in the midst of the 1930s, some of them by farmers turned out by the drought on the southern prairies. Grant MacEwan's diary records a meeting with such a community at Candle Lake, Saskatchewan, where he was told that "if a man brings his equipment with him, he can almost live off the country." Max Foran, ed., *Grant MacEwan's Journals* (Edmonton 1987), 76.

12. J.C. Lehr, " 'The Peculiar People': Ukrainian Settlement of Marginal Lands in Southeastern Manitoba," in David C. Jones and Ian MacPherson, eds., *Building Beyond the Homestead: Rural History on the Prairies* (Calgary 1985), 31-9.

13. This was the economic strategy beloved of agricultural experts and propagandized by the federal and provincial departments of agriculture. There is a delightful discussion in Paul Voisey, "A Mix-up Over Mixed Farming: The Curious History of the Agricultural Diversification Movement in a Single Crop Area of Southern Alberta," in *ibid.*, 179-205.

14. Donald M. Loveridge, "Diversified Farming," chapter 7 of " 'The Garden of Manitoba: The Settlement and Agricultural Development of the Rock Lake District and the Municipality of Louise, 1878-1902," (PhD thesis, University of Toronto 1986), 553-603.

15. For a thoughtful summation of the differences between this and "the quiet frontier of the mixed farmer," see P.L. McCormick, "Transportation and Settlement: Problems in the Expansion of the Frontier in Saskatchewan and Assiniboia in 1904," *Prairie Forum*, 5 (1980), 14-16.

16. Paul Voisey, *Vulcan: The Making of a Prairie Community* (Toronto 1988).

17. Provincial Archives of Alberta, 84.407, W.J. Blair Papers, files 65, 68, 70, 71.

18. J. Shover, *First Majority, Last Minority: The Transforming of Rural Life in America* (DeKalb, Illinois 1976), xiv.

19. W.C. Good, *Production and Taxation in Canada from the Farmer's Standpoint.* Italics and capitalization in original.

20. For innovative use of similar documents for a different time period see D. McCalla, "Rural Credit and Rural Development in Upper Canada, 1790-1850," in R. Hall, W. Westfall & L. Sifton MacDowell, eds., *Patterns of the Past: Interpreting Ontario History* (Toronto 1988), 37-54; D. McCalla, "The Internal Economy of Upper Canada: New Evidence on Agricultural Marketing Before

1850," *Agricultural History*, 59 (No. 3 1985), 397-416; and W.B. Rothenberg, "The Market and Massachussetts Farmers, 1750-1855," *Journal of Economic History*, XLI (June 1981), 283-314.

21. For a similar explanation applied to an American community at an earlier stage in the "Great Transformation," see Christopher Clark, "Household Economy, Market Exchange and the Rise of Capitalism in the Connecticut Valley, 1800-1860," *Journal of Social History*, 13 (1979), 169-89.

22. Chester Martin, *"Dominion Lands" Policy* (Toronto 1973), 240-1.

23. The original questionnaires can be found in the Alexander Begg Papers, Provincial Archives of British Columbia.

24. Wendy Owen, ed., *The Wheat King: Selected Letters and Papers of A.J. Cotton, 1888-1913* (Winnipeg 1985), xvii, xxviii.

25. David Jones has dramatically described this area in *Empire of Dust: Settling and Abandoning the Prairie Dry Belt* (Edmonton 1987).

26. The extent of these activities is sketched in J.G. Rayner, "Adult Education in the Agricultural Field," *Agricultural Institute Review* (July 1946), 414-417, and their importance is considered in L.J. Wilson, Educating the Saskatchewan Farmer: The Educational Work of the SGGA," *Saskatchewan History*, XXXI (1978), 20-33.

27. H.C. Moss, "Mapping our Soils," *Agricultural Institute Review* (March-April 1960), 13-14.

28. For summerfallow to crop ratios, see E.S. Hopkins, "Summerfallow on the Prairies," *Agricultural Institute Review* (January 1950), 19.

29. James H. Gray, *Men Against the Desert* (Saskatoon 1967), 66-83; Grant MacEwan, *Charles Noble: Guardian of the Soil* (Saskatoon 1983), 160-171.

30. T. Isern, "The Discer: Tillage for the Canadian Plains," *Agricultural History*, 62 (1988), 89; Voisey, *Vulcan*, 108.

31. NAC, Canada, Department of Agriculture *Reports*, 1928, 1929, 1930. We would like to thank W. Anderson for research on these issues.

32. J.H. Ellis, *The Ministry of Agriculture in Manitoba* (Winnipeg 1971), 297-301.

33. There is a good description of the necessity and ubiquity of these machines in Robert Miller Christy, *Manitoba Described* (London 1885), 70-73.

34. R.G. MacBeth, *Farm Life in the Selkirk Settlement* (Winnipeg 1897), 4.

35. F.G. Roe, *Tracks Across the Prairies: Homesteading and Railroading in Early Alberta* 197.

36. One bitter personal account may be found in John P. Pennefather, *Thirteen Years on the Prairies* (London 1892), 66-8.

37. *Report of the Saskatchewan Farm Machinery Commission* (Regina 1915), 39.

38. G.N. Denike, "Co-operative Use of Farm Machinery," Alberta Department of Agriculture Extension Branch, Calgary (1942), 1, 8.

39. Ernest B. Ingles, "The Custom Threshermen in Western Canada," in Jones and MacPherson, eds., *Building Beyond the Homestead*, 135-137.

40. A.W. Wood, "A Study of Labour Productivity in Saskatchewan Agriculture" (MSc thesis, University of Saskatchewan 1955), 8.

41. Robert Ankli, Dan Helsberg, and John Herd Thompson, "The Adoption of the Gasoline Tractor in Western Canada," *Canadian Papers in Rural History* II (1980), 15-20.

42. "[Wheat Pool] Contract 339-204" to the *Western Producer* (15 March 1928), 16.

43. University of Saskatchewan Archives, Saskatchewan College of Agriculture Collection I B8, Report of the Department of Farm Management, February 1927.

44. G.N. Denike, "Co-operative Use of Farm Machinery," 1-2.

45. See the account of a "Farmer-Lender Conference" in *The Grain Growers' Guide* (9 August 1916), 14-15. T.D. Regehr's "Bankers and Farmers in Western Canada, 1900-1939" in John E. Foster, ed., *The Developing West* (Edmonton 1983), 303-336 is the best overview available.

46. W.M. Drummond, "From Homesteader to Businessman," in Agricultural Economics Research Council, *Occasional Papers*, #9 (1967), 3-18; Jones, *Empire of Dust*, 157.

47. *Grain Growers' Guide* (1 November 1916), 14.

48. The former was a collection of *Nor'West Farmer* columns written between 1916 and 1918; the latter, credited to former Alberta Minister of Agriculture Duncan Marshall and published by Imperial Oil, borrowed its title from a frequently-cited and much reprinted American book, G.F. Warner's *Farm Management*.

49. Four such Extension Bulletins were published between 1927 and 1931, numbers 37, 43, 46 and 52. The statement is identical in all of them. University of Saskatchewan Archives, College of Agriculture Collection.

50. C. Danysk, "Farm Apprentice to Rural Proletarian: Farm Labour in Alberta, 1900 to 1930" (MA thesis, McGill University 1981).

51. S. Myres, *Westering Women and the Frontier Experience* (Albuquerque 1982), 171.

52. Marjorie Griffin Cohen has explored this idea in a different context in "The Decline of Women in Canadian Dairying," *Histoire sociale/Social History* XVII (1984), 307-34.

53. PABC, Begg Papers, Mrs. A. Bell, Questionnaire #19.

54. *Grain Growers' Guide* (24 October 1917); *ibid.* "Yields and Labour Income" (24 October 1917), 25.

55. C.R. Fay, "Diminishing Returns in Agriculture," *Journal of the Canadian Bankers' Association*, XXXII (October 1924), 22.

56. V. Fowke, *The National Policy and the Wheat Economy* (Toronto 1957), 291-292.

57. *Grain Growers' Guide* (5 June 1918).

58. Report by an unidentified Hart-Parr tractor salesman, May 1926, in the CPR Collection, file 683, Archives of the Glenbow-Alberta Institute. Not all prairie farmers participated in this movement culture of co-operatism. The same report noted that "the successful business farmer, as a rule, has not joined." Although there has been no systematic study of co-op membership, those who did not join the Wheat Pools appear to have been those with the smallest and the largest farms—those at the two extremes of the continuum between self-sufficiency and specialized commercial agriculture.

59. Pool fieldman Tom Bentley quoted in Garry Fairbairn, *From Prairie Roots: The Remarkable Story of the Saskatchewan Wheat Pool* (Saskatoon 1984), 71.

60. Archives of the Glenbow-Alberta Institute, A.H. Rawlins Papers, Rawlins to H.G.L. Strange, 2 June 1936.

61. There are many examples of such problems in the Co-operative Union of Canada Papers, National Archives of Canada. See also B. Fairbairn, *Building the Dream: The Co-operative Retail System in Western Canada, 1928-1988* (Saskatoon

1989) and K.W. Wetzel and D.G. Gallagher, "A Conceptual Analysis of Labour Relations in Co-operatives," *Economic and Industrial Democracy* (1987).

62. K. Wetzel and D.G. Gallagher, "Labour Relations in Co-operatives," *Economic & Industrial Democracy* (1987).

63. See Ian MacPherson, *The C.I.S. Story* (Regina 1974); *The History of Co-op Trust* (Saskatoon 1978); and " 'Better Tractors for Less Money': The Establishment of Canadian Co-operative Implements Limited," *Manitoba History*, 13 (Spring 1987), 2-11.

64. The direct quotation is from Adam Ward Rome, "American Farmers as Entrepeneurs," *Agricultural History*, 56 (1982), 48.

65. These terms and the direct quotations are from Mark Cox, "The Limits of Reform: Industrial Regulation and Management Rights in Ontario, 1930-7," *Canadian Historical Review*, LXVIII (1987), 552-3. Tom Traves uses the terms "promotional" and "regulatory" in his "Business-Government Relations in Canadian History," *History and Social Science Teacher*, 18 (1982), 75-6.

66. A useful and very succinct overview is W.J. Anderson, "Canadian Agricultural Policy—A Review," *Agricultural Institute Review* (May-June 1966), 2-8.

67. Ian MacPherson and John Herd Thompson, "An Orderly Reconstruction: Prairie Agriculture in World War Two," *Canadian Papers in Rural History*, IV (1984), 25-28.

68. Ian MacPherson, "An Authoritative Voice: The Reorientation of the Canadian Farmer's Movement, 1935 to 1945," Canadian Historical Association: *Historical Papers* (1979), 175-181.

69. Two recent articles explore these strikes: D'Arcy Hande, "Parity Prices and the Farmers' Strike," *Saskatchewan History*, XXXVIII (1985), 81-96 and David Monod, "The End of Agrarianism: The Fight for Farm Parity in Saskatchewan and Alberta," *Labour/Le travail*, 16 (1985), 126-143.

70. Authors' calculations based on figures from the *Census of Canada*. The absolute numbers for 1936 are 300,523 farms and a farm population of 1,225,451; and, for 1951, 248,716 farms and a farm population of 963,928.

PAUL VOISEY

24 Rural Local History and the Prairie West

Even a cursory look at local histories on the prairie west reveals some striking features. They now exist in huge numbers—probably over a thousand
and increasing rapidly.[1] Most have appeared since the mid-1960s. Most
concern rural communities and emphasize the period of agrarian settlement.
Amateurs have authored the overwhelming majority, and "semi-
professionals," with some training in scholarly research and writing, nearly
all the rest. Professional historians do not share the tremendous public
enthusiasm for local history. Exceptions exist, of course, but most of them
are recent biographies of large prairie cities that prefer to parade under the
banner of "urban history" rather than the dreary rubric of "local history."
Partly because of professional neglect, then, the general quality of rural local
histories on the prairies is abysmally low. By contrast, local history attracts
highly talented scholars in other parts of the world and their books have
forged important new interpretations.

This article has several purposes: to explain the rising importance of local
history to scholarship generally, to account for its low status on the prairies,
to assess in a general way the nature and quality of those prairie local studies
that do exist, and to suggest new opportunities and the most appropriate
ways to exploit them. Biographies of prairie cities are legitimate members
of the local history family, but because urban historians assess them regularly, they are excluded from consideration here.[2]

A proper evaluation of local history on the prairies requires some understanding of its development elsewhere. At one time, professional historians
mostly wrote about great events like wars and the rise of nation-states, and
about the important people involved in great events. Historians, like other
academics, sprang from privileged classes in structured societies where social
deference still mattered. The illiterate masses seemed unimportant and seldom intruded into studies of great events and great people. Since most

communities consisted largely of illiterate masses, local history seldom received serious attention. When it did, it focussed on places themselves of great importance: London or Paris or New York. And when a learned church cleric undertook a history of his rural locality, the life of the manor house filled its pages while thousands of peasants lived, toiled, and died in the unrecorded shadows.

But the age of the common man slowly dawned and as the twentieth century approached he stood in full sunshine for even the scholar to see. (The common woman would not be visible until much, much later.) This is not the place to explain the sweeping social and ideological changes that elevated the common man to new importance in the industrialized world, but its consequences for local history should be noted. As both the desire and the financial ability to educate the masses arose, they began articulating their views through formal organizations and written documents. Growing scholarly interest in the common man, coupled with the appearance of documents pertaining to his activities, boded well for local studies since almost every community contained people as common and ordinary as those anywhere else, and in a restricted setting they could be found in numbers sufficiently small to invite close scrutiny.

But historians did not lead the way. Social scientists did. They pioneered the "case study," investigating particular problems by using specific communities as (hopefully) representative examples. Sometimes their questions involved such a range of phenomena that a study of the community itself emerged, and for some of them, the very idea of community became important. Historians seldom shared in these adventures because the techniques of the social scientist permitted one to study only the present and recent past. Besides written documents, they relied on direct observations, and later, questionnaires and interviews. But the dead would not speak to historians, nor could the historians literally look into the past. And the time when common man remained illiterate and left no written documents comprised by far the longest stretch of history. Furthermore, the purposes of the social scientists seemed alien. Not for them the great events and great people: they studied population structures, family life, daily work, spatial relationships, and social activities, organizations, and classes. A frank pragmatism often motivated their work; many sought specific solutions to a variety of social and economic problems.

Even when historians did investigate the common man, they remained committed to events and individuals — to the political revolts of farmers and workers and the lives of their leaders. By the 1930s historians of the French "Annales school" wearied of this focus. They argued that the structures of everyday life — the stuff of social science — shaped human history as surely as dramatic events. But unlike the social scientists they sought to measure them over time, to chart the tension between continuity and change.

The Annales school also broke the silence of the illiterate dead. They had, after all, left written records of sorts. Church, census, tax, and legal records listed names, dates, births, marriages, deaths, properties, agreements, and crimes. Studied separately the information told little, but when sorted and linked together, it revealed much. Sifting the new material took endless time and special skills, and the historian, without formal training in statistics, found himself less equipped for the task than the social scientist. As a consequence, some social scientists became historians, and the historians, of necessity, became interdisciplinary in method as well as objective. Because the new data existed in such bulk, some became local historians out of practical necessity. It remained for the English "Leicester school," however, to make local history a focal point for the methods and aims of the Annalists.[3]

The electronics revolution of the 1960s greatly stimulated quantified local history. Although it increased research costs and demanded new technical skills, the computer could link mountains of mass data quickly and spit out complex statistical profiles of almost infinite variety. Although Europe had pioneered interdisciplinary, quantified local history, major activity now shifted to the United States, the nation most advanced in the new technology and best able to finance it. Merle Curti's *The Making of an American Community: A Case Study of Democracy in a Frontier County* (1959), a history of Trempealeau, Wisconsin, marked the arrival of the new local history in North America. Others soon followed. Historians poured from the burgeoning university system in unprecedented numbers, and the social turbulence of the 1960s heightened academic interest in the common man. Local studies espousing the "new history" blossomed across the United States, but especially in New England, where a lot of historians lived, and where excellent local records existed in abundance.[4]

Canada lagged behind. Except for some French-Canadians trained at the Sorbonne or otherwise exposed to its influence, most of its much smaller population of historians received their training in Canada without instruction in the new methodology, and the crisis of Quebec still riveted their attention on the history of French-English relations, nation-building, and regional protest. It took an outsider to launch the new local history, and Michael Katz's *People of Hamilton, Canada West: Family and Class in a Mid-Nineteenth Century City* did not appear until 1975. While other large scale computer projects soon followed, notably on Peel County, Ontario, and the Saguenay region of Québec,[5] in prairie Canada the new local history never arrived at all. The recently published *Genealogy of the First Métis Nation: The Development and Dispersal of the Red River Settlement, 1820-1900* (1981), compiled by D.N. Sprague and R.P. Frye suggests only the most tentative probing in that direction.

But the professional historians of the west did not write much traditional local history either. The long scholarly interest in the Red River region that began with Alexander Ross's *Red River Settlement: Its Rise, Progress and Present State . . .* (1856) and continued in the writings of Alexander Begg,

W.L. Morton, and others scarcely counts, for historians did not study the area as a local community but rather as the focal poir of western history itself. The almost total neglect of local history elsewhere on the prairies seems curious because professional historians often urged its writing,[6] and many directed graduate theses in local history. In fact the bulk of our academic local studies remain buried in that unpublished form.

Why did the professional historians hesitate to undertake the task themselves? Practical considerations may have dissuaded them. Every kind of historical research imposes difficulties, but rural local history offers particularly rugged ones. There are few document collections neatly catalogued and housed in institutions equipped for research and staffed by professional archivists. Instead, the local historian must spend huge amounts of time grubbing for materials in the community itself — if they can be found at all. There is no photocopying machine handy, and no convenient place to work. At night there are no big city amusements. The only hotel in town might be unpleasant, not to mention the local restaurants.

But the professional historians' own ideas about local history shackled them more. They seemed oblivious to its modern purposes, as their advice to local history writers frequently demonstrated.[7] Some argued that local history ought to reflect the major historical developments of the region and the nation.[8] Occasionally that approach is useful. The impact of Dominion settlement policies, the Great War, or the Great Depression can be viewed with profit through the lens of a single community. But if issues attain regional and national significance because they command the attention of politicians and governments, then they can never be satisfactorily explained at the local level. And many national issues must be excluded altogether. A study of Cardston, Alberta, will not illuminate us on the Northwest Rebellion, the Winnipeg General Strike, King's courting of the Progressives, or Diefenbaker's foreign policy. In short, local communities are not simply microscopic specimens of national history, but creatures deserving study in their own right. Everyone belongs to different kinds of spatial communities simultaneously — neighbourhood, town, province, region, and nation — and each shapes human existence in its own and different ways. And the history of the nation is hardly useful to the study of communities as communities.[9]

Advocates of local history as regional and national history writ small often warned the local historian to neglect nothing of "importance," to shake every branch of historical inquiry and harvest everything the local community produced. If limits need be imposed, they should be temporal rather than thematic. But this approach is quite impossible for one can no more discover everything about a small place than about a whole nation. Such advice often stemmed from the notion that local studies should provide historians with factual building blocks to construct more general histories and new interpretations.[10] Reasonable as this argument seems, historiography more often develops the other way around. A general interpretation is proposed, subsequent monographs and local studies discredit it and, finally, another essayist pens a new theory.[11]

The holist approach also defuses any attempt to provide a coherent interpretation. Too often, a bland general survey results. Such books have their uses; students use them to chart unknown waters before plunging into more advanced study, and everybody uses them for references. An important market exists for general surveys of whole nations, and even regions, and perhaps even large prairie cities, but who needs or wants a textbook history of Outlook, Saskatchewan? Professional historians undoubtedly dispensed advice with good intentions, but perhaps they hesitated to write local history themselves because they vaguely sensed that following their own suggestions would result in a book unlikely to raise their professional standing. Besides, so many dramatic prairie events and fascinating individuals still cried out for serious study.

An investigation of those studies that did adhere to prevailing wisdom reveals the severe limitations of the comprehensive, nation as seen through the community, approach. Consider three examples: Margaret Morton Fahrni and W.L. Morton, *Third Crossing: A History of the First Quarter Century of the Town and District of Gladstone in the Province of Manitoba* (1946); Don G. McGowan, *Grasslands Settlers: The Swift Current Region During the Era of the Ranching Frontier* (1976); and Bodil Jensen's recently published *Alberta's County of Mountain View . . . A History*. These examples are particularly interesting for they are among the most scholarly local histories of rural prairie communities. The authors are knowledgeable and competent historians, and all present explanations for community development. And unlike most local histories, each presents a general interpretation. In fact, they share the same interpretation — all agree that their respective communities are products of the transplanted culture of the early settlers. But in their attempt to neglect nothing of importance — to keep mindful of events and themes of regional and national significance — their thesis is soon lost. It is not systematically pursued or convincingly substantiated in any of them. Thus, in spite of many merits, these books seem lacking in purpose; the failure to read them will scarcely impair one's knowledge of the prairie west or of communities generally. Most remarkable is how alike they are even though nearly forty years separate their publication dates, a significant comment on how little the approaches to rural local history on the prairies have changed or progressed.

The foregoing critique itself suggests the earmarks of good local history. Particular questions must be posed and answered as in any good monograph. And the questions themselves must have a spatial component amenable to investigation at the local level. Achieving the proper "fit" in this regard is far more important than arbitrarily deciding how much or little territory legitimately constitutes local history. Furthermore, the topics pursued must have significance that transcends the boundaries of the study area itself. As with good fiction, universal themes must emerge from specific locality. And because such themes largely eschew events in favour of structures and processes, good local history cannot ignore other scholarly disciplines. The number of specific topics that might be suitably explored are almost endless, but the best local histories elsewhere have tackled the following ones in various combinations: property, agricultural production, demographic change, family structure, social class, class relations, social mobility, geographic mobility, social order, community conflict, community development and disintegration, and the impact of urban growth on nearby rural areas.[12] With few exceptions, we know almost nothing of the history of these developments in our rural west.

Some may object that the monographic approach is not local history at all, but really economic or social history. But there is nothing rigid about the sub-categories of history; they are merely convenient labels and the best history often defies easy classification. The last sentence of many book reviews pinpoints a further problem with the case study approach: "More research must be carried out on other communities before we can conclude that (such and such) was typical." Scholars in other countries sometimes heed this advice, especially in the field of historical demography where the same rigorously constructed hypotheses are applied again and again to local communities. This practice has prompted one student to argue that that discipline comes closer to true science than any other social science.[13] But Canadian historians will not likely take pleas for direct comparison seriously. Tradition dictates that one does not earn high marks for borrowing analytical frameworks only to find nothing new or different. Even so, local historians, like all historians, must keep abreast of developments in their field. Ironically, while the themes best suited to local history have little to do with issues of national importance, their universality demands an international perspective.

Sometimes the problem of "representativeness" cannot be overcome, yet the case study approach must be pursued anyway. Many analytical problems arise where comprehensive reporting is more appropriate than random sampling, and some topics simply cannot be studied at all except through the case study. How can the history of community development or neighbourhood social relations be explored except through specific communities?

The foregoing discussion might seem to imply that the Annales school offers an ideal model for the study of prairie communities. But such is hardly the case. Western Canadian historians simply do not have the time span to work with that many Annalists consider sufficient to explore significant social changes (often a century or more). But they do not need it to study many important topics. Nor must superior local history emerge only from quantitative analyses served up by electronic gadgets. A local study of changes in the concept of community spirit, for example, is probably best tackled through traditional methodology. The Annales and Leicester approaches serve better as inspirational designs for prairie research rather than precise blueprints.

Nonetheless, the local historian must pay closer attention to statistics than in the past. Prairie libraries are crammed with local histories that scarcely contain a number, leaving the most elementary questions unanswered. Some historians of the "humanist" persuasion violently oppose quantification, but if at bottom, quantification is nothing more than counting, then all historians count; traditionalists who favour such words as "often, sometimes, rarely, many, most, some and few" are merely being imprecise about it. Thus, there can be no legitimate opposition to quantification in principle, only to its shoddy application and inappropriate uses. The annoying habit of many quantifiers of wallowing in hieroglyphics comprehensible only to fellow cultists is a separate issue. Critics have now sufficiently exposed the pitfalls involved in quantification, and with a little study they can be recognized and avoided.[14] In short, bickering between quantifiers and traditionalists is no longer healthy. History is a difficult craft and it must be attacked with any and all weapons that promise to defeat the problem at hand. The local historian need not become a mathematical mastermind or a computer wizard, nor ever need touch an electronic keyboard; with only a little effort, he can readily put statistical information to good use.

For those who do plunge into advanced statistical analysis, the opportunities are great, for many themes in local history lend themselves readily to the new methodology and most prairie communities are rich in mass data.[15] Until very recently, escalating financial requirements and shrinking funding threatened to end this kind of research, but the microcomputer revolution now promises to sustain it. Home computers and new software packages useful to historians are rapidly coming within the financial grasp of most professional historians.[16]

If superior local history, then, has limited and definite purposes, shuns events, and individuals in favour of structures and groups, and is interdisciplinary in theme and method, do any of the existing local histories on the prairies qualify? Unfortunately, none approximate the highest international standards. Indeed the best examples are not history at all. Few local studies on the prairies match Jean Burnet's *Next-Year Country: A Study of Rural Social Organization in Alberta* (1951), about the Hanna region, for descriptive insight, but the book conveys little sense of how social organization in the 1940s originated and evolved. Emerging from history originally, the social sciences in Canada have steadily drifted away from the mother discipline. Thus, Burnet's book does not demonstrate the historical sensitivity of the sociologists and political economists who contributed to the "Frontiers of Settlement" series in the 1930s,[17] yet it is more historical than such recent offerings as John W. Bennett, *Northern Plainsmen: Adaptive Strategy and Agrarian Life* (1976), about the Maple Creek, Saskatchewan area; or

Travis W. Manning and George Buckmire, *Economic Growth in Agricul-ture: A Comparative Analysis of Two Agricultural Areas in Alberta* (1967), two books practically devoid of history. By the same token, most prairie historians have not embraced the social sciences either.

Historical geography and ethnohistory provide the most common inter-disciplinary exceptions; several such studies have made important contri-butions to prairie scholarship, especially for the pre-settlement era. Although few are local histories, the merits of the approach are recognizable in J.F. Nelson, *The Last Refuge* (1973), a history of the Cypress Hills and surround-ing plain, or John Tyman's *By Section, Township and Range: Studies in Prairie Settlement* (1972) which examines southwestern Manitoba. Tyman's book also exemplifies a popular theme that has stimulated the best research in prairie local history: the settlement process. But much of this work lies dormant in theses or can only be sampled in widely scattered articles, some of such recent vintage that they are still in press.[18]

No general assessment of local history on the prairies should fail to note the phenomenal appearance of community-sponsored local histories.[19] The anniversary celebrations of Canada and the three prairie provinces in 1967, 1970, and 1980 ignited much of this growth because governments urged everyone to become more historically minded and provided funds for local history projects. Yet the roots of this popular genre run deeper. Individuals derive much of their personal identity from where they live, but after World War II extensive rural depopulation and the homogenizing force of mass communications and centralized bureaucracies threatened the existence of local institutions and identities on the rural prairies. Since most communi-ties dated from the late nineteenth and early twentieth centuries, death began claiming the last of the early pioneers at an alarming rate by the 1960s and 1970s. A desperate sense that important links to the past would soon be obliterated launched many local history societies. Not surprisingly, their attention focussed on the settlement period, the era most clearly threatened with loss and the one believed most important in fostering local identity. Thus, the purposes of community-sponsored local history differed radically from those of the scholar.

Residents of rural communities scarcely knew how to proceed with their projects. In most places no one had ever researched and written anything as long as a book, but they turned to the prairie tradition of cooperative enter-prise; coordinating committees asked members of the community to write brief histories of their own families, and they did so largely from oral tradi-tion rather than documents. Sometimes the committee also asked contri-butors for brief institutional biographies; local teachers wrote about schools and local ministers about churches. The typical history book committee solicited four hundred contributions, two-thirds of them family biogra-phies.[20] Professional historians scoffed at the results, but local history soci-eties wrote for themselves and did not expect anyone outside the community to read their books, save former residents. And the books fulfilled local purposes admirably. Packed with names, landmarks, incidents, anecdotes, and pictures, they preserved grandmother's story, drew personal links between past and present, and bolstered local identity.

It is pointless to list all the shortcomings of the community-sponsored local histories, for they commit virtually every sin known to scholarship. A more useful approach is to ask if they offer anything of value to the academic historian. Hugh Dempsey has argued that foraging through them can uncover useful scraps of information. He offers by way of example an eyewitness account of the mood and condition of Sitting Bull's followers as the Mounted Police escorted him back to the United States border. [21] As Dempsey points out, the search yields more if one sticks to typically favoured themes: land settlement, transportation, agriculture, schools, churches. Anyone interested in architecture, technology, or other material history can also benefit from the thousands of photographs they contain.

It is also possible to distinguish the kinds of information most free from error. Memory can easily forget or confuse events and chronology, but emotional reactions are often more vividly remembered, if somewhat coloured by time. No one has written a book on the social psychology of prairie settlement or on the psychological impact of the Great Depression based largely on community-written local histories, but valuable books on such topics could be produced. Indeed, recent claims by some historians that launching new oral history projects will unearth hitherto hidden dimensions of the past seems curious considering that a tremendous body of oral tradition lies already transcribed, and unread, in a thousand prairie books.

Admittedly, scanning these local histories for buried treasure is painstaking work. Nor can the process be shortened much by seeking out the better books. In general, they vary little in quality, hardly surprising considering that the value of individual contributions varies enormously and that each book may contain hundreds of contributions. The rare book that stands out as a whole sometimes owes its success to professional assistance. A good example is *Our Foothills* (1975), on the Millarville-Priddis area of Alberta, which benefitted greatly from the aid and contributions of L.G. Thomas and Sheilagh Jameson. Occasionally a superior one arises because some outstanding feature of the community inspires perceptive local contributors to work harder and more enthusiastically than usual. An example is *Sons of Wind and Soil* (1976), a history of the Nobleford-Kipp-Monarch districts of southern Alberta. This area once boasted one of the largest grain farms in the world, the Noble Foundation, and it also spearheaded the search for new techniques and technology to combat soil drifting on the southern prairies. Conscious of these developments and proud of them, the community produced a superior local history of interest to agricultural historians.

But the greatest value of community-written local histories lies in their potential contribution to quantitative research. And for that purpose, the typical books serve as well as the superior ones. They contain all sorts of random facts about individuals of no apparent significance in themselves: names, dates of arrival in the community, previous and subsequent occupations and places of residence, precise settlement locations, and the dates of births, marriages, and deaths of family members. These are the most commonly included items in each family biography, often because local history societies specifically ask for such information. Here is mass data on a significant scale, and with or without computerized sophistication, it can be linked to homestead files, railway land sales records, land titles, tax rolls, and court records to provide analyses of dozens of themes now commonly pursued in local history elsewhere. Ironically then, while community-written local histories are far inferior to existing academic ones in scholarly merit, their potential value for further research may be greater.

Single author memoirs set in particular communities constitute another form of non-academic local history. Since the authors are often professional writers with varying degrees of scholarly training, their books are more satisfying as history and certainly less painful to read than the community-written local histories. These characteristics are readily apparent in such superior examples as Wallace Stegner, *Wolf Willow, A History, A Story and a Memory of the Last Plains Frontier* (1955), James G. MacGregor, *Northwest of Sixteen* (1958), and Sarah Ellen Roberts, *Of Us and the Oxen* (1963). Richer by their length and articulate expression than the community-written family biographies, they are, like the best prairie fiction, more valuable to the historian for conveying the psychological climates of particular eras, but they seldom provide more in the way of new information. Indeed, lacking the vast quantities of minutiae found in the family biographies of community written local histories, they open no new avenues for research.

The number of publications pertaining to rural prairie communities is huge, yet modern, scholarly local history has not yet reached infancy. It is still experiencing birthpains, and it is too early to tell if the small number of works in progress will produce healthy offspring. The opportunities are nonetheless great, and if more talented people can be attracted to local history, it might be rescued from the stagnant backwaters where it now resides and thrust into the mainstream of prairie scholarship.

NOTES

1. Gloria M. Strathern, *Alberta, 1954-1979: A Provincial Bibliography* (Edmonton: University of Alberta Press, 1982), lists 463 titles for Alberta alone up to 1979: Joanna E. Krotki. *Local Histories of Alberta: An Annotated Bibliography* (Edmonton: Division of East European Studies, University of Alberta, and East European Studies Society of Alberta, 1980), with an expanded definition of local history lists 813.

2. See Gilbert A. Stelter, "Urban History," in *A Reader's Guide to Canadian*

History, vol. 2: Confederation to the Present, ed. J.L. Granatstein and Paul Stevens (Toronto: University of Tornnto Press, 1982), 96-113. Stelter's article also guides the reader to many other assessments.

3. Traian Stoianovich. *French Historical Method: The Annales Paradigm* (Ithaca: Cornell University Press, 1976); H.P.R. Finberg and V.H.T. Skipp, *Local History, Objective and Pursuit* (New York: Augustus M. Kelley, 1967).

4. See J.M. Bumstead and J.T. Lemon, "New Approaches in Early American Studies: the Local Community in New England," *Histoire Sociale-Social History*, 2 (November 1968): 98-112.

5. Ian Winchester, "Review of Peel County History Project and the Saguenay Project," *Histoire Sociale-Social History*, vol. 8. no. 25 (May 1980), 195-205: David Gagan, *Hopeful Travellers: Families, Land, and Social Change in Mid-Victorian Peel County, Canada West* (Toronto: University of Toronto Press, 1981).

6. For early examples see W.H. Atherton, "The Study of Local History," *Canadian Historical Association Annual Reports* (1924), 45-47; D.C. Harvey, "The Importance of Local History in the Writing of General History," *Canadian Historical Review*, 13 (September 1932): 244-251.

7. Most advice is directed at the non-professional. See in particular Gerry Friesen and Barry Potyondi. *A Guide to the Study of Manitoba Local History* (Winnipeg: University of Manitoba Press for the Manitoba Historical Society, 1981); *Proceedings of the Local Archives and History Conference* (Regina: Saskatchewan 1980 Diamond Jubilee Corporation, 1980); Hugh A. Dempsey. *How to Prepare a Local History* (Calgary: Glenbow-Alberta Institute, 1969); Eric Holmgren, *Writing Local History* (Edmonton: Historical Resources Division, Alberta Culture, 1975); Jane McCracken, *Oral History: Basic Techniques* (Winnipeg: Manitoba Museum of Man and Nature, 1974). American guidebooks frequently urged on local historians in Western Canada include D.D. Parker, *Local History. How to Gather it, Write it, Publish it* (New York: Social Science Research Council, 1944); Gary L. Shumway and William G. Hartley, *An Oral History Primer* (Salt Lake: Primer Publications, 1973); and many publications of the American Association for State and Local History including Dorothey W. Creigh, *A Primer for Local Historical Societies* (1976); Thomas E. Felt, *Researching, Writing, and Publishing Local History* (1976); James C. Olson, *The Role of Local History* (1965); Willa K. Baum, *Oral History for the Local Historical Society* (1974); and the many Technical Leaflets published frequently in the Association's journal, *History News*.

8. Hartwell Bowsfield, "Writing Local History," *Alberta Historical Review* 17 (Summer 1969): 10-19; H.C. Pentland, "Recent Developments in Economic History: Some Implications for Local and Regional History," *Historical and Scientific Society of Manitoba Transactions*, 3d. ser. no. 24 (1967-68): 8; Richard A. Preston, "Is Local History Really History," *Saskatchewan History* 10 (Autumn 1957): 97-108.

9. See Finberg, *Local History*, 12-13; David J. Russo, *Families and Communities: A New View of American History* (Nashville: American Association for State and Local History, 1975), passim; Conrad M. Arensberg and Solon T. Kimball, "The Community as Object and Sample," in their *Culture and Community* (New York: Harcourt, Brace and World, 1965), 7-27, argue that a

distinction should be drawn between questions in which the community serves as a case study of a larger problem, and questions about communities themselves.

10. See especially, Harvey, "Importance of Local History," 244-251.

11. David Hackett Fischer, *Historians' Fallacies: Toward a Logic of Historical Thought* (New York: Harper and Row, 1970), 5; Thomas H. Smith, "The Renascene of Local History," *The Historian*, 35 (November 1972), 1-18.

12. See, for example, Kenneth A. Lockridge, *A New England Town: The First Hundred Years, Dedham, Massachusetts, 1636-1736* (New York: Norton, 1970); Stephan Thernstrom, *Poverty and Progress: Social Mobility in a Nineteenth Century City* (Cambridge: Harvard University Press, 1964); Philip J. Greven, *Four Generations: Population, Land and Family in Colonial Andover, Massachusetts* (Ithaca and London: Cornell University Press, 1970); Michael H. Frisch, *Town into City: Springfield, Massachusetts, and the Meaning of Community, 1840-1880* (Cambridge: Harvard University Press, 1972); Arthur J. Vidich and Joseph Bensman, *Small Town in Mass Society: Class, Power, and Religion in a Rural Community* (Princeton: Princeton University Press, revised ed., 1968); Don Harrison Doyle, *The Social Order of a Frontier Community: Jacksonville, Illinois, 1825-70* (Urbana: University of Illinois Press, 1978); Merle Curti, *The Making of an American Community: A Case Study of Democracy in a Frontier County* (Stanford: Stanford University Press, 1959); James T. Lemon, *The Best Poor Man's Country: A Geographical Study of Early Southeastern Pennsylvania* (New York: W.W. Norton, 1976); Richard G. Bremer, *Agricultural Change in an Urban Age: The Loup Country of Nebraska, 1910-1970* (Lincoln: University of Nebraska Studies, New Series No. 51, 1976); Stanley Norman Murray, *The Valley Comes of Age: A History of Agriculture in the Valley of the Red River of the North, 1812-1920* (Fargo: North Dakota Institute for Regional Studies, 1967); Michael P. Conzen, *Frontier Farming in an Urban Shadow: The Influence of Madison's Proximity on the Agricultural Development of Blooming Grove, Wisconsin* (Madison: State Historical Society of Wisconsin, 1971); Michael Katz, *The People of Hamilton, Canada West: Family and Class in a Mid-Nineteenth Century City* (Cambridge: Harvard University Press, 1975); David Gagan, *Hopeful Travellers; Louise Dêchene, Habitants et Marchands de Montréal au XVIIᵉ siècle* (Montréal: Les Presses de la cité, 1974). For the best analysis of local histories and local history technique see Finberg, *Local History*; Russo, *Families and Communities*; Alan Macfarlane and others, *Reconstructing Historical Communities* (Cambridge: Cambridge University Press, 1977); Thomas Bender, *Community and Social Change in America* (New Brunswick. N.J.: Rutgers University Press, 1978); Smith, "Renascene"; Van Beck Hall, "New Approaches to Local History." *Western Pennsylvania Historical Magazine 55* (July 1972): 239-248; Katherine A. Lynch, "Local and Regional Studies in Historical Demography," *Historical Methods* 15 (Winter 1982): 229; Bumstead, "New Approaches"; Robert P. Swierenga, "The New Rural History: Defining the Parameters," *Great Plains Quarterly* 1 (Fall 1981):211-223; idem, "Quantitative Methods in Rural Landholding," *Journal of Interdisciplinary History* 13 (Spring 1983): 787-808.

13. Marion J. Levy, "New Uses of Demography," *Comparative Studies in Society and History* 16 (1974): 104-116.

14. A convenient and readily comprehensible starting point for the non-specialist

that offers concrete examples is Herbert G. Gutman, *Slavery and the Numbers Game: A Critique of Time on the Cross* (Urbana: University of Illinois Press, 1975).

15. Including homestead files, railway land sales records, land titles, tax rolls, and court records. Valuable guides to some of these records include Lloyd Rodwell, "Saskatchewan Homestead Records," *Saskatchewan History* 18 (Winter 1965): 10-29; D.M. Loveridge, "An Introduction to the Study of Land and Settlement Records," in Friesen, *A Guide*, 100-129; Robert A. Doyle, "Land Records as a Source of Historical Information," in Friesen, *A Guide*, 136-141.

16. For the most recent guides, see Richard Jensen, "The Microcomputer Revolution for Historians," *Journal of Interdisciplinary History* 14 (Summer 1983):91-111; Robert McCaa, "Microcomputer Software Designs for Historians: Word Processing, Filing and Data Entry Programs," *Historical Methods* 17 (Spring 1984): 68-74.

17. Although only one volume in the series focusses on a single area, others are based on statistical surveys of a number of specific communities. See C.A. Dawson, *The Settlement of the Peace River Country: A Study of a Pioneer Area*; idem. *Group Settlement: Ethnic Communities in Western Canada*; idem and Eva R. Young, *Pioneering in the Prairie Provinces: The Social Side of the Settlement Process*; W.A. Mackintosh, *Economic Problems of the Prairie Provinces*; R.W. Murchie, *Agricultural Progress on the Prairie Frontier* (all volumes published in Toronto by Macmillan in the 1930s and 1940s).

18. See Donald M. Loveridge, "The Settlement of the Rural Municipality of Sifton, 1881-1920" (Master's thesis, University of Manitoba, 1977); Robin Barrie Mallett, "Settlement Process and Land Use Change: Lethbridge-Medicine Hat Area" (Master's thesis, University of Alberta, 1971); Barry Potyondi, "Country Town: The History of Minnedosa, Manitoba, 1879-1922" (Master's thesis, University of Manitoba, 1978); Bruce Edward Batchelor, "Frontier Near Red Deer and Lacombe, Alberta, 1882-1914" (Ph.D. diss., Simon Fraser University, 1978); Paul Voisey, "Forging the Western Tradition: Pioneer Approaches to Settlement and Agriculture in Southern Alberta Communities (Ph.D. diss., University of Toronto, 1982); R.R. Vogelesang, "The Initial Agricultural Settlement of the Morinville-Westlock Area, Alberta" (Master's thesis, University of Alberta, 1972). For publications based on these theses see articles by Potyondi and Voisey in *Town and City: Aspects of Western Canadian Urban Development*, ed. Alan F.J. Artibise (Regina, Canadian Plains Research Center, University of Regina, 1981); See also articles by Voisey, John C. Lehr, James M. Ricktik, and David C. Jones in the forthcoming *Building Beond the Homestead: Rural History on the Prairies*, eds. David C. Jones and Ian MacPherson (Calgary: University of Calgary Press); and by Jones in the forthcoming *We'll All Be Buried Down Here: The Prairie Dryland Disaster, 1916-1926* (Calgary: Alberta Records Publication Board and Historical Society of Alberta).

19. For many of the following comments on the nature of community-sponsored local histories, I am indebted to Joanne A. Stiles for permission to read her unpublished manuscript, "Popular Perceptions of the Frontier in Rural Alberta."

20. Ibid., 10, 15.

21. H.A. Dempsey, "Local Histories as Source Materials for Western Canadian Studies," in *Prairie Perspectives* 2. ed. Anthony W. Rasporich and Henry C. Klassen (Toronto: Holt, Rinehart and Winston, 1973), 171-180.

XI

URBAN SOCIETY AND LABOUR
IN PRAIRIE CANADA

Until recently western Canadian historians have emphasized the agricultural aspect of western development. Yet at least a third of the immigrants who came to the Prairies prior to 1914 lived in urban centres. What factors led to the rapid rise of cities; what was the nature of their growth; and what impact did they have on the larger region? These are questions which urban historians now address.

Cities developed slowly on the prairies. When Canada acquired the area in 1870, no urban centres existed—only small isolated trading posts and scattered settlements. Yet, cities grew at an astonishing rate in the settlement period from 1870 to 1914. By 1911, thirteen cities with a population over 5,000 existed through the region, plus hundreds of smaller towns and villages. A decade later, one third of the Prairies was urban in composition.

A number of complex factors account for this rapid growth, but two in particular stand out above the others: the railroad and boosterism. To be situated on a rail line was a distinct advantage for a prairie urban centre. Yet there were numerous towns and villages on the rail line, but only a few that succeeded in evolving into cities. What often made the difference was the vigorous promotion of the urban centres by "boosters"—usually civic and business leaders. They worked hard to convince potential residents that their city was the best in the West in hopes of an eventual self-fulfilling prophecy. Alan Artibise discusses the nature of "boosterism" and its importance in the rise of urban centres on the prairies in the formative period from 1870 to 1914 in "Boosterism and the Development of Prairie Cities, 1871-1913."

With prairie settlement came a work force. Initially workers tended to be hired by the two dominant companies in the region: the Hudson's Bay Company and the Canadian Pacific Railway Company. As agriculture developed, especially in the period after Canada acquired the region, farm labour grew, and clearly formed the bulk of the work force on the Prairies prior to World War I. But workers were also needed in the lumber industry, in mining, and in the urban centres. Eventually a working-class consciousness emerged with values and aspirations similar to those of workers in other regions of the country while at the same time displaying distinctive features due to the effect of the unique prairie environment. In "Early Working-Class Life on the Prairies," Joe Cherwinski surveys the evolution of a working class on the Prairies and the resulting rise of a working-class consciousness.

Prairie labour history has shifted its focus. An earlier generation of historians concentrated on the evolution of such institutions as trade unions and labour organizations as being indicative of working-class attitudes, and raised questions about the uniqueness of prairie labour experience—especially its radicalism—in relation to other regions of the country. More recently, prairie labour historians have sought to understand social life among prairie workers in an attempt to delineate the characteristics of a prairie working-class consciousness. Were prairie labourers workers first and westerners secondly? In other words did a class or regional identity prevail? Were the two forces in opposition, or did prairie workers share values and attitudes with their brothers and sisters in other regions of the country? Even within the region did urban and rural workers share any common attitudes and aspirations? What was life like for workers in resource-based towns and did they share in the town's power base? These are some of the questions prairie labour historians are asking, and their answers, although still of a preliminary nature, are increasing our awareness that the prairies were never solely a rural and agricultural society. If we are to understand the region's complexity we must come to terms with its urban and working-class societies as well.

SELECTED BIBLIOGRAPHY

For an overview of urban development in prairie Canada see the articles in A.F.J. Artibise, ed., *Town and City: Aspects of Western Canadian Urban Development* (Regina, 1981), as well as J.M.S. Careless's "Aspects of Urban Life in the West, 1871-1914," in G.A. Stelter and A.F.J. Artibise, eds., *The Canadian City: Essays in Urban History* (Toronto, 1977), pp. 123-41; and A.F.J. Artibise, "Patterns of Prairie Urban Development, 1871-1950," in D.J. Bercuson and P. Buckner, eds., *Eastern and Western Perspectives* (Toronto, 1981), pp. 115-46.

On the important role that the Canadian Pacific Railway played in the evolution of prairie towns and cities, see Max Foran, "The CPR and the Urban West, 1881-1930," in Hugh A. Dempsey, ed., *The CPR West: The Iron Road and the Making of a Nation* (Vancouver, 1984), pp. 89-106, and Paul Voisey, "The Urbanization of the Canadian Prairies, 1871-1916,"

Histoire Sociale/Social History 8 (1975): 77-101. The importance of boosterism in the development of prairie urban centres is discussed further in A.F.J. Artibise, "City Building in the Canadian West: From Boosterism to Corporatism," *Journal of Canadian Studies* 17 (Fall 1981): 35-44, and his "Continuity and Change: Elites and Prairie Urban Development, 1914-1950," in A.F.J. Artibise and G.A. Stelter, eds., *The Usable Urban Past: Planning and Politics in the Modern Canadian City* (Toronto, 1979), pp. 130-54. Studies of three prairie cities are currently available through the History of Canadian Cities series published by James Lorimer and the Canadian Museum of Civilization: A.F.J. Artibise, *Winnipeg* (1977); Max Foran, *Calgary* (1978); and William Brennan, *Regina* (1990).

On labour in western Canada, students should consult the interpretative article by D.J. Bercuson, "Labour Radicalism and the Western Industrial Frontier, 1897-1919," *Canadian Historical Review* 58 (1977): 154-75, as well as Donald Avery, *'Dangerous Foreigners': European Immigrant Workers and Labour Radicalism in Canada, 1896-1932* (Toronto, 1979), and Ross McCormack, *Reformers, Rebels and Revolutionaries: The Western Canadian Radical Movement, 1899-1919* (Toronto, 1977). Specifically on labour unrest and the Winnipeg General Strike, see David J. Bercuson, *Confrontation at Winnipeg: Labour, Industrial Relations and the General Strike* (Montreal, 1974) and his *Fools and Wise Men: The Rise and Fall of One Big Union* (Toronto, 1978). For the strikers view of the Strike, see Norman Penner, ed., *Winnipeg 1919: The Strikers Own History of the Winnipeg General Strike* (Toronto, 1973). On labour in the Alberta coal fields see D.J. Bercuson, ed., *Alberta Coal Industry 1919* (Edmonton, 1978) and A.A. den Otter, "Social Life of a Mining Community: The Coal Branch," *Alberta Historical Review* 17 (1969): 1-11. Life in the frontier camps is vividly described in Edmund W. Bradwin's *The Bunkhouse Man: A Study of Work and Pay in the Camps of Canada 1903-14* (1928) (Reprinted Toronto, 1972).

ALAN F.J. ARTIBISE

25 Boosterism and the Development of Prairie Cities, 1871-1913

In 1871 the prairies had no urban centres. Except for a few Hudson's Bay Company posts, there was no commercial development. The population of the region, some 73,000 persons, was entirely rural. Forty years later, in 1911, the urbanization process on the prairies was well advanced. The region could boast of twelve cities with populations of over 5,000 and one, Winnipeg, with a population approaching 150,000. By this time too the region's population exceeded 1,300,000 and over 35 percent could be classified as urban. Furthermore, the general urban pattern of the prairies was firmly established by 1911, and five cities had emerged as dominant urban centres. These cities — Winnipeg, Regina, Calgary, Saskatoon, and Edmonton — have remained the primary urban concentrations of the region (see Tables 1 and 2.)[1]

In the years before 1911 it was by no means certain that these particular communities would become the prairies' largest cities. It is, of course, unlikely that the region could have supported many more large centres since in this early period urban growth depended to a large degree on the resource base.[2] The rapidity and degree of urbanization was closely tied to the agricultural development of the region. Also, as geographers and economists have pointed out, such factors as locational advantage, agricultural and transportation technology, conscious federal policy in respect to the West, and general economic conditions made it probable that urban development on the prairies would follow a set pattern.[3] Yet, even though all the ingredients for urban growth were present, and even though they all pointed toward a particular pattern, it was, in the final analysis, only the skill and initiative of individuals and groups that translated opportunity into reality.[4] In other words, while the growth of prairie cities cannot be fully explained by internal factors, such as the activities of individuals and groups, neither can the growth process be explained only by impersonal or mechanistic forces. In

TABLE 1   Populations of Prairie Cities, 1871-1916[a]

City	1871	1881	1891	1901	1906	1911	1916
Winnipeg	241	7,985	25,639	42,340	90,153	136,035	163,000
Calgary	—	—	3,867	4,392	13,573	43,704	56,514
Edmonton	—	—	300[b]	4,176	14,088	31,064	53,846
Regina	—	800[c]	1,681[d]	2,249	6,169	30,213	26,127
Saskatoon	—	—	—	113	3,011	12,004	21,048
Moose Jaw	—	—	—	1,558	6,249	13,823	16,934
Brandon	—	—	—	5,620	10,408	13,839	15,215
St. Boniface	817	1,283	1,553	2,019	5,119	7,483	11,021
Lethbridge	—	—	—	2,072	2,936	9,035	9,436
Medicine Hat	—	—	—	1,570	3,020	5,608	9,272
Prince Albert	—	—	—	1,785	3,005	6,254	6,436
Portage la Prairie	—	—	3,363	3,901	5,106	5,892	5,879

NOTES: a) Population is listed according to areas as of 1916.
   b) This is an approximation taken from City of Edmonton records.
   c) The population of Regina in 1882-1883 was between "800 and 900 souls." See
      E.G. Drake, *Regina: The Queen City*, p. 22.
   d) *Ibid.*, p.71.
SOURCE: *Census of Prairie Provinces*, 1916.

TABLE 2   Rural and Urban[a] Population Growth in Prairie Provinces,
   1871-1916 (in thousands)

	Northwest Territories		Manitoba		Total Prairies		
	Rural	Urban	Rural	Urban	Rural	Urban	%Urban
1871	48	—	25	—	73	—	0
1881	56	—	52	10	108	10	8
1891	95	4	111	41	206	45	18

	Alberta		Saskatchewan					
	Rural	Urban	Rural	Urban				
1901	54	19	77	14	185	70	316	103	25
1906	127	58	209	48	228	138	564	244	30
1911	237	138	361	131	261	200	859	470	35
1916	307	189	471	176	313	241	1,091	606	36

NOTE: a) Includes incorporated villages, towns, and cities.
SOURCE: *Census of the Prairie Provinces, 1916; Census of Canada, 1931*, Volume 1.

the case of Winnipeg, for example, location theory does not necessarily provide for the emergence of a single city pattern in the Red River Valley. A more diffuse urban pattern might well have developed.[5] The fact that such a diffuse pattern did not develop is not easily explained, but it can be said with some degree of certainty that one determining factor in the particular pattern that did emerge in Manitoba, and later in Saskatchewan and Alberta, was the initiative of civic and business leaders.

The success of one prairie city relative to another was not determined only by a convenient location or the impersonal forces of urbanization.[6] The residents of prairie cities interacted with the environment, and their hopes, beliefs, energy, community spirit, initiative and adaptability influenced the rate of growth, degree of prosperity, and physical form of the cities. While the role of municipal governments and business organizations in altering the rate and pattern of urban development on the prairies was certainly limited by outside forces, the growth, shape, and character of the five major cities owes much to the policies devised and vigorously applied by these bodies in response to the possibilities and problems that emerged for their communities.[7]

The role individuals and groups played in shaping prairie urban development has already received some attention from those interested in the city-building process in Canada. In particular, such activities as railway promotion, immigration encouragement, industry attraction, governmental reform, municipal ownership, and efforts to attain status as both provincial capital and home of the provincial university, have been studied in some depth and will only be touched on here.[8] But other topics — such as city incorporations, massive boundary extensions, huge public works programs, deficit financing, and land value taxation policies — have received little or no attention. It is these policies, and their impact on the development of prairie cities, that are the subject of this study.

I

An important element in an analysis of the role of individual and group activity is some understanding of the beliefs and activities of the people involved. The vast majority believed in a particular set of ideas about urban development, they shared what can be called the booster spirit, and from this mental set different ways of dealing with particular possibilities and problems emerged. Urban boosterism was both something more than a compendium of super salesmanship or mindless rhetoric, and something less than a precise ideology. It was a broad, general conception that had as its central theme the need for growth; the idea that for a city to become "better" it had to become bigger. This general notion was shared by virtually all members of the commercial classes of prairie cities, although there were, of course, variations in the degree of attachment to the booster spirit. But what is most significant about prairie boosterism is that it existed on a plane above normal social, political, and commercial rivalries.

The vast majority of boosters were Anglo-Saxon Protestants of relatively humble origin who had come West from the small towns and cities of the Maritimes and Ontario.[9] Before migrating, many had gained considerable experience in promoting urban growth in eastern urban centres. But the possibilities in the east were too limited for some elements, particularly, according to a British visitor in 1911, the "restless, the men who were strong and willing to dare, who saw riches around them, but beyond them, and who went West to strive, to battle, to conquer, to gain riches for themselves."[10]

The booster mentality was made up of a web of beliefs and attitudes, but a few stand out above the others. The most important parts of the mental baggage of the boosters were a belief in the desirability of growth and in the importance of material success.[11] To boosters, the challenge presented by the undeveloped prairies was to build there a prosperous, populous, and dynamic region as quickly as possible. They accepted the challenge eagerly, seeing themselves as energetic agents of improvement. They set no limits on the expectations and were intensely optimistic, expansionary, and aggressive. Their interests lay in what has been called the "architectural aspects of society" — the broad lines of its material fabric.[12] Boosters were constantly measuring their city's progress in quantitative terms — numbers of rail lines, miles of streets, dollars of assessment, size of population, value of manufacturing output or wholesale trade, and so on.

Since progress was measured in material terms, prairie boosters directed their efforts toward encouraging rapid and sustained growth in their cities at the expense of virtually all other considerations. This meant for example, that while all prairie boosters wanted the region to grow rapidly, they were especially concerned with the growth of their own communities. Despite the early prominence of Winnipeg, the boosters of the other four cities optimistically envisioned their centre becoming the pre-eminent metropolis of the area. There was, as a result, virtually no cooperation among the five cities in dealings with the railways, eastern industry, the federal government, or any other "outside" force.[13] Each centre zealously competed with the others for economic advantage and prestige. Commenting on this phenomenon, one observer noted in 1915 that

> [western cities had not] quite reached that secure position in which a community can afford to say unpleasant things about itself . . . If Edmonton discovers that it has unemployment, the cry is at once 'Come to Calgary!' 'Invest in Calgary industries!' 'Buy Calgary lots!' If Calgary finds it has slum conditions, Edmonton is ready to profit by the opportunity; Regina pounces with joy on any evil spoken of Saskatoon; and the drift of capital and labour may really be affected. Therefore in each city all citizens possessing property are in a conspiracy of silence, or rather unite in so

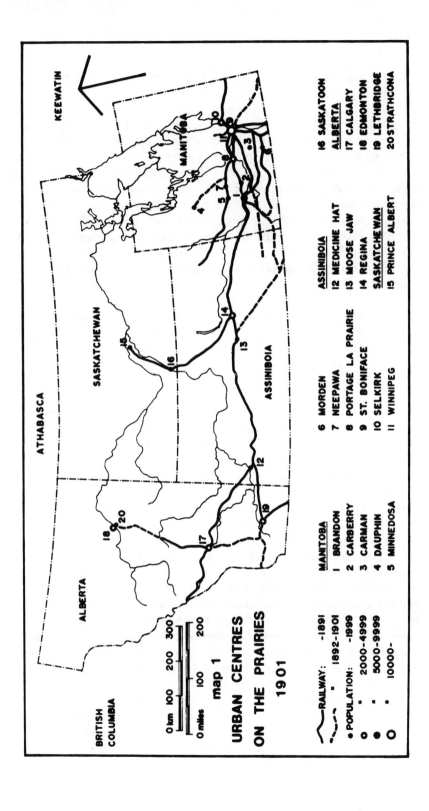

map 1

URBAN CENTRES
ON THE PRAIRIES
1901

RAILWAY: -1891
              1892-1901
POPULATION: -1999
              2000-4999
              5000-9999
              10000-

0 km 100 200 200 300
0 miles   100   200

BRITISH
COLUMBIA

ALBERTA

ATHABASCA

SASKATCHEWAN

ASSINIBOIA

MANITOBA

KEEWATIN

MANITOBA
1 BRANDON
2 CARBERRY
3 CARMAN
4 DAUPHIN
5 MINNEDOSA

6 MORDEN
7 NEEPAWA
8 PORTAGE LA PRAIRIE
9 ST. BONIFACE
10 SELKIRK
11 WINNIPEG

ASSINIBOIA
12 MEDICINE HAT
13 MOOSE JAW
14 REGINA

SASKATCHEWAN
15 PRINCE ALBERT

16 SASKATOON

ALBERTA
17 CALGARY
18 EDMONTON
19 LETHBRIDGE
20 STRATHCONA

hearty a chorus on the glories of their city and district that no other sound can be heard in the neighbourhood.[14]

But while there was a noted lack of co-operation, and sometimes even good-will among the five prairie cities,[15] there was a high degree of co-ordination within each city among the boosters. To prairie townsmen, not to be a booster — not to be part of the team — showed both a lack of community spirit and a lack of business sense. Boosting was essential to progress and prosperity; good citizenship and boosting were synonymous.[16] Successful boosting demanded both collaboration and trust in the pursuit of broad, common goals and priorities on which everyone in the community could agree. An active and positive attitude toward the community was expected and demanded of the "good citizen." As one pioneer Saskatoon merchant put it:

> All were imbued with an optimism that Saskatoon was destined to become an important centre. Newcomers in business were welcomed and encouraged; everyone pulled together to develop and boom the town; there were no petty jealousies of one another. In fact there had already come to life (by 1904) what has rightly been called 'the Saskatoon spirit.'[17]

Boosters saw themselves as community builders in mushrooming cities with unbounded hopes; an environment where personal and public growth, personal and public prosperity intermingled. There was no room for sceptics or, as they were often called, "knockers." Indeed, so powerful was the booster psychology of the civic and business leaders that few in any of the cities rose to challenge their leadership. Throughout the period, the boosterism of the many overshadowed the caution or opposition of the few.[18]

This general lack of overt opposition to boosterism in prairie cities was in part the result of a restricted municipal franchise which did not allow the majority of residents to participate in civic affairs. But the lack of opposition also stemmed from the fact that the boosters effectively used the idea of community solidarity as a purification ritual, a means of discrediting opponents. Advocates and supporters of boosterism were intent on creating a feeling of community spirit on the basis of voluntarism, without any basic revision of the system of economic inequity and social injustice that existed in the cities. They did this by successfully promoting the notion that all classes and groups could be united on the basis of faith in the city, belief in its destiny, and commitment to its growth.

The community spirit promoted by the elites of prairie cities was one that was fashioned more out of will than out of reality, more out of wishful thinking than out of experience. The elites talked about understanding and common ties, about creating a store of wealth to benefit all citizens, but in fact were generally unconcerned about the vast majority of residents as long as they did not disrupt existing relationships. The myth of a shared sense of community was thus a valuable falsehood for the boosters since it enabled them to implement their programs with a minimum of opposition. The booster ethos was calculated not only to meet immediate needs and insure urban expansion, but also to justify social conformity and maintain the existing social and economic system since only a "united" community could prosper. Boosterism as practised in prairie cities even had a tinge of blackmail associated with it. So effective were the booster campaigns about opportunity for everyone, about wealth and greatness available for the grasping, that few residents were not involved. Nearly everyone was infected with the boom psychology, and once involved — whether in land speculation or business promotion — there was an added financial incentive to support the booster campaigns.[19]

Strong beliefs in the virtues of rapid growth, material progress, and social conformity were combined with an equally strong belief in the special role of local government. The boosters shared the view that the active encouragement of growth and business enterprise was the prime concern of a municipal corporation. Local government was purely functional; it was a tool serving personal and community prosperity. Unlike municipal corporations in older, established cities, the governments of the upstart prairies cities had little odour of sanctity; time-honoured precedents that might have got in the way of the uses to which government was put were nonexistent. Prairie city boosters were not confronted with the problem of evading obsolete regulations or dislodging established oligarchies as were their counterparts in the East.[20] In the West, "the dignity of government (was) much diminished, its utility greatly increased."[21] It was merely a device to be used for the benefit of the people who had managed to gain political power or influence. And in all prairie cities it was the businessmen who early gained control of government and who continued throughout the period to maintain that control.

Another element in the booster mentality was the loose degree of attachment to the gospel of Social Darwinism. It is true, of course, that boosters often sang the praises of rugged individualism and competition. But it is also true that "the reality was often at variance with the rhetoric."[22] As one student of the attitudes of Canadian businessmen during this period observes:

> Individualism, though clearly insufficient for business success, was deemed perfectly sufficient for success as a worker or farmer. Business was justified in striving mightily to overcome the laws of supply and demand and the forces of the marketplace; others should bend to them. Co-operation was the keynote of the new business philosophy; hard work and saving were to be others' code. The leaders of trade combines were business statesmen; the leaders of labour unions and farmers' organizations were parasitical demagogues. The price-cutter in business was a pirate, reckless and unethical; the scab worker was a free and honest man.[23]

The attitude of boosters toward organized labour and the poor and disadvantaged was one of scorn, and the cities the boosters dominated spent only
a small fraction of their budgets on such community services as sanitation,
health departments, or welfare — far less than was spent on promoting
growth. In these areas, "survival of the fittest" was the norm.

The individualism of the boosters was selective, influencing only some
of their activities. It often amounted to a philosophy of individualism for
the poor and cooperation for the rich.[24] Boosters not only used the communities' funds for their own ends but went further to become in many instances
firm believers in municipal ownership. It is also noteworthy that one of the
first organizations created in all prairie cities was a board of trade, designed
through cooperation to facilitate the growth of the cities.[25]

One final, general point can be made concerning the boosters' beliefs and
attitudes. While the philosophy or outlook of the prairie booster was sur-
charged with an optimism which sometimes resulted in self-deception, it was
rarely blind to the essentials of urban growth. There was a strong strain of
realism in it. Boosters realized that the development of the wheat economy
would result in the establishment of a large number of towns and villages
linked up with a limited number of commercial cities situated at the junc-
tion points of several railway lines.[26] They also knew that the uniform topography of the prairies placed a large number of small centres on an almost
equal footing as aspirants for the coveted prize of big city status. Only a few
possessed natural advantages as townsites and these were either shared with
others or were not sufficiently prominent to discourage rivals. Every booster
knew, almost instinctively, that the telling distinction would be the initiative and skill of his community's leaders.

II

One characteristic that was shared by boosters in all five centres was an eagerness to attain formal city status for their communities far in advance of that
title coinciding with reality. Winnipeg, unlike the other prairie cities, never
did go through the chrysalis stage of either village or town. When incorporated by the provincial legislature in November 1873, the approximately
1,600 residents of the small hamlet sought and obtained at the outset the
clear and unambiguous title of city — a terminology, however divorced from
reality, they felt would be more respected back East.[27] Regina was not quite
so brash. Although it skipped the village state, it was incorporated as a town
in December 1883 with the distinction of being the first organized urban
centre of the territories.[28] The new town's population was around 900. Furthermore, it was not until 1903 that Regina sought and achieved incorporation as a city.[29] But this uncharacteristic tardiness in seeking city status
is balanced by two significant facts. First, although legally only a town,
Regina adopted the title of city in practice soon after 1883.[30] Second, when

it did apply for city status in 1903, Regina had a population of under 3,000, hardly the numbers usually associated with a city.

Calgary followed Regina's example in immediately incorporating as a town in 1884. It had, at the time, a meagre population of 506.[31] Nine years later, in 1893, with a population of less than 4,000, Calgary received its city charter, the first urban centre in the territories to acquire that status.[32] In Edmonton, members of the Board of Trade, organized in 1889, pushed for incorporation. In February 1892, with a population of only 700, Edmonton became a town. City status came in 1904 when the population was 8,350.[33] Edmonton thus had the distinction of having the largest population of any of the five prairie centres when it formally became a city, though it can be noted that as late as 1901 its population was only 2,626. Saskatoon was the last of the five communities to formally incorporate as a city; it did not attain that goal until 1906 when its population was 3,000. Saskatoon was also the only one of the five to follow the pattern of village, town, and finally city status. It had first been organized as a village in November 1901 with a population of 113. But this lowly status did not long remain in effect since in 1903 Saskatoon became a town.[34]

The manner in which all five urban centres sought and finally achieved city status was very much in keeping with the boom psychology of the pre-1913 era.[35] The arguments used in each community were strikingly similar. Local pride, respect in eastern Canada, and the distinction of achieving the coveted "city" title far in advance of rivals were common refrains.[36] Municipal organization was essentially a technique of boosting — "it advertized the community and gave it a dignity which its physical appearance could not impart;... it was an act of faith, an expression of confidence in the future."[37] The fact that formal municipal organization was also a means to self-government was only rarely mentioned.[38] But these arguments, or the lack of them, were neither the most effective nor the most significant. The most important were that town and city status provided a broader base for borrowing funds for public works and other expenditures, and that the titles presented opportunities for advertising and promotion.

Saskatoon's incorporation experiences are especially enlightening in this regard, although they were not very different from those of other prairie centres.[39] In 1902, the residents of the village of Saskatoon were aware that a group of British immigrants — the Barr Colonists — were scheduled to stop over en route to their new homes.[40] Several local businessmen immediately seized upon this anticipated event as a good reason to seek town status. They argued that to encourage immigrants to remain in the district, Saskatoon would have to carry out an extensive public works program and to do so would have to borrow large sums of money. Since villages could borrow an amount equal to only five percent of the total assessment while town status permitted borrowing double this amount, a campaign for incorporation as a town was hastily begun. To reach the 450 needed for town status, the organizers of the incorporation movement had to include in their census not only permanent residents but also guests in the hotels crowded with the spring immigration rush and everyone else in sight, but it was argued that the visitors would probably settle in Saskatoon anyway. In July 1903, Saskatoon was incorporated as a town.[41] Two years later, similar arguments were used to achieve city status, which allowed borrowing to twenty percent of assessment. This time the increased power was needed to help in the effort to obtain both the provincial capital and the main line of the Grand Trunk Pacific Railway. The success of the campaign for incorporation as a city was never in doubt.[42]

As important as the achievement of city status was to the boosters, it alone did not satisfy their grand visions. In the years prior to the recession of 1913, all five cities underwent vast spatial expansions, bringing huge areas of land within their municipal boundaries. Winnipeg, which started off with an area of 1,920 acres in 1873, had grown to include 14,861 acres by 1913. This was accomplished by two major annexations of territory, in 1882 and 1906, and by several smaller additions in 1875, 1902, 1905, 1907 and 1913. Significantly, the city did not again expand its boundaries until 1963 except to add very small areas of land.[43] In Regina's case, the expansion was completed in one fell swoop. With an area of 1,942 acres in 1883, Regina increased its size fourfold in 1911 by adding 6,458 acres. It, too, found it unnecessary to make any further major additions until the 1950s.[44]

The town of Calgary began in 1884 with 1,600 acres, and through annexations in 1901, 1903, 1906, 1907, 1910, and 1911 it reached a size of almost 26,000 acres by 1912. No further additions were made until 1951.[45] Saskatoon's expansion was more modest. When incorporated as a city in 1906 it included 2,567 acres and, prior to the 1950s, made only one major addition — in 1911 it increased its territory by 5,913 acres.[46] The record for expansion clearly belongs to Edmonton. In 1892 it was a town comprising only 2,162 acres. But additions quickly followed in 1899, 1904, 1908, 1911, 1912 and 1913. With two further annexations in 1914 and 1917, the city grew to no less than 26,290 acres. Again, no further major additions were undertaken until the 1950s.[47]

The "land hunger" of the booster-oriented city councils of the five prairie cities gave them a special status among Canada's urban centres. In 1921 four prairie cities — Edmonton, Calgary, Saskatoon, and Regina — had the lowest population density ratios of Canada's twenty largest urban areas (see Table 3). Edmonton, for example, had only 2.2 persons per acre in 1921 compared to 19.2 for Montreal, 31.5 for Toronto, and 13.6 for Halifax. Regina's population of 34,432 was spread out over 8,429 acres, a density of 4.1 per acre. In contrast, Windsor, with a population of 38,591 had a land area of 2,726 acres and a population density of over 14 per acre.

The boundary extensions of prairie cities were products of the boom psychology of the period preceding 1913 and provided perhaps the best example

TABLE 3   Area and Density of Population of Canada's Twenty Largest Cities, 1921

City	Rank		Population	Land Area in Sq. Miles	Population per Sq. Mile
	By Size	By Density			
Montreal	1	3	618,506	50.24	12,311
Toronto	2	1	521,893	25.89	20,158
Winnipeg	3	9	179,087	23.22	7,712
Vancouver	4	10	117,217	16.89	6,703
Hamilton	5	6	114,151	12.11	9,426
Ottawa	6	2	107,843	6.44	16,745
Quebec	7	5	95,193	8.84	10,768
Calgary	8	19	63,305	40.50	1,563
London	9	11	60,959	10.03	6,077
Edmonton	10	20	58,821	42.50	1,384
Halifax	11	8	58,372	6.72	8,686
Saint John	12	16	47,166	14.31	3,296
Victoria	13	13	38,727	7.25	5,341
Windsor	14	7	38,591	4.26	9,058
Regina	15	17	34,432	13.17	2,614
Brantford	16	12	29,440	4.93	5,972
Saskatoon	17	18	25,739	12.50	2,059
Verdun	18	4	25,001	2.22	11,262
Hull	19	15	24,117	6.25	3,859
Sherbrooke	20	14	23,515	4.85	4,848

SOURCE: *Census of Canada,* 1921, Vol. 1.

of the inflated expectations of the boosters. Large areas were added to the cities far in advance of population pressure; not only did prairie cities have some of the lowest population densities among Canadian cities, but in every case the population was far from evenly distributed throughout the area. Indeed, vast stretches of the city's lands were completely uninhabited or unused (see Figures 1 and 2).[48]

Since population pressure can hardly account for any but a very few of the many annexations of territory, the reasons for the physical growth must be sought elsewhere. They are not hard to find. Among the arguments used by expansionists was the fact that extended boundaries gave the city larger total assessment values, thus increasing both tax revenues and the borrowing power of the municipal corporation.[49] Large assessment figures were also useful when cities went seeking customers for city bonds and

FIGURE 1   Saskatoon in 1912

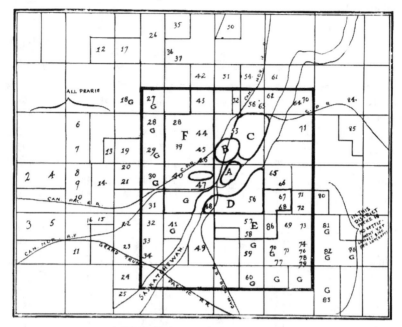

A WESTERN CITY IN THE MAKING.

Map of City of Saskatoon and surrounding territory, drawn to scale, each block representing a section of 640 acres, or one square mile. Saskatoon has now a population of about 20,000, and the official "city" limits contain in the neighborhood of fourteen square miles, or half the area of Toronto, and three-quarters the area of Montreal. The heavy black lines in the form of a square represent the city limits as they now exist. Key to map: A-The select business section, with land at $2,000 per front foot, the price of centrally located business property in Toronto. B-Business section, land $1,000 per front foot. Small oval to left of A is a small business centre. Here land is selling at $350 per front foot. C-Good residence section. D-Land here $80 to $100 per front foot. E-About limits of actual settlement on east side of river. F and G—Open prairie.

It will be observed that the vast majority of these sub-divisions which the easterner has been buying are not now withing practicable walking distance of the business centre of Saskatoon, and, as our Special Commissioner puts it, are for the most part the product of "strong-arm come-ons."

Upper left hand corner—
Crescent Heights
2—Leland Park
3—Industrial Centre and Industrial
Centre Addition
4—Regal Terrace
5—Cordage Park
6—Windsor Park
7—Westward Park
8—National Park
9—St. Charles Park
10—Sunnyside Central Park
11—Union Centre
12—Broad Acres
13—Dundonald
14—Fairhaven
15,16—Shaughnessy Heights
17—Regent Park
18—Glen Arbor
19—Mount Royal Annex
20—Pleasant Hill Annex
21—St. Paul's Place
22—Rosedale Addition
23—Fairview
24—Burnside
25—Fort Rouge
26—Devonshire Heights Annex
27—Tuxedo Park
28. Highbury Park

29—Mount Royal
30—Pleasant Hill
31—Andrews Addition
32—Rosedale
33—Parkview—A
34—Parkview and Transcona
35—Penryn Park
36—Long Acres
37—Saskhome
38—F. Ruskin Place
39—Westmount
G—Riverview
41—G—G.T.P. Addition
42—Lakeview
43—Mayfair
44—Caswell Hill Addition
45,46—Ashworth Hulmes Addition
47—Riverdale
48—IdylwyId Park
49—Bellevue Addition
50—Silver Heights
51—Highlands
52—McVicar Addition
53—Bowerman Survey
54—Highlands Addition
56,63—Schlick Addition and
North Park
56—D—Nutana

57,58—Buenavista
59—Broadway Addition
60—Pacific Addition
61—Richmond Park Annex
62—Richmond Park
64, 70—Parkdale
65,66—University Annex and
Bottom—ley Addition
67,68—College Park
69—Nutana Hill
70—Victoria Park
71—University Heights
72—Alexandra Park
73—University Homes
74—Nutana Park
75—University Park
76—Nutana View
77—Sterling Park
78—Altavista
79—Hampton Park
80—Queen's Park
81—Brevoort Park
82—Utopia
83—Preston Place
84—Sylvan View
85—Sutherland
86—Coronation Park
86—G. Melrose Park

SOURCE: Norman Harris, "What's What in Western Real Estate—Saskatoon and its '57 Varieties' of Subdivisions," *Saturday Night*, Vol. 25, No. 34 (June 1, 1912), p.17.

FIGURE 2   Edmonton in 1912

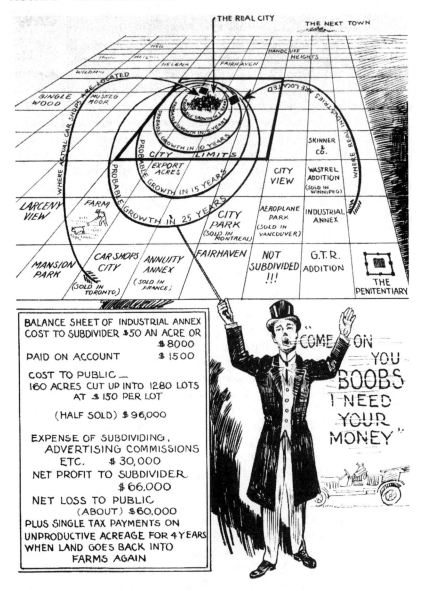

SOURCE: Norman Harris, "What's What in Western Real Estate—Edmonton the City of the North," *Saturday Night*, Vol. 25, No. 40 (July 13, 1912), p.17.

debentures.[50] Another reason for the expansions was the argument that much of the land surrounding the cities was held by foreign — i.e., non-resident — speculators and that by bringing the land within the city's taxing authority, a source of revenue that would be of benefit to local citizens could be tapped.[51] The most important reason, however, was the pressure exerted on city councils by local real estate interests. In every city vast chunks of agricultural land were subdivided and offered for sale.[52] In Saskatoon, for example, there were only twenty-eight real estate firms in 1903; by 1912 there were 267 operating firms with land available for sale in no less than 107 subdivisions. Despite the fact that over 5,900 acres had just been added to the city in 1901, there were, in 1913, forty square miles of agricultural land outside the city limits subdivided for intended urban expansion. Had the real estate bubble not burst in 1913, Saskatoon probably would have expanded it boundaries still further.[53] In Calgary, expansions were urged on by most of the city's two thousand real estate agents who, in 1912, operated out of 443 firms.[54] And in Winnipeg in 1913 there was land for sale in no less than twenty subdivisions outside the city limits. The *Canadian Annual Review* of 1913 summed up the situation:

> Through the Western Provinces . . . everybody had been speculating in real estate, every village and town had been anticipating the days when it would be a city or important centre. Nearly everyone for a time had made money out of selling properties to others in their locality, to the visitor or investor from abroad, to the speculator in another city, to syndicates which further exploited the property or combination of properties as Subdivisions, to the American sharper who bought land for a trifle miles away from the centre of a town and flooded Eastern or English newspapers with flashy advertisements of "a choice residential centre" close to such and such a progressive town, or rising centre, or seat of future railway and industrial development . . . The whole thing was ephemeral, a natural product of exotic progress, an outgrowth of Western enthusiasm.[55]

The advantages, for owners of real estate, that came with the inclusion of their property within city boundaries were twofold. First, it was a decided benefit to be able to legitimately advertise one's property as being in a city, rather than on the outskirts, although it must be noted that this obstacle was often overcome by other means.[56] Second, inclusion within boundaries meant that urban services — waterworks, sewers, roads, streetcar lines, and so on — were likely to be extended to one's property, and this obviously led to increased prospects for both sales and profits. Thus, as with the move to city status, inclusion of land within city boundaries had the effect of raising the value and appeal of real estate holdings.

III

The fantastic spatial growth of the prairie cities, coupled with the rapid population growth that occurred in the pre-1913 period, presented a gargantuan problem for local authorities. Municipal services needed to be expanded at an ever increasing pace. In Alberta's cities, for example, the expenditure and debenture debt increased at a startling pace in the years 1906-1913. In 1906 Alberta's cities spent only $2 million; in 1912 they spent $16.6 million. The total surged to a high of $36.5 million in 1913. The city of Edmonton alone spent forty percent of the 1913 total, or one and a half times the entire provincial government expenditure in that year.[57] Calgary spent $1 million on civic building in 1911 and another $3 million on street railways, waterworks, sewers, schools, electric lighting, paving and parks.[58] In the five years from 1909 to 1913 Winnipeg expended $81,000,000 on buildings alone; Calgary, $50,000,000; Edmonton, $32,000,000; Regina, $20,000,000; and Saskatoon, $14,000,000.[59]

While much of this massive expenditure was made in a legitimate attempt to provide necessary services to a burgeoning population, there was also a good deal of unnecessary expansion during the period — expenditures that added unwarranted burdens to the already over-taxed facilities and resources of the prairie cities. The irony of the situation was that in providing services to new and unpopulated subdivisions far from the city centres, councils neglected to provide adequate services to already developed areas.[60] In Regina, the municipally-owned street railway system was under constant pressure by private real estate firms to build lines into areas "well past the limits of heavy settlement where little and often no housing existed."[61] One result of this policy of creating streetcar suburbs was a loss of over $60,000 on the operation of the system in 1913, in addition to the service charges on the $1.5 million debt of the public street railway company 1913.[62] Yet the obvious lack of judicious planning apparent in the operation and expansion of the street railway system was contrasted with a situation in the city's foreign ghetto of "Germantown" where sixty percent of the houses lacked such basic services as sewer and water connections.[63]

A similar situation existed in Edmonton. In that city, the pressure exerted by private land developers in regard to the extension of city services nearly always had the desired effect. One writer, commenting on Edmonton city council's policies in regard to utility expansion, has stated:

> [Private land developers] bought lands on the periphery of the city but often could not develop or sell them without first having city services extended on them. Nor could they sell for a better price if the services were not first extended to the sites. Successfully they influenced the Council to extend to these areas not only the street-car system but other utilities as well, chiefly water and sewerage, and light and power. In this way

the value of their lands increased and, consequently, the harvest of profits.

Now it has to be admitted that the problem the Council faced was acute and complex. Yet, administrative authorities should not be guilty of favoritism. Moreover, the evidence of mismanagement, as revealed by the Council minutes of 1913, hints at this and suggests that their motives might have been self-interested. The evidence seems also to justify the conclusion that a well-thought out policy in regard to street railway extension was lacking. Before an extension was carried out no thought was given to the expenditure involved, the revenue to be derived that would or would not Warrant the extension, the distance the property was from existing utilities, and the scattered development that would exist . . . Thus the Council of 1913 may be criticized for permitting indiscriminate street railway extensions and by so doing increasing the burden of taxation. The waste was made manifest after the boom collapsed. The City was left with numerous pieces of vacant land, particularly on its periphery, serviced with utilities.[64]

The tremendous sums of money required to pay for the essential as well as the unessential expenditures of prairie cities during these years of rapid expansion came, of course, either from municipal taxes or from the sale of city bonds and debentures.[65] While it is true that prairie cities at one time or another raised some revenue from business taxes, licence fees, poll taxes, and even income taxes, the major source of income for the municipal corporations was property taxation.[66] Furthermore, the property taxes levied by the prairie cities, particularly in the years immediately preceding World War I, were for the most part taxes on the assessed value of land; improvements were either exempted or taxed at only a percentage of their value. While eastern Canadian cities continued in nearly every case to tax land and improvements at 100 percent of their value and to raise significant segments of their revenues from a variety of other sources, prairie cities moved rapidly in the pre-World War I era to an almost total dependence on land taxes. The reason for this situation was the influence of Henry George's single-tax philosophy throughout western Canada.

In its pure form the single tax is a system of taxation by which a community raises its entire revenue from land taxes. The justification given for the scheme is that the value of land is entirely due to the presence and expenditure of the people and the community should therefore receive the benefit through taxation. Through placing all taxes on land, Henry George hoped to nullify the negative effects of land speculation and ultimately eliminate private land ownership.[67] It is ironic then that the adoption of the single tax — or, more precisely, a modified version of it, since it was never followed in its pure form — should have been adopted in western Canadian cities at a time when speculators were making fortunes from land sales.[68] It is even more ironic that among the chief proponents of the modified single tax were the real estate speculators themselves.[69] It is clear, however, that the prairie boosters who supported the modified single tax philosophy did so for reasons that might well have caused Henry George to turn in his grave. For while all the classic arguments in support of land value taxation were bandied about, the adoption of a modified form of single tax in the five prairie cities came about for at least three specific reasons — reasons quite distinct from George's general philosophy.

First, a heavy tax on land values was a means whereby municipal corporations could raise large sums from non-resident land owners and speculators. In Edmonton, for example, the move to a single tax in 1904 came about largely as a way to shift the burdens of taxation to the Hudson's Bay Company, which, at the time, owned a tract of land approximately a mile and a half long by a mile wide in the heart of the city.[70] And even though resident speculators would also have to pay similar taxes, the local businessmen involved in speculation "do not expect to hold their land long, often not even over one tax-paying period" and they thus "do not object strongly to shifting of the (tax) burden to land."[71] The second reason for the adoption of a modified version of the single tax was the belief that it stimulated development by encouraging building. An investigator of the western Canadian tax situation observed:

> [Real estate men] are eager to encourage anything which promises to assist in increasing land values and nothing seems to be more effective for this purpose than the rapid construction of buildings. They are convinced that the land tax stimulates building, and, as one of them expressed it, every real estate man "is for all the single tax he can get." They look upon the plan as a bonus to building, and they, being interested primarily in that part of land which is ripe for building, pay only part of that bonus. Part is borne by the other land owners who had already purchased land when the tax was imposed — purchased it perhaps from these very real estate men. Thus, indirectly, they pay at least part of the bonus themselves.[72]

The third reason for the support the idea of land value taxation received was that it could be implemented in varying degrees without reducing the overall tax base. Since land values were increasing at a fantastic pace (see Table 4), and since prairie cities were continually expanding their boundaries, taxes on improvements and other forms of taxation could be reduced or removed entirely without the tax base diminishing.[73] Land assessment values in Winnipeg, for example, jumped from $11.9 million in 1900 to $53.7 million in 1906, and to $259.4 million by 1913. In Edmonton the increases were even more dramatic. Land assessment value stood at only $1.3 million in 1900; by 1913 it exceeded $188 million. In Calgary, property at the corner of 7th Avenue and 2nd Street West, just on the edge of the main business area, was valued at $150 in 1895. By 1905 the same lot was worth

$2,000; by 1912 the purchase price had jumped to $300,000.[74] In short, the move to an almost exclusive form of land value taxation was very much a product of the western boom.

The actual extent to which prairie cities adopted a modified version of the single tax varies considerably, although no western centre was immune from the intoxicating arguments put forward by single tax supporters. Of the five major cities, Winnipeg was affected least, perhaps because of the relative maturity of its leading businessmen and politicians and because of its dominant position in the urban hierarchy. In 1909 buildings, which until then had been taxed at 100 percent of their assessed value, began to be taxed at only two-thirds of their value.[75] In both Regina and Saskatoon taxes on improvements were reduced by a 1908 provincial statute to 60 percent, but the move toward the single tax did not stop here. Regina further reduced the improvement tax to 45 percent. In 1912 it became 35 percent and in 1913, 25 percent.[76] Calgary reduced its improvement tax from 100 percent to 80 percent in 1909 and then followed these reductions with two further ones in 1911 and 1912. In 1911 the tax was set at 50 percent; in 1912 it was reduced to 25 percent.[77] It was in Edmonton, however, that the single tax philosophy went furthest. In 1904 the improvement tax was eliminated; a situation which lasted until 1918. Several other taxes were also abandoned; the poll and income taxes in 1910 and the business tax in 1911.[78]

The effects these tax policies had upon the development of prairie cities were mixed. Even though the adoption of a modified version of the single tax occasioned numerous reports and studies, the wisdom of the policy remained a matter for debate. Supporters and detractors of land value taxation agreed on only one thing — the modified single tax did not stop land speculation. Single tax proponents argued that the tax did in fact stimulate development; its detractors labelled land value taxation a complete failure and held it responsible for the financial difficulties prairie cities faced in the decades after World War I.[79]

A judicious examination of the impact of the tax policies of prairie cities is, of course, impossible without considering these policies together with the other booster-inspired programs implemented in the years prior to 1914. Furthermore, until a great deal more research has been carried out, the cumulative effects of early city incorporation, massive boundary extensions, huge public works programs, deficit financing, and land value taxation (together with booster policies in such areas as railway promotion, immigration encouragement, industry attraction, and municipal ownership) cannot be detailed except in a very general way. A precise measurement of the effect of boosterism on urban development must obviously await further work, including a study of "losers" as well as "winners." But, even at this point, four observations or conclusions — however tentative — can be made.

It is clear, first of all, that in virtually every aspiring urban centre concerted efforts were made to facilitate growth. These policies took a variety

TABLE 4   Land Assessment Values in Prairie Cities, 1895-1913[a]
(in millions of dollars)

Year	Winnipeg	Regina	Saskatoon	Calgary	Edmonton
1895	11.7	—	—	1.5[b]	1.1
1900	11.9	—	—	1.0[c]	1.3
1902	12.6	1.0	—	1.0[d]	1.7
1904	25.1	2.2	0.4	2.1	3.9
1906	53.7	6.4	2.5	7.7	17.0
1908	62.7	12.4	8.1	10.3	22.5
1910	108.6	12.1	8.6	22.4	30.1
1912	151.7	65.5	35.4	102.2	123.4
1913	259.4	82.5	56.3	133.0	188.5

NOTE: a) The figures are net values, i.e., exempted property is excluded.
b) 80% of net value
c) Includes property owned by city and exemptions.
d) 90% of net value.
SOURCES: R.M. Haig, *The Exemption of Improvements From Taxation in Canada and the United States* (New York, 1915); Province of Manitoba, *Report of the Assessment and Taxation Commission* (Winnipeg, 1919); City of Saskatoon, *1975 Municipal Manual;* P.R. Creighton, "Taxation in Saskatoon: A Study in Municipal Finance," M.A. Thesis (University of Saskatchewan, 1925); Henry Howard, *The Western Cities: Their Borrowings and Their Assets* (London, England, 1914).

of forms, including early city incorporations, massive boundary extensions, huge public works programmes, deficit financing, special tax policies, railway promotion, immigration encouragement, industry attraction, municipal ownership, and efforts to attain status as both provincial capital and home of the provincial university. While booster policies differed in degree and kind from centre to centre, no prairie community was immune to boosterism.

Second, while the promotion strategies pursued by Winnipeg, Regina, Calgary, Edmonton, and Saskatoon were successful in so far as these cities were the largest on the prairies by 1913, there is some evidence to suggest that other centres — including several with greater initial advantages than the eventual "winners" — lost out partly because their leaders' initiatives and policies were not up to those of the competition. And in the absence of sufficient initiative and skill, growth could not be sustained over long periods on the strength of natural advantages alone. In general, leaders in the losing cities were more divided and complacent, and often confined their activities to broadsides in the press.[80]

Third, the policies implemented by the boosters did have some impact on prairie urban development. The decisions made by urban elites were important factors in the determination of the pattern of urban development;

TABLE 5   Rank of Selected Canadian Cities by Size, 1901-1921

Rank	1901	1911	1921
1	Montreal	Montreal	Montreal
2	Toronto	Toronto	Toronto
3	Quebec	Winnipeg	Winnipeg
4	Ottawa	Vancouver	Vancouver
5	Hamilton	Ottawa	Hamilton
6	Winnipeg	Hamilton	Ottawa
7	Halifax	Quebec	Quebec
8	Saint John	Halifax	Calgary
9	London	London	London
10	Vancouver	Calgary	Edmonton
11	Victoria	Saint John	Halifax
12	Kingston	Victoria	Saint John
13	Brantford	Regina	Victoria
14	Hull	Edmonton	Windsor
15	Windsor	Brantford	Regina
16	Sherbrooke	Kingston	Brantford
17	Guelph	Peterborough	Saskatoon
—	—	—	—
36	—	Saskatoon	—
—	—	—	—
73	Calgary	—	—
—	—	—	—
77	Edmonton	—	—
—	—	—	—
97	Regina	—	—
—	—	—	—
110	Saskatoon	—	—

SOURCE: *Census of Canada,* 1931, Volume 1.

in the absence of these efforts a more diffuse or different urban pattern would probably have emerged. Instead, in the relatively short span of four decades five urban centers had by-passed their regional competitors (see Table 1) and all had gained a prominent place within the ranks of Canada's largest cities (see Table 5). Moreover, these five cities together contained 65 percent of the region's urban population (see Tables 1 and 2). Booster policies also affected the region's growth rate. In gross terms, urban growth in the prairie region in the decade preceding World War I surpassed that in all other regions of the country. The urban population of Manitoba jumped from 28 percent in 1901 to 43 percent in 1911, an increase of 15 percent. In Saskatchewan the increase was 11 percent (16 percent to 27 percent), in Alberta, 12 percent (25 percent to 37 percent). During the same period urban population growth in the Maritimes was only 6 percent (22 percent to 28 percent);

in Quebec, 8 percent (40 percent to 48 percent); in Ontario, 10 percent (43 percent to 53 percent); and in British Columbia, 2 percent (50 percent to 52 percent).[81] Of course, the region's relative newness together with the development of the wheat economy of the prairies had much to do with this rapid rate of urbanization. Still, in the absence of such massive efforts on the part of urban elites throughout the prairies it is possible that many of the immigrants and some of the capital investment that did come to the area might have gone elsewhere.

The final point that can be made about the impact of boosterism on the development of prairie cities in the pre-war era is, perhaps, the most important. By 1913 the five major prairie cities had firmly-established framework for future development. This framework included a variety of elements ranging from particular patterns of physical development to special tax policies and government structures. The key element, however, was the attitude of the decision-makers. The pre-1913 experience confirmed in the minds of the elites in all five cities that a booster mentality was essential to continued growth. More than ever before, the elites subscribed to the belief that "cities are made by the initiative and enterprise of their citizens."[82] Not one of the tenets of the booster philosophy had been dislodged by past experience. In their attitudes towards railways, immigration and industrial encouragement, inter-city rivalries, labour, and the role of government, the commercial elites of the cities entered the post-war era intent on following past practices. It was, in many respects, a serious mistake. In the pre-war period, a marked fluidity existed when the opportunities for recruiting the acknowledged attributes of city status — population, major transportation facilities, capital investment — were open to all. In this situation, the leaders of the five major prairie cities acted effectively and were rewarded with rapid growth and big city status. In the subsequent era, from 1914 to the early 1940s, many of the structures, ideas, and routines that had in the past worked to fuel growth were no longer adequate. Indeed, in many cases they became, in themselves, obstacles to continued or renewed growth. The three decades following 1913 were taken up with repeated efforts to alter or overcome the negative effects of earlier decisions. All five cities struggled to regain the initiative they realized was so important to continued success. It was true, of course, that the problems of the inter-war era were aggravated by a long period of depression, but it was also true that the earlier framework of growth could be redefined or reordered to deal with new problems only with great difficulty. By the early 1940s, some of the problems had been overcome and the five centres looked forward to better times. Yet the ability of the cities to take advantage of post-war prosperity was limited; although some changes had been made and some problems overcome, the framework remained relatively rigid. The fact was that by the 1950s prairie cities were in most respects still tied to the structures, ideas, and routines of a bygone era, and no amount of simple manoeuvering could alter this legacy in a major way. Growth in the post-war era occurred almost in spite of the framework and the efforts of urban elites rather than because of them.[83]

This overview of the early history of prairie urban development does not support the idea that local leaders through their actions created their cities, or were alone responsible for their patterns of growth and development. Nor does it reveal the unfolding of a predetermined design whereby a number of prairie hamlets emerged as the major cities of a region. It shows instead the influence of boosterism on urban development. The scope, character, and direction of community policy — conditioned by a complex framework of geographic and economic influences — had profound effects on the rise of prairie cities. It does not propose that "men, not chance" made prairie cities, but rather that the element of urban leadership must be an integral part of any explanation of urban growth.

NOTES

1. The best survey of urban development on the prairies is Paul Voisey, "The Urbanization of the Canadian Prairies, 1871-1916," *Histoire sociale/Social History*, Vol. VIII, No. 15 (May 1975), pp. 77-101. Three of the five dominant cities (Winnipeg, Edmonton, and Calgary) are also discussed in J.M.S. Careless, "Aspects of Urban Life in the West, 1870-1914," in Gilbert A. Stelter and Alan F.J. Artibise, eds., *The Canadian City: Essays in Urban History* (Toronto, 1977), pp. 125-41.

2. For an excellent discussion of resource base and urban growth see N.H. Lithwick and Gilles Paquet, "Urban Growth and Regional Contagion," in Lithwick and Paquet, eds., *Urban Studies: A Canadian Perspective* (Toronto, 1968), pp. 1840.

3. See, for example, K. Lenz, "Large Urban Places in the Prairie Provinces — Their Development and Location," in R.L. Gentilcore, ed., *Canada's Changing Geography* (Toronto, 1967), pp. 199-211; L.D. McCann, "Urban Growth in Western Canada, 1881-1961," *The Albertan Geographer* No. 5 (1969), pp. 65-74; C.M. Studness, "Economic Opportunity and the Westward Migration of Canadians during the Late Nineteenth Century," *C.J.E.P.S.*, Vol. XXX (1964), pp. 570-84; K.H. Norrie, "The Rate of Settlement of the Canadian Prairies, 1870-191 1," *Journal of Economic History*, Vol. XXXV (June 1975), pp. 410-27; G.A. Nader, *Cities of Canada*, Volumes I and II (Toronto, 1975 and 1976); N.H. Lithwick, "The Process of Urbanization in Canada," in R.M. Irving, ed., *Readings in Canadian Geography* (Toronto, 1972), pp. 130-45; A.F. Burghardt, "A Hypothesis About Gateway Cities," *Annals of the Association of American Geographers*, Vol. LXI, No. 2 (June 1971); and T. Kuz, "Metropolitan Winnipeg: Inter-Urban Relationships," in T. Kuz, ed., *Winnipeg: 1874-1974: Progress and Prospects* (Winnipeg, 1974), pp. 7-20. For a contemporary account see E.B. Mitchell, *In Western Canada Before the War: A Study of Communities* (London, 1915).

4. This statement has been discussed in varying degrees of detail in the following: Leonard Gertler and Ronald Crowley, *Changing Canadian Cities* (Toronto,

1977), p. 152; Peter G. Goheen, "Industrialization and the Growth of Cities in Nineteenth-Century America," *American Studies* Vol. 14 (1971), pp. 49-66; and Robert R. Dykstra, *The Cattle Towns* (New York, 1974), pp. 3-7.

5. "The effects of the policies of the commercial elite on the urban geography of the region were striking. By defeating Selkirk in its bid for the railway, by winning freight rate and other concessions from the C.P.R., and by attaining control of the grain trade, merchant wholesalers and traders made possible the emergence of Winnipeg as the primate city of the eastern prairies. Theory does not require the emergence of a single city pattern in the Red River Valley, however. In fact, it can be argued that had the railway been completed earlier and a more energetic immigration policy been followed, eastern wholesalers would have participated more vigorously in the expanded trade of the seventies and a diffuse urban pattern may well have emerged." Donald Kerr, "Wholesale Trade on the Canadian Plains in the Nineteenth Century: Winnipeg and Its Competition," in Howard Palmer, ed., The Settlement of the West (Calgary, 1977), pp. 151-52.

6. This generalization can be made about all five major prairie cities. See Voisey, "The Urbanization of the Canadian Prairies," p. 101; R.C. Bellan, "Rails Across the Red — Selkirk or Winnipeg," *Manitoba Historical Society Transactions*, Series 3, No. 17 (1960-1961), pp. 69-77; and E.G. Drake, *Regina: The Queen City* (Toronto, 1955), Chapter 1.

7. This argument is not a new one. It has been examined in a limited way before. See, for example, J.M.S. Careless, "The Development of the Winnipeg Business Community, 1870-1890," *Transactions of the Royal Society of Canada*, Series IV, Volume VIII (1970), pp. 239-54; and E.N. Dale, "The Role of Successive Town and City Councils in the Evolution of Edmonton, Alberta, 1892-1966," Ph.D. Thesis (University of Alberta, 1966). For an excellent discussion of boosterism in the United States see B.A. Brownwell, *The Urban Ethos in the South* (Baton Rouge, 1975).

8. See, for example, Voisey, "Urbanization of the Canadian Prairies"; Careless, "Aspects of Urban Life in the West"; Alan F.J. Artibise, *Winnipeg: A Social History of Urban Growth, 1874-1914* (Montreal, 1975); Drake, *Regina*; A.W. Rasporich and N.C. Klassen, eds., *Frontier Calgary: Town, City, and Region, 1875-1914* (Calgary, 1975); Dale, "The Evolution of Edmonton"; Jean E. Murray, "The Provincial Capital Controversy in Saskatchewan," *Saskatchewan History,* Vol. V (Autumn 1952), pp. 81-105; Jean E. Murray, "The Contest for the University of Saskatchewan," *Saskatchewan History,* Vol. XII (Winter 1959), pp. 1-22; James G. MacGregor, *Alberta: A History* (Edmonton, 1972); and James D. Anderson, "The Municipal Reform Movement in Western Canada, 1880-1920," in Alan F.J. Artibise and Gilbert A. Stelter, eds., *The Usable Urban Past: Politics and Planning Modern Canadian Cities* (Toronto, 1979), pp. 73-111.

9. These impressions are derived from two indepth studies of elites in prairie cities. See Artibise, *Winnipeg A Social History,* Chapters 2 and 3; and P. Voisey, "In Search of Wealth and Status: An Economic and Social Study of Entrepreneurs in Early Calgary," in Rasporich and Klassen, eds., *Frontier Calgary, 1875-1914,* pp. 221-41. Other studies also tend to confirm this view, if only in a general way. See, for example, Drake, Regina: James G. MacGregor, *Edmonton: A History* (Edmonton, 1967); and D.C. Ken, "Saskatoon, 1905-1913: Ideology of

the Boomtime," *Saskatchewan History*, XXXII (Winter 1979), pp. 16-28. It is clear, however, that more group biographies of elites in prairie cities are still needed.

10. J.F. Fraser, *Canada As It Is* (London, 1911), quoted in L.H. Thomas, "British Visitors' Perceptions of the West, 1885-1914," in A.W. Rasporich and H.C. Klassen, eds., *Prairie Perspectives 2* (Toronto, 1973), p. 192.

11. An examination of any of the promotional literature or annual reports of the various Boards of Trade produced during this period will confirm this fact.

12. A.R.M. Lower, *Canadians in the Making: A Social History of Canada* (Toronto, 1958), p. 364.

13. One exception to this generalization was the issue of "bonusing." After many years of severe competition among prairie cities for industry, competition that usually resulted in the granting of cash bonuses or other similar benefits to prospective business firms in exchange for establishment in a city, the Western Canada Civic and Industrial League was organized at Regina in November 1912. One of the first resolutions passed stated:

> That the practice of granting money or land or bonuses of any nature to, or the guarantee of bonds of, corporations, firms, or individuals, in consideration of their establishing and operating factories, businesses, or industries, in Western Canada is not in the best interests of Western Canada and should be discouraged.

Canadian Annual Review, 1912, p. 626. Similar resolutions were passed by the Union of Manitoba Municipalities and the Union of Alberta Municipalities. *Ibid.*, pp. 627, 624. While this move ended overt competition among prairie cities, it did not end all forms of "bonusing." In ensuing years cities used such incentives as low power rates from publicly-owned utilities as a means of attracting industry. See, for example, *Canadian Annual Review* 1925-26, p. 460.

14. Mitchell, *Western Canada Before the War*, p. 111. For another example of the same attitude see Thomas, "British Visitors' Perceptions of the West," p. 191.

15. Each city, at one time or another, delighted in stories which indicate that their "opponents" were experiencing difficulties. In January 1913, for example, the Regina *Morning Leader* carried a story with a headline that read "GIRLS CANNOT LIVE MORALLY IN CALGARY." The story that followed stated, in no uncertain terms, that no city "the size of Calgary can compare with it in regard to girls living partly vicious lives."

16. See L.H. Thomas, "Saskatoon, 1883-1920: The Formative Years," in Alan F.J. Artibise, ed., *Town and City: Aspects of Western Canadian Urban Development* (Regina: Canadian Plains Research Center, 1981).

17. *Narratives of Saskatoon, 1882-1912* (Saskatoon: University Bookstore, 1927), p. 27.

18. See, for example, Voisey, "In Search of Wealth and Status"; Artibise, *Winnipeg: A Social History*; and J.H. Archer, "The History of Saskatoon," M.A. Thesis (University of Saskatchewan, 1948), chapter V and *passim*.

19. See, for example, J.P. Dickin McGinnis, "Birth to Boom to Bust: Building in Calgary, 1875-1914," in *Frontier Calgary*, pp. 6-19; John G. Niddrie, "The Edmonton Boom of 1911-1912," *Alberta Historical Review*, Vol. XIII (Spring 1965), pp. 1-6.

20. See, for example, Archer, "History of Saskatoon"; Artibise, *Winnipeg: A Social*

History: Drake, *Regina*, p. 156; and Dale, "The Evolution of Edmonton." One example of the situation in the east is G. Bourassa, "The Political Elite of Montreal: From Aristocracy to Democracy," in L.D. Feldmand and M.D. Goldrick, eds., *Politics and Government of Urban Canada* (Toronto, 1969), pp. 124-34. See also Anderson, "The Municipal Government Reform Movement in Western Canada, 1880-1920," in Artibise and Stelter, eds., *The Usable Urban Past.*

21. W.L. Morton, "A Century of Plain and Parkland," *Alberta Historical Review*, Vol. 17 (Spring, 1969), p. 10.

22. R.C. Brown and R. Cook, *Canada, 1896-1921: A Nation Transformed* (Toronto, 1974), p. 145.

23. M. Bliss, *A Living Profit: Studies in the Social History of Canadian Business, 1883-1911* (Toronto, 1974), p. 141.

24. This attitude has been discussed in John Weaver, "'Tomorrow's Metropolis' Revisited: A Critical Assessment of Urban Reform in Canada, 1890-1920," in Stelter and Artibise, eds., *The Canadian City: Essays in Urban History,* pp. 393-418. See also the comments of Max Foran, "Urban Calgary, 1884-1895," *Histoire sociale/Social History*, Vol. V, No. 9 (April 1972), p. 67.

25. Winnipeg's Board of Trade was established in 1879, five years after incorporation as a city. Regina was incorporated as a town in 1883 and its Board of Trade organized in 1886. Calgary became a town in 1884 and set up a Board of Trade in 1891. Saskatoon was still a village when its Board of Trade began meeting in 1903. And Edmonton had a Board of Trade as early as 1889, three years before its incorporation as a town.

26. Thomas, "Saskatoon."

27. Artibise, *Winnipeg: A Social History,* Chapter 1. Municipal government in Manitoba was administered under four types of organization: the city, the town, the village, and the rural municipality. With the exception of Winnipeg and St. Boniface, which operated under special charters, all the municipalities were subject to the Municipal Act and the Assessment Act. From the date of incorporation until 1886 the government of Winnipeg was carried on under the powers of a special charter of incorporation granted by the provincial legislature. In 1886 this special charter was repealed and from that date until 1902 the city's affairs were administered under the provisions of the municipal and assessment acts. In 1902, the city again received a special charter, which arrangement has lasted until the present day.

28. A.N. Reid, "Informal Town Government in Regina, 1882-3," *Saskatchewan History*, Vol. VI (Autumn 1953), pp. 81-88. For general discussions of urban municipal development in the territories and later Saskatchewan and Alberta see A.N. Reid, "Urban Municipalities in the North-West Territories: Their Development and Machinery of Government," *Saskatchewan History*, Vol. IX (Spring 1956), pp. 41-62; G.F. Dawson, *The Municipal System of Saskatchewan* (Regina, 1952); E. Hanson, *Local Government in Alberta* (Toronto, 1956); and K.G. Crawford, *Canadian Municipal Government* (Toronto, 1954), pp. 43-46. In the territorial phase, municipal affairs came under the Municipal Ordinance of 1883. After 1905, Saskatchewan passed the City Act, the Town Act, and the Village Act in 1908. There were no special charters for urban municipalities in the province. In Alberta, towns, villages, local improvement districts and rural municipalities operated under general provincial laws after 1905.

Cities, including Calgary and Edmonton, had special charters.

29. Drake, *Regina*, pp. 24, 116.

30. *Ibid.*, p. 102.

31. L.H. Bussard, "Early History of Calgary," M.A. Thesis (University of Alberta, 1935), pp. 64-88; and Foran, "Urban Calgary, 1884-1895."

32. Bussard, "Early History of Calgary," p. 146.

33. MacGregor, *Edmonton*, pp. 107, 132.

34. M.A. East, *The Saskatoon Story, 1882-1952* (Saskatoon, 1952), pp. 43,50.

35. The five cities discussed above had many rivals. By 1913 Manitoba had four cities: Winnipeg, St. Boniface, Brandon and Portage la Prairie. Saskatchewan had seven: Regina, Saskatoon, Moose Jaw, North Battleford, Weyburn, Prince Albert and Swift Current. Alberta had six: Calgary, Edmonton, Medicine Hat, Red Deer, Lethbridge and Wetaskiwin. Strathcona received a city charter in 1907 but amalgamated with Edmonton in 1912.

36. See, for example, Artibise, *Winnipeg: A Social History*, pp. 15-19; and *Narratives of Saskatoon*, pp. 88-89.

37. Thomas, "Saskatoon."

38. Archer, "History of Saskatoon," p. 79.

39. See, for example, Drake, *Regina*, p. 116; and E. Hanson, "A Financial History of Alberta," Ph.D. Thesis (Clark University, 1952), pp. 1-158.

40. The best account of the Barr Colony is E.H. Oliver, "The Coming of the Barr Colonists," Canadian Historical Association, *Annual Report*, 1926, pp. 65-87.

41. *Narratives of Saskatoon*, pp. 88-89; East, *Saskatoon Story*, p. 43; Archer, "History of Saskatoon," pp. 79-81; and W.P. Delainey and W.A.S. Sarjeant, *Saskatoon: The Growth of a City, 1882-1960* (Saskatoon, 1974), pp. 9-10.

42. The members of Saskatoon's Board of Trade led the campaign for city status. See *Narratives of Saskatoon*, pp. 70-71; J.E. Murray, "The Provincial Capital Controversy in Saskatchewan," *Saskatchewan History*, Vol. 5 (Autumn 1952), pp. 81-105; East, *Saskatoon Story*, p. 50; and Archer, "History of Saskatoon," pp. 95-99.

43. See Artibise, *Winnipeg: a Social History*, Chapter 8; H.A. Hossé, "The Area Growth and Functional Development of Winnipeg from 1870 to 1913," M.A. Thesis (University of Manitoba, 1956); and "Map of the City of Winnipeg Showing Original Corporate Limits and Various Extensions Thereto" (Winnipeg, 1930; revised, 1948, 1949, and 1963).

44. See "City Growth Maps" in City of Regina, *Housing Survey Report* (Regina, 1957), p. 10.

45. See "Map of Boundaries of the City of Calgary and Metropolitan Calgary as of January 1, 1975 and Annexations to the City of Calgary, 1893-1975" (Calgary: City Planning Department, 1975). In 1923, 550 acres were removed from the city of Calgary.

46. See "Map of City of Saskatoon, Expansion of City Limits" (Saskatoon: City Planning Department, 1975).

47. See "Map of City of Edmonton, History of Annexations" (Edmonton: City Planning Department, 1974).

48. See, for example, maps of spatial development in D. Ravis, *Advanced Land Acquisition by Local Government: The Saskatoon Experience* (Ottawa, 1973); Dale, "The Evolution of Edmonton"; and *The Metropolitan Development Plan*

(Winnipeg: The Metropolitan Corporation of Greater Winnipeg, 1968). In 1914, Calgary had 26,763 vacant lots served with watermains and sewers. See W. Van Nus, "The Fate of City Beautiful Thought in Canada, 1893-1930," in Stelter and Artibise, eds., The *Canadian City: Essays in Urban History*, pp. 162-85.

49. In Regina and Saskatoon, the borrowing power of the cities was limited by provincial statute (The City Act of 1908) to twenty percent of the total assessment. The other three cities were not thus limited in their powers by provincial statute, but their city charters did contain restrictions based on percentages of total assessment. See R.M. Haig, *The Exemption of Improvements From Taxation in Canada and the United States: A Report Prepared for the Committee on Taxation of the City of New York* (New York, 1915), p. 112 and *passim*. The boundary extension undertaken by Calgary in 1910 lowered the tax burden to the average taxpayer by about ten percent. See M.L. Foran, "Land Speculation and Urban Development in Calgary, 1875-1914," *Frontier Calgary*, p. 217.

50. See, for example, comments in the *Regina Morning Leader*, 23 January 1913.

51. Of course not all the land surrounding the cities was held by non-residents, and in some cases large land owners protested the inclusion of their land within city boundaries because of the increased taxation. See, for example, Foran, "Land Speculation and Urban Development in Calgary," p. 217.

52. For an excellent description of this situation see "Sub-Division Conditions and Land Speculation in Canada," *Canadian Annual Review*, 1913, pp. 35-42.

53. Ravis, *Advanced Land Acquisition*, p. 13; Delainey and Sarjeant, *Saskatoon*, pp. 22-34; and R. Rees, "The 'Magic City on the Banks of the Saskatchewan': The Saskatoon Real Estate Boom, 1910-1913" *Saskatchewan History*, Vol. XXVII (Spring 1974), pp. 51 -59.

54. Foran, "Land Speculation and Urban Development in Calgary," p. 213. A similar situation existed in the other cities. See, for example, W.C. Mahon, *Real Estate Highlights, 1912-1972* (Regina, 1972); and MacGregor, *Edmonton*, pp. 163-208.

55. *Canadian Annual Review*, 1913, p. 39.

56. See, for example, Kerr, "Ideology of the Boomtime"; and *Canadian Annual Review*, 1913, p. 38.

57. Hanson, "Financial History of Alberta," pp. 156-157. See also Niddrie, "Edmonton Boom," pp. 1-6.

58. McGinnis, "Building in Calgary, 1875-1914," p. 17.

59. *Canadian Annual Review*, 1913, p. 38.

60. See, for example, Artibise, *Winnipeg: A Social History*; and Delainey and Sarjeant, *Saskatoon*.

61. C.K. Hatcher, *Saskatchewan's Pioneer Streetcars: The Story of the Regina Municipal Railway* (Montreal, 1971), p. 15.

62. Haig, *The Exemption of Improvements,* p. 41.

63. Drake, *Regina*, pp. 155-156.

64. Dale, "The Evolution of Edmonton," pp. 99-100, 102.

65. In 1912 alone, according to an estimate of the Montreal *Financial Times,* there were 15 flotations of bonds in London, England by western Canadian cities totalling $27,855,000. *Canadian Annual Review*, 1913, p. 3.

66. Some revenue was also raised from municipally-owned utilities but this was never a major contributor to municipal revenue. Indeed, in many cases, utilities actually lost money. For a good general discussion of taxation in Canada, including material on municipal taxation, see J. Harvey Perry, *Taxes, Tariffs & Subsidies: A History of Canadian Fiscal Development,* 2 Volumes (Toronto: University of Toronto Press, 1955).

67. Henry George, *Progress and Poverty* (London, 1911). See also M.T. Owens, *Land Value Taxation in Canadian Local Government* (Westmount, 1953).

68. Rees, "The Magic City on the Banks of the Saskatchewan," p. 55.

69. Haig, *The Exemption of Improvements, passim.*

70. *Ibid.,* p. 91. See also Perry, Taxes, *Subsidies & Tariffs,* p. 131.

71. Perry, *Taxes, Subsidies & Tariffs,* p. 275. See also S. Vineberg, "Provincial and Local Taxation in Canada," *Studies in History, Economics and Public Law* (Columbia University), Vol. LII, No. 1 (1912), p. 88.

72. Vineberg, "Provincial and Local Taxation," pp. 275-76. See also Owens, *Land Value Taxation;* P.R. Creighton, "Taxation in Saskatoon: A Study in Municipal Finance," M.A. Thesis (University of Saskatchewan, 1925), pp. 31-34; and City of Edmonton, *Special Report on Assessment and Taxation* (Edmonton, 1921), pp. 1-24.

73. Haig, *The Exemption of Improvements,* pp. 266-67. It must be noted that the rapid increases in assessments were not based on realistic increases in land values. This is not only evident in declining assessments in the post-1913 period, but in comparisons made with other cities. Commenting on the situation in 1914, one observer made the following statement: "As evidence of the inflations of land values so as to obtain sufficient revenue on a low tax rate, Edmonton is a most conspicuous example. In 1914, with a population of 72,500 the assessed land value of that city was $209,000,000. Montreal's total assessed land value in the same year was $537,000,000. Had Montreal's land value been assessed at the same ratio to population as Edmonton's, the assessed value would have been $1,874,000,000, or $1,023,000,000 more than the total assessed value of Montreal's land and buildings. In other words, the assessed land value per capita was, in 1914, Montreal $825, and Edmonton, $2,880, or over three to one." J. Hamilton Ferns, "Single Tax or Taxing of Land Values in Practice," *Canadian Municipal Journal,* Vol. XVI, No. 4 (April 1920), p. 119. See also A.B. Clark, "Recent Tax Developments in Western Canada," *Proceedings of the 13th Annual Conference of the National Tax Association* (New York, 1920), pp. 48-69.

74. R.P. Bains, *Calgary: An Urban Study* (Toronto, 1973), p. 22.

75. H. Carl Goldenberg, *et al., Report of the Royal Commission on the Municipal Finances and Administration of the City of Winnipeg* (Winnipeg, 1939), p. 325.

76. Haig, *The Exemption of Improvements,* pp. 40-69; Owens, *Land Value Taxation, passim;* and Crèighton, "Taxation in Saskatoon," *passim.*

77. Haig, *The Exemption of Improvements,* pp. 108-28; Owens, *Land Value Taxation, passim;* and Vinberg, "Provincial and Local Taxation in Canada," p. 83. Calgary also abandoned the income tax in 1911. See Perry, *Taxes, Subsidies & Tariffs,* pp. 134-35.

78. City of Edmonton, *Report on Assessment and Taxation.*

79. See, for example, Ferns, "Single Tax"; J. Loutet, "Taxing of Land Values in

Theory and Practice," *Canadian Municipal Journal,* Vol. XVI, No. 5 (May 1920), pp. 144-45; Haig, *The Exemption of Improvements;* Owen, *Land Value Taxation;* City of Edmonton, *Report on Assessment and Taxation;* and Rees, "The Magic City on the Banks of the Saskatchewan," p. 55.

80. See, for example, K.A. Foster, "Moose Jaw: The First Decade, 1882-1892," M.A. Thesis (University of Regina, 1978).

81. The percentages cited represent population contained within incorporated urban centres and their proportion of the total population. *Census of Canada,* 1931, Volume 1.

82. *Regina Leader,* 16 January 1930.

83. For a discussion of prairie urban growth in the post-1913 era, see Alan F.J. Artibise, "Continuity and Change: Elites and Prairie Urban Development, 1914-1950," in Artibise and Stelter, *The Usable Urban Past,* pp. 130-54.

JOE CHERWINSKI

26 Early Working-Class Life on the Prairies

Even though they are thought of as a single region, the three prairie provinces—Manitoba, Saskatchewan and Alberta—exhibit tremendous geographical variety. There are natural contrasts between their plains, mountains, forests and deserts, and their historical development has maintained huge areas of sparsely populated wilderness while also producing bustling commercial centres. Before World War I, the character of the workforce also differed from province to province. In 1911, for example, agriculture employed 64 per cent of Saskatchewan workers, and only 39 per cent of Manitoba workers; and as Saskatchewan's population became increasingly rural, Manitoba's grew increasingly urban. Manufacturing employed 8.4 per cent of workers in Manitoba but only 3.2 per cent of those in Saskatchewan. The ratio of rural to urban population was stable in Alberta, a province where logging also served an important function in the economy.

While important differences existed, certain generalizations can be advanced about the Prairies and its workers. Once the railway was completed from Central Canada to the West, wheat was the agricultural staple that permitted the settlement and continued development of the region. Though the seasons and the fortunes of a one-crop economy largely determined the experiences of this society of newcomers, the Prairies represented virtually unlimited opportunity during the economic "boom" that lasted very roughly from the mid-1880s to World War I.

During the summer when workers were engaged in long hours of frenzied activity, labour shortages were chronic in all sectors of the prairie economy. Although efforts were made to increase the efficiency of production through technological improvement, immigration was the device ultimately selected to satisfy the immediate demand for more workers. Federal, provincial and local governments recruited immigrants by portraying the Prairies as a region of abundance. The availability of land, resources, and the possibilities for employment were advertised; consequently, male and female workers were attracted by what they perceived as a chance for self-improvement. They came from abroad in the belief that imagination, sacrifice, and hard work would free them from the dismal and exploitative environment they had known. The mystique of the Canadian Prairies was its newness and its promise of prosperity and prestige.

Into the society that emerged on the Prairies, these immigrants introduced the ideas, practices and experiences of their homelands. While these had many practical applications, they were also the source of confusion, division, hostility and conflict. When it became apparent that an instant fortune eluded all but a very few, the remainder found solace and support in their own ethnic community while gradually adapting their cultural baggage to new circumstances.

One of the realities of prairie life was that the wheat economy imposed a seasonal rhythm upon workers so that during the harsh winter, wage-earning prospects were limited. Gradually, a significant proportion of workers came to see themselves as part of a class distinct from their employers. They recognized that there were others in like circumstances, and this awareness became crucial to the development of a uniquely western Canadian working class which, especially after World War I, expressed itself as both a social and political force.

FIRST PRAIRIE WORKERS

The commercial exploitation of natural and human resources began on the Prairies with the activities of the Hudson's Bay Company whose sole objective was the profitable pursuit of the fur trade. A British based monopoly, it dominated its competitors by early in the nineteenth century; as the region's first employer, it hired local as well as imported workers. At its posts scattered throughout the Rupert's Land territory, mostly British employees were engaged in a variety of tasks associated with the collection, packaging and transport of furs. A larger number of common labourers, some from Europe and many from the local Indian and Métis populations, performed dull and difficult work for the company under spartan living conditions. Having few other options, these men generally remained with the Hudson's Bay Company until retirement. The company assumed no responsibility for their welfare once they were no longer employees.

RAILWAY WORKERS

A more systematic exploitation of prairie resources followed Confederation when considerable efforts were initiated to improve communications between Central and Western Canada. The National Policy, with its emphasis on western settlement and transportation, became a vehicle for western integration. Between 1880 and World War I, the railways employed a sizeable percentage of migrant workers as three transcontinental main lines and countless branch lines were constructed. For the immigrant, railway work was often a first job taken to finance another endeavour, usually homesteading.

Railway construction involved jobs ranging from menial tasks to highly skilled work such as that done by surveyors and engineers. Immigrant "navvies" provided the brawn for pick and shovel jobs, whereas the better positions were generally held by those who spoke English. All were subjected to long hours and the extremes of the prairie climate. Accidents were frequent, especially in the mountains where men were killed and injured by rockfalls and the misuse of explosives.

Work camps consisted of tents, rough temporary bunkhouses or residential boxcars. Complaints of overcrowding, poor food and inadequate sanitation fell on deaf ears. In the estimation of Canadian Pacific Railway President Thomas Shaughnessy, "Men who seek employment on railway construction are, as a rule, a class accustomed to roughing it. They know when they go to work that they must put up with the most primitive kind of accommodation." Any protest by the men in the form of work stoppages was easily controlled in the isolated work camps. If necessary, police intervention was used to protect the companies' work schedules from interruption.

Although living conditions were bad and the work was hard and dangerous, wages for railway construction appeared attractive. Yet when the companies deducted charges for room and board, blanket rental, transportation to and from the job site, and medical expenses, the worker had little left at the end of the construction season. When it ended in early winter, the men were dismissed and left to drift to other jobs.

Compared with construction, railway maintenance was less dangerous but it also employed fewer people. The work still involved wrestling with ties and track and shovelling countless cubic metres of ballast, but the men usually worked directly for a railway company rather than a contractor. Living conditions tended to be better as most maintenance workers were able to return to their homes and families each evening.

For hundreds of service and shop workers the railway station or the roundhouse became the centre of their working lives. Usually residing within walking distance of the railway tracks, ticket agents, baggage handlers, express employees and clerks operated out of either small centres with a single station or major divisional points such as Winnipeg or Calgary. In the larger places, shop craft workers like boilermakers, machinists and carpenters were among the thousands employed by the railroads.

Workers in the running trades, including firemen, brakemen and conductors, improved their situation through the development of strong unions, but it was the engineers who smugly considered themselves the elite of the railway workers. Because of the skill and responsibility required by their work, they attained well paid and relatively secure positions through a high degree of organization.

AGRICULTURAL WORKERS

Despite their importance to the economy, seasonal agricultural workers, like the navvies, were considered a necessary evil. Agriculture was the region's primary industry, but farmers viewed farm labour as simply another contributor to the cost of wheat production. Since agriculture was only labour intensive in the spring and fall, comparatively few farm employees were engaged full-time. According to the 1911 census, there was only one farm hand for every four prairie farm owner/managers; moreover, we do not know how many of these were full-time. Immigrant homesteaders relied on their immediate families to keep costs down; therefore permanent farm help was usually kept only by the better established, English-speaking farmers who held more land. (For the role of children as agricultural labourers see *Canada's Visual History*, Volume 32, "The British Child Migration Movement.")

The wages received by the farm hand seldom reflected his skills. Requiring knowledge of the care of livestock, and not only the operation of horse-drawn machines but also the new gasoline-powered devices, a farm hand's work involved long hours in an isolated environment. Working full-time on a farm was often endured just long enough to perfect farming techniques or until more satisfactory employment could be secured.

Farmers' wives contributed significantly to prairie farming without financial remuneration. In 1911 women were still outnumbered three to two by men and were therefore in great demand as companions and to bear children. Young farmers also recognized that the tending of livestock and poultry by farm wives made it possible to expand farming operations. Continental European homesteaders were noted for their assumption that women could toil as long and as hard as men while also fulfilling all the domestic duties associated with the home and children. Sufficiently well-established English-speaking farmers hired domestic servants or home help for their wives; but the demand for these young women always exceeded the supply.

In Manitoba, for example, there were at least two vacancies for each of the five thousand domestics working there in 1908. In conjunction with various church groups, federal and provincial governments responded to this demand by undertaking vigorous recruitment drives. Such concerted efforts brought many women to the Prairies, but like the farm hands, they often rejected the low wages (in 1914, $15 to $21 per month plus board), isolation and boredom of the farm. Since most came from urban centres in Britain, they were attracted to prairie cities by shorter hours, better wages, more comfortable accommodation and greater social opportunities.

The overwhelming majority of farm workers were employed seasonally or part-time. Some short-term tasks, such as bush cutting, stone picking or fence building, were poorly paid, whereas those associated with the harvest were well rewarded. Many urban workers lacking year-round employment depended on money earned during the harvest to support them through the winter. Even railway construction sometimes approached a standstill as workers abandoned it in favour of the harvest.

The successful recruitment and distribution of thousands of harvesters was critical to the economic well-being of the entire region. Cities were scoured for available men, and railway companies ran special harvest excursions from Ontario, Quebec and the Maritimes to meet the demand. In the peak year of 1911, thirty-three thousand came to the Prairies by harvest train. The call for harvesters also went to the United States and Great Britain with over fifteen hundred coming from the latter in 1906. Money was the magnet.

The need for haste in harvesting prairie crops meant that farmers were prepared to offer several times the prevailing wage to attract able-bodied help. Job qualifications consisted of strength, endurance and enough common sense to keep out of trouble. Tedious and exhausting, the harvesters' workday stretched from sunup to sundown, six days a week, with workers moving from farm to farm as needed. Once the sheaves of grain were stooked and the weather began to deteriorate, many harvesters departed. Those that stayed were attracted by the still higher wages offered for the more skilled job of threshing which had to be performed under the ever-present threat of the onset of winter. Provided bad weather had not inflicted long periods without work and the threshing had not been delayed until spring by winter closing in too quickly, most men returned home satisfied with their earnings when the harvest was over in October or November.

WORKERS IN THE LUMBER INDUSTRY

Men who did not return east for the winter or who did not drift into the prairie cities often moved north to the lumber camps. A voracious construction industry intent on creating towns and cities overnight saw up to three thousand men in the Prince Albert, Saskatchewan, area alone produce 177,000 cubic metres (75,000,000 board feet) of lumber in the year 1908. Given the bitter northern climate with temperatures of -30° to -40°C for weeks on end, lumbering was difficult and dangerous. Restricted by heavy clothing, lumberjacks felled trees in deep snow. Even though the winter workdays were shorter, most looked forward to the return of spring and the end of isolation.

Some migrant workers may have been familiar with the ways of camp life, but for the novice the bunkhouses built by the lumber companies offered crude comfort. While they barely kept out the cold, the air inside was heavy with the smell of dirt, smoke and unwashed clothing.

MINERS

Many prairie workers sought winter employment in mining with the result that each spring there was an exodus of workers from mining towns similar to, but not as great as, that from lumbering camps. Migrant workers participated in mining, but the majority of seasonal miners appear to have been homesteaders living in the vicinity of the mine.

Three out of four coal mine employees worked below ground where the work place was a cramped "room" prone to cave-ins and explosions. Boys aged ten to seventeen were employed as slate pickers, greasers, coal car switchers and pick carriers. Considering that the industry was continually plagued by shutdowns and that the probability of miners contracting "black lung", a respiratory disease, was high, their remuneration was modest. The highest wages were earned by contract miners who were paid according to the amount of coal they mined. They were the elite professionals of the mines.

Three quarters of prairie miners worked in Alberta in such places as Lethbridge, Drumheller, Edmonton and the Crow's Nest Pass. There, in 1914, over eight thousand miners produced almost four million metric tons of coal to fuel the trains and heat prairie homes. Although the mines tended to be located in the most beautiful locales, the scene the miner and his family confronted above ground was often as dismal as his place of work.

Mining towns invariably featured small, uniform, company-owned houses for married men and bunkhouses for single men. Ugly utilitarian buildings clustered around the pithead in a landscape composed of mountains of mineral waste. Inescapable was the company store—that exploitatitve institution to which almost every miner owed his soul because there was nowhere else to shop.

Surprising because of the hazardous working conditions and undesirable surroundings, prairie mining communities were relatively stable prior to 1914. Compared with the numerous and protracted coal mining strikes in British Columbia and the Maritimes before World War l, overt expressions of discontent were rare on the Prairies.

THE URBAN EXPERIENCE

Single men in particular were attracted to the cities. One disgruntled farmer, unable to keep help, complained:

The cities were bright; there were people, moving picture shows, taverns, music halls, churches, life and electric light. There was work in the city at good wages; and the hours of such work were regular,—just so many hours per day. Evenings and Sundays were for pleasure and self indulgence.

By 1911, 36 per cent of the prairie population lived in the cities and towns which provided goods and services to the surrounding countryside. As the principal urban centre, Winnipeg served the entire region, while Saskatoon, Regina, Moose Jaw, Edmonton and Calgary met local needs.

For migrant workers, the city was a recruitment point for railway, bush and farm work as well as a social refuge from rural isolation. But, while winter on the farm might be a time of rest for the single unskilled worker, winter in town could mean unemployment. An easy life was not assured, as numerous city residents also found themselves out of work at that time of year. Competition was fierce and the hostility towards non-residents intense. If a migrant was not lucky enough to find short-term employment, he had to stretch his summer savings as best he could. The alternatives— soup and prayer at the Salvation Army hostel or municipal relief until spring—were humiliating.

Language as well as skill determined not only the remuneration and status of the prairie worker but whether or not he might be rehired once work resumed in the spring. While most "foreigners" came to farm, many were obliged to earn money first in lumbering, railway construction or in industry. When in the city to find work, non-English-speaking people tended to seek each other out with the result that most prairie cities developed ghettos of Eastern and Central European immigrants, the most well-known of which was Winnipeg's North End.

Unfamiliar with Canadian customs, such immigrants were vulnerable to exploitation and anti-immigrant abuse; and, after 1913, when the economy began to decline, many were dismissed from their jobs. Newly-arrived Englishmen, distinguishable by accent and clothing, were resented because they were more favourably received and tended to be better off. However, non-English-speaking immigrants often discovered that placing their trust in their own ethnic community did not ensure immunity from the pitfalls associated with getting established in a new country. Newcomers could be easily taken advantage of by people who spoke the same language. Unscrupulous labour contractors and con men saw them as easy prey, and many immigrants found themselves paying exhorbitant rents for ghetto accommodation. Overcrowding and inadequate sanitation facilities promoted disease in such districts with the smallpox epidemics in Edmonton and Winnipeg in 1904 being the most striking examples.

The urban expansion which occurred before World War I created jobs for forty-five thousand men in 1911. Employed as bricklayers, masons, carpenters, painters, paper hangers, plumbers and boilermakers, men who worked in construction were generally well paid due to the demand for their services. Their earning potential must be qualified, however, as the work tended to be seasonal. Reflective of the boom were the large number of firms dedicated to meeting the apparently insatiable demand for construction materials. Sash and door factories and brickyards, for example, all employed half a dozen men or more in production and sales.

Manufacturing employed thirty thousand men (or 5.4 per cent) of the prairie labour force in 1911, but compared with Central Canada the manufacturing capacity of the Prairies was never great. Winnipeg was the only centre producing hundreds of products—from engines and musical instruments to harnesses and overalls—for the prairie market. Other prairie centres concentrated on processing agricultural products. Tanneries, abattoirs, creameries and flour mills employed hundreds of people when there was a demand for their products and when farmers could supply the raw materials.

Women in the cities worked in semi- and unskilled occupations as store clerks, dress makers, miners, waitresses, cashiers, laundresses and kitchen help. Some were employed in small factories producing commodities such as garments, cigars and chocolates. For a fifty to sixty hour work week, a mature woman received between $6.50 and $12.00 in 1914. Girls under twenty-one received less on the assumption that they lived at home, and the wages of restaurant workers took into consideration "free" meals taken at work. Even women in the best paid professions, such as teaching, earned far less than the average male labourer and only about a third of what a skilled tradesman could make on construction. Relatively few had the opportunity to train as nurses and teachers, and the numbers of "clean" jobs, such as working for the telephone company, were limited.

Most workers' pay envelopes provided only enough for shelter, basic meals and modest clothing. Many families relied on backyard gardens or meat and vegetables supplied by farming relatives to supplement what they could buy. With the help of family, neighbours, friends, church agencies and, if necessary, municipal relief, workers and their families made do to the best of their ability.

Every able-bodied individual over the age of fourteen was expected to work; unemployment was viewed as a personal disgrace. While on the job, workers were expected to toil quickly and continuously with few breaks. Hours of work ran from eight in the morning to six in the evening, either five and a half or six days a week. Rest periods were at the discretion of employers who considered idleness tantamount to ungodliness. To avoid on-the-job hazards, employees had to be skilled and alert as few regulations governed industrial health and safety. Compensation was not available until after World War I, and personal misfortunes such as injury or prolonged illness could be economically devastating. Under such circumstances, older children might be forced to enter the labour market by leaving school early.

At least on the Prairies the soot and grime of the older industrialized areas, and their attendant health and social problems, were absent. Despite the clamouring of the three provincial governments for more industry to break the seasonal dependence on agriculture, the Prairies remained an area with few large factories.

In the hope of improving their lot, prairie workers typically drifted between farming and city jobs. Moving to seemingly greener pastures was an easy escape route from the frustration of urban life when the frontier and the farm were at one's doorstep. After being highly mobile for several years, most came to realize that significant social and economic improvement was not within their grasp, and eventually they settled either in the country or the city.

DEVELOPMENT OF WORKING-CLASS CONSCIOUSNESS

Except for Winnipeg, urban areas on the Prairies were small, and the sparse population between them made it doubly difficult for workers to seek and find a common ground. This was only one of the obstacles to the development of a cohesive working class. The nature of the prairie environment and its people created almost as many tensions between workers as it did between social classes.

Communication among the newly arrived was difficult because of the number of languages spoken; consequently, establishing worker strength through unionization was virtually impossible on some jobs. Continental European immigrants were so eager to work, moreover, that they were willing to accept a lower standard of living than those who had been in the Prairies longer. Migrant agricultural workers had a limited commitment to their jobs if not to the region, and some workers, especially recent immigrants, still clung to their belief that the Prairies would provide them with a bright future. The workers were difficult to organize, therefore.

When even landowners periodically worked for others to raise necessary cash, fixed social roles were less apparent than they had been in the old country. Moreover, distinctions recognized elsewhere were reduced by the arrival of many on the same social and economic footing, and people were judged more on merit than on family background—a tendency which baffled those accustomed to a more structured class system.

Despite this homogenizing force, the contrast between the lives of workers and their employers became more apparent as prairie towns and cities cast off their frontier appearance and assumed an air of stability and permanence. The commercial elite built substantial dwellings on secluded tree-lined streets commanding the best views in the community. They joined golf, country, polo and businessmen's clubs where they arranged the affairs of all to their own advantage. They supported mainly the Anglican, Methodist and Presbyterian churches, had their names in the social columns, and accumulated material objects, automobiles and summer homes befitting their status in the community.

Workers' small houses were crowded together on narrow 7.6-metre-wide (25-foot-wide) lots measured out by rapacious land developers. Unable to afford cars, the majority of workers lived close to their jobs in the industrial part of town where land was cheaper and the sound of train whistles and shunting boxcars continued day and night. In these working-class neighbourhoods with their gravel streets and wooden sidewalks, it was pool rooms, hotel beer parlours, schools, churches, stores and playgrounds that became important meeting places.

While environment and lifestyle expressed the social and economic gulf between employer and employee, these differences were also felt in the work place where employers made paternalistic gestures to bridge the gap rather than offering wage increases or other benefits. Company-sponsored picnics for employees and their families, company-supported sports teams, Christmas parties, and year-end bonuses were all provided by employers as acknowledged business undertakings designed to buy worker loyalty to the firm.

Without any real improvement in the situation of prairie workers, an awareness of belonging to a distinct class gradually developed with the help of certain traditional working-class institutions imported to the Prairies early, particularly from Britain. Popular sports such as soccer, and later baseball, provided a common denominator for working people and were inexpensive to play. Similarly, the Orange Lodge and the Sons of England attracted working-class membership, which later shifted to the Oddfellows, the Moose and the Elks, their American counterparts.

TRADE-UNION ACTIVITY

Real worker solidarity sometimes emerged when ruthless employers challenged the dignity of their employees. Desiring to protect themselves against low wages, poor working conditions, long hours and other mistreatment, railway workers were one of the first groups to organize. The militant actions of those hired to construct the main transcontinental railway across the Prairies in the 1880s often faltered and died, however, when strikebreakers and mounted police were brought in to keep construction going.

Somewhat more successful were the attempts of prairie miners to organize and press for better wages and conditions. They had the advantage of greater stability and skill in their work; moreover miners brought with them a class consciousness which already had been developed in Europe or the United

States. The Western Federation of Miners, which first cut its teeth in labour wars to the south, and later the United Mine Workers of America (UMWA), successful in Lethbridge and the Crow's Nest Pass fields, both realized gains for prairie miners, but only at the price of strikes and violence. A lengthy UMWA organizing campaign in southeast Saskatchewan's less valuable coal fields produced frustration in its confrontation with the operators and politicians, and, ultimately, failure in the courts in 1907-8.

Cities were the primary centres of trade-union activity on the Prairies, but labour unrest there never rivalled the protracted disruptions which characterized British Columbia's mines and labour camps in the pre-World War I era. Large-scale resource industries played a lesser role in the prairie economy; therefore skill served as the basis for union strength enjoyed by that region's railway brotherhoods and crafts locals. They were organized under the umbrella of the central Canadian-based Trades and Labor Congress of Canada, which often provided the organizing talent and money to get unions started.

Prairie unions tended to be more conservative in their pursuits than the mining unions to the west. Locals concerned themselves mainly with improving the material lot of their membership. Driven largely by simple self-interest, urban unions sometimes found themselves embroiled in jurisdictional disputes with other unions at the work place. Regardless of affiliation, however, union locals served as mutual insurance and death benefit societies, as fraternal organizations and as social meeting places for kindred souls.

By 1910, most union members were in contact with the entire North American union movement through international journals or local publications such as *The Voice* from Winnipeg, *Labor's Realm* from Regina, and the *Bond of Brotherhood* from Calgary. These papers borrowed from other labour papers and contained lengthy columns of commentary on matters of importance to believers in the class struggle and the socialist alternative. Clearly, some unionists felt it was necessary to transcend the immediate "bread and butter" issues if the situation of workers was to be improved. Unionists formed branches of the Socialist Party of Canada in the cities, and in the Crow's Nest Pass mines the Social Democratic Party drew support from workers, especially those from the Ukraine.

In an effort to wrest control of government from businessmen and developers, labour candidates ran in municipal and provincial elections. Increasingly reluctant to rely only on lobbying to bring about labour-sensitive legislation, unionists and workers did manage to elect some labour or socialist representatives to civic bodies and the provincial legislatures of Alberta and Manitoba. The political results never equalled the effort expended, however.

Union leaders made every effort to demonstrate to the rest of the community that the labour movement was a serious and growing force in prairie society. The yearly Labour Day celebrations included a parade, sporting events and a grand ball as the showpiece for each city's organized workers.

By the end of the first decade of the twentieth century then, the growth of unions indicated that a genuine class consciousness had developed among prairie workers. When the militia was used in Winnipeg against striking street railway workers in 1906, the connection between the role of the state and its support of capital became apparent to many workers. In the years between the opening of the Prairies by the railway and the start of the First World War, harsh actions by anti-union employers also contributed to the awareness that, by definition, workers constituted a distinct and less privileged segment of prairie society. Union expansion in the buoyant economy after the turn of the century attested to a growing self-assurance among organized workers.

THE WORKING CLASS AS A SOCIAL FORCE

Prairie society was a synthesis of the old and the new. Immigrants hungry for freedom inevitably brought many old ways to the new land, but the heady atmosphere before 1913 created a permanent view of the Prairies as a place where there was both the opportunity for financial gain and where innovative and sometimes radical approaches to problems could be entertained unfettered by convention. In time it became apparent that the fate of the region and its workers was inextricably bound to the vicissitudes of the wheat economy. Outside industrial, financial and political forces played with the fortunes of the region, while the toil of both farmers and workers went to fuel the industrial capacity of Central Canada.

When the depression of 1913 wiped out many of the gains made earlier by organized workers, numerous locals collapsed and union membership declined. Some workers found themselves no better off than when they arrived on the Prairies—still chasing seasonal jobs wherever they existed or facing lengthy periods of unemployment. The majority, however, had enjoyed at least some improvement in the quality of their lives in the quarter of a century during which the rough edges of frontier life had been rounded off. They had more of the amenities possessed by workers elsewhere in the country, as well as many of the same problems.

While their motives and aspirations may have resembled those of workers in other places, prairie workers could not help but be aware of the effect the local environment had on their lives and attitudes. From the start, economic, social and geographic realities militated against the formation of a strong, cohesive and independent working class. What emerged was small pockets of strength where certain conditions fostered its growth. These might be where working and living conditions had been especially bad for a long time; where concentrations of people of like background and opinion produced an ideological base; or where many workers were threatened by changes affecting their control of their trades or their work place. Mostly, however, individual self-interest prevented mutual understanding and co-operation. Lacking cohesion, strength and even commitment in some cases, the prairie working class was seldom able to pursue its ambitions. Its response to its general situation and to new threats to workers was sporadic and unsustained.

Only with the catalyst of World War I did the seeds of working-class consciousness planted earlier germinate to produce significant attempts at permanent change. The upheaval and inflation of the war caused all prairie workers to reassess their situation with the result that there were radical expressions of discontent immediately after the war. The creation of the One Big Union and the outbreak of the lengthy Winnipeg General Strike are two examples that stand out among scattered others. Virtually all of these efforts were either quelled by the state or were undermined by the social and economic conditions that characterized the Prairies before and after the war. Though the working class had encountered many formidable obstacles in the pre-war period, it had succeeded in making its presence felt, and after World War I it could no longer be ignored.

XII

AGRARIAN REFORM/REVOLT

The farmers' protest against eastern political domination dates back to the first decades of western settlement. Once here the settlers soon discovered how the National Policy related to them. It required them first to pay a high tariff on manufactured goods, such as farm machinery, coming into the country. Secondly, they had to ship their produce on the government-supported Canadian Pacific Railway. While the National Policy sheltered eastern manufacturers and the CPR, it did not offer the same benefits to prairie farmers who were forced to sell their produce on an open market where the uncertainties of world commodity prices prevailed. At the same time prairie farmers discovered that they had little political influence given their region's smaller population compared to central Canada's and its distance from Ottawa. Farmers attempted to overcome these problems through self-help efforts such as co-operatives and wheat pools. But ultimately they entered politics to change the economic and political system.

Prairie historians have tended in the past to see agrarian revolt in strictly political or economic terms. Yet it was also a social phenomenon and part of a series of social reform movements that arose in the West in the early twentieth century such as the social gospel movement, urban reform, prohibition and women's suffrage. In "The Social Gospel as the Religion of Agrarian Revolt," Richard Allen shows the close link that existed between the social gospel, a socially oriented approach to Christianity that developed among many of the Protestant denominations in the West in the early twentieth century, and the agrarian revolt.

There has been an ongoing interest in defining the ideology of the agrarian reform movement—its myths, slogans and ideas—as a means to understand the outlook of prairie farmers who participated in reform. A study of agrarian ideology can also reveal differences within what might otherwise appear as a monolithic group. In "Crypto-Liberalism," David Laycock analyzes the ideas of one of the groups that made up the Progressive Movement during its heyday as an agrarian reform movement in the period from 1921 to 1926. He claims that this political label best describes the ideas of the leaders and followers of the Manitoba and Saskatchewan wings of the Progressives, as opposed to later reform movements such as the CCF and Social Credit.

The historiography of agrarian reform has undergone significant shifts. Initially the various stages of reform—the Progressives, the CCF, and Social Credit—were studied independently as separate examples of prairie protest each with its own political aspirations and economic concerns. Then political theorists saw them as part of a continuum, manifestations of a common prairie populist tradition. More recently others have defined this populist tradition more precisely to discover within it significantly different assumptions about man, society and the state as well as different aspirations and objectives. The end result is a richer and deeper understanding of why prairie farmers turned to reform and what they hoped to achieve from it.

SELECTED BIBLIOGRAPHY

Students wishing to pursue further the relationship of agrarian reform and other currents of social reform in prairie Canada should see the relevant sections of Richard Allen's *The Social Passion: Religion and Social Reform in Canada, 1914-28* (Toronto, 1971) and the relevant articles in R. Allen, ed., *The Social Gospel in Canada* (Ottawa, 1975). John Thompson examines the prairies' social reform movements of the war years in "'The Beginning of Our Regeneration': The Great War and Western Canadian Reform Movements," Canadian Historical Association *Historical Papers* (1972): 227-45, and his book-length study, *The Harvest of War: The Prairie West, 1914-1918* (Toronto, 1978). An excellent overview of western social reform movements seen in a national perspective is available in Chapter 15 "O Brave New World . . ." and Chapter 16 ". . . That Has Such People In't" of R.C. Brown and R. Cook, *Canada 1896-1921: A Nation Transformed* (Toronto, 1974). James Gray's *Red Lights on the Prairies* (Toronto, 1979) and *Booze: The Impact of Whisky on the Prairies* (Toronto, 1972) are popular studies which deal with the social reform issues of prostitution and prohibition, respectively.

David Laycock's *Populism and Democratic Thought in the Canadian Prairies, 1910 to 1945* (Toronto, 1990) offers a recent and good overview of agrarian reform/revolt. Laycock argues that prairie protest—in the form of the Progressives, CCF and Social Credit—was marked by its diversity of ideology. For a contrasting viewpoint, see John Conway, "The Prairie Populist Resistance to the National Policy: Some Reconsiderations," *Journal of Canadian Studies* 14 (Fall, 1979): 77-91, and the relevant sections of his book *The West: The History of a Region in Confederation* (Toronto, 1983).

The standard work on the Progressives still remains W.L. Morton, *The Progressive Party of Canada* (Toronto, 1950) and, with regards to the American influence, Paul Sharp, *Agrarian Revolt in Western Canada: A Survey Showing American Parallels* (Minneapolis, 1948). William Irvine's *The Farmers in Politics* (1920) (Reprinted Toronto, 1979) is the best primary source on the subject. Reg Whitaker provides an interpretative essay on Irvine in the "Introduction" to the new edition, while Anthony Mardiros has written a biography, *William Irvine: The Life of a Prairie Radical* (Toronto, 1979). W.K. Rolph's *Henry Wise Wood of Alberta* (Toronto, 1950) is a biography of the other major Albertan in the movement. For a discussion of Wood's ideas, see W.L. Morton, "The Social Philosophy of Henry Wise Wood, the Canadian Agrarian Leader," *Agriculture History* 22 (1948): 114-23. We still await a biography of Thomas Crerar, the main leader of the Manitoba wing of the Progressive Movement; a biographical sketch is available: F.J.K. Griezic, "The Honourable Thomas A. Crerar: The Political Career of a Western Liberal Progressive in the 1920's," in S. Trofimenkoff, ed., *The Twenties in Western Canada* (Ottawa, 1972), pp. 107-37. James Gray's *R.B. Bennett: The Calgary Years* (Toronto, 1991) deals with Bennett's years in western Canada.

RICHARD ALLEN

27 The Social Gospel as the Religion of the Agrarian Revolt

Between 1916 and 1926 Ontario and prairie farmers mounted a concerted attack upon the political and economic structure of the nation. Known to history as the agrarian revolt, it toppled three provincial governments, strengthened the agrarian hold on one other, routed one federal party and government and made the life of its successor a tenuous one. Provincially and federally the farmers secured legislation affecting freight rate, tariffs, credit, and marketing. They secured a modicum of electoral and social legislation, and were instrumental in ending federal control of the natural resources of Saskatchewan and Alberta. In the upshot, the agrarian revolt achieved a greater measure of equity for the farmer, and for the prairies in particular, but the balance of its programme — indeed the Progressive party itself — died a lingering death after 1923 amid the cross-currents within the parry and the legislatures of the nation.

The agrarian revolt in the West, like its predecessors and successors, had obvious political, social, and economic roots. Politically the farmers had been underrepresented in Parliament. The West had been the stepping stone of nation-building, and stood on the sidelines of the federal power structure. Socially the older agrarian regions were experiencing a march for the city, and to the newer ones immigration from Europe, Britain and the United States had brought a new fare of reform ideas to feed discontent. Economically, the farmer in the West was disadvantaged by policies of industrialization which forced him to buy in a protected market and sell in an open one, far from the site of production and through agencies entirely unaccountable to him. It was a debtor region. The varied phenomena of the agrarian revolt can be and have been largely accounted for in such terms. However, all of those conditions were perceived and evaluated in terms both explicitly and implicitly religious. It was under the impress of religion that the farmers were rallied to the cause, chose their tactics, and explained their purposes. And religious considerations played a notable role in both their success and their failure.

No man lives by bread — or wheat — alone, and movements with ostensible economic beginnings invariably find themselves clothed with ideas and hopes which provide frameworks for action not reducible to economics or even politics. Patterns of behaviour, individually and collectively, emerge which sometimes owe more to religious concerns of alienation and reconciliation, of guilt, justification, redemption, and ultimate hope than to the cold rationalities of economic interest. The two impulses meet in a framework of ideas, or an ideology, combining self-interest and ultimate aspirations by which a group, class, section or nation, explains to itself and to the world, what its problems are, how it is approaching them, where it is going and why. To a remarkable degree, the social gospel and the ideology of the agrarian revolt coincided.

The identification of western agrarianism with religious motives was even closer than the foregoing implies, for both the leadership and the membership generally espoused religion with a will. Henry Wise Wood, the great Alberta agrarian leader of the time, though not an active churchman in his Alberta days, was a very religious man who viewed the United Farmers in Alberta as a religious movement.[1] The Regina *Leader* described the Saskatchewan Grain Growers' Association as "a religious, social, educational, political and commercial organization all in one, and in the truest and deepest meaning of these several terms."[2] W.R. Wood, Secretary of the Manitoba Grain Growers, wrote that "we are practically seeking to inaugurate the Kingdom of God and its righteousness..."[3] and Norman Lambert, Secretary of the Canadian Council of Agriculture, suggested that the aim of the Progressive party was "to give 'politics' a new meaning in Canada," and "hand in hand with the organized farmers movement on the prairies has gone religion and social work."[4]

Such remarks were in the first instance a consequence of the formative influence of the churches in the years of prairie settlement. Even allowing for the ease with which members were lost in those vast expanses of plain and parkland, the church had been a major educative influence. The leaders of the Grain Growers were often (though not always) churchmen of note and even clergy; and most of the participants were church members who could sing "Onward Christian Soldiers" with great vigour and conviction.[5] Furthermore, many with aspirations to the ministry, others with some theological training, religious workers, and clergy took up positions of influence in one or another of the farmers' organizations: Henry Wise Wood, Percival Baker, Norman Smith, William Irvine, Louise McKinney, G.W. Robertson, R.C. Henders, W.R. Wood, R.A. Hoey. Not infrequently, clergy joined their laymen as members and officers of Grain Growers' locals. The Rev. P. McLeod, Presbyterian minister of Baldur, Manitoba, at the 1916 Convention tried to move the organization from political independence to support for a farmer-labour party.[6] The Rev. W. Kelly was vice-President of the Well-wood local in Manitoba in 1919, and had experience in Australian farmers' movements. The Revs. A.C. Burley, Harold Wildings and J. Griffiths were delegates to the Saskatchewan Grain Growers' convention in 1920,[7] and in 1921 Rev. Hugh Dobson, Western Field Secretary for Methodist Evangelism and Social Service, was a member of the inner policy group of the Regina constituency organization of the Progressive party. In addition, a number of ministers dared to take unto themselves the controversy of running for political office as independent or Progressive candidates with farmer support.[8] The church was not, however, exactly of one mind about such clerical involvement. None of the denominational hierarchies discouraged such social action, but locally it was sometimes a different matter, as one young Presbyterian minister wrote: "Several of the old party men have left the church because of my active association with the Grain Growers' Movement."[9]

This interpretation of agrarian and church leadership, especially in the period of the agrarian revolt, was not of itself, however, only a consequence of the past services of the church in the settlement process. It was still more a reflection of the impact of the social gospel in prairie Protestantism and the farm movements themselves. As the prairie farmer faced the gargantuan task of marketing his ever-growing grain crop in the complex, impersonal international market, the agrarian myth of the virtuous individual yeoman, wresting his due from the soil by his own skill, broke down. Only in combination and cooperation could he cope with the forces arrayed before him: elevator companies, railroads, grain exchanges, even political parties and governments. He was in need not only of new organizations and techniques, but also of a new social faith. The social gospel supplied it.

The social gospel had been rising to the surface of Canadian Protestantism in the decade previous to the founding of the great prairie agrarian organizations. To one degree or another all the Protestant church colleges in the West—Wesley College, Manitoba College, Brandon College, Regina College, Alberta College—became disseminators of the social gospel. Wesley College was chief among them with men like W.F. Osborne and Salem Bland on its faculty, and was the first prairie institution to offer a course in Sociology to its students. As teachers, preachers and laymen, the college students carried the message back to the communities of the West. The flow of the social gospel into the West was multiplied by the migration of British and American mid-western farmers, and then multiplied again when the churches were forced to turn to British recruits for the ministry. Many of them had already been influenced by both the labour movement and the social movement in the British churches, and readily confessed that they were already primed for the message of a professor like Salem Bland at Wesley College.[10]

Bland himself was probably the most vigorous exponent of the social gospel in the West. A cripple, an avid reader, an engaging teacher and a powerful preacher and platform personality, he typified the many connections of the social gospel with prairie reform movements. He had been an ardent prohibitionist. He was on the executive of the Free Trade League, was Honorary President of the Single Tax and direct Legislation Association. He was a representative of the Ministerial Association on the Winnipeg Trade and Labor Council. He was a favorite guest speaker at Grain Growers' Conventions in Saskatchewan and Manitoba. On his first appearance before the former in 1913 he proved to be rather in advance of the leadership, though not of all the members, when he proposed the establishment of third party led by the farmers. When he was dismissed from Wesley College under controversial circumstances the *Grain Growers' Guide* secured his services as a regular columnist, proclaiming: "There is no abler champion of the principles for which the organized farmers stand . . ." His column "The Deeper Life" related resources of Christianity and in particular the social gospel to a broad spectrum of agrarian needs and aspirations. The Chautauqua movement employed him (as well as Henry Wise Wood) in 1918 for its second summer of educational and entertaining programmes in prairie communities. In 1919, the Saskatchewan Grain Growers' Association used him to spearhead the call to political action which the association leadership now considered unavoidable. And the next year, when the *Saskatoon Star Phoenix* reviewed his book *The New Christianity*, it pronounced it to be "a concentrated form of the message which ministers are sending forth from pulpits today," and "just what (one) has thought all his life but lacked the power of expression to put it into words."

But it was not through the formal agency of Canadian Protestantism alone in the west that the social gospel reached its place of eminence in the agrarian revolt. Agrarian leaders had minds of their own; many of them read widely; and the agencies of press, journal and book brought the world to their doorsteps. The *Grain Growers' Guides* book section publicized and sold many of the books like Henry George's *Progress and Poverty* and Edward Bellamy's *Looking Backward* that had made such an impact on the nascent social gospellers of the previous generation. The *Guide* occasionally leaned on the American social gospel, reprinting articles like Lyman Abbot's "My Democracy."[12] In 1916 it used articles by Washington Gladden to provoke discussion of the role of the church in prairie communities.[13] The prairie press at large carried news of notable developments in social Christianity elsewhere. The *Regina Leader* commented favourably upon the proposal of R.J. Campbell, English author of *The New Theology*, that it was the business of the church to profess the religion of Jesus which "was in its inception a social gospel" and by helping erect a socialist Christian state "sweep way those existing conditions which throw a pall over the lives of the larger proportion of our people." And when in 1912 and 1913 the "Men and Religion Forward Movement" was underway in the United States, the *Leader* carried a weekly column entitled "Religion and Social Service."

Primary farm leaders manifested the social gospel early. E.A. Partridge, the greatest agrarian radical of the early 1900s and the most innovative farm leader of the period, came to the West in 1883 with a Ruskinian socialist outlook already formed. It was not necessary to go much farther than Partridge in looking for a definition of the social gospel. In 1909 he wrote, as editor of the *Grain Growers' Guide:* "Christ wasn't trying to save his soul for the next world . . . but was trying to serve humanity by showing men the truth about the proper relations to set up between themselves and God and themselves and others."[14] Therefore, he said, it was necessary to "take your love of God, which in its practical form is love of your neighbour, into politics. Practical religion is for every day, but more especially for Convention day, Nomination day, Election day until our legislative halls are purged of those who represent the most heartless and selfish instincts of the race . . ."[15] Such applications of Christianity were of ultimate significance, because the emphasis on wealth and competition in the present system "checks the march of civilization and indefinitely delays the coming of the Kingdom for which Christ so earnestly laboured."[16]

Henry Wise Wood was not a member of any church in Canada, but brought a liberal leaning religious outlook from an upbringing and training under the Campbellite church in Missouri.[17] Wood was an assiduous reader, both of the Bible and works in social theory, and produced, out of elements of co-operative and socialist thought, social Darwinism, and Scripture, a comprehensive social philosophy for the agrarian movement which can only be categorized as social gospel. Wood held that over the centuries mankind had been held in subjugation by the spirit of animal selfishness, expressing itself in autocratic regimes of government or industry, competition between individuals, businesses and states, and a quest for profit which was nothing less than a worship of mammon. Scripture, the Prophets, and Christ taught another way of social unselfishness which expressed itself in the alternatives of service, cooperation, and democracy. The fulfilment of the social spirit was synonymous for Wood with the achievement of the Kingdom of Heaven.

Tactically, Wood considered that the social spirit was best nurtured in those realms of life where men were closest to each other, namely in the economic realm of occupational groups. In this light, the UFA and the Wheat Pool were as much religious institutions as the church. The primary task of the time, therefore, was to organize those groups on a cooperative democratic basis, and once so organized, to maintain them in the true way. Government might then be built upon the self-government of the groups, and second, upon a legislature and executive representative of all occupational groups. These tactics entailed serious problems in the transitional period when not all groups were organized on a democratic basis, but Wood must have looked hopefully upon the widespread advocacy of industrial democracy after the Great War, when he was advancing his theories.

Because so much was hanging in the balance, not just economically or politically, but religiously, Wood was insistent that farmer politics must be UFA politics, and that UFA politics must not aim primarily at winning elections, but at developing principles. Hence his radical emphasis upon group politics. But he had no doubts about the outcome. How would God who had allowed the perfection of lesser creatures in the natural order, allow his supreme creation to fail? The Supreme Power had this work in hand.[18]

It was possible, then, for the agrarian leadership to appropriate the social gospel and give it forceful expression without a sustained contact with the prairie pulpit although few were without its influence at some stage in their careers. Either way, they sought the support — and sometimes rehabilitation — of the pulpits of the West; and in 1917 created UFA and Grain Growers' Sundays as formal occasions on which to celebrate the social gospel. Not all ministers and locals took up the opportunity, but the farm leaders left little to chance. The SGGA asked ministers to preach on the principles of the association, in the belief, as George Langley put it, that "bringing into prominence . . . our human interdependence will lift us into closer relationship with the Divinity that is the centre of our common brotherhood."[19] Henry Wise Wood was even more explicit in two forceful circulars on the subject. He advised the ministers of the province not to preach on "orthodox things," personal resistance to temptation, or an outdated Biblical view of farming. Rather "tell them that the only thing Jesus ever taught us to pray for, was this reorganized, regenerated perfect civilization. Tell them that this regeneration deals with every element of civilization . . . and that all that cannot pass through the refining fire . . . must be consumed by it." To the UFA members, Wood wrote that, if the church in the past had only offered them a personal saviour, it was because they had asked for nothing more. Now, however, the Church was beginning to recognize Christ as a leader who offered the great social deliverance for which men were seeking. Only on these lines could the farmers and the church find a path through their perplexity. "Is Christ to develop the individuals and Carl (sic) Marx mobilize and lead them? Is Christ to hew the stones and Henry George build them into the finished edifice?"[20] Wood's advice was followed, and in 1920 the *Edmonton Free Press* observed that these Sundays had become established institutions providing an occasion to examine Christ's social teachings, and other press reports of the services convey a simiiar conclusion.[21]

The more traditional holy days were also occasions for the *Guide* and the agrarian leadership to put their activities in religious perspective, or to call on a sympathetic cleric to rehearse the social gospel. For example, J.B. Mussleman's Christmas message in 1918, as Secretary of the SGGA, observed that " 'Peace on Earth and Goodwill toward men' must ever remain a myth while men think of Christ and His teachings only as the means of their personal salvation."[22]

Although at one level, the adoption of the social gospel by the farm leaders brought the agrarian organizations and the church closer together, their heightened religious sense equally provided a severe critique of traditional organized religion. That message could also be read in Wood's circulars in Alberta, in Mussleman's deliverances in Saskatchewan, and W.R. Wood's articles in Manitoba.[23] William Irvine, who was later to become the chief systematizer of Henry Wise Wood's political ideas, urged with respect to the UFA Sundays that there might be more point in "Church Sundays" on which the true spirit and expression of Christianity might be communicated by the UFA to the churches of Alberta.[24] When only one of the ministerial delegates of the SGGA convention in 1919 turned up for a discussion of church union (the others no doubt sick of the subject and eager to discuss headier matters of farmer politics), it was suggested that it was up to the farmers to form a Grain Growers' Church of their own along union lines.[25] Even in the ranks, it would seem, an increasing number were viewing their movements as peculiar sources of social, even religious, regeneration, and expressing in practice what William Irvine was shortly to write in *The Farmers in Politics:* "The line between the sacred and the secular is being rubbed out" and "everything is becoming sacred." First and foremost in that process was the organized farmers' movement.

The social gospel, then, was a power to be reckoned with as the western farmer figuratively took up arms against the national system. But for all that the social gospel could be described as a new development in the religious culture of the agrarian west, once the farm organizations were baptized by the social gospel with the holy spirit, it was possible to make even the resources of the older evangelicalism do service in the agrarian revolt. Were not the farm organizations themselves now the centre of revival, calling the nation to repentance and conversion? Musselman's reaction to the astonishing electoral victories of the fall of 1919 in Ontario and at Cochrane, Alberta, was to quote a hymn that had echoed from revival and camp meeting:

Lo, the promise of a shower,
Drops already from above;
And the Lord will shortly pour
All the pleasure of His love.[26]

And so it seemed as the following three years saw a remarkable harvest of constituencies, legislatures and governments.

Insofar as the western farmer was in need of a social faith for the new commercial age that was upon him, he found it in the social gospel, and for him it provided not only a great manifesto of social justice but also the promise of a great deliverance and the coming of a new time. To say so much, however, and to document it, is not to exhaust the significance of that development. It is necessary as well to ask certain questions: How did the social gospel relate to the enduring ideology of the agrarian myth? What role did it play in the internal problems of the Progressive party, and how did it affect its political tactics? Finally, how much was the social gospel of the agrarian revolt a part of the rampant English Protestantism of the second decade which won prohibition in the West with one hand, while it virtually wiped out foreign language instruction in the schools with the other? Definitive answers to these questions still await substantial research and interpretation, but at least some suggestive inferences can and ought to be drawn from what is already known.

Richard Hofstadter has made much of the inappropriateness of the agrarian myth of the virtuous yeoman to the situation of the western American farmer, whom he views rather as a large scale producer and land speculator, given to an indulgent identification with the common man in times of depression but assuming his entrepreneurial mantle when the going was good. Depending on the season, he ran with the hare or the hounds. Without going into all aspects of the applicability of this image to the prairie farmer, it is evident that in season and out, the social gospel sought to strip away the individualism of the agrarian myth — and did so with some success. Nevertheless, what was lost for the individual was gained for the group; and one might almost say, for the region. While the cartoons of the *Guide* still appealed to the beleaguered individual farmer, they nevertheless taught just that, that the farmer as an individual was no match for the world. In stressing the virtues of association and the common humanity of the farmer, however, the social gospel was far from detracting from the commercial realities confronting him. Each new triumph of organization from 1901 to 1923 was at one and the same time a celebration of the progressive march of Christian social ethics, the arrival of a new breed of virtuous cooperators, *and* an advance in the farmers' commercial sophistication. This enduring sense of his common humanity and the moral superiority of the farmer's response to his word could hardly do other than compound his sense of alienation in the nation in the political and economic crisis of 1918-21.

At the same time, in an apparent contradiction to the social gospel's emphasis upon the brotherhood of man, the overwhelming bulk of the agrarian leadership and a majority of their following were obviously deeply committed to the continuing surge of Anglo-Protestant culture religion, expressed in campaigns for "national schools" with English-language instruction only, prohibition, and church union; the social gospel of the agrarian revolt was closely associated with all that, as can be demonstrated in a number of ways. UFA support in Alberta was strongest — almost unshakeable — in the older settled region of the province south of Red Deer, populated largely by those of British, American, German, or Scandinavian extraction, and devoted to commodity production. This was where those campaigns on behalf of moral righteousness, which the UFA embraced — prohibition, social reform, direct democracy, and smashing the "interests" — had their strongest support. By contrast, these causes — and the UFA — were much less popular in the more recently settled northern area with its heavier concentrations of French-Canadians and Ukrainians.[27] In Saskatchewan, in 1919 the provincial legislators among the ranks of the Grain Growers' Association were with one exception Protestant: half were Presbyterian, a fifth Methodist.[28] And in a study of the Progressive party's middle leadership in 1921 in Saskatchewan all of those on whom significant data could be found were Protestant.[29] In Manitoba, using still another measure, Salem Bland was most frequently called to speak and preach in English Protestant regions west and south from Winnipeg, which was most constant in its support of prohibition.[30] Perhaps, on the one hand, what the association pointed to is obvious. It is not possible to link all social gospellers of the agrarian revolt equally to the status politics of Anglo-Protestantism in the West, but it is not surprising to read of the rousing reception given by the SGGA in convention in 1918 to the call for English only in the schools by Dr. J.G. Shearer, Head of the Social Service Council of Canada and the pre-eminent Presbyterian social gospeller in the land.

What then does one say about the virtuous co-operator of the social gospel of the agrarian revolt? Simply that one man's redemption is another man's alienation? That is not an uncommon pattern with ideologies as the identities of self-interest within them became clearer, and it is evident in the dynamics of the agrarian revolt as well. But that its character can be entirely ascribed to status politics and nativism in the face of new urban — and even rural — groups and classes occasioned by a combination of industrialism and immigration, is not entirely fair or accurate. At a time when it is recognized that there was not, after all, that much to be feared from the maintenance of immigrant cultures, the western agrarian Protestant ought not to be belaboured too heavily for wanting to maintain *his* culture. One might assume that the immigrant was seeking a better country — as were the social gospellers and the agrarians — and were not they offering him its best? In the catalogue of responses to immigration, it cannot be ignored that it was the UFA which provided the House of Commons with its first MP of Ukrainian descent in 1926, or that the Saskatchewan Grain Growers' Association early began using immigrant languages in its publicity and developed a Foreign Organization Department whose staff were able to utilize languages other than English, or that the Womens' Section of the SGGA showed a considerable and continuous concern for the welfare of immigrant families in prairie communities.[31] The culture religion underlying the Social Gospel did not speak an unequivocal word in response to immigration. If in the upshot that response was a mixture of inclusiveness and exclusiveness, it cannot be put down to simple negativism and nativism. Certainly that would not do justice to the literature which Protestant agrarians read on the subject — whether church papers, novels like *The Foreigner* or texts like *Strangers Within Our Gates* — all of which were marked by a complex ambivalence.

If the agrarian's response to immigration was somewhat paradoxical, there was also an irony in his appropriation of the social gospel. Clearly, the social gospel of the agrarian revolt first derived from urban rather than agrarian responses to industrialism. Its framework of thought derived from urban universities, urban civil servants, and urban pastors, and it was popularized by urban-based presses and urban-trained preachers. It could be described as a metropolitan concoction which the hinterland came to share. It provided common ground for farm leaders and urban professionals, whether journalist, cleric, or social worker — and to a lesser degree and in the right season — labourer. It is not surprising, then, that when the social gospel came to prescribe for the countryside, its proposals were extensions of the amenities and social features of urban life.[32] The social gospel had no criticism of the agrarian drive after the turn of the century for the business-like practice of agriculture. The problem was not with business *per se* but with the misuse of corporate wealth and power. What the social gospel of the agrarian revolt proclaimed was that the agrarians had found a way of handling business, wealth, and power, consistent with democracy and Christian social ethics.

Inevitably, the religious dimensions of the agrarian revolt made it more difficult for the movement to function in the given world of Canadian politics. The Progressive party refused to function as an opposition party on behalf of *all* Canadians — which exposed how far it was after all an agency of group interest. Progressives who alone voted overwhelmingly in the federal House against race track gambling and for church union could hardly be expected to make up their minds between Conservative high tariff iniquity and liquor-corrupted Liberal administration in 1925-26. The one affronted their group economic interest and the other their Anglo-Protestant culture religion, both of which were incorporated in the social gospel of the agrarian revolt, even while they were in some measure transformed by it.

The inner problems of the party were likewise an expression of religious sensitivities. From the beginning the UFA representatives had been the bearers of the pure doctrine. They had refused to concede formal organization as a party; they had early separated out, constituting the majority of the 'Ginger Group,' associating themselves with the Labor 'group,' Woodsworth and Irvine; and they survived the debacle of 1926 almost intact. In religious terms of all the Progressives, they had, under Wood's tutorship, come closest to forming a new cult. It should come as no surprise that where post-millenial politics had been most intense, but had failed to avert the disasters and dispel the demons of the 1930s, a virulent pre-millenial politics of the second coming should take its place. The fundamentalist reaction of the 1920s, of course, had intervened and helped that process along.

In embracing the social gospel, the agrarian movement wedded a universal religious perspective to the particular problems of its own condition. The tensions inherent in that marriage were difficult to resolve and revealed themselves most clearly in the crisis of 1925-26. The tension, however, was a sign of the creative, transforming process of true religion at work. The depths of human alienation from the source of being, underlay the experience of agrarian alienation from the national sources of well-being. The enduring human urge for ultimate reconciliation hovered over the desire to be more fully a part of the national community. The perception of alienation and the identification of hope in the particular circumstances of the West in turn victimized some and excluded others, but in the process, the West became a new, mature society, notable for its cooperative structures of business and for what were almost non-partisan service state governments, within a federal system committed to equal opportunity for all regions (however difficult that has been to realize in practice). The universal perspectives of the agrarian revolt helped move Canadian society to a greater measure of justice. The social gospel of the agrarian revolt had done its work.

NOTES

1. W.L. Morton, "The Social Philosophy of Henry Wise Wood," *Agricultural History* (April, 1948), p. 116.
2. 22 February 1919.
3. United Church Archives, Salem E. Bland Papers, letter, 17 April 1919, in Wood to Bland, 18 April 1914.
4. *Presbyterian Witness*, 23 June 1921, pp. 10-11.
5. *Leader* (Regina), 22 February 1919.
6. *Grain Growers' Guide*, 12 January 1916.
7. *Christian Guardian*, 17 March 1920, p. 25.
8. For example, Rev. J.M. Douglas, the Independent Liberal who won the federal seat of Assiniboia in 1896 with Patron backing, followed later by R.C. Henders and W.R. Wood, Thomas Beveridge, the editor of *The Melita New Era* in Melita, Manitoba.
9. *Presbyterian and Westminster*, 8 May 1919, pp. 457-8.
10. Interviews, F. Passmore, 13 December 1960; W. Irvine, 14, 15 May 1961.
11. 19 June 1920.
12. 8 January 1913.
13. 7 June 1916.
14. 28 August 1909.
15. *Ibid.*, 14 August 1909.
16. *Ibid.*, 30 September, 6 October 1919.
17. W.K. Rolph, *Henry Wise Wood* (Toronto, 1950), pp. 9-10.
18. See "Organization for Democracy," *Grain Growers' Guide* 4 December 1918, p. 39; "The Prince of Peace," *ibid.*, p. 23; "Mr. Pepys in the West," *ibid.*, 8 January 1919, p. 47; UFA convention address, *ibid.*, 29 January 1919; also W.L. Morton, *op. cit.*, and Rolph, *Henry Wise Wood*, pp. 9-10, 63-6.
19. Minutes, Board of Directors, SGGA, March 30, 1917, Saskatchewan Archives; *Grain Growers Guide*, 6 June 1917, p. 10.
20. UFA Circulars Nos. 9 and 10, 14, 18 April 1917.

21. 22 May 1920, p. 6; also *Grain Growers' Guide*, 6 June 1917.
22. *Grain Growers' Guide*, 4 December 1918, p. 41.
23. *Grain Growers' Guide*, 5 November 1919, p. 8.
24. *Nutcracker*, 10 May 1917.
25. *Leader* (Regina), 21 February 1919.
26. *Grain Growers' Guide*, 5 November 1919.
27. See Thomas Flanagan, "Political Geography and the United Farmers of Alberta," *The Twenties In Western Canada*, ed. S. Trofimenkoff (Ottawa: National Museums of Canada, 1972), pp. 138-147.
28. *Morning Leader* (Regina), 19 February 1919.
29. Leo Courville, "The Saskatchewan Progressives" (unpublished M.A. Thesis, University of Saskatchewan, Regina Campus, 1971), p. 59.
30. J.K. Thompson, "The Prohibition Question in Manitoba, 1892-1928" (unpublished M.A. Thesis, University of Manitoba, 1969).
31. Guy J. Cyrenne, "The Saskatchewan Grain Growers' Association: Their Educational and Social Aspects" (Honours Paper, University of Saskatchewan, Regina campus, 1973), pp. 20, 25-26; "First Ukrainian M.P. Dies," *Leader-Post* (Regina), April 23, 1973, p. 41 (Michael Luchkovich).
32. John MacDougall, *Rural Life in Canada: Its Trends and Tasks* (Toronto, 1913).

DAVID LAYCOCK

28 Crypto-Liberalism

There are many academic accounts of 'crypto-Liberal' actors during the halcyon days of Canadian Prairie Populism.[1] However, none of these—not even Morton's classic *Progressive Party in Canada*—has systematically analysed the democratic political thought of crypto-Liberalism. This is the purpose of the present chapter.

W.L. Morton coined the word 'crypto-Liberalism' to refer to the politics of a small group of federal MPs from Saskatchewan and Manitoba from 1921 to 1926. The prefix 'crypto' indicated the questionable dedication of men such as J. Johnson, Robert Forke, and of course T.A. Crerar, to a grain grower politics independent of the Liberal party.[2]

I use crypto-Liberalism to refer to a broader pattern of political discussion and thought about issues central to prairie people. The prefix 'crypto' is warranted because, of all four modes of prairie populism we will examine, crypto-Liberalism broke least with contemporary Liberal party ideology and policy perspectives in Canada. Its Populism was thus closest to being a 'disguised' Liberalism. This appellation is most appropriate for the leaders of National Progressive party from Saskatchewan and Manitoba, and of almost all provincial administrations in the prairie provinces from 1905 to 1944. The term 'crypto-Liberalism' is less appropriate for activist elements within the pre-1926 grain growers' organizations, but is none the less more valid (outside of Alberta) than other categories explored in later chapters.

I begin this chapter by considering major ideological influences upon prairie crypto-Liberalism. Then I discuss the treatment of six basic democratic themes within crypto-Liberalism, paying special attention to the Farmers' Platform of 1910, 1918, and 1921.

A NOTE ON IDEOLOGICAL HERITAGE

Several tendencies within national Liberal politics were important to the constitution of crypto-Liberalism. The old free-trade Liberalism of Brown, Blake, Cartwright, and the young Laurier had yielded to Laurier's pragmatic, protectionist, and electorally successful Liberalism. Another pragmatic reorientation involved gradual revision of the *laissez-faire* perspective characterizing pre-J.S. Mill British liberalism. The revision was towards a commitment to state intervention, designed to balance the rough justice of the industrial capitalist economy established in the 'empire of the St Lawrence.' Canadian Liberalism gave political credence to a nascent welfare state in response to many 'interest group' representations[3] made to provincial and federal agencies on behalf of the socially disadvantaged. Also influential in this regard were the perceived attraction of socialism to a working class within an unreformed capitalism, the rise of the farmers' movement, and the undeniable intellectual and social interest in a 'new social order.'[4]

The new Liberalism aimed to recruit the growing labour and agrarian sectors of the population, although the latter proved to be most politically troublesome in the decade following the watershed Liberal convention of 1919. Mackenzie King's idealized vision of peace among social classes complemented the convention's qualified support for some demands by contemporary agrarians and 'progressives.'[5] Among the latter were commitments to tariff reductions (to diminish 'the very high cost of living which presses so severely on the masses of the people'), and use of 'the national credit to assist cooperative Agricultural Credit Associations to provide capital for agriculture at the lowest possible prices.' The 1919 platform promised social insurance against unemployment, sickness, and old age; federal incorporation of cooperative associations; and 'the acceptance of the principle of proportional representation.' Also pledged were 'immediate and drastic action by the government with respect to the high cost of living and profit-earning' and 'a grant to the prairie provinces of ownership and control over natural resources'.[6]

Western producers' experiences with the Laurier and Union governments were sufficiently sobering to prevent naïve acceptance of this program. The 1919 program disguised the likely influence of pro-tariff, socially conservative, and unabashedly central Canadian interests on any future Liberal government's policies. Whether King's 'progressive' 1919 platform was opportunist or not, he had not yet conquered the more conservative elements in the Liberal party. These elements were not simply restricted to the 'famous eighteen Toronto Liberals' who had deserted Laurier over reciprocity in 1911.[7] That the party hierarchy and major funders in central Canada were untrustworthy converts to the 'new Liberalism' of 1919 was not lost on the United Farmers of Ontario, who gave up on their erstwhile political cohorts—with some success, for four coalition years—in provincial politics. Prairie producers' organizations developed a realistic sense of the hidden dangers of the 1919 Liberal platform, and moved rapidly to create the National Progressive party.

None the less, Ontario Liberalism continued to influence western political perceptions. Many prairie farmers were immigrants from Ontario, and were thus affected by the legacy of radical, 'Clear Grit' Liberalism. As Frank Underhill states, 'the old agrarian radicalism of the Upper Canada Grits was coming to life again in a fresh incarnation among the wheat farmers of the new West.'[8] This radicalism had been modified by the Grange and the Patrons of Industry in the late nineteenth and early twentieth centuries, with the Patrons doing the most to recommend democratization of political institutions and processes.[9] The Patrons did in fact make a political beginning in Manitoba and Saskatchewan in the 1890s, but were soon displaced by the Territorial Grain Growers' Association.[10]

All agrarian radicalism in southern and western Ontario after 1837 emphasized policies and political procedures that would simultaneously reduce the power of the metropolitan Canadian business community while advancing agrarian interests. These interests should not be construed in narrowly economic terms. Some leadership elements in the Patrons, in particular, were sympathetic to organized labour, to the extent that they attempted to forge an electoral and movement coalition between farmers and industrial workers.[11] This 'populist' alliance was rationalized on moral as well as strategic grounds. Those exploited by 'monopolists' and old-party politicians were adjured to set their differences aside to work towards a more Christian society.[12] This appeal produced successful Patron candidates in 17 of 56 ridings contested in the 1893 Ontario election. A shift of only 3 per cent in 20 ridings would have given the Patrons the largest legislative representation.[13]

While radical Grit traditions reappeared several generations later on the prairies, it was in the form of a 'fresh incarnation' and not simply a duplication. This was especially true in Saskatchewan and Alberta; in Manitoba, similarities with Ontario patterns were more readily apparent.[14] As one moved west, one found a greater tendency to supplement or replace radical Grit and Liberal perspectives with British labourite as well as 'republican' ideas of American Jacksonian democracy, Populism, and eventually, Progressivism. As Morton says: 'the radical democracy of the Old Ontario Grits experienced a new birth on a frontier less constricted and less subject to conservative influence than that of early Ontario.'[15]

By 1919, Ontario Liberalism included three significant strains, which were by no means organizationally separate. There was the compromise Liberalism of Mackenzie King and those whose vision of national Liberal power prescribed reforms to the party's appeal and perhaps even its operative ideology. A second strain gave radical Grit and Patron traditions more of a home. The United Farmers of Ontario entered political competition with no expectation of winning the 1919 provincial election. Thanks to significant rural overrepresentation,[16] luck in the partisan contests in many ridings, and a widespread dissatisfaction with the two old parties, the UFO formed a coalition government with eleven Independent Labour Party representatives.

The UFO platform was not radical by prairie populist standards, partly because the UFO had not intended to become a continuous electoral force.[17] With the exception of support for public ownership of utilities, its program was not noticeably out of step with that passed by the national Liberal party convention earlier that year. None the less, the 'radical democratic' tendencies of two key leaders, W.C. Good and J.J. Morrison, forced a good deal of more radical talk than one found in the election platform, and the physiocratic orientation in the UFO did not sit very comfortably with Mackenzie King's urban reformism.

Most UFO voters saw it as a moderate reform party for rural Ontarians and others interested in 'honest' government. Like its predecessor, the Patrons of Industry, the UFO was not seen by most as a fundamental alternative to either the established party system or the prevailing economic system. Like its federal 'ally,' the Progressives, the United Farmers of Ontario did not manage to pry the majority of its supporters away from their 'old party' (primarily Liberal) home for more than a political moment. None the less, interesting variations on democratic themes were circulating within UFO ranks, and the conflict between the party organization and legislative leadership[18] was instructive for similar conflicts that would occur in prairie politics, especially those in Alberta several years later. This experience did have one significant impact on the Liberalism that followed the UFO electoral collapse (1923) and subsequent withdrawal from direct political action. Ontario's agrarian radicalism ceased to seek expression in direct political competition, or even high-profile criticism of party politics. Agrarian radicals either turned to co-operative organizations or other 'non-political' means of societal change, such as UFO member of parliament and leader W.C. Good,[19] or gradually lost their radicalism.

Also sharing the post-war Liberal party was a Toronto-centred, business-oriented liberalism. It had made its peace with Liberalism via Laurier's acceptance of the core of Macdonald's National Policy. These rural and urban Liberalisms were the Scylla and Charybdis between which King had to steer. The existence and power of Toronto- and Montreal-based business Liberalism[20] led prairie producers to believe that independent political action was on their agenda by 1919 or 1920. Crypto-Liberals believed that King had been seduced by the sirens of central Canada's business liberalism.

Several of the factors leading to the 'freshness' of prairie Liberalism deserve special mention. The idea of 'the frontier,' with connotations of recent settlement, the absence of the range of institutions that reproduce 'received' patterns of thought and activity, a consequent receptiveness to new ideas and practices, and an unequal relation of power between frontier and established centres, captures several of these factors quite nicely. 'Frontier' also usually connotes a regional economy heavily reliant on a few resource industries. The prairie frontier had all of these characteristics, along with rapid settlement, commercial monopolies (the CPR, elevator companies, implement dealers, and land companies), and resentment of central Canadian dominance.[21]

In this context, it is not surprising that prairie inhabitants were suspicious of conservative Liberalism, or even unmodified rural Grit liberalism.[22] Western provincial adoption of parliamentary government did much to maintain continuities with Canadian experience, and to direct political competition within the channels of the 'national' party system. Still, we should not make too much of the homogenizing power of these political institutions. As the whole prairie populist experience shows, adaptive and creative political thought and practice can occur within and alongside parliamentary institutions, including the party system itself.

As a frontier region, the Canadian prairie West was open to the development of a markedly different political culture or ideological climate than existed in English central Canada. Canada's colonial relation and cultural ties with Britain, and its proximity to the United States, meant that these countries would be the main external sources of ideas with which the regional ideological climate could be shaped.

One set of formative ideas came from the British and American co-operative movements, the former more consumer-, and the latter more producer-oriented.[23] To the extent that they engendered a general distrust of big business and a heightened awareness of class conflict, the British and American socialist movements influenced even the most cautious of prairie populists. Finally, the American populisms of the Great Plains from roughly 1880 to 1900 and American Progressivism between 1914 and 1930 had a major impact on grain-grower politics. These influences were felt via imported periodicals and books and through the pronouncements of local political leaders, publicists, and orators.

The main point to be made about the importation of reform ideas into the prairies is that they were highly competitive with and reconstitutive of those coming from 'empire Ontario.' British and American political ideas had cultural credentials similar to Ontario's. Indeed, in some matters, their credentials surpassed those of 'the centre,' largely because Ontario's practices and perspectives were most obviously associated with specific grievances. Hence, for example, prairie residents lauded the tradition of free trade in Britain as a democratic and properly liberal tradition, which had been abandoned by Canadian Liberals.[24] In addition, prairie citizens often viewed the electoral practices of the southern republic—first male and then universal suffrage, experimentation with instruments of direct democracy,[25] the primaries, and open conventions for leadership selection—as superior to those of their own reluctantly democratic polity.[26]

The enhanced competitive power of radical political ideas from Britain and America weakened the established two-party system in the three prairie provinces.[27] In understanding this weakening, one must grant the importance of relative class homogeneity,[28] physical distance, the break with old family and community political 'networks,' the 1911 reciprocity election, and an agrarian region's disenchantment with Union government and non-agrarian representation.[29] One must still see that plausible alternative perspectives did much to give prairie people a sense that the traditional party system imposed from the centre was dispensable.

Finally, mention must be made of the role of the co-operative movement in the prairie redevelopment of central Canadian liberalism(s).[30] Agrarian producer and consumer co-operatives had made an important mark on Ontario's rural political economy by the turn of the century,[31] but never played the central role there that they did in the prairie provinces after 1901. In the absence of organizational and educational contributions of grain growers' associations and their organs (*The Grain Growers' Guide*, *The United Farmers of Alberta*, and *The Western Producer*), it is arguable that alternative political forms would have largely bypassed prairie politics.[32] 'Third party' and 'independent' politics are by no means inevitable in the absence of galvanizing and complementary social institutions, even in a 'quasi-colonial' context.

Lawrence Goodwyn, a historian of American populism, has emphasized the role of co-operative institutions in the agrarian populism of great plains and southern states. 'To describe the origins of populism in one sentence,' he says, 'the co-operative movement recruited American farmers, and their subsequent experiences within the co-operatives radically altered their political consciousness.' These co-operatives were thus the source of the agrarian populist movement and its culture.[33] While too restrictive for the Canadian case, Goodwyn's major point is still valuable for our purposes. Participation in co-operative enterprises gave hard-pressed farmers self-respect and a sense of the democratic possibilities that eventually sustained a (short-lived) crusade directly into politics (the People's Party). This sense was at the centre of 'the culture of the movement,' initiated by attempts to combat the power of eastern American finance capital.

In the Canadian prairies, several factors complemented and facilitated the emergence at an early stage of co-operative institutions and their characteristic 'cultures' as key determinants of the shape of transferred ideological baggage. Among these were the youthfulness of local and regional political institutions and the predominance of grain production in the regional economy. Also crucial was the speed with which grain growers' associations and farmers' co-operatives, such as the United Grain Growers, became the pre-eminent interest groups with which provincial governments had to deal.

One point that cannot be overlooked in the relation of co-operatives to the fate of liberalism on the prairies is the 'anti-political' perspective that traditional co-operatives communicated to the western political environment.[34] This perspective reinforced western producers' tendency to be nonpartisan and also reduced their enthusiasm for independent political parties. While the former worked against the success of national Liberalism in the West, the latter, ironically, bolstered provincial Liberalism in Saskatchewan and Manitoba.

The relation of co-operatives to 'established' Liberalism was by no means one-way. Just as Liberalism had to adapt to an ideological environment potentially antagonistic to its *laissez-faire* origins, so co-operatives were often initially rationalized in terms compatible with the liberal rationale of the market: organization and concentration leads to power *vis-à-vis* the sellers and buyers encountered in the exchange of commodities. Prairie cooperative institutions engendered an ethos that often transcended this perspective, and sometimes nurtured support for political alternatives embodying this 'transcendence.'

The development of this ethos speaks well both for the democratic potential inherent in co-operative institutions, and for their leadership on the prairies. As prairie Liberalism came to terms with these developments, it developed more easily beyond the boundaries established in the more restrictive Ontario environment than Grit radicals had successfully managed there. As long as it did not embrace the radical implications of the co-operative experience, however, this liberalism remained crypto-Liberalism. This appeared to be the case with the bulk of the United Grain Growers leadership after 1917, partly because T.A. Crerar retained his presidency of UGG during and well after his stint as Progressive leader.

From this brief sketch of the factors conditioning the development of crypto-Liberalism in the prairies, we can look more closely at some of its principal characteristics. Since the fundamental concerns of crypto-Liberalism were rooted in prairie producers' disadvantaged position in the national wheat economy, we shall begin by considering their articulation of economic grievances.

CRYPTO-LIBERALISM AND THE 'NEW NATIONAL POLICY'

The centrality of the tariff issue in western prairie politics from 1890[35] onwards is well known. This issue provides a good entry into crypto-Liberal discourse, but not for the oft-proffered reason that 'Progressivism' was a one-issue movement and that therefore explication of the prairie producers' class interest in free trade tells us all we need to know about prairie protest. The tariff was a grievance that quickly came to symbolize and connote a revealing range of the social and political shortcomings perceived by prairie producers.

To begin with the obvious: a high ('protective') tariff unavoidably drove up the costs of production, the credit costs incurred as a consequence, and the effective cost of living for all prairie dwellers. As low- to moderate-income earners, the farmers found the effect of the tariff regressive as consumers, as did the working class.[36]

Prairie grain producers relied on many imported goods to keep production costs at a minimum. Because the tariff effectively limited the availability of imports, these producers bore the costs of protective tariffs quite out of proportion to both their relative numbers and their contribution to the national economy. To most farmers, there was bitter irony in the fact that the 'spade work' done in the national wheat economy should be rewarded with disincentives to production.[37] It is not surprising, then, that the age-old agrarian theme of distributive justice *vis-à-vis* other primary social classes should have emerged from the grain growers' experience with the tariff. Noting that these producers were, to date, among the most prosperous in Canadian agrarian history does not render their concern trivial or merely self-serving. As a publicly articulated problem, distributive justice is virtually always couched in terms of relative shares and equity within a given polity.

Whether or not an independent national economy could have been sustained if reciprocity had followed the 1911 election, prairie (and rural Ontario) producers were the biggest short-term losers to sustained high tariffs. Their predominantly Liberal sympathies and their pocket-books drove this home, giving their perception of regional injustice and anti-agrarian bias in the national government a major boost.

The tariff issue had been at the centre of Liberal attacks on Toryism long before western settlers came to place it in their pantheon of political demons. Edward Blake, Richard Cartwright, George Brown, George Wrigley, and Goldwyn Smith had captured the hearts of Ontario rural folk with their characterization of protection as the bane of social morality and Canada's 'natural' economic progress. Even before 1896, Laurier had castigated 'protection' as the scourge of the people.[38] Edward Porritt had chronicled the history of protection in two books that remained classics in agrarian circles a generation after their publication.[39] And we find a prominent prairie politician and Patron saying in 1895, 'with regard to reform of the tariff much has been promised, little performed, more, perhaps, from want of power than want of will, for the manufacturers seem all powerful at Ottawa—the manufacturers and the CPR.'[40]

With this background, it is not surprising that the central document in the rise of the farmers' movement, and crypto-Liberalism in particular, should place the tariff at the centre of national government and Liberal party failings. The Farmers' Platform, or 'New National Policy' as it was dubbed by its supporters from 1919 to 1926, went through several incarnations between 1910 and 1921. Presented to the Laurier government during the 'Siege of Ottawa,' in 1910, this set of resolutions effectively announced the arrival of an organized interprovincial agrarian group on the national political scene.[41] The Canadian Council of Agriculture (CCA), established in 1909 as a co-ordinating body for its provincial grain grower and agrarian association members,[42] drafted all of these resolutions, as well as the Farmers' Platform of 1916, 1918, and 1921.

In all versions of the Farmers' Platform, the protective tariff of the old National Policy was the main target of economic criticism and reform suggestions, just as it had been for the Patrons a generation earlier.[43] Given the dependence of the established national political economy on the protective tariff, it is not unreasonable to suggest that implementation of the New National Policy 'would have re-shaped the development of the Canadian economy.'[44] For our purposes, it is important to recognize that the campaign against the protective tariff incorporated a plethora of non-economic and reformist objectives at the core of crypto-Liberal democratic thought. The farmers' platforms were far from dogmatic insistence on the extension of British free trade doctrines to Canada, or a poorly disguised 'republican' plot to subvert Canadian nationhood (a point emphasized by the Conservative press of central Canada).

The tariff section took up approximately 40 per cent of the 1921 platform if one includes preamble and 'demands.' This was considerably more space than was devoted to international relations, treatment of returned soldiers, proposals for settlement, extension of co-operatives, public ownership, or even the twelve-point program for 'other democratic reforms' which ended the document. The CCA clearly intended to nail its colours to the mast with its tariff position. When the platform was 'ratified' by the provincial grain growers associations in 1919, they were equally intent on being publicly distinguished by their position on the tariff.

It is significant that the tariff issue maintained prominence after the platform had been used as a litmus test for political candidates and even for political action by grain growers' associations from 1919 through 1921. Because the tariff was widely recognized to be crucial to prairie agriculture, it came to connote a wide range of apparently unrelated social and political issues in current public discussion. The tariff was given pride of place for yet another reason: it was seen by key Progressive leaders and strategists (such as I.W. Dafoe) as the only issue which could force a realignment of national party politics along desirable lines.

The tariff section of the 1921 Farmers' Platform began with a strategic pitch to those interested in fiscal responsibility,[45] which does not seem likely to have appealed to many in disagreement with the rest of the tariff 'package.' It was argued that the 'huge war debt and other greatly increased financial obligations' could most easily and sensibly be met through a national policy that encouraged veterans and 'the large anticipated immigration' to develop agricultural lands. Only a policy that reduced 'to a minimum the cost of living and the cost of production' could draw this surplus population into agriculture. If one accepted the physiocratic premises of the rest of the document, and the drastic consequences of the old National Policy for agriculture, this new part of the tariff section's preamble would ring true.

The rest of the tariff section's preamble replicates the 1916 Farmers' Platform. Under 'Definite Tariff Demands,' only two novel suggestions appear. They suppose a vigorous pro-tariff campaign by 'the interests' (even in the event of a Progressive victory) and the unlikelihood that governments would regulate tariffs fairly:

> g) That all corporations engaged in the manufacture of products protected by the customs tariff be obliged to publish annually comprehensive and accurate statements of their earnings.
> h) That every claim for tariff protection by any industry should be heard publicly before a special committee of parliament.[46]

Ringing loud and clear in each of these statements are standard prairie producers' assumptions that politicians are manipulated by the 'special interests' protected by the tariff, and that the tariff provides a profit holiday for protected industries.[47]

A more complete sense of the anti-tariff position in relation to non-economic concerns can be gleaned from the 1918 Farmers' Platform. With minor revisions, this version of the New National Policy became the National Progressive party platform in the 1921 election, which clearly marks it as an expression of crypto-Liberalism.

DEMOCRATIC THEMES IN CRYPTO-LIBERALISM

The People

Following Laclau, we can say that the way social conflict is represented within a political discourse tells us much about a populism's general social analysis and perspective. This perception is articulated in characterizations of 'the people' and their antagonists, which illuminates the democratic themes with which we are concerned.

The crypto-Liberal conception of 'the people' tended to be the most general among those of the four prairie populisms and had the least radical connotations. For most purposes, 'the people' was a residual category, referring to all those outside of government who were not a part of the scheming 'big interests.'[48] Thus 'the people' were by definition free from the taint of corruption and class privilege that government and big business carried. In characteristic populist style,[49] 'the people' were endowed with common sense and a heightened sense of justice.

The physiocratic and western regionalist tendencies in crypto-Liberalism gave 'the people' a more precise meaning. The physiocratic orientation was evident in many pronouncements of grain growers' association leaders and publicists, and it constituted the lowest common denominator in the politics of prairie protest.[50] By 1916 physiocratic themes were common to agrarian analyses of the effect of the tariff on party politics, the moral tone of public life, the existence of basic exploitation and inequality in Canadian society, and the prospects of the agricultural economy and its human mainstays.

Particularly forceful instances of these physiocratic themes were found in the Farmers' Platform of 1910 and 1916. The Canadian Council of Agriculture pronounced in its 1910 platform that 'the further progress and development of the agricultural industry is of such vital importance to the general welfare of the state that all other Canadian industries are so dependent upon its success, [and] that its constant condition forms the great barometer of trade.'[51] After laying down five propositions for gradual adoption of free trade, the CCA concluded with a concern for the implications of rapid urbanization. 'Believing that the greatest misfortune that can befall any country is to have its people huddled together in great centres of population,' they said, 'and realizing that . . . the greatest problem which presents itself to Canadian people today is the problem of retaining our people on the soil, we come doubly assured of the justice of our petition.'[52]

The Farmers' Platform of December 1916 was written in light of the defeat of the Liberal reciprocity option in 1911, and after six years of increasing anti-old party, anti-'big interests' agitation in the grain growers' press and organizations. While the physiocratic orientation is still evident, a more radical critique of the national political economy was now the core of the CCA's anti-tariff position. The CCA focused its preamble to free-trade resolutions on the role played by the 'protective tariff' in fostering 'combines, trusts, and "gentlemen's agreements" by means of which the people of Canada—both urban and rural—have been shamefully exploited,' and on the fact that 'agriculture—the basic industry upon which the success of all other industries primarily depends—is almost stagnant throughout Canada.' It was thus manifest that 'the Protective Tariff has been and is a chief corrupting influence in our national life because the protected interests, in order to maintain their unjust privileges, have contributed lavishly to political parties to look to them for support, thereby lowering the standard of public morality.'

Manitoba Grain Growers' Association (MGGA) presidents also gave voice to the physiocratic tendency in crypto-Liberalism. In 1919 and 1921, they claimed that 'the consciousness of the people has now been awakened,' that 'the Grain Growers have within them the potency and power that will make a democratic state,' and that farmers' proposals are endorsed by 'the people' because their policy 'appeals to their genuine sense of justice—the farmers are not selfishly seeking their own interests merely.'[53] Two years later, after the Winnipeg General Strike, the new MGGA president saw 'the people' in narrower terms: 'those who do not belong to the capitalistic class nor to the other extreme, however you like to designate it, but who belong simply to the great mass of the common, intelligent people of Canada.'

Prior to the 1919 strike and increased labour radicalism, farmers' organizations had generally assumed that labour was a natural and sympathetic ally.[54] After the bitter general strike, condemned by the *Guide* as inspired by 'foreign,' 'Bolsheviki' elements, this assumption was rejected by prairie grain grower leadership and much of the rank and file. Social democratic populists were to work hard to repair this rift among 'the people.'

A less physiocratic and more regionalist conception of 'the people' was found in the Progressives' national leadership, provincial Liberal and Liberal-Progressive administrations, and the writings of the classic western Liberal journalist J.W. Dafoe. In all cases, a desire to retain a large constituency, and to prevent divisions within the farmers' movements, prompted a very general usage of 'the people.' The term thus stood for all westerners— local businessmen included—suffering under artificially high living costs and low incomes resulting from federal tariff, transportation, and grain-marketing policies.

Both Crerar and his confidant, Dafoe, were free-trade liberals. Crerar portrayed the western farmers as the principal victims of the protective tariff, but his hope that the Progressives would found a new, anti-protectionist Liberal party[55] led him to portray 'the people' as all those who suffered under protection. Their antagonists were consequently all those (including the contemporary Liberal and Tory parties) who benefited from it. The tariff was 'morally wrong, inasmuch as it permits a particular group of people to enrich itself at the expense of the rest.'[56] It also prevented the natural development of industry based on Canada's natural wealth—land, lumber, and minerals. Instead, the tariff was 'sustaining a long string of secondary and artificial industries which are often merely of the fabricating type.'[57] Western industry was 'natural' to Canada, and Crerar saw those engaged in these occupations as 'the people.' Special interests opposed to the welfare of the people controlled central Canada's contrived and protected industries. They realized that a corrupt relation with government was their only means of distorting the 'natural economy' to their advantage.

Dafoe was equally a booster of the West, and only slightly less physiocratic in outlook. He too associated the federal commitment to 'protection' with the decline of popular interests, and promoted a party of free trade that could advance 'the people's' interests. His support for the Progressives until 1925 (when the spectre of Tory rule led him back to his true political home in the councils of the Liberal party) was predicated on its supposed potential for reforming liberalism along its true free-trade lines, while sending crypto-Tories from Quebec and Toronto into the Conservative party.[58] Dafoe continually expressed the worry that a narrow agrarian appeal, especially one based on the doctrines of H.W. Wood, would destroy the Progressives' opportunity to force a political realignment over the tariff question. He thus saw advantage in keeping 'the people' as diverse as possible. Even moderate labour was encouraged to see that their real interests were contained within a liberal position. Finally, for Dafoe, as for Crerar and the United Farmers of Manitoba leadership by 1922, Winnipeg businessmen were also part of 'the people.'[59]

Liberal administrations in Alberta and Saskatchewan did little to alienate local businessmen, except make it clear that the provincial grain growers associations were their preferred customers. 'The people,' as a result, were portrayed as the whole provincial population, except for hard-core Conservatives. Electoral propaganda of the Saskatchewan Liberal party for 1917 gives us a good idea of how provincial Liberals represented themselves as progressives and the Conservatives as agents of the big interests. On one election handbill, provincial voters were instructed that 'The Liberal Party is the People's Party [which] represents the producers and working classes,' while 'the Conservative Party is the Party of the Big Interests [which] represents the Wealth of Canada.'[60] The remarkable success of the Saskatchewan Liberal 'machine' during even the height of the farmers' revolt testifies to the success of this message.'[61]

Characterizing Tories as the 'party of the big interests' was not displaced as the major facet of crypto-Liberal partisan rhetoric until the CCF presented a threat from the other flank. Even then, however, prairie Liberals presented themselves as the 'people's party.' The major difference, of course, was that the threat to 'the people' (in essence, farmers) in the post-1932 period was purported to come from a farm-confiscating, freedom-crushing state socialism. The 1934, 1938, and 1944 provincial elections in Saskatchewan featured an inflammatory attack on the CCF that set Saskatchewan Liberalism on the dogmatic free enterprise course that led to its victory in 1964 under Ross Thatcher. In Manitoba, a effective coalition between conservative southern farmers and a shrewd Winnipeg business community managed to keep the 'socialists' from the gates of power until 1969. The crypto-Liberal Bracken administrations from 1922 to 1942 laid the solid foundations of this anti-CCF provincial power.[62]

Participatory Democracy and Crypto-Liberalism

Assessing crypto-liberal thought about participatory democracy is complicated by the wide range of relevant statements coming out of the prairie farmers' organizations between 1911 and 1926, and by the absence of systematic approaches to the issue. We can, none the less, distinguish between positions within crypto-Liberal thought: grain grower rank and file were more enthusiastic about participatory democracy than were crypto-Liberal leaders. This difference is noticeable in the support given to direct legislation, the grain growers' associations' moves into direct political action, their critiques of 'partyism,' the varying emphases on local autonomy, and the intrinsic as opposed to politically instrumental value accorded popular participation generally. For a good indication of how leaders and rank and file agreed on basic 'democratic reforms' to Canadian society, one can examine the 'New National Policy' espoused in the 'Farmers' Platform' of the Canadian Council of Agriculture between 1910 and 1921.

When most fervently promoted, the measures of direct democracy—the initiative, referendum, and recall—have been seen as means of bringing the full force of the popular will into a political arena needlessly complicated by élitist, untrustworthy 'politicians.' In this sense, direct legislation is a quintessential expression of the twin attitudinal pillars of all populisms: distrust of all élites and deep faith in the common sense and ethical wisdom of the common people. From the mid-1890s to 1921, there was widespread support for the initiative, referendum, and recall in most agrarian, labour, and anti-old party circles.[63] In the decade prior to the Progressives, prairie grain growers offered tremendous support for the devices of direct legislation.[64] Proposals for these devices of popular democracy were natural responses of a population for whom parliamentary institutions had not brought satisfactory federal policy. Direct legislation was desired as the obvious complement to internal democracy within cooperative and other farmer organizations. It was also viewed as a means of forcing unscrupulous politicians to deliver on their promises on lower tariff rates, most notably.

At one level, direct legislation was favoured by prairie grain growers' associations and those interested in agrarian solidarity as a means of temporarily avoiding internecine, party-defined squabbling, while still availing themselves of the mechanisms of reform. This was the position taken by E.A. Partridge,[65] a later advocate of independent political action for farmers, and by the Manitoba and Saskatchewan Grain Grower associations when they were still informally allied with provincial Liberal parties.

The earliest serious campaign in favour of direct legislation was led by the Direct Legislation League of Manitoba. It soon became a partisan issue, with the premier Tory of the prairies, Sir Rodmond Roblin, excoriating direct legislation as an alien import that ran dead against British traditions of responsible government.[66] The Manitoba Liberal party committed itself to direct legislation in convention in 1910, promptly made it a key campaign plank in elections of 1910 and 1914, and was genuinely dismayed to see its unanimous enactment in 1915 come to naught in a 1916 *ultra vires* ruling by the provincial Appeal Court.[67] This ruling was upheld by the Judicial Committee of the Privy Council in 1919.

The three prairie provinces' grain growers' associations had endorsed provincial direct legislation provisions before the war began. The conviction with which direct legislation was promoted is evident in the following passage from an address of R.C. Henders, president of the Manitoba Grain Growers' Association, to the MGGA annual convention in 1911:

The people of Canada have never abrogated their right to rule. If, therefore, custom has introduced a system of legislation by which our legislators can if they desire place themselves at variance with the wishes of the people, for a period of four years irreparable damage may be sustained, and it is up to the people to correct this error and make such reasonable and proper provisions as the case may demand.

First, by providing that when the voice of the majority has been expressed by petition or unanimous resolution this voice should prevail rather than the preconceived predilections of any member or number of members who may be elected as representatives for the time being. Call this if you will direct legislation.

Second, that when any measure has been passed by legislature or parliament which in its working out is likely to affect materially any class of the people, such measure cannot become law until such time as it has been referred to the people and passed on by them, by a majority vote of all who voted thereon.

Third, when any member elected from any constituency shows himself out of harmony with the wishes of his constituency such constituents shall have the power to force him to explain his position and appeal to such constituents for endorsation and re-appointment.

These, gentlemen, are some of the tools with which the people could rule in fact and not merely in theory. These are the planks that will bridge the gulf and keep elected and electors in closer touch; they will reduce to the lowest minimum the possibility of graft and the use of any pre-election pledges.[68]

Henders further adumbrated this radical stance within crypto-Liberalism in his 1912 presidential address:

The people spoken of by the political stump speakers and election campaign literature as the 'sovereign people' have, I might say, no direct efficient control. They are sovereign de jure but not de facto, except at election times. The actual power experienced by the people consists chiefly in the periodic choice of another set of masters who make laws to suit themselves and enforce them until their term of office expires, regardless of the will of the people. We are governed by an elective aristocracy which in its turn is largely controlled by an aristocracy of wealth. Behind the governments and the legislatures are the corporations and the trusts. Behind the machines, the rings and the bosses, are the business monopolists, the industrial combinations, and the plutocrats; behind the political monopolists are the industrial monopolists.

This, then, in very brief is the state of affairs. What is the remedy? We answer the principal remedy is Direct Legislation, because it opens the door to every other reform. No-one who really believes in self-government can refuse to support the Initiative and Referendum for they merely enable the people to veto laws they do not want and to secure laws they do want, that is, they enable the people to govern themselves.

Did we have Direct Legislation what rapid strides we would make along the lines of civil service reform, proportional representation, the elective ballot, equal suffrage, efficient corrupt practices act, and the popular Recall, all of which are really necessary in order that the people may really own and operate the government under conditions most likely to secure wise legislation and honest, intelligent and economic administration.[69]

The high hopes held for direct legislation here were characteristic of grain growers' associations and the *Guide*.[70] At a minimum, direct legislation would restore party activity to its proper functions, by supplementing or checking policy decisions made by party governments. The New National Policy platform could not be palatable to its grain grower constituency without endorsing direct legislation. Many Progressive candidates signed recall agreements with the constituency organizations that had nominated them.

The records of the three prairie provinces' Liberal administrations in passing direct-legislation bills are interesting. In all three cases, the governments responded rapidly to the grain growers' conventions' support for direct legislation. However, in all cases (Alberta 1912, Saskatchewan 1913, Manitoba 1916) money bills were exempt from direct legislation, the percentage of the population required to initiate legislation was quite high (8 per cent in Alberta and Saskatchewan), and recall provisions were left out entirely. Grain growers were disappointed with the limited scope of these enabling bills in all three provinces, but particularly so in Saskatchewan and Manitoba. In Saskatchewan, a referendum on the direct-legislation bill was held shortly after it had passed through the legislature, with very little positive publicity and a high required approval rate (30 per cent of eligible voters). The Saskatchewan Grain Growers' Association contended that the government had cleverly appeared to sanction direct legislation, while doing little to ensure its implementation.[71]

In Manitoba, an enthusiastic Liberal government passed the Initiative and Referendum Act soon after replacing the Tories, then quickly referred the act to the provincial Appeal Court. The court ruled it *ultra vires* of the province's power to amend its constitution, and noted crushingly: 'In Canada there is no sovereignty in the people; . . . it is in the Parliament at Westminister, and our powers to legislate are such, and only such, as that Parliament has given us.'[72] Morton comments that this decision could not properly have gone the other way: responsible government and direct democracy are hardly to be reconciled with each other without destroying the initiative and responsibility of the former.[73] To this, the three prairie governments would undoubtedly have said 'amen,' but for many rank-and-file grain growers such destruction was not beyond the pale. Their disenchantment with partyism placed them considerably beyond their leading 'establishment' spokesmen and legislators.

Limited support was given to direct legislation by Progressive leaders, the provincial Liberal administrations, and the crypto-Liberal press. The cases of T.A. Crerar and J.W. Dafoe are instructive here, since they were definitive spokesmen of moderate crypto-Liberalism during the Progressives' early period. Crerar had supported the Direct Legislation League before the Manitoba legislation had been struck down, then concluded that it was a lost cause. His 1921 'Confession of Faith'[74] made no mention of direct legislation as a desired political reform or, oddly enough, of the political irrelevance of support for direct legislation in the 1921 Farmers' Platform. His 'Manifesto,' distributed at the height of the 1921 campaign, emphasized the undesirable consequences of the protective tariff, the truly liberal intentions of the farmers' movement, and the need for efficiency in government administration. But direct legislation was not mentioned.[75]

Dafoe supported direct legislation when his partisan support for the Manitoba Liberal party required it (roughly from 1912 to 1916). He backed away when labour and the radical elements in the farmers' movement became its supporters, so as to confound party direction of legislatures' business. His enthusiasm for direct legislation continued only so long as it remained in the provincial Liberal platform and was a clear rejection of the Tory position on the sovereignty of parliament over the will of the electors.[76] By the 1921 election, Dafoe too had come to see tariff, transportation, 'good government,' and party realignment issues as the crux of the Progressive campaign.

Grain grower rank-and-file support for direct legislation was based on a desire to supplement and check the work of representative assemblies. At its most radical, this was to take the form of binding expressions of popular choice, mixed with regulated delegate behaviour in elected assemblies.[77] The logic of direct legislation, if fully extended, could not tolerate crypto-Liberals' ties to the Liberal party. This logic was disguised well by provincial Liberals so long as formal support and, eventually, legislation was provided on this issue.

One might think that prairie Liberal governments would have endured real political travails had the direct legislation statutes remained on the books after 1919. In fact, these governments were on the whole very responsive to demands made at the annual 'farmers' parliaments' of the grain growers' conventions, and tended to anticipate potential policy clashes. The grain growers' real frustrations tended to be with federal matters—fiscal policy, transportation policy, regulation of campaign funding, and so on. Thus, the major object of direct legislation would have been alteration of federal policies, if provision for direct legislation had been made at this level. There is no evidence that such provision was ever seriously considered by a federal administration. Progressive MPs made no sustained attempt to introduce enabling legislation in parliament between 1922 and 1926, probably because economic issues were more pressing, and championing the cause of direct legislation would have been a foregone quixotic affair.

Proportional representation and direct legislation were generally supported as complementary devices in the service of a 'greater measure of democracy in government.' Progressive and labour support for proportional representation was founded on a desire to secure at least minority representation in Canadian legislatures, with seats for farmers and all 'others interested in social reform,' as the *Farmers' Sun* said in 1893.[78] Agitation for this alternative electoral system was neither intensive nor as symbolically significant as that for direct legislation. Ironically, practical successes in implementing proportional representation were much greater than those for direct legislation, even though enthusiasm for the democratic potential of the latter far outpaced that for the former.

At the provincial level, proportional representation had been promised by the Liberal premier of Alberta on the eve of his 1921 defeat,[79] and had not been provided in either Saskatchewan or rural Manitoba.[80] By 1921, all four western provinces had passed enabling legislation for proportional representation in municipal elections.[81] Seventeen cities had taken up this option by 1922, although twelve had abandoned it by 1929 through plebiscites or provincial ordinances.[82] Proportional representation had not attracted much attention in parliament since its first mention in 1913, despite its inclusion in the 1919 Liberal platform.

Our discussion of the adoption of 'direct' political action by grain growers' associations[83] can focus on what these moves tell us about commitments to participatory democracy within crypto-Liberal organizations. We will examine the Saskatchewan Grain Growers' Association (SGGA) experience with provincial political action, and the 1921 campaign of the National Progressive party.

A large minority of SGGA annual convention delegates had favoured formation of a provincial grain growers' party since 1910. Until 1922, the association's leadership was able to convince the majority that political activity would undermine their economic and educational objectives. The leadership also argued that independent political action was a gratuitous undertaking, in view of the Liberal government's responsiveness to the SGGA. The presence of many prominent SGGA members in the legislature and the cabinet (such as C.A. Dunning, W. Motherwell, I.A. Maharg, W.M. Martin) was 'proof' of the identity of objectives. Still, by 1922, after the provincial Progressives had been ambushed by a snap election, a majority favoured independent political action.[84] The 1922 convention instructed its unenthusiastic leadership to prepare for bringing the SGGA into provincial politics. Here is a clear case of the grain grower rank and file forcing an unconventional, that is, anti-Liberal, political project on its leadership.

This grain grower action says a great deal about the passion for 'participatory democracy' in their movement. As at the federal level, grain growers wanted farmer candidates closely connected with an organization of their own.[85] It was not enough to have farmer Liberal candidates committed to responsiveness to the SGGA. There was an irony in this move into political action, however, that suggests a limited appreciation of the difficulties of popular control. After deciding to enter the provincial political arena, the SGGA entrusted preparations to J.B. Musselman, a leader long known as an opponent of this very political project. By leaving the decision regarding political action up to each local, Musselman used the farmers' own commitment to local autonomy to obstruct creation of an effective political organization.

In the full bloom of anti-party sentiment on the prairies, the 1921 National Progressive campaign was characterized by an unprecedented degree of local constituency activity connected to candidate selection. Even before this campaign, local delegates to grain growers' conventions had endorsed the New National Policy of the Canadian Council of Agriculture as the basis for constituency campaigns. Following these endorsements, many Progressive locals designed a method of candidate selection to involve large numbers of local members, as is evident in an excerpt from a guide to candidate selection in the Last Mountain constituency in Saskatchewan:

Any supporter of the New National Policy in the Municipality may hand in the name of a man whom he wishes to have placed in nomination to the chairman or secretary of a polling division, or to the municipal committee man. All these names shall then be sent by the polling division chairman or secretary to the municipal committee man, who shall prepare a ballot or list containing all the names so suggested. The committee man shall then call a public meeting of supporters of the New National Policy which shall be open from 8 P.M. to 10 P.M. or until any other suitable time of day, for the purpose of giving an opportunity to all supporters to vote on the proposed names. The result of the vote in each polling division should then be sent to the municipal committee man, whose duty it would be to tabulate all the votes in the municipality for each candidate. The man having the largest number of the total votes in all the polling divisions in the municipality would be declared the municipal candidate. His name should be sent to the constituency secretary.[86]

Local control over the candidates, over conduct of internal affairs, and over conduct of campaigns once direct political action had been initiated were also sanctioned by the grain grower's organization.[87] A document produced by the United Farmers of Manitoba at their 1921 convention also emphasizes a commitment to autonomy in these spheres, by guaranteeing binding contributions by local constituencies to provincial platforms and 'full autonomy . . . to local constituencies as to the form and conduct of their political organization, the general principle being observed that the constituency recognize itself as one of many working together towards common ends.'[88]

The rank-and-file commitment to local autonomy in organization, campaigning, and candidate selection took away a good deal of the *raison d'être* for a centralized party-like organization. Believing that local autonomy would reduce the Progressives' electoral appeal and increase their public image as a sectionalist party, Crerar struggled to set up such a centralized operation before the 1921 federal campaign began. His attempt was sternly rebuked by the Canadian Council of Agriculture's executive,[89] who recognized that there was little rank-and-file sympathy for such partyish methods. Crerar spoke about the undemocratic character of the Liberal and Tory organizations, but he clearly felt that some of their methods had to be adopted for the Progressives to become a significant political force. Most later commentators have agreed with Crerar on this score.[90]

Academic sympathy for Crerar's position suggests that the more extreme critiques of partyism in the farmers' movement, while understandable, were ill-considered and pre-emptive of feasible yet significant changes in the party system. The Crerar-Dafoe objective of using the National Progressive party to mould national Liberalism into a free-trade, catch-all reform party is thus presented as the only realistic political option open to the Progressives. From this perspective, ridding politics of 'partyism' and party discipline in the context of responsible government is hopelessly naïve and virtually anti-political.

One cannot deny that the Crerar-Dafoe line was more attuned to the exigencies of national campaigning, the potential for lapses in the movement memberships' enthusiasm, and the hazards of a loosely organized party's attempts to play the 'balance of power' game in parliament. However, the Crerarite position on partyism was flawed. At the level of political strategy, one must ask how amenable the federal Liberal party was to Progressive modification. The lesson of 1911 regarding the business community's abhorrence of reciprocity had been well learned by 1921. Potential labour votes would more likely be lost than won on a free-trade platform, at least in Ontario and Quebec. Campaigns were still most easily financed by the 'protected interests.' In addition, being the captive of a volatile and popularly controlled farmers' movement was not an attractive option for any party, as Crerar could himself attest. The Crerar-Dafoe hopes for a 'real' Liberal party were perhaps as naïve as rank-and-file grain growers' hopes for non-partisan politics.

Equally if not more problematic was the effect that soft-pedalling by leadership on political corruption and old-party associations would have had on the rank and file. Given the widespread popular support for local autonomy and non-partisan representation, too many concessions to the old political ways would undermine the Progressive agenda. Among the rank and file, such concessions would engender disillusionment, a willingness to focus primarily on economic organization once again, and eventual grudging acceptance of the inevitability of voting Liberal. As in the case of 'fusion' south of the border a generation earlier, dropping the principled rejection of party politics would rob the movement of its critical edge and its sustaining democratic promise. Neither high prices for grain nor wheat pool campaigns would have damaged the movement in this way; nor, for that matter, would the resignation of Crerar, the creation of the 'Ginger Group,' or the defeat of the UFO government in 1923.

Manitoba Progressives viewed the party system as a machine that, disassembled and relieved of its offensive components, could be put back on the road to deliver good policy mileage with no morally offensive exhaust. For Crerar and his partisans, this new vehicle could be created with the tools of election-financing reform, senate reform, and tariff reductions. These were to reduce the influence of the 'big interests' on the parties. Direct legislation was not seen to be crucial to the outcome. Neither was a democratization within party organization, characterized by local autonomy for constituency associations.

Part of Crerar's 'Manifesto' illustrates this line of thinking. The document presents Progressives as the champions of higher standards of public morality and 'the sweeping away of special privilege in all of its forms.' He then seems to take a radical tack, but retreats immediately into generalities and an exclusive focus on campaign financing:

> The new political movement in Canada is . . . essentially a movement of liberalism . . . that seeks to sweep away abuses in government and to provide policies that will meet the needs of the people. Our appeal is not class, not sectional, not religious. It is to all those . . . who desire to see purity in the government of this country restored who desire to sweep away the abuse of the function of government for the advancement of the interest of the privileged few.
>
> In nothing is the spirit of the Progressive movement more clearly revealed than in the matter of financing election expenses . . . in the past, campaign funds, running often into millions of dollars, have been provided by the managers of the old parties and distributed amongst constituencies . . . for use in ways corrupt and altogether indefensible. These campaign funds have been provided by railway promoters, by manufacturers, or by other interests which were actuated . . . solely by the sordid hope of getting benefits in the way of legislation . . . . The member of parliament elected under this system was not a free agent . . . . If he showed signs of independence the whole weight of the party organization was used to crush him . . . those manufacturers who desired special favors put up the money to pay election expenses, and then, sheltered behind the tariff they had purchased, exploited the Canadian people in

their own environment. Party campaign funds and the sources from which they have come have been the greatest single corrupting agency in the public life of this country . . .

I ask you to contrast this sordid spirit, these selfish, corrupting influences, with the spirit followed by those who are taking part in the new political movement in Canada. We are free men and we want a free parliament, and to that end scores of thousands of voters throughout Canada are providing the funds necessary to carry on the election campaign. This is the business of the people . . . the supreme issue today is whether our government is to be free or fettered, and whether legislation in the future shall be for the few or the many.[91]

A great deal here rides on the idea that the people will be properly served by parties when they replace 'the interests' as the bankrollers of political organizations. While there is clearly something in this, it is hardly a searing indictment of partyism from the perspective of popular democracy. It should, instead, be seen as the belated venting of anti-tariff spleen in the guise of a rejection of 'old-party methods.' No support is offered to the grass-roots desire for a 'new social order' characterized by meaningful participatory democracy.

Comparison with samples of attacks on party politics in the *Guide* and meetings of the grain growers' movement highlights the mildness of Crerar's critique of partyism. R.C. Henders, the Manitoba Grain Growers' Association president,[92] was one of the earlier outspoken critics of the party system. This excerpt from his 1914 presidential address makes his position clear:

The Curse of Partyism

It has afforded the opportunity for the owners of organized capital to secure positions which gave them undue advantage over their fellow men . . . It has converted . . . responsible government into irresponsible government by introducing a system of rabid partyism which has succeeded admirably in removing the government so far from the people that, for the most part, they pay little attention to their honest demands. Partyism gone mad, partyism that cannot see any fault in its own party, and cannot see any good in the opposition party; partyism that would use such insane and illogical reasoning as this, 'Oh well I know that my party has done wrong, but, then, the other fellows will do just as great wrong if I gave them a chance.' . . . My candid opinion, reached after somewhat careful observation and mature study, is that such partyism as I have just described . . . is the great curse of present day politics, inasmuch as it opens the way to all manner of political corruption. Nor do I see any way to cure the ills of our political system until the large class of responsible electors, the stalwart, intelligent yeomanry of our country, combine with the robust and independent labour party and cut entirely loose from the influence of such insane partyism, and judge men and measures on their respective merits.[93]

One would expect an address to the troops to emphasize participation by the people. That this was not hollow rhetoric can be seen from two of the watchwords of the grain growers' organizations (and their journal, the *Guide*), 'education' and 'organization.' The more radical crypto-Liberal leaders wished to transfer these into the political sphere from the economic sphere via 'direct' political action. An emphasis on organization in grain growers' associations did not imply the centralized approaches of electoral machines, but rather a multi-layered, open association of mutual advancement. Organization had to be made a boon to democracy. The same held true for education. The *Guide* was conceived as a means of bringing a democratic movement together, by developing a shared understanding of the political, social, and economic obstacles and prospects facing its agrarian elements.[94]

The provincial grain growers' associations were committed to the educational work that could be carried out on a face-to-face basis in the many locals and district councils.[95] In fact, leaders often opposed direct political action because they expected the educational function of the association to suffer.[96] Another excerpt from a 1918 Henders address indicates the link organized grain growers perceived between education and democracy:

> Democratic rule requires that the average citizen be an active, instructed, and intelligent ruler of his country, and, therefore, the success of democracy depends upon the education of the people along two principal lines, first political knowledge, and second, what is of far more importance, political morality . . . When through the lack of political knowledge, or political morality, citizens fail to realize their responsibilities, when they lose the inspiration which comes through faith in a higher law which neither legislatures nor courts can either justly or safely set aside, then the very foundations of political liberty are swept away, or become a mockery, in which the plutocratic oligarchy grasps the reins of power and the servants of the people become their masters.[97]

In a 1916 speech, Henders combined exhortation to participate in politics with a suggestion that a truly educated farmers' movement would become conscious of itself as a *class* movement:

> Our great source of weakness is . . . that farmers as a class have not in the past and do not even now readily develop the spirit of class consciousness. We pass many important resolutions all carefully planned and well thought out . . . We fail utterly, shamefully fail when we come to the

enforcement of the carrying out of the principles embodied in these resolutions. All other classes, as a result of their combination, and because
of the fact that they place class interests above political preferment, are
able to wield influence in the halls of our legislature. We pass resolutions,
divide our influence along party political lines and so weaken our case
politically that in the great game of party politics we play little or no part.
The banker, the manufacturer, the railway interests, when they have personal interests to serve, know no politics. With them their business is their
politics . . . until we go home and practice that lesson, we need not hope
or expect to succeed in bringing to rural life that consideration which it
merits.[98]

Parts of this argument led in the direction of the 'economic class politics'
of the United Farmers of Alberta. Henders and Manitoba Progressives were
not willing to follow this path. They none the less felt that an agrarian political analysis that owned up to the class politics shaping party competition
was a prerequisite of agrarian political influence at the national level. They
rejected the exclusiveness of agrarian political activity proposed by group
government theory and replaced it with commitment to a catch-all 'people's
party' led by organized farmers. Most Manitoba Progressives were unwilling to see such a party follow the same centralized, élite-dominated route
that the old parties had charted. Uncommitted to constituency autonomy
or principled non-alignment with the Liberals, Crerar and his followers discovered that, even in their home territory (a United Farmers of Manitoba
convention in 1923), proposing a political vehicle too much like the old-
party organization would not be acceptable.[99]

The Grain Growers' Guide was a forum for anti-party sentiment from
1910 to 1925. It had led an intermittent campaign for agrarian third-party
politics since the 1911 reciprocity 'defeat,' fully nine years in advance of the
majority and leaderships of the three prairie grain growers' associations it
served. Editorial and feature writers made criticism of the centralized and
'autocratic' character of old-party organizations a central theme in the fight
against 'partyism,' with the corollary of support for local autonomy. Prominent Manitoba co-operator and *Guide* writer J.T. Hull put this position succinctly in an article on the three 1921 grain growers' conventions:

One feature in the political organization of the movement deserves special mention, and that is the emphasis that is laid upon the local. The value
of this form of organization cannot be overestimated from at least any
democratic standpoint. The curse of the old party system was the grip
that it laid upon the individual. The party laid down the lines of thought
and tolerated no turning to the right hand or the left from those lines.
Over his own mind, declared one of the greatest of Liberal thinkers, John
Stuart Mill, the individual is sovereign. Canadian political partyism

declared otherwise. In making the local the basis of the entire organization, and in stimulating the fullest discussion with the greatest freedom of all questions by the locals, and in bringing the results of that free discussion before the annual conventions, the farmers are doing more to get back to the fundamental basis of real democracy than any other body of men in the country. They are, in fact, the one class that is organizing freedom that the community may gain.[100]

On the eve of the 1921 federal election's announcement, *The Grain Growers' Guide* editorialized on the same theme:

Neither the Liberal nor the Conservative party is democratic in its character nor permanent in its functioning; the organizations of the farmers are democratic in character and they function continuously. They provide channels for individual expression within the movement and the means for keeping the people in touch with the movement in all its phases. These organizations rest on local units; they are built from the bottom up and not from the top down, and it is only by such organization of interest and opinion that partyism of any kind can hope to avoid the evils of an 'odious oligarchy.' And that is not to build on an academic ideal; it is merely recognizing the demand of the time that democracy be more than a pleasant political fiction.'[101]

Guide editor George Chipman refused to let the old parties off the hook as easily as Crerar had. The *Guide* pushed harder on the tariff, campaign financing, business-party ties, and 'class' character of the Meighen government[102] than did Crerar. On the issue of local autonomy and popular control in political organization, the *Guide* and its principal contributors distinguished themselves in an area that Crerar refused to enter.

It is interesting to note, however, that the Progressives' practical commitment to decentralization of the institutions of representation and administration paled in comparison to that of the Patrons of Industry. The Patrons' 1895 platform included the following:

7. A system of Civil Service Reform that will give each County power to appoint or elect all County officials paid by them, except County Judges; . . .
12. Preparation of the Dominion and Provincial Voters' Lists by the municipal officers;
13. Conformity of electoral districts to County boundaries, as constituted for Municipal purposes, as far as the principle of representation by population will allow.[103]

As S.D. Shortt notes, these proposals for reform of electoral machinery and state administration were intended to complement rural political solidarity for the purpose of destroying urban political domination. Farmers, rather than Toronto professionals, would control the functions and administration of most state action bearing upon rural communities.[104] Whether it was the failure of the Patrons to survive the federal Liberal victory in 1896, or the largely federal focus of their policy complaints, prairie Progressives did not see the need to promote so radical a decentralization of state power as did the Patrons. Decentralization of their own representative structures was apparently considered sufficient.

As anti-party sentiment intensified in the West between 1911 and 1921, calls for abolition of 'the patronage system' were central to critiques of 'partyism.' This emphasis meant that the critique was less incisive than the radical democratic critique of party.[105] None the less, it did address a pervasive aspect of party politics, and was an effective means of rallying support within the agricultural community. The attack on patronage was linked to a central Canadian business élite benefiting from the tariff and established patronage network.

A proposal in the 1916 Farmers' Platform for publication of 'political campaign fund contributions and expenditures both before and after elections'[106] followed easily from the preamble's contention that the tariff was responsible for the concentration of industry and inordinate political influence by tariff-sheltered 'trusts.' The suggestion that patronage was the glue for a corrupt political network reflected a widespread prairie belief. There was enough evidence of patronage in federal governmental performance (especially with respect to war-materials contracts and local party 'machines') to make this a very legitimate concern. Patronage was so effectively identified with old-party practices by the early farmers' movement in Ontario and the prairies that all prairie populisms incorporated it into their own accounts of a corrupt political economy.

The patronage issue was seldom treated in isolation from what were seen as closely related practices of party funding by 'big interests' and slick manipulation of public opinion by a pandering party press. Perhaps the most conservative crypto-Liberal account of patronage came from Thomas Crerar. Crerar had left the Union Government in 1919 in response to an unrepentantly protectionist budget, not out of opposition to partyism *per se*.[107] As Progressive leader from 1920 to 1923, he was in fact anxious to organize the Progressives into a centralized political force.[108] Thus, when Crerar attacked partyism, he focused his attack on an uncontroversial target: patronage and bankrolling of old party campaigns by 'big interests.' In his 'Confession of Faith' published in both *Maclean's* and *The Grain Growers' Guide* during the 1921 election campaign, Crerar asserted that 'our criticism is not directed against our federal parliament so much as against the methods by which party managers, fortified by campaign funds derived from the purses of privileged interests, use to manipulate it for their own and their patron's ends.'

The patronage issue figured quite prominently in the *Guide's* attack on old party rule, especially in the 1911 to 1918 period. Even after the Civil Service Act of 1920, any hint of the reemergence of patronage in government personnel appointments was roundly condemned.[109] Unaware of Weber's claim that elevation of the merit principle in government appointments would ultimately subvert democratic control of bureaucracy,[110] the grain growers' organ considered patronage to be the most blatant contradiction of the principles of equity and fairness. Wartime contracts to party-financing businessmen were seen as confirmation of the argument linking government policy to 'the big interests.' Patronage could also be easily linked to the sinister relation between protected industries and high-tariff administrations.

In a dramatic election-eve editorial sheet, *The Grain Growers' Guide* of 30 November 1921 offered two separate seventeen-point scenarios of 'What the People of Canada may expect during the Next Four Years.' 'If the Big Interest Government Wins, . . . Big Corporations, financial interests and tariff barons will be permitted to contribute secretly large sums to the government campaign funds, as they are now doing, and will undoubtedly receive government favors in return.' However, 'if the New National Policy Wins, . . . Special Legislation will be require full publicity for all campaign fund contributions from all sources both before and after elections.' 'Plutocrats' would have no choice but to terminate their illicit relationships with corrupted politicians. Deprived of this support, governments would surely return to serving the public interest (i.e., following the New National Policy). As unlikely as this scenario seems in retrospect, it was entailed by the democratic reform logic in the New National Policy.

The differences between leadership and grass-roots variants of crypto-Liberalism on the issues of party critique, direct legislation, political action, and local autonomy suggest an important underlying distinction. Whereas many of the rank and file in the grain growers' associations of Saskatchewan and Manitoba accorded virtually intrinsic value to participation in political and economic organizations, crypto-Liberal leadership saw participation in narrowly instrumental terms. Participation was necessary to elect MPs who could remake the Liberal party and national fiscal policy. In this instance they were only one step removed from the position of the Liberal party. For the rank and file, participation was an inevitable component of citizenship. This attitude was fostered in the grain growers' associations' activities. Had the SGGA and MGGA been led by activists who pressed the logic of citizenship in a group government and delegate democracy direction, many of their rank and file would have been 'radical democratic populists' and Crerar would have remained a Liberal.

The State and Technocracy

Celebrations of democracy and critiques of 'old party politics' are prominent themes in crypto-Liberal discourse. Conceptions of 'the state' and the idea of technocracy are less transparently so, but they were, none the less, an important part of the overall democratic theory. The pattern of differences between leadership and rank and file exists in this territory as well.

TECHNOCRATIC ELEMENTS OF CRYPTO-LIBERAL THOUGHT

The tension between democracy and technocracy within prairie populisms was not often explicitly perceived as a problem or 'contradiction.' This should not be surprising during a period that combined widespread enthusiasm for the new and democratic social order with enthusiasm for scientific and technological solutions to social problems. To most proponents of progress, new horizons of democratic experience were expanded, not obscured, by expert technical direction of public policies. Such direction was generally assumed to be value-free and non-partisan, and thus even more attractive. Few public figures spoke of a trade-off between the technocratic and participatory-Democratic outlooks.

Crypto-Liberal leaders' thoughts on the democracy/technocracy trade-off may appear unexceptional to late-twentieth century eyes, but they reveal a good deal about both crypto-Liberalism's reformism and its commitments to popular democracy.

Crypto-Liberal leadership at both the provincial and federal levels shared with other contemporary liberals the idea that government's proper function was mediation among various interests in the community. National Conservative claims to the contrary, they did not intend government to implement radical policies. Crerar and sympathetic provincial premiers did not come near rejecting traditional parliamentary governmental practices or party competition for office. Incremental changes in fiscal, transportation, and campaign-finance legislation would satisfy them that Canada was becoming democratic. At the provincial level, democratic credentials could be assured by responsiveness to grain growers', other agricultural, and local businessmen's associations.

Because they demanded little from governments and political life that could not have been provided by 'the system,' these crypto-Liberals rarely questioned the relative strengths or virtues of technocratic as compared to popular-democratic determination of public policy. In Crerar's case, inattention to popular-democratic devices for shaping public policy was complemented by an emphasis on 'sound administration' indistinguishable from the two major parties. His 1921 'Manifesto' included the following passage:

The Progressive movement recognizes that while we need a new moral atmosphere in politics, any government has to meet vast problems of practical administration. A new government, then, must bring to its work not only a measure of ideals, but as well sound, practical business judgement and high administrative capacity. Because of the financial condition of this country and the obligations we are facing, *the great need today is sound business administration of this country's affairs*. The best minds available inside and outside the new parliament must be enlisted for the consideration and solution of these problems, and . . . the Progressive party . . . will apply itself to the discharge of this vast task along the lines indicated. This is a time when patriotism must come before party, when the national well being must be the first concern of every good citizen.[111]

There is nothing wrong with sound business administration or calling on the best minds for policy advice. However, without provision for parallel influence and policy direction from the popular movement Crerar led, this claim concerning 'the great need today' sounds decidedly non-popular democratic. If one substitutes 'Liberal' for 'Progressive' in the passage above, the statement could have been uttered by W.L.M. King in the same campaign. By speaking to a supposed universal public support for 'sound business administration,' Crerar was attempting to 'broaden out' the Progressive party. His grain grower supporters desired sound business administration, but not divorced from clearly defined popular control of governments.[112]

The same tendency was evident in the three prairie provincial administrations during the 1920s. For example, John Bracken's tenure as premier was characterized by what he understood as non-partisan, administratively efficient, and fiscally responsible direction of provincial affairs. Bracken entered politics with no political experience, a distaste for partisan motivations, and a distinguished career as an academic agricultural scientist.[113] To the victorious but leaderless United Farmers of Manitoba in 1922, his renowned expertise and political detachment made him an able premier. Bracken sympathized with the objectives of the UFM, and believed that his premiership might ensure their political success by providing a 'sound, efficient and businesslike administration.'[114]

J.W. Dafoe's support for the United Farmers government was predicated more on its support by the Winnipeg business community and its capacity for accepting 'responsible' leadership than on its enthusiasm for popular democracy. He offered this response to Bracken's acceptance of the premier's chair: 'Professor Bracken is confronted with a business task, calling for powers of organization, foresight, acumen and sagacity—the qualities of the administrator and the businessman. These qualities . . . Professor Bracken has . . . A highly competent agricultural expert has been placed at the head of affairs in a province which, in its wealth-producing activities, are primarily agricultural.'[115]

Bracken did not disappoint Dafoe. Just before his by-election victory in 1922, Bracken announced that 'our purpose, briefly stated, is to give the province an honest, efficient, and businesslike administration; to eliminate waste and cut down expenses to the lowest possible minimum.' In his first legislative speech, Bracken echoed Crerar: 'We are not here to play politics or represent a single class, but to get down to the serious business of giving this province an efficient government.' When up for re-election in 1927, the Bracken government campaigned on its record, and attributed the province's financial standing to 'what may be accomplished when politics is divorced from the business affairs of the government.'[116] 'Brackenism' was thus a very partial reflection of the democratic aspirations of grain grower rank and file.

The point, once again, is not that this approach was exceptional, or contrary to the traditional Canadian conception of democratic government. It was, rather, entirely unexceptional and consistent with these traditions— albeit taking them more seriously than did most patronage-ridden federal and provincial regimes. The popular-democratic rhetoric of the UFM rank and file would have suggested a greater amount of experimentation and unorthodoxy in democratic government. None the less, the UFM rank and file supported Bracken for over two decades; with little indication that they expected government performance to meet the elevated standards suggested by their rhetoric. The obvious alternative, a return to Tory rule, was one they were loath to accept.

The Saskatchewan Liberal administrations of W.M. Martin and C.A. Dunning frequently made the same public commitment to 'sound administration.' David Smith notes that 'Martin found in Dunning a lieutenant who shared his interest in efficient administration. Sound, or as it was much more frequently described, business-like government was a theme which Martin stressed . . . [He was] disposed to value efficient management techniques.'[117]

With our interest in the technocratic tendencies in crypto-Liberalism, we should note the connection between claims about 'non-partisan administration' and the technocratic orientation. The 'non-partisan' spirit[118] was central to early prairie political culture. While non-partisanism was an understandable response to a hinterland wheat economy, it could also offer a beguiling justification for government 'in the public interest' with priorities set by supposedly apolitical administrators. This was especially true at the municipal political level, where the commission-board plan, conceived by American Progressives to prevent corrupt machine politics, was adopted in most prairie cities by 1918.

This form of 'non-partisan' politics was not promoted by principled opponents of partyism, but by local business élites. They felt that by isolating a strong civic administration from party politics, they could ensure that the local 'public interest' could be shaped by business rather than labour priorities. As James Anderson has noted, this kind of municipal reform possessed a corporate and anti-participatory rationale, contending that 'city government . . .

should be run by administrative experts, particularly successful business-men, on business-like principles of efficiency and economy; . . . the adminis-tration of policy should be left entirely to the civic administration or a small executive elected at large, the duties of which [would] correspond to that of the manager of a private business firm.'[119]

These ideas have profoundly shaped public perspectives on municipal politics in Canada. While not accepted so readily in the partisan atmospheres of provincial politics, the underlying logic that government is essentially an administrative, business-like affair, and that politics should be moulded in this light was attractive to prairie administrations. Claims of 'non-partisanship' not only suggested unbiased, fair-handed administration, they also tended to isolate senior policy-makers and bureaucrats from the hurly-burly of 'parochial interests' and 'partisan objectives.' Cloaking a govern-ment in 'sound, business-like administration' was one covertly partisan means of discouraging popular group pressure on governments between elec-tions. This posture enhanced technocratic attitudes at the expense of popu-lar democracy.

Perhaps the most striking conscious presumption in favour of expert tech-nical policy development occurred in the UFA administrations of H. Green-field and J.E. Brownlee. By prairie standards, the UFA administration was no more than ordinarily responsive to its grain grower support. Indeed, Carl Betke argues that the UFA administration under Brownlee 'made its deci-sions on the basis of expert advice, referring regularly to the trust which farmers must necessarily place in such traditionally alien authorities as finan-ciers.'[120] On movement concerns such as monetary and credit reform, the administration arranged a 'replacement of the agrarian wisdom of the UFA by the expertise of special consultants.' This accelerated the decline in UFA participatory enthusiasm and membership.[121]

The UFA administration came to view UFA convention resolutions as unwelcome intrusions into a complicated fiscal and administrative domain. This turned later annual conventions into shadows of their former selves, by undermining rank-and-file belief in the importance of serious policy-shaping contributions by locals and conventions. Their expectations in this regard were undeniably optimistic, but the UFA government did little to accommodate their participatory urge in its policy development processes.

Macpherson, Betke, Morton, and others have explained the relatively low level of direct power that UFA conventions, individual MLAs, and local organizations could exercise over 'their' provincial government. They have pointed to the inherent limits created by responsible government, the fed-eral division of powers, and the party competition in which the farmers' polit-ical representative found themselves.[122] Perhaps these circumstances made the UFA administration's approach to policy development unavoidable. It is significant, though, that the UFA administration developed an early and clear bias against popular interventions, and a presumption that problems raised thereby could only be solved by 'the expertise of special consultants.' While the UFA administration could not have become the direct legislative extension of UFA movement, it did not have to become such a solid example of 'Brackenism.'

These technocratic tendencies in prairie crypto-Liberal administrations indicate that crypto-Liberalism in office was not the popular-democratic operation that grain grower rhetoric might suggest. Provincial crypto-Liberal leaders never wondered aloud about the technocratic flavour of their style of governing, just as Crerar had avoided or not seriously considered the potential grass-roots opposition to his anti-participatory and 'dirigiste' strategy for policy changes. As we have seen, proper governmental practice was often likened to that of successful corporations. 'Business-like government,' 'sound administration,' and even 'scientific management' characterized the hopes and achievements of crypto-Liberal governments. Like other liberals in the early twentieth century, leading crypto-Liberals had faith that science and technology would progressively eliminate the hardships of social existence. Impartial men of science could be relied on to assess the feasibility of requests made by legitimate interests, and then to determine how requests might be met.

Democracy was thus seen in rather narrowly institutionalized and formal terms, with state functionaries and hired professionals viewed as class-neutral and supra-political. It is not surprising that provincial crypto-Liberal leaders saw little conflict between their popular democratic organizations and their technocratically inclined administrations.

Like the national crypto-Liberal leadership, they did not perceive structural or deeply entrenched cultural obstacles in their way. Nor did they carry a passion for collective self-determination rooted in a perception of systematic and sustained exploitation.

The key task of hired experts was not to promote social reconstruction, but to engage in the supposedly post-political administrative business of government. Crypto-Liberal leaders' relatively weak sense of power denied made it difficult for them to see technocrats as another obstacle to greater equalization of power. In these matters, one can see that the crypto-Liberal political leadership was temperamentally and, to a significant extent, philosophically at odds with their grain grower rank and file. This was most obvious in Alberta, but also evident in Saskatchewan and Manitoba. The grain growers' association members and activists supported the use of 'experts' to assist the conduct of sound administration, but they did not accept the priority of 'expert' advice over their conventions' well-considered proposals in matters of basic policy development.

The State

An account of the crypto-Liberal conception of the state follows logically from discussion of its technocratic elements. W.L. Morton puts us on the right track by arguing that 'in the first decade of the century a general reform movement had been growing in the Canadian West . . . [which was] at core a demand for positive state action with respect to such matters as the prohibition of the sale of alcoholic liquor, the promotion of social welfare, and the cleansing of political life . . . In its demand for action by the state against certain evils, it marked an epoch in the development of Canadian democracy.'[123] The strength of this movement helped shape Mackenzie King's decision to have the Liberal party make a formal commitment to nascent welfare-state liberalism in 1919. He saw that, since the onset of the Great War, there had been increasing public acceptance of an interventionist state, which would soften the blow of inequalities created by the capitalist market economy.

In the moral climate created by anticipation of 'the new social order,' the state also came to be seen as an instrument of moral regeneration. Thus all governments were expected to enact temperance, female suffrage, campaign-financing controls, civil-service reform, and other public morality-enhancing legislation.[124] The same state that had protected individuals benefiting from 'corruption' was now expected to heed the public demand to 'reform itself.' Farmers' groups presented campaigns for public ownership of utilities and railways, and of course tariff reform, as means of cleaning up public life.

For many crypto-Liberals, these demands did not imply a comprehensive state regulation of the market economy. Their liberal-physiocratic view of this 'natural economy' held that monopolies, trusts, and the power of 'plutocracy' in the state resulted from unsound fiscal and economic development policies.[125] They assumed that free-trade liberalism would have prevented the growth of 'interests' holding the state to ransom. From this perspective, the state had a moral duty to implement policies facilitating a re-emergence of the 'natural economy,' thereby ultimately reducing its own role and responsibilities in the economy. Crerar, among others, would have cherished such a reformed state, as he illustrated in 1920 by rejecting a grain grower demand for the re-establishment of the Wheat Board.[126] Crerar did not like being seen to favour free trade while asking for special, market-manipulating state support.

Adherence to a *laissez-faire* doctrine did not prevent Crerar from thinking that the federal state in Canada had been the preserve of one 'class.' He did not idealize the federal government as being equally responsive to all social groups' demands. Trying to defuse the old-party attack on the Progressives as a class party, Crerar commented: 'Liberals of the older school have always had a touching faith that popular self-government would prevent any monopoly of the state by any one class, but our electorate has in the past been too gullible and careless of its real interests to make this cure reliable. The one-class domination, which has hitherto existed, has also managed to poison the system of political democracy which was expected to effect the cure for all our ills.'[127]

Crerar promised that one-class domination of the state would be eliminated if the Progressives came to power.[128] The class in question might be best described as 'Eastern urban professional and protected business interests'; crypto-Liberals seldom referred to it as the capitalist class. The state was at fault, then, because it had dispensed its economic favours to the 'urban class.' When Crerar and others spoke of the 'present economic system . . . largely devised for the benefit of a small privileged class,' they were referring to 'financial and manufacturing interests' and their professional hangers-on. 'The system' in question was 'protection,' not capitalism, even though crypto-Liberal discourse contained much anti-capitalist talk.

Most crypto-Liberal rank and file supported an interventionist state well beyond Crerar's wishes. Any number of *Guide* editorial cartoons in the two months before the 1921 federal election demonstrate this optimism regarding the state's potential if the Progressive David could slay the special-interests/Tory Goliath.[129] With their sense of regional mistreatment, they had no ideological problem demanding ameliorative and protective policies for their own industry.

One instance of this was the seventh plank in the 1921 Farmers' Platform. It was clearly designed to benefit the agricultural population, although they argued its implementation would assist all ordinary consumers. This plank proposed 'a land settlement scheme based on a regulating influence in the selling price of land.' To keep land merchants and small speculators honest, and maintain a reasonable price for farm land, 'owners of idle areas should be obliged to file a selling price on their lands, that price also to be regarded as assessable value for purposes of taxation.' If lands simply gathered speculative value, the unscrupulous owners would pay some price for their greed. With more cheap land brought into production, overall production costs would be lessened and ultimate consumer costs reduced. The prosperity of the farmer would thus benefit society, and validate the platform's physiocratic premise. Where the power of the state (provincial or federal) was required for economic or social advance, farmers were prepared to let it play a major role in their salvation.

Most crypto-Liberals felt an ambivalence towards state interventions in civil society similar to that of contemporary trust-busting Progressives in the United States and reform Liberals in Britain. Grain growers on the prairies were keenly aware of these developments in both countries, partly as a result of coverage provided by the *Guide*. They thus felt more comfortable supporting state action to reform industrial capitalism and the Canadian agricultural economy. R.C. Henders noted in his 1912 address to the Manitoba Grain Growers' convention:

An advance in public industry, or government ownership of industry, is not unmitigated evil; indeed it may be advanced in aid of the movement towards good government, because in the first place it helps to do away with private corporations which are chiefly the corrupting influence and certainly one of the leading obstacles to good government today. Secondly, it increases the importance of governmental affairs, and intensifies the disasters resulting from corruption, partisanship, and the spoils system and so arouses the interests of the citizens and impels them to demand reforms that will guarantee pure and efficient management. Therefore, except under especially adverse circumstances, sufficiently powerful to overcome the effects just named, government ownership of industrial monopolies tends towards good government and public ownership, both of which tend, of course, to the diffusion of wealth and power and the realization of a more perfect democracy.[130]

Henders had more enthusiasm for public ownership of utilities and industrial monopolies than most grain growers at this time.[131] None the less, all prairie governments were pressured by agrarian organizations to undertake public ownership of utilities, local railways (in Alberta), and even (briefly in Manitoba) grain elevators.[132] Equally notable was the ninth plank in the 1921 Farmers' Platform, which had been ratified by grain grower organizational members of the CCA in 1919. From a strictly class-interested point of view, prairie producers' support for this plank makes sense. It called for public ownership and control 'of railway, water and aerial transportation, telephone, telegraph and express systems, all projects in the development of natural power, and of the coal mining industry.' They saw public ownership of transportation as the only way to regulate the much detested CPR.

Public ownership of telephone systems was a populist demand accepted early by all three prairie provincial governments. The farming community also viewed cheap and reliable sources of hydroelectric and fuel power as crucial and hence supported public ownership of natural public utilities. State-run monopolies were seen as preferable to private monopolies, which might well influence corruptable politicians (as had the CPR). Support for public ownership of these basic services was thus an expression of distrust in both large private firms and party politicians. Consequently, the campaign for public ownership of utilities and monopolies was widely perceived as an inherently democratic one, transcending petty ideological disputes. Even conservative crypto-Liberals lauded the potential of public ownership to reduce plutocratic power and give agricultural producers the 'square deal' they desired from the state. In this sense, crypto-Liberal support for public ownership may legitimately be taken as evidence of a 'Tory touch' in Canadian political culture.[133]

Unencumbered by a public acceptance of the dogmas of *laissez-faire*, more radical prairie populisms could launch campaigns for more extensive 'social ownership.' By endowing some forms of public ownership with democratic credentials, crypto-Liberalism opened the door to more extensive challenges to the logic of the liberal market on the prairies.

As the rather different case of Ontario Hydro had already demon-strated,[134] public ownership does not necessarily imply socialism. Support for public ownership of 'public utilities' had been a constant of American populism since the 1870s,[135] and has found support in a wide range of agrar-ian political movements since 1921. The fact that many Canadians now think of public ownership as the legacy of Fabian 'gas-and-water socialism' tells us more about collective political amnesia, the shrunken horizons of con-temporary social democracy, and the hegemony of a private-enterprise cul-ture in North America than it does about the nature of the proposal itself.

In view of the mixed results that comprehensive 'free trade' would pro-vide for Canadian grain farmers in the 1980s, it is interesting to review the alternatives to tariffs proposed by prairie farmers' organizations in the era before marketing boards. By 1916, the Canadian Council of Agriculture—dominated by western grain growers—had proposed four forms of direct taxation: 'a direct tax on all unimproved land values, including all natural resources'; 'a sharp graduated personal income tax'; 'a heavily graduated personal income tax'; and 'a graduated income tax on the profits of corpo-rations.'

The first of the revenue proposals shows the influence of Henry George's socio-economic analysis in the prairie West. The direct tax on unimproved land values is presented here as a modified application of George's idea that social inequalities could be largely ameliorated by a 'single tax' on the unearned increment derived by industry and land speculators from land ownership. Under this scheme, taxation of the CPR, the Hudson's Bay Com-pany, and various land companies' holdings would yield major government revenues and maintain manageable land costs to agriculturalists.[136]

The second, third, and fourth tax proposals were relatively radical in 1916. Even the 'progressive' 1919 Liberal platform made no suggestion of income or corporate taxes as devices of wealth redistribution or sources of government revenue. The tax policies broadly proposed by the CCA in 1916 were intended to counterbalance the 'regressive,' hidden tax policy of pro-tection.[137]

It is interesting to note how the redistributionist character of these four complements to 'free trade' contrasts with the corporate power-enhancing logic that pervades the campaign for continental free trade today. Egalitar-ian sentiments and democratized relations of power between classes have little to do with the current scenario for economic rationalization in a con-tinental market, but they were central to the prairie farm organizations' proposals for alternatives to the tariff.

Co-operation

Complicating crypto-Liberal ambivalence about the state was a strong grass-roots commitment to co-operative enterprise. Co-operatives were the preferred instruments of reform. Even if the state at all levels was responsive to grain growers' requests, co-ops would still have several crucial advantages. They were more sensitive to democratic and local control, and more appropriate as educational forms addressing the specific needs of the agricultural community. Co-operative organizations sprang directly from the experience and needs of the agrarian community.[138]

Additionally, the non-partisan and anti-political tradition in Anglo-American co-operation reduced prairie farmers' willingness to depend on the state's 'favours.' The *Guide's* coverage of Britain's co-operative movement[139] retained this anti-statist element, and reinforced the grain growers' tendency to seek shelter from the antagonistic National Policy in their own collective institutions. In the minds of many of their supporters, grain growers' associations and wheat pools had almost assumed the status of an 'alternative state'[140] (hence the title 'grain growers' parliaments' for their annual conventions). In the most radical farmers' political organizations, this tendency was amplified into a syndicalist approach to the state.[141] In a different, non-socialist form, this tendency fuelled the 'group government' scheme. In crypto-Liberal circles, however, it was enough to have separate agrarian vehicles of reform, performing the representative function through lobbying rather than farmers' parties. The Saskatchewan Grain Growers' Association's experience provides the best example of this.

Ian MacPherson argues that there were three basic types of co-operators in the co-operative movement in Canada from 1910 to 1945: 'utopian co-operators,' 'pragmatic or liberal co-operators,' and 'occupational co-operators.' The first group was composed primarily of social democrats and 'co-operative idealists' who 'tried to perceive society as an organic whole and thought that co-operative techniques were ideal for establishing a new social and economic order.' The second group saw co-operation as 'primarily a method to protect the legitimate rights of people on the family farm or dependent upon a weekly wage.' Occupational co-operators viewed co-operatives 'as essentially assistants to the farmers who owned them and not as elements of a wider movement.'[142]

There is little doubt that crypto-Liberalism was influenced primarily by 'pragmatic-liberal' thought on co-operatives, although some of the *Guide's* regular contributors presented co-operation in terms approaching the organic, 'utopian' perspective. MacPherson places 'the bulk of farmers in English Canada' and 'such leading figures as C.A. Dunning, T.A. Crerar, and W.R. Motherwell' in the pragmatic-liberal category.[143] Many of these leaders had cut their public teeth in grain growers' organizations or co-operatives, and worked through the Liberal party when pursuing political careers at the provincial level. The Progressives included 'numerous co-operators who were searching for a political home' during its period of prominence in federal politics.[144] This latter attachment was usually made by those like Crerar who hoped to resuscitate 'real' liberalism after being disappointed by the Liberal party.

For these crypto-Liberal leaders, co-operation represented a hard-headed, group-based approach to securing a 'square deal' for grain growers in an economic environment where other economic interests were well organized and holding market and political power as a consequence. Co-operative organizations were also seen as the best vehicles for community education in better farming techniques and flexing political muscle. Co-operation was not thought of as providing a universal paradigm for economic and social relations, except in a very loose sense popularized by moderate expressions of the 'social gospel' at this time.

Crerar spoke in these terms in his 1921 'Confession of Faith,' when he commented briefly on the need for enabling legislation for co-operatives: 'We believe that there is more real happiness to be derived from the creative impulse and the co-operative impulse than from the possessive and acquisitive impulse and the impulse to authority and dominion over others.'[145] This turned out to be a *non sequitur* rather than an introduction to a passage of 'utopian' co-operative thinking, as Crerar went on to extol the virtues of co-operation as a means of reducing the cost of living for the average consumer. Still, with Crerar as president of the United Grain Growers, promotion of co-operative enterprise by crypto-Liberals at the national level was important.

Provincial crypto-Liberal politicians recognized the importance of enacting legislation conducive to the growth of provincial grain growers' associations and co-operatives. This was true especially in Saskatchewan, where the SGGA and the Saskatchewan Co-operative Elevator Company were virtually 'clients' of the Liberal administration from 1910 to 1929. At this level, the crypto-Liberal political response to the growth of dynamic producers' co-operatives involved formal encouragement of a healthy co-operative movement, co-opting its leaders, and assuring the public that established politcal (and economic) structures could easily accommodate the democratic objectives of the co-operative movement.

Saskatchewan Liberal and SGGA leaders allowed the co-operative movement to feel like a privileged 'pressure group' within the province. For a long time, consequently, the development of a more radically 'co-operativist' or social democratic approach seemed gratuitous to most of their grain grower supporters. Eventually, however, their attempts to neutralize and delegitimize the radical implications of co-operative ideals contributed to the formation of the Farmers' Union of Canada, the United Farmers of Canada (Saskatchewan Section), the Farmers' Educational League, and other populist-socialist alternatives to 'prairie Liberalism.' In retrospect, a clash between the Saskatchewan 'Liberal machine' and the broader democratic vision of the dynamic co-operative movement was probably inevitable.

Within the prairies, co-operation was a veritable religion,[146] and its initiates could thus nod approvingly at the wisdom and progressive implications of the eighth plank of the 1921 Farmers' Platform, which proposed 'extension of co-operative agencies in agriculture to cover the whole field of marketing, including arrangements with consumers' societies for the supplying of foodstuffs at the lowest rates and with the minimum of middleman handling.' For those outside grain growers' associations, it was not evident that producers' and consumers' co-operation, democracy, and a higher moral plane of social intercourse were necessarily connected. Where the spirit of rural co-operation had not left its mark, this seemingly commercial proposal could not inspire. Where it did, rank-and-file crypto-Liberals viewed co-operation as the general philosophical basis on which not just economic security, but also a more complete democracy, could develop. The appeals of the *Guide* and its occasional utopian co-operator columnists—E.A. Partridge in its earlier years, and Salem Bland and J.S. Woodsworth just before the rise of the Progressives—did much to promote this understanding.

A less impressive instance of the crypto-Liberal extension of the principle of co-operation into public life came in the labour plank of the 1921 Farmers' Platform. All levels of government were advised to use 'every means, economically feasible and practicable,' to minimize post-war unemployment. No one was for unemployment, and this proposal committed the Progressives to precisely nothing—as did the Mackenzie King—like recommendation of 'the adoption of the principle of co-operation as the guiding spirit in the future relations . . . between capital and labour.'[147] In the context of the bitter labour-capital relations during and after the war, this appeal beyond class conflict trivialized the concept of co-operations, which had proved its importance in agrarian social life. What farm leaders may have seen as support for the just demands of labour and the legitimate claims of employers was likely seen as pablum by each group.

The standards implicit in the accomplishments of the co-operative movement were transposed into grain growers' political activities. These standards related to 'cleaning up' public life, reducing economic inequality, promoting widespread 'civic education' and moral growth, maintaining decentralized popular control of basic activities, and bringing the common people together. When the Progressives failed to make much headway in these areas during their first parliament, such high standards fertilized grain grower disillusionment with political action. The co-operative movement in the United States and Canada had always displayed a deep distrust of competitive organized politics.[148] This distrust had been partly submerged in the period of the National Progressive organization, but it re-emerged quickly following Progressive frustration at the federal level.[149]

Such distrust was displayed in the career of A.J. MacPhail, the SGGA and later Wheat Pool executive whose public life was chronicled in the *Diary* made famous by H.A. Innis. MacPhail was a 'pragmatic liberal" co-operator in MacPherson's terms, but his anti-political sentiments were shared by many more 'utopian' grain growers. He believed that while some politicians could be trusted, grain growers could not hope to obtain their objectives primarily through political action. Political processes could not alter underlying social and economic attitudes—this was the role of popular organizations such as co-operatives. In addition, state action designed to engineer major changes in society implied compulsion, whereas the co-operation encouraged change through voluntary action by an enlightened citizenry. In these senses, he shared a good deal with Henry Wise Wood.

As noted earlier, the farmers' movement developed within a larger environment of reform in the early years of the twentieth century. In the Canadian West, an important part of this was the 'social gospel' of the Methodist and Presbyterian churches, which did much to build bridges between elements in the reform movement. Its most famous spokesmen are best classified under other populist labels: H.W. Wood as radical democratic populist, and E.A. Partridge, William Irvine, Salem Bland, and J.S. Woodsworth as social democratic populists. All of these men, however, were well known and respected in crypto-Liberal rank-and-file circles, not least for their persuasive account of the indissoluble links between the social teachings of Christ, the co-operative ethic, and the achievement of economic and social democracy.[150] The social gospel established or strengthened connections among the various 'democratic reforms' of the day, and then developed connotative links from these to a broad and potentially radical notion of co-operation. It thus played a major role in expanding the democracy/co-operation relationship within the grass-roots version of crypto-Liberalism. The social gospel did not have to convert its audience into social democrats to place the crypto-Liberal rank and file some distance from their leaders.

The last point to note regarding the idea of co-operation in crypto-Liberalism concerns its implications for political action. Crypto-Liberalism was always distinguished from radical democratic populism on this score by it rejection of 'occupational class politics.' Crypto-Liberals consistently proposed some modified form of 'people's party.' Before the Winnipeg General Strike and the Progressives' rise, grain grower association leaders spoke enthusiastically about the potential for political co-operation between agriculturalists and urban labour, as had the Patrons of Industry leaders in Ontario, Manitoba, and Saskatchewan.[151] The crypto-Liberal desire for such co-operation was squelched by the wave of labour radicalism in 1919. From then on, a more general appeal to 'the common people' for political co-operation on the basis of the 'New National Policy' was made. No concerted attempt was made to court urban support, except in Ontario, where the United Farmers administration lived by the grace of support by eleven Labour MPPs, an arrangement that created considerable friction within the UFO organization.

There was, in fact, no substantial effort put into applying crypto-Liberal notions of co-operation to a political strategy. This tells us a good deal about the limits of even the rank-and-file crypto-Liberal understanding of co-operation: for all of its good intentions and high standards, it did not extend beyond agricultural life. As a result, it could not have much of an impact on a national political economy where power necessitated co-operation among disadvantaged classes. As we have seen, there was a strong anti-political (or at least apolitical) bias within the co-operative movement. When translated into the political action of organized farmers, this bias was very likely to discourage systematic attempts to make common political cause with another 'organized interest.' Thus, despite Crerar's claims to the contrary, Arthur Meighen was correct in saying that the Progressives promoted a class notion of democracy—correct for the wrong reasons, but correct none the less.

Crypto-Liberalism and the Good Society

In sketching crypto-Liberal notions of the good society, we must infer a good deal from the aspects of normative democratic theory and social analysis considered earlier in this chapter. It is wise to begin with some of W.L. Morton's reflections on 'utopian' elements in prairie politics. Morton's comments are meant to apply primarily to the CCF and Social Credit,[152] but they are useful in understanding moderate reform thought as well: 'The reform movement of the first quarter of this century in the Prairie West was . . . tinged with millenarianism . . . The great majority of farmers wanted only to increase the farmers' returns. But all the farmers' organizations, from the Grange to the United Farmers, had some touch of uplift, and used the methods and even the songs of evangelism. The doctrine of the Wheat Pool was preached with apostolic fervour, and received by the majority of farmers with the abandon of converts.'[153]

The instructive point is that there was a future-oriented idealism even in the most pragmatic of prairie populisms. In noting features common to prairie settlers of different origins and eras, Morton referred twelve years later to 'the hope that the west might be a practical, a really viable, utopia,' a hope rooted in nineteenth-century writings and in 'the democratic dream that men might be free and independent, particularly, as transmitted by young women who taught school in Ontario and the west.' Morton goes on to contrast this utopian inclination with the commercial and utilitarian values predominant in Canadian society. He contends that it was 'the most important fact in the creation of the civilization of the west.'[154]

The predominant characteristic of crypto-Liberal utopias was their physiocratic orientation. As we saw earlier, this decisively informed the various Farmers' Platforms. The rural environment was held to be the only one in which free lives could be pursued, uncontaminated by the moral corruption, inegalitarianism, and class conflict of urban life.[155] The prairie rural setting was seen to possess the additional advantage of being new and thus unconstrained by old modes of thought. It possessed a natural bounty of good land and an impressive array of natural resources, the foundation of a prosperous free-trade economy. Given these advantages, prairie populists generally saw no good reason why political and economic institutions and practices should stand in the way of a 'really viable utopia.' There were several bad reasons why this utopia might be blocked.

For crypto-Liberals, the good society could be unachievable if the corrupting aspects of party politics continued, if the protective tariff were retained, and if agricultural production were not given proper recognition by provincial and national governments. For some prominent crypto-Liberal writers, these obstacles added up to a kind of latter-day 'feudalism.'

In these terms, the force animating this new-world feudalism was the dread "Toryism.' The conflict enveloping farmers was thus portrayed as involving Toryism, feudalism, and hierarchy, on the one hand, and 'true Liberalism,' the free market, and democracy, on the other. The promise of the triumph of the latter set of 'forces' was, in effect, the promise of a new Golden Age, where hard-working, God-fearing individuals would have an equal opportunity to lead an honest and rewarding life. The good society would thus prevent a privileged 'plutocracy' from denying a 'square deal' to all those who made an honest effort. Those who worked hard while remaining loyal to the Golden Rule would succeed.[156] The crypto-Liberal conception of justice was thus focused primarily on what an individual merited in return for honest contributions to the social economy. This was qualified by the influence of the 'social gospel,' which bolstered the importance given to charity to the disadvantaged. Still, it is important to see that crypto-Liberal justice was essentially the justice of the 'properly' functioning (and occasionally morally adaptable) free market.

Thus crypto-Liberal justice did not differ significantly from the justice of Anglo-American reform liberalism. If anything, it was less realistic about the prospects for a 'return' to the practices and hence standards of the free market. Paradoxically, this lesser realism gave crypto-Liberalism a more critical perspective on the justice of the modified market society than 'modern' urban Liberalism had, since crypto-Liberalism was less willing to accept the fact and consequences of concentrated corporate power. By itself, this did not push it very far in the direction of generalizing the virtues of collective organization (i.e., of following on the co-operatives' examples). However, one can still claim that 'progressivism should be seen as a step in the development of a Canadian critique of monopoly capitalism,'[157] just as the campaign of the Patrons in Ontario had been a generation earlier. The job of demanding an egalitarian distribution of economic and political power was left to social democratic and radical democratic populisms.

As a consequence, crypto-Liberalism never developed a notion equivalent to that of the 'co-operative commonwealth' of social democratic and radical democratic populisms. Such a notion required that the crypto-Liberal valuation of 'community' be more divorced from the prevailing individualistic liberalism. One occasionally gets a sense of this kind of development from the pages of *The Grain Growers' Guide*, but that is because the *Guide* functioned as a forum for virtually all prairie populism expression.

Clearly, a justice based ideally on a self-regulating market economy and morally self-disciplining population was less in need of a strong state than one that saw neither as 'natural' in human society. Thus, while crypto-Liberals saw a short-term need for strong state action against the organized 'big interests,' their vision of the future good society was decidedly anti-statist and anti-political. Politics had been the most obvious staging ground for corrupt social activity, and had almost always served farmers poorly. Co-operatives had eschewed political involvement, and had seen the state as equally capable of compulsive and voluntary social direction and change.

For all of these reasons, the good society of crypto-Liberalism would have done away with 'politics' as much as possible, while still putting a premium—at least for the grass-roots crypto-Liberals—on participation by common folk in shared public life. The state that became the focus of remaining 'political' activity would be efficient, virtually obsessed with operating economy, and 'non-partisan.' This view suggests a technocratically directed minimum state, if that is not a contradiction. The society it would administer would be characterized by a moral and genuine pluralism, where the interests of the common people would count more than those of traditionally privileged groups. The state would co-ordinate the society that many recent immigrants had believed they were coming to, and would take a modest place in the 'new social order' widely prophesied for Canada.

Finally, to fill out the picture of the normative basis of their democratic thought, it is worth noting that crypto-Liberals were good 'internationalists.' The 1921 Farmers' Platform opens with an endorsement of the League of Nations as an institution capable of guaranteeing national rights of self-determination, fostering international understanding, and 'making the world safe for democracy.' This endorsement complemented nicely their discussion of 'the new social order' for which the Great War was to have been a kind of cathartic prelude. An international organization inspired by recognition of high mutual purposes was welcomed by a variety of agrarian, labour, and political reform groups. This plank was meant as a sign to the public that the farmers' movement's concerns were not 'class-bound,' parochial, or backward-looking, as the Canadian Manufacturers' Association, Meighen's Conservatives, and right-wing Liberals had asserted.

The same could be said of the second plank, proposing 'a further development of the British Empire . . . along the lines of partnership between nations free and equal, under the present government system of British constitutional authority.' Along with this pledge of allegiance to Anglo-Canadian political structures and traditions came a rejection of any overlording by Britain in such a reformed Commonwealth, as it 'would hamper the growth of responsible and informed democracy in the Dominions.'[158]

NOTES
1. The best-known book-length studies are: W.L. Morton, *The Progressive Party in Canada* (Toronto: University of Toronto Press, 1950); Paul F. Sharp, *The Agrarian Revolt in Western Canada: A Survey Showing American Parallels* (Minneapolis: University of Minnesota Press, 1949); Lewis G. Thomas, *The Liberal Party in Alberta* (Toronto: University of Toronto Press, 1959); David Smith, *Prairie Liberalism: The Liberal Party in Saskatchewan, 1905-1971* (Toronto: University of Toronto Press, 1975); Louis Aubrey Wood, *A History of Farmers' Movements in Canada* (Toronto: Ryerson Press, 1924); Ramsay Cook, *The Politics of John W. Dafoe and the Free Press* (Toronto: University of Toronto Press, 1963); and Walter D. Young, *Democracy and Discontent: Progressivism, Socialism and Social Credit in the Canadian West* (Toronto: Ryerson Press, 1969). A recent addition is Charles M. Johnston, *E.C. Drury: Agrarian Idealist* (Toronto: University of Toronto Press, 1986), valuable for its portrait of a key rural crypto-Liberal in Ontario.
2. Morton (1950), 194, 200-1.
3. See Barbara Cameron, "The Transition from Whig to Reform Liberalism in Canada' (paper presented at 1981 annual meeting of the Canadian Political Science Association, Halifax, NS).
4. See Ramsay Cook, *The Regenerators: Social Criticism in Late Victorian English Canada* (Toronto: University of Toronto Press, 1985).
5. The Liberals published the 1918 Farmers' Platform alongside their own 1919 platform in the *Speakers' Handbook* for the 1921 election. C.P. Stacey, *Historical Documents of Canada, Vol. 5: 1914-1945* (Toronto: Macmillan, 1972), 36.
6. Stacey (1972), 'The Liberal Platform, 1919,' 36-40.
7. Frank Underhill, *In Search of Canadian Liberalism* (Toronto: Macmillan, 1960), 41.
8. Ibid, 1.
9. Wood (1924), 109-58; Ramsay Cook, 'Tillers and Toilers: The Rise and Fall of Populism in Canada in the 1890s,' *Historical Papers* (Ottawa: Canadian Historical Association, 1985) and S.E. Shortt, 'Social Change and Political Crisis in Rural Ontario: The Patrons of Industry, 1889-1896' (1972).
10. See notes 7-11, chapter 1.
11. See Cook, 'Tillers and Toilers,' especially on the role played by George Wrigley, editor of the *Canada Farmers' Sun.*
12. On the significance of the social gospel orientation in such radicalism, see Cook, *The Regenerators.*
13. Shortt (1972), 222.
14. See Morton (1950); David Smith, 'A Comparison of Political Developments in Saskatchewan and Alberta,' *Journal of Canadian Studies*, vol. 4, no. 1 (1969), 17-25, and 'Interpreting Prairie Politics,' *Journal of Canadian Studies*, vol. 7,

no. 4 (1972), 18-32; and Nelson Wiseman, 'The Pattern of Prairie Politics,' *Queen's Quarterly*, vol. 88, no. 2 (Summer 1981), 298-315.

15. Morton (1950), 14.

16. With only 22 per cent of the popular vote, UFO candidates managed to win 40 per cent of the seats (45), while the incumbent Conservatives elected only 22 per cent of MPPs with 32.7 per cent of the popular vote. See Loren M. Simerl, 'A Survey of Canadian Provincial Election Results, 1905-1981,' in Paul Fox, ed., *Politics Canada: Fifth Edition* (Toronto: McGraw-Hill Ryerson, 1982), 655-93.

17. See David Hoffman, 'Intra-Party Democracy: A Case Study,' *Canadian Journal of Economics and Political Science*, vol. 27, no. 2 (May 1961), 223-35.

18. Ibid.

19. See W.C. Good's autobiography, *Farmer Citizen: My Fifty Years with the Canadian Farmers' Movement* (Toronto: Ryerson, 1958). For an account of the 'anti-political' orientation in the Ontario farmers' movement, see Ian MacPherson, 'The Co-operative Union of Canada and Politics, 1909-1931,' *Canadian Historical Review*, vol. 54, no. 2 (June 1973), 152-74.

20. On the conservatism of the eastern Liberal faithful ca. 1919-21, see Morton (1950), 77.

21. There is an extensive literature relevant to this subject. One of the best treatments is Gerald Friesen, *The Canadian Prairies: A History* (Toronto: University of Toronto Press, 1984). A classic of economic history that sets the frontier experience in useful perspective is Vernon Fowke, *The National Policy and the Wheat Economy* (Toronto: University of Toronto Press, 1957).

22. Among other things, recent immigrants to the prairies would hardly have concurred with Patrons' opposition to the National Policy's prairie settlement program in the mid-1890s. Shortt (1972) cites one *Canada Farmers' Sun* editorial in 1895, which contended that 'trumping up immigration out of the dissatisfied and ne'er-do-well class in any country is a business for which the people cannot afford to pay.'

23. For a discussion of the flow of American co-operativist ideas into Canada for the two decades following the First World War, see Ian MacPherson, 'Selected Borrowings: The American Impact upon the Prairie Co-operative Movement, 1920-1939,' *Canadian Review of American Studies*, vol. 10. no. 2 (Fall 1979), 137-51.

24. This position was exemplified in J.W. Dafoe's *Free Press* editorials in support of free trade from the early 1900s to the 1930s. In 1911, he put the democracy-free trade relation at the centre of the election: 'Canada comes to the crossroads on September 21. One is the road to democracy, to a larger and freer national life, to wider markets, to the greater happiness and prosperity of the plain people; to the application of the rule of government that the greatest good of the whole nation must outweigh the desires of any one class. The other road leads to privilege, to the administration of the country by a class in its own interests, to the exhaltation of . . . certain special interests, to high protection, . . . restricted markets and trust domination.' (*Manitoba Free Press*, 12 September 1911, editorial; cited in Gerald Friesen, 'Studies in the Development of Western Canadian Regional Consciousness, 1870-1925,' PhD dissertation, University of Toronto, Department of History, 1973). For more along these lines, see the classic writings of Edward Porritt.

25. See, for example, 'Oregon's Popular Government' (editorial) and 'Direct Legislation in Oregon,' *Grain Grower's Guide*, 14 September 1910.

26. These same instruments of direct democracy were promoted by the Patrons of Industry, and even the Independent Labour Party, in Ontario of the 1890s. See Shortt (1972), Cook, 'Tillers and Toilers,' and *Handbook of the Patron Platform* (1895).

27. See Friesen (1984), chapter 14.

28. Macpherson (1953), chapter 1.

29. Morton (1950), chapters II and III.

30. We will discuss particular elements of crypto-Liberal 'co-operativism' later in the chapter.

31. Wood (1924), part II. In 1893, the Patrons of Industry had roughly 100,000 members in Ontario (Shortt, 1972, 212). While most of these members were or wished to become members of co-operatives, most of these co-operatives were consumer rather than producer marketing co-ops (with the exception of co-operative creameries), and few were allied with any larger co-operative organization.

32. As Cook, 'Tillers and Toilers,' points out, electoral political activity by the Patrons in Ontario in the 1890s was stimulated by the ceaseless calls to action of George Wrigley, editor of the Patrons' official organ, the *Canada Farmers' Sun*. When the *Sun* ceased to mobilize the rural constituency for political action, farmers tended to leave active politics. Which is cause, and which effect, is not altogether clear; the *Sun* stopped promulgating this message of independent politics after the federal Liberal victory, and Goldwyn Smith's purchase of majority interest in the paper, in 1896.

33. Lawrence Goodwyn, *Democratic Promise: The Populist Moment in America* (New York: Oxford University Press, 1976), xviii.

34. Ian MacPherson, *Each for All: A History of the Co-operative Movement in English Canada, 1900-1945* (Toronto: Macmillan, 1979), 42-3.

35. See Patrons' *Handbook* (1895); D.S. Spafford, '"Independent" Politics in Saskatchewan before the Non-Partisan League' (1965), 'The Agrarian Movement in the 1890's' (1954), 50-4; and, Brian McCutcheon, 'The Patrons of Industry in Manitoba, 1890-1898' (1970).

36. Organized elements within the central Canadian working class felt that this regressive incidence was offset in their own case by the existence of a greater number of employment-offering 'infant industries' able to survive because of the protective tariff, and were thus, as producers, generally opposed to tariff reductions. This did nothing to endear prairie or Ontario farmers to their urban fellows, or *vice versa*.

37. This point was made in the Patrons' *Handbook* (1895), and all of the agitations by the Patrons in Manitoba and Saskatchewan in the mid- to late 1890s.

38. In 1894, Laurier told a Winnipeg audience: 'We stand for freedom. I denounce the policy of protection as bondage—yea, bondage; and I refer to bondage in the same manner in which American slavery was bondage. Not in the same degree, perhaps, but in the same manner. In the same manner the people of Canada . . . are toiling for a master who takes away not every cent of profit, but a very large percentage, a very large portion of your earnings for which you sweat and toil' (*Manitoba Free Press,* 3 September 1894; cited in Edward

Porritt, *Sixty Years of Protection in Canada*, 2nd ed. [Winnipeg: Grain Growers' Guide, 1913], 316).

39. *Sixty Years of Protection in Canada; The Revolt in Canada against the New Feudalism;* and 'Death of Edward Porritt,' *Grain Growers' Guide,* 2 November 1921, 7.
40. 'Agrarian Movement,' 56.
41. Wood (1924), chapter 20; George Chipman, ed., *The Siege of Ottawa* (Winnipeg: Grain Growers' Grain Company, 1911). For an account of the hopes hanging on the 'Siege,' see *Guide* editorials of 16 November, 23 November, 30 November, and 21 December 1910.
42. See Colquette (1957), Wood (1924), and Good (1958).
43. See especially *Handbook of the Patron Platform* (1895), 15-43 (two-thirds of the *Handbook* is devoted to an attack on the tariff).
44. Morton (1950), 62.
45. Fiscal responsibility was also a major concern of the Patrons in Ontario and the West. It is important to appreciate that this did not reflect a *laissez-faire* desire for a minimum state; as Cook, 'Tillers and Toilers,' points out, and as one can see in the Patron Platform and Declaration of Principles in the Patrons' *Handbook* (1895, 1-2), the economies being proposed by the Patrons were all related to their perception that the urban business élite had usurped political authority, and were living well, through scandalous patronage and wasteful subsidy, at the expense of Canada's farming and labouring population.
46. Morton (1950), 303.
47. Once again, see Patrons' *Handbook* (1895) for extensive argument to this effect.
48. In a 1921 *Guide* editorial, Chipman argued that 'the real issue' in the upcoming election was 'whether the people or the politicians and the big interests are going to govern the country.'
49. Canovan (1981), 294-5.
50. See both Cook, 'Tillers and Toilers,' and Shortt (1972) on the physiocratic element in Patrons' discourse in Ontario a generation earlier.
51. Morton (1950), Appendix 1, 297. For virtually verbatim parallel statements by Patron leaders in Ontario, see Cook, 'Tillers and Toilers,' 13-14, and Shortt (1972), 231-2.
52. Morton (1950), 298.
53. 'President's Address,' *Manitoba Grain Growers' Yearbook*, 1919, 25. William Irvine took essentially the same position regarding the Platform in 1920 (*The Farmers in Politics* [Toronto: McClelland and Stewart, 1920], 222-3).
54. From August 1909 to mid-1910, the *Guide* was in fact entitled *The Grain Growers' Guide and Friend of Labour*. Also significant were the friendly relations between the Patrons and organized labour in Ontario between 1890 and 1896, which failed to result in political alliances, but appeared to be premised on a similar populist critique of business power and the moral evils of industrialized society. See Cook, 'Tillers and Toilers.'
55. Foster Griezic, 'The Honorable Thomas Alexander Crerar: The Political Career of a Western Liberal Progressive in the 1920s,' in Susan Trofimenkoff, ed., *The Twenties in Western Canada* (Ottawa: National Museum of Man, 1975), 114-15.
56. Crerar, 'Confession,' 7.

57. Ibid.
58. Cook (1963), 109 and 116.
59. On the ties of the Winnipeg business community with the UFM in 1922, see John Kendle, *John Bracken: A Political Biography* (Toronto: University of Toronto Press, 1980), 28.
60. 'Liberal or Conservative, Which?' Liberal Party Literature file (Archives of Saskatchewan, Saskatoon).
61. As Duff Spafford, ' "Independent" Politics,' noted, 'the Liberals did their best to portray their government as a committee of delegates performing as a legislative arm of the farmers' organization—as a true 'farmers' government. They were good at playing out the role, and indeed circumstances never permitted them to consider any other . . . The farmers insisted on a government that was responsive and accountable in a very direct way to the electorate.' (*Saskatchewan History*, vol. 18, 1965, 3). See also David E. Smith, 'James G. Gardiner: Leadership in the Agrarian Community,' *Saskatchewan History*, vol. 40, no. 2 (Spring 1987), 42-61, for the way Gardiner saw and presented the Liberals as the party of the people, and minorities, as against the provincial and federal Tories.
62. For anti-CCF and pro-CCF accounts of this, see W.L. Morton, *Manitoba: A History* (Toronto: University of Toronto Press, 1957), and Nelson Wiseman, *Social Democracy in Manitoba: A History of the CCF-NDP* (Winnipeg: University of Manitoba Press, 1984.)
63. See Spafford, ' "Independent" Politics,' Cook, 'Tillers and Toilers,' and Martin Robin, *Radical Politics and Canadian Labour* (Kingston: Industrial Relations Centre, Queen's University, 1968).
64. This support was so great in Saskatchewan by 1913 that a resolution in support of direct political action at the Saskatchewan Grain Growers' Association annual meeting was defeated only because C.A. Dunning (future provincial and federal Liberal minister) tacked on an amendment claiming that direct legislation would be more efficient than party action in achieving the farmers' objectives. See Duff Spafford, "Independent" Politics,' 8.
65. W.L. Morton, 'Direct Legislation and the Origins of the Progressive Movement,' *Canadian Historical Review*, vol. 25, no. 2 (1944), 284, 279-88; see also discussion later in this chapter.
66. Ibid, 285-6; Hon. Rodmond Roblin, *Sir Rodmond Roblin on Initiative and Referendum, a Socialistic and Un-British System* (Speech delivered in the Manitoba Legislature, 27 January 1913).
67. Morton (1944), 286-7.
68. 'President's Address,' *MGGA Yearbook*, 1911, 6.
69. 'President's Address,' *MGGA Yearbook*, 1912, 16.
70. The *Guide* supported the direct legislation campaign in almost every 1909-11 issue, including a detailed account by Robert Scott in four successive feature articles (16, 23, and 30 November, and 7 December, 1910), and coverage of Oregon's experiments with direct legislation. A 14 September 1910 *Guide* editorial, 'Oregon's Popular Government,' argued that 'the corporations have more power than the people and the only way in which this can be overcome is through Direct Legislation, which will place the government completely and at all times in the hands of the people . . . If the people of Canada wish certain

legislation enacted and the legislature refuses to enact it, the people are power-less . . . until [direct legislation] becomes a part of the statutes of each of the provinces.'

71. Elizabeth Chambers, 'The Referendum and the Plebiscite,' in Duff Spafford and Norman Ward, eds., *Politics in Saskatchewan* (Don Mills: Longmans, 1968), 77.

72. *Manitoba Law Reports*, vol. 27, 'In re. Initiative and Referendum Act,' 13; cited in Morton (1944), 287.

73. Morton (1944), 288.

74. 'The Confession' was one of the Progressive leader's two most complete state-ments of objectives to reach a mass audience (in *Maclean's*, January 1921, and reprinted in the *Guide*, 28 February 1921).

75. *The Guide*, 19 October 1921, 7-9. This may have simply been a pragmatic move, in view of the courts' rulings against such legislation. None the less, one still must wonder why Crerar made no mention of the issue, even if it would have been unreasonable to expect him to launch a full-scale campaign on its behalf.

76. Morton (1944), 286-7.

77. In a *Guide* editorial of 20 September 1910, George Chipman argued that "We need Direct Legislation in every province, and when it becomes a part of provin-cial statutes it will be much easier to secure the reforms which the people demand. Direct Legislation injures no party but places all power at all times in the hands of the people. Who else should hold that vast power?' No Liberal party would have endorsed this conception of direct legislation.

78. Shortt (1972), 219.

79. Lewis G. Thomas, *The Liberal Party in Alberta* (Toronto: University of Toronto Press, 1959), 195.

80. In 1920, a ten member 'P.R.' constituency was established in Winnipeg. Mor-ton (1957), 374.

81. J.P. Harris, 'The Practical Workings of Proportional Representation in the United States and Canada,' *National Municipal Review* (Supplement), May 1930, 365. Seventeen cities had taken up this option by 1922, although twelve had abandoned it by 1929 through popular votes or provincial ordinances.

82. Ibid, 367.

83. For extensive accounts of this, see Morton (1950); Sharp (1949); Smith (1975); C.B. Macpherson (1953); Wood (1924); A. Ross, 'National Development and Sectional Politics: Social Conflict and the Rise of a Protest Movement; The Case of the Saskatchewan Grain Growers Association,' PhD dissertation, Univer-sity of Toronto , 1978; Carl Betke, "The United Farmers of Alberta, 1921-35: The Relationship between the Agricultural Organization and the Government of Alberta,' MA thesis, University of Alberta, 1971.

84. Smith (1975), 91-5.

85. Morton (1950), 74ff.

86. 'Appendix I,' in H.A. Innis, ed., *The Diary of A.J. MacPhail* (Toronto: University of Toronto Press, 1940), 59.

87. Once the SGGA opted for direct political action in 1922, constituency organi-zations were given control over the decision to field a candidate, and conduct of the campaign. See Smith (1975), 94-5.

88. 'United Farmers in Politics,' *United Farmers of Manitoba Yearbook*, 1921, 18-9.

89. The executive included UFA President Wood, and United Farmers of Manitoba President J.L. Brown.
90. Morton (1950), 269-70; Sharp (1949), 155-6.
91. 'Crerar's Manifesto,' *Guide*, 19 October 1921, 7.
92. In 1919, Henders the MP was forced to resign the MGGA presidency in disgrace for not voting against a Unionist budget giving no tariff relief (see Morton [1950], 69-70, and the *Guide*, "The Evolution of Mr. Henders,' 12 October 1921, 5). That he later became a rather egregious opportunist in grain grower politicians' ranks does not render his earlier critiques of partyism unrepresentative of grain grower sentiment.
93. 'President's Address,' *MGGA Yearbook*, 1914, 13.
94. See 'Introductory,' editorial of first issue of the *Guide*, June 1908, and "To Whom It May Concern,' June 1908, 11-12.
95. See 1922 SGGA 'Educational Policy Report' by A.J. MacPhail and Mrs. V. McNaughton, in Innis (1940), Appendix II, 62-4.
96. Smith (1975), 67.
97. 'President's Address,' *MGGA Yearbook*, 1916, 20-1.
98. Ibid, 17-18.
99. Morton (1950), 171-2.
100. The *Guide*, 2 March 1921, 7.
101. *Guide* editorial, 12 October 1921, 6.
102. The *Guide* was full of this during the fall of 1921.
103. *Handbook of the Patron Platform* (1895), 1.
104. Shortt (1972), 218.
105. See chapter 3 In David Laycock's *Populism and Democratic Thought in the Canadian Prairies, 1910 to 1945* (Toronto: University of Toronto Press, 1990).
106. Morton (1950), 301.
107. Griezic (1972), 109-11. This judgement, and many others regarding T.A. Crerar, will be challenged in a forthcoming political biography by J.E. Rea. I do not wish to suggest that Crerar lacked integrity, only that his principles were often out of step with those of popular democracy in prairie farmers' movements.
108. Ibid, 125ff.
109. See, for example, 'The Patronage System,' *Guide* editorial, 21 March 1921.
110. C..W. Mills and H.H. Gerth, eds., *From Max Weber* (New York: Oxford University Press, 1946), 224-30.
111. The *Guide*, 'Crerar's Manifesto,' 19 October 1921, 7, my emphasis.
112. Closely related to this concern was one for 'fiscal responsibility.' The Patrons had insisted on a variation of this in 1895, but one that would focus on elimination of unnecessary political appointments that led to meddling in properly local affairs. They argued that 'no reform is so urgently needed in Canada as a reduction in the cost of government in all three spheres, Federal, provincial and municipal. There is a swarm of departmental officials at Ottawa, and a still greater swarm of outside Federal officials, judges, customs and revenue officers . . . and so on . . . while high over all, amid their archaic state and trappings, sit the Governor-General and lieutenant-governors with their considerable retinue, the whole constituting a hierarchy of tax-handlers such as no other five million people on earth have to support out of moderate resources. It is not "revolutionary" for Patrons to declare that this immense edifice of official-

dom ought to be reduced to a footing somewhat in keeping with our means and requirements' (*Handbook of the Patron Platform,* 1895, 13).
113. Kendle (1980) 24.
114. Ibid, 30.
115. Ibid, 31.
116. Ibid, 35, 40 and 39.
117. Smith (1975), 154. Smith notes that Dunning was more willing than Martin to admit his partisanship.
118. See Macpherson (1953), chapter 1; Morton (1950), chapters 1-3; Sharp (1949), chapters 1-4, and Friesen (1984), chapter 14.
119. James Anderson, 'The Municipal Reform Movement in Western Canada, 1880-1920,' in A.F.J. Artibise and G.A. Stelter, eds., *The Usable Urban Past* (Toronto: Macmillan, 1979), 79.
120. Carl Betke, 'Farm Politics in an Urban Age: The Decline of the United Farmers of Alberta after 1921,' in L.H. Thomas, ed., *Essays on Western History* (Edmonton: University of Alberta Press, 1976), 179.
121. Ibid, 185.
122. For a fuller discussion of this, see chapter 3 in David Laycock's *Populism and Democratic Thought in the Canadian Prairies, 1910 to 1945* (Toronto: University of Toronto Press, 1990).
123. Morton (1950), 27-8.
124. See J.H. Thompson, *The Harvests of War: The Prairie West, 1914-1918* (Toronto: McClelland and Stewart, 1978), Robert Craig Brown and Ramsay Cook, *Canada 1896-1921: A Nation Transformed* (Toronto: McClelland and Stewart, 1974), and Friesen (1984).
125. Once again, the Patrons of Industry had stressed this theme a generation earlier. *See Handbook* (1895).
126. Griezic (1972), 119.
127. 'My Confession of Faith,' 14.
128. See cartoon in the *Guide,* 5 October 1921, 6, entitled 'Meighen's Class Government.' A farmer, horrified by the list of cabinet ministers, says to Meighen: 'This looks like a lawyer-corporation-big interests government. I thought you didn't believe in class government.' Meighen, dressed in the plutocrat's tails and top hat, answers: 'Of course I always except my own class and its clients. That's the class I believe in.'
129. See especially 23, November 1921 front-page editorial cartoon, featuring a lumbering Goliath with a right arm labelled 'Meighen Government,' a sword of 'subsidized politics,' a shield of 'protection,' a vest of 'special privilege,' and a club of 'wealth.' Organized farmers, the 'modern David,' are approaching Goliath, armed merely with 'the ballot' in a sling. Meighen was the prime minister responsible for killing the Canadian Wheat Board in 1920.
130. *MGGA Yearbook,* 1912, 17.
131. The first two years of the *Guide* were full of articles praising public ownership, primarily of grain elevators and railways.
132. Morton (1957), 300.
133. See Gad Horowitz, 'Conservatism, Liberalism and Socialism in Canada: An Interpretation,' *Canadian Journal of Economics and Political Science,* vol. 32, no. 2 (1966), 143-71. In Manitoba, the pre-eminent prairie Tory, Sir Rodmond

Roblin, introduced pulicly owned telephones and hydro-power while premier.

134. H.V. Nelles, *The Politics of Development: Forests, Mines, and Hydro-electric Power in Ontario, 1849-1941* (Toronto: Macmillan, 1974).

135. See 'National People's Party Platform' (Omaha, 1892), in G.B. Tindall, *A Populist Reader* (New York: Harper and Row, 1966), 90-6; Goodwyn (1976), Appendix D, 'Ideological Origins of the Omaha Platform'; and Canovan (1981), 56-7.

136. According to Sharp (1949, 69), American agriculturalists were envious of the success with which Canadian grain growers had forced provincial governments to enact some limited 'single tax' legislation.

137. William Irvine endorsed both the CCA critique of tariff and its alternatives for revenue creation, in *The Farmers in Politics* (1920), 217-20.

138. MacPherson (1979).

139. This began with the first (June 1908) issue of the *Guide*, along with coverage of developments in the American co-operative movement.

140. The idea of a co-operative as an almost self-contained society, which provided a model for general social reform, was quite widespread amongst participants in the co-operative movement in Canada in the early decades. See MacPherson (1979), 27.

141. D.S. Spafford, 'The "Left Wing", 1921-1931,' in Spatford and Ward (1968).

142. MacPherson (1979), 46-7.

143. Ibid, 47.

144. Ibid, 78.

145. 'My Confession of Faith,' *Guide*, 23 February 1921, 28.

146. 'Cooperation is a religion pure and simple. It is something which all your senses recognize and long for in proportion to the good there is in you' (*Guide*, 18 October 1911, 20).

147. Morton (1950), 304-5.

148. See D. Laycock, 'Political Neutrality and the Problem of Interest Representation: Co-operatives and partisan Politics in Canada,' in Murray Fulton, ed., *Co-operative Organizations and Canadian Society: Popular Institutions and the Dilemmas of Change* (Toronto: University of Toronto Press, forthcoming).

149. As MacPherson puts it from the perspective of the co-operative movement, 'many cooperators, already exposed to the movement's a-political traditions, had their suspicions reinforced by the Progressive experience. Inevitably, these cooperators became more aloof from political activity, especially at the federal level, during and after the early twenties' (1979, 77-8).

150. See Richard Allen, *The Social Passion: Religion and Social Reform in Canada, 1914-28* (Toronto: University of Toronto Press, 1971), chapters 12 and 22.

151. See Cook (1985), McCutcheon (1970), and Spafford, '"Independent" Politics.'

152. W.L. Morton, 'The Bias of Prairie Politics,' *Transactions of the Royal Society of Canada*, vol. 49, series III (June 1955), 63-5.

153. Ibid, 64.

154. W.L. Morton, 'A Century of Plain and Parkland,' in A.R. Allen, ed., *A Region of the Mind* (Regina: Canadian Plains Research Center, 1969), 174.

155. For a good selection of examples of this aspect of 'country life ideology' in regional periodicals and fiction of the period, see David C. Jones, '"There Is Some Power about the Land": The Western Agrarian Press and Country Life

Ideology,' *Journal of Canadian Studies,* vol. 17, no. 3 (1982), 96-109; and Gerald Friesen, 'Three Generations of Fiction: An Introduction to Prairie Cultural History,' in D.J. Bercuson and P.A. Buckner, eds., *Eastern and Western Perspectives* (Toronto: University of Toronto Press, 1981).

156. This was the theme of most of Ralph Connor's popular stories about life in the new West. See F.W. Watt, 'Western Myth: The World of Ralph Connors,' in D.G. Stephens, ed., *Writers of the Prairies* (Vancouver: University of British Columbia Press, 1973), 7-17.

157. Friesen (1984), 374.

158. Morton (1950), 302.

XIII

PRAIRIE SOCIETY AND POLITICS IN THE GREAT DEPRESSION

The Great Depression of the 1930s was the worst decade in the history of prairie Canada. As wheat prices plummeted from an all time high of over $2.00 a bushel in the late 1920s to 34 cents a bushel in 1932 secondary and service industries in the West and in the rest of Canada were also affected. Unemployment reached an all time high of 20% across the country and as high as 35% in some prairie communities. Natural disasters of drought, wind and dust storms, and grasshopper plagues added to the hardships. Families in towns and cities faced starvation, forcing thousands to endure the humiliation of accepting government relief. James Gray recalls his own experience in Winnipeg of having to go on relief in "Our World Stopped and We Got Off," a chapter from his memoir, *The Winter Years*.

At first, Canadians tried to wait out the Depression, expecting it to be a temporary phenomenon. But it worsened. The two traditional parties at the national level, the Conservatives and the Liberals, offered no new initiatives to deal with the unique situation. Out of desperation new parties sprang up, particularly on the Prairies, offering radical solutions to end the Depression.

Historians and political scientists have long been interested in explaining why such parties as the Co-operative Commonwealth Federation (CCF) and Social Credit arose on the Prairies in the 1930s, and in comparing them in terms of ideology, class composition, and political policies. Nelson Wiseman's "The Pattern of Prairie Politics" offers one such comparison based on the concepts of ideology and ethnicity. He argues that the dominant immigrant groups in the three prairie provinces—Ontarians in Manitoba, British in Saskatchewan, and Americans in Alberta—with their contrasting ideologies—liberal, socialist and populist-liberal respectively—best explain the differing political parties and culture within the three prairie provinces. Wiseman's analysis raises as many questions as it answers. To what extent does the initial group of settlers dominate and shape the subsequent political culture and politics of the province? Do later immigrant groups affect that culture? Is it an exaggeration and distortion to argue that one group dominated the early history of the province? Does a provincial analysis conceal common regional political patterns that underlie prairie politics?

The Social Credit movement/party has undergone extensive revisionist analysis in recent years. Alvin Finkel offers one of the most recent re-evaluations in his "Social Credit Reappraised: The Radical Character of the Early Social Credit Movement." He challenges the conventional theory of Social Credit as a right-wing populist movement based on free enterprise and argues instead that, at least initially under its founder William Aberhart, Social Credit held both conservative and socialist economic theories. In short it appealed as much to workers and farmers as it did to businessmen. Only after Ernest Manning took over as party leader in 1943 did the party purge itself of its left-wing leanings to become a party of free enterprise. This subsequent change has, in the past, according to Finkel, distorted our view of the earlier Social Credit movement.

SELECTED BIBLIOGRAPHY

Students are encouraged to read James Gray's *The Winter Years* (Toronto, 1966) in its entirety for a moving account of a young man's life during the Depression in prairie Canada. In *Men Against the Desert* (Saskatoon, 1967), Gray discusses how scientific experts in the prairie experimental farms attempted to conquer the drought conditions of the Dustbowl. Good general books on the Depression with relevant sections on the prairies are: H. Blair Neatby, *The Politics of Chaos: Canada in the Thirties* (Toronto, 1972); Michiel Horn, ed., *The Dirty Thirties: Canadians in the Great Depression* (Toronto, 1972). See as well the articles in R. Douglas Francis and Herman Ganzevoort, eds., *The Dirty Thirties in Prairie Canada* (Vancouver, 1980), and the relevant articles in M. Horn, ed., *The Depression in Canada: Responses to Economic Crisis* (Toronto, 1988).

There is an extensive literature on prairie protest parties during the 1930s in prairie Canada, but few authors take a comparative approach. In addition to Nelson Wiseman's article, students should consult David Laycock's *Populism and Democratic Thought in the Canadian Prairies, 1910 to 1945* (Toronto, 1990); W.L. Morton, "The Bias of Prairie Politics," in A.B. McKillop, ed., *Contexts of Canada's Past* (Toronto, 1980), pp. 149-60; and David Smith's "A Comparison of Prairie Political Development in Saskatchewan and Alberta," *Journal of Canadian Studies* 4 (February, 1969): 17-25; and his "Interpreting Prairie Politics," *Journal of Canadian Studies* 7, no. 4 (November 1972): 18-32. Walter Young's *Democracy and Discontent:*

Progressivism, Socialism and Social Credit in the Canadian West (Toronto, 1969) is a concise and readable, if somewhat dated account of prairie protest parties.

Social Credit has been well researched. Students should begin with the series of studies on the subject published by the University of Toronto Press, particularly John Irving's *The Social Credit Movement in Alberta* (1959), and C.B. Macpherson's *Democracy in Alberta: Social Credit and the Party System* (1953). A more recent study which emphasizes the decline rather than the rise of Social Credit is John Barr's *The Dynasty: The Fall of Social Credit in Alberta* (Toronto, 1974). Social Credit's founder and first leader has been the subject of a recent biography: David R. Elliott and Iris Miller, *Bible Bill: A Biography of William Aberhart* (Edmonton, 1987). Alvin Finkel's views on Social Credit are presented in greater depth in his book-length study, *The Social Credit Phenomenon in Alberta* (Toronto, 1989).

JAMES GRAY

29 Our World Stopped and We Got Off

From our home on Ruby Street in Winnipeg to the relief office at the corner of Xante Street and Elgin Avenue was less than three miles. It could be walked easily in an hour, but I didn't complete the journey the first time I set out, or the second. If I had not been driven by the direst necessity, the third trip would have ended as the first two had done. I would have veered sharply to the right, somewhere en route, to head down town in one last attempt to find a job. But on the third trip the truth could no longer be dodged by any such pointless manoeuvre.

We were almost out of food, we were almost out of fuel, and our rent was two months in arrears. At home were my wife and daughter, and my mother, father, and two younger brothers. Applying for relief might prove the most humiliating experience of my life (it did); but it had to be done, and I had to do it. The deep-down realization that I had nobody to blame but myself made the journey doubly difficult. In mid-February 1931 I was not yet twenty-five, but I could look back on ten years of psychopathic concentration on getting ahead in life. Then my number had come up and I was confronted with the ego-shattering discovery that there wasn't a single employer in all Winnipeg who would give me a job.

I had been out of work since the end of November, and I was already deeply in debt when my job disappeared. I canvassed the Grain Exchange, where I had worked, from top to bottom every week. I tried door-to-door selling, attempted to leave my application with department stores and the Post Office, but nobody was even taking applications, let alone dispensing jobs. There was no alternative to applying for relief.

At that moment, I was a fitting subject for a sermon on frugality and thrift. Ten years before, at fifteen, I had started out to make my fortune. In our family, the idea of any of us pursuing a higher education was never considered because it was naturally assumed that, as the oldest of four

631

brothers, I would leave school to help support the family as soon as it was legally possible. If I had an educational goal, it was to go as far as I could as quickly as I could before I had to quit. I made it to Grade 10 and then got my first job in 1921 delivering groceries for $5 a week. From that I moved up to delivering engravings for $7 a week. When I landed a job as an office boy in the Grain Exchange at $10 in the early fall, I was convinced I was on the sure road to success. The Grain Exchange was synonymous with unmitigated affluence and was the status place to work in post-war Winnipeg. No one knew this better than I, for I had delivered morning papers to the baronial houses of wealthy Grain Exchangers. Inside these houses lived the men who had come west with nothing and made their fortunes in Winnipeg. If they could do it, I would some day do it. Spinning day-dreams helped take some of the sting from the cold winter mornings.

Money has an overweening importance to anybody who grows up in poverty, and our family knew nothing but poverty in Winnipeg during the First World War. From the time I was nine, and my brother Walter was six, we sold papers, ran messages, delivered groceries and laundry after school. If we never went hungry, there was never a time when what was wrong with our family could not have been repaired with $25 or $50.

The Winnipeg Grain Exchange in 1921 was on the threshold of its last great fling. The brokerage offices were crowded with speculators who bought and sold grain futures on margin. Outside, work was starting on a ten-storey addition that was to make it the biggest office building in the British Empire. The trading floor itself was a forest of temporary wooden beams and scaffolds, for it, too, was being enlarged. Here the shrieking voices of a hundred pit-traders created a din that, when the windows were open, could be heard clear over to Portage and Main. Behind the Monte Carlo façade was the actual business of warehousing, transporting, and marketing the western grain crops. Incidental to the frenzy of speculation, the wheat crops did get marketed. It so happened that the company I went to work for was actually engaged in the marketing business, and my employer never went into the wheat-pit. He was one of half a dozen vessel-brokers who obtained lake freighters for grain exporters and found exporters to charter the vessels.

My first job was running messages back and forth between our office and the telegraph offices on the trading floor. Soon I was helping with the books and learning eagerly how to run a typewriter, operate an adding machine, and make out insurance policies and invoices. The office opened at nine and closed whenever the day's work was done, usually along towards midnight. My job was as exhausting as it was exhilarating and at Christmas time I was amply rewarded with a $100 bonus. I ran all the way home clutching my envelope full of $5 bills.

When navigation ended on the Great Lakes in December, the vessel-brokerage business came to a dead stop. My employer went off to California; I enrolled in a correspondence course in accounting and picked up some extra money as a part-time bookkeeper in an option brokerage across the hall. Thereafter, promotions and pay raises came rapidly. By the time I was nineteen, there was nothing about the business I did not know or could not do, I was making $150 a month, and my Christmas bonus reached $500. Only experienced bricklayers made more, and most bank accountants made less. In those days the banks refused to permit their employees to marry until they were earning $1,000 a year, a level that usually took ten years to reach.

The success I achieved only whetted my appetite for more. I bought a half interest in a couple of race-horses, fell for one swindle after another, sent good money after bad to promoters of oil wells in Louisiana, gold mines in Colorado, and silver mines in Ontario. In between times I took losing fliers in the grain market. That I did nothing but lose never concerned me, because ultimately I would make an investment that would repay all my losses. Besides, by 1926, I was otherwise preoccupied. I had acquired a nearly-new Ford sedan, smoked two-for-a-quarter cigars, and was squiring one of Eaton's prettiest cashiers. Her name was Kathleen Burns, and by that Christmas we were so much in love that we could discover no reason for not getting married. We did so, and I had a further incentive to get on with my fortune-making. Instead of buying furniture or a house, we bought a race-horse, with my employer as silent partner, and for the next year I coupled horse-training with my Grain Exchange employment. As a horse-trainer I was a monumental bust, but it was great fun.

Our daughter Patricia was born in 1928, and her arrival gave me still another incentive. But somehow I had slipped into a rut. My salary had stopped going up, my employer had brought his brother into the company, and my position steadily deteriorated. When a group of grain-brokers decided to finance a new stock-brokerage office on Portage Avenue, I hired on as margin clerk, statistician, and general factotum. Not a single partner or employee knew anything about the stock market or the brokerage business. We even had to bring in employees of other brokers to train us in the simplest procedures such as computing margins. On the basis of this all-pervading ignorance, we were prepared to advise everybody in town how to make and manage investments in the stock market. In the logic of 1928, we should have been eminently successful, but the project never got off the ground and the business closed a full year before the crash.

Instead of going back to the Grain Exchange, I decided the time had come to get into business for myself. The first chance that came along was a candy franchise, and for the first half of 1929 I was in the candy business. I worked eighteen hours a day servicing the candy stands and Kay worked almost as long filling bags with candy. We went broke in six months and I returned to the vessel-brokerage business with a different employer. A few months after the Wall Street crash I was offered a much better job as manager of the grain department of a new brokerage firm that was opening an office in Lethbridge.

I arrived in Lethbridge just before the Solloway Mills scandal broke. Brokers were being arrested all across the country for 'bucketing' their customers' orders during the mining boom. They were more victims of circumstances than anything else. The banks would not lend money on mining shares, and this prevented the brokers from financing their customers' margin purchases at a time when the customers were clamouring for mining stocks on margin. So the brokers sold stock on the exchange against their customers' purchases, a highly illegal action for which they went to jail.

By the time Kay had sold our furniture and brought Patty to Lethbridge, I had discovered some highly unsavoury things about an oil company my employers were floating. The more I probed into it, the more certain I became that the investors would lose their money. I quit in a panic, for fear I too would go to jail, and went back to Winnipeg to the job I had quit only a few months before. It was not until much later that I realized how lucky I was to get any kind of a job then. The brokerage failures turned hundreds out of jobs in Winnipeg. The break of the wheat market below a dollar and then below ninety cents brought hard times for the Grain Exchange, and, outside, the secondary effects of the stock-market crashes were becoming clear. But not to me.

That was the year of the miniature-golf craze. Like millions of others, Kay and I took up the game. The trouble was that the nearest course was miles away from home, and it was always crowded.

'You know,' I said, 'a guy could make a lot of money with a course like this near our place.'

Kay pointed out that she could act as cashier during the day, if my mother would look after Patty, and I could run it at night. Our overhead would be small, and, if we got a quarter of the business the pioneer course was getting, we could clean up. We talked ourselves into it in no time. There was a small impediment. We had no money, or relatively little, compared to the capital required. The original operator egged us on.

'Why,' he said, 'there's nothing to it. Do it on credit! Your course will cost you $2,000. You might even do it for $1,500, and all you need is a couple of hundred in cash. Right now I'm taking in better than $200 a day. You won't do that good. But you could figure on a minimum of $100 a day. In fifteen days you'll pay for the course and you'll be set for next year.'

It sounded wonderful. And it was as easy as that — almost. We rented a vacant lot, installed lights and a shack, and bought clubs and balls. No one demanded payment for the supplies. We were astounded at how good our credit was. Nevertheless, we spent all the money we had and borrowed more before the thing was finished. During the first week business was wonderful and we took in well over $500. Then came Labour Day, and nothing collapsed as quickly as miniature golf in September 1930. We closed the course in October with creditors clamouring for their money. So much of my pay was earmarked to repay loans that there was little left to live on.

Then the blow fell. On November 30 my employer went out of business. Nor was this all. By one of those queer twists of fate, two of my brothers were laid off on the same day. By a momentary stroke of good fortune, I managed to find a buyer for the golf course and he paid me enough to clean up most of my debts. But I still owed better than $300, which was more than I could have repaid even if I had had a job. And I had no job.

I have told this story in detail to make this point: I was a typical 'child of the Twenties'. What happened to me happened to everybody, more or less. What you became in life depended upon the job you settled into. You left school when you had to, though no earlier than fourteen, the legal limit. Then you got whatever extra education you needed at night schools or by correspondence courses. If your first job lacked opportunity for advancement, you quit and went elsewhere. It was not uncommon to make three or four false starts before settling into a permanent position, and no stigma attached to rolling stones.

Lack of education was no handicap in obtaining employment, and it was no bar to advancement for the eager and industrious youth of the Twenties. My educational attainments were at least equal to those of my contemporaries who rose to lofty eminence in Canadian banking and industry. Arnold Hart was fresh out of high school when he joined the Bank of Montreal at eighteen. A. T. Lambert reached the top of the Toronto-Dominion Bank by getting an early start at fourteen. At sixteen, H. G. Welsford got the job that led ultimately to the presidency of Dominion Bridge; James Pearson was only fourteen when he hired on at National Steel Car; G. H. Sheppard got to the top of IBM by starting as a fifteen-year-old office boy in 1929.

Harry Sellers parlayed a teen-age job in a Fort William grain elevator into the presidency of a dozen western grain companies. His feat was matched by K. A. Powell, who began as a minor clerk in the Grain Exchange. George McKeag made it from office boy to the head of Security Storage, western Canada's biggest forwarding enterprise. T. O. Peterson detoured from rural Saskatchewan through the Bank of Montreal to the presidency of Investors' Syndicate. W. M. Currie began as an office boy in Medicine Hat at seventeen and was elected president of the Canadian Imperial Bank of Commerce in 1965.

Rapid advancement was possible on ability alone. The so-called professions had not yet become government-sheltered monopolies, and professional unions were not yet blockading the avenues of advancement. Ours was a bootstrap economy in which you learned by doing. Young men became accountants by enduring the starvation wages of the banks for two or three years. They became mechanics by getting jobs in garages, became carpenters by carrying lumber around construction sites, became railway engineers by starting as wipers in the shops. If they were Harts, Sheppards, or Welsfords, they settled into their first jobs and made them their life work. If they were James Grays, who were driven to running before they could walk, they were willing to try anything once, again and again. There was nothing either in our experience or in our history that prepared us for the Dirty Thirties. Booms and busts there had been—four major depressions in the previous thirty years. But they had passed quickly; and the assumption everywhere was that this, too, would pass quickly. The Dirty Thirties were almost over before governments recognized that a hard core of unemployment had become a permanent fact of economic life. The Dirty Thirties were almost over, too, before the young adults of the Roaring Twenties realized that the world they had known was gone forever; that they had emerged from it equipped only to blunder and flounder through a pathless wilderness.

In the transition between the 1920s and the 1930s, the most persistent and widely held delusion of all was that unemployment was a temporary thing that would soon pass. As I walked to the Elgin Avenue relief office I believed it; the hundred-odd other applicants I found waiting in line believed it. It was a delusion that encompassed all governments and it was the foundation on which the entire system of unemployment relief was erected. The governments simply adopted whatever method there was in existence for dispensing temporary assistance and extended it *ad infinitum*.

The Winnipeg system, like that of all other prairie cities, was designed only to bridge the winter for those who were seasonally unemployed and could prove they were completely destitute. Those who were aided — a few hundred families each winter — worked off their relief sawing cordwood into stove lengths at the city Woodyard. The city Relief Department was an adjunct of the Woodyard — departmentally and physically. Cordwood from the tamarack forests was still a staple fuel in Winnipeg. The city brought it in by the trainload and stored it in great piles twelve feet high and six rows deep around the two city blocks that the yard occupied. At an open corner in the stockade was the yard office, to which the relief office was attached. Least adequate of all the Relief Department facilities was the building itself. It was shaped like a flattened, stretched-out U. The centre section was some sixty feet long and contained the office. At one end an extension, some thirty feet long, jutted out at a right angle and was used as a store-room. The waiting-room was another extension from the other end and it was about fifty feet long and twenty feet wide. Over a door at the corner was a sign:

RELIEF OFFICE

A crowd of several hundred milled around in the yard and I elbowed my way through to the shed. Inside, at the far end of the shed, were three doors leading into the main office. One was marked APPLICATIONS. The next was marked RENT AND FUEL, and a third was marked GROCERIES. There were long lines in front of each door and the APPLICATIONS line extended the full length of the shack and out into the yard. I found the end of it and huddled against the wall with a dozen others while we waited for the line to move up and let us inside. After half an hour in the shack, the one thing we wanted most was to escape into the fresh air, regardless of the temperature.

Winnipeg's North End was home to Canada's largest blocs of unassimilated immigrants, many of whom had only lately arrived. Because of the language barrier they were the last hired and the first fired, so it naturally followed that the bulk of the first applicants for relief were New Canadians. In addition to their arts, music, dancing, and literature, they brought to Canada a folk cookery based upon highly aromatic herbs and spices. Garlic, to race-proud Anglo-Saxons, was something to touch gently to a salad bowl. To the Galicians — a derisive generic term Winnipeggers applied to all foreigners — garlic was an anti-toxin, a medicine, a gargle, a liniment, and a confection to chew while waiting for streetcars. The Woodyard waiting-room that day swam in an aroma of garlic, to which was added the smells of stale tobacco, wet leather, perspiration, and singed rubber and wool from those who stood too close to the intermittently smoking stove.

Overpowering as the atmosphere became, it never reached a sufficient potency to drive anybody out of his place in line. Perhaps it was the narcotic effect of the air, but as time passed so did my panic about going on relief. The closer I got to the door, the more anxious I became to get the thing over and done with. It was as if some impersonal force was moving me inexorably to some mysterious fate. I relaxed and waited, almost impatiently, for the next adventure. The terrible aloneness of the long walk to the relief office was gone. Nobody was alone any more.

I was feeling a lot better when I reached the end of the line that afternoon and a harried clerk took my application and explained the system to me. I became entangled in the regulations before we even got on relief. When we returned from Lethbridge, Kay and I had rented a house with my parents and brothers. The clerk said I could apply for relief for Kay and Patty, but my father would have to apply for his own family. Nobody could get relief for relatives. I explained that my father was partly crippled and could not walk all the way to the Woodyard. In that case, he said, there was no point in his coming. Being unemployable, he was only eligible for social welfare, which was something different and dispensed by the City Hall. I answered that my father was perfectly capable of doing clerical work, only his legs were arthritic.

The clerk went off for a long conference with a supervisor. In the end the supervisor let me apply for everybody, and I went home to await the arrival of an investigator who would come around to inspect us. Two days later an investigator turned up, made a few perfunctory inquiries, and approved my application. He also took the time to make out a special form for my father to sign, scribbled his approval on the bottom of it, and said he would turn the form in at the office and the vouchers would be sent out by mail on a temporary basis. I was to take my approved application back to the Woodyard on Tuesday. Thereafter, save when sickness intervened, I was a regular Tuesday visitor to the Woodyard for the next two years.

When I arrived on the first Tuesday, the system had been somewhat reorganized from the week before. There was now a 'NEW CARD' line parallel to the 'APPLICATIONS' line. The end of the line for new cards was again outside the shack and it took the better part of an hour to get in out of the cold. Eventually I reached the clerk who was handing out the cards. He took the slip the investigator had given me and laboriously copied the particulars onto a printed card somewhat larger than a driver's licence.

Across the top of the card were a number of headings, viz.: 'Groceries', 'Bread', 'Meat', 'Milk', 'Rent'. Under each the clerk inserted code numbers after I had named the store, bakery, meat market, and creamery with which we dealt. I spent the rest of the day going from line to line picking up vouchers. One qualified me to receive seven quarts and seven pints of milk, a second provided for seven loaves of bread, a third was worth sixty-five cents at the butcher's, and the fourth was for $2.38 in groceries. This was the new world of vouchers in which no cash ever passed from hand to hand.

In some cities a different system was used. Regina and Saskatoon gave out food supplies from a central depot. Edmonton and Calgary used vouchers. Regardless of the system, the allowances were about the same everywhere, varying naturally with the size of families. A family of three such as ours was allowed $16 a month for food and $10 to $13 a month for rent. Householders got a winter allowance of $6 to $10 a month in cordwood for fuel. It was possible to live on these allowances because of the collapse in the price structure. Indeed, as prices dropped even these relief allowances were reduced. Regina once cut the food allowance from $16 to $14 a month, until a near-riot changed the city council's mind. Any such episode naturally got economy-minded aldermen in other cities thinking about making similar reductions, 'in view of the drop in food prices'.

In the late winter of 1931, milk was ten cents a quart, bread six cents a loaf, chuck roasts sold for ten cents a pound, hamburger was nine cents, a rib roast was twelve cents, sausage was three pounds for a quarter, and potatoes forty-five cents a bushel. Even these prices would seem high a year later, when milk sold for six cents a quart in Winnipeg, bread was three loaves for a dime, butter sold for fifteen and twenty cents a pound, and eggs were fifteen cents a dozen.

For people accustomed to shopping with money, operating a household with vouchers took a lot of getting used to. Everything had to be bought in small quantities. If we had been given our grocery allowance for the month in a single voucher, instead of once a week, advantage could have been taken of quantity buying. But many months were to pass before the fact was recognized and allowances were distributed on a fortnightly basis. While becoming accustomed to voucher shopping was slow, people settled into the relief system itself with little difficulty.

We had lived in a continuing food-and-shelter crisis for a month, and once these problems were solved by going on relief we were freed from the feeling of being incessantly driven. We relaxed and made a start at sorting out our family problems. On an invitation from relatives, my father and brothers emigrated via cattle train to Ontario to look for work in the textile mills. My mother stayed on with us until they could send her transportation. We found a house we could rent for the $13 a month the relief department would allow and settled down to wait for spring and a job. Two months later I came down with tuberculosis.

NELSON WISEMAN

30 The Pattern of Prairie Politics

Canadian historians and social scientists have usually depicted prairie politics as a response, a reaction, to externally imposed conditions: the tariff, the withholding of authority over natural resources by the federal government, discriminatory transportation policies, etc. This approach tells us substantially about east-west Canadian relations. By itself, however, it tells us little about diversity of political traditions *on* the prairies. What is needed is an interpretive analysis which comes to terms with intra-regional differences. Why, until 1969, was Manitoba politics so dominated by Liberal and Conservative regimes? Why was Saskatchewan so receptive to the CCF-NDP? Why did Alberta spawn such a durable and unorthodox farmers' government (the UFA) then, overnight, become the bastion of an equally unorthodox Social Credit regime and, then, continue its tradition of one party dominance by stampeding to the Conservatives?

Answers to these questions do not lie (although some clues do) in an analysis of the east-west relationship. Nor do the answers lie in analyses which focus strictly on party systems or economic conditions. An economic analysis may be used to explain why, in the landmark federal election of 1911, Saskatchewan and Alberta endorsed the Liberals and freer trade, but it will not explain why Manitoba endorsed the Conservatives and protection. An analysis of party systems may be used to explain why, at the provincial level, Saskatchewan and Alberta rejected the two older parties in favour of third parties. It will not explain, however, why those two third parties are at opposite poles of the Canadian political spectrum. Identifying and accounting for the differences among the three prairie provinces, therefore, is essential. But this too is insufficient because striking diversities are to be located not only among but also *within* the provinces. By the 1890s, for example, Manitoba had been remade in the image of western Ontario. Yet in 1919, Winnipeg exhibited a level of class consciousness and class conflict that was decidedly more reminiscent of the European than the North American scheme of things. In Saskatchewan, until 1945, the federal Liberal party was consistently stronger than in any other English Canadian province. But it was this same province that returned North America's first social democratic government, a CCF government whose ideology was rooted in the British Labour party. Inconsistent political patterns seem no less profound in Alberta where governing parties that are defeated at the polls have faded almost immediately.

The analysis employed here utilizes the concepts of ideology and ethnicity. Elements of Canadian toryism, liberalism, and socialism[1] have been present in varying proportions in each province. Political representatives of these ideological tendencies on the prairies include men as diverse as Rodmond Roblin, John Diefenbaker, Charles Dunning, J.W. Dafoe, J.S. Woodsworth, Tommy Douglas, Henry Wise Wood, and William Aberhart, none of whom were born on the prairies. Because the prairie provinces and their societies were moulded in the late nineteenth and early twentieth centuries this is not surprising. Ideas and ideologies first appeared on the prairies as importations.

It is very unlikely that a Rodmond Roblin or a Tommy Douglas, preaching what they did, could have become premiers of Alberta. William Aberhart would not likely have succeeded in Manitoba or Saskatchewan. Politicians are reflectors of their society, their environment, their times. They may be examined in terms which transcend quirks of personality. Their ideas and actions may be seen as reflections of the popular and ideological-cultural basis of their support.

The key to prairie politics is in the unravelling of the dynamic relationship between ideological-cultural heritage and party. In Manitoba, the imported nineteenth-century Ontario liberal party tradition (with "a tory touch") maintained political hegemony until 1969. In Saskatchewan, the dominant tone of politics reflected a struggle between Ontario liberal and British socialist influences. In Alberta, American populist-liberal ideas gained widespread currency beginning in the very first decade of that province's existence. In all three provinces minorities of non-Anglo-American origins, in their voting, helped make and break governments. These minorities, however, did not determine the ideological coloration of any major party.

Prairie political culture is best seen as the product of the interaction of four distinct waves of pioneering settlers. The first wave was a Canadian one. More precisely, it was largely rural Ontarian. This wave was a westward extension of English Canada's dominant charter group. Ontarians were a charter group in each prairie province but their impact was greatest in Manitoba. It seemed both fitting and telling that one of Manitoba's premiers (Hugh John Macdonald) was the son of Canada's first prime minister. Tory-touched Canadian liberalism was the ideological core of nineteenth-century Ontario and its prairie offshoot.

A second distinct wave in prairie settlement was a new, modern, British group. Coming near the turn of this century, it was largely urban and working class. Transformed and battered by nineteenth-century industrialism, Britain's working class had begun to turn to socialism. Despite the cultural and ideological differences between the Ontario and new-British waves, their social status in the west was roughly equal, both groups being British subjects and Anglo-Saxon pioneers in British North America. The new-British wave had its greatest impact in the cities, most powerfully in the largest prairie city, Winnipeg. In Saskatchewan relatively large numbers of new British (and European-born) immigrants settled in rural areas and they produced Canada's most successful provincial social democratic party. It seemed both fitting and telling that Saskatchewan's premier in this labour-socialist tradition (Tommy Douglas) was British-born and grew up and was politically socialized in Winnipeg's new British labour-socialist environment.

The third wave in prairie settlement was American. More specifically it was midwest, great plains American. Like the Ontario wave, but unlike the new-British wave, it came out of an agrarian setting with deeply rooted agrarian values and settled, in overwhelming numbers, in rural areas. American Anglo-Saxons became the only non-Canadian, non-British charter group of the prairies. The dominant ideological strain carried by the American wave was similar but not identical to that carried by the Ontarians. It was, to be sure, liberal, but its liberalism was devoid of toryism. It was a radical "populist" liberalism that stressed the individual rather than the community or the state as a tory or socialist would. This wave's greatest impact was in rural Alberta, the continent's last agricultural frontier. Populist liberalism expressed itself in an unconventional farmers' movement/government known as the United Farmers of Alberta (UFA) and in the long tenure of Social Credit. It seemed both fitting and telling that this wave's leading representative figure was a veteran Missouri populist (Henry Wise Wood).

The fourth and last wave of prairie settlement consisted of continental Europeans. Because of their numerous national origins, they were the most diverse of the four waves. They were, however, neither a charter group nor did they have a significant ideological impact (the eastern European and Finnish influences in the Communist Party being a minor exception). The non-Anglo-Saxons were "alien" and suspect in the eyes of the other three groups. At times their very presence was attacked and challenged; at best they were tolerated. The ideological and political role of the continental wave became largely one of deference. The continental wave had its greatest urban impact in Winnipeg and its greatest rural impact in Saskatchewan. These areas were also those in which the new-British wave had its greatest impact. The combined voting strength of these two waves was to lead to CCF-NDP victories in Manitoba and Saskatchewan in later years. The Old World ideological attributes of the continentals were dismissed as illegitimate on the prairies. Thus, continentals deferred to the parties based on the other three groups;

but the continentals represented the largest swing factor in voting of the four waves. They helped elect and defeat parties anchored by the other waves; they neither anchored nor led a major party.

The foregoing description of the four distinct waves of prairie settlers is not intended to imply that all Ontarians were tory-touched liberals, that all new Britons were labour-socialists, that all Americans were populist-liberals, and that all continentals deferred ideologically and politically. Furthermore, it should be understood that not all Ontarians voted for the Liberals and Conservatives, not all new Britons voted CCF, and not all Americans voted UFA-Social Credit. The contention here, simply, is that without the new-British impact the CCF would never have attained the stature it did (indeed, it might not have been created at all); similarly, without the American impact the UFA-Social Credit phenomenon in Alberta would not have been anything like what it was; and without the Ontarians, prairie Liberal and Conservative parties would not have gained early hegemony. The conceptual framework underlying this analysis is that Manitoba, Saskatchewan, and Alberta were most influenced in their formative years by the political cultures of early twentieth century Ontario, Britain and the American midwest respectively. What we have here is a bare and simple macrocosmic sketch of the ethno-cultural and ideological bases of prairie politics in the first half of this century.

The evidence for the interpretation presented here is to be found in prairie historiography, but it is generally disregarded. The notion that Ontario, British, American, and continental European people and influences have helped shape prairie politics is not a new idea. But it might as well be, because it is an idea that has never been developed. There are ten excellent books in a series titled "Social Credit in Alberta: Its Background and Development." Not one of these books, however, devotes one paragraph to the American impact on Alberta, an impact unparalleled in Canada.

The impact of transplanted ideas was greater in Canada's west than in the United States because the physical impact of immigrants was greater. In 1914, for example, the year of greatest immigration to the US in the decade, one immigrant arrived for every eighty in the population. In Canada, in contrast, one immigrant arrived for every eighteen in the population in 1913. The bulk of them, whether from Britain, continental Europe or the United States, went west. Moreover, Canada's frontier experience was different from that of the US. South of the border, a soft frontier meant immigrants acculturating as settlement spread slowly westward. North of the border, a hard frontier meant getting off a boat and immediately boarding a transcontinental train. Immigrants and their ideas appeared more suddenly and in greater relative proportions on the Canadian prairies than in the American west.

Initially, Ontarians prevailed on the prairies. They occupied the best agricultural lands and secured homesteads along the new Canadian Pacific

Railway. Their power was most profound in Manitoba which, having entered Confederation in 1870, offered the most accessible frontier. The Ontarians were soon followed by waves of Britons, Americans, and continentals. The British came from the most urbanized industrial society in the world, but one that offered no rise in real wages between 1895 and 1913. More than a century of slowly developing working-class consciousness was represented by this new-British group. The American settlers, in contrast, came largely from the rural midwest. The Jeffersonian physiocratic notion that the soil was the sole source of wealth guided their thinking. Their interest in the Canadian frontier was fueled by Canadian government propaganda which employed the agrarian ideal, the Horatio Alger tradition and the log cabin stereotype, all prominent features of American liberal mythology. The continental immigrants were largely from eastern and central Europe, where land tenancy systems were in some cases only a half-century removed from feudalism. Of these three groups the Americans were the most likely and the British the least likely to homestead. Many Britons and continentals were to find their way into the new and growing prairie cities: Winnipeg, Regina, Calgary and Edmonton.

In addition to differences in immigrant distribution among the provinces there were differences within each province. Although there were equal numbers of Americans and Britons in Alberta, for example, in the 1920s Americans outnumbered Britons in all fifteen of Alberta's rural census divisions, by a ratio of two to one. In a province where the rural MLAs prevailed this meant an extraordinary American political influence. In twelve of the fifteen rural census divisions in Alberta Americans also outnumbered continental-born settlers. All three exceptions were in the northeast—that part of the province that provided the strongest rural opposition that both the American-influenced United Farmers of Alberta and Social Credit encountered.

In Saskatchewan, in the 1920s, Britons only slightly outnumbered Americans. The relative rural homogeneity of Saskatchewan, however, produced a dramatically different equation than in Alberta: the overwhelming majority of Britons settled in rural areas. Paradoxically, Saskatchewan had fewer Britons than either Alberta or Manitoba, but the Britons it did have penetrated rural Saskatchewan in a way that the Britons in neighbouring provinces did not. Furthermore, in Alberta the majority of American settlers were Anglo-Saxons; in Saskatchewan Anglo-Saxons were in a minority among Americans. This was important because a condition for political success was an Anglo-Saxon background. The largest number of Britons who entered Manitoba and Alberta generally headed for the cities; in Winnipeg population quadrupled between 1901 and 1915.

The four distinct waves of immigrants differed in religion as well as political ideology. Methodists and other social gospellers had their greatest impact in places like Winnipeg where the British-born labourist wave was particularly strong. Catholicism, brought over by many continental Europeans,

was strongest in Saskatchewan and contributed to the Liberals' long hold
on power there. Anglicans, with roots in both Ontario and Britain, reinforced Conservative tendencies in all three provinces. Many fundamentalists,
and they represented an exceptionally high twenty percent of Alberta Protestants, came to that province as American Bible Belt populists.

Ethnic voting studies have not been able to provide a coherent interpretation of prairie politics because studying "ethnic" voting by listing "Anglo-
Saxons" as against Germans, Ukrainians, French, etc., fails to appreciate
that some "Anglo-Saxons" were from the "Red" Clyde of Glasgow, others
from Perth County, Ontario, and still others from the populist state of
Kansas. Different types of divisions of course existed within other ethnic
groups. Between the 1920s and 1950s the key distinguishing features in
Anglo-Saxon voting in Winnipeg were class status and birthplace. For example, in one part of Winnipeg represented almost continuously between the
1920s and 1980s by MPs J.S. Woodsworth and Stanley Knowles, large numbers of British-born, low-income residents voted overwhelmingly CCF. The
city's highest income Anglo-Saxon area with relatively fewer British-born,
in contrast, voted overwhelmingly Liberal and Conservative. In both areas
Canadian-born Anglo-Saxons far outnumbered other Anglo-Saxons. This
revealed that second and third generations reflected inherited ideological-
cultural traditions which continued to be expressed in party voting.

Although their demographic impact was great, continental immigrants
did not play a leading role in early political developments. Rather, they
yielded to the politics of the charter groups. Large numbers of them were
isolated in rural ethnic colonies; many were in marginal farming areas where
federal agents had directed them. In response to their new opportunity, and
in their related effort to prove their loyalty to their new country, these minorities voted Liberal in Alberta from 1905 to 1921, and Liberal in Saskatchewan from 1905 to 1944. In Manitoba too the Liberals were the main
beneficiaries of this vote although occasionally, as in 1914, proof of loyalty
expressed itself in a Conservative vote. Winnipeg was an exception to the
rest of the prairies only in that its working-class continentals were sufficiently
numerous, concentrated and class-conscious to form a vibrant Communist
party after 1920. The politics of deference, however, did little to raise the
status of the European minorities. Racist prejudice against the continentals
was widespread.

Ontarian influence seemed dominant in all three provinces until at least
1921. During World War I, for example, all three provincial premiers, their
ministers of agriculture, and a majority of MLAs were Ontarians. In
Manitoba the grit agrarianism of Ontario expressed itself in the selection
of every premier from the 1880s until Ed Schreyer in 1969. Its distinct mark
was reflected in the transplantation of the Ontario municipal system and
in the School Question. In Saskatchewan this same, essentially Protestant
and English grit outlook dominated the Saskatchewan Grain Growers

Association (SGGA), the province's federal and provincial Progressives, and the Liberal party. But in Saskatchewan, unlike Ontario and Manitoba, the dominance of this liberal grit tradition was dependent on support from other elements in the population, specifically non-Anglo-Saxons, of which Saskatchewan had English Canada's highest percentage. Moreover, Saskatchewan's version of grit agrarianism was to encounter a powerful ideological competitor in the form of British-style socialism. The votes of the continentals helped elect a prairie version of the British Labour party in 1944.

American populist influences were greater in Saskatchewan than in Manitoba but they were secondary and not nearly as significant as in Alberta. In Alberta, the American-style populist farmers association (the UFA) determined the complexion of successive provincial governments for years. Alberta populism, like American populism, attracted some socialists, but it rejected socialist ideology. CCF socialism, embraced in Saskatchewan, was rejected by Alberta farmers on the peculiarly American grounds that it represented a repudiation of their "rugged individualism."

MANITOBA: THE ONTARIO OF THE PRAIRIES

Manitoba was the province most true to the values of rural Ontario. In the language rights debates it was more Orange than Ontario. Manitoba imported its early American-inspired farm organizations—the Grange and the Patrons of Industry—only after they had become established in Ontario. Manitoba's Tory farmers rejected any suggestion of possible secession from Confederation and American annexation in the 1880s.

A good representative of Manitoba's tory-touched liberalism was Rodmond Roblin, premier from 1900 to 1915. His toryism was reflected in the debate over direct legislation, an idea brought to the prairies from the United States. Every political party on the prairies supported the proposal except Roblin's Conservatives in Manitoba. Roblin attacked direct legislation on the basis that it was "A Socialistic and Un-British Plan." This permitted him to appeal to a fundamentally liberal but tory-touched rural Manitoba. According to Sir Rodmond, direct legislation represented a form of "degenerate republicanism," much too strong a phrase to use successfully in Alberta, but not in Manitoba.

T.A. Crerar was a typical Ontarian in rural Manitoba. As a member of the dominant charter group on the prairies, Crerar became a spokesman for the west but remained a product of the east. Between 1919 and 1922 he was offered the premierships of both Ontario and Manitoba. Crerar's liberalism was expressed in his leadership of the Progressive party and in his role as the architect of federal Liberal-Progressive rapprochement. He insisted that his party was not appealing to any specific class in society.

Alberta's Henry Wise Wood, in contrast, insisted that it must make a class appeal to farmers by demanding occupational representation or what became known as "group government." Wood's approach was typical of the American left, wholly within the confines of monolithic American liberalism, defining class in liberal (equality of opportunity) rather than socialist (equality of condition) terms. Crerar's liberalism, closer to British liberalism, denied any connection with class politics. Crerar represented the tory-touched rural liberalism of Manitoba; Wood reflected the radical populist liberalism of Alberta.

Although Manitoba Liberal and Conservative governments relied on rural support from continental-born immigrants, few Europeans, of either British or continental origins, were to be found in the higher echelons of either of these parties. Nor were many to be found in the United Farmers of Manitoba (UFM). "Canadian Ukrainians do not have any influence," declared one Ukrainian paper in 1932, the year of the CCF's birth. "We are poor and need political help. Ukrainian farmers and workers depend for their livelihood on the more powerful. This forces us to support a politically influential party. Affiliation with small radical parties brings Ukrainians only discredit and ruin." Such deference, however, did little for continental immigrants in the city. In the 1930s none of Winnipeg's banks, trust companies, or insurance firms would knowingly hire a Jew or anyone with a Ukrainian or Polish name. Nor would Anglo-Saxon premiers pick them for their cabinets.

Labour-socialist politics in Manitoba were as much determined by newly arrived Britons and Europeans as agrarian politics were determined by Ontarians. Winnipeg became the home of Canada's first Independent Labour Party (ILP) and, by 1899, twenty-seven separate unions appeared at the May Day parade. A year later, the editor of Winnipeg's labour newspaper, *The Voice*, was elected to the House of Commons.

Within a decade the labour-socialist sectarianism of Europe was reproduced in Winnipeg. Two groups working outside of the dominant ILP influence were the Social Democratic Party and the Socialist Party of Canada. By 1920-21 the two permanent parties that emerged were the British-led labourist ILP and the continental-based Communist party. Every imprisoned 1919 strike leader, except one, came from Britain to Winnipeg between 1896 and 1912. So too did most of the ILP leadership. The Communists, on the other hand, drew their inspiration from the Russian Revolution and scientific socialism. A small and insignificant British minority, including One Big Unionist and strike leader, R.B. Russell, stayed out of both camps. In Manitoba, as in Britain, labourism won over Marxism and syndicalism. By 1923, when the Ontario ILP was falling apart, the Manitoba ILP could boast that it held more than two dozen municipal and school board seats, the mayoralty of Winnipeg and representation in both federal and provincial parliaments. This modern, turn of the century British labourist tradition had its greatest Canadian urban impact in Winnipeg and Vancouver and, thus, the strength of the CCF-NDP in these cities.

Until at least 1945 much of the politics of the large Ukrainian community in North Winnipeg were still tied to the Russian Revolution and its aftermath. Those against the Revolution supported the Liberals. The CCF, for many virulent anti-communists, was a socialist step in a hated communist direction. Those supporting the Revolution embraced the Communist Party. The CCF, for many communist sympathizers, was a naive, liberal, social democratic, reformist gang. Since World War II, however, ethnic assimilation has contributed to strengthening the CCF-NDP position within both the former Liberal and Communist Ukrainian groups. An example of the shift from the CP to the NDP is the contrast between Jacob and Roland Penner, father and son. The former was for decades Winnipeg's leading Communist, the latter became the NDP's Attorney General in 1981. The CP withered because the older continental-born generation died and the party lost its base. The ideology of British labourism, in contrast, in the form of the ILP-CCF, survived and took root. Other socialist traditions among British and continental immigrants either accommodated themselves to this dominant influence on the left or they generally faded as did the SPC and CP.

Liberal, Conservative and Farmer governments dominated provincial politics. Winnipeg counted for little in the government's considerations and center and north Winnipeg, where the British and European-born had settled, counted for less. It was unpenalized neglect because a rurally biased electoral map ensured agrarian dominance. Between 1920 and 1949, for example, Winnipeg had only ten seats in a fifty-five seat legislature. In the 1922 election labour votes equalled those for twenty-seven non-labour MLAs, but Labour won only six seats. In 1945 the CCF received as many votes as the Liberal-Progressives and almost double the Conservative total, but the CCF won only ten seats to the Liberals' twenty-four and the Conservatives' thirteen.

Successive Manitoba governments reflected an alliance of Anglo-Saxons in the southwestern wheat belt and in south Winnipeg. This alliance went under various labels at different times: Liberal, Conservative, United Farmers of Manitoba, Progressive, Liberal-Progressive, Brackenite, Coalition, and even Non-Partisan. What distinguished it from its main ideological opponent was class and heritage, not ethnicity. In 1919 the warring Strike Committee and Citizens Committee had one feature in common: Anglo-Saxon backgrounds. In working-class Winnipeg the European minorities lined up behind the British-born Strike Committee because the Citizens Committee gave them little choice, condemning them as alien radicals. In rural Manitoba these minorities deferred to the established Canadian-born anti-strike forces.

These divisions were reflected in voting patterns. There seemed little basis for farmer-labour cooperation in Manitoba. They shared little in common. Labour issues, such as the eight-hour day, were ridiculed in the countryside, and every rural newspaper in Manitoba condemned the 1919 strike. Labour's attitude to Manitoba's farmers was also suspicion and, until 1927, UFM members were ineligible to join the ILP.

Manitoba's farm leaders went the way of Ontario's. Alberta's UFA, Saskatchewan's UFC (SS) and even Ontario's UFO affiliated with the federal CCF in 1932 (although the latter disaffiliated in 1934). The UFM, like its forerunners a half-century before, was true to the values of rural Ontario and remained aloof. In the late 1940s agrarian politics in Manitoba began to shift somewhat with the rise of the Manitoba Farmers Union (MFU). The MFU's membership came largely from more northerly, less prosperous, continental-born, and second generation Canadian farmers. By the 1950s, ethnic interaction over the course of forty years made possible the viability of such an organization. To the MFU leadership the Manitoba Federation of Agriculture, like its UFM predecessor, represented the wealthier, established, Anglo-Saxon Liberal farmers. After John Diefenbaker and Conservative premier Duff Roblin left their respective leadership posts in 1967, the provincial NDP capitalized on gaining informal MFU support in certain rural areas. It was a breakthrough that helped the NDP win enough rural seats to form a government in 1969. For a combination of reasons, including the fact that he was the son-in-law of the first president of the MFU, Ed Schreyer was the only figure in the Manitoba NDP who could attract such support.

Manitoba was ripe for an NDP victory in 1969 in a way that Ontario was not. In Ontario the impact of Anglo-Saxon voters, most of them long established in Canada, was more powerful than in Manitoba. This is another way of pointing out that Ontario is ideologically older than Manitoba in its conservatism, particularly in the rural areas, but in the cities too. There was a significant new British labourist impact in Ontario (e.g. Toronto mayor Jimmie Simpson in the 1930s) but, because of Ontario's relative oldness, it was not as profound as it was further west.

Manitoba had enough of Ontario in it to have sustained the only provincial Conservative party west of Ontario that has never collapsed. But it also had enough of modern Britain and continental Europe to provide CCFer J.S. Woodsworth and provincial Communist leader Bill Kardash with parliamentary seats between the 1920s and 1950s. Manitoba also had enough of the prairies in it to produce national and provincial Progressive parties in the 1920s. Their Ontario-born liberal leadership, however, led both of them back to the Liberal party.

SASKATCHEWAN: BRITISH LABOURISM ON THE PRAIRIES

As in Manitoba, provincial politics in Saskatchewan initially meant transplanting Ontarian politics. The provincial Liberal government operated at the pleasure of the Saskatchewan Grain Growers Association, the dominant political and economic organization in the province. Both the Liberals and the SGGA were led by the same figures and most of them had Ontario roots. The Progressive debacle in Ottawa, however, and the inability of the SGGA to break with the Liberals fuelled the formation of a rival agrarian organization: the Farmers Union of Canada. It was founded and first led by L.B. McNamee, a former British railway worker and trade unionist. This difference between the SGGA's Ontarian leadership and the Farmers Union British leadership broadly represented the difference between Ontario liberal and British socialist influences. The division became a central feature of Saskatchewan politics.

The success of the Farmers Union led to the formation of the United Farmers of Canada (Saskatchewan Section) and that, in turn, led directly to the Farmer-Labour party, led by British socialists and Canadians sympathetic to socialism. It then took three elections and ten years, from 1934 to 1944, to catapult this party to power under a CCF label. This became possible because enough continental-origin voters transferred their preferences from the Liberals to the CCF.

Liberalism at first seemed unbeatable in Saskatchewan. Although it came later than in Manitoba, the Ontarian impact was the first in Saskatchewan and it was, as in Manitoba, generally Liberal. While the national, Manitoba, and Alberta Liberal parties were rejected in the early 1920s, the Saskatchewan Liberals carried on. All six of Saskatchewan's daily newspapers supported them. A key factor for the Liberals in Saskatchewan was the province's large numbers of Catholics and eastern and central Europeans. In the European rural districts the provincial Liberals reaped the rewards of the federal government's immigration program.

In Saskatchewan, however, unlike Manitoba and Alberta, there was a significant new-British *rural* presence. Although Saskatchewan attracted fewer Britons than either Manitoba or Alberta, it had almost as many British-born farm operators as the other two provinces combined. This British influence, coming later than the Ontario influx, took a longer time to assert itself. The farmer-labour connection in the Farmers Union was unique among prairie farm organizations of any significant size. Much of its support came from farmers in continental-based areas, areas that switched from the Liberals to the CCF between 1934 and 1944. The SGGA, like the neighbouring UFM and UFA, had largely ignored the non-Anglo-Saxon farmers and had almost no following in areas settled by Europeans. All three organizations were rooted in the oldest and most established areas.

The United Farmers of Canada (Saskatchewan Section), a product of a merger of the growing Farmers Union and the declining SGGA in the mid-1920s, was socialist in a way that no other Canadian farm organization had ever been. That socialism, like Saskatchewan's early made-in-

Ontario liberalism, was imported. The two most important permanent officials of the new UFS (SS) were former members of the British Labour party and the Socialist Party of the United States. The UFC (SS)'s socialist, British, labourist, and agrarian heritages could be summed up by isolating two planks in its 1930 platform: "Abolition of the competitive system and substitution of a cooperative system of manufacturing, transportation, and distribution," and "Free trade with the mother country." The UFC (SS) endorsed a land nationalization scheme, one patterned on the British Labour Party's rural program. The UFC (SS) also forged a political alliance with the Saskatchewan Independent Labour Party. Formed in the late 1920s, the ILP was largely composed of teachers, some unionists and British socialists. It was patterned on the successful Manitoba ILP. When the UFC (SS) and the ILP came together in 1932 they formed the Farmer-Labour party and elected a British-born Fabian, M.J. Coldwell, as their leader.

A contributing factor to the rise of socialism in Saskatchewan was that the cooperative movement was stronger there than in any other province. Moreover, Saskatchewan's cooperators were more socialist than their provincial neighbours. The cooperative movement became an integral part of the CCF's constituency in Saskatchewan and the movement's growth in the province was aided by a provincial government branch headed by a British immigrant experienced in the British cooperative movement. This "British" link reappears often in Saskatchewan history.

The story of the CCF's success in Saskatchewan need not involve, as most sources do, a discussion of the Depression. When the Farmer-Labour (CCF) party ran in 1934 it was largely an unknown entity in politically cautious and deferential continental-origin areas. It had to contend, moreover, with the Catholic Church. Catholic opposition to the CCF was important in Saskatchewan because it was the most Catholic of the prairie provinces. A papal encyclical and a 1934 statement by the Archbishop of Regina attacking socialism as contrary to the Catholic faith aided the Liberals. The Liberals swept both the Ontario-anchored regions and the continental, particularly Catholic, areas. Voting among Anglo-Saxons divided, however, between areas that were largely Ontarian in origin and areas that contained large numbers of British-born. In both the 1934 and 1938 elections cultural rather than economic factors provided the clues to unravelling the voting patterns.

The CCF succeeded because it was British-led and ideologically British-based. The CCF's Britishness, its cultural acceptability, made it difficult to attack as alien. Its cultural legitimacy made it politically acceptable. It could therefore become an alternative to the Liberals for Saskatchewan's continental-origin citizens. Even more than in Manitoba, continental-origin citizens represented a large potential swing factor in voting. This helps explain why the CCF-NDP's success in Saskatchewan came twenty-five years before it did in Manitoba and why it was more profound in terms of votes and seats. The large rural British presence, combined with a large rural continental presence relative to Manitoba and Alberta, made it easier for continental-origin citizens in Saskatchewan to attach themselves to the CCF. This was further facilitated in 1943 when another barrier to CCF aspirations was lowered: the Catholic Church declared its support for the cooperative movement, expressed concern respecting social welfare, and told its members they were free to vote for any party that was not communist. The CCF victory in 1944, therefore, was no surprise.

The surge in CCF support in 1944 was most dramatic in the previously Liberal, continental-origin areas. Many CCF rural leaders were of non-Anglo-Saxon origins, a dramatic contrast to the overwhelming Anglo-Saxon character of the Liberal and Conservative leaders. The swing among continentals from the Liberals to the CCF was no less pronounced in urban areas. Between 1934 and 1944, for example, support for the CCF rose 218 percent in the most European part of Regina.

American influences in Saskatchewan were secondary to the Ontario and British influences. In contrast to Alberta, however, the Americans in Saskatchewan tended to help the fortunes of British-led anti-Liberal organizations such as the Farmers Union and the CCF. In Saskatchewan, unlike Alberta, the majority of Americans were non-Anglo-Saxons. Moreover, few of them in Saskatchewan had English as a mother tongue. Among these European-Americans in Saskatchewan were large numbers—larger than in Alberta—of Scandinavians. European and American Scandinavians in Saskatchewan were much more receptive to socialism than Anglo-Saxon Americans—the majority American group in Alberta. Therefore, European-Americans, such as Scandinavians, encountered a powerful, legitimate and culturally acceptable ideological ally in Saskatchewan in the form of the British-influenced CCF. In Alberta, in contrast to Saskatchewan, there were both fewer British farmers and fewer European-Americans. British labour-socialism, moreover, was not a leading ideological force in rural Alberta as it was in Saskatchewan. In Alberta, European-Americans represented a minority among Americans in rural areas. Moreover, they had no corresponding powerful rural British labour-socialist strain to attach themselves to. Thus, in Alberta, there never arose a socialist agrarian rival to the UFA as there was to the SGGA in the form of the Farmers Union.

The connection between British birth and labour-socialist politics has been demonstrated in Manitoba. It was also reflected, as late as 1942, in Alberta where four of five CCF provincial executive members were British-born, and in British Columbia where nine of the fourteen CCF MLAs were British-born. In Saskatchewan, in slight contrast, there were four Americans yet only three Britons among the eleven-member British-led CCF caucus at this date. Some of the Americans elected as CCF MLAs in 1944 had voted for Socialist Eugene Debs in the United States. In the United States, as the Socialist Party withered, socialist supporters of European origins on the American great plains returned to the established American parties. In

Saskatchewan, in contrast, as the socialist-farmer-labour movement grew, American socialist sympathizers of European ancestry, not overwhelmed by American liberalism as they were in the US, had alternatives not restricted to the established parties.

In the late 1950s Saskatchewan produced another political phenomenon, John Diefenbaker, who made it possible for the Conservatives to become a national party for the first time since 1935. In the 1940s, Manitoba preferred the Liberals, Saskatchewan the CCF, and Alberta Social Credit. Diefenbaker, unlike other national leaders, was neither Anglo-Saxon nor was he identified with Central Canadian financiers. This made it possible for European-origin farmers to flock, for the first time, to the Conservative banner. Ethnic interaction and the passing of earlier prejudices no longer crippled the Conservatives in Saskatchewan's European-origin areas. At the same time, Diefenbaker's toryism and commitment to agricultural interests made him equally acceptable to rural, Anglo-Saxon, prairie farmers. They recognized him as an established, Ontario-born Canadian not as a European, naturalized one. Diefenbaker's populist image, another side of this phenomenon, helped him in Alberta where agrarian populism, as in the United States, eased its way into agribusiness. The prairies could therefore embrace the federal Conservative party after the 1950s because it was a qualitatively different party under Diefenbaker than it had been under Arthur Meighen, R.B. Bennett, John Bracken, and George Drew.

Seymour Lipset's *Agrarian Socialism* is something of a misnomer in reference to Saskatchewan. The Saskatchewan CCF-NDP consistently fared better in cities than in the countryside. More precisely, it had been a case of British-style socialism succeeding in an unexpected agricultural setting. M.J. Coldwell, Tommy Douglas, Woodrow Lloyd, and Allan Blakeney were never farmers. Nor was British-born and longtime Toronto MP Andrew Brewin who drafted Saskatchewan's "showpiece" labour legislation in the 1940s. Saskatchewan did produce one British-born non-socialist premier: Charles Dunning. But he represented an older part of Canada's British heritage. Dunning succeeded as easily in Prince Edward Island, which he went on to represent as finance minister in Mackenzie King's cabinet. The only part of the Maritimes that would have sent a Tommy Douglas to Ottawa was Cape Breton because it had been subject to the same type of new British influx as Saskatchewan. This connection between British-birth and socialist inclinations was revealed in the 1970s when Douglas represented Nanaimo (British Columbia) as an MP. In the 1920s, Nanaimo was the most British city in Canada, almost half its residents having been born in the British Isles. The British labourist-socialist connection became, paradoxically, most successful in Canada's most agrarian province.

By the late 1970s, the Liberals disappeared from the Saskatchewan legislature for the first time. Liberals defected in droves to the Conservatives who went from two percent of the vote in 1971 to fifty-four percent in 1982. This represented no ideological realignment; the Conservatives, who were by now free-enterprising liberals indistinguishable from the Liberals, merely replaced the latter as the preferred anti-socialist standard bearer in Saskatchewan's bipolar political system. Saskatchewan's Liberals, like their Manitoba and Alberta cousins, suffered from their identification with the federal Trudeau Liberals with the result that there was only one elected provincial Liberal in all of Western Canada in the late 1970s. More than ever, the Saskatchewan NDP appeared as an unmistakable urban party. As such it lost power, its rural weakness becoming the major impediment to its return to office. The provincial Conservatives, moreover, had been remade and recast, calling themselves populists and opening their membership so that they were no longer an anathema to the ethnic minorities.

ALBERTA: THE AMERICAN MIDWEST ON THE PRAIRIES

The politics of rural Alberta were as much influenced by the values of the American great plains as the politics of rural Manitoba were influenced by the standards of rural Ontario. In Alberta the various cultural waves, from Ontario, Britain, continental Europe, and the United States, came closest to arriving simultaneously. Early Ontario settlers in rural Alberta, as in Saskatchewan, encountered another ideological strain. It was not, however, a socialist challenge as it had been in Saskatchewan. It was, rather, a more militant, more radical, less tory form of petit-bourgeois liberalism, than was the Canadian norm. It was not so much a challenge as a reinforcement, a radicalization, of the natural liberalism of transplanted Ontarians. There seemed little need, as there had been in Saskatchewan, for two rival agrarian organizations or for an ideologically distinct opposition party. The older parties simply re-oriented themselves. The Liberals and Conservatives became competitors vying for support from the American-influenced UFA. An MP remarked in the House of Commons that Alberta, "from the border northward to Edmonton, might be regarded as a typical American state."

American populism pervaded Alberta politics. Many Canadian- and British-born settlers, to be sure, were found in the vanguard of the agrarian movement. But Americans and American ideas played an influential role in Alberta that was unparalleled in Canada. An early example of this in the UFA was that both sides in the debate over whether or not to enter electoral politics argued their cases with references to experiences south of the border, one side referring to the sad end of the People's party and the other side pointing to the Non-Partisan League's success in North Dakota.

When Social Credit came to power in 1935 there was no significant shift of ideological allegiance in rural Alberta. UFAers had been nurtured on inflationary monetary theories in the United States and at UFA conventions throughout the 1920s. The overwhelming majority of UFAers found socialism alien and voted for a technocratic, "pragmatic" remedy in Social Credit. It was a response with American (Free Silver, Greenbackism), not Canadian, antecedents. Social Credit had much in common with American monetary reform schemes like the Townsend Plan which, in 1936, claimed over three million adherents. Although the Social Credit label originated in Britain, Alberta's version of Social Credit had stronger material links to the United States. In Britain, Social Credit's appeal was strongest among the Catholic, the urban, and the cosmopolitan. In Alberta, in contrast, Social Credit was viewed most suspiciously in Catholic areas and was most popular in the rural and Protestant, particularly American fundamentalist, areas.

The American influence in rural Alberta expressed itself in many ways. In sheer numbers, more than one in five Alberta residents at one point was American-born while the national ratio was less than one in twenty-five. Canadian branches of the American Society of Equity, containing large numbers of transplanted Nebraskans and Dakotans, were the core of the UFA when it was formed in 1909, and about one-half of the directors on the UFA's board were American-born, outnumbering both British- and Canadian-born.

In sharp contrast to T.A. Crerar and Manitoba's farmers, Henry Wise Wood and the UFA's break with the Liberals was to be final and complete. The division between the UFA brand of third-party populism and the Manitoba brand of third-party parliamentarism, one longing for a reconciliation with the Liberals, came at the very founding convention of the national Progressives in 1920. Wood intended that the UFA govern Alberta with no reference to the older parties. This never happened in Ontario-anchored Manitoba. This difference meant that the Liberal party was doomed in Alberta. In Ontario, Manitoba and Saskatchewan, in contrast to Alberta, most of the federal Progressives who had been elected to replace Liberals became Liberals.

American-style populism prevailed in Alberta because a heavily rurally oriented electoral map, like Manitoba's, meant agrarian dominance. The new British labour-socialist impact in Calgary and Edmonton was insufficient to offset American populist-liberal dominance in the rural areas. Although one-third of Calgary was British-born and it served as the site of the founding conventions of both the OBU and the CCF, as well as being the constituency of Labour MP William Irvine, Calgary was in the largely rural province of Alberta and was thus also subject to an American impact: it became the headquarters of the Society of Equity, the Non-Partisan League, the UFA, prairie evangelism, and Social Credit, all of which had American roots.

Alberta's preoccupation with monetary theories was a result of the American influence. Low agricultural prices in the United States led American farmers to fight for the free coinage of silver and an inflation in the money supply. When J.W. Leedy, the former populist governor of Kansas, and US

credit expert George Bevington and many other Americans emigrated to
Alberta, they brought along their monetary theories. Throughout the 1920s
and 1930s UFA conventions became debating forums for the monetary theorists. The monetary issue was second to none. In Manitoba and Saskatchewan, in contrast, it was rarely debated. When C.H. Douglas's Social Credit
theories appeared they had much in common with notions already present
in the UFA. The UFA had contributed to this link by distributing Douglas's
books throughout the 1920s. Social Credit, therefore, could be regarded
as a supplement rather than as an alternative to UFA thinking.

Wood's retirement from the UFA presidency led to a crystallization of
the majority and minority positions in the UFA. The American-influenced
majority was occupied with monetary reform; a British-influenced minority
was more interested in socialist efforts at the national level. Both positions
gained recognition at the 1931 UFA convention: Bevington's annual inflationary money resolutions were endorsed and British-born, socialist leaning Robert Gardiner became the new UFA president. Gardiner led his federal Ginger Group caucus into an even closer working arrangement with
J.S. Woodsworth's Labour group. When the UFA's federal leadership in
1932 took the UFA into the CCF, Gardiner's caucus in Ottawa became isolated from the majority sentiment in rural Alberta. Neither Wood, nor UFA
Premier Brownlee, nor his cabinet ever endorsed the "farmer-labour-
socialist" alliance as the CCF described itself.

Social Credit was the political heir of the American-influenced monetary
reform wing of the UFA. William Aberhart succeeded only because the monetary reformers in the UFA had tilled the soil so well for him. It was the UFA,
he continually reminded his audiences, that had introduced Social Credit
thinking into Alberta. By 1935 UFA locals throughout the province were
clamouring for some form of Social Credit. During the election campaign
Social Credit was really not a partisan issue: few dared attack it. It became,
rather, an assumption. Even the Liberals promised Social Credit and the
Alberta Federation of Labour indicated enthusiasm as well. Aberhart's Social
Credit message was consistent with Alberta's populist history. The American monetary reformers had done their work well. Social Credit's sweeping victory in 1935 was therefore no surprise. Had Social Credit not
appeared, another party would have arisen preaching much the same gospel.

American analogies are logical in Alberta. There is something to the argument that Aberhart comes closest among Canada's premiers to looking and
sounding like a radical, populist, American governor. Many of his supporters
referred to him as Alberta's Abraham Lincoln. But no one could compare
prairie CCF leaders such as Douglas, Coldwell or Woodsworth to American populists. One could identify them with a Norman Thomas but, to be
more accurate, one would have to look to a Briton like Ramsay MacDonald,
Labour's first prime minister.

Alberta's voting patterns may be related directly to the patterns of settlement and to the ideological-cultural heritages of the settlers. Initial Ontario settlers in the south, particularly those who came before 1896 and settled along the CPR line, voted for the party of the railroad, the federal Conservatives. The early twentieth-century American influx altered this. The American impact was most pronounced in southern and eastern Alberta, an area representing the key to political power in the province just as the southwest represented that key in Manitoba. The southern, American-settled parts of Alberta which were most favourable to prohibition in 1915 became the most favourable to the UFA from 1921 to 1935 and to Social Credit from 1935 to the early 1970s. Those areas in northern Alberta that tended toward the UFA were those whose population most closely resembled the American-anchored south.

Continental-origin and French Canadian voters in northern Alberta represented a Liberal electoral base for the same reasons as in Saskatchewan and Manitoba: the Liberals were the party of immigrants and Catholics. The UFA, in contrast, was overwhelmingly Anglo-Saxon, composed of Canadian-, American- and a sprinkling of British-born farmers. UFA and Social Credit majorities were produced by an electoral map which ensured that the party that swept the south was the party that won elections. UFA and Social Credit vote totals were never as high in the continental and French Canadian north as in the Ontarian and American south. These patterns reflected how much the UFA and Social Credit had in common with each other and how little either had in common with the CCF.

The new British labour-socialist element in Alberta was largely isolated in the urban centres. Consequently, the CCF floundered. The British-anchored provincial CCF never managed to win more than two seats in Alberta. Significantly, both CCF MLAs in the 1950s were from the north and were second generation Ukrainians, as were large numbers of their constituents. These northeastern areas were among the very few where, in the 1920s, continental-born farmers outnumbered American-born ones. The CCF success here confirmed the shift, in a much less dramatic fashion than in Saskatchewan, from the Liberals to the CCF among non-Anglo-Saxons of continental, particularly eastern European, origin. In Saskatchewan, large numbers of rural continentals had swung their votes to support the party of large numbers of rural Britons, the CCF. In Alberta, however, there were both fewer continentals and fewer rural Britons. Thus, the CCF was a relatively minor force in Alberta's rural areas.

Manifestations of the American influence in Alberta abound. One example of a republican liberal tendency was the Alberta government's refusal to appear in 1938 before the Royal Commission on Dominion-Provincial Relations, addressing its comments instead to "the Sovereign People of Canada." Parliamentary government was described as a form of state dictatorship. Another example was the complaint of a Nebraska-born MLA who called the caucus form of government undemocratic and criticized the

Speech from the Throne for making more of the 1937 coronation festivities than of Social Credit. Could such a sentiment respecting the coronation have been expressed at Queen's Park or in any other English Canadian provincial legislature? Solon Low, Alberta's treasurer and then the national Social Credit leader in the 1950s, was the son of Mormon immigrants from Utah. In the 1980s, when the Western Canada Concept elected an MLA in the constituency of the departing Social Credit leader, that MLA was a graduate of Utah's Brigham Young University.

Although prairie politics continue to be tied to prairie history as the twentieth century draws to a close, the passage of time has brought changes. In the late 1980s, Conservatives formed the governments of all three prairie provinces. Once the anti-immigrant party, they refashioned themselves over time and succeeded among many of the grandchildren of the ethnic pioneers. As ethnic differences count for less in prairie politics, other cleavages such as class, may count for more. The politics of deference on the part of the ethnic minorities are no longer practised nor anticipated. The European-origin minorities became established economically, culturally and politically. In the 1970s, for example, Jews served as leaders of Manitoba's Conservative and Liberal parties and as the provincial chief justice. When the latter retired, he was replaced by a Franco-Manitoban. This would have been inconceivable in the 1950s, unlikely in the 1960s. Slavs made up one-third of Howard Pawley's first NDP government and were present, in increasing numbers in influential positions, in the administrations of all three provinces. One became the leader of the Saskatchewan NDP, another was the runner-up for the Alberta Conservative leadership and the premiership. One served as a lieutenant governor, another became the deputy prime minister and, in 1988, Manitobans elected a Conservative premier of Romanian-Ukrainian ethnic heritage.

The increasingly active role of those from the ethnic minorities was fostered by their integration, acculturation and assimilation. Urbanization, mobility, as well as changes in laws, education and values have also played a role. "Multiculturalism" became part of the national constitutional fabric with all the parties courting rather than excluding the minorities from active participation. The older British or Anglo-Saxon charter group, moreover, decreased in relative numbers, making up just over a third of the populations of Manitoba and Saskatchewan in the 1980s. Today's new ethnic minorities include diverse groups of Asians and natives who are not as numerous or established as the European-origin minorities. Nevertheless, they too have today relatively easy access to the political system, contesting and winning ridings for all three parties. In the 1990s, unlike the 1920s, it is Ontario and not the prairies that is home to most new immigrants. Ethnicity and foreign birth are today perhaps more clearly expressed as factors in party politics in metropolitan Toronto than on the prairies where a population that was once more than 40 percent foreign-born is now overwhelmingly Canadian-born and socialized. The ethnic minorities are in the mainstream, rather than at the periphery, of prairie politics.

Ideological differences among the parties continue to be reflected symbolically and in public policy agendas. Although parties of different stripes behave similarly once in office, differences in nuance, style, and substance persist. Sterling Lyon, for example, exhibited a trace of toryism in objecting in 1980 to a revised constitution that entrenched individual rights at the expense of parliamentary sovereignty. Peter Lougheed, in contrast, offered historically more populist and liberal Alberta a referendum bill in 1980 that could be used to settle constitutional as well as non-constitutional matters. Allan Blakeney's career as a civil servant and then as a socialist politician in Saskatchewan reflected the NDP's ideological concern with building a professional civil service, one sensitive to social democratic values.

The successful persistence of the social democratic NDP has fed a continuing ideological fissure in a way that is absent, in contrast, in Atlantic Canada. Lyon regularly referred in the 1970s to the need to "throw out the socialists who follow alien doctrines laid down in Europe in the nineteenth century" and the Manitoba legislature in 1983 became the unlikely venue for a debate on American policy in Nicaragua. In the context of Alberta's more radical liberal environment, the WCC depicted the reigning Conservatives as crypto-socialists. And, in an echo of Aberhart's Social Credit, the WCC's leader suggested that all who voted for his party would receive $1,000 from a WCC government.

Protest parties continue to sprout on the prairies, but they have not flourished or established a secure beachhead. The Reform Party, led by the son of a Social Credit premier, the WCC, and the Confederation of Regions party which ran second in a number of Manitoba's federal ridings may fail and fade. In part this is due to the institutionalization of the established parties through new rules that range from party finance legislation to free access to broadcasting. But it is also a product of changes in the constituencies that once fed and sustained protest. Rurally based and led parties, once the driving forces in prairie politics, have bleak prospects because electoral maps have become more representative and because farmers are fewer and count for less: Saskatchewan, for example, had 170,000 farms in the 1950s but only 70,000 in the 1970s. Today there are more university students than farms in Manitoba, more government employees than farmers and one city, Winnipeg, has as many ridings as the rest of the province. Prairie politics are, like prairie society and economy, in continuing flux.

ENDNOTES

1. See Gad Horowitz, "Conservatism, Liberalism, and Socialism in Canada: An Interpretation," *Canadian Journal of Economics and Political Science* 32, 2 (May 1966).

ALVIN FINKEL

---

31 Alberta Social Credit Reappraised
The Radical Character of the Early Social Credit Movement

When Orvis Kennedy resigned in 1982 as president of the collapsing Alberta wing of the Social Credit party, the ancient party warrior reminded Albertans that the party had been founded to "save free enterprise" during the depths of the Great Depression of the 1930s.[1] Such a view of the party's origins was shared by the aged handfuls of party faithful who had remained with the party for five decades, and had watched sadly as the party failed to recruit younger members after World War II[2] and finally fell from power in 1971. Historians, concentrating largely on the implausible monetary theories of the party founders, have also largely accepted the view that Social Credit was, from the beginning, a right-wing populist movement hostile to government economic intervention except with regards to the evil bankers.[3]

In fact, however, Kennedy, the retrospective free-enterpriser, secured a parliamentary seat (Edmonton East) in 1937 with the acknowledged aid of Communist campaign workers.[4] And many early Social Crediters were at best ambivalent on the question of socialism versus free enterprise. An examination of the behaviour of the party in its early years, and of the first Aberhart government, demonstrates considerable openness on the part of early Social Crediters to government interventions of various kinds outside the field of banking. What follows is an analysis of the early Social Credit movement which de-emphasizes the well-documented party discussions regarding the banks, and concentrates on the attitudes and prescriptions of the party and government on broader economic and social issues. It also assesses the views of the opponents of Social Credit and notes that their fears of Aberhart and his colleagues went well beyond concerns for the fate of the bank branches in Alberta — whose safety from Aberhart's clutches had been established by the courts before the end of Aberhart's first term in office.[5]

The Social Credit party, which swept the provincial elections of 1935, had enrolled over thirty thousand members before the election was called.[6] Yet the Alberta Social Credit League had made the decision to enter the electoral arena only six months previously.[7] Before then, the League had spent its time organizing social credit clubs and lobbying the provincial government to implement William Aberhart's schemes. Aberhart, as all historians of Social Credit agree, dominated the Alberta movement despite his inability to comprehend the intricacies of Major C. H. Douglas's social credit theory.[8] Aberhart, a radio evangelist with a loyal following, and a Calgary high school principal, became the symbol of the struggle to secure a more just social order. His correspondence shows him to be what his detractors claimed: a vain, authoritarian, short-tempered man whose oratorical abilities far exceeded his intellectual capacities.[9] Aberhart was, however, also deeply distressed by the poverty and hopelessness which surrounded him and genuinely committed to seeking solutions to Depression conditions.[10] While he remained convinced to his death that public control over the financial system was the key to ending poverty, he proved willing at least to consider other options as it became clear that only the federal government had the constitutional authority to regulate banks and currency.

Aberhart and his followers did not commit themselves to a thorough criticism of the capitalist system such as the Cooperative Commonwealth Federation (CCF) had made in the Regina Manifesto of 1933. But the early party avoided attacks on the manifesto and on the CCF, preferring to paint banks rather than socialists as the enemies of prosperity. In part, this can be explained by the lack of a socialist threat in Alberta. Despite Kennedy's protestations that Social Credit was needed to save free enterprise in Alberta, the political forces of socialism in the province were weak at the time Social Credit decided to transform itself into an electoral party. While the United Farmers of Alberta organization (UFA) had affiliated with the CCF, the provincial UFA government took little notice and governed indistinguishably from a Conservative or Liberal government. Because of the affiliated character of the CCF organization, no attempt was made to establish a new organization composed of UFA members and others who rejected the orthodox economic policies pursued by the provincial government. The provincial Labour party was avowedly socialist, but it lacked organization outside of the two major cities and some of the mining districts; by 1935 it was, in any event, on the decline.[11]

The CCF's weakness was not the sole reason why both that party in particular and socialism in general were not attacked by Social Credit. The Social Credit leaders and members were ambivalent about market-based economics and, before the early forties, did not reject out-of-hand notions of a planned economy or even of public ownership. They did not embrace state planning and public ownership as central doctrines as the CCF did; "funny money" — government printed-and-distributed "social dividends" meant to boost purchasing power — provided the party's fundamental platform. But Social Crediters also toyed with CCF doctrines.

Aberhart's *Social Credit Manual,* which was widely distributed through-out the province during the 1935 provincial election, reflected his party's confusion about the extent to which the state should be involved in economic life. The manual's opening comments indicated that the party rejected the traditional views of political economists that the marketplace rather than the state must act as the guarantor of economic justice. The party's "basic premise," it claimed, was that:

> It is the duty of the State through its Government to organize its economic structure in such a way that no bona fide citizen, man, woman, or child shall be allowed to suffer the lack of the base [*sic*] necessities of food, cloth-ing, and shelter, in the midst of plenty or abundance.[12]

The state, it argued, should not confiscate the wealth of the rich and dis-tribute it to the poor. Party doctrine recognized individual enterprise and ownership, but the party also believed the state must outlaw "wildcat exploi-tation of the consumer through the medium of enormously excessive spreads in price for the purpose of giving exorbitant profits or paying high dividends on pyramids of watered stock."[13] It could prevent such exploitation by sys-tematically controlling prices "for all goods and services used in the province" and fixing minimum and maximum wages for each type of worker.[14] This was hardly a prescription for saving a market-based free enterprise econ-omy, though it substituted state regulation of pricing for the socialist solu-tion of state control of industry.

Aberhart's proposals were riddled with contradictions. Though he proclaimed that Social Credit would not take from the rich to give to the poor, he also promised that a Social Credit government would "limit the income of the citizens to a certain maximum" because "no one should be allowed to have an income that is greater than he himself and his loved ones can possibly enjoy, to the privation of his fellow citizens."[15] While he insisted that Social Credit recognized individual enterprise, he promised to break up the large oil companies' control of the oil industry and to allow new entrants into the field.[16]

On the whole, then, Social Credit anticipated using the state as a lever to restore a smallholders' democracy. It was less interested in free enterprise — indeed it was hostile to the market system — than it was in a wide disper-sion of business ownership. While Aberhart's rhetoric against capitalists was relatively moderate, he appropriated the CCF's phrase, "fifty big shots," to describe the country's ruling economic clique.[17] Some of his supporters were more strident. The *Social Credit Chronicle,* the party's official journal, editorialized in September 1934:

How many of these capitalistic lions will support Social Credit? Not one of them. How many of them will try and obstruct the bringing in of Social Credit principles? Everyone of them . . . . They know that if ever Social Credit is adopted in Alberta it will only be the beginning of a new era, it will be the overthrow of their power . . . .

Let the supporters of Social Credit stand firm on this issue, let Alberta take the lead in showing the country that the people have broken away from the old yoke of the capitalistic system.[18]

The capitalists did indeed try to obstruct Social Credit's progress. Their attack was led by the boards of trade in Calgary and Edmonton. Before the provincial election of 1935, the boards had decided that businessmen should set up an organization whose sole purpose was to oppose Aberhart's social credit movement. As J.H. Hanna, secretary of the Calgary Board of Trade, commented to his counterpart in Drumheller, direct opposition by boards of trade to Social Credit would be regarded with suspicion because "those who take so readily to such schemes as Social Credit look upon our organization as having the capitalistic viewpoint."[19] But the founding of the Economic Safety League by the businessmen was unsubtle and it is unlikely that many were deceived that this was a broadly-based organization.[20] Nor were the businessmen deceived about public feeling towards them. Commenting on the election results, Hanna observed:

We should keep in mind that the majority of the people who support these new and radical plans blame the so-called capitalist class for their troubles and are prejudiced against Boards of Trade because they believe they are the servants of the capital class and are not interested in the welfare of the people generally.[21]

From the businessmen's point of view, then, Social Credit was hardly the saviour of free enterprise which Orvis Kennedy retrospectively claimed it was intended to be. Nevertheless, Hanna noted that many small retailers who had kept their opinions to themselves during the election openly applauded the Aberhart victory. To some extent the division of business opinion on Social Credit was between big and small business, between successful operations and those forced to the wall by Depression conditions. But organized business as a whole opposed Social Credit from the beginning and only relented in the 1940s when Aberhart abandoned the reformist plans which his government and party embraced during the Depression. The opposition was not restricted to the boards of trade in the two large cities. The boards in smaller towns such as Drumheller, Stettler, and Medicine Hat went on record in opposition to Aberhart's plans during the election of 1935 despite the professed non-partisanship of boards of trade.[22]

In general, Social Credit attracted the support of the poor and was rejected by the better-off. In Claresholm, for example, the president of a men's club in which businessmen predominated observed:

> We are composed of a membership of about 75, perhaps 60 being businessmen or associated in a business or profession and perhaps 15 being farmers, retired farmers, etc. I think 75 per cent are opposed to Social Credit including myself and all our executive. Among the affiliated legion members, many of whom are in poor condition financially the percentage of those supporting Social Credit would be considerably greater. There are I think four merchants, one lawyer, one dentist and one medical man here supporting Social Credit.[23]

During its first term in office, Social Credit appeared uncertain about how far it wished to go to implement election promises in the face of implacable opposition from most of the provincial economic elite as well as local elites in most rural areas. Aberhart's procrastination with regards to banking legislation and the promised social dividends of twenty-five dollars per adult per month have been well-documented.[24] So have the government's broken promises to treat the unemployed with greater humanity than the United Farmers of Alberta government had demonstrated.[25] Nevertheless, from the start, business found much to be alarmed about in Social Credit actions and their fears seemed to grow throughout Social Credit's first term.

The first session of the legislature under Aberhart opened early in 1936 and passed several pieces of legislation that were denounced as "fascist" as well as "socialist" by the Calgary Board of Trade, which was not known for precision in its use of either term. Among the offending items of legislation were male minimum wages (minimums for women had existed since 1920), compulsory membership of teachers in the Alberta Teachers' Association, motor vehicle licences for all drivers, and legislation restricting various trades to licensed individuals.[26] While male minimum wages and restricted entry into trades offended employers, they won the government considerable support among workers. The unions, we shall see, were largely hostile to the Social Credit administration during its first term; but, unlike the business groups, their objection was that Social Credit was doing too little for the province's workers.

The businessmen feared not only Social Credit's legislation but the government's intentions regarding legislation already passed by the United Farmers of Alberta administration, especially the Department of Trade and Industry Act of 1934. This act allowed businessmen in a particular industry, whether in manufacturing, wholesaling or retailing of a product, to combine to write a "code of fair practice" for the industry, which could include price-fixing and the setting of production quotas; the code regulations would be enforced by the government.[27] While the legislation proved generally attractive to small businessmen, it was greeted with hostility by large retailers and wholesalers who claimed that it would keep small, inefficient firms afloat at the expense of the consumer. While the UFA, which had unsuccessfully attempted to win consensus for codes before imposing them, had implemented few, Social Credit proved more daring. Within a year of taking office, it had established codes for retailers, wholesalers, and a variety of service industries. These codes included price schedules, hours of work for employees, hours of operation for firms, and proscriptions against such practices as offering loss leaders. They were warmly greeted by small business and attacked by large firms who claimed correctly that they made the government, rather than the marketplace, the arbiter of prices and business practices.[28]

The opposition to "codes" was mild in comparison to the opposition to the Licensing of Trades and Industry Act passed in October 1937. The act gave the Minister of Trade and Industry sweeping powers to determine who could operate a business in the province. The minister could "provide for the registration of all persons engaged in or employed in any business or any description or class thereof so designated and prohibit the carrying on of that business or the engagement in that business of any person who is required to be licensed and who is not so licensed."[29] The minister could impose whatever license fees he regarded as appropriate for firms in particular industries and could prohibit licensed firms from engaging in operations other than those which they had been authorized to perform. A license could be cancelled if a firm or individual contravened more than once the Department of Trade and Industry Act, one of the Minimum Wage Acts, the Hours of Work Act, or the Tradesmen's Qualification Act. Stiff fines would be imposed against violators of the Act's provisions.

Predictably, boards of trade, in which the small businessmen who supported Social Credit appear to have lacked influence, unanimously opposed the legislation. So did the provincial branch of the Canadian Manufacturers' Association.[30]

A legal challenge to the Licensing Act, launched by a Calgary automobile dealer with financial aid from boards of trade,[31] stalled the government. The Honourable Mr. Justice Howson, who had been leader of the provincial Liberal party during the 1935 provincial election, ruled in favour of the dealer because the Attorney General's department had made technical mistakes in its drafting of the legislation.[32] So the legislation was re-drafted and reintroduced; a second appeal by the car dealer was dismissed by a justice of the Alberta Supreme Court. The federal government had rejected business pleas that the legislation be disallowed.[33]

The government meanwhile had fulfilled the business community's worst fears by giving itself the absolute right to broadly regulate all industries. A Provincial Marketing Board was established in 1939 with the power:

to buy and sell and deal in any goods, wares, merchandise and natural products, or any of them whatsoever, either by wholesale or by retail, or both by wholesale and retail, and to act as a broker, factor or agent for any person in the acquisition or disposition of any goods, wares, merchandise or natural products, and for the purpose to do and transact all acts and things which a natural person engaged in a general mercantile business had the capacity or the power to transact.[34]

The Board was also given the sweeping power "to engage in any or all of the following businesses, namely manufacturing, producing, processing, handling or distributing of any goods, wares, merchandise or natural products," and in the process, "to acquire by purchase or otherwise any land or any other property required by the Provincial Board for the purpose of or incidental to any such business."

The Edmonton Chamber of Commerce warned ominously:

The full exercise of such powers will transform Alberta into a corporative state; the partial exercise without any safeguards which do not appear in the bill, will endanger democratic freedom and private enterprise, and discourage investment in all lines of industry.[35]

The frustration of the government's efforts to restore prosperity by monetary tinkering had led to a reawakening of its interest in the "just price" and the result was a piece of legislation which would have enabled a socialist government to nationalize and operate any industry it wished. Social Credit preferred to leave businesses under private ownership, but despite its later professions of total opposition to public ownership and regulation, it was prepared in the late thirties to consider a giant leap to the left, as the Marketing Act demonstrates. Government officials had at least toyed with the idea of establishing a complete enough control over industry to yield the funds needed to provide the chimerical social dividends that had proved so alluring to the electorate in 1935.

Alfred W. Farmilo, the secretary-treasurer of the Alberta Federation of Labour, recorded notes of a meeting in July 1937 with the powerful emissaries to Alberta of Major C. H. Douglas, the founder of Social Credit. Both G. F. Powell, and L. D. Byrne were interested in finding ways that the government could secure the funds to begin paying social dividends.

He [Powell] then said do you not think productive industry could be controlled in a manner similar to the pools and cooperatives.

We then discussed the possibility of the Province of [*sic*] setting up an institution similar to the Savings Department into which the flow of currency or money might be diverted through the control of industry. Powell looked over to Byrne, and asked if he had considered this phase and the answer was in the affirmative. It would therefore be as well to keep in mind that the treasury department may eventually be used along these lines.[36]

Byrne and Powell and some of the Social Credit MLAs, however, were devotees of Douglas and their views at any given time shifted as the views of the unstable founder of Social Credit shifted.[37] One can over-emphasize the extent to which the Social Credit government leaned towards interventionist solutions in its first term of office. Certainly, however, there were enough statements made and actions taken to justify the anxieties of the business community that an anti-capitalist government was in charge of Alberta's affairs.

Within the party at large, socialist and left-wing reformist views were certainly influential. Historians have over-stated the extent to which devotion to Aberhart and the simplistic lure of the twenty-five dollar social dividends attracted members to Social Credit.[38] An analysis of the resolutions of provincial conventions of the party, and of local Social Credit clubs indicates that party members sought reforms beyond simplistic monetary experiments promised by Aberhart; and municipal alliances with Communists and CCFers demonstrated the rank-and-file feeling that Social Credit's natural allies were the collectivist parties rather than the free-enterprise parties. State medicine, which would be viciously denounced by Social Credit from the mid-forties onwards, was part of the platform approved by the convention of the Social Credit League in 1935 that sanctioned the League's entry into the electoral arena.[39] Every convention from 1937 to 1940 reaffirmed the party's commitment to prepaid coverage of medical and hospital bills for all citizens. The 1938 convention, for example, resolved "that we request the Government to immediately formulate a scheme of state medicine and hospitalization and state insurance to cover time lost while sick."[40]

Provincial Social Credit conventions from 1937 to 1940 also called for free enterprise textbooks in Alberta schools, producers' marketing boards, the eight-hour day in industry, and direct and generous relief for single men on relief (as an alternative to soup kitchens and bed tickets for bunkhouses).[41] The 1940 convention also endorsed a resolution on war profiteering that paralleled CCF resolutions on the issue. The resolution said party members:

> are opposed to profiteering out of the sale of armaments and also opposed to profiteering out of the sale of foodstuffs, clothing and the necessities of life. Be it therefore resolved that conscription of capital and finance must precede any other form of conscription that the exigencies of war may make.[42]

Many local constituency groups went beyond the resolutions of the provincial conventions to call for government initiation and operation of

manufacturing firms to put the unemployed back to work and for government ownership of the petroleum and hydroelectric industries.[43] Such resolutions usually came from Social Credit clubs in the cities and in the mining
areas where Communist influence among Social Credit members was
pronounced. Communist influence led to the formation of a number of electoral united fronts at the municipal, provincial and federal levels from 1936
to 1939. The Communists, who had initially denounced the Social Credit
movement as "fascist,"[44] were aware that a considerable number of unemployed individuals who had joined Communist-led unemployed groups had
also joined the Social Credit party. It feared that strident denunciations of
Social Credit would alienate these individuals and ruin the party's long-term
chances of exposing Social Credit as a fraud and then recruiting Aberhart's
former supporters.[45]

Rank-and-file Social Crediters proved friendly to the Communist
embrace, though Aberhart did not. The Lethbridge constituency organization, dominated by the unemployed,[46] declined to nominate a joint federal
candidate with the Communists only after pressure from senior party officials.[47] The Crowsnest Pass Social Credit groups, which included many
miners, worked closely with the local Communists.[48] It was in the two major
cities, however, that close Communist-Social Credit links caused Aberhart
the greatest concern. In 1936, the Social Crediters of Edmonton agreed to
a Communist plan for a joint nomination of "progressive forces" in a city-
wide provincial by-election, and the candidate chosen by a joint Communist-
Social Credit meeting was Margaret Crang, a left-wing Labour alderman.
Crang was expelled from the Labour party and the CCF for accepting the
nomination and the CCF candidate polled enough votes to deprive her of
a victory.[49] But a united front of Communists and Social Crediters in the
municipal elections of 1936 convinced some Labourites that the progressive vote was being unnecessarily divided between two groups. They cooperated with the Social Credit-Communist alliance in Edmonton and Calgary
in municipal elections in 1937, but afterwards returned to their former go-
it-alone policy.[50] Communists, however, worked in front groups with Social
Crediters for another two years, and a Communist alderman, Patrick Leni-
han, was elected in Calgary in 1938 with Social Credit votes.[51] Orvis
Kennedy's election in a federal by-election in 1937 on the Social Credit ticket
resulted from a joint Social Credit-Communist campaign.[52]

Aberhart made clear to the Calgary Social Crediters that he opposed their
political alliances and their municipal platform. He wrote Ethel Baker,
secretary-treasurer of the Calgary provincial constituency association (Calgary and Edmonton both formed single constituencies with five seats each),
to register his disapproval of the platform which Social Credit had approved
in 1938 in conjunction with its Communist friends. The platform pledged,
for example, "to help and develop trade unionism in every way in the City
of Calgary." Commented Aberhart: "This is a pure labour plank to which

Social Credit could not wholly subscribe. The beliefs of trade unions are not altogether in harmony with the program of Social Credit." To the platform call for a "humanizing of relief rates and relief rules; clothing allowance to be increased," Aberhart retorted: "This will give the person who supports it very great difficulty in carrying it out."[53] The Calgary Social Crediters, however, ignored Aberhart's misgivings and stuck to this platform during the municipal election.[54]

The willingness of urban members of Social Credit to support policies that went beyond the official monetary panaceas that were the original *raison d'être* of the party demonstrates the fluid character of radical thought in Alberta. Many individuals had joined the Social Credit League because they regarded Aberhart as a champion of the underdog; but they remained open to influences that suggested monetary reform was insufficient to make the economic system work for the poor. As we saw earlier, some actions of the Aberhart government indicated that its members also recognized the need for other reforms if only because a constitutional straight-jacket inhibited them from making monetary adjustments.

Rural members of Social Credit, like their urban counterparts, supported non-monetary reforms and at times made alliances with socialists and Communists. As noted earlier, party conventions had supported producer-controlled marketing boards. Social Crediters were also behind the establishment of the Alberta's Farmers' Union (AFU), a rival to the United Farmers of Alberta. The AFU manifesto adopted by the founding convention in 1939 announced that the organization intended to:

> initiate a policy of direct action in the way of non-buying of machinery strike; and the non-delivery of grain strike . . . . In other words to adopt the same methods as the organized labourers, and withhold our production from the industrial set-up the way they withhold their services from the industrial concerns for whom they work, and a definite, direct way of protest against the lowering of their living standards.[55]

Such a stance reflected a far more militant posture than the UFA adopted. Many Social Credit farmers regarded the UFA as too cautious and objected to its leadership's continuous stream of anti-Social Credit rhetoric.[56] The AFU's early leadership included a large contingent of east Europeans and many of the early members were sympathetic to Communism as well as Social Credit.[57] Their views on the efficacy of militancy in obtaining results were reminiscent of the attitudes of the Communist-led Farmers' Unity League in the early thirties.

While Aberhart did not share rank-and-file willingness to unite Social Credit with other reformist elements, some Social Credit leaders viewed positively the possibilities of an alliance with the CCF. E.G. Hansell, the secretary of the federal Social Credit caucus, wrote Aberhart in March 1939, of the caucus's interest in including the CCF within a coalition for the upcoming federal election for which Social Credit had already made an alliance with W.D. Herridge's New Democracy movement.[58] The CCF, however, proved as unwilling as Aberhart to form such an alliance.

Indeed, the philosophical underpinnings of the CCF and Social Credit and even more so of the Communists and Social Credit were so different that alliances between them were, not surprisingly, short-lived. But the rank-and-file of Social Credit were generally unconcerned about philosophical differences between their party and socialist parties; they wanted unity against the "big shots" whom they believed were oppressing them and appeared little concerned about the discrepancies between socialist theory and Douglas's monetary reform ideas.

Party rivalries, in the end, as much as philosophical differences, prevented unity among the anti-establishment parties in Alberta. The Communists largely abandoned united-front politics when they proved unable to win significant support outside their own ranks for Canadian neutrality in World War II (a position they set aside when the Soviet Union was invaded in June 1941).[59] The CCF leadership meanwhile was dominated by provincial labour leaders who regarded Aberhart as hostile to unionism and wished to see him deposed.[60] Labour interestingly was as suspicious of the Social Credit regime as business — though the post-Aberhart period demonstrated that it was only labour that had legitimate long-term fears about Social Credit's aims.[61]

Labour's attack on the Aberhart movement however had always had contradictory threads. On the one hand, the leaders of the Alberta Federation of Labour charged that Aberhart's announced intention to control the banks and currency in the province had scared away investors[62] — a charge also made by organized business.[63] On the other hand, as leading members of the socialist CCF, the same labour leaders denounced Social Credit for not having nationalized the hydro-electric and petroleum industries,[64] hardly moves that would have endeared a government to investors. The labour leaders' main reason for opposing Social Credit, however, was fear that Social Credit's policy of establishing wages by government decree would destroy collective bargaining and trade unionism.[65] Aberhart had ignored the question of the role of trade unions in his discussions of wage-setting and thereby contributed to labour fears.[66]

His government did pass several pieces of legislation which labour had requested, most notably legislation establishing collective bargaining contracts as legal contracts.[67] But the premier, short-tempered with all opponents, proved particularly cantankerous to the labour leaders[68] who had been accustomed to friendly relations with the UFA administration from 1921 to 1935.[69]

Despite the labour leaders' close alliance with the CCF in the provincial election of 1940, Social Credit retained the loyalty of most workers and farmers who had turned against the old-line parties. As *People's Weekly,* the unofficial CCF organ, conceded, "the progressive voters of the province are remaining loyal to the government they elected in 1935."[70] The days when the left-wing parties and even the old-line parties could attack Social Credit as a small-c conservative party were still in the future.

Indeed, the old-line party supporters were sufficiently determined to overthrow Social Credit to unite in so-called "People's Leagues" that nominated a single anti-Social Credit candidate for each constituency. The unity on the right produced a close contest in the popular vote though Social Credit retained a comfortable majority of legislative seats.[71] The losers were not especially gracious. A year later the boards of trade of the two major cities were still condemning the Alberta administration as hostile to the private sector. The secretary of the Calgary Board of Trade wrote: "it is evident that the Government's interpretation of social credit is merely one of an autocratic state socialism."[72] The secretary of the Edmonton Board of Trade added uncharitably:

> You may wonder how such a Government was re-elected but you must take into account that we have a very large foreign population that will believe anything and is responsible for this result. Even a rudimentary knowledge of economics and monetary science will demonstrate the infeasibility of such fatuous policies.[73]

The premier's response was characteristically strident:

> It is unfortunate and yet not surprising that the organizations from whom the attacks originated have been consistently and bitterly opposed to any movement of social or economic reform. Dependent as they are, however, upon the good will of the banking institutions and subject to the undemocratic control of the present money system, their attitude is not unexpected.[74]

Fifteen years later, these organizations were among the most vocal supporters of the Social Credit government led by Ernest Manning, William Aberhart's protege and his successor as premier. The Edmonton Chamber of Commerce, for example, praised government policies in a submission to the Board of Industrial Relations in 1956:

> The prosperous condition of the province is, in large measure, due to the fact that the Government and the Boards of Government have supported free enterprise, and have followed the positive policy of the minimum of interference with business.[75]

Clearly, circumstances had changed. Social Credit had become the free enterprise party which Kennedy wrongly claims it had been all along. What had caused the change? Historians who have concentrated on Social Credit's monetary fixations have had little difficulty with this question. From their point of view, once the courts had ruled out the possibility of provincial tinkering with monetary policies, Social Credit was prevented from taking action in the one area where social credit doctrine proposed radical interference in the free market.[76] As we have seen, however, Alberta Social Crediters, including both rank-and-file and some leaders, had an eclectic approach to economic reform that did not limit them to seeking monetary changes. So, some explanation is required of why these people turned from reformers into reactionaries.

In part, the answer lies in a change in the character of the party from 1935 to 1943, the year when Aberhart died and was succeeded by Manning. In 1935, the party was a broadly-based and growing organization of about 30,000 members. Its membership peaked at almost 41,000 in 1937, but in 1942 it registered only 3,500 members. Membership was so low in 1943 that the Social Credit League decided against holding the annual convention and instead simply held a conference open to all League members.[77] In part, the League's loss of over 90 percent of its 1937 membership can be seen as a reflection of better economic times; just as the majority of the UFA's 38,000 members in 1921 had retreated from politics as prosperity returned,[78] many early Social Credit activists abandoned politics as their individual economic situations improved. But the slide in party membership had begun in 1938, when party membership dropped by half despite a continuation of Depression conditions.[79] That drop was partially the result of the disillusionment that set in when it became clear that the courts would not allow the provincial government to carry out its promised monetary reforms. It was also, no doubt, a reaction to the government's unwillingness to brook criticism from the Social Credit groups. Aberhart's letters in response to criticism from party groups were as tactless as his responses to criticisms from other sources. It is unlikely that members remained after being told by Aberhart:

> I am very surprised at anyone calling himself a social crediter who appears to be so far out of touch with what the government is doing or attempting to do that a letter like the one referred to should be written.[80]

Alberta's Social Credit League, as C.B. Macpherson has noted, gave unusual power to its leader, including the right to choose candidates (constituencies drew up a list of five names, from which Aberhart and a handpicked board chose a candidate). Although the Social Credit clubs and constituency organizations as well as provincial conventions made constant attempts to influence government policy, Aberhart proved aloof from the organizations whose existence had been spawned by his rhetoric. Increasingly, what had been a broadly-based secular reformist party became the political home of the Douglas dogmatists and of fundamentalist Christians who supported Social Credit less because of specific policies than because of the party's leadership by radio evangelists, that is Aberhart and Manning.[81] With the purge of the evangelical Douglasites in the late forties because of their professed anti-Semitism,[82] Manning's control of the party and government was unchallenged.

When Manning took over the party and government, the party was no longer a mass party and Manning reasoned shrewdly that the government could be re-elected by stressing its good administrative record rather than by embarking on a new anti-establishment course that would rekindle the initial populist spark that had put the party in office. Profoundly conservative himself, Manning was, like his predecessor, a religious man whose entry into politics had not altered his fundamental otherworldliness.[83] He assumed not only Aberhart's premiership but also his weekly Bible hour and continued to do the Bible show for many years after he had resigned as premier. Manning had never been part of the Social Credit alliances with socialist groups, and he took a hard-line stance against socialism, equating all forms of socialism with German "national socialism."[84] The CCF had become the major opposition political force in the province during the war,[85] and Manning was prepared to pull all stops to beat back the socialist challenge.

The business community, once so repelled by Social Credit, embraced the Manning administration as the only alternative to the CCF, and Manning proved willing to welcome successful businessmen into a party which previously had largely been the domain of plebeian elements. The Licensing and Marketing legislation, while it remained on the books, became a dead letter.

Left-wing resolutions still occasionally made it to the floor of provincial Social Credit conventions. So, for example, the 1951 convention debated resolutions in favour of state medicine (which had formed part of party policy at least until 1940), an increase in old-age pensions, state automobile insurance, state ownership of hydroelectric utilities, provincial subsidies to cooperative building associations, and the establishment of old-age homes by the province in each constituency. Significantly, all of these resolutions were defeated, some without even coming to a vote.[86]

Indeed, Social Credit conventions, once the scene of endless speeches denouncing bankers and profiteers, now became the scene of endless speeches extolling the free enterprise system and denouncing socialism of every description. Prosperity, Ernest Manning, and the growing political apathy which had induced most of the early Social Crediters to leave the party even before Manning's accession to power, had produced a spectacular political transformation. Social Credit, a monetary-reform party, which had attracted to its ranks workers and farmers who held a variety of reformist views, had become a party beloved of the financial establishment with which it had once tangled. The determination of the first Aberhart government to establish state control over the cost of living had given way to a solemn rejection of interference in the marketplace so thorough that the party rewrote its history to make it appear that it had always stood for rigid free-enterprise principles.

NOTES

1. *Edmonton Journal,* 9 June 1982, p. 1.
2. The lack of young faces became a constant theme of Social Credit conventions after the war. The conventions proposed programmes to stimulate youth interest in the party but in vain. Ernest Manning to Mrs. Marion Krough, 5 December 1947, Premiers' papers, Provincial Archives of Alberta, File 1461; "Resolutions of the Seventeenth Annual Convention of the Alberta Social Credit League, 1951," Premiers' papers, Files 183 and 1846 B.
3. This view is expressed, for example, in C.B. Macpherson's classic history of the origins of Social Credit in Alberta, *Democracy in Alberta: Social Credit and the Party System* (Toronto: University of Toronto Press, 1962). Macpherson concentrates on the social credit monetary doctrines, the conspiratorial theories of Major Douglas, the Social Credit founder, and the authoritarian aspects of both social credit theory and Aberhart's practice. He ignores Social Credit government interventions in non-monetary fields and fails to analyze party demands for bolder programmes of intervention. Macpherson's analysis is unchallenged in more recent accounts such as Walter Young, *Democracy and Discontent: Progressivism, Socialism and Social Credit in the Canadian West* (Toronto: McGraw-Hill, 1978), 83-108. One recent article that raises the question of Aberhart's vaunted conservatism is David Elliott, "William Aberhart: Right or Left?," in *The Dirty Thirties in Prairie Canada: 11th Western Canada Studies Conference,* eds. D. Francis and H. Ganzevoort (Vancouver: Tantalus Research, 1980), 11-31. But Elliott deals only briefly with the Social Credit administration and not at all with the Social Credit organization. His view that fascism and socialism are similar ideologies (both are allegedly authoritarian) creates some imprecisions in the article.
4. Ben Swankey, "Reflections of a Communist; 1935 Election," *Alberta History* 28, no. 4 (Autumn 1980): 36. Swankey notes with reference to the late thirties:
    It was in this period that close relationships were established between the Communist Party and sections of the Social Credit movement including its MLAs which included, for example, Communist support for the election of Orvis Kennedy in an Edmonton by-election in March, 1938, where the victory parade following the election included Leslie Morris, western director of the Communist Party, in its front ranks.
5. The major account of the constitutional battles regarding the Alberta government's schemes to control finance is J.R. Mallory, *Social Credit and the Federal Power in Canada* (Toronto: University of Toronto Press, 1954).
6. Premiers' papers, File 1124.
7. Macpherson, *Democracy in Alberta,* 147.
8. Young, *Democracy and Discontent,* 88-89; Macpherson, *Democracy in Alberta,* 149-50.

9. Typical of Aberhart's responses to suggestions for changes in government policy is this reply to the provincial secretary of the Alberta Motor Association who forwarded to the premier the organization's resolution that revenues from gasoline taxes and motor licences be earmarked for highway construction and maintenance.

> We have answered this type of resolution so many times that it seems to us we are wasting our time and paper in replying further to them. We do not believe that the Calgary Branch of the Alberta Motor Association has any right to direct this Government in what it shall do with its unexpended revenue.

Aberhart to S. W. Cameron, 2 March 1942. Premiers' papers, File 1221 B.
10. Elliott. "William Aberhart," 12.
11. Alvin Finkel, "Populism and the Proletariat: Social Credit and the Alberta Working Class," *Studies in Political Economy* 13 (Spring 1984): 118-20.
12. William Aberhart, *Social Credit Manual: Social Credit as Applied to the Province of Alberta* c. 1935, p. 5.
13. Ibid., p. 7.
14. Ibid., pp. 21, 41-43.
15. Ibid., p. 55.
16. Ibid., p. 62.
17. Ibid., p. 13. Aberhart wrote somewhat incoherently: "At the present time this great wealth (machinery and natural resources) is being selfishly manipulated and controlled by one or more men known as the "Fifty Big Shots of Canada."
18. *Social Credit Chronicle*, 21 September 1934, p. 2.
19. J.H. Hanna to John Mackay, secretary, Drumheller Board of Trade, 27 May 1935, Calgary Board of Trade papers, Glenbow-Alberta Institute (hereafter CBT, GAI), Box 2, File 13.
20. The *Edmonton Bulletin,* which had supported the Liberals in the election, complained afterwards that the Economic Safety League campaign proved counterproductive for the anti-Aberhart forces.

> Its grotesque campaign methods and lavish expenditures gave credence to this campaign (whispering campaign against the League) as its radio and publicity material was considered of the most reactionary kind, while the fact that its membership was anonymous, as was the source of its funds, gave Mr. Aberhart and his followers a priceless opportunity to point to it as being a glaring example of financial control from the East.

Edmonton Bulletin, 26 August 1935, p. 3.
21. J.H. Hanna to E.C. Gilliatt, managing secretary, Winnipeg Board of Trade, 12 September 1935, CBT, GAI, Box 2, File 13.
22. John Mackay, secretary, Drumheller Board of Trade, to Hanna, 3 May 1935; Stettler Board of Trade to Calgary Board of Trade, 12 August 1935; Medicine Hat Chamber of Commerce to Calgary Board of Trade, 9 August 1935: CBT, GAI, Box 2, File 13.
23. P.J. Carroll to Hanna, 10 August 1935, CBT, GAI, Box 2, File 13.
24. Young, *Democracy and Discontent,* 98.
25. Alvin Finkel, "Social Credit and the Unemployed," *Alberta History* 31, no. 2 (Spring 1983): 24-32.

26. "Report of Legislative Committee to the Council of the Board of Trade," 15 April 1936, CBT, GAI, Box 1, File 1.

27. "An Act for the Establishment of a Department of Trade and Industry and to Prescribe its Powers and Duties" (Assented to 16 April 1934), *Statutes of the Province of Alberta,* 1934, Chapter 33.

28. Among the organizations supporting codes, the Alberta branch of the Retail Merchants' Association was prominent. Premiers' papers, File 921A; the large chain stores opposed the legislation: P.W. Abbott, legal representative of "T. Eaton Company and several others of the larger retail establishments in Edmonton" to Aberhart, Premiers' papers, File 921A.

29. "An Act to Amend and Consolidate the Licensing of Trades and Business Act" (Assented to 5 October 1937), *Statutes of the Province of Alberta,* 1937, Third Session, Chapter One.

30. Among the boards whose opposition to the bill is recorded in the Premiers' papers are the boards in Edmonton, Calgary, Red Deer, Medicine Hat, High River, and Lacombe. Premiers' papers, File 922; F. Ashenhurst, secretary, Alberta Branch, Canadian Manufacturers' Association, to Aberhart, 29 September 1937, Premiers' papers, File 922.

31. CBT, GAI, Box 1, File 5.

32. H.J. Nolan, lawyer with Bennett, Hannah, Nolan, Chambers and Might to L.A. Cavanaugh (the automobile dealer), 8 November 1938, CBT, GAI, Box 1, File 7.

33. *Calgary Albertan,* 9 September 1939, p. 1; Hanna to W.L. Mackenzie King, 13 January 1938, CBT, GAI, Box 1, File 7.

34. "An Act Respecting the Marketing of Natural Products and other Commodities and to Provide for the Regulations Thereof Within the Province," *Statutes of the Province of Alberta,* 1939, Chapter 3.

35. Ibid.

36. "A meeting with Messrs. Glen L. MacLachlan, Powell, Byrne, July 9, 1937," Alfred Farmilo papers, Provincial Archives of Alberta, Box 1, Item 44.

37. Macpherson, *Democracy in Alberta,* 193.

38. Ibid., 162, for example, claims: "The social credit political theory and the inspirational quality of Aberhart's leadership, which demanded and received the complete submergence of his followers' wills, combined to put any problem of the popular control of the legislature out of sight, or at least in abeyance."

39. *Edmonton Journal,* 5 April 1935, p. 1.

40. Premiers' papers, File 1105.

41. Ibid., Files 1105, 1106, 1117B.

42. Ibid., File 1117B.

43. Ibid., Files 1068A, 1119, 1128.

44. *Edmonton Journal,* 27 March 1935. p. 14.

45. The Communist change of heart regarding Social Credit was expressed in various issues of the *Western Clarion,* a Communist party organ, during 1936 and 1937.

46. Herbert Clark, secretary-treasurer of Lethbridge (provincial) constituency organization, to Aberhart, 2 May 1938, Premiers' papers, File 1125B.

47. A.E. Smith, chairman, Lethbridge federal constituency, to William Aberhart, 22 April 1939; Aberhart to Smith, 28 April 1939; Smith to Aberhart, 29 April 1939, Premiers' papers, File 1055.

48. W.B. McDowall, president, Castle River Social Credit zone, to Aberhart, 1 May 1938, Premiers' papers, File 1109. McDowall enclosed a resolution passed at a mass meeting called by Social Credit "in deference to the wishes of a number of our supporters who are not or only a few of them members of the group" and who "have a leaning towards communism ever since they belonged to that party when miners." The meeting was addressed by two Social Credit MLAs and the socialist mayor of Blairmore. The resolution said in part:

> The meeting feels very strongly now that our common enemy has been brought out into open view and the battle joined that all progressives should close their ranks in a united front. It would be suicidal at this time to allow differences of opinion to the best final solution to divide them.

49. *People's Weekly,* 13 June 1936, p. 4; and 27 June 1936, p. 1.
50. Finkel, "Populism and the Proletariat," 125.
51. *People's Weekly,* 26 November 1938, p. 1.
52. See footnote 4. The cooperation with the Communists later proved embarrassing to a militantly anti-Communist Manning government. Elmer Roper notes, that as CCF leader in the legislature, he retorted to Manning's charges of Communist sympathies in the CCF by showing the legislature the photograph of Communist leader Leslie Morris on the running board of the Social Credit victory vehicle alongside the victorious Kennedy. Finkel interview with Elmer Roper, Victoria, 21 February 1984.
53. Ethel Baker to Aberhart, 4 October 1938; Aberhart to Baker, 7 October 1938, Premiers' papers, File 1115.
54. *People's Weekly,* 26 November 1938, p. 1.
55. In H.E. Nichols papers, Glenbow-Alberta Institute, Box 7, File 42.
56. *People's Weekly,* 5 October 1946, p. 1.
57. Nichols papers, Box 4, File 28.
58. E.G. Hansell to Aberhart, 17 March 1939, Premiers' papers, File 1055.
59. Ivan Avakumovic, *The Communist Party in Canada: A History* (Toronto: McClelland and Stewart, 1975), 139-40.
60. Fred White, president of the Alberta Federation of Labour, had been a Labour MLA from 1921 to 1935, representing Calgary. Defeated by Social Credit in 1935, he ran again unsuccessfully in the 1940 provincial election under the CCF banner. *Canadian Parliamentary Guide.* Aberhart and the union leaders were on poor terms. Responding to a letter from a United Mine Workers' local protesting the premier's dismissive treatment of an Alberta Federation of Labour delegation, Aberhart wrote in part:

> I was rather surprised to hear that the leaders of the Alberta Federation of Labour have evidently decided to make a political instrument out of the Federation.
>
> Ever since the Government came into office it has given the greatest consideration to the resolutions of your Federation, notwithstanding the fact that Mr. White and Mr. Berg have been bitter political opponents of our policies . . . .
>
> Now it would appear that these same leaders, who were treated so courteously by us, are now sending out circular letters to try to stir up the members of the Federation in a political way. Surely it should be understood that no Government can be expected to meet with or discuss its policies with any

other political party. I should therefore suggest that since your Federation has not entered the political field and since it can in no way be considered a political party this course of action by your leaders in attempting to infuse political flavor into your Federation should be resented by you.

Aberhart to A. Orlando, secretary, Cambrian Local Union #7330, District 18, United Mine Workers of America, Wayne, Alberta, 3 March 1939, Premiers' papers, File 1227.

61. On Social Credit-labour relations in the post-war period, see Warren Caragata, *Alberta Labour: A Heritage Untold* (Toronto: Lorimer. 1979), 140-42.

62. AFL executive members Carl Berg and Alfred W. Farmilo are quoted to this effect in the *Edmonton Journal,* 31 May 1935, p. 17.

63. *Calgary Herald,* 8 August 1935, p. 1; *Edmonton Journal,* 8 August 1935, p. 1.

64. *People's Weekly,* 10 February 1940, p. 5.

65. Carl Berg made this charge publicly — *Edmonton Bulletin*, 8 August 1935, p. 1. Farmilo expressed this view in his outline of a meeting between labour leaders and government officials. "A meeting with Messrs. Glen L. MacLachlan, Powell, Byrne, July 9, 1937," Alfred Farmilo papers, Provincial Archives of Alberta, Item 44.

66. The *Social Credit Manual* (1935), pp. 41-43, asked "How can just wages be fixed?" and answered:

Just wages are fixed today by the Minimum Wage Act. Experts would fix the minimum and maximum wage just as they could fix the price of goods. It is understood, however, that wages must not be reduced on account of the issuance of the basic dividends.

67. Labour's gratitude for this legislation was expressed at the Alberta Federation of Labour annual convention in 1938. "Proceedings of the 22nd Convention of the Alberta Federation of Labour, November 28-30, 1938," Farmilo papers.

68. See footnote 60.

69. A Labour party member, Alexander Ross, was a Cabinet minister in the first UFA administration. On relations between Labour and the UFA, see Finkel, "Populism and the Proletariat," 117-19.

70. *People's Weekly,* 30 March 1940, p. 7.

71. The best account of the 1940 provincial campaign is Harold J. Schultz, "A Second Term: 1940," *Alberta Historical Review* 10, no. 1 (Winter 1962): 17-26.

72. T.E.D. McGreen to Auckland Chamber of Commerce (as reported in an unidentified newspaper and sent to Aberhart, 16 July 1941), Premiers' papers, File 1089.

73. J. Blue to Auckland Chamber of Commerce, Premiers' papers, File 1089.

74. No date, Premiers' papers, File 1089.

75. "Edmonton Chamber of Commerce submission to the chairman and members of the Board of Industrial Relations for the Province of Alberta," 11 January 1956, Alberta Liberal Association papers, Glenbow-Alberta Institute, Box 35, File 174.

76. Macpherson, *Democracy in Alberta,* 206.

77. Premiers' papers, Files 1117A, 1124, 1129.

78. Macpherson, *Democracy in Alberta,* 64.

79. Premiers' papers, File 1124.

80. Aberhart to William Holowaychuk, secretary-treasurer, Paulus Social Credit

group, Chipman, Alberta, 16 December 1938, Premiers' papers, File 1128. Petulant letters of this kind abound in Aberhart's correspondence as premier.

81. For an analysis of the latter-day Social Credit party, see Owen Anderson, "The Alberta Social Credit Party: An Empirical Analysis of Membership, Characteristics, Participation and Opinion" (unpublished Ph.D. dissertation, University of Alberta, 1972).

82. Macpherson, *Democracy in Alberta,* 211-12.

83. As one commentator observed after interviewing Manning, the Alberta premier's strong opposition to socialist philosophy rested on religious doctrine. Socialism to Manning "deemphasizes the individual struggle for salvation" and the attainment of grace by placing responsibility for the individual on the shoulders of the state rather than the individual himself. Social benefits such as medicare and guaranteed incomes breed idleness and permit "the evil tendencies of the individual to come to the fore, thereby causing a breakdown of his relationship with God." Dennis Groh, "The Political Thought of Ernest Manning" (unpublished M.A. thesis, University of Calgary, 1970), p. 65.

84. For example, Manning wrote to one correspondent in 1944:

    . . . it is an insult to suggest to the Canadian people who are sacrificing their sons to remove the curse which the socialism of Germany has brought on the world that their own social and economic security can be attained only by introducing some form of socialism in Canada. The premise embodied in your proposed resolution, namely, that there is such a thing as democratic Socialism, contradicts itself in that it attempts to associate together two concepts of life which are diametrically opposed and opposite.

    Manning to J.B. Hayfield, Bittern Lake, Alberta, 3 February 1944, Premiers' papers, File 1242.

85. CCF membership of twelve thousand in 1944 in the province exceeded Social Credit membership by four thousand, Alberta CCF provincial office to Margaret Telford, CCF national office, 4 November 1944, Alberta CCF papers, Glenbow-Alberta Institute, Box 5, File 42. The CCF received 25 percent of the provincial vote in 1944, almost double the vote of the third-place Independents. *Canadian Parliamentary Guide,* 1945, pp. 381-82.

86. Premiers' papers. Files 1843 and 1846B.

XIV

THE MODERN WEST:
POLITICS AND ECONOMICS

The discovery of oil at Leduc, Alberta in 1947 is often seen symbolically as the beginning of the modern west. Oil and natural gas development in Alberta and mineral development in Saskatchewan and Manitoba contributed to both economic and social change. They have made possible affluence undreamed of by the generation that had experienced the Depression.

Resource development, mechanization in agriculture, and improved transportation contributed to another important change—urbanization. The urban population of each of the provinces increased dramatically in the postwar era. By the mid-1970s, the urban population was 70% in Manitoba, 55% in Saskatchewan, and 75% in Alberta. The image of the western interior as a rural hinterland was clearly outdated. The swiftly changing skylines of rapidly growing cities (particularly in Alberta) had their counterparts in the less visible realm of social structures and values, which have also undergone tremendous alterations since the Second World War.

During the late 1950s and early 1960s, westerners tired of experimenting with third parties. Inspired by the vision of John Diefenbaker, many began to see the national Progressive Conservative party as a new vehicle for regional protest. In Saskatchewan and Manitoba the CCF remained a viable force but only by transforming itself from a protest party into a broadly based party, the NDP. In Alberta, Social Credit has disappeared as social and economic change eroded the underlying conditions which had given it life.

Politically, each province continued to go its own way at the provincial level; but on the national level they all shared, for most of the postwar era, a common rejection of the national Liberal party (which remained in power at the federal level during most of the period). The Liberal party was widely seen as being tied to the interests of Ontario and Quebec and insensitive to western interests.

Many westerners continue to feel resentful that given the numerical dominance of Quebec and Ontario in the game of national politics, the deck seems stacked unfairly against them before the play even begins. And yet given the dependence of the west on international markets and transportation, many of the major decisions affecting the prairie economy are made in Ottawa. The lack of political power at the national level leaves many westerners feeling powerless and frustrated. In "Political Discontent in the Prairie West: Patterns of Continuity and Change," political scientist Roger Gibbins discusses the nature of western alienation during the 1980s. His discussion focuses primarily on Alberta, where western alienation has been strongest since the 1920s, where various separatist movements have emerged in the late 1970s and early 1980s, and where in the late 1980s and early 1990s a new populist movement, the Reform Party of Canada, developed its greatest strength. Gibbins looks at western alienation as a political ideology of regional discontent, and touches on the facts of economic dependency and the resultant boom-bust economy which has contributed to alienation.

How justified are the economic grievances of the west? To what extent do the grievances stem from an unfair application of national economic policies, and to what extent do they reflect the inevitable concerns of residents of small, resource-based regional economies? In his article, "A Regional Economic Overview of the West Since 1945," economist Ken Norrie writes in support of the latter interpretation. He argues that the economic characteristics of the region largely explain both its economic structure as of 1971, and the nature of the economic adjustment to the terms of trade after that date. The existence of large public sector resource revenues provides a degree of uniqueness to the experience, in that they were used to promote a series of province-building measures.

Whatever the validity of Norrie's arguments, there can be no question that political alienation remains an important fact of life in the western interior. To what extent will changing party fortunes at the national level increase or decrease alienation? To what extent could western alienation be overcome through new institutional arrangements federally—such as the introduction of an elected senate that would give a much greater voice to the west?

SELECTED BIBLIOGRAPHY

For a stimulating overview of political, economic, and social change in the prairie provinces in the post-World War II era which compares the "old" west of the wheat economy with the "new" west of resource development, see Roger Gibbins, *Prairie Politics and Society: Regionalism in Decline* (Toronto, 1980). For an overview of changes in the prairie political culture see J.F. Conway, *The West: The History of a Region in Confederation*

(Toronto, 1983). There are valuable essays in A.W. Rasporich, ed., *The Making of the Modern West: Western Canada Since 1945* (Calgary, 1984). For a discussion of resource development and "province building" in Alberta and Saskatchewan, see John Richards and Larry Pratt, *Prairie Capitalism: Power and Influence in the New West* (Toronto, 1979). For an analysis of the decline of the Liberal Party in western Canada see David Smith, *The Regional Decline of a National Party: Liberals on the Prairies* (Toronto, 1981). For a good overview of Saskatchewan in the post-world War II era see the relevant sections of John Archer's *Saskatchewan: A History* (Saskatoon, 1980), and the articles in N. Ward and D. Spafford, eds., *Politics in Saskatchewan* (Don Mills, 1968). For a recent look at Saskatchewan politics, see James Pitsula and Ken Rasmussen, *Privatizing a Province: The New Right in Saskatchewan* (Vancouver, 1990). Dennis Gruending has completed a biography of Saskatchewan premier Allan Blakeney entitled *Promises to Keep: A Political Biography of Allan Blakeney* (Saskatoon, 1990).

For an economic analysis of the impact of oil wealth on the Alberta economy in the 1970s and of the Alberta Heritage Savings and Trust Fund see the special issue of *Canadian Public Policy* 6 (1980): 141-280. For a popular account of the impact of oil on Alberta and on federal-provincial relations see Peter Foster, *The Blue Eyed Sheiks, The Canadian Oil Establishment* (Toronto, 1979). Carlo Caldarola, ed., *Society and Politics in Alberta: Research Papers* (Toronto, 1979) is a useful collection of articles on Alberta politics. For an analysis of social and political change in Alberta during the 1970s and 1980s see the relevant sections of Howard Palmer with Tamara Palmer, *Alberta: A New History* (Edmonton, 1990). On the Alberta economy, consult R.L. Mansell and Michael Percy, *Strength in Adversity: A Study of the Alberta Economy* (Edmonton, 1990). On the oil industry, the NEP, and Ottawa-Alberta conflict, Peter Foster's, *The Sorcerer's Apprentices: Canada's Super-Bureaucrats and the Energy Mess* (Toronto, 1982) and G. Bruce Doern and Glen Toner, *The Politics of Energy: The Development and Implementation of the NEP* (Toronto, 1985) are helpful.

Larry Pratt and Garth Stevenson, eds., *Western Separatism: The Myths, Realities and Dangers* (Edmonton, 1981) contains a series of articles on alienation in Alberta. On the provincial election of 1986 and shifting trends in Alberta politics, see Allan Tupper, "New Dimensions of Alberta Politics," *Queen's Quarterly* 93 (1986): 780-791. On Alberta political culture and the NDP in Alberta, Larry Pratt, ed., *Socialism and Democracy in Alberta* (Edmonton,1986) should be consulted. Forthcoming is *Government and Politics in Alberta*, edited by Allan Tupper and Roger Gibbins (Edmonton, 1992).

On political change in Manitoba see J. Wilson, "The Decline of the Liberals in Manitoba Politics," *Journal of Canadian Studies* 10, 1 (February, 1975): 21-41; Tom Peterson, "Manitoba: Ethnic and Class Politics in Manitoba" in M. Robin, ed., *Canadian Provincial Politics* (Scarborough,

1972). Russell Doern's, *Wednesdays are Cabinet Days: A Personal Account of the Schreyer Administration* (Winnipeg, 1981), and James A. McAllister's *The Government of Edward Schreyer, Democratic Socialism in Manitoba* (Kingston, 1984) assess an important phase in Manitoba politics. For analytical essays on the political economy of Manitoba see Jim Silver and Jeremy Hull, eds., *The Political Economy of Manitoba* (Regina, 1990).

On the Meech Lake Accord and the west, consult Roger Gibbins, with Howard Palmer, Brian Rusted, and David Taras, *Meech Lake and Canada: Perspectives from The West* (Edmonton, 1988). On Alberta and senate reform, Roger Gibbins's "Senate Reform: Always the Bridesmaid, Never the Bride," in Ronald Watts and Douglas Brown, eds., *Canada: The State of the Federation 1989* (Kingston, 1989), pp. 194-210 is very helpful.

For developments in aboriginal western Canada since 1945, see Donald B. Smith, "The Original Peoples of Alberta," in *Peoples of Alberta,* edited by Howard and Tamara Palmer (Saskatoon, 1985), pp. 50-83, 476-86; and J.R. Miller, *Skyscrapers Hide the Heavens: A History of Indian-White Relations in Canada* (Toronto, 1989, revised ed., 1991). The Metis experience is reviewed by Murray J. Dobbin in "The Metis in Western Canada since 1945," in *The Making of the Modern West: Western Canada Since 1945,* edited by A.W. Rasporich (Calgary, 1984), pp. 183-93.

32 Political Discontent in the Prairie West
Patterns of Continuity and Change

The 1980s have proved to be very tumultuous times on the western Canadian political stage. The decade was ushered in by the 1980 general election, in which the federal Liberal party won a national majority while being all but shut out of western Canada, capturing only two seats in Manitoba and none further west. The Liberals defeated Joe Clark's short-lived Conservative government, which had not only enjoyed strong support from the west, capturing 74 per cent of the region's seats in 1979, but was led by the first prime minister to be born in the west. The election was followed nine months later by the National Energy Program, which touched off protracted intergovernmental conflict between Ottawa on the one hand and the provincial governments of Alberta and, to a lesser extent, Saskatchewan and British Columbia on the other.

The energy conflict coincided with nearly two years of intense and often abrasive constitutional negotiations set in motion by the 1980 Quebec referendum on sovereignty association and culminating in the proclamation of the Constitution Act on 17 April 1982. The early 1980s also witnessed a precipitous decline in the western Canadian oil and natural gas industries and the spread of recession across a regional economy that a few years earlier had been the most buoyant in the country, the "growth pole" of the national economy. Not surprisingly, then, it was during the early 1980s that western alienation came to a boil and that, for the first time, vociferous separatist parties commanding significant levels of support emerged in the prairie west.[1]

Then, in 1984, the political climate changed dramatically with the landslide election of the progressive Conservatives led by Brian Mulroney. For the first time in two decades, apart from the brief tenure of the Clark government, the west was on the winning side of a national election, with 58 western MPs on the government side of the House and strong regional representation in the federal cabinet. The 1984 election was followed shortly by the Western Energy Accord, which at least temporarily brought an end to the protracted energy dispute between Ottawa and the provincial governments, and in more general terms by a marked improvement in the tone and civility of intergovernmental relations. Western alienation waned while separatist parties fell into internal disarray and were all but driven from the political stage. In Alberta, the west's preeminent regional warrior, Peter Lougheed, retired from political life, and in the wake of his retirement opposition parties finally succeeded in cracking the Progressive Conservatives' recent monolithic grip on provincial political life.[2]

The fact that Alberta has now emerged as the Liberals' bastion in western Canada drives home the extent and rapidity of political change during the 1980s. The rapidity of change, however, should not obscure underlying patterns of continuity in western Canadian political life. The objective of this paper is to place the events of the 1980s in perspective by looking at such patterns of continuity in western Canada and, more specifically in the prairie west since the turn of the century.[3] My thesis is that despite quite dramatic changes in the political landscape that centre on the 1921, 1958, and 1984 federal elections, there has been an underlying pattern of regional discontent that has not dissipated and will continue to shape political life in the prairie west. The continuity of regional discontent springs from the west's inability to escape the bonds of economic dependency. This underlying and at times overarching economic dependency has fashioned a distinctive regional orientation to political life, commonly referred to as western alienation.

WESTERN ALIENATION

Western alienation has become an important if ill-defined component of the Canadian political vocabulary.[4] Elsewhere I have described western alienation as "best seen as a political ideology of regional discontent . . . [encompassing] a sense of political, economic, and, to a lesser extent, cultural estrangement from the Canadian heartland. [It expresses] the interlocking themes that western Canada is always outgunned in national politics and *that as a consequence* has been subjected to varying degrees of economic exploitation by central Canada."[5] However, in discussing alienation it is useful to distinguish among three quite different targets: political authorities, the political regime, and the political community.[6]

In a broad sense, *political authorities* are those individuals and parties who hold power at any particular point in time — for example, Pierre Trudeau and the federal Liberal party during the early 1980s. Not surprisingly, political authorities have provided the principal target for prairie discontent, as western Canadians have given their votes to both national and

regional opposition parties in an attempt to dislodge incumbent governments. The fidelity of prairie voters to the Progressive Conservative party
through two decades of Liberal national dominance stretching from 1963
to 1984 can be seen in this light. More dramatically, western Canadians have
fashioned a variety of regionally based protest parties, which have emerged
in opposition not only to particular federal parties but to the party system
more broadly defined, a system that in the past at least was seen to be stacked
against the regional interests of western Canada. Examples here include the
Progressive party of the early 1920s, Alberta support for federal Social Credit
candidates, and, to a lesser extent, support in Saskatchewan and Manitoba
for the Co-operative Commonwealth Federation. However, while such parties have at times enjoyed considerable regional success, they have not been
successful in wresting national power from the Liberal and Progressive Conservative parties.

The *political regime* refers to the rules of the game — the institutions,
constitutional norms, and traditional mores than govern political life within
a country. The political regime in Canada would thus encompass our
parliamentary system, the federal division of powers, the conventions of
responsible government, and traditions of strong party discipline and executive dominance. Over the past century western Canadians have mounted
a sporadic, inconsistent, but nevertheless often intense attack upon the political regime. Included in this attack have been efforts to decrease the role of
partisanship and to strengthen the role of private members within the House
of Commons, to reform the Senate, to devolve greater constitutional powers
to provincial governments, and to change the electoral system in order to
prevent western Canadians from being shut out of the national government,
as was virtually the case through the 1970s and early 1980s. The most recent
attempt in this long and, in the final analysis, unsuccessful assault on the
political regime came during the constitutional negotiations of the early
1980s, when the lack of regional consensus precluded any significant institutional reform.[7]

The term *political community* refers more generally to those people who
live within a politically defined territory and who share a distinctive set of
political institutions. While authorities are the most transitory component
of the political system, it is the political community that provides the essential foundation upon which the regime infrastructure is constructed. Unlike
the nationalist movement in Quebec, western alienation has only rarely
extended to a rejection of the political community. Western alienation springs
from the continued frustration of a regional community that seeks not
independence but rather more complete integration into the Canadian political, economic, and cultural mainstreams. At least through western Canadian eyes, it is the frustration of outsiders wanting in rather than, as in the
case of Quebec, insiders wanting out. Thus we find empirical evidence that,
within the same individuals, regional discontent can coexist quite easily with

continued allegiance to and a strong emotional bond with the national community.[8]

In recognizing that western alienation can be chanelled towards quite different targets, we should also recognize that such discontent is not fed from a single stream. The litany of western discontent is extensive in the extreme and embraces a complex and interwoven set of political, economic, and cultural grievances. Certainly there is not the space, nor probably the need, to repeat that litany here. There is, however, one factor that stands apart from the rest in both its centrality and its continued importance over time. It is the dependency of the regional economy on external market forces beyond the control of western Canadians or their provincial governments that provides the essential grit at the heart of the western alienation pearl.

ECONOMIC DEPENDENCY

From a political perspective, the outstanding characteristic of the western Canadian economy has been its dependency on external markets for agricultural products and natural resources found beneath the soil.[9] To paint with a very broad brush indeed, a staples economy has been created in the west which, due to the region's rather sparse population, is dependent upon external markets usually found outside Canada. This dependency has in turn been associated with economic instability. When the demand for western Canadian products has been strong and the prices high, the region has prospered; when demand has faltered and prices have fallen, the region has suffered.

In many respects, of course, the western Canadian situation is similar to that of the Canadian economy more broadly considered. Certainly that larger economy has also been very dependent upon external markets. However, the national economy is more diversified, enjoys a proportionately larger domestic market, is less dependent upon a transcontinental transportation system, and is placed less at risk by the vagaries of the Canadian climate. As a consequence, market-induced swings in the regional economy tend to be more pronounced, and thus have a greater political impact than do such swings in the national economy.

Dependency on unstable foreign markets was most pronounced during the first three decades of this century, the heyday of the grain economy, and had catastrophic consequences with the onset of the Great Depression. This was a time when over 50 per cent of the prairie labour force was engaged in agriculture and when the production of a single crop — wheat — dominated the grain economy.[10] The result was a roller-coaster, boom-and-bust economy that destabilized the political system, producing both the Progressive revolt of 1921 and the political turmoil of the mid-thirties.

Although the prairie economy today is much more diversified than it was in the past — less reliant upon the agricultural sector and, within that sector, less reliant upon a single crop — the pattern of dependency still persists. The growing agricultural price war between the United States and the European Economic Community over agricultural subsidies, weakening export demand for Canadian agricultural products, and increased international competition from other agricultural producers all pose major threats to western Canadian producers and to the regional economy more broadly defined.

The dependency of the west has been most dramatically illustrated by the history of Alberta over the past fifteen years. In the early 1970s OPEC-led increases in the price of oil touched off a dramatic economic boom in the province. Individual Canadians and corporate capital poured into Alberta in pursuit of a rapidly expanding natural-resource pie. While growth was most explosive in Calgary and Edmonton, it was also felt across the province and indeed across the region as world markets improved for a wide range of western Canadian natural resources, including coal, natural gas, potash, and uranium. Then in the early 1980s softening natural-resource export markets, coupled with the impact of the National Energy Program, led to a crippling recession. By the thousands people began moving out of the province rather than moving in. After a brief recovery from 1983 through 1985, the economy again sagged as the world price for oil all but collapsed. Once more, then, the regional economy is experiencing deep distress, while, it should be noted, lower oil and natural gas prices are perceived to have at least a short-term positive impact on economic growth in other regions of the country.

At this time there is no need to belabour what is undoubtedly a very simple and even simplistic economic analysis. The basic point to stress is that throughout this century western Canadians have been forced to grapple with economic dependency. In so doing they have turned to the political system for some protection from an unstable and at times threatening economic environment. Unfortunately, the dependency that has confronted western Canadians in the economic arena has also confronted them in the political arena. It is indeed the interaction between economic and political dependency that has shaped western Canadian political life.

THE POLITICAL RESPONSE TO ECONOMIC DEPENDENCY

To understand the political response of the west to economic dependency it is important to keep in mind the federal nature of the Canadian political system. Federalism has provided western Canadians with provincial governments that they control, governments that are necessarily sensitive to regional concerns and responsive to regional interests. Thus provincial governments have provided the first line of defence for assaults from an unstable economic environment. Here we might note, for example, what has become the Holy

Grail for provincial governments in the west — economic diversification. Provincial governments have tried consistently, and without a great deal of luck, to diversify their economies in order to escape reliance upon a single crop or a single sector of the economy.[11]

However, while western Canadians may control their provincial governments, the constitutional division of powers has not given those governments much leverage on the basic problem of economic dependency. The powers that count tend to fall to Parliament rather than to the provincial legislatures. Thus we find that Parliament has exclusive jurisdiction or at least paramountcy in the areas of international and interprovincial trade, interprovincial transportation, banking, and finance. As a consequence, many of the critical concerns that western Canadians have had in the past and continue to have today — concerns about access to foreign markets, about tariffs, interest rates, freight rates, and the health of the country's transcontinental transportation system — are concerns that must be addressed first and foremost through the national political system.

This is not to say, I must stress, that the constitutional division of powers in some way conspires against the regional interests of western Canadians. It would be difficult to imagine how the Canadian federal state or indeed any federal state could survive if ultimate control over such things as international and interprovincial trade were not lodged with national authorities. It is worth noting none the less that western Canadians find themselves in a somewhat more difficult constitutional position than do the residents of Quebec. Whereas the primary concerns of western Canadians, concerns which are by and large economic in character, are constitutionally lodged with the national government, the primary concerns of Quebecers, concerns which are by and large but by no means exclusively cultural in character, tend to be lodged with provincial governments. Thus the provincial government is a far more powerful instrument for protecting the cultural interests of Quebecers than it is for protecting the economic interests of western Canadians. This is not a conspiracy perpetrated on western Canadians but rather a constitutional fact of life.

Drawing attention to the impact of the constitutional division of powers should not suggest that provincial governments in the west have been powerless to act in the economic interests of their constituents. To note but two from a multitude of possible examples, the debt-adjustment legislation brought in by the United Farmers of Alberta during the Depression provided some relief to hard-pressed farmers, and in more recent times the Alberta government has used money from the Alberta Heritage Savings and Trust Fund to finance the construction of a new grain elevator in Prince Rupert, British Columbia, and to purchase grain cars for use on the national rail system. Provincial governments in the west have also become very active in the pursuit of international trade by setting up provincial offices abroad and by supplying infrastructural support for provincial businessmen pursuing foreign markets.

The fact remains, however, that provincial governments can act only at the margins of the economic concerns that confront their constituents. When they try to act more directly, as the Alberta Social Credit government did in its attempts to regulate banks and financial institutions during the late 1930s, they run afoul of the federal division of powers. Therefore western Canadians must turn to the national political arena, in which their clout is much less.

Western Canadians have argued that the national political process exacerbates rather than alleviates regional problems. The central difficulty, however, springs less from any deliberate attempt by the national community to frustrate the interests and ambitions of western Canadians than it does from a flawed set of political institutions. Because parliamentary institutions tend to inhibit rather than to facilitate effective regional representation, they yield national policies that are not as sensitive to regional interests as they might and should be. Although not by design, parliamentary institutions have become part of the problem faced by western Canadians rather than the means to any solution.

The problems Canada's parliamentary institutions have with regional representation can be brought into focus by the distinction between *intrastate* and *interstate* federalism.[12] In this context *intrastate* federalism refers to the representation of regional interests *within the institutions of the national government by national politicians. Interstate* federalism refers either to the protection of regional interests through the constitutional division of powers or to the representation of regional interests *to the national government by the political executives of subnational governments.* Intrastate federalism directs our attention to regional representation within such institutions as the House of Commons, the Senate, the federal cabinet, and the Supreme Court. Interstate federalism directs our attention to the constitutional division of powers and to intergovernmental relations.

To paint once again with a very broad brush, it can be argued that intrastate forms of regional representation do not work very well in the Canadian case.[13] Effective regional representation in the House of Commons is inhibited by tight party discipline, by executive dominance and the very limited power exercised by individual MPs, by a committee system that is lumbered with both executive dominance and party discipline, and all too frequently by regionally imbalanced party caucuses that flow from distortions introduced by the electoral system. While the Senate may have been seen initially as a forum for regional representation, this promise was stillborn when the decision was made to appoint rather than to elect senators and when the power of appointment was placed in the hands of the national government.[14]

It should also be noted here that, to some extent, western Canadians have been the architects of their own parliamentary misfortune. It can be argued that western Canadians crippled their own influence in Ottawa by electing

Progressive, Social Credit, and CCF MPs, who were excluded from the government caucus and, more importantly, from the federal cabinet. Too often western MPs were embittered outsiders looking in at a parliamentary process that they could neither control nor influence to any significant degree. Then, in 1958, John Diefenbaker swept the Social Credit party from the western Canadian political stage and all but destroyed the Saskatchewan-based CCF, leaving its remnants to re-emerge in the New Democratic Party, in which western Canadians played a much less important role than they had played in the CCF.[15] Diefenbaker brought the prairie west into the Progressive Conservative fold and thus *temporarily* into the Canadian political mainstream. Unfortunately, while Diefenbaker held the prairies for the Conservatives, he lost both Quebec and national power to the federal Liberals, who were to dominate Canadian political life until the early 1980s. Diefenbaker brought the prairie west into the Canadian political mainstream but not into the corridors of power.[16]

All this is not to say that Canadian parliamentary institutions or for that matter the national political parties should be condemned, for they have done many things very well indeed. It is just that providing effective regional representation for western Canadian interests has not been one of those things. As a consequence, western Canadians have fallen back upon interstate channels of regional protection. However, as I have noted above, the constitutional division of powers has not offered much protection for western Canadian interests. The principal economic concerns of western Canadians fall largely under the jurisdiction of Parliament, and it is difficult to imagine alternative constitutional arrangements in which provincial governments would have paramountcy in such fields as interprovincial and international trade.

This leaves intergovernmental relations, or *executive federalism,* as the first and, in the eyes of many western Canadians, the only line of regional defence. Provincial governments become the conduit for the flow of regional interests into the national political process, and provincial premiers rather than MPs and senators become the champions of regional interests on the national stage. Given the scale of contemporary provincial governments and the vigour of recent provincial premiers, this is not an inconsequential line of defence. However, it also entails some serious problems. In waging battle with the federal dragon, provincial premiers have inflamed rather than moderated western alienation. In asserting that they and they alone represent regional interests in the national arena, the premiers have further eroded the political authority of MPs and senators. Intergovernmental conflict has become both intense and chronic. Last but by no means least, western Canadians are alienated from the national government when their premiers battle Ottawa from the outside rather than MPs and senators from the west fighting the good fight from within national parliamentary institutions.

The political situation in the prairie west prior to 1984 can be summarized as follows. Western Canadians, faced with chronic problems of economic dependency, sought assistance through the political process. However, the region lacked sufficient demographic weight and thus electoral clout to ensure that national parliamentary institutions would be sensitive to regional interests. In short, intrastate federalism failed to work or failed to work well enough to ward off a growing sense of regional alienation. Repeated regional assaults on both political authorities and the political regime failed; new parties were unable to acquire significant leverage on the national political process, and the institutions of the Canadian federal state proved resistant to change.

Western Canadians therefore fell back upon the defensive mechanisms of interstate federalism. However, as the constitutional division of powers provided little assistance, they were left dependent upon their provincial governments to protect their regional interests within the national political arena. This was a role that the provincial governments took on with enthusiasm because it inflated their own importance and contributed to their electoral success by enabling them to fight "fed-bashing" campaigns against Ottawa rather than having to campaign against provincial opposition parties. Yet it was also a role that further eroded the stature of federal politicians from the west and further estranged western Canadians from the national government.

In closing I shall indicate how this picture has been altered by the 1984 election, in which western Canadian Progressive Conservatives swept emphatically into power and, in so doing, apparently completed the movement of the west into the national mainstream that had begun with John Diefenbaker in 1958.

LOOKING FORWARD FROM THE 1984 ELECTION

The 1970s opened up three important "windows of opportunity" for western Canadians. First, it appeared that surging economic growth in the west might offset the region's demographic weakness in Canadian political life, that in a crude sense western Canadians might be able to buy their way into the national decision-making process. While this opportunity was most apparent in Alberta, where rapidly rising oil and natural gas revenues gave the provincial government more money than it was able to spend, it was also present across the region, given strong international markets for western Canadian natural resources.

Second, it appeared that the region's economic prosperity had ended the West's long-term demographic slide. While the prairies' share of the national population had fallen from approximately 23 per cent in 1931 to just over 16 per cent in 1971, it had risen slightly during the 1970s. With in-migration picking up during the boom, it appeared that the region's demographic weight might continue to increase. If this trend continued, then parliamentary institutions could be expected to become increasingly more sensitive to regional concerns and aspirations.

Third, the national-unity crisis with Quebec opened up the constitutional framework of the Canadian federal state to substantive change and reform. The independence challenge from Quebec and the determination of the Trudeau government to ward off that challenge with constitutional change provided the opportunity for western Canadians to restructure national institutions so that they would be more receptive to regional concerns.

Shortly into the 1980s these windows had largely closed. The recession of 1982 and the deepening economic crisis of the mid-1980s crippled the economic power of the west. The demographic tide into the west peaked and began to recede, leaving little doubt that the 1986 census will show a smaller proportion of Canadians living in the prairie west than was the case in 1981. Finally, the proclamation of the Constitution Act on 17 April 1982 brought the process of constitutional renewal to a halt, leaving parliamentary institutions and the federal division of powers essentially intact.

The closing of these three windows made the 1984 election all the more critical. The election results enable us to put to the test what might be termed the "western Canadian political hypothesis." The essence of this hypothesis is that parliamentary institutions, and therefore the mechanisms of intrastate federalism, are inherently flawed with respect to the representation of regional needs and aspirations, and that such institutions will continue to foster regional discontent. Now, with a truly national government in place enjoying strong support from all regions of the country, we can ask whether the parliamentary system might work after all. Given the right circumstances — the right party in power and a leader committed to national reconciliation and intergovernmental cooperation — changes to the political regime may in fact not be necessary. In seeking changes to the political regime, perhaps western Canadians have been barking up the wrong tree all these years.

Given that the Mulroney government has been in office for less than two years, it is still too early to predict whether the western Canadian hypothesis will be rendered inoperative by the 1984 election results. I would argue, however, that the prognosis is not good, that there is little chance of any fundamental change occurring in the patterns of political discontent sketched in above. The acute economic problems that the west is currently experiencing will tax the capacity and resolve of even the most supportive national government. The free-trade negotiations with the United States will focus attention on regional tradeoffs and strain Ottawa's ability to be all things to all regions. There is also a growing chance that the Progressive Conservative government may not survive the next election, in which case western Canadians could once again find themselves cast into the political wilderness unless the Liberal revival laps ashore in the prairie west. Finally, there is some concern that the 1984 election results have shifted the centre of gravity of the federal Progressive Conservative party away from the west, that the Conservative party has been nationalized by Mr. Mulroney and re-oriented to the central Canadian heartland, that western Canadians have gained a government but lost the party that John Diefenbaker made their own.

If this admittedly gloomy prognosis holds, western discontent can be expected to follow essentially the same patterns that it has followed since the turn of the century. This is not to say, however, that western alienation will pose a major threat to the Canadian political community. The appropriate medical analogy for western alienation is not cancer but arthritis. The condition is not one that kills but rather one that impairs the body politic, one that responds to short-term changes in the political climate but continues none the less to hamper the effective operation of political life. The country will survive, but its health will be less than we might expect or deserve.

NOTES

This paper was originally presented to the symposium "The Prairies and Canada," University of Manitoba, 2-4 June 1986.

1. In the 1982 Alberta provincial election the Western Canada Concept captured 11 per cent of the popular vote although the party's one sitting member, Gordon Kesler, was defeated.
2. Prior to the provincial election of 8 May 1986, the Progressive Conservatives held 75 of the 79 seats in the Alberta Legislative Assembly. The New Democrats elected 16 members, an increase of 14; the Liberals elected 4 members, and the Representative party retained its 2 sitting members. The Conservatives none the less won a majority, with 61 seats in the 83-member Legislative Assembly.
3. While the prairie provinces and British Columbia are frequently lumped together as "western Canada," the two regions have experienced quite different political histories. For a discussion of this point see R. Gibbins, *Prairie Politics and Society: Regionalism in Decline* (Toronto: Butterworths, 1980), chap. 1.
4. For an extended conceptual discussion see *Prairie Politics and Society,* chap. 5. For a more critical discussion of the manner in which the term has been used, see Donald E. Blake, *Two Political Worlds: Parties and Voting in British Columbia* (Vancouver: University of British Columbia Press, 1985) chaps. 4 and 7.
5. *Prairie Politics and Society* p. 169.
6. The distinction originates with David Easton, *A Framework for Political Analysis* (Englewood Cliffs, N.J.: Prentice-Hall, 1965).
7. For a more detailed discussion of this point see Gibbins, "Constitutional Politics and the West," in Keith Banting and Richard Simeon, eds., *And No One Cheered: Federalism, Democracy and the Constitution Act* (Toronto: Methuen, 1983), pp. 119-32.
8. Donald E. Blake finds that "a wide variety of Canadians in B.C. can express reasoned disagreement with their federal government, its leader, and his party without calling into question their affection for Canada or their belief that in other ways the federal government can be trusted to perform many activities

passably well." *Two Political Worlds*, p. 131. For further evidence on this point see David Elkins and Richard Simeon, *Small Worlds: Provinces and Parties in Canadian Political Life* (Toronto: Methuen, 1980), chap. 1.

9. For an insightful analysis of the western Canadian economy see John Richards and Larry Pratt, *Prairie Capitalism: Power and Influence in the New West* (Toronto: McClelland & Stewart, 1979).

10. For a more extended discussion of this period see *Prairie Politics and Society*, chap. 2.

11. The pursuit of economic diversification in Alberta and Saskatchewan has been documented at length in Richards and Pratt, *Prairie Capitalism*.

12. The distinction between intrastate and interstate federalism has been advanced in the Canadian context by Donald V. Smiley, *Canada in Question: Federalism in the Eighties*, 3rd edn. (Toronto: McGraw-Hill Ryerson, 1980).

13. For a greatly expanded discussion of this point see R. Gibbins, *Regionalism: Territorial Politics in Canada and the United States* (Toronto: Butterworths, 1982).

14. Appointment by the national government also introduces some representational strain with respect to the Supreme Court, although in this case it is not clear to what extent representational needs can be served by a judicial institution.

15. For a discussion of the "nationalization" of the CCF-NDP, see *Prairie Politics and Society*, pp. 112-15.

16. It could also be argued, of course, that Diefenbaker marginalized the federal Progressive Conservative party as much as he brought western Canada into the political mainstream.

KENNETH H. NORRIE

33 A Regional Economic Overview of the West Since 1945

The broad theme suggested for this paper would, if it included government policies in addition to narrowly defined economic events, be a truly staggering task. Consider the number of major economic and political developments since 1945. The period has witnessed, first of all, major structural changes in the key agricultural sector, with all that these have implied for the economies more generally. Fewer but larger farms, rail-line abandonment, the decline of small towns, net outmigration and even absolute population losses for Manitoba and Saskatchewan, and the diminishing political influence of the farm vote[1] are all direct or indirect consequences of increased mechanization. In addition, and still within this sector, there have been significant fluctuations in prosperity over the period, ranging from the near depression conditions for wheat in 1969/70 to the boom years of the mid-1970s.

The third major development has been the emergence of two new staple industries, oil and gas[2] in the three westernmost provinces and potash in Saskatchewan. The former event has, obviously been the more dramatic, completely transforming the economic, social and political structure of Alberta and to a much lesser extent Saskatchewan and British Columbia. Edmonton and Calgary replaced Winnipeg as dominant growth points within the Prairies, as Alberta became the primary destination for labor displaced from agriculture in Manitoba and Saskatchewan. Potash has had a much less pronounced effect, although the construction spinoffs together with the government revenue it has provided have altered the economy somewhat. In many ways, the political controversies generated by this staple base, ranging from public versus private ownership debates to a Supreme Court challenge to provincial taxation and regulation powers, have been its most interesting legacy.

The fourth significant event in the postwar period has been the turbulent economic events occurring in the energy sector since 1971. The large increases in crude oil prices after this date were significant for western Canada in several respects. The conventional oil industry was directly affected, and natural gas prices and hence exploration activity soon followed suit. The perception that supplies of these conventional energy sources would soon be exhausted led to a frenzy of activity in substitutes such as oil from enhanced recovery techniques, oil sands and heavy oil. Even further removed along the substitute continuum, there was renewed interest in coal and uranium, both of which the West possessed in abundance. Finally, and obviously, all of these developments were accompanied by serious and divisive political controversy, between public and private sectors, consuming and producing regions, and the various levels of government.

A fifth and often neglected event has been the accompanying boom in the other resource sectors of the region. The industrial expansion in the early years of that decade in the face of limited inventories of industrial raw materials meant that more than just grain, livestock and petroleum prices rose significantly. Metallic minerals, potash, lumber and forest products all benefited as well. These upswings were of limited duration, relative to that for energy products, and had much less overall impact. They are, nevertheless, an important part of the economic history of the last decade.

The final two noteworthy events are political in nature, although they either stem in large part from economic developments or lead to them. First, the postwar period has seen the continuation, and even intensification, of the tradition of economic and political alienation in the West. The economic bases of this growing disenchantment are perhaps best exemplified in the position papers prepared for the Western Economic Opportunities Conference in 1973, where the traditional concerns over tariffs, freight rates, monetary policy, commercial bank behavior and central government purchasing policies were evident. To this list must be added the natural-resource jurisdictional disputes of the last decade. The oft-cited sense of political powerlessness relates to the long tenure of the Liberal party federally, to the virtual disappearance of direct western representation in that government, and to the extinction of the several provincial Liberal parties.

The other significant political-economic development has been the emergence, or more correctly perhaps the explicit articulation,[3] of province-building strategies. The motivation behind these is complex and varied, but it certainly includes some mixture of genuine provincial loyalties seeking a political outlet, a defensive response to the alienation discussed above, and the use of the apparatus of state by regional elites to advance their own economic and political interests. Whatever the basis, the result has been a host of economic policies designed to stimulate economic growth and diversification. Taxes, subsidies, infrastructure projects, regulatory powers, and nationalization have all been used to promote new activities and to expand the scale of existing ones.

Given the number of important developments, and the inherent complexity of each of them, it is not obvious how to structure this overview. One strategy would be to attempt to survey all of these developments in a general way. The resulting product, though, would be lengthy, descriptive and largely superficial. A second tactic would be to focus on one or two key developments. This is done to some extent in other papers in this collection, however, and it would miss the essential task of synthesizing postwar developments.

There is a third strategy which I intend to follow for the remainder of this paper, namely to provide a conceptual overview which attempts to link together these economic and political developments. The hypothesis advanced here is that the staple or export base theory of economic growth, appropriately applied to a regional economy where economic rents are appropriated in the first instance by the local government, and supplemented by a few simple concepts from public choice theory, is both necessary and largely sufficient to understanding economic and political developments in western Canada since 1945.

The first part of the argument stressing the export-base approach to economic growth is not new, at least to those somewhat familiar with Canadian economic history. The full implications of using such an avowedly deterministic model in a regional context are not always fully appreciated, however, so it is worth drawing them out more fully. The concurrent focus on public sector rents, both as a development tool and as a key link between economic and political variables, is perhaps more novel.[4]

The following discussion is organized around two general issues in regional economics. First, how can one explain the structure of a specific regional economy at any given moment in time? Second, how will this economy, given this economic base, adjust over time to changes in its economic fortunes? The first question is static in nature, and is akin to stopping the action on an instant replay of a hockey game and explaining the positioning of the players. Some conceptual or "theoretical" points will be needed as well as some reference to the preceding action. The second query is dynamic, with the obvious analogy of letting the replay run again and explaining the subsequent action. Again "theory" will be needed, but now of a different type.

The following section takes up the first or static question with respect to the western economies as of 1971. The dynamic analysis, covering the decade of the 1970s through to the present, is contained in Section III. The year 1971 is used as a reference point because of the widely-held view that the West entered a new phase of political and economic development about that time — the westward-shift hypothesis to be precise. Section IV discusses the political economy of province-building in the West, while a final section makes some brief concluding comments.

THE ECONOMICS OF A SMALL, RESOURCE-RICH, REGIONAL ECONOMY

The argument advanced in this section is that the economic status the West had achieved by 1971, after more than seven decades of extensive development, was largely a product of its geographical and institutional environment. The region throughout its history was a classic example of a small, resource-rich, regional economy. Each of these characteristics individually imposed a particular constraint on the type of economic growth that could occur, and collectively they forced the economy into the only development pattern that was feasible in the long run. To see this, it is necessary to consider each of these features in turn.

Looking at the appellation "resource-rich" first, the obvious implication is that a region endowed in this manner will have an initial comparative advantage in producing raw materials and semi-processed products for export. The economy will thus develop around the leading sector or sectors, at least initially, with ancillary or linked activities forming locally to the extent that location considerations are favorable. The condition that firms locate so as to minimize total costs typically means that service activities will be drawn to the region while manufacturing other than simple directly-linked industries will not. Construction, personal services, retail trade and the like must be consumed on site by definition. In this sense, they are like the primary resource sectors in that they use an industry *and* a geographically-specific factor of production, in this case urban land. Relatively large primary and tertiary activities together with relative underemployment of the manufacturing sector is, of course, an oft-cited feature of staple economies.

This much is just conventional staple or export-base theory, supplemented by classical location concepts.[5] Two points emerge immediately, however. The first is that this conceptual approach provides a remarkably complete explanation of the basic economic structures of the West *circa* 1971. Primary industries that export a large portion of their output did dominate each of the provincial economies; service industries were relatively large; the manufacturing sector was noticeably small; and what industrial activities were present typically involved further processing of primary products prior to export or provision of specific inputs for the extractive sector.[6] On a cyclical basis the obvious link between agricultural, energy and timber profitability and the macroeconomic performance of the four western provinces further establishes the relevance of this classic export-base model.

The second point follows logically from the first. If economic and geographical determinism can explain industrial structure in the West adequately, there is no need to resort to more nebulous and ill-defined assertions such as the following recent statement (Sahir and Seaborne, 1982, 92), "The failure of the prairie region to significantly diversify its economy is, in part, a reflection of its continued role as a hinterland economy and its domination by the national heartland." If "hinterland economy" and "heartland" are meant to distinguish between regions with a comparative advantage in primary and manufacturing activities respectively, this is simply a restatement of the export-base theory. If the term "domination" is to be the key one, however, the quotation ceases to have much meaning. Space limitations preclude more than an assertion that the basic industrial structure of the West has been very little affected by the mix of tariff, transportation, monetary, taxation and purchasing policies pursued by central governments over the decades.[7] The scale of the economies has undoubtedly been affected, and some of the policies have certainly reallocated income interregionally. But the basic point remains. The West is relatively dependent on primary industries because it has a strong comparative advantage in these, due to: favorable endowments together with a relatively late and sparse settlement, geographical remoteness, the prairies' lack of access to lake and ocean shipping, and harsh climate.

The two other characteristics that act to define the economies of the West are their smallness and the openness that stems from being a regional economy within a larger national one. To assert that an economy is small is to say that it is a price-taker on all items that are transportable. This applies to goods such as raw materials or processed products, some services such as finance or insurances, and factor inputs such as capital, labor and technology. In technical terms, Westerners face virtually perfectly elastic demand curves for exports, and horizontal supply curves for imported goods, services and factors of production. As with a basic resource orientation, this does not represent any failure or shortcoming within the region, or any perfidy on the part of the central government or eastern Canada. Rather it reflects the small size of the regional market, the number of close substitutes for most of its output, and the technical difficulty in effectively exploiting whatever small degree of market power it might potentially possess.

Openness refers to the ability of goods and factors to move into or out of an economy in response to any initial price differentials, and as such really only reinforces the characteristic of smallness discussed above. The latter establishes that there will be an exogenously determined world price for wheat to the region for example, while the former ensures that the local price will be equal to this world rate less shipping and handling charges. To give another example, the West has no influence over the going rate of return on an asset in any given risk class, while the free movement of capital ensures that the reward to investment locally cannot long deviate from this given rate.

For the West, the combination of small and open means that nearly all prices are set externally. Given that provincial governments cannot in principle establish migration or investment quotas, interregional migrations of capital and labor will determine local factor prices. Since the regional exchange rate is fixed at unity, there is no possibility of having local prices of traded products behave differently than those in other, larger economies.

The only exception to these statements, an important one as it will turn out, is that with respect to non-traded outputs and the associated industrial and geographically-specific factor inputs. In these instances, prices are set by regional supply and demand by definition.

Recognizing the small, open nature of the western economies is important in several respects. The first is that the economic fortune of the region will lie largely beyond its control. Events in national and international markets will be paramount, with the region having no recourse but to adapt accordingly. While this dependency is an inevitable outcome of overall endowment, it does typically generate sentiments of economic and political alienation, including a tendency to associate periods of instability with perceived shortcomings in existing national and regional institutions. Hinterland economies are thus very often politically restive ones, always in search of an elusive "better system."

Secondly, real factor incomes in the region cannot deviate very much, or for very long, from those available elsewhere in the national economy. Thus aggregate real per capita income, once adjusted for industrial structure, will approximate the national average. Put another way, changes in the economic fortunes of the region, coming from whatever external stimulus, will be resolved by adjustments in extensive variables such as investment or labor migration rather than in intensive ones such as rates of return or real wages.

The exception to this statement is the one noted above; namely, that real returns to owners of geographically immobile assets such as urban land will vary directly with the extensive growth of the region. Economic booms will increase the demand for the output of non-tradeables, generating economic rent for the owners of the specific factor. The converse is true for downturns. These income flows become the residual payment in effect, adjusting to equalize, the variation in the differences between exogenously-given output and factor input prices. What this means, politically, is that this group of property owners will have a vested interest in promoting extensive growth internally. Since regional politicians and bureaucrats are also typically assumed to favor extensive growth, for by now familiar reasons,[8] the result is a powerful, political alliance motivated to use the powers and resources of government to direct the province's economy.

The argument to this point has been that the economic development of the West to 1971 is adequately explained by noting that the region is a classic example of a small, resource rich, regional economy. Falling within the general survey of the theory are: the key leading sector role played by a few primary industries; limited secondary manufacturing activity; relatively large service sector; a pattern of extensive rather than intensive growth in response to external stimuli; approximately national-average per capita incomes; tendencies toward regional dissent; and activist economic strategies by politically influential local elites. By extension then, one need not resort to vaguely defined notions of dependency or conspiratorial theories to explain the present economic structure of the region.

These considerations lead to hypotheses about the structures of the western economies at any given point in time. By extension though, they should also be useful in predicting the nature of the economic adjustment within the region to any exogenous disturbances. Specifically, they should provide a basis for analyzing the western response to the energy price shocks of the last decade. These events were seen by many, both within the West and outside it, as a vehicle for developing and diversifying the western economies, and thereby shifting economic and political power in Canada westward. Western political leaders clearly expected this at the outset, and they did create these expectations in the populace more generally. This raises an obvious question then, and an important corollary. Has there been structural change in the nature in the western economies over the last decade? If not, why not? These topics are taken up in the following section.

ENERGY AND REGIONAL ECONOMIC ADJUSTMENT

The reason for singling out the last decade for analysis is that these years have been among the most crucial and interesting in the entire history of the region. All the grand themes of western economic and political history — primary sector volatility, export-led growth resulting in large swings in investment and migration, a quest for economic diversification, and political and economic alienation — have all been present in pronounced fashion. These events should, therefore, provide a good test of whether the general themes introduced above carry over to this turbulent decade as well. The argument is that they do, once public-sector resource rents are brought into the picture.

There are three key facts to be kept in mind when looking at the economic and political history of the West over the past decade. First, the increase in energy prices in 1973/74 and again in 1979/80 represented a significant shift in intersectoral terms of trade. Left alone, a market economy will undergo a predictable response to this disturbance. In Canada, the fact that energy sources are located primarily in the West while the bulk of population and industrial capacity is in the East, means that the inevitable intersectoral reallocation of resources will at the same time be an interregional one. This complicates the simple mechanics of the adjustment slightly, and the politics of it immensely.

The second fact is that unlike the wheat boom seventy years earlier, much of the economic rent generated over the decade was appropriated in the first instance by provincial governments. This revenue, combined with regulatory control over energy resources, gave the provinces considerable scope to intervene in the economy to promote economic diversification. The final point is that these rents and powers came at a time when there was increased concern within the region about the long-term implications of remaining tied to the traditional economic base. The need to develop new economic bases to offset an expected decline in the conventional petroleum industries became the theme of Alberta's then Opposition Leader Peter Lougheed, for example.

The analysis of an adjustment to a shift in the intersectoral terms of trade in favor of energy within a closed economy (i.e., assuming a fixed supply of factor inputs) is straightforward. The potential for higher returns in petroleum and petroleum-related activities (including substitutes such as coal, uranium, synthetic fuels, etc.) means an increased demand for capital and labor inputs to these sectors. Prices for these factors start to rise as expanding sectors begin to bid for a larger share of the given supplies of productive inputs. Average costs of production increase and local firms begin to lose out to competing suppliers, both in export markets (e.g., forestry products) and through increased imports of manufactured products. The service sector is able to pass along cost increases in the form of higher prices, which together with an income elastic demand means it typically rises slightly overall.

The net result is a wealthier economy, but one even more specialized in energy and service activities. It is wealthier in the sense that one unit of petroleum output will now exchange for a significantly greater amount of other products than before; i.e., a greater consumption is possible from any given production effort. But it is more specialized in that this very increased value of petroleum has now induced a reallocation of the region's productive resources toward this sector, and away from other traded activities. If energy output is to expand, and there are fixed supplies of capital and labor, some other sectors must decline to release these factors. Since nonpetroleum exports and secondary-manufacturing products face highly elastic external demands and competing supplies respectively, it is they who perform this function. This establishes the important proposition that in the absence of offsetting factors the energy prices boom of the 1970s could have been expected to increase the economic specialization of the region, rather than to provide a once-in-a-lifetime opportunity to escape as it was often alleged. For the latter to be true there would need to be further, offsetting factors.

The first such qualification is provided by the fact, noted above, that the West as a small, regional economy faces a highly elastic supply of capital and labor from other jurisdictions. As excess demands for these factors appear: due to expansion of the energy sector, they are met by increased supplies from outside rather than price adjustments within. The result is that the energy sector can expand without having to draw as much upon other, traded industries in the process. In the extreme, if all factors are perfectly mobile with respect to price incentives, there will be only extensive growth; rewards to mobile factors will not change at all. The regional economy will simply be larger by the amount of the expanded energy sector, plus whatever output growth it has induced in other, linked industries. Note again, however, that the economy will still appear more specialized, even in this limiting case. Energy production has increased absolutely as have service and more directly-linked manufacturing activities. The only difference now compared to the closed economy case is that the other activities have only declined relatively rather than absolutely.

This limiting case is too extreme even for a small regional economy such as the West, however. In point of fact, not all factors are perfectly mobile. Services require a geographically-specific input, the final output cannot be traded interregionally, and they are an important input to production and a key item in consumption. Thus as energy and other outputs rise, and labor moves in response to higher wages, the demand for services will rise. Since production is constrained to follow an upward-sloping supply curve because of a limited supply of the specific input, and imports are ruled out by definition, prices must rise. This means increased production costs for the traded sectors, causing them to lose sales to competitors as before. It also contributes to a higher regional cost of living, meaning that nominal wages will need to rise to continue to attract workers. Again, this puts upward pressure on production costs overall, and the consequent absolute decline of some activities.

This realistic case, intermediate between the extremes of a completely closed economy and a completely open one, predicts increased specialization in energy and its directly-related activities together with services. The point may be seen belabored, but it is an important one given the widespread view in the West and elsewhere during the 1970s that the energy boom *per se* would be the means whereby the West would escape its traditional dependence on primary activities.[9] In fact, exactly the opposite would be true, all else being equal. Natural market forces would operate to increase the region's relative[10] dependence on its now more valuable energy sector. This is the additional[11] constraint which regional policy makers faced over the decade in their quest to diversify the provincial economies.

The energy boom did provide some offsetting scope for economic diversification in two other important ways, however, and herein lies the interesting political economy of the decade. First, provincial governments have broad constitutional authority over natural resources. The western provinces have used this provision to guarantee supplies of feedstocks to locally-based processing firms, at the expense of exports if necessary. Thus in the early 1970s, when security of supplies of natural gas was a dominating locational consideration, the Alberta government managed to lure petrochemical firms to the province upon the promise of a guaranteed long-term supply of feedstock. Attractive feedstock prices also apparently played a role in this development, although no formal subsidy was ever acknowledged.[12]

By far the more significant factor, though, was the huge economic rent captured by the provincial governments, especially Alberta, after 1973. These revenues provided a unique opportunity to intervene to alter the basic structure of the economy. Normally, the ability of a regional government to tax factor incomes in excess of value of services provided in return is effectively precluded by the mobility feature. Hence there is little scope for offering subsidies to attract industrial activity to the area. Economic rent, by definition, is free of this problem. Intramarginal units of land and resources can be taxed without having their services withdraw, and the revenue used to provide fiscal incentives to attract capital and labor from other jurisdictions. It is this feature more than any other which gives some substance to the claim that the energy boom provided a once-in-a-lifetime opportunity to reverse the staple orientation of the western economies.

This opportunity did not come without cost, however, both economic and political. Economically, the cost would be the dissipation of some or all of the potentially available natural resource rent. An industrial diversification beyond that already evident by 1971 would need to be subsidized and, because of the locational disadvantages discussed in Section II, this could be expected to be costly. In addition, as seen in this section, whatever natural disadvantages the region already possessed in this respect were magnified by the nature of the internal economic adjustment to the terms of trade shift. The political cost, at least in Alberta, was that the government was being forced to compromise its declared adherence to free-market principles in order to make good its economic promises. Diversification was only possible, if at all, through active intervention in the economy. Yet, the only western government in any real position to affect the basic allocation of resources significantly had constrained itself politically not to do so. It is to this complicated political economy of province-building that the paper now turns.

THE POLITICAL ECONOMY OF PROVINCE-BUILDING

The complete story of province-building efforts in the West over the last ten years has yet to be told.[13] There are two economic questions to ask in this respect. First, what in principle might a revenue-rich provincial government have done to promote industrialization and diversification, and to what effect? Second, what did they actually do in this regard, again to what effect? The interesting political question obviously is why did they choose the policies they did, or indeed any at all? This section takes up each of these issues in turn.

There are a variety of subsidy programs that a regional government can in principle employ to affect industrial structure, from the very specific to the very general. The former refers to grants directed to specific firms or industries with a view to offsetting natural disadvantages. Examples are: subsidized feedstock prices for petrochemical plants, performing research and development for private forms in certain areas, relocation or modernization grants, and low or no cost loans. These would be effective to the extent that the subsidy actually covered the extra costs of locating the activity within the province rather than its most preferred site. The cost would be relatively straightforward to compute, being equal to the value of the revenue expended in this manner.

There has been remarkably little recourse to industry or firm-specific subsidies, even in Alberta where the financial wherewithal certainly exists. Rather the typical procedure has been to funnel resource revenues through the existing taxation-expenditure system so as to provide a general subsidy to any capital and labor located within the province. Low corporate and personal taxation rates, special treatment of small business profits, the absence of a sales tax, and the recent mortgage subsidy schemes are examples of these policies. They all have the effect of increasing the real, after-tax return from any given nominal payment. As an example, an individual earning $20,000 per year in Alberta is better off in a real income sense than his identical counterpart in Ontario, since he will receive a much greater value of government services per tax dollar (net fiscal benefit) thanks to the subsidy provided by the resource revenue.

Higher real-after-tax returns in the West can be expected to attract capital and labor from other jurisdictions for as long as the differential persists. This immigration proceeds, and drives down nominal returns in the West below those in the East, until the point where the net fiscal benefits expected are just equal to the private-sector real income foregone. At that point there will no longer be an incentive to relocate, and the interregional capital and labor markets will be in equilibrium. Note however that now costs of production within the region have fallen, due to the lower nominal factor payments. This allows all sectors to increase their hiring and expand output until these cost differentials are again eliminated. The final result is a regional economy that is bigger in the sense that Gross Provincial Product, the capital stock and the labor force are all larger than they would be in the absence of the general subsidies. The government has used its resource revenues to promote extensive growth, without resorting to specific subsidy schemes.

This policy of providing general locational incentives through the taxation expenditure system has received considerable attention recently under the heading of fiscally-induced migration.[14] The reason for the interest is that a movement of capital and labor from higher to lower tax jurisdictions can be shown to be socially inefficient, even if privately rational. In essence, the notion is that too much capital and too many workers end up in the resource-rich region. The contribution each makes to total national output in the new location is less than that foregone by leaving the old one. For the individual migrant this is acceptable, even if it is reflected in a lower private-sector wage, since the difference in made up by the net additional fiscal benefits enjoyed. For the economy as a whole, however, there is a social cost in that total output is lower than if factors were allocated more properly across regions.

There was considerable concern over the last decade that the large fiscal surpluses enjoyed by the resource-rich western governments were causing this type of distortion within the Canadian economy.[15] If true, this would mean that the western economies are currently larger and more diversified than they would have been in the absence of this particular use of resource rents. Unfortunately, there is little firm evidence on this yet one way or the other. We (Norrie and Percy, 1982, 1983a, 1983b) have looked at the question in a more general way by developing a stylized model of a small, resource-rich regional economy, calibrating it roughly to Alberta data, and performing a series of experiments designed to simulate the economic adjustment to an energy-price increase under a variety of rent-disposition schemes. The basic conclusion that emerges from this work is that it is certainly possible to use resource rents to promote the growth of either specific activities or of industries more generally. The manner in which the public sector revenues are distributed turns out to be important; under some scenarios, for example, the main effect is an expansion of government activities and a partial crowding out of the other sectors. The extent of the induced diversification is also shown to depend crucially on a variety of technical parameters such as the sensitivities of export demands to price changes, the degree of responsiveness of migration to economic incentives, and so forth.

The next logical step in this type of research has not yet been done. That is we (Norrie and Percy) have simply simulated the implication of alternative, *possible* uses of natural resource rents. In actual fact, the western governments have adopted a variety of rent disposition schemes, ranging from potash nationalization in Saskatchewan and tax relief in Alberta through specific industrial incentives and mortgage assistance to Heritage Savings Trust Funds. To date, no one to our knowledge has attempted to estimate the actual effect any of these has had on growth and economic structure in any given province. One suspects the impact has been marginal at best, for the reasons given above: viz, the region has a large natural disadvantage to begin with; the simple economics of the energy boom exacerbated this condition; and the key province, Alberta, has been notably recalcitrant to use much of its resources in this manner, until recently that is. Supporting this conjecture is the evidence given in our report demonstrating no significant structural change to 1979 at least (Norrie and Percy, 1981).

What is clear from the existing research, however, is that each of these subsidy programs leads to a dissipation of economic rent to some degree. That this must be true can be seen by recognizing that the general object is to use resource revenues to make up the difference between (a) the maximum amount that industrial concerns will pay for factors and still locate in the West and (b) the total income these same inputs require to come to or remain in this region. The greater the disadvantage is in this sense, the higher the costs. Subsidizing specific projects is the least costly, but it has the least effect on overall extensive growth. More general subsidies through the taxation-expenditure system have a larger overall impact, but use up much more of the resource revenue.

Herein lies the fundamental political economy issue for the western provinces. Developments in world petroleum markets have given the current residents of the West an unanticipated real income gain. Under existing institutional arrangements much of this appears in the first instance as provincial government revenues. The government then has to decide how to allocate this windfall. The options run from distributing the proceeds as an equal per capita dividend payment to all current residents[16] to spending the entire amount on province-building activities. The former would maximize the gain to current residents, but leave the region increasingly specialized in its traditional activities. The latter option can introduce a measure of extensive growth into nonpetroleum sectors, but dilutes the real income gain to "pioneers." Measures in between the two extremes will have an element of both.

Why might a provincial government pursue province-building activities, if the cost is forgone real income gains to current residents? There are three possible, not necessarily mutually exclusive, answers to this question. The first is that the subsidy process will eventually produce an industrial and service sector which will be nationally and even internationally competitive in its own right. This is certainly the position that many in the Alberta government hold, for example. It would be credible if one could demonstrate that any of the following are true and important: national economic policies are largely responsible for the current lack of industrial development in the region such that a few key policy measures by the provincial government can offset these distortions; agglomeration economies exist, and the West is on the threshold of being able to exploit them significantly; locational considerations for the next generation of industrial development (e.g., high-technology industries) have shifted away from traditional centers, putting the West at less of a disadvantage now. A quick response to this would be that the first has already been discounted above, while the jury is still out on the second and third.

The second explanation is that these activities are costly and conceded to be so, that a diversified economic base is sought nonetheless for noneconomic reasons, and that this represents the expressed and considered will of the populace. Residents may equate a more diverse economy with greater economic stability, regional political power, or a greater choice of jobs, now or in the future. The society then "invests" its resource revenue in creating this economic structure.

A final explanation is suggested by a public-choice theoretical approach along the lines used to explain why protective tariffs, which are known to reduce real income, are nevertheless an almost universal policy. The basis of the explanation lies in recognizing that tariffs reallocate income from the population as a whole to specific groups within the economy. The gains in total are less than the losses, with the difference equal to the efficiency loss. But the fact that the gains are relatively concentrated, and hence appropriable by a specific group, makes them highly visible. Groups will be formed to lobby for the measures, and politicians will receive political credit for implementing them. The very diffuseness of the losses, on the other hand, makes political action against such measures unlikely. No one will take the time and effort to lobby against them, since the individual cost is so little relatively, and politicians will not lose much from being identified with them. Thus economically inefficient measures can still be popular policy options.

Province-building strategies based on resource rents seem to fit this model well. As shown above, there are groups that gain from extensive economic growth even in a small, regional economy; viz, the owners of geographically immobile factors in the service industries. This group, Richards's and Pratt's (1979) new urban elite, will thus have a strong incentive to lobby for policies which will draw additional capital and labor into the region. The costs, like those from tariffs, are borne by the population as a whole. Individuals already in the region may perceive that they are not sharing in the province's resource wealth to the extent they might, and that they do not appear to benefit much from the extensive growth that is occurring, but the incentive for taking political action is small.

The costs associated with using resource revenues are even more obscure than this, however. In the first place, they are not so much costs as foregone potential gains. That is, any revenues expended on province-building efforts do not come from direct taxation of the population, but from government resource royalties. Thus, no individual resident is actually worse off as a result of the policy; he or she simply does not receive the capital that would otherwise have accrued. Even further, however, few residents expect to receive any direct share of these resource revenues, due to the manner in which they have always been collected and utilized. In effect, provincial governments levy a 100 percent tax on each resident's share of royalty income. These same authorities then decide how much of this shall be saved, how much to provide government services at subsidized rates, and how much devoted to other objectives such as sponsoring extensive economic growth. Since this has always been the procedure, there was little awareness over the last decade that there was an individual cost to such policies. With benefits concentrated and appropriable, and with costs nebulous and diffuse, there is little wonder that province-building was a politically appealing policy over the last ten years.

CONCLUSION

The main arguments of this paper can be summarized very briefly. The post-war period has witnessed several significant economic and political developments within western Canada, but the basic structure of the region is unaltered. The West was born a small, resource-rich economy, and it has remained so through to the present. This endowment has provided the region with average or above average living standards, and with a unique economic and political structure. Resources and linked sectors dominate the economy, with more traditional secondary manufacturing activities being relatively underdeveloped. The openness of the economy means there will be swings in extensive growth, with rewards to mobile factors never deviating much from national variables. This inevitable dependence on external conditions in both product and factor markets generates sentiments of economic alienation, while the small population and hence relative underrepresentation federally creates a feeling of political isolation. Geographically immobile factors and public-sector resource revenues are the key indigenous variables which provide a degree of uniqueness to the regional political economy.

The intent of this paper has been to argue that these considerations explain both the economic structure of the West circa 1971 and the nature of the economic adjustment to the favorable terms of trade effective after that date. Before the disruptions in commodity markets some ten years ago, the economic history of the West in the postwar period was essentially one of adapting to labor-saving technological change in agriculture in the face of some rather severe swings in its profitability, and to the extensive economic growth resulting from the new staples. The economic structure of the region thus displayed every characteristic that one would expect of a richly endowed but small and geographically-remote regional economy.

Analysis of events since that date must necessarily focus on two conflicting tendencies: the increased returns in the energy sector pushed the western economies (primarily Alberta's) toward increased specialization in these industries; while at the same time the obvious volatility of the current structure provided the incentive, and with the revenue and regulatory powers the apparent means to achieve exactly the opposite outcome. The result was a series of policy measures destined to have little real impact on economic structure, but guaranteed to dissipate much of the real income gains potentially available. Compounding this conflict was the fact that such policies would, nevertheless be politically popular, given the concentrated and obvious nature of the benefits compared to the diffuse and nebulous perception of the costs. Indeed, the dynamics of western political economy over the last decade have revolved around this theme of perception versus reality.

Three brief comments which follow from the above are offered in conclusion. First, it must be stressed that western provincial governments have been admirably restrained in the use of natural resource revenues, at least until recently.[17] This is all the more commendable given the magnitude of the revenues they had to work with, and the political ease with which more ambitious development projects could have been pursued. Ironically, the Alberta government is currently bearing the wrath of editorial writers among others for not having followed a more activist policy in the last ten years. This paper has argued that province-building strategies, always costly because of natural economic disadvantages, would have been doubly so if pursued in the heat of the energy boom.

The second point concerns the phenomenon of regional economic alienation. The crux of what has been discussed above is that the basic economic structure of the western economies is effectively explained by geography, history and market forces. The implication is that federal economic policies, with the possible exception of the Crow rate distortion, have played little or no role in determining this structure. In particular, they have not made the West less industrialized or diversified than it might have been otherwise. This is not to say that some of these policies have not reallocated income among regions within Canada to the detriment of the West. Indeed they have done this, the National Energy Program being the most obvious instance. The point is, however, that the cause of good policy analysis would be well served if western spokesmen were to begin with a more rigorous appreciation of the binding constraints.

Finally, the considerations raised here support the view that, barring further major disruptions in energy markets, the long-term future for the western Canadian economies may well involve a slow and orderly reversal of the pattern of extensive growth.[18] This means GPP increases of less than the national average, net outmigration, and so forth. The process will be slow, because, contrary to current alarmist reports, that economic base will clearly not collapse. It will be orderly, because past experience has shown that product and factor markets in the West adapt rather efficiently to changes in relative returns. But it will mean that the West will not play the leading role in Canadian economic and political affairs that many inside and even outside the region had come to expect.

NOTES

1. Howard and Tamara Palmer (1983) argue that the relative decline of rural Alberta was a primary factor in the defeat of the Social Credit by the Lougheed Tories in 1971, for example.

2. There was an oil and gas industry in Alberta prior to 1947, of course, but of insignificant scale until the Leduc and subsequent discoveries.

3. Province-building strategies in one form or another are as old as the region. For a survey of earlier efforts see Owram (1982).

4. Much of the argument in this paper is based on work done by the present author in conjunction with my colleague Michael Percy (Norrie and Percy, 1981, 1982, 1983a,b,c).

5. The best reference to the staple theory are Watkins (1963) and Stabler (1968).
6. See Norrie-Percy (1981) for a discussion of the economic structure of the West in 1971 as it related to primary export industries.
7. This point is developed further in Norrie (1976, 1978). The Crow or Statutory Grain Rate distortions are a possible exception to this view. See Norrie-Percy (1983c) or Harvey (1980) for a discussion of the impact of these freight rates on prairie manufacturing.
8. See Cairns (1977) for a discussion of province-building and regional elites.
9. The possible exception to this pessimistic view is if the energy boom were to increase the absolute size of the economy sufficiently that agglomeration economies came to be important. Little is known about this phenomenon, however, theoretically or empirically. Norrie and Percy (1983a) do incorporate it in some simulation experiments.
10. There would almost certainly be absolute expansion of these sectors, it should be stressed. The discussion here is in terms of structure, not total output.
11. Additional to the existing natural disadvantages as discussed above, that is.
12. Natural gas is relatively expensive to transport, so there is a significant wedge between western and delivered eastern prices. The presence of long-term contracts at very low, preboom prices added to this advantage.
13. Indeed, much of it is yet to happen, given the concern over the current economic slump in the region and the consequent pressure to use Heritage Savings Trust Funds to bolster growth.
14. See Economic Council of Canada (1982) for a summary discussion of this literature.
15. Purvis and Flatters (1980).
16. See McMillan and Norrie (1980) for a discussion of this point.
17. The mortgage subsidy schemes introduced recently by both Saskatchewan and Alberta are examples of the worst possible use of public natural-resource wealth.
18. The paper by Schweitzer (1983) is the most recent example of this view.

REFERENCES

Cairns, Alan C. "The Governments and Societies of Canadian Federalism." *Canadian Journal of Political Science* 10:4 (December 1977), pp. 695-725.

Economic Council of Canada, *Financing Confederation.* Ottawa: Supply and Services, 1982.

Harvey, David R. *Christmas Turkey or Prairie Vulture? An Economic Analysis of the Crow's Nest Pass Grain Rates,* Montreal: Institute for Research on Public Policy, 1980.

McMillan, M.L. and K.H. Norrie. "Province-Building vs. a Rentier Society." *Canadian Public Policy* 6 (Supplement 1980), pp. 211-24.

Norrie, K.H. "Western Economic Grievances: An Overview with Special Reference to Freight Rates." *Proceedings of the Workshop on the Political Economy of Confederation.* Institute of Intergovernmental Relations and Economic Council of Canada. Ottawa: Supply and Services, 1978, pp. 199-237.

Norrie, K.H. and M.B. Percy. "Westward Shift and Interregional Adjustment: A Preliminary Analysis." *Economic Council of Canada Discussion Paper No. 201,* 1981.

_____."Energy Price Increases, Economic Rents, and Industrial Structure in a Small Regional Economy." *Economic Council of Canada Discussion Paper No. 220, 1982.*

_____."Economic Rents, Province-Building and Interregional Adjustment: A Two Region General Equilibrium Analysis." *Economic Council of Canada Discussion Paper,* 1983a (forthcoming).

_____."Province-Building and Industrial Structure in a Small Open Economy." Prepared for the Second John Deutsch Roundtable on Economic Policy (Kingston: Queen's University, November 11-13, 1983b).

_____."Freight Rate Reform and Regional Burden: A General Equilibrium Analysis of Western Freight Rate Proposals." *Canadian Journal of Economics* 16:2 (May 1983c), pp. 325-49.

Owram, D. "The Economic Development of Western Canada: An Historical Overview." *Economic Council of Canada Discussion Paper No. 219,* 1982.

Palmer, Howard and Tamara Palmer. "The Alberta Experience." *Journal of Canadian Studies* 17:3 (Fall 1983), pp. 20-34.

Purvis, Douglas D. and Frank R. Flatters. "Ontario: Policies and Problems of Adjustment in the Eighties." In *Development Abroad and the Domestic Economy.* Toronto: Ontario Economic Council, 1980, pp. 129-65.

Richards, John and Larry Pratt. *Prairie Capitalism: Power and Influence in the New West.* Toronto: McClelland and Stewart, 1979.

Sahir, A.H. and A.A. Seaborne. "Economic Diversification in the Canadian Prairies." *Prairie Forum* 7:1 (Spring 1982), pp. 91-4.

Schweitzer, Thomas. "Migration and a Small Long-Term Econometric Model of Alberta." *Economic Council of Canada Discussion Paper No. 221,* 1983.

Stabler, J.C. "Exports and Evolution: The Process of Regional Change." *Land Economics* 44 (1968), pp. 11-23.

Watkins, Melville H. "A Staple Theory of Economic Growth." *Canadian Journal of Economics and Political Science* 29:2 (May 1963), pp. 141-58.

XV

LITERATURE AND ART

Many writers and artists have tried imaginatively to capture the prairie West. Their images have varied over time, yet underneath the changing perceptions has been a continuity which has perceived the Prairies as a cohesive region.

Early images of the West, often expressed by people who had never visited the area, preceded large scale settlement in the region. These perceptions affected settlement and growth of the prairies almost as much as political decisions and economic factors. As the region evolved so did the images in the minds of artists, writers, social critics, and propagandists. Douglas Francis examines the various perceptions of the West from the fur trading era to the present in his article "Changing Images of the West."

In attempting to understand the essential images of the prairie region, analysts have often contrasted the area to the American West. Since the two regions have shared similar geographical features but contrasting historical traditions, it is possible to understand the Canadian prairie West's unique cultural values and milieu through a study of how its values differed from those of its neighbours. One area of contrast is fiction. Novels about the American and Canadian wests begin with different assumptions about the nature of man, society and even the natural world. The result is two contrasting types of fiction which can tell us a great deal about how prairie Canadians and western Americans perceive themselves. Literary critic Dick Harrison examines the divergent forms of fiction in the two Wests in "Fictions of the American and Canadian Wests."

Intellectual and cultural historians of prairie Canada turn to literature and art as sources for understanding the intellectual and cultural milieu of the region. While it may be debatable whether a regional culture exists, it is true that literature and art can and often do reflect the values of the regional society of which the writer and artist are a part. What values did these literary writers and artists express? Have these values been consistent over time or has there been an evolution in perspective over time? Answers to these questions will offer us insights into the mindset of prairie Canada.

SELECTED BIBLIOGRAPHY

The most comprehensive overviews of prairie literature are Dick Harrison, *Unnamed Country: The Struggle for a Canadian Prairie Fiction* (Edmonton, 1977) and Laurence Ricou, *Vertical Man/Horizontal World: Man and Landscape in Canadian Prairie Fiction* (Vancouver, 1973). E.A. McCourt's *The Canadian West in Fiction*, revised edition (Toronto, 1970) and D.G. Stephen's *Writers of the Prairies* (Vancouver, 1973) should also be consulted. Douglas Francis's work on images of prairie Canada can be examined further in his *Images of the West: Changing Perceptions of the Prairies, 1690-1960* (Saskatoon, 1989). Useful articles on prairie literature include Eli Mandel's "Images of Prairie Man," in R. Allen, ed., *A Region of the Mind* (Regina, 1973), pp. 201-9 and his "Romance and Realism in Western Canadian Fiction," in A.W. Rasporich and H.C. Klassen, eds., *Prairie Perspective 2* (Toronto, 1973), pp. 197-211; Henry Kreisel, "The Prairie: A State of Mind," *Transactions* of the Royal Society of Canada, 4th series, 6 (June 1968): 171-80; and Gerald Friesen, "Three generations of fiction: an introduction to prairie cultural history," in D.J. Bercuson and P.A. Buckner, eds., *Eastern and Western Perspectives* (Toronto, 1981), pp. 183-96.

Students wishing to pursue further the subject of Canadian-American prairie/plain literature should consult Robert Thacker, *The Great Prairie Fact and Literary Imagination* (Albuquerque, 1989); Dick Harrison, ed., *Crossing Frontiers: Papers in American and Canadian Western Literature* (Edmonton, 1979); and Carol Fairbanks, *Prairie Women: Images in American and Canadian Fiction* (New Haven, 1986).

On prairie art, students should consult the relevant sections in J. Russell Harper, *Painting in Canada* (Toronto, 1966). Ronald Rees deals with images of the West in prairie art in "Images of the Prairie: Landscape Painting and Perception in the Western Interior of Canada," *The Canadian Geographer* 20, no. 3 (1976): 259-78, in his book, *Land of Earth and Sky: Landscape Painting of Western Canada* (Saskatoon, 1984) and in sections of his *New and Naked Land: Making the Prairies Home* (Saskatoon, 1988). Lorne Render, *The Mountains and the Sky* (Calgary, 1974) discusses painters of the prairies and the mountains. Patricia Bovey, "Prairie Painting in the Thirties" in R.D. Francis and H. Ganzevoort, eds., *The Dirty Thirties in Prairie Canada* (Vancouver, 1980) pp. 111-24 looks at that important decade in prairie painting.

R. DOUGLAS FRANCIS

34 Changing Images of the West

At times one has the impression that the historians of western Canada have assumed that the best way to understand the evolution of their region is to compile study upon study of the most intricate and minute historical detail. Yet the history of the West* is more than a total of its parts. There is an aspect of its history which transcends the decisions of politicians, the intricate workings of the economy, and the daily activities of its people; it exists in the mind. The history of the West has often been governed as much by what people imagined the region to be as the "reality" itself. This paper will explore the changing images of the West by examining the secondary literature on the subject — to look at studies which attempt to explain the image in a particular time period — in an effort to discover what research has been done and what still remains to be done.

Historical geographers of western Canada have argued that prior to 1850 the North West was viewed as an area unsuitable for agricultural production and settlement. The image was first projected in Henry Kelsey's poetic report to the Hudson's Bay Company which resulted from his 1690-1692 expedition into the interior of western Canada. The report included such terms as "desert" and "barren ground" to describe the grassland region. John Warkentin notes that this negative image also prevailed in later fur trading accounts.[1] Another historical geographer, D.W. Moodie, demonstrates the difficulty faced by such opponents of the Hudson's Bay Company as Arthur Dobbs, a spokesman for British commercial interests, in refuting this negative image prior to 1850, even with the use of accurate scientific information.[2] As Wreford Watson points out, the terms "barren" and "desert" were equated with the lack of trees in the minds of Englishmen and eastern Canadians.

In Canada the matter did not end with semantics. People came actually to believe that where trees did not grow the soil could not produce. There was a mental equation that ran: bareness equals barrenness equals infertility equals uselessness for agriculture. Kelsey's report came out in a mental context which led to the illusion of a western wasteland.[3]

An equally unpopular view of the British North West existed in the United States. Warkentin notes that as early as 1820 the American explorer, Stephen Long, mapped the existence of a "Great Desert" north and east of the American Rocky Mountains which, it was believed (although not scientifically proven), existed from Mexico northwards into the Canadian West.[4] That image prevailed well into the 1850s and influenced John Palliser's perception of the area. Thus the Canadian West was viewed in negative terms from both a northern and a southern perspective with a resulting loss of interest in the agricultural potential of the region and an acceptance of the Hudson's Bay Company's undisputed control.

In the 1850s there was a marked change to a more positive image of the West. Douglas Owram's extensive study, *The Promise of Eden: The Canadian Expansionist Movement and the Idea of the West 1856-1900,* documents this changing perspective.[5] He leaves no doubt that a few visionary and aggressive individuals in a mid-nineteenth century Canadian expansionist group helped to mould a new and positive image of the West in the mind of the British and Canadian public which in turn contributed greatly to Canada's decision to acquire the North West.

Owram attributes the rising interest in the North West in the early 1850s to changing economic conditions. The prosperity following the Reciprocity Treaty of 1854 and the optimism of the railroad age made it feasible for the first time for Canadians to consider acquiring an economic hinterland of their own. The idea interested businessmen in Canada West, and they provided the financial backing necessary for such an enterprise to succeed. The expansionists also appealed to the agricultural interests of the United Canadas by warning them of the rapidly declining good agricultural land within their own boundaries and thus the need to look to the North West for further growth. Adding weight to the economic arguments of the expansionists were moral ones. The North West was seen as "the basis of power for the whole British Empire." Thus even before Canadians had had an opportunity to assess the potential of the land in the North West in order to judge its intrinsic value for agricultural settlement, there existed in the mind of powerful eastern commercial, political and expansionist interests an image of the North West. They saw it as a great agricultural hinterland which one day would make the united colonies of British North America a great and powerful nation and indeed the vital link in a greater British Empire. As a result, when the Hudson's Bay Company's charter came up for renewal in 1859, tremendous pressure was put on the Company to relinquish its hold on the North West and to sell it to Canada for settlement purposes.

Owram's study can be supplemented by other available materials on the period. L.H. Thomas has compiled a useful collection of primary sources on "the Mid-Century Debate on the Future of the North West" which includes helpful introductions and a good balance of excerpts from scientific reports, political speeches and newspaper editorials. F.H. Underhill's early article on the Clear Grit Movement is also useful because of its liberal quotations from George Brown's *Globe* concerning western expansion. The geographer G.S. Dunbar has shown the importance of Loren Blodgett, the noted American climatologist. Using the concept of isotherms as conceptualized by the European climatologist, Alexander von Humboldt, Blodgett compared the Canadian North West to similar regions in northern Europe for agricultural possibilities and concluded: "Climate is indisputably the decisive condition, and when we find the isothermal of 60° for the summer rising on the interior American plains to the 61st parallel, or fully as high as its average position for Europe, it is impossible to doubt the existence of favourable climates over vast areas now unoccupied."[6]

An important development in the mid-fifties was the sponsoring of two scientific expeditions to Rupert's Land: John Palliser's British expedition, and Henry Youle Hind's Canadian Expedition, both of which resulted in extensive and comprehensive reports. Two articles by John Warkentin already mentioned offer good insights into the images of the West in the two expeditionary reports. In addition, Irene Spry's valuable introduction to *The Papers of the Palliser Expedition, 1857-1860* discusses the background to the expedition and the image of the West which emerged from it.[7] W.L. Morton's recent biography of Henry Youle Hind partially fills a large gap in our knowledge of this man who so greatly influenced the perception of the West in British North America in the mid-nineteenth century. Morton devotes two chapters to discussing Hind's expeditions to the West in 1857 and 1858. While the chapters are more narrative than analytical, Morton does judge Hind's importance in popularizing the positive image of the West as a region with an extensive "fertile belt" — as a phrase which unlocked the North West. "Fertile belt" was the positive side of Palliser's negative image of the "desert" region conjured up by the term "Palliser's triangle." Morton notes:

The *Narrative* is first rate of its kind as a perceptive description of lands which, if known for over half a century, were to most people only vaguely known. Particularly was this true of the Canadian prairies. The fur traders had kept to the northern forests and explorers such as Franklin and Richardson had followed the routes of the fur trade. Hind had first presented, with the vividness which was his peculiar gift, the wide spaces and deep valleys of the grass and aspen country of the west. The *Narrative* was like a ship bursting into unknown seas. As such it remains at once a source of much and various detail and brilliant description of the plains on the eve of settlement.[8]

Owram's The *Promise of Eden* gives the impression that the expansionists of the 1850s were working in a vacuum, without the support of other groups — politicians, businessmen, artists and literary writers. In fact, their sudden success owed a great deal to the romantic image of the West as depicted in the artistic works of Paul Kane, the literary writings of John Ballantyne, and the propaganda of Captain William Francis Butler. Romanticism in the mid-nineteenth century was a strong force which inspired individuals and nations to open up new vistas of exploration. J. Russell Harper argues that Paul Kane had a tremendous impact in arousing interest in the West and its native people through his romantic image of the land and his depiction of the "noble savage." Harper notes:

> He painted the grass of the wildest regions trimmed like an English green sward. Trading boats descending the Saskatchewan River have the dignity of Roman galleys, and buffalo hunts are like wonderful tableaux on some gigantic stage . . . The stiffly posed warrior chieftains have a noble bearing. His personal romantic nature . . . was consistent with the spirit of the age.[9]

Kane was not the only artist to paint or sketch the region. Lesser known artists were making their contribution such as Peter Rindisbacher, George Brodie, George Frost, R.B. Nevitt and William C. Hind. These artists, notes Lorne Render in a chapter on "The Expeditionary Artists" in *The Mountain and the Sky*, were usually amateurs with some training who painted for practical purposes — often as members of a scientific expedition so as to provide visual information for official reports or illustrations for scientific journals.[10] Thus their paintings need to be judged not only on their aesthetic merits but also on their historical importance. As historical documents they reveal less a West actually seen than the romantic image of the West in the painter's eye before he actually saw the West. Ronald Rees notes that their early prairie scenes "were viewed through a filter of Victorian optimism with the result that most of the drawings and paintings presented an unforbidding, even cheerful image of the West."[11] J. Russell Harper draws the same conclusion in his biographical sketch of W.G.R. Hind: — "While William portrayed the factual elements of Indian life, he also must have had some feeling for the exotic and unknown . . . life, a feeling which was rooted in a romantic strain that was an integral facet of the Victorian age."[12] These romantic scenes greatly influenced subsequent perceptions of the West with the result that the "real" West for many people was the image perceived through the eye of the artist. Rees concludes: "As the first pictorial interpretations of the West they were instrumental in helping to establish images of the region in eastern North America and Europe."[13]

The romantic literature of the period had the same popular impact. Dick Harrison devotes part of a chapter in *Unnamed Country* to discussing the difficulty early travellers and settlers had in seeing the West on its own terms. Their eastern bias dictated what they wanted to or would see, and that bias was a mixture of romanticism and realism. It was a pastoral ideal moulded by perceptions of the West popular in Europe, the United States and eastern Canada. Harrison describes writers like R.M. Ballantyne and J.C. Collins as giving "the prairie a distinctly Walter Scott or Fenimore Cooper cast."[14] Ballantyne's image of the West as the home of great adventure coloured his own self-image, and he spent the latter days of his life in Scotland "lecturing about his experiences in Rupert's Land, striding purposefully across the stage, black-bearded and handsome, and dressed in the colourful coat and leggings of a North American trapper."[15]

This new positive image of the Prairie West in the 1850s contributed to the decision of the Canadian government to purchase Rupert's Land in 1869 and to incorporate it into the Dominion. What image was in the mind of the Fathers of Confederation when they thought of the West? Unfortunately little work has been done on the subject, but in the late 1960s and early seventies a lively debate developed on the West and Confederation which centred on the image of the nation as reflected in the issue of language rights in the Manitoba Act of 1870 and the North West Territories Act of 1875. Stated simply, the question was whether the Fathers of Confederation envisioned the West (and ultimately the nation) as unilingual and unicultural, or bilingual and bicultural. Donald Creighton, in "John A. Macdonald, Confederation and the Canadian West," argued that the Fathers of Confederation, particularly the nation's first prime minister, did not favour a bilingual West but were forced into recognizing the two languages in the Manitoba Act by a dictatorial Louis Riel. Macdonald's image was of a West which was a reflection in language and culture of Ontario, very much in line with expansionist views as outlined by Owram. Ralph Heintzman rejoined with a persuasive argument that the Fathers had a "spirit" of cooperation and goodwill at the time of Confederation which extended to the view of the North West's constitutional structure. A third article on the subject, by David Hall, attacks Heintzman and endorses Creighton's position.[16]

Less controversial was the image in the minds of individual English-speaking Canadian politicians, and in the collective mind of Ontarians, of the West as a colony of central Canada. W.L. Morton, the dean of western Canadian history, first presented this argument in his ground-breaking article "Clio in Canada: The Interpretation of Canadian History," and extended it in "The Bias of Prairie Politics" and in his excellent study, *Manitoba: A History*.[17] J.E. Rea speculated further on the implications for western attitudes.[18] Using Louis Hartz's model of fragmented cultures, Rea argued that the West (particularly Manitoba) was a fragment of the dominant culture of Ontario. The early migrants implanted their Ontario culture on the West so successfully that Manitoba adopted a more Ontarian perspective than the original province itself. The image was "rural Ontario West." L.H.

Thomas and Donald Swainson agree with Rea on the dominant image of a colonial west. Two other historians, Greg Thomas and Ian Clarke, claim that the human landscape of the early fur traders with their palisaded forts, and the first British-Ontario farmers with their tree-walled homesteads was an attempt to recreate the West in the image of the eastern landscape from which they had come; it belied the reality of the existing landscape.[19]

The Canadian artists of the late nineteenth century reflected this central Canadian vision. In his recent study, *Our Own Country, Canada,* Denis Reid contends that the artists of the period 1850 to 1900 were driven as much by "a sense of advancement and self-improvement" as by visions of national grandeur, but that the two concepts — the ideal and the reality — became indistinguishable. Their artistic renditions of the Canadian drive to the West were depicted in "romantic and naturalistic images of the noble adversary, the strong and resistant land itself." Reid makes the link more explicit:

> In the mid-eighties this romantic involvement with the land found con-crete manifestation in the ribbon of steel that sought to physically bind the nation together. The promoters of the CPR understood the force of images, and they encouraged the associations artists made between their road and the picturesque wonders it opened. If they saw themselves as nation-builders, they were also eager to be seen as enriching the cultural life of the nation . . . The remarkable success of the CPR programme in promoting interest in artistic views of the Rockies and the West Coast represents the first significant instance of a widespread acceptance in Canada of the myth of the land as the basis of a national art.[20]

No individual is more identified with the CPR and the optimistic vision of the West than John Macoun. He played an important role in projecting an image of the North West as "the greatest agricultural region of the world." In a study of John Macoun's writings on the West, W.A. Waiser argues that the botanist's optimistic image was simply a reflection of the prevailing view of his time. In the United States, for example, "the Great American desert became known as the Great American Plains—what was termed as 'an imaginative conquest'. Men's illusions about a new environment were more important than the real geography of the land itself." In Canada, the West was linked to the national potential of the new Dominion. Macoun provided the bond in his exaggerated vision of the entire region — even the southern grasslands — as having agricultural potential. In *Manitoba and the Great North-West* Macoun wrote:

> Want, either present or future is not to be feared, and man living in a healthy and soul invigorating atmosphere will attain his highest develop-ment, and a nation will yet rise on these great plains that will have no superior on the American continent.[21]

It was Macoun's optimistic image of the southern grasslands that helped persuade the Canadian Pacific Railway Company to build its line via the southern route rather than follow the North Saskatchewan River Valley.

Two articles offer some insight into the romantic images in the literature of the late nineteenth century. The first, Irene Spry's "Early Visitors to the Canadian Prairies," introduces a multiplicity of writings of early visitors to the West and the images they portrayed. The second, Patrick Dunae's " 'Making Good': The Canadian West in British Boy's Literature, 1880-1914," explains the romantic vision of the West which inspired "the immigration of youthful and ambitious British males to western Canada in late-Victorian and Edwardian times," and thus goes a long way to explaining the large number of young, single British settlers in western Canada at the turn of the century. Dunae notes that:

. . . western Canada was a popular setting for much of this literature. The region offered a hardy climate plus an impressive landscape and, with a little embellishment, boys' writers could readily introduce hostile natives and a population of struggling white pioneers.

Of related interest is an article by the western Canadian historian, L.H. Thomas, which examines the increasing interest in the West after 1885 by a growing number of middle-class British visitors who for the first time could afford the journey west thanks to cheaper and more efficient transportation.[22]

This positive image contrasts strikingly with the negative one in the mind of Quebecers. Arthur Silver offers evidence that French Canadians were discouraged from going West because Quebec politicians, newspaper editors and parish priests convinced them that "western settlement was the sole concern of Ontario." These formulators of public opinion established three major images of the Canadian West: that the land was infertile and "agricultural failure was almost certain"; that it was unsafe for a French Canadian to live outside the province of Quebec for "in the rest of the dominion his national identity would be endangered"; and that Manitoba could never be considered "part of their country."[23] This Quebec image of the West — more mythologized than factual — had tremendous implications for the cultural tradition of the West.

Robert Painchaud has added a new dimension by looking at the image of the West in the minds of those French-Canadian priests who were already in the West. He argues that despite a concerted effort by these priests to persuade Quebecers to come West, they failed because the Quebec priests and politicians saw the West as a weakening influence, with its separate school problems and multicultural immigration, on a strong French-Canadian identity. Better for French Canadians to remain in a strong Quebec.[24]

What still remains somewhat of a mystery is the way in which this central

Canadian image of the West in the minds of the early western settlers was transformed during the late nineteenth century into a western Canadian consciousness. Indeed, many of the Ontario expansionists later became the strongest exponents of western regionalism and led the struggle of the West to liberate itself from alleged eastern oppression. Owram devotes a chapter to the question, and attributes the shift in loyalty to the economic depression of the 1880s and the resulting tarnished image of this land of opportunity. As Gerald Friesen has shown, "the myth of the West" which lay at the base of its regional consciousness in the late nineteenth century was rooted in

> . . . an emphasis upon the new society which would be created in an 'empty' land. Environmentalism, pastoral and agrarian myths, physiocratic beliefs, and elements now associated with the 'frontier' thesis — democracy, egalitarianism, individualism, co-operation, virility, opportunity, innovation — were aspects of the new society in popular estimation.[25]

Friesen, however, does not explain how these images became part of western consciousness nor how they affected the way westerners saw themselves.

Paul Rutherford argues that "the western press was the chief exponent of western regionalism" in the late nineteenth century and that the press instilled into the minds of its readers a strong regional image based on the myth of the superiority of the West:

> The myth presumed that the west was destined to become the granary of the world, the last and richest frontier of European expansion . . . [The press] argues that the 'new Canada' would be a better society, free from the mistakes of other lands. By 'better' they meant more simple, more individualistic.[26]

It was an image based upon a suspicion of eastern interests and a feeling that the West was a region with its own ideals which, paradoxically the press argued, were still "Canadian." Hence Rutherford concludes that "western regionalism seemed based upon two opposed concepts, regional alienation and 'Canadianism.'"

The positive image of the West in the formative period of western development in part stimulated the large-scale surge of American, British and European immigration at the turn of the century. There is no definitive study of the various images of the Canadian West presented in the extensive immigration propaganda distributed by the Canadian government, the Canadian Pacific Railway Company, and private land companies. Klaus Peter Stich has made a beginning from the literary perspective by analyzing five samples of propaganda literature *qua* literature. He denies that such literature was simply "distortions and lies" but was, rather, one genre of popular *fiction* — "realistic-cum-romantic" — which, like all literature, helped to shape "western Canada's cultural image at home and abroad."[27] It was an optimistic vision of "Canada's Century."

An offshoot of this immigration propaganda was boosterism — a deliberate attempt by urban leaders to present an inflated image of their home town in hopes of an eventual self-fulfilling prophecy. Urban historians are only beginning to examine this side of urban growth, but Alan Artibise speculates that boosterism was as important a factor in urbanization on the Prairies as were natural physical factors. He notes:

> . . . explanations of prairie urban development cannot be carried on entirely in terms of the usual factors of site and situation . . . . The physical and economic environments are inert and unimportant until human effort is applied to them. Urban centres and regions do not grow in the organic sense of the word; they are rather, the product of thousands of individual and group decisions. These decisions, in turn, are a product of a particular cultural milieu and reflect the biases and knowledge of the actors.[28]

Boosterism was particularly strong in the West because of the underdeveloped prairies, the lack of natural physical advantages, and the uniform topography. In such an environment, the mental component — the positive image in the minds of a city's elite and citizenry — was often the deciding factor in urban success or failure.

Ethnic historians have often neglected the role of imagery in evaluating the conditions that caused immigrants to leave their native land and to react as they did in Canada. There are two notable exceptions. In his study of Dutch immigration to Canada in the years 1892-1940, Herman Ganzevoort devotes a chapter to the role of the emigration agent "who depended on myth rather than fact to recruit. And it was all too obvious that myth and not reality was the great drawing card for potential emigrants."[29] A further chapter discusses the images of the West projected by emigration societies and in governmental propaganda. Anthony Rasporich's study of western Canadian utopian settlements examines the vision which inspired a significant number of ethnic, religious and social groups in the pre-1914 era. He concludes:

> The ideals of social cooperation and of work as a creative act of self-fulfillment, and the concept of the garden city were all essential components of these strains of late-century liberal-imperial thought which shaped the Anglo-Canadian mentality of the early Northwest before the First World War.[30]

This idealism, he implies, was a strong force behind the agrarian protest which followed the war. When the initial idealistic utopias were inevitably unfulfilled in the harsh economic and physical realities of western Canada, these individuals simply substituted their earlier more naive image with one more closely rooted in the economic and political realities of the time. Yet it can be argued that the agrarian ideology of the twenties was no less idealistic in its fundamental perception. The western farmer premised his fight against the East, big business and urban encroachment on the image that "God Made the Country, Man Made the Town" — that farmers were God's Chosen People, and that the family farm was the ideal social unit. Unfortunately, the ideology of agrarian reform has received less attention than the politics and economics of western protest.[31]

Utopianism was only part of a much broader image of the West as "the new and ideal society," so popular in the first two decades of the twentieth century. This vision sustained the farmers' protest movement; it also inspired the Social Gospel Movement — which drew much of its leadership and support from, and had its most significant impact in, the West. As the newest region of settlement, the West held out higher hopes than the older and more established areas.[32] This image of a "new society" was reflected in the early western Canadian literature. Whether one is discussing the tremendous popularity of Ralph Connor, R.J.C. Stead, Nellie McClung, Emily Murphy (Janey Canuck) or lesser literary figures, there is a sameness in their romantic image of the Canadian West as "the garden of the world." As Dick Harrison notes in *Unnamed Country*:

> Like Eden, their West had no past, only a present beginning when the settlers arrive, and a better future. This was, of course, a time of boom and optimism and, for the writers at least, a time of agrarian ideals . . . . There is no doubt that at this stage the literary imagination was out of touch with certain hard realities of the plains, though no more so than the practical minds that planned the agricultural expansion in the West.[33]

Gerald Friesen, a cultural historian, indicates that this image was transformed into "reality" by associating the pastoral ideal directly with the physical locale of western Canada in the minds of both western writers and politicians.

> Whether described as a former garden or an untouched land, the west was to be the home of a new society; the pastoral ideal as thus moved from literature into history, from form into reality, and become both a place and a mode of belief . . . . The 'West', which in post-confederation Canada had a precise geographical location, had become an idyllic region.[34]

This early group of western literary figures described their region in terms of its contrast to the East. They imagined the West to be "young, not old;

free, not restrained by convention; egalitarian, not caste-bound; virile, not feeble; close to nature, not urban. It offered a new start, not enslavement by history." The explanation for the contrast was environmental; the land itself moulded an individual's character. One of Ralph Connors' characters explained: "How wonderful the power of this country of yours to transform men."[35] The ideal West lay in the future, a Golden Age, when the "good guys" moulded by their western environment would prevail over the "bad guys" who came West contaminated by their eastern environment.

This image was reinforced in the historiography of the West in the period up to and including the 1920s. Doug Owram examines the historiography of western Canada up to 1900 and concludes that there emerged during this period an interpretation of history which emphasized the uniqueness and strength of western Canada in contrast to the region to the East. Owram concludes:

> Resentful of their treatment at the hands of the East and Ottawa, westerners had rejected the eastern interpretation of their place within the nation and had looked to the land around them for a new definition of their role. In so doing they developed all the necessary prerequisites for a strong sense of regional identity . . . . The West was no longer merely an adjunct of the East or an annexed land; it was, westerners felt, something more than 'a new Upper Canada', and something better.[36]

The frontier school of thought which was borrowed from F.J. Turner's thesis in American historiography and which became popular in Canadian historical writing in the 1920s, reinforced the image of the West as superior to the East. The West was seen as the home of democracy, the inspiration for reform, and the seed-bed of individualism, radicalism and freedom, in contrast to the more privileged conservative and reactionary East. As J.M.S. Careless concluded: "Canadian environmentalists frequently displayed the compelling mood of the frontier school, with its moral implications of a struggle between sound native democratic forces [in the West] and elements that cling to privilege, exploitation, and empty Old-World forms [in the East]."[37]

The emphasis on environment affected the image of the West in Canadian literature as well. In the 1920s, a new "realistic" image emerged (in contrast to the earlier romantic literature) with the publication of three notable prairie novels — Martha Ostenso's *Wild Geese* (1925), Robert Stead's *Grain* (1926), and Phillip Grove's *Settlers of the Marsh* (1925). All three depicted a hostile and alien prairie environment. The strong emphasis on environmental influences on the characters in these and other prairie novels has led some literary critics, notably E.A. McCourt, Henry Kreisel, and Laurence Ricou, to conclude that the image of the West must be sought through an understanding of the impact of environment on perception. Kreisel writes: "All discussion of the literature produced in the Canadian west must of necessity begin with the impact of the landscape upon the mind." Similarly, Laurence Ricou concludes that prairie fiction illustrates "both the prevalence of the myth of the land in Canadian writing and the regional qualities which derive from the encounter with a specific distinctive landscape."[38]

Western Canadian artists in the 1920s — L.L. Fitzgerald, W.J. Phillips, Illingworth Kerr and Robert Hurley — also looked to the landscape to create a new regional consciousness. They were doing for the West what the Group of Seven was doing for Canada in general: namely, discovering images of the land which could become symbols of identity. One of the best known was Robert Hurley, an English painter who came to Saskatchewan in 1923. He broke with the romantic tradition in western Canadian art by shifting the iconography from streams and wooded valleys — uncharacteristic prairie landscape scenes — to flat prairie, railways, telephone posts, grain elevators and an expansive sky — images that he stereotyped as representing the essence of the prairie. Ronald Rees describes Hurley's technique: "By suppressing detail and by using hard, clean outlines and bold, exaggerated colours, Hurley was able to convey a sense of the simplicity and emptiness of the landscape and evoke the clarity and harshness of the prairie light."[39] Hurley inaugurated a new era in western Canadian art by shifting the artistic image of the West from a promised land to a harsh environment, and hence forcing the artist to seek its meaning in abstraction or symbolism.

The onslaught of the Great Depression erased the remaining vestiges of the West as a promised land. As the hardest hit region, the West came to symbolize all the worst aspects of the Depression. The very phrase "The Dirty Thirties" conveyed the new image and conjured up

> . . . awesome pictures of defeat, long lines of unemployed; boxcars covered by men 'riding the rods'; the boredom of relief camps; windfall apples and surplus cod; whirling plagues of dust and grasshoppers; the interminable bitter heat of the unrelenting prairie sun.[40]

A useful study for a cultural historian would be to examine the image of the West in the popular literature of the decade. One would expect to find a similar view to the negative one in the classic novel of the prairie West in the 1930s — Sinclair Ross's As For Me and My House, "the most severe of the Depression novels." According to Dick Harrison:

> . . . we see the complete progress of the prairie from beneficent to indifferent to hostile environment. What is new is a strain of desert imagery, with its inevitable suggestion of spiritual sterility extending to characters like Philip and Mrs. Bentley.[41]

Not surprisingly, the Great Depression witnessed a new environmentalist approach to Canadian history which was as harsh in its image of the West as that depicted in the literature of the time. The Laurentian thesis argued that the metropolitan centres of central Canada formed a commercial, political and cultural empire that dominated and exploited the hinterlands, like the West, which came under its influence. Thus the West ceased to be seen as the creative centre of the nation which had constantly thrown up new ideas and democratic movements (as in the frontier thesis) and was depicted instead as a region subordinate to the East and one essentially conservative and even reactionary in its ethos. Careless summarized the idea this way:

> The Laurentian School . . . looked not from the forest-born frontiers for its perspective of Canadian history but from developing eastern centres of commerce and industry. Indeed, it primarily studied the effects of the East on the West, and largely regarded business men and conservative urban political elements as agents of national expansion who might well be more far-sighted in their outlook than were their agrarian opponents.[42]

Out of the West there arose in the post-World War II era a voice of protest. The western Canadian historian, W.L. Morton, accepted the validity of the Laurentian interpretation for an understanding of Canadian history but objected to the negative image of western Canada it implied. This image, he believed, could only lead to an inferiority complex among western Canadians which would ultimately be more pervasive in influencing the history of western Canada than the impact of the environment itself, a case of mind over matter. Truth is how an individual perceives it, which in the case of a western Canadian would be that of a second-class citizen of Canada.

Morton set out to dispel this negative image by attempting to create a new self-image in the minds of westerners through an appreciation of their history. He would have agreed wholeheartedly with his colleague, A.R.M. Lower, who argued that history is myth and the historian a myth-maker.[43] Morton described *Manitoba: A History* as "a history that informs and shapes our minds." The history — and therefore the image — of the West that Morton created was one which saw the region as attempting to be like, not different from the rest of Canada. He argued in fact that the West has been germane to the Canadian experience and that its history could be seen as a miniature replica of the nation itself.

Yet Morton's image of the West had its own limitations. J.E. Rea has observed in an appropriately entitled article, "Images of the West,"[44] that Morton could not get beyond his own image — moulded by his personal experience of growing up in a British family on a prairie homestead — of the West as an essentially rural, agricultural and British society; his vision could not incorporate the European immigrants and the urban West. Morton reveals the roots of his agrarian image in "Seeing an Unliterary Landscape," an article characterized by imagery. It can also be argued that, by emphasizing the constant struggle of western Canada for equality with and recognition by the rest of the nation, Morton has reinforced the subordinate position of the West while ironically trying to dispel it. In "The Bias of Prairie Politics," for example, he argued that "the subordinate status given the West in Confederation was the initial bias that set in train the development of prairie politics towards an increasing differentiation from the Canadian standard."[45] To Morton this initial bias explained all of western Canadian history, from the struggle for political equality in Confederation in the period 1870 to 1905, to the rise of agrarian revolt in the years 1905-1925, to the utopian period from 1925 to the present.

What Morton did for the historiography of western Canada current literary critics, such as Eli Mandel, Dick Harrison and W.H. New, have done for its literature. They have challenged the "environmentalist approach" with its belief that literature is a product of the landscape. In "Images of Prairie Man," Mandel characteristically reverses the earlier association of environment and mind, to argue that the landscape is itself nothing more than the image which exists in the mind of the beholder. Thus writers are also "conscious myth-makers" who do not simply reflect the region itself but help to create it. Robert Kroetsch expresses the idea this way: "In a sense we haven't got an identity until somebody tells our story. The fiction makes us real." Social mythologies — the myths of history — create the mind-set which in turn superimposes a form of reality on the particular place being mythologized. With respect to the prairies, Mandel expresses it thus: "What isn't clear is whether the prairies themselves are a form that imposes itself on the resistant self or whether it goes the other way around: we possess these stories, not even our own, and try to put their shapes on a world which resists fiercely."[46] A study of regional literature becomes a search for identity — a search characteristic of Morton's search by means of history for his identity — his image of the West as his homeland, his cultural roots.

A similar internalizing of the landscape has occurred among Canadian geographers, resulting in a new interpretation of regionalism which in turn has affected their image of the West. Some current geographers have argued that there are no "natural" regions in Canada based upon formal physical features. Instead regions should be defined according to the perceptions and use that man makes of his particular physical environment at any given time, which in turn changes over time. As Wreford Watson explained the concept:

. . . physical geography should be brought into regional geography, as something which, when perceived by man and translated into certain images based on the aims and powers people have at their time, then becomes a cogent, meaningful reality: but always a reality in terms of man's perception. The real "reality" is the image in the mind, rather than the pattern on the ground.[47]

Thus man's changing images of the land become the primary concern of geographers.

This new approach has led geographers to argue that a region must be understood according to man's perception of its *function,* i.e. its relation to other regions or to the nation as a whole, rather than its *form,* i.e. its natural environment. Hence J. Howard Richards has seen the uniqueness of the Prairie region not in its physical form but in its functional role as the economic hinterland of wheat production for external metropolitan centres — a view very much in keeping with the metropolitan-hinterland concept of Canadian history. The image he depicted was an isolated region — isolated not only nor primarily by vast spaces and sparse population but by an attitude — a perception — which has kept the West distinct from the urban and industrial growth of the rest of the nation. The physical and political isolation of the West has been, in Richard's view, further "reinforced by a sense of psychological separateness and difference which modern communications have not removed." It is this perceptual isolation in particular that

> . . . has helped to create a special identity, and common acceptance of this has induced a conceptual frame in which popular characterizations such as 'bread basket' and 'colonial economy' are frequent, and vague ideas exist of second class economic status *vis-à-vis* the rest of Canada.[48]

Wreford Watson raised the further question:

> . . . to what extent the Prairie People, having found in wheat a commodity that in a sense defied isolation, entrenched themselves as wheat producers, thereby isolating themselves from the incentive and the opportunity to engage in industry? Perhaps we have blamed the natural environment for what the environment of the mind really caused.[49]

The image of an inferior region in its historical relationship to the nation reinforced a way of life and a perception of the landscape which become a self-fulfilling prophecy. This has led Watson to appeal to his fellow geographers to study "mental images of our environment" — the internal landscape — as the most fruitful means of understanding the geography of a region or the nation. "Somehow the mental images of our environment must be measured by geographers and become part of geographical study because they affect the actual way in which men use their world and make their geographies."[50]

Prairie painters also turned to the internal landscape by means of abstract painting as the best means to capture the image of the West. Patricia Bovey claims that the prairie landscape has been particularly suited to abstract painting because of its common denominators of sky and land.[51] Illingworth Kerr, Saskatchewan's native-born professional painter, was one of the first prairie artists to attempt abstract painting, claiming that "abstract was the answer to Western space with its vast scale, its power of mood, rather than tangible form."[52] Abstraction has done for the western Canadian artist what the search for universals did for its literary writers or what functional regionalism did for historical geographers or historians: freed him from the restrictive search for the image of the West in the physical landscape and enabled him to search within himself. Northrop Frye observed in a different context:

> The effect of stylizing and simplifying is to bring out more clearly not what the artist sees, but what he experiences in his seeing. Abstraction sets the painter free from the particular experiences, and enables him to paint the essence of his pictorial vision.[53]

The "real" landscape is within the mind of the artist, and it changes as each prairie artist paints his own West anew.

The underlying premise in the metropolitan interpretation of Canadian history, in the functional approach to regionalism in Canadian geography and in the mythical concept of Canadian literature, is of a region that has been predominantly an agricultural hinterland in its nature and in its association with the rest of Canada. Yet western Canada has undergone tremendous economic and social changes since World War II which have led to increased urbanization and industrialization. Have these changes resulted in new images of the West? Only recently, in the past two decades, have historian, geographers, political scientists, artists and literary critics addressed themselves to this question.

A number of historical geographers argue that the social changes have had little impact because the prevailing image of the West as an agricultural hinterland has continued to exert a powerful influence on the development of the region long after it ceases to be valid. Despite the increase in urban population and the development of new primary industries based on the new staples of fossil fuels and potash and the resulting increase in tertiary industries, there has been no change in the western image of itself as an economic hinterland. Prairie urban centres still see themselves in relation to metropolitan centres in the East rather than as foci for national centres on their own. Within the West itself, the towns and cities continue to function as "service centres for farms and ranches" long after agriculture and ranching have ceased to be the dominant economic activities of the region. Hence Kaye and Moodie conclude, in "Geographical Perspectives on the Canadian Plains," that the historical evolution of the West as an agricultural hinterland has given the region a uniformity and a sense of uniqueness even after it has become urbanized and industrialized like the rest of the nation.[54] Past images still dictate present developments. In a study of architecture in small towns of Saskatchewan, the historical geographer, Ronald Rees, reinforces the view. Rural values — thrift, industry, pragmatism and sobriety — still dictate prairie architectural styles:

> The small frame buildings, the unpaved streets, the false fronts, and the general air of seediness and decay give the small towns a look of impermanence which is only slightly offset by the occasional brick building such as a bank, station or municipal office. The larger and sturdier centres are more reassuring. But in these, too, the visitor is conscious of only a partially developed urbanity, for the general aspect is an expression of utilitarian rather than social or aesthetic values.[55]

Kaye and Moodie conclude as well that "the cultural patterns established during the classic period of plains agricultural occupance are still the dominant ones today."[56]

This hypothesis is consistent with recent work by Alan Artibise on the impact of boosterism on current trends in prairie urban development. He argues that the image of tremendous growth of urban centres within the context of an agricultural hinterland role, which was so much a part of the booster mentality in the pre-1914 era, continued to exert a powerful influence in subsequent periods including the post-1950 era when the West ceased to be a predominantly agricultural region. "By the 1950s prairie cities were in most respects still tied to structures, ideas, and routines of a bygone era, and no amount of simple manoeuvering could alter this legacy in a major way."[57] Thus the image the elites attempted to foster tended to retard rather than to stimulate growth.

These conclusions differ markedly from that of the political scientist Roger Gibbins in his recent study, *Prairie Politics and Society*.[58] He claims that the prevailing image of the West as a rural agricultural hinterland victimized by eastern interests is no longer applicable in the urban industrial West of today. The result is a decline in regional consciousness and a rise in provincial power. Yet Gibbins fails to explain why modernization should lead to an even narrower base of identity than the region itself. One would expect a similarity in economic, social and demographic trends in the West to that of the nation in general to foster a national identity. Westerners should become more like other Canadians in attitude and political behaviour, yet Gibbins concludes otherwise. It would appear that images of injustice, victimization and inequality still prevail as "western" traits in all three provinces of the West (although Gibbins' evidence emphasizes Alberta); they are simply linked to the provinces rather than the region as a whole.

Yet has this not been 'traditionally true'? The West has never been a common political region to the same extent that it has been a common economic, cultural or social region. If regions are defined in functional terms, as geographers have argued, then the West can have different boundaries if one is speaking in political terms as opposed to cultural or economic terms. Thus the traditional images continue to exist and to assert the influence they did in the past. This conclusion is reinforced in a recent article, "Political culture in the West." David Smith argues that throughout the history of the Prairie provinces there have been certain ideas which have prevailed, in spite of the changing nature of western Canada, and which have become part of the political culture of the West: a rejection of English-French dualism on the prairies, a distrust of central control, either public (governmental) or private (corporate); and a need to struggle consistently to protect regional resources and to assert regional autonomy against central domination. The image of the West as a victimized region lives on.[59]

Prairie writers have been sensitive to the changing nature of the West. To contemporary writers the old agrarian West is gone, the subject of reflection and reinterpretation. More than this, it has become, according to Dick Harrison, a subject of rediscovery since it is necessary to discover new images of the West in order to free it from the restraints of the older images which no longer fit. This required "re-naming the past," the title of the last chapter of Harrison's *Unnamed Country,* which deals with the views of contemporary western Canadian novelists. In a prairie world out of touch with the images of an agrarian West, the past events can no longer be real but must be symbolic acts. As Harrison writes: "The prairies become less a thing 'out there' which must be shaped physically as well as imaginatively and more a territory within the psyche which must be explored and understood . . ."[60] Eli Mandel explains it thus:

> . . . it is not place but attitude, state of mind, that defines the western writer — and that state of mind, I want to suggest, has a good deal to do with a tension between place and culture, a doubleness or duplicity, that makes the writer a man not so much in place, as out of place and so one endlessly trying to get back to find his way home, to return, to write himself into existence, writing west.[61]

To be western is a way of perceiving that becomes "real," independent of the physical place itself. Still it is the myths, legends and feelings of the region, evoked by its geography and history, which will decide the imagery that writers use in recapturing their lost home. For the search for home is but an understanding of self which, in turn, is a product of time and place. The search must continue to be pursued within the traditional framework — the altering image — of the region itself. But these entities no longer have a narrow, restrictive role; they are fluid entities which influence each individual differently and hence make the West very much an image within the mind of the beholder. There continues, therefore, to be a healthy and creative tension between "perception" or "imagery," and "reality."

The search for home, for self, the need to define oneself in context of time and place — to discover images of the West — which have concerned contemporary literary writers, have also been the subject of western Canadian art, particularly the paintings of William Kurelek. In a penetrating analysis of Kurelek's paintings, Ramsay Cook notes that the artist's "farm paintings and his religious paintings were the product of the same imagination."[62] It was an imagination moulded by the Prairies — the product of a particular time and place. His paintings are part of "Kurelek's creation of a new past, part of his search for himself, a coming to terms with his own past by recreating it." It was a search within for the images which best captured the West that was so much a part of himself — a journey taken by a number of western Canadian writers, including W.L. Morton. His images of the West have become part of our perception of it, as much a part of the West as the physical landscape itself.

In conclusion, it is evident that the West has changed over time, and that the change has been due as much, if not more, to the altering perceptions or images of the region as to the changing physical environment. The change has been within the mind. The West is, as Richard Allen notes, "a mental construct."[63] And the image has imposed a form on the external entity which has transformed it into the identity given to it at a particular period in history. Each generation searches anew for an image that gives meaning to its perception of the physical locale and historical evolution of the region. Hence the changing images of the West.

ACKNOWLEDGEMENTS

I wish to acknowledge my appreciation to Anthony Rasporich, Howard Palmer, Donald Smith, Herman Ganzevoort and Robert MacDonald for their helpful comments on this essay.

NOTES
*   The term "West" refers to the North West in the fur trading era and the Prairie provinces in the post-confederation era.
1. J. Warkentin, "Steppe, Desert and Empire," in A.W. Rasporich and H.C. Klassen, eds. *Prairie Perspectives* 2 (Toronto: Holt, Rinehart and Winston, 1973); and *The Western Interior of Canada: A Record of Geographical Discovery: 1612-1917* (Toronto: McClelland and Stewart, 1964).
2. D.W. Moodie, "Early British Images of Rupert's Land," in R. Allen, ed., *Man and Nature on the Prairies* (Regina: Canadian Plains Studies Centre, 1976).
3. W. Watson, "The Role of Illusion in North American Geography: A Note on the Geography of North American Settlement," *The Canadian Geographer*, XIII (Spring 1969), p. 16.
4. J. Warkentin, "The Desert Goes North," in Brian Blouet and M. Lawson, eds., *Images of the Plains: The Role of Human Nature in Settlement* (Lincoln: University of Nebraska Press, 1975), pp. 149-63.

5. Douglas Owram, *Promise of Eden: The Canadian Expansionist Movement and the Idea of the West, 1856-1900* (Toronto: University of Toronto Press, 1980).

6. L.H. Thomas, "Mid-Century Debate on the Future of the Northwest," in J.M. Bumsted, ed., *Documentary Problems in Canadian History*, Vol. 1 (Georgetown: Irwin-Dorsey Ltd., 1969); F.H. Underhill, "Some Aspects of Upper Canadian Radical Opinion in the Decade Before Confederation," in Canadian Historical Association Annual *Report* (1927), pp. 46-61; G.S. Dunbar, "Isotherms and Politics: Perception of the Northwest in the Rasporich and Klassen, *Prairie Perspectives* 2, p. 94.

7. Irene Spry, Introduction to *The Papers of the Palliser Expedition, 1857-1860* (Toronto: Champlain Society, 1968).

8. W.L. Morton, *Henry Youle Hind: 1823-1908*, Canadian Biographical Studies Series (Toronto: University of Toronto Press, 1980), p. 86.

9. J. Russell Harper, *Painting in Canada* (Toronto: University of Toronto Press, 1966), p. 150.

10. Lorne Render, *The Mountain and the Sky* (Calgary: McClelland and Stewart West for Glenbow-Alberta Institute, 1974) p. 18.

11. Ronald Rees, "Images of the Prairie: Landscape Painting and Perception in the Western Interior in Canada," *The Canadian Geographer*, XX (1976), p. 261.

12. J. Russell Harper, *William G.R. Hind: 1883-1889* (Ottawa: National Museum of Canada, 1976), p. 19.

13. Rees, "Images of the Prairie," p. 260.

14. Dick Harrison, *Unnamed Country: The Struggle for a Canadian Prairie Fiction* (Edmonton: University of Alberta Press, 1977), p. 24.

15. Eric Quayle, "R.M. Ballantyne in Rupert's Land," *Queen's Quarterly*, 75 (Spring 1968), p. 70.

16. D. Creighton, "John A. Macdonald, Confederation and the Canadian West," *Historical and Scientific Society of Manitoba*, Series 3, No. 23 (1966-67), pp 5-13; R. Heintzman, "The Spirit of Confederation: Professor Creighton, Biculturalism, and the Use of History," *Canadian Historical Review*, 52 (September 1971), pp. 245-75; D.J. Hall, " 'The Spirit of Confederation': Ralph Heintzman, Professor Creighton, and the Bicultural Compact Theory," *Journal of Canadian Studies*, 9 (November 1974), pp. 24-43.

17. W.L. Morton, "Clio in Canada: The Interpretation of Canadian History," *University of Toronto Quarterly*, XV (April 1946), pp. 227-34; "The Bias of Prairie Politics," *Transactions of the Royal Society of Canada*, XLIX Series III, Section II (June 1955), pp. 57-66; *Manitoba: A History* (Toronto: University of Toronto Press, 1957).

18. J.E. Rea, "The Roots of Prairie Society," in D. Gagan, ed., *Prairie Perspectives* (Toronto: Holt, Rinehart and Winston, 1970), pp. 46-57).

19. L.G. Thomas, "Introduction" to *The Prairie West to 1905: A Canadian Sourcebook* (Toronto: Oxford University Press, 1975); D Swainson, "Canada Annexes the West: Colonial Status Confirmed," in B. Hodgins. D. Wright and W. Heick, eds., *Federalism in Canada and Australia: The Early Years* (Waterloo: Wilfrid Laurier Press, 1978), pp. 137-57; Greg Thomas and Ian Clarke, "The Garrison Mentality and the Canadian West," *Prairie Forum*, 4 (Spring 1979), pp. 83-104.

20. Denis Reid, *Our Own Country, Canada: Being an Account of the National*

Aspirations of the Principal Landscape Artists in Montreal and Toronto, 1860-1890 (Ottawa: National Museums of Canada, 1979), p. 68.

21. W.A. Waiser, "Macoun and the Great North-West," M.A. Thesis (University of Saskatchewan, 1976), p. 125.

22. I. Spry, "Early Visitors to the Canadian Prairies," in *Images of the Plains*; Patrick Dunae, " 'Making Good': The Canadian West in British Boy's Literature, 1880-1914," in *Prairie Forum* 4 (Fall 1979), p. 166; L.H. Thomas, "British Visitors' Perception of the West: 1885-1914," in *Prairie Perspectives* 2.

23. A. Silver, "French Canada and the Prairie Frontier, 1870-1890," *Canadian Historical Review*, L (March 1969), pp. 11-36.

24. R. Painchaud, "French-Canadian Historiography and Franco-Catholic Settlement in Western Canada, 1870-1915," *Canadian Historical Review*, LIX (December 1978), pp. 47-66; also "French-speaking Settlers on the Prairies, 1870-1920," *Canada's Visual History Series* I, Vol. 19 (Ottawa: National Museum of Man, 1974).

25. Gerald Friesen, "The Western Canadian Identity," Canadian Historical Association Annual *Report* (1973), p. 15.

26. Paul Rutherford, "The Western Press and Regionalism, 1870-96," *Canadian Historical Review*, LII (September 1971), pp. 291-92.

27. Klaus Peter Stich, " 'Canada's Century': The Rhetoric of Propaganda," *Prairie Forum*, 1 (April 1976), pp. 19-30.

28. A.F.J. Artibise, "Boosterism and the Development of Prairie Cities, 1817-1913," in *Town and City: Aspects of Western Canadian Urban Development* (Regina: Canadian Plains Studies, 1981), p. 206; in the same volume see Max Foran, "The Makings of a Booster: Wesley Fletcher Orr and Nineteenth-Century Calgary," pp. 289-308.

29. Herman Ganzevoort, "Dutch Immigration to Canada: 1892-1940," Ph.D. Thesis (University of Toronto, 1975), p. 154.

30. A. Rasporich, "Utopian Ideals and Community Settlements in Western Canada 1880-1914," in H. Klassen, ed., *The Canadian West: Social Change and Economic Development* (Calgary: Comprint Publishing Company, 1977), p. 61.

31. On agrarian reformers see W.L. Morton, "The Social Philosophy of Henry Wise Wood, the Canadian Agrarian Leader," *Agricultural History* 22 (April 1948), pp. 114-23; and Reginald Whitaker, "Introduction" to W. Irvine, *The Farmers in Politics* (Toronto: McClelland and Stewart, 1978).

32. R. Allen, *The Social Passion: Religion and Social Reform in Canada 1914-1928* (Toronto: University of Toronto Press, 1971). On the early social reform movements see J.H. Thompson, *The Harvest of War: The Prairie West 1914-1918* (Toronto: McClelland and Stewart, 1978).

33. Harrison, *Unnamed Country*, p. 33. See as well Patricia Roome, "Images of the West: Social Themes in Prairie Literature, 1898-1930" (M.A. Thesis. University of Calgary, 1976).

34. Gerald Friesen, "Three generations of fiction: an introduction to prairie cultural history," in D.J. Bercuson and P.A. Buckner, eds., *Eastern and Western Perspectives* (Toronto: University of Toronto Press, 1981) p. 186.

35. Quoted in Friesen, "Three Generations," p. 187.

36. Owram, *Promise of Eden*, p. 216.

37. J.M.S. Careless, "Frontierism, Metropolitanism, and Canadian History," *Canadian Historical Review,* XXXV (March 1954), p. 12.

38. E.A. McCourt, *The Canadian West in Fiction,* Revised Edition (Toronto: The Ryerson Press, 1970); Henry Kriesel, "The Prairie: A State of Mind," *Transactions of the Royal Society of Canada,* 4th Series VI (June 1968), pp. 171-80; and Laurence Ricou, *Vertical Man/Horizontal World: Man and Landscape in Canadian Prairie Fiction* (Vancouver: University of British Columbia Press, 1973), p. 4.

39. Rees, "Images of the Prairie", p. 270.

40. D. Francis and H. Ganzevoort, eds., "Introduction" to *The Dirty Thirties and Prairie Canada* (Vancouver: Tantalus Research Limited, 1980), p. 5.

41. Harrison, *Unnamed Country,* pp. 270.

42. Careless, "Frontierism," p. 16.

43. W.H. Heick, ed., *History and Myth: Arthur Lower and the Making of Canadian Nationalism* (Vancouver: University of British Columbia Press, 1975). Lower writes: "A myth is not a false story but that which is generally believed to be true" (p. 1).

44. J.E. Rea, "Images of the West," in D.J. Bercuson, ed., *Western Perspectives* 1 (Toronto: Holt, Rinehart and Winston, 1974), pp. 4-9.

45. W.L. Morton, "Seeing an Unliterary Landscape," *Mosaic,* III (Spring 1970), pp. 1-10; "The Bias of Prairie Politics," p. 66.

46. Eli Mandel, "Images of Prairie Man," in R. Allen, ed., *A Region of the Mind* (Regina: Canadian Plains Study Centre, 1973), pp. 201-09; R. Kroetsch quoted in Eli Mandel, "Romance and Realism in Western Canadian Fiction," in *Prairie Perspectives* 2, p. 198; Eli Mandel, "Writing West: On the Road to Wood Mountain," *Canadian Forum,* LVII (June-July, 1977), p. 28.

47. Wreford Watson, "Canada's Geography and Geographies of Canada: Review Article," *The Canadian Cartographer,* 5 (June 1968), pp. 27-28.

48. J. Howard Richards, "The Prairie Region," in John Warkentin, ed., *Canada: A Geographical Interpretation* (Agincourt: Methuen Publications, 1968), p. 396.

49. Watson, "Canada's Geography," p. 31.

50. *Ibid,* p. 36.

51. Patricia Bovey, "Prairie Painting in the Thirties," in *The Dirty Thirties in Prairie Canada,* p. 116.

52. Quoted in Rees, "Images of the Prairie," p. 271.

53. Quoted in *ibid.,* p. 272.

54. B. Kaye and D.W. Moodie, "Geographical Perspectives on the Canadian Plains," in R. Allen, ed., *A Region of the Mind,* pp. 17-46.

55. R. Rees, "The Small Town of Saskatchewan," *Landscape,* 18 (Fall 1969), p. 29.

56. Kaye and Moodie, "Geographical Perspectives," p. 35.

57. Artibise, "Boosterism and the Development of Prairie Cities," p. 230.

58. Roger Gibbins, *Prairie Politics and Society: Regionalism in Decline* (Toronto: Butterworths, 1980).

59. David Smith, "Political culture in the West," in *Eastern and Western Perspectives,* pp. 169-82.

60. Harrison, *Unnamed Country,* p. 189.

61. Mandel, "Writing West," p. 26.

62. R. Cook, "William Kurelek: A Prairie Boy's Vision," *Journal of Ukrainian Studies,* 5 (Spring 1980), p. 34.
63. R. Allen, "Preface" to *A Region of the Mind,* p. ix.

35 Fictions of the American and Canadian Wests

If asked to describe the sound of a clock, most of us would probably say "tic-toc," thus creating a fiction by which to humanize the thing, make it talk our language. Frank Kermode, in his literary study *The Sense of an Ending,* says that experimental subjects, having imposed this fiction, register measurably higher success in predicting the interval between tic and toc than between toc and tic even though the sounds are indistinguishable.[1] Because of the fiction, the interval between tic and toc is charged with significant duration; it is structured meaningfully. Kermode concedes that as fictions go, "tic-toc" is not very interesting, nor very significant except that it illustrates an important psychic need and our way of satisfying it. In our everyday perception it is by such fictions that we order the chaos of sensory experience, and on a larger scale it is by fictions that we structure our experience in order to assign meaning to it. In this extended category of fictions Kermode includes the hypothesis by which the natural scientist organizes his investigation of physical phenomena, the theory by which the historian attempts to make the events of the actual world comprehensible, the fiction through which the novelist seeks a reality of another kind, and the popular myths within which we assign value to the material and immaterial worlds. Truth is stranger than fiction because it is by such fictions that we understand our world. At the mundane level the average man is expected to buy his house and car, marry and divorce his mate, select his career and cast his vote according to prevailing myths. In the more rarified atmosphere of literature, the historical tradition is commonly more important to the novelist than the historical facts. A Frederick Manfred may crawl across the prairie to recapture imaginatively the ordeal of Hugh Glass, but the form and significance of his *Lord Grizzly* owes more to Turner's frontier thesis than to Ashley's expedition up the Missouri.

The fiction of the American and Canadian Wests has been very different partly because the fictions through which those Wests have been perceived have been very different. Setting aside, for the occasion, all personal and literary influences, consider the historical traditions which influenced the novelists most profoundly in the first half of the Twentieth Century. Canadian historian W. L. Morton compares them in his "Clio in Canada" (1946), a germinal essay in western Canadian historiography in which Morton laments the effectiveness of the Laurentian thesis as self-fulfilling prophesy:

> In the frontier Turner found the American quality of American history. It was, according to his thesis, in virtue of the frontier experience that the American people became American. But, according to the Laurentian thesis, it was the commercial system of the St. Lawrence which made Canada, not a folk movement wringing from the harsh, common life of the frontier a national character and way of life, but a scheme of commercial exploitation, Hamiltonian in its politics, imperialistic in its methods, aiming not at political justice but at commercial profits.[2]

Obviously these theories would not only imply different sets of values for the two Wests but assign them entirely different positions in the national consciousness. The ready acceptance of these theories suggests a reasonable correspondence with public opinion, and there is some evidence to confirm the suggestion. Edwin Fussell, in *Frontier: American Literature and the American West,* claims that journalistic publicists of the mid-Nineteenth Century were fond of saying that the American mind would be brought to maturity along the chain of the great Lakes, the banks of the Mississippi, the Missouri and their tributaries in the far northwest.[3] The contrasting Canadian attitudes of the time can be found in Douglas Owram's *Promise Eden: The Canadian Expansionist Movement and the Idea of the West, 1856-1900.* Owram cites influential spokesmen of the time who held to the belief that the northwest was "both unsuitable for settlement and worthless," and that "'no British colony will ever approach nearer than twelve or thirteen hundred miles' to the Red River."[4] Such professional and public "fiction" would have an influence on what kinds of fiction would be thought appropriate to the two Wests.

Of course, historical theories, unlike Kermode's "tic-toc," have substantial bases in fact. The Wests always *have* been different, culturally and institutionally, in ways characterized by the two theories. Canada's West was not a frontier in the sense of the advancing edge of a more or less continuous settlement. Separated from settled Canada by several hundred miles of intractable precambrian shield, it was not the "frontier" or border *of* anything. Because of its isolation it had to be colonized in a more deliberate way than if it had been contiguous with the settled colonies. Any influx of settlers was preceded by the structures and institutions of society, including traders, missionaries, Indian treaties, railroads, land survey and law enforcement. This was one of many circumstances encouraging attitudes toward institutions and the sources of order unlike those characteristic of the American West. And the differences have been profound and permanent beneath the homogenizing effects of mass media. Suffice it to say that the people of a West which can elect Ronald Reagan do not see the world in quite the same way as those in a West which can elect democratic socialist governments in three out of four provinces. The inundation of both regions by the same popular culture is likely to change rather than eliminate the difference. When an American and a Canadian sit down to their T.V. sets, they may tune in the same American western, but the American is watching something domestic, in some sense his own, while the Canadian is watching something he knows to be exotic. The pictures are the same but the experience is quite different.

Probably none of the regulative fictions applied to the Wests are without some basis in fact, but what we were actually doing to settle the two Wests — and continentalists and post-Turnerians would argue that it was not that different — may be less important to the novelist than what we thought we were doing. The differences in that perception find suggestive parallels in the basic ideals upon which the two nations were founded. If we postulate a kind of national mythology growing from our origins, it should be no surprise that a republican democracy created by a Declaration of Independence and a revolutionary war should nurture different myths than a hierarchical dominion created by an act of someone else's parliament which has repeatedly and with force of arms rejected the revolution. Compare the founding documents:

> When in the course of human events it becomes necessary for one people to dissolve the political bands which have connected them with another, and to assume among the powers of the earth, the separate and equal station to which the Laws of Nature and of Nature's God entitles them, a decent respect to the opinions of mankind requires that they should declare the causes which impel them to the separation. — We hold these truths to be self-evident, that all men were created equal, that they are endowed by their Creator with certain unalienable Rights, that among these are Life, Liberty and the pursuit of Happiness, — That to secure these rights, Governments are instituted among Men, deriving their just powers from the consent of the governed, — That whenever any Form of Government becomes destructive of these ends, it is the Right of the People to alter or abolish it . . . .[5]

This is poetry, and its themes are those of the frontier: egalitarianism, the Laws of Nature, radical faith in individualism and the primacy of the individual conscience, the fallibility of institutions, the legitimacy of civil disobedience and violence, freedom, pursuit or questing.

The preamble to the BNA act contrasts sharply:

Whereas the Provinces of Canada, Nova Scotia, and New Brunswick have expressed their Desire to be federally united into one Dominion under the Crown of the United Kingdom of Great Britain and Ireland, with a Constitution similar in principle to that of the United Kingdom:

And whereas such a union would conduce to the Welfare of the Provinces and promote the Interests of the British Empire: etc.

Be it therefore enacted and declared by the Queen's Most Excellent Majesty, by and with the Advice and Consent of the Lords Spiritual and Temporal, and Commons, in this present Parliament assembled, and by the authority of the same, as follows:

Including: "The Executive Government and authority of and over the Dominion of Canada is hereby declared to continue and be vested in the Queen."[6]

You might wonder why we would exhaust ourselves in attempts to bring this document to Canada. It is bureaucratic prose. Its themes are order, hierarchy, profitability, expediency, and others, commonly summed up as "Peace, Order and Good Government." Note especially that the theoretical source of power and authority remains at the top rather than the bottom; the model of order is deductive rather than inductive. Words such as "Life, Liberty and the pursuit of Happiness" would seem almost frivolous in such a verbal context. I have sometimes thought that the solution to any impasse in Canada-U.S. relations might be derived from a close rhetorical analysis of these two documents.

It is easy, perhaps even unnecessary, to identify the correspondence between the ideals voiced in the Declaration, those evident in Turner's frontier thesis, and both the popular mythology of the nation and the popular fictions of the American West. As Richard Slotkin says in his *Regeneration Through Violence,* "In American mythogenesis the founding fathers are not those eighteenth-century gentlemen who composed a nation at Philadelphia. Rather they are those who (to paraphrase Faulkner's *Absalom, Absalom!*) tore violently a nation from the implacable and opulent wilderness."[7] The popular mythology finds its most direct expression in popular fiction which, as John Cawelti says in his *Six-Gun Mystique,* "has the important functions of articulating and reaffirming the primary cultural values."[8] The formula western, in particular, has served as "a kind of foundation ritual," a dim reflection — or perhaps an unwitting parody — of America's struggle for independent nationhood. The pattern is clearly visible from Owen Wister to Zane Grey to Max Brand or Louis Lamour. Central is the frontiersman as Henry Nash Smith describes him in *Virgin Land,* a figure torn between the lure of anarchic freedom in Nature and the comforts and responsibilities of civilization, half-reluctantly helping to carve a nation out of the virgin wilderness, to establish a society which his own heroic gifts preclude him from enjoying. The rich dramatic potential of this half-savage figure explains the eternal vitality and almost universal appeal of the popular western. What is more significant is that the writing and reading public have consistently chosen a particular phase of settlement to embody their ideals of nationhood, whether the stories are studiously historical or totally a-historical. The good rogue cop on television is still a frontiersman: "Baretta" is a cryptowestern.

The correspondence between popular fiction of the Canadian West and the British North America Act is by no means as obvious. In the hierarchical, centralist mythology (and historiography) of the nation, the West would necessarily appear not as the living edge of society but, at worst, a hinterland providing markets and raw materials, at best a purified model of Ontario. The adventure stories, romances of pioneering and sentimental romances of early twentieth-century writers such as Ralph Connor, Nellie McClung, Robert Stead and Arthur Stringer do, however, articulate the primary values of peace, order and good government in an hierarchical dominion. The dominant myth is not the frontier but the garden, specifically an imperial garden in which the adventures justify a hazy identification of the human order of empire with the natural order and the divine order. The central figure is not Smith's half-savage frontiersman but a teacher, a minister, a policeman or a respectable homesteader, firmly entrenched within the cultural order and devoted to demonstrating that order is also natural and divine.[9] There is no extra-legal justice, no salutary application of violence, no individualistic hero in the American sense. Even the North West Mounted Policeman, that chivalric figure riding into danger to maintain the right, derives his power not from anything inherent in his personality but from what he represents — an abstract "right" descending from a remote centre of Empire. He is the knight, not as hero but as champion, invincible not in his powers of self-assertion but in his powers of self-abnegation. So much for Freedom, egalitarianism, the laws of nature, individualism, the fallibility of institutions, the legitimacy of civil disobedience and violence. Northrop Frye once said that a Canadian was an American who had rejected the revolution.

Here again the phase of settlement emphasized by the fiction is significant of national perceptions of the West. A couple of decades at the height of the cattle industry in the American West inspired mountains of popular fiction. The fact that two centuries of fur trade which preceded settlement in the Canadian West have inspired little fiction suggests how slight an interest the Canadian imagination has taken in the frontier and its attendant questions of primitivism and civilization.

The serious or literary fiction of the Wests is, by its very nature, more difficult to generalize about. Its relationships to the regulative fictions through which the two Wests have been perceived are also more subtle, complex, often ambivalent; it would be misleading to suggest direct correspondence of the sort evident in the popular fictions. But at the risk of appearing to do just that, I would like to single out some typical features of theme, form and mode which are suggestive of connections with the other fictions, including the popular. The serious fiction, for example, is distinguished by a tendency to scrutinize and question those primary cultural values affirmed in the popular. Thus while Wister, in *The Virginian,* offers a glib justification for a lynching by appealing to democratic principles, Clark, in *The Oxbow Incident,* uses a lynching to explore the nature of justice, of responsibility, and of individual and communal authority in a democratic society. Serious fiction of the Canadian West began as a conscious reaction against the romances of pioneering. While Robert Stead's early romances celebrate the harmony of man's agrarian order with the orders of nature and of God, Frederick Philip Grove, in his *Fruits of the Earth,* explores a profound spiritual alienation from the land arising from that very presumption of harmony. The Anglo settler, seeing familiar institutions in place, assumes that he can transplant his Ontario culture intact without regard to the character of the new land.

To some extent, then, the serious fiction returns to the themes of the popular fiction not to affirm the popular mythology but to engage at a more profound level the paradoxes inherent in the national ideals. In this respect both Wests have a distinctive value to the literary artist by virtue of being large, recently and sparsely populated, and above all, settled not by foreign powers but by the United States and Canada as nations. The writers can find in the traditions of the Wests the literary symbols appropriate to exploring certain fundamental aspects of the North American condition of being an immigrant culture coming to terms with a vast and often inhospitable continent. The Wests, in effect, offer the extreme case of the individual caught in the collision between an old culture and a new land. The setting seems particularly useful in developing themes of individualism and community, man's spiritual relationship to nature and ethical relationship to society. The ways in which American and Canadian writers have developed these themes seem to me to diverge in nationally distinctive ways. Take, for example, the treatment of man's spiritual relationship with nature — and, by extension, with the entire created universe. In the work of major western writers such as Ferguson, Guthrie, Clark, Fisher and Manfred, some version of the frontier experience remains central. The hero is a frontiersman like Sam Minard in *Mountain Man* or Boone Caudil in *The Big Sky,* caught between the freedom of the wilderness and the bonds of human society. In a sense, he is a protagonist of the national psyche; by virtue of his revolutionary tradition he is freed from any fixed commitment to traditional social bonds, moving with freedom of choice between the natural and human orders. The result may be tragic, as when Caudil discovers that his savagery has violated the bonds of human brotherhood and isolated him from his kind. Or the quest may be successful, as when Sam Minard experiences the wilderness as a vast symphony, provided the frontiersman establishes a spiritual bond with nature, freeing him from any weak dependence on society. Max Westbrook, in his monograph on Clark, interprets this aspect of the hero's quest as a search not simply for freedom but for contact in nature with a primordial reality which will unify and complete his psyche, fragmented by the forces of civilization. Only with a wholeness of the conscious and the unconscious, the rational and instinctual sides of his being, can the hero be an effective force in creating the new kingdom out of the wilderness. The terms of the quest, as Westbrook interprets them, are reminiscent of the familiar American struggle against the tyranny of the conscious intellect which D. H. Lawrence describes in his *Studies in Classic American Literature.* They also suggest a search for moral authority in a society which, by embracing a revolution, has rejected traditional authority. The values expressed in the Declaration of Independence are clearly evident: freedom, the laws of nature, egalitarianism, individualism, the fallibility of institution, etc. In his essay "Mountain Home," Westbrook goes further, to make an explicit connection between the pattern of the frontiersman's quest and the ideals of the revolution: "Briefly stated, this pattern is a devotion to values beyond the law, located, somehow, in nature."[10]

If the protagonist of the American psyche is at large between the natural and cultural orders, his Canadian counterpart, by virtue of having rejected the revolution, finds himself confined within the social structure of his cultural inheritance, and his access to his immediate natural environment is defined and distorted by encompassing cultural patterns developed to accommodate life in a very different place. Grove's Abe Spalding, in *Fruits of the Earth,* confined within the rectilinear world of European man which has been blindly imposed upon the prairie, discovers that ignoring and suppressing external nature has the dangerous consequence of repressing the instinctual nature within himself. The two aspects of nature can threaten to destroy his consciously created world. Northrop Frye describes one reaction to this tension manifested in Canadian literature:

> It is not a terror of the dangers or discomforts or even the mysteries of nature, but a terror of the soul at something that these things manifest. The human mind has nothing but human and moral values to cling to if it is to preserve its integrity or even its sanity, yet the vast unconsciousness of nature in front of it seems an unanswerable denial of those values.[11]

The terror Frye describes is only one effect of the problematic and unstable relationship with nature implicit in a culture which rejects natural law in favour of traditional human wisdom. The more general condition of the protagonist of the national psyche, as seen in the work of major western Canadian writers such as Grove, Edward McCourt, Sinclair Ross and W. O.

Mitchell, is one of seeking yet fearing contact with that natural environment which at the same time represents the immediate present experience (denied by the undiscarded culture) and the unconscious, intuitive side of his own being. Above all, he is seeking to understand what his relationship to that environment should be, within the terms of his inherited culture. The very different ways in which the two literatures develop the universal theme of tensions between the conscious and unconscious aspects of the psyche are consistent with the national ideologies.

Differences in the treatment of common themes inevitably generate differences in form between the American and Canadian western novel. Because of the importance America has ascribed to the frontier and to the process of "westering," the novels, as John R. Milton says in *The Novel of the American West,* favour questing motifs and forms related to epic, romance and myth.[12] The mobile hero's questing through nature implies a loose equation between physical movement and spiritual transformation. The West is recreated as sacred space through which the hero moves toward an archetypal experience of a primal reality.

In the Canadian western novel, the protagonist is inclined to be static, seeking inward for an understanding of his spiritual relationship to the place in which he finds himself. In effect, the West is of interest not as space but as place, and journey motifs are a less common structural feature. Take, for example, such central novels as Grove's *Settlers of the Marsh,* Ross's *As For Me and My House,* or Mitchell's *Who Has Seen the Wind.* Even though Grove is writing about the immigrant experience, his settlers do not journey west; they merely arrive there. Ross's Bentleys have been shifted from one small town parsonage to another, yet the dramatic tensions of the novel are generated not by movement but by the rigid immobility of their lives. *Who Has Seen the Wind* dramatizes the passage of a boy from childhood without the traditional journey motif. Underlying the fact that journeying could have been but was not chosen as a main narrative strategy is the less obvious fact that movement and westering do not carry the implications they have in American fiction.[13] Rather than epic and romantic, the fiction is inclined to novelistic and confessional forms. The frequency of involuted forms with a high degree of technical sophistication may grow out of the fact that the novels are a search for ways of understanding the ambivalent relationship of the individual to his environment. If the philosophical thrust of the American western novel could be said to be moral or ethical, that of the Canadian might be described as epistemological.

Considering the divergent forms of fiction developed in the two Wests, it is not surprising that the American epic and romantic fictions are finally more affirmative of national ideals. The relationship, that is to say, between the literary fiction and the other fictions through which the Wests have been perceived is more amicable in the American West. Even satiric writers such as Thomas Berger in *Little Big Man* and Ken Kesey in *One Flew Over the*

Cuckoo's Nest are ultimately less concerned with criticizing frontier values than with lamenting their passing. But then, the ideals themselves are fundamentally more optimistic. The differences in the fictions attaching to the two Wests reflect the contending assumptions of unfallen and fallen man upon which the two nations were founded. If, as Leslie Fiedler says, "America had been unremittingly dreamed from East to West as a testament to the original goodness of man,"[14] then the Canadian West has been the product of stern reflection upon the need for just institutions to contain the impulses of unregenerate man.

NOTES

1. *The Sense of an Ending: Studies in the Theory of Fiction* (New York: Oxford University Press, 1967), pp. 44-45.

2. "Clio in Canada: The Interpretation of Canadian History," reprinted in *Approaches to Canadian History*, ed. Carl Berger, Canadian Historical Readings 1 (Toronto: University of Toronto Press, 1967), p. 45.

3. *Frontier: American Literature and the American West* (Princeton: Princeton University Press, 1965), p. 11.

4. *Promise of Eden: The Canadian Expansionist Movement and the Idea of West 1856-1900* (Toronto: University of Toronto Press, 1980), p. 7.

5. "The Unanimous Declaration of the Thirteen United States of America," 1776. The copy from which I quote is a facsimile produced for the American Bicentenary.

6. G.P. Browne, ed., *Documents on the Confederation of British North America*, Carlton Library No. 40 (Toronto: McClelland and Stewart, 1969), pp. 302-304.

7. *Regeneration through Violence: The Mythology of the American Frontier, 1600-1860* (Middletown, Conn.: Wesleyan University Press, 1973), p. 4.

8. *The Six-Gun Mystique* (Bowling Green: Bowling Green University Popular Press, 1975), pp. 31-33.

9. This feature of the fiction is examined more thoroughly in my *Unnamed Country* (Edmonton: University of Alberta Press, 1977), chapter III.

10. "Mountain Home: The Hero in the American West," in *The Westering Experience in American Literature*, eds. Merrill Lewis and L. L. Lee (Bellingham: Western Washington University, 1977), p. 9.

11. Conclusion to *Literary History of Canada*, gen. ed. Carl F. Klinck (Toronto: University of Toronto Press, 1965), p. 830.

12. *The Novel of the American West* (Lincoln: University of Nebraska Press, 1980), p. 59.

13. This subject is explored in more detail in my "Imperial Heritage in Prairie Fiction," *Kunapipi* vol. 2, no. 2 (1980), 107-116.

14. *An End to Innocence: Essays on Culture and Politics* (Boston: Beacon Press, 1955), p. 132.